HARDCORE SOFTWARE

Steven Sinofsky • *Learning by Shipping* • *Microsoft 1989–2012*

HARDCORE SOFTWARE

INSIDE the RISE and FALL of the PC REVOLUTION

{ Steven Sinofsky }

A Learning by Shipping book

Supported on the Substack, Inc. platform.

Learning by Shipping, LLC, Seattle, WA and www.learningbyshipping.com

Enjoy the free online supplement and audio narration at hardcoresoftware.learningbyshiping.com.

Text and design by Steven Sinofsky, with editorial and design support. Cover by the publisher.

Author welcomes reports of any typographical errors, omissions, or fact errors to hcsw@learningbyshipping.com.

Printed in the United States of America on recycled paper.

Revised print April 2024

10 9 8 7 6 5 4 3

ISBN: 979-8-99038-850-5
eBook ISBN: 979-8-99038-851-2

To M.W., Z. & C.

Without everyone at Microsoft, customers, and partners around the world, nothing described here would have been possible or nearly as fun. Thank you.

Special gratitude to W.H.G., P.A., S.B., S.K., D.H., L.B., M.A., T.G., J.B., and J.L.G.

To be hardcore is to be wildly optimistic about what can be achieved tomorrow while harshly pessimistic about what works today. Creating software is an art. It is computer science and engineering. It is inspiration, and perspiration. It is inherently individual yet relies on a team. Most of all, building software is a group of people coming together to conjure something into existence and turning that into a product used by billions.

That is hardcore software.

CONTENTS

About the Author **1**

Author's Note **2**

Prologue: Making of a Hacker **4**

1989-1990 .... **7**

001. Becoming a Microsoftie 8

002. SteveSi 12

003. Klunder College 17

004. Everything is Buggy 22

005. Keeping Busy with Cross-Platform OOP 26

006. Zero Defects 29

007. Windows 3.0 Buzz 33

1990-1992 .... **37**

008. Competing with Steve Jobs (the First Time) 38

009. Password is NeXTStep 41

010. Our BillG Review 47

011. Strategy for the '90s: Windows 53

012. I shipped, Therefore I Am 62

013. End of the Beginning 70

1993-1994 .... **74**

014. Executing on the Expansive Vision of Bill Gates 75

015. Every Group Is Screwed Up 78

016. Filling the Void Left by IBM 81

017. Eyes On Competition, Architecture, and Whitespace 86

018. Microsoft's Two Bountiful Gardens 91

019. BillG the Manager 97

020. Innovation versus Shipping: The Cairo Project 103

021. Expanding Breadth versus Coherency: The EMS Project 110
022. Injecting New Ideas and IQ: The Information Superhighway 117
023. ThinkWeeks 122

1994 128

024. Discovering "Cornell is WIRED!" 129
025. Trapped 132
026. Blue Suede Pumas 138
027. Internet Evangelist 143
028. Pivotal Offsite 148
029. Telling of the Untold Story 152
030. My Performance Review (and an Expense Report) 160

1994-1995 162

031. Synchronizing Windows and Office (the First Time) 163
032. Winning With the Suite 168
033. Creating the Office Product Unit, OPU 174
034. Office94, Office96 180

1995 185

035. Windows 95, August or Bust 186
036. Fancy Wizard and Red Squiggles 192
037. Capone and Email Without Typos 198
038. Designed for Windows 95 203
039. Start Me Up 206

1995-1997 210

040. Creating the First Real Office 211
041. Scaling the Office Infrastructure and Platform 217
042. Clippy, The F*cking Clown 226
043. DIM Outlook 234
044. Our First Big M&A Deal (Beating Netscape) 242
045. Incompatible Files, Slipping, Office 97 RTM 249

1998-2000 256

046. Prioritizing a New Type of Customer 257
047. Don't Ship the Org Chart 262
048. Pizza for 20 Million People 269
049. Go Get This Rock 277
050. The Team's Plan in the Face of Disruption 286
051. HTML: Opportunity, Disruption, or Wedge 293
052. Alleviating Bloatware, First Attempt 300
053. Strategy Tax: Outlook Storage, First Attempt 306
054. Steve and Steven Get New Jobs 313
055. Office 2000 is Good to Go! 318
056. Going Global...Mother Tree 323

1999-2001 329

057. Enterprise Agreements 330
058. That Dreaded Word: Synergy 336
059. Scaling...Everything 345
060. ILOVEYOU 355
061. BSoD to Watson: The Reliability Journey 366
062. Split Up Microsoft 377
063. Managing the Antitrust Verdict 384
064. The Start of Office v. NetDocs 386
065. SharePoint: Office Builds Our Own Server 395
066. Killing a Killer Feature In Outlook, Again 409
067. MYR-CDG: Product Meets Sales 414
068. The XP eXPerience 422

2001-2003 429

069. Mega-Scale, Mega-Complexity 430
070. Office.NOT 438
071. Resolving NetDocs v. Office 452
072. Notes on Tablet PC Innovation 462
073. **DO NOT FORWARD** 473
074. Outlook Pride, Finally 480
075. Scaling and Transitions 488

2003-2006 497

076. Betting Big to Fend Off Commoditization 498
077. What Is Software Bloat, Really? 507
078. A Tour of "Ye Olde Museum Of Office Past" 516
079. Competing Designs, Better Design 525
080. Progress From Vision to Beta 532
081. First Feedback and a Surprise 540
082. Defying Conventional Wisdom to Finish Office 550

2006-2007 561

083. Living the Odd-Even Curse 562
084. Who's On the Team, Exactly? 571
085. The Memo (Part 1) 580
086. The Memo (Part 2) 586
087. Reorg! Why Are We Together, Exactly? 598
088. Planning the Most Important Windows Ever 606
089. Rebooting the PC Ecosystem 619
090. I'm a Mac 630
091. Cleaning Up Longhorn and Vista 637

2007-2009 .... **648**

092. Platform Disruption...While Building Windows 7 649

093. Netbook Mania 661

094. First Public Windows 7 Demo 668

095. Welcome to Windows 7, Everyone 675

096. Ultraseven: Launching Windows 7 684

2010 .... **691**

097. A Plan for a Changing World 692

098. A Sea of Worry at the Consumer Electronics Show 702

099. The Magical iPad 711

100. A Daring and Bold Vision 720

2011-2012 .... **735**

101. Reimagining Windows from the Chipset to the Experience: The Chipset 736

102. The Experience 756

103. The End of Windows Software 772

104. //build It and They Will Come (Hopefully) 782

105. New Ultrabooks, Old Office, and the Big Consumer Preview 798

106. The Missing Start Menu 814

107. Click In With Surface 828

Epilogue. The End of the PC Revolution **851**

In Our Memories **867**

Extended Bibliography **868**

Index **879**

EndNotes **897**

ABOUT THE AUTHOR

A respected technologist and business leader, Steven Sinofsky is an investor, adviser, teacher, and writer. He began his career at Microsoft in 1989. Sinofsky joined Microsoft fresh out of graduate school as a software engineer when only one in ten US households had a desktop PC, almost no one had email, the internet as we know it had not yet been conceived, and smartphones and tablets were science fiction. Starting in Development Tools, the software used by programmers to create software, Sinofsky worked on the first version of the new programming language C++ for the nascent Windows platform. He was Bill Gates's technical assistant during the development of Windows 95 and Windows NT and the rise of internet as we know it today. He then joined the newly formed Office Product Unit and, for twelve years and six releases, rose to senior vice president leading all of Office product development. Sinofsky was tapped to bring order—and innovation—to the Windows division as president. He served as president of the Windows division through 2012, delivering two major releases of Windows, Windows 7 and Windows 8, as well as the creation of Microsoft Surface and online services such as Outlook.com and OneDrive.

After Microsoft, Sinofsky began serving as a board partner at Silicon Valley investment firm a16z. He serves on corporate boards, as a mentor to employees, from founder and CEO to recent graduates, and adviser to a broad range of companies from seed stage to public.

He earned a Bachelor of Arts in both computer science and chemistry from Cornell University and a Master of Science degree in computer science from the University of Massachusetts, Amherst. Sinofsky was a visiting scholar at Harvard Business School. He lived in China while working for Microsoft. He traveled extensively through Asia and Africa learning about society and technology.

With Marco Iansiti, the David Sarnoff Professor of Business Administration at Harvard Business School, Sinofsky co-authored *One Strategy: Organization, Planning, and Decision Making* (Wiley, 2009), a compendium of blog posts authored internally at Microsoft during the creation of Windows 7 combined with context and analysis by Iansiti.

Sinofsky maintains an active online presence of over one million follower-subscribers writing about a wide range of technology industry and business topics on LinkedIn, Medium, LearningByShipping.com, and most actively on X and on Substack.

AUTHOR'S NOTE

I have always loved reading books about building and managing complex projects. When I first became a manager in 1992, I began a tradition of gifting books in this theme to team members. Soon, I started to see those I'd worked with for several years building out a shelf of books in their offices. It was touching. While many books have been written about Microsoft, most were written about the earliest days, before Windows, or with a focus on the monopoly litigation, and none were written by those who worked on the products through many product generations. The book missing from that shelf is one about building software at Microsoft.

In more ways than I can count, I was lucky enough to find myself an enthusiast, participant, and, in some contexts, leader of Microsoft projects from the early times of Tools, Office, and Windows through the growth and then mature days of the *PC Revolution*. My hope is that this book conveys the human side of building software at a scale never seen—putting software on every desk and in every home, literally. This book is about the interplay of individuals, organization, technologies, and products that happens when all the parts are moving. Individuals are learning and growing while new organizations are built around them for the first time, and technologies are invented and turned into products accomplishing what has never been done before.

There are thousands of people I wish I could have written about, each of whom made incredibly valuable contributions to the teams and products described in these pages. Equally, I wish I could have shared all the stories of the highest highs and lowest lows. To those individuals I was not able to include or those I included but did not share the story you wish I shared, please know that I wanted to and probably even tried but could not include everything I would have liked.

I worked hard to tell the story of what I saw at the PC Revolution, from the vantage point I was given, and to capture the people, culture, and organization that created products used around the world by a billion people. Since most contemporary readers will have experienced Office and Windows, I intentionally did not shy away from product features and technologies as elements and actors in the story.

This is a first-person account from my memories and memorabilia along with research based on public sources. I endeavored to achieve the highest level of accuracy possible. It is a cultural history not a deep dive into corporate archives. Quotes from print journalism were taken directly from online or print, and quotes from video my best effort at transcribing. Corporate sales and other metrics were taken from annual reports or SEC filings, though team-specific numbers were my own recollections. Industry-wide measures, such as PC sales, were sourced from contemporaneous first-party press.

Any errors are my sole responsibility. Despite the amazingly detailed and heroic efforts of numerous reviewers and fact checkers, I want to preemptively apologize for any fact errors as I know that no matter how trivial mistakes sting. The events described in this book were experienced deeply by tens if not thousands of people and most certainly some had differing recollections, and in reality, all of our experiences are equally true. In writing this book, I intentionally waited several years in the hopes that my own truth would become more settled, but still I recognize that when it comes to experiences and perspectives, especially those as personal and dramatic as shared here, the truth evolves over time—as wounds heal, bruised egos recover, and importantly as more people share feelings they did not share at the time. Errors will be tracked and recorded with my intent to set a record of facts straight as needed.

In writing this I was often asked why I waited "so long" after leaving Microsoft to tell this story. There were two reasons. To do justice to the narrative, time needed to pass and to provide a filter for what is important versus what was exciting. Too often, books tell stories of companies before the ending is clear. Those books don't stand the test of time that I hope this one does. Second, I set out to gain perspective on the PC journey by relocating to Silicon Valley and immersing myself in the whole other world. It was only two years into that journey when Microsoft changed CEOs and brought a clear transition to a company that plays a different role in the technology world.

The title of the book, *Hardcore Software*, comes from the college recruiting tagline used when I was recruited to Microsoft and for some time after. The poster read, "Stop fooling around. It's time to get hardcore about software. With Microsoft." In today's context, this would not be the most inclusive language for recruiting, but it captures the 1980s and later *zeitgeist* of computer programming.

S.S., 2024

PROLOGUE: MAKING OF A HACKER

In 1982, *Time* magazine named the personal computer *Machine of the Year*, marking the first time a non-human was awarded *Man of the Year*. It was a fascinating read, but like many nerdy kids across the country at the time, I'd already become captivated by computers.

My best friend Dave Crotty and our other best friend, Neal Fordham (collectively, the three of us were known as *the boys*), spent the previous year making mixtapes of '80s punk and new wave on Dave's father's Bang & Olufsen component system.

When Dave's brother Kevin got an Atari 800 computer, my curiosity piqued. I was mesmerized by this new machine—not by the video games I could play on it but by the presence of BASIC, the first programming language experienced by most everyone in the early days of personal computing. BASIC was thanks in no small part to Bill Gates and Paul Allen and their start-up originally known as Micro-Soft.

I gave up Space Invaders for rows of numbered lines. The timing turned out to be great.

Our family business was a retail store in Orlando, Florida. My Saturdays were spent calculating sales tax, doing inventory, and making change while chatting with customers.

Dave's Atari gave me an opportunity to create my first program:

```
10 PRINT "Amount of sale?"

20 INPUT sale

30 LET tax = sale*.04

40 PRINT "Merchandise: " sale

50 PRINT "Tax: " tax

60 PRINT "Total: ", sale+tax

70 GOTO 10
```

As the family business evolved, my father, David, realized that turning it into a wholesaler was a great opportunity for the family. He decided to buy a computer to run it. I have no idea where the motivation for this came from and certainly knew the expense was significant, about $1,800 then or about $5,000 in 2020 dollars. While our family had been early adopters (to some degree) of many modern household items—we had a fancy 35mm camera, a microwave, a Betamax, and even a big-screen TV—a computer, however, was puzzling. It was also an enormous privilege. Rather than a "toy" computer, of which the Apple][, Atari, and the new Commodore 64K (64 kilobytes) were viewed at the time by those who claimed to know, my father invested in a *business* computer. He went to a computer store, staffed by people in suits and ties, and bought one of the earliest Osborne I computers.

The Osborne was a remarkable machine at the time and in the history of the personal computer. A nearly 30-pound "portable" that didn't even have a battery as portable meant you could relocate it. Described as "the size of a sewing machine" it had a 5-inch CRT screen that wasn't large enough for a full 80 characters across, so using the CTRL key and arrows that panned the screen would allow someone to see the rest of it. It came with two 90K 5.25-inch floppy drives and 64K of memory. It ran the CP/M operating system, Control Program/Monitor, which at the time was vying to become the *de facto* standard.

It came with a bundle of "free" business software, including the WordStar word processor, the SuperCalc spreadsheet, a copy of the remarkable VisiCalc on the Apple][, and two (!) different BASIC languages, MBASIC, which I later learned was Microsoft BASIC, and a faster variant, CBASIC. Notably, a "database" called *dBase II* was promised but did not arrive until later, or "real soon" as the dealer told us.

Magazines were the early fountain of knowledge about the new computer because computers were not connected to anything else or any other computers. The monthly *Portable Companion,* the first issue free with the computer, was filled with tips and tricks for using the Osborne and the bundled software. I dutifully filled out reader response cards and soon had a library of code samples I could type in and printer configuration codes. I read *Dr. Dobb's* and *BYTE* at B. Dalton Bookseller in the mall instead of playing games.

I set up the computer in the tiny extra room that served as the TV room for my sister and me, much to her chagrin. The noise created by the combination of typing on the full travel keyboard and the constant grinding and clacking of the floppy disk drives, not to mention the loud beep at power-on and whirring fan, took a toll on my younger sister, Jill. Through our lightly constructed 1970s Florida ranch house, I heard her repeatedly whine, "Stop clicking…stop beeping."

I was undeterred.

My father and I spoke twice about the computer. The first time was when we bought the computer for the business and I was left to figure out how to "put it to work," whatever that meant in 1981. Second, after a few months, when I was not making enough progress, he basically said he was firing me and he was going to hire a professional, whatever that meant. But that second conversation lit a fire under me.

I spent a month or two using CBASIC to build an inventory program for the wholesaler. I had no idea how a database worked, what a database table was, or anything like that. There were enough example programs for managing "lists" in CBASIC for me to figure out how to modify them.

Probably just in time for my father's loss of patience with me, I was rescued by the delivery of disks and manual for dBase II. After a few hours of using it and going through the typewritten photocopied documentation that came with it, a whole new world opened up for me. I immediately began building an entire system for the business.

A tribute to the power of dBase II more than to any skill I had, it took only a few weeks to get accounts, inventory, payables, and invoicing up and running. My father was relieved. I began the job of manually inputting the names and addresses of hundreds of customers and thousands of products.

To store all the data that did not fit on a 90K floppy, I spent weeks evaluating a 10-megabyte hard drive to add to the second Osborne bought for the business while one remained at home for me to program and the other ran the business. The 10-megabyte drive was the size of our Betamax and sounded like a small aircraft, but it dramatically changed how the business could be run. Imagine something like 100 floppies running all at once. It was magic. And it was fast!

Along with dBase II, the "300 baud modem" that promised to unlock the world of connecting to other computers over telephone lines was also delayed. When it finally arrived, I added a new sound to the clicking and clacking, the audible modem handshake that later came to symbolize "online."

At first, there wasn't much to dial-up except expensive per-minute professional services that were out of my price range and required a credit card I did not have. After a lucky meeting at the local CP/M User Group, or *CPMUG,* as it was called, where I was the youngest by at least 10 years and the only person there not yet working at Martin Marietta or Kennedy Space Center, I learned about FIDONet.

I was finally online. And then I was online all the time using the second home phone line I received for my Bar Mitzvah.

That connected me to user groups, forums, and others writing and exchanging programs. I felt like I was on a new learning curve as every night led to another discovery. Sometimes I learned the arcane aspects of CP/M, such as how to edit the OS code to disable the File Delete command to make using the computer safer for my father or to customize WordStar for our printer so it would print "double wide" characters for fancy headings. Other times, I learned some sophisticated dBase II constructs like keeping multiple tables connected and in sync for reporting. It was also in an online forum that I learned about the IBM PC and how it was going to be the winner between it, CP/M, TRS-80, and Apple Computer, the other ever-present computer systems.

So much was changing in such a short amount of time. That year fewer than two million PCs built by dozens of companies were sold, each computer running different and incompatible software, as if early automobiles needed different roads for each car maker. A year earlier, IBM introduced the IBM PC and was welcomed to the PC Revolution by five-year-old Apple Computer in a full-page advertisement in *The Wall Street Journal.*

It was early in the PC Revolution.

Cornell University's computer science program, one of the first in the country, started in 1965, the year I was born. As 1982 wound down, I was admitted to Cornell.

Prompted by that *Time* article, my mother, Marsha, told me that computers were a fine hobby, but she reminded me that I wanted to be a doctor. I received a good talking to once she read the descriptions of "hacker" culture—flannel shirts, no shoes, and working late at night in the solitary computer room of the nation's colleges. It all sounded too close to late-night beeping and clicking. She wanted assurance that I was attending Cornell to study something more in line with what was expected, what I wanted. She was concerned that I might become a "hacker."

Too late.

1989-1990

PCs and software barely work, but the ascent of the IBM PC powered by Intel processors and Windows is underway. It is the start of the modern PC era as PC sales (from all manufacturers for the year) exceeded 20 million units worldwide, which is about half the worldwide sales of all personal computers to date including those from Apple, Tandy, Atari, and more. Looming, however, is platform competitor NeXT, the new computer company started by Steve Jobs. The dramatic extent to which that company will alter the technology landscape is decades from revealing itself. While Apple's Macintosh is a competitor, it is also the foundation for Microsoft's Applications business. The group I was hired into was squarely in the middle of both the new and old Steve Jobs platforms.

001. BECOMING A MICROSOFTIE

The whiteboard in my graduate school lab read, "Steven, Bill Gates called. Call him back."

It was super weird to see that written because Microsoft wasn't on our collective academic radar and most people didn't know who Bill Gates was. Someone was clearly playing a joke on me. My college friend Brent grew up in the Seattle area and I had mentioned to him that I was interviewing at Microsoft, so it was probably him.

Later that day, I got home to find my PhoneMate microcassette answering machine flashing. There were two messages recorded. The first one was left earlier that morning as I started walking to the Lederle Graduate Research Center at UMass-Amherst where I was a second-year PhD student in computer science. A somewhat squeaky and distracted voice said, "Steven, um, this is Bill Gates calling. Can you call me back at…um…206-882-8080?" The second message had been recorded later in the day. "Steven, yeah, this is Bill Gates calling again. I guess I called you at your lab like your message said, but you weren't there either. When you get a chance call me back." My outgoing message at home gave the number of the lab since that was the only other place, basically, that I spent time.

Brent's ploy seemed rather elaborate. He kept it going for a couple of days as I kept getting voicemail messages claiming to be Gates. I did nothing.

As an undergrad I had written a program called MacMendeleev after the father of the periodic table. I had been dying to write a Mac program after the incredible Super Bowl launch advertisement. MacMendeleev was the result of landing in an encouraging chemistry lab—thanks, Professor Clardy. As much as computer science classes made me finally feel like I was in the right place in life—thanks, Professor Teitelbaum—my chemistry classes were the exact opposite where a B+ fall of freshman year was the highest grade I'd receive in chemistry in four years. The Mac was not a business computer, especially according to the advertisements by IBM, and they weren't used in my classes. There wasn't dBase II yet, as I had used earlier on my Osborne from high school, and I wasn't going to use Microsoft BASIC to write something from scratch. The Mac was, however, focused on education. The one thing I loved in chemistry was the periodic table. I dreamed up the idea of an interactive periodic table that could chart or graph the elements according to different properties to see what exhibited periodicity. I got some help from my lab mate, Tom Ball, to help me with the graphics.

Surprisingly, MacMendeleev achieved a small amount of success. We signed up with the ever-present photocopy store Kinko's that maintained an in-store kiosk that made copies of library programs. It was a software vending machine. The program was used in a few classes, and we made enough money on it to fund a cruise on Cayuga Lake.

The program also scored me an invitation to the 1988 Association of Computing Machinery regional gathering on Computers in Education. The conference loaned me a Mac to use, instead of the luggable PC I started using that I had acquired from my summers at Martin Marietta. The PC ran MS-DOS (Microsoft Disk Operating System), the software required for a PC to run and provide capabilities for other companies to write programs. It was the defining product for Microsoft in the 1980s and became the business engine that powered the company prior to Windows and Office.

I had never been to a conference and was not sure why I was there or what was going on, but I found myself sitting at a table talking about the periodic table, doing my first demos and booth duty. Apparently, I impressed the organizers enough to win an award. My prize was a just-released Color Macintosh. It was a huge score.

A representative for Microsoft approached me after my win, offering me some software, and asked me what I wanted…BASIC? I was heads down building Smalltalk on Unix, using TeX for papers, and using all GNU tools, but we agreed on a copy of Microsoft Word. I was excited but thought it was weird because everyone used WordPerfect on PCs and MacWrite on Macintosh, and I used LaTeX.

My first year of college I worked the night shift at a public computer lab filled with all sorts of new computers. There were PCs people could use (mostly grad students) for word processing and spreadsheets using WordPerfect and Lotus 1-2-3, an odd Apple Lisa the predecessor to Macintosh, several highly advanced computer graphics workstations used by physics students, in addition to the mainframe terminals, punch card readers, and refrigerator-size line printers I maintained. By early 1984, the first public Macintosh computers arrived, and I spent my Friday night shift helping people recover documents after the notoriously flaky MacWrite crashed and ate them.

Later, when I was applying for jobs (with the resume of a student who never really had a job), on a whim, I applied to Microsoft using the address on the Microsoft Word box I'd received. It was 16011 NE 36th Way, Redmond, WA 98052. I also sent my resume to Apple Computer. Like everyone I ever knew, I never heard back. They were like that back then and still are, I am told. I think about a year later I got a postcard with a yellow Post Office sticker forwarded from Amherst to my current address letting me know my resume was on file.

I was fairly certain I was going to work in government service, as it was a popular trajectory for engineering graduates, especially those like me with some Russian language skills. There were multiple trips taken to undisclosed locations in the metropolitan DC area talking to the high-tech parts of three-letter agencies.

But then, two days after mailing it, a Microsoft recruiter named Cris Wittress called about having me come out to interview. She overnighted a plane ticket and a hotel booking. I was off.

The taxi ride to the hotel had a cutting edge feel to it. I was used to seeing important technical companies on Boston's Route 128, like DEC, Data General, Apollo, and Banyan, but in Seattle, the names were all different: Apple, MicroRim, Egghead, Tektronix, and more, and oddly a McDonnell Douglas Aerospace building right next to Microsoft.

I stayed in the new Residence Inn, which was only a few minutes from the Microsoft *campus,* as it was called. It was a dreary February. I didn't have a car and couldn't figure out where anything was, but there was a Houlihan's next-door so I had potato skins and fried cheese, as if I was still in high school. I got back to the room and decided to try out the fake log in the fireplace. Apparently, there was a chimney door or something, as I quickly set off the smoke alarm and caused a minor incident.

First thing in the morning, I put on my blue Brooks Brothers suit and headed over to building 1. I signed in in the lobby and was promptly greeted by Cris Wittress, who introduced herself as "Cris Wit" as though it were a nickname. The first sign of cool: She had an office. Come to think of it, everyone had an office—with a door. Fancy.

Cris briskly walked me through the day, describing the people I was going to meet and explaining that they were going to ask me technical questions and that was my interview. In one-hour slots, back-to-back, I met with a phenomenal loop of people who asked me coding questions, grilled me on architecture, and challenged my core assumptions. There was a fancy lunch and a fancy dinner that were typical of job interviews in the go-go 1980's. Not so typical were the offers of beer at lunch and sake at dinner, at Benihana. Most everyone on my interview loop was a recent graduate of Waterloo or Toronto. Along with the elite schools in the US these two schools were well represented in the Microsoft ranks.

I flew home the next morning. Cris called right away to tell me I had a job offer and sent me a rush version followed by a formal letter. The offer arrived overnight via Mailgram, an expensive, old-fashioned telegram except it could be a full page. Mailgrams were used by big business before the internet, when the fax machine dominated offices, though students did not have one.

It happened fast. The offer was to work in the Applications Tools group. It was for $37,500 and had 1,500 non-qualified stock options, plus moving expenses. I called my uncle, who worked in investment banking on Wall Street, to ask what a stock option was. He told me and said mine were probably going to be worthless, but someday maybe they'd be worth $10,000.

Still undecided but leaning toward government work, one evening, late, I got a call at home.

"Hello, Steven…finally great to get a hold of you. My name is David Pritchard and I work in college recruiting at Microsoft. Bill Gates has been trying to get a hold of you, but it has been difficult. Can we set up a time tomorrow for you two to talk?"

David was one of Cris's managers and leader of the college recruiting program. The success of that program is owed to his early efforts.

Oops, I guess that really was Bill Gates before and not a prank.

When Bill and I finally spoke, the conversation was awkward, since neither of us were exactly good at chit-chat stuff.

"Hi, Steve, this is Bill Gates."

"Hello. Thank you for calling, and so sorry for the confusion. I thought a friend of mine…"

"So, David gave me this list of like ten people and I'm supposed to call all of them and convince them to work at Microsoft. You should come work at Microsoft. Do you have any questions?" I always thought this was the best part of the call—him telling me he was just cranking through a list. Transparency.

"I'm definitely excited and thinking about it. I don't really have any questions."

"Well, why haven't you accepted yet? You have a good offer."

"I'm considering other things. I have been really interested in government service."

"Government? That's for when you're old and stupid."

No, really, he said that.

"At Microsoft we have amazing things going on in multimedia. Have you seen all the things we are doing with CD-ROMs and video? We are going to make a whole encyclopedia on a CD-ROM, 650 megabytes with videos, maps, quizzes, and more."

"I haven't. I use a Macintosh and workstations. I used MS-DOS at my summer job and Windows 1.0, but it was pretty slow."

"Well, Microsoft makes more money on Macintoshes than Apple does because of our apps—our word *prosser* [*sic*], Word, is super good. OS/2 runs in protect mode, which the Mac does not do. Do you have any more questions?"

"Not really."

"I'm glad we got to talk. The offer is super good. Bye."

After some failed negotiations on my part for more salary, I accepted and joined the Applications Tools group with Scott Randall as my manager. My start date was set for July 10, 1989.

The *Seattle Times* wrote an article in 1989 called "Inside Microsoft – A 'velvet sweatshop' or a high-tech heaven?" Cris mailed it to me, along with a flurry of fancy Airborne Express overnight envelopes I would receive over the coming weeks containing items meant to woo me including the *Annual Report*, a Microsoft Press Desk Calendar (with an ASCII table in the back), issues of The Seattle Weekly (to remind me of the cool music scene), and glossy data sheets on Microsoft products. The *Times* story chronicled the long hours people worked, including evenings and weekends. It talked about former employees referring to themselves as "recovering" Microsoft workers, but it also painted the picture of a creative, challenging, prankster-geek culture. The contrast and the controversy didn't bother me.

What could be so bad about hard work that came with a private office, free Coke *or* Pepsi, and Lipton Soup?

Whatever was going on there, it was working well.

Microsoft finished fiscal 1989 as I was crossing the country to start my job. Despite a global recession and a market crash leaving company stock close to its IPO pricing three years earlier, it closed the books with more than $800 million in revenue (1989 dollars) and a market capitalization of about $3 billion. The company was already doing business in 50 or so countries with dozens of sales offices around the world—a testimony to the growth mindset of Bill Gates. The company had approximately 3,000 global employees. I was the latest of about 1,200 hired in research and development, mostly in Redmond, Washington.

When I joined Microsoft, I knew little about the company and even less about the corporate world in general. I was a kid fresh out of school, impatient and *gung-ho* to be a part of my new world, but equally inexperienced and a bit overconfident about what I was in for.

In the computer world Microsoft was well known but it wasn't IBM or RadioShack. But most people I knew, including my family, were extremely fuzzy on what I was going to do and where I was going to do it. My grandfather was the only person in my family to have ever been to Seattle, and that was by stow-away train rides during the depression. I spent most family gatherings explaining what software was and that Seattle was not just a forest.

002. STEVESI

When I first arrived in Redmond, I lived about three blocks from campus, in company-provided temporary housing at an apartment complex called Bellevue Meadows, a block from the Residence Inn I had almost burned down during my interview. It was still light out at 9 p.m. on my first night (welcome to the Northwest), so I walked over to campus to check it out.

Microsoft's three-year-old campus was made up of the *original* X-wing buildings, 1 through 6, and the recently completed double X-wing 8 and 9. There was no building 7. Nobody knew exactly why, though there were a bunch of theories tossed around over the years. Sending a new person to meet up at building 7 was an ongoing prank. The real buildings surrounded a fountain and the small-but-infamous Lake Bill, which looking back, is much smaller than I recalled from that first night. There was a basketball court near the lake, which always seemed to be in use. The buildings, connected by tree-lined sidewalks, were known for their design, which was meant to maximize the number of private offices with windows.

In a nod to Microsoft's culture of self-reliance, the next day, my first day, after a two-hour orientation session that felt like forever, I and about 20 other college hires were left to fend for ourselves. While I had been told how to set up direct deposit (paychecks were still hand delivered for many) and learned some details about my healthcare plan, I literally had no idea where to go. Fortunately, a more studious fellow new hire noticed, buried in the paperwork, that there was a map and an old-style printout with name (Steve Sinofsky), telephone extension (x67768), manager (Scott Randell, listed as SCOTTRA), and an email ID and password—yes, printed. The floor plan and numbering system made MIT's infinite corridor look understandable.

As I flipped through the paperwork, I noticed my assigned email name was STEVESI on the printout, which immediately irked me as I was *steven* in all my previous systems, all lowercase because of Unix which preferred that. Obviously, I was not going to complain.

As I came to understand it, SteveSi was officially, and forever, my new name, usually written in mixed case. Email names were how people wrote and spoke about others. Where a previous generation might have used only a last name out of casual respect or mister in person, Microsoft used email from BillG to SteveB on down. Aside from the free drinks, private offices, and khakis with button-downs, email names remained one of the iconic cultural identifiers of those days and still used among alumni. Given names no longer mattered at Microsoft. I was SteveSi. Cris Wittress was CrisWit—I finally got what she meant.

Before I started, Steven Schwartz had landed the name StevenS, a fact for which I was always jealous. After he left, I even tried to secure the name, but there was a no-recycle policy. A coworker named Bill Gallagher was given BillGa, and for years he got crazy mail intended for the real BillG. As the company grew, it began to wrestle with the complexities of people getting married (or divorced) and how to deal with email name changes—much trickier than they'd imagine. Ultimately, in the late 1990s with the move to Microsoft's email product, we finally moved to *friendly* names like steven.sinofsky@microsoft.com.

There was a list of email aliases (an early Unix-ism) to get help, like *benefits*, *sickday*, *vacation*, *supply* (office supplies), *recept1* (*recept2*, *recept3*, etc. for the receptionists), *stock* (stock option sales), *espp* (employee stock purchase plan), *payroll* (for help with direct deposit), and, best of all, *pcrepair*, which could help with computer hardware. Perhaps that was second best, as I soon discovered *library*, which mailed the Microsoft librarians any topic to research or a request to send copies of articles or locate any book needed for work. There was an actual library filling most of one arm of an X in building 4, where I spent a lot of time as well. Everything was an email away.

Microsoft made about 35 different products back then, and I had personal experience with almost none of them. Importantly, by the mid-1980s, Microsoft moved beyond being a single-product company. It had substantial businesses in each of the major categories of the day: languages, operating systems, and applications. No single product represented more than half the company revenue. This early diversity was critical to Microsoft's growth. In many ways, early software companies emulated record or book publishing by having many licensed titles for sale, and while early Microsoft followed this model it was now building most software in house.

The Systems group was the big group and was made up of the grown-ups. It felt to me the most like my summer aerospace job because there were people who were married. Gasp! Some even had children. This was the group that made MS-DOS, which was the single biggest moneymaker. They were also making OS/2, which was a massive joint project with IBM. There was a much smaller side project called Windows that was increasingly interesting. Unique to the Systems group was a much larger number of people who had joined Microsoft with years of prior work experience. There were people from IBM, DEC, ATT, HP, and a host of other computer companies from a previous era. Dave Cutler (DaveC), a legend with over 25 years of experience, had recently joined from DEC along with many of those colleagues. This made sense since building an operating system was something done at other big companies.

Languages was the history of the company and the oldest group. This was the group that made BASIC, as well as programming languages and tools from C to Pascal, Fortran, and, importantly, Assembler. The Languages products were for MS-DOS, Xenix (the commercial version of Unix, the ancestor of today's Linux), and an expansion to OS/2, an ill-fated joint development between Microsoft and IBM.

I thought many of the people I met in Languages seemed old. Some owned houses and had new cars. Some had been at Microsoft more than five years already.

Apps was the colloquial term for Applications, which is how the computer industry viewed programs used by end-users, versus the Operating System, which was required by the machine, or Languages used by developers. The Apps group was less tenured as it was both a newer business for Microsoft and seemed to have more college hires. Apps was almost a sleeper business even back then. Most of the products it made were for the Macintosh, like Word, Excel, and File, all of which were on the first or second version. Apps for MS-DOS were almost as numerous, but all were a distant number two in the market relative to software giants Lotus, WordPerfect, Ashton-Tate, and Software Publishing that I had used in my summer job during college.

I walked over to building 5 to find the private, interior office in which I'd begin my career. It had no exterior window but had one to the hallway. As I searched for my office, I passed the kitchen and saw the giant glass-door refrigerators filled with cans of every variety of Coke and Pepsi products like a convenience store.

It would be decades before I paid for a beverage.

Just across from the kitchen was the mail and copy room. This room had *everything* one could imagine needing for work. It was like a CompUSA and Office Depot all in one. Along with a big laser printer and a copy machine, there were 5.25-inch and 3.5-inch floppy disks by the case, notebooks of every size writing paper as computers hardly existed in portable form at this time, printer paper, pens, tape (transparent and masking), thumb tacks, and more. There were boxes of colored pencils—legend had it that BillG used those to annotate code with different colors, but I later learned that was a myth. There were rulers for scanning across lines of code in landscape. Best of all were the staplers with the Microsoft logo on them. This was like a gift shop, and anyone visiting left with a box of floppies and one of those staplers.

After a few wrong turns, I finally saw the engraved door placard, think *Mad Men*, that read STEVE SINOFSKY. Not Steven. I was peeved. While I did not meet him for a few years, *Steve* Ballmer (SteveB) had something to do with this, I'm certain.

Later that morning, I met a fellow college hire named Antoine Leblond, a French-Canadian who was in a far worse position than me, as the powers had reduced him to TonyL. That only lasted until his then-girlfriend visited and, as an even more ardent Québécois, Lucie Robitaille somehow managed to get it changed to a cool alias: Antoine.

Offices back then were furnished in what could be described as *Native Northwest*. Think a solid wood oak 60-by-30-inch-deep desk with a 24-inch typing return and a swivel chair with matching oak arms. There was a matching 60-inch-high solid oak bookcase. A whiteboard and cork board were attached to the white walls. A 12-button analog phone in corporate brown was on the return, featuring my personal phone number, 206-936-7768 or x67768. The furniture reminded me of the *make it as indestructible as possible* stuff that filled the freshman University Halls at Cornell. Even if I was motivated to rearrange the layout of my nine-by-twelve-foot space, I could not because everything was so heavy. The setup was also horribly non-ergonomic by today's standards. Still, by any measure of an entry-level office, it was amazing.

My bookshelf was pre-populated with, I later learned, standard-issue books for every new software design engineer hire. There was an Intel 286 and 386 reference along with a Motorola 68000 reference—everyone in software engineering understood machine architecture and instruction sets. A phone-book-size MS-DOS encyclopedia weighed down the shelf. There was also a dictionary and thesaurus, and a copy of the same Microsoft Press desk calendar featuring important milestones in computing and an MS-DOS technical reference card in the back that CrisWit had sent as a recruiting gift.

Importantly, there were two seminal works on programming, Fred Brooks's *The Mythical Man-Month* and *Programming Pearls* by Jon Bentley. The former, I learned, was the most epic of all Microsoft struggles, which was trying to release products on time—by the summer of 1989 Windows was on the second version, having shipped 1.0 almost two years after public announcement. The latter book represented the *hardcore* ethos of Microsoft software engineering, which was *tight code*—what code could be written to solve the problem with the most clarity and fewest lines, least amount of memory, and fewest CPU cycles.

There was also a copy of *The Hacker's Dictionary* by Guy L. Steele, a famous computer scientist partly responsible for the programming language Scheme used and developed at MIT. The book was a 1980s version of what was often called *computerese* though Microsoft had its own unique language. One other book seemed rather strange to me, Stewart Brand's *The Whole Earth Catalog*, which seemed useful if I was intent upon producing my own energy or building a yurt, but definitely represented the tail end of the hippie culture of computing from which we all originated.

There was a Compaq PC and a terminal in the office. The Compaq was an Intel 386 chip running at 33 MHz with an extended memory card and hard drive. The terminal was hardwired to Xenix servers via a different network and where the email system was hosted. It was Xenix email, which itself was just a port of Unix mail. I was right at home shelling out to "vi" to edit mail as I had been doing since college. *vi* as in *visual editor* abbreviated. There was also an HP-16C Computer Scientist calculator, for handling all the hexadecimal and binary conversions I would need to do, but I already owned one.

I signed on and changed my password to one I used for the next 10 years or so until password policies came into vogue. I fired off emails to some old lab mates who were the only other people I knew using email. I didn't hear back right away, which was weird. That was when I learned outbound mail was batched and sent/received twice a day. I was told Gordon Letwin (GordonL), the legendary MS-DOS and OS/2 engineer, was not in favor of being connected to ARPANET or BITNET due to security concerns (he was certainly ahead of his time) so this was the compromise. Emphasizing this, our first business cards had only phone and fax numbers and TELEX numbers! By special request, a UUNET address could be added. UUNET was one of the first commercial internet provider of email addresses. That summer uunet!uw-beaver!microsoft!stevesi. Don't ask. Microsoft used email for everything inside the company, but externally email was not yet a thing.

Turning on the PC, I was immediately greeted with a hung machine (back then we called them *machines,* not devices) unable to make it through the boot sequence. I received my first lesson in *corpnet*, or the corporate network. The network was reliable, but the software on the PCs was not. Hangs were frequent and the only fix was a power cycle. I was only familiar with Novell Netware and had not yet experienced a product in the same space that Microsoft had just released, LanManager, a.k.a. LanMan. I wasn't alone. Almost no one had bought the product because it mostly didn't work.

This brought my first experience with emailing *helpdesk*. By email, they asked me if I was an SDE. I wasn't sure, and then I realized my title was software design engineer. The next mail said they were on the way.

A nice man with a pushcart filled with tools and gear to keep PCs running and connected showed up. He pulled a 5.25-inch floppy out of a plastic disk holder and began the process of a network boot, which was a fancy way of using a floppy disk to boot a computer and connect to the network. After a minute or so of grinding floppy noise, I saw the magic "C:>" prompt.

The tech began some magic incantations that were new to me, like NET USE to connect to a shared network drive. Then he began to install OS/2 1.1 and then applications, but there weren't many. I asked where the printer was, and he laughed. I learned OS/2 didn't really print yet, and to do so I best use MS-DOS and those apps, which he then set up, also using some new magic like *mapping LPT1* to the nearby printer in the copy room.

Once my computer was set up, I still wasn't sure what to do with my day, but it was lunchtime. I was never really good at lunch or spontaneously meeting new people, so I began to get stressed. I finally resigned myself to passing on lunch and futzing in my office. Then I heard a knock on my door.

"Hi, my name is Andy Craze…AndrewCr."

We were both new, though Andy had started the week before, and we were both joining Apps. The team would soon move to Development Tools in my first of many re-orgs. As recent grads do, we exchanged where we were from, college, and major information. Andy was from Cleveland. Went to Stanford. Studied computer science. He was outgoing and suggested we get lunch.

What I didn't know, until Andy explained it, was that we weren't technically working at our actual jobs yet, or even sitting with our teams. Instead, we were in Apps Developer College. ADC was where new Apps SDEs learned how to be Apps SDEs. We would be there for an indeterminate amount of time while we learned the ropes—meaning learned the tools and techniques of the Apps division. If those few sentences sounded like a bunch of jargon, that's essentially what every conversation sounded like.

Unlike today's start-ups in Silicon Valley, lunch was not free but marginally subsidized by Microsoft and operated by an institutional food company. We went to the pizza station, and I ordered by the slice.

I sustained myself on pizza for a decade.

003. KLUNDER COLLEGE

ADC, Apps Developer College, was more a curriculum than a college, run by Dan Newell (DanN) and Doug Klunder (DougK.) It was called *Klunder College* because Doug created it. ADC was basically a couple of three-ring binders of assorted documentation and memos and a bunch of self-paced coding exercises that constituted a new and unique approach to on-boarding at Microsoft at a time when most everyone who programmed was self-taught. The idea of a programming orientation or bootcamp seemed unnecessary, perhaps even insulting. I would take away much more than I could really understand at such an early juncture in my career as I immersed myself in my first lessons in culture.

Most teaching was done during a meeting with Dan, and usually by stopping by or hovering at his office. Even though we had offices, there was a constant roaming of the hallways and stopping by unscheduled to see people. This, I would soon learn, was the Microsoft management and learning culture—self-sufficient, informal, and interrupt-driven (a specific computer term that became one of my first Microsoft-isms — "What's the best way to meet them? …Oh, they are interrupt-driven.") It was a big change from the structure of universities but also consistent with how most everyone there had learned PC programming in the early days.

DanN's office was filled with vinyl records, a stacked stereo system, and a few early '80s music posters. He was an experienced Microsoft SDE and was half the leadership of ADC. A few doors down was DougK. In contrast to Dan's office, Doug's office was completely spartan, as though he had only recently moved in. Doug looked like a member of the Doobie Brothers, with a long beard, flannel shirt, cords, and no shoes. He was exactly what my mother had warned me about.

Doug was a programming legend at Microsoft. After graduation from MIT, he joined Microsoft as the first college hire and subsequently an informal leader in the quest to hire directly from college, especially in Apps. He was one of the earliest Apps SDEs and had written much of the code in an early spreadsheet for MS-DOS that Microsoft released as Multiplan but called *Electronic Paper,* or EP, while under development.

Dan told me that BillG decided the company's future was on graphical user interface (GUI) like OS/2 and Macintosh so the company chose not to bring an updated MS-DOS (CUI, or character user interface) spreadsheet to market. Doug was so frustrated by this decision that he quit Microsoft and went off to work on a farm in California. Doug's innovative work was critical to Mac Excel 1.0, which ultimately shipped for the original Macintosh. Later, he returned to help finish Mac Excel 1.0 and contribute broadly to Apps in the transition to GUI. Doug was the ideal person to indoctrinate us into the ways of Microsoft Apps.

My first day had been a success, or at least not a failure.

After a few weeks of ADC, I finally received an email from ScottRa. He suggested we meet the next day *first thing*. "How about 11 a.m.?"

Microsoft SDEs bordered on nocturnal in those days. This was consistent with how college programmers coped with the scarcity of computers. It was always best to work late at night when fewer people were trying to get to terminals and, if on a shared mainframe, slowing it down. Everyone was working nights at the office back then. There was no way to even do email from home and certainly not any coding. The old Xenix email system made it easy to see if a person was logged on, and rumor was that BillG was always checking in on key people to see if they were connected. These were all traits of the original hacker ethos that had worried my mother.

When asked if Microsoft had "flex time" (an '80s buzzword) by prospective college hires, we always said, "Yes. You can choose to work whichever 80 hours of the week you want to work." That was, essentially, true for the '90s. Our views later matured as did the company, much to the chagrin of new old-timers like me. Mostly we were in our 20s and loved what we were doing.

Scott explained what was in store for me for the next few months. Before programming anything I needed to learn the unique dialect Microsoft used. While I knew the programming language, Microsoft had a unique style called *Hungarian,* named for Charles Simonyi (CharlesS), one of the rarified level 14 architects in the company and the only one in Apps. CharlesS was recruited by BillG from Xerox PARC where he had built the first GUI word processor. Hungarian was the secret handshake used between programmers at Microsoft and it was unlike anything I'd ever seen. In college programming or in books, one might use a name in code such as **FormatLine**. In Hungarian, we used names like **FFormatLineFspec**, which were chosen to make code more manageable for large teams.

I also needed to learn the tools used to build Excel and Word. There was a proprietary programming language called CSL, also named after CharlesS. This language, based on C, had a *virtual machine,* which made it easier to run on other operating systems (in theory) and also had a good debugger—attributes that were lacking in the relatively immature C product from Microsoft. I also learned RAID, the database tool that the product groups used to track bugs in products, complete with backronym of *Reporting and Incidents Database*. And, most importantly, I learned SLM, pronounced slime, the source code tracking tool, like today's GitHub. Through this I used shipping code and coded up features and fixed bugs as exercises, never checking them into production. It sounded pretty cool. It was pretty cool.

I loved talking with Doug. He was not like anyone I had spent a lot of time with—he was truly the hippie/hacker *Time Magazine* described in the *Machine of the Year* issue in 1982. As I got to know him, I learned of some of his relatively extreme perspectives. He was obsessed with privacy. He didn't have a driver's license, bank account, telephone, or anything, but still lived among us. I often saw him outside of work. We lived in the same Capitol Hill neighborhood, soon the heart of grunge music, where he always paid cash at one of the restaurants in the neighborhood. This dedication to privacy proved even more ironic, and prescient, as he went on to build Microsoft Money, which he used to track his cash transactions. In his post-Microsoft career, Doug became an attorney and, admirably, went on to work for the ACLU on issues such as privacy. He was ahead of his time.

Importantly, for my own future, Doug instilled in me a sense of principled product development. Throughout my time at ADC Doug shared his account of the decisions around building Mac Excel instead of a new MS-DOS spreadsheet, including a famous Red Lion Inn offsite where the strategic decision was made to bet on the graphical interface. BillG insisted on prioritizing GUI over CUI even with a potentially killer MS-DOS spreadsheet close to complete, causing DougK to ultimately quit out of principle. Doug's principled lessons followed me through my career.

Doug was an incredible programmer, the first of many amazing ones I met. He had a full map of an entire body of product code in his head and a deep understanding of the data structures and code paths—more than encyclopedic but organic as though his brain had merged with the code. In hindsight, I came to understand that great programmers have the same relationship to code and products as great writers to words and complete works, or filmmakers do to camera shots and complete films. Every line of code, every data structure, was not only deliberate but deeply related to the other choices one makes.

One issue we spent an enormous amount of time discussing was memory management, which was an acute problem in PCs those days—how to fit more information in less space. This was not simply about data but also the amount of code in an application—how to do more with less. Doug recounted how he had developed *minimal recalc* for Excel originally for the unreleased spreadsheet product, which was a way of only recalculating the cells in a spreadsheet that needed to be calculated when something changed. Previously every change in a spreadsheet recalculated the entire sheet, which was slow and memory intensive. It is difficult to overstate the brilliance in Doug's approaches. It would be equally fair to say that Doug wrote code only Doug could understand, very much how great products were built then.

Many of the conventions or techniques used in Apps were pioneered by Doug and *taught* or, more correctly, *transfused* to us in ADC. Even though software products were often late (very late), and quality was spotty (very spotty), that was only in hindsight. In general, Microsoft's Apps, particularly MS-DOS Word and Excel, were generally among the most robust and highest quality. DougK and DanN instilled several key lessons about being an Apps software design engineer:

- Scheduling and estimating work. Individuals needed to be really good at scheduling their own work and coming up with estimates that were not only precise to the day but accurate as well.
- Bulletproof code. Developers were responsible for building code beyond their features, including the code that ran in "debug mode" that was constantly checking the integrity of the data structures and ensuring that assumptions made by programmers were validated. During any code review in ADC, the code was sent back if it was not fully defined by what were called *debug ASSERTs,* or code that was run to verify the values of variables and integrity of data structures while running a special build of the product for this purpose.
- Self-documenting code. Schools taught that good code had comments or annotations that were not code but English that explained the code. Doug *hated* comments and insisted that code should be the ultimate comment itself. This was a bit ironic because he was known for developing some insanely efficient code that was also difficult to read and would have benefitted from comments. His view was that comments were always out of date and far less precise than the code itself. I really had to unlearn commenting, a practice I had embraced.
- Performance in speed and minimal memory. CPUs were slow and memory was extremely scarce, so there was a big focus on writing efficient code. This was rooted in BillG and was an important part of Microsoft's early developer culture and key contributor to success. Code written this way was *hardcore.*

During ADC, I built a memory allocator, code that handled requests from a program to provide memory to store data and later free memory. Early programs, especially written in C or CSL, were notorious for mismanaging memory, which caused program crashes and in turn crashed the entire computer along with it.

Doug had developed a set of ideas for building a bulletproof memory allocator, one that tracked allocations and reallocations and made sure memory was properly initialized before it was used in the code. These were super common bugs in PC software.

It was a huge learning experience. But I had also been working on modern, automatic memory allocation called *garbage collection* (GC) in graduate school. After a few days of hacking away on my memory allocator project for Doug, I worked up the guts to approach him and ask why Microsoft did not use GC.

It didn't go so well. Doug literally laughed at me. Still, after I persisted, he suggested I go meet Jon DeVaan (JonDe) on the Excel team who could go through every bug in Excel (it was up to version 2.x and ran on Windows) and explain how many came from bad memory management code. Doug knew that his memory allocator, also my programming exercise, was a significant barrier to creating memory allocation bugs in the first place. He wanted me to see for myself.

JonDe didn't laugh at me like Doug had, rather he listened then indulged me by going through 30 minutes of RAID searches looking at memory management bugs to see if GC fixed them. GC prevented perhaps eight of 7,500 in Excel. That made for a convincing argument that GC was not remotely worth the tradeoff in memory and performance. GC would eventually become standard practice on the web and on Apple's iPhone, but I was a decade too optimistic.

JonDe was among the best Microsoft had ever produced, in addition to being one of the best engineering managers to have ever worked at the company. We worked together for the remainder of my time at Microsoft, each with unique strengths, making each other better at what we did.

I spent an inordinate amount of time installing Microsoft products and using them. I developed my own method for using a network boot disk and getting a "clean" PC up and running. This skill seemed to be both a necessity and something each person reinvented on his or her own. PCs still barely worked.

One product I spent a lot of time on that was still under development, Windows 3.0, a year away from finishing but was already the buzz of the developers running it. At the time, the mainstream SDE machine was running OS/2 because it was able to use more memory and handle more programs gracefully, but it also had a lot of limitations, such as a lack of apps and the inability to print. There was always much cafeteria discussion about how lame OS/2 was, wondering what was going on over in Systems with our partnership with IBM.

Windows 2.x was already in market and had some early pioneers supporting it, including Ray Ozzie at Lotus, who had developed the innovative Notes product. The biggest supporter of Windows 2.x was Excel, which was also developing version 3 of Excel to be on both Windows and Mac (and OS/2) at the same time, using an innovative cross-platform layer of software.

Back then, buyers did not get a PC with Windows. PCs came with MS-DOS. Using Excel meant buying Excel, and it came with Windows. According to branding and packaging, Windows was an *operating environment,* or more like an *app* on top of MS-DOS. This became the subject of antitrust consternation years later. As innovative and successful as Excel was on the Mac, Excel on Windows was not competitive with the MS-DOS Lotus 1-2-3. Microsoft's older CP/M and later MS-DOS spreadsheet Multiplan was a distant number two.

Windows 3 was a bit of a skunkworks project and was a bet on a new architecture called *protected mode,* which enabled multiple programs to operate at the same time and share a larger amount of memory. In many ways this was also what OS/2 was supposed to do. OS/2 had much grander visions as well as a difficult engineering partner in IBM, or IBM might say it was Microsoft that was the difficult partner. Windows 3 was beginning to look more like an operating system and less like an add-on to MS-DOS. It was interesting to install and play around with, which all of us did. Actively under development were versions of Word and Excel and several other products. We spent the summer trying everything.

DanN shared with me what he was most excited about—one of the key "secrets" of Windows 3, which was how the product enabled protected mode but could also remain compatible with old MS-DOS programs. David Weise (DavidW) and Murray Sargent (MurrayS) had invented some novel uses of the Intel chipset that even Intel did not anticipate, which enabled these efforts. One programming trick called PrestoChangeoSelector was a key "hack" they developed and later became an absurd symbol of "secret" application programmable interfaces (APIs) in Windows. This was absurd because it was supposedly secret, when in fact it was right there to see. Dan told this story with great Microsoft pride, as the development of Windows 3 and these techniques represented much of what Microsoft did so well in those days. Hack.

I admired Dan. What Doug brought to ADC in insights for coding, Dan brought in big picture about how products were built and team dynamics. Dan knew everyone at the company and was definitely a cool kid. Because of Dan I got to meet quite a few of the senior people across both Apps and Systems. Systems was pretty OK to Apps people and vice versa, but there was clearly both an organizational and cultural divide between the two—a theme that I would experience for many years to come and also be the subject of many "battles."

A few months in, Scott came by and said he was anxious for me to join the team. My time in ADC was abbreviated so I could get cracking on our project. Unbeknownst to me, I was joining a newly formed "tiger team" created to build an entirely new product to streamline building applications.

Object-oriented, GUI, and Microsoft's next killer product (*killer* was Microsoft jargon), plus Scott told me our project was "super important to BillG."

004. EVERYTHING IS BUGGY

As the summer of 1989 turned to fall, the shipment of Windows 3.0 was looming. When not working on a Mac product or trying to get OS/2 stable for daily use, most of us in Apps were dealing with getting something to work on Windows and reporting bugs back to the Windows team.

Far away in Systems, Windows, what started as a side project was now a full team of people grinding away on a *death march* to get Windows 3.0 done. Typically, in those days, this period of heightened work hours and intense cycles of bug fixing marked the last months of any project. The cafeterias were not usually open for dinner ushering in a mostly Systems tradition of *ship meals*, featuring a buffet much fancier than the cafeteria offered. The idea of serving dinner as part of routine death marches became a decidedly Systems approach that was so formalized it became a budgeted line item as I would later learn when I joined Windows. Windows 3 was still months from shipping, but the activity was going on around the clock.

Windows was in Systems, which was the *big dog* half of Microsoft. While the history of the company was in Languages where BASIC and other tools were made, the center, and at the time the economic engine of the company, was Systems where MS-DOS was made. MS-DOS was the brilliant product born out of a commitment to IBM to deliver a product that didn't exist and wasn't yet under development. It was subsequently acquired and modified to meet the deadline, with the twist that Microsoft was free to license the product to other computer companies.

In other words, while IBM was the first contract for MS-DOS it was not exclusive.

Out of that, the entire PC industry was created. And not for one second was that lost on the Systems people.

From those early first days, Microsoft felt like two different companies: Apps and Systems. A buzzword in modern business, these two *cultures* could not have been more different, at least that's what I was led to believe by listening to stories at lunch. Even though the company was made up of only about 3,500 people, with half in Redmond, I had not yet met anyone in Systems. While I could have easily walked a few hundred feet over to one of the buildings they occupied, that wasn't something that people did. Apps and Systems didn't exactly intermingle.

The one thing we knew about Systems, despite the anonymity, was that as buggy and late as Apps products were, the Systems products, I was informed, were buggier and later. Windows 3.0 was coming down to the wire. There were no real secrets—many people had builds and were installing the product, and the weekly industry tabloids, *InfoWorld* and *PC Week*, were tracking the latest rumors, test releases, and gossip. The actual delivery date was not well known, not by the team or anyone else.

From the time I arrived at Microsoft and installed that first build in ADC in the summer, the launch of Windows 3.0 was always *real soon now,* often abbreviated RSN in snarky email. That had no impact at all on the enthusiasm as the buzz that Windows 3.0 would be a breakthrough was pervasive through the hallways. The industry was equally anxious for what appeared to be a showdown across a plethora of operating systems including MS-DOS, Windows, OS/2, and Macintosh.

In hindsight, it was easy to make fun of the fact that everything seemed late and hardly worked. The entire industry was like that. From the earliest days of PCs none of us knew anything else.

The expression *vaporware* was commonly used to refer to software that was well known and frequently discussed but not yet shipping. The phrase was used first as far back as 1983 by Esther Dyson in the industry thought-leading newsletter *Release 1.0*. In some sense, most everything was vapor. I remember sitting in my ADC office having just received a Goldman Sachs analyst report on Microsoft from the library. In the report was a table of all our company's products under development and estimated ship dates. The dates were far in the future and all wrong by many months or even years.

In fairness, it was challenging to simply get a non-trivial product built, have it work on the wide variety of PC configurations that existed, and then ship it in dozens of languages. That's because there was no internet, no diagnostics, or telemetry, and anything that went wrong simply crashed the whole computer, requiring a power cycle. And, most importantly, the field of software engineering was nascent to the point of not really having the institutional knowledge of building and testing software for mass distribution. Before the PC, there were many complex systems, but each one was custom and staffed by full-time people to keep it running. PCs were different. Everything was new. And that was before the complexity of coding for a graphical interface like Windows and Macintosh.

One of the biggest differences with PCs was that the PC operating system ran in such a way (called *real mode* compared to *protected mode* that would be introduced later in Windows and still later in Macintosh) that any bug in a program generally did one of two things, but probably both. First, for certain, whatever file was open and being edited probably became corrupt and data was lost. That was a heart-stopping given. Second, there was a good chance that the crashing program also caused the computer to crash, hang, or otherwise stop working. Thus, the cardinal rules of the early PC era were born: First, frequently save work and make backup copies, and second, if something goes wrong, reboot the machine.

I learned this firsthand too many times. In college when I operated computers in the lab, an entire shift could often be consumed by trying to help a classmate salvage the remains of a term paper off of a floppy after a crash. Those were the most horrific bugs because work was lost that people assumed they were saving. Such were early PCs, and Macs.

Because of this, it was extraordinarily super-human to even get programs working in the first place. By definition, a mistake in the code caused everything on the computer to stop working, including the tools being used to diagnose the bug. The best programmers, like Duane Campbell (DuaneC), ScottRa, and others, were able to figure out how to step through each instruction carefully and monitor whole blocks of memory for changes at the lower levels to figure out what was going on.

DuaneC was already a legendary programmer within the ranks, a *tech lead* as I would learn. He was a few years older but seemed more grown up simply because he was married and had a maturity level that most of us lacked. DuaneC had a slight Southern accent, having grown up in rural Tennessee, and a speaking tempo I was familiar with from the people I grew up with in Florida. He was a musician but also studied computer science at the

University of Tennessee. He was one of the earliest members of the MS-DOS Applications team and a key contributor to Word. He was also one of the kindest and most thoughtful leaders I had ever worked with.

The most difficult bugs were those that crossed from the application into the operating system. That meant it took knowledge of not only your own code, but also code in MS-DOS and probably code from a video or print driver as well. Lunchtime discussions often dove deep into the details of bugs and the techniques used to find the mistake, and almost always the mistake was one of a small number of common flaws, such as forgetting to check for null pointers or using uninitialized variables.

The tools and techniques that were being developed across the engineers at Microsoft to build software at scale and to make reliable products proved to be a competitive advantage. That was an important fact. It was state of the art. The 1990s saw an incredible advance in building software at scale. And no company did that better than Microsoft. Microsoft's ubiquity and scale did not allow for gloating or even acknowledging the progress, but it would have been deserved.

The world outside of Microsoft was different. Outside, the computing landscape was marked by a period of extreme heterogeneity. While IBM lorded over the PC, which dominated business, Compaq and Dell were becoming leaders in making PC clones and even racing ahead of IBM in areas like portables and using the new Intel chips. Apple Macintosh was not viewed as a viable alternative in business but captured the hearts and minds of students, educators, and creatives. While Microsoft was busy making MS-DOS and Windows 3.0, and was already shipping Windows 2 with Excel, it was also deep in a partnership with IBM to develop OS/2, a much more sophisticated and reliable (protected mode) operating system. From the outside, Microsoft looked confused or at least lacking a clear strategy. Caught in the middle were companies trying to bring software products to market. Which operating system would they come to rely on for their products? Some viewed the duality of Windows versus OS/2 as an elaborate scheme by Microsoft to distract potential future competitors. The age-old conspiracy theory, which lacked any foundation other than IBM's poor execution, was that this was some sort of head-fake to distract developers with OS/2 while Microsoft could dominate Windows apps. The partnership with IBM was the highest priority, but it wasn't working out well.

The ever-present industry trade magazines seemed not to miss a beat over the rift between Microsoft and IBM. The raging debate over the cost and benefits of moving to a 32-bit operating system, specifically OS/2, was front and center even though OS/2 for 16-bits had not taken off at all. This put Windows 3.0 at a perception disadvantage as it was a 16-bit operating system that could take advantage of 32-bit Intel processors. The industry disliked this lack of purity but loved the complexity of the debate. Something I learned early is just how much the PC era was marked by bringing complexity front-and-center to debates that had little to do with customers but served to keep analysts and pundits busy. Our job was to hide complexity, but it seemed others were constantly surfacing it. Though to be fair we did our share of talking complexity, not usually passing up a chance to demonstrate our nerd credentials.

More importantly for customers, there was the constant coverage of quality problems with software and hardware. If programs were not slow, they took too much memory, or hard drive space. At the same time, every week seemed to bring more news of faster processors hoping to finally make yesterday's software fast enough to use. Except we were busy building more software, requiring even faster processors and more memory. We were under constant pressure to build software that ran on PCs customer had while also taking advantage of the latest processor and hardware. In hindsight, what saved us all was that at any given time the installed base of PCs, existing PCs in use, was being dwarfed by the run rate of new PCs sold to new customers or to replace older slower PCs. The velocity of this dynamic was key to our ability to constantly ship software that outstripped the PCs people already owned.

The industry saying was something along the lines of "what Intel gives, Microsoft takes away" in reference to increasing hardware capabilities constantly outstripped by more demanding software.

The early and successful Microsoft strategy of developing applications that ran on multiple platforms, remained the cornerstone of the Apps strategy. Only now Apps was busy enough just developing for Microsoft's own platforms consisting of the mature MS-DOS where Apps never gained a lead, the nascent Windows that few were buying (yet), the non-existent, mostly non-functional but strategically critical OS/2, and the monster money-maker Macintosh that was competing with all of those. As crazy as the strategy (or lack thereof) seemed to the press and Wall Street, it was even more taxing for us developers in Apps.

Cross-platform development was not only impractical but the answer to a question no single customer had on their own. Yet that did not stop the search for a magical solution, and thus my first real programming work. Microsoft, BillG in particular, always believed there was a software solution to any problem if enough "IQ" was applied. BillG used IQ as an expression of currency, such as "how much IQ is in that group" or "he brings a lot of IQ to the problem". This optimism and faith in IQ was a gift to Microsoft, but also caused a lot of problems because not every problem required a high IQ solution and those with high IQ could not always apply it in a practical manner.

Finding such a magical solution was my first project and the first project of our new team.

005. KEEPING BUSY WITH CROSS-PLATFORM OOP

As part of the Apps Tools group, we were set up to provide the tools to make it easy to build apps that worked on any platform, regardless of the differences or details of each platform. Isolating app developers from platforms was our job. The industry called this *cross-platform development.*

Historically, such an approach was at the core of Microsoft from the beginning, simply because computing had always been heterogeneous. The makers of computer hardware customized the operating system, which in turn meant that apps needed to be modified to run on each different computer system. This was not any sort of evil plot, as some believed, but simply something that was in place because the *hard* part of making a computer system was the hardware. Hardware engineers, naturally, chose to modify the software if it meant making the hardware easy. In Microsoft's earliest days, PaulA and BillG made the BASIC language for many different computers. Microsoft early apps, like the Multiplan spreadsheet, ran on many different personal computer systems at the time, a variety of 8-bit microprocessors and operating systems. Developers like JonDe and DuaneC were experts in the underlying technologies used to get Microsoft apps running on systems from DEC, Tandy, Zenith, Data General, and a host of other names from a bygone era, as well as IBM and then Hewlett-Packard, Compaq, and Dell. PCode and the virtual machine that DougK talked so poetically about in my summer training were in part about making it easier to run software on multiple platforms.

It was natural, therefore, that with Microsoft looking to grow the graphical interface apps business while also itself building multiple operating systems, there was a need for cross-platform tools that were more sophisticated than the 8-bit character mode tools that were already in place. Microsoft needed cross-platform tools just to be able to develop its own applications for its own operating systems. Let that sink in. It was common practice in the industry at the time for every major independent software vendor to also develop their own cross-platform toolset, designed to optimize for their own app and their own view of the platform landscape. Microsoft was unique in creating its own need for cross-platform tools, with multiple operating systems and its own applications.

Cross-platform product development was the elusive brass ring of development that accompanied each generation when there was no clear platform winner. From mainframes to minis to the increasingly popular Unix variants to microcomputers, and now the rising graphical interface. Each new platform promised to be the one to end all platforms, and it might have been, until the cycle repeated. Cross-platform tools are one of those developer problems that everyone believes they have an answer to, certainly early in software lifecycle.

This did not stop even Microsoft from getting caught up in building cross-platform tools. As platforms and applications mature, cross-platform becomes increasingly difficult and the customer experience decreasingly good. Microsoft was still in the early days of cross-platform, so it was looking workable. Given the early success with BASIC and 8-bit character mode, it was no surprise that BillG thought the next generation of such work was *trivial,* a term he loved to toss around. The difficulty—the lack of a trivial solution—was that more and more work was shifting to operating systems away from apps. In other words, as Microsoft (with IBM, and Apple) invested more into making the operating system feature-rich, it made building cross-platform applications more difficult. In fact, that was the strategy, even if it pertained to its own operating system products.

Still, the industry believed the key to making cross-platform trivial was a programming technique, one that wasn't too new dating back to the 1970s Xerox Palo Alto Research Center (PARC), called *object-oriented programming*, or OOP, sounds like *oops*. OOP was everywhere. A trip to the Tower Books on NE 8th Street in Bellevue, something I routinely did on Friday nights because it featured a necessarily deep section of programming and technology books, yielded new books every week with *OO* in the title. OOP promised to make programming an *order of magnitude* easier, which was another common phrase, meaning 10 times better or more, but with no specific units or ability to measure.

OOP was also deep in my own bones. My lab in graduate school was the *Object-oriented Systems Lab*. We spent the better part of a year recreating the original OOP platform from Xerox PARC, Smalltalk-80, so we could build our own OOP projects using that as a foundation. It is where I came to believe garbage collection was an important part of OOP. I came to Microsoft already an OOP zealot, which in part was why I was hired I was later told.

Aside from abstract computer science concepts, a new innovation for OOP was a new programming language pioneered at AT&T Labs, which, despite the breakup 10 years earlier, was still functioning and a leader in many fields of research, still winning prizes and medals. C++ was the OOP version of the widely used and taught C programming language. That meant it held the promise of not only making programming an order of magnitude easier, but also through its OOP techniques making it possible to be cross-platform, all while maintaining compatibility with the industry standard C language, the language used across Microsoft at the time. OOP as expressed in C++ would make not just cross-platform programming easier but make all programming easier.

Imagine that? No, really. *Imagine that*, because that's all that could be done at the time, or ever.

The buzz around OOP reached epic, or comical, proportions even making its way into mainstream business press. The cover of BusinessWeek magazine featured a baby in diapers at a keyboard and monitor introducing OOP to readers as "a way to make computers a lot easier to use." It was no longer just a magical tool that would make cross-platform programming trivial or a technology that computer scientists believed would lead to more robust and maintainable code. OOP was even going to make resulting applications easier to use.

Object-oriented programming and C++ represented my introduction to the hype cycle of the technology industry. In experiencing this now, I was fortunate in two ways. First, I was still early in career, so I was more mystified than cynical. Second, I was surrounded by already seasoned managers focused on "shipping" who helped our group to navigate the St. Elmo's fire of OOP.

The industry would undergo a tectonic shift over a multiyear journey to demonstrate the utility of OOP when it comes to mass market software, especially for GUI platforms. Today, most anyone can build GUI applications, but early on the complexity made that extremely difficult. While we could not make it possible for an infant in diapers to program, we could make it much easier for the typical professional or college student. The degree to which OOP or other developments contributed to making it easier will always be the subject of debate, as programming tools and languages always seem to be. There is no doubt, however, that OOP is deeply rooted in the evolution of the graphical user interface, going all the way back to Xerox and forward to today's smartphones.

Making progress in my new job, however, had one big problem: There was no C++ for the PC. In fact, there was barely C++ at all as it was primarily a research project at AT&T. The only tools around took C++ code and transformed it into C to then be compiled by a C compiler. Normally, one thinks of programming as typing in one language and then converting that into the raw numeric code for the PC, straight from English-like to binary numbers. C++ was so new that using it was akin to translating to German by going from English to French to German. C++ was first translated into C that Windows tools could understand, then finally translated into binary.

Like every other Microsoft project, we were already late and behind schedule though I didn't realize it or even really internalize it. But how could I have? I had no idea what product we were supposed to be building. All I knew was we were supposed to be working on cross-platform GUI and that meant OOP and C++. We did not, however, even have the software development tools to use the C++ language. There was a team in Languages working on a compiler, but first they were busy releasing the latest version of C, which was late and buggy and did not include C++ support.

ScottRa cleverly decided that we needed to keep busy. I was too young and naïve to really understand how deliberate this strategy was as Scott was essentially stalling while the company figured out larger strategic issues, such as Windows versus OS/2 versus Macintosh, and while the Languages group finished up C and could move full time to C++ tools.

Were we soldiers, doing battle and training, or were we the TVA just digging ditches to keep busy? I had no idea. Nevertheless, ScottRa devised a simple master plan. We learned the ropes of getting C++ code to work by being pioneers within Apps and using a crazy library of C++ code from researchers in Switzerland, ET++, and a commercial product Glockenspiel C++. The latter was a port of the AT&T C++ tools to OS/2 designed to work with Microsoft's industry-leading C compiler, C version 5.1, that was already in market. ET++ was something called an *application framework*, not unlike parts of Smalltalk-80 with which I was very familiar—a framework was a collection of prewritten *objects* or code that helped programmers to write applications quickly because they could reuse previously written code. ET++ too was cross-platform, but it was just a research project at a university. ET++ was presented at a paper that came out when I was in graduate school and compared itself to MacApp, an application framework for the Macintosh that I was also quite familiar with from my MacMendeleev days. It was a given that we would someday build our own application framework. ScottRa told me it was just too soon.

That meant, however, at least there was a project. We spent our days trying to get ET++ to work on OS/2, which basically no one else on earth was even thinking about. Days turned into weeks, and months.

I was glad to have a project to work on. Like so many new hires into big companies, though, I struggled to figure out how what I was doing fit into the big picture. Actually, I wasn't quite sure of the big picture just yet.

006. ZERO DEFECTS

When it came time to write my first performance review, it simply read "attended ADC" and looking forward my only goal was to "make ET++ work."

Still, I was nervous about writing mine. So, I shot off an email to Melissa Birch (MelissaB) asking for some tips. She was on the Word team, which was in the very final stages of shipping the original version of Word for Windows 1.0, code name Opus and another long and late project. She graduated from Brown University in 1987, the same year I graduated Cornell. Melissa was tall, polite, and formal. We shared the East Coast rhythm and sensibilities. MelissaB was an astute engineer, tuned into the challenges of making projects work. I knew she could help.

Thanks to fellow Apps Tools developer Kirk Glerum (KirkG), I'd made my way through the gauntlet of a seemingly cliquey lunchroom of regular tables, seated at a table with MelissaB, KirkG, DuaneC, Jodi Green (JodiG), and many others on the Word dev team.

Kirk was a hacker's hacker. He spelled his name Glærum (which wasn't spelled that way by the facilities name-changers and was quite a trick to type on US English keyboards in MS-DOS) in reference to his family's Nordic heritage. KirkG was as Northwest as one could get. He grew up in Oregon. He attended the University of Washington and was a die-hard Husky fan right down to his purple Converse sneakers. When meeting coworkers, where someone went to college was often the first fact Softies revealed since so many of us were straight from college. Most interesting was how he ordered a sandwich at the cafeteria. When asked what he would like, he always said, "Surprise me." I could never have ordered like that. I later learned his business card listed his title as "Software Alchemist"—back then you could make up your job title and mine said "Computer Scientist" since I was convinced I would eventually go back to graduate school.

A New Yorker, JodiG joined Microsoft early on. It was immediately apparent that she was a manager because at lunch she was always asking other members of the team about their bugs and progress. She was another graduate of Brown. It was common for graduates of the same school to find each other at Microsoft, even if they weren't classmates, because alma mater recruiting was something developers did, mostly because they knew the department, classes, and professors. I would soon be making recruiting trips to Cornell.

To help me with my review, MelissaB, over lunch, talked about the new mantra at Microsoft called *Zero Defects*. We would continue this discussion over a long email thread, as was all too common.

Zero Defects was a memo that was circulated by the leading development managers (the most senior engineering managers) in Apps and Languages. It was an effort to attempt to get a handle on product death marches and ever-increasing bug counts that were contributing to a broadening view of inevitability as products became more complex.

The underlying argument put forth was that we were rewarding developers for checking in new code and declaring a feature done, even if it was not. Testers then found a lot of basic bugs. That meant they were preventing more interesting testing from taking place and that more code to fix those bugs was quickly written, delaying the new work, and testers would continue find even more bugs.

In any software project, adding or changing code had a good chance of introducing a bug approximately 10 percent of the time (a number floating around in academic circles for decades), whether it was fixing one line of code or adding whole new capabilities. The cycle of trying to complete a feature by finding bugs could never really end—this was called *infinite bugs* and was plaguing the development of Omega, Microsoft's first Windows database, and to some degree Opus Microsoft's first Windows word processor, which began in 1984 but did not RTM until 1989.

RTM, *release to manufacturing,* was a phrase heard constantly. Everything was about getting to RTM. RTM was the ultimate goal. RTM was shipping. For the first decade or so of Microsoft, RTM literally meant to a factory, a Canyon Park facility about 10 miles north of Redmond where there was a shrink-wrap assembly line of boxes, manuals, and floppy disks. At the end of every product, at RTM, teams took a trip to Canyon Park and watched the first boxes roll off the line. We might have made software, but we shipped it in boxes to retail stores.

The specification for Opus from BillG famously was "build the best word processor ever" and finish by October 1985, to align with the release of Windows. This was likely the first edict for Apps to align with a Systems schedule, a topic that emerged again and again. It was also as likely as two golf balls colliding mid-air.

Zero Defects was probably one of the most profound engineering documents I had ever read, and yet it was also common sense and blindingly simple. I remember one sentence well: "The hardest part is to decide that you want to write perfect code." This was an impactful memo, in part because it was my first exposure to the collision between the idealized world of hacking and the pragmatic world of engineering products for millions. It was so practical and made so much sense, yet it was such a dramatic change from the hacker ethos that the most and fastest coding *wins.*

It might sound over the top to call a single memo that is literally about how to code without bugs as something "profound." Certainly, for me it was profound because it was the first business memo I read that was also about why we are doing what we are doing, not just how. In a broader context, however, the memo was about the novel enterprise that was Microsoft at the time. Apps was building software for millions of people that were not trained computing professionals. That was new, for everyone. This memo was a realization that the company was at a crossroads and the old way—the way of hackers and hobbyists—was no longer acceptable.

This memo also marked a change in the entire Apps division, now numbering hundreds of people. With two big projects that were late *and* buggy, Omega and Opus, and several other challenging projects such as the recall of Macintosh Word for quality issues, Apps needed to do something different. No other company was building software at scale across so many categories and so many platforms as Microsoft Apps was doing. While all this was going on, Excel version 3.0, for both Windows and Macintosh, was under development and would soon ship merely 11 days late and with rock solid quality—a feat that would not be bested for a decade or more.

From my vantage point, *Zero Defects*, marked the start of Apps culture of shipping. A culture that included an organization structure to scale development teams, a process to plan and schedule products, techniques to maintain engineering throughput, along with methods for ascertaining quality through the entire development schedule. Excel 3.0 would be proof that projects could be on time and have superb quality. Apps would iterate and hone this process for years to come, but it is neat to have a sense for when it all began.

That is somewhat hindsight. The memo would have been more profound to me if I ever experienced a death march or worked on a large and complex shipping code base. I had no experience shipping a product, so what did I know? As MelissaB shared her perspective with me, I came to understand what *ZD* as we called it really meant. There was no system-wide integrity (in an engineering sense) and that the wrong people were writing too much code. Some developers wrote a lot of code to make it look like a feature worked, even if all the boundary conditions weren't handled or if the code was *fat*. "Fat" a Microsoft expression for verbose code that took too much memory or was too slow—a reminder that PaulA's and BillG's original Microsoft BASIC fit in four kilobytes of memory, or about two pages of this book. Worse, those developers received high praise for getting "so much done." System-wide, the schedule was used not as a tool to get work done but more as a system to stretch goals without reflecting the complexity and interdependence of the work of the team.

Something MelissaB said to me during one of our lunches and many emails on the subject resonated for decades and proved to be a cornerstone, not only for me but for how the entire Apps division (and later Office then Windows) operated. Her reading of *Zero Defects* and her own observation was that everyone should be focused on clearly communicating what work they did and be measured by achieving that. No games. No stretch goals. No race to check off things that were not yet done. No doing the minimal work to make a feature demonstrable. Later, we came to call this *promise and deliver.*

Melissa also connected some dots for me and explained that the way groups were rewarding people who ultimately contributed more bugs than code was in practice rewarding some men and penalizing some women on the team. Teams that were small had few women. There was no hiding that fact. Melissa's view was that the women were routinely delivering the code they said they would, when they said they would, and at the same time getting feedback about the need to do *more*. As potentially controversial as such a statement was, it was simple to demonstrate by looking through the schedules and at the RAID database. While Microsoft was just starting to appreciate how different developers worked, Melissa's explanation of ZD in the context of specific people and their approaches to work (and rewards) made everything far more concrete. The specifics Melissa shared became a rallying cry for me later in my career as a manager and I would often share what she taught me.

Underlying this memo was the beginning of the idea of continuous quality. Every day the product should be shippable and of high quality. Work that was not yet completed was not part of the *checked in* (completed) code, but that code was kept in sync with the main product. This is something analogous to today's *continuous integration and continuous delivery,* and it took decades for Microsoft to achieve this level of engineering, which began in a moment of crisis and self-reflection. Although this seems obvious today, software projects were not typically run in this fashion, certainly not PC software.

That's the long way of explaining that MelissaB's answer for my performance review question was to "make sure you put in that you will practice *Zero Defects* in everything you do." That was a bit cynical, but it worked for us, and everyone. Those were performance reviews circa 1989.

With those goals in hand, we spent the fall of 1989 and winter of 1990 hacking away at ET++ and making it work on OS/2 and Windows. Little sample programs, like a calculator, worked. Along the way we found a lot of bugs in the new version of the Microsoft C compiler. And we continued to test out the programs we created on Windows 3.0.

In many ways, those early months were a second ADC or an ADC *practicum*. The opportunity to be on the ground floor of a new computer language was great, and the added challenge of trying to make it work on a bunch of operating systems that didn't work only added to the fun and, also, the frustration. I guess I had not really considered that my job might be frustrating. It had not yet occurred to me how truly *messy* the company was.

Nevertheless, experiencing this while waiting for other groups to finish so we could collaborate seemed better than any alternative. Once performance reviews were complete and thinking about all my friends *shipping* Windows 3.0, Word 1.0, and Excel 3.0, left little doubt my project was busy work, and it was dragging on.

007. WINDOWS 3.0 BUZZ

With spring 1990 approaching, the buzz for Windows 3.0 was becoming deafening within the halls of Microsoft. One of the most exciting things was seeing the visual appearance of the product. Windows 1.0 and 2.0 were, to put it kindly, garish, or at best excessively blocky and utilitarian. Much of this was out of necessity as computer monitors only displayed about the equivalent number of pixels of one app icon on today's iPhone and only had access to 16 colors or no colors at all. Windows 3.0 also added overlapping windows like on Macintosh which made a huge difference in how the product felt.

Windows 3.0 was the first integrated release of Windows, meaning sold along with MS-DOS on a new PC. The notion that Windows was an "operating environment" added on to MS-DOS was giving way to Windows the *operating system*. While seemingly arcane technical jargon, the change in vocabulary was also a change in how the product was sold to computer makers and how software developers should think about Windows. Windows coming with a new PC meant it was no longer a question developers would need to ponder when deciding how to write software. The landscape was changing from IBM-compatible PCs to Windows-compatible PCs. This was huge.

To emphasize this point, the company scheduled a major (for Microsoft) press event in New York in May 1990. What was months earlier a side project was now front and center for the whole industry. While Microsoft had previously held launch events at trade shows, this was one of the earliest examples (and certainly the most expensive) of a major event for a single Microsoft product.

This event was going to be monumental for the entire company, except perhaps for the people working on OS/2. We were all using OS/2 every day as a main development machine, and many people were working hard but struggling to get Word and Excel working on it. But it was also viewed with a good deal of skepticism internally. Much of this was because of the stories that made their way over to Apps from Systems about working with IBM and the disconnect between engineering cultures, but also our own experience in the poor quality and difficulty in using the product.

There were many stories of IBM's *dysfunction* that were common knowledge. IBM used to measure their programmers on lines of code produced; more lines meant higher productivity. Except Microsoft believed fewer lines of code to create the same feature was better. IBM thought Microsoft engineers were less productive while Microsoft thought IBM engineers produced bloated code. Microsoft was young and confident. IBM was…experienced.

While IBM was a few decades into writing software, their experience was rooted in making highly custom and highly reliable mainframe software, over very long periods of time. The reality was Microsoft was at peak productivity for new lines of code being written for PCs, but we were still very early in figuring out a reproducible process for releasing products and of course we continued to have quality problems and scheduling missteps. BillG even noted our challenges in releasing software on time as he walked on stage at the event, saying that today Microsoft is announcing the completion of Windows 3.0 and had the product not been done hosting such a big event would have been a bit of an "extravagant way to announce a delay in the schedule."

The deep tension between Microsoft and IBM was hardly visible to us and, frankly, the industry was geared toward a world with many competing computing platforms. Nearly every article about Windows viewed the product as a steppingstone to the more modern OS/2 that would shed its connection to 8-bit MS-DOS. No one was anticipating Windows 3.0 becoming a *de facto* standard, certainly no one at our daily lunch table. We increasingly knew Windows 3.0 was an exciting product, but we also knew that Microsoft had committed to a joint development project with IBM, a company perhaps 100 times the size of Microsoft. None of us really had a clue just how tense the relationship between Microsoft and IBM was becoming while we continued to find ways to absorb the complexities of OS/2, Macintosh, and now Windows 3.0.

Along with Windows 3.0, Microsoft demonstrated a new release of Excel for Windows, Excel 3.0, an updated Word version 1.1, and the first version of PowerPoint for Windows version 2.0. The PC software industry was a version number machine—literally everything was a 1.0 or a 5.0, or debating whether a product was a .1 or a .5. It was the source of marketing games such as "big upgrade in version 2.1" and notorious for cynicism such as "avoid a 1.0" or "wait for the 'a' release." Microsoft was a varsity player in this world of confusing version numbers (and product names), and we were just getting started.

Those updates were just the software from Microsoft. The platform marketing team, which in the software industry had become known as *evangelism*, a term pioneered by Apple, had successfully wooed hundreds of independent software vendors to show off their latest products on Windows. The Windows 3.0 event included mentions of many of the biggest names of the day including Corel, Aldus, Iris (makers of what would eventually become Lotus Notes), and Crosstalk. Noticeably absent with Windows products were WordPerfect, Ashton-Tate, and Lotus, the leading applications for MS-DOS. Lotus announced it would support Windows, which was viewed as a big win at the time, but the product would not arrive for some time.

Also, at the ready were hundreds of hardware companies ready to deliver a range of fully compatible computer systems, components, and peripherals. While often overlooked, the ability to have hardware and the required software to make printers, displays, and a host of accessories work with Windows was an achievement equal in magnitude to applications.

Windows 3.0 seemed to have everything that OS/2 did not. There were compatible PCs. There were new applications. There were supporting peripherals. It had the pricing and distribution too. The fact that it ran on as little as one megabyte of memory (though really two was better) and also ran all existing MS-DOS applications even better than they ran before made for an incredibly compelling launch.

Windows 3.0 represented a step-function change in the PC. The clunky world of obscure commands and text-based screens would give way to colorful overlapping windows and a mouse, something that Macintosh had for the past five years. While the PC was catching up in capabilities it was still outselling Macintosh by more than fifteen to one. What the PC lacked in ease of use and elegance, it more than made up for in lower cost hardware, a much broader base of support from software makers, and a wide array of peripherals.

The launch event was satellite broadcast to conference rooms around campus. For most of us, the idea of seeing Microsoft on a video stream like this was kind of crazy. While certainly the company was one of the biggest and brightest stars around, the world of technology and software was still a relative blip in the economy. Bill Gates was hardly a household name. About 15 percent of US households owned a personal computer in 1989, and worldwide about 17 million PC compatibles were sold. The year 1989 was the first time more than one million Macintosh computers were sold—the Macintosh always had an outsized influence. It's worth noting that Word and Excel were selling to most of those Macintoshes, which was not the case for Microsoft apps on PC compatibles.

The trade press, which we devoured every week in tabloid sized print magazines at the library. Senior executives were permitted to have their own subscriptions, but regular folks had to make their way to the library, covered every development of Windows and OS/2 as though both operating systems were inevitable.

Since we knew the Systems teams were hard at work at both, we had no other source of information to counter the narrative in the trade press. It is interesting to consider how much we were influenced by what we read in trade press when there was little else for us to go on. Little did we know that BillG, and the executive teams, were deep in an enormously complex "divorce." The company was on the verge of moving away from a partnership with IBM and would go it alone with Windows. This would not happen quickly.

In fact, in the months leading up to the launch event, Microsoft and IBM famously issued a joint communication emphasizing that long term their collective efforts are squarely on OS/2 and urged independent developers to follow. When we read about this in the trade press it seemed exactly like what we were doing as Microsoft followed this advice too. Many of my friends were working super hard on OS/2 versions of Word and Excel. We were working hard to make ET++ work on OS/2 as well. At the same time, making applications work for Windows was ongoing, and going very well. The work on OS/2 was definitely not fake as many would say in the years to come, but it also wasn't progressing. Everything was confusing and messy to those of us just doing our jobs.

Windows launched in May 1990 and sold four million copies in the first year. That was all the market proof the company needed to know that Windows was the future. The complex partnership yielding a complex OS/2 product was also looking less and less strategic. The fact that progress on the product was slow and the rapid sales of Windows were attracting all the interest of third-party developers, made the positives of OS/2 mostly theoretical. Who needs a better file system if all the interesting applications are on Windows?

In hindsight, that day in May was somewhat surreal. I had not yet even started to internalize the scale of Microsoft or its potential. To me things still seemed so approachable. The Microsoft I knew was not much larger than my high school and I felt like I knew all the people in Apps.

A few weeks after Windows 3.0 launched, Microsoft closed the books on fiscal year 1990. It would be the first year the company would report sales over one billion dollars, $1.18 billion to be precise. That was almost double the revenue of either Lotus of WordPerfect, the two largest software companies. Microsoft became the first pure play PC software company with more than one billion dollars in sales.

The inevitability of Windows was starting to sink in over the summer. BillG always used to tell the interns, and by now we had perhaps 100 that summer, that he worried Seattle summers were so nice that people would not work. In fact, there was an incredible amount of energy that summer, but we were in desperate need of strategic clarification. I needed it for my own job, the company needed it too. The industry, it seems, had already decided.

As far as reviews of the product, *BYTE* magazine concluded "on both technical and strategic grounds, Windows 3.0 succeeds brilliantly. After years of twists and turns, Microsoft has finally nailed this product. Try it. You'll like it." Still, the technology enthusiasts were fretting about OS/2.

There was definitely a feeling that we were at some sort of new beginning with Windows 3.0, and at the end of the first era of the personal computer.

1990-1992

The big bet on Windows begins to pay off, but Microsoft struggles to win over developers who were enamored with object-oriented programming and C++ to build GUI programs more easily. Within Microsoft, differing cultures emerge between groups, and eventually define the company.

008. COMPETING WITH STEVE JOBS (THE FIRST TIME)

Microsoft was starting to lose its edge, even with Windows taking off.

The company got its start with languages and developer tools, but by the early 1990s tech enthusiasts and hobbyists were moving away from BASIC toward more advanced or professional languages and tools. Developers were being wooed by an exciting upstart, Borland International. Led by an energetic Frenchman, Philippe Kahn, Borland captured the hearts and minds of enthusiasts with a line of TurboTools that integrated a compiler, code editor, and debugger into one slick package. It was fast, really fast—fast the way that got under the skin of BillG. With support for both Pascal and C, and priced favorably, the products and the company became a favorite among independent developers. It also didn't hurt that Borland expanded its product base to include a killer spreadsheet in Quattro Pro (get it, it came after Lotus 1-2-3) and Paradox, an industrial-strength database for MS-DOS.

Microsoft secured the professional end, particularly with Microsoft C 5.1, the product we were using for our ET++ experiments. The successor product, Microsoft C 6, re-upped the professional standard but was late (as everything was) and lacked the pizzazz of Borland. Microsoft responded to Borland with Quick C, a similarly integrated all-in-one product for MS-. With C 6 a Windows version was added. Quick C was viewed as a defensive move. It was. We were focused on the high-end commercial developers, not the hobbyists or solo developers.

Being squeezed from the low end was one thing, but the high end was becoming problematic for Microsoft. Not only was the C 6 product late, but it was C and neither C++ nor object-oriented. This challenged Microsoft's perceived leadership. In addition, Borland's products performed better than the anticipated C 6. Internally, the teams, particularly Excel, began testing whether they could move to the Borland tools. This was especially noteworthy because it was coupled with a move away from Microsoft's proprietary C-like language CSL.

As if this wasn't enough, the growing importance of the graphical user interface would soon require a wholesale reinvention of tooling. Microsoft was way behind. Windows was our platform, but we lacked convincing and competitive tools. Squarely between Windows and OS/2, the Tools teams all but sat out developing new tools for GUI programming and focused simply on the programming language. The additional tools for developing the interface of menus and dialogs, as well as the complexities of making a GUI program, were left to the respective platform teams. These teams shipped tools in a software development kit (SDK), which was complete but not as polished a product as Borland sold.

This was my first experience with *disruption*, though that word was years away from business vocabulary. In 1990, we just called it competition. And losing.

While our marketing team talked all about revenue and market share, like any good business, in reality Tools was not really a business. An important lesson about Tools and platforms that I was learning in real-time was that a robust platform company invests (that is spends money on) Tools at an irrational level to support the platform. The reason Borland could have a Tools business was because it was spending much less than Microsoft, and so could be profitable. Microsoft was spending more money and making a worse product. In other words, I was part of an irrational investment that wasn't paying off. We were a poor business, and we were failing at building tools professionals wanted to use. Losing control of the Tools was akin to losing control of the platform.

Apple invested heavily in tools for the Macintosh, just like a winning platform should. There was also a vibrant market for many different languages and tools for creating apps for the unique graphical platform. This was well known within Microsoft because so many of the Apps engineers got their start writing Mac software in college, including me. There was always a sense of envy regarding the elegance of building GUI applications with a GUI toolset on Macintosh—*bootstrapping* was when programming tools created themselves. Historically, programmers viewed bootstrapping as an important, if mostly symbolic, step in developing a platform. Microsoft was far from bootstrapped, as it was still using Xenix and OS/2 to develop for MS-DOS and Windows. Worse, most developers at Microsoft thought this was a superior way to build software. All that marketing we were doing explaining that a GUI was easier to use had the effect of telling programmers that GUI was how lesser programmers worked. Worse, that is what our own marketing team was telling us about our own customers.

Besides, even with those great tools and a lead of several years, Apple was still far behind in PC sales. Steve Jobs was no longer at Apple and his new company, NeXT, was top of mind for BillG and the industry. As successful as Windows was for Microsoft, there was a strong belief that no single system would dominate. NeXT was new. NeXT was led by Steve Jobs. And most of all, the product was clearly innovative and setting the bar by which BillG would judge our product and technology.

Microsoft had to do something, something about Borland and NeXT.

Moving offices at Microsoft was a constant. It was time for our first move, to new buildings that were even bigger than the big double-X layouts. These were the new buildings for Apps: 16, 17, and 18. Rather than low slung grey these new buildings were 3 stories of glass and brick and featured their own courtyard and fountain, which would be the site of our future ship parties. The buildings had huge atriums of open space and skylights while still maintaining the sacred 9x12 foot single office with a door. The three buildings were connected by an enclosed tube system that looked like a Habitrail. The uniqueness of these tubes meant that they were frequently used for photo shoots and videos.

The night before a move (my first of a dozen I would experience), MSMOVE dropped off a stack of boxes, a roll of tape, and a move form. A paper form was used to draw placement of the huge oak desk, return, guest chair, and developer-issued folding table. The movers showed up at the end of the day, unplugged phones and computers, and put everything on carts and trucked them to the new office. Unpacking could happen 12 hours later. The MSPHONE person eventually showed up to make sure the newly hooked up phone worked with your assigned number.

This was going on every night in every building at Microsoft. It was like a giant nine-square puzzle, where at any given time an entire group existed in the moving trucks in the parking lot because there was never enough space for everyone, even with the new buildings.

My new office was right around the corner from a connecting tube and for the first few months I could hear the door slamming every time someone entered the tube. There was a design defect that turned the tube into a wind tunnel, making the door difficult to open while also forcefully closing it with high-speed wind. Eventually some vents were added solving this problem.

As with every hallway of developers, there was a deep sense of personalization that came with the private office space we were each allotted. Since most people were not yet grown-ups, there were no family photos, or traditional memorabilia. Rather, offices were filled with some form of personal collection representing youth. I saw a collection of vintage car license plates, a wall of album covers, and a beer can collection sitting on a custom shelf high up on the wall. And most every office featured a pyramid of used beverage containers, usually Mountain Dew or the ever-present Washington apple juice, and the occasional chocolate milk containers like the ones from elementary school.

Next to each door, there was a full-length window, a relite, about one foot wide, made with that type of institutional glass from high school with wires inside that gave a sense of involuntary confinement. While designed to let light in form outside, it often served as an outward-facing sign of personal expression. Usually, the first thing decorated in a new office, relites were covered in stickers, signs, news articles, Dilbert comics, jokes, and bad code examples or bug burn down charts, all expected to be updated with some frequency.

Like the first day of high school, people wanted to stand out, but they *didn't* want to stand out. I nervously attached a few items to my glass, mostly American tourist-trap kitsch from my recent cross-country drive: a Wall Drug sticker, a Corn Palace postcard from South Dakota, and a copy of Elvis Presley's death certificate I had acquired in Memphis. Road and street signs were popular, and my "Slow Children At Play" road sign also followed me around for a decade.

I didn't realize it but our ET++ team had just been reorganized. Not only did I move offices, but I found myself on a new and bigger team with a clarified mission.

009. PASSWORD IS NEXTSTEP

NeXT, founded and led by Steve Jobs, developed new hardware, a new OS, and, importantly, entirely new object-oriented tools to build programs for their platform. The computers were not selling well (yet), but there was a growing belief that the technology was unique and forward-looking. Due in no small part to Jobs himself, the industry stood up and took notice.

One person really noticed. That was BillG.

Steve Jobs was famously separated from Apple in 1985, and later created NeXT Inc. along with several key members of the Apple Macintosh team. He also started Pixar but that's another story. NeXT produced three main products that had recently the refreshed with new models after the 1988 launch.

First there was the NeXT computer which was a blazing fast *workstation* class computer along with an incredible display, fancy optical drive, and a laser printer. Second, was the operating system that ran on the computer, object-oriented (of course) with a graphical user interface, called NeXTStep. And third, an incredibly rich set of tools for programmers to build object-oriented GUI programs for the hardware and OS, called Interface Builder. The whole product was launched in 1988 as almost a "super Macintosh" or at least was viewed that way by many. It was covered broadly across mainstream press because of the fascination with new home computers and of course Steve Jobs. By this point, many local newspapers were covering home computers as a regular section, something that seemed inconceivable just a few years earlier.

NeXTStep, while object-oriented, did not use C++ but a different object-oriented language which only made it seem cooler. BillG who believed strongly in having complete ownership of a programming language, thus his general reservations around C++ as I would soon learn, and his favorable views of Objective-C.

On my first college recruiting trip to Cornell in search of more Microsofties, I visited my old lab where many of the Macintosh computers were replaced with NeXT computers. Steve Jobs's new company followed the same marketing plan that Apple followed with the launch of Macintosh, convincing a number of computer science departments to make a bet on NeXT. This would not be the first time a recruiting trip to Cornell would show me something unexpected.

ScottRa procured a NeXT computer, the new *pizza box* form factor (like a true workstation) and we would explore it late into the night, sharing our discoveries with each other and the rest of our team. It was truly a marvel of engineering and experience. It was amazing to me that a computer and software built from scratch could do so much. Technically, much of the core operating system was built on a research project foundation from Carnegie Mellon University, known as Mach, which becomes important later in this story.

It ran at full 32-bits and running a variant of Unix under the graphical interface it rivaled the workstations I used in graduate school. It featured a level of sophistication in software and features that made Windows 3.0 PCs seem almost toy-like while having an ease of use of a packaged software product. It cost almost $10,000 1990 dollars and had minimal support from mainstream software makers who were already busy navigating MS-DOS, Windows, and OS/2.

Still the capabilities were so significant that NeXT was viewed as a major strategic *threat*. Microsoft, as I was learning, frequently used that word to describe competitors. ScottRa explained to me the importance of competing with NeXT, but I had difficulty grokking what that meant for our little team tasked with building cross-platform tools.

It became increasingly clear to me, however, why our source code server was named \\OBJECTS. Scott cleverly named the share \DART, a joke that was lost on me for years. I'll never forget the first time he told me the password. He said, "the password is 'nextstep', capitalized correctly." Everyone by then knew it was "NeXTStep" or perhaps "NeXTSTEP."

While I had no first-hand knowledge, the idea was in the air that BillG was frustrated at trailing a product by Steve Jobs. NeXT appeared to be a better product than anything Microsoft was about to ship or had planned for the foreseeable future. One of the things I am thankful for is having a direct competitor at such an early stage in my career. While how to compete was fuzzy, it was clear what we were supposed to compete with. Rumors of what BillG thought were cool or competing products or features would race around the company, and NeXT was one of those products. Microsoft was a product company, so the fact that it cost so much money or sold so few units was no excuse for not knowing what a product did or why it was viewed as good, and what we would do about it. BillG was (and remains) fiercely competitive and would often drive conversations about competitors in a relentless fashion, never allowing a team to dismiss one aspect of a competitor simply because of some relative weakness, no matter how overwhelming a weakness it might be. A product that is fantastic but not selling at all is every bit as formidable as your actual number one competitor, at least that is how we had to treat it when it came to BillG.

The rivalry between Bill and Steve was real. Everyone knew about it. We'd been through yearly company meeting updates on the litigation between companies and could read the trade press reviews of Macintosh versus Windows. That's why our little team was funded. It was why our conference room had a NeXT computer costing as much as four developer PCs.

The Systems division was responsible for delivering the SDK for the platform, though they relied on the Tools team to deliver the underlying compilers and other tools. The SDK was supposed to make it possible to build GUI applications. Unfortunately, the tools were mostly the bare minimum and lacked the elegance seen on Macintosh and NeXT.

The Systems team, aware of NeXT and the high bar it set, staffed an additional, smaller team to build much more innovative and competitive tools for OS/2 and Windows.

I had no idea what they were up to. BillG did of course. But now Microsoft had two small teams chartered to compete with NeXT while the much larger teams in Windows and Tools were not focused on NeXT as a competitor. This struck me as weird, but what did I know?

Jeff Harbers (JeffH) had firsthand knowledge of the BillG–Steve Jobs rivalry. Jeff was the engineering manager for Apps and led many of the earliest Apps products back when the team was merely one group of developers assigned to projects as needed, much like a typical start-up. He was hired to bring a level of experience and engineering quality to Apps and was part of the founding Apps team at Microsoft. Jeff was the first person hired by CharlesS. He had been in the middle of many technical conversations between BillG and Steve Jobs during the development of the Macintosh and Microsoft's commitment to delivering Word and Excel with the release of the Mac in 1984. Above all, though, Jeff had a well-earned reputation for being direct and accountable, with a strong commitment to excellence in engineering and quality—owing to his background in traditional mechanical engineering more than the hacker ethos.

Jeff's email name did not have the first letter of his last name, because there weren't any other Jeffs when he arrived. I thought this was kind of cool. But it drove BillG kind of nuts. Still, Jeff insisted on maintaining Jeff as his email, so BillG created an alias that directed email sent to JeffH to his Jeff account, just so he didn't have to see "Jeff." Years later with Microsoft's more friendly email system, the alias JeffH was spelled out as "Jeff Harbers forwarding alias for BillG." That was what happened when stubborn met stubborn.

Given his skill and experience and his understanding of Apps development, BillG tasked Jeff with merging the two teams and creating a new group to take on NeXTStep and to bring innovation and object-oriented tools like NeXTStep to Windows and OS/2 development. OS/2 was still top of mind in 1990.

This marked the start of a Microsoft entry into object-oriented development tools.

Because this team spanned both Apps and Systems and Jeff was an Apps person, the team reported to Mike Maples (MikeMap), vice president of the Applications Software division. Little did I know, but this spanning of Apps and Systems, while reporting to Apps, was quite a crazy structure and was a "condition" upon which Jeff would run the team. Microsoft was still a startup in the sense of the CEO creating ad hoc organizations around an individual.

MikeMap transformed Microsoft and set it up to be the product company it is today, quite literally. He joined Microsoft in the summer of 1988, as one of the earliest VPs at the company. So much of Microsoft culture today—that of Office, the quality of the products, and most of all the scaling of Office from a chaotic, infinitely buggy, siloed organization to one of the largest and most profitable software engineering product teams in the world—is a debt owed to MikeMap.

Mike was the opposite of the Microsoft archetype, older than most, having graduated from college in 1965, the year I was born. He grew up in Oklahoma and attended Oklahoma City University and earned an MBA as well. Prior to Microsoft he worked at IBM for more than two decades. The news of his hire caused a lot of worry about blue suits, white shirts, meetings with "foils," and even songs as IBM had official corporate songs. The stories of IBM's *process* were legendary at Microsoft because of the close working partnership between companies in Systems. Instead, Mike, with his disarming Oklahoma accent, showed up in plaid button-down shirts.

Both MikeMap and JeffH would become two of the most important mentors at Microsoft, for me and for many others.

Under direction of BillG, Jeff assembled a new founding team. It included two developers who I was in in awe of, Brad Christian (BradCh) and Rick Powell (RickP), and from Systems, Microsoft legend Neil Konzen (NeilK) and Garth Hitchens (GarthH.)

Plus, me, the new kid. ScottRa reported to Jeff. He would quickly attract more from inside the company, and we were soon about ten SDEs. BradCh was one of the main developers on Windows Word. RickP was likewise a key developer on Excel. NeilK was an original original, joining Microsoft while in high school biking over to the offices. He worked on the Apple Z-80 SoftCard, Multiplan, Windows, and was leading the graphical subsystem of OS/2, and much more. Famously, Neil wrote the BASIC game DONKEY that shipped with MS-DOS originally. His initials, NK, were also embedded in every Multiplan file as an identifier.

The charter of this new group was defined by the aggressive mission to *utilize the latest in object-oriented C++ technology to provide tools and libraries for developers writing the most advanced GUI applications on the market*. In the context of the time, this was wide-open and, importantly, had all the buzzwords that mattered—object-oriented, GUI, C++, and for Microsoft, *developers*.

I was new to corporate organization tensions, but they were readily visible. Alone, and having not done much for a year, I felt it. Between the two parts of our new team, the Apps Tools part and the Systems part, there was somewhat of a rivalry given we were *jammed* together in a typical corporate reorg. Add to that a concern about having Jeff as our manager—at least that's what I was hearing in the late-night hallway chats.

A big deal at the time, though one that had played out before my arrival, Jeff came with some history that made some people uneasy. Back when Jeff was as an overall engineering manager in Apps, the most significant and somewhat out-of-control project at the time was the first version of Word for Windows. This project became legendary as both an incredible success after the fact and an incredible death march while it was happening. The project was in a Harvard Business School case study that detailed the frustration the developers had with management. Photocopies of photocopies of that case study seemed to be in everyone's metal file cabinet. While not referenced by name, the case study stated that "upper management" referred to the Word team as the "worst in Applications development."

The "worst" team description came from Jeff around the time he reached a breaking point that led to a 12-month leave, which was uncommon at the time, but his decision. His characterization of the team ruffled feathers even when he returned one year later. But in truth, the development of Word for Windows caused several people to reach their limits. Many moved on. As I learned from *Zero Defects*, the early "big" projects had a lot of problems and those had a lot of causes. Jeff was more of a symptom than the cause, at least that is what I came to conclude.

While we were eager to start, Jeff insisted we first come together as a team at a retreat to help alleviate the angst. The retreat felt like one of those *Dilbert*-esque corporate team building offsites. Jeff was always a rugged individualist, but his return from leave came with a of a spiritual side that led to the offsite. Other than resident adviser training in college, I had never participated in anything like this. Our team went to the Westin Hotel in Seattle (cool because I walked to the hotel from my Capitol Hill apartment) and we stayed overnight.

Professional facilitators took us through a series of forgettable bonding and exploring exercises. We even lined up and passed oranges to each other from under our chins. It was like a scene from *The Office*. We spoke in pairs about our feelings and goals. We did trust exercises. JeffH talked a great deal about renewal, alluding to his Word experience.

At the end of the day, we had a fancy hotel dinner. It was the first time I ordered wine on Microsoft's tab (actually ever, but that's another story), a bottle of red, which I then promptly tipped all over the table onto BradCh. Later in the evening, KirkG suggested we raid the minibar. It sounded like a good idea at the time, so we did, but I was reprimanded by Jeff once he saw the bill afterward. It was so terrifying that I thought I would get fired, but it also instilled, for the *first* time, my sense that Microsoft was indeed a start-up when it came to spending money. The company had completed its first $1 billion sales year. I got a stern talking to over the minibar.

Back at work, job one was NeXTStep.

We started building a *cross-platform application framework*, basically the starting point for using C++ and being object-oriented. The ET++ experiment we trained on was such a framework, but the marketplace was already flooded with such frameworks that aimed to make it easier to create GUI programs that worked easily on any GUI operating system. Borland, our real competitor, had such a framework, called *Object Windows Library*, or OWL.

NeXTStep was based on the Objective-C programming language, and not C++. The NeXT system was alone in embracing this language and that was the subject of much debate on the USENET discussion forums—USENET was among the earliest internet services where mostly grad students exchanged ideas, often likened to today's Reddit. The main differentiator, and key point of conflict on USENET, was that Objective-C had garbage collection (via reference counting to be technically specific)—that memory management technique I favored in graduate school and then abandoned once I was schooled in the real world by JonDe.

Because we were to compete with NeXT, we needed to have everything NeXTStep had, but better. That was only logical. Our framework also used automatic garbage collection, which we were going to add to C++ (going against the grain of the C++ language purists and the most experienced people I knew, JonDe and DougK.) Given the construct of our group—RickP, NeilK, who built the windowing system, ScottRa with experience in architecting applications, BradCh, GarthH, and so on, we were like the *X-Men,* each with a superpower destined to be part of one significant framework.

Except me. I had no experience doing anything. I brought to the table my academic background in data storage and what was known as *object persistence* and garbage collection, so I worked on the ability of the framework to save and load objects from memory to disk. Everything we were doing was our own invention—it was neither Windows nor OS/2; it was not standard C++; it wasn't built using standard PC graphics. It was a perfectly consistent and well-architected system, unrelated to everything. To be fair to ourselves, that is how every application framework was done at the time.

Our project needed a name. We referred to it by the generic name *af* for application framework. One night, ScottRa and I were talking, and I mentioned that I saw an exhibit at Boeing about a new fighter jet, the FX or something. We joked about how there's always an X in cool products and thus we christened the project *AFX*. Over the years we would make many jokes about what it stood for, like *application frameworkx* or *application framework eXtentions,* but it was never an acronym.

We spent about nine months building our framework. We were a product team. We were writing code, checking in code, building tests, and doing all the things I thought a product team did. I certainly was naïve.

Jeff didn't see us making progress and the experienced product people on the team knew this. RickP bemoaned this fact to me in his straightforward and honest manner at some of our nightly chats. We were spending a lot of time fighting the tools that didn't help us to do the non-standard things we were trying to do, as well as debating esoteric, almost academic object-oriented philosophy all while NeXTStep was getting better.

To prove our work, Jeff declared *App Month*, which meant taking time to use our framework to build apps ourselves to determine if our product made it easy for developers to create apps. Though we didn't realize it at the time, there was a method to Jeff's madness. Jeff was obsessed with getting customer feedback and understanding the customer we were building product for, something already baked deeply into Apps culture. He told us to come up with an app on our own and spend a month building it, using our framework.

For my App Month I chose to build a personal finance app. I figured with our great framework and a month I would be able to beat the Microsoft Money team led by DougK, which at the time was only two of three developers. Really, I thought I could beat DougK because I had an application framework. I worked day and night, but I struggled with tools.

After a month, I created a bloated, slow, flaky program that only drew a check on a screen and saved it to a disk for a later reload. It didn't have a check register. It didn't print checks. It didn't do any math. It didn't have accounts, payees, categories, or, well, anything. I disliked it and I got the feeling everyone else did too.

I wasn't alone. My teammates all experienced the same problems in their apps—games, utilities, and productivity apps alike. None of us achieved anything impressive.

Our mood sat somewhere between humiliated and disappointed. I was now 18 months or so into my career and was staring at the second time a project went nowhere.

010. OUR BILLG REVIEW

Jeff scheduled a *BillG Review* for a week or so after App Month. Bill was anxious for our progress and Jeff, having learned some valuable lessons about overpromising, was careful to moderate Bill's expectations. But the prospect of a looming BillG Review was intense, I quickly learned.

In 1990, a BillG Review was a big deal, a really big deal. The company was large enough that teams were not having routine in-person contact with Bill, but it was also small enough that he knew most of the key developers and program managers, especially on the main products. AFX was a main product, sort of. It had the attention of one. Even though our team was small, I was too junior and never shipped anything so obviously wasn't invited. I felt left out, but I also relieved. I was too new to be called stupid or to say, "the dumbest thing" BillG ever heard. I had not established my "IQ." These were all examples of well-known BillG-isms, right up there with rocking back and forth in his chair. Still, I felt I was missing out.

The team was supposed to show Bill our progress and how close we were to state-of-the-art tools for GUI and beating Steve Jobs at his own game. All indications of progress were poor. Our code was big and bloated. Our tools were not revolutionary. We could not create GUI programs quickly. But we understood the existing tools well. We wrote many memos on how NeXTStep, Borland, ET++, and several other commercial products were superior to Microsoft's lack of products.

Jeff knew Bill and understood how he worked better than most anyone. Jeff asked us to put together our materials—literally printouts of code, APIs, benchmarks of memory usage, competitive product briefs, and more—and assemble them into a binder. Back in those days a "good" review came with a big binder of papers that were sent over a day or so before the meeting so Bill could prepare. Bill read everything. Bill remembered everything he read. Jeff knew we had to be buttoned up, of course.

We also knew we had been poor engineers.

I spent many evenings standing in RickP's doorway talking and learning from him. Rick was the nicest, most thoughtful developer and, at the same time, he was unbelievably *hardcore*, the ultimate Microsoft accolade for a developer, focused on every line of code, every byte of memory, and every CPU cycle.

Ahead of the BillG Review, he did a group presentation summing up his App Month. He had slides—everyone was flummoxed! Rick never made slides or even led meetings. Our conference rooms had overhead projectors so when we used slides (which MikeMap referred to as the IBM word *foils*) we prepared them in PowerPoint (or Word), printed them out, and then photocopied them onto transparency pages.

The title of Rick's talk read, "What Would Make Rick Happy?"

Through a series of slides, Rick took his perspectives of building real shipping apps and his hardcore focus on performance and reliability and defined a broad set of criteria for how a reusable framework should be built. He played back all the choices made on the Excel layer system but applied them broadly. This presentation hit me like a 16-ton weight. He converted me to a performance zealot in 20 minutes—a transformation of the highest order. Whenever I encounter a buggy, slow, fat product I think back to how unhappy that would make Rick and ask myself, "What Would Make Rick Happy?"

In addition to being hardcore about performance and bloat, Rick made several incredibly astute observations that would carry great weight moving forward in terms of distinguishing our product. First among those was that we tried to "fix" the operating system. We took building a cross-platform framework as a chance to cherry pick the best concepts from each target operating system, or more likely simply our favorites. We thought of that as making a new and better OS. In fact, it was just different.

Jeff had a great way of describing this both to BillG and back to us. He would remind us that the OS groups were huge teams of 100 engineers compared to our team. How could our tiny team possibly "compete" with those big teams at designing an operating system. Even more straightforward, was how could our team of one contract documentation writer compete with the dozens of books about programming Windows, Macintosh, or OS/2 that filled Tower Books. There would never be enough to learn about our framework. What is amazing about this point is that literally every framework was doing this same sort of fixing of operating systems. Even more amazing, this tradition of cross-platform tools inadvertently creating new platforms without the resources to maintain or document them, or even to be competitive continues to this day.

Rick also had some other observations about working with an operating system that proved especially important as our strategy would unfold after the BillG review. In particular Rick cautioned about redundancy and reimplementing concepts already in the OS. A common example was how the OS maintained a list of windows but so did the framework. Not only was that more memory, more code, but it was a chance for the two lists to disagree and introduce bugs. The whole concept of not maintaining copies of information the OS already had was critical to performance. If an app needed to know something, then there needed to be only one place to look.

In general, these observations, rules if you will, formed the foundation of what was to come. They were more than observations or theories, however, as we learned them from our experience building the framework that didn't work. Jeff felt leading with what we learned was a key strategy to engage BillG on failure. These concepts proved the core of what we learned.

Up until that point, I had almost exclusively only interacted with other software design engineers, developers or *devs* as we called ourselves. A unique role, particularly in Apps, was Program Management or PM. PM originated in the Excel team as a role responsible for making sure the product being built was easy to use, met the needs of customers, and achieved business goals. The role came about as a way to make sure developer schedule time would be used more efficiently by avoiding false starts and rework, while connecting the dots between the ever-increasing number of features.

Prior to the introduction of PM, most debates about what to build were settled by the developer writing the code and based on what they felt was *right,* however they defined right. If it didn't work out, then it would be rewritten. If developers did not agree, an endless email thread ensued, and continued until someone got bored or more likely the most forcefully expressed point of view would *win*. We called this pre-PM era "testosterone-based development."

PMs created processes reflecting customer needs in the product, at least something more than just asking friends in the hallway which constituted feedback and planning in the early days. PMs also represented the product to other teams and was generally viewed as the face of the team, even though they were peers with development and software test engineering.

Generally, PM led the BillG Review. Clif Swigget (ClifS), who joined from the Macintosh apps team where he worked on a well-known database product called *Microsoft File,* jumped right in. What a challenging way to begin. ClifS and the team were as ready as they could be for a meeting where we basically had nothing but a year's worth of learning to show. BillG was not likely to be impressed by mere learning.

To sum up our learning we referred to our "condition" as *oopaholism.* That's how we described ourselves to BillG.

We drank far too much of the object-oriented programming Kool-Aid, using techniques and approaches that might be good in academia or look great on paper but were wholly inappropriate for building industrial-strength, commercial software at scale. Maybe this was naïve, but every new wave of technology comes with it a certain amount of religion and zealotry, even if it isn't immediately practical. There was an optimism that the new way would solve all the old problems and be better, faster, easier, and cheaper. In reality, things almost never worked like that. OOP proved itself to be more of a passing fad and a lot less than a whole new approach. OOP influenced everything to come but was not the change-agent the zealots believed it would be. A recurring theme in new technologies is how often the first try at something serves, to a much larger degree, as inspiration and influence rather than as a foundation for implementation.

My contribution, entirely a failure, was about to go through my first BillG Review, and it terrified me. Not only was I not at the meeting, but I would be out of town when it took place. That was a blessing, as it turns out.

While it was happening, I attended the *1991 USENIX C++ Conference* in Washington, DC. As conditions for attending, Jeff insisted that I fly coach, book a cheap room, eat no elaborate dinners, and, above all, I was to write a trip report and lead a group meeting on what I learned when I got back. It wasn't just that Jeff believed we should spend Microsoft money like it was our own last dollar, but that spending should result in a contribution to the group not for the benefit of one. The worst part: I was OOF for a couple of days. OOF is common tech community jargon originating back with mainframes meaning *out of facility* that had a specific implementation in Unix email where you could leave an automatic reply message with the details of the absence. I edited my .oof file saying I'd be back by the end of the week and detailed the conference I was attending. Before the broad use of mobile phones and laptops—a ubiquitous Compaq LTE laptop was still more than a year from reality—I was able to check my voice mail using my Microsoft AT&T calling card, something I'd do at the inevitable layover at the ORD United terminal. Those were the days?

The conference seemed small, and everyone seemed so grown up. They had big titles, like chief scientist and vice president, and they were with big companies, like AT&T, IBM, General Electric, and Texas Instruments, but unlike me, they were real adults. It terrified me. I made the rounds, booth to booth, sporting my first ever conference badge with Microsoft affiliation, and in the small hotel ballroom used for the main session I quietly sat in the back row, quiet and intimidated.

Over the course of the conference, about twenty papers were presented, and all were extremely relevant to what I was working on. Long before there was Linux, there was UNIX, the famed operating system from 1970s AT&T Labs favored in academia and research. USENIX was more of a bottom-up conference of system administrators, programmers, and scientists, all working on the leading edge of the UNIX system, not a highbrow academic conference. The C++ language originated from this community, and the first gatherings focused on C++ language design were hosted by this group. Unlike the strictly academic conferences I followed in graduate school, the USENIX conferences were geared toward industry or at least non-tenure track faculty.

The debate at the conference centered around the controversy over evolving the C++ language, which at the time seemed premature. This was a language almost no one was using commercially and with almost no tools support beyond UNIX, but that's the world they worked in. Contributors debated the use of "proposed" C++ features such as multiple inheritance, templates, and even my old favorite, garbage collection. All the while there were reports about new class libraries being developed everywhere.

In one small session, Martin Carroll, a well-known AT&T C++ proponent, gave a talk on some detailed aspects of the language, and toward the end in Q&A someone asked about using the feature in their code. The answer was something I would use for years. "You're writing code for your product, not a compiler test suite," meaning the presence of a feature in the language didn't mean it had to be used. There was no reason for code to touch every language feature. This presentation later led to my own version of "What Would Steven Like?" My thoughts were racing with ideas to develop a set of rules to govern our use of C++ while making sure RickP got what he wanted for performance.

When I got back to the office, I was anxious to hear how the BillG Review had gone. Unsurprisingly, my voicemails had gone unanswered.

Was BillG in a good mood? Did anyone say the "stupidest thing" BillG had ever heard? Was there yelling? Did anyone get called "random"? Maybe someone was called "high IQ"?

A BillG Review was generally viewed as an exercise in survival more than an opportunity to shine. At least that's how we, the broad base of people who only heard about the meetings after the fact, perceived them.

I walked the hallways in search of the scoop. Given that we had nothing to show, and that Bill was anxious to compete, ScottRa, who attended the meeting, said that it went "as well as could be expected." He said there was no yelling but a strong sense of disappointment. Jeff, I was told, took the brunt of the negatives, and discussed many of the challenges—tools that didn't yet exist, cross-platform development, new team, and new technologies. ScottRa said we needed to come up with a plan.

Finally, in a hallway chat, Jeff later reiterated that the meeting was rough, and Bill was disappointed but he "behaved," and that Scott and others did well. The meeting was replayed a dozen times that day pairwise. Each of us must have heard the story several times from each participant, trying to gauge the tone and every nuance. It was like hearing about an amazing concert that I didn't get to attend, but instead of music it was my future career at Microsoft.

Jeff detailed the meeting summary from BillG. It was not the kind of summary anyone expected.

He said that Bill concluded the meeting by saying something like, "It is disappointing that we haven't made the progress we would have hoped. But it sounds like the team has learned a lot while making many mistakes. The thing we can't do is make those same mistakes again while we come back as soon as we can with a product that is competitive."

That sure didn't sound like the BillG we were all terrified of.

As Jeff explained, Bill appreciated learning and understood, if not embraced, the failure that could happen while learning. While at events like intern parties or new hire gatherings he often told stories about appreciating failure (like Xerox not capitalizing on the invention of the GUI), he never seemed to use examples of failure from within Microsoft.

It was a relief. It would also foreshadow that the caricature of BillG was not always the same as BillG the manager, leader, and CEO. At least I had one counterpoint.

I still had to give a presentation on my trip. My presentation about what I learned was presented as a series of new rules for using C++ that we should follow. I won't dull down this exciting story with a diatribe about programming language design but suffice it to say we took to heart the idea that as powerful as OOP was, using C++ as a better C would be our hallmark. We would apply RickP's and the Microsoft hardcore ethos to OOP. I don't really know what made me assert all this stuff in what was supposed to be a trip report. In hindsight, I think I was just totally jazzed by attending a conference and in a bit of a panic over what was now coming up on my second anniversary with no shipping code. Maybe it was just that we made it through the BillG review, though that was all Jeff's doing.

From that point forward, we became *reformed oopaholics*. AFX was the hardcore OOP group.

Not only did we survive what should have been a horrible meeting, but at least by Microsoft standards it was motivational. We were given license to regroup, plan what to do, but to execute quickly. We needed a focus.

Focus was difficult to come by given how many operating systems or platforms we were on the hook to support. NeXT only had to support one. Apple Macintosh only supported one. Microsoft was, on its own, building MS-DOS, Windows, OS/2, and supporting Macintosh, and more…

Shipping would clarify things. Shipping was everything. This was just sinking in for me. If you're not shipping, you're literally not doing anything. Excel 3.0 had just finished. This was the version of Excel that took advantage of Windows 3.0 memory management and worked on the Macintosh. It was an amazing product.

It also shipped 11 days later than its *original* schedule. A noteworthy event. A memo was circulating about a talk Chris Peters (ChrisP) gave as a summer *TechTalk* to interns, something I would come to love. I did not know Chris personally, yet. He was already a legend in the hallways and JonDe's manager. His talk was "Shipping Software On Time" and by all accounts he was the master of the new shipping software religion in Apps based on leading the Excel 3.0 project. The memo hung on my relite for years. My relite was crowded. This memo meant everything and was also everything we were not doing.

The essence of the memo was commitment and accountability to a *ship date*, not a target ship date, not a date like "first half" or "second quarter." Those were, as Chris would say, "180 dates" or "90 dates". There are many variables in a project, the ship date cannot be one of them. He went on and on about shipping. Everyone on the team has one job, "SHIP PRODUCTS." And to really hammer the point he explained how everyone else comes to work trying to prevent a team from shipping. Hardcore. Hardcore Software.

We needed to ship. Something. Fast. On time.

011. STRATEGY FOR THE '90S: WINDOWS

With our BillG review completed we needed to regroup. We knew what we did wrong technically, but we lacked a strategy to build a product that involved target customers and product goals. We were a technology team in search of a problem. Microsoft's strategy was coming into focus and Jeff set our small team up to be the glue by amplifying our efforts. We needed to ship. Shipping is everything.

The traditional C compiler team was working on C++ after the death march release of C 6. They were making progress on what was an enormous task. The team of about two dozen brilliant compiler and code-generation expert developers added Martin O'Riordan (MartinO), who pioneered the implementation of many of the esoteric features of C++ in the Glockenspiel compiler, the one we had been using for ET++ and AFX. The team was making significant progress at the core compiler technology and immersed itself in the language standardization process ensuring Microsoft had a front row seat for C++.

Windows 3.0 shipped and exceeded any and all expectations. Pre-installed sales in its first few months shot up to more than one million copies. By the time our BillG Review happened, Windows 3.0 sold twice that or more. Work was well underway for the successor, Windows 3.1, which would make substantial progress in using the latest Intel processors, significantly improving networking and file sharing, and adding new user interface APIs that would make building Windows programs easier.

Its success meant that our strategy was handed to us. With all the conflicting goals and external relationships, knowing what to do or having a feeling about what made sense from a technology perspective is not the makings of a strategy. Strategic shifts, like the one BillG orchestrated with the transition to GUI in the first place, take clear, top-down, direction. We had anything but that, still.

Windows morphed into Microsoft's main strategy, from a side project. While the Apps team was already heavily invested in Macintosh, when it came to Microsoft's operating systems, we were inconsistently spread across MS-DOS, Windows, and OS/2.

Often, in times of strategic turmoil or doubt, a few simple observations on the state of the world expressed plainly can lead to an effective strategy, removing ambiguity and doubt.

Our team knew we needed something to compete with NeXTStep and we knew we were going to use C++. We had two big problems.

First, AFX was given the mission to develop tools for all of the platforms Apps might build for, which included Windows (which at the time would always mean some of the older versions and the newest ones), Macintosh (where the money came from), OS/2 (because that was the company strategy), and even MS-DOS, where most of the customers still were.

Second, we had been strategically focused on professional developers, which might not sound like much but implied many things about the product such as using character-based tools instead of GUI and not worrying much about how easy it was to write programs. The most important apps of the new era were being written by professionals, not hobbyists, but now Borland was attracting professionals.

We were hamstrung by the perceived need to cater to professional developers who were focused on the complex Microsoft platform strategy of MS-DOS, Windows, and OS/2. How could we pick one without breaking the strategy? Who were we, the small group in Apps, to make such a decision?

The answer was right in front of our faces. Windows 3.0 sales surpassed Macintosh sales. In the entire first year, Windows 3.0 sold about 4 million units, almost twice the number of Macintosh computers sold and over twice the number of all Windows units sold previously since 1985. Windows sales were doubling in months and Macintosh was growing sporadically but about 30% per year on average. The rest of MikeMap's Apps organization turned to focus boldly and clearly on Windows (and Macintosh) at the expense of MS-DOS and OS/2, which led to only one conclusion: Focus our efforts on Windows. Borland was already doing that. Many application vendors were starting to do that, except for the largest ones. The situation for programmers was rapidly becoming one where if someone was building a new app, then it would be on Windows. For existing companies, the question was not if the focus would shift almost exclusively to Windows, but when. Even Macintosh started to be questioned in some commercial circles, simply because of the growth rates and urgency around Windows.

This change happened in the span of months and was as dramatic for us as it was for everyone, including our friends and co-workers in Systems. In Systems they were still trying to get OS/2 to work and executives were still navigating a relationship with IBM. That relationship had cooled substantially in public with increasingly political statements being made about who would support what and when. Rather than clarify a partnership, these began to clarify a reality. Windows was the breakout. Everything else was going to be left behind.

This was a classic case of the internal situation making something seem bold, but from the competitive marketplace the choice was obvious. Windows.

The summer of 1991 would prove to be a pivotal time for Microsoft and the industry. In hindsight, this was most decidedly a moment along with a memo to prove it and decisions around that. Rarely in corporate evolution do incredible successes so easily connect to specific dates and choices, but Microsoft's early years seemed to be marked by several BillG moments. Microsoft, just a decade earlier, closed the deal with IBM and the single decision to codify Microsoft's right to license MS-DOS to other PC makers was documented in a succinct business plan memo. And just a few years after that, Microsoft stopped building new applications for MS-DOS to focus on GUI at an offsite led by Bill. It is amazing that the most early and key strategic choices the company made could be connected to specific events and moments in time.

In the Spring of 1991 BillG set aside a week, as he was doing regularly, to get away and update himself on the latest technical developments, called "Think Week." As I would learn personally in just a few short years, most of the time was spent deep in reading, but he would also commit to writing. This particular week, deep in the success of Windows 3.0 and ongoing development of Windows 3.1 and the ongoing frustrations of OS/2 development, he took a step back to consider, and decide, Microsoft's big platform bet.

As I would come to learn this was a prototypical BillG memo. It was a series of seemingly unrelated points, usually detailed in a bulleted list, each with a block of strongly imperative and candid text. It was also, for lack of a better word, a bit paranoid, especially in hindsight when one considers all the issues. Yet when reading the memo in the context of the moment, it is clear that while these might be a bit of a laundry list of everything he was worried about, it is just as much a list of all that must go right for a strategy to be successful. Bill knew more than anyone just how fragile the world of software can be to companies. While I'm forward referencing a bit, he was fond of saying that a company's most difficult times are seeded when things appear to be going perfectly well. The list of just PC software companies in decline or that vanished was already long.

Bill detailed this strategy in the widely read email he originally sent to only the executives, but quickly raced around the company and is now online[1] due to leaks and the discovery phase of litigation where some of our best emails are now available. Microsoft had always been an exceedingly open culture when it came to mail forwarding or including others in email. This was from the top-down. BillG, more than anyone, overshared, whether on the CC line or simply forwarding and asking for views then forwarding those views to others. I did not personally know this yet, though had already seen many BillG mails.

> *In the same way that DEC's strategy for the '80s was VAX—one architecture, one operating system—our strategy for the '90s is Windows—one evolving architecture, a couple of implementations. Everything we do should focus on making Windows more successful.*
>
> Bill Gates, May 16, 1991

This was the first *BillG Memo* that I saw, and in hindsight it showed the deep thought that Bill put into focusing the company on Windows in a time of change. The May 16, 1991, mail also made it into the *San Jose Mercury News* and *Wall Street Journal* and then even into some of the trials and tribulations with regulators. I was too naïve and too much of a true-blue believer to even consider the negatives or theories in the press on what was significant. I took the memo at face value. The memo was abundantly clear. "In the same way that DEC's strategy for the '80s was VAX—one architecture, one operating system—our strategy for the '90s is Windows—one evolving architecture, a couple of implementations. Everything we do should focus on making Windows more successful."

The press mostly focused on the sections of the memo expressing concerns about competitors. The *Wall Street Journal* headline was "Microsoft Founder Gates, in Memo, Warns of Attack and Defeat by Rivals" and discussed the widening rift with IBM, even saying Microsoft "lashed out" at IBM. The memo's ever-present competitive tone using war-like terminology such as "attack" and thinking through competitive battle scenarios were too exciting to be omitted from coverage.

> *The simplest summary is to repeat our strategy in its simplest form — "Windows — one evolving architecture, a couple of implementations and an immense number of great applications from Microsoft and others."*
>
> Bill Gates, May 16, 1991

In fact, the memo codified what the market had seemingly decided—the winner was Windows. Bill was clarifying, crystalizing, and emphasizing that point with specific calls to action. He made sure that everyone knew OS/2 was no longer a priority and that we now had a strategy that was entirely Windows. In concluding he restated this as "The simplest summary is to repeat our strategy in its simplest form – 'Windows' – one evolving architecture, a couple of implementations and an immense number of great applications from Microsoft and others."

For most of us in Apps, the part that seemed more newsworthy was a clear mention of what until then was simply known as "Advanced Windows" or usually OS/2 3.0, was now a full bet on Windows and that Microsoft was no longer committed to making the imminent release of OS/2 2.0 a priority. The memo acknowledged that the relationship with IBM would be difficult but optimistically noted that Microsoft would come out a bigger and stronger company no longer successful simply because of support from IBM.

> *The "a couple of implementations" is a somewhat humorous reference to the fact that our NT based versions and our non-NT versions have a different code in a number of areas to allow us to have both the advanced features we want and be fairly small on the Intel architecture. Eventually we will get back to one implementation but it will take four years before we use NT for everything. I would not use this simple summary for outside consumption—there it would be more like "Windows—one evolving architecture with hardware freedom for all users and freedom to choose amongst the largest set of applications.*
>
> Bill Gates, May 16, 1991

In hindsight there is a fun section in the memo where Bill points out the reality that Microsoft currently has "a couple of implementations" of Windows technologies, and it would take "four years before we use NT for everything." It would be almost ten years and eight or so releases of the two different main code bases to get to one operating system code base, Windows XP.

The bet on Windows, the bet on what was now becoming known as simply Windows NT internally was now clear. While initially NT was an abbreviation for "New Technology" it was common knowledge that we were not to confirm that brief history and to say it is just the two letters, something about lawyers and trademarks was the hallway talk. Literally overnight the efforts around OS/2 and MS-DOS fell from most everyone's plate and certainly all new projects reset their focus to be Windows.

Where did that leave our AFX effort and competing with NeXT? The memo also pointed out that the most important differentiator between operating systems and most important criteria for winning in the market would be "hardware freedom for all users and freedom to choose amongst the largest set of applications." It was our job in AFX to build the tools to enable the largest set of applications to exist.

Our challenge was that the C++ product team, managed in a different group reporting to MikeMap, did not have it so easy. Unlike AFX, which had no existing code or commitments, the C++ product group was committed to delivering the C++ compiler which was becoming essential for the creation of NT and to deliver C++ for Windows 3.1 and later. That support was for the professional tools, professional in the sense that they were character-based command line tools.

Oh, and Windows NT already had a target ship date towards the end of the year. This was an experienced team that was making progress. There was a real urgency to have C++ tools for the upcoming Developer Preview release of NT. Microsoft was already planning a big conference for professional developers and part of that conference would be a preview of Windows NT and the tools required to build applications.

There was a lot going on and while the strategic shift was clarifying, the next level of detail when it comes to figuring out the ordering and priorities of projects still needed to be worked out.

At the same time, there was no way for us to build, from scratch, an entire suite of GUI tools competitive with NeXTStep in the months remaining in 1991. Jeff was a master at schedules and understanding where groups really stood relative to where their optimistic plans were—he lived through 10 years of app schedules and death marches. Plus, the C 6 team just shipped after their own march and they needed a significant update, C 6.0a, to address concerns that the initial product was buggy.

A key insight Jeff brought was directly connected to his experience working with Apple and Steve Jobs, most recently reflected in ChrisP's "Shipping Software" tech talk. The idea that being grand architecturally is a distant second to being pragmatic and shipping product. Steve Jobs famously rallied the Macintosh team with the mantra *real artists ship,* a play on Picasso's famous saying, "Good artists borrow, great artists steal."

Jeff told us to put our oopaholic problems aside and said, "Enough is enough. It's time for us to ship."

Like all lofty goals, we needed to break the project down. There was an obvious step to take. First get C++ done, which was necessary since our tools were built in C++. From there, we could build the Windows GUI tools in C++ and fully bootstrap or self-host. This two-step plan also created an opportunity for our AFX team to ship "something" or "anything" with the forthcoming character-based C++ compiler.

The C++ compiler also needed something as well. Borland was busy building an application framework. Microsoft had none. Borland led the way in telling a new generation of programmers how to use the latest in object-oriented tools to build Windows programs, on Windows. That meant Microsoft was ceding control of the actual platform it was creating to Borland.

When it came to class libraries, we still needed a philosophy or point of view that helped to guide us—all we had was a failed oopaholic view. That's where my experience at USENIX came in. Returning to the slides I presented, as per the JeffH requirement, after laying out the context of the conference one slide was all that mattered.

Restating my conference lesson, I put on a slide "C++ is a programming language not a religion." Certainly obvious, but not to anyone on the leading edge of technology who believed that C++ *required* a new way to think about programming. I went on to say that the lessons I took away from the conference were that C++ was a better C, not a new way to do everything. The most effective way to use C++ was to stick to a "sane subset" of the language, which was basically heresy to all the people advocating for adding new features and complexity to the language. While the Languages team was required to implement the public standards (which were being developed at the time and we were active members of the ANSI committee), there was no reason for our own class library to serve as a "compiler test suite."

This philosophy of C++ minimalism was the first step in building our class library. The second was the impetus of ScottRa and RickP. Both had built many layers to insulate people from variations in different operating systems and platforms and both knew the cost in memory size and code complexity that comes with that. While it always seemed like a good idea at the time, eventually the team building the layer found itself having to do as much work as each of the operating systems. That meant a small effort turned out to require two or three times the effort of some large teams, which were, effectively, competition.

Given the realignment of MikeMap's Apps division around Windows versus being everything to everyone along with our newly minted religion around C++ minimalism versus oopaholism, we had a strategy. We would build tools for Windows, running on Windows, and a class library that was dedicated to building Windows apps, not an academic exercise in OOP.

During a doorway conversation with Jeff, we discussed how we would ship. We were trying to find a way to break down the problem to give the team time to build our NeXTStep competitor. Jeff asked if there was a way to ship part of the class library with the forthcoming C++ compiler and then ship the rest with an update that included the new GUI tools.

In hindsight, I think Jeff knew the answer. *Yes, we could.* Still, I gave him that answer. Our ideas for a minimal class library could easily be partitioned into parts applicable to Windows and parts that were more in line with the focus on the first C++ release that was about character mode. We sketched out what was known as the *class hierarchy* based on what we called *foundation classes* and Windows classes. These foundation classes would be the minimal product we could ship in time for the developer conference and would simply give a bit of a flavor of the class library to follow. They weren't even all that helpful for writing Windows programs…yet.

Jeff asked if I would lead the near-term project—the first release of AFX that was aligned with C++ 7.0, the obvious next name for the compiler product.

I had no idea what *lead* meant except that I was being asked to *ship*, and that was exciting. I still reported to ScottRa, but Jeff promoted me to manager. One day I was not a manager. Then I was. At first, I thought, *Wow, everything is going to be different.* Except at Microsoft in those days, especially working for Jeff, that was not the case. Jeff's idea of a manager was to take people who were so productive that they could do the previously required work but also have enough extra time to manage. The management part was an add-on. There was no such thing as a manager who didn't also code. ScottRa was a full-time developer. So was GarthH. Everyone was writing code. Managers just did some extra stuff for a half a day a week or so.

My first direct reports were RickP and Eric Schlegel (EricSc.) Eric recently graduated from Dartmouth and knew everything there was to be known about Macintosh. RickP, a pioneering engineer on the Excel team who created much of the layer of code that helped Excel work across Windows and Mac, was a legend. While we became great hallway friends, the idea of me managing Rick was absurd. I had literally *nothing* to offer him. Rick wasn't looking for anything, though, and it ended up being a great chance for us to officially hang out. He knew the work that needed to be done and wanted to do it. He was better at it than anyone else. Eric was going to work on some Mac-specific tooling as part of a broader project that remained in place.

We defined a project and built a schedule. Next, we needed to ship. We needed to create a source code project, an SLM project. In a symbolic gesture of ridding ourselves of the past evils of oopaholism, we created the new *afx* source code project, deleted the old project, and, for good measure, I deleted the last copy of the code: "rm – rf afx." That wasn't quite the command for the source control system but became how we symbolically told the story of becoming recovered oopaholics by using the well-known Unix terminology. I deleted all the files from our failed project, which we started referring to as *Old AFX*.

We had a clean slate.

But first things first, we needed a T-shirt. Without a T-shirt there was no way to start a project, and frankly that explained a lot about the previous years. Getting a shirt in those days was no easy task. First, it had to only be one color because silk screening multiple colors was prohibitively expensive. Second, a big deposit was required as was a commitment to a certain quantity. There was a place by the Kingdome, in industrial Seattle, where we went to check proofs. It was crazy.

I needed a design. The lesson that came out of the BillG Review for us was that we had not been in tune to the market while at the same time we were sloppy. At the time my uncle, a banker, was working at Prudential, which had the slogan, "Rock Solid. Market Wise." I called him up and asked him to send me some letterhead or a poster or something. There was no internet. I received a big Federal Express tube the next day (!) filled with all sorts of slogan items. At the Microsoft library I made a scan of the logo using the public scanner. Using Windows Paint, I added "Microsoft Foundation Classes" across the top of the Rock of Gibraltar along with the (trademarked) Prudential tagline. Then our group's administrative assistant, Kathleen Thompson (KathT), who later contributed to the thousands of pages of documentation as a writer, guided me through the process of getting a T-shirt made.

There was one problem. I did the classic Microsoft thing of acting first and not asking permission. Thinking about the minibar incident, I chose to pay for the shirts myself and work it out later. I wrote a check for $450. Two weeks later, we had T-shirts. And apparently, we also named our first product. Microsoft Foundation Classes (MFC), which I came up with for the shirts, had stuck. We were building MFC 1.0.

I proudly gave Jeff a shirt when they arrived. His first comment was not "Did you get permission for the logo?" but rather "Who paid for these?" My answer was "I did," and before I managed to ask for reimbursement he smiled and mouthed, "Good answer." It was a different era. People thought of company money differently, as if Microsoft was still a start-up, and as crazy as it was to pay for T-shirts, I understood Jeff's point as we started to see the spending all around the company increase. A few weeks later, a reimbursement check (a physical check) arrived. Jeff worked the amount out with KathT.

Coding the project was a whirlwind through the next few months. The Languages team worked under a deadline that wasn't realistic, but we were only a small deliverable to their big project and were not in a position to play *schedule chicken*, a common description used when two groups shared an unrealistic deadline.

Surprisingly, decision making clarity came from having a clear point of view, a tight deadline, and constraints. This idea of a clear point of view was something Jeff instilled in me during one of our many conversations. He would use the expression to highlight a unique perspective or belief that defines a product, or guiding light. It was new to me, though years later I understood why it was referred to as a North Star.

While this was all happening to me, it was also changing me. While I was on the job for almost two years, I had not really transitioned from graduate school to industry. And then I did, and it happened fast. Big and small things were happening to the product quickly too, seemingly all at the same time.

We had to choose naming conventions for objects in our source code—what the code looked like in books and what happened when thousands of programmers typed each day. This was essentially a life-or-death struggle and picking wrong could be legitimately alienating. Microsoft Apps championed a specific and rigorous naming convention called *Hungarian*, which we learned in ADC. It was pioneered by CharlesS and was his Stanford PhD dissertation. Windows took Hungarian and basically broke it in ways that made Apps people cringe. MFC was both a new language with many new idioms and straddling the world between Apps and Systems. But time, pressure, and clarity of mission made it simple, and we picked a few conventions that came to define C++ for a generation of programmers: Classes start with a *C* as in CString; member variables start with an m_; and everything starts with our main class CObject, which was super lean and had no memory cost. That was the whole oopaholic philosophy swung 180 degrees from conventional wisdom. Also, when it came to tabs versus spaces, we chose correctly.

What previously took weeks, we dispensed within a day.

Scott and I worked on diagrams for the class hierarchy, sort of a family tree of the product. We drew them in PowerPoint, which only had basic shapes then and didn't even have good alignment tools, and then at night I took them to the all-night Kinko's on Capitol Hill where they could make copies the size of posters. Class hierarchy posters were the currency of the C++ world, and we had the best.

Sticking with the RickP philosophy of not duplicating code from Windows, we made a lot of choices that went against what people hoping for cross-platform code would have liked. We used existing Windows OS implementations for most everything in MFC 1.0, including files, strings, and more. If the intention was running this code on another OS, then it meant basically implementing those parts of Windows. It wasn't about being sneaky, it was about being efficient for people writing Windows programs, which we felt was where the world was heading. It was our strategy to make Windows programs efficient and easier to write.

We decided that for credibility with developers we would ship our library source code. Microsoft never shipped source code and guarded it closely. In this case, though, Jeff thought this was important and supported us. This meant, however, that we needed to make our code pretty and free of the kinds of things that routinely peppered the code of Microsoft products—comments like //BUG or //DON'T TOUCH THIS CODE. As part of this we also chose to use the Afx prefix in the code as well, which ended up being the source of many rumors trying to discern its meaning.

Finally, we were absolute zealots about performance and memory usage. We were running on 16-bit computers with Windows 3.0 and memory was tight. RickP taught me a bunch of ways to measure and report on memory usage that I not only implemented but reported out every single day. Every night, late, I mailed out the changes to the project in lines of code, size of compiled code in bytes, and size of the most trivial program, "Hello World."

Displaying Hello World on the screen was a technique pioneered by the creators of the C programming language. It allowed programmers to compare programming languages (which they loved to do) by looking at the simplest program.

If something went in the wrong direction, we were required to explain it. Every. Single. Day.

While this was going on, we were helping the compiler team to ship. There was a massive amount of work to build a C++ compiler and we were one of the only products under development using C++.

Since we still needed to compete with Steve Jobs, our team was simultaneously working on an even bigger project. Version 1.0 of the Foundation classes were a fraction of the scope of what we needed to get done.

012. I SHIPPED, THEREFORE I AM

"Who are you and why are you here?" –Dave Cutler (DaveC)

By July 1992, it seemed like the whole of the industry gathered in San Francisco at the Moscone Center for the first Professional Developers Conference which came to be known as the *Win32 PDC*, named after the 32-bit Windows APIs that were unveiled and the cornerstone of the event. For the first time Microsoft also mentioned *Chicago*, the code name for the successor to Windows 3.11, which would become Windows 95, real soon now. More than 5,000 developers attended this event, an enormous number, and were introduced to Windows NT 3.1 Preliminary Release Build 297, dated June 28 and provided to attendees. As I recall, something like 25,000 developers ultimately received the first CDROM.

Windows NT was a next-generation operating system, aiming for the professional workstation and high-end data center markets to compete with Unix and VMS, from Digital Equipment Corporation, DEC. The project leader and architect was the legendary Dave Cutler (DaveC) and included a group of experienced industry engineers also from DEC, collectively the key members of the original VMS team. Windows NT was a 32-bit (and soon 64-bit) operating system designed from the start to run on several of the latest microprocessors, including those from Intel rival AMD and Silicon Valley upstart MIPS. When it was under development, it was always scheduled to ship *real soon now*, though the project was always under control and managed with military precision and discipline. The task of building NT was immense. Like every project, it just took longer than people thought it would, even the most experienced people.

At the PDC the OS was referred to as a beta by most. Not quite a beta, officially it was labeled *Preliminary Release for Developers*. It was a build, basically the most current version that worked. The team was extremely hardcore about maintaining daily quality. Every day a build was created that was reliable enough for the team to self-host. The NT daily build was as solid as anything Microsoft was doing at the time, and it was a new OS built from scratch running on brand-new hardware. It was impressive, even in its early stages.

Along with the compiler and tools from the Languages group, a major effort, we released a beta version of our entire MFC application framework, which eventually became version 2.0. This included the ability to create Windows programs for NT on MIPS and '386 chips (by this time the industry was calling chips '386 because the *i386* from Intel had a competitor in the AMD *Am386* which was fully compatible), and Win32 and also Windows 3, now referred to as Win16. For the sake of completeness, I should mention "Win32s" the implementation of the Win32 API on Windows 3.1. It was viewed as potential way to expand Win32 applications to existing PCs. In the end it sounded better than it really was. We even considered using it for the C++ product, but at the time it was comforting to developers who thought it would expand the reach of new Win32 applications and a classic Microsoft approach of trying to include existing hardware and code in a new strategy.

Reaching this milestone was huge for our AFX team, all 18,692 lines of code.

Our team shipped our first product! I shipped a product! It was a beta and all, but still. It was on a CDROM and everything!

It was also my first time speaking at an industry conference. This was a huge conference with many tracks and a wide range of developers. C++ and OOP were extremely hot topics, so I ended up giving a talk to what seemed like the largest room I had ever been in, certainly bigger than the USENIX ballroom and bigger than any meeting on Microsoft's campus. By this time, we had a great story to tell about being reformed oopaholics and "hardcore", using C++ as a better C, and, importantly, about our class library being all about Windows and not competing with Windows or duplicating it.

A funny thing happened along the way to the PDC—I got to meet DaveC. It was terrifying. And then gratifying.

As soon as it became clear that MFC and C++ would ship with the PDC release of Windows NT we were introduced to the NT "ship room." This was a conference room, but one where the team met every day to discuss bugs and propose changes to the product. The NT team (and many other teams) preferred to call it the "War Room" as a source of pride, sometimes even officially with an officially engraved door sign. I always hated that term and wouldn't use it. Building software is not a war, at the very least. It was lorded over by the most imposing engineer I ever met, DaveC. Everyone was terrified of Dave. No one wanted to be responsible for slowing down progress or worse introducing an error somewhere that caused problems for others. The ship rooms in Apps were challenging but nothing at all like this one. During the NT project, Dave famously put his fist through the wall. The team memorialized the hole by writing the date next to it with a marker and putting a wood frame around it. Things were different over there. My role was to attend these meetings regularly and not say anything, and if I was asked something, to say that "MFC was on track and had no issues." And then go back and do everything to have no issues. Keith Rowe (KeithRo) had the job representing the compiler to the ship room and was constantly given a much harder time at these meetings. I am certain his Canadian disposition served him well in these moments. I just sat in the back and wasn't allowed to make a mistake.

There was just one thing. I thought the Windows NT team was making a mistake, and a big one. We were building MFC to make it easy for programmers to create apps for either 16-bit Windows 3.0 as it was shipping millions of copies and for the new 32-bit Windows NT. We were committed to using the Windows APIs and not fixing them or changing them. Unfortunately, there was an organizational and philosophical schism between the 16-bit Windows 3 team and the 32-bit NT team. The resulting divide created a difference in the APIs for each Windows, a difference in expression (in WINDOWS.H to be specific) that made it difficult for the APIs to work in C++. Ostensibly, this was due to expanding the APIs to handle twice as many bytes that is "widening" from 16 to 32 bits. But much of it was also rooted in assumptions for how compilers worked which were not correct. The functionality was the same, but it would have made it tricky for developers and would not have worked if there was ever a world where we would move from 32 bits to 64 bits, which of course happened a decade later. The idea of a seamless and scalable API from 16-bit to 32-bit (also 64-bit) Windows was a key strategic initiative and it felt like we were at ground zero showing it was not coming together nearly as clean as it could. There were also a good number of gratuitous changes in Windows APIs, among the 350 or so that existed at the time, that were made by the NT team, likely "fixing" some irregularities or inconsistencies in the original Windows APIs.

Jeff thought this was a great opportunity for me to show leadership—an opportunity for advancement as they say in the military. He sent mail to DaveC subject line "Win32 issue" and copied me suggesting that I meet with DaveC.

Once again…terrified.

I was a newly minted lead who had never shipped. I hid in the back of the ship room. I was trying to ship our product for the first time on the biggest train at Microsoft. I was supposed to meet with a larger than life *General of Windows NT*. On some level, I wanted none of this.

I went over to meet DaveC though. It was just the two of us in one of the tiny conference rooms with a single 60-inch round table that made up the interior ends of the single X buildings. I was sitting there. He walked in and looked at me and in an annoyed tone barked, "Who are you and why are you here?" I was prepared with all sorts of printouts and descriptions of the problem and began to explain. There was an argument of sorts but mostly he kept asking me why I waited so long to bring this up. This would be a massive change, when every change was scrutinized, even without the PDC deadline. Like every good engineering manager, I would come to understand figuring out who messed up was far less important than the stress over fixing it so late in the process.

I went on to explain that we were a new project and the first people doing C++ programs on top of both Win16 and Win32. I explained how we modified the code in question and tested it and it works fine—of course everyone always says that about changes. I tried to steer the conversation, to the degree you could call it that, to where Win32 varied from Win16. I didn't understand why things changed or assign blame. There was some more yelling, though not clearly at me as much as at the situation. I recall sticking to my ground only because it seemed so obvious and even trivial. In hindsight, I had no experience with how off-the-rails things can go by making small changes toward the end of a project. These would be changes in the mother of all files, WINDOWS.H. I really can't believe I advocated making that change. I'm pretty sure later in my career when sitting in the other seat I never would have accepted it so late.

Nevertheless, the change happened. I didn't ever get the benefit of an admission of my correct view in person. Rather on my way back to building 17 (while I was feeling like throwing up), DaveC sent an email to Jeff that read, "fine" or something like that. Jeff was proud of me, and I was relieved and felt I accomplished something but really it was just weird. To be honest, I felt best when RickP, someone I thought so highly of, said months later, "I heard you went and fought with Dave Cutler [emphasis in his voice] over this change and won."

Shortly after the PDC, *Microsoft C/C++ version 7.0 Development System for Windows* released to manufacturing in August 1992. It took time to *manufacture* and distribute to stores because the box weighed over 42 pounds in shipping and included 23 floppy disks and over 10,000 pages of printed documentation in 24 books. The box was so large that Microsoft's own manufacturing facility could not handle it and it was ultimately packaged at a plant in Oregon that handled sporting equipment. This was physically the heaviest product Microsoft ever shipped and the last time a developer product was released on floppy disks.

With C7 shipped MFC 1.0, a subset of the pre-release product from the PDC. It was a set of "helper" classes that could be used to make some aspects of C++ easier. It was not a framework for building an application, but rather simply some reusable code. Importantly, it was our team shipping and that is what mattered. At Microsoft, shipping equated to being relevant, plus *real artists ship.*

MFC 1.0 was constrained, and everything Jeff (and ScottRa) thought would happen did, which was that the product helped our team figure out how to ship. The biggest lesson a new team can have about shipping is that once you ship, it gets easier to do it as a team the next time.

We had work real to do to compete with the NeXT system.

We hardly had time to catch our breath. While we were shipping MFC 1.0, the bulk of the AFX team, about 15 of us, was building an entirely new tool for creating Windows apps, with the code name *Composer*, playing off the idea of art and artists creating and shipping.

Composer was the tool to compete with NeXTStep Interface Builder, where a developer arranged the dialog boxes and menus of their app using a mouse and GUI. Composer was also going to be the first large-scale Microsoft app written in C++, using MFC. We were self-hosted or, as the Windows NT team called it, *eating our own dogfood.* This expression was rooted in the 1970s commercial for Alpo dogfood—"the kind dogs love to eat"—and later used in an email from PaulMa extolling the virtues of using pre-release software ourselves. Composer was using the complete class library we shipped in beta at the PDC.

We still needed magic though. Composer already had a competitor recently acquired by Borland shipping with their C++. *Borland Resource Workshop* (BRW) became a favorite among developers. There was also a Borland Class Library called *Object Windows Library*, OWL. To me, OWL seemed a lot like Old AFX, bloated and different than Windows. With these tools, however, Borland was making significant headway with professionals.

ScottRa was the magician. The key challenge with Windows programming was that it was finnicky and verbose. There was a lot of bookkeeping and rote code that was error prone. Doing simple things, like putting up a dialog box for the user to make some choices and acting on those choices, was hundreds of lines of code, all with ample opportunity for mistakes. For most professional programmers who honed their skills in character mode and MS-DOS, this stuff was maddening.

Visual Basic pioneered the concept of making it easy to code GUI programs. The problem was that it was not viewed as a professional tool and was much more geared toward business app developers and not commercial C programmers. In use, NeXTStep looked like Visual Basic but used what was considered a more professional (albeit obscure) language.

ScottRa previously worked on something used across the big shipping products in Apps (Word and Excel) called SDM, *standard dialog manager*. It made it easy to design user interface and get information to and from the end-user. He cleverly took those same techniques and built a way for MFC to accomplish this same task. Instead of designing the interface by typing text in an editor, a programmer used Composer to connect windows, buttons, and checkboxes (controls) to MFC C++ classes. The programmer added any extra required code, like if the input needed to be a valid phone number or something. Even better, if the developer needed to add another control, that could be done without any worries about breaking what was there.

We believed we created the first graphical tool for C++ programming that allowed code to be created and modified and then later changed without breaking it. Programming tools that created code were common, but they were usually limited to only creating code once or creating very fragile code that was difficult for programmers to modify or incorporate into large-scale projects.

Composer was slick. Super slick. Thanks to the program management from ClifS and the coding artistry of BradCh, the app itself was pioneering user interface techniques for Windows soon seen across the industry. A favorite example was the small *property inspector* window that floated on top, always showing the details of what was being worked on. It had a cool little thumbtack to keep it locked in position.

This wasn't all a theory, either. It was being used in practice. Composer was being used to build Composer, which was itself built with MFC. We were building GUI tools using a GUI framework. Having said that, there was one challenge. We did not have a GUI code editor or debugger. Those tools were still the old C 7 character mode tools. It was not at all clear we could make the tools run well on Windows 3.0, while Windows NT was still not going to be a broadly used commercial product for some time. On the other hand, the next C++ product wouldn't be ready for some time. This was, again, a classic schedule chicken between two big teams with their own agendas.

The Languages team previously shipped the Quick C compiler for Windows, but it was a different code base from the professional compiler. The editor and debugger, collectively called an *integrated development environment* (IDE), were not nearly the same level of professional tool as the character mode ones. The challenge was if we as a big team could bring the IDE together with Composer and MFC to create a professional development environment in and for Windows, then we would have something to compete with NeXTStep.

It was rather contentious. The idea of being on Windows 3 was technically problematic because Windows was not robust enough for development. If the program crashed while being written then the programming tools crashed too, probably losing work. Since programs always crashed when being built, Windows was pretty useless as a programing host. That didn't stop Borland though. Many professionals were on OS/2 and anxiously awaiting (or moving to) Windows NT. For better or worse, there were many fans of the C6 and C7 character mode tools. While the need and wish were obvious, the technical limitations were plentiful.

Schedule chicken is never fun, and generally at this point in Microsoft's evolving engineer culture, everyone was wrong about their dates. I think many on AFX felt the Languages team was too conservative on making the bet on GUI. Many on the Languages team thought the AFX team was naïve and was not being pragmatic about what could be done or the risk to losing to Borland if we got caught not shipping for a long time while we waited on Windows. There were deep concerns on all sides about performance such as speed to compile a program, which reviewers measured in exhaustive multi-page reviews. There was tension and frustration, and we were still behind both Borland and NeXTStep. The Languages team was much more concerned about Borland, especially with the various teams at Microsoft continuing to make noise about performance relative to Borland. We were just as concerned about NeXT because that was the charter of our group. With no prior product experience and no connection to existing customers, the choice to build GUI tools seemed abundantly clear to me. In reality, I had a lack of empathy and experience upon which to base my opinion.

We needed a decision across the teams, so Jeff scheduled a meeting with MikeMap, who by now was leading all of product development at Microsoft in a sprawling role as executive vice president of the Worldwide Products Group.

This was my first senior executive meeting. I am sure MikeMap had already heard all sides of this in previous discussions with various leaders, as should have been the case. I was a new lead sitting in the outer ring of chairs—the observer seats. Many people were in the meeting, which began with a slide outlining the big decision to be made. The decision was whether to make a big leap to a Windows/GUI integrated development environment on NT or to stick with what we knew to be a favorite among high-end professionals especially those in Apps, which was a character mode IDE, or could we make something work on Windows 3, but how. There were schedule questions (and chicken) and technology questions.

There was an enormous deck with insane levels of detail across marketing and engineering. Right at the start the first slide was labeled, "Decision" and an indication that the team was looking to Mike to lead the way.

MikeMap had a sage and entertaining way of disarming any room and imparting wisdom at the same time, and he was about to do that. He looked around the room and said, in his Oklahoman accent, "There's a lot here…much more than I can absorb in an hour. How long have y'all been working on these foils and this problem?"

The room looked perplexed. MikeMap was still fairly new to most people, especially Languages. Everyone sort of mumbled in their own way, an indication that basically this is all we'd been working on for weeks or more.

Mike then said, "Y'all been working on this longer than me, and know more than I will ever know. Why don't you just tell me what you decided to do and then we can move the project forward?"

It was an incredible moment and frankly the opposite of everything I'd been culturally prepared to hear. We all envisioned executives as people we went to for answers, especially BillG and the big architects. Here was the newest but most experienced senior person at the company, telling us to decide on our own. Classic Mike, as it would turn out. That single interaction made a profound impression, and it was the first of many lessons from Mike in this same spirit.

Nevertheless, we debated vigorously among ourselves in front of Mike, a mistake. At one point, from the gallery, I overstepped my bounds and pushed too hard and in too negative a way in favor of moving to Windows. At least in my head I thought what I was saying was obvious. Microsoft was a contentious place, but it also wasn't in-your-face aggressive, especially around Apps, which had a far more refined culture than Windows especially Windows NT. And definitely wrong to do in front of Mike. And from the gallery.

With all pros and cons aired, the team committed to building a Windows hosted toolset and to find a way to make things work for Windows 3.0, committing to a separate project optimized for NT later. Composer would be one part of a complete Windows development toolset, including a compiler, code editor, debugger, and so on. We were, at least we thought, on a path to have something credible to compete with Borland and NeXTStep. The meeting was tough and what people were really looking for was the right to own the target ship date if they were also being asked to create a new product. That's what Mike could assure the team.

After the meeting, someone told Jeff that my participation in the meeting was poorly received. He summoned me and insisted that, by the end of the day, I personally go and apologize to the leader of the C++ dev team, Dave Weil (DaveWe) then report back. Sheepishly, I did what I was told. I most definitely learned my lesson.

Jeff was cool like that, perhaps due to his own experiences. At a time when Microsoft barely had any people management at all and most of HR was recruiting, I was getting a lesson. As I would soon appreciate, especially after Windows Word and with the arrival of MikeMap, an incredibly strong and maturing management culture had developed in Apps but still needed to make it to new people like me and to Windows.

It would come to define the teams I later worked on and how we (and I) aspired to lead.

With the tension behind us, we were in the final stages of shipping a Windows IDE, a new Composer, a complete class library MFC 2.0, and a tool for creating apps. This last tool was known as *App Wizard,* or AppWiz as we liked to call it.

AppWiz was our big demo. In an era where creating a Windows app could take days and required a 900-page book, a developer could with a few clicks and without ever leaving the comfort of Windows create an app. It was industrial strength and professional. We still had to prove to pros that this was not a toy app and was as powerful as writing a C app in the style of Charles Petzold's *Programming Windows* book, the bible of Windows programming.

Taking a lesson from shipping MFC 1.0, we tracked daily the lines of code and size in bytes of MFC 2.0 but also the number of clicks, lines of code, and size of the "Hello World" app created with AppWiz. Our goal was to fit Hello World on a single page, or even better a single slide, without cheating or breaking the purity of the MFC app framework. We achieved this goal, and it really wasn't a hack or fake. In a just a few clicks, a fully functional program capable of having multiple windows, file open/save dialogs, help menu (that was important back then), and even an About…box, which was important since that is where the name of the programmers often went. The killer feature, which was even eventually employed by Netscape for Windows, was printing with print preview, notoriously difficult features. We made them essentially "free"—all the programmer needed to do was add the code for drawing his or her content on the screen.

Given the compelling nature of the demos, I was about to experience hand-to-hand combat in the world of software and developer tools. Borland was going all out to gain the upper hand, and with the beta release of what was being called C 8 (and what was in the NT PDC build) there was starting to be some grumbling about how efficient and "compliant" MFC was with industry standards.

The way this was done back then was two-fold. First, companies wrote detailed technical white papers of 20 to 30 pages and circulated them to the press and influential analysts. These papers served as background material and were used by writers as sources. They rarely saw the light of day because by reusing the content in them rather than quoting them directly all the analysts and writers seemed more objective and smarter. These white papers amounted to "gentlemanly trash talk." This was sort of the air war of competition.

Second was the use of the old USENET newsgroups at a grassroots or hand-to-hand combat level. This was much more direct and much less polite when going after each other. USENET was a massive trove of the internet's first worldwide bulletin board system. It was organized into groups much like today's Reddit. There were several interesting groups for MFC and C++ with names like comp.lang.c++.standards or comp.os.ms-windows.programmer. Technically this was pretty much all that was on the internet in 1991. Getting on the internet from within Microsoft wasn't easy back then so often I dialed up from home or went downstairs to the Microsoft lobby and used the fax line and then went through my own dial-up service, crazy as it sounds. Eventually the groups were available internally through a mirror site.

On these groups people posted arguments or rants about topics, and then a long argument thread ensued. I spent hours debating people, some anonymous and some from Borland even, over the esoteric aspects of C++ language syntax and rules or topics like the performance of MFC Windows programs. The old internet devolved the same way today's internet does, only the tools change. Most discussions eventually end up in a stalemate or name-calling.

Eventually, I took matters into my own hands. Back from the Borland Developer Conference (BDC) in San Diego that I attended under an assumed name since my original registration was rejected as a Microsoft employee. Borland was like that. I wrote my first guerrilla marketing and technical buzzsaw taken to a competitive product. A *buzzsaw* was a favorite Microsoft technique used to look at a competitive product (or even code from another team) and quickly find all its flaws or weaknesses. At the conference, they were vicious and trashed the current release of C++ and the beta with MFC 2.0. All fired up, I wrote my first white paper, *Borland C++ & Application Frameworks 3.0 vs. Microsoft C/C++ 7.0: An Exposé / A Draft Response Prepared by Microsoft Development*. I did my best work to shred the Borland competitive assertions in a whitepaper they distributed at their conference.

This was the start of writing missives late at night in hotel rooms, which became a pattern for some of my best work, said humbly.

We just needed to ship. At least I shipped once, finally.

013. END OF THE BEGINNING

As we closed in on release mid-1992, the product needed a name. Naming products at Microsoft was known to be somewhere between painful and traumatic. That proved to be so for my first experience.

I already learned that my accidental naming of Microsoft Foundation Classes caused two problems. One was a cease and desist from a French bank over the use of the acronym MFC as software and banking were the same trademark category. This made us spell out Microsoft Foundation Classes everywhere which led to the second problem of absurd complexity and grammatical gymnastics in our volumes of documentation. Oh well.

It was clear the compiler was going to be version 8 because compilers just get version numbers and continue to. C8, as everyone called it, ultimately became the world's best and most industrial strength C++ compiler. It was an achievement.

MFC 1.0 (I'm stubborn about the acronym here) was officially bumped to version 2.0. Class Wizard and App Wizard names remained. Composer became the visual centerpiece of the product and gained the name App Studio, which was how we competed with NeXTStep Interface Builder.

Naming the individual pieces was easy. What to call the entire product was tricky. Microsoft was notorious for finding it difficult to arrive at simple names. In this case, calling the whole collection of tools C++ 8.0 or something descriptive, and the logical successor to C/C++ 7.0, seemed lame and not all that competitive with Turbo from Borland. As we debated, some advocated reusing the Quick moniker, but that represented the low-end or amateur programmer. It was complex.

In the meantime, Microsoft Languages had a huge hit product on its hands, Microsoft Visual Basic or VB. VB came from out of nowhere—it was a combination of Microsoft's BASIC language runtime with a Windows-based "forms" editor and runtime, an idea originally seeded by an email question from BillG. A runtime or runtime library provides programmers with additional capabilities that can be accessed by the programmer as a form of reusable code. Some runtimes provided simple capabilities such as basic math functions while others can provide sophisticated capabilities for creating games or connecting to databases. Runtimes were in many ways the heart and soul as well as a secret ingredient of the early PC era. Basic had a runtime. dBase had a runtime. Runtimes were even a vibrant market where developers could buy special purpose ones for use in their applications. These runtimes presaged the world today of APIs and services.

GUI forms were windows with buttons, checkboxes, menus, and more associated with them—BillG loved forms and would spend the next decade pushing for more and better implementations from many different groups. VB pioneered the ability to rapidly draw a form then use the BASIC language to program all the logic of an application, called *code behind forms*. VB 1.0 released approximately 18 months earlier but took the world by storm, particularly among professional developers inside of corporations. In code name shorthand, VB was *Ruby plus EB*, EB was short for the embedded BASIC runtime, and Ruby was the code name of the forms package, and together had the code name Thunder. A version of the forms portion was created independently by Alan Cooper and acquired by

Microsoft. Alan was later honored as an original Windows Pioneer and is known as the *Father of Visual Basic* for his work.[2]

Coincidentally, Visual Basic was also loosely an ancestor in the Quick family of products and the original editor and development environment derived from QuickBASIC. It seemed logical then that the new C++ product should take on a similar naming scheme.

There were a lot of meetings, a great deal of consternation, and even some lawyers. It turned out that the success of VB spawned a cottage industry of people registering product names derived from Visual before Microsoft. The various Languages marketing teams agreed to start a family of products, first with Visual Basic and then Visual C++. Microsoft also worked to secure a few other visual names, though Visual COBOL from Microsoft never made it to market. While we called the product *VC++*, BillG stubbornly insisted on calling it VC for some reason.

Just before we launched Visual C++, I attended a fall 1992 meeting hosted by Microsoft at the original Northup building (Microsoft's second Bellevue location after moving from their downtown location in the early 1980s) down State Route 520 adjacent to Burgermaster, then home to *Microsoft University* (a.k.a. MSU), which created books and training materials for Microsoft products. At this meeting, local commercial companies talked about their experience using the new C++ compiler and tools from Microsoft—specifically, why they chose Microsoft over Borland, which was all we cared about.

Seattle was home to a couple of large independent companies building Windows software back then. The largest among them was Aldus, creators of PageMaker and inventors of the desktop publishing software category. PageMaker was an early Windows app and one of the first to require a mouse, and it was also a big product with a lot of code. Winning them as a customer over Borland was a big deal.

When it came time to present, the PageMaker engineering manager made a strong case for why Microsoft's product was solid. Aldus presented benchmarks for compile time (the time to produce a running program from source code) and runtime performance for key operations. Aldus PageMaker was computation-intensive and highly dependent on how well C++ created code. Finally, joining at the podium, the leader of PageMaker's C++ rewrite presented and went into depth on the adherence to language standards and completeness of implementation. Sitting in the back with a few members of the team, we were beaming with pride.

After the presentation I went to thank the speaker. She introduced herself as Julie Larson. We talked for quite a bit in the parking lot about their internal C++ library (which sounded surprisingly Old AFX like), and after a while she mentioned it was late and "I need to get off my feet" as she glanced down towards the ground. I was a bit confused by that comment and then realized she was pregnant, something I might have noticed at first and then did that awkward thing one might do to avoid looking down or commenting. Microsoft would soon experience its first baby boom, having just gone through a first wave of thirtieth birthday parties. I mention this only because while on leave with her new daughter Katie, she was recruited by Denis Gilbert (DenisG), the new general manager of VC++, to join the team. This chance meeting and Denis's strong recruiting work began an incredibly important Microsoft career. JulieLar would go on to be a key leader, along with many alumni of the VC++ product cycle, in the elevation of Visual C++ to the Visual Studio product line. Later, she became arguably the company's most significant leader and manager in building human-centric Microsoft products. For me, meeting her was the start of an incredibly important product development partnership.

Leading up to the launch event, I was quite busy learning the ropes with the press—something that I would end up doing a lot more of for the rest of my time at Microsoft. The focus of the VC++ product messaging ended up being the ability to create Windows programs, and that made me a good spokesperson. We spent a lot of energy trying to move the evaluation criteria for "compilers," from compilation speed and code size to how fast a Windows program could be written and how easy it was to modify it.

The state of the art in evaluating products, perhaps represented best by the elaborate labs at *BYTE* magazine or *PC Magazine*, was to have dozens of PCs running all sorts of automated tests dozens of times, averaging the results, and compiling endless tables of comparisons. These labs were incredible and rivaled our own in-house testing labs. There was a strong desire to distill results down to quantitative measures that readers loved, which always posed a challenge when working to tilt evaluation criteria towards what we were strong at. Ultimately, VC++ did well in reviews but still took a few years to win over the hearts of developers even if we won over the minds.

In the early 1990s, the press reviewed products in two waves. Usually at RTM the next issue of a monthly or weekly would have a *first look* short form that was usually not much more than the voice of the company, perhaps with a little doubt as to execution or a bit of wait and see. Then after a few months and an editorial calendar opening an in-depth review would appear. These reviews were often the work of a full team and weeks or more of dedicated work, from benchmarks to real-world usage across the leading products in the category.

The most fun was the trek up to *BYTE* magazine's offices in rural New Hampshire in what was a converted agriculture or bovine research facility of some kind. No really, it had huge elevators to move cows around. The trip there always included a stay-over at the famous Jack Daniels Motor Inn and the Peterborough Diner. Today, the only equivalent of reviews like we used to receive are those that run in *Ars Technica.* A typical review would be ten or more pages, with several full-page tables. Part of visiting each publication, usually for a half day or more, was an attempt to influence the *rows* of all those tables—what criteria would be evaluated. While we were adversaries in a sense, I made a ton of great friends on those trips across editors and writers.

I mention these trips and the reviews because Jeff had instilled in me an absolute obsession with reviews and digging in and reading them in depth. This was quite different than what you hear about people in other creative fields that stay away from the potential criticism of reviews or reviewers who aren't necessarily skilled, or whatever. Jeff's view and that of Apps was the opposite and reviews were everyone's job to understand, read, and absorb, and not just our reviews but the competition as well. BillG read all the reviews too and he was always current and up to date. Losing a review was almost a guarantee that you'd receive email asking why.

Everything was in the home stretch. That meant that while people were coming to work to triage and investigate, it always appeared as though they were not doing much but postponing issues and re-running tests. In the projects of this scale and duration, there was an irony that productivity dropped to effectively zero at the end of projects. Making any change was always riskier than shipping whatever was being fixed.

The Group Product Manager in charge of marketing for the Languages business picked a launch date and venue at the Software Development Conference (SD93) in February at the Santa Clara Convention Center. The event featured black-tie presenters and an orchestra theme—Visualize Your Masterpiece. This venue was generally where big tools for developers were launched, the newly recruited marketing leader Jim McCarthy (JimMcC) pulled out all the stops for a huge event.

Back in Redmond in our AFX hallway there was clearly a well-earned sense, from Jeff, of mission accomplished. He had led the creation of a new team, alignment of strategies across the historically strong-minded Languages group, and created a new category of professional development tools for Windows and in Windows. To some, he redeemed himself from that Word experience. We accomplished the BillG goal of not making the same mistakes again. The two years went by quickly and even though I felt like I had wasted a lot of time early on, looking back, at what we accomplished would not have been possible without all we had endured. I learned the classic engineering lesson that every failure is simply practice for success.

The introduction of Windows 3.0 and products like Visual C++ for Windows marked the end of the first era of personal computing and the start of the transition into the next—while Windows 3.0 and 16-bit successors were the overwhelming customer choice, attention already shifted to full, or native, or real 32-bit computing as shown by Windows NT previews. Win32 is where developers wanted to be. In fact, a quick turnaround of Visual C++ 1.0 specifically for Windows NT was in the works.

The GUI revolution was about to kick off a colossal expansion of computing throughout the workforce and home, and then the internet accelerated that, or perhaps it enabled the internet, beyond anything imagined in Redmond.

Culturally within Microsoft, I came to understand that in a sense I completed my schooling in the worldview of Apps, and I fully embraced that culture. This was almost certainly pre-ordained by my path to Microsoft having started out in computing building business apps, and at each step I saw the product built through the lens of the end-user or business problem rather than from the bottom-up or technology perspective. The Microsoft Apps culture was also one that held a distinct view of how teams are led and managed and products planned and executed, distinct from the traditions I saw in Systems and Languages. Jeff created a little Apps “island” in the sea of Languages and Systems when he created the AFX team. My Apps perspective would stay with me for the rest of my career. I owe everything to Jeff, and he was not done supporting me.

Having said that, while that perspective would prove transformative for me as a future manager, there were also times it would test me.

With 1993 coming to an end, the team geared up for future releases, including the transformation of VC++ to Visual Studio. I too was ready to build on our successful product. My mentor Jeff and HR leader Natalie Yount (NatalieY) had different plans for me as I was about to find out.

1993-1994

After almost five years at the bottom of the Microsoft organization learning the ropes, I am given the opportunity to see things from the very top. I take on the poorly defined role as "Technical Assistant" to BillG. No one is quite sure what that might entail, but there is so much going on. Microsoft is at the start of developing a new future operating system, eventually Windows NT. At the same time, Windows is also in the midst of the development of "Chicago" or eventually Windows 95. Office is making huge progress and so is the new Server business. I learn firsthand how BillG sees strategy and running Microsoft.

014. EXECUTING ON THE EXPANSIVE VISION OF BILL GATES

I blew off Bill Gates the first time I was supposed to meet with him—well, at least the first 20-plus minutes of our meeting in the fall of 1992.

I had been in AFX group leader Jeff's office talking about some last-minute ship details for VC++ when I realized, "Oh crap, I am supposed to be meeting with BillG."

Days earlier, Natalie Young (NatalieY), at the urging of Jeff, spoke to me about taking a job that I knew nothing about, working for a person I had never really met, doing…I had no idea what. It was called technical assistant.

NatalieY represented a rarity at Microsoft. She was a core torch-carrier of the company culture, but not a technical person. She came from the famed Xerox PARC where she worked as a research librarian in the labs during some of the most innovative years at one of the most innovative places in technology or anywhere. At Microsoft, she quickly captured Microsoft's culture and became the leader that bridged fresh-out-of-college technologists and the real world.

During our meeting, she and I talked for a bit about me, my least favorite subject, but our conversation did not feel like an interview. Then she described the job. There had only been one other official technical assistant and that was Aaron Getz (AaronG), another college hire who had worked with DougK on Microsoft Money as the only program manager. Carl Stork (CarlS), a college classmate of BillG's, had previously unofficially held the job very early on where he worked with Bill on the organization of commands for *Multitools* apps. Richard Brodie, the original Word for DOS developer and former Xerox PARC engineer held the job for a year in what he described as a lousy choice for the role. Jabe Blumenthal (JabeB) had as well. JabeB had joined Microsoft as a college hire in the early 1980s. JabeB was the original program manager at Microsoft and had led the design of Microsoft Excel before leading efforts in the newly formed Consumer Software Division, where multimedia CD-ROM products and other *home* software was being developed.

It sounded like the job was "assist BillG with technical stuff" I thought to myself. In other words, there was no real job description. Jeff later described it as BillG's "eyes and ears" on a deep technology level so he could continue to be engaged in a way he wanted to. That helped slightly. One thing was clear: The previous holders of this job were Apps program managers, while I was more of a Tools software design engineer. A concern (BillG had, I was told) was that as an SDE I lacked a big picture view and was too focused on the code, but that was not how I had been trained. JeffH told me not to worry.

Natalie later sent me a note and copied BillG's assistant to schedule a meeting.

In thinking about what this sort of *meeting* would be like and how to prepare, the realities of Microsoft began to sink in. Not the product realities, those I understood well, but the realities of the company and that it, and BillG, were changing.

Jeff, my mentor who clearly arranged for this meeting to happen, offered me some of his insights. First and foremost, he confided in me that the company was now at a scale that Bill can't keep track at the level of detail that he wants to. This was not to take away from his IQ or anything, but just simply that Microsoft had a lot of stuff going on. Jeff talked about how he could not put a finger on it, but Bill was "different" during the formation and shipping of AFX products—different in the sense that his input was more abstract, strategic for sure, but not at the level of detail he engaged on the evolution of Word or the first versions of Windows. Bill wanted to and believed he could continue to engage at a deep technical level, but Jeff felt he needed tools, or a person, to scale that effort. That's how he came to suggest me to Bill.

Second, the company was clearly entering a new phase. The release of Windows 3 and the subtle but deliberate changes to how NT was evolving were clear signs that Microsoft was no longer dependent on IBM nor was Microsoft's forward-looking success due to IBM. Bill said as much in his email on *Strategy for the '90s*.

The first few years after Microsoft's IPO had been kind to Microsoft. Whether on the cover of *Time Magazine* in 1984 or the cover of *Fortune Magazine* in 1986, the image of the youthful and brainy nerd cemented Bill as a leading innovator of our age. Heck, it seemed like the whole country was embracing khakis and button-down shirts. It was like the ten-year old film *Revenge of the Nerds* had become reality.

Then came the book *Hard Drive: Bill Gates and the Making of the Microsoft Empire* by two reporters for the local *Seattle Post-Intelligencer* who had covered Microsoft for some time. The book had just come out, Spring 1992. Everyone at the company knew Bill, allies, and employees did not cooperate. It was clearly intended to portray events in a negative light and was trying to be the first to do so and succeeded. Writing today, I've learned that books like this are written too soon and amplify (or even get incorrect) events that are still happening and still unclear, the *fog of war*. Even today reading the book's stories of hidden bugs designed to disadvantage customers or third-party developers seem as patently absurd, and false, as they did back then, even if the book spun a yarn saying otherwise. The arrival of the book began to color interactions with the press that to this point had been even-handed or even celebratory. Microsoft and Bill seemed to be entering the bad part of the cycle of build you up, then tear you down.

The real difficulty was the cloud of regulatory oversight that was just starting to form. While there were one-off stories, there began to be a critical mass of what might be called *business practices* that were claimed to be at the root of the success Microsoft was achieving. In other words, with the success, people were looking for the cause. Microsoft's aggressive business practices were starting to be viewed as crossing some line. There had to be a way to explain the success that was not rooted in building great products, or so it seemed.

The way that employees could see this were through stories in trade press most often with quotes from who we viewed as competitors, or perhaps even bitter competitors that had lost. The primary dynamic going on that we talked about at lunch endlessly was how the success of Windows even caught Microsoft off guard compared to the determination to make OS/2 and the IBM partnership work. What Microsoft did was not pull back or even sacrifice that partnership to bolster Windows, but rather was just quick to recognize the product was not working and to find a different path. Unfortunately, most of the leaders in the industry chose to stick with IBM even longer than Microsoft did. That caused a lot of bitterness among the software leaders of the first era of the IBM PC, all of whom were under increasing pressure to have similar success on Windows. My old friend from drinks at the *Software Development Conference*, Philippe Kahn the founder and CEO of Borland, was one of those who led the charge, even advocating for IBM.

What was so weird was that in the lunchroom we were mostly relieved. It was not a master plan, but a master pivot.

There was then the constant stream of opinion pieces in the trade press criticizing Microsoft for products that were late or buggy. Every product was late and buggy. While we might argue at the very least our products were less buggy, given the financial success the industry and customers were expecting better.

Across the industry trading barbs in the press nearly continuously for the past year or more over the future operating system platform was now routine. Analysts and executives on all sides would say the others are spreading "fear, uncertainty, and doubt" or *FUD*. FUD is a tactic, or theory about a tactic, designed to prevent customers from buying rival products by sowing negative views. In an ironic twist that really gnawed at Microsofties, often it would be said that Microsoft was employing a FUD strategy just as IBM had done before and perhaps even Microsoft, in the early 1990s, had become the new IBM—a recognition of the declining influence of IBM in the personal computer industry and Microsoft's rising influence, or even dominance. NT was viewed as the center of claims of FUD because it was shipping *real soon now*, and at the same time Microsoft was indeed putting forth a pretty grand vision for the product that would take years to materialize.

Internally both now and for quite some time, Microsoft felt and acted like the insurgent. The computer companies we knew growing up were being left behind and many companies we knew from just a few years ago were struggling with the transition to PCs from mainframes and minicomputers. It was not difficult to imagine that fate for us if we just missed a few beats, executed slowly, or failed to deliver. At the same time, we were just struggling to keep the wheels on trying to deliver products, fix all the bugs, and make things work.

The narrative outside of power and influence simply didn't match our day-to-day experience of fragility and challenges. We'd read about power and did not feel it or even understand what it felt like. Certainly, no team returning from a BillG review felt power. They felt the same pressure to achieve technically.

It was all super weird.

These were all really big issues, the subject of lunch time gossip. I could never hope to have an intelligent conversation with BillG about them.

I was more worried about Bill asking me questions about technology I would not know the answer to. Or pushing me on flaws in our products that I had been part of creating. Maybe even saying something that was "the stupidest thing" he had ever heard. I wanted to be "high IQ" even though it was still unclear if I was interviewing for a job or just doing some sort of informational meeting. I had no idea what it was like to change jobs inside of Microsoft and almost no one I know had even done that yet, save for OS/2 people moving as the project started winding down.

I set up a time to meet with BillG.

015. EVERY GROUP IS SCREWED UP

"Nice of you to show up." –Bill Gates (BillG)

I was hyperventilating by the time I got to BillG's office, having raced from building 17 to the double-X building 8 overlooking the fountain. Being late was out of character for me. I never missed anything. At the time, it was entirely typical for BillG to be late. Bill totally changed this later in life and became maniacal about being on time.

Once I made it to BillG's office on the second floor (there was an executive suite, but no special receiving area or security or anything), his executive assistant, Julie Girone (JulieG), gave me the look one would expect to receive for showing up late. Still, she pointed to the open glass door, where I got another look, this time from BillG, that basically said, "Nice of you to show up."

BillG's desk was a giant pile of memos, papers, magazines, books, a lot of three-ring binders for BillG Reviews, and two old school leather travel suitcases were by the door. I would soon learn that Bill traveled with one suitcase of clothes, and one used as an over-stuffed briefcase and laptop bag. The bookshelves were jammed with more books and older review binders. He had the same oak desk that we all had, but he had the deluxe version with a credenza and a long bookshelf on the wall above. On the few bare walls, there was a framed poster of the layout of an Intel microprocessor and another of a radio wave spectrum map, and on a narrow column was a photo of Henry Ford. Behind the spectrum map was a secret white board.

We sat on the standard-issue Microsoft couch. I tried an icebreaker by mentioning that I had been difficult to get ahold of during college recruiting season three years earlier. BillG un-hunched himself and laughed a bit too loudly and then said, "And you were late to this."

OK, this was going well.

What was left of our hour was a blitz of questions—deep technical ones about Windows, C++, and Excel. The former surprised me in a sense because even though he had pushed so hard on NeXTStep, he was not as deep into programming Windows as I might have expected. The latter was interesting since he knew I didn't work on Excel. As we talked about Excel, the questions were much more about user interface and topics such as handling text in the product, connecting to databases, and new features (at the time) such as toolbars (the rows of icons representing commands, that previously were hidden in menus or complex keyboard sequences) and automatically generating better charts and graphs.

At one point, he said, "You seem to know a lot about Excel."

This surprised me and I wasn't sure what to make of it. How could I not know about Excel as it was a flagship app? I was surrounded by the Excel team from ADC including DougK through that talk with JonDe as well as AFX with both Jeff and RickP. And I used it every day for computing all the stats about MFC.

When we discussed Windows, his concern was performance as well as the difficulty of writing software for the platform compared to NeXT. I was super prepared to talk about that. While I was talking Bill would engage in his characteristic rock—a little hunched over, elbows on knees, rocking back and forth in his chair, lifting his toes in an almost choreographed manner, pausing only occasionally to push his eyeglasses back into position.

He talked about C++ at length, without asking any questions, about extending C++ in a proprietary way to make it easier to write Windows programs. While this could, in hindsight, sound nefarious, it was not. First, Borland had not only done this but was touting it in the press. NeXT had essentially taken over a programming language, Objective-C, which was much more appealing to BillG than using an industry language like C++. And second, Microsoft had a long history of essentially owning a language going back to BASIC. This was how the industry worked. IBM owned COBOL and Fortran. Sun and the Unix world owned C. PCs owned BASIC. It seemed like a natural evolution waiting to be exploited to improve the platform. Over the years, we ended up having many debates about when and where proprietary languages and APIs made sense.

Obviously, with our meeting cut short, a second one was needed. For this one, at Jeff's suggestion, I brought some of the patents I had applied for in developing MFC and we talked about those. BillG loved patents and was interested in what I had filed as a result of working on C++. Patents were new to the company, and we had heard the first mention of them at a recent all-company meeting where BillG said we would file patents more often going forward, but they would only be used defensively. This was a big deal because the libertarian streak among programmers was quite real and patents were viewed as almost anti-software by many developers, including me. This was also a response to ongoing litigation with Apple and a lawsuit between Borland and Lotus over whether user interfaces were patentable or simply copyright protected.

I got the job and accepted it. I never really thought about the decision, almost entirely because Jeff told me I needed to do the job for the good of Microsoft. So yeah, that worked.

I was never really sure how much thought Bill put into the role. My sense then and now was he was very happy with the way Aaron had provided a sounding board but remained lukewarm on the role. He was still scaling (as we say now) with the company and was still reluctant to let go.

Later, I learned that after bumping into BillG prior to my official start while at Jeff's wedding, and having little to say to one another, BillG sent a note to NatalieY expressing concern that I might be too "shy" for the role. At least he didn't say something about my tardiness.

I started in the new year, after we completed VC++ (RTM!) and our old AFX team was integrated with the larger C++ team in Languages. Right before I left for the holidays, I moved into my new office—my fourth office in three years. Tucked in the back of the *executive suite* was a supply closet and a small (smaller than typical) window office overlooking the fountain, so that was nice. I had the same oak desk and bookshelf but no room for a guest chair. I shared a wall with BillG on one side and Greg Maffei (GregMa), Microsoft's then treasurer, on the other. The walls were thin. Greg talked loudly on the phone a lot.

Aaron was still cleaning out his office when I arrived. It was a huge job as there were papers, boxes, books, magazines, products, and piles of stuff. While Aaron was finishing up packing, I began contemplating a trip to Fred Meyer for 409 and Lysol. I was always a bit finnicky between office moves.

The first and most well-formed thing Aaron said to me was, "Look, you have to understand that every group is totally screwed up."

OK. Well, that was good to know.

Coincidentally, BillG said this same thing to *The Wall Street Journal* in May 1990 when asked about a late product that year. "I'd say there's as much screwed up now [at Microsoft] as there always is."[3] This was in an article at the launch of Windows 3.0 that chronicled all of Microsoft recent failures including OS/2, LanMan, and even optical drives, CD-ROM.

Aaron explained that a big challenge in the job, one I still did not yet understand, was that there seemed to be an endless series of meetings. In each, every group presented what was going wrong. Even if they didn't offer what was going wrong, the meeting would turn into a forum to find out what was going wrong. This focus on what was not working was a hallmark of not just BillG meetings but email and other interactions. There was little time to waste on what was working.

He offered a second piece of advice. "Bill knows everything about every group and never forgets what they told him at the last review meeting."

Aaron said, "I thought he knew what was going on because they told him the last meeting and he remembered it. Then after meeting with some groups for a second time I realized he remembered *everything*—things I didn't remember and even things the team didn't remember (or wanted to forget) going into the meeting."

Good to know. My notetaking skills would be put to good use.

With little additional guidance, he summed it up by saying the job would be what I wanted to make of it and to be helpful to BillG. His parting words were, "Start looking for your next job now because it is going to take you forever to decide which screwed-up team to join."

In hindsight, all of Aaron's advice, what little he offered, proved correct.

016. FILLING THE VOID LEFT BY IBM

Getting settled in my new office was pretty much like each of my previous moves. Unpacked my boxes, placed my developer-issued books on my tall bookshelf, and began to setup my new Compaq LTE laptop. This was my first corporate issued laptop.

Trying to figure out what I was supposed to do was a bit weird. It wasn't like I could check in with my manager, or should I?

BillG was generally free from ceremony and rather spartan in executive presence, including minimal staff. He had JulieG, who handled scheduling, travel (commercial and in coach), direct inbound calls, and everything else, literally. His small reception area had the same oak receiving area that was in the front of every building and it was staffed by an administrative assistant, Debbie Stanley (DebS.) She handled all the calls from the main switchboard, primarily calls to 206-882-8080 requesting, "Connect me with Bill Gates, please", as well as all the inbound postal mail and packages, which would eventually get screened, but only later in my tenure as tensions around the world increased. And then there was me. My title was technical assistant, but it became apparent I was really assistant for everything else. I kept his home and office PCs running, mail connected, slides made, and anything else that kept us efficient, especially when we were on the road, and it was just the two of us. Bill had not grown a dedicated staff, nor had any executives in the company really, and instead leaned heavily on the team he was working with for any event, sales call, or other external work. If he was giving a speech about Windows, for example, the Windows marketing team and DRG (Developer Relations Group) would make the slides and iterate with him in a meeting before leaving for the event. I'd end up in most of these meetings.

No sooner had I moved into my office than I was off to Semiahmoo, a golf resort near the Canadian border, for the Management Conference. Semiahmoo had become the site of all the official executive offsites, though few of us knew anything about golf, especially me. This was my first time at a fancy offsite with executives and my first opportunity to spend time with about 35 people in jobs I had no familiarity with, including sales, subsidiaries, corporate functions. I was told I was invited to attend because of my work on C++ but now attending as TA had the effect of setting me apart, preparing me for how people would react differently to me.

The format of the offsite was straightforward and, as I learned, the canonical Microsoft offsite format. Upon arrival, we had a small mixer that included the most basic of matchmaker games. We each previously provided an interesting, yet unknown, bit of trivia about ourselves and we matched trivia to people by meeting and talking. The fun tidbit we recalled for years was that one attendee had "just met Sting." That was BillG and he was excited about it.

During the mixer I encountered the first time I had to introduce myself as Bill's TA. I wasn't sure how to answer the most basic questions about my new job. Did I say, "I'm Bill Gates Technical Assistant" or "I am on BillG's staff" or maybe "I work for BillG." No matter what I came up with I was answered with a pause and then a follow up question asking what I *really* did. Since I'd been on the job just a few weeks, my answer was always vague, but not on purpose. Even at this offsite, my fellow Microsofties were circumspect or even a bit put off by the role. It became awkward for me. For external use, I ordered business cards that simply said "Technical Assistant to the Chairman" which turned out to mitigate things believe it or not. It was saying Bill's name that got the attention, not the title. For Japan, I was told I must have a Japanese language card and it must have Bill's name on it. Internally I quickly came to realize people I was not close to always thought I was eavesdropping or something. To say the role was isolating would be true, but at the same time I found myself in most every meeting with people ten years and 5 stops above my actual pay grade.

We then convened in the small auditorium at the resort. BillG and the new VP of Human Resources, Mike Murray (MikeMur), who moved from Marketing to Human Resources. Before Microsoft was the legendary head of Mac marketing at Apple who led the launch and creation of the famous 1984 commercial. Mike explained that the offsite was basically the same offsite the executive staff had held, and the idea was to see if a "select group of up-and-coming" *Softies* would come up with better or different answers to the questions posed to executives. There were nine executives in attendance, which was about one-third of the worldwide executive staff at the time. There were only eight executives in the product or technology part of the company and half of them were at the retreat.

We were divided up into five teams of five and, after a brief discussion with a relevant vice president sponsor, we were given a challenge to resolve over the following day and a half.

By design, none of us had firsthand knowledge of the topic at hand and we were 120 miles north of Seattle, practically in Canada. There was no such thing as the internet and no Microsoft library. We could, however, call the library in Redmond to have articles and answers faxed to us. But mostly, we were supposed to brainstorm and use the knowledge we already possessed to extrapolate or divine an answer.

Some people (me) seemed more stressed than others.

It would be a few years until Andy Grove, then CEO of Intel, would write his seminal book on management, *Only the Paranoid Survive*, though he had written *High Output Management* years earlier. But long before that or perhaps always, BillG was paranoid. It is no surprise then that most of his brief 30-minute introduction to the offsite was focused on all the ways everything at Microsoft might collapse. In hindsight, as good a management approach as this was, it was arguably a ludicrous proposition that embodied the deep conviction of paranoia that permeated our collective thinking. To those that had been around for the 8-bit PC era and now the struggling mini-computer market, technology companies simply disappearing like a once active geyser at Yellowstone was not in the least bit paranoid.

Still, in 1993, there were already more than 30 million computers running Windows, and over 27 million IBM-compatible PCs were shipped compared to more than 3 million Macs. That statistic obscures the fact that Microsoft was still making much more money for each Mac than for each PC simply because of the dominance of Word and Excel on the Mac compared to the nascent success of Microsoft Apps on Windows, which was still dominated by customers running (primarily) MS-DOS apps like Lotus 1-2-3 and WordPerfect. Those numbers represented a growth of about 30 percent year-over-year, which had been going on for several years already. Microsoft was definitely not on the verge of collapse.

Still, the first breakout topic BillG introduced was "Doomsday," and that group was assigned the task of outlining a doomsday scenario for how Microsoft's growth and/or leadership could be attacked by competitors.

Another topic, which would become increasingly important in my role as TA (and later in Office), was how Microsoft could move away from licensing perpetual software and become more of an *annuity* business. This would also become exceedingly relevant decades later in a world of Software as a Service (SaaS) and subscriptions. When I think about this topic, one I spent many more offsites trying to crack, I realize just how far ahead BillG's thinking was. Or, admittedly, how far back he was looking since IBM had long since pioneered leasing computing resources rather than selling them.

Owning software was an aberration in the beginning and middle of the PC era. It seemed inevitable that it would end, though many considered computer software to be the logical successor to music or VHS tapes without the rental.

Our group's topic was, "How to fill the void left by the demise of IBM." It was 1993 and Lou Gerstner had not yet been named CEO, which was just a few weeks away. IBM was on the verge of insolvency. This was not something looked at from afar as IBM and Microsoft were linked by a Joint Development Agreement for OS/2 and IBM remained a leading maker of PCs. The JDA would be wound down but would take some time to do so completely.

Our group's executive sponsor was Brad Silverberg (BradSi), who was leading the product development and marketing for Windows, including the new version under development code-named *Chicago*, which would become Windows 95 and later consume a huge amount of my attention as TA. Brad was relatively new to Microsoft but joined at a senior level with a great deal of experience, having worked at Apple on the predecessor to Macintosh, Lisa, and then at my nemesis Borland, but at least not on C++. I would be lucky to spend a lot of time with Brad over the next few years and fortunate to have learned from him early in my career, first as an assistant and then as a member of his team.

After the remaining topics were introduced, we broke into groups. Our group could not have been less prepared for discussing the IBM enterprise business. We had a finance person who worked on the costs of software licenses, a Product Support Services (PSS) leader, the general manager of Microsoft Hong Kong, a manager from the consumer software division, a leader from Excel marketing, and a manufacturing specialist who worked at the packaging plant north of main campus.

Not one of us in our group understood the IBM business all that well. My personal experience was with the IBM mainframe at Cornell, loading punch cards and changing the ribbon on the giant IBM printer while wearing arm-length rubber gloves. I sat next to the "ladies" that coded IBM reports when I worked at *Martin-Marietta* during the summers after my first two years of college where I learned some of the ins and outs of COBOL and RPG.

Collectively, we knew three things: First, IBM was in dire straits in early 1993 and on the verge of bankruptcy—a rather stunning decline from where it had been a few years earlier when I was working at Martin Marietta, and it was on the verge of one hundred billion dollars in revenue. Second, a few of us had read the best seller *Father, Son & Co.: My Life at IBM and Beyond* by Thomas J. Watson Jr., a personal history of IBM. Third, we had all heard the expression, "Nobody was ever fired for buying IBM." Our task was to stitch those together into a coherent view of turning Microsoft into a reliable business computing brand.

We sent off an email to the library for a briefer on the IBM business and received back a faxed Annual Report and writeups from financial analysts. We certainly learned things were bleak. Then we also received materials from industry analysts that were looking at IBM mainframes and topics like account management and how many MIPS per year IBM was selling. MIPS are a measure of CPU power used by IBM to measure sales, representing the quaint notion of millions or machine instructions per second. We had about 50 pages of material to go through. None of it seemed all that relevant to Microsoft's products or sales efforts.

We were up late and were making progress on the whole idea that Microsoft maintained an arm's-length relationship with customers, whereas IBM had big account teams assigned to customers and in many cases, they worked on site full time, which seemed just crazy to us. Those that worked in the Microsoft field and finance had familiarity with these teams and I realized the people in full suits in the hot Florida summer that occupied our hallways at Martin Marietta were those very account teams.

In the introduction, BillG had pointed out that most of our sales still came from retail sales—literally from people going to the store or ordering multiple copies from a reseller. While we had volume licensing, this was a program about to roll out developed by a member of our team.

Today when I talk about the idea of transitioning Microsoft to the enterprise business, most people can't believe that was ever a "thing." Microsoft is perceived to have been born into selling enterprise products. In reality, the company grew out of two other ways to sell software. Bill and Paul pioneered the idea of an OEM relationship with computer makers to include BASIC for a small fee, and later MS-DOS. This proved incredibly profitable at relatively low prices but with very high penetration to each computer sold. Second, products like Word and Excel were sold one copy at a time through retail sales outlets for what seem like incredibly high prices, such as $495 for Word. There was even resistance to "bulk discounts" or "site licenses" because those clearly would end up with much less revenue from customers that used the product the most. While each sale was profitable, perhaps only 10 percent of new PCs owned (legal) copies of Microsoft applications. Microsoft was just figuring out the idea of how to sell just the software (not the hardware) to large businesses. Steve Ballmer moved to lead worldwide sales and was just beginning to build Microsoft's efforts to be the colossus that it is today. He wasn't at the retreat. The driving product force behind this transition was Windows NT, which was still months from RTM. The transition to building and selling enterprise products would occupy the next decade of Microsoft's evolution. This offsite was clearly my introduction to this transition and by proxy, Bill was getting the executive staff broadly familiar with the topic.

We concluded that to fill the void left by IBM we needed to have account teams and build better customer relationships. We needed to de-risk the notion of the PC and PC software. We also needed to be in the networking business, which was dominated by Novell. We had a big project underway called *LanMan* that was the "red killer" as red was the Novell corporate color. Much of what we concluded might seem obvious in hindsight, but in a sense, Microsoft was learning this in real time.

We pulled together a deck and I ended up doing the typing. The person most closely resembling program manager at an offsite always made the slides, which, surprisingly to me, somehow meant I was going to lead the presentation. I was a bit intimidated. I made our group listen to me do a dry run late the night before. That was probably too much, especially since they had all been to a wine reception before.

We were only given a few minutes to present and so there were only about a dozen slides. See what I did there, way too many slides. I vividly recall using some of the now vintage PowerPoint clip art. When describing how demanding IT was, I used "demanding guy," which was a cartoon of a bald man pounding his fist on a table. In describing how IT thought of Microsoft, I used the cartoon of a mainframe computer reaching out and strangling someone.

We presented the idea that IBM was much better at articulating a vision for computing than Microsoft. Microsoft needed to present a more forward-looking vision. The irony was that everything the company talked about was mostly considered *vaporware* by the press and customers since most of our products were perennially late and released with fewer features than we originally talked about. The idea of not overpromising was a core MikeMap belief, which he instilled in Apps, and which was most decidedly a pillar of my own value system. I would struggle with articulating a vision versus overpromising for my entire career.

BillG sat in the front row, hunched over, elbows on his knees, rocking back and forth. With every rock backward his toes would lift up and every rock forward his heels would lift up. That was his trademark that I was growing accustomed to. It meant he was listening. Occasionally, he grabbed his yellow pad and wrote something down with his felt-tip pen, usually circling or putting a box around whatever he wrote. Before we could even finish, he was asking me (or us) to explain how this elaborate plan would escape creating customer expectations we could not meet. IBM basically promised to deliver no matter the cost, and the best part about Microsoft's business was that everything we sold was sort of "as is." We had no idea what was going on with the customer and had the margins to prove it. One could argue this was going to be a lesson that would take a decade or more to learn. BillG was at once concerned about setting higher customer expectations while also failing to provide a compelling vision. That was probably my first and most visceral experience of BillG taking something most think of as an *or* and turning it into an *and*.

The offsite essentially wound down as the teams presented. Throughout the two days the other execs came and went. They all had clipboards and were taking notes. Years later, when I possessed a clipboard, I would learn that while the goal was to produce a presentation and enrich yourself, the execs were basically evaluating your performance in the group.

Sneaky.

Back at the office, I started to find a bit of a rhythm though was still unsure of when to participate or not. Given my newly minted expertise one of the strangest things I did just as we got back to the office was to sit in Bill's office when he and newly appointed IBM CEO Lou Gerstner had a phone call. For Microsoft this was a call to a big customer who made very good PCs that needed an operating system. For IBM, this was a call to a former partner now a supplier or vendor to the PC business, and a competitor with OS/2. The industry was buzzing with how IBM should be broken up and sold off for parts. Conventional wisdom was also pondering a non-technical outsider leading IBM. The most vivid memory I have is Bill articulating how the strength of scale IBM possessed was the reason *not* to break the company up. Gerstner of course went on to an incredibly successful run, though he did eventually spin off the PC business.

I continued to learn how to work with BillG. More than anything I was absorbing his focus on competitors.

017. EYES ON COMPETITION, ARCHITECTURE, AND WHITESPACE

Unsure of exactly how to interact with BillG or what to do at all, I got some insight about a week after the offsite as I was summoned to his office. Holding a Microsoft supplied steno pad like I was going to take shorthand, I headed through the glass door to Bill's office, where we had our first discussion of expectations and process. He suggested I look at the schedule and be sure to attend review meetings, which sounded easy enough. He told me he didn't need notes summarizing the meetings (as I had sent him a few times previously) but he told me that I should be on the lookout for any interesting follow-up items. He also did not seem interested in being briefed before the meeting, which seemed fine to me, but later in life I would come to appreciate that this was unique to BillG because he was able to dive into any topic. Rather than briefs, I would develop a process of sending notes on what I had learned about the broader concepts prior to meetings.

Bill then rattled off a list of topics that were top of mind: text strategy and code reuse, forms, indexing, image editing, multimedia authoring, Microsoft research, Lotus Notes, architecture, and more. Bill seemed to think in two dimensions.

First, lists. Everything was always a list. The list of technologies was consistent over time and rarely did something fall off the list. Instead, something was either making progress or something was in a bad state. Usually, these technology lists had a single team in mind that owned (or should own) each item or worse there were several teams with competing and suboptimal implementations. The lists were two columns, the problem area in one and the people or teams in the other.

Second, calendars. Everything was always viewed through a time dimension. Bill would routinely sketch out a calendar with a black felt tip on an ever-present legal pad. This would map out the next weeks of meetings or next months of milestones, relative to that list of technologies or perhaps speeches or travel. While Bill was always keenly aware of his time, he often ran late or over in meetings. That would change later in life. We did not have fancy Microsoft Exchange schedules back then with delegate access or anything. In fact, there was no personal Schedule+ calendar for BillG, the Microsoft scheduling product we used at the time. Everything was kept in JulieG's Schedule+ to avoid moving things around or removing appointments "accidently." The real source of truth was an old fashioned large-format appointment calendar where appointments were written in pencil and the pages archived at the end of the week. If I ever really needed to know what was going on, that calendar was where I looked.

It quickly became clear that redundancy and inefficiency in code and the use of *scarce* developer resources was top of mind, all the time. Bill was worried about redundancy across groups and, while this was inefficient in headcount, more worrisome was the inefficiency in code and thus memory. Everything always came back to memory because Bill squeezed BASIC into 4K, over the weekend as he would remind people, still. Redundancy also created a suboptimal user experience because no single group devoted the resources to do an excellent job on one code base and every group just built a *random*, a classic BillG word, subset that was just enough for them. Something like text editing drove him crazy. Everywhere in Windows apps people were building little mini text editors with varying levels of capability. Some supported basic formatting like bold and italics. Some others might support Japanese characters but not right-to-left languages. Others might support editing but did not have good support for copy/paste across apps, and so on.

Several of the topics on that list were places where this inefficiency existed, and it was *super annoying*, another BillG phrase, that no group (specifically Windows) was solving this problem. Which meant that we needed a group that was *hardcore*, more BillG vernacular, focused on text editing. Apple Macintosh had one extremely good text capability, why couldn't Windows? Office eventually solved this with the RichEdit project leveraging the incredible typography and typing from Word, but it ended up being too late for the internet and so now we're all using the editing and rendering capabilities of HTML, which are still trying to catch up. Text editing, forms, graphics, storage, and more were all places where from Bill's vantage point most everyone was building incomplete subsets of what should be much bolder and more reusable offerings from Microsoft, and Windows.

A constant tension existed between groups trying to keep up with cross-group synergy (loved that word) while being given the latitude to determine their own destiny and a strong desire for a highly leveraged, efficient, and centrally executed plan. BillG meetings were a place where the downsides of empowered execution would constantly bump up against the perceived benefits of coordinated and centralized strategy. There were always more ideas on ways to leverage grand architectural plans than there were practical ways to implement them.

A key role I ended up playing was to represent the execution side of these observations or debates. I always felt it was easier to have the grand unified theory than to execute on something, especially when everything was already late and not quite working. BillG's strength was in letting go—providing the input and knowing when to push and when to pull back. The execution focus that I brought (that I didn't quite realize I had) would become closely associated with me, both positives and negatives as I will write more about.

What I came to realize over time was that BillG was not using these meetings to confirm or affirm the direction of a team but rather to push them to do more or to do better. While teams would view a successful meeting as one that did not get redirected, there was rarely praise that matched the confrontation. Unlike leadership and CEO books, or what might get taught in business school, BillG was not asking to look at metrics or hear a presentation on the validation of strategic goals. He also was not there to provide emotional support to the team, at least not yet. He had three tools and he used them: competition, architecture, and (what always seemed to be) some wild card or "whitespace."

First, how did the product shape up against the main competitor? Every product had a main competitor and BillG is a very (very) competitive person. One of the oldest traditions at the company was the *Microgames,* an annual summer party up at Hood Canal where teams would compete in a summer camp sort of environment. It was not unheard of for BillG to seek, let's just say, an advantage for himself. He also assumed competitors would flawlessly execute, and any attempt by a team to claim otherwise was a tactical error in the meeting.

Regardless of having a plan to compete or not, failing to know the competition inside and out meant a meeting was going to go poorly. BillG was a voracious reader of all the trade press and product reviews, and when he wanted to make a point, he would take them at face value and not let groups debunk the claims or test results. Every weekend he read *The Economist,* which was sent to his house via some sort of VIP subscription. Monday he would devour *PC Week and InfoWorld*, every day he read *The Wall Street Journal* and *The New York Times*, and every month he read *BYTE* and *PC Magazine* which at that time were the size of the fall *Vogue*. Product groups that would attempt to point out that a given review gave a competitor too much credit or were too harsh on Microsoft would find themselves in a debate as though they were talking to the reviewer or an executive from the competing company.

In meetings, Bill would often be provocative to the point of over-stating the strength or capabilities of a competitive product. He would exaggerate the performance of a competitor or even claim a product was faster or easier to use, sometimes without personal knowledge. After a while it became easy to tell he was doing that because I knew if he had used a product but also because he had a bit of a *tell* in the meetings, often looking at me as if to seek validation. I made it a point of being able to amplify these points from personal experience of some kind. Unless the meeting was not going well, and then I would use up some of my own credibility or competitive experience to bring the meeting back into focus and off the defensive.

Second, and this was a moving target, but how architecturally sound was the product? Was there strategic code reuse? Where did the product make use of native Windows features versus rolling its own implementations? Where did a product have a proprietary advantage? How was the product extensible by developers or customizable by end-users? Was the product redundant at a deep technical level or overlap with another product?

Third, assuming that a product had answers or at least credible discussions for the previous two, BillG always maintained the option to bring up something that seemed from out of left field—but in practice this was his way of making the team think about its product in an entirely different context. The most common way of doing this was to point a product group at another team, usually somewhere in Windows or Microsoft Research, that was doing something BillG viewed as more innovative or had a broader vision or could be connected in a way that the whole was greater than the parts.

Bill thought a great deal about "whitespace", or new opportunities that were important or critical and fell in between different teams rather than completely within a team. Perhaps it was dealing with IBM all those years, Bill clearly understood that the best way to compete with any company is to build products that fall between two teams or executives. In a big company, both teams will usually fight to claim a competitor is in their sights, but rarely will they execute directly. Then when the company is losing the organizations will turn around and say they never intended to compete directly. Some companies were deliberate in hedging bets and having multiple competitors in the labs, so to speak. To Bill this was inefficient and wasteful. He wanted the best group owning competing, which sounded great. At the same time, however, he wanted all the necessary other groups to contribute to a new competitive offering. That, as we will see, was almost always where Microsoft ended up under-performing relative to a focused competitor with only a single organization.

The reason the discussions about unseen opportunities were always the most difficult in meetings was that a team was working on the area, or more likely that some team was doing a little bit of the area, but they did not have a big enough view of the opportunity, or they were thinking too tactically to really get ahead. Most of the frustration that would emerge from product meetings would be rooted in the misalignment between what appeared strategic to BillG but meant an overwhelming amount of work and collaboration to a product team for a relatively minor win, and on the unacceptable time scale the work would take place.

I quickly found myself getting into the rhythm of these meetings. As one might expect, not being on the receiving end was far more enjoyable than having to put in tens of hours of preparation and showing up hoping for the best. I essentially bucketed groups into three categories.

There were groups that were executing and had a good story. Fortunately, these were the big groups. It wasn't like the meetings were always happy time, but by and large the meetings would go as expected. Whether it was the NT team that would show up with performance numbers needing work, or the Office team needing to be easier to use and reduce overlap, the conversations often were tense but not crazy. Whether the group was executing or not looked different in these early days—everything was late so a group that was executing well was just simply late, but not out of control. Most of the time the dates were not even the subject of the meeting and for many projects it could be said it wasn't even clear what the target dates meant or how reliable any dates were. Generally speaking, just getting to the next milestone (a beta test usually) was all that mattered. As much as it hurts to say, these groups did not need Bill's help. That was difficult to admit. It was, however, an incredible achievement that the most important products (still very early in their lifecycle) were already staffed with leaders and executing in an autonomous way.

Second there were groups that were executing but their story was not compelling or did not appear to be achieving any sort of escape velocity to speak. Many groups were capable of "shipping", but the problem was that shipping was not going to add up to much in terms of a competitive win or substantial revenue. These meetings in many ways were difficult. Many were products that were started (often by Bill personally) with the best intentions but somehow ended up being less interesting as they closed in on becoming a product. Perhaps the area of "consumer" software meetings, rooted in the innovative work of CD-ROM titles was the most like this. At one point there were dozens of new "titles" for the holiday seasons each with wonderfully rich photographs and text, unlike anything ever seen on a PC, covering topics such as the pioneering *Encarta* encyclopedia, *Dogs*, *Cats*, *Musical Instruments*, *Isaac Asimov's The Ultimate Robot*, and the much-loved *Cinemania*, like today's IMDB. The challenge with these groups was that the meetings would inevitably focus on that framework of competition, architecture, and whitespace. Those are where Bill was most effective, but not really where the problems were with the efforts.

Third, the groups that were not executing but had wonderful stories to tell. This, as it would turn out, was where I would spend the most of my time and where Bill was spending most of his time. The challenge for me was how to be constructive—how to encourage more execution while not being the one to take away from or deflate the story. There were so many of these projects that I might even say that the early 1990's was a time when Microsoft had far more great stories than it had execution. In many ways this was the expansive vision Bill had for the company firing on all cylinders.

The next year or so I would spend trying to do my part to help Bill help more teams get from their fantastic stories and lack of execution to a bit more focus on execution. Perhaps what I ended up learning more than anything, was just how much the initial seeding and DNA of a group end up defining the outcome.

I was still getting my rhythm with Bill and earning his trust. I had to figure out how to have a *high bandwidth* relationship with him and wasn't there yet. I needed to ramp up more quickly as there were some of the biggest projects in company history underway and these would prove to be the foundation for everything to come over the next decades.

018. MICROSOFT'S TWO BOUNTIFUL GARDENS

I had to figure out how to have a *high bandwidth* (a BillG word) relationship with BillG and the key execs in his orbit, known as the *Office of the President* created in early 1992. I felt I should reach out to leaders and meet with them to see if they had any idea how to do this job. Microsoft was organized into a triumvirate or *troika* of executives (something about using a Russian word just after the fall of the Berlin wall seemed exciting to the press): Steve Ballmer (SteveB) leading Worldwide Sales Support Group (WWSSG), MikeMap leading the Worldwide Products Group (WWPG), and Frank Gaudette (FrankGa) leading all the financial and administrative functions. Collectively, this was the Office of the President, which Microsoft promptly turned into the acronym BOOP for *Bill and the Office of the President.*

The BOOP filled a gap left by the retirement of Jon Shirley (JonS) who, from 1983, served as president and chief operating officer through 1991. JonS brought a level of scale and discipline to Microsoft's execution that established the solid foundation upon which everything was subsequently built. Jon remained on the board through most of my time at the company. I, and many others, benefited enormously from his wisdom. After Jon retired, Michael Hallman joined to fill Jon's role. His tenure was only two years and was not a match from the early days. The reports at the time focused on that failing and to some degree viewed the new organization as Microsoft giving up on hiring external executives. As it would turn out, that was probably true.

It was no surprise, but MikeMap reached out even before I had a chance to reach out to him. He was like that. Walking over to his office I was running through the scope of his job in my head.

As I became Technical Assistant, TA, MikeMap was almost a year into managing all product groups and organized them into divisions: Systems, Desktop Applications, Database and Development Tools, Consumer Software Division, and Workgroup Applications. This was an enormous job by Microsoft standards, but relative to Mike's previous employer IBM ($60 billion in sales, 250,000 employees in 1993) this probably didn't seem so huge. It was the first time all product development was under one executive who was not BillG. That was actually huge.

WWPG was a sprawling organization. Fiscal 1993, which was only half over at this point, brought in more than $3.75 billion in product revenue, with more than half coming from Applications, $2.17 billion, and about 34 percent from Systems, $1.27 billion. The remainder from hardware and consumer. It had 14,000 employees. While Microsoft did not break out the profitability of each group, the reality was (and for years remained) that the operating systems were more profitable because of the OEM model, the original equipment manufacturers or PC makers. Few inside or outside would realize the revenue size of the applications business relative to MS-DOS and Windows, a theme that would be consistent for another 20 years. By most every account and every action, the operating systems group came first, and applications were the gravy. BillG understood the brilliance of developing both and building the network effect and ecosystem, but emotionally Apps played backup to Systems regardless of revenue, perhaps because of the profit.

Taken all together, this was MikeMap's WWPG world. The Research & Development budget was $470 million that year, or more than 4,000 people. He also had the marketing for all the WWPG, though there was a significant shift in budget, ownership, and accountability for marketing with SteveB leading sales—distributing much of the spend and accountability to country managers.

Mike brought with him a wealth of experience from IBM. Many believed that wealth of experience demonstrated what we should *not* be doing or copying. This was decidedly true for the Systems teams who had forged a beneficial, albeit dysfunctional, relationship with IBM over the past decade, most recently with respect to OS/2, which by this time was circling the drain along with the IBM-Microsoft Joint Development Agreement. In practice, MikeMap's experience in managing organizations at massive scale was not only relevant but essential for Microsoft at this point. He had seen it all when it came to org dynamics and dysfunction. Not only was he in the right place at a much-needed time, but he was exactly the right person.

Mike didn't fear change. In his first year, he restructured his Apps division from a largely *functional organization* (for example, one large team of engineers and one large team of marketing) to a group of independent *business units*. The reason was clear—these were independent businesses. They had distinct customers, with distinct product schedules, and distinct competitive dynamics in the marketplace. There were some shared resources for localization and tooling, but they essentially operated independently.

Leading up to this change in 1989, MikeMap created a brilliant vision presentation, outlining at a deep technical level a vision for the evolution of Office. This was simply a presentation, but the slides and notes remained relevant for years and many, me included, were greatly influenced by it. As a seasoned exec, he knew the necessity and value of repetition, so in many ways this became his stump speech for Apps as he created the new organizational groups. As a result, everyone in Apps knew the vision and reasoning behind the organization Mike put in place and the future direction of products.

The names of these groups are seared into my memory as they became the lingua franca when talking about Apps for many years. Each business unit, BU, represented one product family of Mac and Windows plus some secondary products: Analysis or Excel, ABU, Office, not what might be thought of as Office down the road but Word and the nascent email business, OBU, Graphics or PowerPoint, GBU, Entry or Works, EBU, and the new Data Access or database, DABU. Conversations were littered with the use of ABU, OBU, DABU, EBU to the point of sounding like a language unto itself, or maybe a Beatles song, *aboo, ohboo, daboo, eeboo*. The leaders of these groups, known as a *business unit manager* (BUM), were ultimately the key product leaders in Apps and were responsible for the product in every aspect. Mike chose these leaders with care, making sure they came from a variety of backgrounds, not only engineering or marketing.

To my surprise, one thing Mike knew well was my TA job. In fact, he seemed to have more insight than even BillG or NatalieY about what the job could be. IBM had a long history of the TA role going way back. Mike offered me a whole framework for thinking about the role that was not unlike *Rumsfeld's Rules*, the famous Washington DC insider memo from the former Secretary of Defense.[4] Mike seemed acutely aware of the risks that could befall me as TA, of which I had no clue. In short order he offered some crisp guidelines that I wrote down (I was always taking notes) and stuck to religiously, even expanded upon and passed to future TAs:

- ☒ You are not BillG and don't pretend to be. People will try to get you to pretend to be BillG or channel him, which you can't do.

- ☒ Avoid talking about what BillG wants or what BillG would like to see. In other words, I should avoid speaking as though I know that.
- ☒ Remember that people don't care what you think; they care what BillG thinks. Your opinion isn't the one people are after. They might act like they care what you think, but don't be confused.
- ☒ Bring an outside perspective rather than more inside baseball. Mike suggested I could be BillG's eyes at events and meetings he could not attend, like conferences.
- ☒ Don't waste BillG's time and find ways to help him to be more efficient.

Specifically dealing with meetings and reviews, Mike said something that made me think: He said that at review meetings, people are hoping to be and do their best, but in reality, they are often at their worst. Even after my first few meetings this was already clear, but it was also awful because for most people a meeting with BillG was a career moment, at least they believed that to be the case, and something that might happen once in a year at most. The smartest, most thoughtful, and hardest working people freeze up or talk gibberish at meetings. The pressure to perform was real. Nothing makes one more acutely aware of the theater of meetings and management than sitting and observing the meetings of others. Conversely, not having to be on the hook at meetings also comes with a decided lack of empathy.

Mike's advice was to get to know people so I could serve as a bridge or lifesaver in meetings by restating or even redirecting an interaction to get to a more productive spot. Nothing would become more important to me over the years than thinking about executive meetings this way. It became almost second nature to me to jump on bad moments and try to diffuse them or pull people out of those horrid tailspins that can happen in reviews.

He also said his experience with BillG was that he loved email and so maybe that would be the best thing to do. Mike was varsity at email but never warmed to tiny laptop keyboards, even on his beloved ThinkPad. This was concrete and actionable for me.

No meeting with MikeMap was complete without a story, allegory, or colorful metaphor, and this introduction to WWPG would be no exception. I asked him for some guidance on working with the Windows teams or understanding the culture a bit, having briefly mentioned my experience with NT when I met with DaveC to explain why the NT APIs were broken. Windows was clearly front and center for Bill and other than being at the receiving end, so to speak, in Tools I was short on experience and insights.

In a colorful manner that only MikeMap would choose and doing my best to capture, he said:

> *Microsoft is like a home with two amazing gardens; one is the OS and one is Apps. Each is a beautiful garden, a very successful garden, in its own right. One of these gardens is maintained by people who are always in the dirt, with tools flying around, dirt everywhere, scraped knees and cut fingers, and in general just chaotic. But you look over to them when they are done and there is a nice garden. The other garden, well, you just look and there are nice flowers, and they are just tended to calmly by people. The first garden is the OS. The second is Apps.*

His view, which I ascribed to, was that the origin of each business contributed to this differing culture. To build an OS required being way ahead of yourself—the need for getting OEMs (massive giant companies) to make bets, device makers to build drivers, firmware, and more all require a level of evangelism that forces a level of aggressiveness that is akin to swinging tools around quite a bit. Building an operating system and computer while also creating an ecosystem of partnerships is a massive bootstrap problem. At the start, there's no computer and no operating system and everyone just wants to wait and see what happens—no one wants to be first and risk the opportunity costs. While individuals used an operating system, the paying customers were PC makers and to a considerable extent the wide array of independent hardware and software makers that were critical to fostering an ecosystem. Successfully bootstrapping created MS-DOS and later Windows, and that first garden.

Apps, which was making huge amounts of money and just recently closed in on the scale of Lotus and WordPerfect, had to start with individual customers and win them over, almost one at a time. This end-user appeal—specifically when it meant getting on a plane and visiting banks on Wall Street to woo them to Excel or government lawyers to get them to switch from WordPerfect—required a much more subtle approach. The culture of Apps was one of building, learning, and refining. It was often self-described as almost Japanese-like, which at the time was a high form of praise given the incredible rise of Japan's electronics and manufacturing industries. In the Apps market, it wasn't the absence of products that drove the culture, but the presence of so many alternatives. While people were using Word and Excel for the workplace, the paying customer was an individual or small department that was making a choice about what software to use and winning over these *influential end-users* were critical to gaining early momentum. Successfully winning over customers created Excel and Word, first on the Mac and then on Windows, and the second garden.

Neither culture was wrong or right in isolation, but in the context of the need for the business to be successful each culture made sense. I would spend the next two decades bouncing between each of these cultures trying to bridge them, work with them, and even transform them. It is why when people believed Microsoft was made of up fiefdoms or organizations out to get each other that I take strong objection—each culture had problems, self-realized shortcomings, or systematic issues, but each was what was needed and what was right at the time for what needed to get done. Conversely, those who saw Microsoft as one Borg-like entity were far removed from the realities of what it was like to make products inside the company.

This analogy and description fit my reality. It was vastly different than the politics or power portrayed over the years. Cultures evolve, but to experience the two gardens was to experience teams that were the culture of the work that needed to be done and not politics or pettiness.

While there were two cultures and Apps was making a lot of money, there were no doubts about the "high order bit," more BillG talk, and that was Systems, which was slowly becoming known as *Platforms*. Apps was still a few years from becoming known as Office given the Office product was only about 15% of sales in 1993. The company, and BillG himself, saw everything from the perspective of the Windows product and ecosystem. It was the big bet, and it was the primary engine. The success of Windows would enable the success of Apps, from Microsoft and third parties, and the growth of many companies making PCs. Seeing the choice of software and PCs would make Windows more attractive and further attract customers, developers, and hardware makers.

Culturally, Systems dominated. The culture of Systems was the culture of Microsoft and in many ways the culture of BillG himself. The outside world was beginning to see all of this. Internally, there was most decidedly a hierarchy, with Systems at the top and by and large the NT team, even though the product had not yet shipped, at the top of the top in terms of perceived product technical leadership.

The Apps teams, as strong as they were and as market leading as they were, did not seem to have that technical glow that the Systems always had, business results notwithstanding. It was not unusual for topics to come up where a Systems person was asked or might volunteer to opine about the best way to solve an Apps issue. It might be extreme, but the general view could be distilled down to the belief that Systems was *truly difficult* engineering work and Apps were *mostly trivial*. Such characterizations would often surface at review meetings where Systems would be proposing or discussing a new operating system feature that would replace something in Word or Excel with a few OS API calls. As a builder of a framework and on a team that straddled Systems and Apps, I found myself in the middle of many of these discussions. I became somewhat of a shuttle diplomat explaining to Apps why the OS felt it could add value by building an API and not remove a competitive advantage and describing to Systems the complexity of the implementation in the apps should they hope to replace code. From toolbars to standard dialog boxes to database connectivity and later HTML and networking, as it turned out both Apps and Systems were doing a lot of the same work, only differently. And BillG hated redundancy.

Whether Systems had a superiority complex, or Apps had an inferiority complex, and whether either was appropriate, would be a matter of perspective. But when it came to resolving differences, there were no doubts where the definitive opinion would come from.

I continued my *Meet the BOOP* and executives tour, talking to Paul Maritz (PaulMa), who with the creation of WWPG was managing the Windows product line.

Previously at Intel, Paul had enough experience with new projects at companies to know it was important to allow something time to reach maturity rather than subject it to an internal dialog too soon. NT had been nurtured essentially off on the side, which had worked well for Windows 3.0 previously—meaning it was making progress without a great deal of meddling from executives or other product groups. NT was in the final, intense stretches of what ultimately became a four-year project from inception to shipping the first release. NT was originally begun to compete with Unix as a distinct high-end offering from Microsoft. The major change that was announced at the 1992 PDC a few months earlier was how the 32-bit Windows API would be scalable from the low end with Chicago to the highest end with Windows NT—this was called *Windows 32,* usually shortened to *Win32.*

Since the release of Windows 3.0, a major update was in the works and about to release. Windows 3.1 would add support that would greatly improve the ability to run several programs at once and support a lot of memory, very helpful for VC++, by running only in protected mode. Importantly, a significant update was also planned that would add workgroup networking. The "workgroup" buzzword, pioneered by the billion-dollar revenue Lotus Corporation, had infected Windows as well. In fact, it was in large part the concerns over Lotus that led to releasing an updated SKU of Windows called *Windows for Workgroups.*

Whereas the Apps division was organized around business units that had an easy mapping from boxes on a retail shelf to top levels in the organization, the Platforms organization was mostly a cluster of technology focused teams, often overlapping to some degree. There were many projects spinning at different velocities with competing interests between different product release timelines. The org structure was not inherently a challenge, but the high variance in actual versus planned ship dates was a challenge. Again, this relates to the challenges of bootstrapping a wide range of ecosystem partners and the constant flow of new technologies and industry standards that might make it into whatever release of the operating system might be on the horizon.

Paul suggested that I could help to do my part to assist in keeping BillG informed enough to minimize *random* inbound commentary. I was beginning to get a sense of the different relationship BillG had with Systems as compared to his relationship with Apps. While Bill, perhaps through MikeMap, had already put some distance between himself and Apps, with Systems they were trying to figure out how to best channel his efforts and avoid being *randomized.*

I spoke with Nathan Myhrvold (NathanM) who had the most fluid and continuous contact with BillG. Microsoft Research (MSR) was also only a few months old and getting off the ground. It was exciting to BillG. MSR became an increasingly important part of Microsoft and my role as TA given how much BillG was personally working on the new division. Nathan proposed MSR to BillG in 1991, and with much fanfare MSR was created with the hiring of significant research talent in Speech and Natural Language from IBM. Later in 1992, Rick Rashid (Rashid) joined from Carnegie Mellon University in a major statement of the importance that MSR would bring. Nathan's memo on MSR aimed to structure MSR to avoid the most common failures, particularly around technology transfer from lab to product group, that had come to define computer science research, notably, the failure of Xerox to capitalize on graphical interface and more.

Microsoft had two bountiful gardens, and BillG's goal with MSR was to create a third. There was little doubt as MSR grew where Bill believed the highest IQ people in the company were. He was well-versed in the history of all the corporate labs and in how opportunities were missed or squandered and was determined to do something different and better.

After meeting with many senior people, I became obsessed with not wasting BillG's time. Though, I got off to a slow start trying to figure out how to "add value" without asking. I began what would become our tradition of many late-night email threads about various topics. Sometimes BillG would kick off a thread asking about a product or technology. Other times I would share something I learned and that would kick off another thread. We had many threads going in parallel.

Understanding the products and technologies was not the difficult part of the job. Figuring out the realities of management was the challenge. BillG never really talked about management or process or schedules or customers. He talked about products and technology.

I'd often ask myself if he was even managing or if he was, was he doing so consciously?

019. BILLG THE MANAGER

At 38, having grown Microsoft as CEO from the start, Bill was leading Microsoft at a global scale that in 1993 was comparable to an industrial-era CEO. Even the legendary Thomas Watson Jr., son of the IBM founder, did not lead IBM until his 40s. Microsoft could never have scaled the way it did had BillG managed via a centralized hub-and-spoke system, with everything bottlenecked through him. In many ways, this was BillG's product leadership gift to Microsoft—a deeply empowered organization that *also* had deep product conversations at the top and across the whole organization.

Bill honed a set of undocumented principles that defined interactions with product groups. The times of legendary BillG reviews characterized by hardcore challenges and even insults had become, mostly, a thing of the past excepting the occasional sentimental outburst. More generally, they were a collective memory of hyper-growth moments any start-up experiences, only before the modern era when such stories were more commonly understood.

Much later in 2006, when BillG announced his intent to transition from full time Microsoft and part time philanthropy to full time philanthropy, many reporters surprised him by asking how Microsoft would continue without his coordination of technical strategy and oversight. But even in the early '90s, at the height of the deepest and most challenging technology strategy questions, he never devoted the bulk of his time to micromanaging product development. He spent a good deal of time engaged with products, but there were far too many at too many stages of development to micro-manage them. In many ways this was the opposite of the approach Steve Jobs took, even if both were known for their own forms of challenging interactions. The most obvious contrast between the two was the breadth of the product line and the different market touchpoints.

Having grown up through Development Tools and Languages, I was familiar with Microsoft's product line, but only as TA did it become clear how comparatively broad Microsoft had so quickly become. The software world was thought of through a lens of major categories: operating systems, tools and languages, networking, and applications, roughly mirroring Microsoft's org chart. The latter was thought of as word processing, spreadsheets, graphics, databases, as well as assorted smaller categories. It was easy to identify leaders in each of those areas—names that were tip of the tongue at the time and most of which are no longer in the PC software space: IBM, Borland, Novell, WordPerfect, Lotus, Aldus, Ashton Tate, and many more. The ah-ha moment in the early 1990s was the realization that no company on that list was competing in more than one category. Microsoft was hardly winning in every category. In fact, in most categories it was new entry, a distant second, or even third place, but the company was in every space. Bill was committed and patient. Microsoft was relentless. And Microsoft was focused on Windows.

BillG had fostered Microsoft with a grand vision to compete in every category of PC software, from some of the earliest days. With rare exceptions, no other company set out to do that. BillG led a deep technology strategy. It started with the operating system, supported by tools and languages, and then using those to build applications. This seemed simple enough. In fact, it is what IBM built for mainframes and DEC built for minicomputers.

There was a crucial difference. Microsoft did not build hardware and was not vertically integrated to reduce competition. Microsoft built an operating system on an openly architected PC (the same Intel-based architecture that came to power both Macintosh and Linux years later) and published APIs so that anyone could build tools and applications for the operating system—an open hardware platform and open operating system APIs. This approach simply addressed all the early challenges Microsoft itself faced trying to figure out how to build winning applications—it was so busy dealing with dozens of proprietary computing platforms, each with their own tools and APIs just different enough to make things difficult, but not so different as to be valuable. Bill saw the value in software and in openness at key points in the overall architecture. At the formation of the company, he and PaulA saw the immense and expansive value of software and, essentially, the liability that being in the hardware business carried. Building Microsoft's software-only business on an open hardware platform where many players competed to drive prices down while maintaining compatibility with the operating system was one of the all-time great strategy choices. The idea of building hardware seemed like a sucker's bet, with low margins, manufacturing, and inventory—the baggage of the physical world. While Microsoft would dabble in peripherals or hardware that could bootstrap new PC scenarios, building whole computers was a headache better left to others.

Expanding the impact of that breadth software strategy was BillG's day-to-day operating model, not micromanaging the specifics of any given project. I am painting this with a broad brush, intentionally so. Part of the difference between the then dominant cultures of Systems and Apps was that during the MikeMap era (and arguably during the earlier JeffH era), Apps weaned itself from Bill's intense and constant scrutiny whereas the Systems culture more clearly embraced that dynamic. That was largely true until PaulMa took a more hands-off (or walled-off) approach to the nurturing of the NT project.

In his May 1991 email, "Challenges and Strategy," BillG set the company on the Windows strategy, clarifying the foundations for every product and group, solidifying what had been complex platform choices every team faced. Regardless of whether Bill was a savant when it came to the technical details of projects or he simply remembered everything each group sent or told him, he operated the company at a higher level of abstraction than reporters believed to be the case in 2008 when he ultimately reduced his full-time commitment to Microsoft.

I had a glimpse of this when our AFX team had our pivotal review. Later as TA I was there to connect the dots and amplify the Windows strategy. By and large the company was still wrapping itself around the details of what it really meant to embrace Windows, exclusively. That, and coping with the myriad of choices and decisions that come from the tension between aligning with a Windows strategy and having some control over your own destiny as a product. Which version of Windows? When is that shipping? Will the APIs our product needs be in Windows? Will those APIs work on older versions of Windows? What about Windows NT? On, which microprocessors? What about the other parts of Microsoft? The questions were endless. This was truly big company stuff—the strategy at a high level is one thing, but execution across a $600M (1994) research and development budget was another. The fascinating thing was how products so quickly scaled beyond what Bill personally experienced as a programmer, both in size and technology specifics. This was to be expected—by any measure the company was huge—but people and Bill himself still expected to interact on product details as though he was a member of the product team. I often found myself looking for ways to help Bill engage at that level, even if just for show.

In addition to the Windows strategy, with the late 1993 launch of *Office 4*, Microsoft also declared 1994 "Year of Office." It was the biggest launch for Apps and represented a major pivot of the organization to the opportunity of selling a suite of products. This too was in the earliest days of a strategy, one that I would end up spending significant time on as TA and then later as a member of the team.

Just because Bill operated at a level of abstraction across products groups did not preclude product groups from engaging on what might seem like relatively small, non-technical matters. One of the more entertaining meetings I attended was preparing for the launch of Office 4, which was a worldwide event complete with a reporter given permission to shadow the team. A key differentiator would be how the user would experience "intelligence" in the product, so that it understood what was intended and how to achieve it in the new Office software. The development team built a series of features along the lines of what was termed "basic use" such as AutoCorrect in Word, AutoFilter in Excel tables, and a host of Wizards (guided step-by-step flows such as for creating charts), and more. To bring them together and communicate with the market and on retail packaging, the marketing team came up with an umbrella term. Pete Higgins (PeteH) came over to brief BillG on that choice in a small meeting in Bill's office.

PeteH was by then the spiritual leader of the business side of Apps. He rose through the ranks of Excel and was clearly MikeMap's lead executive. Pete was the kind of calm and in control leader that everyone enjoyed working for—he was at once clearly the boss, but also a member of the team. Pete was a native of the Seattle area, high school football star, and Stanford graduate. He was a new generation of Microsoft product executive, coming from the business and not the coding side. For me in my TA role, Pete was one of my biggest supporters and mentors and made connecting with Apps super easy.

Sitting at the little couch under the Intel chip poster, after going through the details of the launch, Pete said the proverbial "there's one more thing." Bill rocking in his chair shook his head, given that the meeting was mostly an uneventful recap of the upcoming press tour. Pete went on to explain the problem of communicating all the features and how Microsoft needed a term to market and describe them. Pete was dancing around this because he knew well enough that Bill was not a fan of "marketing." Ever so delicately Pete said, "this is your chance…we want to go with this term but if you don't like it…"

Pete then said, "IntelliSense. Microsoft Office introduces IntelliSense."

Bill's reply, "Intelli…what?"

Pete again tried to position the positioning, his instinct about resistance proving correct. "It is IntelliSense…it means that Office has built-in intelligence, and it understands what you need and how to do it."

Bill still not warming up, went full pedantic, "what intelligence…is there a Prolog rules engine, a neural network…". He was also making the scrunched up surprised look that he does, which turns out (once you realize it) to also be a bit sarcastic. It meant he was warming up.

A few more times back and forth, and Pete just made Bill say IntelliSense in a sentence one more time, which he did with kind of a devilish smirk.

Done.

Looking back this all seems absurd. Consternation over a single phrase. Literally seeking approval to use it from the CEO of a billion-dollar company. All on the heels of what was no doubt months of preparation, including getting SteveB's approval which was actually critical. Finally, the theater that Pete would pull the plug a few weeks before the tour. In some ways this was the Apps way of bringing decisions to Bill—it wasn't really a choice and it had been broadly vetted and was buttoned-up. Any debate would probably be theater more than anything.

On average, there was one product-focused meeting on most days. Most teams saw Bill once or twice a year. NathanM saw Bill most every day or at least in most every technology context, present day or far out there. Most executives, like PaulMa, PeteH (leading Apps), and Susan Boeschen (SusanB leading consumer), saw Bill in product review contexts several times a month because each had many ongoing projects or, in the case of the big projects (like operating systems), many large components. Everyone was in constant contact over email. Bill was always forwarding emails across the company, adding relevant people from all levels of the organization to the CC line, and never backed off a good *reply-all* opportunity. Phone or in-person 1:1s were not the typical way of interacting across the product executive team. For the most part, work happened in groups or at least with an audience, with outcomes and flare-ups quickly disseminated by email. I found myself constantly on the move walking around campus from one building to the next to meet people in person, rarely was I in my office, a pattern that continued my entire career.

I was often asked to meet with teams before they met with Bill. They hoped for insight into how BillG might think about choices and decisions or even the presentation overall. I often disappointed teams in these pre-meetings since I was hardly a stand-in for Bill, and I was hardcore about leaving any such impression. Pre-meetings gave me a chance to better understand the issues the team was struggling with and to make sure those were brought forward in an objective and transparent manner. The fastest path to failure was to structure a conversation so Bill discovered an issue rather than having it revealed to him. To be fair, an equally fast path to failure was a first slide listing a slew of problems and issues in the hopes of inoculating the remainder of the meeting. In that case, I would caution teams that they were exposing themselves to the inevitable "How can this be so difficult?" comments. Getting this balance right was the essence of leading an effective meeting.

For most meetings, I wrote a summary meeting preview. Even though Bill said he did not want this, I could not help myself. While he was always effective, I felt that a little bit of specifics could go a long way in making the meeting more effective and less *random*. I could tell he had read my mail if he raised a point verbatim from my note, and frequently he would kick off the meeting doing so, never crediting me of course. In these, and all mails talking about other teams, I always tried to separate the facts of the meeting, the team's analysis, and my own opinion. Bill was transparent with email and thought little of forwarding an entire thread. I learned the ramifications of that the hard way.

As an example of where I failed to follow my own rules about fact versus opinion, I totally offended Jim Allchin (JimAll), leading the *Cairo* project, on the role of a specific technology in distributed programming. Not only did Jim inform me that my opinions were wrong, but also that I stepped all over his own PhD dissertation as a leading expert. In hindsight, this was terrifying—Jim's reply was brutal—but it proved a good early learning experience, so to speak.

While the product line was already broad, the expansion to entirely new areas was unstoppable. On most any product area, we were forming an opinion, beginning work, or already in the market. There was not a booth at a tradeshow, a focused conference, or a major company looking to partner that Microsoft was not already connected to or connecting with in some way. While Microsoft was in the earliest days of achieving a PC in every home (about 25 percent of US households in 1993) and on every desktop (about half of US workers in 1993), every day in this job was either furthering that or expanding beyond homes and desktops from data centers to handhelds to airplanes. The first in-flight PC-based system was an early partnership between Microsoft and an airline, including certification for Windows Server.[5]

Product meetings had no set format or structure and usually reflected the culture of the organization. This might be a surprise to some as many CEOs, or perhaps their staff, might have imposed some more rigor on meetings. Microsoft had two bountiful gardens, but there were micro-cultures throughout out the company. While one group did slick and well-rehearsed presentations, another might present research-heavy deep dives. Bill often pushed a team outside its comfort zone, deliberately pushing the team to discuss places they were less prepared, or even less interested. It was a technique he employed. He once said to me, "Why spend all the time with the Windows team talking about architecture, if that was their predisposition anyway?" This was also a strategy to level the playing field—talking about architecture to Windows or ease of use to Excel was too lopsided and Bill was disadvantaged.

The reality of BillG Reviews never lived up to lore.

Most meetings progressed without incident—meaning without yelling. Sometimes, though, there were comments such as "That was the stupidest thing I ever heard" or "That is brain-dead." The worst was "That's trivial…let me show you." Those were all the clichés that teams anticipated but then wore as a badge of honor. They happened with far less frequency compared to how much they were talked about. Even over the short period of time I worked as TA, Bill became more intentional in his use of meeting dynamics. Still, the first seconds of a meeting remained a bit of a mood thermometer, pity those for whom it was clearly a bad day.

When meetings ended up "bad" it was always because the team was poorly prepared, or they came to talk about the project in a way that diverged from expectations. There were typical capital offenses in the meeting, such as failing to understand a product strategy of competitors or downplaying a competitor's potential. Worst was coming across as though a product was making mostly tactical decisions driven by schedule or failing to understand the architecture of the product relative to the evolving platform and related teams across Microsoft. PivotTables were just making their way across most teams, so many were still making the common errors of using static charts and graphs that always seemed to have the data oriented or filtered in the least useful way. Those moments always held potential for a *lively* discussion.

Part of my role was to reduce the potential for such liveliness ahead of time. I tried to alert teams about potential issues without acting as a surrogate for Bill, and to make sure meetings did not save the difficult or bad news for the end. I was also there to throw myself on the grenade, so to speak, and get meetings back on track by helping the team through a tough moment—usually by restating or interpreting what they were saying or by redirecting the topic at hand to a follow-up discussion.

By far the biggest strategic error one could make was knowingly duplicating code outside core expertise, and then compounding that by attempting to explain why in this particular case it is justified. Microsoft Publisher was a new product in the desktop publishing category. It was being built by the Consumer Division under the leadership of Melinda French (MelindaF.) The product aimed for the small business and non-professional market, compared to the incumbent Aldus PageMaker. It differentiated itself with ease-of-use features, pioneering Wizards, and other user interface innovations. But it also produced printed pages that looked a lot like what one should be able to create with Microsoft Word. This overlap was the source of endless consternation—why can't they share code, why can't Word do all these features, and then ultimately why does Publisher even exist. Yet, customers loved it. At one point, a meeting went down a rabbit hole over bullets and numbering and how Publisher was basically writing all the same code Word was and wasting everyone's resources. There was little actionable in this kind of rant, but it did establish the norm of being called out for redundancy and the need to be prepared to cope with the feedback.

Bill maintained a deep commitment to evaluating a portfolio of efforts, and even within a single product he believed in the portfolio approach of features—not every product nor every feature was a winner or a breakthrough, but on the whole, something needed to be working. As much as Bill might give a group a difficult time (as happened with Visual C++), he knew there was always more to the product and more products to the company. It was not just that Bill was building a product portfolio for Microsoft, he was managing the teams as a portfolio of efforts. This portfolio approach created a resiliency in the company—resilient to the unpredictable nature of technology bets and to the ability of the people on the team to execute. Not everything went as planned nor did every planned bet ultimately make sense.

Whether deliberate or not, BillG had three axes that created a constant state of balance, of push and pull, across the hundred teams creating software. Bill's approach of constantly balancing the tension between *innovation and shipping*, *expanding the portfolio* while maintaining coherency, and the *injection of new ideas* while also executing on existing work proved to be the most interesting "management" lesson. The next three sections are examples of each of these dimensions.

020. INNOVATION VERSUS SHIPPING: THE CAIRO PROJECT

It wasn't like Microsoft's operating system strategy was ever simple, at least to me. Perhaps it was asking too much for a cleaner or more straightforward strategy to emerge with the move away from OS/2 and the early success of Windows 3.0, and now 3.1. Being complacent or content was not in Microsoft's DNA—a bold vision for Windows was, however, and with that came even greater product complexity.

Microsoft had a simple external message of "Win32." The problem was the product had not yet caught up to that message. Windows NT was just shipping its first version while the market was predicting NT would soon dominate the desktop. Microsoft was also anxious for that, first almost always talking about Windows NT after selling Windows 3.1. The "real" 32-bits, advanced networking. client-server developer strategy were all great selling points, but Windows NT was a new code base and lacked compatibility with huge numbers of applications and devices that represented the richness and key strategic value of the 16-bit Windows (and MS-DOS) ecosystem. Beyond that, Windows NT had the capability to run on non-Intel microprocessors which only fueled more punditry over the future of the PC. This left many believing the operating system market still seemed up for grabs and buying a PC remained a complex decision.

In the meantime, Microsoft had fallen woefully behind Apple Macintosh when it came to ease of use and the day-to-day effort required to keep a PC working—not behind in sales, but that was not what counted for currency with BillG. Microsoft had yet to release a simple files and folders experience that matched Macintosh and was still mired in the vestiges of MS-DOS, such as file names restricted to "8.3" or eight dot three, as in eight characters plus three for the file type. It is a cliché even today, but Macintosh just seemed to work, and PCs always seemed to be crashing, hanging, or flaking out, or just much more difficult to use. Just as PCs became common in schools and the workplace, "the dog ate my homework" was replaced with "my PC crashed and ate my work" or something like that.

Microsoft's core Windows project for consumers was Chicago, eventually *Windows 95*. Chicago would bring the compatibility and ecosystem support enjoyed by Windows 3.1 together with the new Win32 API, while at the same time addressing ease of use shortcomings of Windows compared to Macintosh. Chicago had the goal of being a PC that was better than Macintosh plus bringing with it all the benefits of Windows that had cemented leadership in the market. The project was still early enough that most attention was on the just released and bolder Windows NT, primarily because so many believed that the 16-bit heritage of Chicago was a fragile legacy code base ill-suited for the modern 32-bit world. Microsoft's own efforts around marketing NT only emphasized this point.

For any company that would be enough of a big bet, not for Microsoft or BillG though. Chicago was just one part of an all-out assault on the operating system market, one Microsoft already dominated: Chicago for consumers, Windows NT Workstation for professionals, Windows NT Server for the *back office*, along with numerous early-stage efforts on both living room and handheld computing devices going on in NathanM's advanced technology group. These all came about as a direct reflection of BillG's scalable Windows strategy best expressed by a slide from the Win32 Professional Developers Conference showing one Windows scaling from the smallest devices to the biggest computers—a slide that would in some form carry Microsoft's vision for the remainder of Bill's leadership.

Then there was *Cairo*. Whereas the major axis that defined everything along the scalable strategy was simply how much computer horsepower a device had, Cairo set out to redefine how people interacted with computers and how developers wrote programs. Cairo was to be a new paradigm from user interface to data storage, to networking computers together.

In an era where computers hardly worked and every developer at Microsoft was struggling to figure out how to write reliable code, ship that code, and meet a schedule, Cairo was by any measure an audacious bet, and that is probably an understatement.

Exactly where Cairo fit in and how, and even if that was possible, would occupy a huge amount of Bill's time and thus my time. Given how I had just navigated the operating system strategy to do my little part to ship tools, I was fortunate to be well-versed in the technology and the teams. But where I found myself was in the awkward and impossible spot of having to help evaluate the practical realities of shipping for a CEO who wasn't generally focused on those aspects of projects.

Landing on my desk early in 1993 was the first of many drafts of Cairo plans and documents. Cairo took the maturity of the NT product process—heavy on documentation and architectural planning—and amped it up. Like a well-oiled machine, the Cairo team was in short order producing reams of documents assembled into three-inch binders detailing all the initiatives of the product. Whenever I would meet with people from Cairo, they would exude confidence in planning and their processes. The confidence took on such a level that people began to refer to Cairo unofficially as the updated version 4.0 of Windows NT.

At a college recruiting trip at Cornell, I remember spending an evening at the Statler Hotel bar with one member of the NT team and one member of the Cairo team (both fellow Cornell graduates) debating over schedules. Would Cairo be NT 4.0? Would NT 4 beat Chicago to market? Would Chicago be dead on arrival because of Cairo or its MS-DOS legacy? Or would "real" NT 4.0 beat Cairo to market? This was engineering bravado at its best. It was also Microsoft's operating system roadmap at its worst.

While any observer should have rightfully taken the abundance of documentation and confidence of the team as a positive sign, the lack of working code and ever-expanding product definition seemed to set off some minor alarms, especially with the Apps person in me. While the Cairo product had the appearance of the NT project in documentation, it seemed to lack the daily rigorous builds, ongoing performance and benchmarking, and quality and compatibility testing. There was a more insidious dynamic, and one that would prove a caution to many future products across the company but operating systems in particular.

Technology was moving very fast and new products were appearing across the industry at a rapid pace. As a brand-new product under development, it was tempting to look at every new development and wonder how it might be part of what is being built. This is especially true for an operating system which tends to lack any traditional product boundary like one might see in a word processor or spreadsheet. What is an operating system after all? Purists might say it is a kernel, but then what about the graphical components? Others would be quick to point out that networking or storage are not always considered part of an OS except at some basic level.

Cairo tended to take this as a challenge to incorporate more and more capabilities. New things that would come along would be quickly added to the list of potential features in the product. Worse, something that BillG might see conceptually related, like an application from a third-party for searching across all the files on your hard disk, might become a competitive feature to Cairo. Or more commonly "Can't Cairo just do this with a little extra work?" and then that little extra work was part of the revised product plans.

Along with this BillG *reinforcing function* of feature additions, there was the internal dynamic between the three major operating systems teams. Each team navigating the external competitive landscape, the ongoing BillG input, and a desire internally to be seen as both the leading OS and the one that will ship first and ultimately "win." The idea of being first to market turns out to be a compelling way to measure success. This was especially interesting in a world of fluid or even non-deterministic ship dates where there were few absolute dates for shipping but a plethora of relative milestones. Who had a beta first? Who had a preview before that? Which product would get sent to OEMs for review before that? When was the next PDC and what code would be distributed there?

This led to a rise in one of the more classic *Microspeak* expressions, as we called them, or jargon as it is called elsewhere. In our little Seattle area bubble, disconnected from most of the world and not yet connected by the internet, Microsoft developed a vocabulary that to this day dominates discussions between alumni. *Cookie-licking* is when one group would lay claim to innovate in an area by simply pre-emptively announcing (via slides in some deck at some meeting) ownership of an initiative. Like so many expressions this one seemed rooted in something long lost, but the basic idea is that teams wanted to keep features to themselves by declaration or fiat, almost always independent of a schedule, resources, design, or any concrete steps. Cairo by its own efforts and, frankly, by Bill doing his share of pushing features to them, licked a lot of cookies. Even calling Cairo NT 4.0 out of the gate was cookie-licking as a high art form. The team was hardly alone. Other parts of the OS landscape would take the grand ideas of Cairo and lay claim to much more pedestrian implementations and state they would deliver the innovation sooner and more practically, with the caveat there were future plans (slides) to deliver the rest of the vision.

I was often caught in the middle of these debates. Who was going to deliver what and when were the questions of the day for nearly everything that came up in every discussion about Microsoft's next operating system. The larger-than-life leaders of these projects intimidated me, at least early on. I decided on a very practical approach which was I just bought a lot of hardware and installed a lot of daily builds and let the code speak. It was what JeffH had taught me about shipping and it was the easiest way to prove or disprove what was going on. Windows NT was by this point very solid and building out on the promises of the workstation and data center, with many developers running it as their primary work computers. Chicago was just starting to deliver builds and you could experience significant changes in the user interface – files, folders, long file names, and earliest form of what would become the Start menu. Chicago followed a series of scheduled milestones M1, M2, M3, and then M4 which was the first build that made it to the outside world and was also usable on a daily basis for the incredibly brave like me. I remember showing it to BillG when he commented on how "Chicago seems to be marching along like a British highway system, M1, M2, M3, M4." I'm not sure why that comment stuck with me. Maybe he thought it was super funny.

Cairo was a different story.

Cairo was announced and demonstrated at the December 1993 PDC, but no code was provided. With that came almost impossible to describe internal tensions and angst. While there was always tension between OS/2 and Windows, the skunkworks nature of Windows and the outside forces of IBM proved ample outlets for frustration. With Cairo, everything going on internally was self-inflicted. At every level of the organization and across the product teams, the constant back-and-forth between Chicago, Cairo, and the next NT. NT did not lack for code names at this point, going by the moniker Daytona, a nod to the efforts to improve speed and the affinity for fast cars among the leaders of the team. Pick any two and there was an ongoing knock-down, drag out battle over schedules, performance, architecture, or user interface. The Apps group, third-party software developers, and the hardware ecosystem were all caught in the middle.

Chicago was a big team. NT was an even bigger team. Cairo quickly grew to be even larger. For those looking for reasons to see the potential for failure, ever-increasing team size was a good proxy. Frankly, the divergence of documentation and slides from the daily builds was an even bigger indicator. That was the factor I focused on. I often had to pull Bill back from reading about what was being developed to see what was actually in code and at what pace that was changing.

The only saving grace was the steadfast and relentless evangelism of the Windows API and the Win32 vision. That held the company together as a practical matter, at the time and for another decade.

In my own small way, I lived through a variant of this vicariously through my lunchroom friends working on Word years earlier. After the debacle that was Windows Word 1.0 (if you can call winning a debacle), a project was started to build a new more robust and refined, a modern, code base for word processing. The *Pyramid* project went on for a couple of years before the realization that the existing code could be made to work fine and new code brought with it new problems. It was quietly and quickly shelved. The tension and confusion were real and ongoing.

IBM was famous for having competing projects and many in technology thought companies should build new products with multiple efforts, in some sort of *coding Darwinism*. Maybe it had worked before, but the human and customer costs seem out of proportion. It is one of those business school ideas that looks great on paper. I probably did not need more proof that I was living through a case study in the making.

If meetings and my TA efforts with Chicago were focused on the relatively narrow or mundane topics of performance and the number of bits in use in the kernel (should Chicago be 16 or 32-bits and in which subsystems was a major ongoing point of consternation), Cairo was expansive. Cairo, like Chicago, had a new shell (Microsoft's favorite word for the user interface for launching programs and managing files) and a new file system, but the innovations were to be radically different. Where Chicago aimed to commercialize broadly the graphical operating system, a concept understood by most, the goal of Cairo was to commercialize two of the biggest buzzwords in computing: object-oriented and distributed networking.

Cairo aimed to advance personal computing with dramatic changes in how we thought of files—rather than single files and folders, Cairo intended for files to have the capabilities of a database. Everything on your PC was to be stored in a database to easily search, find, and show relationships between items: files, email, contacts, photos, documents and more. Advancing storage was a long arc of innovation Bill favored.

The graphical interface for manipulating these objects had elements of traditional files and folders but enabled more operations. A folder, for example, might not have anything in it until a user indicated the folder should contain "all objects from 1992." The folder would be filled as though everything matching that description had been copied to that folder, but it did so without making copies of the files. It seemed slick at the time.

The object-oriented nature of Cairo was not just dreamed up but paralleled several efforts across the industry, some even going as far back as Xerox PARC research work. Specifically, Apple was building a system called OpenDoc that promised to bring object-oriented files to Macintosh. It would never make it to market though. IBM had a project known as *system object model* (SOM), which aimed to bring objects to every size IBM computer, from PCs to mainframes. It too would fail to materialize. All this object-oriented stuff was developing a pattern.

Object-oriented storage would have been impressive if it all happened on a single PC. The true magic of the promise of Cairo was that everything that took place on one PC could work across networked PCs. The notion of a network was still new, and the first web browser was just being released while we were busy building what some might call a weblike system. JimAll, leading Cairo, was a pioneer in distributed computing, inventing a system called *Clouds* for his PhD dissertation.

The Windows NT team was also steeped in distributed computing, having seen the Digital Equipment VMS operating system gain distributed capabilities a few years earlier. Similarly, the distributed capabilities of Sun computers running Unix and NeXT from Steve Jobs, were gaining popularity on Wall Street and in academia.

The biggest impact Cairo had on Microsoft's technology direction was in the adoption of a technology called *component object model*. COM started in part of my original team, Apps Tools, as a way for productivity applications to talk to each other, the earliest work invented by the PowerPoint team to make it easy for PowerPoint to include charts from Excel or pictures from other apps. The Cairo architecture used COM for every aspect of the system—it was object-oriented at every layer of the system. In fairness, I am intentionally glossing over a good deal of complex technology history about COM and technologies included under this umbrella including Object Linking and Embedding, OLE, Automation, and DocFiles.

This seemed like a good bet, but then as the system started to mature it became clear that being so object-oriented had downsides when it came to performance and even managing all the code in the system. As it turned out, those building operating systems were equally susceptible to *oopaholism*.

At one point, things became so fragile that JimAll asked for a meeting with BillG to discuss the future use of COM, questioning even moving forward to perhaps reset and find a more robust approach.

I quickly pulled together all the background and made a list of pros and cons. My own history on C++ came in handy as we had gone through our own education and reform as oopaholics. I asked my old manager, ScottRa, to attend this small meeting to detail his experience with COM and objects. I was definitely on the side of abandoning COM, having seen the cost of being excessively object-oriented.

The meeting took place during the Software Development Conference when we were launching Visual C++. I booked a flight for a day trip, something not usually done, and arrived at the meeting just in time. Bill questioned my judgement of a one-day turnaround. The meeting was a first and one of the few times I saw a clear choice and decision being made. I mean this in a good way because most often meetings that claim to decide things, really don't. Bill was well aware of that and used meetings to arrive at consensus rather than force choices that would need to be revisited at some later date.

There was a good discussion for quite a long meeting, and ultimately JimAll decided to stick with COM, but there was a commitment to be sure to use it at higher levels of the system and to avoid oopaholism. In other words, the OS itself would limit using COM and objects while pushing the use of that technology to developers. This seemed practical but the "do as we say, not as we do" aspect of this proved to be problematic for a long time.

COM went on to become an architectural anchor, like on a boat, for nearly everything else Microsoft did for decades. I think often about this particular meeting—the stakes seemed so high, though had an alternate decision been made, things may not have ended up all that differently. COM was an anchor, which was true, but the value was so much higher level and in so many other parts of the system. COM had all the architecture, complexity, and proprietary elements that the company seemed to be craving at the time.

The number of companies with projects potentially competing with Cairo continued to increase, which only caused the scope of Cairo to broaden. At the same time, the value that Cairo provided to other teams made the effort worthwhile—pushing the Chicago shell to have a leading-edge design, encouraging the Database team to think more about storing different types of data, and creating the precursors to networking advances that drove the client-server computing revolution. Some would say the influence of Cairo is less reality and more putting a shine on the ultimate failure of the project. Perhaps that was the case at the time. Does it matter?

Ultimately, the human toll of Cairo was high in the sense that so many people spent so much time early in career working on a project that not only didn't ship but was viewed as squandering resources, at best, and misguided at worst. It was a bit of a black eye for Microsoft among the press and analysts who believed Microsoft would deliver on the idea of object-oriented the way that NeXT had done but at scale. The magnitude of the project would leave many people with Cairo war stories for years to come. I wish I could say that the lessons learned would prevent another experience like this from happening, but that isn't the case as we shall see.

The success Microsoft was having with Windows and the failure of competitors to do better in the market created an environment where even mistakes as significant as this seemed not to slow things down. Importantly, and I think this is a good thing, it did not cause Microsoft to back off audacious goals and big visions for technology. It is easy to see a world where a setback like this would force Microsoft to reconsider big bets and to aim for less lofty goals. I am glad that did not happen, as difficult as the next years would be.

The entire time I worked to amplify Bill's efforts at steering Cairo, I felt caught in the middle between innovation and shipping, not that those were mutually exclusive. To the contrary, I naturally tilted toward shipping and believing that was innovation. The dichotomy between shipping groups and non-shipping groups was too often portrayed as a dichotomy between execution *or* innovation. That proved to be the root of the feeling that every group was screwed up—the innovative groups weren't shipping enough, and the shipping groups weren't innovating enough. Sometimes I felt that groups that were shipping were almost never given the benefit of the *innovation* moniker, and groups that were innovating seemed to be unburdened by shipping. Perhaps this was the Microsoft way of having competing groups.

021. EXPANDING BREADTH VERSUS COHERENCY: THE EMS PROJECT

Microsoft was an early and intense adopter of email.

Nearly all my job as TA involved email—long, detailed, memos written as email. BillG routinely emailed weekend or late-night missives prompting response chains that would go on for hours. *Not* missing a "thread" was part of the culture.

Microsoft did not use its own product for email. Well, it *sort* of did. Microsoft's email ran on Xenix, a precursor to the Linux operating system, and typically a *mail PC* was issued that was a dumb terminal connected directly to Xenix computers. Mail was simple plain text with no formatting. Using attachments could be awkward. To alleviate the annoyance of using command lines for email, product team developers wrote mail programs to use in MS-DOS and later Windows that copied mail from Xenix and made it easy to use mail in character mode, WzMail, or GUI mode, WinMail. Given how much time we spent in email, there was no shortage of efforts to build mail programs as side projects. I was a hold out and continued to use my Xenix terminal for as long as they were supported. The big disadvantage to these tools was that all your mail was copied down from the Xenix server to a PC—if your PC hard drive crashed you also lost your mail. Clever people figured out all sorts of ways to avoid this failure point, only pointing out just how important email was and how much time and effort typical employees put into just keeping it working. Windows hanging in the middle of drafting a long message or reply was the sort of thing that ruined your day and happened all too frequently. Everyone had email horror stories.

The rest of the corporate world was light years behind Microsoft and almost never used email outside of the technology teams or other companies in the software and technology industries. IBM was the leader in corporate email, using an arcane mainframe system, Professional Office Systems (PROFS), made famous by Oliver North in the Iran-Contra hearings. Since nobody in the PC industry had mainframes, email was a collection of ad hoc tools and systems that worked well only for relatively small companies, like the one mail product Microsoft had called *Microsoft Mail*. Microsoft Mail competed with a Lotus-acquired product called *cc:Mail*, which dominated the email category to the degree it existed. Microsoft Mail was based first on a licensed Macintosh product and then subsequent versions were based on technology acquired from a Canadian company called Network Courier, held by Consumers Software.

There were many other products. I installed and used several of them during my summer internships when simply connecting the computers together was difficult. These early products were built on basic infrastructure of sharing files over dedicated networks—a mailbox was simply a file on another computer and sending mail was for all practical purposes reading data from one file and copying it to another. I'm simplifying for effect.

Because email relied on connecting one set of mail products to another, there was a time when the big telephone companies believed they would provide email service much the same way that they provided voice connectivity, especially since mail between companies involved phone lines. This led to attempts to standardize email using Byzantine standards that only phone companies could love.

While all this was going on, one of the first substantial Windows programs, designed by Ray Ozzie at a company called Iris, owned by Lotus but kept independent in a nod to the difficulty of developing innovative products within an established leader, increasingly gained momentum. The product, Lotus Notes, was a platform for building custom applications that could run on several different operating systems as well as being a rich graphical application. It was *also* an email program. Notes created a new category called *workgroup computing*. Even though Notes competed with Microsoft, Ray Ozzie and the team received a *Windows Pioneer Award* in 1994 at a ceremony honoring the most significant third-party contributions to the creation of Windows.

Notes had an architectural appeal that cut right to the core of everything Microsoft valued. It ran on PC hardware. It was designed for Windows. It worked whether connected to the network or temporarily *offline*. Most of all, it was a platform with a database and a programming language, a flagship product for the PC era. The capabilities of Notes touched on every group in the company—effectively competing required Microsoft to marshal teams, and, more importantly to change plans, for most every division. There's a great lesson in big companies competing—the best way to compete is to build a product that spans business units or divisions as Lotus had managed to do. Ideally the core of the product would land squarely between two business units, creating a standoff of sorts between those groups as they decided how to compete.

Microsoft needed to compete. Microsoft, however, had nothing. That's an overstatement in sense. We were selling Microsoft Mail, but we weren't even using it internally. To complicate our internal mail architecture, we used the companion product for scheduling meetings called *Schedule+* even though we did not use the mail product. In *Microspeak*, when scheduling a meeting people would often say "send me an S plus" or "Schedule plus me" – lingo that would stick around years after that product was no longer used.

A new team under MikeMap was created to build email for corporations with the acquisition of Network Courier in 1991. The importance of email was certain, though it would be five or even ten years until corporations saw email as a workplace standard. More important than email itself was building email to take advantage of the new Windows Server platform. Windows Server was still very new and part of the dual mission of NT in addition to Workstation. Version 1.0 (officially named 3.1) did not ship until mid-1993, and it would be 1996 before the first broadly used release was completed, NT 4.0. BillG's strategy for a platform was to build the platform strength by also building apps and create strength in apps by making a singular bet on a new platform—deliberately creating the virtuous cycle. This was especially important in the early days of the platform when it was difficult to get existing companies to bet on something that might not be commercial for years. That was exactly the goal of the new EMS team—Enterprise Mail System, or sometimes Messaging, with an early code name *Mercury*, as in messaging.

No one had ever built email on Windows Server using the new architecture approach called client-server that Windows was designed to support. Significant internet standards for email did not yet exist reliably. The familiar @ sign was decades old, but routing email around, use of anything more than plain text in messages, attachments, and more were still flaky. Windows Server did not yet exist. Tom Evslin (TomEv) was brought to Microsoft via an acquisition, Solutions, Inc. which made Mail software used in Mac Office in 1990, ultimately to lead EMS engineering. He brought with him detailed knowledge and experience in email and experience with the challenges of scaling email to hundreds or thousands of people. Microsoft, with its history of personal computing, had yet to internalize how different computing and data storage would be when running on servers or meeting the needs of thousands of simultaneous users using PC servers, and how different it would be to sell and deploy mission critical data center software.

There was a lot for me to dive into as TA. I had to figure out how to frame the challenges the team faced so that BillG was effective in driving his strategy. Given how much the team needed to do—and I was empathetic—it would have been easier and more straightforward to minimize the reliance or *dependency* on other parts of Microsoft. As Bill reiterated on many occasions, that was not the sort of strategic approach Microsoft benefited from—in fact, Lotus Notes was already succeeding by *not* relying on Microsoft all that much, even emphasizing its cross-platform capabilities.

Just as word processing and spreadsheets were the anchors of the Windows ecosystem flywheel, Bill decided that email and database were the anchors of the server flywheel under development. The database efforts were spearheaded by David Vaskevitch (DavidV), a longtime enterprise advocate within Microsoft and database expert. The database under development was Microsoft's variant of an industry standard known as SQL, a category dominated by giants like IBM and Oracle. Oracle in 1993 had $1.5 billion in revenue, growing 30 percent or more per year.[6] SQL was designed to handle highly structured information like inventory or financial transactions, which was different than the relatively arbitrary information in email. In other words, SQL was not designed to handle email. SQL had become so dominant that there was not a data storage problem that advocates of its core technology were not working hard to solve using SQL.

The third triad of the server ecosystem was the *directory*—or, basically, the list of all the users and computers that were part of the network. The directory, from the earliest days of NT, was an integral part of the system known as simply as *NT Directory*. The name Active Directory would come later. The key competitor to Windows NT was Novell and they sold a separate product as a directory, so Microsoft's strategy would be to integrate it with its new server product as was typically done in technology. The NT directory was, however, not designed to handle all the capabilities required for email. In practical terms, Microsoft was in the earliest days of *deploying* NT Directory, which was proving to be enormously complex and extremely difficult to operate.

In the ideal, EMS would be architected to use SQL to store email and the Windows NT directory to keep track of all the user email addresses. To compete with Lotus Notes, EMS should use Visual Basic to create the user interface for customer-developed applications. Discussion along these lines happened almost continuously. Every time the EMS team mentioned some product feature or engineering challenge, it seemed like they received feedback over how much easier it would be if they would just use SQL and NT Directory. When those were not the answer, then building on the enhanced capabilities of Cairo would serve as a placeholder for solving problems in the best architectural manner. The easiest way to characterize this is that every time EMS showed something that looked like a hierarchy of folders with items (mail messages), they would get feedback about how they should be representing that in SQL the way business applications routinely do for sales by region, country, district, etc. And failing that, they would then be told to "go talk to Cairo" who was building a way to view folders and files using SQL, so they were solving the problem. Predictably, every time the EMS team came back saying it would be better to implement something on their own, it was received as a justification for failing to think strategically. It was messy and uncomfortable, and slowing progress to compete with Notes, which did not use either SQL or the file system.

At some level of abstraction such a technology approach made sense. Building the product this way, however, amounted to crazy talk. That is what I heard as I practiced reconnaissance and shuttle diplomacy across teams. I found myself between two entirely different cross-team debates. Cairo debates seemed somewhat academic compared to EMS debates, which were rooted in getting a more practical product to work at scale.

For storage, EMS had no intention of using a commercial SQL database. Attempting to represent mail in such a structured manner had been tried before. Oracle was famously trying and not delivering. The allure was great—the industry rallied around SQL and was investing heavily in tools and infrastructure to standardize on SQL as data moved off mainframes. At the same time, the SQL team was lobbying hard for reusing all this effort knowing that building for scale and reliability was a full-time job and they were certain that EMS would end up duplicating their work, while also trying to build email. In a sense they were correct in that any storage technology EMS used would also require them to build capabilities to scale to huge storage requirements across many computers, tools to manage all those computers and disks, as well as backup and restore should anything go wrong.

This dynamic happened so many times. A team building something new appeared determined to rebuild something that already existed because the requirements for what they needed could not be met by the existing product. At the same time, the existing product team was busy trying to win in their market and didn't have time to take on the special requests from the new product team that had never shipped anything. As a result, Microsoft dev teams got very good at articulating reasons why some piece of code was not good for what they needed and at the same time product teams got very good at explaining why their schedule did not permit them to add special features. We never seemed to master having a rational discussion. Over many talks, BillG would admit to me that part of his reason for staking such extremes was his hope of making some progress. He knew realistically teams would end up somewhere less than he hoped, but if he started there they would end up with even less. Hearing this kind of bugged me because it sounded like everyone was playing a game of some sort. It did not sound like JeffH "promise and deliver" that I had been schooled in.

I wrote endless late-night emails summarizing the pros and cons of different data storage approaches for BillG, and there were many meetings and discussions that followed. This topic came up at almost every meeting where developing applications for NT was discussed. I was in a database group in graduate school and sympathetic to the realities outlined by SQL. But I was also part of a team looking beyond the 1970s SQL model to a new object-oriented data model (there's that buzzword again) and was sympathetic to the new styles of usage. EMS opted for being in control of its own destiny, a decision that was not difficult for them to defend on technical grounds. EMS spent the better part of the next decade scaling the product, officially named Exchange, and working on scale and reliability, exactly as the SQL team predicted. Likewise, every limitation that Exchange faced when it came to building applications on top of the platform were exactly like the SQL team predicted. To the credit of the Exchange team, SQL did not end up being the right solution for email. In fact, huge email systems today were built using something called *NoSQL*, decidedly not SQL. My intent is not to start a database war as I am sure some will argue semantics over what constitutes SQL versus NoSQL.

The debate over the directory was quite different. In this case BillG had two groups, each on a path to ship and each deeply strategic. The sales proposition to customers could not be that there was one place to store all the employee names for when they signed on to the network to print or share files and an entirely different place for when employees used email. The entire purpose of a directory was to have a single source of *truth* for security and identity within an organization.

Windows NT was on a mission to ship, with the RTM months away and the beta already out there. The product was still quite early for customers and the directory worked in specific ways but was not yet all it had promised to be, as was typical with a 1.0 product of the era. Microsoft IT was in the process of architecting and deploying the directory for the company and wrote a huge white paper in collaboration with the NT team on how that would work. I showed this to BillG and we both marveled at the complexity—not in the positive way, but more like *yikes*. It was page after page of graphs showing servers in different countries required with backups, redundancy, and overnight processes to keep everything in sync so there was one master copy of the directory. It was a massive undertaking.

That proved to be a defining moment because deploying a directory was hugely complex and there was no way EMS could do it twice. In one of the rare times an architectural choice was pushed to a team, using the directory from NT became a requirement for EMS. Many others supported this, including the Server leadership. It was to them as natural as pushing Excel to use Windows—the directory was that core to NT Server—while sharing files and printers was the baseline scenario, it was the directory that brought deep enterprise value to customers. For the better part of the following year or more, EMS would not speak well of using the NT Directory, and conversely the NT team felt that EMS was trying to use the Directory in ways it was not designed to be used. This sounded to me a lot like getting Excel to work on Windows, and it played out exactly that way. Had EMS not used NT Directory, it is likely Directory never would have achieved critical mass as the defining *app* for the client-server era and remains the cloud anchor for today's Office 365. And conversely, had the NT team not met the needs of EMS, then the NT Directory would have likely been sidelined by the rising importance of the email directory in EMS. Forcing this issue, while it might be an exception, only proved the strength of a strategic bet when it is made and executed. Still, it was painful.

Developing applications for EMS turned out to be an endless series of missteps in strategy. Notes had risen to popularity as a platform for building applications. Customers buying Notes were building incredibly cool applications for tracking all sorts of line of business processes and corporate knowledge management, which also happened to be key buzzwords in business at the time. Everywhere our sales teams engaged, they saw customers piloting applications they had written internally or with help from the giant consulting firms. These applications were often the highlight of Chief Information Officers and used to show how cutting edge a large enterprise was. While they ran on Windows, they did not use any strategic (and new) Microsoft software except maybe Word and Excel files. They did not use SQL Server, NT Server, and Notes was a substitute for EMS. Even worse, Notes had its own programming tools so Visual Basic was not even part of these applications. It was a nightmare!

My contribution to the mess was a long memo outlining how to "package up" EMS, Visual Basic, and Microsoft Access (the database in Office) to compete with Notes. It was the kind of memo I wrote knowing that it was exceedingly tactical and would never win in a competitive review. Importantly, none of the teams thought doing a project like I described was their job. Everyone was busy with their own category. I worked super hard, creating screenshots, architecture diagrams, and more. Bill really wanted a team to run with this. No one was interested. I felt this left us totally exposed to compete with Notes, and Bill agreed.

What neither of us saw was that the market for custom applications built on top of email was not nearly as interesting to customers as simply getting email to all employees. In a sense, Notes had made the same miscalculation. To Notes, email was one kind of application to be built with Notes that happened to be built by the Notes team itself. With EMS, email was *the* application, and the only one until the Outlook email program came along to add integrated scheduling. The grander vision for the category fell victim to the near-term needs of customers. Microsoft's sales teams would use the techniques I outlined in my memo over the coming years to sell against Notes, but few customers built and deployed applications that way. Email was the killer application for Windows NT Server and the Directory, at least until the internet came along. Importantly, email was the killer application that every company needed to roll out to every employee. It didn't hurt that NT Directory was itself a killer application just for rolling out shared folders and printers. The virtual cycle between these products was unlike anything, perhaps even greater than Excel and Windows.

Perhaps the biggest and in many ways most painful experience in building out EMS was Microsoft's own transition to using the product internally. Email was the most mission critical software at Microsoft, probably even more important than any billing and accounting software. Every single employee used email. Part of building EMS was figuring out how to get it deployed to all of Microsoft, and by SteveB goal to do so before the product shipped to customers. In other words, Microsoft needed to be self-hosted on EMS before paying customers. Makes sense.

The EMS team (and of course the NT team because everything ran on NT Server) were pioneers in the idea of dogfooding products and created a whole new infrastructure where the team itself ran on the very latest builds, then a large set of partners and friends ran on slightly older but more stable servers, and then ultimately Microsoft's IT department supported the rest of the company through a migration from the old Xenix system to EMS. The team was incredible at keeping servers running and keeping mail delivered. While there was downtime, when that happened pagers went off and people ran to the office to fix bugs. The team put these same skills to work with a small set of first external customers which received the highest level in support so they too could be part of the initial launch of the product, validating how it worked reliably and seamlessly for hundreds of thousands of mailboxes. When people ask me the true start of Microsoft's enterprise approach to building *and* selling products, this dogfood process was absolutely ground zero and key to Microsoft's long-term success. The process was heavy-handed and brutal on the partner teams (as I would learn building Outlook) but it is not clear there was another way. Running Exchange email turned out to be one of the most complex asks of our enterprise customers and something that was by all accounts nearly impossible to get right including being secure, reliable, and so on, unless you were the dogfood team. At the same time, there were no alternatives. The reality of software hardly working at all moved from the desktop to the data center. EMS dogfood before shipping the first time went on for about two years until the product finally shipped in 1996, long after I left my role as Technical Assistant.

Ultimately, BillG was entirely correct about the architecture required for email. Microsoft Exchange continued to struggle as a platform beyond email for decades. The lack of structured storage like SQL and programmable forms like those in Visual Basic made it difficult or even impossible to build additional applications. Microsoft would produce tools and languages for Exchange for the next 15 years, none of which gained critical mass or long-term adoption. On the other hand, Exchange dominated email without question—it arrived with global scale email at the right time and even transitioned that email capability to the cloud, forming the cloud portion of today's Microsoft 365.

Where most executives in charge and accountable for results would have kept pushing knowing they were right (and he was), what Bill routinely did was make his point of view clear while giving room for teams to execute and deliver, when it was clearly the right thing to do. Cairo had a backup plan (actually, two) so it was the right call to keep pushing on innovation. EMS did not have a backup plan. If EMS did not become a product, then Lotus Notes had too much opportunity. The bet on NT Directory proved to be critical to the entire product line and server initiative. Bill had the foresight to believe and operate as though email would become the anchor of enterprise computing for knowledge work, and it certainly did.

022. INJECTING NEW IDEAS AND IQ: THE INFORMATION SUPERHIGHWAY

Whenever I was feeling caught between shipping products and big vision or hearing about a product that was deep in bugs and had an unpredictable ship date, I could be rescued from my supply closet of an office by a demonstration from Microsoft Research (MSR) or the Advanced Consumer Technology group, ACT.

Bill viewed the gathering of the level of "IQ" and experience in these groups with great pride and a good deal of personal effort, as he often personally recruited them. Icons filled the rosters of the two teams over the years: Jim Gray, pioneer in databases; Chuck Thacker, coinventor of ethernet networking; Gary Starkweather, inventor of the laser printer; Alvy Ray Smith, Academy Award winner, cofounder of Pixar, and inventor of alpha channel in graphics; and Butler Lampson, founding member of Xerox PARC and inventor of the personal computer—and those were just the people hired in the early 1990s. I sometimes had to pinch myself that I even got to meet these legends. When Butler Lampson (BLampson) was being recruited, I was asked to take him to lunch, but I was mostly starstruck.

NathanM and Craig Mundie (CraigMu, who at the time reported to Nathan) were a yin and yang. Nathan brought an eclectic background in physics and science, though he founded a PC software company acquired by Microsoft that brought him to the company, among others including DavidW the pioneering Windows engineer. CraigMu was an industry veteran, having seen the entire arc of computing. He got his start at legendary Data General then ultimately started a well-known supercomputer company, Alliant. The company fell victim to the advances of Moore's Law, which brought him to Microsoft, "having seen failure," as BillG used to say. Officially Craig was leading the Windows CE project, Microsoft's first efforts in mobile, but he often managed, formally or informally, advanced projects and an ever-expanding portfolio. Part of the yin to Nathan's yang was that Craig was a former CEO of a larger company and a technology industry veteran.

The *information superhighway,* as it was called, was front and center of all the *future* discussions BillG and NathanM were involved in. The internet, as we think of it today, was more than a year away when I first started as TA, though the first version of the Mosaic browser was released in the summer of 1993. The highway was how the phone companies and cable television companies described accessing information over their respective networks. Bill's first book, which he began writing around this time, was titled *The Road Ahead* (1995) and spoke quite a bit about this metaphorical highway. The cover photo by Annie Leibovitz even featured Bill on a lone stretch of highway. In public, Bill was a bit of a realist about the timeline and who would "win." The highway was the first time as a public company that Microsoft faced a huge mainstream *hype cycle*. Part of this cycle were alternating predictions about how Microsoft with come to dominate the superhighway or how Microsoft was missing out.

Prior to the internet, much of the discussion in BillG meetings looked like the internet, only it used proprietary software and required dedicated hardware devices from Microsoft, phone companies, or cable companies, and mostly worked only over private networks of leased lines running proprietary protocols or archaic phone company standards. The *Information at Your Fingertips* vision (more on this in a future post), first articulated in 1990, looked a lot like the internet would come to be in a very short time, but with an entirely different implementation.

While there was no single definition of the Superhighway, the common articulation was the idea that a wide variety of consumer services would be available directly to home computers using a new type of data connectivity offered by phone or cable companies, the obvious incumbents with wires to the house. Common examples offered were news, weather, sports, stock market, movie listings, shopping (like at a mall), along with communication services over voice and video. So basically, not unlike a local newspaper.

Cable companies were extremely interested in offering one of the most forward-looking services one could imagine at the time, video on demand. Imagine watching any show anywhere, anytime. Most of us were still kicking ourselves if we forgot to put a blank tape in the VCR to record *Seinfeld* or if we had to go to Blockbuster in the rain in the hopes of finding a movie to rent. The early time shifting digital recorder from ReplayTV was not yet released. In fact, there was not even an electronic program guide to know what was on television. Some cable systems had a guide on a separate channel that scrolled by continuously.

No one really had any idea how to deliver video on demand, especially in a world where there was intense fear that a movie could be recorded, or stolen, and copied on to videotapes and sold on the street corner. The technology required to digitally encode a video was enormous. It had to store a massive amount of information and transmit the video to households reliably, provide program listings and remote control, such as pause for breaks, and so on. In 1994 we were a long way away from home DVRs or DVD movies. Even HDTV remained years off. By comparison, CD-ROMs held about 700 megabytes, which was about seven minutes of TV-quality uncompressed video.

Yet, somehow, one day I walked into a conference room with BillG and we saw a demonstration of all those pieces working. A program guide of movies to choose from, select a movie, *instantly* begin to watch it. It was one of the more impressive demonstrations I had seen—it wasn't a fake demo made with Director or AuthorWare but real code from Microsoft Research. NathanM called the product *Tiger*,[7] which was a code name for an MSR lab project developing a file server that could reliably move files around in real time. For this demo, the Tiger file system was used to deliver compressed video streams to a PC. The demo showed many PCs receiving different movies, each with their own pause/rewind/fast-forward controls. Mind blown.

Nathan detailed how this system worked, using a dozen or more Windows NT Servers connected to large collections of high-speed disk drives, connected together with the highest speed networking available. The architecture he spoke poetically about was the biggest problem they could foresee. Storing thousands of movies required a lot of disk drives, and unfortunately disk drives on PC servers were not particularly reliable. Nathan walked through the math for us—computing the mean-time-between-failure of drives, number of drives, and number of movies. His eyes got bigger and bigger as he got to the punchline, which was that a system like this would see failing disk drives as the bottleneck and "we'll need people on roller skates—like in the old days when computers had vacuum tubes—replacing disks as they failed." It was a colorful metaphor for a system decades ahead of its time.

Tiger generated a huge amount of interest from cable companies. Many wanted to immediately deploy it, but while they had been counting on networking capabilities into homes, there were none yet. Tiger also represented the collective view of Microsoft's immense industry power—if it could conjure a remarkable system like this and extend the control of the PC to the living room, what could Microsoft *not* accomplish? The press reports of Tiger simply stated as fact that Microsoft would control of the information superhighway, too.

Tiger, which really was a research project and had no product team structure around it at the time, became somewhat of a lynchpin in multi-way discussions Bill, Nathan, and Craig found themselves involved in. On the one hand, there was an industry that made cable TV tuner boxes each of them jockeying for a role in making the device that would sell millions to the cable companies to replace low tech CATV tuners. On the other hand, were the carriers, cable and telephone, who were trying to out-maneuver each other to gain the upper hand in being the pipeline to the home, and with that the ability to control the flow of information, the services offered, and to earn incremental revenue for everything on the system. There were also the content providers who owned everything interesting. For months, Bill, Nathan, and Craig met with CEOs across these industries. At one point Microsoft entered into a pilot project with Time Warner that garnered ongoing national news about the rollout of the superhighway.

Microsoft found itself in a new position. By some accounts it was poised to dominate the future of information services to the home. By other accounts it was going to provide plumbing to the massive companies already providing cable and voice services. But with announcements from all those companies almost constantly about pilots, prototypes, partnerships and more, many thought Microsoft was behind because it wasn't in all the announcements. Microsoft was at the same time in the early days of being one of the most dominant US companies, including early investigations by the Federal Trade Commission. Microsoft the nerdy tech company found itself front and center in entirely new industries. It was crazy. And all we had was Tiger and Windows PCs. What product would Microsoft even make?

Like so many of the innovation-oriented projects, Tiger was so far ahead as to be unable to connect to the *here and now*. Customers were not prepared to deploy and manage thousands of Windows Servers, consumers did not have high-speed networking, and even Hollywood was not ready to distribute video this way. The path from Tiger to today's streaming services (that Microsoft is not part of) does not represent a series of missteps by Microsoft but rather a series of additional technologies and marketplace expectations that completely discounted how Tiger approached the difference with streaming as we came to know it. It is fun to think about how early the vision was, but as is so often the case when you dive in you realize all the assumptions made were the wrong ones and all the technologies needed were generations away from being ready to solve the problem.

Fumbling the Future: How Xerox Invented, then Ignored, the First Personal Computer, a book detailing how Xerox invented the PC but failed to capitalize on it, was top of mind for BillG. It was a tragic story, and one Microsoft did not want to repeat. Being aware of the challenge and avoiding falling victim to it are different things. Nobody wants to be wildly underestimated or misunderstood when history is presented.

The technology world eventually solved Nathan's disk drive problem, but it wasn't Microsoft's answer.

Microsoft and the world around Windows NT followed the path of IBM mainframes and continued to work to make disk drives and the software more reliable—redundancy, quality control, and more increased the costs per megabyte and made it even more difficult to scale to huge data volumes. A new company came along to solve this problem, taking the exact opposite approach. Google, not even a company for another five years, would invent what came to be known as GFS, which stood for the Google File System early in the millennium. It used cheap commodity disks (like the kind in a home PC, not those used for data centers) and designed a system that assumed the disks would fail. As such, the idea of replacing them quickly like vacuum tubes was unnecessary. Coincidentally, the lead inventor of GFS was a classmate of mine from Cornell who also worked on the Cornell Synthesizer project—that revolutionary programming tool that influenced many of our ideas in Visual C++. Small world.

In hindsight, it was easy, especially during the down times of Microsoft, to become cynical over the company's inability to commercialize legitimate inventions such as Tiger. Beyond Bill's expansive vision for the role software and computing could play, it was also a management and organization approach that allowed projects to incubate. In particular, the very experience that influenced both Apple Macintosh and Microsoft Windows, visits to Xerox PARC, the birthplace of the PC and graphical operating system, was front and center of Bill's efforts to develop innovative projects and to commercialize them.

What I learned, and only in hindsight, is that visualizing the future and even providing working prototypes of it cannot account for the ability of the marketplace, customers, or even the most cost-effective technology approaches to make something a reality. The technology industry is littered with *ideas before their time,* and to find fault in those companies or leaders for not capitalizing is almost always in error. Tiger was not on a path to be a commercial streaming service. Deploying it, as we saw it in 1994, wasn't remotely possible.

Years later, as Microsoft hit rough patches in innovation and leadership, people pointed to many of the projects from the 1990s and asked what happened. BillG led and empowered visions across nearly every computing domain, but the under-pinning of them was the assumptions that built Microsoft—PCs, Windows, Win32, and then Windows Server held together with a client-server architecture. If those weren't the right ingredients, then building with them didn't create a path to some future. At the time, however, those were the only ingredients, so it made total sense to be using them. Faulting Microsoft for building with Windows in the 1990s would have been as crazy as faulting IBM for using mainframes in the 1970s or criticizing Detroit for building cars with internal combustion engines in the 1990s. What is impossible to see is when those ingredients cease to become assets and turn into liabilities. What really does happen is that those new entrants seeking to invent a new future deliberately take different approaches to solving problems and in doing so intentionally avoid following in the footsteps of the incumbent. They too often fail, but the world hardly notices…until one succeeds.

The pattern of Microsoft being early to so many innovative spaces often omits the challenges that existed at the time. When you're early many of the ingredients required—like the internet, high-speed networking, faster processors, long battery life, touch screens, pen digitizers, and so on—are simply not there. That means the products aren't ready to be built. When a new generation of product takes off it is rarely an invention; rather, it builds on the many early failures that came before.

In my role I was supposed to be eyes and ears, but I struggled with how to overcome what I saw as potential blind spots. It was never difficult to show new technologies to Bill and he was ready, willing, and able to absorb new information and incorporate it (or not) into his world view. At the same time, he seemed to over-index on the complex or sophisticated, seeing those as a moat or strategic advantage. Simple solutions did not have the appeal that a complex solution did, one that required the IQ of MSR or "deep architectural thinking." The researchers also valued complexity. The product teams tended to avoid complexity, seeing edge cases and boundary conditions as the enemy of shipping. This aversion to complexity looked almost lazy, as though there was a fear of taking on the hard problems and solving them. Worse, simplicity looked expeditious as though there was an attempt to get full credit for a solution by doing only part of the work. Seriously though, who was I to raise these questions? What did I know?

Bill saw products as built out of components of technology and each of those components needed to be the most sophisticated and singular across the company. The best text control, the best forms package, the best directory, and the best database each were ingredients that allowed him to take a product like the information superhighway or Lotus Notes and break it down and assign those components to the very best people to build the parts. There was a blind spot there.

Who would stitch those pieces together to make a product? Was Lotus Notes really a database, forms package, and a programming language? Was video on demand really Tiger plus some user interface code? The hands-on experience on MS-DOS and Windows seemed to have enshrined the lesson that building components was the winning strategy and developers would provide the rest of technology to create a full product experience. The Applications teams were learning the exact opposite lesson—that winning was about the complete experience and having the most advanced high-tech pieces without stitching them into a product was not all that useful.

The two cultures at Microsoft (MikeMap's two gardens) yielded different results for different reasons, and they both worked.

What I did have a handle on was shipping and products. In my (only) five years and innumerable stories about shipping I had heard, I definitely believed I could tell the difference between something that was real and something that was mostly slides. Bill did not always see things this way. He gravitated towards the technology view and was less interested in the process and mechanics of shipping. When a project like Cairo or Tiger needed him to push on shipping he was more comfortable continuing the technology discussion. The NT and EMS teams were happy to engage on the technology discussion, but in a sense kept those at arm's length while they dedicated themselves to making the tradeoffs for shipping.

Most any leader setting this tone would have had far more projects ultimately end like Tiger, but Bill had one enormous strength that made the company what it was. He did not hire only people in his image. Rather he balanced his technology leadership with product, sales, marketing, operations leadership and empowered those people to get their jobs done. They just had to put up with those deep technology discussions and have good answers to them. MikeMap, PaulMa, PeteH, BradSi, ChrisP, JonDe, and on and on filled out the product building ranks and were given the latitude to execute. I soon found myself spending my time as a TA trying to amplify those voices, while too often showing the effort required to go from technology to product.

023. THINKWEEKS

Microsoft's overall rhythm, the "rhythm of the company", as SteveB later called it, was still in the formative stages. In the early 1990s, the company fiscal year budget drove most of the rhythm for executives. The performance review process tended to set a yearly rhythm for product groups, though the product schedule was the real master often trumping work on reviews. For BillG, who was always obsessive about planning out a calendar for himself, the rhythm that seemed to matter most to him was the twice-yearly *ThinkWeek* times he set aside. They weren't a full week, but close. ThinkWeek had been mostly an informal time for Bill to catch up and to get away from the day-to-day of the CEO job and Redmond. Given the scope of thinking, it seemed an opportune time to up-level the process.

Bill's family vacation house, *Gateaway*, was located on the Hood Canal, about two hours by car or by ferry from Redmond. The Canal was a favorite place for Bill and his family, and where he vacationed with his grandparents when he was young. It was peaceful and isolated.

Learning about ThinkWeek from AaronG, the previous TA, I decided to make it a much bigger deal than simply gathering materials from teams for Bill to read. ThinkWeek was a fascinating way to immerse Bill in the details of what was going on, not just at Microsoft but across the industry. I spent a month preparing (overachieving) for each of the three ThinkWeeks we had together. Bill offered some guidance each time, such as the topic of a memo(s) he wanted to write, or if there was a theme he wanted to explore. He would suggest I speak with specific people for ideas. I discretely pinged people 1:1 who I knew would not start big email chains with subject lines like "BILLG THINKWEEK!!!" The frontline leaders in program management offered the best suggestions that came without agendas.

I created a spreadsheet (of course) to track ideas for content across a wide range of formats: product plans, books, magazine articles, memos, and demonstrations. I had a field day at an office supply store buying filing boxes, color-coded folders, and labels to create banker's boxes of ThinkWeek materials.

One of the ground rules I established was that I tried to avoid the use of ThinkWeek as a deadline or forcing function to rush to get something written just for the week. I generally insisted on memos and product plans that were already written for the normal course of work, and not special ThinkWeek pieces. I always felt these would confuse more than enlighten since there was no way of knowing if something was or would ever get connected to ongoing product development. Interestingly this is something that would completely reverse in a few years, when ThinkWeek would become more of a wide-open all-company brainstorming event.

The demos presented the most difficulty. In the early 1990s before software was released, it was almost always the case that a given product required a bunch of random hacks to work, and those hacks meant nothing else would run on that PC. Preparing a demo of something like a new version of Excel meant preparing an entire PC to demo *only* that version of Excel. This was also before laptops, so each ThinkWeek also meant there were a half dozen or more PCs that I had packed into my Jeep Cherokee (I was in my Northwest phase) along with reading material, all of which I delivered after he'd had one full day on his own.

Our first ThinkWeek together was in April of 1993, a few months after I started the job. The contents skewed toward the present, with the whole company immersed in the development of Chicago, Cairo, and finishing the first major release of Windows Office with new versions of Word, Excel, PowerPoint, and the Access database. Microsoft Research was getting started as well.

Bill was fixated on the need to gain more alignment and synergy across the product lines with respect to 32-bits, the shell, and more were still being settled. Execution plans were being put in place. Bill used ThinkWeek as a chance to delineate all the places where Microsoft could have a stronger strategy and leverage shared code more, to be more efficient in engineering effort, use less memory on running systems, and provide a more consistent experience for customers. He made a lot of lists. There were many core technologies to be developed and for each group to contribute to and use, rather than create more suboptimal redundancies.

An example of combining the high-altitude view with the ground-level perspective was demonstrated when we walked through many of the products under development and considered all the ways *text* was used and used inefficiently. Each product, Word, Excel, Publisher, Visual C++, Windows (itself had many places where text was used), and then all the CD-ROM products required what was called *rich text*—text with formatting, bullets, colors, numbering, alignment, fonts, and more. Each of those products built their own text capabilities, limited to what they believed they needed in the moment. Over time, each had many customer requests to improve that—examples, such as how Excel customers wanted to use multiple fonts within a single cell or how Publisher wanted to use bullets and numbering like Word. It was early enough in PCs that each product also had a different strategy for displaying text in languages with characters beyond the basics used in English and European languages. Some could handle Asian, some right-to-left, some vertical, but none could yet handle complex scripts like Arabic. We spent a few hours making a list of all the text inefficiencies while firing off mail to lots of people who then scrambled trying to figure out how best to say they were just doing what customers demanded or schedule permitted.

A little back story is that the 1994 film *True Lies* was to feature not-yet-shipping Arabic Windows and Word in the opening scene and had just contacted Microsoft for help in making that happen—for the company meeting that year I helped get a copy of the ¾ inch video tape to use at the meeting to highlight worldwide innovation. The clip was the opening scene of the film when Arnold Schwarzenegger uses a rendering of Arabic Windows and Word. It was very exciting.

It was easy to look at this and ask, "Doesn't a CEO have better things to do?" The company was maturing operationally and technologically, and the combination of the pace of change and the empowerment across teams meant topics like cross-product architecture were not yet part of the fabric of the company beyond Bill. Even within just one group, Desktop Apps (where I would work next), there was almost no code-sharing to facilitate the scenarios we experienced, just for text. If architecture didn't matter to a CEO, problems like this could go on for years and no one would notice or even be rewarded for thinking them through. It was a key differentiator of Microsoft that the company was thinking across the broad product line at such a level of granularity, even if not everything was acted upon it served to reinforce a culture of alignment and synergy while maintaining a level of empowerment. All of this was contrasted with the absurd cross-company process IBM used, whose disenfranchisement was all too familiar to Microsoft—the *Management Committee(s)* or the crazy *Common User Access* interface standards that burdened (crushed) OS/2 before it even started.

This first ThinkWeek was also the first time Bill looked deeply at infrastructure for the information superhighway. The nascent internet would prove to be a time for very important memos from many people. In the next chapter I will cover the internet and the impact on Microsoft, including Bill's first ThinkWeek impressions in late 1993.

I collected materials on all the ways the telco and cable companies believed consumers would connect to "the net" including X.25 dial-up, Asynchronous Transfer Mode, ISDN, and so on. I set up accounts on AOL and CompuServe, and we even dialed up to the original multiplayer game network Sierra Online, which Bill found intriguing. AT&T also found the company intriguing and acquired it and made it even more intriguing. The email threads that followed these demos dug deep into the ways consumers would get high-speed connectivity to the home that was not cost-prohibitive or whether consumers got stuck at dial-up speeds. These challenges became important as the ideas for *Marvel*, the code name for the new Microsoft Network online service to be released with Chicago, were solidified, work that was newly under investigation and a big part of these discussions.

Product demos contrasted with deep technical reading and strategic discussions and offered a bit of a respite. The demos were extremely important to me as I felt I was representing the teams and wanted their work to shine. Normally a demo for pre-release products was a nail-biting experience even for those working on the product. They were using the product day in and day out and knew the landmines. I was given a script and told not to veer at all from the script. Good luck doing that with Bill.

One demo was for the forthcoming release of Microsoft Word for Windows, version 6.0, code name *T3*, a nod to the film *Terminator 2* that had been released when the project started. Word built a sort-of sophisticated *rules engine* into the product, eventually marketed as *machine learning*, to implement features that would automatically format a document, such as look for headings or numbered lists. I followed the demo script, but the feature did not seem to work, so we typed a basic letter including "Dear Bill" and "Sincerely" and then selected the Auto Format command from the Tools menu. A second or so later, nothing seemed to happen. Then Dear Bill turned into *Dear Bill* and Sincerely became **Sincerely**. That was it. Bill fired off mail and a scramble on the Word team ensued. Additional demo steps were provided later in the day.

The Chicago product was making progress. Pre-release builds leaked over the summer. Without the internet, leaks did not go far, but the trade press picked up on screenshots and extrapolated from there. The core question moved from synergy and alignment to whether Chicago was going to be competitive with Macintosh.

In subsequent ThinkWeeks, I structured most of the reading and materials and demonstrations around operating systems or applications taking advantage of the latest operating system capabilities like networking, storage, and multimedia.

The ACT (Advanced Consumer Technology) group was in the early stages of one of the earliest tablet computers Microsoft considered, code-named *WinPad*, running on the Windows CE operating system, which was under development. Windows CE was the precursor to Windows Phone and was an implementation of parts of Windows for low-powered ARM chips, instead of Intel, and designed for stylus input. This was before the Palm Pilot that debuted in 1996, giving new life to the category of *personal digital assistants*, or PDAs, pioneered a decade earlier by devices such as the Psion. The primary competitor that was much more intriguing was from a company named General Magic with a product spun out of Apple by some of the original Macintosh developers. As General Magic was developing its product, Apple released the Newton, which, while ultimately a failure seemed competitively *scary* during ThinkWeek.

The external focus on indirect competitors was a hallmark of Bill's approach to competition. The ACT team was thinking about the Newton and General Magic, but no one else at Microsoft was. For example, General Magic had invented a programming language called TeleScript, core to the way the platform could be extended. Historically, PDAs were more purpose-built devices and not rich platforms, and certainly not platforms with their own programming languages. From Bill's perspective, BASIC was a key part of the early PC era, and it followed that a new platform with a pioneering new language would be a powerful combination. In poring over the documentation for TeleScript, it became clear that Microsoft would need to up its game in creating applications for a more connected world as envisioned by both Newton and General Magic.

The more traditional PC competition was much more focused on the direction Apple was taking Macintosh. Apple, under CEO John Scully, had repurposed a faltering project started years earlier called Taligent. The project had become the punchline for jokes about vaporware, but Apple sorely needed a more modern operating system. Chicago would be vastly superior to the current Macintosh in how modern it was relative to running more than one program at a time. Apple seemed stuck. Strangely, Taligent morphed into a partnership with IBM. In some ways, that made it difficult for Bill to take seriously the Taligent materials I provided for reading as there was no software—he knew well the risks of a deep partnership with IBM, as did BradSi and the Chicago team. Bill did his best, though in classic style, to make the most of the risks that could come from Taligent executing. They had a much broader vision than Chicago that would never materialize. That did not stop Bill from using it as a competitive threat or risk when talking to the Chicago or Cairo teams.

Sometimes things didn't always go as planned and one topic ended up taking up a big chunk of time. One ThinkWeek, we spent a good deal of time on the competition with Lotus Notes. The EMS project was starting to gain engineering traction and had sent over product specifications. The memo I previously wrote on using Visual Basic and Access with EMS was the topic of many email threads. Evenings were often spent watching videos. We watched a videotape of a keynote from Lotus CEO Jim Manzi with a demo of Lotus Notes that was definitely something that pushed those competitive buttons.

Bill wrote a detailed memo on competing with Lotus Notes, sharing his views of what he had learned, again using his perspective to stitch together the Microsoft organization. Up until that point, the field sales organization had only been raising the competitive risks of Notes but had nothing to respond with. Bill provided some guidance but mostly motivation to get our collective act together. He pointed out that selling email and workgroup software was a long process and required partners, industry analysts, demonstrations, and more. It was a good and specific *motivator*.

ThinkWeek would come and go. Emails would get responded to. Some people priding themselves on pulling together what was needed (and then some) in super short order and replying. Other replies would trickle in a week later. Memos would always fly around campus email even if they were only moderately interesting, they were still BillG memos. A few times a memo would be critically important to a group or the company.

The April 1994 ThinkWeek was my third and last. Bill devoted a good deal of time to writing his first strategic internet memo, which set the tone for the strategy the company would take going forward. We were fresh from the offsite on internet strategy and the memo was a chance to reflect on the important initiatives coming out of the gathering.

Bill was keenly aware of the ability for groups to craft unique strategies around a technology shift. He set out to make sure that teams across the company would not slow down the transition to an internet-centric strategy. Over the next couple of years, many would document Microsoft's transformation from a desktop company to an internet company—this April 1994 memo was the *moment* that happened.

We spent a good deal of time going back and forth over what I saw as the risks that each group would "interpret" the internet differently and try to absorb different parts into their plans at different times and in different ways. Many groups were skeptical about the internet, including the new online service, multimedia and consumer, and the enterprise teams. The memo crafted a great line to open: "Product groups do not have to spend time studying the future of the Internet or researching this phenomenon. We want to, and will, invest resources to be a leader in Internet support, fully understanding that if we are wrong about this it will have been a mistake."

About a year later, Bill repeated and amplified much of this memo in a loftier and more intentionally external missive that would receive wider distribution and wide acclaim, *Internet Tidal Wave*. While the April 1994 memo was a more standard list of technologies and owners (in other words, a memo to get work done), *Tidal Wave* a year later was an exciting narrative and combined with the imminent Windows 95 release, served as a much more dramatic moment in time.

There was more that year though. In fact, the company-changing products for 1995 were on the way. Chicago builds complete with the Start menu, as we would come to know it, began to work well-enough to at least demonstrate, along with the 32-bit version of Office and a slate of soon to be *Designed for Windows 95* products. The press visibility of Chicago energized the whole of Microsoft, still more than a year before shipping. We spent a good deal of time using the most recent Chicago builds, which was hugely motivating for Bill.

Given the rise of the internet and discussions fresh on our mind, ThinkWeek dove deeply into consumer and home computing, in particular content. The industry view at the time was *content is king*, an expression driving consolidations, mergers, partnerships, and more across the telephone carriers, cable companies, Hollywood, and online services, especially AOL. The idea that the internet would be used to operate businesses was not mainstream at all, with the focus on the internet as a potential consumer information superhighway technology.

The Consumer division invested heavily in creating CD-ROM *titles*—applications that required a CD-ROM on a PC along with capabilities to play video and audio, which were relatively new—having these titles was an important differentiator for Windows. Chicago promised to make using multimedia even easier and more reliable with better hardware support and less of a need for consumers to struggle just to get sound to play on a PC. I assembled a *portable* multimedia computer, a suitcase-size PC weighing 20 pounds, and loaded up over 40 multimedia titles.

We spent hours exploring a wide variety of topics from *Autos* to *Strauss*, from the *JFK Assassination* to *Earthquake Preparedness*, as well as a variety of games for all ages.

Bill wrote detailed feedback on these titles, not from a user review perspective but from a strategic perspective. Could these titles be repurposed on the Marvel online service? Shouldn't titles have more quizzes, reference materials such as maps, and always more videos, tiny little postage-stamp sized videos? Many of the titles would transition to be part of Marvel in some form or another, and all would be important parts of articulating the broader internet message beyond simply protocols and formats.

ThinkWeek was intense, but it was also fun. We would sit upstairs in the loft of the vacation house drinking endless Diet Coke. Bill was just starting his Cherry Coke phase under the influence of Warren Buffet, whom he'd met two years earlier at Hood Canal[8]. In his thirties, Bill had many such phases. One of the most famous was his vegetarian phase despite his long-held love of Dick's Burgers, especially the Queen Anne sit-down Dick's. We had a great time hacking away at all the pre-release software, making lists, diagramming on the whiteboard, and keeping an eye on email threads. Even for Bill, connectivity was dial up. There was no pretense and truly no distractions other than the weather, which I had to keep an eye on because of the ferry ride. We spent perhaps 12-15 hours each day with breaks when mostly we'd just do our own email.

Sometimes the "thinking" would be interrupted by some Microsoft issue of urgency, such as the FTC or DOJ, or even something personal, like getting engaged or planning a bachelor party. There was always something to distract and I had to do my best to help focus on the memo writing goals or making it through demos. The expected disappointment from teams who put together demos only to find out that we didn't have time sometimes forced me to stretch the truth a bit about going through the demo.

One unique experience was ultimately documented in a January 1994 article in *The New Yorker*, "E-Mail From Bill" in which John Seabrook documented his ongoing conversation over email with Bill on topics ranging from personal job satisfaction to innovation. There were a lot of highbrow conversations about the information superhighway. Mostly the article is a time capsule trying to explain the Microsoft culture and even the culture of email to readers of *The New Yorker*, most of whom were years away from email.

At the end of each week, I'd pack up all the desktop and laptop PCs, boxes, and books and come back to the office to return everything. The folders of photocopied articles and memos organized by topic would travel around with Bill in one of his two carry-on bags, sometimes for months. Then one day an email out of the blue would reference that lone article on ATM or micro-payments or something.

The real legwork was going back and thanking all the people that put together demos and materials and doing my best to give them a play-by-play of any interactions while being careful not to have that influence anything other than morale.

1994

The greatest change in computing lands on a world that is still figuring out what a PC does. Welcome to the world of the Internet or World Wide Web, WWW. In 1994 Microsoft goes through the most significant strategic shift any successful company has ever gone through and does so in an incredibly short time as we "pivot" the company around the Internet.

024. DISCOVERING "CORNELL IS WIRED!"

As Technical Assistant at the time I found myself in the middle as a facilitator but also an activist and champion. The personal growth that I experienced during this time would prove to be an incredible blessing that led to enduring friendships and amazing memories. At the same time, this was a period of remarkable turmoil and angst, mixed in with an unrelenting corporate urgency.

The pending storm was all anyone was talking about as I completed the last few interviews at the end of my annual (or more) recruiting trip to Cornell in February 1994. As snow, and more snow, piled up, I knew I was not getting out that day as planned. This happened every other year or so.

What I did not know was that getting stuck would turn into a lesson on what it takes for a large and successful organization to change course and rally around something new.

Microsoft, and BillG in particular, were thinking about the opportunities *online,* as it was called. Russ Siegelman (RussS) focused on the opportunity. As a recently hired fellow TA, he was exclusively looking at the existing world of online information services and connectivity.

The biggest online service by far was America Online (AOL); the dial-up service had membership of over two million households, and notably was equally accessible from both Windows and Macintosh. AOL along with CompuServe and Prodigy were collectively a sort of *big three* of online services and gave a bit of a feel that they were like TV networks and in some sense, they operated that way with various forms of *channels*. In 1992, AOL released a Windows version of the software, which previously ran on MS-DOS, putting it at parity with Macintosh. I used AOL in graduate school with the screen name SHNOWZ, it's still mine but that's another story. Apple even had a deal with AOL that offered online services for Macintosh users on the AOL platform, and that in turn gave them leverage to develop exclusive *online content* deals with major media brands. That's the kind of thing that would concern Microsoft.

Millions of people sent email to each other on AOL, participated in communities, and explored deep information services on finance, sports, entertainment, and more. All of this was done from within the AOL application.

Few, if any, at the time thought this approach, a so-called *walled garden*, was bad. In fact, most people thought it was the only way to "package up" a variety services and information sources. AOL uniquely combined services with an application that handled the complexities of connecting a computer modem to the service over a landline. It was slick. To attract customers, AOL was spreading floppy disks everywhere, through magazine inserts, cash register checkouts, and direct mail. It was growing fast, approaching $100 million in revenue.

AOL was so exciting that Microsoft cofounder PaulA became a major investor, much to the chagrin of the Microsoft competitive spirit. He even tried unsuccessfully to acquire controlling interest of the entire company. Paul correctly recused himself for several Board meetings during this time because of the ownership stake.

BillG was spending a great deal of time on the earliest stages of working with the "carriers," or the phone companies, trying to navigate the right partnership model. Dial-up made these companies essential to the online world. Household high-speed connectivity was still years away with many predictions of timelines and technologies, but no approach seemed like it would take hold any time soon. In Europe, somewhat faster ISDN was useful to business customers, but globally connectivity was rooted in the traditional phone companies over dedicated connection-based lines, and slow.

The phone companies, and later the cable companies, were motivated to achieve more than their pipeline or carrier status. Both wanted to play in the world of content and services and own more of customer experience, especially for consumers. This led to a long series of discussion and eventually pilot projects between various players including Microsoft. The spectacle of giant companies navigating a new space while simultaneously partnering and competing (frenemies, or coopetition, terms that became popular in the increasingly intertwined PC industry) was a sight to be seen.

AT&T created a series of television commercials known as the "Someday you will…" ads. These were slick visions of the future directed by David Fincher (*Fight Club*) and starring Jenna Elfman (*Dharma & Greg*), and narrated by Tom Selleck of *Magnum, P.I.* fame. They pitched a world in which one might borrow a book from thousands of miles away, watch any movie on demand, or even send a fax from the beach. That's AT&T for you!

Bill loved to talk about these exact concepts when meeting with various digital highway partners, so when I showed him the commercials I had taped at home, he seemed irked at the feeling of having his concepts "stolen." The truth is everyone was talking about these broad ideas. AT&T happened to do a great job visualizing them. As we would learn, the part of the company that created these videos had nothing at all to do with the part of the company delivering products and services. It was pure vision marketing. There was a lot of that going on.

Microsoft was investing heavily in creating CD-ROM content and was in the early stages of a robust line of multimedia titles including *Encarta* encyclopedia and a whole series of interactive versions of beautiful books by Dorling Kindersley, from *Dinosaurs* to *Dogs* and *Musical Instruments*. We talked a great deal during ThinkWeek about how this experience could translate into a programmed online experience, though the limitations of bandwidth were obvious, especially after the compromises faced to get these to work on PCs.

Broadly, Bill's *Information at Your Fingertips* (IAYF) vision loomed large. Unveiled at COMDEX, the massive computer industry tradeshow (COMDEX is a portmanteau of Computer Dealer Exchange), in November of 1990, IAYF presented a vision for computing years in the future that put important information in an integrated and seamless fashion a click away. To articulate IAYF, Microsoft made its first visionary video based on the fictional coffee company *Twin Hills* with an oddly familiar green logo. *Twin Peaks* filmed east of Seattle was as big a Northwest hit as our local coffee. Many of us, me included, made it over to the library to watch it or secured one of the video tapes that were widely distributed. There was also a very fancy brochure which I kept at the time as a reminder of our vision. I was definitely giddy about the future. It was a future where we moved seamlessly between applications, just pointing and clicking, editing rich documents filled with charts and graphs, connecting to rich information, and more. It was graphical. It was easy. It was what we loved to call a *North Star*.

The company would update to IAYF to be shown at the November 1994 COMDEX more than a year away. Recall those demonstrations from ThinkWeek about devices like General Magic, that would become the focus of this vision.

The roots of IAYF brought together two famous visions from the history of computing. In the July 1945 issue of *The Atlantic,* Director of the Office of Scientific Research and Development Dr. Vannevar Bush authored "As We May Think," in which he described a futuristic information tool for the workplace:

> *Consider a future device for individual use, which is a sort of mechanized private file and library. It needs a name, and, to coin one at random, "memex" will do. A memex is a device in which an individual stores all his books, records, and communications, and which is mechanized so that it may be consulted with exceeding speed and flexibility. It is an enlarged intimate supplement to his memory.*[9]

The idea of having access to the world's information was a key part of IAYF. Bush took it a step further and connected aspects of the information together:

> *All this is conventional, except for the projection forward of present-day mechanisms and gadgetry. It affords an immediate step, however, to associative indexing, the basic idea of which is a provision whereby any item may be caused at will to select immediately and automatically another. This is the essential feature of the memex. The process of tying two items together is the important thing.*

This notion of tying two items together was widely present in the multimedia titles. This action became known as *hypertext* as originally described two decades after Bush's essay in a seminal work by information theory pioneer Ted Nelson published in 1965 as *Project Xanadu*, the second major technology brought into IAYF. On the subsequent project *Hypertext Editing System*, Nelson worked closely with legendary computer science professor and founder of the computer science department at Brown University, Andries "Andy" van Dam, who later became among the first advisers to Microsoft Research.[10]

Hypertext formed the foundation of multimedia titles and the training and help materials in Windows and Office, known as *WinHelp,* likely the most mainstream use of hypertext, which was about to become incredibly interesting to Microsoft. It's notable that Apple *HyperCard* for the Macintosh, released in 1987, made extensive use of hypertext and was a widely used modern commercial system that influenced a generation.

AOL was the reference point for online services and defined the experience we collectively believed was relevant. The idea of an online service that had the feel of a television network for the information superhighway while also working as a PC application seemed to check all the boxes.

The snow kept falling as I looked out the window of Cornell's Statler Hotel. I was about to have my whole understanding of online services turned upside down.

025. TRAPPED

Feeling nostalgic, and trapped, I decided to go visit old lecture halls and campus sites. Cornell was used to the snow and even with all the warnings of a big storm, most students were going about their evening. From the career office in Hollister Hall, I made my way over to the Upson Hall basement where I had worked the terminals and the mini-computer room for computer science majors.

It was still early enough in the PC revolution and connectivity that most students were still doing their work in these shared facilities.

The layout of Upson had changed dramatically from my time there. Walled cubicles of VT-100s with a shared line printer were replaced with long tables of Macs. There were new NeXT cubes that were getting a lot of use. There were even laser printers that had magnetic *Vend-a-Card* readers that stored cash to pay $0.20 a page for printing. When I worked in the Uris Hall computer room, I was lucky enough to have the only public laser printer on campus, but alas it was only connected to the IBM mainframe.

It was the end of the day. The room was buzzing. People were racing in, spending a few minutes at a Macintosh, and racing out. At first, I couldn't tell what they were doing, and with no student ID I wasn't able to use a machine. After watching a few students, I realized they were all following the same flow.

Each quickly sat down at a Mac and pulled out a floppy disk from a backpack, slung over one shoulder, none of this both-shoulder thing the kids do these days. Shaking the mouse to wake the machine up, the Macs were set to launch only one program called *Bear Access,* Cornell's mascot. Students typed in some ID, inserted a floppy disk, and then quickly navigated to mail. I later learned the students were storing their mail on the floppy because the Cornell mail servers were running the POP protocol and were not storing it after the initial download to save on costs.

As dinner approached, Upson vacated, and a quick look outside made it obvious that everyone was hunkered down in dorms and apartments for the evening. I asked the operator if they were closing due to weather as we would never have done that, and he assured me he would be around because he needed to get the hours in that week. I was staying across the quad at the Statler Hotel, so I headed into Collegetown to eat.

After a quick stop at Souvlaki House, I went back to Upson. It was completely empty. The operator was reading from Foley & van Dam, the standard text on computer graphics.

"I know this will sound strange, but I used to work here about 10 years ago," I said. He looked annoyed.

"I see you are taking Graphics…is it Professor Greenberg?"

While I had not taken the class, all my friends did and I was also friends and classmates with Professor Greenberg's son, which I was quick to mention. He remained bothered.

"Well, I work at Microsoft, and I am here interviewing students for internships next summer…"

He interrupted me, grabbed his backpack, and pulled out a resume.

After a few minutes of typical discussion about opportunities and how to interview and more, I asked, "Can you maybe show me how Bear Access works and tell me how you are using computers these days?"

We pulled up chairs at a Mac. He logged on. I stopped him and asked where and how students got an ID, thinking back to the punch card with TGUJ@CORNELLA.EDU I received orientation week freshman year. Cornell IT (CIT) had built an identity system such that it maintained the canonical mail address for students and faculty and routed mail to the appropriate mail server. The email system in use at the time, as was typical in most organizations (academic or otherwise), was distributed and heterogenous. Different departments each ran their own mail servers of different types along with different ways of assigning email IDs. CIT created login IDs so students could always be referred to by a single @cornell.edu mail address no matter where their mail went. Every single member of the university community had a login ID.

This was the first example of a solution to a problem that was a product under development at Microsoft, Windows NT.

The business or enterprise version of this problem was known as *directory service* and was a rather heated battle between Netware and the new entrant, Windows Server along with the EMS project described previously. But at Cornell, this was already working. Most companies in the early '90s were not yet using email and definitely did not have a directory.

Launching Bear Access, I was immediately struck by the similarity to AOL or Prodigy. Here was a Mac running graphical software (and TCP/IP networking, another technology that PCs did not routinely run) where the icons were all information sources. The resources available, all a click away, included email, library, the university bursar, chat, access to the directory for finding people, campus store, and something I was totally familiar with, CUINFO.

I got excited. "Tell me about CUINFO!" Ten years earlier CUINFO was a magical behemoth. It was thousands of lines of IBM 360 assembly language, among archaic languages such as REXX to massage the data feeds, running on the mainframe out at the airport accessed via VT100 kiosks throughout campus with no logon required. With CUINFO, text-based information, such as the weather forecast, course roster, and campus events, were available. It was years ahead of its time.

Instead of accessing it via a terminal, clicking on the Bear Access icon I launched something called *Gopher*. Then right before me was something vaguely familiar. Instead of typing menu numbers like a phone tree, I was navigating an information service with double-clicks. And there was the same NOAA weather forecast I remember being coded by my fellow operator a decade earlier.

But what was Gopher?

A few months earlier, Cornell migrated the entire CUINFO system from the mainframe to running on the open-source project Gopher, developed at the University of Minnesota. The IT effort involved took the CUINFO information and organized it into a Gopher hierarchy: Academic Life, Administration, Dialogs, Library, Student Life, Campus, Ithaca, and so on. And within each of these there were further hierarchical topics, such as under Library there was schedule, information, electronic books, and the online catalog. I learned that the CUINFO hierarchy itself was over 800 pages—that's the outline of the information not the information itself. Gopher looked a lot like the early builds of the new *Explorer* in Chicago.

From my Microsoft vantage point, adding insult to injury, the CUINFO Gopher server was connected to a slew of other like-minded Gopher servers around the world. In other words, it wasn't only that Cornell was doing this or even that other places were, but there was a network. That network on the internet was growing at a rate of 3 percent *per week*.

Information was searchable using WAIS, an early internet, open-source content indexing and search platform. Search was a key, but theoretical, part of IAYF in Cairo, but this was an area where literally no one at Microsoft was working on a product.

While hardly today's Facebook, I was treated to demonstrations of search across the *Who Am I* service. What used to be entirely impossible was routine. "Find the person Pat in Arts [and Sciences] school, class of '96, who lives on College Ave." Using the information students voluntarily put into the directory, the results appeared. There was an ongoing debate on campus about privacy and soon thereafter searching was curtailed.

The early internet was rather quaint that way.

Chat was another service accessed from Bear Access, using the newly familiar (in tech circles) *Internet Relay Chat*, or IRC protocol. Later that evening in my old dorm, Founders Hall, I watched as a group of about 10 students in one computer room chatting all together with other people around the world. Chat wasn't for fun, as I learned; TAs were using it for study and course-maintained IRC rooms as well.

This was all incredibly exciting. But it was also humbling. And scary.

My baseline experience was AOL (a walled garden with a monthly fee) or the barren enterprise network, which best case was fairly heavy email running on clunky shared file servers, as Exchange was still years away. A revolution had taken place.

Back at Microsoft, RussS and others were working to define an online service for Windows, and yet here was one that was already rivaling AOL, built entirely on free software at a university and growing much faster than AOL.

This snowstorm was turning into the biggest surprise learning experience of my early career. More importantly, it was opening my eyes to speed of change. I had been at Cornell less than a year ago and yet everything I was seeing was new. It wasn't only the software but the students and faculty and how they interacted with computers and information.

My new operator friend was on the ball. We went through how difficult it was for them to keep the Macs running. Like many places, after each use the Macs were "reset" and all the files and programs deleted and restored to a new state. This happened dozens of times a day. This hack was clearly an opportunity for Windows. At least it should have been.

After almost three hours, it was getting late—close to 11 p.m.—but before I left, we looked up my old boss who ran CUINFO and IT, Steve Worona, in the directory. I sent him a "Hey, I am in town" note. We set up a meeting the next day at Day Hall.

Late that night I went to the Hot Truck on west campus. I ordered a "double PMP Pep" (Poor Man's Pizza—Johnny's Hot Truck invented French bread pizza, so the lore goes) and waited in the blizzard. Two students in line were busy talking about the new Visual C++ that had recently come out. It was surreal.

I said, "Hey, I know a bit about Visual C++," trying but failing to remain composed and with some hint of modesty. The students seemed excited. One told me about writing his first Windows program. It was like an advertisement. After some back and forth I told them what I did. He asked if he could run back to his dorm and get his copy of the product so I could sign it.

I was not sure who was more excited by this conversation. This was the strangest thing that ever happened to me.

The excitement of the moment was soon awash in the nausea that comes from eating Hot Truck at midnight as an adult.

The next day, the school was knee deep in snow and mostly shut down. I wasn't getting out. I headed over to Day Hall to see Steve Worona, who was then the assistant to the CIO of the university. Steve was the original programmer for CUINFO with an office right inside the small computer terminal room in G20 Uris Hall where I worked freshman year.

For about an hour we talked about how far things had come since he originally wrote CUINFO. Hearing Steve's acknowledgment of the many challenges that lay ahead was super interesting. The university was wrestling with privacy, independent organizations had different ideas about information sharing, and even labor unions were concerned about how access to information might impact employment.

Steve then set up a small camera to show me a demo using, as I recall, one of the earliest pre-release Connectix QuickCams, which was a Macintosh-only peripheral. It was super frustrating that it did not run on Windows. I had only seen the camera in the press. Interestingly an Excel product manager had just moved there so I was able to secure one at the time back in Redmond. It was an amazing technology in search of a use. Then it met the Internet.

He launched a program on his Mac called *CU-SeeMe,* fiddled with it a bit, and then a window opened. This was a small black and white moving image of a classroom in North Carolina. A few minutes later more windows opened up of other classrooms, two in New York and one in Washington, DC.

Suddenly, I was looking at a five-way video conference made up of tiny *postage stamp* black and white windows at about 10 frames per second. Live. From around the country. Everyone dialed into the same traditional voice conference line. For half an hour, students did what students do in a learning environment as teachers asked questions of each other. Watching them share information was incredible. For Steve it was new but becoming routine. The project was called *Global Schoolhouse,* supported by NSF and the Department of Education.

After the classroom, Steve spent a good hour explaining the technology they developed. The project created a video protocol, a multicast network server, and the client software. They were already doing "student exchange" programs with Europe even. IBM was even helping to make a Windows version. Everything was on Macintosh.

It was almost more than I could take.

Video conferencing built on the PC, as we showed in IAYF, seemed forever away and for sure no one was really working on it at Microsoft. Microsoft NetMeeting was still yet to be conceived and would not include video conferencing for years.

Steve showed me one more demo. Switching to his Windows 3.1 computer, he launched a program called *Cello*. Cello was developed by the Law School at Cornell and was the first "world-wide-web browser," or just *browser*, for Windows. A web browser looked like Gopher and CUINFO but used a different protocol and different format for information. Where Gopher looked like a file explorer or Mac Finder, Cello used hypertext and links to pages with nice formatting and looked more like Windows Help or HyperCard. Because of Cornell's mixed computing environment, Steve explained they also used *Mosaic* on Macintosh. Steve was super clear that he expected the browser to supplant Gopher even though he loved the information hierarchy; the browser's use of images was too good.

Cello and Mosaic were the world wide web, WWW.

At the time, Marc Andreessen and Eric Bina were developing *Mosaic* at the University of Illinois, which was the first graphical HTML browser. By the end of 1993, it was running on all the major platforms in early beta form. On the internet, it seemed not only was everything free, but everything was in beta and was developed by students at a university somewhere. That was something I had to get everyone back in Redmond comfortable with, along with the reality that everything ran on every operating system.

That afternoon, February 13, 1994, I went back to my room at Statler and wrote a fairly breathless memo entitled *Computing at Cornell and the Internet*. After apologizing for being a Cornell cheerleader, I detailed my personal history of computing at the school and the evolution of what I had seen.

Along with the memo, I shared series of recommendations—specific things we could be doing to improve Windows (and servers) and Desktop Apps to make them internet-friendly and even great for the internet. Most of them were directed toward Chicago, the Windows 95 project that was under development.

I sent the memo as a Word attachment in email to BillG with the subject line "Cornell is WIRED!" to get his attention. *WIRED* was the new magazine at the time and "wired" was synonymous with cool. I also backchanneled the memo to BradSi and John Ludwig (JohnLu), who was one of the two lead Windows executives. I did this to make sure no one was blindsided by my report since it could easily be seen as me saying, "Add even more stuff to Chicago that is already late."

Bill, doing what he always did, immediately forwarded the email to a set of key execs working on Chicago and platforms, proving it was a good idea to backchannel people. The thread was sent to PaulMa, who sent it to the email exec, TomEv, and even to the Windows evangelists in hopes of getting them to drive an engagement with developers to use Windows. Pretty soon I was getting emails from university relations, Microsoft's connection to schools and colleges. And they told two friends…

I was comfortable with my emails being forwarded around, but this one had taken on a life of its own.

It clearly touched a nerve.

The most actionable response I received was from JohnLu, who told me I should talk to a "guy over in NT" who was working on this "stuff." He copied J Allard (JAllard.) J sent me a note saying something along the lines of "Where you been?" and attached a memo he had just started circulating called *Windows: The Next Killer Application on the Internet.*

I read J's memo while still trapped at Cornell. It was everything I could have hoped it would be after getting so amped up over the internet for 48 hours. Even the title of the memo was so subtly clever—it said that Windows would be part of the internet, decidedly not the other way around. While too many came to remember this memo for the use of "embrace, extend, innovate," the reality was always the other way around for J, and I agree. The internet was larger than Windows and could not be contained by an operating system—Cornell was already proving this. Windows was an application on the internet.

Also misunderstood was the use of "killer." "Killer app" was a phrase used broadly to lend legitimacy to a new platform. A necessity for a platform to gain traction was that it have a so-called killer application. VisiCalc was the killer application for Apple. Lotus 1-2-3 was the killer application for MS-DOS. Excel was for Windows, and so on. The turn of the phrase was that Windows would be what could accelerate the internet.

There would be much truth in that.

026. BLUE SUEDE PUMAS

Back home, I went to J's office in one of the single X buildings just across the walkway from Building 8. He had a typical Microsoft interior office for a junior program manager, but his had an aquarium with some reptile in it. Yuck. We were both wearing blue suede retro Puma Clydes. Because of our footwear, I was able to forgive the reptile which even after showing up at his office 100 times made me uncomfortable.

J graduated from Boston University in 1991 and Microsoft was his first job. At BU he worked in the computing facilities the way I did at Cornell and we bonded over that. He described the job he was given by SteveB as "make this TCP problem go away." He joined the networking group at a time SteveB was still running Systems, which included the always struggling LanMan product. TCP referred to the customer problem Steve was seeing where Microsoft did not support the technology that was rapidly becoming the preferred protocol in business networks, TCP/IP. This was a time when the choice of a network protocol was a strategic business decision guided by IBM, DEC, and hopefully Microsoft someday, and few would think of using what was generally considered a research platform.

This was one of my first lessons in Microsoft challenges in developing an internet-centric strategy. It was new to me, but for J, it was the daily "battle" he already faced. Microsoft thought it would develop a connected PC by also developing the networking protocols that connected the PCs. There was a great deal of work that had gone into many "layers" of the networking software. Microsoft could do a better job if all the parts of the network were running Microsoft software. Microsoft was not unique in thinking this, but it was late to the party.

The internet didn't work that way, though. The protocols themselves were openly developed. Vendors developed their own implementations of those protocols, but they needed to interoperate with all the other parts of the network. J's job was to make sure Microsoft had great support for TCP/IP, the base networking layer for the internet. Some big commercial and government customers were early in adopting TCP/IP, including money center banking and defense departments which were very large Microsoft customers.

To the Windows and NT teams, TCP/IP was one of several ways of connecting. Windows NT was designed from the start to be networking agnostic but solidly favored and made a bet on TCP/IP, which was a significant departure for a Microsoft product, and also evidence of the difference between NT and LanMan. Chicago was working hard to support Netware's protocols, which were the current business leader, but not TCP/IP. The speed at which networking switched to TCP/IP was stunning. The reality was that it was vastly superior to any other solution for running corporate networks. As I recalled from my first day at Microsoft, the beeping death due to network failure was still all too common and not something I experienced in graduate school where TCP/IP dominated. TCP/IP addressed that with a much more robust approach. J re-explained all of this to me.

He was tracking the public sources of data and was seeing the exponential growth in the use of the internet. This is really what got everyone's attention, including, and especially, BillG's. BillG gravitated toward the exponential.

The internet was over two million connected "nodes" at the time. Today, a node might be a house with dozens of devices on the internet or a business with tens of thousands. Then, a node was a single computer, a Mac like at

Cornell or a Gopher server. It was estimated that 25 million people were using the internet, and it was growing at a rate of more than 5 percent *per month*, 70 percent per year. Importantly all the companies that offered networking over phone lines and leased lines were starting to offer internet or packet switched connectivity to businesses.

The numbers were breathtaking.

By way of comparison, about 37 million PCs were sold in 1994. But growth was slowing to about 12 percent per year. Given the lack of internet capabilities of Windows, there was a clear challenge in that Macintosh might become the preferred internet PC and, with the internet growing much faster from a similar base, the numbers could be substantial. Simply by growth metrics, the internet was going to swallow PCs.

During our discussion, J offered more technical details on the services Windows required in order to be a first-tier internet device, on both the desktop and the nascent Windows server market. The largest volume by bytes was email, but the newest service, the one used by Mosaic, was growing at an astronomical rate. At the time there were just over 600 web servers (or sites) worldwide and estimates that over one million people were using Mosaic, which users downloaded from the university site by FTP, a geeky and wonky tool if there ever was one.

That wasn't a lot on the internet compared to what AOL or CompuServe offered, and like so many things that ended up being disruptive shifts, it had a toylike feeling. The WWW server that concerned J and team the most was that their biggest competitor, Novell, had already put all their networking documentation on the internet on novell.com.

J showed me a larger tower PC with a network cable going up through the ceiling where a tile had been pushed aside. J introduced me to two members of the team, David Treadwell (DavidTr), a developer on networking, and Henry Sanders (HenrySa.) I already knew David from common connections in college recruiting. Henry went to Cornell and was a terminal operator at the same time as me, though he graduated a year ahead. I remembered him. He did not remember me at all. Henry had a good deal of fun in college.

The three of them formed the bulk of the TCP/IP networking team. They were building out Microsoft's TCP/IP layer and additional services required for the internet, such as FTP, for transferring files and TELNET for connecting to other computers—the bare minimum required to claim any entrée into the internet world compared to the Mac or especially Unix, as there was no Linux yet.

The large tower computer was an important demo. The team had created an FTP server so people could download Microsoft software. Microsoft made a version of MS-DOS freely available but did not have distribution beyond the private services like CompuServe. J said that with no "marketing," tens of thousands of people were downloading free MS-DOS from this one computer sitting in a hallway running pre-released Windows NT and one of the earliest and most arcane internet apps, FTP. Software patches and updates were also placed there. Over 50,000 people per week visited ftp.microsoft.com, essentially as customer support, in lieu of getting the same materials at CompuServe for a connection fee. A local company provided internet connectivity for Microsoft HQ, and we were nearly all of their volume and Microsoft's traffic was the equivalent of 25 percent of the largest provider on the internet.

It was crazy.

In a big company, the first step of solving a cross-company problem was to make sure there was someone working on it. Usually, a bunch of people say they are, but they really aren't—big companies love to stake a claim on an area but digging in reveals little more than a hobby or side project. On a good day, only one person was working on the problem.

Systems had a phrase for this, *cookie-licking*, or laying claim to a technology area without actually working on it.

J *really* was working on Microsoft's internet strategy.

His only challenge was that he was in the networking group and working on the low-level plumbing, not on the consumer experience that was on display at Cornell. That's where my role as TA came in. It was to bring together the right people with the right level of both technical understanding and management responsibility to create a coherent strategy. That was all.

Jumping to a conclusion and the main tool I had as a TA, the power of convening, we needed to have a big *emergency* offsite. I told J, after hearing about the opportunities and challenges, that I would push BillG for one. Bill loved offsites. At the end of an unrelated meeting, I told him we needed to do an offsite on the internet. He grabbed his pad and felt tip and sketched out the calendar, an actual calendar, for what remained of March and April, identifying travel dates, important meetings, and the like—he was always obsessed with his use of time and calendar constraints. A few scratches and arrows and we had a date.

Before I could begin my adventure, though, I had one problem. I could not get "on the internet." J fixed that by connecting (a pun) me with Dave Leinweber (DaveL), an old-timer in Microsoft Information Services (MIS), the IT organization that ran the company network. I emailed DaveL right away, subject line "DTAP," which was how one described a direct access to the internet.

DaveL arrived at my office having not really been summoned before. Before connecting me, he talked at great length about how risky the internet was for network security and what a big problem this could be. He also talked about how much it cost in internal billing. After some negotiating, and me explaining I understood the company's concerns, we agreed I received authorization for my DTAP, a bright red network cable in a separate jack with a warning label. The rule was that I could not connect a machine to both networks at the same time, and any machine that was connected to the red plug could never be connected to the regular corporate network ever again without first erasing the hard drive.

I needed a new computer for my new setup, fortunately just as Apple released the PowerBook Duo laptop. It was a *slick* portable with a fancy motorized docking station that inhaled and exhaled the computer with a lovely *whirr*. It had a trackpad! The bulky Compaq LTE with a goofy trackball mounted vertically on the screen was an embarrassing contrast. Plus, most of the internet software I'd seen to date was Mac first or Mac exclusively.

I set up the Mac with an IP address as per DaveL—my Mac became one of the two million nodes directly on the internet. On the front of the Mac was a sticker with the IP address that was assigned to both me and the jack in the wall. I immediately began to download software. I first had to find an FTP client, which I did via transferring a floppy from my Windows PC after downloading the client from CompuServe on Windows. From there, I connected dots.

I felt like I was in graduate school again. Back then my DEC workstation was assigned an IP address, and I went and added that to the university's HOSTS table which then communicated that to all the other computers on the network at the university and everywhere. The current mechanism of having a private internet address (those 192.168.*.* addresses) was still a year or so away from general deployment.

Using Gopher from the University of Minnesota, I located programs for IRC (Internet Relay Chat, which was the successor to the Talk a program I used in college) and reading USENET News. Then I finally got to Cello and eventually Mosaic. Soon, I had a folder full of internet applications, which I labeled *Information Superhighway*. I also learned that AOL could use an internet connection if it existed (instead of a dial-up connection), so I was experiencing AOL, except it was *extremely* fast. How fast? Well, that DTAP running on a shared T1 line I had was about the speed of a 3G mobile phone, or less than 1 megabit per second but substantially faster than dial-up's maximum of 56 kilobits per second.

That first day with the internet stretched well into the early hours of the morning. I was downing Diet Cokes and making notes in a text file of cool "places" to visit on the internet. "Surfing the web" was not yet a term, but that's what I was doing. I built a list of favorite links in a text file, which was precisely what every early user did. I felt like I was back in my high school TV room exploring FIDONet all over again, but everything was faster, in color, and much more fun.

The biggest, peaceful world event happening at that time was the Lillehammer 1994 Winter Olympics and it had an internet presence. I was able to find a page that had a camera pointed at the main Olympic stadium. Every minute a tiny still black and white image, like CU-SeeMe, refreshed. I downloaded a separate program that made it possible to watch the live "feed." Unbelievable.

I found MTV.com, which was a rogue and unofficial page maintained by legendary VJ Adam Curry. It became a favorite of mine, given that I tuned in to MTV constantly in high school when we first obtained Cable TV. Curry set up the site a few months earlier without getting permission, including taking the domain name. It was all about music and musicians, but also had audio clips that could be downloaded. These required a separate audio player for the format that was common at the time. Apple was still charging for QuickTime and Windows formats had yet to be developed; MP3 was still a year away. I found several sites with song lyrics and routinely showed people R.E.M.'s "It's the End of the World as We Know It (And I Feel Fine)," comparing different interpretations of a song with rather fluid lyrics. MTV sued Curry and eventually he surrendered MTV.com to the corporate masters.

A few years later, streaming arrived, but at the time what we were seeing was mind-blowing.

Think of the most mind-blowing product experience you ever had. The product experience that left you speechless, hyperventilating, with a million questions and a million ideas. I had already experienced that with so many of the *firsts* in my own computing life: Atari, dial up BBS, IBM PC, Sun workstation, Xerox Star, Macintosh, Windows 1.0, and on and on, but none of those compared to the Internet in 1994. Talk about the luck of timing. I experienced all those things when they were firsts, so at the very least I could calibrate my own reaction to the Internet.

While it was swell that I could see this stuff, I needed to get more people excited and soon. I felt Microsoft was behind and as soon as people saw this stuff, they would see the same level of urgency I did. I quickly became an internet evangelist. First stop was BillG.

I was about to begin a huge lesson in how to change a large company. I was excited, and scared.

027. INTERNET EVANGELIST

The Securities Exchange Commission (SEC) made public company filings available on the WWW. This was interesting because the information had been previously difficult to obtain and was only available with a subscription fee.

That would get BillG's attention.

In the early stages of a technology, users are also the builders. As a result, there was a lot of easily accessed material about the WWW itself, a sign of a healthy movement. Many individuals tracked metrics such as number of servers, connectivity speed, and volume of major protocols. Part of my research was building up a data set to explain the growth and diffusion of the WWW and associated technologies.

I went to the Kinko's on Broadway on Seattle's Capitol Hill and once again used their crazy copy machine to make a big poster of the NSFNet internet backbone map of the United States. This would often become a main talking point for business-oriented discussions.

For technology discussions, I also started building my own library of important internet technical documents. These were called *requests for comments* (RFCs) and were the specifications for how different internet technologies worked. RFCs began with the research network itself in 1969 and continue today. While many other standards bodies started contributing to internet and networking, such as IEEE, ISO, and W3C, much of the important work for the internet still takes place via this process. These documents are as important culturally as they are technically. When you read about email, domain names, network address translation (NAT, this was brand new at the time) you not only understand the implementation but gain a whole appreciation for the culture of openness and collaboration. These were the exact opposite of the rigid specifications from IBM or the NT team.

After meeting with JAllard and hearing his excitement and also concerns, I scheduled a few more meetings. I met with people on the Chicago networking protocol team and the team working on higher level user features for networking. I also got an earful from my new friends in the Microsoft Information Services group about security concerns and also risks of leaking intellectual property, at the same time they were anxious to find ways to offer secure connectivity as a service to employees.

My first demo was with Bill. It was very intense and probably lasted two hours. As fast as I could click on the screen, Bill had deep questions about technology, business models, ownership, intellectual property, and more. I jotted down notes of questions I knew nothing about and kept the demos moving. I was less than a week into learning the internet. Bill was two hours in.

What kind of questions did Bill ask? Though I was able to show BillG a lot, he stumped me asking to explain the difference between WinHelp, Microsoft's relatively new online help engine, and the WWW. They were both formatted text with hyperlinks and the user experience was similar. The formats even looked the same. WinHelp used Word's Rich Text Format (RTF) which was also a tagged text format. In fact, WinHelp looked world's ahead of HTML because it was richer and compressed, so it took fewer bytes. On the face of it, distinguishing between WinHelp looking at Visual C++ help and Cello looking at the Novell site was not easy. Bill immediately saw WinHelp as Microsoft's "competitive response" or counter to the new WWW.

It took a few minutes for both of us to converge toward a shared understanding, but this was important learning. WinHelp at the time could not access links between different files, let alone different computers on different networks. This was a key innovation in HTTP and the invention of URIs. Uniform Resource Identifier, then often called the more specific URLs, *uniform resource locators,* referred to web addresses.

There were challenges that we discussed. It was going to be difficult to add more features to WinHelp. There was no WinHelp server. In fact, there were no servers anywhere. Microsoft was just starting to build servers. If someone working on WWW (HTML and HTTP) had stumbled into the conversation, they would have laughed at us thinking WinHelp was anything at all like the WWW. Just because there were links did not make them similar—the technology implementation mattered, and this theme kept emerging.

Navigating a Gopher site looked like the developing Chicago Explorer or Windows File Manager. At least that included networking sites. But in this case Windows even lacked the basics of long file names, except on Windows NT. The similarity to directory browsing took on a more nuanced differentiation because the Windows servers were "connection based" and Gopher servers were stateless/connectionless like everything on the internet. This was a key discussion and differentiating point that, while sounding a bit esoteric, represented the challenges Microsoft faced technically in working with internet technologies.

One of the things I concluded was that as I showed different aspects of the internet to Bill, such as gopher, WWW, ftp, telnet, and HTML. He was quick to map those to existing or envisioned capabilities in Windows or in Information At Your Fingertips. I was struck by this because, well, I did not see that at all. I saw everything on the internet as totally new and different. I saw everything we had as kind of clunky and unrelated, or at least different. As I reflect on this and now have the benefit of the vocabulary of *disruptive technologies*, I can see how I had an insurgent view of the technology whereas Bill had the incumbent view. As the insurgent I had nothing to lose and everything to gain by embracing the new and seeing it as different. As the incumbent, the natural inclination is to see new things from the perspective of the existing work.

To emphasize this point I found myself making printouts of screenshots of some internet technologies as well as their comparable Windows technologies. Again, back to Kinkos for their color printer since we did not yet have those in the copy room. For example, I made a screen shot of WinHelp and compared it to a screen shot of WWW. I had a sample of HTML and a sample of RTF from Word. I did the same for the envisioned File Explorer in Windows and Gopher, and so on. I had these handy because as I spoke with different people, I routinely found myself needing to explain what was new grounded in the reality of Microsoft's technology platform.

The excitement around this first "new" internet demo was tangible. I repeated the demo later and we exchanged questions and answers over email. Bill had seen various bits and pieces of the earliest (pre-WWW) internet demonstrations at ThinkWeeks. Then, the internet still seemed like a competing mechanism for accessing proprietary information services—using TCP/IP packet switching instead of X.25 dial-up connections. These new demos quickly changed his view. The internet was changing faster than twice a year ThinkWeeks.

I reminded Bill we agreed to have an offsite—that was a good thing to do I figured. I wasn't sure what we would accomplish but needed to get a bunch of people in the same place thinking about this at the same time, importantly, with the same inputs, which would be our goal for the offsite. We had set a date for April 5, which gave me about 6 weeks to pull together the right people, meet and pre-brief attendees, and prepare pre-reading materials.

While offsite preparation was going on, I dragged anyone I could into my office to demonstrate the WWW and discuss the internet. The program manager in me put together a standard demo script that was flashy but also explained what was going on. If you've ever seen the *TODAY Show* clip in which the anchors asked, "What's the internet?" and then debate how to say the @ symbol (about? at? around?) and internet addresses, that almost exactly sums up what it was like to demonstrate the internet even at a leading tech company. Most Microsoft people weren't even using AOL because most of our work activities were on CompuServe, with its clunky text interface and overpriced access to interesting information sources. There was a uniform interest and even excitement.

In big companies, however, everyone is busy. At Microsoft (and with software companies in general) every project was already late. That meant it was always the wrong time to show people something new, and most times my attempts were met with skepticism and concern.

"Will this impact our schedule?"

"Is it really a big deal?"

"We have something similar."

J and I needed to up-level the conversation while we balanced schedules, the understanding of the technology, and the reluctance to take on new work. It wasn't pushback; everyone understood the technology. There was a lot happening at Microsoft already between Windows Chicago, Windows NT, a new version of Office, and every other product building on those.

Every person and team, from Chicago to Cairo, reacted differently. Was the internet an app or a platform? What exactly were we worried about from a competitive perspective? Did we care about formats, protocols, or implementations? These abstract questions became fundamental to how Microsoft evolved its perspective.

Chicago was already late. Originally Windows 93, we were well into 1994 and still 15 months from finishing. Most everyone on that team said of the demo, "We have the plumbing," but apps would come from third parties.

Cairo reacted differently. The skepticism mirrored that of corporate customers who viewed a body of free, university-developed software as risky and unreliable at best, or toylike at worst. The Cairo project was aimed at commercial implementations. The internet was difficult for the Cairo project to wrap itself around as it was a direct "competitor."

NathanM and CraigMu embraced the technologies. Nathan and Craig were leading the idea of partnering with the large telecom and cable carriers to deliver home services for the information superhighway. How the internet as I was showing it related to these became interesting. As an example, AT&T viewed the internet as a "home endpoint," like a phone. A big project they had underway was to think about how everyone could have an email address and then list that in a big directory. If that sounds like the email version of a phone number plus 411 that's exactly how a carrier like AT&T thought of new technologies—through the lens of proprietary services and protocols.

RussS had already transitioned to work full time on the online service Marvel. Russ set out to build an entirely new network, a new dial-up service, to ship with Chicago. He went from researching an opportunity to critical path for the release of Chicago in the span of a few weeks. He saw the potential of the internet but was going to need time to absorb what impact, if any, it had.

Rob Glaser (formerly RobG) left Microsoft to form an exciting new company called Progressive Networks. It was going to be a distribution channel for politically progressive content. Rob had spearheaded Microsoft's multimedia strategy and collaborated with Bill on many projects during his time at Microsoft. Rob was the first to ask me a lot of questions I did not know the answers to. Rob wanted to understand who paid for the internet and how it was going to be a viable model. Part of my demo "kit" was a map of major nodes on the internet and the connectivity speed. Rob wanted to understand much more about the journey of bits over the network and how that worked. He had a lot of interesting questions. Rob later renamed his company RealNetworks, which became content streaming pioneers. In September 1995, RealNetworks livestreamed a Seattle Mariners game. Rob was well ahead of almost everyone.

SteveB was overseeing and creating the global sales and support organization, the "field." He was in Japan working at MSKK, but he still managed to catch a demo on a trip back. He was immersed in the growing needs of enterprise customers—Microsoft was still overwhelmingly an OEM and Retail business. He was well versed in and played back many of the typical concerns voiced by corporate customers regarding the maturity and readiness of "free" software from universities. One WWW site I showed him was the Novell Networking site, which was already far ahead of any Microsoft presence. Well, we had no presence at all except the FTP server outside HenrySa's office. The availability of Netware documentation in a WWW browser made an impression immediately and riled up SteveB's competitive spirit, as if that needed any help.

Living in Japan and traveling all the time, Steve was acutely aware of the difficulties connecting to Redmond HQ for resources. Microsoft's products, collateral, and demos were growing exponentially, and downloading all these over paltry connections was a hot button. The field created a monthly CD-ROM, which was DHLed to the subsidiary offices around the world. Maybe the internet could speed this up. Steve also wanted me to connect with someone in Product Support Services, which was managed by PattyS, to see how we should use the internet for providing product support.

I also offered demonstrations to any guests that were in the office to meet with BillG or NathanM. They were meeting all the time with people from the telecommunications industry, Hollywood, and cable television. In spirit these were a lot like the Microsoft meetings in that people were quick to try to map new technologies or experiences into the world they knew, but unlike the Microsoft technology stack I was ill-equipped to explain how NSFNet related to leased X.25 lines or how HTML might evolve to be good enough for Hollywood productions. One well-known director was thankful for the demonstration and sent a 6-foot Jurassic Park cardboard cutout that remained in my office for my tenure.

Perhaps the most fun I had were the demonstrations for my friends and peers. Erin Cullen (ErinCu) worked in corporate communications and had been poking around all the new stuff. She soon made a case to the larger team that Microsoft needed a web presence and helped to make Microsoft's first WWW home page.

Soon, I was getting mail from all over the company requesting demonstrations. I wish I kept a list of how many times I went through my expanding and improving demos or how many times I had to explain who pays for the internet or who wrote the software we were looking at. While everyone to a person was intrigued and excited, what exactly should come next was totally unclear. I was incredibly happy that there was so much excitement. I was equally nervous that people did not "get it" like JAllard insisted needed to happen. I did not quite understand it at the time, but I was facing that ever-present corporate force that just wants to keep doing what it was doing. I had an over-abundance of misplaced confidence and a cool demo script.

I also had an offsite to prepare for and what was beginning to sink in was the opportunity to use the ability to convene the leaders who could really embrace (and extend) Internet technologies.

028. PIVOTAL OFFSITE

Microsoft loved a good offsite. We loved a chance to "wallow" in the minutiae of technologies, implementation, and competitors. We also enjoyed tearing apart ideas and approaches with our proverbial tech buzzsaw. In setting up the offsite I had no idea how critical it would become.

BillG famously redirected or pivoted the company away from character-based MS-DOS products to the graphical user interface products in a retreat just a decade earlier. Platform shifts in technology seem to come in these decade waves, though perhaps that is a retroactive timeline. Was the Internet the next platform shift, even though GUI had just started? Was this offsite going to be as pivotal to Microsoft's future as when the bet was made on making Excel for Macintosh? I certainly hoped for that but had no idea how the company's leaders would see things when they were all assembled to discuss it. I thought about that as I remembered DougK, the inventor of minimal recalculation in spreadsheets, told me the story of leaving Microsoft after that offsite because he disagreed with the new direction.

The offsite was schedule for April 5, 1994, coincidentally the day after the incorporation of Mosaic Communications Corporation—later to be renamed Netscape Corporation—created by legendary founder of SGI, Jim Clark, and original Mosaic programmer Marc Andreessen. I prepared the mother of all briefing books for the offsite. No offsite was complete without an elaborate briefing book. I hand carried the entire thing to the copy center (MSCOPY) and ordered 30 copies, doubled-sided, bound, with tabs. They called me an hour later and told me I needed two volumes, so I headed back and removed enough pages to keep it at the 300-page limit.

Looking at the book now, it serves as a great reminder of just how small the whole of the internet was back then. One of the books I ordered for many people was by Ed Krol, *The Whole Internet: User's Guide and Catalog.* How crazy to think that the entirety of the Internet could be represented as a book and cataloged, but that was sort of what it was. Similarly, the technology underpinnings were perhaps 100 pages of protocols and formats that everyone at the offsite could easily absorb.

One of the most popular prep materials was a copy of a video tape episode of *The Computer Chronicles*, the award-winning Public Television show hosted by Stewart Cheifet from 1983-2002. The video was essentially the entire briefing book in a one-hour television segment. It is a remarkable time capsule of the 1993 Internet. It was already a bit out of date by the time of the offsite, but it was easily absorbed, especially for those who did not come by my office for a demo.

Perhaps I got a little carried away.

About 20 people gathered at Shumway Mansion in Kirkland about 8AM, early for developers. In his introduction without any slides, Bill improvised the term "mania" to describe the internet and emphasized a core company value, which was that exponential phenomena cannot be ignored. The internet was exponential. He said something that I thought was critically important and returned to time and time again over the years that followed. He told us the internet was not to be "studied." It was already decided that it would be a critical part of our next wave of products. We were kicking off the process to decide what to do, not *if* we should do anything. His choice of words and body language was as strong as his email a few years ago declaring Windows our strategy.

In order to develop a plan, we divided into three groups, each given a set of questions:

- *Systems*. How do we make Microsoft platforms the preferred choice for internet as both a client and server? How do we make internet applications available given that most everything is free? What is the internet experience missing that we could provide? How does Cairo/EMS (the next, next generation OS and the new mail server, both very early in development) complement or conflict with the above?
- *Tools and Services*. Can Microsoft use the internet for customer support? How do we connect with developers using the internet? If we use the internet for support, will we get credit for providing better support compared to what we do on CompuServe? How do our existing tools such as WinHelp and Word relate to/benefit from/compete with internet formats? Where do the new tools being developed for Marvel (notably a tool known as *Blackbird*) fit in?
- *Online Strategy*. Should our online service Marvel embrace the internet? How do we make our clients the best internet clients? What value do we bring to the internet community?

The natural reaction to such a situation at Microsoft was not to push back because of schedules or capacity, but rather to go after the other side on technical grounds. The technique of arguing against a new technology (competitive product and alternative architecture, for example), not on the basis of one's own constraints but on the lack of merits of another approach—the technical buzzsaw. The basic goal was to find all the flaws on the other side to avoid admitting lacking the engineering agility to get it done.

As an example, with respect to the HTML format, there were two schools of thought. Blackbird was chartered to create a high-end authoring tool to enable content creators to make rich, interactive content for the Marvel network, like our CD-ROM titles. It cast a very long shadow and was a widely feared (and misunderstood) product, even without ever shipping. In a relative sense, HTML was a trivial subset of what "Hollywood" or magazines needed to bring their brands to the WWW. Marvel was embracing that class of content owner as a core potential partner, so HTML was broadly deficient. At the same time, a divergent view came from the Word team that embraced being able to edit HTML from within Word—Word routinely dealt with formats with lower fidelity, so it seemed perfectly fine to think of HTML as a supported format. In fact, HTML was even a subset of a just released add-on for Word called SGML Author. SGML was a mega-standard upon which HTML was loosely based.

Connectivity to AOL and CompuServe used the X.25 telecom standard—that is, connectivity provided by analog, dial-up phone lines—so ubiquitous and reliable that it was a stronghold for the telecom companies. The idea that consumers had access to the internet outside of that network or even that the packet-switched network (TCP/IP) would mature to be reliable and widely available seemed crazy. Others, seeing the exponential growth in internet users connecting with local connectivity providers using new packet-switched protocols, believed it was investing in legacy to even consider worrying about old-style connectivity and partners.

This led to a good debate over how and if Marvel should be focused purely on internet protocols for the service or not.

There was also an interesting conversation taking place surrounding various new projects intersecting, with no real way to reconcile the overlap between them. The relationship between new mail service EMS and the new online service Marvel was one example, and a topic that continued to smolder. Marvel, competing with AOL, would clearly have email and discussion boards. Marvel was already working to understand a potential relationship to USENET and the NNTP protocol it used. EMS was an enterprise mail service just starting to be able to handle email for a few people at Microsoft. A big and differentiating feature of EMS was going to be Public Folders, or essentially shared email boxes that looked a lot like the USENET experience, and, like Marvel, EMS was also trying to figure out the relationship of its feature to USENET. The EMS design point was enterprise IT and a highly managed environment for intense email usage in the workplace, not the mass-scale lightweight consumer mail Marvel envisioned. Some things took decades to resolve, and the email strategy was one of them. Blackbird, Marvel, and EMS, overlapped with each other and also with the internet. It was both stunning and kind of ridiculous. These products didn't yet exist, and the internet did. It is impossible to catch up to something growing exponentially. That doesn't stop debates at a big company, though, as I was learning.

Considering the Internet within the halls of Microsoft and for most attendees was months old, there was a broad consensus that change was in the air. The closer a group's products were to the internet the more the discussion was about schedules and constraints. The further away from shipping a team was, the more the internet seemed like a great idea. That's the opposite of what we needed, though.

The critical exception to this observation was Systems, as the first team to use the day to validate and expand plans already in place and to express a strategy. Systems intended to ensure both OS projects underway were the best client and server for the internet. The details mattered, though.

At the base level the forethought from the networking group on NT *Daytona*, the code name of the next release of Windows NT, was paying off. They were well down the path of implementing the required networking infrastructure. These were the essential ingredients to "get on the internet" with a Daytona computer. There were many implementation challenges to reuse this work on Chicago, which was still debating how fully 32-bit the operating system was, and also how much low-level compatibility existed between Chicago and Daytona for code like networking drivers.

The group concluded that implementing applications that made the internet interesting was critical. Those responsible decided building news, mail, Gopher, and a WWW browser, were goals.

In early 1994, the internet was not *just* the WWW. The internet was made up of many different services, each a combination of server code, client code, and then ultimately one or more viewers. For example, Gopher had a server that maintained the hierarchy for the site, a Gopher client that navigated that site, and then any number of viewers that could be launched to view the "leaf" of the Gopher tree. For example, there might be a Gopher site that eventually led to photos, or a bunch of Word documents, which launched an image editor, or Word to view them. The WWW had rich text, links, and images all in one "viewer," and a simple server setup. But as I was showing off in my demos, many WWW sites were simply navigations to content that the browsers did not understand, such as music or video files.

As the debate and discussion of solutions continued, my feeling at the time was there was a lot of wheel spinning considering the galactic shift that the internet appeared to be. Perhaps because I was relatively early to the space, I had become a zealot? Or maybe I was so down on such inward-facing debates given what I had seen firsthand. It was a challenge to relay the experience I had on Cornell's campus to teams—I sounded like a crazy person, like a junior person back from his or her first customer visit or conference. I sounded like I sounded when I came back from USENIX with a changed view on C++, though that worked out pretty well.

Looking back, by the end of the offsite, some converted to internet zealots. In many ways the zealots, me included, left that day with the feeling that Marvel was going to either happen or it wasn't, but that there wasn't much that could really be done since it seemed so *different* than the direction we should have been going in. Marvel felt like taillights, competing from behind and not vision-setting. It is certainly easier to say that today seeing where things went.

One of the most difficult challenges to understand, until you have lived through it, is the pressure to keep moving forward even in the face of disruption. The biggest lesson I learned in just the short time between getting trapped in the snow and this first week of April 1994 was just how much of what happens in a company is a result of the momentum of a product (or technology) and the structure of the organization in place. Make no mistake, as a manager I would have my very own challenges in this regard even though I lived through this experience.

The offsite did not come to a dramatic end with the key developer quitting as the bet on graphical interface, but it was an incredible day. There's no doubt it was very important to urgently bring everyone together and for Bill to make it abundantly clear just how much we were betting on the Internet, and he did so without hesitation. Many would look to the *Internet Tidal Wave* memo years later as the clarion call when in every respect this was the pivotal day in the journey to an internet-centric company.

029. TELLING OF THE UNTOLD STORY

The clock really was ticking, and to get things done for Chicago meant starting *immediately*. Chicago, originally planned for early 1994 or maybe 1993 depending on who you ask, was not yet in beta and so practically speaking was not going to finish in 1994 given the time required for broad beta testing, recalling my previous Cornell recruiting trip and the debate over whether Cairo would ship before "Windows 4" aka Chicago later in 1993.

Evangelizing tactical work items for the internet strategy and making sure they landed with owners was my job as TA. With regards to the "Internet mania", our mantra as per BillG was two-tiered: embrace and extend.

Much like *killer app,* the phrase *embrace and extend* proved to be far more loaded an expression than intended. Computing evolved by companies constantly finding ways to uniquely extend existing software and hardware, elements viewed as commodities, while at the same time always bowing to the existing investments of customers by claiming an embrace of any standards or winners. That was the view of how value was created—everyone built on all that came before. That was how everything worked. In a sense, each new product somehow related to the product it would supersede while extending it in uniquely valuable ways.

What had changed was the open-source movement that viewed everything as embrace with no advantage bestowed to any party, with any extensions going back to the community. As it would turn out, embrace and extend is precisely how nearly every open-source innovation was commercialized, particularly as software moved to the data center. Not everyone believes that is good, but it is what happened. In 1994, embrace and extend was synonymous with evil. Admittedly, it didn't help that the phrase was sometimes attributed to Microsoft as "embrace, extend, and extinguish."

With specific action items outlined, for the next couple of months I made sure the company was embracing the key protocols I had seen at Cornell (and that our brave corporate customers were beginning to demand): TCP/IP, email over SMTP, HTML for online documents, NNTP for discussions and bulletin boards, HTTP and Gopher on the server, and IRC for chat.

In doing so, I found myself in the role of shuttle diplomat or "glue" as we said looping around the cluster of single-X buildings, the location of the Chicago team, and the next version of Windows NT under development and over in building 16 where Peter Pathe (PPathe), the general manager of the Word team, sat. Many days I found myself almost in a constant swirl running between buildings in the misty drizzle of Redmond.

My agenda was to help identify issues and bring teams together to arrive at the common goals outlined at the offsite. I was to help, not do. It is a confusing a difficult spot to be in, especially as a self-described zealot, and particularly as someone with no responsibility for a product schedule.

Chicago was on a mission, a new mission to embrace the WWW. The team quickly came to its own point of view and strategy, which included the *get on the internet* capabilities, as well as coming up with a viewer and browser strategy. During the offsite the Chicago team affirmed this point of view, but the commitment was for after the initial Chicago release. The realities of the Chicago schedule meant that work that did not impact the product directly had a chance of being delivered simultaneously to customers because of the way OEMs ship new PCs, known as a *service release* in the OEM process—taking advantage of the ability to add features to Windows on new PCs even after the retail boxes of Windows were manufactured for upgrade customers who would later download those same changes or purchase the same-day add-on for Windows 95 called "Plus!" which in addition to those same internet capabilities including Internet Explorer 1.0, included games, screen savers, and other *extras*. While much would be made by regulators of these small changes in dates and what the "final product" was, this is what agility looked like in the age of massive software projects, a multi-month manufacturing channel required by ecosystem partners, and a schedule that was always a bit fluid until it wasn't.

This became the plan of record led by a longtime engineer, Ben Slivka (BenS.) In the short term, the strategy was to make sure developers around the world understood the underlying technologies provided by Chicago that made it easier to build viewers and browsers and to evangelize those—if Chicago could not have its own then at least it should have the widest range of choices from third parties. This was a tried-and-true strategy Microsoft had always followed—the best of first and most of third parties. The same type of work, meaning a combination of built-in capabilities as well as evangelizing third-party capabilities, was going on with all sorts of extensions to the operating system from networking to USB support to Wi-Fi, but none of those would be contentious down the road.

Originally BenS was planning the features of the follow-on release, but seeing the situation of enormous growth in the internet, the already strong base infrastructure in Chicago, and the Chicago schedule, he devised a plan that involved licensing browser code as a way to kickstart the efforts for higher level viewers, especially WWW. In a series of negotiations (and after looking at some alternatives), the Chicago team ended up licensing the code to build Internet Explorer from Spyglass. In parallel, others looked at whether to expand on offerings for FTP, Gopher, or any number of other viewers/protocols.

With every passing day, it became abundantly clear that the WWW was the only viewer or internet technology that really mattered. The pace of adoption and growth of WWW servers compared to Gopher servers made this obvious.

Coincidentally, and unknown to Windows, the Word team had established a contractual relationship with a company called BookLink, which also made a browser. I had seen BookLink at the Spring COMDEX show and it seemed like a reasonable commercial implementation of the current WWW (HTML viewing and HTTP protocol), and I noted such in my trip report. I pointed the Chicago and Word teams toward it. I knew Word needed HTTP protocol work, as Word was busy building HTML authoring, described at the offsite. Part of that required the ability to traverse URLs and fetch the WWW page. To do that, Word licensed the BookLink code, which bugged the Chicago team that thought Word was trying to build a browser versus just read in an HTML file to edit. There was some combination of cookie-licking and "stay in your lane" going in both directions, but also the technical reality that to edit WWW pages (HTML) required the ability to use those protocols, and the Word team had no intention or desire to start from scratch.

Roughly in parallel, the Chicago team was in negotiations with BookLink for their entire browser, but those talks ended when BookLink was acquired by AOL, among other reasons. At least in part my fault, there was a bit of the right hand not knowing what the left hand was doing across the Windows–Apps boundary, which was not uncommon, much to the chagrin of people who believed the relationship was much more orchestrated and sinister. The fact that both teams were moving aggressively was good, though I have to think the BookLink people got a kick out of our org chart.

The tension between Apps and Platforms was not rooted in people or organization like far too many believed. It was rooted in the approach to building products—there was a reason MikeMap's two gardens description reflected an operational reality. Building a platform meant focusing efforts on creating opportunities for developers by offering abstractions in the form of APIs, application programming interfaces. APIs provide services that programmers use to the build applications. For example, the Windows browsers that were being built did not write their TCP/IP code from scratch. Rather, they used the Windows APIs called *WinSock* that provided a higher level of abstraction, so it was easier to build the browser. Windows did not, however, have any reusable code for rendering HTML as an example. That was something for later. Success for Windows might look like having many FTP and Gopher applications built using the Windows platform, something JAllard, along with the Chicago team, and I spoke about quite a bit.

If the Platforms approach could be thought of as bottom-up technology problem solving, then the Apps approach was top-down starting with the user problem. Apps looked at a problem and wrote the code to solve the problem for the end-user, rather than a developer. There was less flexibility in how much to accomplish since, to an end-user, an app either solved the problem or it didn't. Developers on a platform always had the option of building more code themselves or finding other code to use that helps. On the other hand, app writers did not have to worry about what other programmers thought about how their app is built or structured since that remained relatively opaque. Success for an app was having the most users, and that's it. A platform saw success as having the most apps in a given category, even if some were not so great or all the apps did the same thing, so long as there were unique apps for the platform. I'm writing this as an either-or, when in practice it is a spectrum. At least it was viewed that way at times, which made any cross-group efforts that much more challenging. Knowing exactly when an app was an application and when a platform was a platform, and not the other, was often only determined in the context of a specific feature at a moment in time. That indeed is the true tension.

It would have been nice if Platforms and Apps teams were as cleanly separate as their description. In practice each took on characteristics of the other. Platforms built apps all the time, such as the Windows Explorer, Reversi, or Write—parts of Windows that to end-users felt like whole solutions and tools, even if under the hood these had APIs for developers. Apps routinely provided platform APIs for developers as well. Many developers used Excel as a platform to build custom financial or data access software, for example.

App creators were developers and they made choices all the time about using APIs from the platform or building their own simpler or faster solutions because they only solved specific problems. Platform developers routinely provide more than APIs, building out the first steps of an experience. When a new, exciting area comes along, the natural tendency for everyone is to adopt the technology, from their perspective. It was at these times of newness that the more standard traits of Apps and Platforms got tossed aside in the zeal to be first adopters.

The introduction of the WWW browser was such a time.

From all outward appearances, WWW browsers were apps. They were installed on Windows. They came from third parties. There were a bunch of end-user features. Even something simple, like printing a web page, seemed like a feature better done on the Apps team, since almost nothing in the platform supported printing. They were even a "category" in that there were several competing apps one could choose from, like word processors or spreadsheets. Most of all, if you wanted one you just went to an FTP site and downloaded *that thing*. A browser was clearly a thing, an app even.

That's why many in the Apps group thought it was a good idea for an Apps team to build a browser. Apps were great at working from the end-user down, even if there were some APIs for developers.

The Systems team saw things as a platform. They saw the browser as a platform that Apps would target. The address bar in the browser could be thought of as almost a Start menu. The URLs were like the names of apps. The fact that browsers ran across many platforms and were the same was the kind of thing that platform creators don't like to see—they want apps to be unique on their platform. The real problem was that the platform was woefully incomplete compared to Windows. They saw parts of the browser from navigating a URL to rendering HTML as reusable components that could potentially be used by others to build other browsers (the way developers built more games using graphics APIs in Windows) or even entirely different apps with browsers built into the app. The browser just needed more APIs.

That's why many in the Systems group thought it best for a Systems team to build the browser. Systems were great at working from the APIs up, even if there was some user interface for end-users.

While those, like me, who favored the Apps approach thought this was a good discussion, it wasn't much of one at all. There was little doubt that Microsoft's browser was going to be a Windows offering, a platform and an app. Microsoft was a Windows company, and Windows was still in the earliest days of trying to win, as strange as that sounds. The superiority of Macintosh for the internet was not lost on anyone, and competing servers from Sun and Oracle were dominating a Windows Server that had not yet made a market impact.

The responsibility of authoring HTML falling to Apps with viewing owned by a new browser in Windows might have made sense to some. It definitely made sense early on when there was little hint that browsers would have editing. Things could not be so clean, however, because of a very strategic *rich-content* creation tool being developed. Blackbird for the new online service Marvel was being talked about broadly and externally with partners, especially print newspaper and magazine publishers. Blackbird enabled such partners to maintain the fidelity of their physical products online and even enhance the experience. At least that was the strategy. Blackbird cast a long shadow because of the early concerns from some of the country's largest and most established media companies. Concerns were everywhere. Would Microsoft become a dominant media company? Would Blackbird prove to be a monopoly printing press? How would publishers make money on the WWW and was Microsoft going to be a gatekeeper? This might sound like crazy talk, but this is exactly what I heard at a time when no one questioned Microsoft's dominance or ability to execute. For many industry insiders, Blackbird was some kind of shorthand for Microsoft's future expansion into owning all content creation. It was more than crazy talk. It was just crazy.

It is entirely possible for a company to have exactly the right vision for a technology future but, by virtue of market position in a totally different market, be exactly the wrong company at the wrong time to try to realize that vision. This burden or curse of market leaders is a history that repeats. We were experiencing this for the first time.

Apps focused on being viewers at the "edge" of the WWW. For example, a professor with a course web page might post the lecture slides as a PowerPoint file on the page, which you might get to by clicking from the university home page to a department to current courses to a specific course page. This was all incredibly novel at the time when you consider the alternative was to pay cash to a student notetaking service for the notes for a lecture you missed.

Such a strategy left little room for Apps to participate in the WWW. This might have been perfectly fine if the WWW ended up being primarily about navigating to "files" the way Gopher had. The attraction of the WWW experience was being in a browser (an app!) and never leaving. Thus, Apps saw HTML as potentially the way for productivity documents to be rendered simply so they could be seen in the browser with the least amount of friction, almost like a new way to print. The idea that anyone could create web pages by simply using the tools they were already using seemed cool enough—for the time being creating web pages was akin to programming so this seemed like progress.

The Apps team was almost in the exact opposite position as Windows. Rather than a project that was late and getting later, Apps was on a much more constrained path. Apps was in the final stages of wrapping up the Office 4.x product, the last release of 16-bit Word, Excel, PowerPoint, and Access. The product began shipping many months earlier, but not everything was complete, and the first version of Office 4.0 shipped with older versions of some of the products. Shipping "Office" as one product was a challenge for the next release.

During the relative downtime of the Office products finishing, Word continued to polish the HTML authoring features. Surprisingly, PowerPoint was also at work on HTML. In a visit I made to the PowerPoint team in Cupertino to hear their views on the WWW, I received my first dose of Silicon Valley outside of attending conferences in Santa Clara.

At lunch at a Pizza Hut on Stevens Creek Boulevard in early 1994, surrounded by badge-wearers from Apple, Sun, and other companies, Lucy Peterson (LucyP), the program management leader, shared with me how customers were doing all sorts of crazy things to take slide decks and post them to the WWW. They were taking screenshots of each slide in slideshow view and then adding buttons for next/previous slide to use the minimal capabilities of a browser to show slides. It was crazy. I was caught off guard by how "informed" the distant PowerPoint team was about the internet. I hadn't thought for a minute that this recent phenomenon originated there. Duh!

To save slides to the WWW, they planned to automate the manual process and make it much better and faster. This came later than the Word feature but proved incredibly popular in the early days of the WWW. If you spend time on the internet wayback machine, you'll see old presentations with bubbly forward and backward buttons under a slide saved as a single image file, which were output with the PowerPoint Internet Assistant.

As Microsoft was making the transition to an enterprise-focused software company, top of mind was building out the global account management process. Account teams have an insatiable demand for information (translated into 30 or more languages) from Redmond including information sheets, demonstration scripts and tools, technical details, reference documentation, and more. In the early 1990s, a great deal was prepared for print production as well. To distribute this information around the world, a group in the *Enterprise Customer Unit* (SteveB's newly formed worldwide HQ team that supported the account teams) collected information on CD-ROMs, which were airlifted by DHL to all the field offices around the world once a month. Using CD-ROM seemed leading edge and consistent with the direction of multimedia computing…at least until the WWW.

SteveB wanted me to meet with the team that did all the production and talk to them about using WWW. I did my standard demo but emphasized the distribution of information from tech companies like Novell and Sun. The team remained unconvinced. They raised a series of, in their view, insurmountable challenges, from power of formats to the effort it took to copy all the information to a local server, the lack of bandwidth to even download the materials in a timely manner in most offices. This was my first encounter with WWW meeting someone's job reality. They didn't see a path "right now." Over time, the organization came to embrace the WWW and became some of the largest contributors to Microsoft content. It took time.

My experiences in meeting with Microsoft's Product Support Service (PSS) faced the same challenges. PSS was tasked with dealing with tens of thousands of customer contacts every day. Most were from individuals calling up Microsoft, wading through a phone tree, and getting help with how to get something done with a product. People called asking how to format documents, install a printer, or, the most dreaded calls, of computers that were slow, crashing, or wouldn't start. Operating PSS was extremely costly—all of us in product groups tracked call volumes, called generators, and had explicit goals to fix the top issues of the product. It was common knowledge that a call cost Microsoft something like $100, quickly eroding the margins on a sale.

For that reason, meeting with PSS came with the hope of making it cheaper and easier to solve customer problems. PSS loved the idea of distributing software updates over the internet. Taking names and addresses and fulfilling floppy disks was expensive and time consuming. This was already happening with ftp.microsoft.com and CompuServe.

PSS maintained an enormous online system called the *knowledge base* or KB. PSS engineers were goaled on writing articles that populated the system. These *KB articles* were the recipes for solving problems. While it seemed natural to just post these on the WWW, the early feedback and challenges showed how difficult it was to search. Beyond that, knowing if an article applied or not was the job of the human agents. Much of the dynamics of a call involved matching what a customer was saying to whether the KB article applied. KB articles are often nice steps preceded by a "do not try this at home" warning or caveat. Throwing these out to the WWW made PSS feel that the presence of the articles was to be *call generators* not cost reducers. They might have been right.

The use of newsgroups and USENET seemed like another opportunity. PSS was loath to engage with online chat with customers as it was extremely time consuming. On the phone incidents could be resolved in a few minutes. With online messaging or email-based support (already a top customer request) the back and forth could span days. Agents could go off shift or even on vacation and new processes would need to get established. Worse, providing these online contacts probably meant that after an issue was resolved, people returned to the "thread" and used it for other purposes months later.

They were probably right, even though in the moment I thought they were resisting the march of technology. Having been an avid USENET poster for Visual C++, and finding myself caught in many email threads, the concerns were in line with my experience.

When did Microsoft figure out the internet and when did it *pivot* to be an internet-centric company was the source of much industry chatter. From a Wall Street perspective, Microsoft adapting to, or adopting, internet technologies was generally viewed as one of the most significant corporate strategy changes in recent history. From a regulatory perspective, it is fair to say it was not only viewed with some skepticism, but a more sinister eye. Regardless, it made for an exciting narrative and in a sense a perfect place for a BusinessWeek cover story.

We received word from the most senior public relations people at Waggener Edstrom that a story was in the works, utilizing senior reporter Kathy Rebello. JAllard, BenS, Chris Jones (ChrisJo), and I kicked off a quick email thread and agreed on a timeline—we knew the press loves these kinds of timelines. ChrisJo, a new recruit to Windows after working on Microsoft Publisher, was leading program management on the browser. The three of us had become sort of joined at the hip in our efforts and hit it off well. What did we know and when. I was using a predecessor to the Palm Pilot I had purchased in Japan to take notes and had a text file with the timeline that served as our script.

After a series of calls with many executives and participants across Microsoft and a lot of PR handholding, the cover story ran. The story covered exactly what we had experienced in many ways, at least from my perspective. The article had a photo of JAllard, BenS, and I. Ben was in his characteristic Hawaiian shirt. I was clearly in my grunge phase with perhaps the only plaid flannel shirt I ever owned. The story, in the July 15, 1996, issue, and the timeline amounted to an official record of a major corporate turnaround. The BillG memo, *Internet Tidal Wave,* a year earlier was viewed by many as the start of the turnaround. As we've seen here the work began much earlier. It takes time for the work to surface and for a story to come together so a broader community understands it. It also takes time for us to figure out how to tell the story.

The story started with a letter to the editor from the weekly *MicroNews* newsletter that was still printed and distributed every week:

> *Oh, our eyes have seen the glory of the coming of the Net,*
>
> *We are ramping up our market share, objectives will be met.*
>
> *Soon our browser will be everywhere, you ain't seen nothin' yet,*
>
> *We embrace, and we extend!*
>
> *Battle Hymn of the Reorg*
>
> *Anonymous Microsoft Employee in MicroNews*

The story went on to say "Microsoft, already the ultimate hardcore company, is entering a new dimension. It's called Internet time: a pace so frenetic it's like living dog years—each jammed with the events of seven normal ones." It also featured thoughts from ever present analysts such as "Until six months ago Gates & Co. appeared lost in cyberspace. It was so far behind...might be sidelined in the new age of Internet computing." It was all very dramatic and compressed two years into a few pages and some great photos. It was difficult not to feel a sense of accomplishment from my perch, even knowing all I contributed was email and meetings. No matter what all the books and trials might come to say, the company really did a whole bunch of work in a very short time and a lot of it was really good.

Still, it is interesting in hindsight to consider that frequently when facing *disruption* (still a few years away from existing in business context) incumbents view disruptive forces (products or business models) as additive to what is already being done rather than either orthogonal or full replacements.

On the one hand, we did not abandon any products and start from some notion of "pure internet," and on the other, most every product that needed to change was a 1.0 product under development or at least early in the classic adoption curve. In fact, the 1.0 internet products such as MSN and Blackbird would come to represent the parts of the strategy that were not at all successful.

Whether or not much of what we ended up doing was too much about adding some internet to things we were already doing was years, maybe decades from revealing itself. Regardless of any product or market realities, the sales force and broader ecosystem around Microsoft fully bought into the dramatic change.

Across the company product, sales, marketing, and more embraced the newness of the internet and WWW. The company went from a small locus of activity to a cross-company buzz of efforts of all kinds. My job as TA was to take Bill's guidance and evangelize new technology. The internet was an obvious high point for me, though I still believe I received far more from this role than I provided. In that respect, my job was winding down, and it was time for me to go build something.

030. MY PERFORMANCE REVIEW (AND AN EXPENSE REPORT)

In July 1994, after almost 18 months as TA, NatalieY, head of recruiting but also in many ways the emotional leader of Microsoft, sent me an email reminding me that BillG needed to fill out the spreadsheet with my *review score*, which was Microsoft's performance review system, and, more importantly, my salary and bonus. Yes, the review system in place was a spreadsheet managers filled out with a rating, raise, and bonus. Because of all the work and excitement of the job, I had totally spaced and not even thought about that. Natalie reminded me because she also knew I would be changing jobs soon and any new manager would want to know what Bill had thought of my work. I later referred to my time with BillG as "the two most expensive years of my life" because I missed out on the material compensation that I might have earned had I filled out the performance review form and received typical salary and stock awards. The non-material compensation was priceless, so, obviously, no complaints.

Most everything I did was well-documented because mostly all I did was send email about meetings I had with different groups or write memos about the lessons learned from conferences, using software, or other trips. I really took to heart the early advice I received, which was not to take up or waste too much of Bill's time. In fact, we never met about what I was doing or should do. Except for ThinkWeek, I don't recall meeting with him one on one except for when he would occasionally dart into my office to follow up on something or fix some beta product that stopped working. Even when we flew to the same place, I would take a different flight knowing that someone else would find more value in bugging him on the trip. Though I should note, Bill's routine for flying was to sit in a window seat with a blanket over his head and not talk to anyone, often disappointing those hoping for a discussion.

For my review I wrote a memo, rather than use the performance review form, which wasn't something BillG was familiar with. Rather than waste his time, the memo detailed all the projects I worked on and the memos I had written. I noted all reports I'd written for learning trips I had taken as Bill's *eyes and ears*.

Except for one.

PaulMa asked me to go with him to London on short notice to help document what was going on with a sizable enterprise customer. PaulMa was the most enterprise-focused of executives and with Windows NT beginning to gain traction this type of customer learning was important. Having never taken overseas travel for Microsoft, I emailed Paul's executive assistant, Kay Barber-Eck (KayB) for help and she obliged, booking a plane ticket and a hotel. I packed my blue suit and off we went to visit with several UK banks.

When I got back, I took the plane ticket (the red-backed carbon paper kind) and the hotel receipt (one night) and filled out the standard expense report in triplicate and gave it to JulieG like I always did. The following Monday morning when Bill signed things for the week he refused to sign off on the expense because "he flew business class" as per the note on the form. I panicked. The ticket was thousands of dollars, and I could not afford that on my own. I emailed KayB and she said to submit it again and tell him it was the policy, and it was OK. She let me know the employee handbook included the travel policy, which said flights of eight hours or more could be optionally business class. I copied that policy page from the employee handbook and printed out a note explaining myself. A week went by. The report came back unsigned, noting that the flight was seven hours 45 minutes. At that point, I was about to be overdue on my credit card bill. I panic-telephoned KayB. She said to bring the expense report over and PaulMa would sign it. Phew.

Microsoft was still a start-up in Bill's mind. How could one not respect that, I asked myself?

Out of protest, I never sent Bill my trip report on the future of ATMs and banking from home in the United Kingdom.

Natalie insisted that I schedule a meeting with Bill to go over the review even though we both disliked scheduling time to talk. Bill read the memo and agreed with my self-assessment but zeroed in on one line, which to this day we still joke about.

In my performance review memo, I said that in an effort to be efficient and not waste his time I never asked for feedback about how I was doing or even what to do. Instead, I wrote stuff and sent it to him, such as the pre-meeting notes or trip reports, and then watched to see what he repeated to teams or forwarded to others. It was like training myself as a neural network. He got a real kick out of that. So much so that for the next few weeks in a meeting if he knew he was repeating something I had said to him, he would look at me and sort of grin a bit.

Everything in my career that followed can be traced to my time working for BillG as his technical assistant. The ability to think broadly while applying that to building products, balancing innovation and execution, treating innovation as a portfolio of work, and always keeping a focus on competition are a few of the skills and approaches I modeled and developed based on working in this role.

I got a small raise and no promotion.

But at least the expenses for my trip to London were approved.

One thing I mentioned in the review was how difficult it has been to figure out what to do next. Bill wanted to direct me to a specific job, but these did not feel like jobs. They felt more like problems. I would later learn in talking to many people that served similar roles at other companies, this is almost always how product/technology leaders think of staffing for valued contributors, which is the exact opposite of how people think of their own careers. This notion of putting a person on a problem reflected the Systems way of working, which was that the execs maintained a list of people and a list of problems and there was a constant juggling of assignments between those lists. As I came to learn, the Apps way of working was much more about assigning people to products and thinking first about what products needed to be built and who would be best. As always, this reflected Microsoft's two gardens.

It also did not help that as AaronG, the previous technical assistant, told me the day I moved into the office, "every group is screwed up." From this vantage point, all you see are the problems and there's no shortage of those.

A vacation spent deeply immersed in some competitive software would change my trajectory and outlook.

1994-1995

The rise of the internet dramatically accelerates the growth of the PC. The Windows PC in particular, becomes a must-have home appliance and an essential business tool for most every profession around the world. Windows PC unit sales have doubled since 1989 to over 40 million units per year and the growth rate was increasing.

031. SYNCHRONIZING WINDOWS AND OFFICE (THE FIRST TIME)

During a visit to my family in Miami, I was bored with the July heat and endless trips to the mall to avoid the heat, so I went to the local CompUSA to buy the newly released Lotus SmartSuite version 2. Wanting to spend time with it firsthand, I loaded it floppy-by-floppy on to my Compaq LTE laptop running Windows 3.11 and used the better part of the vacation diving deep into the product.

The main messaging for SmartSuite was consistency and the way in which each of the programs worked together. At Spring COMDEX 1994, the booth had been a relentless chorus of a *work together* jingle. The promotional materials offered up *SmartIcons*® shared across applications as supporting evidence—basically toolbars with customization. As I began to use the 1-2-3 spreadsheet, Ami Pro word processor, Freelance graphics/slides, Lotus Organizer personal information manager, and Approach database (the latter four were acquisitions), I saw a fairly sophisticated suite of products, but I didn't see a lot of user experience consistency.

It was weird. It felt like we were being marketed to. We were.

A *normal* person would have taken screenshots of the user experience and compared them. But I was a developer tools person, so I groveled around in the compiled code looking clues to see how *shared* SmartIcons were in reality. This was a big deal to my Apps friends because performance was everything and loading Word, Excel, and PowerPoint meant a good deal of *duplicated* code. Surprisingly, all those buttons took a lot of memory and used scarce graphics resources in Windows. Office was a bundle but not an architected product, yet.

Much to my surprise (but given the acquisition history of the product it should not have been), not only did each Lotus app have its own copy of icons, but each frequently varied across apps.

Busted. We *were* being marketed to.

I quickly put together a nearly 30-page memo, detailing inconsistencies and inefficiencies in the product. I made a giant table of copy/paste between apps to see how each was handled. In hindsight, decades later, nobody would think this was even a problem, but in the early days of cross-application scenarios, simply moving information between products was hit and miss. It had been an area Office 4.x had worked hard on, especially using the new Object Linking and Embedding (OLE) technology. I also detailed the disk footprint, memory utilization, and even the number of help topics.

Consistency was all the rage in the world of applications. There were two historic drivers of this. First, there was a strong belief, in part encouraged by Microsoft and Apple, that a graphical interface was inherently consistent across applications. Apple relentlessly touted their extensive documentation, *Human Interface Guidelines* or HIG, as a sort of rules of the road for building graphical apps. The HIG provided specific, almost Talmudic, rules for how to display commands, dialog boxes, and menus. Windows was just beginning to recognize the importance of this kind of effort and with Chicago would release a major set of guidelines, the Windows Application Design Guide or

WADG, pronounced wad-gee. Unlike MS-DOS where every application made up its own user interface, graphical products should all be very similar as a result.

Second, consistency was supposed to make it easy to move from one application to another without learning an entirely new and equally arcane command system. Most people used only a single application and what easier way to get more out of a PC than if moving from one application to another did not require learning a bunch of new user interface, especially in suites of products that were coming to dominate sales. In reality, developers would be developers and most every application went in its own direction, all justifying that by saying customers had specific needs, a topic we will return to with respect to Office.

To that end my competitive memo was a source of pride. Whether or not any of my findings were relevant to sales or competitive positioning was unclear. My own lens was not particularly broad at age 27. But, up until that point, reviewers of SmartSuite had been quite impressed with the integration and I was growing increasingly disappointed in the lengthy product reviews that failed to reveal all the details.

While I wielded a great technology buzzsaw, I was also applying Microsoft's perspective, not necessarily what Lotus was looking to accomplish or what reviewers would see. For example, my focus on shared code came straight from BillG as that was his hot button. The Lotus products clearly hadn't focused on that at all. I thought they were "wrong" not simply different. This mismatch was something I had seen in the evaluations of Borland C++ versus Microsoft VC++. For example, Borland had a compiler optimization switch "/O" that was, basically, "make this code as fast as possible by enabling all the best optimizations." To us compiler-heads at Microsoft, we thought of this as technical nonsense because each of the myriad potential optimizations meant something unique to the programmer (literally the entire alphabet of command line switches), but it had captivated reviewers. I came to champion (and push) the addition of "/O" for our complier and it turned out that it *worked* with reviewers. When Ami Pro, the Lotus SmartSuite word processor, demonstrated its new ease-of-use features under the umbrella of *working together*, it similarly captured the attention of reviewers, even if deep down in technical details it didn't make much sense.

This lesson really stuck with me.

In distributing the memo, which as Bill's TA garnered attention, and talking with the Office team it became clear that we saw things the same way—Lotus was doing a great job marketing—but the Microsoft team needed to do better with Office architecture. It needed to do a version of "/O" but one that was consistent and marketable. My writeup on SmartSuite offered some fuel for that work. Pete Higgins (PeteH) even emailed me to ask about the memo.

PeteH was the leading protégé of MikeMap and the spiritual leader of newly named Desktop Applications Division, DAD. He rose through the ranks, eventually leading Excel and then all of Office. Pete represented the kind of leader, manager, and team member we all aspired to be, representing the very best of the MikeMap value system and intense focus on customers and the business. On my Lotus memo he casually asked me rhetorically, "Why didn't our team write this up first?" I loved that but also felt badly about it. My intent had not been to make the DAD team look bad. I found myself sending around apologies each time someone asked for the memo. It made me think about the lessons JeffH had imparted, about managing across teams when people perceived me to be in the "power position," which as TA they certainly did even though I felt like a junior assistant.

The DAD teams were busy finishing Office 4.0 which started in late 1993 with a launch event but lasted until the summer of 1994 when the last product would finally ship. It was crazy—it took almost 9 months to complete a launched product. In fact, the first boxes (the physical boxes with floppy disks) came with a new version of Excel, but the older releases of Word and PowerPoint. Buyers were given coupons for the updates to the other applications which would dribble out over the coming months. Internally, the team referred to this as an "air box" because customers got coupons instead of new software. Finally, the much-promised Office Professional with a new version of the Microsoft Access database shipped in the summer of 1994. Office was the team that shipped on time! It was just that organizationally each of the component applications was a different team operating at a different velocity. Lotus even capitalized on this by running advertisements in the trade press pointing out the IOUs.

Over in Systems, products were also late, but the strategy was confusing as well. The industry seemed to be questioning whether the future (there was always just one future, *the future*) was going to be Windows NT or Chicago.

The organizational split underlying the technology differences was front and center for me as I was looking for a job. I would talk to the Chicago team and hear about how they were the natural evolution of Windows and how Windows NT took way too much memory and was not compatible with all the software and devices that customers used, especially all the new games and multimedia on the Internet. The NT team mostly thought the Chicago product was fragile and toy-like and lacked the architecture to ever achieve the required security and robustness the PC needed. There was also the Cairo team that felt everything was rather pedestrian until they would ship. Meanwhile the industry was just waiting and waiting for Chicago. In many ways, Windows 3.11 was old news. Microsoft had been touting 32-bit computing long enough and now the market wanted a product. In particular, all the new Internet tools really needed the connectivity and multi-tasking capabilities in 32-bit Chicago.

The number of new products under development across Microsoft was stunning. I'd seen them spring up in meetings with BillG. These new teams were attracting seasoned developers and program managers and provided new opportunities for career growth. Though at the same time there was a growing tension between the major teams like Applications and Platforms (or Systems in older terminology) and these new teams, be it Online Services, Consumer, or the new Advanced Consumer Technology groups. The prevailing view was that people were drawn to these new *shiny objects* teams to "rest and vest" because somehow the work was perceived to be easier than slogging through compatibility bugs and increasingly difficult memory and disk constraints. Such a characterization was decidedly rude, but it was in the air. Microsoft was developing a bit of a cultural pecking order. Increasingly groups began to talk about metrics like revenue per employee as a way of distinguishing the ever-growing list of teams that were in *investment* mode.

I needed to find a "real job." There was not much precedent to this transition, but my self-imposed 18 months was almost up. Months after writing the Lotus memo, as Office 4.x was near complete, I started looking. The memo served to discuss the potential of working in DAD. It was not my first choice given my roots in Tools and focus on databases and programming languages in grad school. Plus, Bill had clearly demonstrated that from his perspective Windows was central and where the "hard problems" that required "IQ" existed. Still, my mentor and previous boss, Jeff Harbers, was an original in Apps and built our AFX team around that culture and he insisted and brokered a discussion.

That first stop was with Chris Peters (ChrisP.) At the end of 1993 with the launch of Office 4.0, ChrisP was promoted to vice president of the newly formed Office Product Unit (OPU) reporting to PeteH in DAD, who reported into MikeMap's expansive WWPG. OPU sounded redundant—why did Applications need an Office Product Unit to make Office? I was confused and intrigued.

When ChrisP introduced himself he always said something like, "I grew up on Bainbridge Island, went to the University of Washington, didn't have a car when I started at Microsoft in 1981 then worked on DOS 2.0, Windows 1.0, Mouse 1.0, DOS Word 1.0, and then Excel development manager (DM) and Word BUM [Business Unit Manager]."

His Microsoft pedigree was legendary. He was one of the few people to have worked on most of the major products, including hardware and in Apps, holding senior roles on both Word and Excel in development. That was a big deal. In reality, it was only part of ChrisP's contribution—he was also among the most creative leaders at the company with a true fondness for art (he championed the acquisition of an M.C. Escher work as an original member of the Microsoft Art Committee and went on to become a professional artist) and at any given time he would concurrently and deeply be immersed in a new hobby like rockets, robots, architecture, bowling, or film photography. ChrisP was most well-known for instilling the culture of shipping—the idea that shipping software trumps everything—memorialized with the ever-present quote "shipping is a feature." This shipping focus was elevated to historic levels with Excel 3.0 shipping a mere 11 days late from its *original planned* ship date.

For this newly formed group, ChrisP was thinking about picking a key direct report as group program manager. The current and talented leader the group inherited did not want to manage a large team. I had not managed a big group before, but then again, most people had not. He was not as interested in whether I had all the answers myself as he was interested in if I could manage and lead the team. I was, in a sense, interviewing to join the DAD family, as much as to work on Office. Sitting in the courtyard between buildings 16 and 17, a patio with commemorative *Ship-It* tiles celebrating the release of each Microsoft product, we both started to realize DAD was the right fit.

DAD was organized by business units as a result of MikeMap's transformative organization in 1988. Each of Word, Excel, and PowerPoint, and also Microsoft Project, were headed by seasoned general managers and had all the resources to plan and develop products. There was a single marketing organization which divided resources across the products, with dedicated leaders for each application. This organization worked spectacularly well and resulted in the leadership of Word and Excel on Macintosh and the increasing success of the new Office bundle.

My first work would be figuring out what "Office" meant—both the product and the newly formed team. Why was there a new organization to build the product people knew about? Or did they? The Office product was not close to as widely known as Excel on Windows or both Word and Excel on Macintosh. PowerPoint was light years behind. The Lotus compete memo gave some clues. All the meetings the Office team had held with BillG were about code sharing and consistency, something that customers wanted to buy but Microsoft was yet to sell.

ChrisP later offered me the role of group program manager (GPM) in the newly formed Office Product Unit. I reported to him. The initial Office PM team, called OFFPM, was 14 people mostly made up of the team that managed the setup and installation program. We would be growing quickly, but deliberately.

Two lessons really stuck with me in what would essentially be my last job search. First, I decided to *run towards the fire* and joined the relatively large and mature organization rather than join one of the exciting new businesses. Applications in 1994 was $2.9 billion in revenue compared to Platforms revenue of $1.5 billion. The success of Windows 3.x had driven sales of Microsoft's own Windows applications to account for 85% of revenue by 1994, after years of dominance by Macintosh platform revenue. Joining Desktop Applications meant I was joining a team with a great deal of responsibility to Microsoft on the business side, and at the same time the team was established and had a very strong culture. It was exactly the kind of job many people at Microsoft were *not* gravitating towards at the time.

Second, the conversations with ChrisP about management were very difficult and had the direct effect of shaking my own confidence. It was entirely true that I had hardly managed anyone prior to this job and stepping up to manage a team of 14 with two levels of management was unheard of in DAD, where people worked their way up as ChrisP had. The company was being forced to make these leaps because of the explosive growth in headcount, but DAD generally resisted that. In discussing this with Chris he explained what a leap this was for me and how in taking this job I was not signing up for a passive role in learning how to manage. I would need to rely on the strength of the team around me and also recognize the level of trust the organization was placing in me. While it was humbling, it was far more terrifying. Years later I would learn just how much of this was based on the newness of the Office Product Unit and DAD in a sense trying to create a new culture as well. There was no doubt a bet on me.

A note about today as I write this. I rarely ever gave direct career advice even for relatively routine internal moves at Microsoft. This transition for me cemented two things that I always do offer. First, run towards the fire in a big company, especially early in career. This is so much harder than it looks—the seductive roles are always the new technologies and new teams. It always seems like there is more opportunity there but there is also more opportunity to get little done because of the very forces of a big company that tend to draw all things towards the existing and critical businesses. Second, always make sure the team is making the same level of bet on you that you are capable of making on them.

The reason I was offered a such stretch job was because the team (ChrisP and my peers) were going to support me and essentially train me for the role. It wasn't that I was unqualified, but that the strategic view and the technology perspectives I brought were only part of the job. Managing people and leading a team at that scale were new to me. ChrisP reminded me with his final words, being a manager of a team this big is always new the first time. One day you're a lead or not a manager and then the next day people are lined up outside your door asking you what to do. He assured me that he had the confidence I could do the job, but also that he and others were there to support me.

I was very excited to have a real job. In just about every way this would be the last job change I would make where I was worried about fitting in or if the job was right for me. I found a home and family in DAD as I would quickly learn. For the next ten years and six releases of Office and innumerable service packs and bug fixes I would feel as though I was on a mission and part of something much larger and more important than myself. I felt as though any efforts I made would return so much more because of the strength of the team I was fortunate enough to be part of.

032. WINNING WITH THE SUITE

There were two major shifts taking place in the early 1990s together altering the market landscape for business software. The most visible was the move by the business market to Windows, beginning with Windows 3.0 but picking up the pace dramatically with each subsequent release, Windows 3.1 and Windows 3.11. Bringing networking to the operating system, a seemingly simple ability for PCs in an office to share files and printers, was becoming a force.

By 1993, Windows/DOS PCs were outselling Macintosh ten to one and Windows was on 30 million of the 120 million PCs worldwide, with Windows dominating new PC sales.

That transition itself did not instantly shift the Applications market, though. The leaders of each category, particularly WordPerfect for word processing and Lotus with its 1-2-3 spreadsheet, as well as Borland with both Paradox and dBase databases, were not only entrenched but generally had passionate customer followings. Law schools were using WordPerfect and newly minted lawyers were proficient in the inner workings of the mysteries of formatting a brief with reveal codes. WordPerfect's mysterious *codes* that showed formatting before *WYSIWYG*, or *what you see is what you get* in GUI. MBA students were masters of the 1-2-3 *slash* commands for navigating a financial model. That Windows 3.x ran these products extremely well, because compatibility with MS-DOS was a key design point, only solidified them. Windows 3.x made running MS-DOS products even better by supporting multiple programs running at the same time.

However, the graphical interface was beginning to put pressure on existing MS-DOS leaders. The improved support for printing, such as supporting more printers from various manufacturers, as well as the ease at moving information from one app to another with the clipboard were tangible benefits. With the rise of laser printers, the era of producing business and school reports that included charts, graphs, and tables in-line with the text—all prepared camera ready—was a new baseline expectation. This was vastly easier with GUI apps.

As a result, product reviews began to evaluate the MS-DOS and Windows products in the same category. The word processor category, for example, included Word for Windows and WordPerfect for MS-DOS. The reviews would compare features but also compare ease of use at complex scenarios, often including the ability for documents to incorporate information from other sources. Even though the Windows applications were behind on features and had different user interfaces from MS-DOS, there was an uptick in perception based on ease of use of GUI.

To be fair, the tech elites of the time greatly resisted the GUI—often claiming the mouse and all those graphics were counter to productivity. I had witnessed this myself in 1984 at Cornell when people looked at the mouse and shook their heads, referring to it as a *toy,* and to the inefficiency of lifting their hands from the keyboard. Working within the disconnect between evolving technology and entrenched elites proved to be a theme throughout my career.

At the same time, existing software leaders resisted or at least paced themselves with the move to Windows. Many over the years tried to either explain or rationalize this and much has been written. Microsoft committed a ton of energy trying to get the likes of Lotus and WordPerfect to be launch partners with Windows versions or to just commit to Windows, even as Microsoft was building Windows versions of its own apps. There was no head fake on the part of Microsoft—it was believed that Windows would be best with Windows versions of leading apps and the Microsoft apps would, as they had been on MS-DOS, do everything they could to compete and win. Even with all the effort, leading vendors viewed Windows as yet another platform and most were also not wild about adopting the Mac (this was the opening that was created for Microsoft) and were still focused on character mode platforms. The reluctance of betting on a platform Microsoft controlled with its apps was real, but in hindsight proved... limiting.

Ironically, the success Apps achieved on the Mac provided a winning strategy roadmap for Windows—both the applications and the operating system—in creating the right ingredients to take advantage of the market change from individual products to suites, the second shift of the early 1990s in business software. Whereas the *killer app* on MS-DOS was Lotus 1-2-3, on Windows it was really Office that proved to be that. The Excel team might say that they created the *defining* app, and that is arguably correct.

On the Mac, both Excel and Word had proven successful products on their own. In modern terminology, these products had clearly demonstrated *product-market fit*. PMF was coined by Andy Rachleff, cofounder of the legendary venture firm Benchmark. Product-market fit means a product so clearly satisfies a market need that the market literally pulls the product from the company, no matter any incidental flaws or execution challenges. I wish I had the term PMF to work with as so much of what I experienced is rooted in an understanding of what it means to work on something before, during, and after PMF.

PMF for Office on the Mac was a statement about the role of GUI in business (then only on the Mac) and the feature set of each of these products. Professionals were as passionate and committed, perhaps more so, to Word and Excel (and PowerPoint) on the Mac as professionals were to 1-2-3 and WordPerfect on MS-DOS.

The interesting business challenge was that a majority of customers were not purchasing both Word and Excel, and fewer were purchasing PowerPoint. We weren't sure why that was—market size or price. Did fewer people need a spreadsheet than needed a word processor? Probably not. More likely, the retail price of $395 per product was the problem. The computer cost about $3,000 at the time. The notion that the software would become a significant portion of the price of the computer was perplexing at the retail counter, no matter how much Microsoft was spending on Research & Development or how much that metric might not make sense. The industry was not quite ready for software to become a bigger business than hardware—it was the *computer business*.

Creating the Office Suite was a brilliant move by Apps marketing. It created a new category of product while building upon the strengths of the existing products, and at the same time was a fantastic value for customers. The fact that no other company had all the elements of the Suite was a competitive bonus that would mostly not matter on the Mac but prove to be a significant advantage on Windows. The pricing for Office was an incredible bargain at $949 suggested retail. I remember buying copies for a professor back at Cornell from the Company Store where software sold at a steep discount to employees, essentially for the cost of goods. I don't remember the exact price, but it was less than $100 though shipping it was costly as the box weighed ten pounds and was huge. Still, it was a popular holiday gift in 1990.

Windows Office followed Mac Office but with a slightly bumpier journey. Externally, with Windows, the challenge was first winning critical acclaim and customer love over the category competition. The journey would take years for some customers—not only were the MS-DOS leaders loved, but those products were hard to learn and customers invested a lot in the keystrokes, macros, plugins, and in the existing files, which were difficult to import and export with Excel and Word. The MS-DOS PC era was characterized by investing in a PC and software to the tune of $3,000 ($7,000 in 2019 dollars) or more, and then literally taking classes and buying books to learn to use the computer. I spent two summers in the mid-80s at Martin Marietta teaching people how to use WordPerfect and 1-2-3, though never both to any one person as "secretaries" learned WordPerfect and managers learned 1-2-3.

For each customer, this would have to happen at least twice, but perhaps three or more times for Office to win. In other words, it wasn't enough for Word or Excel alone to win, but both had to. In any given business organization, there were many lawyers using WordPerfect and finance people using 1-2-3 that made this challenge significant.

In evolving Apps to sell Office for Windows, the launch of Office 4 was a watershed moment. It wasn't exactly a moment, rather a rolling series of releases that started October 1993 (while I was still Technical Assistant) and a massive wave of marketing and PR, including getting some major mainstream business press. The software was available as Office 4.0 for Windows. It contained the new Word 6.0, the third release, and the existing releases of Excel 4.0, PowerPoint 3.0, Mail 3.1. It was the fourth version of Office that began with Mac Office 1.0 in June 1989 containing Word 4.00, Excel 2.20, PowerPoint 2.01, and Mail 1.37. It took until the summer of 1994 and Office 4.3 for the full suite to be updated to include Word 6.0, Excel 5.0, PowerPoint 4.0, Mail 3.2, Access 2.0, and for it to also be available on the Mac. Including the time to translate the software into other languages, Office 4 released over the course of almost a year. I was still signing off on the releases at the tail end as GPM of OPU in late 1994 months after I joined the team. The version number chaos described above is intentionally included showing just how random it was for customers.

The idea of releasing all the updated products at the same time seemed to be a combination of impossible and undesirable from the perspective of each individual product following different schedules and with different category dynamics in the marketplace. The closest any product got to a ship date was Excel 3 by 11 days but imagine trying to get every product to hit the same date—it boggled the mind. More importantly, the GMs for each of the apps didn't see any benefit to even trying such a feat.

The early days of the PC Revolution were characterized by two major product development forces. First, making things work at all was a huge accomplishment. Second, getting anything done on any sort of reliable schedule was not only difficult but almost an anomaly. Everything was riddled with bugs and late. What doesn't get enough credit was how much DAD was beginning to figure out, and uniquely so, how to accomplish both quality and schedule. Excel, under ChrisP's management, led the charge across the division.

Simply getting software out the door, *releasing*, was exhausting, and most of the burden for releasing Office fell to part of the new OPU program management team I had just started to manage. It was labor intensive and frustrating trying to create one product release from multiple product lines moving at different velocities with different engineering processes and levels of schedule precision, across both Windows and Mac. While the teams might have used the same words, the meanings differed, and the cultures built up attached a high value to those differences.

Releasing Office meant combining all the floppy disk images across products on to a minimal set of disks (for cost reasons) and building a single installation program, while also maintaining efficiency in producing the standalone category products.

While Microsoft managed to create an Office release, we did so without a shared understanding of the basic steps each engineering team maintained. For all practical purposes, each of the product teams was almost like an independent tribe within DAD. Worse, OPU was viewed as just another tribe. Worse than that it was not even a major app on its own, just a bundle. Early adopters might have purchased Office, but they were clear they used Word and Excel, rarely mentioning Office by name.

All of this was happening under the constant scrutiny of product quality, the second major challenge facing DAD. Word, as solid as it was, continued to have perception issues (or a reality) regarding product quality. Like many products Word 6.0, for example, was known to be a one where customers were better off waiting until the first servicing update or *point release*, Word 6.0a, before it was deemed reliable. It was not uncommon for industry press to get caught up in anecdotes about bugs and quality. There was little a product team could do about that given that the *only* data that existed was what Microsoft recorded in private bug databases and haphazard customer reports or press anecdotes. Huge amounts of energy were spent by the marketing team to manage the perception of product quality. Often one reviewer would have a bad experience and for months did not miss a chance to mention that in a weekly column. The fact that most writers in tech had started to use Word (along with Windows for the first time) and most had personally run across data-losing bugs, only increased the frequency and gravity of this challenge.

Across Microsoft and the industry, every product went through a similar release cycle including the market confusion over the quality of a new release. Every new product released later than some expected, certainly later than the original schedule. Bugs were reported and word spread that the new product still had bugs as though a product could ever have no bugs. NT was rumored to have thousands of bugs even when it shipped. Interviews and calls to reporters with the company followed, making clear the product was the highest quality ever. An announcement of an update always followed. Professionals concluded it was important to wait for the update. The press concluded the product was rushed to make a deadline that had passed. Marketing entailed a significant effort remind potential customers that there was no need to wait, and the quality was high. Then a release or point release shipped, and the product was ready for market. In practice, it was quite typical for a product to become substantially better with these first updates. Such was the climate of these early days.

Creating the suite, as difficult as it was, had started to transform the business, and the bet being made in late 1993 with Office 4.0 for Windows and creating OPU was that the future of the business was the suite. Over two million copies of Office were sold in that fiscal year, and half of the overall DAD business (which was itself half of Microsoft's revenue) came from suites compared to sales of single products. Office was itself a $1 billion business. An actual $1 billion dollars, not an accounting gimmick or allocated revenue. Each license of Office that was sold was essentially a retail sale counted on that day—it would be a few years before multiyear licenses would become the norm.

The creation of OPU, described in the next section, was a major effort in DAD and came a few years after MikeMap's enormously successful and effective Business Unit structure. Still, any time something that people loved and was working changed, things became difficult. This was no different. Incredibly, what started as a marketing experiment transformed the business and the industry.

During this time, Lotus had finally and fully committed to Windows with a major update to 1-2-3 for Windows. Lotus had, through acquisitions, a full complement of products to create a suite known as Lotus Suite first releasing it in early 1992. Building Office was no longer a nice way to sell more stuff, but had, seemingly overnight, become a key entry in a major competitive battle.

Unfortunately, this meant BU leaders were in both a suite war and a category war. Or did it? The market was transforming, but how quickly? Would focus on competing come at the expense of competing in traditional categories? How could we tell if we were making a lot of money selling standalone products as all the competitors to DAD were doing? The answers were not readily apparent. Any time a business is in transition, decision makers can lose sight of the cause and effect of actions. *Are today's numbers secure? Are they relevant to the future? Did last year's choices still matter? Is today's revenue predicated on doing more of the same or a bet on the future?*

There were some issues to consider. The industry had not yet bought into suites. While there was a wave of broad reach press about the transformation of the industry being fed by both Lotus and Microsoft, the product reviewers and industry analysts were rather undecided. Should customers get all their products from one vendor? Would customers be happy with a suite when one or more of the elements would not win reviews in a category? Why don't the vendors focus on making their individual products interoperate? Would customers come to value consistency and integration across products more than specific innovations and experiences within a category? At the extreme, there was a view that suites were somewhere between marketing gimmicks and attempts at locking customers into inferior products that can't stand on their own. The constant grumbling was "suite versus best of breed" and "most people don't need so many products."

Second, the category battles on Windows seemed to be just getting started, unlike on the Mac where it seemed Microsoft had little risk of losing on word processing, spreadsheets, and presentations. To those working on the categories, particularly BU leaders, the Windows competition and market situation felt decidedly different, and more precarious, than the Mac. Some believed betting on suite consistency and integration felt like a way to make a worse spreadsheet competitor just so it could do some stuff with the word processor—a feeling shared by many in the industry, not just the hallways of building 17.

Third, the notion that somehow magically all the products and BUs would agree to ship their products at the same time and meet these schedules with good quality seemed, well, laughable. The Office 4.3 nine-month lead up had been nothing but staggered releases of products so there was ample evidence to suggest such an alignment would be impossible. Nobody wanted to hold back the shipping of a single product because another product was out of control. We were there to ship not to stare at the finished work and admire it.

Strategically, one would have to make a leap to agree that suites were the future, especially on Windows and especially as a BU leader being held accountable for success against one category competitor. Operationally, the leap to designing these integrated scenarios and shipping them at once seemed nothing short of wacky. To each BU, it seemed like a case of taking on the most *external* dependencies possible and hoping for the best at a time when the culture was to reduce all external dependencies. The fact that this was teams at the same company in the same division in the same business did not make it feel any less *external*.

In the waning days of stand-alone apps versus the suite, a widely distributed memo emerged from the Excel program management team by Lisa James (LisaJ) outlining a process to "manage" dependencies from the perspective of Excel. The approach was structured and hierarchical, with Excel sitting at the top of the hierarchy. Every other team was a dependency to Excel and Excel had the right (and obligation) to fully manage that process. It was the hallmark of shipping and *hardcore*. Ultimately the goal was to minimize dependencies whenever possible and if not then tightly managing a dependency using a rigorous process was required. This model worked for Excel and was critical for innovations such as Visual Basic but would prove challenging to scale. To any team on the receiving end of this process, it felt a bit intimidating, as in don't mess with Excel intimidating. But it worked.

In building a suite, there were countless external dependencies as everyone involved was an external dependency to everyone else. The BU approach could not be operationalized for this to happen. Plus, it was suffocating. The rule of thumb was to basically have one dependency per project, which was impossible in building a Suite that was filled with dependencies. The idea of *dependency management* would ultimately grate on me so much we effectively banned the term and renamed all such relationships *partnerships*, while also changing the tone to be more congenial and less authoritative.

In our first Office-centric effort to shape the team, we actively evangelized the idea of partnership over dependencies with a new memo and training, along sweeping change in operations and even our vocabulary. In the process our team pioneered many of the approaches used to build products spanning divisions. We did away with dependencies and introduced the idea of partnering.

As it would evolve, the idea of betting on collaboration and partnering across the teams would prove to be a huge cultural shift within the Desktop Applications Division and the new Office Product Unit.

033. CREATING THE OFFICE PRODUCT UNIT, OPU

The year 1994 marked the first time a new organizational structure also signaled a new product strategy for DAD. This was disconcerting to the existing BU structure as it created an unsolvable problem up front: What comes first, the suite or category?

It was challenging.

Just prior to when I joined the team, OPU was formed at the end of 1993. The leadership of the team was put in place and designed to make a statement by choosing Chris Peters (ChrisP) to lead the team as the division's first product leader vice president. In 1994 there were 29 vice presidents among the over 15,000 employees. This was a huge deal at the time—an actual Microsoft engineer hired directly from college made it to product group vice president for the first time. ChrisP's no-brainer choice to lead development for OPU would be Jon DeVaan (JonDe), who just finished up Excel 5.0 for Windows and Mac. Leading testing was a new hire and a rare industry hire for DAD, Grant George (GrantG) who started on the team just before me. He joined Microsoft from a major project—huge in scale and in failure—the legendary Taligent project at Apple, which was cancelled in favor of Apple acquiring NeXT and thus returning Steve Jobs to the company. It wasn't immediately clear, but Grant's leadership and the elevated role of testing would be one of the most major contributions to making Office a reality of a product.

Staffing the team was a non-trivial choice. Do you *draft* people by skills and need or do you take only *volunteers* in the hopes of keeping everyone happy? Drafting people would have the effect of sending a clear message about priorities but no one performs well in a job they don't want. Taking only volunteers would make OPU a happy place while all but guaranteeing the individual apps teams would lobby for people to stay in their jobs and solidify the discord between the apps and OPU. There was some experience in these staffing choices that came from the gentle *persuasion* that was used by leaders to nudge people from Excel to Word for example. The code bases, development processes, and cultures were different enough that changing jobs was viewed as a bit of a reset. Plus, why would one want to go from Excel to Word when a word processor is nothing more than a spreadsheet with one cell, as ChrisP used to say. Chris moved from Excel to be GM of Word prior to leading OPU.

The undercurrent of the staffing choice was that resources were being reallocated from individual apps to OPU. The apps teams were getting smaller to fund OPU, at least in the immediate term. This was a huge issue. The apps teams had plenty of work to do and could not understand how they would get all that work done while reducing staff size. Plus, this all seemed insane to do right on the cusp of potentially winning in the market. The market in this case meant the market for stand-alone word processors or spreadsheets, not the suite market. The apps were not only committed to winning only in their category, but they had ample evidence the industry was not quite there yet as well. The feeling was at any minute Lotus could release a killer Windows spreadsheet or WordPerfect could release a Windows product that would lure all those existing MS-DOS customers to Windows. This was a legitimate concern. It was also not the bet Microsoft was making—the bet was on the suite.

Meanwhile every team continued to hire as many graduating engineers as we could, so we would have plenty of people to do all the work. In software development, the number of engineers is literally everything, perhaps except for schedule time. The WOBU (Word Business Unit, renamed from OBU when the Mail product was moved to the new Messaging Business Unit) team had grown to over 65 software engineers plus an equivalent number of Test Engineers and about 25 program managers. The Excel team was not quite as large and finished Excel 5.0 with about 50 software engineers. The new strategy and organization called for creating an OPU with 60 more engineers but seeded with 30 or so engineers from Word and Excel.

The reduction in the individual Apps team headcount immediately and decidedly created a negative view of this process. Teams felt they were being told to do more with less—there was no indication that OPU would be contributing to the mission of winning in categories or even adding useful features. When engineering teams are put in this position, they resist everything. In the case of Word and Excel, their default answer for everything asked of them was along the lines of "go ask OPU as they have all the resources." At the same time, the apps assumed that OPU would in reality contribute little and what it did contribute would need to be reworked to perform well inside Word and Excel. In other words, OPU was viewed as a net negative, while resources were being taken away. At least that was the emotional argument at the time. It fell to JonDe to deliver and change this debate among developers.

Second, OPU was going to take the lead in orchestrating a planning and engineering process that would result in all the products shipping at the same time. Navigating the fine line between planning for a winning suite product and planning winning category products would be the main challenge. While resources had been set "from above," what precisely to build and for how long were still open questions. This is what I needed to do.

Had the product plans been left to the business units, each would have chosen a release timeline of about 18 to 24 months with an error rate of perhaps three to six months. People always said, "plus minus" when talking about dates for projects, but in the history of software nothing finished early. Still, we continued to humor ourselves.

In some sense then, the suite could have come together if everyone hit the starting line at the same time and had planned on the same length of project, give or take six months. This sounded good enough, but Office was a retail business and that meant products needed to launch in time for retail purchasing waves like holidays, back to school, or new PCs in the spring. If one app missed the target then it would be back to the "air box," which was costly and frankly embarrassing.

Alas, none of that mattered because the current products for the Office 4 release continued to hit the finish line at different times. Excel 5.0 was having a tricky time at the end, having integrated Visual Basic for Applications (VBA) and finding challenges in getting the Mac version done. Word 6 had employed a different technology for the Mac version (a top-secret feature we created in AFX to enable Windows programs to run on the Mac, which later proved to be a big mistake) and was having even bigger challenges. PowerPoint, and not enough credit was given, had done a fantastic job at their Windows and Mac versions for PowerPoint 3 (shipping the second Windows versions based on their original Mac product), but was about to embark on a major C++ rewrite of the entire product for PowerPoint 4. The third release of the Microsoft Access database was shipping for the first time as part of Office 4. Turning from the final phases of shipping to starting again took time, thus getting to the starting line all at the same time would be difficult.

Rather than try to negotiate both a start and finish, the best plan was to develop some constraints and get moving. In any project, the most calendar time was burned by postponing difficult and somewhat arbitrary choices (choices that wouldn't become more informed with time) such as picking a schedule. The focus of the new OPU were choices like that. There were objections to any approach and with the competing interests of four major category apps each with different engineering goals, there was no process to converge.

The biggest constraint was to ship at the same time—in the art of shipping software, the first thing is to pick a date and carve that in stone. But picking that date was not such a simple task. How much time for each engineering milestone? How much time for testing? How much time for localization? Not only were the process models different for each app, but these were also viewed as different for reasons that mattered. Looking back, it was kind of amazing how hard everyone fought and how much debate we had over these schedule issues, all while not even coming close to finishing on time.

DAD had to simplify things—the endless long tail of releases, shipping coupons for promised but late updates, and the constant re-releasing of Office with updated bits were exhausting and expensive. Not counting the specific language/country releases, *the year of Office* released at least five times to keep things up to date and complete. The market, it seemed, appreciated seeing new versions of Windows and new versions of apps at the same time. Seeing apps from Microsoft on Microsoft Windows was especially validating, for both Systems and Apps. A number of data points reinforced this view, even going back to Excel on Windows, including the updates tuned for Windows 3 and soon 32-bit versions of Office supporting Windows NT.

There was a group of evangelists on the Windows team charged with doing everything they could to get the major vendors to work on the latest Windows release and ship the same time or at least commit to doing so. Many, many did. What was always so odd about this being in DAD was that we didn't really get a choice but also didn't benefit from the evangelism efforts. Whenever there was a chance, the reference products, keynote demos, and even advertising would show off other vendors more than DAD, at least that is what it felt like as were overly sensitive to each mention of our competitors. This was a perfectly valid strategy, but often counterintuitive to the outside world, if not scrutinized as the subject of conspiracy theorists who believed in some inherent advantages held by the Apps team within Microsoft. The only advantage we held was our Windows strategy was not up for debate, whereas our competitors continued to debate the priority of Windows.

The alignment of the next Windows release, Chicago, and a release of Office was the topic of many meetings while I was winding down my BillG role. I spent a great deal of time bouncing between the developers in Apps and those in Systems trying to understand the value of synergy and strategy as well as engineering challenges at the time. Aligning dates was one thing, but what about the implementation of apps and taking advantage of Chicago? What were the features of the platform that mattered to apps?

Suffice it to say, this was not a slam dunk for anyone. Chicago ran 16-bit applications perfectly well, a major selling point, and the integration with Windows was still relatively nascent. Some things were known, such as that Chicago would support long file names (finally!) rather than FILENAME.DOC "8.3" names, but that was easy for Apps as the Mac had always supported those. In fact, as was often commented on from the outside, many of the important features for applications on Chicago were catching up to the Mac such as long file names, high-color displays, more extensive use of drag and drop, and so on. Much of the innovation in Chicago was about working with a wide array of hardware and peripherals, which didn't exist on the Mac but for the most part would come for "free" to applications simply by being Windows applications.

There were, however, a great many deep technical challenges in the combination of apps, Chicago, and the recently announced Win32 API yet to be uncovered. Addressing these and reconciling them would come a bit later.

When would Chicago ship, though? In mid-1994 when all of this was being planned, Chicago was going to release to OEMs for spring 1995 PCs, which was not far off, but the schedule had already shown the standard levels of accuracy for the time. Remember this was originally Windows 4.0 shipping in 1993, according to my friends debating this while sitting at the hotel bar on a 1992 recruiting trip. Should the Office product aim for a release less than a year away? In boardroom discussions, I'd already seen Chicago slip several times.

When Office picked a ship date they meant a date, like June 24. When Systems picked a date, they usually said something like "first quarter." Earlier into projects, the dates were expressed as "first half," which is approximately 180 potential dates as ChrisP used to say. Dates had a different meaning and "religion" across Systems and Apps.

The Windows team was not only shipping its own product but had a whole ecosystem of hardware and software they would line up to provide to PC manufacturers. The uncertainty in any one part was significant and chaotic, making MikeMap's "gardening" analogy accurate. Aligning with this meant Office was one moving part in the equation. Given that Office was also viewed as easier or at least secondary to Windows, simply fixing the date of Office was enough. In other words, the idea would be at the company level to treat Office as an external dependency on Windows. Strategically this made sense. But given that Office also was a business and had at least some history of shipping, this seemed weird.

Regardless of the reliability of the end date of the schedule, the overall length of the schedule was going to be short by the standards of a "full" product release. While these product schedules of two years or longer might seem absurdly long by modern standards, in practice the amount of code and complexity of what was being changed and shipped was comparable to what was done in the same period of time decades later. Distribution was the challenge—there was no way to get code to customers, so the only choice was to make it as right and complete as it could be for the one opportunity to ship. The ability to provide updates and more incremental features to customers over the internet was still 10 years away.

At the same time, the need for a longer, more traditional schedule was clear. Importantly the leaders in applications, Lotus and WordPerfect, were committed to Windows and had released products, but they were not yet ideally taking advantage of Windows. The market, however, seemed patient and that was the biggest concern among the BU leaders. On the one hand, each app continued to be locked in a competitive battle within the category and the BU leaders were clear about those needs—Word still had not won over lawyers, Excel was still winning over bankers, PowerPoint was still creating the category (meeting rooms were still not using projection from PCs), and the Access database was just starting out. In addition, the email and calendar categories had yet to make a real dent and Lotus was challenging with the inclusion of Organizer in their Suite. Additionally, Microsoft had yet to make a bet on building and developing a "truly" integrated suite—what did that even mean? Ideally there would be a good

24-month schedule of three full milestones of development for a "real" entrant into the suite market, enabling full releases across Windows and Mac with deep architectural changes.

The evolution to the Office suite was a major cultural change. I remember the progression of discussions speaking with the GMs. My first meetings, while I was still working for BillG, were about how close the battles were with competitors in categories. Then as months passed and the competitors seemed to have lost their way, the discussion became more about execution and asking if we could really build a suite, or it would still be more efficient to brute force the needed synergy. The reviews at the time seemed to support that. Then one day after I joined the OPU team, PPathe, GM of Word, told me what he had started saying to the Word team. Whenever people complained about OPU he reminded the team "[T]he best feature we have for competing with WordPerfect is Excel." He finally had his messaging that appealed to the Word-first zealots—they would win by having Excel be a great feature of Word. Brilliant.

The new OPU leaders knew they needed to have a schedule to accommodate Chicago and to develop the depth product work for the Suite. The plan decided among DAD leadership seemed impossible on paper—Office started on two releases and worked on those in parallel—yes, two releases at one time beginning from a somewhat staggered start given the tail of Office 4.x. Everyone *knew* that parallel releases did not work and wasted resources and created false expectations. At least that was conventional wisdom. We set out to prove it could be done. We did not have any other choices that made sense. This was such a big decision that even as I was interviewing with the team, the debate still raged. While my interviews were mostly informal, the most difficult discussions were asking me to *pick* an approach—knowing that the choice had already been made and BillG had been informed. Schedules and mechanics were never his focus, so long as there was a release with Chicago and a vision for the next release, he was fine.

The first release of Office, Office94, would ship with Chicago, at least "within 30 days of Chicago's release to manufacturing (RTM)", which at the time this schedule was picked was November 1994. This date for Chicago was nine months away at this point and would soon slip to February, then April, then tail end of June 1995. The project started at the end of 1992 shortly after Windows 3.11 completed in August of that year with an original date of December 1993.

The cultural differences between Systems and Apps could be ascribed to many things, but at the core it was the difference in philosophy and operations over dates. In Apps, dates were the core tool of the entire organization and the high-order bit for decision-making, execution, and accountability. Systems had equally strong beliefs around the ecosystem and partners. One measure of this was that Chicago would have six external releases prior to RTM, which was five more than Office, and those releases would go to more than a million people, compared to thousands for an Office release.

The second release, Office96, would then ship two years from the shared start. During the planning this became known as *12/24* for shipping one release in 12 months and the second release 12 months later. Culturally, not every team used code names, and so began the era of innocuous code names for Office releases as the two releases would be known as *Office94* and *Office96*, respectively, based on the year they were scheduled to ship, which is how these will be referred to here until the names become official in the story.

To anyone in the final stages of the last releases of Office 4.x this seemed not only impossible once, but impossible twice. First, the general view of developers was that "nothing" could be done in 12 months—literally, working backward there would be almost no time to write code and develop new features of any depth. Second, the fantasy of each app hitting this same schedule for Office96 remained.

It wasn't just that the team had signed up for the next release, but it also signed up for the *next* next release. Crazy talk.

034. OFFICE94, OFFICE96

The use of year-of-release code names was not arbitrary but reflected a broad consensus within leadership that Microsoft needed to move to product releases that reflected more of an annuity or subscription relationship with customers. The idea of using the year moniker was based on how car companies used model years. We had yet to prove software could be released in this fashion, reliably, and we still lacked a way to distribute products so quickly, but the idea became a cornerstone of planning what to build and how to articulate value. The early naming research for Chicago was heading down the path of using a year name, and similarly Office 4.x would be the last "version number" release.

Marketing had mixed feelings about the year names. The biggest issue was that for some period of time customers would hold off purchasing a product knowing the current version was old. It was also quite stressful for the development teams that had no idea how to ship so much software on real deadlines.

Taking the idea of one release in 12 months and a second one 12 months later, both starting from the same date in late 1993 led naturally to naming the releases 94/96, or Office94 and Office96, typed without spaces since this was all for file names and source projects. The 94/96 plan was in place. Sync within 30 days of Chicago in the spring of 1995 or thereabouts. Then Office96 12 months later.

The team's passion was around Office96, with Office94 being somewhat of a strategy tax while at the same time being viewed as an excellent opportunity to prove out Office as a product and OPU as a team. The plan covered what was necessary and sufficient, albeit with a huge risk—what if Office94 took too long as Windows slipped, bumping up against Office96? You can see the schedule chicken already being played with the assumption that Windows would slip their schedule but Office would not, though there was little history across Word, Excel, and PowerPoint to think Office schedules were that robust and zero experience shipping the entire Office suite at once. History would show that no matter how far off Apps might be, Windows was going to be further off.

To execute required employing a great deal of finesse and some game theory. A plan emerged prior to me joining the team but one I sold to BillG as his TA. The Office team's 94/96 plan split the resources across releases substantially in favor of Office96. Each Product Unit (Word, Excel, PowerPoint, and OPU) devoted one "feature team" to Office94 and the remaining teams were on Office96. A feature team was the organizational unit of a dev team, and it is made up of a software development lead and anywhere from three to seven software developers. There was an equal amount of testing and two to three program managers. This was phrased (marketed internally) as "15 percent of the resources dedicated to Chicago" or "85 percent of the resources on Office96." See what was done there? Everyone got something. When talking to Windows we emphasized the dedicated Chicago team. When speaking across DAD and especially to marketing, we emphasized the 85% on Office96.

Depending on perspective, this was either a relief, albeit still a high cost to pay to get moving on Office96, or a total snub aimed at Chicago. "What, only 15 percent of the team!?" One view was that the unreliability of the Chicago schedule was such that to "sacrifice" any more resources would not be prudent. The worst case would be, ironically, if Chicago did hit the date, then too many people trying to do too much in Office would never finish within 30 days.

A different view was that 15 percent was hardly sufficient. Chicago was aiming to be the most important release for consumers (Windows NT was for business) and since the Office business was still a consumer-driven phenomenon it didn't make sense to be so frugal. In the 15 percent there was a lot for Systems to dislike. If the requirement was to ship simultaneously and reliably with Chicago, then a small team doing the minimal amount was the most prudent, though such thinking was never in line with how Systems worked, which was an "all in, or not in" mindset.

More importantly with DAD, the major with the Office96 part of the plan was the general view that 15 percent of the resources, reductions on top of the shift to OPU, would significantly impact the ability to be competitive within categories, a further reminder about the teams being reduced to "fund" OPU.

If your head is spinning reading this, then you can see why the whole plan of 12/24 was causing heads to spin and adding in the animosity (or just complexity) of the new OPU and shift to suites only made things worse.

We still needed a way to structure the detailed schedule. Normally we would have three milestones of about 10 weeks each. Given the mandate to sync with Chicago the schedule worked out to a single development milestone, instead of the traditional three-milestone schedule. Not only was a small portion of the team on the project but they would be doing a lot less work. Aside from syncing up the final date, the other issue was being available for pre-release testing on the Chicago schedule as they were going to want reviewers to see proof of 32-bit applications. This requirement further justified the schedule and resource constraints. That did little to appease Systems that felt we were totally hedging.

Without a feature list or specification written, things seemed shaky. Picking dates with resource levels set is the first rule of shipping.

Up until this point, most Apps releases had been dictated by the improvements in *ease of use* while adding productivity features that were the most logical next steps—there was innovation in category features across Word and Excel, but there was also a decade of history in the category, whereas PowerPoint was still establishing the category and faced different challenges. While most of 94/96 was chosen on business and customer grounds of the apps, the prioritization of what to do was heading in a new direction with the emphasis of the suite. There was a great deal of momentum in both the organization and the processes. It was easy for apps, even with fewer people, to keep going down the same path, and it also seemed right from a business perspective. A new product category demanded new investments and new priorities.

Office94 was about Chicago, that was clear, but what did that mean for the category? It would also be the first release of Office to ship all the products on time, which was unique. Office94 would provide marketplace evidence of an integrated suite of products by shipping at the same time with some specific work aimed at demonstrating its suite nature. Reviews were still written by category, though that now included a new category called suites. By and large the yearly magazine issue devoted to word processors or spreadsheets was one of the top sellers of the year. It would seem we needed category features to fill those pages and indirectly meet demands of customers and win reviews.

Times were changing, though. The key insight for building a suite, versus selling a suite, was that customers were placing value on the integration and consistency across the component products. Given the origin of suites as product bundling plus discount and the penetration of business software at the time, it was no surprise that the early value propositions from all the vendors centered on ease of use just as the category products did. For suites, however, ease of use was evaluated by user interface consistency, the idea being that consistency made products easier to learn and thus easier to use. Technologically the idea was that if the products shared code between them to accomplish consistency, then using more than one product would also consume fewer system resources, like memory. It was still all too common for Windows users to see "Out of Memory" error messages and those became more common as users were encouraged by suites to run multiple products at once. There was the architectural synergy, minimal memory footprint, and code-sharing that BillG championed.

Office94 had no time for any major architectural investments. In need of constraints, another constraint was added: Office94 would not change the file format (.DOC and .XLS) and would rely on the same format as just released for Office 4.x. This became the mother of all constraints, as both a positive and negative. Today I recognize this seemingly obscure issue, the details of a .DOC or .XLS file seem far removed from anything that could matter, but in reality, that was not the case at all.

Here's why: Through the entirety of applications on PCs from the start, new releases of products nearly always meant new file formats. With that change came the pain of making sure old files could be read and displayed and the experience of saving new files as the old format (to a floppy, for example, to give to someone) and alerting users when something would not work on the old version. While many assumed this was a conspiracy and some sort of theory of obsolescence, in reality changing formats was directly related to the underlying implementation of files. For the most part the file formats of apps represented a direct mapping of the internals of the product and what was stored in memory—in fact, in Word the file format was literally a type of *virtual memory*. There was neither a level of abstraction nor a mechanism to interpret data that the app did not know about. This clever invention was from CharlesS and something he brought with him from Xerox PARC and was a huge favorite of BillG, who knew all the details of the architecture.

Decades later, the idea of a file format seems rather arcane or even crazy. For the first two decades of the PC era, files were everything—files on hard drives, files on floppies, files on network drives, files on the Windows desktop and in folders, files on USB memory sticks, files in email attachments, files burned on to CD-ROM discs. Files were synonymous with work and files required a program. Thus, file formats created a virtuous cycle for users or network effect in modern jargon. The more people used an app and shared files, the more their coworkers benefitted from using the same updated version of the product. And yes, Microsoft benefitted too. To many in the regulatory world this looked and smelled like locking in customers. To us it seemed like a natural and beneficial *feature*. Over time there would be diverging views internally at Microsoft over how critical or even appropriate *leveraging* this feature would be, as we shall see.

Today many have probably tried to explain *files* to a student who has only used Google applications and found doing so about as awkward as explaining linear television or fax machines. Except for the occasional PDF or those companies still operating with attachments in email, files are seemingly extinct for non-engineers.

What this constraint implied to the members of the Office suite was that Office 95 would not have any features significant enough to justify a file format change. People could hardly imagine what features might be dreamed up without a way to save them to a file—every interesting feature was tied in some way to saving it in the file.

Fortunately, the needs for Chicago started to echo the needs of 32-bit native applications on Windows NT. The list of work was short and easy to articulate and measure. Everything seemed doable, though there were many concerns about the customer value beyond validating Chicago. I spent a lot of time shutting across the street to the Chicago dev hallway sort of reverse engineering what would ultimately become the "Windows Logo Requirements" or the minimal set of features that an application needed to implement to pass a third-party certification and receive a "Designed for Windows" logo for the box. Bill was anxious about the specifics of a list of features that apps would implement to be purpose-built for Chicago. The next chapter goes into details.

Apps needed to move to 32-bits. Chicago was going to represent the transition, requiring 32-bits and a 386 processor, which could come from Intel or AMD. While this sounded easy enough, there was a big problem.

Requiring 32-bits and an '386 meant that Office94 could *only* run on Chicago and new Windows NT PCs. Much of the market and marketing for Office was to get existing customers to upgrade—that consumed most all of the outbound efforts. The cost of a new PC was significant and adding on the cost of Office *at the same time* seemed exorbitant. For example, upgrading a 2MB of memory machine to 4MB might cost $200 in chips often specific to the computer plus the time and effort to install and configure. PCs required screwdrivers to open and often memory was tricky to install, resulting in blood-drawing scrapes from sharp metal within the PC case. This added up to a release without many new features that required a new computer purchase, which felt like a loser, or at least risky. Fortunately, it was only 15 percent of the team. Office96 continued on this level of commitment as well, which created a good deal of angst. So, 100% of our resources were committed to 32-bits.

In order to believe in this choice, one had to believe that the number of new PCs and the number of people new to computing with Chicago would be so great that the upgrade market opportunity would be much smaller. That was an enormous bet. In the world of business this was the kind of bet known as *burn the bridge*. Once placed, there was no turning back. It was also the kind of bet BillG loved to make for Apps, as he did with Excel on Windows and with the internet. What we (and everyone at Microsoft) did not know at the time, was that getting a first PC with Windows 95, specifically to "get online", would be a generational force that would make all of these conversations and concerns look downright silly.

This was a huge choice. Importantly, it was not the same choice our primary competitors were making. They were collectively still seemingly reluctant to go all-in on 32-bit Windows the way we were in Office. Chicago to most established vendors represented yet one more operating system from Microsoft they needed to deal with.

From summer of 1994 through the release of Office94, the DAD leadership team, sometimes called the *gang of 10,* wore two hats, Office94 and Office96. Every day, every moment seemed to be a context switch between releases.

What we did not anticipate was how that 15 percent would consume so much of the team.

What I didn't anticipate was that we somehow ended up being so successful at convincing people not to worry about 12/24 that soon people like NathanM were suggesting a far better strategy was something like 12/24/48/60—that we should be building four different products in parallel including one that was 5 years out. It was too soon to be intoxicated with our own success, but such fantastical discussion was just getting started.

Far more important was actually delivering Office 95 as **one product for the very first time**.

1995

Sharing code and processes to build Office pays off and the concept of the suite takes hold in the market. The Windows schedule becomes a death march to finish what is hoped to be a revolutionary new operating system. Netscape IPOs in the summer of 1995, weeks before the public availability of Windows 95.

035. WINDOWS 95, AUGUST OR BUST

Office94 had a plan in place, with a date and resources, as well as the major architectural bets of 32-bits and suite. There was so much focus on getting started and the resource constraints so extreme that, while this was the first release of an Office *product,* it would also be the last release for which the planning was fully distributed to each team with little centralized effort.

The organization was set with a feature team for each product and one in OPU. For the most part, the feature team leads were running this project, at least from the start, as the more senior leaders were supposed to focus more on Office96. Putting in place the plan for Office96 happened in parallel with a different set of people and a lot more attention from the BUMs. Unless there was something specifically troubling, for the most part Office94 was flying under the radar of DAD and had almost a skunkworks feel to it, at least at the start. That did not last long, for me.

As the new PM leader in Office, I was wearing two hats juggling both releases—in hindsight the first 12 months in Office were probably the time I put in the most hours working as I was learning how to manage managers for the first time, not to mention learning the DAD ways of working.

While I was juggling, among our team of about 15 program managers Mike Conte (MikeCon) was the primary program manager on OPU driving Office94. Mike joined the Excel team after experience running his own Macintosh startup. On Excel, he was a key to Excel gaining adoption at large customers, especially banks. A true New Yorker, Mike wore all black and had a no-nonsense attitude. He laid the groundwork for the release, but early on moved to a new role on the Windows team. He easily transitioned the release work to Heikki Kanerva (HeikkiK.) Products had a formal management team that was ultimately accountable, but each release saw people step up and take on the informal leadership required for complex cross-group work. This was Heikki's release to step up.

Heikki was a Finnish Olympic-caliber skier who found his way to Microsoft by studying business and computer science on a scholarship to the University of Alaska, after mandatory Finnish military service on a submarine. He joined DAD in the shared interoperability group and cut his teeth on shipping the enormously complex OLE technology. As it turned out, Heikki had absolutely the perfect demeanor to lead all of the teams through shipping the first synchronous release of Office. He was unflappable and possessed a military precision and the dedicated work ethic of an Olympian. And when needed, he could make light of a situation with a Finnish submariner expression that did not translate well at all into business English or, frankly, polite company.

Heikki led the newly formed Office-wide project meetings—the first time that key managers across all the apps assembled routinely to make progress on work. These meetings started off weekly and then as milestones approached, daily and then twice daily. While this was only a few people at the beginning, it was the organizational and cultural shift required to begin to operate as a suite, not as a bundle. These meetings became the operating heartbeat of the team, not a tax while the real work happened elsewhere.

I know it seems ridiculous to mention that we scheduled a weekly meeting for a new project, but up until this point creating Office essentially flew under the radar without an operational motion.

From an engineering perspective, the move to 32-bits was fairly smooth especially since much of the work had been done earlier in the side projects of making native apps for Windows NT as proofs of concept and to make them available for sale later. From a practical perspective, however, the transition to 32-bits hit Microsoft where it cared the most, performance. If there was one thing deep in the culture of the company, it was squeezing the most out of the scarce compute resources of CPU and memory. The move to 32-bits was inevitable, but the impact on performance was counter-intuitive.

In moving all the apps to 32-bits, no surprise but all the code got twice as big. And much of the data stored in memory got twice as big. Moving all that around made things slower. Crazy. For Office, 32-bits didn't mean very much—Word already handled long documents, and spreadsheets could be pretty big. These products grew up in extremely limited memory. In fact, many of our own tests were showing that the 16-bit versions of apps performed better on Windows 3.1 and were even a bit slower on Chicago. That's because Chicago was also going through this widening experience with the operating system code. Everything was expanding. Except the *system requirements*, the amount of memory a PC required for Chicago and Office as printed on the box.

It didn't take long for fingers to start pointing. That's natural. The real issue was not necessarily the benchmarks which over time would tend to work themselves out (we hoped) but just how much memory was required to get reasonable performance. The key market promise for Chicago was that customers could upgrade their Windows 3 systems to Chicago and things would get better, but if those systems had only 4MB of memory or yikes 2MB then these systems would be horribly slow, and even more so if they also upgraded Office.

PCs were not only expensive in the 1990s, but they were also treated as capital expenses by companies. They had 5-year lifecycles, amortization schedules, and an expectation that the software could change over time without expensive and very difficult or impossible to implement hardware upgrades. Upgrading memory required a day or more of downtime, a "truck to roll" with a tech, and probably hundreds of dollars of hardware.

There was not much we could do about this but continue to work to reduce memory usage. There were some significant efforts in tools and analysis and some amazing work across Windows and Office to make things work on 4MB, but ultimately 8MB was "recommended" versus "required." This fell short of the 2MB Windows 3 required. As it would turn out, doubling the system requirements for each release of Windows became the norm as I would point out in about 12 years when we launched Windows 7. Office trended remarkably well and for many releases, the typical Office application of Word, Excel, and PowerPoint did not substantially increase requirements.

While reviewers and people in stores immediately noticed the system requirements as that was often the first aspect of a new release to check out, the main feature visible to people using Office would be long file names. In hindsight, it is hard to believe that for the first 15 years of MS-DOS computing, human beings tolerated naming their work with cryptic 8-character names. Still, Microsoft email names continued to be 8 characters.

Dealing with these 8.3-character names forced people to create all sorts of algorithms for naming files. While the convention was that the three characters after the period would determine which product created the file, there was nothing in MS-DOS or subsequently Windows or Chicago that required that, an area where Macintosh continues to be better, even to this day. As a result, companies created rules for how files should be named. For example, all the reports for the fourth quarter might be BUDGET.Q4, DETAILS.Q4, SUMMARY.Q4 for the spreadsheet, word file, and presentation instead of the default .XLS, .DOC, and .PPT. Chicago was moving to a model where the final characters of the name, the creating program, was hidden in the interface as had been done on the Macintosh from the start.

Even though such a change was long requested or desired, as with everything Microsoft did the pain of the *installed base* and embedded resistance to change always seemed to make a showing. A major bank once sent me a long feedback memo explaining how the pre-release test of Office for Chicago made their convention difficult to use and considered it a "showstopper" bug—long file names broke how they sorted all their quarterly documents in folders. A showstopper was a bug believed to be so bad that a product could not ship, and in our case meant it would not be purchased. Being able to use hundreds of characters to name a file was at first viewed as a negative by some, despite being so liberating. The feature of not needing to worry about the last three characters of the name was a feature, or so we thought, not a bug as the customer thought. Ultimately people adjusted, but this served as a reminder of how difficult transitions are even when the benefit is readily apparent.

Between 32-bits and long file names we believed we had landed most of the critical features to support Chicago. There was a long list of small changes as well, which we often tagged in our RAID database with the source "TT" for "tiny and trivial." As Chicago made more progress the list seemed to grow in scope. And everything that came up was viewed as a "Pri 1" (priority 1 in RAID) work item by the Windows team for Office to do. There was a strong belief that if Office did not implement something then no other developers would—and within Microsoft there was no confusion over who was driving the agenda.

As the schedule marched through 1994, it became clear that the features we were implementing to be more of a Chicago application were helping us to become more of a consistent suite. Even though we were struggling across the Apps and OPU to become consistent the even bigger stick of Windows made it possible to drive some features that we otherwise would not have done.

Working with Chicago

While not central to the product experience but very visible the Microsoft Office Manager (MOM), a tiny little bar of buttons that floated in the upper corner of the screen that enabled one to switch between apps with a single mouse click, was a surprisingly popular feature of 16-bit Office. This feature came about when a college-hire program manager, Dean Hachamovitch (DHach), quickly prototyped this solution to a common problem on Windows 3.x before there was a Start menu or taskbar, and it proved so interesting that it was completed using contract developers and shipped with Office 4.x, becoming something of an early symbol of Office and later copied by Lotus—by demonstrating that Office was more than a bundle but a seamlessly integrated set of tools. With Chicago, this feature had dubious value because of the enhancements to the OS, but removing it was certain to be a customer pain point—it was common for IT to build lessons and documentation around features to be used in training, and every major change involved reworking such in-house curriculum.

A new Office program manager, David Tuniman (DavidTu), spent most of the release trying to devise a useful and appropriately strategic evolution of MOM. He was constantly running back and forth from building 17 to the old single-X Windows buildings to find some way to integrate and show off Chicago. Ultimately, he arrived at the Office Shortcut Bar, OSB, which did the same thing as MOM but took advantage of the new Chicago feature called *shortcuts*—and once again turned out to be rather popular with IT, much to our surprise. We know this because when we removed it from a future release we received a lot of complaints.

We worked across Windows and Office to build on the new capabilities of Chicago. That was the win-win. OSB was a feature that just kept expanding and adding significant complexity and exposing a ton of issues in Chicago. Reviewers and customers were enamored with OSB even though in the end it almost entirely overlapped in capability with the Windows Start menu.

After the "work on Chicago" features, there were two major themes for the product release, though to be fair none of this was determined before the products were being built—the constraints of time and not changing the file format dictated what work could be done and the themes arose by packaging those ex-post. The themes were *consistency* by showing off the suite and IntelliSense, or a doubling down on doing things *automatically* introduced in Office 4.

Extending AutoCorrect from Word 6.0 to Excel and PowerPoint marked some of the first shared user interface and functionality across the suite, and keeping with the idea of making the Suite paramount for everyone the Word team took the lead on making this work happen. This did not come without battles. As expected, Word had ideas for expanding the feature beyond Word 6.0, given how wildly popular it was. PowerPoint was fine with the feature but could have easily done without shared code. Of course, the Excel team put up a fight because not only did they resist the shared code, but the whole concept of AutoCorrect scared the team—the potential to introduce errors as text was automatically inserted that was different than the person typed, by accident perhaps. The result was a shared AutoCorrect feature that was a subset of the new implementation in Word, but importantly the list of customized entries was shared across the product. In hindsight this seems so small today, but monumental at the time. When we did the first all team demonstration it registered with a round of applause.

Consistency was something many had identified (including me with my memo on SmartSuite) and seemed relatively easy enough. But doing the work bumped up against how different the users of each product were, or so each product team liked to mention.

We did not embark on sharing a lot of new code to achieve user interface consistency and would save that for Office96. There were several initiatives that proved critical to market reception (and perception) as well as developing a suite muscle in program management. Importantly, the constraints pushed us to pick "high-value targets" for consistency.

The most visible user interface in the products were the two main toolbars—the one with all the basic commands (file open/save, print, and clipboard) and the one with all the common formatting commands such as bold, italic, and center. For the most part, what goes on these toolbars was the result of studying people using the product and what resulting documents looked like and reverse engineering the commands used. While everyone might be different, the top commands are consistent enough that we could design toolbars to be the same. Right out of the box we had a big step forward in consistency. Each app could also have room for its own tools as well. For example, Excel had tools for drawing borders and using the new Maps feature, Word would have some buttons for new IntelliSense features, and PowerPoint emphasized the ability to include content from Word and Excel in slides. In many ways, the choice of these buttons were the earliest days of today's "growth hacking" as we primarily populated the toolbars with common features, but every once in a while included something new or strategic in hopes of driving awareness.

I am skipping a lot of steps. Achieving consistency in toolbars was a historic battle that took years and several releases to get us to even some marketable level of consistency in this release. Originally, even the icons used were points of pride across different applications. For example, Word originally chose a piggy bank icon for the Save. It was only after realizing that such an icon did not share the same meaning around the world that Save was immortalized as a now obsolete floppy disc. There was a debate over little text bubbles appearing above buttons providing a long description of the graphical button, called tooltips, should they be yellow or white, and how big? Excel and Word each had different ideas on using color in icons—was color useful, necessary, or a distraction would occupy program manager battles for a full product cycle. The teams could not agree on how many pixels toolbars should use, should they be 15 or 16 pixels? While seemingly nitpicking, the premier demonstration of Office 4 routinely showed off this disagreement when switching between Word and Excel and a little 1-pixel shift would cause the demo to jitter, intentionally so to speak. The newly formed OPU led the charge towards a consistent and unified experience starting with toolbars, but it did not end there.

If the toolbar was the most visible, then the file open dialog was the most used dialog and also was horribly inconsistent across products. In the MS-DOS era, the experience of opening a file was viewed as primary competitive advantage and major topic in product reviews. The Mac made this relatively obsolete because apps used a file dialog provided in the Mac operating system. Interestingly, Windows did not have a common interface for this available to developers until Windows 3.11 so the idea of competing on this interface still existed. Windows 95 had built-in interfaces to use, but by then there was a challenge in that competitors to our apps were not using them and all apps needed more advanced capabilities. For any other vendor, the idea would be to win and not worry about what Windows was doing. For Office, what Windows was doing mattered, and we had a mandate to consistently use the Windows dialog and to win in reviews. Having the Windows feature pushed on us in such a critical area was annoying, especially with so few on Windows committed to helping us win competitively.

We created a separate team to build a superset of the existing experiences across Word, Excel, PowerPoint and then use the ability to customize the new Chicago File Open to build a robust and consistent File Open user interface. In addition, they would inadvertently create a small feature that would become one of the all-time great areas of complexity for Microsoft across Office, Windows, and Server—an accomplishment few small teams could match. The feature came about because WordPerfect had done a fantastic job with search for MS-DOS and was certainly going to bring it to Windows—and Chicago.

The team built a mechanism that indexed the files on a hard drive and made it easy to quickly retrieve files based on searching for content. Internally, we called this *personal Lycos* after the earliest internet search engine. For Office94, it was a small button in the new File Open dialog and a small utility program called *Find Fast.* When the PC was not being used, the program started up and read through files and built the index—this was a great way to make use of all the unused processing power of a Chicago PC. But it also became one of the first features that stressed the performance of early battery-powered Chicago laptops, with slow hard drives and limited memory.

The problem was twofold. First, people thought their PCs were possessed by demonic forces or, worse, a virus because the disk activity light popped on and the PC started making the grinding hard drive noise even when not being used. Second, laptops generally had about two hours of battery life at best, and this reduced that even more. We were fast running into trouble with this feature, but at the same time we received tons of positive feedback from early users, especially reporters and writers where the feature worked best. Down the road this would cause more "trouble" because it was clearly something that Windows should have for all apps, not just Office, and Windows Server should do something to compete with Lycos. Things were newly getting started with this technology, and it would follow me all the way through to my time in Windows.

But we had a great and consistent File Open dialog with a new way to search for all the files gathering on ever-growing hard drives.

There was a lot more to the release. One thing we learned is that when you build a product out of a bundle, no matter how hard you sell the *sum of the whole is greater than the parts*, people want to see innovation in the parts. We also learned people like to see whole new parts of the bundle.

036. FANCY WIZARD AND RED SQUIGGLES

Using a PC mystified most people, even in the workplace. Features designed to assist or help customers were almost always viewed positively even necessary as part of product reviews in magazines. *Answer Wizard* was our first attempt at using *natural language processing* and early artificial intelligence techniques to provide assistance in using ever more complex products.

The early days of PCs were days filled with in-person courses to learn the products, and these had given way to 600-page books that filled the shelves at Barnes & Noble and Tower Books, regurgitating every feature, menu, and dialog box in alphabetical order. We had written thousands of pages, provided reference materials, created online "computer-based training," and more, but still the first days of the PC era were marked with too much complexity and too high a hurdle to begin to use. Most people buying a new computer were also enrolling in courses that met for a couple of hours every week for a month. Such courses were the upsell much like today's extended warranty.

One of the core problems was jargon. There are dozens of phrases in the user interface that look like words a normal person would know but used in a way only a techie might grok, a common techie expression for "to understand" that comes from *Stranger in a Strange Land*. For example, PowerPoint, a tool few were comfortable with or had any understanding of, defied any logical English (or other language) word. What is a "slide master" or a "meeting minder"? What's a "snap to grid"? The worst were features that were not so obscure but used English words in ways that most people could not understand, such as Word's "mail merge" or Excel's "lists." We used to joke that we could probably put the version of Office with German language menu commands in front of English speakers, and they probably wouldn't even notice the difference.

Answer Wizard was designed as a bridge between humans and computer jargon. If someone typed, "How do I send letters to a list?" Answer Wizard would find the Mail Merge feature without literally going through all the menu items trying things at random as a human might. Sometimes commonly used symbols in Word such as the pilcrow, ¶, were totally unknown to regular people who would type questions into Answer Wizard such as, "How do I get rid of the elephant character?"

Answer Wizard was a collaboration with Microsoft Research and proved to be the foundation of future work in Office96 being developed in parallel. Answer Wizard was the underlying technology of the natural language interface to what would become the Office Assistant, or Clippy. The official name was Clip-It but in this work we will use the informal and much more widely known name. The earliest research group at Microsoft was the natural language research group where they were working on big hard problems of translation and understanding. That technology was more than a decade away and ultimately delivered by Google. Instead, we collaborated with the MSR's first group of AI researchers using Bayesian mathematics to probabilistically select from among a set of choices. Basically, we tried to add an element of probabilistic guessing to the solution rather than relying on a traditional full text search or index.

The guessing was based on a small database of words not already in the index or help database that we could map to the various articles in the help system. We called these metanyms because they were not precisely synonyms but somewhat close in meaning. We brought together those who wrote documentation, called *User Education,* or UserEd, and for the first time they were working on much more technology baked into the product. We renamed the team and the effort and called it *User Assistance,* or UA. It would be a few more years until we stopped referring to customers and humans as *users,* as we would often remark that only one other industry called customers users.

One of the seemingly minor changes we made was that hitting the universal help key, F1, would always bring up Answer Wizard. We designed the new experience with a flashy animated icon, the first use of animation in Office, and even broke our own style guide with the font in the interface. Answer Wizard arrived as a feature just as people started typing queries into web search engines looking for help. Surprisingly, we quickly learned how much easier it was becoming to find answers to usage questions on the internet than it was within our own assistance features. Nevertheless, Answer Wizard proved to be one of our first suite-wide features and reinforced the commitment we had to making Office, not just the apps, the easiest to use product.

While the marketing story of Office94 was told through the lens of the suite and consistency and the few significant changes to the product we made in order to emphasize the suite, the constraints of not changing the file format and a small team led to some of the most innovative and memorable app features, under the guise of IntelliSense. Some of these seemed so small and trivial, yet they had to be invented at some point in history, and when they were they were often the work of a small set of people with a clever idea and the runway to get things done.

IntelliSense had become the branding moniker describing the intelligent features in Office 4. The canonical IntelliSense example was the newly introduced AutoCorrect, first released in Word 6.0 but brought to all the products in Office94. The feature was such a big part of Word 6.0 that the print advertising campaign for Word 6.0 often featured a large "teh" changed to "the." As with so many things that are incredibly helpful, it wasn't much work. The genesis of the feature was a remarkable story as it set a tone for developing data-driven features for years to come while also learning a great deal about global scale and sensitivities to users of vastly different backgrounds and cultures.

DHach joined the Word team straight out of Harvard's Math department as a program manager on the "basic use" team of Word, which was the part of the team tasked with making the product easier to use for core functionality versus improving use of long documents or fancy magazine layout features. Word already had many fascinating unused features. One of those features was the "glossary," which was a way to type a short phrase, hit a keystroke, the F3 key, thus explaining why no one used this feature, which would then replace the short phrase with the longer text. Dean's insight was that in English the spacebar could replace the awkward F3, and then he realized that he could prepopulate the list of glossary entries with a library of common typos and misspellings. This was the origin of correcting "teh" to "the" and hundreds of other words. Other insights included replacing the accidental caps lock key. For example, "dEAR sIR" turns into "Dear Sir" with caps lock turned off.

One of the more aggressive uses of AutoCorrect was turning off the "sticky" shift key, which caused typos at the start of sentences such as "THis is the start." Because so many acronyms were used in business and often with plurals, such as PCs, this feature was held back from Word 6 until an elegant solution could be devised for Office94.

As the first *do what I mean* feature, AutoCorrect was revolutionary. The key lesson in building automatic features was their value…when they worked. And when they did not, the frustration level soared. This tension over doing more for people while also not introducing errors and mistakes, or breaking muscle memory, was a theme in the evolution of IntelliSense and also proved to be a wedge issue with other products. For example, Excel resisted the idea of AutoCorrect for common formula typos because of the potential to insert the wrong formula or wrong reference to a named cell. This was a real concern but at times seemed somewhat stubborn from the OPU perspective. It was a classic example of "Excel users are different," to which the OPU refrain was "Why, because they don't make typos?" These would be worked out, but navigating these cross-group opinions was always time-consuming.

Given the success of AutoCorrect, it became a star feature of Office, embraced by all the applications with some app-specific constraints. Importantly, this feature was one of the first features shared across all the apps—the same typos got fixed the same way no matter where they were typed.

AutoCorrect could not catch everything, though—a lesson from Word 6.0 was that being too aggressive and making mistakes was far worse than leaving extra work for the user. As a result, AutoCorrect didn't replace traditional spellcheck, but the idea of helping automatically when possible informed us on ways to introduce a dramatic improvement to spelling correctly. In developing IntelliSense features, we learned that our corrections needed to be right 100 percent of the time—being wrong even a little bit felt to customers like we were wrong all the time. This is a lesson the industry continues to learn with today's autocorrect on phones.

Spellcheck was the original feature that distinguished word processors from typewriters. At first, most companies that sold word processors sold companion *spell checkers* often costing as much as the word processor itself. These largely competed among products by the size of spelling dictionaries and the ability to add custom dictionaries, such as legal or medical terms. Using these (and Microsoft's) spell checker was a *modal* experience, that is the user would invoke the spell checker and begin to identify and correct spelling errors one at a time unable to do anything else. This was time-consuming and frustrating—the process was stopped when a correction was needed and then restarted, and every falsely flagged word required the user to click on an "Ignore" button. A spelling error resulting in a substantial change often reset this process requiring a full scan of the document again.

Office94 took two major steps in spelling, AutoCorrect and background spelling, which became iconic Office features.

Originally, spellcheck was a feature of Word. There was never any thought given to using it in Excel, where there weren't a lot of words—another case of *Excel users are different*. Excel users had been evolving in their desire to use Excel all the time. On Wall Street, Excel was such a hammer that it was being used to nail nearly everything. One of the biggest new scenarios was using Excel to create *pitch books* for financial products. By removing grid lines and making clever use of fonts, borders, table widths, and the sophisticated macro programming that was a hallmark of Excel, one could create a pitch book without ever leaving the comfort of a spreadsheet. In Excel 3.0 there was even a presentation template that made Excel look like PowerPoint complete with animated transitions between slides which were really ranges of cells. It made sense, therefore, that adding spellcheck would finally become a useful feature.

Word, Excel, and PowerPoint adding robust spellcheck proved to be a nice addition and emphasized the suite. Word had created a breakthrough idea, which went on to be a universal feature anywhere people typed, background spellcheck or the ubiquitous little red squiggles under (mostly) misspelled words.

The origin of the feature was a product of multiple small ideas and thoughts that piled up over time, starting with an incredibly novel research approach the Word team had done using Word 6.0. Reed Koch (ReedK), a longtime program manager in DAD, was one of the early proponents of studying how people used the product in the real world. This was not as easy as it sounds before the internet and cloud computing. To study the product "in the wild," the Word team created a special variant of the product, called the *instrumented version,* or IV, which was the same product in the marketplace except it recorded what Word commands were used (menus, toolbar buttons, keyboard shortcuts, dialog box choices, and more) and in what order and frequency. Data was gathered from a small set of selected informed volunteers who knew that their actions (but none of the content) was being collected once we installed this special version on their computer. After a few weeks we returned to the customer site and collected the data, using a stack of floppy disks, and replaced the IV version with the regular product. This use of real-world data was a pioneering effort and formed the foundation of how the applications would collect and use data on the internet in just a few short years.

Program managers pored over the data and analyzed it (using Excel of course as well as Access because the datasets were so large), trying to understand patterns and places where customers were getting stuck, using too many steps, or failing to use a feature that would have made things easier. The wealth of insight gathered from this approach could not be underestimated and building IV versions became a significant part of customer research that led to many of the internet and cloud innovations in future releases.

Aside from learning things, like the fact that Print was the most common command more so than Save, or that as many people used each of the menu command, keyboard shortcut, and toolbar button for cut/copy/paste, or that features for assembling long documents (table of contents, index) were not frequently used—all of which most might think obvious—some important things were annoying users. One of those was the message that would pop up: "The spelling check is complete" with an OK button. It was a pointless message that did nothing but interrupt workflow, thousands of times.

In addition, the IV helped to inform the team that with great consistency, if during a spellcheck a suggestion for a misspelling was chosen as a correction then it was one of the first suggestions listed or it was ignored. This insight would form the foundation of one of the biggest advances in IntelliSense, spellcheck while typing. Getting to that feature required connecting a few dots.

Invisible to users, Word did work behind the scenes to keep the document up to date for printing while typing or reading. For example, if a document had page numbers and added text in the middle of a document caused flow to the next page, then in the *background,* without slowing Word down, page numbers were adjusted to *repaginate* the document. In a world of operating systems with limited memory and CPU, this was a nifty engineering trick. Essentially Word was its own mini operating system. Today we take for granted the ability of computers to do work in the background, but prior to Chicago this wasn't supported and took incredible trickery to pull off.

This was called the *idle loop*, because it was where the program looped or did nothing while a person was taking those tiny little breaks when typing or thinking. Could this background processing capability also check the spelling of documents without taxing the system and slowing everything else down? Writing code to take advantage of this idle processing power was somewhat of an art and the developers often referred to it as a devil's playground of sort—one wrong addition or ordering of background tasks and the whole thing would grind to a halt and be very difficult to debug.

PCs were getting more powerful, so much more powerful than when the original spellcheckers were programs purchased separately from word processors and run after typing simply because there was not enough memory on the computer. The first word processor I used was called WordStar and it came with a separate program called SpellStar to check spelling. It was cumbersome. Integrated spellchecking was a big improvement, but it was still *modal*—a separate step and manual operation. PCs were 100 times faster since SpellStar, but word processing documents had not grown at the same pace. What could the team do with the power that was otherwise sitting there idle?

Running the spellcheck in the background while typing was simply taking the idea of background processing to the next level. It was so important that background processing was a key part of the patent application. The implementation frustrated our partners on the Chicago team and at Intel who were evangelizing the idea of using Win32 *threads* as the way to add background processing. It also happened to be a feature of these modern operating systems and chips, but the overhead and complexity of rearchitecting for threads to support background spelling, printing, and pagination. was far too high for such a critical capability, especially when processors were already becoming far faster than required for editing.

The lesson from the IV was that showing the closest matching words from the dictionary using a convenient right-click menu would have a high likelihood of being correct. The red squiggles were simply reflective of a proofreader's style of mark, which was one of the early uses of color in the interface. Just in case, Word left the existing interface in the product for good measure. It also made use of the right click menu, which had been introduced across the products in Office 4 and had become a defining feature for power users.

The feature did need a way to communicate to users that "something was happening," and so a small animation was placed in the status bar of Word at the bottom of the screen. Originally the team wanted to use a tiny buzzing bee, as in "spelling bee." But as was quickly pointed out by the diverse team that made up Word, such an iconic representation did not translate to other languages and cultures. The result was a little notebook with a squiggling pencil. Whimsy was difficult at global scale.

The feature was not without critics. There was an unintended side effect of opening a document which was as soon as the background processing kicked in the misspellings were identified. Maybe it was a company name, or a city, or a product name but these all looked like misspellings particularly in a world of sharing email attachments when the custom dictionary was different on the other end. Word introduced a number of subtle tricks to help with this, such as not marking words until an edit and providing for an easy ignore button that would unmark the incorrectly flagged text.

Still some people were so frustrated they wrote letters (actual letters) to BillG to complain and those would invariably end up in my inbox. Often these were just irate at proper names being flagged as misspellings, such as from members of the Phenis family who often exchanged letters and did not like to see their name underlined, and they especially did not like the suggestion. We quickly removed the offending suggestion in the next update. The letters back and forth continued for some time as the product update took a while to reach all customers.

Sometimes things got a bit over the top. A public radio broadcaster hosting a music show from Oregon was rather irate each week as the playlist was assembled. Every time they cued up their favorite Queen of Soul the red squiggles offended them. Again, not just the squiggles but the alternate suggestion for Aretha Franklin was really what got them going. As you can sense from these two examples, the words referring to anatomy had to be reviewed even though Word was used by medical doctors and scientists all the time. The host threatened to "unleash the indignation" of their viewers if it was not fixed. The broadcaster was so annoyed they started sending the letters to their congressional representative claiming that Microsoft's monopoly power was to blame. That got me in a long thread with what I assumed at the time was a zealous intern. Once again, we removed the words and added names to the dictionary. I only had to endure one last broadcast where the host read the letters of the campaign's success on air.

While such letters were obviously not representative, they proved extremely important to Microsoft's culture. Most every product hallway had a wall of letters from customers, usually at the extremes of loving the product or incredibly awful experiences. Other than the instrumented versions in Office and the samples of telephone support calls, anecdotes were the primary real-world inputs. While there was a special product support phone number that executives could use to escalate an incident, the company did not have a systematic approach to the onslaught of problems that came from millions of customers, whether a problem was Microsoft's creation or not. Nevertheless, I enjoyed these letters and the dialog that came from replying, including the dozens of times I refunded the price of a product for whatever reason brought great frustration to a customer.

Background spelling with red squiggles ultimately became a showcase feature for the product and made the lofty phrase IntelliSense make sense to reviewers and customers. Groups all around the company asked for the IntelliSense code so they could add it to their products, not even realizing it was marketing. IntelliSense spawned endless jokes for wanting red squiggles under things in real life, as in "This idea should have red squiggles." In brainstorming sessions at a whiteboard, someone would invariably put red squiggles under a misspelling or lame idea. Scott McNealy, the founder and CEO of Sun Microsystems, famously joked that Microsoft had a whole team of people deciding on red for squiggles and an option to change it—his attempt at making a joke (misguided and incorrect) about bloated features people don't use. The feature became commonplace in every word processor and every browser and more.

037. CAPONE AND EMAIL WITHOUT TYPOS

Leading up to Windows 95 shipping was probably the most explosive era in product development in Microsoft history. Whole new divisions, lines of business, and products were springing up so fast it was often difficult to keep track. It wasn't just the strategic clarity of focusing on Windows, but also expanding Windows into new areas from automobiles to televisions, from markets as far flung as hospitals to passenger aircraft, not to mention the global expansion of the ever-expanding sales force.

Compounding this was the Internet. It wasn't just that every one of these new efforts was capitalizing of the Windows strategy that was finally approaching market readiness. It was also, and perhaps more important, that each effort also lead the way in embracing the Internet.

While most everyone outside of Microsoft would aim their concerns at the "The Internet" icon on the Windows 95 desktop (appearing first in the OEM service release), the ownership and strategy behind that was all contained within one team in one division, Windows. The real battle, or more appropriately consternation and endless debate, would take place over a much less discussed desktop icon, "Inbox"—the email client application that could connect to Microsoft's two email products, the legacy MS Mail and the not-quite-finished enterprise mail product, Exchange, as well as what was then called *internet mail* or email that used standard internet protocols such as POP3 or IMAP.

Unlike a WWW browser, building the company's email strategy lacked a singular organizational focus. Rather, it was more of a classic strategy of permissiveness and letting many flowers bloom, an approach that Microsoft would employ repeatedly for product areas such as photos, messaging, collaboration, and more. When something was cool or the next big thing, it always seemed as though every group would somehow manage to find the resources to squeeze it into their strategy. Eventually, in the 1990s every part of the company had an email strategy: Windows, Online/Consumer, Servers, and Applications. Those didn't always align or even work well together.

Windows, like OS/2 and Unix and soon Macintosh, was like every operating system and assumed that connecting to standard internet protocols for email was important. Even though by email accounts, most consumers were reading email in America Online (AOL) or one of the other online services, these protocols were wildly popular with Internet Service Providers (those providing dial up access directly to the internet without the information services of an online company) and small businesses. About a year after Windows 95 shipped, the team released "Microsoft Internet Mail and News" (code name Athena) which would go on to become one of several extremely popular email clients for customers using internet protocols.

Online/Consumer was building the Microsoft Network which of course had email. The email experience relied on a purpose-built mail server, custom protocol, and mail interface that would power the @msn.com email addresses. In a short time, the same group would acquire Hotmail, which provided free email directly through any WWW browser with an internet connection. The team would spend quite some time reconciling the implementation of this strategy.

Servers, the division building the back-office products powering the client/server strategy for business, was the home of the team building EMS as previously discussed. The team was primarily made up of hardcore server or backend developers focused on scale, reliability, and performance. EMS had many more email features than could be supported through internet protocols, such as calendaring, sharing mail folders, and enterprise-level security. To support those EMS had its own proprietary protocol or API, which meant it needed to build its own email client. So, they did.

Applications, specifically the Office team, ended up part of this effort by a re-organization in mid-1994. There was a second email client effort going on code-named *Ren & Stimpy* (mail and scheduling) to be a full replacement for MS Mail and Schedule+. Since these were mostly distributed as part of the Office product, it seemed to make sense that the team should move to Applications. This was an early version 1.0 product and far from shipping. The EMS team grew increasingly frustrated with the product compared to their own Capone effort. Ren seemed to tax the EMS server significantly more than Capone. So, out of sight and out of mind.

From a business perspective, the largest competitor in email appeared to be Lotus Notes, which was gaining traction and with the recent 4.0 release showed a revamped user experience and focus on email and strong connections to the internet. I attended the yearly conference in Orlando and left suitably concerned. Ultimately, IBM acquired Lotus just a few weeks before the Windows 95 launch, cementing Notes as the premier competitor to both Office and Windows. *The New York Times* front page covered the deal along with several adjacent stories about the magnitude of this deal, financially and strategically.

Notes created the workgroup or groupware category, something Microsoft could not seem to get right. A variant of Windows, *Windows for Workgroups*, offered some networking features but had little to do competitively. Office had several packages done as add-ons to Excel to enable workgroup activities such as budgeting, but those too missed the mark. Visual Basic was being used to create collaborative applications and was going to be a key part of the EMS strategy, but that was far off and not the focus of the Languages team. The addition of *Inbox* to Windows 95 would be yet another attempt at turning up the competitive heat against Lotus with something neither core to a product team nor complete in execution.

What Lotus had done with Notes was create a product that was not squarely aimed at any existing Microsoft product. In fact, it landed between all of the groups. That meant on some days any group could simply ignore Notes and on others it could claim it was aiming straight for it in a competitive sense. Ultimately no one was accountable, and everyone could point to someone else.

In many companies, people look to executive management to clarify overlapping or incoherent strategies, especially in technology companies where we love to have all the pieces fit together well. In times of rapid change and high uncertainty, however, most leaders prefer to maintain optionality and prefer the costs of internal organizational scuffles to the potential cost of having the wrong solution. This was decidedly BillG's approach, which for all the bravado of review meetings he avoided at all costs making a binary choice between two groups and preferred to leave the differences to some natural course. It was as if he had hoped a Notes competitor would magically appear from within a group already tasked with competing with an entirely different company or product.

This drove me (and many) crazy, but as I reflect on this in hindsight it is only hindsight or *told-you-so* recollections that allow people to say they knew we should have done something different. No one knew how email would turn out, we just knew we wanted to be a big player.

Office had yet another view on email. It wasn't as much an interest in building an email client as it was that email seemed to be positioned to replace the core use of our product, which was creating documents, spreadsheets, and presentations. In 1994, email was in the early days of making its way through the corporate world. When email was in use, as it was at Microsoft, it was clear that the role of the traditional 10 – to 20-page business memo was declining. Our instrumented version of Word confirmed a gradual decline in short documents once email was in use. What used to be done as short memos printed and circulated in interoffice mail was being replaced by email.

At first this was somewhat terrifying for the most used anchor of the suite, but additional research showed that Word was still used for the most important and valuable documents, and often longer documents, created by multiple authors. In the pre-internet era this was some comfort for the team. The question remained, though, what, if anything, should be done about short documents? How could Office participate in email without being yet another group developing an email client application? We were just getting our minds wrapped around Ren & Stimpy, but that did not yet have a schedule and seemed more like a far-off project.

The Capone client was basic and while it was primarily (some would say exclusively) about EMS, it was also being pushed to be a stellar example of a Chicago application. By stellar, it meant that the user interface for mail needed to look like the Chicago file explorer and reuse as much of that code as possible. While there was little top-down direction over reducing the proliferation of email clients and servers, there was an intense focus on Capone being a great Windows 95 application.

This design, appearing to users like the file explorer, had been a key goal of BillG's for years and was at the heart of his mission for a universal *shell* as sought after in the Cairo project. I was never a fan of building shells—they aren't that important and frankly people make too big a deal out of them, but I was in the minority and much of Microsoft embraced the idea of shells. The shell was "just a place people have to go to in order to launch Excel and Word," something ChrisP always said. I would later experience firsthand the high levels of emotion people attached to launching programs when introducing Windows 8.

Capone was far behind the proposed Chicago ship dates of early 1995, primarily because the mail server product was as well, though Capone could theoretically connect to other mail servers, which would justify inclusion with Chicago. In Chicago, Capone was named Inbox and received an icon on the desktop (that was really difficult to delete) representing the importance of mail for Chicago. Capone had a relatively simple text editor for creating mail messages, supporting only the basics of typing and formatting.

The Word team, especially Peter Pathe (PPathe) and Ed Fries (EdF), were fascinated with the idea of replacing the email editor with Word. PPathe (or his nickname Blue, which was also an email alias) originally joined Microsoft to lead what became all of the efforts around typography and printing. A veteran of the Boston tech scene (and both Caltech and MIT), Blue was a rarity in that he had experienced all of the ups and downs of the PC industry outside of Microsoft while at the same time came to the company with deep domain expertise, having worked on innovative PC software before Microsoft.

EdF was carved out of the same mold as ChrisP and JonDe, and often the three of them were thought of in the same breath. EdF joined Microsoft in the mid-1980s and was already an Apps veteran who had famously created fish-themed software including co-authoring a famous screen saver. He was leading the Word development team, which was the largest Apps team, and had successfully led the team through the groundbreaking Word 6.0 release. Ed would later go on to become a pioneer in Xbox and a legend in the gaming industry.

EdF routinely described his goals for Word and mail as, "What could be more magical than, all of a sudden, my email didn't have typos and it was easy to add bullets?" Routine today, back then it was magical—and costly.

Mike Angiulo (MikeAng) was a new hire in OFFPM, assigned to design this feature and to make it work. That put him at the center of storm between WGA, Chicago, Word, and the Office test team measuring performance. WordMail, as it was called, was the ability to use Microsoft Word as the editor for email messages. It ultimately became a grand slam of cross-group coordination, but also of finger-pointing.

Over several months, there were more complexities than one could count. The API to reuse Word's editor was known as *DocObject* and was part of broad plans to enable Office apps to be used in web browsers. If a link opened a Word document, then Word could open up inside the browser like if it was an HTML page. This approach was countered by the Netscape *plug-in* API, announced after weeks of negotiations over whether Netscape would freely license this API for use in Navigator. This was my one experience with Netscape that would play a tiny and mostly irrelevant though memorable part of the future antitrust trial. In 1998, the Department of Justice (DOJ) and twenty State Attorneys General would sue Microsoft, resulting in a long-running regulatory dispute. DocObject itself was based on the enormously complex OLE interfaces, which JonDe and team tried to make perform in 4MB of memory after the decision was made to stick with OLE when I was working for BillG.

The Capone client was not ready for primetime, and the interfaces and capability to extend it were no more ready than the rest of the product, including EMS. The problem was identifying where the problem rested. The Capone team had been benchmarking performance with EMS, measuring both memory used on Chicago and a somewhat mysterious item known as an RPC. An RPC, *remote procedure call,* was a request to the Exchange server to do something—retrieve a message, sort an inbox, or lookup an address. Using Capone generated RPCs, and every RPC was one too many as the server was trying to scale to hundreds of users. In other words, the best way to scale the server was to avoid calling on it to do work, at least that is how it seemed.

During the project there was a puzzling discontinuity between the development team and the executives who expressed increasing frustration over the tension between Office and WGA. Executives, it turned out, were insulated from the product performance challenges because their mail was hosted, *dogfooded*, on a special dedicated server named OXYGEN, that had far more capacity per user than the typical employee experienced. This special executive treatment gave the false impression of progress when we were, in fact, struggling.

Capone had gotten the number of RPCs to an acceptable level, and it didn't hurt that Capone was also on the same team as Exchange. When WordMail, coming from a different organization, was integrated into Capone the number of RPCs went up, mail messages got bigger because they had nice formatting not plain text, and a lot more memory was used because Word was running. The number of RPCs went up, and it was all WordMail and was unacceptable to EMS. MikeAng along with the dev and test teams spent months tracking down and removing what they could, and justifying what remained, to deliver Word as a mail editor.

The result was an insanely cool demo. Mail messages looked like fancy printed documents—so that one-page meeting agenda looked, once again, like what used to arrive by interoffice mail. Ultimately, the feature was too early for Exchange and too soon for 4MB or 8MB Chicago machines. The groundwork proved incredibly useful for Microsoft's next email product in Office96, as Capone led a short life. There was great vindication of this strategy by the end of 1995 when widely read and highly respected analyst Bill Gurley wrote about the arrival of rich email with color, graphics, and even letterhead. We were just early with a crazy implementation.

Coming into the summer of Windows 95, we had little to show to compete with Lotus Notes. The Inbox, with WordMail, would have little to do with the competitive battle for the backend of a modern enterprise. The parallel releases of Office94 and Office96 gave us a second chance for Office to compete with Ren & Stimpy, as we will see. The pain this optionality foisted on the product, marketing, and sales teams and even customers might eventually pay off. That is why when I reflect on all the craziness of the strategy, it is difficult to say it would have been easier—yes it could have been easier if only we knew the future.

038. DESIGNED FOR WINDOWS 95

By early 1995, the most important elements for the launch were determined. Chicago had picked an early summer RTM date. For Office, what had been "no more than 30 days later" was simultaneously shipping, which was awesome for the retailers and for the business. Windows had chosen the name Windows 95 and the idea of using the Rolling Stones's *Start Me Up* in future ads was floated. Things were really hopping, and everything went from uncertainty to terror in the sense that we truly needed to finish. We transitioned from a software team to a team gated by duplicated CD-ROM discs, assembling boxes, and distributing palettes of them around the world.

Office94 received the name *Microsoft Office Professional Designed for Windows 95 version 7.0* in a classic Microsoft naming bonanza, and to compound that there were other editions such as *Small Business* or *With Bookshelf* on the box. Everyone on the planet called it *Office 95*, including all of Microsoft at launch events. But there were real forces at work, such as the fact that the Product Support systems relied heavily on the actual version number of the program to route and track support calls. It was also kind of a funny name since the apps were each on different versions: Word 6.0, Excel 5.0, PowerPoint 4.0 Version 7.0 came from bumping the highest number product, Word 6.0, to the next version. In what was a big deal, we versioned all the apps to 7.0 (Excel 7.0, PowerPoint 7.0, Access 7.0), which seemed like a weird and often used marketing gimmick from the past era. In fact, it was to be Office for the first time and to simplify all the downstream systems that required real version numbers. And, because the company wanted only one 95 and that was Windows. All the clouds were visible on the box, but it was challenging to find a "95" without looking closely.

For the development team to fully feel the terror and pressure of the deadline, Robbie Bach, (RobbieB), the head of marketing for all of Desktop Apps, suggested I attend his weekly meeting where all the planning for the launch was being coordinated. My first reaction was rather immature, and I thought between Office 95 and Office96 I had enough to do on the product. In addition, we had a team reporting to ChrisP specifically set up as the interface between marketing and development, known as Product Planning and led by Mark Kroese (MarkK), who had been doing all the work to make sure the product SKUs, naming, and branding were accurately reflected in the software coordinating with product design as needed.

Despite my resistance, it proved to be a critical learning experience as the scale and complexity of an Office launch was nothing at all like the nice little events we had in Languages, and this was truly going to be, to date, the biggest of all launches and in hindsight the biggest one ever. Every week, I learned more small but important product issues—demo scripts that were not right, feature names that needed to be changed, concerns about localization, and good things to know like how much lead time one needed to rent out venues and the importance of mobilizing a global sales effort with the right sales tools and information. Everyone always says that PM and marketing need to work closely together, but until you experience the myriad of details marketing needs to get right it is abstract. What no one could have prepared me for was just how many of these details came crashing together under crazy deadlines at the end of the project. There was a great deal of learning.

One recurring theme in the marketing meeting was a desire for "more" evidence that Windows 95 and Office 95 [*sic*] were designed to work together. This was particularly frustrating because by far the biggest features were 32-bits, long file names, and shipping the whole thing on time. Nevertheless, as soon as we had a ship date, we also had a long list of Windows 95 integration feature requests. The list was not only long, but like a cake rising in the oven it seemed to be alternating between collapsing under its own weight and flowing over to make a total mess. Many of these details fell a growing list of "must have" features from the Windows team about what makes for a great Windows 95 application.

I was going back and forth every day between building 17 and the old buildings of the Chicago team—the shell team, networking, setup, and more—trying to figure out how important, how real, and what was the least amount of work needed to get things done. Seeing what was going on in our marketing team and knowing the realities of getting the code done, I felt I was mostly caught between these two incoming trains. Shipping big projects is as much a battle to say no and keep things in control as it is a schedule and crossing off work items. On the front lines, one always feels lonely—as though everyone else, every single other person from marketing to testing to PM to VPs, was coming to work every day to prevent the product from shipping on time. That's how I felt in these discussions.

Much of this late work was coming about because the specifics of integrating with Windows 95 were, finally, coming together. For a Windows 95 app, the basics of installation and, more importantly, uninstalling or removing the product, was a defining area. Removing a product from a PC was hit or miss until Windows 95 when it was required. Today I realize the idea of installing and uninstalling software is archaic, but before Windows 95 putting software on a PC was a one-way adventure. It was close to impossible to remove a product, uninstall it, and return the PC to what it used to be like. This was a huge source of customer frustration and PC flakiness.

In order to make sure that third-party products were well designed for Windows 95, the Windows team created a program called *Designed for Windows 95*. This program allowed third parties to have their products certified by an independent test agency and, upon passing, the products could be branded and marketed with a Designed for Windows 95 flag logo on the box.

This, as it turned out, was enough for marketing to feel like things worked together. Primarily this was because it seemed arduous and time-consuming enough that not everyone was going to have the logo on the first time.

On the other hand, there really wasn't much of an option. Office 95 had to pass these logo requirements. Windows was making a huge deal out of the logo. Historically, app developers looked to Office for ways to support Windows, but suddenly Windows was trying to tell Office what to do. App developers were looking to Office to be the first to support the logo and get the *Designed for Windows 95* flag. We didn't think it mattered much, but boy the Windows team and marketing thought it was important.

Because of our scale, the boxes were being designed and printed assuming this would happen. Looking at the final box it is kind of funny in that "Designed for Windows 95" appears five different times on the box plus it is in the detailed system requirements.

Logo requirements were somewhat of a moving target and many of them involved significant work. The logo program used an outside testing agency to verify products seeking logo approval, and companies had to pay for each test (and re-test)…even Office. The outside testing agency was particularly literal and nitpicking with Office 95.

There were dozens of requirements tested throughout the project, and the details of what was acceptable was refined all the time. Each time we ran the test we had to pay something like $1,000 to the agency. It was driving HeikkiK (Heikki Kanerva, the former Olympic telemark skier and Finnish submariner on the team) crazy. The closer we got to the deadline the longer it took to get results back because the agency was overwhelmed. The Windows team had rallied many independent vendors to earn the logo as well.

In Office we always felt there was a conspiracy against us in that we were held to a higher standard than third parties. It certainly felt through the whole logo test like we were aiming for a moving target. We wondered if our competitors had such a hard time.

Heikki, the ever calm, cool, and collected leader, by sheer force of will got us through this process, and we eventually received a passing mark. It was such a crazy experience that I had framed copies of the certification letter made for each of us. They remained on our walls for years.

The logo was one of many unplanned events that would mark the final six months of the project. Every day Heikki was convening the dev, test, and program manager leads for a status meeting. Heikki had no time for issues without resolutions and calmly kept moving the conversation forward. Every meeting people would bring up issues regarding our ability to ship, starting with the beta release or OPP, Office Preview Program. Heikki would look at them and calmly ask in his Finnish baritone, "Is that an OPP-stopper?" The answer was invariably no, and thus the issue was resolved.

No whining was allowed.

On July 14, 1995, just six weeks before launch we passed the logo requirement. I framed the letter we received for HeikkiK and we were relieved the frustration was over. This was literally under the wire because the scale of Windows was absorbing all the manufacturing and logistics available. Combined we ended up using a lot of air freight and overnight shipping to get boxes of both Windows and Office to the thousands of retail endpoints and distribution centers around the world for August 24.

039. START ME UP

By late July, Word, Excel, PowerPoint, the Office 95 suite (called *Office Standard*), and a number of other products from all over Microsoft were off to manufacturing. This only left four weeks for the manufacturing and airlifting of retail product all around the world. The baton had been passed to marketing and logistics.

Just after sign-off, I got a call from my mother that my grandfather was ill. I flew back to Miami immediately. Pop was 90 years old and up until then had been perfectly fine, walking miles every day around his North Miami condo complex, Point East. *Seinfeld* fans picture *Del Boca Vista*. Sitting beside his hospital bed, we talked about a lot of stuff. His biggest frustration was that Microsoft was not paying a dividend. He was a depression-era person with little faith in the rise of equity. He would often send me newspaper clippings and earnings press coverage via postal mail, something many of us experienced from our Greatest Generation relatives. That said, he also would place a bet on anything with a starting line or a clock and we had spent most of my vacations at the Hollywood Racetrack betting *his* numbers, 6 and 7 or 4 and 8, the birthday he shared with Grandma. His winnings paid for my nursery school and summer camps growing up. When it was time for me to leave, lying in his bed, he wished me a happy birthday, my thirtieth, and flicked his wrist at me and said, "Get out of here, don't worry about me." Two days after the Windows 95 launch event, I flew back for his funeral. We celebrated the full life he lived.

Planning the launch event was all consuming for DAD marketing while development team was still mostly working on Office96, finalizing product availability, newspaper and magazine ads, tools needed for retail point of sale, and especially for public relations. By 1995, the tech press had become a mainstream phenomenon and all major newspapers, magazines, and even television networks had dedicated technology reporters. I had no idea how much time I would end up spending supporting our marketing team as the "product" person in all sorts of interviews, demos, lunches, and more. This was the release at which I met most of the industry beat reporters and established relationships that still exist.

Everyone was writing stories and reviews of Windows 95 and Office 95. Everyone.

Shipping Office 95 as a single product was a huge accomplishment for the Desktop Applications division, and it was only fitting that it was a small part of the myriad accomplishments under the leadership of Mike Maples. As the previews were going out, Mike announced that he was going to retire from Microsoft and live full time in the Hill Country of Texas. While many of us stayed in touch with him for decades, in 2016 I had the privilege of coteaching a class at Stanford with Mike—teaching alongside my teacher was a great joy.

Without Mike, Microsoft would have become a different place. Mike brought to Microsoft, especially to Apps and Office, a culture, attitude, and strategy that perhaps more than most any other person were responsible for the success of Office, a success still felt decades later in Office 365.

The Redmond, Washington, launch event was set to be the biggest and craziest event ever hosted on Microsoft's campus. The entire sports and grass area, about two football fields, was tented that third week of August. Most Microsoft people ended up watching it in the conference rooms all around campus.

For all the tech press, the event was the culmination of months of writing about the ever-expanding impact of Windows 95 on computing. For most, however, the rise of the internet and Microsoft's new and more critical competitor, Netscape, fresh off its public offering a few weeks earlier and worth over $3 billion was getting equal, if not more, attention.

Even the conversations we had with each other were internet related. At one point I ended up in a conversation with BillG and his new technical assistant over "internet search." Because of the work in the Office 95 "personal Lycos" feature, there had been a newfound interest in internet search. Google was still almost five years down the road, and many "search engines," including Lycos, came and went. I was making a strident argument with Bill that the future of search would be full text indexing and not the currently dominant index hierarchy of Yahoo, which was all the rage. Bill loved libraries and hierarchy and he asserted there would be a hierarchy. We went back and forth on this for months, but there's some irony that we debated this at the launch of Windows 95.

My official role at the launch was tech support for the demonstration of Office 95.

The demo fell to Office product manager Sarah Leary (SarahL.) Sarah joined DAD marketing straight out of Harvard and was already a veteran of several major launches. Sarah was mostly focused on the business motions and strategy for the launch, and she also happened to be the best demo showperson, probably in the company.

This was not just any demo. She was flanked on one side by BillG, a frequent demo companion, but on her other side was Jay Leno, who was then the relatively new host of *The Tonight Show* and the clear leader of late-night TV.

Sarah scripted the demo to show off the key integration between Windows and Office. There was a nail-biting moment when it was time to bring up a print dialog. Normally, a demo would never include anything that could possibly "hang," like printing, but she pulled it off and skillfully showed some of PowerPoint's new animations and used PowerPoint's new Top 10 animation to create a Jay Leno Top 10 list.

We didn't hire professional writers like a giant company might—we wrote the jokes ourselves. My contribution to *Top 10 List: Windows 95 and Office 95* was "OJ Says, 'Office 95 fits Windows 95 like a glove.'" Cringeworthy years later, but Leno loved it since OJ was a late-night staple. The crowd laughed and that joke made it into a box on the front of the *USA Today* newspaper.

There were countless parties all around campus as the launch event was, in fact, the ship party for all of Microsoft. The evening after the main launch event was filled with parties, dinners, and drinks all around Seattle. I had dinner twice with two different groups of reporters. Then at the old Capitol Hill home of B.P.O.E., the coolest after-party was hosted by the marketing and dev evangelist team, many of whom were the first people I demonstrated the Internet to just 18 months earlier. In the most hyper-self-aware fashion, the party was a sea of blue and white cloud-covered cups, plates, napkins, Koozies, frisbees, and more, each labeled appropriately in Franklin Gothic, the official font of Windows 95. There was Plate 95, Cup 95, Napkin 95, all while hip Seattle grunge music (mixed in with '80s cover band fun) played late into the night.

Ultimately, as the reviews revealed, Office 95 represented the last release where individual apps would be evaluated versus suites. Word, Excel, PowerPoint, and Access more than held their own in category reviews by and large, handily winning the roundups. When it came to suites, the combination proved even more formidable. We achieved this using only 15 percent of our development resources, something that was not lost on me. The reviews treated the release like a big deal, even though it was almost a side project to our team.

As we were finishing, Hank Vigil (HankV), the leader of DAD marketing, told JonDe and me he was so excited that his biggest worry was that Office96 would finish too soon, frustrating customers who would be asked to buy another release. Because Office 95 was *delayed* by the Windows 95 schedule, he was worried that 12/24 would end up being 18/24. Jon and I shrugged, knowing the realities of our schedule at the time. But to think there were business worries we could release too much new code was *interesting*.

It is difficult to imagine today, but the idea of an excess of software was top of mind of most corporations. Customers were overwhelmed by the quantity of software being produced by vendors. And to be honest, customers were underwhelmed by the quality. The burden was not as much new features and fixing problems, but the dreaded *Total Cost of Ownership* and the ability for customers to deploy and manage PCs and train end-users who were still not always computer capable. While it is difficult to imagine this predicament, it would also profoundly influence the next ten years of how we built and released products and how Microsoft established relationships with customers that would supplant those built by IBM over the past 25 years.

Despite some low-level rumblings of best of breed versus suites, customers moved on, preferring an integrated set of applications. The suite competition simply wasn't there. Lotus delayed building apps for Windows 95 and was the only vendor with a full suite. Borland and WordPerfect teamed up, but two companies building an integrated suite proved to be challenging, and Corel would soon be the owner of the assets, choosing instead to focus on the low price and individual market.

In competition it is said that it is not enough for the competitor to drop the ball, but someone had to be there to pick it up. The strategic bet on Windows 95 and the strong execution of Office 95 were a great combination at the right time, when competitors were focused elsewhere. Windows 95 and Office 95 provided further evidence of the virtuous platform-apps cycle that was such a part of Microsoft's history.

The internet and shift from document creation to communication and collaboration was next for Office and would prove challenging for Office96.

Windows 95, even with the unpredictability of the development cycle, proved to be arguably the defining product for Microsoft and the PC industry for the next decade. Reviews around the world were fantastic. The only people who didn't like it were in Cupertino and a few in Armonk. The explosion in computing at home and work could be directly attributable to the ease of use of the product, ecosystem of partners, and availability of multiple varieties and price points of PCs. Just as BillG had strategized, adding Office 95, despite the reservations of our team, to the launch further validated not only the capabilities of Windows but Microsoft's commitment to GUI, Win32, and the developer platform overall. With Windows 95, the PC ecosystem or flywheel as it was frequently called was in full effect. The economics of hardware, peripherals, software, training and consulting, custom business software, and support for all of those were present and growing at a scale that was unprecedented in business.

With Windows 95 and Office 95 shipping that day along with probably a dozen other new products, the event was really the launch of Microsoft 95.

On that day, August 24, 1995, Steve Jobs was still a couple of years away from returning to Apple, and what was once Microsoft's most intense competitor, the PC, left the adolescent era of computing and was entering early adulthood. The fact that Apple chose to make a brief appearance with a full-page ad in *The Wall Street Journal* (and *Financial Times* and their hometown *San Jose Mercury News*) mocking the old 8.3 filenames of MS-DOS saying "C:\ONGRTLNS.W95". I still have my copy framed. was looking like a rout. Oh, and a giant sign in tow behind a truck also made its way past the soccer fields, and to be safe the Sea-Tac airport also had a few billboards.

I walked (or stumbled) a few blocks home from *Party 95* feeling a strange sense of completion but realizing that Office96 awaited me as my year of multitasking would give way to a chance to focus completely on what was ahead.

Windows 95 was a new start for PCs. The PC emerged from a hobbyist tool or a tech novelty, to truly something for every desk and every home just as BillG and PaulA envisioned. We were so focused on making everything work and get out the door that for many of us it would not sink in until we went back to visit family for the holidays. Those were the holidays nearly every one of us would forever remember as the start of family tech support

1995-1997

As PC sales surge, growing at a rate of 60 percent in 1996, the enormity of the internet becomes widely realized and will soon dwarf the impact of everything that came before it.

The Apps and our Office team were 110% focused on what should have been the last months of Office96 as part of our 12/24 plan of parallel releases. The product turned out to be much more difficult to finish and the new Office-centric organization met with much more resistance than planned. On top of that, Office 95 took our entire Test team to get out the door, putting us behind on quality. In other words, the 24-month project was going to take longer but we did not yet know how much longer.

Something about Windows 95 shipping changed Microsoft, especially at the top and how the company thought strategically. It was as though with the success of Windows 95 came the need, though not necessarily the ability, to think big thoughts and to develop big plans for the future. The products we were working on we assumed, but just not interesting. Everything interesting was yet to begin.

040. CREATING THE FIRST REAL OFFICE

It was as though we had not been working on Office96 for the past year. With all the excitement of Windows 95 (oh, and Office 95) the conversation quickly turned to asking what Office would do next, after the release we hadn't even finished and was late. It was kind of weird.

In a relatively short time, many things changed. MikeMap retired and with that a slight change in the organization to accommodate that. Microsoft Research was a few years old and occupying more and more of BillG's headspace. Windows NT 4.0 was on a path to completion and with that a solid spot in the minds of IT leaders, especially for the most anticipated business product of all, Microsoft Exchange email. The much-anticipated Cairo project began to fade in interest and what became more interesting, and ultimately much more important, would be bringing the Windows 95 user experience to the Windows NT operating system kernel. The browser war between Internet Explorer and Netscape, and the broader competition over back-end server technologies for the Internet, was well underway. Windows would kick off a series of updates to Windows 95 primarily for the benefit of holiday or back-to-school PC Sales including Windows 98, Windows 98 SE, and finally Windows Me. For Office, by many accounts it appeared as though Office had successfully taken the leadership position in the new product category of suites. We were still paranoid about competition, especially that Lotus was now owned by IBM and had a huge sales motion behind it.

That seems like a lot of work going on and it was, but from a company strategy perspective it was as though that was all known and thus, for lack of a better word, boring. The real excitement and interesting work was answering the question from BillG "What is Next?" There was an almost insatiable demand to know our plans for a few years from now, not our current development efforts. It was rather sudden, but soon the altitude of our company dialog was less about the products under development and more about what products should be under development. The concern or even fear was not losing in the next release cycle but in the ones that came later. Intellectually that seems prudent, but practically it is enormously frustrating as I would alternate between significant execution challenges and vague discussions about an infeasible future.

There were people in parts of the company that had what were considered great visions for where to go, but it always seemed to me like there were practical ways to get to 90% of that in much less time. Others had ideas for how things should be done, but clearly there was no way to build those now because of some limitation like how different everything else would need to be to be able to build that. Innovations like work from General Magic captivated BillG and everyone but were not selling well even with a big IPO. As I'd become accustom, a failure in the marketplace was not a failure for BillG so that meant we needed to treat it like a potential competitor. I needed to find a way to engage in this dialog and to represent applications and productivity effectively as "thought leadership" which was a rather popular and vacuous buzzword.

We were still deep in building Office96, the second part of the 12/24 strategy of working on a pair of releases in parallel. In fairness to me, this was occupying every cycle I had. We were almost two years into the project by the end of 1995 and it was clear we were going to ship much later than planned. Yet, no one really wanted to talk about

Office96. Rather, everyone wanted to talk about what would be next. What would be big and bold. To us, Office96 was **huge.** The scale of the product was greater than anything we had ever done, greater than anything done in the industry.

Office96 did not have any of the *a priori* constraints of Office94, other than shipping as a suite all at the same time. At the start of any release in early 1994, product teams were thinking big. This time, in addition to each app, there was also the new OPU (Office Product Unit) team thinking big. Aligning these big thoughts would be add to the challenges.

Our Desktop Applications process was a unique expression of a product development lifecycle. It is not the historic and inappropriately applied moniker of "waterfall"—a legacy process where first requirements are gathered then specifications written, and then code developed until testing signs off. It is also not what would be thought of as agile, in more current terms, when products are increasingly built up over time constrained by short cycles or sprints. This was primarily because we took a long time, though some also would say because we did not change the software in response to external inputs along the way as well. Throughout the development schedule the product was kept stable and usable by the team but not in a shippable state until defined milestones or beta tests.

The Apps/Office process of setting large aspirations that span 18 to 24 months and scaling implementation as the project evolves was unique at Microsoft and clearly the source of the stability of the products and the position in the market that continues to benefit the company today. Apple remains a lone exception and has brilliantly mastered a delicate balancing act of consistent yearly releases (unbelievably amazing) and long-term product plans patiently released over multiple years. Business is a social science and as such drawing causal relationships between processes used at different companies is risky thinking.

Most attribute the definition of the *waterfall* development approach to the classic 1970 article by Winston Royce "Managing the Development of Large Software Systems."[11] A careful reading of the article shows that Royce was critical of this, and the Apps approach was much more like what he prescribed. Alas, the rise of agile and in particular *internet time* 1996-2000 all but eliminated the idea of holistic product planning and replaced it with shipping and iterating on feedback. This would be an ongoing skirmish between some groups in the company but would become a major challenge for me in about 10 years when I moved to Windows. More on that to come.

Whatever one might call this process (it just became known as *the Office process*), the assumption BillG had was that whatever we were able to articulate to him was already booked. On the one hand, this was great, and it meant he could count on us to deliver. On the other hand, it was incredibly frustrating for him for two reasons. First, the ability to articulate a product extremely concretely—literally with early working code that he knew would ship, screen shots, and endless specifications—meant it was going to feel done and immune to his tweaks and inputs. Second, the very existence of a working and reliable product meant that it was time to move on. It was almost a curse of being perceived as reliable and focused on execution. Still, we were very late and didn't even know how late we were.

BillG and NathanM leading Microsoft Research were focused on 5 years out or more. There was nothing special about that time, other than it was longer than anyone was already working. We used to joke that if from the very start a project took 3 years to complete then everything beyond that was infinity years away. A project that someone said would take 5 years would never finish. The world would be so different by then and the choices we would make so different why solidify plans now. That argument did not hold water at all. We had to do something to move this discussion forward. We started writing more and taking risks in talking about the future, a future we were not quite working on yet. It was uncomfortable.

First, we set out to cast Office96 in more futuristic language and goals. In other words, re-skin Office96 not as what we were doing but as what we could be doing next on top of it. We called this *Project X.* Nothing about Project X existed at all. It was simply a name and a memo to have a discussion. BradWe and the design team even mocked up the ideas in Project X and we demonstrated it at the Company Meeting and in a vision presentation at COMDEX in 1995. Brad began hiring designers from the new programs in interaction design popping up in Europe, particularly in UK and Netherlands, including from the Royal College of Art where Apple's Jony Ive has long been affiliated. To kick off the process I made my own concept—a single screen showing off the concepts I thought we needed to show off. It is comical in the use of clipart and PowerPoint but it was a good conversation starter with design.

Project X took over the desktop with a series of new metaphors. There were filing cabinets that contained binders that could be constructed by searching across all your documents, not just physically storing them. Calendaring with a timeline view and task management would be easily accessible. It would be easy to have small notes, Post-It like, attached to any item in the system. People were the center of activities not just documents, with easy access to contact cards. The little teddy bear was always there to help you as an *intelligent agent.* There were also virtual desktops so each project a person might be working on could have its own set of tools organized appropriately and quickly switch between them. All of these were rooted in Office96, but projecting out years if we had more operating system services and synergy.

Working from this sketch the designers, after deservedly mocking me, created an interaction sequence that was an ultra-modern skin, so to speak, on the features of Office96. The designers were the same ones designing the real menus and dialog boxes, so it made sense. And like that, everyone was far more excited in what was to come than in anything we were currently working on.

That might seem like a success, but in fact it quickly blew up and many across the company became either concerned or needed to know more so they could adjust their plans to fit in with Project X. In some parts of the company this would be viewed as huge win. For Office this was a problem. We not only had to finish Office96, but we were a big business and the last thing we needed to do was to need to explain to customers that the Office 95 they were thinking of buying would be obsoleted by the new cool Project X. So, I quickly wrote a memo explaining Project X. While I spent most of the memo explaining the features shown at the Company Meeting and how they related to the real work of Office96, I also used it as a chance to try to align the work of Windows ("Systems") and Apps.

> *Although this sounds totally drastic, this memo will make it clear that we were really building Project X all along, though we lacked a shared vision of how it all fits together. In this memo we will detail the various technologies and architectural components that make up Project X, who is responsible for the design, and who is tasked with building them.*

While a lot of people were excited by Project X, they were less excited by the prospect of trying to align all of our products again after Windows 95 given all the work already going on. In particular, I was learning that the job of aligning fell to Office to align with Windows, not the other way around. Office needed to do a better job of using the new underlying technologies in Windows to build applications. Except there weren't any new underlying technologies. What BillG wanted to do strategically was repeat the GUI Windows-Excel innovation cycle, but what was the next GUI, the next app?

So back to writing. Realizing that the problem seemed to be not as much a lack of big thoughts, but a lack of ideas for evolving the whole of the platform, meaning Windows and Office. In "On the Evolution of Office" the key thing I put out there was that while we just finished 12/24 of two releases in parallel, then why not "12/24/48" and start working on something four years from now! I wrote that while the Office96 was slipping, and the team was reeling from the trauma of trying to do two releases in parallel. We weren't being *political* as much as just trying to put forth some framework for talking about the future that was infinity years away. NathanM loved it!

> *By betting all or a portion of a team on building 48 month developments into the current product, we are doomed to failure. No group is smart enough about our industry to know what bets to make now in our products today in order to have them pay off in four years, all in the same product. One way to think about this is to ask what features were worried about four years ago in Excel and compare that to what ended up in the product. Although there are some things that have been perennially on the list of adds, and then cuts, the marketplace clearly did not miss them (though perhaps we regret not having done them for development efficiency reasons.) We can continue to explore how to just "extend" our 24 month cycle to a 48 month analogue, but it would be hard to convince me that we would find a process by which we can work on meaningful features in parallel with our current products.*
>
> *What is needed, though, is a redefinition of the 48 month aspect. Instead of thinking of it in parallel to our current process, we should consider the 48 month time frame to be an independent bet on something that we think (strongly believe) will pay off handsomely in the four year time frame. In other words, while we should continue to bet largely on the code, process, and architectural aspects of 12-24, we must look hard at the current state of the marketplace and products and spend some of our efforts on a completely different effort. As PeteH likes to remind us, we must be sure that the "generals are not fighting the last war."*

What was most important to me was helping not just BillG and NathanM but the rest of our team to see that we were not crazy. So, to do that we took a concrete technology approach to describe all the places in the applications that we made assumptions about how PCs worked and why those needed to change. The reason assumptions needed to change was because Moore's Law was firing on all cylinders across CPU, RAM, disk space, while Metcalfe's Law on connected networks becoming increasing powerful clearly described the growing internet. Designing our software for an old world was just dumb. I really like the idea of documenting the context and assumptions of a product to force a rethinking of what still makes sense, or not.

The analogy I used was that "code is like a dinosaur" implying that the comet that hit our codebase was the Internet. The assumptions, baked into Word, Excel, and PowerPoint make for a long list of potential points of competitive weakness. The term *disruption* was not yet a word in business vocabulary, but that would be appropriate. These assumptions included:

- *Stand-alone applications dominate*
- *Categories consisting of spreadsheet, word processor, presentation graphics, database*
- *Testing software was an afterthought, or a small portion of development at best*
- *Teams were started with 2-3 programmers, but we reached a limit at about 40*
- *The product architecture was really the work of "one guy"*
- *Sharing code is hard*
- *Disk-based file formats*
- *Networking limited to file/print sharing*
- *CPU bound applications are the norm*
- *Virtual memory not available*
- *Operating system services are slow*
- *Users can run setup on their own*
- *Documents are primarily printed*
- *Images in documents are primarily adornments*
- *Macros were run in process and for a single application*
- *Most information is stored locally*
- *Document structure manipulated and created by the user*

The dialog now shifted. These were topics we could discuss across teams and meetings. In a parallel list, the memo offered some ideas for new assumptions we could make about building productivity software. I realized that Project X had not done enough to incorporate the Internet and so we focused much more on how that changes everything:

- *Drawing and graphics are the norm, not an exception*
- *Virtual memory replaces disk-based file formats*
- *Multi-stream documents are the norm, along with progressive rendering*
- *Interoperating with Internet protocols is a requirement*
- *Programmability should start from higher abstractions than the user interface*
- *Documents will be viewed on-line*
- *Documents will contain more active, user-encoded behavior*
- *Applications need to be easier to setup and install*
- *Knowing the structure of a document is of paramount importance*
- *File formats need to be tagged for upward compatibility*

A few more months would pass, and the Internet would be more solidly represented in our products. In fact, we were well into building and innovating in Internet Explorer, Internet Information Server (Microsoft's web server), and more new products than we could name. This led to a final manifestation of these ideas with a decidedly web-centric view. So, a final memo before we got around to actually shipping Office96, was "Web-Centric Productivity."

In this memo we articulated many ways that we could build applications to take advantage of the web, across storage and management of documents, personalization, collaboration, and annotations, solving our setup and deployment problems, and more. We did yet another prototype called *Project Stretch* to visualize these ideas. As mentioned many times before, I had a disdain for code names, so this is a tongue-in-cheek reference to a famous IBM project that was not commercially successful but led to many core technologies for later mainframes.

Stretch envisioned an Office available all the time, from any device, running in an industry standard browser. It was mid-1996 while Internet Explorer 3.0 was being developed, and as such it predates technologies that became essential for creating richer, desktop-like, user experiences. Even scripting was only months old, technologies like DHTML were years away. HTML as it currently stood had only the most minimal text rendering capabilities, which we found troubling in Office though we were determined to adopt it. The most interesting strategic bet being made (in Internet Explorer 3.0) was what became ActiveX, which was rooted in OLE and thus something that concerned me while also saluting the strategic flag. The prototype became a way to articulate what would eventually lead to products such as SharePoint and OneNote, as well as underlying technologies for sharing and collaboration.

With this executive, long-lead effort going on in the background, the real work of building Office was taking place. Each and every day was a new challenge in the face of ever-increasing scale. What was once three independent application teams in Word, Excel, and PowerPoint, along with a new product for email and a new team called Office building shared code, had to grow to be a single, well-functioning product team. We were not there yet.

Office was late. The team was not gelling. It was painful.

041. SCALING THE OFFICE INFRASTRUCTURE AND PLATFORM

In shipping at scale, it is not enough to agree on what needs to be done. There also needs to be agreement on how it gets done.

While the big apps were successful in their own right, won reviews, sold incredibly well, had high customer satisfaction, and were made by teams that were exemplars of the MikeMap value system, they evolved with different engineering systems. Differing in detail, they all accomplished the same: shipping a high quality (for the era, or at least higher quality than everyone else), while striving for a ready-to-ship product every single day of the process.

To developers and testers on each team, the micro details of how this worked across teams for committing changes, check-in tests, unit testing, localization, and more were highly evolved. Each step in the process was tuned to the "unique" needs of each product's engineering organization, or perhaps tribe is a better description. Minor differences would be amplified both at scale and across teams. A common example was how and how much time in the schedule was reserved or buffered for the unknown. Excel with its record of getting closer and closer to on time RTM, could be seen as either extremely hardcore or excessively conservative, but managing the day-to-day progression through the schedule was critical and very much a key part of the culture.

It is a statement about Microsoft culture that the better Excel got at hitting projected ship dates and shipping award-winning products, the more the discussion across Microsoft (outside the Excel team) centered around how conservative the team was getting. To Excel, they were just being hardcore. This was best symbolized by the leather biker jackets developers earned as a ship gift, or perhaps it was the jacket's *Recalc or Die* logo. Times were different.

The idea that getting better at daily engineering and hitting scheduled milestones was somehow a sign of being less aggressive or grandiose in plans gets to the heart of the divergence of Microsoft cultures across the company. The Apps teams not only wrote but received the *Zero Defects* memo and internalized a cultural attribute of over-promise and under-deliver. Much of the rest of Microsoft seemed to have succumbed to the idea that such a process (or philosophy) was somehow less hardcore or even wimpy. There was a strong belief among the over-promise side of the house that building a platform was simply more difficult than building applications (never mind that the applications were also platforms, but I digress) and that there was a real difference in impact if a platform cut features the ways Apps did in order to ship. I can say this because many times when it came to collaborating across the company I was on the receiving end of comments along the lines of "yes, but that's only because it is *just* an app." In my weaker moments I would say the quiet parts aloud, such as "yes, but you'll never ship."

Apps, meaning Office, was the more fragile growth engine of the company, and bigger opportunity for profits. Office depended on customers choosing to buy Office over an existing product they already owned or competitor, and that decision benefitted from a new version of Office drawing interest to new capabilities and over time would come to depend on much more profitable corporate deals, as we will learn in the next chapter. Windows, on the other hand, was going out on most every new PC at a much lower price than Office but a much higher attach to PC. Whether an updated version of Windows was on the PC or not, PC sales were going up primarily due to businesses buying first PCs for many employees, and in a bit of a twist those customers often preferred the current or even previous version of Windows anyway. There was certainly a pop that came from a new Windows, especially when timed with updated PCs for back to school or holiday, but no one was confused over the revenue drivers. These differences in the business models directly led to the variation (and tensions) in development processes, and also to the differences in how each business evolved and innovated well into the future. We were all products of our environment.

As an example, within Office each program management team (Word, Excel, PowerPoint) developed unique approaches to overall design and feature selection. When there were differences in design or prioritization the discussion would inevitably turn to a claim along the lines of "Excel users are different [than Word or PowerPoint users]." Each team was focused on ease of use, or what we often called "basic use," yet maintained a different idea of the prototypical personas using the product.

Putting these together, there were three tensions at play in building Office96:

- Enlisting support across executives for an overall plan. The normal process of each formerly Business Unit then Product Unit doing this on their own no longer sufficed.
- Developing a plan with buy-in from the dev managers and test managers for how Office96 was to be built—the tooling, day-to-day dev process, and the overall testing and verification, through to localization.
- Deciding what to build that represented a suite while continuing to recognize that to the outside world, customers and press, the category battles might not be yesterday's news even if the Microsoft strategy was all Office.

I wish there was a lot of a story to tell about how this played out, but in reality, "decisions were made" in a bottom-up or distributed manner. The rest was going to be in execution. The Office Product Unit was created while the product plans were created in parallel, thus much of Office96 would be characterized by OPU and the Apps in a state of tension over planning and execution. Ultimately, this made for a bumpy Office96 release filled with many new execution challenges, but it also built the foundation for an execution machinery that would become unprecedented and largely responsible for what ultimately became the largest and most secure business at Microsoft.

The Office96 plan had two main pillars:

- The Apps product units embarked on deep, category-defining features, continuing to make inroads against legacy MS-DOS competitors and to win against Windows competitors. At the outset the suite included Word, Excel, and PowerPoint within the DAD organization and Access in the Tools group. These products underwent significant architectural work consistent with a full 24-month schedule. The initial plan was to continue to ship Mail and Schedule+, though this would change completely as we will see.
- The Office Product Unit built a set of features shared across the apps and integrated those features into one or more apps (this is a key tenet about creating shared infrastructure), leaving the other apps to do integration work on their own. In addition, OPU would, by nature of code and also influence, make sure the suite was designed for consistency and integration across the apps.

The OPU features ranged from a lot of heavy lifting, but straightforward, to some of the most sophisticated refitting of features envisioned by the apps. In contemporary terms, OPU was both an infrastructure team and a platform team. In terms of infrastructure, OPU drove a new shared engineering and quality process (led by JonDe and GrantG) and created shared components essentially representing a platform upon which to build Office applications, providing the code (APIs) for many common application paradigms across user interface, text handling, graphics and drawing, and much more.

As a successful product engineering team scales and a product line grows, there is an inevitable desire to gain efficiencies of engineering scale and an ability to expand the product line efficiently. This all sounds perfectly reasonable until you realize doing any of this strongly runs counter to the very forces that got the teams to success in the first place. Changing processes sounds risky when it took so much work to get to the current state. Sharing code always sounds much more difficult than not sharing code.

Sharing code always means either replacing something that already exists in a winning product with new code from someone else or adding code that does not completely and fully understand the unique needs of the winning product or its customers. As is almost always the case, the shared code is viewed as bloated, overly complex, or simply does more than needed. Despite the recent success in using shared open-source code, the more established a product is the less likely it is to see code from the outside as a preferred path. In 1996, it was always about performance, memory management, or simply complexity. The technical buzzsaw would evolve to include security, manageability, and even privacy/safety—the reasons might change but the goal of avoiding shared code remained. Shared code is a way of ceding your autonomy to another group. Developers have traditionally maintained an attitude of *NIH,* not invented here, as shorthand for the distrust of *OPC*, other people's code.

The benefits to sharing are enormous, and that is what leads teams to take on these challenges. If a product team can create infrastructure and platform assets, then more engineers can focus on category-specific work while also making it easy to add entirely new products to the business with substantially less effort. Office had Word, Excel, PowerPoint, and now Access, but the world of productivity software was vast and it made no sense not to try our hand at drawing, personal information management, note-taking, project management, desktop publishing, or a host of new categories. OPU would be a key part of how to scale both out and over in productivity, and Office96 would be our collective growing pains.

To best illustrate this, let's look at some of the specifics of what OPU did. The diversity, breadth, and frankly aggressiveness is due to JonDe and his engineering leadership that pushed to do a lot in the first release of shared code out of the gate in early 1994 a few months before I joined the team. The body of code was packaged in a Windows DLL. A dynamically linked library is a Windows mechanism for packaging executable code to be shared, and also the source of endless frustration in the world known as *DLL Hell*, but I digress though will return to this topic soon enough. The DLL file was ultimately named MSO97.DLL, though sometimes called *mee-so* in conversation. Along with MSO, there were a few other files as well as a test harness that could exercise many of the capabilities called Lime. Lime would grow over time and eventually prove out just how much of a platform we were building.

MSO contained code designed to be shared across applications, bringing with that engineering efficiency, experience consistency, higher quality (doing something once brings that), improved performance, and even more features because generally that is what happened with a dedicated effort.

Features were the currency of Apps teams. Features defined contributions. The more visible and customer facing, generally speaking the better. Therefore, it was important for OPU to have its own features, not just be a dumping ground for the grunge work that the big teams traditionally farmed out or de-prioritized. An example of this was Setup, the code that copied bits from floppies to hard drives. Almost always getting this done was a last-minute sprint and shunted to new hires or even contractors. Apps teams were more than happy to have OPU take this over without giving up any resources of course. Creating OPU was not going to go that way, so the portfolio consisted of a fair share or more of grunge, cool features, and even an app of its own, the Binder. This type of portfolio was critical to the successful creation of an OPU team and culture, giving it an identity beyond simply the plumbing team, so to speak.

Over time and several releases, MSO would be viewed by the entire organizations not as a tax or effort bolted on the side, but as an asset and more importantly a starting point. The journey of building the Office platform would start with the tension and difficulty described herein, and end with new features defaulting to shared efforts, new apps spinning up quickly with MSO, and the organization finding a balance between platform-infrastructure, and category-specific innovation.

Every product or even organization at scale finds itself at some point of the swinging pendulum of centralized versus distributed efforts. Often this is viewed through the lens of what is good for the broader business, but at each end of the pendulum is an *on-the-ground* view of challenge. These views are as predictable as the broader swings. When moving from a distributed to centralized effort (or resources), the formerly distributed accountability will find every reason to doubt the capabilities and necessity, and ultimately viability, of a centralized effort. Over time, the same people and organization comes to rely heavily on the shared team and actively pushes work to centralized efforts.

This dynamic characterized most everything in OPU.

In the work I do with companies today, the topic of scaling, sharing, and building new products efficiently over time is one of the most popular lessons I have the opportunity to share. My own experience was a journey of a career, in a sense, as scaling, sharing, and collaborating, occupied the next 15 years of work. We spent a good deal of time in 2000 describing some of this for a Harvard Business School case, which for many years was used to teach a combination of customer-informed product development and shifting an organization to sharing.[12]

At the sophisticated end of the platform features was a shared drawing layer, code-named *Escher*. The Microsoft art collection, which had a significant job to do to fill the reception areas and lobbies with something, mostly featured Northwest contemporary artists but had one original M. C. Escher hanging in the building 17 atrium. The acquisition of that was championed by Art Committee member and first Office vice president, ChrisP. Sometimes even Apps had cute code names.

Escher was a big effort spanning all the apps and especially PowerPoint, where much of the lower-level graphics code would be implemented. The integration of Escher into Word was done by a new OPU team, staffed with developers from across Apps. Having engineers that had worked in each of the apps code bases was critical to building shared code to work across those products (again these were the massive products and code bases of Word, Excel, and PowerPoint) and a key decision JonDe made in staffing the teams.

Like all of the new shared features, there was a constant debate across the apps and OPU as to the value of the feature for each team. OPU was in a constant state of *selling* the value of shared code and the idea that sharing enables teams to get more than they might need, basically for free. Except in practice nothing was free as each app inherited compatibility and complexity that it decided it did not *need*. Drawing was a great example of that, but it was not even the most controversial.

Every app in Office had some support for drawing, but none were particularly deep, and all seemed to serve category specific use cases. Word was able to embed drawings as rectangles within a document, much like a photo, which is how most people thought about adding illustrations to business documents, if they could draw. Business memos and other documents having basic drawing tools that could float on top of a document, much like an acetate layer, greatly enriched documents were recently added to Word but still relatively limited. Even more exciting was the ability to use broadly the fancy text that became known as *WordArt,* which was new but constrained, as with drawings, to be embedded in regions and not used arbitrarily throughout a document. The complexity of creating feature-rich and deeply integrated drawing tools was daunting in Word. To mitigate this, the lead engineer, Peter Engrav (PeterEn), volunteered to lead the integration of Escher into Word from within the new OPU. A key tool for managing the shared features was that OPU would lead the integration into one of the main apps, thereby learning firsthand the complexity and also minimizing the work to the app.

Excel had elaborate tools for charting, such as candlestick, donut, 2.5 dimensional in addition to the classic line and bar, and some minimal tools for doing callouts and basic graphics on sheets. There was a great deal of resistance to features that were deemed "not something Excel users requested" or even features that were viewed as less than professional or business-like. Whether that resistance was genuine or simply a sort of buzzsaw didn't really matter. The Escher team constantly received inbound "doubt" over any features simply from the perspective of it not being interesting to Excel users.

At the other end of the need spectrum was PowerPoint, which was basically a big drawing program. Why would a drawing program want to use a shared code base, as that was their entire domain? As though to emphasize the maximum complexity of sharing code across these apps, PowerPoint's main concern was that Escher wasn't enough for them competitively, simply because they were spending time putting drawing in Word and Excel—neither of which appreciated drawing as much.

See how that worked? That's the "middle" that OPU found itself in as a platform team for already successful products.

Escher would go through many rounds of adding features for compatibility with what was there and removing features because of schedule constraints, along with challenging debates over features versus integration. The end-result, however, was a tsunami of graphics features across the product. Every product picked up integrated capabilities previously found only in high-end and rarely-owned professional tools from a broad array of drawing shapes, modern graphics files formats including transparency, photo handling, shading, and even an integrated and vastly richer variation of WordArt, the curvy, glowing, bubble-text so popular with grade school children and small business signs. A huge part of Escher was that much of the shared work was also done from within the PowerPoint team itself. PowerPoint was also located in Silicon Valley and this was the first time we had embarked on sim-shipping deeply integrated code across a plane flight.

While the debate over Escher was intense, the debate over the core or primary user interaction (meaning the user interface) in apps was even more so. The core user interaction in Office took place through toolbars, which were a primary source of app innovation—so much so that the image on the box and most screenshots in the press were of the toolbars. In an effort to build a suite, one sold with a value proposition of consistency and memory efficiency, it was only natural that we tried to share toolbars—do them right, do them once as Lotus claimed to do.

In modern context, this might seem trivial, but at the time this was a key innovation. With the different teams on different schedules, but with a shared DNA and understanding of potential solutions, it was no surprise that there was some common evolution, along with opportunities to be a little bit better, or different, depending on perspective. Toolbars proved legendary in this regard.

One of the first "battles" we found ourselves in was over the design of toolbars. Word and Excel had each designed and tested their own toolbar implementation and arrived at different heights—15 versus 16 pixels. Trivial to mention, but research done separately by Word and Excel, surprisingly, showed that Excel and Word users had different preferences—obviously due to test design or some other factor since it is ludicrous to think this differed by app. This might not have mattered except that the main marketing demonstration of Office showed Excel embedded charts within Word. Clicking on the chart loaded the Excel toolbars and caused a one-pixel shift in the document. As if that weren't enough, there were equally divergent views over the design of the tooltip, the little text that appeared when the mouse was held over a button explaining what the icon might be. This invention had those that believed the tips should be white and those who fought for yellow, not to mention debates over the delay, stickiness, amount of text, whether the keyboard shortcut should be there, and whether there was a choice to disable them. Even the simple features, no matter how new and clever, were impossibly difficult to coordinate.

Ever the diplomat, Andrew Kwatinetz (AndrewK) spent the better part of the product cycle ironing out (negotiating, pleading) consistency issues. Andrew was already deeply experienced, as an intern and college hire, in both Word and Excel user interface design and had already proven himself to be one of the next-generation leaders of OPU. Early in the product cycle, Andrew sketched out all the places across the product that lacked consistency and coherency as an original volunteer in the newly formed OPU (and its prior form, the Apps Interoperability Group), and he had begun to map out plans to bring the product together and innovate in user experience.

Having committed to sharing the code, we finally had in one place all of the buttons, menus, and commands for all of Office—thousands of entries in a single place. Pete Morcos (PeteMor), a recent college hire, arduously managed them all by maintaining a database of every icon, command name, tooltip, menu string, and keyboard accelerator in the product. The difficulty and attention to detail required was only matched by the long-term value for consistency, localization, user assistance, and most of all ease of use. One of the most significant differences between

Office and most other tools is the sheer breadth and simultaneous depth of features, something that would become even more apparent as web pages came to the forefront. Each application had over 1000 commands (buttons, menus, keyboard commands) with something over 2500 unique commands in Office96. The scope of the product would be further amplified by the platform APIs available through VBA, another major shared effort that enabled developers to build custom applications based on Office.

The sharing was enormously difficult, taking a toll on the OPU team and frustrating the Apps teams. We were a year or so into the project and, while we were clearly making progress, we were also moving more slowly than we needed to. We had not taken the time to adapt the organization to sharing nor did we really consider the breadth of the undertaking.

The team was so frustrated that JonDe and I decided to have a meeting with ChrisP and PeteH to discuss "the situation." It was a combination of us asking for help and us being called to the carpet for the situation bubbling up to them from the apps teams.

My own memory refers to this meeting as the one when JonDe said, "People think Jon has lost his marbles" and thus I recall the meeting as the *marbles meeting*.

I had put together slides with some basic philosophical problems we had been dealing with across primarily OPU, Word, and Excel. There was nothing really new in the deck. I had previously sent a couple of really long emails basically warning that things were challenging, and progress was slow. PeteH was hearing the other side of this from the Apps leaders—how things were slow because of OPU's shared code that wasn't needed and features they didn't want slowing things down, making the products bigger and slower, while taking time away from doing features that could win customers and reviews. I'm not exaggerating.

The key moment in the meeting was when JonDe explained how crazy things had become. A year earlier, Jon was leading the Excel team through a hugely successful release and prior to that he had been a key leader for the entire history of the product. He epitomized everything about DAD culture. Yet all these developers that idolized and looked up to him suddenly believed he'd lost his mind and somehow gone crazy, drunk off the Kool-Aid of shared code. His old team stopped believing his schedule estimates or even architectural approaches. Jon had clearly "lost his marbles." We were deadlocked by the "Word users are different," "Excel users are different," and "OPU is wasteful" mindsets.

We vented and PeteH listened. Still, it felt like there was not going to be any immediate change. I had hoped they would do something simple like send mail to everyone saying to listen to us and this is the way it is. In hindsight, that was desperate and totally the wrong way to solve the issues, but our frustration levels were intolerably high.

Somehow, things did change, though. PeteH and ChrisP worked quietly in the background doing more to reinforce both the strategy and execution of Office96, the focus on shared code, the consistent experience, and the notion of one team working together to make Office. This happened in all the right ways through mostly small or 1:1 meetings. That was the DAD culture. Pete was savvy enough to know the team would not react positively to some sort of commandment or over-the-top edict about sharing. The subtle persuasion and repetition were what the team needed and got. Eventually, the Apps leaders were reaching out more, and over the following weeks we saw the climate changed.

Our view was that BillG would be quite proud of the sharing. We thought for sure the idea that breaking down the barriers between apps and improving the architecture of everything would be viewed extremely positively.

The product was still impossibly difficult to run, though we had stable daily builds due to sheer force of will from JonDe, GrantG, and the development and test managers, but there was two years of work ahead as things started feeling better. Even with bumps on the road ahead, I was feeling good about it all.

Every month, I gathered up the status from across the project for an email report. Each team (Word, Excel, and PowerPoint as well as Escher and the all the OPU contributions) contributed a section with information on progress—the PDL, or product development list, in reference to the spreadsheet of all active projects. The individual apps also created PDL reports, even though our goal was a single product release. There were two important items to cover. First was the project on time. Office96 appeared to be generally running on time, at this point, so the update was benign.

The second part of this update included the process that was near and dear to Apps, which was adds/cuts. Throughout the development, particularly after an eight – or ten-week milestone, each team, at a granular level (individual developer), reevaluated the list of work items (tasks taking about a day of development or so) and considered the progress made versus progress required. The result was almost always feature *cuts*—removing proposed features from the product. There was also learning along the way. There were also *adds*: enhancements, new options, or reworked d features. JeffH had always taught me that transparency and completeness were critical to how BillG thought, so my PDLs were works of art in those attributes. I worked super hard to bring the product to life with some clarity.

Upon receiving one PDL for Word, BillG replied to let us know two things:

First, we were cutting too much. "The number of cuts is truly amazing to me" he asked in red text. In fact, in the effort to be honest, my PDL looked like we were gutting the product every month. That was not the case. In DAD, the basic approach was *cutting is shipping*, so in order to ship things would be scaled back as we learned more. That was how the process worked and everyone was comfortable with that, at least within DAD.

I felt horrible for the team and certain the email would result in people quitting and Apps using it as a chance to say, "OPU was a bad idea." That concern was followed by worry that I was going to get fired. Were we on a path to a bad product? Was I leading us in the wrong direction? Was I messing up? Or perhaps this was all a communication problem.

Separately, Bill chose to highlight some specific features that he felt strongly about. This inadvertently (honest, it was unintentional) allowed the apps teams to say that the OPU efforts and resources were robbing the apps of features that Bill would prioritize. Ugh.

The right thing to do was to show BillG some progress, but without the ceremony of a full review.

We were early in the development of Office96, and most features were merely crawling. Most of us were not running the product on a daily basis as it was not ready (called *self-hosting*), and certainly it was neither ready for BillG to use nor was it a polished demo. Nevertheless, I took it upon myself to set up some time and march over to BillG's office with my laptop, talk through the PDL, and show him some carefully curated features. It was a risk, but so was debating in email or letting the issue fester.

It was a quick 30-minute "drive by," and one of many that I routinely did over the years. I made clear I was not showing features specific to Word, Excel, of PowerPoint—the dynamics of the DAD organization would not have looked kindly upon that as I had no responsibility for those features. Rather my goal was to put Bill at ease over the investments of shared features. I showed off the toolbars (called command bars) as they brought unification of both toolbars and menus), Escher drawing, highlighting the depth of the work we were doing. This was enough to put people at ease for the time being. It was a good lesson on how the verbose nature of the email status report was mostly undermining the goal of showing off progress.

The demo went so well that we separately held another demo session at the end of the milestone. In this one we filled the room with members of each team, and everyone got to show off the work of their team. It also served as a reminder that while there were plenty of shared features, a large part of value of the release came from the domain or app-specific features across Word, Excel, and PowerPoint. We had a new saying now, which became "we're selling Office, now we're making Office, but people use the individual apps."

After the meeting, I nudged Bill to send a nice note summarizing what he saw and served to solidify the progress we were making across the team and undo some of the earlier nonsense.

And it was a good lesson that working software beats a status report. Onward.

042. CLIPPY, THE F*CKING CLOWN

In early discussions, we attempted to explain how we had learned from the abysmal failure of Microsoft Bob and that we had a plan. At one point, the conversation turned from stepping through a complex task in Excel to BillG bringing us to tears in playing back what he heard. They were both tears of joy and tears of pain. It went something like this:

> *Demo: The Assistant will then appear and offer each step in sequence to create a chart, as the user interface does today. But it will be more friendly and approachable and have easy access to help content.*
>
> *Bill: So, when I want to create a chart the clown will pop up and say, "I'm here to help" and...*
>
> *Demo: Not clown, but assistant.*
>
> *Bill: The clown pops up and then I'm like clicking on the clown saying clown next, next, clown next or something just to create a chart.*
>
> *Demo: The Assistant is just a more approachable and helpful version of the same number of clicks and steps you always had.*
>
> *Bill: Next...next...next, and pretty soon I just want the fucking clown to get out of the way.*

Bill often had these routines or short skits that he would play out over and over—if you were the target, it was painful the first couple of times then it was for show for other attendees then you had to assert yourself. This was one of those. Through the entire rise and ultimate fall of the idea of an animated character or agent, which he referred to as a "clown", this pattern complete with the escalating high-pitched frustrated BillG voice would make an appearance. I lost track of how many times he ridiculed the feature this way. Still, he doesn't get the right to say told-you-so.

This started with the earliest products based on an animated helper that were developed in the early 1990s and released while I was working as Technical Assistant, so I was quite familiar with the above routine. Then Microsoft's focus was on bringing software and PCs to children and like all products for children, the general theory of education told us that products needed to be fun, engaging, and immersive, and different from business-oriented or grownup products.

A pair of products were developed together for Windows 3, *Creative Writer* and *Fine Artist*, a kid-oriented word-processor and drawing program. While these products were nominally about the basics of productivity, they were part of an entire animated world called *Imaginopolis* hosted by the ever-present guide, *McZee*, a lanky purple humanoid. It is easy to be dismissive of the products, but in fact they contained enormous feature-depth for the time. McZee was more than just a helper, but essentially the full user interface for the products. All the actions were directed through McZee.

Measuring success in the new *Microsoft Kids* line was difficult because the unit sales weren't spectacular and also because everything was new, and the company was determined to stick with it. Recall the Microsoft reputation for taking three versions to get something right dating back to at least the original Windows. The spiritual successor to these two products was an even greater product risk as it was not just for kids, but for the home. The problem that needed solving was that people were buying home computers, but lacked software to do home things, like keep lists, write letters, track to-do items, and calendars. While there were business packages that did that, the general theory was that software for the home needed to be more friendly and approachable, especially because those not skilled in business computers would use it.

The Consumer Division where Microsoft Kids software came from was filled with people on a mission to bring software to a broader audience. One of those was Karen Fries (KarenFr) who was the lead advocate and pioneer for the use of what was widely known in academic circles as social interface. Karen was co-leading program management for these new products and was deeply immersed in the cutting-edge technology. She was a co-author of a 1994 paper "Seductive interfaces: satisfying a mass audience" with some of the early work in the area. Other authors on the paper were Stanford researchers, Clifford Nass and Byron Reeves. This was serious work with some depth. Nass and Reeves (who would later consult with our efforts in Office) developed the work into a book *The Media Equation: How People Treat Computers, Television, and New Media Like Real People and Places.* Their research developed and provided evidence of a core thesis that humans "treat computers, televisions, and new media as real people and places" and beyond that, humans develop models for interacting with technology and media based on how those works are designed. At the extreme, this explained frustration and fear of computers because of the general belief that computers are smarter than people and so interacting with them took on the traits of interacting with a much smarter and less tolerant human. This is what Karen, along with her co-leader (and designer) Barry Linnet (BarryL) set out to fix in developing *Microsoft Bob*, code name *Utopia*. No strangers to making easy to use software, Karen and Barry co-led the creation of Microsoft Publisher, a very successful and much-loved entry into what was known as desktop publishing, a tool for creating newsletters, certificates, menus, signs, etc. aimed at home and small business users.

Like McZee, Microsoft Bob was an immersive environment. The experience, however, was less kid and more home. It was still animated, and it was still fun. Bob was the smiley face that occupied the middle letter O of the name, though within the software an ever-present puppy acted as the assistant and guide for using the many modules of the product. Each module was depicted as a place to click on in the home—click on a phone index for contacts, a pad of paper to write a letter, a checkbook for finances, a globe for a geography quiz (gosh, that was such a BillG thing), and so on. The software had even more depth than the previous products. As an example, a typical home letter-writing effort might be a complaint to an airline for lost luggage. Bob not only contained samples, but even maintained a list of airlines and addresses that it would use to pre-populate a complaint letter as this was long before the internet.

At the January 1995 Consumer Electronics Show, Bob was launched to immense fanfare and broad media coverage across print and even morning television. There was so much enthusiasm about home computers but before the internet people were just not sure what to do with them, at least broadly. That said, the product was unfortunately not well-received and ran into the buzzsaw of technologists who simply didn't buy into the shell or veneer Bob created around Windows.

Why was Microsoft going through all this and making these risky, or even edgy, products? Many seemed puzzled by this at the time. In order to understand that today, one must recognize that using a PC in the 1990s, and earlier, was not just difficult, but it was also confusing, frustrating, inscrutable, and by and large entirely inaccessible to most everyone unless you had to learn how to use one for work. In fact, using a computer usually meant signing up for an in-person class that would meet at night for a few hours over the course of several weeks—often buying a computer came not with an extended warranty upsell, but one of these classes. It was this era when businesses would put out job opportunities for people that had 1-2 years of experience using a PC, preferable Lotus 1-2-3 and WordPerfect. These products with their dizzying array of keystroke commands and chorded combinations of ALT, CTRL, and SHIFT keys were difficult if not bordering on impossible for most people to master.

As written previously, Windows and the graphical user interface were supposed to fix all this with its easy-to-use menus and direct manipulation with a mouse. Yet the exact opposite happened because while those made accessing commands easier, the number of possible commands was growing at a rapid pace. It wasn't just that Word added bullets and numbering, but it added the myriad of options to stylize, format, and order paragraphs. And footnotes, endnotes, pagination, hanging indent, and on and on, then Excel and PowerPoint too. In order to mitigate the growing complexity of the products, Office developed an array of bolt-on utilities from massive printed and bound books, wizards (pioneered in Publisher), tutorials, getting started (like a tutorial but shorter), even a friendly tip-of-the-day that offered a quick refresher lesson when you launched a program. It got to the point where even these various forms of help needed an overview to explain them. Ironically, an after-market developed which packaged up all that information and the expertise of authors to create even more help. Typically, owners of Office (or even those considering owning the product) would invest in phonebook sized softcover books further explaining the use of the product. At first this seemed cool, then we started to realize the futility of our own product development efforts.

The one constant, as we studied the landscape of people using Office, was that getting anything done involved tracking down the nearby Office *guru*—the person that invested the time and effort to master the software more than the rest of the people in the office. Need to create a table, figure out a formula, or draw an org chart then go down the hall and get help from the guru.

Chances were high that the product did what you thought you wanted to do, but the path through the maze of commands was not only difficult but fraught with the risk of destroying your work or getting the document into a state that would make further work even more difficult. We often would receive letters detailing specific features or outcomes a customer would like to achieve, only to learn that the feature was already in the product.

With Office96 we set out to build the guru into Office to solve this growing problem and dissatisfaction with the product. The early love of Office was turning into early signs of resentment as the customer-base grew. Early adopters loved the power of the product, but increasingly new customers felt overwhelmed by their lack of mastery. We had a genuine customer satisfaction problem on our hands.

As we knew from Nass and Reeves research, people had confidence in the tool to get things done but lacked a way to interact with it to understand how unless the right human guru was helping. Our challenge was to build a software equivalent to the guru.

That software equivalent would start with the clown as BillG called it or Assistant as we called it. The name of the internal implementation of the Assistant, *tfc* in our Hungarian notation, was a hat tip to BillG's "the f*cking clown." Even though Bill had ridiculed each social interface product, we were deep in the problem we needed to solve and optimistic we could figure out an approach. We needed to look no further than the computers on *Star Trek*, which enabled Captain Kirk and Spock to tap into the vast resources with vague questions and open-ended problems. Similarly, the industry was buzzing with the idea of *agents* that would be able to do work on your behalf such as find cheap airline flights or schedule meetings. Everywhere from Apple to the MIT Media Lab were talking about agents. There was ample evidence this was not simply a weird vision in our corner of the tech world. In fact, by some accounts we were in a race to have the first and best guru in the box.

The lesson from Bob was clearly that an entire immersive environment would not work, plus there was no way we would do that for Office. We also knew that rewiring the entire interface to do everything through the step-by-step interactions with the assistant would not work. Instead, we wanted to combine the warmth and comfort of a social experience with the kind of help the guru provided in real life. While many would ultimately conclude that the paperclip was simply bolted on the side of Office to provide cuteness, we made three big technology investments, even bets, to bring Clippy to market.

The first step in asking a Guru for help was to ask a question in your own language. The guru then maps that question to the typical answers or FAQ (frequently asked questions) that were known. You might ask "how to print sideways" and the guru knows to check the landscape option in the print dialog, or "how do I hide the elephants in Word" and the guru knows you are talking about the pilcrow symbol, ¶. A typical question might be even more abstract such as "how do I format alternating rows in a spreadsheet" which a guru might point to more sophisticated features of Excel rather than some of the direct formatting tools. This is precisely the technology we had developed and released for Office 95 as the Answer Wizard. In fact, we back-ported Answer Wizard to Office 95 because it was working pretty well and did not disturb the rest of the product. As mentioned previously, there was a collaboration with Microsoft Research (also a group from Stanford) that led this first pillar of the guru.

Next, one of the things a guru does, at least a good guru, is watch over your shoulder when you are struggling. Often diagnosing a problem, like trying to align two boxes in an org chart or get the columns of a table to be the right width, is not so much being told the right answer as much as being told which step was where you went astray. We knew many tasks in Office were composed of multiple steps that needed to be done in the right order, and often people would try something click undo and try something else. We posited that if we could track the activities as the product was used, we could either proactively or on request (hitting the help key, F1) offer a suggestion from our library of help topics for how to get the right thing done. For example, if a user seemed to be clicking around paragraph formatting and indenting, the system might know enough to suggest a help topic on formatting headings or paragraph spacing. And if a user was stuck, simply hitting F1 was a way to summon the guru using the context that was accumulated over the most recent few minutes of use. This was another collaboration with Microsoft Research based on some of early 1990s work using Bayesian math to build a model for making these guesses based on contextual cues. This work came out of Stanford's artificial intelligence lab and formed the early AI efforts in Microsoft Research. It too was all the rage at the time in academic tech circles.

It was this part of Clippy that proved to be the most challenging to deliver on the promise. Deciding when to fire off the assistant, finding that balance to being helpful versus annoying, is precisely what the human guru finds challenging when looking over your shoulder. Too little help and the product remains frustrating. Too much help and the user just wants to hand the keyboard over and say you do it. The artificial intelligence approach may or may not have been the right technology, but it proved inadequate at the time. The product had too many commands and entry points, or simply too many decisions to make at any given time to be truly helpful.

One mistake, well really the mistake, was firing Assistant on the most simple and obvious effort in Word. The sequence of starting a new document, typing Dear <name> and pressing return would cause the assistant to say, "Looks like you're trying to write a letter." And with that Clippy was forever sentenced to memedom. Is that a word? In our heads we thought this was OK because we were already doing a tip (a yellow bar across the top of the screen) to alert the user to the letter writing feature. This was really a step too far. It did not help that if you clicked "Yes" the software would launch an incredibly complicated wizard offering all sorts of options for a letter, most of which went unused. A few years later, the Microsoft researcher who contributed the Bayesian technology even turned on us in an interview with *The Economist* and said it was all because we didn't use enough of the technology. That really hurt—it was as much their work as our work.

The third pillar of bringing the guru to Office was to offer the user the calming and comforting personality of a guru. Using a computer was difficult and frustrating, and we set out to bring some levity to the daily grind. Leaning heavily on the work of Nass and Reeves, we developed the actual character to represent the guru—to attach a personality to the source for answers and tips that would encourage help. We also went a step beyond that and decided that the Office Assistant would be where messages (or alerts) would come from. The ever-present "Do you want to save this file" or "The spell check is complete" would emanate from the assistant. This was the biggest and highest risk bet of the entire feature. It is also what separated the feature from the previous dozen attempts at providing help—it wasn't yet another bolted-on tool, but it was in the flow of usage and there to help everyone. Internally we called this *IntelliAssist*.

The minute we had an animated Assistant it was obvious that any opinion or controversy about the feature would stem from the clown or character itself, not the assistance provided. Starting in early 1994 we began the most intensive usability research testing we had done to date on a feature. The number of tests, the number of locations and languages, and design ideas we iterated on was kind of mind-blowing. At one point people were flying to Japan and Europe to rerun tests to see how the results might differ. How big should the assistant be, how much noise should it make (if the user even had a sound card), how often should it appear, how animated should it be, and on and on. The iterations were seemingly endless, all with the goal of making it friendly and approachable while tapping into the fancy underlying artificial intelligence technology.

Choosing the actual character was incredibly controversial. It became immediately apparent everyone had an opinion, and importantly every major sales geography had their own view of what would work locally. It didn't matter that many animated characters worked globally, there was a strong demand for input and oversight. The risk, after all, was very high. For example, Japan accounted for nearly one-third of Office profits because of the unique market there. The lead program manager, Sam Hobson (SamH), an experienced member of the Excel team who joined

OPU (also a college hire like the rest of us) had the perfect demeanor for managing all the connections across the company.

Perhaps we were naive, but we never sat around contemplating the risk the business of doing this feature. In 1995, Platforms revenue was $2.36 billion, and Applications revenue was $3.58 billion—even a small hiccup in Office would be a huge deal. We weren't comforted in the past sales of the product, but rather sought the comfort of believing we were on a mission to solve an acute customer problem—a problem left unchecked that could materially impact the business. How could a product remain successful if people increasingly dislike it?

Sam created huge boards of potential characters for everyone to look at and pick their favorite. He would lead tests at shopping malls and markets around the world understanding preferences. Meanwhile, Nass and Reeves reminded us of these preferences were rather predictable and also not as crucial as maybe the salespeople who saw this more as branding than utility believed. In one hilarious early use of these boards, Sam invited the spiritual leader (and then Microsoft board member) Mike Maples to pick his favorite character. Ever the rancher and Oklahoman, everyone thought Mike would pick the big dog or maybe the lion or something. Instead after browsing the dozens of choices, Mike went with…the pink bunny rabbit. He smiled and said it reminded him of the rabbits on the ranch. This kind of reaction is what led to the full gallery of choices. While the paper clip, Clippit aka Clippy, would be the default, we featured a dog, a cat, a happy smiling dot reminiscent of Bob, and several more including a really boring Office logo for marketing purposes. The scale of Japan's business required us to take their input and from that we ended up with the highly controversial *Office Lady* or Saeko Sensei, which to many at HQ was less than appropriate. Japan also came to love symbols of nature, and guided us to a Kairu, a dolphin and again there was irony in that choice that made us uncomfortable. We kept those characters to the Japanese version of the product. We would later add a small Macintosh-like computer called Max for Mac Office. Being Microsoft, we had an SDK and even a third-party partner that could (and would) create additional assistants.

The character, like the artificial intelligence behind the first two pillars, had a depth of capabilities that often go unappreciated and certainly did at the time. We were severely constrained in disk space and memory, not to mention graphics capabilities, yet wanted to provide a reasonable animation experience. This proved extremely difficult as the expectations for animation had been set by cartoons.

At one point we had a most memorable opportunity to meet with the legendary animators from Walt Disney, Frank Thomas and Ollie Johnston otherwise known as Frank and Ollie. Together they were involved with everything from *Pinocchio* to *Fantasia* to *Bambi* and more. An example of a constraint that frustrated us was the window the character was trapped in. We wanted to do a borderless Assistant like in Bob, but the platform constraints were too much when overlayed with regular Windows apps. Frank and Ollie not only relieved us of that but explained how we should use the window as their stage to allow for entrance and exit and directional animations. They also pushed us to add a sidekick (think Thumper) which was something they had pioneered in animation. They suggested Clippit have something like a little eraser friend. That was well beyond the two dozen or so animation sequences we could have but really brought us optimism for how the feature could evolve with more platform support.

Sound was still nascent in most PCs, constrained by the original MIDI sound capabilities. Windows 95 and multimedia were changing that. We also added a set of sounds that came along with animations which if a user had them on made a real difference in the experience.

These capabilities were coded throughout the product. The Assistant would occasionally just blink or smile or take note of work. If you stopped typing for a while it might perk up and notice you. Using a more technical feature would come with a more substantial animation. The assistant was also programmed to get out of the way while you were typing or scrolling, which led to a fun game of chase-the-paperclip using mouse and the Excel grid as was commonly shown in demonstrations.

As we tested the character in various stages behind one-way glass or in focus groups, there was almost always surprise and more frequently than most would believe today praise and support for the feature. It is a cliché for a failed feature to say that it worked in early testing, but that was genuinely the case.

Still as the project progressed there were many that were nervous or outright hostile. As we showed the product to the hardcore technical audience, the reactions were often visceral and immediate. Either people wanted to immediately turn it off without much consideration or they would be thoughtful and suggest that it is not for them, but they could see others (read as less technical) people benefitting. As we would learn time and gain, when core technical users say that something isn't for them but for others it too often means that the feature might be good, but it is going to need to get past these gatekeepers. We made a very difficult decision to provide an array of settings to control the various capabilities of the Assistant. In other words, we made it possible to turn it off. At the same time, we provided full programmability with VBA so that developers could create custom solutions with full control over the Assistant, including adding custom text in the balloons and choosing animations. Imagine how much fun that budget template in Excel could be with custom chatter from the Assistant!

The Assistant was one part of an enormous release of Office. The remainder of this chapter details some of the other challenges in building Office 97 on the platform and infrastructure described in the previous section. The product reviews were ultimately mixed, but hardly universal, as we will see in the end of this chapter.

We stuck with and improved the Assistant in the next release of Office. By the second subsequent release we retired the feature, albeit in a humorous way. In parallel with Office 97 an effort began to bring the Assistant to Windows for use by third-party developers. *Microsoft Agent* had much richer interactions using early speech recognition and voice but lacked deeper integration with applications unless coded by developers. Agent was used in Windows XP and remained available for some years.

The journey of Clippy (in spite of our best efforts that was what the feature came to be called) was one that parallels the PC for me in so many ways. It was not simply a failed feature, or that back-handed compliment of a feature that was simply too early like so many Microsoft features. Rather Clippy represented a final attempt at trying to fix the desktop metaphor for typical or normal people so they could use a computer. What everyone came to realize was that the PC was a generational change and that for those growing up with a PC, it was just another arbitrary and random device in life that one just used. As we would learn, kids didn't need different software. They just needed access to a PC. Once they had a PC they would make cooler, faster, and more fun documents with Office than we were. It was kids that loved WordArt and the new graphics in Word and PowerPoint, and they used them easily and more frequently than Boomers or Gen X trying to map typewriters to what a computer could do. It was not the complexity that was slowing people down, but the real concern that the wrong thing could undo hours of work. Kids did not have that fear, yet. We needed to worry less about dumbing the software down and more about how more complex things could get done in a way that had far less risk.

The other lesson from the Clippy experience is clearly how amazing it was that Microsoft even considered such a high-risk feature. Imagine doing a feature that you know at launch will have some people significantly annoyed with you but doing so also knowing that you could reach some other new customers or bring joy to customers that were otherwise worried. The whole business relies on upgrading existing customers and attracting new customers when all of them have an option of doing nothing or going to one of several competitors. The Microsoft that made Clippy is the risk-taking company that I admired so much. It was the failure of Clippy and the lack of repercussions that in a sense that cemented my own connection to the company. I got way more grief outside the company than inside.

And I needed that because for the next five years of college recruiting trips, I would have to answer snarky questions about Clippy from college students. The deepest pit in my stomach came when I was in New York on a trip at a low point in the Microsoft versus DOJ trial. I turned on the hotel television for some *Late Night with Conan O'Brien* and his opening monologue took a swipe at Microsoft, "Come on Bill, Microsoft got off easy compared to what the Government did to Clippy, that *annoying paperclip* in that pops up in Microsoft Word" [emphasis added] followed by a gruesome violent act perpetrated against poor Clippy. That hurt. A lot. The cheers from the studio audience hurt even more. I was totally signed up for the risk and reviews but being mocked on my favorite late-night show. Ouch.

Then one campus season, perhaps in 2002 or 2003, those snarky comments turned into an expressed love of Clippy and comments like "I remember Clippy on my mom's computer at work" or "I miss the Dog." That was amazing. Only that was outdone when about a decade later, Clippy transitioned from nostalgia to a high-tech feature that was somehow ahead of its time. I wish I could say that was the case, but it was simply an idea, not an unreasonable one and not one with a particularly bad execution. The implementation, however, was decidedly 1997.

043. DIM OUTLOOK

When we started the 94/96 plan, Office was Word, Excel, PowerPoint, and (for about half our customers) the Access database in the premium edition, Office Professional. By the time we shipped Office96 we added two entirely new products, FrontPage (acquired from Vermeer corporation) for website creation, and *Ren & Stimpy* (the code name for what would become Outlook) for email and scheduling. It is rather remarkable in hindsight that by some measures the Office product nearly doubled in size and complexity along the way. Bringing two products into Office proved to be equal parts learning and terror, and my first experience dealing with the role bundling plays in our business execution.

Through the whole Office 95 product cycle, I was maniacally focused on all things internet. One of the fastest rising uses of the internet turned out to be the oldest, and that was email. Microsoft tended to view email through the lens of the nascent yet growing server business because of Exchange Server, still under development in the Workgroup Apps team, WGA. With the release of Windows 95 (and WordMail), Exchange Server was front and center for all of Microsoft and the growing enterprise business, and still a year away from release to the public but deploying inside Microsoft and a few select customers.

Being a server team, the end-user experience for the product would characteristically receive less attention. The Exchange-created mail client program, Windows 95 *Inbox* (previously Capone, but still called that in discussions), and the calendaring program, called *Schedule+*, which was ported from the legacy MS Mail system, constituted the Exchange clients. None of these clients (client as in client-server architecture) were particularly good at connecting to internet mail.

The industry, in general, had a blind spot for internet mail. New entrants like Netscape were the exception, as everything at Netscape was *native* to the internet. Lotus Notes, the primary competitor to Exchange, was aggressively building in Internet capabilities. They already had a successful product in market and recently executed a big launch of internet connectivity at their conference, all with the backing of IBM ownership.

Surprisingly, within the Workgroup Apps team there was a second mail client being built with the code name Ren & Stimpy. Originally the team planned two releases, Ren a lightweight product to include in Windows, and followed by a more full-featured product, Stimpy, to include potentially in Office. Work had been going on for quite some time already.

Brian MacDonald (BrianMac), leading the team, was legendary in his ability to project a monstrous and all-encompassing vision for a project and recruit and rally an ever-growing team to go after the vision. Brian was well known within Apps, having created Microsoft Project as a start-up acquired by Microsoft 1989, growing it to a business of hundreds of millions of dollars. Project was a traditional project management tool used to manage timelines and resources for big projects such as construction. It was one of several market-defining and significant revenue-generating products from the expanding product that were often over-looked in telling the story of the Apps business.

Sometimes people with BrianMac's set of skills, aspirations grow faster than the execution. Perhaps through no fault of their own, they find the product positioned between one or more teams who alternatively believe they are competitors or depend heavily on the product for their own success. In the case of Ren (the shorthand name), it was clear the team achieved a combination of most of these.

The Ren vision was extremely broad—to encompass the whole flow of daily work on a PC from mail and contacts to scheduling to tasks and *to do* all the way, including managing your files and even custom business apps like Lotus Notes could create. It is this breadth that at once caused it to become an essential part of every team's strategy and also a competitor. Without having shipped a line of code and without anyone outside the team even close to using the product, Ren had become central to most every conversation within Microsoft. When Ren wasn't licking the proverbial cookie of some team, it was the cookie being licked by another team.

Ren was heavily dependent on Exchange features and performance. Ren also bumped up against (or even surpassed) capabilities of Inbox/Capone and Schedule+, Windows Explorer for managing files and the successor called the Cairo Shell, Lotus Notes, and even Excel because of the pivot-table like UI it had for viewing data stored in Exchange. Yes, this was a confusing lot and meant it pretty painful to go to any meetings on these topics. Was Ren partaking in cookie-licking or was it going to deliver was a common theme and that meant groups had no problem articulating plans that bet against Ren. In other words, there was no shortage of pessimism about the product to counter its own expansive and optimistic vision.

While we had not made any packaging choices for Office, in the latter part of 1994 the Ren team was moved to the Desktop Apps division, specifically within the Office Product Unit. Adding an entire product to OPU was awkward, as our mission was shared code, but the state of the product was such that it would benefit from the hands-on management that would presumably come from BrianMac working side-by-side with the rest of us in OPU.

As an alternative to Capone and Schedule+, Ren was clearly going to be integral to the success of Exchange. Early on, however, there was a great deal of resistance within the WGA team to an outside group that did not understand the intricacies of the email server being so core to the success of the product, as we learned building WordMail. Yet the server team's focus and execution on clients remained a relatively narrow expression of the space, aiming to expose the server functionality in a somewhat linear manner—meaning a focus on email messages, not a general database as both BillG and BrianMac were pushing. Ren had much grander visions for taking advantage of all the server might possibly offer in ways the server team had not really thought of doing—something experienced frequently by platforms.

The product team that most immediately placed Ren in the crosshairs was the even larger and more ambitious operating system, Cairo. Cairo was a fundamental rethinking of the operating system from the ground up, with two aspects of it that ran up against Ren. The challenge here was not aligning products or technologies, but how to foster such an alignment when both projects were so exceedingly early and ambitious that really this was less about one code base pitted against another and more about one slide deck going against another.

Cairo aimed to reinvent the interaction with the desktop, files, folders, and programs. This new model, an object-oriented shell, encompassed two *third rails* in one description. First was the buzzword *object-oriented*. As I learned in C++, this was a phrase that meant everything or really nothing, depending on your perspective. When it meant everything, as it did to Cairo, it meant that it was likely that Ren was doing everything *wrong*. There were going to be many OS techniques that Ren should take advantage of that were entirely different than those available on Windows 95 and beyond. That's what reinvention is all about. Navigating this would be quite difficult since most capabilities didn't yet exist, and Ren was trying to sync up with Exchange Server and also Windows 95.

The concept of the shell as the one place for everything is essentially what the "desktop" is on an operating system, or on today's mobile phone home screen. Since it is the most visible part of the OS it receives a lot of attention, especially during reviews and evaluations. In practice, most customers who aren't tech enthusiasts see the shell as a place to launch the programs they care about and copy files around and not too much more. As an OS-first company, though, Microsoft and BillG were very much shell-first in thinking. This meant that Ren's self-described mission to be a shell was important and thus would bump up against the actual operating system.

Every team aimed to be a shell. In tech evolution in general, each mini-epoch can be thought of as a time when all software generally converges to one type of application. In the early days of the PC basically everything became a word processor—most all programs were about typing in some way or another and would add features over time to be better at typing such as spelling, printing support, and fonts. With the GUI, most every application aimed to become a shell and place where other programs could be launched, and files opened. The Microsoft Office Shortcut bar is an example of this as was the investment in overly featured file open dialogs across most commercial software. Future epochs would be defined by convergence to web browsing, later photo editing and sharing (which became a routine demo joke during the early 2000s when it seemed every product demo at the company meeting showed photos), and in the late 2010s every product eventually became a text-based messaging product.

The second rail of Cairo was an entirely different underlying storage model—where mail and other data should be stored. So again, even before getting too far down the process, the Ren team was doing everything either twice correctly or once correctly for the present and incorrectly for the future. This dilemma routinely faced Microsoft, as during this period of rapid expansion things were being duplicated at many different parts of the company and with varying levels of execution capabilities.

The Ren versus Cairo struggle is not unlike so many of the classic struggles at Microsoft, which could be summed up as asking the question "Why did Microsoft have two (or more) groups trying to do the same thing?" To outsiders this can look wasteful at best, or plain stupid at worst. To insiders, this looks confusing and strategically lacking. Basically, everyone on the collective teams just thought executives were clueless and needlessly torturing everyone. Oh, to be young again.

To the execs, they knew that they wanted the sum of the work across all the teams. They might want the user interface skills of the Apps teams and the server programming skills of the Server division but had no way of doing both easily. The naïve view was to just create a team with all those skills and let them go at it. That was what almost everyone in product teams argued for, but to execs doing that created a ton of organization friction not the least of which was even deciding where to put that team. Frankly, there's enough experience to know that even if you created a whole new team with all the valued skills and perspectives, wherever the team lands was going to be the high-order bit of the new team and determined its fate.

Something I came to appreciate as I gained experience was that organizations are not a substitute for strategy. In fact, the organization ultimately defines what the strategy will be. Capone sitting in the Exchange team guaranteed a minimalist mail client that expressed the viewpoint of the Server, as an example. Years later I would often approach strategy questions being debated through the lens of potential re-organizations by asking rhetorically "tell me the outcome you want, and I can craft an org" knowing that was exactly the decision execs did not want to make. Usually, the answer to that was something along the lines of "the teams will work out the optimal solution" to which I would reply seriously, not rhetorically, "tell me who will manage the team and we'll know the decisions they will make." Even though that was right, I could be frustrating.

With such a grand vision and sandwiched between two groups, Ren had an even bigger challenge, and that was executing. There was simply too much to do. ChrisP, master of shipping, was asked to *manage* the Ren team and help find a way to get it to ship with the Office96 product release. In the best of circumstances this would have been a crazy challenge. Our team already had too much going on, and the urgency ChrisP was asked to inject into the team was not welcome. Rather, the Ren team continued to expand its scope, further raising the eyebrows of both WGA and Cairo.

Once Ren was moved to Office, it was going to ship. That instantly became the high-order bit. In Office we shipped, and strategy and vision were scoped to shipping, not ever-expanding. That was going to frustrate some (including the Ren team) but putting the team in OPU determined the next steps. As part of moving Ren to Office, part of the Cairo team also moved to Office. That was really BillG hoping that those magical Cairo features would ship sooner. While I'm sure some people believed that could happen, I was certain that moving the team to Office made the actual outcome abundantly clear.

Moving the responsibility for developing Ren to DAD made sense as it could compete with SmartSuite on the desktop, leaving Exchange to compete on the server with Notes. Still, this was controversial since the strength of Notes was that it combined both a server and a desktop client in one integrated product. In a sense it was taking a contrarian view of competing—having a distinct client and server communicating over a well-defined API, rather than having an integrated client and server placing code where it made the most sense. Or it could be viewed as relying on the strength of the Office desktop versus SmartSuite. Would the email client pull in a new set of productivity tools for Lotus/IBM, or would the leaders in productivity tools be able to pull through a new entry to mail servers with Exchange?

ChrisP and I developed a "get focused" management approach that was both straightforward and rather gutsy. Since I would be on the front lines in daily/weekly cross-group meetings, to downplay the expanding visions we developed a series of questions that we would have at the ready every time the Ren team looked to be slipping out of "get-done" mode and back into vision mode. We called these the "Get Serious Seven":

1. Is it 100% Compatible with Capone?
2. Is it 100% Compatible with Schedule+?
3. Is it 100% Compatible with Chicago Explorer?

4. What is the working set [memory usage] when using it to read mail? When using it to browse files (not logged onto mail)?
5. When is it going to be used by all of Office? All of DAD? What are the code complete, ZBR, beta dates?
6. Is everyone running and testing Ren on Chicago?
7. Does it browse FAT [file system]? Cairo OFS [file system]?

There was nothing magical about these questions as they encompassed the ChrisP and DAD methodology and also represented the claims the Ren team was making about the product across the company. In that sense this was rather straightforward. The details do not make much sense today since many of these features never made it, but the idea was to constrain the vision talk and emphasize execution talk.

A second action, and gutsy one, was to add a person to the mix. ChrisP asked Jodi Green (JodiG), the longtime Word engineering leader (also cafeteria tablemate) and fantastic project leader, to take on a role as the development manager for Ren. The thing was there already was a development manager and the org was not going to change. Jodi was looking for something she could take on part time where she could use her expertise without the overhead of line management, so this was a perfect match. JodiG convinced herself, along with support from all the OPU managers across dev, test, and PM, to sign up to be the *adult supervision*—or a *spy*, depending on your perspective. The truth was she was going to be an asset to the team if they could just realize it.

Jodi and I often talked about the challenges—the lack of specifications, the churning of ideas and code, and general absence of discipline. The team was in a situation that we saw all too often in both "version 1" products and projects that did not feel the hunger to get to market but were seeking perfection—the enemy of the good is the perfect. As a version 1.0 product, Ren also had its share of trying to use all the latest tools and techniques. Ren was first big application to be *object-oriented* and to use C++ and even started from my old MFC libraries. There was nothing inherently wrong with this (in fact, I was super proud and excited, albeit a bit nervous), but when you're already long on vision and short on execution these become evidence points and, worse, part of the blame game in the hallways. It is worth noting, that the Ren team was made up of many people who had shipped a lot of products, but something about the vision and leadership had caused an expanding appetite for vision.

The plan was starting to work, and after a few months things really started to solidify. While Jodi deserves a huge amount of credit for putting herself in the middle of the team as an influencer, she drove a more refined team culture and helped to bring them into the DAD fold. As one might expect, projects that churn and change a lot also begin to fatigue the team or at least create some frustration or friction. One engineering leader in that camp was Don Gagne (DonGa), new to Microsoft but with 20 years of experience at start-ups shipping software, growing companies, and more. He joined with significant experience in the email space and had risen quickly to become the go-to leader of the team. With JodiG from the outside and leaders like DonGa rising from within the team, Ren began to look more and more like it could be part of Office96.

The depth of features in Ren was kind of mind-blowing. Early in the product cycle, after using the product for a brief time I sent AndrewK, the user interface leader for OPU, a note bemoaning my "exhaustion" in using the product because it had so much "stuff on the screen." While that sounds like an insult, I also said it was a "goldmine."

I wondered though how customers would react when the vast majority were not yet using email and almost none had email in their corporations. Email growth was, however, exponential and with Exchange driving that there was an enormous opportunity for Microsoft.

Ren not only had a very feature-rich email capability (such as a new inbox that showed the first few lines of a message) and incredibly rich scheduling capability (including delegate access, numerous views for day/week/month/workweek, time zones and more), but a host of other modules including rudimentary task management, little yellow sticky-notes, browsing regular files in Windows, and even a kind of journal that kept track chronologically of all the work in Office. Beyond that the user interface was, for lack of a better word, object-oriented. Every one of those features could create custom views of items that worked like Excel pivot table, or display items as a calendar (tasks viewed in a calendar for example), or even dragged and dropped to create mail messages, such as mail a task to someone. Beyond that was a whole new user interface element called the *Outlook Bar*, which was like the Office Shortcut Bar but inside Outlook for switching between the different modules of Outlook plus tons more features. The Outlook Bar was itself the subject of intense debate and endless consternation over the design and whether it had enough! The product was a fountain of snazzy, but incredibly difficult to discover demo features.

While all of this was going on, the big competitive issue for DAD and Microsoft in general remained Lotus SmartSuite. The resurgence of Lotus Notes, arising from IBM's aggressive acquisition of Lotus in late 1995, put a spotlight on the enterprise threats facing Microsoft—competing with Notes became much more of an issue for Office. IBM's enormous sales force selling Lotus Notes for workgroup and email with SmartSuite on the desktop would be formidable and scary.

Ren was christened *Outlook* after an elaborate and expensive search for a product name. The marketing team defined Outlook to be in a new category, *desktop information management* or *DIM*. This somewhat puzzling choice was the source of endless puns from the groups that still bet against Outlook ever finishing. In moments of frustration, the Exchange team loved to remind me of "DIM Outlook."

I was worried. Shipping is difficult in the best of times. We were behind in Office96, with an original ship date of end of early 1996, it was becoming clear that even making 1997 was a challenge. Blaming Outlook would be easy, but also incredibly unfair. Across Office we had too much work to do. The question was not, however, if we would finish but simply how late we would be. Still, I was not immune from worrying Outlook would be the "long pole" as we would say with respect to shipping.

Outlook was the first of several newly created products used not to grow new businesses (revenue streams) but bundled with Office (or given away for free, depending on perspective) to sustain the existing business. Jim Barksdale, the CEO of Netscape, was famous for his comment, "There are two ways to make money in business: bundling and unbundling." Microsoft, and SteveB in particular, were squarely on the side of bundling new capabilities into our existing efforts to sustain them and deliver more to customers.

Much like the strategy versus org question, the bundling question is one that had easy answers when I was young in career and over time the answer became more subtle and nuanced. At this moment, I was decidedly against bundling but entirely for operational reasons—I was just worried Outlook would slow us all down while also dramatically increasing memory requirements. Additionally, without Exchange server Outlook was all but useless. It would not be until later that rudimentary support for the basic Internet mail protocols would get added, but many of the core demo features of the product required Exchange, which was exactly the point, strategically speaking.

The other naïve perspective I had was that if we wanted to grow the business, then clearly selling a new product for a real dollar price was better than just giving it away for free. Given that Outlook wasn't useful for most customers or so I thought, how could a free product grow our business. Our old friend exponential growth is important here because the growing in mail was so explosive, that the idea of email not applying to customers would be dated and plain wrong less than a year after shipping.

What I truly failed to grok, however, was the role of having an incredibly simple and efficient message for an expanding army of salespeople. The cost of adding a new effort to sell Outlook was enormously high and didn't scale around the world like I might think it would as an engineer in Redmond. Having a simple message "Office" everywhere is something that scales. The couple of SKUs were there to just fill in basic price points and offer negotiating leverage for sales, but the message everywhere was "Office Pro." Guess what sold? Office Pro. Lesson learned.

This lesson would really hit home to me just a bit later when I visited the newly opened Microsoft Vietnam subsidiary. The General Manager met me at the hotel, and we took a scooter to the office. It was a single open space in the capital city. When we entered the whole office was lined up to greet me—all three people plus the GM. After introducing ourselves by name, he smiled when I asked who worked on which parts of the business. I was expecting abstract assignments like Public Sector, Enterprise, Small Business, Education, and so on. Instead, he proudly pointed left to right "Windows, Office, and our administrative assistant." Back in those days, a GM could add a person to the subsidiary for each incremental $1M in sales. Owing to the recent success of the business, the administrative assistant was recently added.

I wish I could say that lesson would cause me to love bundles. The choices became more difficult over time as the pressure for incremental revenue increased in the face of slowing sales to new customers. That didn't change the complexity of selling something new or the pressure to develop whole new products. It did make the debates over packaging choices much livelier.

The early packaging choices, Word + Excel + PowerPoint, and later adding Access and Outlook, were so enormously successful that it tended to confuse later decisions. In the market, Word and Excel were undeniably successful, each on their own, and in many ways supported PowerPoint (at least for a while until PowerPoint gained equal footing) and later Outlook in achieving success. Outlook being the required client for Exchange, included at no extra charge whether customers bought Office or Exchange, as IBM was doing with Notes, helped everyone including customers, sales, analysts, and reviewers.

From the product development perspective, the challenge we faced was an inability to understand market success with such a strategy. Was the whole product winning? Were we winning just because of sales and marketing? What was the right way to measure winning? Was winning about product reviews or customer satisfaction? Or was it much more about the efficiency of pushing product through our new sales channels? These challenges added complexity to our ability to plan and deliver features and products while coordinating releases with sales.

We had a great deal of work to do to ship and to learn how this decision played out. What we knew now was that Outlook had a lot of features, it was a new "puzzle piece" in the Office family logo. Outlook was going to ship everywhere Word, Excel, and PowerPoint shipped…just as email was exploding. If we were right, then Outlook would have the potential to redefine the suite. If we were wrong, Outlook would be an albatross that could impact the adoption of new versions of the core money-makers.

044. OUR FIRST BIG M&A DEAL (BEATING NETSCAPE)

We enjoyed a very fancy and atypical dinner at Daniel's Broiler on Lake Union. Chris Peters and I were hosting the co-founders of a Cambridge, Massachusetts startup, Vermeer Technologies, Incorporated. It was awkward. Only after would we learn that none of us knew what we were doing, and we were all nervous and kind of terrified.

If email was the biggest application on the internet, the technology that was causing Office the most strategic concern was HTML publishing pages to the web. When it came to web publishing, figuring out the role, if any, Office would play was much more difficult. The internet was quickly splitting into two camps. There were those who were hand-crafting sites in HTML. Using basic text editors, they pushed the limits of HTML to do everything in the browser—going all in on native HTML, which at the time did not even support basic tables or much of anything. Then there were those who would navigate with HTML until at the very end a link pointed to non-HTML documents such as PDF files (almost like the eventually extinct Gopher application), particularly inside the earliest corporate web servers called *intranets* or the new consumer web sites from print magazine publishers.

Our approach was to find ways to use Office to create HTML content so it could be viewed in browsers even without Office—in a sense the idea was to turn the World Wide Web into the next generation printer or workgroup file server for Office. Except we had two big problems. First, HTML was too minimal to support any common business documents, even as a "printer" so to speak. Second, from a PC there was no way to emulate the Save dialog to save a file to a web site. As much as we had a vision for these intranets, the technology was not there yet. We had to invent something.

The Internet Assistants across the apps bringing HTML add-ins to market for this "print-to-the-web" scenario was a level of agility that Office had not yet exercised, with much of the work happening while both Office 95 and Office96 were under development. A key person in those efforts was Kay Williams (KayW), a program manager on the Word team who had worked on getting Word's first Internet Assistant to market just in time to beat Netscape 1.0.

At one of the internet conferences in Boston, Internet World, in the fall of 1995, Kay spotted the demonstration of a product called *Vermeer*, named after the artist, by the company cofounder Randy Forgaard. Kay fired off mail to the Word team highlighting Vermeer's WYSIWYG HTML Editor. A *What You See Is What You Get* is an editor that showed what the end result would look like while the document was being created and edited. The product was especially clever. It not only edited HTML pages, but it had a new model for managing a full website collection of pages.

Nothing like that had been done before.

The technical challenges of typing a web page were understood, but no one had invented a way for less technical people to create a whole site. A site needed a home page, navigation aids, and a way to link all the pages together. This was something that many of us were experimenting with at the time as we all raced to register domain names based on our last names or other pet projects. Creating web pages was tricky enough but managing a collection of pages and especially doing basic things like collecting information from a form were equivalent to programming. Vermeer seemed to address this. I had been using early versions of the HTML assistants to share digital photos. For the photos I used the Epson *PhotoPC*, one of the first consumer digital cameras, which I had found for BillG to give as a gift to the exec staff one holiday. I pulled together a bunch of photos and created a PowerPoint HTML slideshow. I did this for a trip we took to the USS *Ohio* nuclear sub in Bremerton hosted on my original sinofsky.com. That was the early world wide web.

As we all raced to become our own independent web site publishers, Ed Fries (EdF) leading Word development, sent around a timeless mail that continues to become more relevant. In a quick joke he said:

> `Subject: thought for the day`
>
> `Truth is stranger than fiction.`
>
> `Fiction: In the future when computers are everywhere, evil forces will be able to discover everything there is to know about you by snooping computer records.`
>
> `Fact: In the future, when computers are everywhere, everyone will create personal home pages filled with boring details about their lives with the hopes that someone will pay attention to them.`
>
> `-EdF`

Several of us tried the Vermeer product and were all impressed. We later learned Vermeer was keenly aware from its server logs that Microsoft people had downloaded the product, decidedly something we were not used to. Sitting in ChrisP's office he was pondering the idea of approaching the company to see what could come of a relationship with them. Chris was many things but not usually spontaneous, so for at least an hour we rehearsed a "cold call" to the company CEO with an offer to simply meet and see a demonstration. It was kind of exhausting and very ChrisP.

After some discussion and rehearsing the call, ChrisP picked up the phone and dialed directly to Charles Ferguson, the CEO. Much to Chris's surprise, Charles picked up the phone. At first, I don't think Charles believed the vice president of Office was calling. Chris was probably more nervous, even though he joined Microsoft when it was tiny he had mentally transitioned to being used to Microsoft scale. Since PowerPoint, the Office team had not done any M&A, and it was certainly new to Chris and me.

After chatting for a bit about how excited he was to see the product, "HTML for the masses" and describing how much the design and feel of Vermeer reminded him of an Office product, Chris invited Vermeer to Redmond. We would have gone to Cambridge, but they were just as happy coming out here. By this time, we had already demonstrated the product to BillG and Chris made a point of telling that to Charles. Chris was convinced Microsoft should acquire the company.

Microsoft was not a particularly acquisitive company. Since going public, Microsoft averaged less than one deal per year. The Applications group had done only a single deal, but it was a huge winner—acquiring Forethought, Inc., the makers of PowerPoint. That $14 million dollar deal (Microsoft's revenue at the time was $345 million) and the way the product was integrated into the company, set the bar very high for Apps.

None of us were well versed in the intricacies of venture capital nor did we know at the time two important facts. First, Vermeer was in the process of fundraising, which might not have mattered except it had a big impact on the purchase price of a company, I vividly remember having this explained to me. Second, one other company had called and expressed interest and that was Menlo Park–based Netscape. Marc Andreessen was also going to be visiting the company.

Charles Ferguson and co-founder Randy Forgaard arrived in Redmond. It was nerve-racking for all of us. The two were as awed by the scale of Microsoft as they were petrified of the Microsoft reputation that preceded. It turns out Charles was somewhat skeptical of Microsoft as a company. Prior to co-founding Vermeer, Charles authored the book *Computer Wars: The Fall of IBM and the Future of Global Technology*, which among its chapters describes Microsoft as having a strategy focused on locking customers into products.

Nevertheless, the demonstration and the team were a hit. We had arranged a fancy steak dinner at a Seattle institution, Daniel's Broiler. The conversation, at least our side, was rehearsed and practiced days before. We had no intention of trying to extract information or anything more than size of the team and so on—we had decided the product was exactly right, "105% of what we had been thinking" Chris repeated from the phone call. We were trying to get to the next stage of a deal. Chris had developed a salvo that went something like, "We would love to work with you more closely. We might consider anything ranging from a lightweight marketing arrangement to a source code sale or perhaps all the way to possibly the *full meal deal*." Much to our surprise, Randy and Charles did not skip a beat and were open to acquisition, even downplaying lesser options.

And like that, Chris and I found ourselves totally in over our heads negotiating the purchase of a company. We enlisted the help of Microsoft's treasurer and soon-to-be CFO Greg Maffei (GregMa)—my former office neighbor when I worked for Bill. Greg quickly educated us on all sorts of things we did not know about: Series B financing, percent ownership, pre-money, and more. Greg even came up with some clever idea of a bridge loan in case they needed payroll, in an effort to reduce the need for them to raise the next round.

With the help of Greg, we met in the fanciest boutique hotel I had ever seen in New York City (GregMa picked it out) and negotiated over a pot of coffee that cost $80. It was an amazing experience to watch Greg negotiate the deal. We did not reach a final offer in the room, which was Greg's strategy. We flew back, agreeing to send a new offer in 24 hours. The response to the next offer was not a yes. We were worried. We did not know it at the time, but Vermeer was worried too.

In the midst of the negotiations, on December 7th Microsoft held a briefing, *Internet Strategy Day,* for the press at the Seattle Center. It was a huge event with international press, not a single one could resist the Pearl Harbor theme. The big news was the licensing deal for Java crafted by the platform team. Among the many demonstrations and strategy slides, Office would demonstrate the role *intranets* would play in the modern workplace. Our team had prepared a "vision" demonstration that I did on stage with BillG. The key features included publishing to websites from future Office tools.

The Vermeer team saw exactly how committed we were to web publishing and the internet. They also concluded, though did not share at the time, that joining forces with one of these companies would be a better way to achieve their vision than competing head-on.

We started to get worried and knew they were also in talks with Netscape. That was enough to pique the interest of PaulMa in Platforms. Charles pressed Chris that a deal could be had and offered to fly back to Redmond to do a demo for BillG, PaulMa, and other key executives. Charles was specific. He did, on December 8th. That demo by Randy sealed the deal, probably as much as the body language and Randy's impressive demo skills and passion as it was about the interest from Netscape.

A little more back and forth and we had a deal, and Netscape lost out or passed or whatever. For a brief moment, it seemed very cool to us that we had won out even if we kind of also felt it was our deal to lose. I mean we were Office. It felt a bit weird to be so focused on such a tiny company among all the scale of Office, but we were deeply convinced that web authoring was a future for Office.

Just after the papers were signed, I flew to Cambridge with Chris to help to make a good impression with the team, at least we hoped. The success of the deal relied on successfully hiring almost everyone and also moving to Seattle. That's how deals were done then. I had previously visited companies at this stage and knew how tense employees could be. The fact that Microsoft was viewed as a cross between *The Borg* and a *Death Star* did not help. When I visited Intuit at this stage, some things our group said about culture did not go over well, so at least I had those lessons. Chris of course was masterful, as he was one of the most tenured and respected engineering leaders who had progressed to lead the biggest business at the company. I filled in with details of strategy and other details, most of which I said Chris would be handling and no one had to worry. Most of the team had read mainstream press and certainly everything in the industry was skeptical of Microsoft on many dimensions. The just-published Douglas Coupland book, *Microserfs*, was making the rounds and that didn't help either. *Generation X* was much better, but I digress. I found myself trying to unwind serfdom and settled on ordering copies of the just completed *Microsoft Secrets: How the World's Most Powerful Software Company Creates Technology, Shapes Markets and Manages*, even though I disliked the title. We cooperated with the professors writing this book and I found it to be an accurate and detailed description of how products were built at Microsoft at the time.

Most all of the engineering team ended up making the move, which was a huge success. Several could not relocate due to family reasons and were offered roles in the regional office.

The deal was announced on January 16, 1996. It was announced for $130M, almost ten times the PowerPoint deal and an enormous deal for Microsoft at the time. We watched the stock price that day, though we rarely did, and it was up enough at the announce to pay for the deal. Having just finished the crash course in venture funding and deal-making, we then began our crash course in M&A regulation and learned about all the FTC filings and the process. Microsoft was under investigation for antirust and everyone was quite worried, as just a couple of years earlier a deal to acquire Intuit, makers of Quicken, was scuttled due to regulatory concerns. We worked through the process and won approval. We got a real kick out of the requirement that Vermeer would need to remain an independent company, in other words Vermeer.com for email and the web site, and other accommodations such as which entity would own the source code.

ChrisP decided it was time to dive back into code and return to the engineering and product scale he loved. He dedicated himself full time to Vermeer, leading the team as VP of FrontPage, complete with a new Vermeer business card. He was incredibly energized and even wrote code. He quickly added an Insert Hyperlink dialog to match the one in Office.

What ChrisP did was an example of a *golden rule* of any acquisition—always have someone of seniority willing to bet their career on the outcome of the deal. That means someone willing to change jobs, integrate themselves into the appropriate place in managing the deal, and signing up to be there until the next logical step. Almost always further integration into a broader organization or the separation of the business into something needing a distinct CEO role. To his credit, ChrisP signed up for that role. To many it looked like Chris walked away from a big job in Office. Though to Chris—developer on DOS 1.0, Mouse 1.0, Windows 1.0, and so on—this was a logical progression and Office was the diversion from his path of shipping and innovating entirely new to Microsoft products.

The strategy was to quickly turn around a released copy of FrontPage, packaged in a standard Office box, and get that on shelves as soon as possible, which they did. This FrontPage 95, Vermeer 1.1, made it into market and in short order became the leading web authoring tool, selling over 150,000 copies in a few months, substantially more than the 275 copies Vermeer had sold as an independent company.

Once that release was complete, ChrisP began the long-term integration of FrontPage. The biggest concern was losing momentum in what he believed was a next big category for Office. In some ways, PowerPoint offered a good lesson in integration. For the most part the team continued on their mission, only prioritizing getting a Windows release out quickly. The whole divisional transition to Office also changed PowerPoint from an independent, so to speak, operation to one more integrated. Even then it was a peer to Word and Excel, albeit remote.

In the short history of acquisitions, Microsoft could be said to have roughly three modes of venture integration. The most common was to simply **absorb** the code and team into an existing group or product. Microsoft just completed a series of acquisitions in graphics, for example, and those in some form (or not) went on to become parts of or team members of the underlying graphics technology for games on Windows. Similarly, several acquisitions were done in email and networking, landing in their respective teams.

A second type of integration, far less common, was to acquire a company in a space Microsoft hoped to lead and to put forth the product as the **new leader**. These tended to be less successful during this era, perhaps because of the way the sales efforts were transitioning to business licensing from either retail or distinct sales motions for each product. The company was becoming a Windows, Server, and Office machine and whole new products would struggle to fit in if they were not part of these efforts. A big challenge with these deals was the ever-present goal of synergy across Microsoft. The pressure on visible leaders to also show integration with Microsoft, especially to leverage sales efforts, was rather intense. Additionally, there was the pressure to build more on the next generation technologies Microsoft was building. SoftImage was acquired to enter the television production space for $130 million, but Microsoft lacked a structure that could capitalize to grow the asset. Hotmail was acquired for over $500 million in 1997, and from the start it was a leader in free email but also in constant synergy negotiations with Exchange and ongoing pressure to build on Windows server. This pattern would repeat many times for many future acquisitions. The logic behind this integration strategy is always something along the lines of "this is a great company, but we can make it even greater." In reality, most leaders seemed drawn to this approach, declaring the acquired product a new leader, because that brought with it all the attention and glory of being a leader having simply done a deal.

A third type of integration, and by far the most difficult, was what I would call **sheltered**. The company was acquired, and the product nurtured as though it was going to be a new leader, with a specific integration agenda and a strong sponsor that tightly controlled all the inbound requests for synergy. I hate to describe it this way, but you could picture essentially building a bubble around the team and offering outsiders (to the team) very specific points of integration. Executing on this strategy while not simply telling every other group to drop dead was both an act of diplomacy and heroism, and enormously self-sacrificing. As we know today, this is almost always the right way to do venture integration and when everyone agrees, the painful bubble is replaced by standard operating procedure. The logic of this mode of venture integration is easy to see— "this is a great company and we acquired it because it is great and the team should keep making it even greater, just ask where Microsoft resources could help." The emotional costs of such a strategy in a company dominated by strategic synergy and sales efficiency were high and few had the clout to pull it off.

ChrisP had the desire and clout to build a bubble around Vermeer. Inside the Office team we knew to basically leave FrontPage alone and unless Chris or one of the senior people came asking, we just assumed they were doing what was right. As the development of FrontPage 97 continued, many points of integration came about, but with few exceptions these were done via the negotiated portals through the bubble.

Chris and the team found themselves drawn to many potentially strategic discussions, however, and those created quite a bit of stress. It is easy to imagine that everyone had their sights set on either leveraging one part of FrontPage for their product or expanding the strategic importance of their technology by convincing FrontPage to adopt it. At the same time, few teams saw the beauty of the whole of FrontPage, an integrated view of designing, creating, and managing web sites.

Some teams wanted to use the incredibly novel ability of FrontPage to publish pages and content to the web. This resulted in a technology that many of that era remember, the FrontPage Server Extensions, which became a standard offering on most web-site hosters. These even ran on Unix back in the day, which was quite controversial at a time when helping Windows NT to win in web hosting was key. Other teams wanted to add HTML editing to their tool and so it was natural to request the editor component of FrontPage as a chunk of reusable code, something that BillG would be proud of. Things are rarely that separable. Internet Explorer was also working on adding editing at the time, as was Netscape. Many meetings were held explaining how much more difficult WYSIWYG editing was, even if it was for simple HTML. It was clear the FrontPage team were probably the world leaders in Office-level HTML editing, which made these conversations awkward.

The team soldiered on working within the bubble that Chris had so carefully crafted. He was under enormous pressure and at the same time was happily coding away his features in the product. It was amazing.

To help to scale the team, ChrisP also built out the program management (product management in modern Silicon Valley vernacular) function of which Vermeer came with none, say for Randy the co-founder as is common with most startups today. ChrisP assembled a PM team from several members of Office, with a lead from Word who had originally detailed the depth and richness of FrontPage. Chris also brought in a leader to build out the test function and a marketing leader, thus making Vermeer equivalent to a well-staffed Office application along the lines of the old product unit model, before Office. Vermeer was a self-contained unit with the functions needed to create a stand-alone product and business.

As the team would learn, bringing PM into a development centric startup was not nearly as easy as one might think. Our view was always that PM was there to help make development more effective and not to waste time, and importantly Apps viewed the approach to PM as something that contributed significantly to the success of Word and Excel. PM would often handle all those inbound requests for help and so on. The Vermeer developers, however, felt pretty good about their ability to select features, prioritize, and specify interaction models—after all they got this far and did well enough to be acquired. There was a tendency to think of PM as process over substance, a not uncommon view among many outside of how Apps had evolved the role. Building out the PM role while continuing to build the product, was one of the more challenging aspects of venture integration.

For many years, the integration of Vermeer would be the case study for Microsoft in how deals could be discovered and executed. Harvard Business School had a six-part case taught over two days to first-year students. Reading the entire case is one of those times when the case method is able to tell a great story and anyone wanting to read all the details as told to a Harvard Business School professor and researcher would find it enjoyable and worth the effort.

As it would ultimately turn out, however, the viability of a stand-alone web-authoring tool would be subsumed by many different categories and brought to market as a part of a variety of products. The web was still young and moving fast in many directions. While FrontPage did not endure as a stand-alone product, most all the members of the team went on to remain and contribute significantly to Office and as leaders in both editing and web technologies. In that sense, Microsoft got an even better deal than originally envisioned.

045. INCOMPATIBLE FILES, SLIPPING, OFFICE 97 RTM

Office96 was quickly becoming the biggest slip to an Office or Apps release in years, and that was extraordinarily disappointing. We reached our Zero Bug Bounce milestone (ZBB, because for a brief moment the product would bounce around a mythical zero bug count) in July 1996, and that was great. We were also behind our original schedule by months, and we knew there was no way to catch up. We needed more time. We felt like shit.

I did not always go to lunch in the building 17 cafeteria but happened to go one summer day. I was waiting to pay, holding my two slices of Marriott cheese pizza, when I heard, "SINOFSKY! SINOFSKY! WHAT DO YOU MEAN YOU ARE CHANGING THE FILE FORMATS?? WE CAN'T DO THAT!"

SteveB was yelling across the cafeteria at me, and all of a sudden, I felt like a few hundred people got quiet and were watching to see how I reacted. His voice seemed to come from everywhere, so it took me a moment to locate him. A 10-minute conversation followed that started in earnest as he made his way toward me about the reality that Office 97, as it had been officially named, had a whole new architecture with loads of new features for document creation like drawing and fancy Word tables, animations in PowerPoint, and new charts with top-notch graphics in Excel. Word and Excel changed the file formats to support these features. A changed file format meant a customer file such as FOO.DOC or FOO.XLS on disk was only compatible with the version of the app that created the file, or a newer version. Trying to open FOO.DOC created with Word 97 on a Word 6.0 setup would give an inscrutable error message. This message would often terrify the user into thinking they had a corrupt file or the computer had eaten all their work. This horrible experience was perfectly normal for state-of-the-art software. I kid you not.

Well, it turned out that the strategy of *not* changing the file formats in Office 95 (at least for Word and Excel) was a huge hit with the field sales force. So much so that they thought it was our new strategy to maintain the same file formats forever. When, in fact, we thought of 95 as the exception and only way to sync up with Windows 95—we had spent a ton of creative energy arriving at sellable features that did not require a file format change but were severely constrained in doing so.

I never really thought of mentioning this because it was so obvious, or so I thought. Steve thought we were totally screwed and had misled his sales team.

The file format changed probably within the first weeks of the project and was *standard industry practice*. The success of Office 95's unchanged file formats caused a bit of a crisis as we were working on Office96. It was obviously both too late and impossible, regardless, to reverse course. HeikkiK coordinated what could best be described as a crisis mitigation plan involving format converters for existing applications and *Save As* capability within the new versions to produce *down-level* files, with the risk of losing new features. This was a reasonable solution but would require organizations to install software on every PC, whether it was just a converter for existing computers or the whole new Office 97 on new PCs. In other words what we thought was reasonable was a huge pain. SteveB was right.

The Apps culture was tuned to avoiding crisis moments, usually by rewarding prevention, and a low tolerance for avoidable drama. When a crisis did hit, self-inflicted or otherwise, the Apps approach aimed for cool, calm, collected. ChrisP often described this like listening to the cockpit recordings of Naval aviators landing jets in difficult circumstances. That calm was accompanied by an executive team that did not view a crisis as an opportunity to micro-manage or upend existing processes.

As a result, we thought this through in excruciating detail. All of the test managers and PMs from each team had developed a complete plan to support the new file formats in old products and deliver product updates to existing products, even using the novel approach of internet downloads. This did not solve the physics problem that we could not make the new features of Office96 show up in Office 95 or Office 4.3, but we could ease the pain and prevent people from being unable to open files they received due to the growing use of email.

One bit of good news was that the biggest motivator for changing the file format was to support the new worldwide standard for representing text in computers, called *UNICODE,* that Microsoft had contributed a huge amount to. Up until then, PCs had a difficult time representing many of the world's languages and mixing several languages at once was almost impossible. UNICODE was a major step forward and for multinational corporations, the ones complaining loudly to SteveB, easing the pain of multilingual documents was a significant win. A decade later, UNICODE would become familiar to everyone as it supported *Emoji.*

This was a rare crisis for the team and a good learning experience to the degree that foisting incompatible files across a corporation could be called a learning experience. As an organization this did bring us into the modern, Office-focused world in two ways. First, the crisis created a new *muscle,* which was driving change to core behavior across all the products. That had to happen. It was the first of what could be called *suite-first* problem-solving and coordination.

Second, this was such a pain for every team that it served to be an early dose of the enterprise business and what would be different for the team. The needs of enterprise customers became paramount as we moved to future releases, and the solutions to those needs were addressed across the entire team.

Still, this was my first of many, many lessons in the difference between consumer products and enterprise products, between selling at retail and selling through account managers. Because every product always changed file formats, this should have been viewed as routine. But the world had changed—seemingly overnight documents were being emailed around, and all of a sudden it was all too common to get files that could not be opened. In a sense this was really a crisis for the Office business and one that would cause a sea change in how we viewed files. It also happened to be the strength of the internet and world wide web—one single format that could be read by any browser, and soon one language that could be used to write a program once and run it anywhere.

Beyond that it was a lesson in how Microsoft's customers were changing. The technology enthusiasts who embraced changes and had a high threshold for the pain that random changes caused were being replaced by system administrators and IT professionals who were not only change averse, but often barriers to change. The file format incident was a warning sign for what was to come, not just for Microsoft but for me personally as I had to reconcile innovation with a customer base that was becoming less interest in technology changes, which we thought of as cool innovation, and more focused on the costs of those changes, which we thought of as simply necessary.

Strategy changes don't always come with a moment, but it was clearly this moment when it became clear we would move Office files to be *open* and to use the format of the internet, HTML. This would prove to be enormously controversial with BillG as the very origin of Apps, specifically Word, was the invention of the Word .DOC file format, which was a key, and proprietary, competitive advantage. It was also a technology Bill knew well.

By the Fall, Office96 was approaching the finish line. The team was tired. We were nine months late off our original schedule. We felt it. Nine months late was kind of inexcusable, but relative to the rest of Microsoft and the industry still well within norms. More than the feeling of exhaustion, we were feeling that as much as we accomplished, we had also not executed as hoped.

We were hard on ourselves for the slip. The routine *post-mortem* that would follow was filled with genuine discussions of trying to figure out how not to repeat this slip, even if it was also the last release we would talk about Office versus the Apps.

Even with exhaustion there was much to be proud of. The product cycle was difficult, but we did not experience any sort of death march. Yes, many people put in long hours. While many teams would do a "bug bash" one night in a week, we were not catering food every night as was common practice in other parts of Microsoft. Babies were born. People were married. There was all the life experience that happens within a group of 1,000 people over three years. Relative to the rest of the company, we ran the project with a sense of balance and normalcy. The core tenet of our process was that we arrived at the schedule and dates from bottom-up estimates, and when those estimates were wrong, the individuals worked extra or we scaled back features—both of those were viewed as acceptable. We did not seek out heroes. We were proud of that. And we would get better at estimates, accountability, and balance each release going forward.

The release to manufacturing, which came about six weeks before launch, was on a cold and rainy November 16, 1996. A few of us were at COMDEX in Las Vegas doing press when HeikkiK led the team through the final ship room meeting and signoff. He was kind enough to call in and I spoke from my flip phone but might as well have been in outer space—the connection was horrible. Still, the sense of accomplishment was as real as the relief. From afar I wished everyone well and knew there would be one heck of a party on campus. And there were pictures to prove it.

Marketing was gearing up for a launch and did a fantastic job creating awareness and a retail presence, and for the first time gearing up an ever-growing enterprise sales force. The industry had grown so much creating a massive demand for press coverage unlike any we had experienced. Every paper in every town in every country seemed to have a tech section. The summaries of press coverage were growing ever longer, and the skills the Office marketing had to get the word out in a consistent and clear way were growing with demand.

The launch was subdued relative to Windows 95, and that was by design. Late 1996 was mostly about the enterprise and servers so Office focused on those elements of the product.

While Office 95 was viewed as a significant release, the realities of a 200-page *Office 97* reviewers guide detailing all the features of the product really sent the message that Microsoft was all-in on suites and had unparalleled depth and breadth to offer. The plethora of features in the product and breadth of tools kept the technology press busy and excited. The phrase shock-and-awe was routinely used to describe the overwhelming depth and breadth of the newest Office suite.

The reviews were extremely positive. Office 97 garnered nearly all the major awards across magazines, which at the time were a big deal. *BYTE*, *PC World*, *PC Magazine,* and more each recognized the suite and individual applications as editor's choice or world class.

Clippy became the most controversial feature, even to this day, in productivity software. Even the reviews were controversial, with key mainstream reviewers citing both innovation and acknowledging the problem needed addressing. The late Steve Wildstrom, the widely read and deeply respected columnist at *BusinessWeek,* wrote, "I was deeply skeptical about these omnipresent artificial-intelligence devices. But to my surprise, I found the animated assistants useful—and a feature that sets the new Office apart from competing software suites." Quite a few reviews were initially skeptical, and then using the product turned them around. For example, PC Week said, "Office Assistant exceeds my expectations: It's not only visually effective, but also more than superficial in the help that it offers to even a veteran nerd." These comments gave us hope. gave me hope.

Still, there was a love/hate relationship with our assistant friend. Clippy immediately became the stuff of legend when it came to the reception among the core technical customers in IT and tech enthusiasts—the kind of users that know all the keyboard shortcuts and don't want anything to get "in the way" of their work.

I learned something in how this type of customer chooses to express distaste for a feature. Rather than directly say, "I do not like it" or "I will not use it," these customers generally stepped up and claimed to speak broadly for "typical end-users," often talking about their mothers or grandmothers, always female, to represent someone who is not fully versed in the product. In the case of Clippy, we would often hear that this is not the right feature to help "those users like my mother or grandmother needing help." This *projecting* of product concerns rather than owning them directly would be a valuable lesson and something I would carry with me when bringing new features to market that must make it through these gatekeepers.

The negative reviews of Clippy were fairly brutal. I think everyone used the cuteness of Clippy as an invitation to spice up the language used to insult the feature. Stephen Manes in *The New York Times* wrote, "…help is presented solely in the form of dialogue balloons attached to one of eight cartoon characters, most of which make irrelevant, distracting movements and sounds until you turn them off. But these toon-zombies are as insistent on popping up again as Wile E. Coyote."[13]

That really hurt.

Most unfortunate, though, was how the feature could be construed as a symbol of Microsoft losing touch with customers, especially in this era of heightened scrutiny on the legal front. We were wrong, but not because we had lost touch—we were wrong because we went overboard (and in the wrong direction) trying to make computers easy to use for a much larger audience.

Still, we had pushed through a final design change to enable the assistant to be turned off. The change was easy technically, but difficult emotionally. Our goal was for Clippy to be an ever-present but unobtrusive assistant (Agent was the term at the time, today that would be Bot), thus turning Clippy off was an admission of failure. Making this possible was quite hard on the team given how far we had come from Bob through "tfc" and beyond. That is all the techie crowd needed, and with that most of the business deployments of Office 97 had no ever-present Assistant.

These reviews mattered. Reviews of products might seem old school in a world of instant hot takes in social networking and especially with products where bugs or errors can be fixed on the fly. In an era when software could not be so easily changed, publications assigned several people over the course of weeks or more to dig deep into a product, and our own marketing touted excerpts. These reviews really carried weight. We had a reviews team in marketing, 3 or more full-time people plus a reviews team at our PR agency working broadly with all the outlets, and this was repeated in most major subsidiaries, especially Japan, Korea, Germany, and UK. At the peak (over the next product cycle) there were easily 100 reviews being executed in the US. The marketing team was on a plane for two months meeting in person with all of these. I would visit dozens myself. There was a constant stream of communications fielding questions, dealing with bugs and compatibility, and offering support for demos and more. There was a growing parallel effort working with the rising importance of IT industry analysts, such as Gartner Group that would soon eclipse the traditional tech reviews in importance to our business.

It was not without controversy that we focused so much on reviewers. This was an era where they could be characterized as a form of *gatekeeper*. It was no doubt limiting as any one reviewer represented a narrow perspective compared to all customers. There were no real alternatives. In many ways the internet would come to save us and enable a product as broad as Office to reach many more customers directly with more tailored messages, content, and calls to action. The changes in how we reached customers coincided with the maturing PC and PC industry.

Two reviews really stood out as defining, not defining the product in market as the product went on to great success but defining for me personally as a "product person" and also a leader. Stephen Manes, who had obliterated Clippy, was by most descriptions a curmudgeon and it would be difficult for me to say something he liked. We once debated whether a specific Sony laptop (the 505) was good compared to an Apple PowerBook in a session that went on for most of a press event at CES. His complete review, however, of Office 97 had a headline (keying off his description of the product) "An Upgraded Leviathan Sets Sail." This was a brutal shot. It characterized the product as, in a sense, just another release while also describing it as, well, a leviathan. The text of the review is painful for me to read even today.

I will say for the record that one part of his review I often talked about was that he called out the addition of word and character count in the status bar of Word. While it surprises many professional writers, most people using Word never used the word count feature because most writing is not tracked by that metric. We did, however, add it to the status bar by default for the press who lived in Word. We have no shame about that. They were an important constituency. True to form, I think most reviews mentioned the feature.

While I hung that review on my Office door as I did many others, I also went to the office supply store and purchased a portfolio case—a plastic folder with a dozen or so clear sheet protectors in it. The first thing I put in the first page was the leviathan review. After that I put a few pages that I would carry around all the time and update as needed—the list of teams, senior managers, total headcount, ship schedule and milestones, data sheets on competitors, top support calls, and so on. It was this review and the next one below that I would talk about and hold up at team meetings when describing our challenges as a business, especially as we planned future products.

Much more problematic was Outlook's reception as it was not a single feature to turn off after making fun of it—but rather a marquee addition to the suite, a new "puzzle piece" in the product line. The Office logo was a puzzle with each app taking on a different color. The absence of support for internet standards as well as the overall complexity of a version 1.0 product led to a series of fairly brutal reviews. Perhaps the one that stung the most came from *The Wall Street Journal* with the title "Microsoft Introduces Personal Organizer That's Unorganized" and zingers such as:

> *The combination is so tempting that Microsoft incorporated Outlook in its showcase $190 Office 97 suite of software, and rejected the PIM [personal information manager] label for it, calling Outlook a "desktop information manager," or DIM. Sadly, that unfortunate acronym is apt. Outlook 97 doesn't live up to its potential. It's a great idea, poorly executed.*

What was an internal joke between the now rival Exchange team and the Outlook team was a review. The review concluded, "Microsoft has a history of doing a poor job on the first version of new products, and Outlook fits that pattern."

The reporter, Walt Mossberg, had a broadly read and widely discussed column, *Personal Technology*, aimed at taking on the *techies* of the world and makers of overly complex products. He was the clear leader in the point of view that, in his words, "Personal computers are just too hard to use, and it isn't your fault." He would challenge us, consistently, repeatedly, and objectively. He played no favorites and was perfectly straight in dealing with us and any vendor. There was no way to exert undue influence over him, no special treatment, nothing. We showed him the product, answered his questions, tried to fix any issues, and waited for the review, then he returned the product and loaner laptop to us promptly.

Walt's contribution to encouraging or pushing Office do a better job is something I have shared with him many times. I have enormous respect for him and what he accomplished in his column, and later the conference he cocreated as well as a media and technology web publication. His keen reviews profoundly influenced buyers and makers alike.

The complexity of Outlook and Walt's experience ironically deepened our ties. Walt began sending me questions and comments from his readers and I would often answer the myriad "how-to" or "why" questions he received. I never resented or tired of receiving these, and later felt nostalgic about them.

Walt was right about Outlook, and we had a lot of work to do.

I can't exactly compare what our team went through to a battle or a traumatic experience, but we did have a shared experience that changed the team dynamic. It also came at the right time as the industry was changing dramatically right before our eyes. Teams are built by going through a journey together. When I reflect on Office 97 I am convinced that the journey to build the product is what created the team and culture that have been so enduring, even today.

Office 97 was the last release to be sold primarily to individuals at retail. It was the last release to be marketed significantly as app features. And it was also the last release to be built as independent applications with shared code versus a shared strategy.

PCs were the new onramp to the information superhighway. The internet had become a global phenomenon driving PCs into every home, as Bill and Paul had envisioned more than 15 years earlier. No longer did demand need to be created for PCs; it needed to be met. For Office, all those PCs getting on the internet were being used for schoolwork, homework, and work at home using Office.

PCs were also standard on every desktop in the business world, as Bill and Paul had hoped. The race was on to equip workers with all kinds with PCs, to get them email, and to provide them with the tools needed for the creation and dissemination of knowledge. Office was a standard part of this.

We needed to scale our product development approach to meet these needs and scale.

In terms of PCs, dollars, documents, and customers, millions would turn to hundreds of millions and hundreds of millions to billions.

We were at the "end of the beginning" of the PC Revolution—the first part of the journey dominated by hobbyists, tech enthusiasts, and early adopters. The PC was now front and center in a revolution taking place in business and Office was destined to be a foundational element of the computerization of work. Over the next twelve months, PCs would sell more than 100 million units and more than half of those were bought directly by businesses. The PC was no longer a hobby or a luxury, but an essential element of business.

For me personally, Office 97 marked both an end and a new beginning.

1998-2000

While Microsoft battles software bloat and explosive growth, both in market cap and headcount, the world is introduced to computer animation. USB connectors, and the hybrid car. Everyone is buzzing about the year 2000 and how it could translate into a global technology meltdown. AOL stars in a romantic comedy and becomes a household name. It also becomes a target for Microsoft as the company endeavors to dominate in every single market.
The internet-connected PC ushers in the middle of the PC Revolution as the information technology profession shifts their focus from mainframes to the PC and PC servers.

046. PRIORITIZING A NEW TYPE OF CUSTOMER

Since the organization was still in the early stages of creating Office first, rather than apps first, there was pressure and challenges that came from the race to start planning the next release. Apps figured if their plans could be put in place then they would be harder to unwind in favor of other ideas from the Office Product Unit. And so, the planning for the next product release began in an uneven manner prior to RTM for Office 97.

But over the next three product releases, almost seven years, the Office team and the business transformed. The era of apps, each operating independently, gave way to a coherent Office suite. The single user of productivity tools on a personal computer was the toehold upon which Microsoft built an organizational productivity toolset that became an integral part of IT infrastructure in *large organizations*, LORG. The focus on LORGs and the transformation of the business to multiyear Enterprise Agreements (EA) resulted in an increase in revenue, profits, and ubiquity of Office and set the stage for the business for years to come.

Although Office was sold as a bundle, it was built as independent, and award-winning, products. The next step was to build the product we were selling, an integrated productivity software suite.

The journey, however, was difficult and repeatedly pitted our efforts to build innovative and empowering software for individuals against the demands by IT professionals to reduce change and maintain a level of control over the ever-sprawling, always-connected personal computer.

These changes in the business and role of Office required the team to transform from a set of reasonably well-executing but independent entities, OPU and the app product units, to a single, execution engine. We needed LORG product development machinery to match the LORG business that was growing. Building software, at the time, was still too hit or miss, quality too uneven, and predictability lacking. These were all qualities that our new, and extremely large, customers were demanding of Microsoft. If we were to sit across the table from General Motors, the Department of Defense, or Proctor & Gamble we needed to operate at scale as effectively and maturely as they operated their organizations, even if we were making relatively newfangled PC software.

PaulMa was leading Platforms and had recently returned from one of his many trips visiting with CIOs and enterprise customers. PaulMa, more than any other product leader, was responsible for Microsoft embracing the dialog with CIOs most of whom were not from the PC generation but began their careers on mainframes. Paul pushed across teams to engage with CIOs and even upgraded the Microsoft Executive Briefing Center against BillG's wishes to provide a very deluxe setting for CIOs (and government leaders) from around the world to visit Microsoft and learn the latest in technology from the newly crowned leader. Upon returning from this trip, Paul wrote up his notes as he always did and proclaimed that he heard very little about "open systems" or Unix as it was called. In fact, customer dialog had dramatically shifted away from open and towards "making Windows work."

The root of the problem was a phrase *total cost of ownership* or TCO coined by the industry analyst firm Gartner Group. TCO measured the real cost of computers and servers in organizations, not just the cost of hardware and software licenses, but all the internal costs for training, management, upkeep, helpdesk, upgrades, and more.

The numbers were astounding when we saw them. One of the first TCO reports from Gartner concluded that a Windows 95 PC connected to a network in a business costs almost $10,000 dollars **per year**.

Strategically, the Network Computer, NC, was a huge topic of discussion. The NC was a form of PC championed by Oracle and Sun that only ran a browser. That seemed crazy to us at the time. To the benefit of the PC, Gartner did not find these to be radically cheaper in terms of TCO. That did not slow down the conversation at all.

Paul immediately declared a war on TCO. As we'd come to expect from the Platforms culture, this was the new crisis. Suddenly there were meetings, offsites, slide decks (lots), and more. Platforms seemed to always love a good crisis. The thing was this was a real crisis.

Office 97 was very exciting for end-users, but between broken file formats, tons of new features requiring training, and especially because of the addition of email, we found ourselves essentially the enemy of IT professionals. Windows 95, so loved by consumers, was proving exceedingly fragile in an enterprise environment. There was great hope for *NT 5* (no code name, which I totally loved), if only there was an Office to go with it. NT 5, however, lacked all the consumer features of Windows 95 and the follow-ons Windows 98, Windows 98 SE, and then Windows Me. In other words, we had a product crisis on our hands due to TCO.

The people buying our product were IT professionals with an entirely different lens on product needs and capabilities. The buyer and the user were no longer the same person. Importantly, almost no one building products on the Office team had even the slightest experience working in an IT controlled environment.

Across the company this challenge could be looked at as a call for Microsoft to "grow up", probably for the third time. Jon Shirley (JonS) joined Microsoft in 1983 after 25 years at Radio Shack, a great Microsoft customer. He came as the company was growing rapidly to bring a classic model of experience in scaling a small company. MikeMap and PaulMa brought a product development maturity five or so years later.

Now Microsoft was at a scale where no single person could up-level the company. Instead, we began an era of formal management and training as a way of instilling at least some common set or baseline experiences. These "HR courses" (Human Resources), as we called them, would become both objects of ridicule (I mean who doesn't make fun of HR courses) and also brought a lingo and way of talking about Microsoft that we could at least share across the three different cultures in the headquarters product groups: Apps, Platforms, Online.

We experienced enough challenges building Office 97 in how different parts of the team worked together or even communicated with each other. Across the company these difficulties were compounded to the point that cross-company work was often hit or miss, as I personally experienced going as far back as building tools for NT 3.1. By the late 1990s, it had become all but impossible for people to even move across cultures and when they did often successful people would experience a form of *organ rejection*. As an example, one of the strongest leaders in Apps was asked to move to NT to bring a bit of apps program management to the team. He ventured over to NT and lasted only months before he roundtripped back to Apps, both sides convinced it was a horrible idea. Multiply this by dozens of people, the need to collaborate on code, and now the customer demand for products to work together in new ways and this was a huge problem.

Leading this charge for HR was NatalieY. Natalie who was the cultural beacon of the company and had recruited me to work for BillG was determined to help Microsoft mature. She hired many people who developed a broad curriculum and took so much grief for the work they did, though ultimately it was Natalie who convinced a skeptical BillG, SteveB, PaulMa, and many others to endorse, participate, and encourage the formal training.

This was not without a few early disasters, at least a disaster as far as a group of us were concerned.

Forming, Storming, Norming, Performing

When it came to these HR classes, I reacted as anything but supportive and open to them as was the case for most engineering brains. I always felt I had my fair share of touchy-feely training as a *resident advisor* in college, where I underwent countless hours of introspection and sharing.

In fairness, however, I learned vocabulary that proved useful over the next years as a manager and leader. Like almost any of these *extracurricular* experiences (they were never required), what tended to make them most valuable was not necessarily the content but the timing of the content relative to what was going on.

One straightforward class was on organizations and teams. Its singular takeaway was the framework for how teams evolved. *Tuckman's Stages of Group Development* was from the mid-1960s, but outside of an HR class there was no chance I would have been exposed to this. The timing of the class was perfect.

As the research described, a team goes through phases of *forming*, *storming*, *norming*, and *performing*. With this framework we discussed examples from our jobs. It was simple and non-controversial. It helped me to put the conversations JonDe and I had with ChrisP and PeteH in context—that idea that the Office team had lost its marbles.

The OPU and Apps teams were all in different stages of team formation, and at the same time individual perception of where the team was might not have coincided with an objective measure. While Excel as a team might have thought it was performing, that was only the case so long as building Excel was the goal. Excel was clearly our highest performing team at the time. The Office team finally shipped features in Office 97, but to say it was beyond the early days of norming was an exaggeration.

I walked away from the class believing all of DAD, which we continued to called Office, though that name would not be our official division name for a couple of years, OPU and the Apps, were organizationally much earlier than the business results would have us believe. In many ways, we were still storming. Looking at the reviews of the product and where customers were, we could also say that Office suites were slightly ahead and customers were beginning to see suites as normal, especially customers that adopted Windows. The class was a wake-up call to not assume anything about how the team operated as we developed the organization and plans for what would come next.

Each one of the spinning plates of Office maintained a process for ideation, planning, and execution, but we needed a process to bring these together and to scale from teams of dozens to a single team of hundreds. There was no playbook, and we knew that at this point while other parts of Microsoft were having their share of enormous success, there were no repeatable processes to emulate.

We needed to invent a new *Office process* while also building a new Office.

Another HR class became an accidental legend and provided endless entertainment and stories after the fact. A selection of about two dozen people from the product groups, including JonDe, ChrisP, me, and many across major divisions, were invited with few details to a training offsite. NatalieY picked a selection of cool kids or influencers as we would say today, assuming we would endorse the experience and more would choose to participate.

We were sent reservations for travel with no lodging, just a flight. We flew to Boston, rather mysterious, and then took a small plane (like *Wings*) to Cape Cod.

There was a lot of eyerolling.

Upon arrival in the tiny airport, our luggage, wallets, ID, laptops, and new Motorola StarTac and Nokia 6110 phones were *confiscated*. We learned that before our arrival, leadership for the United States Postal Service had just experienced the retreat and loved it, which seemed to worry us. We were taken to a primitive location, a sort of religious summer camp where we were divided into three groups. The first were "tops." I did not make up these names. They received instructions prior to the training, arriving a day earlier. JonDe was a top. The tops were assigned nice rooms. The second were "middles," who were given group accommodations. The largest group were "bottoms" of which I was one. We were given what appeared to be the kids' bunks with no linens.

Over two days, the middles were given various goals from the tops and some resources to carry them out, such as clearing dirt paths or washing picnic tables. In turn, the bottoms worked to accomplish the goals in exchange for provisions, such as sheets or food. Our first assignment, we spent a few hours clearing leaves in exchange for lunch. We were trapped on the Cape without any communication tools at all, not even a payphone.

It was not going well for me—while I spent many summers camping in a tent, it was by choice. Being forced into this, with no idea what was happening, was not cool. I began plotting my own escape but couldn't even find a phone, plus I had no money though I had my AT&T calling card number memorized if I could just find a pay phone. I was not alone. In fact, one person actually escaped by hiking to a nearby gas station and using a payphone. He caught a flight back, abandoning his luggage and laptop. He wasn't just complaining like me, he literally escaped the island.

At one point, I was serving dinner to JonDe, as a way to secure linen for the evening. We were told that the next day we would receive richer tasks and be given more exciting things to do. After sleeping in a bunk bed with a sheet and using a washcloth for a towel, the next morning we were given tools to create an economy, so to speak, and we could do things for money and stop bartering.

It felt absurd. ChrisP, also a bottom, devised a coup in hopes of ending the farce. We took the supplies for the "town", and everyone started creating art—paintings and drawings, and such, and selling them to the tops at inflated prices and then buying each other's products at even higher prices. In other words, we flooded the economy with money. We ended up with more money than there were provisions to buy, and the game literally collapsed. The organizers were alternating between laughing and crying. Hungry and stinky, I took to yelling at one organizer, who eventually shut down and walked away.

We broke the entire system, cutting the entire simulation short by two days. We thought we were clever. Really, we were kind of a bunch of jerks. Just horrible. When I think of how I behaved at this course, I have nothing but regret. Forget needing to mature for CIOs, as a group we needed to mature as human beings.

Game over.

We learned that the workshop was a famous organizational behavior workshop based on some important academic research. They conducted this exercise (at this same location) *hundreds of times* before and never anything as crazy had happened. Suffice it to say, there was a sense of old-school Microsoft pride in having hacked and destroyed the entire training exercise.

However, all was not lost. We walked away with a set of important lessons about organizations—though to be fair they could have interoffice mailed us the pamphlet and skipped the trip. The essence of the experience was to better understand the power dynamics across different strata of an organization. We tend to think of tops being in charge, middles balancing the needs of the bottoms and tops, and bottoms as victims. In practice, every individual can take on the behavior traits, beliefs, and coping mechanism of each layer. Every role is a bit of each layer or caught between competing layers.

As crazy as all of this was, the core idea of bottoms as victims, tops as all knowing, and so on being highly context dependent did in fact have an impact on me. Years later, a friend in HR begged me to go to a three-hour version of this workshop held at Microsoft. For years I forbade anyone on the team from participating in this class out of retaliation for my suffering. I conceded and found the short version to be quite beneficial, and I recommended it for many.

In reflecting in several email threads, the most important lesson for me was that while a group of us really hated the training, there were people that did not mind it or even liked it. In fact, some of the people from Platforms wanted to have a follow-up. Perhaps that spoke of the diverse cultures more than anything.

Still, the legend of breaking *Power Lab* is one for corporate history.

047. DON'T SHIP THE ORG CHART

With the start of our company-wide transition to becoming enterprise-focused, the product group organization seemed to be in a state of flux as we began a new release to follow Office 97. Churn across the senior leadership was a defining element of middle age for Microsoft.

Over the next decade or more, at least for me, it seemed as though we were always fluid at the top. We were either restructuring or leaders were being moved around, and sometimes both at once.

By the time Bob Muglia (BobMu) was my manager, starting in March 1999 and right around the release of follow-on to Office 97, Microsoft had gone through three major restructurings over the course of seven years—changing first to five main operating units then to seven and then back to three. Just keeping track of division acronyms was impossible, and as fast as we could distribute T-shirts and logo items, the acronyms expired. It wasn't uncommon to enter an office with moving boxes that remained packed in anticipation of the next move.

Desktop Applications had four different executive leadership structures during planning and delivering a single release of Office over 30 months. From the end of Office 97 until we shipped the next product, the larger division containing Office would change names numerous times: ACG (Applications and Content Group), AICG (Applications and Internet Client Group), ATG (Applications and Tools Group), BPG (Business Productivity Group.) The groups were each defined as Office and other stuff, often not particularly adjacent in the market. Each one of those changes came with some feeling that even after the successful launch of Office 97, some things needed to be done differently. But what?

While never explicit, the executive changes all had one thing in common. Each was a gradual move towards Apps being managed by executives from Platforms. There was a subtle reminder that the company was a Windows company, and importantly that when it came to the senior executives, it was the Apps teams that needed leadership from Platforms, not the other way around. It always felt like we were getting a message that we needed help in some way.

A level below these new executives, Applications had been fairly stable for quite some time. As described previously, from the earliest days until Mike Maples' business unit re-organization in the late 1980s, the teams were organized by job function. The business unit function served well through the rise of the Macintosh business leading to Office and the creation of the apps for Windows, until the creation of OPU in 1994, the Office Product Unit. This relative organization stability coincided with a growing execution capability on the team. While products were late, they were (with few exceptions) never out of control. Individuals became strongly committed to the individual apps teams and finishing what you started became a key element of the strengthening culture of Apps.

By way of comparison, Windows ran with parallel teams through much of a release, with one team focused on shipping the current product and another team focused on the next release. Culturally, there were *starters* and *finishers*. The starters were the big thinkers in terms of ideas and architecture, and the finishers were the closers who drove a project to completion and managed the complexities of closing down ecosystem contributions.

That meant that at any given juncture there were always two buckets, with code names: Chicago/Cairo, Nashville/Memphis, and Whistler/Blackcomb, for example. When a product finished, there was a changeover in leadership. The finishers came in and the starters moved on. It was their culture. The presence of a future team seemed to me to almost distract executives providing a team to meet with and a place for all the new ideas to go, while the shipping team worked heads down. The handoffs were never that clean and with some frequency the future product failed to make it to market or would change substantially with the shipping leadership.

Office, on the other hand, was predominantly *single-threaded*—focused on one release at a time. Office believed firmly in a culture of engineers finishing what they started, program managers owning features from start to finish, and testers being involved from the start of a feature. Most of our performance evaluations and promotions were based on understanding complete product cycle contributions. The idea that features that did not fit in one release rolled into the next release did not work for us, simply because we started each release from a clean slate and awaited feedback or learning from the market. It was almost never a good idea to begin a release with what was not finished previously—a lesson that is even more applicable in today's continuous delivery model. Planning for the next release began informally around beta and then ramped up—a process that I worked a great deal on developing and honing. Our view was that shipping was learning and that assuming what was not complete needed to be finished was not the right place to start.

The Office team's single-threaded product development proved frustrating to BillG and Platforms over the years, and given the change going on with the internet, browsers, and even org changes, the pressure to be talking about the future was greater than ever. LORG customers also demanded more information about the future, a constant source of tension for Office that lacked a second team building the next release. Because software was always in a constant state of deployment, LORGs wanted assurances that what was being deployed today would remain relevant in the future. Thus, with LORGs came an ever-increasing demand for long term product roadmaps. Accountability to those roadmaps was another issue entirely.

As much as a LORG customer might wish to standardize on a single version of Office and Windows for their standard PC, the realities of release schedules, product updates, evolving PC hardware, and their own desire for new features made that impossible. Like painting the Golden Gate Bridge, the deployment of Office and Windows was always a work in progress.

The execs felt that without a second team available for ongoing conversations, they had no ability to give input. My own experience, especially in watching this from my role as Bill's TA and in seeing the hand-off between several versions of Windows, was that much information gathered from those meetings was lost in the transition between starters and finishers. The hand-off was a loss of team momentum as well. I was never convinced that it was possible to execute parallel releases. Our experience on Office 95 and Office 97 only cemented how difficult and consuming that could be, and we were extremely constrained and disciplined.

In order to gain more visibility for what appeared to BillG and others to be a *secret Office planning process* we began planning with more people from other parts of the company—company-wide thought leaders. I documented the offsites with memos and notes and distributed them. This, in turn, created more demand for participation and sharing, which concerned me because we had a strong desire to keep release plans confidential. The business still relied on exciting launches and reveals to drive upgrades. We had not yet reconciled the demand for product roadmaps from customers but were already familiar with the ability for any forward-looking materials (especially) slides to find their way to the field, customers, and even the press.

These offsites were an integral part of building a shared view of a product's future. As much as offsites were loathed, I witnessed their effectiveness (and not) when working for BillG. As such, I put them to use in Office. The offsites were a weird match between people who knew all the details and people who knew none of the details, but everyone had strong opinions often stated as facts when in reality we had very little data about the world as it existed and none about where things were heading. These offsites were useful in bringing a common dialog forward and at the very least when criticism was offered, we knew from where it came.

By this time JonDe was the VP in charge of the whole Office product, OPU and the app teams. He reported to several different executives in a short time. During the transition to the next product release, JonDe and I were determined to embrace a new mantra, "Don't ship the org chart."

Collectively we saw too many examples of this in Office 97 and across the company, where the organization mirrored the code architecture and that constrained what could be built, thus determining what would be built, regardless of broader goals. Developers naturally want to own code. Managers of developers want to know which code they own and control the flow of data to and from their code and what other parts of the system can use this code. Over time, for us, this created a code boundary that was enforced by the organization. Products ossify and it becomes difficult to branch into new areas. These boundaries define resource allocation requirements—if a team took a certain number of people to code one release, then it needed to have the same number, or more, next time.

Creating software is always a process of layers, each more abstract than the next. In an ideal world, there are clean layers of abstraction communicating only with layers above and below through pre-determined programmer interfaces. In the real world, not only is it exceedingly difficult to create these nice layers, but it is also nearly impossible to maintain them as the needs of the product evolve over time. In fact, innovation mostly happens when a new product comes along and has a different view of these layers, creating an innovative (better performing, more secure, easier to use) product by busting through layers.

Examples such as integrating charts in Excel, background spelling in Word, or the whole of the graphics features in Office 97 broke through existing or traditional code boundaries. Failing to recognize the power of breaking existing abstractions and, more importantly, not letting the organization determine how code is built is key to innovation. Having fluidity in layers and in ownership of code over time creates innovation and enables flexibility in the organization to take on new problems and bring new perspectives to how features should be implemented.

Planning the release after Office 97 was a chance to step back and create a new process for a new Office product, and a new organization.

We started with the defining characteristic of an Office product planning process—*the best combination of top-down, bottom-up, and middle-out planning*. This was straight out of the Cape Cod experience, credit where credit is due. It contrasted sharply with the prevailing approaches to product planning that were used across the company and most industries. Historically, the plans for products were driven by the "smart person" or staff who owned pulling together a slide deck. They presented this for review to executives. Over time, the decks became increasingly denser, but the overall integrity of a schedule, engineering plan, or iteration about the plan was all left for *after* planning. Much of this approach explained the difficulty of finishing a product on time. This worked well when the product plan was a known programming language or a known specification like a video driver. We had far too much iteration in what we were doing, not just how we were doing it, for such a centralized handoff or waterfall approach.

Each App team maintained a sense of rhythm of planning and there were many inconsistencies. In leading Office Program Management, I needed to find a way to bring synergy and consistency across the teams as we moved resources from App teams to OPU to create more suite-wide features. We de-emphasized app – or category-specific investments. This strategy remained controversial for years but was abundantly clear to the market and well supported by JonDe.

In order to talk about a new release, we needed a name for it. We settled on calling the next release *Office9*, complete with a logo from the design team. The name was simply the next version number, not anything more. Recall that Office 95 was the first time we bumped all the app versions to be 7.0, the successor to Word 6.0, followed by Office 97 as version 8.0.

We spent a good hour one day brainstorming potential code names. While Word had used clever code names, such as *Spiff* and *T3*, by and large I and Office shunned codenames. Flashy codenames when leaked were fodder for the press. We considered boring codenames like the government uses. My favorite example was *Beige*. In the end sanity prevailed and for the next decade or more Office stuck to version numbers.

I wrote a memo, *Priorities and Processes for Office9*, intending for it to be the planning kickoff, sent while the team was in the last days of finishing Office 97. This meant only a few paid attention. The memo was a call for us to work together across teams. From a feature selection and prioritization, it was too little too soon, but it was the first stake in the ground on what came to be known as a *framing memo*, a step in the process for creating products.

Most merely wanted to know the release timing, since that was historically the first guidance from management. Office96 slipped nine months, painful and disappointing. Parallel releases proved brutal, and the team wanted to make sure not to do that again. The memo announced one release, one ship date, and one product cycle.

The rest was mostly lost on a team focused on shipping a product that was later than we planned, though it was less of a debate across teams than when we began 12/24. The memo said we would have one of everything: one milestone schedule, one feature planning process, one specification process, one engineering process, one beta, one ship date, and so on.

Writing any memo always presented challenges, especially when the organization took everything in it as a requirement or an absolute, or the opposite, random musings from OPU. Starting a tradition, the memo explained itself and what it did and did not mean—it was a framework, and any examples were examples, not specific mandates. At the same time there was a lot of subtlety because the absence of a mandate did not mean anything was possible. The polite way of saying this was that the spirit of the articulated direction needed to be followed. The impolite way of saying this was that the DAD organization was extremely empowered in a bottom-up manner, but this empowerment did not give the team the right to do dumb things or anything they wanted.

As a manager, writing a framing memo became an exercise in making sure I had a direct contribution at the start of every product cycle. Memo writing from execs and at length, other than from BillG, was something few did on the product side, though in marketing and sales, yearly memos created by the staff were the norm. It was important to me to put myself on the line like this.

The Office9 memo set a goal of a product plan memo in a few months called a *vision memo*. This was the first use of the term *vision* as denoting a product plan. Historically, a vision was more aspirational and less concrete, but I chose to call it such because I wanted us to feel that a release was itself an aspiration even if the document itself was supported by a concrete plan. It was a play on words for sure and some, particularly outside the team, were confused by the level of commitment to the vision. The vision represented our collective performance objectives and review goals, as an organization and individuals.

The vision was the plan. The vision memo became a signature process, and the hallmark of the machinery that became Office and later Windows through the middle-age of PCs. The process of creating a vision and series of offsites, memos, and communications became the subject of both emulation and some mystery. Teams always wanted to know who wrote the memos, when did I "approve," or how were "decisions made." While teams across the company looked to the artifacts such as memos, spreadsheets, and slide decks, the reality was it was the team that came together, and those artifacts simply reflected the collaboration versus driving the collaboration. Simply copying the artifacts ended up like the replicated food in the *Squire of Gothos* from Star Trek, knowing of "all of the Earth forms, but none of the substance" as Spock remarked.

A unique characteristic of the vision is that it came from the product engineering team, and not a staff planning organization or the marketing team, as a market requirements document or product requirements document as they were often called in Silicon Valley. This was a key part of building a plan that was a combination of top down, bottom up, and middle out, again using those terms from Cape Cod. We were still a technology-driven company or organization with plans emanating from the engineering function. Incorporating the business aspects of the plan was an equally important part of the process, thus presenting a unified view of the entire business.

For the next months, teams brainstormed about what to build or what code to write. I was struggling with how to bring about a more unified approach to planning. I zeroed in on the vestiges of the product unit organization. Each of the GMs of the product units was still focused on a single product. I proposed to JonDe that we combine multiple apps into teams, broadening the scope of a GM while reducing the hierarchy of the organization by having fewer GMs.

We shipped one Office *box*. In fact, while we had many SKUs of Office, the overwhelming focus and majority of business customers chose Office Professional: Word, Excel, PowerPoint, Access, and the new Outlook. This core product remained unchanged though different apps, or *modules*, as BillG called them, came and went over the next few years. Given that, each release began by deciding which combinations of products would be managed by each GM.

Sitting in the small conference room across from the big executive office on the third floor in building 17, JonDe and I worked to converge on a plan.

We settled on having an organization made up of *Authoring* (responsible for both Word and PowerPoint), *Data Access* (Access and Excel), and *Office* (OPU.) This might seem simple but gave us two benefits. First, each of the general managers had oversight for two distinct types of customers, for example lawyers and consultants. Second, the opportunity for code sharing would present itself given the overlap in scenarios, for example the mechanisms for connecting to databases in Excel and Access.

With JonDe now leading all of Office, the logical successor for leading Office development was Duane Campbell (DuaneC), who was leading Excel through Office 97. Even though he was a development manager overseeing almost 50 people through Office 97, he still coded features in the product. He knew the code across every product better than most anyone and was clearly among the best engineers in the company. He also appreciated my Elvis Presley wall clock in my office. Grant George (GrantG) continued to manage Office-wide testing. Grant had proven himself during Office 95 and 97 as a supreme leader of large-scale testing. He single-handedly advanced Office in new ways.

We shifted more resources to OPU, and for DAD we continued to hire as many people from college as we could—everyone was involved in recruiting. Office became the *onboarding* group for the company and was brimming with the new-hire enthusiasm of hundreds of college interns and hires every year. We easily hired over one hundred full-time people from college every year, or as many as we could get allocated from the recruiting organization. I was taking two or three recruiting trips every year and would continue to do so for the rest of my career. I loved college recruiting.

One organizational problem we faced was that the newest member of the Office box, Outlook, was not even part of this organization. After the heroic efforts to get the first version shipped, the product was moved to be part of the new Internet Client and Collaboration division (ICCD) within the Applications and Internet Client group (AICG.) After years of saying Microsoft would not have an internet division ("that would be like having an electricity division,"[14] according to BillG), an internet division was formed with responsibility for Internet Explorer, email, and many internet-focused products and technologies.

Org chart separations have the potential to take on a life of their own. Outlook was put in organizational proximity with the mail program, called *Internet Mail and News,* bundled with Windows 95, and eventually and confusingly renamed *Outlook Express,* code-named *Athena.* Recall this was the replacement for *Inbox* from the Exchange team. The problem was that Outlook was designed for Exchange server. Outlook Express was designed for consumer mail and only worked with the internet protocols used by internet service providers and universities. In product reviews, Outlook's support for consumer email was rightfully called anemic. Reconciling the strategy for the new Outlook product family became a high priority, especially since we already chose to name them as though they were related. The code bases shared almost nothing technically.

Outlook 97 was placed on a rushed product cycle to fix the deficiencies in internet support. This was a classic strategy that almost always backfired, as would be the case in this instance. What was supposed to take a short couple of months stretched out for more than six and resulted in Outlook 98 shipping in June 1998. Office 97 shipped in November 1996. While the rest of Office was planning the next release, a key part of the product was working on what was termed an "out-of-band" release. Worse, the release was rather a hack in how the internet was supported. Running Outlook for the first time offered up a choice to run the product in *Internet Only* or in *Corporate or Workgroup*. The whole product had basically been split into a giant *if* statement. As a bonus, the product switched to a different installation technology, playing havoc with our total cost of ownership story. Outlook also missed out on planning with the suite. Yet we had just finished launching and selling LORGs on Outlook as an integral part of the Office suite.

The deficiencies of Outlook caught the eye of a future college-hire, Jensen Harris. He found the time to create add-ins for Outlook 97 that enabled it to do some of the things possible in Outlook Express and expected of any internet mail application. Jensen would go on to become one of the most significant contributors to the design of Outlook, Office, and then Windows.

It was all quite messy and the kind of crisis development that was rapidly becoming incompatible with the LORG focus of our business. We quickly regrouped with the Outlook team for the next release of Office, though as a result fell behind on the integration of Outlook with the suite.

This was literally shipping the org chart. We had to live with Outlook in this state as we planned Office9 and as we created and announced the Office organization.

If the framing memo was the first step of kicking off planning, the second was putting an organization in place. The planning efforts informed the choice of the organization, while at the same time the changes being considered, especially resource changes, inform the planning. Iteration of a feedback loop is crucial to moving forward while also avoiding lock-in based on organization.

We announced the org structure and had our first experience realigning the team and resources for a new release. That was easy. Not really, but it was done. Rolling out the changes and announcement was incredibly stressful for most everyone in management, on every side of the change. We even did a post-mortem on the announcement itself and collected feedback from a survey.

Everything felt new. New organization. Hiring many new people. New product mission. Even a new business with enterprise licensing and LORG customers.

I did learn one thing though as I walked around the halls and the cafeteria after the org change. By and large, most people didn't really notice or care. They just wanted to know the ship date. milestone schedule, and most of all who their direct manager would be. That was a particularly good lesson for me. It reminded me of a story my Russian teacher from college told me at my 5-year reunion when we caught up. With the fall of communism, I asked him what his friends back in the former Soviet Union thought. He smiled a bit and just said, "Well, everyone still had to wait on line at the GUM department store the next day to see what was in stock." A good reminder, that even in times of significant change, the local effects are what people pay attention to.

All the teams switched to using a variant of "9" for the names of the apps and we looked and acted like a single team, Office9. At least so far. At least so far.

048. PIZZA FOR 20 MILLION PEOPLE

A characteristic of the early computing era was how much of it was created and built simply for our collective enjoyment or our view of what the products should do and how they should work. Looking back, it is easy to see the limitations of such an approach. How could a bunch of math and computer science majors with no previous work experience build a word processor for lawyers or a spreadsheet for bankers? This was even more true in tools and operating systems where just doing the work to make other stuff function was not only miraculous enough to constitute a product release, but also kind of fun. Even Microsoft's biggest bets, such as the graphical user interface, were not based on any sort of "what the customer wants" or even customer problems, as much as building it because we (or more correctly conventional wisdom among hackers) thought it made sense or simply because we could.

This approach, which I previously referred to as *testosterone-based development*, hinged on the most assertive argument or fastest to write code dictating what we did, served the company and industry extremely well. Then one day we looked around and the universe of people buying computers was much larger than our fellow techies. The people with all the money were interested in a more nuanced approach to software, and that included meeting what they perceived were their needs. They wanted computers to contribute to the business bottom line, and to do so cost-effectively.

Our approach to building the platform and apps led to a complexity that even we could not understand at times. I recall once struggling in my office to build a histogram with Excel. I just couldn't do it. There was no internet to ask. I finally asked a teammate who was one of the original Excel developers to help me. We spent hours that night, some of it in the Excel debugger, trying to figure out how to make Excel do something we knew, or so we thought, it could do. It was a weird moment that left a real mark on me but in hindsight it was no surprise that even an Excel developer wasn't an expert in actually using Excel. This pattern repeated itself across the whole Microsoft product line. Our "power users" and those that authored the 1000-page how-to books were far more expert in what we were doing and the limitations than we were. One group in particular had raced well ahead of us in understanding Office, the corporate IT administrator of our new LORG customers—those tasked with putting a PC on every desk. Much to our surprise, the complexity of issuing a PC to every worker was vastly more than going to the store and buying one for home or even managing the 5 PCs in a typical developer office. It was, in a favorite Microsoft-ism, *non-linear* complexity—the more PCs a company had the ever more complexity each additional PC created.

We needed to wrap our collective minds around both the suite and LORGs in a new way. What did it mean to build Office for LORGs? To be concrete, what features would sell? What were customer pain points that if we solved would cause more customers to upgrade?

Teams like Windows Server and especially Microsoft Exchange fully embraced the complete trappings of LORG product teams. The leaders were showing up in the newly renovated Executive Briefing Center where potential customers came to spend a day learning about our strategy. Teams engaged with the industry analysts at firms like Gartner Group, Meta, and Forrester. These groups acted almost as referees of enterprise product strategy and roadmaps, charging enterprise IT, our customers, handsomely for interpretation and explanation of vendor strategies. Microsoft even paid to have their strategy heard and critiqued knowing customers were paying for an objective interpretation—this was the enterprise game, or racket. These activities spun up and were driven by a newly LORG-focused Office marketing team with dedicated leadership for LORGs, staffed with people who previously worked in field sales. Server groups spent considerable energy on these efforts, particularly from program management.

It would be impossible to overstate the effort and results from the Server and Exchange teams deeply embedding themselves into customer environments. Organizationally from the top-down there was a melding of the minds with the deeply technical IT leaders that were making career bets on deploying Windows servers and Exchange email. There were people on the Exchange team, for example, which spent far more time at Boeing than they ever did at Microsoft. There were LORG customers that were so frequently seen in the Server hallways that one could mistake them for full time employees or vendors, and some even had Microsoft credentials.

Office needed to find a path more suited to the products we were building. The server products were both purchased and used by IT professionals. Office differed between the buyer and the user. BradWe, of Office design, was fond of saying we needed to be building products that were "useful, usable, and desirable," and then reminded us of that when the purchaser and the end-user were different people or organizations. IT people were both end-users of Office and also corporate gatekeepers. The most fascinating thing about working with them was keeping track of which hat they would be wearing for any given conversation. We had plenty of inputs and a much deeper understanding of end-users, but it was not uncommon for IT people to flip from talking about deployment or performance to suggestions for formatting features or ease of use. That was always the tricky balance for us.

The Apps teams pioneered smart processes for learning from end-users. Word used instrumentation to learn from individuals while also learning from specific customer types such as lawyers to understand the nuances of multipage footnotes, specific formatting of tables of citations, or the crazy complexity of nested numbering in briefs. Excel mastered getting inside the heads of the power users of Wall Street and the sophisticated models they created. PowerPoint from the start understood consultants, trainers, and even preachers, in addition to the art and science of graphical presentation. These techniques formed the foundation of learning from customers in a systematic manner that helped avoid product design by *feedback* and *anecdotes.*

With the rise of a highly engaged sales force and the deeply connected product teams, we had an onslaught of anecdotes. Executives were fanned out around the world "visiting customers" as we would say when referring to the highly stylized ritual of an executive hopping on a plane and visiting a few countries and 8-10 customers in a swing through a geography account teams in tow. Execs would routinely share the horror stories from these visits about products that didn't work, competitive threats, or simply customer demands for must-have features. The target for these visits were the Fortune 500 or even the Global 2000, and the leading government agencies in most every country of the world. Quickly we were knee deep in forceful anecdotes—a new form of testosterone-based development. Sifting through these often-conflicting inputs not to mention a tendency to *most-recently-heard* feedback being the loudest was stressful.

We needed some sort of systematic process. We needed to treat LORG customers as a category of customer, the way we had for lawyers, consultants, or bankers. They were indeed a customer segment, and now the most important one.

There was a gaping hole in the Office team's knowledge of LORGs—understanding information technology professionals (IT Pros) and system administrators (sysadmins)—the individuals at a company responsible for pushing Office out to thousands of desktops and maintaining Office on PCs. Office assumed one person bought the product, ran setup, and was responsible for their own PC. There were features, white papers, and support personnel to assist sysadmins, but basically, they used the same Office products. We dutifully produced the *Office Resource Kit* to assist these IT professionals, but most of the content was related to training and usage. With our file format crisis in Office 97 we had an early trial by fire and substantially increased the content related to deployment. Still, these additions were objection handlers and not primary design points. For the first time, we were designing Office for IT Pros and sysadmins.

Peggy (Stewart) Angevine (PeggySt) led program management on *setup*, the program that copied Office from floppy disks to the hard drive, a contribution considered somewhat mundane, though technically challenging. Originally and proudly from Wisconsin, PeggySt joined Microsoft a few years earlier after graduate school. She and the team created the first integrated Office setup feature, streamlining a laborious and manual process. The lists of the thousands of files that made up Office were maintained in large text files that were so big (and the lines so long) that even Word was not a good editor for them. In contributing to this, Peggy became well versed in the way that LORGs took these text files and customized them. When Office was installed on thousands of PCs at a big company, it was customized with the exact set of features that the company wanted, trading off on disk space and complexity. LORGs viewed the customization of Office setup as a key part of deploying Office and important *features*. Our first LORG feature for Office was enabling custom setup.

Setup was a major pain during this era of software. Originally setup meant copying files from floppy disks to the hard drive. Over time, setup became an enormously complex task that, in addition to being customized by admins, might, for example, detect what language or locale Windows was running and then copy over the right spellers. For example, in Canada both French and English needed to be installed. It might also do all sorts of things for our business such as check for existing versions of Office or validate the serial number typed in. This work was done by a couple of people on the team who maintained this sorcery in their heads because we had few tools other than a text file to codify the solution. Program managers Teresa Fernandez (TeresaFe) and Jennifer Cockrill (JennC) managed this complexity. I had 15 years of programming languages experience, yet when I stopped by Teresa's office and looked at her screen filled with thousands of lines of *code* I was mostly overwhelmed by our creation—each of the thousands of lines in the file were hundreds of characters long with dozens of commas and semicolons and one character misplaced might be a disaster. We had no tooling or debugger other than using a text editor. Outside of Microsoft, a small community of people reverse-engineered this expertise, against our recommendation and support policy, becoming resources (on internet newsgroups) to the sysadmins of the world customizing Office. This system was called *ACME,* and we were on version 1.1. Everything about this crucial step in delivering software was mostly an afterthought.

Embracing LORGs meant embracing setup and the process of upgrading software on an existing PC. PCs were significant capital investments and companies wanted them to last a long time, even forgoing the benefits of upgrading Office that they had purchased if it meant introducing complexity or incompatibility to an existing PC. HeikkiK, with his command-and-control military background, spent the last part of Office 97 working on a *hardcore* upgrade initiative called *Upgrade or Die*—intended to overcome the inertia among customers to stick with old versions of Office. Without upgrades our business was dead or suffering.

As trivial as it sounds in hindsight, setup and upgrades were the heart of how our new friend TCO (Total Cost of Ownership) was measured. The high costs of bringing even one PC into a business was increasingly dragging down what looked like an enormous upside. For the first time, business customers were telling us they simply could not deploy more PCs. Each PC they sent out was costing them thousands of dollars in internal help desk, slowing down the company, and just creating headaches all around. Worst of all, the internal measures of satisfaction with IT were very low and IT was starting to look like the punchline to jokes in most every venue from *Saturday Night Live* to *Dilbert*.

HeikkiK and PeggySt took on TCO from two different perspectives, HeikkiK as a program management leader figuring out what features best reduced TCO, and PeggySt with the product planning team where customer research and learning took place. The first thing the pair did was to hop on a plane and go visit customers—our default response to enterprise customers, a direct result of the TCO crisis mails flying around from field sales after reading the latest Gartner report on TCO. The field was more than happy to host members of the product team for a lashing by their accounts. Whether through English as a second language or a translator, these immersive visits were enormously difficult for a group of us that, frankly, thought we'd done a pretty good job building apps that customers loved.

Learning trips like this involved meeting with a combination of our closest, biggest, toughest, and most open to talking customers. SteveB was the permanent Ford Motors account manager so they were top of the list. SteveB grew up in the Detroit area and his father worked there, as did my grandmother during WWII making tank parts in New York. There were other companies that were tour regulars, but Ford always carried the most weight internally because of that connection.

Heikki returned from Detroit having seen the light, so to speak, but his learning sounded like a dystopian future where the very tools of empowerment, the PC, were controlled by the dark forces of IT. Talking with the sysadmins at Ford, Heikki received an earful about the difficulties of the file format transition and customizing Office setup that he knew all too well. Ford wanted to minimize the disk space used and the number of features in the product to reduce the support costs of Office. As was typical at the time, Ford created a helpdesk that employees contacted for PC assistance, including help for basic tasks like creating and formatting documents. This type of support was factored into the Gartner costs for owning a PC. As the people building the product, we thought we provided a great deal of help within the product, which was designed for this situation. As far as Ford was concerned, we did not create easy to use products, at least not for their employees.

Sysadmins typically thought the best way to make a product easy was to remove a lot of features. For example, many end-users wanted more clip art and images for their presentations. That was a common support telephone call topic: "how to get more." There was no internet inside of Ford or most any company and this was years before using the internet to search for images was possible. Office shipped with tens of thousands of images, but still, the perfect one might not have always existed. IT's answer was to remove all the images and thus save on disk space and phone calls and not give the impression that images were even available within the product at all. Problem solved.

Not actually.

The real problem was not only Office, but all the cool things people could do with their PCs on their own. They could add a printer, buy more software and install it, play DVDs from home (wasting time!), attach a modem and dial-up to use AOL, or even plug in disk drives and other storage. From a sysadmin perspective these were distracting and costly. From a Microsoft perspective these were precisely what a PC was good for. In Heikki's tour of Ford, his contact was sharing stories about how PCs were getting used for "too much." Heikki learned they were buying sleek multimedia-capable PCs on the cheap online. The PCs arrived and all the software was removed. Ford customized Windows and Office, adding Ford's other business software to the standard image. A hard drive image was a copy of all the files that could be easily transferred to a new hard drive in a single operation, creating an exact copy of a new PC, just how PCs were manufactured at Dell or IBM.

To reduce cost of ownership, Ford removed the DVD drives, and the USB ports were sealed with epoxy. Heikki's new friend proudly showed an entire storage closet filled with DVD drives that were removed from brand new PCs, along with a supply of epoxy. Heikki was also told, "And, believe me, if we could put the keyboards in this closet we would."

The pattern repeated across the largest and best customers. The details differed, but the goals and basic hacking at Office were consistent.

I joined in the learning and visited a large Wall Street bank. My experience was just as concerning. I was shown the tool that IT created to simplify the creation of in-house documents like meeting agendas and interoffice communication. They determined that Word was too complicated, and it distracted people from their important work because it had too many features, or "options," as they told me. To address these needs IT made a small place for Word in the traders' desktop—a program that took up the full screen, dividing it into regions for different banking activities—and created a tiny little window to type a memo into. There were no menus or toolbars so no ability to format the document. There was a single custom toolbar designed with Save, Print, and Open commands and basic formatting. The customer took all of Word and cut it down to WordPad. They were proud of this work. I was mortified. Later in the day, when I managed to have a quick side conversation with an employee who was using this setup, they were quick to tell me how much they hated it and how they wrote all their letters on their PC at home. I had my anecdote.

The team heard dozens of similar stories as it fanned out around the world. We understood that IT was under siege. The PC went from volunteers requisitioning one at a time to companies mandating they be deployed to every *knowledge worker*, the newest hip term for white-collar work filling weekly business magazines. If a PC owned and managed by IT was a bit finicky or occasionally troubled, that meant that at any given moment someone could not get work done and needed hands-on help. That's where the thousands of dollars were going.

How could we reconcile this? We could obviously see the complexity of managing tens of thousands of people using PCs, each unique in some ways. At the same time, we saw the good work we were doing, across Windows and Office, scaled back or even disabled. Worse, to simplify the product, Office was being turned into something it was not and was being made more difficult to use, the exact opposite of our design goals and past decade of designs.

To be fair, we simply didn't believe in the idea that Office merely needed to do less. We understood and empathized, but the desire to do less was the solution as the customer saw it, and we could do better than that. It is not difficult to see the customer view. People are calling unable to do things in the product, getting tripped up figuring out how it works, or simply spending too much time on one task. The simple answer was to have less there for them to get lost in.

We felt we could provide empowering tools for creativity that were manageable and usable in a LORG. Doing so required us to integrate a LORG perspective into the product design process.

We aimed for the feature design process to be participatory and include IT—we wanted professional IT to feel a part of the design process for the features they cared about. PeggySt suggested we bring representatives of IT, those responsible for Office, together for an ongoing partnership to inform feature designs. While the server products deeply engaged with early customers, especially for deploying the product, and held design reviews, the idea of Office starting from a blank slate with a small set of well-informed customers, outside the sales and support process, was innovative. Peggy developed a straightforward plan and called the forum the *Office Advisory Council*, OAC, creating the first *participatory design* effort for a major product. What was different about the Office approach was how we combined the participation of IT professionals with our existing process for planning and scheduling a release. We intended to invite participation, but we were not taking direct orders or dictation for what to do, because we had millions of other customers we had to design for. That was the big difference.

Except nothing was ever simple.

Using her contacts across sales and marketing, Peggy solicited input for OAC membership—we intended to create a council that would meet quarterly in a systematic way. We believed if we assembled about 20 representatives from across countries and industries and spent enough hours with them then we would have a unique perspective to incorporate their needs into the product.

Peggy immediately ran into the sales organization wanting to understand what we would tell *their* accounts—the concept of "account control" was new to all of us, having zero experience selling. The regional VPs insisted on veto authority over the accounts we chose, and the sales team wanted us to work with accounts that were difficult deals to close and thus swayed by more attention from headquarters. The account managers insisted on being present. The lawyers on both sides were concerned about disclosure and intellectual property. The technical account manager teams (TAM) were upset that the customers learned more information about the product than they did. Other product teams wanted to align customers so that the best Exchange customers were also part of the OAC, or perhaps the worst SQL customers would become better customers if they saw the power of Excel working with SQL. Marketing was worried that these customers might leak information to the trade press. Even I expressed concern to

Peggy that simply talking to customers before features were complete might commit us, especially if the customers communicated what they learned from our meetings to their Microsoft account teams.

It is often said that the hardest thing to do in a big company is *to do something*. We were used to the technical buzzsaw, but this was a process buzzsaw. What seemed like a simple idea of learning from customers turned into an avalanche of stakeholders and special interests. It was one of those times we just put our heads down and ignored the noise. We knew what we needed to do.

The OAC was a two-way learning forum, not a sales or support tool or a perk for good customers. We trusted the participants and they were going to trust us. The tone was a partnership. Customers thought their input was being taken seriously, not just documented.

Shortly after the vision for Office9 was completed, we held the first OAC forum. This might sound backwards or even disingenuous. What I observed with the Platforms engagements was that bringing customers in too early led to input and feedback that was all over the map and difficult to work through with clarity of purpose. Starting off with asking what to do, even with technology professionals, was still only as good as the solution set they were aware of. For example, we would receive lots of input on fixing the syntax of our setup customization language, but no one would suggest an entirely different approach. By having a high-level plan and features to discuss we were able to prioritize, refine, and validate the intended product—the discussions were far more constructive. Most importantly we knew that the resulting input could be mapped to a robust product plan and the feedback truly made a material difference.

The first meeting we held involved an exercise in budgeting the product engineering resources. We created lists of dozens of features for the product across each of the key areas we intended to innovate in for the release. Normally discussions would then take place about those—platforms would bring in experts and present those features and there would be a feedback session. We did that, but we also gave the OAC members a budget. They then got to spend a few hours with sticky notes allocating resources across the team, deciding what features they would choose to do. The most fascinating part of this exercise became the debates between the OAC members themselves over what Microsoft should do. By participating in this way, we learned the value customers placed on different features while at the same time the OAC came to understand that there are inherent trade-offs in all we would do. Even they came to the conclusion that releases with no features other than TCO-reducing work would be boring and not have the business value justifying a deployment.

To broaden the impact across the OAC had across the team, we scheduled *atrium talks* where members of the OAC presented their view of Office and the challenges they faced and the needs they had. The atrium was the large open space in building 17 where we often held large group meetings. They presented how they rolled out PCs, deployed new software, maintained stability and robustness, and supported their own users internally. In a way, this was giving everyone on the team their own version of executive customer visits, knowing that customers had no interest in hosting every engineer on our teams the way they would host execs. As we made this more systematic it became common to hear people talking, actually empathizing, with customers over the problems they had and the unique ways they deployed and managed PCs.

Peggy introduced this exercise by saying building Office was like ordering pizza for 20 million people, without a big enough budget and no way to make everyone happy. It reminded me of the limited budget we had in our dorm for ordering pizza and the debates we had for that one time I got to spend my resident advisor budget. In hindsight, 20 million does seem like such a quaint number. This also became the title of my standard college recruiting talk that I would give for the next 5 or more years.

BillG even joined. He was never super enthusiastic about the needs of IT, especially when it came to tailoring products for the specific people who wanted to turn all the features off, so to speak, but the result of the session was interesting: Both Bill and the OAC members gained a strong sense of empathy and commitment toward a common goal. By this time, securing a small conference room meeting with Bill was not even something many of their CEOs would have been able to do, which made it all the more special.

OAC continued to grow to be an increasingly important and significant evolution of Office planning. Every member of our team working with the OAC could point to specifics in features they worked on that were improved, rethought, or prioritized because of those interactions. On the other side, members of the OAC became long-time friends of Microsoft and us personally. As members of the OAC progressed in their own careers, often to CIOs. it was not uncommon for me to hear from them about how much being in the OAC helped them to better understand product design and how to relate to product makers. Each release the competition across the field to get their favorite customers into the OAC increased and the visibility of the program became its own sign of success. Still, maintaining the core function of participatory design and not turning it into another sales pipeline or marketing tool remained a (sometimes difficult to maintain) priority.

Personally, not only was the OAC a cool part of learning and process innovation at Microsoft, but it was also a learning experience for me when it came to enterprise selling and an appreciation for the incredible complexity the PC was bringing to business even while empowering employees to be more effective and creative.

I consider the OAC one of the most important contributions we made to building Office for this middle part of the PC revolution. Over time, enterprise thinking became baked into product design. That presented a new set of challenges as we will see.

049. GO GET THIS ROCK

Planning Office9 was going to be difficult because it was the first time we would plan a release from the start as a suite. We soon realized most other groups thought Office was being disrupted by the Internet. As I will explain, disrupted was all the rage in business jargon, having replaced thought leader. To address this challenge, or I should say inevitability, Office needed to navigate external competitive forces and internal strategies that conflicted with each other, even before taking into account what Office might do for customers strategically or technically.

Windows existed in a parallel world where the Windows 95 consumer code base was almost entirely engrossed by the Internet, while the NT code base designed for business and IT was working to add a modern graphical interface and then build up compatibility with the consumer ecosystem, a project that would take three releases and 6 years.

The server products such as Exchange and SQL were built around IT as the buyer and the user, which led to a world view exclusively about the enterprise, where embracing internet technologies had a less urgent need. Windows Server, the core platform product, had a clear mandate to be a great WWW server, building on the early work of Internet Information Server which was itself in a bare-knuckle competitive race with both Netscape and the open-source Apache web server, both of those primarily running on Unix and increasingly Linux.

Office 97 finished the last consumer release and as a team we were in the process of figuring out how to focus on enterprise customers, while also recognizing that our buyer was IT, but our user remained the individual or workgroup. Our internet plans were based on what we had started years earlier, apart from Outlook which was in the process of its sudden embrace of internet protocols resulting in the off-cycle release separate from the Office suite. Nevertheless, in many markets Office was going to remain a consumer or retail business for some time to come, especially Japan which was approaching half of our business.

With the organization above me in flux and the executive overseeing the Office organization during Office 97 changing a couple of times, I discovered that sometimes there was opportunity in chaos. During this time, I experienced my own evolution as a leader, learning to be focused on the team and getting the product built, while stuff above me just sort of happened. I began planning the release in my role as program management leader for the Office Product Unit (OPU) but finished the release as the General Manager and then VP for the entire Office suite, though the team experienced none of the "big reorg" issues. My manager was JonDe for the entire release as he endured the changes above him, and diligently worked to minimize the impact of the chaos on the Office team. There's no way we would have finished Office9 without that support.

As a program management team, we held offsites for several months prior to Office 97 shipping. I scheduled one to kick off the process of buy-in from upper management. I structured it in the way I believed the Platforms culture (our new executive leadership) preferred, which was a series of slide decks presented by area experts with interaction and discussion including a deliberate description of architecture. This differed from how Office usually handled offsites. I saw these cultural differences in working across teams and as BillG's technical assistant and knew how important it was to have discussions culturally in sync, even if I did not always do a good job myself.

The plan was to have BradSi (now JonDe's manager and Senior Vice President *Applications & Internet Client Group*) and PaulMa (Brad's manager and Group Vice President of the new *Platforms & Applications Group,* which was everything but MSN) attend, as well as my manager, JonDe, and his reports, plus the group program managers (the product leaders across Office and also several teams from Windows and across Platforms) and of course marketing.

But then a wrench was thrown into the planning. JonDe told me the Office9 plans were creating angst among execs. This was a bit puzzling and somewhat scary because the plans were not known broadly. Actually, we didn't have any plans at all, and the product hadn't even officially started the schedule yet. How could they already be concerned and about what?

In JonDe's office on the third floor in building 17 we grumbled about the challenge of Office being managed by Systems execs. We felt similar to a couple of years earlier sitting together in that very same office pondering the idea that the Apps teams said we in Office lost our marbles, before we finished the successful (but late) Office 97 product. This was different though because, as Jon relayed, Office9 wasn't exciting enough or soon enough so it seemed. We were told the "rest of Microsoft" felt like Office didn't get the internet and was not embracing the future—it was those kinds of vague assertions that made their way to us. I felt certain that I had credibility when it came to internet religion. What could such feelings about the team be based upon?

There were forces at work, or, more aptly worded, criticisms of Office based on nascent technologies that might prove competitive. *Innovator's Dilemma*, the seminal 1997 book by Harvard Business School's Clayton Christensen, was fresh off the presses and like every large company facing the internet, the book's lessons were immediately extrapolated to the strategic challenges posed by the internet. The original article upon which the book was based, "Catching the Wave", was widely distributed among teams at Microsoft. The book was not without controversy when it was released and increasingly so as time passed. The disruptive force, as it related to Office, was the internet and what it brought to productivity and document creation. Unlike the concrete examples in the book (such as the switch to 3.5" hard drives from 5.25" ones) there was no lower-priced, less-functioning product competing with Office…yet. Office did not understand the internet, so our bosses seemed to suggest. I had, apparently, lost *my* marbles. Every discussion would somehow come back to the new and ever-present theory of disruption, though everyone seemed to have a different interpretation of the book.

Yet, there we were facing our own management team. In the context of planning Office9, we were being told Office was being disrupted. It was not a question if or when, it was happening right now.

In the Systems way of developing a strategy, problems were generally distilled down to specific technologies or architectures that would be used to out-architect Microsoft. The conversation almost always started from the technology end-state and from that basis one countered. Communication challenges would arise when the discussion turned to or started from scenarios or customer perspectives. Disruption facing Office was not a specific product, but the way future products were being built or contemplating being built. Somewhat like Christiansen's steel minimills, Office faced a technology challenge.

Our technology approach was customer focused, not technology focused. Still thinking from a customer perspective did not preclude technology. Rather, we faced the belief that technology defined the starting point and context for the conversation, not the end point in solving customer or market problems. It should be no surprise, but technology driven is what makes sense for much of an operating system. This different focus is not a problem, rather it is why Microsoft had two wildly successful businesses. Even to this day there remains a nuance to this heated topic. Every company, especially mature and successful ones, claim to first and foremost listen to customers. Whereas every new startup is almost always highly technology driven. As we will see, Office was and remained customer focused while making significant and seemingly anti-customer bets on major technologies. Systems would continue to be primarily technology focused which both served it well and also created challenges within the team and for Office.

There were numerous technologies in play that were, as we came to say, poised to disrupt Office. Key among them were the browser, network computers, Java, and *components*. This might all sound like jargon or at some level interchangeable buzzwords of the era—and to those who know the jargon these might not sound like particularly discrete choices—but the importance of having a strategy discussion based on these technologies was key. Each one of these technologies was deeply important to a different part of the overall product organization. Each was viewed as the most important competitor for at least one part of the company.

As I discuss these, it is important to consider that the technologies while related were at an important level mutually exclusive—we could only build Office once and had to pick one technology approach to build the product. Office was being disrupted, but by which technology? It also meant we were by definition currently building Office on the wrong technology for the internet—could it be that using Windows was wrong, in 1997? The problem was not just that we were wrong at the start, but we would have to pick one approach from several and in the process, we would still be wrong for some executives and their view of disruption. How would we possibly align? Importantly, every division wanted Office to align with and validate its strategy.

As the flagship application for Microsoft, independent software vendors would take their lead from Office, thus strengthening our new internet strategy, whichever one that might be. It is impossible to overstate the strategic need and value of Office making a technology bet in the 1990s. Office betting on a technology in Microsoft Windows (or not) was a massive signal to the market about that part of Windows and equally about the bets we did not make. We took this responsibility very seriously. Even small things like what version of Windows was required by Office were galactically important—the teams building new versions of Windows wanted us to require the latest version because doing so drove new PC sales through PC makers with a one-two punch of a new Windows and new Office together. The newly powerful enterprise sales teams wanted Office to run on the existing OS and installed base of PCs.

At any given moment, about 30% of our customers were on the one before the previous version of Office (in this case Windows 3.1 and Office 4), 30% on the previous one (Windows and Office 95), and then in about 2 years the rest would be on Office 97 (probably with Windows 98 and a little bit of Windows NT in the enterprise), just in time for Office9. Repeat this for every new technology and you can start to see how difficult it became to release new capabilities that required a new OS, a new PC, and a new version of Windows. We were already stuck and didn't even realize it.

First among technology equals was the browser. There were advocates that believed productivity tools like Office hosted in the browser were imminent and Office's days running on Windows were numbered. In early 1997, HTML was made up of a collection of about 20 formatting elements and the programming language JavaScript that was about 18 months old, both experienced over 56k dial-up connections for most people. Internet Explorer supported both JavaScript and of course Microsoft's own VBScript. Microsoft would tiptoe around the most strategic choice for scripting and the launch of JavaScript was one of the earliest "Anyone But Microsoft" (ABM) moments in the browser. The market made its choice of scripting languages clear with JavaScript the obvious winner. Office was already iterating on saving documents to HTML and making progress. Still, many thought the combination of the latest HTML 3.2 and scripting along with future browser enhancements meant the replacement for Office was looming.

PowerPoint was a canonical example of an Office app to be replaced by HTML. As it turned out, a dozen different sites were doing pages that from 10 feet away looked like a slide-creating program. The ability to make big title text with bullets was grabbing attention. Unlike PowerPoint in Windows, where most people used the default look reminiscent of color television of a blue gradient with yellow text. These new browser slides had cool texture backgrounds (like fabric) and blinking title text Thank you, Netscape, for that one! These were absolutely trivial *slides* and there were no real tools for editing. In fact, these worked by typing lines of text into a form or series of five text boxes and clicking "submit," and the slide came back as an image with bullets added. The image didn't scale to full screen and most of the time picking the size of the image was done at create time. PowerPoint, however, was going to be the first victim of the browser, or so it was suggested.

Reading this, one might say that of course this happened, evidence today's Google Workplace apps. Two decades is a long time—that is like saying the iPod was going to come along and disrupt the Walkman so the Walkman team should have just given up, long before the iPod arrived. Still, Google today has not commanded more than a small slice of the productivity tools business dominated globally by Office. Whether that is still changing or not, only strengthens the point about the timescale we are talking about. As this book shows, and will show, frequently being early is not always the best path.

Netscape was already building email and that was going to displace Outlook, as it was put bluntly. There was more credibility in this only because Outlook lacked support for standards and was still far from the most loved product in Office, or "Byzantine" as it was called in reviews. Netscape was building an internet native email client, not unlike the current favorite *Eudora* that the Internet Mail and News app, Outlook Express, was going after. Rumors were swirling about a word processor and tools for collaboration based on a significant acquisition Netscape made. I was concerned. Netscape was a force. We were already on edge about word-processing with the rise of email, which is why we did so much to integrate Word and Outlook. A word processor that shipped with the browser was exactly the strategy the Office team proposed at the company's very first Internet offsite.

For the rest of our Internet Division, however, the browser was everything. Having Office commit to the Microsoft browser was not only good for Office but would enhance the unique, proprietary aspects of Internet Explorer that Office would use to deliver a product in the browser.

I was not alone in questioning the maturity of browsers to build document creation tools. Sun Microsystems introduced a new programming language called Java that addressed the lack of power in the browser to create full-featured applications. Java was getting a great deal of attention from enterprise IT strategists because it came from Sun, leaders in the server world (and main competitor to NT), and because Java more closely resembled the client-server world they were used to. In many ways, Java was viewed as the successor to Microsoft's Visual Basic with the added benefit that Java was touted as "write once, run anywhere," which meant it worked on any computing platform. Enterprise IT loved to hear about technologies that avoid platform lock-in, and the theory of Java was just that. Adding to the strength of that message was the rebirth of IBM under CEO Lou Gerstner as a company free of the shackles of proprietary technology and open to supporting all the popular platforms. IBM was "all in" on Java and emphasizing it as a key technology across their product line. The embrace of all competitive or alternative technologies as a way of leveraging account control was now the IBM playbook, and one that threatened to slow down Microsoft's emerging opportunity in enterprise accounts.

JonDe and I grappled with the notion that writing programs in Java was a significant risk to Office. It wasn't just technical reservations, but our life experiences. Java was an *interpreted language*, which meant that the programs were represented by code that was converted to native machine code as it ran, unlike Office, which shipped as fast *compiled* native code, as most all modern software did. For JonDe the idea of using an interpreter for programs was close to home. His first job at Microsoft used an interpreter (PCode as previously mentioned) specifically to write apps once that ran on many computers of the day using as little memory as possible—Microsoft had its own proprietary dialect of the C programming language and an interpreter for an array of different computers. Over the past few years, all interpreted code was removed from Office products as modern operating systems made using an interpreter unnecessary and slow. Interpreted programs made sense when the scarcest resource was memory, which was no longer the case.

Finally, the GUI programming model of Java was strikingly close to the big fat AFX class library that was thrown out and a huge failure much earlier in my career. The idea that the way to work seamlessly across multiple platforms is to invent yet another platform seemed doomed to failure. In the case of Java, Jon and I sat in his office reliving years of our shared experiences, making it difficult to think there was any reality to this technology. Cross-platform, interpreters, big class libraries—what a horrible foundation. Add in the promise of *write once, run anywhere* and it seemed obvious that Java was set up to fail as a tool for writing client apps. We'd seen these movies before. Or was that a warning sign to us to be cautious in fighting old battles again?

There were at least a dozen different companies building what were casually called Java Office products including consumer favorite Corel. There were suites of tools, attempted clones of Word, Excel, PowerPoint, and integrated products like Works. There was a huge investment from Silicon Valley venture capitalists to fund Java-based companies and many of those were going after Office. Like JavaScript, Java was supported by the loose consortium of anyone but Microsoft.

Therefore, Java was enormously important to the Developer Tools division where maintaining the mindshare of developers was their key mission. In another aspect of embracing technologies, Microsoft released Visual J++ as part of the family of Visual tools, side by side with Visual Basic and Visual C++. Visual J++ was a technical *tour de force*, but Microsoft was strategically conflicted over embracing it because of the loss of control on the client where Win32 was strategic and on the server where Java could lead to a stronger position for Sun. Microsoft .NET was still a few years away. Office was a big user of Visual Basic and enterprise customers were deeply committed to it for client-server development, at least for the moment. It was clear that Office could not bet on Java for those reasons, but then again what if Java were to win in the market?

The *network computer,* or NC as it was called, was particularly troublesome to the Windows operating system team. Larry Ellison at Oracle championed the NC, a simple computer that only ran one program, a web browser. For the NC to disrupt Office, browser-based applications offering some functionality like Office were required. The real fear of the NC was that enterprise customers would adopt it simply because managing Windows PCs was so painful and expensive. PaulMa and the people on the Windows team thinking about TCO spun up an initiative *ZAW* for zero administration Windows. It was a classic sales tool to solve a deep technical problem. While I was as worried about the NC as anyone, from an Office perspective it still required HTML Office (or potentially Java Office), which was, at the very least, a stretch. The NC was a strategic threat for every aspect of Microsoft. The question was on what timeframe and again with what technologies?

The fourth technology movement to navigate was the idea of *components.* Components were not a specific programming language or even technology, but the concept that component technology would replace tools such as word processing and spreadsheets with much *smaller and lighter* components. Components might be viewed as an expression of *object-oriented* concepts in the context of resulting products rather than programming techniques. Components could best be thought of as basic building blocks of applications from which a customized version of a full-featured application could be easily created with the benefit of having only the capabilities required resulting in a reduced need for system resources like memory and disk.

Components were a response to the feeling that suites were bloated with too many features no one used, making them inefficient for the enterprise. IBM, who did not have a competitive suite even after acquiring Lotus, was the leader in touting components. IBM repurposed Lotus SmartSuite as components, more sleight of hand than technology. Components were attractive to industry analysts like Gartner who believed that enterprises might construct purpose-built desktops tailored to workers by using components. This type of design was exactly what I saw at the bank in New York when I went to learn about total cost of ownership. Java was the new way to implement components. We were sort of going in circles. That was sort of the point—the proponents of Java did not want to compete with Office so they created a product strategy that was something Office could not do even if it wasn't something humans wanted to do.

To cover all the bases, a newly created alliance of various Java vendors announced a component architecture called *Java Beans*, to fill the architectural holes in using Java for components. This technology was aimed squarely at Microsoft's own ActiveX or earlier technology COM. Many in the Microsoft platforms ranks viewed COM as something of the crown jewels of our overall architecture approach. This made competing in component technology even more important. Office already used COM and it was tightly integrated with Visual Basic. This was good for strategy, but again if Java or Java Beans became the defining technologies to disrupt Office then we would lose out.

In addition to technology, the concerns about Office included cultural and process issues starting with the length of time Office was going to use to create a new release. The Internet Explorer team became quite enamored with the concept of "internet time." Internet time was a key element of the ongoing *browser wars* (as they were called)[15] between Microsoft and Netscape.

Unlike Office, where releases took 24 to 30 months, browsers were being released every nine to 12 months, at least for the past two versions—any two data points can make a trend. On the face of it, releasing the browser that quickly did not seem risky—the main characteristic of browsers was that they were viewers, and if they crashed a user could revert to what they were previously reading. No work was lost, unlike if Word crashed. Plus, HTML was designed in a fault-tolerant way, so any coding mistakes in displaying it on the screen were minor annoyances more than anything else. This relaxed a huge constraint on engineering and certainly made release velocity possible—that and the fact that these were not big programs yet. HTML and the browser user experience were maturing rapidly—there was so much low-hanging fruit to get right just looking at how other browsers worked. Basic, and known, features like clipboard, printing, accessibility, and more needed to be added. Most of all everything was new so there were few pre-defined criteria for features, other than what Netscape was doing.

To some, this was another point at which Office didn't get the way the world changed. Office needed a new architecture and to release faster.

Office9, the product that few knew about and that even we had not developed full plans for, was not exciting enough because Office was being disrupted. It was also taking too long to get done, even though we didn't have a schedule. To thwart the disruption, we needed to build a new Office that was more exciting, but to do so meant solving a complex web of technologies and competitors, none of which seemed remotely up to the challenge. Every time I said something like that I was literally the punchline or punching bag? of *Innovator's Dilemma* or sent another link to a press article about a new startup building Office in HTML, Java, Components, or Network Computers.

My emotions ran from angry to upset to frustrated as I tried to figure out how to have this conversation without being the person who said, "All the new technologies won't work," while also being the person who said, "Office won't change." That was a dangerous combination when the phrase "disruption" was being tossed around because such a reaction was literally the one written about in the book. In other words, everything I might have said was going to be viewed through the lens of me playing the role of the executive with his head in the sand. Oddly, I was one who helped get everyone excited about the internet in the first place. More than anything that stung, being painted as a luddite so soon after running around the company trying to get people excited about the internet.

The feedback felt to me was like an allegory of *Go Get This Rock*, that was told to me by members of the original LanMan team, the failed but legendary networking project that was originally managed by SteveB.

> *Elder: I wish to be clear and helpful. Go get me a rock.*
>
> *Student: (runs to riverbed to get a rock and picks out a nice one) Here is a rock.*
>
> *Elder: No, not that rock. Try a bigger one.*
>
> *Student: (runs again) Here's a bigger one.*
>
> *Elder: Yes, but that isn't smooth enough.*

To the elder (the manager), this was the process of managing by "I know it when I see it," which was certainly one valid school of management. To the student, this was unwanted insanity.

The kind of feedback we were getting felt like getting rocks. No product approach was right. No technology choice was right. Nothing was soon enough. And it was frustrating. It was, unfortunately, also the default executive management approach. At the time I was miserable from this and of course did not handle it well. This manifested itself in endlessly long email threads, which I feel I achieved a varsity letter in writing. With the benefit of hindsight, this was a product of the uncertainty. No one knew what to do and everyone was kind of worried. We simply entered a period where the prevailing view was knowing what to do once the right answer was presented, and at the same time there was a belief that the right answer was higher in the organization where there was more context about the risks to existing businesses. In many ways, this was the *innovator's dilemma* we faced (all of us)— the question was if the new technologies could be fit somehow into existing strategies, or we needed a whole new approach. There was also a great deal of Microsoft's universal cultural attribute, paranoia.

Writing memos in addition to email became my tool for processing my own thoughts and, in a way, getting my act together for confrontation, at worst, or at least a strategic discussion. Writing was my way of saying, in detail, "Here's a rock," and a way of documenting promises and commitments in one place for all audiences. It was also a way of saying "This would be a dumb rock and here's why."

I wrote a dense 20-page memo called *High Hopes for Office9*. This set a tone that was, in hindsight, overly defensive. Caffeinated on Diet Coke and wound up, I banged out this memo in an evening. It served as a precursor to the strategy offsite for Office9, detailing the main product pillars. I took on all the technologies and strategies I could and did not hold back.

In the abstract, I needed to find a way to at least suggest that the main technologies being talked about as disruptive to Office might pose a threat but not in any reasonable time, even though this was tilting at windmills. We already planned to embrace internet technologies. Primary among these were saving documents as HTML, using HTML as a native file format, connecting Office apps to servers using internet protocols, even using the internet for help, assistance, and content like clip art and templates. Most importantly, we were shifting our resources and efforts to building a collaborative server capability using FrontPage. All of these relied on internet technologies to solve problems within Office, which was decidedly different than rewriting Office in internet technologies.

Second, I showed that I understood that the attraction of these new technologies was due to deficiencies in Office. I then demonstrated how we could dramatically improve the cost of ownership, ease of use, and management of Office on PCs by simply doing a better job in areas we had previously paid little to no attention to.

I also knew that no matter what happened, someone always said it would. Microsoft was at the scale where regardless of how something played out, someone always wrote the memo predicting it. NathanM was even famous for writing multiple memos with conflicting predictions.

I was not naïve, but I was optimistic. Our plan was strong, an internet-savvy plan, but we also knew that the zealots who were convinced the internet was the undoing of Office would not be pleased. As I learned from BillG, there was a benefit to balancing the opinions of the zealots with reality. Balancing the extremes while executing well was, for better or worse, my sweet spot.

With my memo presented as a deck at an offsite, and the goal of not hurting the morale of the team, which would undermine plans and execution, for better or worse, the team appeared to feel the same way that I did. Looking back, it was more that the plans for Office were given reluctant acceptance by executives without much actionable feedback. In hindsight, there really was a high degree of uncertainty about what to do, really, and no one, especially executives from Platforms new to managing Office, wanted to hinder the Office business out of the gate.

At best if the project went well, then we could say we agreed, but if things did not go well, it was obviously my/our fault. I was fine with that level of accountability. In fact, it served us all well.

The next step was to have an actual plan. The kind of plan that the Office team was skilled in delivering and executing.

050. THE TEAM'S PLAN IN THE FACE OF DISRUPTION

Leading the plans for Office9 placed me decidedly in the role of the incumbent in the context of "technology disruption," as was being thrown around the hallways or thrown at me. We were moving forward with a plan that was either going to work or prove to be one of the biggest cases of disruption ever, not to mention the biggest mistakes ever made for an incredibly successful business on a huge upswing. Therein is the most counter-intuitive aspect of this plan—almost no one on the outside would think we needed to do anything to "save" Office, and everyone on the inside had wildly different theories on how we must save Office, all relying on nascent (at best) technologies.

I committed to create a document outlining the plans, a vision, for the whole Office9 product and my self-imposed deadline approached. The *High Hopes* offsite and memo turned out to be a draft, which was helpful. When I wrote the *Priorities and Processes for Office9* that declared there would be a unified plan for the release I didn't quite know what I had signed up to create. The offsite and accompanying memo were clarifying.

The bet the product team made was on transforming us from a machinery adept at making new productivity features for individuals—IntelliSense, formatting, document creation and editing—to a new execution machine aimed at creating tools for a whole business. The cost of entering that market as a leader was to significantly improve deployment and manageability, or said another way reduce the total cost of ownership. The features we would aim for were not personal productivity features that saved minutes, but business features that saved teams hours and saved IT headaches and dollars.

In other words, the plan for the product—the vision—would completely upend the historic priorities for the product. This was a big change years in the making but faced with a single moment, the distribution of the plan to the complete team, to most the change would happen suddenly. While we were busy easing a group of 50 or so senior managers, the other 1500 people were mostly hearing rumors while they were busy working on their own team's features. There's no easy way to make a big change in a big company.

I took what I wrote for *High Hopes,* removed the defensive tone, and made it much more forward looking, focused on what we planned to deliver to customers, detailing the state of the business, and how we would work. It was an exciting document, if not a bit overly poetic as I'd not yet found a style for these. I wrote it using Word's Internet Assistant and would eventually post it in HTML to our new http://officeweb running FrontPage sitting on a machine in my office. In 1997, almost nothing was written for an intranet website. The text was in the new sans serif Verdana font, blue with a muted yellow background, as I tried to make it look cool like a web page. It was rather unreadable and mostly unprintable, and with Office 97 copy/paste from the browser really did not work yet. We learned quite a bit from forcing ourselves to use web technologies in this way.

It is important to the process to understand that the past few months were spent in offsites and meetings, and a host of cross-team efforts, arriving at features that would be done by each app and the shared OPU team. *High Hopes* itself was a summary of what we had iterated on up until that point. This is the heart of what is meant by the Office process of "the best of top-down, bottom-up, middle-out." The vision is not a news event when individuals see their own work and their features, but a chance to see what the rest of the hundreds of people will be up to. It is also a tool for the all-important process of adds/cuts—when each team (or feature team, the smaller unit of a team within an App team or OPU) figured out what they could really do with the resources they have. Thus, the document also served as a check on resource allocation—ensuring the people where the work is needed.

This ongoing iteration within a decision-making framework is sometimes depicted as a funnel in consulting diagrams—lots of ideas come in and a process narrows them down. I think of it as a refinement with increasing levels of specificity. This refinement is also what leads to accountability. By the time the vision document is in the hands of the team, not only is it a reflection of the best efforts of the teams but it is also an execution plan, and it is also the accountabilities for the team. There's a development schedule, at least the first cut, and a target ship date. The vision document itself is not a refinement but a summary of the refinement that has been happening all along.

That's the view on paper. In practice, this first attempt would be a bit rough and contentious. The lessons learned would be super valuable the next time we went through this when the team would understand collectively that we were serious about the process. It is fair to say I brute-forced this first vision document through.

I wrote the vision on my own, circulating it for feedback first to OPU program managers and then to senior leaders and forging ahead without really considering the immense implications of what we were up to. Unfortunately, people reading the draft were reading for how it changed or affirmed what they already thought they were doing, not to learn what we were doing together. This was the first attempt at building a shared plan. While we were making progress, the Apps teams hardly surrendered their autonomy. The good news was that I captured most of what everyone was working on and laid the groundwork to unify the expression of why we were doing all that we were doing—that was the goal. The vision was a leading, but also lagging, indicator. The later steps of resource allocation would help to make sure the plan was executed as intended and agreed. This step, resource allocation, is what was almost always omitted in transforming a plan to execution.

The multitude of offsites and planning discussions paid off. Collectively, we were close to being on the same page, at least as close as could be for a team of senior managers who previously were working autonomously with OPU trying its best to be the glue across teams. The rest of the organization was starting to worry, something I heard in hallway grumbling.

Our team administrative assistant CollJ booked the big conference room, Kodiak Room, for March 15, 1999, for an all-hands meeting for the team including satellite/tape for Asia and Ireland where we had large teams. The last time we did this was for developer demo day when each independent app showed off features of Office 97. The night before the presentation I had an idea to make a cheat sheet or one-pager highlights. I quickly excerpted the 12-page vision document, choosing the goldenrod paper stock from the building 17 first floor copy room and made 1000 copies. I was there late in the night and most copies ended up crooked. I had to finish in a second copy room because the machine kept jamming. It makes me smile now to look at the crooked paper that remained on my cork board, adding subsequent cheat sheets each product cycle.

The *Office9 Vision* began by stating that Office 4 through Office 97 changed the way people worked, but that was the past. A paradigm shift was underway. Microsoft, especially BillG, loved the word *paradigm,* in the Thomas Kuhn sense. This shift was toward the internet. Office9 declared itself to be "the best execution of an integrated suite of

Internet-centric communication and productivity tools for creating, editing, sharing, synthesizing, and analyzing business information."

This was my way of pushing back on the idea that the internet, by definition, implied new productivity tools. My point: The internet could make existing tools better and more relevant. The team liked this, or at least reacted positively to it, even if the implications were unclear. Office9 declared Office 97 the end of an era of individual productivity and the start of a new one.

Later, I realized it was the beginning of the middle of the PC era, an era defined by expansion into business combined with a shift to enterprise features and sales motions.

An interesting note relative to disruption is that one response incumbents have to new technologies is to attempt to absorb them into an existing product, failing to recognize the substantial changes the new technology might ultimately imply. This was something I did not consider but thought a good deal about a decade later in Windows.

In order to outline the strategy shift, the vision explicitly stated the six priorities:

- Migration, Administration, Deployment, and Management
- HTML Document Creation
- Outlook and Outlook + Application Integration
- Web Collaboration and Solutions
- Web-Based Corporate Reporting
- Personal Productivity

Of note were the first and last. In the vision I used a bulleted list (HTML tag <UL>) and went back and forth myself over whether to number the items (HTML tag <OL>) to further emphasize the priority. As it would turn out, everyone mentally numbered the list anyway and I got the benefit of the full effect. I explicitly rejected the traditional business notion of having one single priority, say the internet. Such an approach only looks good on paper. In reality a single priority leaves most everything to chance as it is necessarily too abstract. Eight or ten priorities seemed too many so this release and others would arrive at five or six.

Migration, Administration, Deployment, and Management declared the most important thing we were doing—making Office a LORG product. Suddenly, the thing that was always last, always assigned to interns, always fixed as blockers in later product updates, was moved to the very first priority. The problem was that by talking about migration, administration, deployment, and management, I made Office9 seem like the dullest product ever. These features were always the last to get completed. The thought of doing this work as a first-class effort became an eye-roller. The vision called this the *TAO of Office*, or totally adminsterable [sic] Office.

HTML document editing was the second major area. Much of this work was already underway in the form of Internet Assistants for Word and PowerPoint. There were two controversial elements to this. First, Excel had done little by way of HTML and pushing an investment there would ultimately drive a great deal of effort on performance, rendering, and capacity in Internet Explorer, which loved web pages they could display but would crush

Netscape. Second, we had not put much effort into ingesting HTML, versus outputting HTML By developing the ability to open HTML files, as difficult and not particularly useful as that was, we laid the groundwork for using future HTML as a native file format (instead of our crazy binary formats that had caused us so much trouble in Office 97) and importantly for a format to interchange data between applications and the browser using copy/paste. This was the start of a multi-year, multi-product investment that would pay off immensely over a long period of time. The controversy around this choice will be explored in the next section.

In the past, the buyer and user of Office were the same person—the individual productivity user or the power-user/developer we called *influential end-users*. Apps previously segmented customers by end-users and influential end-users, also commonly called power users or techies. Excel segmented bankers. Word segmented lawyers, and so on. Office needed to mature and build a product for segments the way we were selling software. The vision made a case for this level of importance by highlighting different customer segments and the value each would see from Office9.

For the first time, we declared that administrators and CIOs were users, not just buyers—they just wanted entirely different features. We also made a consistent appeal to developers, something we had done unevenly across the product.

The team understood this and making a case with the financials and sales of the company reinforced the new reality for the business. This information also reinforced the dominance of the suite in defining the product.

What turned out to be *unacceptable* was the last priority, *personal productivity*. Historically, personal productivity meant *features* customers liked and made the product easier to use and demonstrate. Anything and everything could be personal productivity since we made personal productivity tools. The personal productivity bucket consumed all development schedule hours and made the product appear as a long list of features to marketing, rather than any theme. That was old-school personal productivity, priority 1 and beyond.

The plan constrained the definition of personal productivity to features that were unique to each app—features unique to spreadsheets or word processors, not general user experience or ease-of-use features. By allocating development resources to productivity features shared across Office and reducing app resources to focus on each app, the plan was to have a more coherent product to communicate to the market, and one that emphasized the suite nature. Most of the personal productivity features in Word and Excel in the past were similar ideas done differently, inconsistently. Office9 moved that work to OPU and away from Apps teams.

Immediately, program manager leaders across Apps threatened to quit, even raising the issue to BillG. It was not the reaction I expected. They felt disempowered and felt that I had kneecapped the apps. The need to build a suite for LORGs seemed like the obvious plan—to me. Also obvious to me was that Office 97 won. I was experiencing a reality of management: Everyone went along until something changed—they were in favor of change, and even change advocates, until the actual change.

I was disrupting Office not with a new technology but with a high-priority focus on a new customer segment and target. Disruption does not always have to be about a new and unproven technology.

It was one thing to declare the need to build a better LORG suite. It was quite another thing to choose to build one at the expense of other features.

Word, Excel, Outlook, Access, and PowerPoint believed that the battle to win in the categories still raged. Outlook had been poorly received and was now busy on their own interim release that would stretch out much longer than planned. PowerPoint was consistently viewed as the weak link. The general utility of the Access product, and our move to upsell Office Professional, which counted on demand for a database, was still too early to declare a success. Lotus and WordPerfect were rumored to be releasing Windows versions that transitioned their MS-DOS product leadership to Windows. From an app perspective, there were plenty of reasons to worry about losing category reviews, should there be any.

Winning in each of these categories, the PM leaders told me, required freedom to innovate in the base experience. There was no way for Excel to beat Lotus 1-2-3 unless they could build an experience tailored to the unique needs of spreadsheet users.

Repeat for each app.

We were right back to "Excel users are different."

Independently, Excel was planning a unique user interface re-architecture that was "weblike." This sounded crazy to me and was the exact opposite of an integrated suite. It was also something that had not been broadly shared or considered across the teams. I could not imagine how we could be a productivity suite if the flagship product, alone, had a new user interface just as we finished launching on the merits of consistency across the suite.

The two weeks from presenting the vision at the all-team meeting we were consumed almost entirely with defending *Personal Productivity Is Priority 6,* as it became known. My inbox was filled with subject lines like "#6," "Priority 6," or "Why such a low priority?"

What seemed easy, took a turn toward the impossible.

To make the most difficult even more difficult, BillG appeared in my inbox. He asked me why Office was going to have a plan that did not advance productivity and was not going to innovate in user interface. It was a direct shot at the plan even though he only knew a small piece of the story. Clearly, he had heard from a leader on the Excel PM team.

Here I was again on the defense, though, logically, I was *certain* he was going to be OK with it. He knew the importance of the suite and LORGs, intellectually but not emotionally. Bill had not really faced a product team intentionally constraining a release up front. Of course, that is why so many things were late.

Once he read the vision, BillG switched from being concerned about the product to being concerned that all the smart people would leave the team if they weren't allowed to innovate. I went from preventing productivity features from making it into the product to the manager who smart people did not want to work for. This felt personal and more of a character trait assault than a list of adjustable features.

This wasn't the first time in my tenure as a manager and later an executive that I would defend the team that was in place over a single person leaving. One of Bill's most enduring and appreciated traits was the loyalty he felt to those committed to Microsoft. This trait surfaced when someone telegraphed that they might potentially leave. In this case, Bill's first reaction was to go to the manager assuming something was wrong in the environment that was *causing* this. Almost always, this was difficult to handle because the information was one-sided (regardless of how BillG found out) and the only thing a manager (me) could do was then talk about all the ways that the team was trying to move forward and how the disaffected person wasn't on board.

I had been defensive in this case. It was early in my career and leading OFFPM, which had grown to about 65 people. And BillG was concerned about any *thought leaders* (a great 1990s word) leaving. After some back and forth, however, he was supportive of the bigger picture. Despite all the changes in the vision and the *demotion* of personal productivity, the team was overwhelmingly in place as we planned and only one PM leader of about 15 bailed, and that had worked out best for everyone.

The rollout of the vision kept moving.

By spring of 1997 we still had two or more years of tight collaboration ahead of us, much tighter than with Office 97. We could not afford a misstep. We rephrased a section in the vision, tenets, which defined the cultural priorities for the release. We made them explicit in the vision document so we could refer to them later in the project:

> *All members of the Office9 team, regardless of the reporting structure, are responsible for the innovations in the Office9 product. By corollary, the shared feature teams are responsible for the integration of their work in each application.*
>
> *Development and process efficiency is critical to the success of the Office9 schedule, and therefore it is better to do things the same way once rather than doing things in multiple places. This refers both to features and process. In other words, it is better to be the same rather than different.*

We took this as a chance to create a new employee orientation for the Desktop Apps division. By instituting a small amount of informal training during new employee onboarding, we were able to show employees the vision document and detail the organization and priorities. Almost immediately, the vision document took on an even broader role than originally intended.

The vision even included specific tenets when it came to the product, schedule, and how we would manage the team. The goal was to have a set of non-negotiables across the App teams and OPU to effectively centralize what mattered. Even something simple like which non-English languages we would focus on (German and Japanese) was previously a big headache that we just decided up front. Similarly, we committed to the platform requirements for the release which included working on the new 3-year-old Windows 95 and also that we would make sure our HTML worked on Netscape Navigator, which was almost heretical, further detailed in the next chapter.

Rolling out the vision for the first time to the entire team was stressful. There was the ever-present fear of leaks, leaving someone out by accident, typos, and oversights. Most importantly, the people who didn't agree wouldn't tell the sender (me) but would create a negative vibe across the group. We saw some of this in the original 12/24 plan.

People who didn't agree stayed on the lookout for what wasn't working and were right there to call this out. For Office9, we knew those who wished to prioritize apps would do the same. All of these were signs of an organization still finding its way from storming to norming.

Given how late Office 97 was, a significant concern was any doubt about the overall schedule. Those manifested as schedule chicken between apps, with each app betting they would just finish ahead of another, rather than working to be first.

The key to a robust schedule was buy-in from the test and dev managers. GrantG already harmonized the schedule across the test discipline when he wasn't personally testing the latest build or filing bugs. While there were differences in style, they really snapped to the same page under his leadership.

DuaneC rallied the dev managers behind the schedule. Duane's style, much like JonDe's, was quiet, understated, factual, and exceedingly straightforward. While directly managing nearly 100 engineers and having responsibility over the full team of over 350 engineers, he still managed to own code, fix bugs, and add features.

It all worked. Following the team meeting, the dev schedule was in motion. Code was being written. We officially started coding in May of 1997 (about 8 weeks after the vision meeting), with a beta scheduled for a year later after three milestones. We planned an RTM of July 1, 1998. There was a big risk to a summer RTM—another DAD rule of thumb along with not releasing on a Friday or before a holiday was avoiding an August RTM. If we missed it, there was a cascade (summer and global holidays that broke up the work calendar, followed by end-of-year) that almost automatically pushed us into the following year.

We were off.

One final note, the group program manager for PowerPoint, BrendanB, was so amused with the vision process and especially the cheat sheet that he went one step further and made a version I could hang from the rear-view mirror of my car along the lines of *Repo Man*, "there's one in every car". This became his tradition and I have a whole collection of these that I maintained on my cork board.

051. HTML: OPPORTUNITY, DISRUPTION, OR WEDGE

First thing Saturday, 9:44AM December 5, 1998, so might as well have been 5:44AM, I received an unsolicited mail from BillG subject line "Office rendering" and copying the full management chain in case they weren't busy that morning. I joke, this was normal even though Bill had been increasingly focused on broader issues lately. For some reason (no context provided), Bill read something somewhere that gave him concerns about the use of HTML in Office. We already had a plan, which he knew about but was now having second thoughts or something. It was not unusual to have to back up and go through our logic and approach to get to an admission that we were not nuts, or perhaps to tweak something. This was a big issue though and cut to the core of our second highest priority in Office9, "HTML in Office9." Bill had some concerns, to put it mildly.

When we changed the traditional binary file formats in Office 97, we caused a real disruption in work. Suddenly files were being emailed within and outside the company and they simply couldn't be opened if the recipient had the wrong version of the application. Worse, even if a converter was available there was a pretty good chance after a few edits the document returned in email would look funny or even wrong. What had served our industry so well—the binary format that represented the internal data structures of each application—had hit a wall with the combination of email and slow deployment of the latest version of software. Without new file formats we were really stuck because every new feature was represented as a change in the data structures and file formats. That's just how things were done.

The browser and HTML were the cool new thing, but they also held out a promise of a *universal* platform for viewing documents. Enterprise customers and industry analysts were enamored with the idea that HTML was a resilient, text-based format. If people used different browsers, they could still read documents with just a few formatting hiccups and all they needed was a browser and not some expensive new version of a productivity tool. Plus, everything just seemed better in a browser, better than the old File Open dialog, connecting to network drives, endlessly navigating folders in hopes of finding something. Just click on a cool blue link and up pops the most current sales numbers or marketing plan. Little details like being connected to a high-speed internet from a laptop, something that was nearly impossible outside large office buildings in major cities, would take years or a decade to address.

We knew all this. Solving these problems was our plan. The big problem? No one knew how those cool documents that were so easy to read, so resilient, so friendly, so snappy, and so much better could be made. What tools would typical knowledge workers use to create *web pages*? What server would they be stored on? Our strategy: Office and FrontPage.

Even if we had some ideas, there were many questions about the role of Word and PowerPoint, and to some extent Excel, given the increasing preeminence of browsing. In a world of browsing web pages created with the relatively simple formats in HTML, where and how would tools designed for sophisticated print-formatted documents fit in?

The most complex cross-group feature of Office9 was the second pillar of the vision, HTML file creation. Demonstrating that these large apps could be relevant in the face of the WWW was a major part of our strategic challenge, especially within Microsoft.

Our choice not to do browser Office, Java Office, or components of Office was a big miss for many in the company who saw those technologies as synonymous with embracing the WWW. The answer in the vision (and in *High Hopes*) was using Office to participate in the WWW, using the apps to create HTML documents that could be viewed in the browser. In a sense, this was turning the WWW into a giant online printer or document repository for businesses. FrontPage powered this ability to publish documents from the desktop PC—we called it the *two-way web*.

A response to potentially disruptive technologies is for the incumbent product to do a bit of a jiu-jitsu move and attempt to turn the disruptive technology into a feature within the product—rather than build a whole new product out of the new technology, embrace the technology as part of the existing product. That's what we were doing with HTML. Rather than rewrite Office in HTML, what if we made HTML a feature of Office? Strategically, some might view this as defensive and certainly not as dramatic as turning the existing business inside out or upside down, as championed by some. The bet was as theoretically cool as Office in HTML might be, and realistically we were a long way off from browsers being able to do that. Even with Internet Explorer rapidly gaining share and Netscape seemingly unraveling, we were years from Internet Explorer dedicating their efforts to building productivity tools like Office on the browser platform.

Our Office Advisory Council was extremely positive about HTML. There was a huge wave of effort at large companies (the OAC represented over one million desktops) surrounding questions about how to use the browser for intranets for collaboration and document sharing, like our http://officeweb. OAC members loved the idea of having a focus area beyond deployment and administration aimed at LORGs because it gave them a seat at the strategy table, not only operational efforts. They were excited to be evangelists of creating documents with Office that could be viewed in a browser and easily saw potential for solving their document distribution challenges.

To make this work, we needed to do a crazy amount of work to twist HTML into representing as much of Office capabilities as we could, no easy task. We knew ultimately our goal was to move to HTML as a fully *native* file format, meaning it could be used in place of the *de facto* standard .DOC, .XLS, and .PPT. The capabilities of HTML were rather spartan compared to Office and difficult to work with. HTML was designed for minimal online documents in a browser. Office handled the myriad capabilities for print documents and sophisticated online presentation. Myriad is an understatement. Typically, people think of Office in terms of document formatting commands, but that leaves little room for even basic formulas in Excel, or presentation template semantics in PowerPoint, or even the simplest of page footnotes in Word, just to name a couple of examples out of thousands I could list. All of those would need some representation in HTML as well.

This is where my view diverged with BillG's view. Having gone through the painful Office 97 transition and not wanting a repeat, I saw our file formats as a liability—something to mitigate. BillG saw them as a significant asset, a proprietary asset, and he loved proprietary assets. File formats raised the switching costs for customers who would move to a competitor. He was right. Unfortunately, our biggest competitor was our old version and what we were inadvertently doing was raising the barrier for customers to upgrade (also known as buy and deploy) the new version of Office.

While we often had disagreements, we didn't often see things as so starkly opposite. BillG had historically focused on those proprietary levers because that's how the industry grew up. All products were open because everyone was building a platform, while at the same time those points of openness were "protected" by proprietary defenses. An API, user interface, data formats, programming language, were all combinations of wide-open platforms and proprietary elements.

When the topic of HTML as a file format came up in strategic conversations, especially with BillG, the discussion quickly turned to a view that HTML implied ceding strategic control of file formats to either a competitor or to what might become a standards body—that was the worst of all outcomes. Seeing this type of situation as an advantage or risk, was something BillG was always good at. While I might have personally recoiled at the idea of having something *proprietary* simply to have those control points in the product, it was not just good business, but the kind of business routinely practiced across technology. In an era of open source, proprietary innovation is often viewed as old school or passé, when in fact it is more vibrant than ever. Behind today's *cloud* is all open-source software made proprietary by remaining in data centers.

The debate for Office9 was far more grounded because the current state of the art for HTML was so limited. The most recent innovation in HTML was the addition of tables, enabling many scenarios, such as presenting financial data in a spreadsheet fashion, though they still lacked most of the formatting used in Excel. More interesting was a great lesson for me in how rapidly new technologies diffused when there was an incredibly strong demand to improve them *immediately.* Every content website, those trying to show stories like a newspaper or magazine, struggled with the most basic formatting problems while trying to get something, anything, that looked reasonably professional to display in a browser in a reliable way. With the original specification of HTML, most sites looked a bit like ransom notes—lots of colors, font sizes, bullets, and that awful blinking text. That's all that people had to work with.

Tables were designed for presenting data, tabular data. Quickly, web developers realized tables were perfect for placing text on the screen in precise spots. They could be used to create columns like a newspaper, or place photos such that text wraps around them, or even nifty tricks like headlines that span columns. Suddenly, sites were using tables to make fancy documents. These did not look like tables one might see in a statistics book or financial report with bordered rows and columns, but what could be seen were aligned text, spanning headlines, and images with wrapped text. Many web purists were troubled by this because the purity and simplicity of HTML were lost. In practice, this *abuse of HTML,* as I called it, also made it difficult to realize many of the benefits of the web like processing documents on servers, automatically generating documents, or even searching and indexing documents as Yahoo was doing. Tables made HTML more complex, but they also made sites look great in the browser. In a sense, HTML was evolving to be a complex file format tuned to online documents. Not what the original creators intended, but it was the browser makers who started calling the shots.

Tables were an opportunity for us. They made web pages more complex, making things more difficult for everyone but nicer for humans reading pages. Office tools were perfectly tuned to handling complex user interactions to create nice-looking documents, which could be seamlessly represented in HTML all while editing in Word as one normally did.

Much to the dismay of purists, HTML was quickly becoming an implementation detail that few humans would deal with directly. Computers could easily absorb the complexity while the human just worked with a tool. Office was a great tool. We received many requests to *convert* Office documents into HTML documents, especially from small businesses and students. While HTML was originally simple to use, perhaps even a bit like using WordPerfect because of tags or *codes,* as WordPerfect called them, doing anything one could do in Office was impossible. Professionals were using tables and creating increasingly difficult-to-code sites. There was room for Office to make this easy.

Our strategy was to make the most we could of HTML to *publish* documents, essentially thinking of HTML as an online print command. Program management fanned out across the products to map formatting capabilities of each product to capabilities of HTML. At one end of the spectrum was PowerPoint, which could always save an entire slide as a single image, as was done by early third-party tools. For PowerPoint, though, this lost out on animations, scaling or selecting text, and the richness of the tool. Tables were a perfect way to maintain the layout of slides in a way that worked much better with browsers. PowerPoint had an early start on converting to HTML and was already pushing the limits of what could be rendered in a browser, but it was fantastic. Slides that acted like real web pages where you could select text, resize the window and scale the slide, and even use full screen presentation view.

At the other end of the spectrum, Excel saw little value. Was this another case of "Excel users are different" and trying to foist a one-size-fits-all OPU consistency on to Excel, or was there real utility? One look at what was being published on early websites and one could see the same type of needs that the print world saw, which was that Excel was used to create charts, graphs, and numeric tables that were then incorporated into Word documents. Some of the first uses of the WWW were sharing corporate financial filings, tables of income statements, and balance sheets. While we could push all this work to Word with copy/paste, most of the time that rendered Excel tables as images, making them difficult to print, select, and scale to different size screens. We decided that Excel needed to be an equal citizen in saving HTML. This also made our Office consistency story stronger.

Word's opportunity was larger, primarily because most people saw what was in the browser resembling Word documents. Just as most of what we read in print was originally created in Word, the early internet was taking on those same characteristics. Leading the efforts on Word's program management team were KayW, who had early on recognized the power of web authoring for Office, and Eric Levine (EricLev.) EricLev started his career at Microsoft in marketing after college where he was coxswain on the Harvard crew team. A giant oar adorned the wall of his office which always a pain when he moved offices. Together, KayW and EricLev drove much of the strategy across Office for HTML. Coincidentally, my office was between them, putting me literally in the middle of the HTML strategy.

Kay and Eric were strong proponents of developing what was called *round-trip* HTML, which meant Word created brand new documents (or read in old documents) and saved them as HTML and later opened them again to make changes. HTML as a *first-class* format, not only a publish-only format, was as brilliant as it was difficult. As an example, consider something simple like a page header. On a printed page it is obviously a header centered, but how it got there could be the result of many different paths, and to open a file for editing later we needed to preserve that path. A centered heading could be created by hitting the center button obviously, but it could also be centered using tabs, changing the margins, or even putting it inside of a table and then adjusting the table. The text itself could be formatted using the bold button and font size, or it could be adjusted with the *Heading* style. Looking at an entire printed document and thinking about the permutations for every bit of formatting quickly boggled the mind.

The complexity of simply copying and pasting formatted text from one product to another was already mind-boggling—and an ongoing source of frustration, product support calls, as well as a competitive problem. HTML was an opportunity to improve because all the products worked on supporting the format at the same time. The clipboard, where information is temporarily stored, relied on an age-old format called RTF (rich text format) that many tools supported, but unevenly. If all the tools supported HTML natively, there was a good chance sharing data across tools would improve. That was our plan.

Solving any problem in Office across the main applications was an enormous task because there was so much history. The product, even in the late 1990s, had thousands of features. But HTML and keeping track of all the formatting and how features were saved in files was a *next-level* effort. KayW and EricLev amassed an incredible amount of knowledge about how HTML was implemented across the products. It worked so well we found many places that browsers were not ready, or, according to the browser teams (including Microsoft's), we used features in unintended ways. For example, saving a spreadsheet could easily create a table that essentially caused the browser to choke on too many rows or columns. New browser features used by PowerPoint were unevenly implemented across different browsers, making slides show up incorrectly depending on the vendor or version of the browser. Professional web designers were experiencing these same problems in their handcrafted web pages, which they would debug by trial and error in different browsers.

These problems led to the rather heated and ongoing debate between BillG and me. He was itching to tell me, "Told you so." He saw an opening because he believed we were limiting ourselves to a lame foundation. I saw the foundation as moving rapidly and one we could exploit. He saw the foundation as one that would constrain us and commoditize our product.

Bill was nervous about using HTML because of the loss of proprietary features. Would HTML be slower? Would files be bigger? Would it be easier to clone Office if we constrained it to only features the browser could render? Would fewer people buy Office and rely on a small set of licensed users to do document creation while others skipped buying Office to use a browser? These were not just good questions, but they were all answered in ways that made the strategy appear flawed. My view of the strategy was simply that the browser was happening, and either Office created content for the browser and remained relevant or other tools, not Office, created documents when they needed to be viewed in a browser. This was a *ride the horse in the direction it is going* strategy.

Bill's mail to me that Saturday morning generated a response from me. That's how we always worked together. Writing long detailed responses to even polarizing assertions was kind of my thing. Bill's thing was poking staccato style with a list of assertions, an argument. My replies were many paragraphs with context, pros and cons, and conclusions. I often included screen shots or supporting information. I did that quickly. If Bill's approach was to "shock" then my response was to "awe."

In this case, Bill's shocking email was more than enough to garner interest by the antitrust regulators and our trial—one of hundreds of mail threads that were entered into evidence of Microsoft's monopolistic behavior. We weren't thinking about that on Saturday morning. My reply only showed the tension and, in a sense, amplified the negatives of his comment. This thread was just one of so many like this. The most mundane conversation memorialized in email just never goes well. Mark my words.

Bill's provocative statement was definitely dramatic, but typical:

> *[A]llowing Office documents to be rendered very well by other peoples [sic] browsers is one of the most destructive things we could do to the company.*
>
> *We have to stop putting any effort into this and make sure that Office documents very well depends [sic] on PROPRIETARY IE.*
>
> *Anything else is suicide for our platform. This is a case where Office has to avoid doing something to destroy [sic] Windows.*

Things were not that bad. But I somehow managed to make them worse, especially in the eyes of the regulators. Because of the variances in browsers and our desire to use HTML, we were working well with the Internet Explorer (IE) team as we looked for ways to maintain an edge over Netscape in rendering documents, and maybe Netscape was not all that keen to work with us. The potential flood of Office documents seemed like an opportunity. On the other hand, rendering better in IE than in other browsers could also be perceived as a corporate initiative.

One person's strategy, however, is another's nefarious plot.

My reply:

> *For all practical purposes, Office 2000 requires Windows and IE. We started the project trying to be great on all browsers, and even greater on Internet Explorer (from our vision and presentation we did for you), but the momentum inside the company essentially prevents that message from making it through development.*

That was what every observer's worst nightmare might have been. The momentum inside the company was solidly behind IE, as naturally expected—no one was thinking about helping Netscape. Office didn't require IE. Rather, IE was the only browser interested in what amounted to standard use of HTML in Office. The trial offered up some of the many times Office and Netscape tried to work together, but it is not difficult to imagine that went nowhere.

BillG would almost always default to a proprietary solution as I had learned in our very first meeting when we discussed C++ and his desire to extend C++ to make it easier to create Windows programs. That point of view was most effective when the playing field was level. The tables had turned, and Microsoft benefitted from the use of open standards. The risk was low as I tried, but not so successfully, to explain.

We finished the release with an incredible implementation. The demonstration included being able to have incredibly rich documents in Word, Excel, PowerPoint (and Outlook with fancy email that could read by any HTML mail client) saved out to a web site running FrontPage. We did have endless debates with HTML purists who absolutely hated how we "abused" HTML. In demonstrations with that crowd, I was routinely asked to show the resulting HTML which was not human readable. This aspect of our implementation was well ahead of its time, as today even the source to the simplest web page is impossible for a human to digest without tools. Everyone abuses HTML.

For much of the project, BillG and I went back and forth in email. History was not entirely kind to either of us in this debate—while we both got elements right, ultimately where HTML and Office ended up was kind of boring, albeit successful. Given that most reading this never directly experienced Office using HTML, I should fast-forward a bit and finish the story.

To this day, Office is as widely used as ever, and it continues to dominate any other document creation tools. Word, Excel, and PowerPoint ended up contributing massive amounts of information to the WWW, as neither .DOC/.XLS/.PPT but rather as PDF, Adobe's ancient *portable document format,* which is essentially a printed version of the document.

Nobody expected PDF to dominate. It was some combination of the deployment cycle of new Office apps that supported HTML, lack of awareness that Office could produce HTML, and especially a lack of ways for regular people to share Office as HTML. The biggest thing PDF brought to the solution was a single file, that always looked the same and looked exactly like it would look when printed. The problem we could never solve (and we tried) with HTML was how to deal with the explosion of files such as pictures, charts, illustrations, and so on typically found in Office documents and intrinsic to the browser.

There is some irony in this endpoint. These portable document formats were my first project when I was Bill's technical assistant, a hand-off from my predecessor. AaronG and I both thought PDF was potentially super useful. The Adobe Acrobat product was new when I became TA. Bill disagreed then for the same reasons HTML with Office was considered not the best idea—he wanted to see Office's native formats. For any number of reasons, PDF never became the liability he thought it could become. My dream of HTML documents created in Office, showing up in browsers, never quite materialized. Neither of us got to an end-state we wanted, but Office remained relevant. That is an advantage to product-market fit.

HTML proved to be enormously beneficial as the underpinnings for an entirely modern and newly designed Office file format, Microsoft Open XML, which became an open standard and eventually used by other products and was regulator friendly. HTML was also instrumental in making copy and paste across Office, and from browsers, vastly more reliable. Word can still publish to HTML, and it is still pretty nifty.

We were both partially right. We were both also quite wrong.

052. ALLEVIATING BLOATWARE, FIRST ATTEMPT

Features. That's all we ever talked about. Adding features. Fixing features. Missing features to be added or fixed. Office achieved the position it achieved, as precarious as it seemed, now with the rise of the WWW and Internet, by adding more features with more regular releases of new versions than competitors. Reviews focused on features, and we won reviews. We had built a team, an engine to add features.

As fast as Clippy could appear after hitting the F1 key, it seemed as though our greatest strength and our most significant asset—features—had become a great weakness. We went from dominating with more well-executed features to being crushed by the *perception* of the weight of our products. The industry latched on to the expression *bloatware* to describe products that seemed to have too much—too many features, too many megabytes, too slow, too difficult to use, or simply too much.

It was one thing to develop a strategy to address a customer problem we had created, albeit inadvertently, when it came to total cost of ownership. We even committed to building fewer productivity features, despite the internal backlash over personal productivity moving to priority six. It was entirely another thing, however, to look at what we built and be pressured into admitting customers didn't want or need it. Still, customers were buying Office by the tens of millions of copies.

Were customers, press, and analysts right? Did we have a product problem, a technology issue, or a marketing challenge, or some combination? Of course, the development team was certain marketing wasn't convincing people how amazing the product was. Marketing was certain the dev team was not delivering business value. Press and analysts were relentless. What could we do?

Our hometown *Seattle Times* reporter, Paul Andrews wrote "already some have nominated Office for Bloatware of the Year." While unclear who "some" were and knowing there was no actual award (thankfully), that was a sharp dig in an otherwise positive Office 97 review.

Worse, however, was the headline in *The Wall Street Journal* that simply stated "Microsoft May Face Backlash Against 'Bloatware'" right on the front of the Marketplace section. The article used every possible way to explain the scale of Office as big from "two years and several hundred million dollars [in R&D]" to "appetite of companies for such programs" it did not let up. The requisite quote at the start of the article from an IT professional was brutal "couldn't care less…there was nothing from a business point of view that was a compelling reason to upgrade." To this day I still get a sick feeling in my stomach from the box in the story stating, "Microsoft's Office 97 contains 4,500 commands for features both useful and arcane." Each of those features meant something and we were so proud of and represented real effort. Plus, during the interview the reporter kept pushing for ways to talk about how big Office 97 was. I resisted and let this slip in a moment of pride, only for it to be used against me. I added this article to the binder I carried around and had it at the ready whenever the topic of bloatware came up.

Bloat was a constant source of strain in conversations with field sales, in the Executive Briefing Center, and with the press. Each time the topic came up I used my go to answer, which was that there is a set of features that everyone in Office uses and those are easily understood such as open, save, print, copy and paste, and a host of basic formatting commands. Everyone nods. Then I would talk about how each application has features that a few people use, perhaps footnotes, financial formulas, or animations in PowerPoint. Most would agree with that.

A common variant of this discussion was "your bloat is my crucial feature" or "yes this is bloat, except that one time a year I need to use it." Most PowerPoint presentations are minimal when it comes to production values, except for that one time a year when the stakes are high and huge effort goes into making a great show. A favorite example is that few claimed to use *Mail Merge* in Word, until they find out they need to send out holiday cards or invitations to a large group. And yes, it even worked with email. Bloat rarely considered the frequency of use and often presumed infrequent use meant no use.

I would often point out the significant business value of Office was that any person could use their set of features in any one tool and seamlessly share files and collaborate with someone way more advanced than they were. For example, I don't know how to draft a contract and use "red lining", but a lawyer could use those tools and send me the contract for review. Intellectually people understood, but almost always would shrug and still say that the software is "bloated."

To each constituency, bloat implied something different. There were mundane answers like how much disk space or RAM Office took up. These Moore's Law measures were easy to complain about but were especially incorrect relative to competitive products, Office was far and away the best. Unfortunately, no one ever experienced more than the one product they used so if Office seemed slow and all conventional wisdom was about needing to upgrade hardware with more memory or a laptop that ran out of disk space, then bloated Office was to blame.

Some believed that literally having too much stuff on the screen is what made the software slower or bloated. There was some truth to this in that the user interface of Office—the menus, toolbars, wizards, and more—was rapidly growing and exceeding the available pixels on the most common screen sizes, especially on new laptops. While desktop computers were getting larger monitors, laptops, still uncommon, were also a generation behind in the amount they could fit on the screen.

The industry analysts believed in something of a combination of all these factors. There was a view that the older legacy features of the product were weighing the programs down with old code, or cruft, and that if the product could just be "factored" [a technical programming word, to break the code up into smaller pieces] then we would have much sleeker and more tuned products that took less memory, less screen real estate. Analysts viewed the disruptive technologies of Java, HTML, and components discussed previously as somewhat magical answers to bloat. Frustratingly, many thought these new technologies not only made better products, but the results would be bloat-free as if by the magic of the programming language. In moments of frustration, I would point out the obvious, that if a product didn't do very much it would of course be less bloated. There's a good lesson in potentially disruptive technologies in how all the positives flow to them and none of the negatives, with little proof along the way.

These stories and definitions of bloat were endless. I received letters, emails, and every Briefing Center visit offered more anecdotes. It was exhausting. Perhaps the worst part about every one of these encounters was that after complaining about bloat, the customer would invariably start talking about new features in the product they so desperately required. And as if to rub salt in the wound, a good portion of the time these requests were already somewhere in the product submerged in the user interface.

We had a good deal of intuition about bloat but not a lot of hard data. While we had our instrumented studies and knew without a doubt that much of the surface area of the product was used in practice—in total, not by any single person—we were working with limited data sets. It would not be until the next release that we would greatly expand our use of the internet to understand real-world usage.

When companies in the 1990s needed to understand customers, they did focus groups. Researchers fanned out around the world on a series of focus groups to better arrive at a shared meaning of bloatware. While we did not learn anything new, we did obtain some more anecdotes and lots of hours of video tape of people complaining about the product.

We had to do something.

One way we reduced the perception of bloat was to not install less frequently used bits of Office on the hard drive, and rather to install them on demand. This was a feature designed specifically for IT professionals who were touting the advantages of disruptive components. In every story about components, especially those built with Java, the idea of loading features as you need them "on demand" was an advantage. The Total Cost of Ownership efforts built an entire infrastructure to load less frequently used features in this manner, conserving disk space, not bothering anyone. IT professionals hated this in practice and immediately loaded everything on the PC to avoid any "on demand." Exasperated, we learned the idea that someone (mostly an executive) might be on an airplane wanting a template or a help file that was not loaded on the PC and seeing the "Please Insert Your Office CDROM" error message was unacceptable. Why take the risk, they would ask, it was just some extra disk space!

We really wanted to do something about the feeling of bloat. How could we make Office feel lighter weight, less overwhelming, and more approachable? Hanging on an interior office relite near DHach's office the whole release was an old cartoon from a tech magazine titled *Office 2000* proclaiming what a future word processor might look like. The drawing was of a Word document surrounded on every side by toolbars, buttons, widgets, and more—almost the entire product screen was consumed by interface widgets with a tiny little spot to type. This really was the bloat we needed to fix. But how? We knew the features were used and we couldn't just delete them.

A common refrain from focus groups and our own intuition was that customers really wanted Office to be tailored to their own usage patterns. It seemed obvious that if Office just knew what customers wanted to do and only presented those options then it would be more valuable, rather than pushing a bunch of features that might confuse or slow down work.

Rooted in our own history was a hint at a possible answer. A decade earlier, as the early Macintosh and first Windows versions of Word and Excel were being built, the teams implemented a feature known as *Short Menus*. This was an early answer to a common PC paradigm of sort of a beginner and expert mode. Even Macintosh had two modes for the desktop, a standard one and a simplified one called *Simple Finder*. Short Menus would show only the most common menu commands. One could easily choose a menu command (the irony was not lost)

Full Menus to show off all the possible commands in the product. Switching back and forth could be done by just choosing the menu.

This was supposed to make the products more approachable. Instead, it just introduced another menu command that made little sense and added a step to using many commands, assuming one even knew to consider this modality in the first place. This idea came and went with the early PC era, along with the idea of expert modes. As the products evolved and added toolbars, the idea of simply hiding menu commands made little sense given the importance of toolbars. But toolbars also contributed to a bloat perception.

DHach who was leading the user interface program management team in OPU, along with a college hire from Cornell, Mike Arcuri (MArcuri), created a new interaction model based on an idea originating on the development team. We were certain they helped reduce bloat. We called this *IntelliMenus* (as in IntelliSense) or smart menus as a working name, and ultimately marketing referred to them generically as *intelligent menus*. The implementation was a smarter take on Full Menus/Short Menus, and also applied to toolbars. It built on our investment in the unified codebase for menus and toolbars that was working so well for us. It was clever, intelligent, and used our code architecture well.

The Office9 feature was subtle. First, it was always on. By default, the product curated short menus; based on the instrumented studies. We were confident of what was used frequently. Second, MArcuri created a series of heuristics to determine if a user might be intentionally browsing for a command or lost trying to find a command, and at that time the short menus or toolbars automatically expanded to full menus. A user could also click on what looked like an arrow key to manually expand to full menus. *Intelligent menus* were an IntelliSense answer to the age-old idea of having special modes that were hard to find and often confusing, and instead they learned from how the product was used and adapted over time. We built a personalized Office.

The feature proved attractive in early previews. In press briefings, we were lauded for taking on bloat and no longer ignoring the rampant problem. While most feedback was positive, as we expected, in beta feedback those who understood the product felt this was a bit of a *who moved my cheese?* scenario. Interestingly, the OAC representing LORG desktops had a unique take—there were some views suggesting that the shorter menus be permanently on so as not to confuse people, along the lines of the old short menus feature. Others were concerned about the training costs and, in particular, what a *how-to* call would be like if the person at the other end of the phone could not be certain of which menu items or toolbar buttons were visible. Hypothetical calls were always based on a VP calling at odd hours on some important trip with little time to spare. Again, as with the trendy on-demand, the reality of the enterprise IT world aimed for stability and completeness over anything dynamic or adaptive.

Smart menus were a solution to take on bloat of known features. They did not solve the challenge of discovering new features. We were keen to add new features as well as make the existing features easier to use. That included how Office could better support creating documents by gathering up information from the web to create a document. Researching a topic of interest changed dramatically with the WWW. Instead of writing memos or slides from paper notes or cards, research was increasingly based on browsing web pages and stealing bits and pieces from around the WWW. The *workflow* for this was incredibly difficult: see something on the browser, select and click copy, and then go back to the document to click paste, over and over again. Taking a few different parts from the same document was a window-switching pain. DHach's idea was to be able to just keep clicking copy, select more content, copy again, over and over without returning to Word to paste every single research find. Then when ready, the user went back to Word or PowerPoint and clicked paste, paste, paste over and over. This was also a great use of HTML because the formatting from the web could be maintained, at least with Internet Explorer.

The *Office clipboard* was a fantastic demo showing integration across Office and any browser and even other applications. The brilliance of the feature was that it created a whole new scenario without adding more menu commands (no bloat) or new features to learn, sort of. The feature activated if the user copied twice in a row quickly and no one did that by accident. We were, however, quite stuck on how to make this feature more discoverable so the user would know all those bits were sitting in a magical clipboard. We were constrained by perceptions of bloat, yet like so many new features, we needed a way to surface it to customers and decided to take the same route as AutoCorrect, which was a minimal user interface.

The Office Clipboard was a notable example of a feature already in one product (Word at least) and then added to all of Office but was routinely requested by customers. The feature was demanded so frequently that there were dozens of separate add-ins, products, and downloadable tools that offered a shared clipboard feature. As was often the case, when a feature was part of a large and complex product bundle it was often easier to find a separate, standalone tool that did what was needed instead of finding the feature in the big suite.

The struggle of discoverability and bloat continued to be enormously challenging for Office. It was fascinating how our skills at creating features exceeded our ability to make those features discoverable or create a product overall that remained easy to use for the broadest set of customers. This was an existential problem for our business as the WSJ pointed out— "One worry is a market nearing saturation"—if people have the product and feel it does everything they need, then our business is shrinking.

This kept us up at night, but not for business reasons as much as the reality that we just knew people were constantly asking for Office to do more and to make it easier and faster to get work done. I used to say "Office 97 is hardly the ultimate achievement in creating, analyzing, and presenting information. We know we can do better." We were primarily competing with our previous version—also bloated with all anyone might ever need—and that proved to be a most difficult situation. This was especially difficult in the enterprise market where the benefit of any new feature was weighed against the cost and challenges of deployment and re-training. Given the investment customers made in that prior version, we were limited in how much we could market against it. It was not lost on me that the competitors we did have (StarOffice, SmartSuite, Perfect Office, and Arae-A Hangul and Kingsoft WPS outside the US) were consistently adding features we already had and touting them as new. Each was making the mistake of competing head-on with us. It would be years before a product would take web-based productivity tools in a different direction.

Otherwise, there were no lean or *unbloated* alternative products people could point to that were in use. There's much more going on to bloat that we would need to discover. What was the relationship between Office to Windows, and the rest of the PC? How were PC problems such as grinding hard drives, degraded performance over time, or just flakiness, bugs, and instability related to bloat? How much of the problem of bloat was being caused by enterprise IT software that people disliked (who *likes* their work software?) and worse the security and management tools that took ever-increasing control of the PC. The problem of bloat is bigger than just Office. It was the product's ubiquity and, frankly, high customer satisfaction (no matter how we measured it) that made it a symbol of a much broader challenge for Microsoft.

In this work, I want to share the lessons with plenty of context and not a lot of certainty about how lessons might apply in a different context. The notion that products get easier to use and more approachable simply by hiding or deleting features is something I've seen disproven repeatedly. Rarely can simplicity come from simply hiding capabilities that people use, and in fact as we saw in this story, often in the process of obscuring features the product becomes more difficult to use. Lesson learned.

I wish I could say that slowed our feature machinery, but it did not. We were doing more than ever, faster than ever, but we were at least more aware of the challenges we were faced and every day becoming more empathetic. The dialog around adding features changed from how fast to how well, from must have to will it work. We were maturing as a team. This became more important as the demands for features to support broader, and much less clear, strategic initiatives increased as we built Office9.

053. STRATEGY TAX: OUTLOOK STORAGE, FIRST ATTEMPT

During a visit to Japan, I ran across a new Sony laptop, the VAIO C1 PictureBook. What a wonderful machine. Crammed into a half a sheet of A4 paper in length and width was a laptop processor, 64MB of RAM, a 1024x480 screen, and a PCMCIA slot for wired or wireless networking. It also had a port replicator to support the new USB connector, CDROM, and floppy drives. It ran Japanese Windows 98. One of most distinguishing features aside from size and weight was that it was one of the first portables to have a built-in webcam. It was my new favorite computer.

I spotted this machine at Yodobashi Camera at Shinjuku Station, which was always my first stop after landing at Tokyo's Narita Airport. In order to be prepared to meet with the Japan team, known by the corporate moniker MSKK, I needed to see first-hand what was on display at the world's largest electronics store. Each year more people visit Yodobashi than Disney World. Among the hundreds of computers, cameras, home appliances, and everything imaginable, Sony reigned supreme. Something stood out this year. Sony products, including PCs, were starting to support a new kind of removable storage card, like the CompactFlash cards in use by the first digital cameras, but smaller and proprietary to Sony. I learned it was designed to compete with a new standard memory proposed by all the other Japanese electronics companies. It was called the Memory Stick. Sony had been trying to create proprietary formats and consumables ever since it lost the Betamax battle, and this seemed the latest effort.

What was more interesting was how it caught BillG's eye on his own trip to Sony meeting with Idei-san and Morita-san among others. He too learned about Memory Stick (and the associated digital rights protection technology called MagicGate that he really loved) but more interesting than the storage technology was how Sony seemed to rally around adding new memory stick support to every product, whether it needed it or not. Camcorders, cameras, mobile phones, music players, televisions, and more were all outfitted with Memory Stick slots.

At some big meeting I was using my PictureBook during a conversation about Microsoft's own storage technology, then known as *Web Store* (as in web storage, as it was going to be a place to store files in Exchange mail server that would make it act like a web server), and the desire for it to be used across all products. The topic wasn't new, and we'd been going in circles for quite some time already because it was clearly too early and the technology was, as far as I was concerned, far in the future at best. My skepticism frustrated BillG and those making the technology, primarily in the Exchange team where they were building the next release called Platinum. If that's all too many codewords, don't worry you weren't the only one confused.

This might be one of the few stories that even those that lived through it cannot agree on the precise terminology used and code names as the technology evolved.

Web Store ran on Exchange. Local Store was a similar technology that ran on laptop and desktop PCs providing symmetry between the server and PC. It was at first a generic term and then morphed into a project called *LIS*, local information store. These all represented the same concepts at different points in the evolution from 1998-2001, sometimes on the PC and sometimes on the server.

I made a semi-serious/semi-sarcastic statement about how we should all have to use Web Store the way that Sony was putting Memory Stick in every product.

Bill jumped on that comment in a way I did not quite expect, proclaiming something along the lines of "Yes, that's called strategy. Why can't we have that?" He wasn't really asking. Oops.

The specifics of this technology weren't as interesting as the fact that the company was really in a new phase. We began to have huge technology projects that were just getting started and before they were fully defined it was important for all the biggest groups, like Windows and Office, to sign up to use these technologies and make big bets on them no matter how irrational that might seem. There were faint memories of how Excel bet on Windows, but long gone were the realities of what it took to get that done and importantly that neither Windows Excel nor Windows itself quite existed when those bets were made. Now the bets were about replacing huge swaths of existing products—billion-dollar products—with unproven technologies with far-reaching, often abstract computer science goals. A key part about this new phase was a technology like LIS was talked about with customers and analysts, and even appeared in the press, long before there was even a plan or code, just boxes on "architecture" slides. LIS was solving problems long before it existed, so it seemed.

In the case of LIS, the vision was for all of Microsoft's products, especially Windows and Office, to store data in a new kind of database that provided capabilities going well-beyond what the existing operating system for storing files could support. Eventually this storage system would replace files itself. In the meantime, the first goal was to store all the kinds of data routinely stored in Outlook, such as email, contacts, tasks, and calendars. This storage system, the APIs and protocol, would be built so it could run on a single laptop PC but also scale up to run on the huge Exchange server as well. LIS with Outlook was simply the first, and most important, step. Using LIS would imply a wholesale replumbing of Outlook.

Exchange was incredibly early in its evolution but was doing extraordinarily well. It was exactly the product every enterprise wanted and the synergy with Windows Server (as detailed in Chapter III) was proving an enormous business and strategic win. Exchange was building their next version, code-named Platinum, with a major focus on scale and performance as customers were deploying the product to huge corporations with hundreds of thousands of mailboxes around the world. Web Store supported a new range of sophisticated data features, on the server, and was making real progress in development. In theory, the desktop/laptop LIS and the server Web Store would support the same features. This is how the main competitor Lotus Notes worked, called client/server symmetry. This theory was not supported by the way Microsoft's efforts were being organized and built, but it would take a long time to surface.

Outlook was critical to Exchange success, and it too was very early in its evolution. While Exchange was experiencing growing pains in scale, Outlook was simply experiencing pain. It was a complex product that received lukewarm reviews at best, but it was the way to use Exchange, so customers put up with it. Outlook was called Byzantine in reviews, complex by our own Product Support Services team, and was taxing on the limited and expensive memory in typical PCs. Email was not just about Exchange, however, and Outlook also had failed to live up to the needs of the broader Office customer base that used AOL, internet mail, and more.

LIS was to be built by a partnership between the Exchange team and the SQL database team to replace the storage technology created for the initial release of Exchange. The fact that two big teams were building one piece of code for use by a third big team is noteworthy. One can begin to get a sense of how taxing this situation was on the individuals simply trying to ship their respective products by a predictable date with acceptable quality and performance. For all the institutional memories of Microsoft and IBM trying to coordinate building software, we seemed to be immune to thinking such problems would arise internally at Microsoft.

Those old enough to remember using Outlook might be familiar with an infamous file type called PST, which was the file that stored all the Outlook data. It was infamous because it was the precious place with all your email and yet also a file so big it was difficult to backup or copy. While Exchange was working at one end to scale mail storage to massive data centers for terabytes of mail, they were also busy trying to squeeze some subset of that technology onto the lowest power mobile computers of the day, such as the new Sony VAIO. Outlook was supposed to simply replace what already worked with an implementation from LIS—replace the code that handled the most important and difficult to manage file on your PC with an entirely new technology. Sure, in a computer science sense with all the right layers and architecture, "it should just work." Whenever someone says that you know it isn't really the case.

This kind of architectural replacement is exactly the kind of thing BillG loved to hear. With the right API or interface, the new code just plugs in, and everything gets much better. Yeah right.

Was this what corporate strategy is like? This was still the only place I'd ever worked, so I had no idea. If Sony was an example, it seemed kind of dumb. It felt like a tax on every group, not something useful. When you think of something you're forced to do and have no say in, you think tax, and so this definitely felt like a tax.

For example, digital cameras were using standard CF cards, and this meant Sony cameras would use a different card, and cards were expensive. If I was at Sony and was trying to beat Canon or Fuji, this sure seemed more of a problem than an advantage. Regardless of the quality of the idea or ability for a team to execute, they had much bigger problems like megapixels. Implementing a Memory Stick card added cost and complexity to a product but did not help it win in the market or solve existing customer problems, at least from the perspective of the team making a product. It was (and would prove to be) a *strategy tax.*

The biggest challenge of the release proved to be right where we left off with Office 97—getting Outlook to the finish line. That had nothing to do with replacing PST files and the vague scenarios that might come from the new technology.

The enormous effort to release Outlook 97 was followed by the organizational split and Outlook turning to a short release (independent of the Office product it shipped with) to gain traction with features required by the huge and growing number of internet email customers. Ironically, this was completely off-strategy relative to addressing the needs of Exchange customers, the very focus of our sales efforts and business strategy. In other words, the strategy Outlook was executing was disconnected from the overall corporate strategy. The short release, called Outlook 98, shipped eight months after Office 97 (and Outlook 97), in mid-1998. The internet support was beefed up, but that came at the expense of enterprise customers who got little from Outlook 98 even with a long list of issues and complaints. The immediate strategy for Outlook was working against the strategy from Office 97 of making Outlook an integrated part of Office. Go figure. This was very difficult.

The rest of Office9 completed our scheduled coding milestones just as Outlook was joining the project—right as we were winding down the project, Outlook was ready to start. The rest of the calendar for the project was supposed to last about five months and include two betas releases. All the Office teams, as a practical matter, were behind schedule, though Outlook proved an easy scapegoat. Unfair, but the last to finish received the bulk of the blame even when everyone was late. Symbolically, I struggled to maintain the hardcore shipping culture of DAD while letting Outlook slide through, breaking the spirit of the process by doing new work after the coding milestones. For me personally, this made me look like I wasn't serious about shipping and importantly the Office product unit, OPU, was not serious. We didn't have a choice. Besides, everyone was late. The risk was just making everyone even more late by acting so careless about Outlook.

Office9 declared *code complete* in March 1998, only about four weeks later than planned. Code complete meant coding milestones were complete, features were finished, and all that remained were performance and quality issues. But we were kidding ourselves. The project wasn't code complete. Declaring code complete when it wasn't was a violation of our own process. We spent a great deal of time figuring out how to adjust and what needed to be cut, focused, and rethought. We were not out of control. We knew what needed to be done. We needed more time, but a knowable amount of time. Any notion of slipping, even though the product would be what we had said it would be, had implications within the team, primarily schedule chicken. This is a lot of words to say that our execution was sloppy.

There were also deep concerns from marketing and ultimately the field sales organization. The business was in transition. In huge numbers, customers were moving to sign 3-year agreements with Microsoft where instead of buying just one version of Office (the current one) they would own all the versions released during the 3-year term. We were still working out the implications of this. For now, this seemed to imply that many newly signed deals were waiting for Office9. This meant a late Office9 was delaying deployment of a new 32-bit Office as those customers were still figuring out Office 97 after slow-rolling Office 95. What a mess.

With the development team declaring code complete, all of marketing became fully engaged transitioning from supporting the field on Office 97 to preparing to launch the new release. Immediately the press, and our own salespeople, dubbed it *Office2K*, or O2K. Internationally some would call it "Office 2 oh oh oh" or "Office two zero zero zero". That irked marketing. We considered Office 1999, but Y2K, year 2000 preparation to make sure computer systems were able to properly handle dates in the year 2000 without causing mayhem was everywhere. An ill-prepared sounding name wouldn't work. Though all I could think of was *Space 1999*. So, Office 2000 it was.

Just as we named Office 2000, Outlook made a heroic transition from finishing Outlook 98 to figuring out how to quickly build Outlook9 (aka Outlook 2000) and align with all the initiatives, especially deployment and cost of ownership. For example, we rebuilt the installation and setup program for Office9 and had to find time to integrate Outlook, which ironically had rebuilt setup for Outlook 98 to use another new and different setup technology specifically for internet products. For Microsoft trivia buffs, this was called Active Setup, and the new Office technology was called the Microsoft Installer (MSI), code name Darwin, which is still in use today.

The team hardly caught its collective breath. The whipsaw with which we treated Outlook's strategic direction was in full force. Straight from focusing on consumers and internet protocols, Outlook swung the opposite direction to be entirely focused on enterprise features, which meant being a great mail and calendaring client for the next Exchange Platinum release. Kurt DelBene (KurtD), leading Outlook, partnered with Gord Mangione (GordM) on Exchange. Kurt switched the team from a crisis of internet protocols to a new crisis of Exchange protocols and storage: LIS, WebStore, and a protocol known as DAV, Distributed Authoring and Versioning.

The huge technical problem for Outlook and Exchange to address was called *always offline*, which is an odd sounding phrase for email, which was all about being online. This meant changing the original model for using Exchange to a more internet-savvy architecture. Originally, Exchange was designed to work exceptionally well when connected to robust, high-speed networking. Unfortunately, that was almost never the case. When using a dial-up modem or a flaky emerging-market connection over ISDN or X.25, Outlook and Exchange routinely hung or often crashed. The internet, especially the WWW, was designed for a less reliable network and much of the success of those designs was this architectural decision and associated implementations.

Perhaps the most expensive possible way to demonstrate this design failing of Outlook and Exchange was when KurtD was offered a flight (actually summoned by the then CEO of Boeing, Phil Condit) on a Boeing Business Jet—the kind of plane used by CEOs and billionaires. The privately owned jet was a custom-outfitted Boeing 737 that cost something north of $30 million at the time and designed to seat ten or so people in posh comfort rather than the normal 150. One of the new features offered then was internet access, which over satellite was the perfect torture test for how bad Outlook plus Exchange could be. Kurt took a trip to Montana and back. A $100,000 trip for an owner, just so Kurt could experience Outlook *not* working over a satellite link. Boeing was one of the earliest and biggest Exchange customers.

The design and implementation proposed to address this involved reworking the way networking and mail storage worked in Outlook, which also loosely coincided with BillG's strategic goal of building a fancy proprietary storage technology across all the products. The networking part was relatively understood. Rebuilding storage was made enormously complex by coupling the fix to a new storage architecture to the Web Store/Local Store or LIS. From a competitive perspective, such storage functionality was the major advantage Lotus/IBM Notes held over Exchange. It was, therefore, a critical advance. In other words, the solution to this problem and to beating the main competitor were both wrapped up in what seemed to be a strategy tax.

The Exchange Platinum Release delivering this, also behind, was originally scheduled for some time in 1998/1999 around the same time as Office9. LIS work had been underway for quite a while. When people study large organizations and want to understand why and how it is so difficult to do projects that span those organizations, a feature like LIS is a case study in great intentions, positive working relationships, but differing methodologies and approaches that make these efforts difficult to nearly impossible.

The Exchange team built out their processes for building and releasing software such that working extremely closely with a small number of customers early was the primary test of readiness. That work was relatively unpredictable because there was no way to ship without those customers signing off, so the process ceded control to a set of independent customers who held out for all the promised features for however long it took. This was the classic

Systems, particularly *Server*, methodology that made any changes, specifically cuts, to the product plan costly in relationships with customers, prioritizing features over the date.

Outlook, as part of Office, was part of a methodology that made a product plan upfront and reevaluated the details at milestones, scaling back as needed in order to deliver on dates, even if these dates were never perfect. This date-focused methodology was rooted in the need to regularly update the product for retail customers or for business customers with multiyear agreements.

Neither of these were wrong or right in absolute, but relative to the major customers and business models each was appropriate. Outlook was caught in the middle.

This was especially difficult for BobMu, the new senior VP of our team, renamed to *Applications and Tools Group*, ATG. While most of the Server products worked in the Platform division, Exchange was organized in ATG specifically to bring synergy between Office and Exchange for email, and other products as well. Literally the organization was put in place to deliver on this strategy tax and that put me in the middle of it.

In reality (meaning in the code) solving this problem had little to do with using LIS. Many developers on the team thought using LIS to address this critical challenge was off base and simply wrong. The strategy, however, was about using LIS everywhere and using LIS in Outlook would somehow contribute to a much easier solution for flakey Outlook. This was a prime example of a strategy tax—being asked to take on a significant technical dependency while facing enormous product challenges knowing that this dependency doesn't help solve those problems while those making the strategic call actually believed they were helping. One person who was not helping was me and I felt, well, helpless to support the team's view that this wasn't going to work or help Outlook. With the new organization the management chain was unified with the Systems view that the right way to solve this was for Office to just make the bet on the platform technology. It was my first time as a manager having to keep up the appearance of making this work while the team struggled. It was disempowering to put it politely.

Not only was there a shared Systems view of how the products should evolve, the recent executive organizational moves, in the midst of product plans already in place, only served to up the ante on this level of collaboration between Exchange and Outlook. The fact that the field sales group was briefed on the potential for LIS was another part of the overall squeeze on Outlook, Office, and me. Every time I expressed doubt about LIS, I was told to head over to the Executive Briefing Center and "learn from customers."

No amount of business strategy or management saying we needed to work better together could change the reality that LIS was simply not far enough along to support Outlook, especially with such a short schedule. The chosen design was too far away from being even functional, let alone performant. It was super tough, but it was the kind of effort where the further away from management the questions were asked, the more definitive the answer became "no way."

Collectively, we needed to cut LIS integration with Outlook, and in doing so lose a significant competitive feature versus Notes, a strategic initiative for the company in data storage, a commitment to engaged LORGs, and a cross-group collaborative effort that many worked hard on. Any time a choice like this is made, the people close to the work feel a sense of relief, but those (almost always organizationally above) continue to blame others for the miss or assert it will eventually work. We collectively cut LIS. We were collectively relieved. To be completely fair, the actual engineers on Outlook invested little code in making this work and mostly went to meetings for a couple of months before this idea was abandoned. The real waste was minimal. We would not be so lucky the next time this strategy would be required. We took up the storage discussion again for the next release of Office, and the one after that. Stay tuned.

The decision put the entire Office9 product back on track. Outlook9 moved forward with both feet firmly planted in Office9. Outlook wasn't in the first beta release, Beta 1, a fairly limited test anyway. A few press leaks and *first looks* commented on "missing" Outlook. The larger issue was unwinding the communication with the Microsoft enterprise sales machinery, which briefed and effectively pre-sold LIS for some time. We received a good deal of heat for this type of change. The cost of winding up and then winding down the sales force on a feature that was high risk became a worthy lesson. It was especially problematic for the Boeing account team.

LIS was the first strategy tax for me and the team that also crossed into the field sales force, the press, and enterprise customers. It would not be the last. The company was changing, and the appetite for such unifying themes and grand bets across products was growing, even as our ability to deliver them was not. In fact, the strategies were becoming more complex and less likely to get delivered. It would have been good to have a single success at scale. To date, the most significant win (and it was huge) was the delivery of VBA throughout Office 97, which became a model of cross-division collaboration. We in Office would use this as the template for how things should work, while we continued the quest to make other strategies demanded of us live up to that example.

In Office we remained conflicted between making features that were easy to explain to individuals creating documents and investments that played well at the enterprise strategy level, even at the expense of individual end-users. In that sense, LIS felt a bit "too strategic" for me as I would often joke. Saying something was too strategic was my way of saying that it felt a combination of too abstract and too focused on the CIO slide deck, and also probably not achievable. The company was not confused. We were all in on enterprise, all in on strategy. We'd made that bet. Could we deliver?

054. STEVE AND STEVEN GET NEW JOBS

The full-page story in InfoWorld July 27, 1998, began ominously "Most new presidents can count on a 100-day honeymoon...but for newly appointed Microsoft president Steve Ballmer, that blissful period is probably going to be something less than 100 hours." This wasn't the typical coverage.

In fact, most of the coverage reflected the broadly shared internal view that Microsoft was growing up and needed an executive structure to match. It was growing up in precisely the way Steve had orchestrated and been leading—Microsoft was becoming an enterprise company. The coverage was by and large friendly and reminiscent of the close connection Bill and Steve had and the natural evolution of the role he had been playing in the company.

Previously, Microsoft had a legendary President/COO Jon Shirley (JonS) who brought 25-years of experience from Radio Shack and was responsible for building out Microsoft's business infrastructure through 1990 and was still an active board member. Microsoft brought on several other senior leaders, but like many growing companies had a difficult time helping them to fit in and thrive. Bob Herbold (BHerbold) joined from P&G in 1994 and remained as COO reporting to Steve through 2001. Steve, with his connection to Bill and his strong role in shaping the new Microsoft, was a more certain appointment.

SteveB was named president of Microsoft in July 1998. Microsoft's fiscal year ended June 30, and frequently big changes happened either right before or just after the end of the year. For many, me included, this was viewed as a natural progression and one that most felt was entirely right for the company. Steve was managing worldwide sales and support and was promoted to lead the product groups and all the operational groups.

BillG emphasized that he still planned to devote time to product issues, and with so much to do he saw himself spending the next 10 years as CEO, perhaps to put people at ease, but to be clear, this was a huge change for Microsoft. For the first time, we had a non-product/technologist managing all product groups. In a 1:1 with Bill he emphasized to me this "10 years as CEO" talking point, which was in most of the press, countering an oft-repeated assertion that Bill might be making room to spend more time on the looming regulatory challenges Microsoft faced. Bill assured me that he was going to continue to spend time, now more time, immersed in product development. After the recent debates over HTML, it wasn't as clear to me that was a positive. I kept that thought to myself.

Steve orchestrated perhaps the largest *pivot* (a phrase that became deeply rooted in Microsoft lingo due to Excel's successful feature) to enterprise an sales operation ever seen, expanding and building out a global sales and support organization that easily matched in quality if not scale any of Microsoft's competitors, from Oracle to Sun to IBM. From databases to networking to directories to email to productivity, SteveB's sales machinery across LORGs, MORGs, SORGs (large, medium, and small organizations), governments and education, and industry verticals from finance to health care all were covered. Operationally, the enterprise sales force was a machine. It was present. It was loud. It was visible. And mostly it was all new, as if synthesized from thin air. *The field*, the collection of account managers (sales and technical), country general managers, and business segment leaders, is often hailed as Microsoft's biggest asset, and what has certainly fended off many competitive challenges, even if product people like me like to think the product did the heavy lifting. It is the field operation that carries Microsoft today.

SteveB never approached a job with tepidness, often employing a saying from his father, "If you're going to do a job, then do a job." He began his tenure as president by a widely known (and followed via backchannels) series of *100 1:1s* with leaders across the company. Mine was scheduled for the end of August. It was not like a list was published or anything, but among many there was a desire to know, "Did you do your meeting?" I knew SteveB from working with Bill. I figured our meeting was intended for Steve to get to know me and my role and for me to understand the role of Microsoft president.

Shortly before Steve's promotion, I was named general manager of Office—meaning I would be managing all of product development for Office. Word, Excel, PowerPoint, Access, Outlook, and the *Shared Office Team* as we were now calling OPU, all together were approximately 800 full time engineering. While it was a natural progression, though not one I sought out, and a huge promotion, we were mid-cycle, and I was hesitant to change anything or distract from the work being done. Plus, I was only 32 and was deeply worried about losing connection with product and technology. Still, this management consolidation, especially bringing Outlook with the rest of Office under one manager, was clearly going to happen—with me or without me. At the time, taking on the job was at least as much about the opportunity for me as the worry about who they would pick instead.

I walked over to Steve's office which I hadn't been to since I was doing demos of the internet a few years earlier and immediately noticed it was different. The apparatus around him was much larger than the one around BillG, PaulMa, or MikeMap. He had a chief of staff, multiple executive admins, communications people, finance, and more. The worldwide sales team was much larger than the product group, spanned the globe and time zones, and involved thousands of customers and partners always seeming to need or want SteveB's attention, of which he loved nothing more than to offer. So, this all made sense.

When I walked into SteveB's office I received my familiar greeting, a bellowing "Sin-AHFF-skeee." I remember the meeting vividly for no particular reason other than the ceremony around it was so grand and it really was a big transition for Steve and the company.

Without much small talk or easing into the conversation, SteveB started by offering me feedback about how I needed to be easier to work with. That my reputation was such that I ran Office [note, I was not running Office except for the past few months] in a way that made it difficult for people *to get things from Office*. To be sure it was a tight ship, but Office was hard to work with, or maybe I was hard to work with, or maybe I was hard to work with, so Office was hard to work with, or perhaps the other way around.

It was a lot to take in, considering I thought I was there for a quick reiteration one normally sees at announcements like this. I expected to hear nothing would change, everything needs to keep going, and so on.

What I did not know was Steve's context for saying this. What was he told he needed to do in terms of hitting the ground running? What were the immediate big problems? I knew for certain that BillG would always be pushing on more architecture, deeper alignment between Office and Windows, and starting work on the next release. I also knew that BillG would not have pushed him on the slipping or fantasy ship schedules that plagued the company. Perhaps there were already doubts about me in the general manager role?

I did fail to appreciate that Steve did not need guidance. He ran the field. He spent every day with enterprise customers. He was feeling their pain. In hindsight, and knowing Steve even better over time, I should have realized what he wanted to do was fix that pain as soon as he could. In a sense, he had been given the keys and wanted to drive. How often it is that a new manager or someone new to role takes such an approach?

I wasn't exactly making a first impression, but rather I was being told what the first impression of me was. It was bad timing. It felt baseless or at least lacked actionable evidence. That's almost always the way everyone sees unanticipated negative feedback—make it specific, make it actionable.

While I didn't agree, I understood where he was coming from. Mostly what was on my mind was how screwed up everything was that the field was being told was going to make the next killer fiscal year: Exchange Platinum, Windows NT 5.0, Office9, plus our collective effort to compete with Lotus Notes, the field's number one priority. Beyond that were a host of new enterprise products for systems management, knowledge management, database and storage, development tools, and more that were far from shipping let alone deployed by customers.

Everything we in the product group were working on had one common thread—it was late, off schedule, or worse not even on a path to ship and no one was fessing up. Maybe I was the only one who cared about ship dates, though highly doubtful, but for sure I was going to be the one to say we're living a fantasy if we think FY99 was a big product year. That's right, everything the field was literally gearing up to plan to sell from July 1998-June 1999 was not going to be available. I was on firm footing because by now I was fully aware that the original planned ship date for Office9 was already upon us and we were going to finish March 1999. In other words, just a sliver of FY99 would remain and hardly enough time for enterprise deals to complete based on Office. And Office was the very best case among products it seemed. Windows 2000 shipped February 2000, Exchange Platinum/November 2000, SQL 2000/August 2000 and so on.

Everything was out of control precisely when the field was expecting a tight ship. The processes Steve had pioneered—the budgets from the field, the forecasts from headquarters, the business plans for each product that had been run up, down, and across the company, all culminating the country managers meeting followed by the global sales meeting—all presumed a banner year of products, though many of the plans and communications from HQ were the kind that looked like tempering expectations without exactly saying so. The way this was done in the new enterprise model was to talk about the next milestone such as a beta test release or big customer event, instead of RTM of code.

Additionally, Steve was dealing with product quality problems directly from customers such as performance, reliability, early days of security. The flagship Windows 98 product was buggy. The flagship next operating system was very late, impacting server and client. Even with new products, new versions required time to deploy. Realistically, he was about to hear how nothing was going to get substantially better until at least FY00. All this, on his first weeks on the job.

And he was going to hear that from me, the new GM of Office, 32 years old.

In real time, I figured that the best course of action was to be more abstract than pick on my fellow product groups and to filibuster on the complexity of software projects. Steve was not new to big software projects, though the scale we were operating at was new for everyone. He personally oversaw Windows in the early days and then later LanMan. All projects back then were also late. I hardly needed to remind him, but it was on my mind. Recent Windows projects including the current NT5 were all late as well. NT5 was in development and ultimately shipped as Windows 2000 but took four years to finish, August 1996 through February 2000, an important and big release, but late.

My view, expressed to Steve, was two things. Microsoft products shipped late and that had to be fixed, especially in the world of LORGs. I was trying to show empathy for where he was focused. Office was the best of major products, but with Office9 we were already plus five months and that likely meant we were as much as a year away from shipping, which meant Office 97 to Office9 was 30 months from shipping, or the outside limit of the delta between releases acceptable to customers. Outside of Office, Windows was late with every release after Windows 95 which was late enough that most long forgot the original target date. Often projects were so late there was not even agreement on the planned ship date or typically all that mattered was the next milestone such as completing a public build, beta test, or release to be distributed at a conference.

With late products came quality issues. With quality issues came the need for larger service packs and updates. With those updates came additional slips to new products under development, and so on. With those came even more disgruntled customers. The company was in a quality and execution tailspin, I believed.

Second, I really wanted to express my view of how fragile our Microsoft product processes were compared to other industries. We lacked a process to plan and commit that was uniform enough to enable collaboration across products. The plans that were in place were hardly more than sketches. When collaborations between groups did happen (I used Office 97's work on Visual Basic as an example), they were efforts where personality overcame the organizational and planning hurdles.

Beyond that, the enterprise sales efforts took it as a given that selling the EA platform meant selling the *next* release, making the release of the product, as marketed, even more important. This introduced a fragility into the product development process. If something was discovered or learned, or a new customer understanding, then it was added to the schedule, but without changing any of the milestones or goals. If a product is late, it should be obvious adding more only made it later—every single developer new-hire received a copy of Frederick Brook's *Mythical Man-Month*, the established canon on software development processes. Yet the most critical teams were solving key customer satisfaction problems by just adding more code, later in the project, and dealing with that issue even further down the road. The new inability to cut features to make room for other features of a higher priority was a guarantee for even more fragile schedules.

It was this type of work process that made everything going on seem to hang by a thin thread, on the verge of spiraling out of control, if it was even under control in the first place. I tried to paint a picture for SteveB of "You want on that wall. You need me on that wall." I would not be exaggerating to say my tone was not that far off from the courtroom speech immortalized in the film *A Few Good* Men that every team probably saw for movie night.

I left the office feeling that what I said did not resonate. In fact, I felt like the idea of hanging on by a thin thread, which I viewed as a negative, was seen by SteveB in a more positive light. Almost like living on the edge was cool. Years later, the Windows Vista project frequently reminded me of this conversation, and frankly any number of projects between that summer of 1998 and the next decade.

Still, the tone that was set was not great. My monologue had not helped. I was already in a penalty box, it seemed. The rest of the meeting was uncomfortable for me. I did not do well.

As the conversation continued and Steve started talking more about the organization and how he saw things, it was abundantly clear (even) to me that he was already planning a reorg. It would have been naïve to think there would be no reorg with such a big change at the top, especially since the field organization all but formalized a yearly shuffle to align for the fiscal year. I thought to myself, when your new exec offers observations on the organization, the next step is an org change. Words to live by in the corporate world.

There would be a reorg halfway through the fiscal year, but it would be talked about for months leading up to it.

I walked back to building 17 to focus on shipping Office9.

055. OFFICE 2000 IS GOOD TO GO!

Not only were we five months late by the end of 1998, but we also faced the lag time that would happen on the other side of our pending a holiday break. It became clear our end-of February completion date for Office9 was going to be a challenge.

At least we were on the glide path to completing the product before we left for the holidays. As far as the enterprise sales team was concerned, we were going to finish in the first quarter, which was important for customers buying or renewing volume license contracts. Office 2000 was shaping up to be a significant release for the end of the millennium. And yes, Office 2000 was Y2K ready.

As I prepared to head to Florida for holiday vacation to see family, JonDe let me know that I was being promoted to corporate vice president. This was truly a big deal personally, and as I look back, I realize it was a big deal for the company. Along with BrianV leading Exchange a press release would go out announcing our promotions in about a week—the ranks of executives were small enough then that not only did we do press releases for promotions, but we became named officers in the company and the two latest additions from the product development teams. If you've ever been part of a rocket ship, what you experience is growth in executive promotions when you start to wonder if this is a worthy promotion or will people outside your immediate group roll their eyes. NatalieY, the spiritual and cultural leader of the company in human resources, sent me an incredible note telling me how "real" the promotion was which meant everything. These insecurities come with what does seem like one of the most significant milestones in a career and for me, I will always think of this as the most significant, owing much to JonDe and all of the Apps people before him.

While everything was the same organizationally, what was simply a title change in the Exchange address book was the start of being treated differently, particularly by those I did not yet know, especially in the field sales org, and, perhaps even more entertaining, by the various Microsoft systems and services.

In short order, Colleen Johnson (CollJ) was being briefed on the exec travel desk (EXTRAVEL), executive tech support (EXECSUPP, yes, there was special on-call PC and tech support for executives), executive shuttle (sort of an Uber for VPs to go between buildings that I almost always walked anyway), and even the special team that helps make PowerPoint slides for execs, and so on. I knew these existed, but I thought they were for Bill, Steve, the CFO, and Board, not all the VPs. Oh, and my card key worked in all sorts of places it used to not work, like weekend access to the Executive Briefing Center! I did have mixed feelings about special treatment for run of the mill execs in product groups. The teams were all incredibly nice, but this felt like excess to me.

CollJ was a key addition to our team who had an outsized impact on our operational excellence and culture. Hired as an administrative assistant, she quickly and quietly assumed the role of indirectly managing the dozens of administrative/group assistants across the team (on average one for every 100 people) which was the front line of our culture of careful management of resources. She also took on the role of formalizing all our headcount tracking which was a key enabler for how I would manage the team. A dumb example was instituting a code in our SAP-based system for what individuals worked on (Word, Excel, Office and so on) and what functional group they were in such as dev, test, and program management. Amazingly our systems did not track that and yet it is *all that mattered* in managing a significant team. For decades neither she nor I managed to coach other teams into managing this way, even after the yearly visits from teams being told to learn from a best practice how we managed things. There's a lesson in there—*you can't manage a big team at scale if you don't know what people are working on and how humans, not dollars, are allocated!*

Colleen also led our efforts at developing a new more scalable Office culture. Too much of Microsoft was still acting like it was college when it came to team outings or now operating like a fancy Wall Street bank when it came to using company resources for events. From figuring out how to get a huge discount on team movies by renting all the theaters for morning shows and offering family friendly and alternatives to the current sci-fi release, to helping teams to know about $250/day offsite locations including a stop at Fred Meyer for snacks instead of the $2,500 locations before the required hotel catering, Colleen instilled a broad sense of fiscal and cultural responsibility across the team of admins. She helped to create whole classes of events such as our product vision meetings, the "tradeshow", and especially our launch events. As the team grew, the tradeshow became a hallmark event where every member of the team had a chance to experience all the other teams building Office as though we were at a tradeshow. Years later, Microsoft Research would adopt this format for what became the Microsoft TechFest event.

As a VP I quickly learned people I did not know would no longer email me directly and even people I did know would soon also employ the level of indirection afforded by CollJ. The Microsoft culture had developed an arm's length VP culture, where contacting a VP meant going to the Exchange address book and looking up the direct reports of a VP to find their Executive Assistant to contact about "getting time with" or "what is the best way to email them." Exchange had a unique feature where you could offer an assistant direct access to an email account as a delegate. Suddenly VPs were having admins screen email and even respond on their behalf. How quickly we became "big." Along with helping people to email me directly, Colleen had to remind people of one other quirk of mine I insisted on, which was I managed my own calendar. I was hardcore about this because of what I'd gone through in terms of the ripple effect of scheduling. A meeting was scheduled with an exec, the executive assistant moves the meeting for something important, then everything dependent on that moves as well. Soon the one person who needs to get out of the way, the VP, is the barrier to making progress as a *routine* course of business.

I think I spent the rest of my years trying to hold on to a feeling of small, and avoiding the distant feeling new hires (and we had hundreds every year) would have towards execs. I think I had varying degrees of success at doing so and certainly made my mistakes at trying, but with Colleen's help I worked hard at that for my run, even as we scaled.

The press release went out while I was on the way to Miami. I was expecting an uneventful time in condo haven, North Miami, aka *Del Boca Vista*. Working to avoid the tourists in the city, I was reading the pre-holiday *Miami Herald* newspaper, scoping out a holiday movie to see. The paper contained a story of tragedy at Disneyland. Anything to do with Disney received a great deal of attention in Florida and caught my eye having grown up in Orlando. A guest was seriously injured on a ride, through no fault of his own, and later reporting said he died on Christmas Eve. The first coverage did not have a victim's name but soon the details emerged.

Almost at the same time as the first story, an email arrived from Jeanne Sheldon (JeanneS), who was leading Word testing at the time, asking me to call as soon as I could, which was not routine. Over the phone, I learned from Jeanne the victim was a senior test engineer on the Word team who, like me, also started at Microsoft in July 1989, after first emigrating from Vietnam to attend university in Paris. His wife was also injured though expected to recover. Their son escaped injury. JeanneS took it upon herself to craft a note that was to be the first email I would share as a vice president to the entire division. The subject line read, "Sad News."

Microsoft was still young enough that we did not have in place the big company processes that eased these tragic situations. Much of the grieving happened in email over the holiday. It was an awful time for such an awful tragedy. I was starting to learn that at a certain scale, every kind of life experience, joyous and otherwise, would be part of our team. Microsoft had a few sad times before, and even some close to home in Apps, but this was difficult in its own way.

As we returned to work the project was winding down and we were in bug fix mode where only critical bug fixes were "taken" meaning only the most serious bugs were addressed with code changes.

Despite being a team always worried about engineering productivity, we were in that phase of a major software project where 2,000 people came to work every day and basically did nothing, if the measure of something was making changes to the product. Testers ran and re-ran tests. Developers investigated bugs and decided if the code change risk was greater than the risk of leaving a "bug" in there. Program management was fielding endless inbound requests for *just one more thing* or digging into one last potential oversight. Documentation and Localization were working on producing international releases. Lawyers were combing through marketing materials and documentation, and of course adding more words to the end-user license agreement, EULA. We were all using the product as end-users and testers on every computer we owned.

The biggest disappointment we were having about the new release was the lack of excitement within Microsoft. Whereas people were beating a path to the servers to install Office 97, we struggled to get Office 2000 deployed in large numbers across the company. This was, in reality, a sign of changing times.

Broadly pushing, perhaps forcing, internal use prior to shipping was another cultural difference between Apps and Systems. The Systems view was always hardcore—hardcore about pushing internal use, sometimes even too early, and hardcore about not using competitive solutions. The first was enabled by the long end game of shipping a Systems product, for example, Exchange Platinum (Exchange 2000), which began use inside Microsoft in 1998 and did not ship for almost two years. SteveB even apologized at an all-Company meeting one time for the bumpy Exchange pre-release. It was in beta for most of the entire Office 2000 product cycle. Competitively, Systems often rooted out competitive products and made it a goal to remove them, like Oracle server or later Google search.

The Apps view was always a bit less aggressive. The time from the product working until shipping was much shorter—there was less time when the product was usable by the typical employee, and by then a typical Microsoft employee was not much different than a typical employee in most any large company. We always viewed the use of a competitive product as a failure on our part, but one to learn from not to force away. If an individual or team wanted to use an alternative, then we would not object but want to understand why. The biggest example at the time was the growing use of Adobe's PDF instead of using the native file formats that BillG had insisted upon.

Our testing and release process did not rely on an extended period of internal testing or external beta tests. The nature of our products and process enabled us to achieve a high level of quality, even during these maturing days of the PC. Perhaps this was misplaced confidence as there was little data to base this on, but we closely tracked support calls and enterprise customers to have a good "feeling." In the next chapter we will have an eye-opening experience when it comes to data informing these decisions.

In the case of Office 2000, we were starting to see a sea change in Microsoft and the industry. Office was not the only place (or even a place) for excitement at the time. Browsers were really exciting. Consumers were excited by new MP3 players, not laptops. Most of all, enterprise IT was not excited by anything that caused them work—their *cycles* were being used trying to stabilize internal infrastructure, convert legacy client/server to the web, and prepare for Y2K.

We were losing competitively but to different competitors, not the alternatives to Office we feared.

The biggest competition for Office 2000 was…Office 97.

We were so heads down finishing Office 2000 that we didn't realize how well received, and how good, Office 97 was. Everything we announced at our Office 2000 enterprise event in New York was solid and the feedback from the beta was good, but we faced resistance to upgrade because it took work. While customers already owned and paid for Office 2000 with their multiyear agreements, the cost to deploy, including the costs of change, support, and labor had to be considered. To deploy Office 2000 or not was a major decision point within IT.

The sign-off for Office 2000 took place on a sunny April day in 1999. The product was eight months late from our original schedule we picked in March 1997. Unlike Office 97, however, the team was not frazzled, but tired. We faced the complexities of pulling everything together, but we improved the process and came together as a team. Still, an eight-month error is big on a 24-month schedule. We would conduct a detailed postmortem and make a series of changes.

CollJ and the admin team commandeered the fountain area between buildings 16-17-18. The makeshift stage and a megaphone were ready. Continuing with the theme of a maturing culture, Colleen instituted limits on alcohol and all went smoothly except for a minor champagne incident inside Building 17 that the Art Committee was rather upset about. We grew up a little bit more this ship day.

Earlier in the day we met in the ship room, with one representative from each of the 20 or so teams. Going around the horn like Mission Control at Cape Kennedy (1999 was the 30th anniversary of the moon landing so space was everywhere), we proclaimed Office 2000 "ready for the web" and "good to go."

I missed signing off on Office 97, but this time, as the VP of Office, I was going to get the "special treatment," meaning I was going to get thrown in the fountain. To everyone's surprise, I came prepared, wearing a bright yellow rain suit and goggles to protect from flying corks. CollJ printed out a giant copy of the paperwork that went to the manufacturing plant that duplicated DVDs and we did a ceremonial sign-off with BillG, who made a fast getaway to avoid the celebration.

The surplus air raid siren, a desktop applications cultural touchstone, sounded (though technically illegal to set off in the city of Redmond), as was DAD tradition for every ship party and sign-off. The next thing I remember was sitting in a fountain soaking wet.

The events of the day were memorialized with a videotape, an actual cassette, which each member of the team later received, including a congratulations from BillG at the end after rolling the credits for the release. Almost 2,000 names scrolled by while the Office Assistant PowerPup looked on. Still always looking to save money, we didn't do anything fancy for the credits—it was a Word 2000 document that I scrolled using support for the wheel mouse, first introduced with Office 97.

Our growing business with enterprise customers and the arrival of the internet introduced a new step in releasing the product. Enterprise customers would now begin deploying Office 2000 right away and would not have to wait for the retail arrival of boxes. We announced RTM for enterprise customers with a press release. In a few weeks we would actually launch the product for the retail market with a global series of events. I was off to Japan.

It wasn't just mission accomplished. It was my first mission as a general manager and executive, and it did feel different. Standing on the makeshift stage in my protective gear and signing off on the product—the first release of Office as a single team—was an emotional product moment.

056. GOING GLOBAL…MOTHER TREE

Everything about participating in our launch event in Japan was as orchestrated and as on time as the JR subway. For weeks before launch, I received down-to-the-minute updates. I could not have been more excited to attend.

My friends (co-workers) in Japan were frustrated that I flew there by myself, navigated the city on my own, and declined being met at Narita Airport to be shuttled into town, a 2-hour trip. In the '90s my ways were not how American executives did Japan, even though it was not one of my first trips Please see Michael Lewis's *Liar's Poker* for how bankers did business in Japan. They were so concerned I might get lost that someone prepared a camcorder recording of the entire transit route for me from customs at Narita to the hotel, which they sent to me on a CD-ROM to view.

Using my video directions, I arrived in Tokyo. The head of East Asia R&D, Akio Fujii (AkioF) met me at the hotel—he insisted, no, he really insisted. He drove us in his car with a TV in the dashboard (!) to the *Windows World Expo/ Tokyo 99* event, which was a 1000-person venue that we would fill. Oddly, a bright yellow Lamborghini was parked practically at the front door of the expo hall. Fujii-san explained that the launch event creative manager drove that car and that he was (very) big in Japan event circles. I was already off to an over-the-top start to the event.

We arrived and met with Susumu "Sam" Furukawa (SamF.) SamF, a tech legend in Japan, was an original leader of the Microsoft subsidiary, MSKK, and served as Chairman of Microsoft Japan. He was a relentless champion for the PC, Microsoft products, and an advocate for Japan in the United States where he kept a home by Microsoft. In addition to his passion for every conceivable electronic gadget, audio/video tool, or handheld device, Sam was famous for his love of model railroads and elaborate scale scenes often featured in the magazines. He was also known as one of Japan's leading gadget gurus and had deep relationships with Japanese consumer electronics companies. His enthusiasm was so remarkable and infectious I often failed to keep up with him in meetings because his excited English ran together and sounded like one long word or sentence. Then once BillG mentioned to me that he was pretty sure no one could keep up with Sam in Japanese either, which was quite a relief.

The stage seemed rather stark. Draped over most of the front of it was a plain gauze curtain, a scrim. Puzzling. SamF arrived and was his incredibly excited self. He secured "the brightest high-definition projector in existence from a best friend at Hitachi." The Hitachi crew in matching jumpsuits and hard hats was up on the catwalk calibrating the projector.

They gave me staging for the next morning's event. There was no room for improvisation. The translator was briefed. I was to say *only* what I was told to say—"*Konichiwa,* Sinofsky *desu*" and then recite the English script, ending with "*Arigatou gozaimasu.*" That became my Japanese business vocabulary that served me for decades. It was *Lost in Translation* happening to me as I was staying at the relatively new Park Hyatt. It took hours to get everything right. At least I thought it was right.

They told me that after my rehearsed words, music would play and the scrim would drop, revealing a Hitachi projection of Office 2000. Sam had me leave the stage so I could see it all from the audience's perspective. We headed to the back of the room by the control board that must have been twenty feet long staffed by six people.

The stage lights dimmed, a spotlight lit up where I'd been standing, and Sam said, "Pretend now you are finished."

A rising crescendo of strings and wind instruments, like Yanni, rose in volume to almost an ear-crushing level. Then the scrim dropped in rather dramatic fashion. The stage lights went up. There was a giant backdrop projection of a single huge Bonsai tree brightly filling the brilliant and enormous screen that spanned the stage.

Over the tree in white letters, it read *Office 2000* with the new logo. There were some Japanese words that I could not read and in the Japanese font used for English letters the words *Mother Tree.*

Sam was blown away. He said, "Isn't it amazing?!"

I said it was. "Amazing. Beautiful. Brilliant." But I had absolutely no idea what *Mother Tree* meant.

I bowed to everyone I could make eye contact with. I said, "Arigatou," while deeply expressing appreciation.

I had no idea what was being said on the giant display.

When I asked Sam for the meaning, he said, like he often had before, "It can't be translated." I asked Fujii-san, and he said the same thing. I even asked the head of Office marketing, Nobuyoshi Yokoi (NobuY), who in MSKK was known as *Mr. Office,* and he simply pursed his lips, pulling in some air, creating a Japanese *thought-bubble* implying *difficulty*, and said, "So sorry, Steven-san, but there is no translation."

The best I could gather was that it was marketing the importance of Office and how it was a strong collection of tools growing from a solid and enduring foundation.

Maybe?

While I never truly learned the full meaning, I loved it. It represented the hard work and dedication of MSKK and the incredible effort they put into the launch. I brought back a giant poster of the image (they packed it incredibly well) that must have been four feet high and six feet wide and hung on my office wall for years. Like every single thing I experienced in Japan, the poster was magic and evoked the warmest of emotions.

In Japan, as in the rest of the world we coupled the launch of Office 2000 with the long-anticipated beta release of Windows 2000, in a campaign informally called *Desktop 2000,* aimed at defining a new standard enterprise desktop PC. The launch event was a mix of enterprise and consumer though it was clear the emotional connection was to retail customers. This should not be a surprise because of how the business was structured in Japan.

Unique to Japan, Office at retail was a huge business because it sold for the full retail price with newly purchased PCs. Japan had not yet embraced the top-down IT model of purchase and deployment, which was OK because the retail model was more lucrative for Microsoft Japan, so long as new PC sales kept growing. Originally offered as a service by PC stores, the idea of installing Office for customers—*pre-installed PC,* or PIPC—was a special offering of Word, Excel, and Outlook (with an option to upgrade and add PowerPoint) that was offered with a new PC for what amounted to full retail pricing. This offer was wildly successful and popular, though could never be replicated elsewhere. For years people would assume Office came "bundled" on new PCs, but really that was only true in Japan where the price stickers on new PCs made it entirely clear what the price was with or without PIPC Office. So successful was this business in in Japan that it was a significant part of the overall subsidiary, so profitable that it was a noticeable part of all of Microsoft's earnings.

BillG's investment in and focus on the Japanese market is not often appreciated. Very early in Microsoft's journey BillG began a partnership with legendary Japanese technologist Kazuhiko "Kay" Nishi founder of ASCII Corporation (a magazine publisher), eventually partnering to bring MS-DOS based PCs to Japan. In the 1980s, Japan was innovating in PCs in an isolated way but also represented a huge market. Japan was the world leader in electronics and had a powerful government ally known as the Ministry of International Trade and Industry (MITI) that was often in the news here in the US because of concerns the US was falling behind in computers, chips, and software due in part to the intense involvement of the government in directing innovation. In the 1990s, the specter of the Japan economic engine was vast, from chips to New York real estate to autos.

It took a great deal of partnering and Japan-specific development to break into the market and ultimately win over in-country rivals. For many years until Windows XP was in stores, it was not uncommon to see DOS/V compatibility indicated on products, the variant of DOS supporting Japanese characters and video devices spearheaded by IBM. Working with Kay Nishi, Microsoft collaborated on PCs with Japanese companies and eventually sold Basic and then DOS to Japanese companies. In 1986, Microsoft opened the Japan subsidiary. BillG hired SamF to lead it. Sam immediately began hiring among the very best recent graduates and software people he could find to lead Microsoft's first international research and development office.

Among those hires was Akio Fujii. AkioF, or Fujii-san, as I generally preferred—in an interesting twist, Microsoft's email people wrestled with reversing Asian names to be more proper but could never quite get that right, especially in Chinese where to IT the first and last names were often not obvious, much to the frustration of employees. Under the leadership of Fujii-san, the Desktop Apps development team in Japan coordinated the development of most all of Microsoft's products for Japan and led development across East Asian products (Korean, Traditional Chinese, and Simplified Chinese) with teams in several locations, known as East Asia R&D. Fujii-san was one of the earliest employees hired by SamF. Many of the people working at MSKK today trace their own lineage directly to SamF and AkioF and the original opening of the subsidiary, which has grown to thousands of employees and just celebrated its 35th anniversary.

In the early days, simply getting software to work with the mysterious *double-byte characters* used to represent Japanese in DOS and 16-bit Windows was a huge technical challenge. While standard practice today, almost no code from the early days of the personal computer was written to be localized or translated into other languages, and certainly not work with the alternate characters or vertical text used in Asian languages. Many early Asian-language products were created by taking the English/European source code and hacking away at it for an entire product cycle without much help from Redmond, often taking more than a year to release.

The financial motivation and advancing technology brought this "delta" (the time between the US release being complete and localized variants of the software being complete) down to a predictable number of weeks. Aside from making the code simply function with Asian language characters, there were thousands of user interface strings and many thousands of pages of help files that were translated each release as well.

Even after all that, early products were simply wrong for the market, wrong as in customers were often puzzled by the missing features or the type of documents that were extremely difficult to create with Office, even as late as 1995. Fujii-san and team would perennially raise issues about the missing features or difficult to use features in Office for the Japan market, but these would often fall on deaf ears—not deaf for lack of empathy but simply because of the ongoing competitive battles just trying to win in the US.

A symbolic example in Excel was the lack of *donut charts* which are used routinely instead of pie charts but did not exist in Excel. After much consternation, donut charts would make it to Excel albeit much later. I could make many excuses from being too busy to too complicated to have developers in another time zone on the same code base (a real challenge back then), but it really was a failure at making a distant market a priority. I previously faced this when I first met the MSKK development team trying to build Visual C++ for Windows, which also had local market challenges.

The Word team set out to address this, in particular by hiring native or near-native Japanese speakers on to the team in Redmond. Several other members of the team took Japanese lessons as well. This began a long and sincere effort to fully adapt the product to the needs of Japanese users, working closely with and often with contributions from the engineering teams across East Asia. With this came extended visits to Japan to learn directly from customers and upon returning to Redmond, educate the team on the cultural differences. The hallways were filled with Japanese documents illustrating the differences in how features were used and what the difference was in printed output.

One of the most memorable examples was when the team explained how many Japanese customers preferred to use Excel as a "word processor" to create standard forms and templates rather that Word, which seemed a bit crazy to us. What followed was an endless series of example documents that were far more focused on grid-layout than anything we'd see in the US. As any English-native who has flown to Japan, checked into a hotel, and filled out an exit visa can tell you the documents are filled with boxes and lines, as well as vertical text. Word simply couldn't create those documents and Excel was great. This changed in Word 97 when a feature known as *table pencil* was added, which let users draw (and erase) grid lines in a table and create documents that were literally elaborate tables.

Following this and several other lessons, the team got much better at integrating feedback and eventually features and entire market-specific products the Japan. The East Asia R&D team developed some of the most innovative and earliest linguistic features for Office and Windows, features few today can imagine living without. Asian languages based on characters and not finite numbers of letters that fit on a keyboard require input via phonetics that translate that into suggested characters, which the user then chooses from. This is called the Input Method Editor, IME, and was one of the most significant innovations in the PC era for Asian languages. Starting with Japanese, then adding Korean and Simplified and Traditional Chinese, the team created the user experience for typing. In many ways, today's mobile phone experience we share with autocorrect and fixing mistakes resembles what Asian language users have been experiencing since the earliest days of the PC. Early on they shared many of the same complaints about incorrect guesses and awkward suggestions that we still live with today.

While most new software companies were content to battle in the US and expand to Western Europe, Microsoft was early and aggressive about expansion into Asia. For me personally, the Office 2000 product launch marks the start of strong devotion to working in Asia and elevating that work. I had many fun product launches and visited multiple times per year, creating many strong friendships that continue today on social networks where these stories are shared. In 2004, I spent my Microsoft *sabbatical* (technically the Microsoft Achievement Award, MSAA, a three month break to do what you'd like, earned after seven years of service) living in Beijing and working with the subsidiary on local market issues with the government.

Back in the US, the product launch was decidedly enterprise focused. In fact, much of the fanfare would wait until the arrival of Windows 2000. The enterprise sales team geared up for a massive push of Windows 2000, Windows Server 2000, Exchange 2000, and Office 2000, then even added SQL Server 2000. The launch of all this software—perhaps the release that came to define the company as an enterprise provider of software—was inspiring. Microsoft was indeed firing on all cylinders as an enterprise company. It would take a few years for customers to digest such a wave of software while at the same time we were relentless in releasing even more.

The enterprise launch of Office was held at the newly opened Sony Metreon space in downtown San Francisco, featuring the long-forgotten first Microsoft retail store, *MicrosoftSF*, which featured displays of products you could look at and not buy. Steve Ballmer, in his first major launch as President of the company, brought his undeniable enthusiasm to an enterprise product launch. San Francisco Mayor Willie Brown also proclaimed it "Microsoft Office 2000 Week" saying he can do that because he's the "Bill Gates of San Francisco."

The event was also the first of many of a new style of Microsoft event that reflected an enterprise level of information density. Every keynote or launch featured strategy slides, multiple demonstrations, video testimonials from customers and partners, and then a long-term vision for the industry by a senior executive. At this event in the IMAX theater, we even had Q&A with the customers and partners in attendance. It was quite a show—in length and density.

If the wave of products defined success in the enterprise, it was decidedly the opposite for consumers or just regular people, even small businesses. Across the board our traditional reviews were underwhelmed or even perplexed by the focus on collaboration, web standards, reducing cost of ownership, and other big company features.

With two launches and availability dates, the reviews came in two waves. The enterprise reviews for Office 2000 were extremely solid. I don't think we could have wished for better enterprise evaluations. With enterprise availability that April, *InfoWorld*, the go-to source for enterprise computing news, said:

> *Its many enhancements should ease IT administration headaches, reduce overall ownership costs, and improve the workgroup collaboration experience. For companies who are already standardized on the 95 or 97 versions of Microsoft Office, the move to Office 2000 should be a no-brainer. And even for those who are not, moving to Office 2000 offers some compelling benefits.*

The consumer launch in June brought another wave of coverage. Only this time, the words were not so positive. As successful as we were at orienting the business around enterprise, we clearly did not deliver what the consumer reviewers were looking to see. Walt Mossberg, with whom I personally met several times during development, wrote in an article headlined, "Microsoft Updates Office Suite, but It's Not for the Little Guy."

> *However, I may be able to save you the trouble and expense. I've been testing Office 2000 for months now, and I believe that most individuals and small businesses that already use one of the last two versions of Office will gain little or nothing by upgrading. It's not that the program is a dog. It works well, in fact. But this version has been engineered almost entirely for big corporations with speedy networks. Its most significant new features are aimed at helping people who collaborate over a network and post a lot of documents to the Internet or a corporate intranet...Some new features look great on paper but work well only for corporate users...The bottom line for consumers and small businesses is this: If you have a very old version of Office and a fairly new PC, or you need to post a lot of business documents on the Web, it makes sense to upgrade to Office 2000. Otherwise, forget it.*

The sting was real.

I was hurting. Was *Personal Productivity Is Priority* 6 the wrong approach? Did we really mess up? Should we have seen this coming and adjusted along the way? It seemed so obvious in hindsight. On the other hand, we did exactly what we set out to do. In Microsoft performance review lingo, this was a 4.0. Our scale at the time was 2.0-5.0 in 0.5 increments, where almost no one ever got a 4.5 or 5.0 and 70% of large teams received a 3.5 or 4.0.

The answer, regretfully, in some ways, was that we (or specifically I) did not mess up. The Office business depended on building a product for business customers. The reviews were positive in that regard. The consumer reviews were not the key to the success we were achieving and needed to achieve going forward.

We built what could sell. And we were selling what we built.

We should do both was a constant refrain over many discussions—we should have a great consumer product and a great enterprise product. On paper that is the ideal situation. In practice it was not that the needs and desires of each type of customer were diverging; they were increasingly in conflict. It was not that consumers wanted different features; they also explicitly did not want the enterprise features. This worked both ways, as the enterprise IT view decidedly did not want more *features*, but rather fewer.

Practically, anytime one tries to take on two conflicting perspectives in one product, the product comes across as a compromise. It is neither one nor the other, but a displeasing mess. The hope I had at the start was that by making personal productivity Priority 6 we avoided the messy middle. We succeeded at that, but I was struggling with how unsatisfying this felt.

The middle age of the PC was upon us. The age of designing for the individual, the lone hero using the PC as a tool of empowerment, was over. The tinkerer and influential end-user moved from the garage or basement to the office of the chief information officer, the new power seat in the boardroom. The PC was a tool of corporations, and Office needed to deliver that if it were to stay relevant. With Office 2000, the business results suggested that we were spectacularly relevant.

I still held out hope that we could find a path forward that was more appreciative to the individual sitting in front of Office with a job or schoolwork to do.

1999-2001

The world realized just how dependent it had become on email and the PC and when viruses became a mainstream part of the technology vernacular. In the halls of Microsoft, it became apparent that being early was as strategically deadly as being wrong. PCs sell more than 100 million units for the first time in 1999. Things start to heat up on the antitrust front. We are learning to plan a release in the context of a massive change in the business of selling software to the enterprise.

057. ENTERPRISE AGREEMENTS

Enterprise wasn't just the direction of the business—it was the only business.

But could we listen to customers and still fail? That's what it felt like was happening.

Office 2000 had become entrenched in the enterprise, if not yet deployed it seemed inevitable. In the process, we left end-users behind. Those concerns over too much enterprise focus that were pushed aside to make way for Office 2000 became front and center. From a product development perspective, we were failing in the reviews that we had been trained to want the most to win. Starting with "nothing in it for the little guy" to "thousands of features, some useful and most not" the product was not something end-users wanted.

Business results told an entirely different story. Most quarters our Office finance lead would come to a senior manager meeting and discuss the earnings announcement and put it in context. As a public company these discussions were not news, but at least helped the broader team to understand where the money came from and how much we were spending. Each quarter of results had a new entry in the filings and disclosure that went something like this from Microsoft's 2000 annual report:

> *At June 30, 1999 and 2000, Windows Platforms products unearned revenue was $2.17 billion and $2.61 billion and unearned revenue associated with Productivity Applications and Developer products [Office] totaled $1.96 billion and $1.99 billion. Unearned revenue for other miscellaneous programs totaled $116 million and $210 million at June 30, 1999 and 2000.*

It would be an understatement to say that finance was almost giddy over the unearned revenue number. It was growing at a crazy rate and the numbers were billions of dollars. Sometimes it felt like the world's largest rainy-day fund (even though Microsoft's cash on hand was also astronomical) or that we could stop selling software and run the company on unearned revenue for a couple of years. The company came a long way from BillG's founding principle of maintaining a full year of cash on hand to weather economic uncertainty.

Revenue was no longer as simple as how many copies of Office were sold. The turn of the millennium was about selling multi-year contracts for Office and other Microsoft products, often all together. While Office for $100 or even $150 dollars per desktop PC seemed historically low, gone was the angst over upgrades. The largest companies in the world were buying our software for every PC and committing to keep buying it for the next three years, called an Enterprise Agreement or EA. It was effectively a massive increase in revenue per customer, in exchange customers received the full enterprise treatment of support, sales teams, strategic partnering and more. *Software Assurance* or SA was the enterprise version of the traditional retail model of receiving a discount when buying an upgrade but did not include rights to all past or future versions.

Wall Street had to find new ways to think about earnings. Instead of booking the revenue for one box of Office entirely in the quarter it was sold, revenue was formally recognized over the life of the contract, usually three years. Contractually the revenue was guaranteed, but accounting rules meant Microsoft had to wait to recognize revenue.

It is easy to see why this is a good idea, as absent from that we could conceivably have monster quarters only to fail to sell more products in the future.

This created a radically new problem for how we thought of the business. Microsoft created a virtual line-item *unearned revenue* representing all the future payments yet to be recognized or received. Instead of the top line, Wall Street was now focused on the rate of growth of the unearned revenue. Very quickly billions of dollars from Windows and Office were piling up in the unearned revenue line item. Unearned revenue would convert to plain old revenue on a schedule based on the length of the agreement and would be added to the revenue line of reported earnings. As quickly as these agreements took over, we had to change how we thought about product development.

Unearned revenue (almost an oxymoron, and certainly not a phrase coined by marketing) could sound like an accounting gimmick and was especially tricky for the teams in headquarters that had no real insights into pricing, number of agreements, or even the promises and terms. We only had one important rule, which was that we could not (ever) disclose the future release date of a product. Doing so would potentially turn unearned revenue into earned revenue as the rights to buy an upgrade went from "if" one was available to "when" one was available. Disclosure would also cause customers to attempt to time their deals so as to maximize the number of upgrades they received. It felt super weird to be involved in this dance, but it was also very straightforward. There was even a regulatory investigation at one point because we started to deliver more software online and had to adjust the portion of revenue recognized immediately versus over time.

The problem was that selling Office to retail customers was a big business but going nowhere compared to enterprise licensing. Easily half the business was new volume licensing products, and the switch from retail, especially for medium and larger businesses, was progressing rapidly. Soon the bulk of all revenue would be volume licensing/EAs, and retail would simply be, for lack of a better word, rounding error.

Still, the Office 2000 product felt too enterprise. I was determined that Office maintain both end-user excitement and broad horizontal appeal —those were our roots and people sat in front of Office hours every day. Microsoft was rapidly becoming a company of extremes, with Xbox and internet services targeting the latest consumer trends and Servers at the extreme of enterprise. Office, used by most everyone with a PC it seemed, occupied a broad space in the middle as products used by individuals and teams, at home and at work, but purchased and managed by IT professionals. This was our product design challenge—how to build a product where the buyers and users differed so dramatically.

We were years away from phrases such as "consumerization of IT," or the idea that people wanted enterprise software that felt and worked like the cool consumer software they used outside of work. Office, however, always occupied that space. Used by individuals, even if sometimes purchased by organizations, the software was decidedly built for people who had better things to do. Office was unique software designed for *work* but used up and down and across an organization in a myriad of ways. Almost no enterprise software was used the way Office was, by every single person in an organization.

Creating the Enterprise Agreement was one of the most brilliant decisions in all of Microsoft history, right up there with the MS-DOS license or committing to Macintosh applications. It is why the company today could so easily transition to selling Office as a modern software as a service offering. Microsoft developed and used a muscle, so to speak, for changing the business terms while maintaining product compatibility. Once again, we see the foundation of the company today form decades earlier. The EA, which got its start in the late 1990s, was also quintessential SteveB, combining exactly what the customer wanted with just enough nuance and complexity that Microsoft could stay ahead on the business side, and yes it was also ahead of where we were in the product groups. The EA started as an "offer" as Steve would say, and then we worked backwards and filled in the details.

Office was not like a magazine, utilities, or cable subscriptions with regular flows of some consumable resource. Office never stops doing what it was purchased to do. It keeps going and going. PCs got messed up (all too easily) with poorly behaved software, but corporate IT figured this all out and created processes to *clean install* a PC and refresh it with known versions of software but none of the bad stuff gumming up the system. Tech enthusiasts knew this too. In fact, the internet became a hotbed of tips and tricks to cure a sluggish PC of ills caused by downloading software from the internet or playing around with the registry. The constant need for security updates had not yet become a reality, but that challenge is just around the corner and as we will see, the enterprise model only made it that much easier for Microsoft.

Key to all of this when it came to product development was that new releases seemed to be able to bypass market validation to appear successful. Customers have already purchased the next and latest release, which meant we could easily fool ourselves into thinking the product was a hit by looking at the revenue numbers. Customers were buying a sales and support relationship with Microsoft, as much or perhaps more than the software itself, even when running old releases. While this was not a short-term issue, over time the lack of individual buyers acquiring specific products seriously clouded Microsoft's collective product judgement. In many ways the mostly captive Windows OEM model, selling to a very small number of enormous accounts, would presage this product-market challenge.

Unaware of what was possible, end-users never really demanded specific new features, but IT professionals did, and what they wanted was not necessarily representative of what individuals valued. Individuals, however, seemed to have a decreasing voice in what software a company used as IT gained control of the chaos that PCs unleashed. EAs were the tool IT needed—in their mind they paid, so they dictated every aspect of the PC.

The divergence of the target buyer from the target user increased with each new Enterprise Agreement. The success created a new kind of problem—when people at Microsoft talked about "the customer" we needed to calibrate to better understand who we were talking about. Windows meant PC and hardware makers, the OEMs. Server products meant enterprise IT infrastructure. Tools meant developers. Office meant individuals and teams. Most of all, the sales force always meant the C-suite sponsoring a sizable deal with Microsoft, the higher up the better. By and large, customer really did mean the high-ranking executives with a direct line to the account team, the Executive Briefing Center, and SteveB.

The complexity of Enterprise Agreements was often comical. There were hundreds of thousands of different deal and price permutations. There was no easy way to sell billions of one thing, just like Coca-Cola didn't only sell 12-ounce cans of Coke—so went the conversation I would have with those on the team tasked with implementing and tracking seemingly endless and ever-changing SKUs. Not all companies (customers) were on the current release; in fact, most were not. Not all customer EAs started in the same year or at the same time. Collectively, customers were equally spread into three cohorts expiring in a given year, and each of the following two. This meant that any given release was deployed by at most one-third of customers. When buying new PCs, the oldest customers upgraded from a version two releases back, a version none of us were running that Microsoft had long forgotten about. Seemingly overnight, EAs created a complexity matrix based on the outside chance that the most out of date customers might upgrade to the latest release. We were committing to upgrading from software potentially six or seven years old because at any given time, the current and previous two releases of Office were each used by about one-third of customers—a fact that remained stubbornly true for a very long time.

PCs were also starting to last longer. There was another decade or more left in Moore's Law, the idea that computer power doubled every 18 months. The law, really an observation and prediction, was named after the cofounder of Intel and pioneer of microprocessors, Gordon Moore. It was Moore's Law that kept people buying a new PC every other year or sooner, which was shifting to more like three years and, in the blink of an eye, to five. The first decade of the PC was marked by software consuming every bit of hardware that could make it to market including CPU, memory, and disk space. By 2000, typical PCs had ample specifications for business productivity. Laptops were just a couple of years behind in terms of the price and performance curves but were getting there quickly in a highly competitive market. The guideline most businesses followed was that new versions of software rolled out commensurate with new levels of hardware. Many companies were trying to get on a cycle to regularly update hardware, but they were finding that doing a refresh of the software load got another year or more out of a PC. Windows gained the most by creating an incentive for new hardware, but they were more focused on the consumer and building a successor to Windows 2000, what would become Windows XP, that equaled the legacy Windows 95 product and their product cycles were much longer. Whereas people previously wanted a new PC at work so much they would spend their own money, a practice eventually not allowed, everyone seemed content with whatever their workplace provided. PCs and software seemed good enough. There was only one customer segment larger than EA and that was OEM which meant by and large Windows continued to focus on OEMs and less so on enterprise customers, at least with the release under development.

This dynamic was entirely appropriate of the *middle age* of the PC era. Instead of moving to a new home it seemed far simpler to repair the existing one. As central as the PC was to the workplace environment and health, slowly businesses were making different choices. EAs were the perfect way for a business to make one decision and not worry about it again, even if it meant paying a bit more.

EAs also created a crazy environment where concerns over hitting a ship date for retailers and OEMs were secondary to those of IT professionals trying to time the start date of their Enterprise Agreement. They knew they owned the current version, but if they delayed purchasing for as long as possible the two next versions might be released and ready to ship as they signed. They deployed the current release and owned the next one, and if Microsoft hit a target ship date, then they'd also own the third. As the renewal dates for a given customer approached, the pressure from that account team to the Redmond marketing team for a public commitment to a ship date only increased. This was all invisible to the broader market, but the idea of renewals was front and center for the sales and business leadership.

Wall Street analyst interactions were similar. Analysts maintained an unearned revenue number in their forecasts. They would work hard to extract from me a target ship date which gave me the uneasy feeling that I was just filling in a cell in their spreadsheet model for Microsoft earnings.

My own ability to interact with customers in settings like the Executive Briefing Center (EBC) became its own game of schedule chicken. Customers assumed that Office continued to improve but were only marginally interested in the product strategy. They really wanted to know if a new release was due within their EA subscription window. Every EBC I attended turned into a contest of *how many ways can I get asked about the ship date without answering*. Often the sales team prepared me for a strategy briefing only to find myself on my first slide dodging questions about ship dates. My standard line was, "We aim to ship a new release of Office every 24 to 36 months, and we last shipped…" This was wholly unsatisfying to customers, especially to a specific customer with a specific date in mind for their EA, asking a VP, technically by then a senior vice president. Account managers and country managers were getting increasingly frustrated with me and Office in general for not being more open and committing to ship dates.

Then there were those pesky accounting rules, so I just couldn't say anything. Still, if I were to give a more specific range to customers (or to the analysts, for that matter, who as a proxy for customers also *needed* to know) then I had to be right. The problem was we were never right. For customers, even a one-month error was a massive dollar-value issue. If we were a month late and a customer didn't qualify for the product then every impacted customer sought compensation. Plus, a date range was a joke. Inside Microsoft if someone said "first half" of a year, as they often did, then other product groups might assume June 30. Customers hearing the same range likely assumed January 1.

A ship date is a date, not a range. A quarter is 90 dates. Half of a year is 180 dates. I hated this game.

It felt as absurd as it sounds. Yet, it was the reality. It made me look clueless at best, at worst, coy. I hated pretending not to know. I hated acting like we were ineffective at our jobs. So many customers commented, "In our industry we make a big giant complicated *thing* and if we told our customers we didn't know when it would finish, we'd have no business."

Every time, I thought about industries from Boeing planes to Ford cars to Bechtel bridges and how late they were. I repeatedly bit my tongue.

Then I stopped putting myself in the EBC. It wasn't the best practice, but I just wasn't wired for this type of tap dance. I have some regrets.

EAs came about to maximize an available revenue opportunity and customer relationship (thinking back to that 1993 Management Conference retreat where we talked about filling the void left by IBM—this was it), even if the product or product development process had not caught up to that opportunity. As we bundled already successful Word and Excel into Office even though the products were not yet integrated, we were selling enterprise licenses even though our processes (and product) had not yet matured to that level. We were selling subscriptions long before subscriptions were cool, or even built—this is an important and hugely significant legacy of SteveB's enterprise sales leadership. Eventually these EAs would be called *recurring revenue*.

Given this, Office needed to create features that delivered so much value to IT professionals in the enterprise that they outweighed the cost of deploying and training employees. Simply making Office more enterprise friendly and easy to deploy were nice, but it was still more difficult to deploy than to do nothing. We needed to accomplish this on time and within the magical three-year window.

I genuinely believed that we had created an unsolvable problem—creating enough business value to justify an upgrade in the eyes of the gatekeeper. Imagine trying to make Word, Excel, and PowerPoint so much more valuable that the new features were worth more than the sum of all the old features? Difficult enough, but what made this even more absurd was that the IT people were actively customizing Office to disable features they deemed to be of low business value. It was not surprising to see companies disable access to HTML, templates, Visual Basic programming, or data connectivity features simply for concern, or fear, that they might get misused, waste time, or generate support calls. While this was acute for Office, upgrades were an industry-wide challenge.

Failing to create value, some in the industry moved to *upgrades by force*, by changing the file formats, creating proprietary connections between servers such as Exchange or the Windows web server, or by requiring the new version for patches or updates. Office generally resisted these artificial *growth* methods.

This ran counter to new internet era companies, which were not about *tightly coupled* software but about *loosely coupled* software. This philosophy was the exact opposite of how Microsoft created new features—the connection between Exchange and Outlook was as tightly coupled as could be—each required the other and without both there was no value at all.

Enterprise Agreements were making it look increasingly difficult to build the right product. How ironic.

Grinding out relatively on-time releases that shipped on a certain date and doubled down on enterprise features seemed perfectly achievable. There was little risk that we could mess things up with such a plan—I would achieve all my performance goals relative to EAs. The product would probably stink, though, for the people that used it for their jobs every day. We would try to create metrics across the company, incentives to achieve customer upgrades, but no teams controlled anything that could dramatically alter customer behavior. From the product group our job remained the same, to build a great product. We could make a better Office, but that would not dramatically change how fragile a PC was, especially one loaded with IT software and customizations. This wasn't an excuse. It was reality.

If there was one lesson building the apps business, it was that great releases empowering individuals and helping them to create compelling documents pulled Office into companies. There needed to be some balance. Achieving that balance was our goal for planning would become Office10.

058. THAT DREADED WORD: SYNERGY

Sync with Windows 2000. Sync with Whistler, code name for Windows XP. Sync with Windows Server. Sync with Exchange Platinum, code name for Exchange 2000. Sync with Exchange Titanium, the one after that. Sync with SQL 2000. Sync with the one after that that didn't even have a code name yet. Sync. Sync. Sync. That was what we heard from every corner of the company when it came to building the next release of Office. Sync wasn't just about schedule. Sync implied deep strategic connections in the code and user experience—it was all about product synergy.

A remarkable accomplishment of Microsoft's earliest days was entering all the major lines of software at the time. In a c. 1981 video produced by Microsoft, "A Hard Line on Software", the company touted its product line.

> *A full line of system software not just one or two products, and all of our products are designed to work together...a full line. Microsoft products cover all three areas of system software: languages, operating systems, and end-user tools.*

Microsoft's core DNA was having products in all the major areas of software while also committing to products worked better together. This was BillG to the core.

By the late 1990s, Microsoft had spawned two businesses greater than $10 billion in Windows and Office and breaking those down further one could find multiple businesses closing in on $1 billion in revenue from Visual Studio and developer tools to the various servers such as Exchange and SQL to the new business of MSN and games. The breadth part of the DNA was firing on all cylinders.

The other part of our DNA was proving to be more difficult and at the same time the demands for products to work together were only increasing. This was happening as product complexity skyrocketed and the predictability of product releases was not improving. More importantly, each of these big products began to have significant overlap: Exchange and SQL, Basic and C++, Word and Publisher (and anything that edited text), Excel and the Access database (and Visual Basic), Internet Information Server and Windows file server, and the list goes on and on. Mind you, the overlap was not entirely obvious to most as the market clearly saw these as different products. Inside Microsoft, however, the overlap was at some deep architectural level worthy of debate and ultimately synergy and unification.

As enterprise customers came to dominate the business, strategy was no longer just about features. Strategy was how products were deployed, managed, and integrated into business scenarios. Something entirely clear at a usage level such as email, a database for line of business data, and file storage became a galactically hard strategy problem when customers wanted to deploy and manage one scaled "place to store data."

The technical leaders of the company spent most of our executive time on the collisions between products when it came to deployment and management and the seams between them when it came to user-experience and scenarios. Having more than one way to do something or failing to have clarity in prescriptive guidance to the field sales organization was reason enough for a big meeting or offsite.

Call it what you will, synergy, strategy, unification, consistency, or simply efficiency were the key attributes everyone was to aim for. It was assumed achieving this was part of the schedule, though this operational aspect was almost never discussed or even challenged. Unify was definitely BillG's favorite way to describe his goal.

For better or worse, those of us with our experience in Office made oft-repeated calls that synergy comes from synchronizing ship dates across products. Surprisingly it seemed to have sunk in now that a big wave of server products (Windows 2000 and the 2000 servers) were nearing completion. So now everyone wanted to know when the next Office was shipping and importantly, would that date align with what they were planning on for the next releases. Such scheduling was of course impossible. Not only was no one in the company hitting ship dates but having any two groups first agree on a target and then hit that target was akin to bullets colliding mid-air downrange, on purpose. Important here is that we're not talking about new groups or small teams, but massive billion-dollar products and customers spending tens of millions of dollars per year on their Enterprise Agreements. Each of the product teams approached 1,000 people at this point. The scale was immense.

As it would turn out and much to our collective surprise, the next releases of both Windows and Office (the releases being planned in the timeframe of this chapter) would in fact hit their target ship dates. Both of our teams came to the exact conclusion, independently, in the heat of synergy overload—shipping was all that mattered. Windows put in place a plan to add all the key consumer support missing from Windows 2000—the last features that remained from the 16-bit code base—along with a broad range of features and technologies from around the Windows team. This plan was code-named Whistler, nominally named after the Canadian town and ski resort favored by many Seattleites. It was both remarkable and commendable to see this *little* part of Windows carved out and allowed to be, given all the strategic initiatives going on. To be honest, for most of the time we were working on Office it always seemed like the other shoe would drop and the product would slip. In hindsight, that was probably unfair. On the other hand, it might be the first release of Windows to *ever* ship on time.

In Office we were smarting from the lukewarm reviews for Office 2000, despite the groundswell of support from our enterprise customers for the complete *Desktop 2000* that was just starting to deploy. Knowing that most customers were just beginning to deploy we could have taken out time with the next release, but I felt a strong need to get back in the market with end-user appeal and to bring some focus and attention to innovation in productivity and of course the internet. There were still deep concerns about the potential for relevancy of Office in an internet-centric world.

All this pressure about synergy and synchronizing pushed us to start planning for a new release in the summer of 1998 which turned out to be seven months before finishing Office 2000. My reluctance to even provide a code name, which would then probably leak, excite the field sales force, make it into the press, and so on, caused me to plainly title the memo "Next Release of Office." Cleverly, the team immediately took the code name of the release to be the ambiguous "NRO." I admit it now, but I kind of liked that. Security by obscurity. In short order the team started calling the next release *Office10*, because it was the one that came after *Office9*. That was good enough for us.

There was much we could focus on. There was also a great deal of low-hanging fruit we could pick off in terms of enterprise customers. This was in practice our big challenge. How can we find a way to balance all the various forms of feedback, knowing that the bulk of revenue came from enterprise IT, but nearly everyone sitting in front of the product for hours per day were just regular people? In NRO I wrote the following, accompanied by a fancy new OfficeArt diagram showing the full spectrum of feedback.

Getting the right kind of customer feedback integrated into the product is always a challenge. As Microsoft has grown the bias has been towards fewer people interacting directly with customers and towards over-representing the feedback from large and vocal customers. The following picture illustrates the current paradox for getting the right kind feedback. Today we tend to over value and over-practice customer "feedback" that is actually more valuable to the customer as pre/post-sales support than it is valuable to the product team during the design phase. This is not to say we should not practice things like EBC visits, or one-to-many presentations like the Global Executive Roundtable, but we should consider them for what they are which is a self-selected and large company focused effort. The more inputs we gather from the right side of the diagram the better off we will be at understanding the true problems we are solving. One way to consider this spectrum is that the left side of the diagram is where our decisions are validated and the right side is where ideas are elucidated. Despite the pressure in the company to focus on one-off customer contact from LORGs, we must not lose sight of getting the right feedback through the right mechanisms.

The competitive landscape remained clear. Our number one direct competitor remained previous releases of Office, and for Enterprise Agreement customers it was the still not deployed versions of Office customers *already owned.* To make this point clear, the memo detailed the fact that we could never ever again change the file format:

We must not lose sight of the fact that our biggest competitor continues to be our existing products and the inertia they have. The cost and pain of upgrading still overwhelms any sense of benefit we seem to be able to communicate to customers. We learned that if we ever change our file formats again we can kiss the upgrade good-bye. Literally no one will ever upgrade if we change the Word and Excel file formats-I hope that fact is engrained in everyone's thinking. We must always consider the major competitor to be the Office release that is already deployed and running.

It became increasingly apparent that our competition would be new tools and new ways to be productive. In detailing the competition, NRO described a new category of products known as *virtual office.* These products were web sites that promised to have all the files and other interesting project information readily available from anywhere on the internet from any PC with a browser, primarily focused on collaboration. Somewhat related was the new area called *software as a service* (a surprisingly early use of the term) which aimed to provide similar functionality but to offer it as a pay-for-use license hosted by an internet service provider or partner. Already the industry was split between on-premises and what would eventually be called cloud computing but known as *hosted* or sometimes *application service provider.*

> ***Virtual office products****. The area of virtual offices has garnered a lot of attention for both small businesses and large corporations. These products such as eRoom, IntraNetics, Netopia, Visto allow for group collaboration over a web site. They can be thought of as both software and a service and it is the fuzziness between the two ends of the spectrum that make these products interesting. In terms of the product, the need for teams to organize and create "places" for the work and results to live is not new, but the web makes this a more immediate need with a much clearer solution for customers. Everybody can imagine a home page for their project, but few can imagine how to create one or keep it up to date.*
>
> ***Software as a service****. The virtual office products are also offered as a service. Two that have received a lot of attention are HotOffice and Visto. Today these are all tend to focus on integrating Office's binary file formats and thus leave out the innovations in Office 2000. These services are clearly the value add that people are looking for-how can I share my files, how can I backup my important information, how can I have a secured customer relationship, etc. Another perspective on software as a service is the role of very targeted web sites that allow customers to create certain types of documents. For example, if you visit the Kinko's web site they have a multipage wizard that walks you through creating a draft of a resume that a Kinko's representative will then fully typeset for you. It is not hard to imagine an array of services like this perhaps all being offered under one umbrella at AOL for example.*

Over the subsequent months a growing set of program managers, then developers contributed to creating a product vision. The processes we used for Office 97 kicked into gear with much less fuss. There was almost no fuss at all. The lessons of building a team by forming, storming, norming, and performing were apparent.

That was within the Office team. Outside the team, it was proving much more difficult to arrive at a strategy that worked uniformly across the company. Partnering with one group would leave out a competing group. Aligning schedules with one product would preclude alignment with another. The crux of this alignment challenge was the server infrastructure which was also the lead dog in talking strategy with IT professionals. The constant pressure for one single answer, one product, one solution flew in the face of our disparate products, schedules, and technology approaches. And most of these did not align well with the rapidly expanding internet.

Every product was in early days of developing an internet strategy and was looking to develop that strategy by connecting to Windows or Office in order to design, develop, validate, and then distribute the product or more likely portion of a product such as APIs to be included as code shipped with Windows or Office. Across the company groups were always asked what work they were doing with Windows and Office. And Windows and Office were asked what they were doing with each other. The goal seemed to be to connect every team to each other team—just as we had joked about a few years earlier.

When it came to the internet, our Office strategy was to use HTML for Office files so they could be viewed in any browser, connecting to internet services for content like clip art and templates, and sharing files and collaborating with the web server tools based on FrontPage, which became *Office Server Extensions* which were implemented using standard web extensibility. We planned on an expansive role of the server extensions to build an "Office server" as we called it, a one-stop shop for all the collaboration needs for typical Office users. Many across the company looked at these technology bets and felt they were too open or did not represent a truly *better together* strategy with the rest of Microsoft, servers that longed for a world of tightly coupled and proprietary integration, while always promising a bit of openness. Enterprise customers were extremely skeptical of new internet technologies, viewing them as woefully inadequate for hardcore enterprise needs. Internet technologies were simply too immature, almost toys, compared to the industrial strength products the enterprise was just starting to deploy such as Windows Server, SQL Server, and Exchange.

Integrating with those servers epitomized this conflict—Exchange for email, SQL storing data, plain old Windows server for files and web serving, and even Internet Explorer connecting to those servers. BillG would constantly ask how there could be exactly one copy of a file on a network, no matter if it was mailed, used in a database, or stored on a team file server, not to mention a new web server. SteveB once cornered me in the cafeteria (this happened often) and scrambled to find something to write on (and settled on one of his business cards) to draw a picture of all the places he needed to look to find out "tell me what's going on in Microsoft France" and begged me to solve the "where do I go?" question. This problem persists.

While we were busy pondering unification, customers were making long-term, strategic choices and there was a *zero-sum, win now or forever lose information infrastructure* being laid down in corporate America. A loss to Netscape, Oracle, Sun, or IBM/Lotus was not just a loss for the quarter, but almost certainly a loss for a decade. The stakes could not be higher, and Microsoft was playing catch-up.

Pondering pure internet technologies could be construed as evidence undermining the goal of winning with integrated products. That is a dramatic way of saying what was going on—everyone wanted to build great products, but what defined great had many dimensions.

Many in the industry loathed proprietary approaches but at the same time sought the prescriptive and coherent strategic value a partner like Microsoft could provide, *especially* in a time of rapid change such as the internet was foisting on CIOs. The chaos of the internet was far more concerning than keeping promises of openness. In fact, there were clear signs that the standard-bearer torch was handed over to Microsoft from IBM and customers were seeking out Microsoft's guidance on how to implement IT. We were happy to oblige, just as we had hoped at the 1993 offsite where we role-played a world after IBM.

To most of the world of Fortune 500 CIOs, Microsoft was being looked to as a place of comfort and reliability, in a chaotic world. Microsoft had replaced IBM as the safe bet to make and many of the new generation of CIOs were betting their careers on Microsoft's strategy. The dividends of this change continue to pay off today.

Exemplifying this was the web server skirmish brewing between Windows and Linux—ground zero in the war over proprietary versus open-source software. This put Microsoft's soup to nuts approach to building web server infrastructure and tooling up against the chaotic but customizable and fast-moving Linux (and Apache) server community. In the first years while the web was being built out, Microsoft gained mindshare and product traction. Over time, however, new technology layers that were being used by startups and the broad public internet came to dominate. Microsoft ultimately lost the server battle with Linux, in the short term for web servers and in the long term when it came to the operating system for the cloud. Customers might say one thing in the short term but over time competitors often acquire the attributes that appear initially absent as early adopters iterate and build out a more complete and cohesive solution. As we will see, complexity was also a key culprit in our loss.

Competition between IBM/Lotus Notes and Microsoft Exchange was intense because of the millions of dollars at stake, but more importantly the winner was certain to cement email infrastructure for decades. This latter epic battle came to define Microsoft's enterprise culture. In hindsight, winning was also the defining product win for Microsoft in the enterprise—Exchange became proof of Active Directory and Windows Server, and with those pulled the whole client/server compute win to Microsoft. Client/server architected in this manner was relatively short-lived as the web dominated, but the long tail of the Exchange (and Outlook) win paid off for a generation. Even Microsoft's future in the cloud with Office 365 was anchored by Exchange in the cloud.

Email infrastructure was slow to move, the battle having started five or more years earlier. Beyond just email, IBM successfully continued to raise the enterprise discourse from email to *knowledge management*, consultant-speak for the kind of work done by most PC users that involved writing, analyzing, presenting, collaborating, and sharing information primarily with email and Office. IBM did a better job positioning Notes to use Office than we did using Exchange and Office, except for the role of Outlook. This battle was far from over. With Exchange a peer to Office in our organization, Exchange became the *right answer* for anything to do with collaboration—right with customers, the field, and product groups. The implication was that the web and HTML were decidedly wrong. Also, using SQL Server or the Windows NT file server was the wrong approach. Storing data in Exchange was the most strategic approach. Technically, however, it was way off base.

As was too often the case, the Office team found itself in the middle of internal strategy debates. While no one could dispute the importance of competing with Notes, how exactly to compete was at issue for the Server and Tools teams. Many of the server and database thought leaders, such as David Veskevitch (DavidV), believed strongly that competing with Notes meant using a real database not an email database, whatever that meant—a debate itself. SQL is an industry-standard for databases—literally every major computer system in the world from financial to retail to customer service was built with SQL, usually from Oracle and sometimes IBM, but not yet Microsoft. Winning the SQL market was as important to Microsoft's future as winning Exchange.

In other words, Microsoft enterprise server strategy required winning in both Exchange and SQL. There was an elegance to SQL architecture and scale that most found quite appealing. Others were equally attracted to the flexibility and lack of forced structure that email provided. BillG was a big fan of SQL, something that remained true for a long time. Not surprising, what Notes accomplished, through the brilliance of Ray Ozzie's architecture, was to develop a storage system that was a unique combination of attributes of both SQL and Exchange for storing data—called an *object-oriented database,* which by coincidence was what I had studied and built in graduate school. Because Notes was a hybrid, it landed squarely between the Exchange team and the SQL team, who routinely debated the merits of their approach to achieving competitive parity with Notes. Caught in the middle was Office, which was constantly being evangelized to support one or the other for the collaboration scenarios, and mostly to validate one product over another. In Office, however, we saw the choice of where to store data as an important implementation detail irrelevant to customers compared to solving the collaboration scenarios that were top of mind for us.

While this saga continued for 10 years at Microsoft, the first couple of years into it, Office made at least one wrong bet. There was a strong desire to see Outlook support SQL to store email, something Exchange did not yet do. At the same time some suggested using Exchange to store Office files for collaboration, something better suited to SQL as was done for the new OSE. In other words, it often seemed what the Server teams wanted was for us to do everything twice. To avoid going further into the weeds, I'm leaving out the fact that Outlook used only Exchange, and Excel and Access connected only to SQL. We frequently met with both teams trying to arrive at plans to unify in some future release—they were anxious to have the distribution of Outlook driving the use of and validating their server. To those readers deeply familiar with Microsoft's developer API strategy for data, the parade of data access APIs (ODBC, DAO, ADO, CDO, RDO, OLEDB, ADO.NET and more) were a symptom of this unification fiasco.

Outlook was the team that seemed to do everything twice. Making email, calendaring, scheduling, and more to work with Exchange consumed the team for almost six years and it was still fragile and unreliable. When it came to broadly competing with the IBM message of knowledge management, Outlook plus Exchange was not competitive with Notes because it was not a full database platform to build applications like expense reporting or information tracking solutions. To build those applications, IT needed a SQL database and it needed to be both on the Exchange server and on desktop Outlook—that symmetry was the Notes innovation. Since Exchange server did not run on a desktop (nor was it SQL) a new *Local Information Store* was being developed—yes, that same project from Office 2000 was revived to become a key part of Office10. *Local* because it ran on PCs (versus a server, which was remote) and *Information Store* referred to data storage, abbreviated LIS. LIS would finally make it possible for Exchange and Outlook to compete with Notes.

Still, we had to write down what we were going to do. The process for building a product was now something of a cultural touchstone for the Office team. The next step for us was to develop a product vision document—a list of priorities, a set of scenarios, detailed value propositions, and above all a schedule.

Input and strategic direction like this led to a complex and gerrymandered Office10 vision, which made it seem like we were doing everything twice. I felt stuck. The foundation was moving under us, whether it was Exchange or SQL or Windows NT file server. Collaboration, however, remained a key strategy bet for Office. The Enterprise Agreement selling motion required synergy and strategy across all of Microsoft, which ran right up against the Office view that customers *just wanted things to work.* A key challenge with strategy and unification is that most of our competitors did not have all these assets to coordinate and unify, making customer choice seem easier and more often than not the products seemed less complex. Little did we know directly, but at the time IBM was pushing this same level of unified strategy on our primary competitor, Lotus Notes. Over time, the Notes team found itself deep in execution challenges because of strategy initiatives.

In order to write the vision, we found ourselves pivoting the whole collaboration message around choice—customers could choose the infrastructure that worked right for them in their environment. Customers and industry analysts loved this kind of message. Customers always love choice because it is the opposite of lock-in. Industry analysts love choice because it creates an opportunity to help customers untangle the messy strategies of vendors.

In reality, choice is confusing because competing products are no substitute for each other even if an analyst says they are in the same category or *magic quadrant,* the tools used by the firm Gartner to explain relative strengths of vendor strategies. Beyond that, and it should be entirely obvious, a strategy based on multiple choice is wholly unworkable. Given two options to do something, customers will create a third option composed of the best attributes from the options. That third option will be impossible to build and thus out of the gate the product will be unsatisfactory.

The choices in the vision became *Office and Exchange for Corporate Groupware* and *Universal Web Documents and Web Sites*. Customers with Exchange got what they wanted through Outlook, unless they wanted something universal or they didn't have Exchange, and then they got the parallel implementation that happened to use SQL Server. Not surprisingly, customers preferred something like a *universal web with Exchange*, which didn't exist. This frustrated BobMu, so we incubated a third project to build web-based collaboration using Exchange, headed by the former head of Outlook development, Mike Koss (MikeKo), a pioneer Excel developer. It was not just words, but even within the Office product we were literally building many scenarios twice, with different and incompatible implementations.

It was a mess.

The team lacked clarity, and my primary job was to provide it. Everyone was nervous going into the release because the main pillars were so sloppy. The gerrymandered concept isolated the work on each of the three approaches to separate teams. In private, I was fairly convinced that only one approach would ship, and the web would win out, but could never have said such a thing that early.

It was messy for BillG, PaulMa, and BobMu as well—it was messy up the entire management chain. They were uncomfortable waiting for the work to get done when the new Exchange and other new servers were so close to shipping. Seemingly out of nowhere, there was a strong demand for a different product plan than we were closing in on.

I was enormously frustrated. Like every product-centric person I wanted a plan that was well-defined, tight, and efficient. The idea of duplicate solutions or scenarios was the opposite of unification that we so strived for. I would come to realize, partially through many conversations with BillG, such a perfect plan was also fragile and leaves little room for failed execution. I needed to get comfortable with a product plan that represented a portfolio of ideas. On the other hand, such an approach meant during development no one was sure where we would land, resulting in groups working against each other. It felt *Darwinian*. I did not like that. We had a way to move forward, and I needed to get comfortable in my own role as leader of ambiguity.

Then one day at a meeting I got asked point blank if Office could do a *quick* release of Office to synchronize with the new Exchange followed by an *even more strategic* release later? Crazy talk. This would have put Office on the two-release treadmill that was so common in Systems, so it was a reasonable ask from that perspective, ignoring that the second longer-term release never seemed to happen.

For a team having sworn off the idea of doing parallel releases *ever again,* this was a nightmare. For the execs, this type of planning and *doing* parallel releases was normal. It fell to me to somehow demonstrate that the second of the parallel releases never happened. While this was *their* culture, I felt a personal commitment to defending the, and now my, Office culture. The next Exchange scheduled to finish *soon* did not ship until months before the planned schedule of Office10 but spent most of Office10 trying to finish and unable to do new features that might help this strategy. The other servers were also late.

I spent most of the release defending our schedule.

To counter the complexity, the vision planned on more concrete areas, each to be stewarded by the appropriate leader on the team. Of note were two somewhat *classic* investments. First, *everyday tasks made easier through innovation* was our catchphrase used to get back in the personal productivity game—repayment for when I made "Personal Productivity priority number 6." In this area, AndrewK led the charge across the apps in toning down our approach to automatic features that got a bit out of control (the Smart Menus in Office 2000 that moved commands around unpredictably) and broadly adding a new user interface to present commands right when needed without having to navigate menus and toolbars. Office10, for the first time, shipped Microsoft-developed speech and handwriting recognition, incorporating pioneering work by Microsoft Research. These generated applause in demos, especially when reviewers considered their own use cases.

Second, *nailing the fundamentals* was a broad focus on product quality. Our experience with Office 2000 was that rallying the team around total cost of ownership (TCO) was boring and difficult to measure, but Microsoft culture loved performance. We rebranded TCO as fundamentals and it became a bit more interesting. In truth, enterprise-ready deployment (including *setup* and more) became a fundamental business need.

As a sign the product team was maturing, we rolled out the *Office10 Vision* with much less fanfare, and angst, than Office9. We held a team meeting with prototypes and fast-paced slides from each of the leaders. Everyone on the team received a one-page printout with the key product plans and a mock press release announcing the availability of Microsoft Office10 on "3/2/01," ushering in a product cycle dominated by themes of rockets blasting off. Antoine and GrantG signed up to land this release on time. Antoine, finally, moved over to OPU to lead development after successfully leading Word 2000.

We changed the structure of the schedule to have only two development milestones, each 12 weeks duration rather than three shorter ones. The complexity that it required to exit, and then enter, a milestone grew over time, and we felt we could get more done if people worked longer, and continuously. We built on a growing *maturing* of the organization that kept the product in a working state and continuously integrated new code into daily builds.

With the completion of the vision, AndrewK chose to focus on features for end-users and joined a newly created team to build worldwide internet-connected features for all customers, marking the first time we built features assuming an internet connection. Obvious in hindsight, but at the time we even came up with new wording on the product box to explain that internet connectivity with a modem might be required.

HeikkiK stepped up to lead Office-wide program management. His no-nonsense shipping sensibility and embrace of enterprise customers further solidified the intent of the product and the culture of PM.

Work began with an incredible focus on shipping. The intense friction across the team over the shared work in Office versus the apps largely receded. I faced a new kind of stress, and that was all the strategy going on across the rest of Microsoft.

The team finally graduated from storming and forming to norming and even performing.

059. SCALING…EVERYTHING

Increasingly, our newly minted enterprise customers grew frustrated with Microsoft's readiness as an enterprise partner. When an enterprise customer is frustrated, they describe the company as a vendor rather than a partner. A vendor is what we used to be, or so we thought. We had to up our game.

Customers were sitting on a mismatched pile of software from Microsoft, some of which was by all accounts being ignored by us in the product groups. There were ATMs running OS/2, which we long ago turned over to IBM. Banks in Europe were running Word and Excel on OS/2, which we made as essentially a one-off. One of the leading business magazines had a publishing system that used Word 2.0 and Windows 3.0, from the early 1990s. That was 8 years ago, an infinity in software years. We had moved on from those products. Our customers had not.

Business is business and Microsoft needed to change. While it took us more than a year of meetings, in 2002 we finally announced a *Support Lifecycle Policy.* To much press and customer outreach we announced that Microsoft products would now have a minimum of five years of product support. In the Microsoft blog post describing the new policy, the CVP Product Support Services, Lori Moore (LoriM), explained that we "worked closely with customers, business and industry partners, leading analysts, and research firms." Noticeably absent from that were the product groups that would be on the hook to deliver bug fixes and updates to customers covered by Software Assurance or Enterprise Agreements as part of this new policy.

It should be no surprise then that Microsoft's fully distributed and empowered product groups interpreted this policy with differing levels of enthusiasm. Did it apply retroactively? What about products designed for consumers? What if we have multiple releases over five years? What if product releases took more than five years? What if Exchange has one interpretation and Outlook another? The intended effect of this effort was to do good by enterprise customers.

Instead, it was just an early step in making the transition to a new operating model. Customers interpreted the Lifecycle as a license to deploy what they could or would and then freeze the infrastructure for at least five years. Imagine in our fast-changing technology world, just freezing a company's information infrastructure. Five years was the minimum. Customers could even buy longer support contracts and they did so in droves. It meant that even five years from now, product groups were on the hook to support products that no one was actively working on.

That said, in Office we created a team that grew significantly over-time of full-time engineers dedicated to what we termed sustaining engineering. The team, Microsoft Office Sustaining Engineering (MOSE), originally envisioned by Excel test manager Carl Tastevin (CarlT) and then led for many years by former Word test manager Jeanne Sheldon (JeanneS), prided itself on being a direct connection to customers. They would spend the time to understand the context and customer environment driving problems and were reliably the best source of information anywhere for how the product was performing in the market with customers. The team was not an outsource model for quality and fixes because the product team developers that created the problems were accountable for fixes. It was a fantastic model for us and one we would later replicate in Windows which had gone full outsourcing after Windows XP shipped, which turned out to be less than ideal.

It would not take long, not even eighteen months, and the policy would again be updated. The feedback was less than positive on the first policy, mostly because it was uneven across the company and hardly long enough compared to traditional enterprise partners. This time the product groups were deeply involved in the process, in what grew to a major corporate undertaking. Since the first announcement, most teams released major new products, and all had built out engineering teams that were able to handle the new volume of support issues from enterprise customers. I attended many of the meetings of the product leaders who were trying to agree on a more uniform policy. The group was working well together but not converging. Microsoft's multiple billion-dollar businesses each serving distinct customer types and each with substantially different release schedules were struggling to arrive at a more uniform policy that was also longer. Some product groups aimed for very long support terms and others wanted nothing to do with previously released products. Office was in the middle. The position depended entirely on the primary buyer such as IT professionals, OEMs, or general corporate buyers.

In a moment of frustration for how long this was dragging out, I, probably the most senior product group person in the room, suggested (with some force) we should all settle on a ten-year support offering. This would make customers happy and would put this issue to rest. Our competition, such as IBM, supported products for decades. How much support would customers really expect nine or ten years from now for a product long forgotten? What a huge mistake I made. In hindsight, I was intoxicated with the idea of making sure the field (and SteveB) knew we "got it" in the product groups and also over-confident with the idea that we could execute on such a commitment. I really can't believe I thought this was a good idea—not only for Microsoft but for customers to rely on it. Think of all that changed ten years prior or all that would change from 2000 to 2010, especially considering how most customers were still far away from deploying email and the internet. Yet, SteveB and the field support and sales teams were incredibly happy and thankful for the teamwork and support from the product groups it took to make the updated policy a reality. Ten years.

You could feel the bubbles and the froth everywhere as the end of the millennium approached in the Fall of 1999.

Microsoft was in the midst of an all-out frenzy of activity in late 1999. First and foremost, the company's main business drivers were firing on all cylinders. Combined, Windows and Office were on pace for almost $18 billion in revenue and enormously profitable. Microsoft was growing at a rate of nearly 30 percent per year in revenue and would end the year with over $20 billion in cash on hand—truly unfathomable numbers. Wall Street responded with an unheard-of market valuation of over $600 billion and a position as one of the (if not the) world's largest and most successful companies. BillG's wealth was valued at over $100 billion dollars, personally.

The Microsoft vision was expansive. No software escaped Microsoft's attempts to enter and redefine a market with PCs and software. It was a crazy time. Anything that came up in the news or could be read about had a project and team somewhere at Microsoft working on it.

As if that wasn't enough, the burgeoning online division spun out home-grown Expedia as a separate company with an initial public offering that leaped 282 percent on the first day of trading. Microsoft acquired LinkExchange for $250 million to bolster online advertising. The Applications and Tools Group, of which Office was a part, acquired Seattle neighbor Visio, makers of a business drawing application, for *one point five billion* dollars, making the previously huge Vermeer acquisition look trivial. When we weren't making money, we were spending it. New buildings were going up. Morale events, offsites, and endless ship meals (for all those late products) were getting more elaborate. Unopened PCs laid in hallways waiting for new hires to show up. Servers piled up in our ever-expanding online data centers waiting to be racked and stacked.

The focus on the enterprise was paying off handsomely and we were in middle of a profitable and maturing PC era. Growth in units and revenue for Windows and Office were not slowing, but the revenue growth outside of those was increasing faster. BillG recognized this, and in the early fall 1999 authored a widely distributed memo with the priorities for the following year. Windows 2000 was the priority, and it was going to ship *real soon*. It shipped to customers six months later. The other priority was what Bill was referring to *software as a service* in a September 1999 email to all employees with the subject "Changing the World Together":

> *The other very significant focus for us in the years ahead will be providing software as a service. This won't in any way change our commitment to the PC. But adding to that focus, we will be developing exciting new technologies to provide software as a service across a range of devices in the enterprise, to small business and to consumers. The goal is to maximize simplicity, flexibility, manageability and responsiveness to customer needs and interests. Software as a service reflects a fundamental change in the way we will be designing, integrating, deploying, licensing and supporting technologies, so there's lots of exciting work ahead.*

In terms of history, while IBM leased software for years, the phrase was first used by BillG in reference to the company strategy and quickly followed up by articles describing this across major news outlets. Silicon Valley was using the phrase *Application Service Provider* or *On-demand Software.*[16]

It was not lost on me that Bill's memo did not mention Office. Office was fading into the background as senior executive leadership was increasingly formed from Windows and Server alumni. In a big company when the most profitable and highest revenue team doesn't get a shout-out, people notice. The team noticed. I do not think the omission was intentional, but rather a byproduct of where he was focused and was spending time.

The early projects for software as a service were incubated by a cross-section of systems and online services senior architects and engineers. Across the company we had countless offsites, meetings, memos, slide decks, and more working to develop a plan, all while the Office team was busy planning and executing a new release of Office while most of the company was just finishing releases. In many ways the first software as a service efforts followed the *Innovator's Dilemma* playbook by not sharing connections to the main product groups. For time being these incubations were under the radar, but that would change soon enough—Microsoft couldn't help itself.

Notably absent from the flurry of activity were competitive concerns. Microsoft appeared to have won the battles that a just couple of years earlier seemed existential. The internet did not end up dominating Microsoft's traditional business, but rather Microsoft's traditional business morphed into internet businesses; Wall Street certainly thought so. Windows laptops became the preferred gateway to the internet for consumers, with AOL purchasing

Netscape for $4.2 billion on the heels of poorly received products, such as Netscape 4.0 compared to a winning Microsoft Internet Explorer 4.0. Windows NT Servers (eventually updated to Windows 2000) were becoming a corporate standard. Nobody else was making much of a dent in the Office business—not Office competitors, Java, components, or in the browser space. Sun even acquired a clone of Office, a Win32 suite of desktop apps, and then subsequently made it available for free, yet even that was not having an impact.

The antitrust cases continued, but day to day this was a matter for the legal team and not the product groups. The business press heralded Microsoft's success as one of the great turnarounds of business history, a pivot, as in *Microsoft pivoted to an internet focus.*

One layer below all of this was a significantly different story.

Microsoft's success in transitioning to internet technologies was financially successful but strategically weak. Microsoft lost the mindshare of developers—while Windows was a great place to run a browser, it was no longer the preferred platform for writing software. Microsoft was using many internet standards, such as HTML and HTTP, but our influence on those standards was minimal.

It is abundantly clear today as I write this, that the decline of relevance of Win32 as a developer strategy began as early as the early 2000s. Except for the big software companies like Adobe and Autodesk, and the vast array of line of business client-server applications written by in-house IT, there just weren't any new and exciting applications written for Windows natively. Windows Server was new, but again never really saw a level of investment in unique apps on par with expectations, especially compared to the internet. The most exciting developments going on were browsers, web servers, and software built on those, and there was little at all specific to Windows. It was just that at the time and for the next five years or so most everyone happened to run Windows and Windows Server, giving the appearance of a vibrant Windows ecosystem. There is a subtle but important difference between success and relevancy in the technology world.

Windows Server was great for sharing files and printers inside the confines of a company, but the product was failing in the world of web sites and *hosted services*, even with significant marketing and programmatic support—today we call this *cloud computing*, but back then we called it *ASPs or ISPs* (internet service providers) or just *hosters*. The challenges didn't stop with the operating system. The server programming models used on any of the exciting new consumer web services were not using Windows. Our own Hotmail continued to resist the Windows platform. Even among the best LORG customers, Windows Servers were mostly used internally, and Linux, a free implementation of the Unix operating system from another era, was the preferred operating system for corporate internet sites, especially commerce and commercial sites. There were strong architectural and technical reasons, limitations, and costs associated with Windows, that facilitated the rise of Linux. Microsoft's existing business made it impossible to compete with free without taking a major hit to revenue, or so the logic went.

MSN (short for the Microsoft Network), a collection of web-based information services emanating from RedWest (Redmond West Campus), was front and center of the industry, but the financial losses kept mounting with no end in sight. In this sense, Microsoft was consistent with the rest of the internet world. Internet competitors weren't making a lot of money, especially in comparison to Windows, Server, and Office. For example, market-leading and era-defining Yahoo booked about $600 million in revenue in 1999 while losing money to being marginally profitable—it was unclear whether that concerned or excited us.

Microsoft's enormous success selling a business vision was hiding the fact that these core products were failing in equipping the new internet platform. While Microsoft was making the most money, the internet was increasingly being run and programmed using non-Microsoft and, worse, free technologies.

Nothing made these aggregate challenges clearer than the enormous COMDEX tradeshow (historically an abbreviation of COMputer Dealers' Exhibition) in November 1999. It was perhaps the largest tradeshow event ever at the time and still a record-holder in the United States. The show had come a long way since the *Halt and Catch Fire* era just 15 years earlier. Every hotel room, convention space, and taxi were fully occupied for the week. The convention was electric, and massively, painfully crowded.

A funny thing happened as over 220,000 people made their way there that year: PCs became somewhat irrelevant. If this sounds frustrating, surprising, or even puzzling it was. Those very feelings consumed me as I definitely did not think we had ceased to be interesting or that the business we were in was boring.

The *consumer internet* took over COMDEX. Historically, the PC had been the heart and soul of COMDEX, but it suddenly faded in importance, and with it so did COMDEX. This marked the biggest and, effectively, the last of the show, as all the major PC makers left the following year. So, it goes. The Consumer Electronics Show, CES, would become the go to show as COMDEX sputtered.

I saw the rise of the consumer internet during frequent trips to Silicon Valley and to PowerPoint, the 1987 acquisition that was based in Silicon Valley (with offices on Sand Hill Road no less) and remained there, never relocating to Redmond. The billboards on Silicon Valley's highway 101 shifted away from networking and databases, the foundations of client-server, to the likes of Flooz, Pets.com, and Excite. These were the precursors to the dot-com bubble and the stock market crash that was still months away. Seattle wasn't immune. Seattle's newly hip Belltown neighborhood (where I had moved to a new apartment) was constantly circled by Webvan.com grocery delivery vehicles and one building was painted with what became an infamous logo for MyLackey.com, a concierge service summoned by a website with a retro-butler graphic.

The dot-com era was not about enterprise software but about consumer services delivered over the web. PCs were too complicated, and the industry, as I witnessed at COMDEX, was responding with a sea of *internet appliances* that were simpler, easier, and more reliable to use than PCs. The market spoke. PCs were too complex and bloated for the new *e-conomy*.

The result was that BillG's keynote at COMDEX that year was all the more divergent. He spoke at length about Windows 2000 and Office 2000 improving reliability and getting work done, topics for the most part lost on the audience and even the press. Microsoft was not immune from the consumer internet though, building on WebTV, an acquisition Microsoft made in the appliance category. I was a huge champion of it, having been an early adopter and buying them for family. Microsoft introduced *MSN Companion*, an internet appliance for connecting to the internet over a phone line much like the dozens of devices on the tradeshow floor. The device ran Windows CE, a subset of 16-bit Windows that was about to become legacy code that ran on microprocessors from ARM. Compaq, eMachines, and others manufactured the devices, licensing the software from Microsoft in a business model (and code base) that presaged how Microsoft would enter the mobile phone business. These non-PC devices as we called them were big news.

MSN Companion came from the Online Services division. Microsoft, historically two cultures of Apps and Systems, spawned a third—Online Services, Microsoft's foray into the consumer internet. As if to further emphasize the cultural divide, the online groups were located in a new campus, RedWest, about a mile down the street from the main campus. The brick buildings, identified by letters and surrounded by streams and pathways, were in contrast with the utilitarian stucco facades of the main campus with the lone Lake Bill in a near random series of numbered buildings.

The Online world was indeed a new culture, even though so many on the team came from Apps and Systems. There was arguably a degree of superiority emanating from RedWest, or perhaps inferiority from main campus. Everything seemed more exciting. Everything seemed more relatable to friends and family. Celebrities routinely visited RedWest and these visits were dutifully covered in *MicroNews*, the employee newsletter that eventually became an online intranet site. RedWest was to old-timers everything that the previous Consumer Division hoped to be, but instead of CD-ROMs it was web sites.

No surprise, the PC presence at COMDEX was brutal. I walked the show floor, systematically as usual. It was much more crowded than expected though the contrast from the previous year could not have been more dramatic. The effort to equip booths with *Windows 2000 Ready* signage was hopeless because the booths running Windows were on variants of Windows 95 for compatibility or simply because of laziness, as the much beefier Windows 2000 was still in pre-release and had been under development for so long most stopped paying attention. In fairness, Windows 2000 was not aimed at consumers, but at businesses—a necessary narrowing of focus due to the consumer hardware ecosystem that remained unsupported. Productivity tools such as printers were repurposed to show printing photos or CD labels. Email was shown but only when running on new internet appliances. Even digital signs that used to be PowerPoint running in loops were replaced by a new favorite gadget, digital picture frames that were all running Linux and the latest ones natively connected to the internet.

Back in Redmond, after COMDEX, Microsoft was better able to compartmentalize the ongoing challenges. External stimuli can be disorienting if you're a giant, successful company that has just successfully transitioned to a new era. At least that was what the press was telling us. And we believed them.

A favorite saying of mine is from Hemingway's *The Sun Also Rises*:

> *"How did you go bankrupt?" Bill asked.*
>
> *"Two ways," Mike said. "Gradually and then suddenly."*

This is how technology change (or bankruptcy or disruption) happens to the successful. At first, changes take place slowly and mostly go unnoticed. In reality, they do not go unnoticed, but rather, they seem insignificant—especially in a large company where there is always someone shouting or emailing that "the sky is falling." To paraphrase a line from the 1984 film *The Adventures of Buckaroo Banzai Across the 8th Dimension*: "No matter what happens, someone always said it would." It seemed there were quite a few people readying themselves to be able to say, "I told you so." Memos were flying around, and choice quotes from *Innovator's Dilemma* made their way into every slide deck. Every week someone would pull something out of their *Sent Items* folder to remind others of their predictive wisdom.

Then much further out in time than anyone thought, the accumulation of these small, unnoticed changes pile up and compound into a huge, seemingly unstoppable wave. When faced with these small changes, the natural reaction is to look inward, brushing them off as…small and insignificant. There's always plenty to do, and usually that seems really important, and customers are demanding it. The outside world is shut out and the focus turns to self-determined goals and activities. You enter a bubble. It is a really big $500 billion bubble, but a bubble.

I constantly worried about the increasing distance between what we were doing and what seemed interesting to the world beyond Microsoft and business customers.

For us, it was the constant drumbeat of enterprise customers that was difficult to match. Microsoft expanded to tens of thousands of enterprise sales and support personnel in a strong, aggressive, and empowered field organization, a number that greatly outnumbered the product team. On the Office team, about 200 people were in the position to interact effectively with sales and customers, but they were busy designing, building, and marketing Office and customer demands greatly exceeded our capacity to interact.

It is a cliché to read business books and hear of success stories about product teams that get close to customers. I dove headfirst into every book I could find on learning from customers—from *In Search of Excellence* and *Crossing the Chasm* to books about customer-obsessed companies like *Wal-Mart* and *General Electric*. I quickly learned that those were almost always stories that did not have a natural analog with Microsoft's products. Our products were complicated, like IBM or GE products, but they were used directly and differently by hundreds of millions of people. Even if a large company used Office, within the company Office was used as though each customer was unique.

The challenge we faced was that the Systems approach much more closely resembled the IBM or GE model of listening to customers, and the field loved that. While each MRI machine might be used and configured differently, there are only thousands of them in the United States. Each email server installation of Exchange had many unique elements, but there were only hundreds of them at the time. Product groups like Exchange were the same size or bigger than Office but could easily develop high-touch relationships with the largest customers, and further support those with the dedicated field support being built up around the world. Even Windows had a *level of indirection* in that by and large the view of being close to customers from the Windows team meant being close to the 10 major computer makers, not to hundreds of millions of new PC buyers. The PC makers even handled the cost burden of offering customer support for Windows.

By contrast, Office was not only unique at the company level, but each company might have dozens of configurations, plus each individual might have a different type of PC, and certainly might have different software, printers, or other peripherals. It was the use cases that grew rapidly—companies generally converged on best practices for using and managing servers, but when it came to Office, diversity was the rule and hands-off was the support policy.

That was our strength. The Office team embraced that. The rest of Microsoft, especially field sales and the server products, did not see things the same way.

The lack of direct enterprise engagement looked like Office not listening to its customers, and that was a constant tension on the team and between organizations. We (specifically, me) were not quick to jump to the customer crisis of the moment or to dedicate resources to understanding the latest hot customer scenario or problem. There was always a desire to dedicate resources as a show of customer love. At any given time, there were thousands of these that we knew about, and countless individuals struggling somehow with the product.

By listening to what percolated through support or executive escalation, we risked having the product team be driven by anecdote and squeaky wheel. Customers and partners were rewarded if they escalated, no matter what connection they would use. Every time SteveB or a senior exec returned from visits with the field, the escalations would follow. I always knew who was visiting customers as a trail of emails would land in my inbox.

Office continued to maintain the highest satisfaction ratings among products (and among product development teams), a fact I resorted to sharing. The brand consistently stood for "ease of use" in the eyes of customers. We continued to win head-to-head reviews. The Office Advisory Council, OAC, was our key enterprise customer learning tool and our OAC members loved the depth of engagement.

Becoming an enterprise company was a journey. In the late 1990s, the enterprise companies were Netscape, IBM, Oracle, Sun, HP, and SAP, and in Japan companies like Fujitsu, NEC, and Hitachi ruled the landscape. Wall Street made up fun names for these two groups. *NOISE* referred to the US companies Netscape, Oracle, IBM, Sun, and *everybody else*. The Japanese tech industry referred to *FNH* for Fujitsu, NEC, and Hitachi. Take that *FAANG*. Microsoft was not a consumer company but more of a vendor to enterprise companies than a partner, especially Office. In a sense, Office became part of the enterprise fabric or infrastructure but not part of enterprise decision-making.

One view was that we were not invested in the dialogue. We were, though not with every customer and that was a problem.

Another view, and what I believed, was that the dialogue was about server infrastructure and Office was personal productivity. The IT world was about servers, just as they were about mainframes. They viewed the desktop as far less strategic. Servers were strategic buys. Office was a must-have, but also a transactional purchase, except for Outlook which was strongly connected to Exchange Server. IT provided email as a service to employees, so it was held in high regard.

The question was whether my view was limiting, convenient, or expansive.

Starting with Y2K planning early in 1999, company-wide efforts on building enterprise trust dramatically increased. The company was rapidly shifting. In SteveB's words, we were out there "selling what we built" as enterprise salespeople, but we needed to "build what we could sell" as enterprise product makers.

With SteveB's appointment to CEO in 2000, Microsoft was, as he said, "all in" on enterprise. BillG was completely and deeply engaged in the design of future products as Chief Software Architect (CSA), his newly created title. Our company-wide processes from planning to budgeting, and especially marketing, changed dramatically with the shift to enterprise leadership. SteveB was the sales leader and that permeated company operations.

The implications were broad. Aside from choosing features that enterprise customers valued, several separate yet significant enterprise-level *initiatives* were in flight, and each required cross-company product team collaboration and a connection to the global sales and support teams. While any might have taken place before (and many did), with SteveB as CEO these had sales urgency and top-down processes. I could see in all the communications an element of "as chartered by SteveB" or "we committed to get back to SteveB in 120 days" as, let's say, reinforcement. Taken together they presented an opportunity for Office (and me) to be seen as an equal partner to enterprise customers along with Server teams.

These initiatives included getting ready for the changeover to Y2K, improving PC security, privacy, viruses, malware, crashes, and reliability, and the previously described support policy. These special projects were happening in parallel with building Office10 and stretched through the next release as well.

The Y2K changeover mobilized just about everyone at Microsoft as we saw across the entire tech landscape. Microsoft was almost giddy in preparation. We seized on the opportunity to have a crisis that seemed like a fun technical puzzle. Every product we released going as far back as you could imagine, and every company system were exhaustively tested and verified. We had a Y2K operations center, complete with generators and food supplies. Every communication system was made redundant for the rollover. What seemed at first to be a big headache was kind of fun for everyone that spent a year in preparation. The virtual team took great pride in tracking down obscure products and finding compliance issues, documenting them as part of the elaborate classification of Y2K readiness. Microsoft was as surprised as anyone that the new millennium got off to a glitch-free start.

Microsoft already had a few run-ins with regulators regarding privacy of early online services, but the growing internet was creating a whole new set of concerns especially when considering some of the services we were running at massive scale such as Hotmail. Similarly, computer viruses that were once nothing more than an annoyance had become business critical problems. The next section is dedicated to the history and building a company-wide response to this challenge.

Y2K was one class of potential bug, but in practice our products had not made much progress in terms of quality over the past ten years. Office was incredibly solid, but if there was a problem then invariably all the customer's work was lost. Such catastrophic loss was very bad for one consumer but entirely unacceptable to enterprise customers. Server products had their challenges with scale, configuration, and network management. Windows made significant improvements going from the 16-bit to the new 32-bit code base, but for new computers Windows 2000 lacked support for most consumer software and required more memory and disk space than PC price points could support. In a follow-on section, the innovations Microsoft introduced that radically changed not just our products but how developers thought of using the internet to improve software quality and reliability will be detailed.

Working on each of these brought a level of cooperation and collaboration across the company that we had not seen previously. Soon we were sharing best practices and thinking more broadly about how to be proper engineers more than hackers. As one indication of the importance of this change, JonDe, who had led Office for so long, would take on a broad role of creating an *Engineering Excellence* organization to formalize this type of cross-company maturing.

Individually, each of these initiatives seemed, especially in hindsight, seemed trivial or even obvious and basic work we should have been doing all along. It wasn't so simple. So much was going on and everything was happening so fast, with so much potential for failure on much larger issues, that it took time to catch up to understanding the situation. From a team perspective, these were milestones or perhaps tests on the journey moving from products for tech enthusiasts to a platform for enterprise computing. Taken together, these represented a step-function change in the perception and reality of product quality and business readiness. Tech enthusiasts were not only more tolerant of these product quality issues but often embraced the foibles and prided themselves on knowing the ins and outs of products. On the other hand, LORGs were not only less appreciative of what they termed product *defects* but pointed to the very existence of them as proof that Microsoft was not ready, or even capable, of serving the enterprise. Industry analysts chided Microsoft for a lack of enterprise chops and often scored products lower because of this.

The special cross-company projects were meant to serve customers and were decidedly strategic for our existing customers. At the same time, they were not going to address the potential disruption from the changes we saw at COMDEX. It was easy to look inward, but I tended to view these as essentially taxes on the team. All "just work," as we said. Others with a more near-term focus viewed these as innovation in the context of enterprise.

We were both right. We were both also wrong.

We needed to walk and chew gum at the same time. That need was not always clear. But more often, the whole of Microsoft was still more focused on these activities rather than what might happen in a few years.

060. ILOVEYOU

One morning during the first week of May of the new millennium, I received a call at my apartment while I was getting ready for work. I heard a reporter tell me their name, and then listened to hyperventilating and (apparently) proclaiming their love for me repeatedly, "I love you. I love you."

That's what I heard, anyway. The call. A reporter. Early morning. It was all weird.

Unfortunately, LOVE broke out all over the internet. Over the span of a weekend, inboxes around the world of Outlook and Exchange email users were inundated with dozens of copies of email messages with the subject line, "ILOVEYOU."

I learned from the reporter that the LOVE email incident was deemed so serious that the PR lead gave them my home number and simultaneously sent me a briefing via email. In the era of dial-up, I could not read the email and talk on the phone because I only had one analog phone line at home. I had no idea what was going on, so I agreed to return the call after I dialed up and downloaded my email.

That's when I realized the magnitude of the issue.

For all the positives of the PC in business, IT professionals still wrestled with the freedom of PCs, not only the freedom to create presentations and spreadsheets but the freedom to potentially wreak havoc on networks of connected PCs because of computer viruses. Viruses were hardly new, part of PCs from the earliest days. As a new hire in the Apps Development College training, I completed a unit on early MS-DOS viruses. The combination of many more PCs in the workplace, networking, and then email created a new opportunity for those wishing to do harm with viruses. By their nature, and by analogy to the word *virus*, most viruses are not fatal to a PC, but they could cause significant damage, loss of time, and take a good deal of effort to clean up.

By the late 1990s even amongst government and academia, the risk posed by viruses to the nation's infrastructure were front and center. Fred B. Schneider, a Cornell faculty member, and former sponsor of our chapter of Association of Computer Science Undergraduates, chaired a working committee going back to 1996 on the topic of *trustworthy information system*. The word trustworthy will make an appearance in much of Microsoft's reaction to the stories shared here. The committee included faculty from many universities and representatives from across industry, including Microsoft's George Spix (GSpix.) The work was convened by Computer Science and Technical Communications Board of the National Research Council whose members included Butler Lampson (BLampson), Jim Gray (Gray) and Ray Ozzie. The effort resulted in a 300-page report that was widely influential, once the commercial world caught up with these challenges.

Enterprise IT was increasingly uneasy about viruses and had the expectation that Microsoft must do something. The openness of the PC platform was a hallmark feature responsible for the utility and breadth of the PC ecosystem, even if some *bad actors* (as they were called) might exploit that openness. Microsoft took a *laissez-faire* approach to this annoyance.

Office shared this permissive attitude until the mid-1990s and the rise of networks when sharing files became common. With everyone connected, an annoyance morphed into a virus that shared itself automatically between computers. A virus infected Microsoft Word 6.0 called *WM/Concept.A*—viruses often had cryptic names. In this case the WM stood for Word Macro, and presumably Concept referred to the fact that this was testing a new concept for viruses.

This was a new type of virus. It did not exploit bugs or programming mistakes in Word. Concept used Word *macros* as they were designed. Macros were present in software for ages, going as far back to the MS-DOS days of WordPerfect and Lotus 1-2-3. Macros, called *programmability* or *extensibility* in Microsoft lingo, were a prized accomplishment and something BillG believed in pushing extensibility for all products. Programmability made a product sticky when customers invested time and effort to write macros. Macros were used to automate repetitive tasks, for example, if a company wrote similar letters to customers for past due notices, one could write a macro, which generated letters with all the right address fields and salutations. Another example might be to automate collecting sources in a document and creating a bibliography. The uses for macros were endless and an entire industry developed consulting and training in Word automation. Word macros used a derivative of BASIC.

Some macros were written to automatically run as soon as a file was opened, making systems appear more automatic to end-users. The WM/Concept.A virus took advantage of a combination of features to create an exceedingly simple and yet maximally annoying experience including macros, automatic start-up, and networked file sharing.

The original author of WM/Concept.A probably crafted a tantalizing document with the virus and shared it on a network knowing others would open the document, sort of a patient zero. Once anyone opened that document, every document they created or opened became infected. Any document they shared became infected and infected every PC that opened that document. Like the old shampoo commercial, "...and they told two friends, and they told two friends, and so on, and so on." Well, that is exactly what happened. WM/Concept.A circled the globe relentlessly.

Contrary to what was commonly believed, successful viruses didn't usually do anything harmful like delete all your files or format your hard drive. If they did, the viruses failed to spread and serve their purpose. WM/Concept.A did only one annoying thing other than propagate, and that was to display a message that looked like a broken Word error message—a simple window with the character "1" and button labeled "OK." That was it. The message showed up once during the initial infection.

While there was no direct harm to PCs or any documents, the obvious implications of this *Concept* virus were that viruses could easily spread and, if the author wished, could do significant harm or at the very least truly interrupt workflow, and at most, do heinous things like delete text at random times or worse. Removing WM/Concept.A from an infected system was a chore. A cottage industry of virus removal and disinfecting was born, as was a cottage industry of using the Concept techniques to do more harm.

With this virus, General Manager of Word, PPathe (Blue), decided to take the first steps on Microsoft's antivirus crusade. Blue and team changed the way macros worked. They added a warning noting that a document contained a macro installed, and also made it more difficult to run macros automatically when simply opening documents.

These were small steps and were, in spite of the awfulness of WM/Concept.A, greeted with much pushback by fans of Word and IT managers because these changes *broke* business systems and workflows. Blue stood his ground and Microsoft's PSS team proactively worked with customers to get the word out, so to speak.

WM/Concept.A was our first lesson in the incredible balance between building an extensible and customizable system and the need to maintain security and reliability on PCs, and how customers push back when making products more secure means making changes in how they work. But the virus scared me in a much broader way. I wrote another frantic twenty-page memo, *Unsafe at Any Megahertz*. The title was a reference to the Ralph Nader book that shook up the auto industry in the 60s. It was meant to be a call to action for our product engineering. The software industry grew up from the counterculture 1960's. Steve Jobs wore no shoes. Bill Gates hacked his high school computer system. Both were college dropouts. What the PC industry lacked was any formal notion of what it meant to be a software engineer. My clarion call was that our lack of formalism, reproducibility, and external validation would only result in heavy-handed government regulation. I pondered a sort-of *Underwriters Laboratory* for software. That would be scary. I never sent the memo for fear it would be viewed as just too controversial in a company and industry that was the epitome of informal. Instead, the memo was a good exercise for me in *writing is thinking* and it made me double-down on how Office would operate with respect to product quality.

The ability for *bad actors* or even pranksters to wreak havoc on the growing and newly connected PC infrastructure became a major liability for Microsoft. Yet our products were behaving exactly as designed and customers appreciated those design patterns—extensibility was a major selling point of Office and a major part of our product and engineering efforts. As soon as we introduced the functionality changes, new viruses were created that circumvented what protections were in place.

While in the midst of creating the vision for Office10 in early 1999, our PR firm, Waggener Edstrom (often called *WaggEd*), received an inbound request from John Markoff of *The New York Times*. Markoff was one of the most respected reporters in technology with a deep history in reporting on all aspects of the industry, especially on intensely technical topics. He received broad acclaim for two books on hacker culture and in particular the effort that led to the identification and capture of Kevin Mitnick, who was convicted of several computer-related crimes.

In our case, Markoff inquired about a feature in Office 97, Office 2000, and a related feature in Windows 98. He was following a tip he received, which we later learned was from a programmer, well known to Microsoft, who built tools for MS-DOS. He was told that documents created with those versions of Office seemed to have been stamped with what the tipster referred to as a "digital fingerprint." Related to this, it appeared as though the programmer discovered that Windows 98 was also creating what amounted to a fingerprint for an entire PC using similar technology. The combination meant both documents and PCs seemed to have fingerprints.

Kim Bouic (w-kimb, now Barsi) of Waggener Edstrom called me right away. Kim was the PR executive leading the Office business and was exceptional at handling crisis situations like this. On the one hand, she talked me down from lecturing reporters about how they didn't understand, and on the other gently reminded reporters that things might be more complex than they seemed. Her skills were needed more than ever as "digital fingerprint" was rapidly becoming a crisis.

Markoff was chasing two lines of inquiry and they were leading to the same conclusion, which was that Microsoft created some sort of fingerprint or serial number in Windows and Office—if so, this constituted a major risk to privacy because documents and computers could be traced using this technology. As if this weren't enough, Intel announced the new Pentium III chip and it contained a unique serial number, which Intel said was for security use but fed right into the narrative of serial numbers for tracking PCs. To make this all the more ominous, in one of the early discussions with Markoff on Windows someone referred to the technology as a GUID (pronounced goo-id), an acronym for *globally unique identifier*.

Big Brother was suddenly part of the story.

GUID was the name of the Windows functionality that did, in fact, create what was intended to be a unique number—something useful for a broad range of programming tasks. The origins of Microsoft GUIDs were buried deep within the system but the value of a number that was for all practical purposes unique beat people trying to create a number on their own, something that eluded computer scientists for years—in fact, the origins of GUIDs went back at least to early 1980s Open Software Foundation work and were originally called UUIDs, for *universally unique identifiers*. To create the unique number, the GUID creation function combined several pieces of information. One of them was the serial number of a network card called the *MAC address,* which was relatively unique and required for networking. That serial number remained visible in the GUID. So, someone with a GUID and access somehow to serial numbers of network cards could identify a computer. The fact that there was no database of MAC addresses or even that anyone kept track of them, or that MAC addresses were part of the lowest level of how the internet worked, were all facts lost in the moment. Much to Kim's frustration, I continued to try to explain.

Pro tip: *If in a PR crisis you find yourself explaining some deeply technical thing, stop.*

I could not stop. Kim was annoyed.

The specifics of how Microsoft ended up using GUID technology made this look bad, and that was what Markoff was on to.

This conspiracy theory ran deep.

In Office 97 we introduced hyperlinks as a native feature inside documents. It was part of our push to make Office great for the web. From within any Office document, clicking a link opened the browser. We were especially interested in links between Office documents on a web server. One problem with Office documents is that if files are renamed or moved then the link breaks. The WWW was already well known for broken links. In the corporate world, with reorgs and project name changes, files moved around a lot. We decided that by using FrontPage on the server we could keep track of links used in Office documents and detect when a file was moved, and then repair the links. We thought this was a great way to prevent what was becoming a huge web problem of broken links. We needed something more than a file name, since in a company, files might frequently have the same name. A clever idea was to use the new feature of Windows to create GUIDs, and when a link was created to a document a GUID was also recorded. Links in HTML used the file and folder name, so if the file was moved or renamed the link broke. Having a GUID also gave us a chance to fix the link and find the file using FrontPage server. We thought this was a useful and solid plan.

Will Kennedy (WillK) was the development manager on the feature in Office 97, though he moved to Outlook shortly after we began Office10. An Alabama native, college hire, standing 6-foot, 6-inches tall, Will was the epitome of a calm development manager. I forwarded him some of the mail from Markoff describing the feature. He walked through all the Office code with the test team and ascertained we did store the GUID in a document. To further the conspiracy, the GUID was not visible to end-users in any way and was hidden in the file. However, as Office 97 progressed, albeit late, we never implemented the fix-up feature but the GUIDs remained. That seemed benign at the time. Will said it was trivial to remove the code that wrote the GUID to files. He prepared a quick fix for Office 97.

Simultaneously, but coincidentally, Windows 98 implemented a product registration tool that, in the process of registering the PC, collected a set of information about the hardware, such as how much memory, disk space, and CPU. It was also optionally collecting personal information like any registration process. At Microsoft, the hardware information went to the development team and the optional personal information went to marketing's customer database. As it turned out, the bits of hardware information needed a *unique identifier.* Windows chose to use a GUID.

GUIDs contained that network MAC number, which could link the Windows 98 registration and documents created with Office, no matter where those documents ended up being distributed.

The tipster, and Markoff, came up with a scenario by which Microsoft could, if it wanted, maintain the capability of knowing if a document was created on a PC and who registered that PC. In fact, the theory implied that given a random document, it might be possible for Microsoft to determine who created it.

All Microsoft needed to do was connect each of the new databases, and no one could stop us.

Kim needed me to get on the phone with Markoff and explain this theory away. I told her the theory was baseless, and therefore harmless, plus, we would never do what was being suggested.

But it was a conspiracy theory and those can't be explained away.

Microsoft at the time (early 1999) was not exactly the most loved company and certainly not the most trusted, especially by those outside of technology. Combined with a lack of trust was a perception of power that rivaled governments.

On the other hand, the idea that somehow the Windows and Office teams could connect their databases and execute this scenario seemed laughable to me. We had enough difficulty connecting our bug databases and sharing code, even though we fully understood and had a use for those things!

Kim scheduled a call with Markoff. She reminded me once again to take Markoff seriously, and that I could not dismiss his concerns no matter how wild they were. On the call, I walked through the feature in Office, but there was no way to deny what Markoff was asserting. Microsoft did have these databases. There was a serial number of a network card in a GUID. Files had GUIDs. The story was ultimately filed and was, according to Kim, factual and accurate. As was almost always the case, I took the story personally. Kim reminded me that it was a win, considering where the story started and where it could have gone.

We issued patches to Office. We changed Office so that it did not create GUIDs (that we never used) and we also released a tool to remove GUIDs from existing documents. Windows also changed the product registration tool and the way the GUID creation capability worked. GUIDs are widely used today on the internet in browsers, websites, and mobile phones in almost every application.

The GUID story was also the introduction of the word *metadata* to the general public, data about data, not generally seen by end-users, but used to describe data. The GUID in an Office document was an example of metadata. With the rise of web browsing, web browser *cookies*, and mobile phone records, public awareness was just being raised. Privacy advocates were in force challenging metadata collection and analysis. We were truly entering a new era of privacy.

Whereas WM/Concept.A was the Office team's first experience in dealing with networked viruses, GUID was our first experience dealing with privacy. These both came as we were planning Office10 and changed the way we thought about security and privacy. In fact, security and privacy moved from defensive capabilities to main tenets in our product vision.

We weren't finished learning.

Just a few days after *The New York Times* ran Markoff's story on GUIDs, I received an interesting message in Outlook with the subject line "Important Message from Jon." And another interesting message with the subject line "Important Message from EJ." And another. And another. In fact, my inbox was filled with "Important Message from..." messages.

That was no good.

Each message contained only the text

```
Here is that document you asked for ...
don't show anyone else ;-)
```

and a file attachment called LIST.DOC.

I wasn't the only person getting these emails. It felt as though everyone with Office running Outlook was receiving them, seemingly at the same time.

Then, suddenly, I received no more messages. I couldn't send messages either. Email was down.

Microsoft shut down email service as did companies and email providers around the world. The internet was under attack by a virus, a replicating email virus. This virus was quickly analyzed by many across the internet—it was named *W97M.Melissa.A* as it left a signature containing the name Melissa on an infected PC. Melissa was a Word macro virus much like WM/Concept.A but one extended to use Outlook in order to replicate.

Office had been weaponized. This virus also did not harm the infected PCs but was generating so much email that servers were getting gummed up in what is called a *denial-of-service* attack, or DoS. The system administrators in charge of mail servers were angry. More importantly, for the first time perhaps hundreds of thousands or millions of white-collar workers were without email all at once, heading into a Monday morning of a work week.

If there had been any doubt, we immediately learned how important email was to the workplace.

Our customers and offices around the world were angry.

News reports were everywhere (though reporters resorted to phone calls to report), and the number of mail servers impacted was in the tens of thousands, which was hundreds of thousands if not more PCs. This was huge.

What was going on? This was a new type of virus. It introduced the term *worm* to the general population, named such because it could automatically spread itself to other PC users without any action, *worming* its way around the internet. In the press the terms worm and virus were used interchangeably. Once released *into the wild* via a deliberate simple email, Melissa virus spread when a recipient opened the file attached to the "Important Messages." The message was designed to look familiar and so the file was almost always opened.

That was *social engineering.*

The attachment contained a Word macro and was written in a way that not only bypassed any protections added to Word after WM/Concept.A but immediately disabled the macro protection features. In this sense, it was the same as the Concept. When using any mail program but Outlook, Melissa was like Concept both in how it spread and its high annoyance level.

If a user was running Outlook, then Melissa went one step further. The code in the Melissa virus used the macro capabilities of Outlook—yes, Outlook had those too, and customers really loved them—to automatically send the same "Important Message" to the first 50 people in the Outlook address book. Instead of telling "two friends," each infected PC was telling 50 and each of those who opened the attachment told 50 more. That's how the virus spread across the whole planet in a weekend.

If there was any humor to it (there was not), after mailing 50 people the virus, the code checked if the current day of the month was the same as the minute. If by chance it was, it added the following text to the currently open Word: "Twenty-two points, plus triple-word-score, plus fifty points for using all my letters. Game's over. I'm outta here." This made no sense until there was a deep dive into where Windows kept program settings (called the *registry*) where it recorded that Melissa infected the PC. There, text could be found reading "Kwyjibo." Together those were a reference to an episode of *The Simpsons,* "Bart the Genius," where Bart tries to cheat at Scrabble with that word.

Hunting down the propagators of viruses and worms was an internet hobby and a profession going as far back as Robert Morris and the infamous worm unleashed from Cornell in 1988 while I was there for my first homecoming, sleuthed, and then documented by Clifford Stoll in the incredible book, *The Cuckoo's Egg: Tracking a Spy Through the Maze of Computer Espionage.* Immediately the internet tried to find clues to the origin of Melissa. In some ways this was similar to the Centers for Disease Control trying to find patient zero. With email this was possible because of the accurate time stamps and journey information in every message—the digital DNA of a computer virus.

Melissa offered up one other clue, unbeknownst to its creator. The LIST.DOC file had a GUID, the kind John Markoff wrote about and the same feature that we had just removed from Office. The tipster assisting Markoff, who we then knew to be Richard Smith, the CEO of Phar Lap, found the GUID and posted it online with the virus code. A graduate student in Sweden said the code looked familiar and pointed Smith to a user named *VicodenES*. Smith then began to connect the network card address (the same one he complained about as part of a GUID) and records of internet servers. Eventually, Smith was able to connect the whole trail of network card addresses to the actual creator of the virus. He was arrested in New Jersey at his parent's home a week after releasing the virus.

The metadata in Office 2000 made that possible.

I wish I made that up.

We assisted IT managers and sysadmins in getting their systems back online and removing the virus. This was a criminal investigation, and for the Office team this was the first time we were involved in one at this scale and in real time. The week was filled with remorse, grief, anger, and finally, when we heard that metadata was involved in finding the criminal, pure disbelief.

The macro capability of Outlook, as used by Melissa, developed a huge following and was a strategic aspect of the product. We were in the same spot as we were a few years earlier with Word—a key feature enterprises valued was being weaponized by virus creators. For Word, we added a series of warnings and administrative controls. Our first steps in dealing with Melissa did the same.

As soon as we implemented these and put out updates, we heard from enterprise customers and the community of consultants, authors, and the Microsoft *Most Valued Professionals*. MVPs were a group selected by Microsoft's support professionals to represent the broad external community. We "broke" their solutions built on top of Outlook. Whether these were time management, scheduling assistants, customer relationship management tools for salespeople, or email automation (to name a few), the user was prompted by Outlook every time macros ran. It was annoying, but it needed to be that way because we did not have another readily available solution.

When people using software are in a flow going through some tasks such as from opening email, to booking tickets, to opening a program, to browsing web pages any warning messages that pop up are essentially ignored, and therefore meaningless.

This lesson was learned repeatedly by every generation of software. A warning message simply got in the way. No one reads text when there is an OK button right there.

As with Word, there was a gradual chipping away of the extensibility of Office. Our products (and customers) were put at risk due to an increasingly connected world. The design approaches we took that worked fine for tech enthusiasts no longer worked for typical office workers with relatively limited knowledge of the inner workings of PCs, and especially not for the administrators who supported them.

Once a virus is thwarted by any means, the community of bad actors works to find similar patterns to exploit, but ones that work around the fixes. In the meantime, an even larger community of copycats duplicate the existing exploit and take advantage of unpatched software or software protected by relatively unsophisticated antivirus tools that did not pick up on small changes to the pattern used. That's how viruses work.

We briefly secured the product.

The press in the first week in May 2000 when I received that exhilarating call at home on Sunday morning were reporting billions of dollars in damage, computer users around the world blocked from using email or even working. The reports cited the previous Melissa exploit and the much earlier Concept virus in Word, and many in between.

That's when I realized the magnitude of the issue.

In reporting, once there are three points of evidence then there is a trend. In this case, the trend was the escalating risk of using Office and the escalating costs to business IT professionals maintaining corporate desktops—TCO, our old friend total cost of ownership, was again a critical issue.

In an online story posted the first evening of the spread, industry "experts" anticipated that by morning half of all PCs in North America became infected and more than 100,000 mail servers in Europe were infected or taken offline as a precaution. The United States Senate was infected, as were important news outlets such as Dow Jones. The infections reached worldwide telecom and television outlets in Denmark and employees of Compaq Computer as far away as Malaysia.

The impact was profound. Billions of dollars in immediate lost productivity and money spent to eradicate the virus. Customers were livid. If and how we responded to this was clearly going to be a test of empathy for the pain customers were experiencing.

The creators of the ILOVEYOU worm, dubbed "Love Bug" in the widespread press, exploited a hole in the warning messages that ran when Outlook's data (such as contacts) was accessed. As with Melissa, the worm used the contact list and replicated itself, but instead of just the first 50 contacts it automatically (and silently) sent mail to *all* the contacts in an address book. This infection also installed itself on the computer, so it continued to run all the time and did damage by deleting files and replacing them with copies of the virus. The infection was started by an email attachment with the name "Love Letter," which was a hidden program and not a letter at all. Any email program would have been vulnerable to this method of transmission, which simply required the user to open the file on their PC, but Outlook was not only the most prominent, but it was also the most easily programmable.

It was bad. Really bad.

The team was trying to figure out what to do and began exploring options.

Microsoft Office was having a Tylenol moment. While the human suffering of the computer virus was dramatically less than that of the 1982 product tampering that left seven people dead from poisoning, the brand suffering was comparable. Could Outlook be trusted? Could Microsoft? Tylenol's parent company, Johnson & Johnson, took unprecedented and drastic measures to save lives and rebuild consumer confidence in the brand. They removed all medicine from distribution and encouraged the destruction of all pills. In addition, the company diagnosed and improved their systems, including the development of tamper-resistant packaging. In doing so, they developed the modern playbook for crisis management.

Acting with uncharacteristic haste, the US Congress House Science Committee, Technology Subcommittee held hearings on May 10, 2000. Witnesses testified about the "love bug" computer virus that infected over 10 million computers worldwide, shutting down Internet servers and corrupting files. Testimony centered around how the virus spread so quickly, the impacts and damages, and what steps could be taken to prevent similar attacks in the future. The witnesses were third-party experts, and not from Microsoft. The testimony, I believe, stands in contrast to the hearings in the present day on social networks in how relatively calm and rational, even in the midst of a crisis, the dialog was. Still, it is worth noting that the hearings made numerous references to the ongoing investigations into Microsoft and the global market "power" the company maintained.

Like so many crisis situations in management, at first managers (like me) think they will show up and save the day with some brilliant idea that no one thought of. Failing that (as is almost always the case), the next approach is to take several options and combine them into what seems brilliant but is ultimately unworkable. That's assuming you don't show up and just wish the whole thing wasn't happening. That too is never the case.

Rob Price (RobPr), Outlook's PM leader, and WillK led the discussion. Their view was clear. First, we would disable sending a bunch of file types of attachments that people routinely sent or opened if they showed up in an inbox. Essentially, this meant not sending executable code or files that ran when opened. Second, we would guard Outlook such that any programmatic access to the address book or attempt to send email silently generated a warning and disabled access. Finally, although wonky, we would treat all email as untrusted, which basically meant no matter how code was snuck into email it did not run without a lot of warnings. We would effectively quarantine email messages and isolate the user's important Outlook data from any code.

These actions or guards could be enforced and customized by administrators in large companies.

The team wanted to talk about exactly how much "stuff" would break in the process. KurtD and Martin Staley (MartinSt), Outlook's test manager, said that no matter how much or how little we broke customers would complain we broke either too much or too little. Some things were super simple. For example, large companies compressed their files before emailing them as attachments to save storage and bandwidth. A common way to send them without requiring a separate program to decompress them was to have the compressed file sent as an executable file, which was automatically decompressed and saved on the local hard drive when opened as an attachment. This extension to Outlook was popular. And it would be totally broken, rendering attachments invisible to recipients.

The debate was not whether to make these changes as soon as possible, but whether we should even enable companies to turn them off or somehow reduce the scope of protection. As veterans of the past few rounds of viruses, there was reluctance to enable IT pros to reduce the protections on a PC. Their assessments weighed the risk of an important boss or stakeholder not getting work done with the support costs across an organization if a virus were to surface. We knew with any option that some percentage of customers would side with more pain in after-the-fact remediation than the pain of prevention. It was the wrong tradeoff, but the kind that is often made in IT organizations when they are put on the defensive because of weaknesses of the products they are supporting.

What the team really wanted was permission to cause the pain. They knew what needed to be done but knew there would be pushback. They wanted to know I would support them. For that, I did not hesitate given how much pain we had already caused and how much they clearly understood about the problem and solution. There was so much going on to suggest this significantly undermined the whole value proposition of Office that I wondered if we would have to introduce Outlook-free versions of Office with reduced pricing—everything always came back to pricing.

In four weeks, on June 8, 2000, the team completed the patch and made it available for download—the now infamous *Outlook Email Security Update*. It went out for Office 97 and 2000, Outlook 98, and Outlook 2000 and for all sub-versions of those products all around the world.

Four weeks might seem like a long time, but cleansing PCs of the problem was time-consuming and occupied IT. The antivirus vendors and email security products did their part. We notified PSS and field sales. Marketing prepared a library of materials, as did Support, who wrote detailed technical articles for the Microsoft *Knowledge Base*. We issued a long "interview" with me, as a news release, detailing all the fixes. We did calls with the major press outlets.

The rollout was bumpy. With every virus, the knowledgeable PC enthusiasts tend to take a blame the users stance when faced with an update that diminishes PC capabilities. We saw this with both Concept and Melissa. In the case of LOVE, features like mailing around code were precisely what enthusiasts did frequently, so they were rather irate. In forums they complained, "Who opens attachments from people you don't know?" People are busy and expect PCs to work. They don't view using a PC in the same vein as walking down a dark alley in a strange city. Quickly, the community took to trying to find workarounds for the security changes, but to no avail. Several declared that end-users should change a few IT settings we did provide to return to "normal."

Enterprise admins behaved as expected. Some optimized for the near term. Others took the pain in changing workflow and incompatibilities. Outlook, with the email security update, was the new normal and eventually accepted. While in hindsight it all seemed easy, the idea of breaking an important ecosystem, for a new product especially, was antithetical to Microsoft's focus on compatibility. What the team proposed and then delivered was gutsy.

Office continued to have fewer and mostly less severe viruses for decades to come. At least a part of that was due to the *Outlook Email Security Update*.

Tech enthusiasts, IT Pros, and even our beloved MVP supporters complained for years and wrote many articles pejoratively referring to the Email Security Update as they adjusted to a new normal for Outlook.

The world moved on. And it was a bit safer using Office and Outlook.

061. BSOD TO WATSON: THE RELIABILITY JOURNEY

PCs used to crash a lot, a whole lot. PCs routinely crashing, freezing, hanging (various ways to describe a computer that has ceased to function) and losing work were the norm. Over about twenty years of engineering and iteration, the PC experience changed dramatically for the better, with vastly more reliability and higher quality. Now I recognize even typing that should make for a protracted thread on *Hacker News* or Reddit where everyone shared the crashes that just happened today or happen "constantly." This is the story of going from a world of nearly universal quality and reliability problems to a literal world-changing innovation that dramatically altered the path of PC quality.

My first semester in college staffing the shared computer facilities where nearly everyone used minis, mainframes, terminals, and card readers. If there were problems, it was almost never something IBM did and almost always some form of "error between the chair and keyboard" as we used to say. When I returned to the Spring semester, Macintosh invaded the terminal rooms. My job dramatically changed. Now I was full time on Friday nights helping people to recover corrupt files from floppy disks after the new Apple MacWrite crashed and "ate" their work. After a few weeks, our team of operators started to share best practices: save your work every hour or so, save to a new file, keep papers under about 10 pages, print drafts if possible, don't use too many fonts and sizes, and finally if you're doing a big restructuring then save those deleted sections to another file to reuse. Using MacWrite to write a term paper at the end of a semester was, quite honestly, a risky proposition. I dealt with more than a few classmates who lost their 10-page papers hours before deadline. Lost. Gone. Evaporated. The only thing to show for the work was a useless file and an error message on the screen "Sorry, a system error occurred" with a little cartoon bomb as if humor was appropriate.

That was state of the art. Windows wasn't far behind. By 1990 with the release of Windows 3.0, Microsoft would introduce its own brand of crashes to the world. Given the rapid rise of PC sales, it was the PC that assumed the mantle of king of crashes. Frustration with PCs crashing, losing work, or just being hard to use was entirely the norm. As we learned from the Stanford researchers who provided the inspiration for Clippy, the precision and exactness of the PC led PC users to assume when something went wrong it was their fault. The PC itself was not the problem.

It was certainly our fault. We were making the software, but we were also making crashes seemingly as fast as we were making features.

Any visit to watch someone use Microsoft Office illuminated the nail-biting, edge-of-seat, stress-inducing experience of using a PC. Our difficult to understand user interface and faulty software engrained a generation with defensive usage patterns: save, copy, backup, print, and so on. Even the most basic operations such as reorganizing a long memo, or rearranging slides came with a preamble that involved saving the file "94MEMO2.ORI" or some other equally obscure name. Using a command that you weren't sure of, then of course save your work first because you had no idea what might happen.

A series of changes in how we designed interface and engineered products led to a markedly improved experience and a step-function improvement in product quality.

The journey starts with the most simple and obvious command: *Undo*.

Most software in the '90s only worked in one direction, making changes, or *destructive changes* as we called them. To revert back to what was there previously, an opposite command had to be applied. Clicking again un-bolded a word and it went back to normal, for example. Same with text pasted in one spot: delete and paste again. As programs became increasingly complex, operations were becoming more destructive. Importantly, reversing an operation could be entirely unintuitive, such as changing a chart, a notoriously complicated task or simply moving text with the mouse instead of copy and paste.

People developed ways to cope with this complexity. Prime among them was the use of saving a copy of a file before embarking on big changes and learning how to hit save often. This too had drawbacks. Keeping track of copies of files or saving and then losing old changes that might be useful—it all added to the mental overhead of defending yourself against the whims of software.

Inventing Undo seems lost to history. there were many approaches over many years including Microsoft's CharlesS when he was at Xerox PARC and earlier Andries van Dam at Brown University, pioneer in hyperlinks and world-renowned teacher to many and original advisory board member to Microsoft Research. Many specialized products such as Adobe Photoshop and Autodesk AutoCAD introduced undo relatively early. In Office, many people developed Undo—a feature that differentiated Office from most all other software especially considering the complexity of Office across words, pictures, and numbers. Not only did Office create Undo and implement it across products, but for each release it improved.

Office10 introduced *multilevel undo* across products, extending Undo to a nearly unlimited number of commands—like opening a file, making many changes, and then reverting back to the original just by clicking Undo. All of which could be undone with Redo. Undo and Redo, two simple buttons, represented thousands of hours of work, reducing untold amounts of stress and angst. Office was not the first with the capability, but it was the most widely used, most broadly implemented, and perhaps the most thorough.

Some of the best innovations, like Undo/Redo, while undramatic are both obvious and seamless and often taken for granted, missed only when absent. The early web browsers, though they touted ease and simplicity over Windows and Office, lacked the kind of safeguards being built into Office like Undo/Redo. The analogous buttons in a browser, Back and Forward, failed to correctly work most of the time, and still often don't.

Undo/Redo also reduced phone calls to corporate help desks. As PCs were being deployed across industries and jobs, companies were pushed to provide support, and that meant on-call telephone support for employees. Windows and Office were sold to LORGs in such a way that the support burden was maintained by the customer, not by Microsoft. Much to the surprise of most individuals at big companies, they could not call Microsoft for help, and if they did, they were routed back to their own company or offered a paid incident. Microsoft created a large support staff, but it was only for retail customers. Undo/Redo changed the paradigm of learning how to use Office. Instead of fear, people learned they could try something and if it worked, great, and if it didn't work it could be undone, or redone. We reduced the risk of using features and the need to ask another person for help. Just try something and if it didn't work, undo it. The oft-repeated sequence of undo/redo would become a substantial blip in our instrumented studies and when watching people use Office in our usability labs.

Undo/redo did not, however, change the scariest part about using a computer: a crash. Crashes happened at any time, leaving a user staring hopelessly at the screen, often a blue one, hours of work lost to the ether. The lucky person didn't lose much if they happened to have just hit the magical Save button, but nobody ever expected a crash. The worst type of crash lost the entire file, not just the changes since the last save. A so-called *corrupt file* became the worst of PC nightmares—you know your work is in there somewhere in the file, but you can't get it out because Office just fails at trying to open the file. A whole cottage industry of file recovery services grew up around PCs.

The loss of work was so profound and such a part of the fabric of using a PC at work that "my computer crashed" replaced "my dog ate it" as an excuse. Crashing computers and lost files were the subject of internet jokes (we didn't call them memes yet), newspaper cartoons, and an all-too-common film and TV plot device. Who among us has not stopped to snap a photo of a crashed kiosk at the airport or supermarket? Crashes were also the leading single subject of calls to Microsoft's Product Support and a major cost to customers. These calls were futile at best and there was little a support engineer could offer. Whether senior government officials, expensive lawyers facing court deadlines, or famous authors escalating their way through support, there was almost nothing we had to offer them, VIP or not.

As if crashing weren't bad enough, the way software handled a crash was, well, laughable, especially in hindsight. I don't know how many years it took for carmakers to give up and create a red *Check Engine* light, but the first two decades of PC software were a journey of absurdity, making every crash a bit of a mystery.

When software tries to do something that is literally impossible the processor simply stops and the whole PC ceases to work. That's a *bug*, a crash. It is the most severe kind of bug, and it comes from programmers writing incorrect code. Technically a bug is any time anyone believes the software behaves differently than expected, even if it does not cause a crash. There are as many ways to crash as there are programmers. The program is trying to do something that doesn't make sense, such as fetch some data from a location in memory that does not exist or invalid math such as divide by zero. These failures are routine, but not all programs handle them gracefully. Good programmers write defensive code. That means they always check to make sure operations make sense before trying them and after they execute. Even with the best intentions, not every line of code is defensively programmed as DougK ingrained in us in Applications Developer College—it isn't always practical, and it doesn't always come for free.

Crashing bugs can be difficult to find and fix. Many times, a crash happens intermittently or appears because a different series of steps are used. The bug may depend on the information being processed—how big a document is being edited or maybe the series of formatting commands, how much free memory the computer had, what else is running at the same time, or even what type of printer or display is in use. Bugs appear anywhere, not just in the code in an application. They could be in the Operating System code, such as MS-DOS or Windows, in the application, like Word, or even in the code that makes a certain model of printer or video display work, but what the end user sees might be totally unrelated to where the coding mistake happens to be.

These conditions make finding bugs an enormous and time-consuming challenge. One of the greatest programmer skills is finding bugs in other people's code. Legendary programmers in Apps such as JonDe, DuaneC, JodiG, RickP, ScottRa, and DougK were held in high esteem, not only because of the bug-free code they wrote but also for the bugs they diagnosed in other's code.

I created many bugs on my own before Microsoft and learned how to find bugs planted in Microsoft code during my training in ADC, but I learned about my first commercial bug during my first summer at Microsoft. DanN my lead in ADC shared (JonDe refreshed my memory of the specifics) the story of the infamous "Sindogs" bug in Excel 2.0, which was the first Windows version that shipped with Windows 2.0 about 18 months before I arrived. The bug manifested itself when an important part of Windows, a plain text file with all the system settings, was corrupted—in the file where it was supposed to say "[Windows]" it somehow was changed to "[Sindogs]." Neither the word *Sindogs* appeared in any code nor did any code write that string, so its appearance was rather mysterious. The bug took days to materialize and was only discovered after Excel testers ran an automated test to create and print charts over and over, for many hours. Eventually, through a significant amount of sleuthing, the team narrowed it down to a bug in drawing code in Windows, which was called when adding arrows to charts then printing them on old-school dot-matrix printers. There was a memory corruption, which changed the contents of the settings file that was in memory before it was saved to the disk. Stories were told about it for years. The Excel team even renamed their file server after the bug, and through Office 97 we connected to the server "\\SINDOGS\REL" (REL was short for release) for release builds of Excel.

Imagine tracking down a crazy bug after the product was in market and trying to figure out what caused it, then multiplying that by all the possible printers, video cards, and programs involved. Looking back, it was an engineering marvel that anything worked at all. In moments of frustration, or desperation, that is what we told ourselves.

In the early days of PCs before Windows, crashes *froze* the computer—nothing worked, not even banging on the keyboard. The only recourse was to turn the computer off and start over, losing unsaved work and causing a potentially extreme emotional moment. In the earliest days of automobiles, drivers had to be mechanics for fear of getting stranded by flaky engines—PCs were sort of like that.

As PCs evolved, so did crashing. Windows developed a new way of dealing with crashes. Rather than freezing the computer and doing nothing, Windows 3.0 offered the first crash-handling experience known by the friendliest of names: *Unrecoverable Application Error*, or *UAE*. Instead of freezing, a crash offered a big white message box that read:

```
UNRECOVERABLE APPLICATION ERROR
Terminating current application.
```

The message offered a single "OK" button, which was ironic because nothing was actually OK.

Not only was this not helpful, but it also offered no solutions to fixing the problem. Useless, yes, but Macintosh did not do much better, offering a similarly useless message, albeit one with a nice sound and a newly famous graphical bomb exploding. The text of the message apologized, "Sorry a system error occurred" and the one button offered not OK but "Restart" as a worse reminder of the state of affairs. In either case, there was effectively nothing to do other than "don't do that again," even though no one was ever sure what they did to cause the crash.

That was the state-of-the-art PC experience until Windows 3.1 in 1991, which introduced an innovation that began a 10-year journey into making software more robust in the face of crashes. While a little nicer and equally useless to end-users, the new UAE message was at least useful to software developers. Though, in hindsight, it was laughably hostile given customers were about to lose work:

> Application Error
>
> `WINWORD.EXE caused a General Protection Fault in module KRNL386.EXE at 0002:4356`

This message had a single Close button. The sequence was meaningless to anyone who did not design microprocessors for a living. Who was this "general" and from what army? As expected, the company quickly abbreviated this as *GPF,* and we entered a new era of tracking these GPFs and certainly talking about them in the cafeteria all the time as a new Micro-speak term.

Over time there were many variations of these crash messages. None were particularly helpful. In fact, they became more techie and contained a broader array of techno-language. Meanwhile, Apple stuck with their exceedingly simple and apologetic system bomb.

In Product Support Services (PSS) and in our bug databases (called RAID) we tracked these snippets of data. When customers called, they read this screen and jargon to the support engineer who then entered it into a tracking system. PSS would diligently record all the numbers and produce a monthly report detailing all the crashes. After a while they could talk about some of the crashes happening more frequently than others because of the similarity in the memory locations of the crash. Because so many crashes were due to settings and configurations unique to a customer environment, PSS became adept at walking through a whole series of potential changes in an effort to simply alter something in the environment to remove the crash. All of this, from the lists of crashes to the sorcery of changing settings, was entirely inadequate but it was the best people doing the best they could. There was almost nothing we could do on the development team with these mere nuggets of data as we searched tirelessly for more information and steps to reproduce crashes.

The primary problem was a lack of information, such as what steps preceded the crash or what else was running. We needed the full state of the computer at the time of the crash, not just the place it crashed. What else is in PC memory, and what else was going on at the time of the crash?

Windows needed a flight data recorder (a.k.a. *black box*), like on an airplane. A member of the Windows team developed a tool called *Sherlock,* which was just that, a flight data recorder for PC crashes. Right away, companies ran the program, eventually renamed *Dr. Watson* due to the discovery of a naming conflict with a commercial product. Shipping with Windows 3.1 Dr. Watson featured an icon of a doctor and a magnifying glass, cementing a new level of approachability for Windows crashes. If customers called PSS with a crash, PSS directed them to restart their PC with Watson running (which could be downloaded from AOL or CompuServe) and try to crash again intentionally to gather additional information to email to Microsoft.

The information was entirely gibberish to customers but super helpful to developers. After the crash, a file was left on the PC and could be sent to Microsoft. The internet was still not in widespread use, particularly with LORG customers, but enough people had email. From there developers and testers could combine that with some information about what a customer was doing at the time of the crash. This helped PSS to help product teams fix real-world crashes.

The relentless march of non-actionable and awkwardly worded crash messages from Windows continued with Windows 95. This revolutionary product aimed to make PCs easier to use, but it did not put a stop to crashes. Windows 95 did update the experience to put much more information in front of the user:

```
This program has performed an illegal operation
and will be shut down.
If the problem persists, contact the program
vendor.
```

Following this screen was what could only be defined as a wall of numbers and letters, which a user could select and copy to email to Microsoft, after they hung up with PSS because they had dial-up.

Unlike General Protection Fault, which was funny, Illegal Operation was scary. We were telling people that their computer did something *illegal*. I was recruiting at a university outside the United States when a bilingual student asked me if anyone reviewed the translation of this message, because in her native language the translation sounded like the authorities were on their way to confiscate the computer or at least issue a fine.

Over time to become more friendly and perhaps offer a choice, the *blue screen* was, by some measures, improved as it became the primary crash experience:

A fatal exception 05 has occurred at 0026:D00564F. The current application will be terminated.

```
* Press any key to terminate the current application
* Press CTRL+ALT_DEL again to restart your computer.

You will lose any unsaved information in all applications.

Press any key to continue
```

The modern 32-bit Windows NT product took the new blue screen to a whole new level. When Windows itself crashed the screen would be filled completely with the numeric contents of memory. The only indication that nothing good was about to happen was the "*** STOP:" that appeared at the top of the screen indicating that the computer needed to be restarted. This is by most accounts the original Blue Screen of Death, the BSoD.

While an improved Dr. Watson tool was available and helpful, most customers came to loathe the BSoD experience, which became a meme for PCs. In hindsight, this was a particularly hostile design. BSoD also became Micro-speak but rose to a higher level of pop culture, appearing as the de facto method to represent a crashed computer on TV and in movies.

Windows NT, with its modern operating system design, did not remove crashing from the PC experience, but at least crashes no longer required a full computer restart. That was good. Users still lost their work but only for the program that crashed, as if that was any consolation. For IT professionals, the Dr. Watson information was always saved on the PC and could be fetched remotely and shared with Microsoft.

We were making progress. The additional information and the inclusion of Dr. Watson technology with the broad use of email and new online support meant that development teams received detailed information about crashes. Tracking down a single crash was time-consuming, but we gained an understanding of the real-world product experience.

We increased our level of commitment to eliminating crashes but were only making marginal progress. As Office usage grew, the absolute number of crashes also grew, and the sheer number of them was increasingly noticeable. We continued to double down on taking reports from PSS of the top crashes and fixing them, proudly announcing in a service pack that we removed top crashes. Still, LORGs were complaining and sharing stories of those mission critical documents that were lost in the wee hours of the morning before the big meeting or contracts that were lost just as the final changes were made, and even within Microsoft the stories of lost documents and spreadsheets were too numerous to count. Yet we also knew Office was among the highest quality—least crashing—software on the market.

We desperately needed a breakthrough.

Over the holidays in December of 1998, as we were in the final bug-fixing stages of Office 2000, KirkG (one of my first Microsoft friends) sent me a note saying he wrote up an idea. He banged out the note on his preferred 83-key Compaq keyboard from the 1980s. He had posted it on http://office10 in the *total cost of ownership* team section. It was shocking because I had known Kirk a decade and could not recall him writing a memo or even a long email about anything. He was a hacker's hacker who preferred low-level assembly language whenever possible.

Two pages, the *memo* featured a graphic at the top of D. W. (Dora Winifred) from the animated TV series *Arthur.* Kirk and Melissa (who recently retired as MelBG) gave birth to their first child and thus were steeped in the children's culture. The use of D. W. was a play on Dr. Watson, eventually only *Watson.* Kirk wrote:

> *DW is an update of Dr. Watson. Its purpose is to extract information about a crash, and establish communication with Microsoft.com. If the bug is known to have been fixed in a service release, DW will assist in installing the SR. If the bug has not been found or fixed, DW will transmit necessary information (stack trace, etc.) to Microsoft.com such that we can fix it.*
>
> *Why. Customers hate crashes. Of all the things wrong using PCs, nothing is more in-your-face frustrating than a crash. Microsoft has a reputation – rightly or wrongly – for shipping buggy software, and to a large extent, buggy == crashing. We should make every effort to find and fix crashing bugs, and we don't. We make every effort* before shipping *[emphasis in original], but once out the door it drops precipitously. With web-based communication, this needn't be.*

Kirk was clear, to the point, and he was right. What Kirk proposed was a sweeping change in how we handled crashes. Using the web, all of about three years old, to create a closed loop from the moment a PC crashed until the bug was fixed. Updated software could be downloaded after we diagnosed and fixed the problem.

Kirk built his idea from an architectural feature in PowerPoint 2000, an attempt to handle crashes more gracefully by giving users a chance to save a file when a crash occurred. While a huge improvement, it did not address the root cause. In a few sentences, Kirk extended PowerPoint's idea of handling a crash straight from the customer's PC into the debugger at a developer's desk.

Instantly, this was a profound change in software. While excited, everyone underestimated exactly how this changed software development. For years to follow, I gave a recruiting talk to college students, detailing the innovation in Watson as among the biggest changes to programming and computer science I experienced.

It truly was.

Like any feature, going from spec—generously calling Kirk's two-pager a spec—to a full-fledged feature was a journey. In this case, DW was the first time Office connected from a PC to the internet, to Microsoft specifically, and that had repercussions. During the late 1990s, trust in Microsoft was not exactly in abundance given the cloud around the company from trials, viruses, GUIDs, Y2K, and so on. We were gaining traction with LORG customers who would raise deep concerns about PCs "phoning home."

Microsoft designed a feature that automatically sent information back to Microsoft, which seemed scary on the face of it. The world was starting to realize the implications of the internet and how it could be misused even while serving so many positives.

Unlike many features of Office, this feature had little by way of user experience but did require a great deal on the back end in Microsoft's new data centers. The sheer force of will needed to stand up a set of servers and connect them to the internet was incredible—the whole company seemed to fight against it. Changing assumptions of what and how teams operated within a big company was a lot of work.

Watson was a small bit of code that was always running in every Office application. When an app crashed (it wasn't supposed to, but if it did) Watson gathered the state of the program (what was going on in memory) at the time and packaged this up into a small *minidump*, technically a CAB or *compressed cabinet file*. In contrast to a *fulldump* of everything in the system, it was much smaller and could be sent to Microsoft when and if the PC was connected to the internet. The first step was to make sure CAB files were anonymous, containing no identifying information. This sounded easy. Thinking back to GUIDs and metadata covered by *The New York Times*, there were challenges. Basic items like the serial number of Office or the hardware address of the network card were omitted. Identifying the PC or human submitting a crash was meaningless to us, but we needed to find a way to convince people that was the case.

The memory and state DW gathered might have contents of a document entirely private to the user or information like a name and address or worse. Even though we could not trace back to a person or PC, the mere presence of this information could be perceived as troubling. EricLev, who moved to OPU after working on Word HTML, designed a user interface that allowed customers to see every single byte of information transmitted to Microsoft. It was one click away from the crash dialog. We appreciated designing for full transparency, but we knew people would be reluctant or even creeped out.

The combination of the location in memory of the crash, the program, and a few other items made for a unique crash signature, or as it was called a *Watson Bucket*. We enabled Watson early in the development cycle for testing. There were tons of crashes that happened then and mostly we were exercising the system, trying to understand how the flow from crash to bucket to debugger to fix worked.

We learned how quickly crash reports fell into buckets representing a single bug. The more hits a bucket received the more frequent the crash. We began to see that while there were many different crashes, the majority of them could be attributed to a small number of buckets. In other words, if we fixed a few bugs we eliminated a huge number of crashes, dramatically improving the reliability of the product for everyone.

Watson buckets were such that the 20 percent or so of most frequently occurring crashes accounted for more than 80 percent of all experienced crashes. This 80/20 rule is known mathematically as a *Pareto* distribution, but we lovingly called it the *Watson Curve*.

Soon in the development of Office10, thousands of CAB files were uploaded. Watson upended our development process. Testers saw crashing bugs in real-world experiences and, as a result, directed testing efforts to features causing the most buckets. Development managers were looking at bugs in the bug database and trying to understand the source. Was the bug found by testing, a person elsewhere, or Watson? Watson streamlined our own bug workflow so that engineers could go straight from the crash to the CAB file details to the debugger in one step. The internal website http://watson became a major part of the engineering process—anyone could visit the site and see the details on a bug. All information was unidentifiable, and the site was secured to members of the development team.

During early beta testing of Office10, Adobe released an update to their popular Acrobat product. In the update they added a toolbar to Office apps to make it easy to create PDF files. Unfortunately, there was a crash in their toolbar for those running the beta of Office10. Fortunately, this crash happened so frequently, and Acrobat was so popular, we immediately saw the Watson bucket and got in touch with Adobe. We knew about the crash because of Watson before Adobe even heard of it. Watson soon expanded so independent software makers could easily see how their software was performing in the real world as well.

Watson continued to evolve after finishing Office10, and somewhat in parallel the Windows team developed a companion service for diagnosing bugs in Windows. These systems were combined in a one-plus-one is greater than two combination to become *Windows Error Reporting*. The Office team continued to operate the internet service and soon became somewhat of a locus for the product groups running full-scale web services. I found myself signing off on huge purchase orders for servers and storage as we were receiving tens of millions of crashes. All of this starting from KirkG's idea and a server under his desk.

In 2011, the results of this cross-company work received one of the first Engineering Excellence Awards, created by JonDe, to reward significant milestones. Raising the visibility even more, the work received a Chairman's Innovation and Excellence Award from Bill Gates. Finally, in 2011, the work was published in the Association of Computing Machinery journal *Communications of the ACM*, as *Debugging in the (Very) Large: Ten Years of Implementation and Experience*, with nine authors across the company including KirkG as a top author, with OPU program manager Steve Greenberg (SteveGr) and others listed. EricLev left Microsoft and was by then a successful founder of *CellarTacker,* an oenology website he started as a hobby.

People used to ask if clicking on that "Send Error Report" button did any good. It absolutely did.

While having a flight data recorder was helpful to the product team, customers were still losing data when Office crashed. EricLev's team designed Office10's Document Recovery, extending PowerPoint's innovative crash recovery to Word and Excel. When a crash happened Office automatically saved the file to a new location and automatically restarted showing the last version of the original file as well as the file just before crash. This lifesaving feature was dubbed "airbags for Office" by the marketing team when describing it to the press.

The period through building Office10 and the following releases saw an unprecedented pivot to building enterprise class software. While we started selling enterprise software with Office 97, it took time to catch up in the product team. We changed our engineering practices and built out engineering processes that were as mature as anything IBM might have used for mainframes. A decade earlier, if someone suggested we might become more like IBM, I would have been insulted.

The response to Y2K, viruses and malware, crashes, and long-term support were some of our enterprise trials. On the heels of these, Microsoft built out the internet infrastructure to deliver product updates to a billion PCs around the world. This was known as *Windows Update.* Since that time, everyone has taken the ability to update devices (and machines) for granted, but it was a project years in the making, designed on the heels of scaling to an enterprise company.

Having passed these tests, we had, in the eyes of customers, moved much closer to the coveted trusted enterprise-ready product organization. The industry took note. I could feel the difference with customers and industry analysts and see the difference in how Microsoft was portrayed in trade press when it came to product quality. Expectations rose, but so did our ability to deliver, and to do so proactively. Office markedly improved product quality and we could quantify the improvements with the number of bugs fixed before shipping and with the real-world crashes experienced by customers declining.

Over future releases the role of telemetry would expand dramatically, first to better creating help and how-to content and then to measuring the usage of the product at an extremely granular level including each command, keyboard shortcut, toolbar button. Watson was even used to further our efforts at securing the PC by tracking crashes that were used as vulnerabilities by bad actors. Through this evolution we maintained a rock-solid privacy approach and by and large the role of this telemetry was accepted. We had gone from essentially guessing about product quality to reacting to being proactive and understanding at a very deep level how our products were used by nearly everyone. While it might sound like hyperbole today, I stand by the language I used on college campuses and this work was a huge step in applied computer science.

We executed well through Office10 M1, M2 approaching the tail of the release. We were a team of 1,500 full-time engineers at that point. Gradually, code stopped changing, and bugs triaged. Execution and precision were at all-time highs. The product was stable. Everyone was using it all the time. This felt great.

I still worried that we could spin out of control—projects at scale do that. Or maybe forces outside the company work to spin us out of control?

062. SPLIT UP MICROSOFT

On June 7, 2000, the verdict, known as the *Final Judgment*, was delivered. I read the PDF (itself a scanned copy of a fax from the legal team) on my BlackBerry flying back from a Windows conference. In-flight connectivity didn't exist, but the BlackBerry magically worked over the pager network, downloading a few sentences at a time while I avoided looking like I was using prohibited electronics in the air.

> *The Plan shall provide for the completion, within 12 months of the expiration of the stay pending appeal set forth in section 6.a., of the following steps:*
>
> *The separation of the Operating Systems Business from the Applications Business, and the transfer of the assets of one of them (the "Separated Business") to a separate entity along with (a) all personnel, systems, and other tangible and intangible assets (including Intellectual Property) used to develop, produce, distribute, market, promote, sell, license and support the products and services of the Separated Business, and (b) such other assets as are necessary to operate the Separated Business as an independent and economically viable entity (Final Judgement June 7, 2000)*

Judge Thomas Penfield Jackson ordered the breakup of Microsoft into two companies, though there was a debate over whether it should be two or three companies, after listing all the federal and state laws Microsoft violated. The punditry (and press) all but declared victory. The dragon had been slayed. Magazine covers across mainstream and industry press featured all varieties of *busted* and *gotcha*.

The litigation began way back in July 1994 when I was working for BillG as his technical assistant with a lawsuit by the Department of Justice, DOJ. Microsoft and DOJ entered a consent decree to resolve the case, but then in 1998 the DOJ sued Microsoft in civil court for violating the terms of that agreement as it pertained to how Microsoft licensed Windows to PC makers. Microsoft initially lost the case, but on appeal it was ruled that Windows 95 bundling Internet Explorer did not violate the agreement. There was a catch though. The resolution of this case did not preclude further action for violating antitrust law.

Filed May 18, 1998, the US Justice Department and 20 state attorneys general sued Microsoft for violations of the Sherman Antitrust Act. The suit charged the company with abusing its market power to impede competition, especially Netscape. Running over fifty pages, the initial complaint read like a *greatest hits* of emails, comments, and things we probably should not have said. All the classics were there from "We are going to cut off their air supply. Everything they're selling, we're going to give away for free" to "You see browser share as job 1…I do not feel we are going to win on our current path. We are not leveraging Windows from a marketing perspective" to "Integrate with Windows [to] increase IE share."

The trial and subsequent rulings were low points for Microsoft. While the Office team was not part of the offending acts it was very much part of remedy being tossed about. From BillG's deposition performance to the botched courtroom exhibits to the lack of voices of support from so many that benefitted from Windows, there were plenty of moments to feel awful about. The industry tracked the trial, but the pace of coverage was nothing like we see today with instant commentary and analysis at the speed of Twitter. By and large most employees did not follow the trial day to day and even the daily summaries that went out to some execs were not the most important thing. Even with all these negatives, the team of people at the trial were working incredibly difficult and long hours with a strong sense of purpose and pride. At an exec staff meeting, a Windows executive returning from the trial said to me they genuinely believed it was Microsoft's "best people doing some of their best work." There was optimism throughout the trial, until we lost.

Some aspects of the case stuck with me more than others. One in particular was the finding about bundling Internet Explorer with Windows. The judge wrote in the *Conclusions of Law*, April 3, 2000, that "Microsoft's decision to tie Internet Explorer to Windows cannot truly be explained as an attempt to benefit consumers and improve the efficiency of the software market generally, but rather as part of a larger campaign to quash innovation that threatened its monopoly position."

I felt that being explicitly called out for building products to "quash innovation" was particularly brutal. With the passage of time, I have come to recognize that if you have faith in the system that governs us, it is fine to disagree with a particular ruling, but one must accept it as a fact because the system does. Even if I disagree, most everyone else will go by what the court held to be the facts determined through the process. I held (and continued to hold) a product person's view of product development, which is that the work of product development is somehow a higher calling and done for the benefit of customers, partners, and the market. It is fair to say this is a horribly naïve view that doesn't consider the realities of running a business in a brutally competitive market. This belief of mine would be put to the test later in my career when I found myself managing Windows.

In the *Findings of Fact* in November 1999, the judge found that the company held a monopoly—an important finding that forever changed how Microsoft was viewed. Following that was a lot of back and forth about the penalties, but once the company is labeled a monopoly, something was going to happen.

> *Viewed together, three main facts indicate that Microsoft enjoys monopoly power. First, Microsoft's share of the market for Intel-compatible PC operating systems is extremely large and stable. Second, Microsoft's dominant market share is protected by a high barrier to entry. Third, and largely as a result of that barrier, Microsoft's customers lack a commercially viable alternative. (US v Microsoft, Findings of Fact November 5, 1999)*

It was in that Final Judgment in June 2000 that the judge ordered a structural remedy and the splitting of Microsoft into two companies. One company was to be the Windows company, and the other was to be made up of the rest of Microsoft including Office. The case had finally hit close to home.

Looking back this was a very long road. The investigation started more than six years earlier, after the Federal Trade Commission (FTC) dropped its case in a deadlocked vote and passed the authority to DOJ. I remember the early meetings from when I was working for BillG and how "crazy" all this felt at the time. While perhaps at the highest level the complaints did not change, the details and reasoning changed as the company saw more success. There was a subsequent case focused on violating the original settlement that lasted well into 1998. There was even a moment of daylight in that case when an appeals court ruled in May of that year that Microsoft could indeed integrate any software it would like into Windows so long as consumers benefitted. Then came this massive antitrust lawsuit on the heels of that small victory, often referred to internally as "the big day."

It was amazing to think how much the industry changed over this time—Windows 95 and the internet came to be—and many said the industry shifts were just starting, yet the case was still there. The arguments put forth by Microsoft insisting that market forces were already at work to "disrupt" Microsoft fell on deaf ears and were viewed as self-serving. The consensus was that Microsoft had reached an invincible, all-powerful stature that needed to be corrected.

As a practical matter, once a trial started little would change for Microsoft unless, well, we lost. Losing took a much longer time for both sides. Plus, there was always an appeal. Litigation at this level is a slog and a true test of patience. In high school we once had a guest speaker in social studies class who had a role in the AT&T breakup lawsuit which had just concluded with the breakup of AT&T. He told us he had worked his entire legal career on that case. We were dumbfounded. I now know plenty of lawyers who worked nearly their entire professional career on the Microsoft case.

That day in June, it obviously felt like we lost…badly.

Microsoft had always been comfortable in the context of litigation, perhaps owing to BillG's upbringing as the son of a prominent Seattle attorney. The earliest days of the company were characterized by a lawyerly *Open Letter to Hobbyists,* penned by BillG in 1976.[17] In the letter, he argued that software should be a royalty-based product like music. The letter was controversial in a world where all the money was in hardware with freely bundled and shared software but ushered in the pure-play software company we now know. In all fairness to Bill, the hardware side of the industry was characterized by secrecy, patents, and its own litigation.

The early software industry wrestled with how law applied to this new type of product, a product required for hardware, dreamed up like art, and manifested in a proprietary digital encoding.

In 1988 (a decade before the antitrust suit), Microsoft found itself in what it would describe as a straightforward contract dispute, and what Apple would characterize more broadly as an intellectual property dispute in Apple versus Microsoft.[18] Apple agreed to license elements of the Macintosh software for use in Windows 1.0, partially in exchange for an effort to secure Microsoft applications for Macintosh, Excel in particular. The case was front and center of the industry as Apple claimed a right to the "look and feel" of the Macintosh, which seemed to many rather unbounded, though obviously their product was unique on many levels. In a key ruling for all of software the court stated that, "Apple cannot get patent-like protection for the idea of a graphical user interface, or the idea of a desktop metaphor." While ultimately resolved in Microsoft's favor in 1996, based on contractual terms, the litigation served to condition employees to the *hurry up and wait*, and the ups and downs, of the winding nature of the US legal system. For years at the annual company meeting someone inevitably submitted a question for BillG about the case and every year he would say there is nothing new but that we felt good on the merits. In between those times, the various motions and courtroom events were rather baffling to non-lawyers, somewhat like trying to watch a cricket match for the first time and not being sure if something good was happening or for which team.

Litigation was a significant part of the industry in the early days of software as the rules of the road were established for software patents, copyright, and contracts. Another closely watched case was Lotus Corporation, a giant, suing Borland International, an upstart, for copyright violation in 1990. Borland had essentially cloned the interface of Lotus 1-2-3 and expanded upon it in its Quattro Pro product, to smooth the transition from 1-2-3 to Quattro by providing a compatibility mode. This case had profound impact on the ability for upstarts to enter an existing market because whether it was user interface or API, providing compatibility by reverse-engineering (without having access to source code or trade secrets) was key to expanding the industry. This case was decided in Borland's favor, allowing for the copyright of the Lotus implementation but not the expression of user interface in Borland's product.[19]

These as with other legal matters were often discussed more as curiosities than existential risks to the company, at least among us less senior people that had no inside scoop on the matters. Even when working with BillG, a time when many of these issues were front and center for the company, he did a remarkable job of compartmentalizing the challenges. Importantly, except for the yearly question at the all-company meeting, these topics were hardly discussed within product groups or large forums and we were always cautioned to do what we believed was in the best interests of the product and not to try to think like lawyers, a cultural challenge I would face when I moved to the post-antitrust Windows team years later.

As these suits were winding their way through the system, Microsoft's rise to the largest software company and its new power position as an unabated leader continued. From the outside, Microsoft had all the appearances of a growing software empire. From the inside, Microsoft was paranoid and felt everything was fragile and could evaporate at any moment—just as we had seen happen to the fortunes of nearly every technology company before us.

I can't emphasize this point enough. Microsoft saw all the previous microcomputer companies, many application companies, stand-alone word-processing companies, and of course the mainframe and mini companies all but vanish in the blink of an eye, falling victim to a new generation of technology. I mean Marc Andreessen himself had predicted that Netscape would render Windows a "poorly debugged set of device drivers" (he later attributed the statement to Bob Metcalf) and Microsoft's nemesis Scott McNealy at Sun Microsystems never missed an opportunity to ridicule the quality and utility of Office. Disappearing was one thing, but from a business strategy perspective, Microsoft was deeply concerned about having our competitive advantage removed by non-market forces. We'd seen what happens when a company like IBM or Intel are made to surrender their earned advantage, or in business school terms, their moat. Somewhere between fragile upstart and unstoppable force was the truth. It would take more than a decade from the first regulatory inquiries until resolution reaching some sort of détente with regulators around the world.

In hindsight, it shouldn't have been a surprise that a company could become the most well-capitalized company in the world and as a result be subject to regulation. Microsoft's views that we were just selling software at very low prices that customers and partners put to good use seemed rather quaint and naïve. The government was struggling to wrap itself around how such a huge success could come to exist without any involvement of regulators. The rise of the internet, originally funded by government research, only served as a reminder that something huge was shaping our economy and was essentially free of any government oversight. Normal issues that governments oversee such as product quality and safety, sales and marketing practices, even employment procedures had all gone unchecked. That a company maintained unfettered influence over massive societal changes was basically unacceptable.

It was always difficult to separate out the problem needing to be solved. Was it the problem of what Microsoft did? How Microsoft did that? Or was it simply the scale of success Microsoft achieved?

This mismatch of perspectives—Microsoft as a paranoid upstart just trying to keep up with the popularity of its products and a government blindsided by unregulated corporate growth and power—created a difficult situation, which required the legal and regulatory systems to resolve. Analysts, pundits, former regulators, and competitors can propose "remedies" (as if the success of Microsoft was an affliction) faster than the system can understand the problem (few in government had any expertise in software) and address it in the context of the existing laws.

Competitors complained about one set of problems. Consumers complained about another. Partners had their own issues. Economists and academics had views too. The law had its own definitions of problems. Two things were notable about this early time in Microsoft's massive success and "power."

First, parties were seeking a remedy for this problem that was not yet defined as we often liked to say. We lacked specifics, even with the 50-page complaint. Was it simply the scale of Microsoft? Was it that Windows had come to dominate the operating system market for PCs? Was Windows a monopoly? Were PCs to be treated like common utilities? Was Microsoft's business model of low-price, high-volume problematic? Was it unacceptable for one company to sell operating systems and to sell applications? Or was this about some other type of product integration such as browsers and media players? These questions did not have obvious or consistent answers back then, even among third parties. The complaint said Microsoft could not integrate a browser into Windows, but few complained when Windows added networking, file management, or game graphics. There were examples of common business practices to counter every complaint.

Second, assuming agreement was reached on the problems being solved, what would the right regulatory framework be? How do you solve the problems identified? The experts in regulation (and antitrust) were themselves products of the incredibly long-running cases of IBM, AT&T, and others. In the technology industry we looked at the IBM case and saw litigation solving the problem long after it mattered—the whole industry moved on to mini-computers, workstations, and then PCs from mainframes and it seemed this case was still going on, a condition that created a view that regulating the fast-moving technology industry did not make sense the way it might for the industrial economy. The AT&T case seemed remote as it was created by the government as a monopoly and primarily involved physical cables, and much of the unleashing of competition that took place came about not because of the new regulatory framework as much as what AT&T fought for. For example, AT&T quickly sold off the cellphone operation for a small amount to focus their win on long distance lines. But the breakup of AT&T was on everyone's mind and that led to calls to breakup Microsoft—it seemed clear if there's a monopoly it needs to be broken up into pieces. The debate over whether regulation simply stifled one of the most inventive and successful companies in US history continued.

This set up for a confrontation as the process wound through, with each side articulating extremes, and neither side particularly good at stating problems or matching problems and remedies. Microsoft, especially from its paranoid mindset as an upstart, insisted that it had done nothing wrong but make products people bought and so any interference was paramount to killing off innovation just as had happened to IBM. The punditry would opine about the need for choice and alternatives in products and suggest that Microsoft was itself already stifling innovation.

All of this activity changed the company's narrative. A few years earlier, BillG was a boy wonder, the under 30 founder who had grown a new industry for the world through the magic of software. By the mid-1990s, Bill and the company were ruthless competitors who rolled over every other entity, dictated terms for the industry, and above all could enter any market and dominate. It was this fear of what Microsoft might choose to do next that drove the most extreme views of regulatory remedies—the government needed to do something to prevent Microsoft from becoming a real-world RAMJAC, from Kurt Vonnegut novels.

Regulatory norms over a new industry were unavoidable. Governments are empowered to provide oversight and there was simply no way the newest and seemingly largest and most important industry would escape regulation. It did not matter how we thought of the fragility of our industry or even how much evidence the IBM case offered as to the futility of regulating technology.

We generally learned what little we knew about antitrust in school as it seemed to originate, in industries where a physical lock on a limited supply existed. Microsoft was a company that created an industry with none of those physical barriers, pioneering a licensing and business approach never used before (open licensing versus closed integration), even among the first to charge for software. There were many times we thought it odd that laws written for an entirely different set of circumstances would simply apply. To legal scholars and regulators, such a view was naïve and self-serving. Of course, laws could apply the lawyers would tell me.

We wished someone could have made a good argument as to why technology was different than say banks, telephones, farms, oil, autos, theaters, or shoes. But technology was not different. We quickly learned that trying to tell the regulators or those immersed in the legal system that technology was different was poorly received at best, and destructive to the dialog at worst. Simply being new was not a free pass through the system, not matter how techno-optimistic we might have been. Rather, we were naïve.

On the other hand, it would have been equally fair to have asked for those calling for remedies to do a better job articulating the problem being solved. And therein lies the challenge. Jumping to remedies that so clearly did not address the problem only made one question motives and create the appearance that parties were further apart. Championing remedies that seem to be designed to simply kneecap a single company don't serve an industry, or an economy. The political (versus legal) nature of proposed remedies only gets worse when we experienced the grandstanding in the halls of the Capitol or in endless quotes and op-eds in national publications.

Given the inevitable, but also the wide gap between parties, the process took a long time. It wasn't debilitating as some might have suggested. There was learning, discovery, and socialization. The process was more like having a chronic condition with relapsing-remitting pathology. Long periods of time went by without symptoms, then suddenly and unexpectedly there was a flare up, like the opening of new complaint by a regulator, a country getting involved for the first time, a legal filing, or even a dramatic courtroom moment. We were in an ongoing state of "hurry up and wait" as Bill Neukom (BillN), Microsoft's chief legal strategist during this time would tell me. The process often felt like those NASA drills where you knew at any moment the lights would turn red, steam would fly out of pipes, and a siren would sound signifying a crisis, but you just never knew when that would happen.

Even after all that, the conclusion of the case felt anti-climactic.

With these kinds of cases, the results are rarely as dramatic as early predictions and tend to be far more specific and, well, rational solutions to identified problems. Regulation does work when it is eventually created through the system. It might not be ideal for a newly formed company or for one hoping for more extreme remedies, but it ends up designed to solve the problems that regulators can solve. The problems Microsoft ultimately showed to have pertained to how business was conducted, in a sense these were understood to be problems of monopoly maintenance. Being declared a monopoly was certainly not fun, but in many ways, it was reality—Windows had, in fact, won. It was time for Microsoft to admit that.

Time would show that Microsoft's argument that technology winning in one era will have a hard time winning in the next was decidedly true. Continuing to debate the end-state wasn't only futile, but not done. Once a company loses in these cases, it becomes necessary to make way for the winners to own the new narrative. This might be the most difficult part to live through in the near term, and over the long term these same patterns will again play out because to the victors go the spoils, or the narrative.

063. MANAGING THE ANTITRUST VERDICT

We received little guidance regarding how to talk about legal matters. I was never under orders to avoid speaking about the trial, though that seemed like common sense. Once the verdict came down, teammates were starting to ask questions, wondering what the case meant for Office. I knew enough to know that absent anything official, people made up their own reality. I was worried that this could become a local press issue, with people talking to friends and friends talking to friends, ending up in the *Seattle Times*.

I organized an impromptu all-hands in the atrium of building 17. Anyone who wanted could attend. This was the largest space we had without going off campus, also where we presented the Office10 vision. Using a single speaker audio system, I spoke into a handheld corded microphone like a lounge singer. I walked the team through the trial and what had happened, not adding anything that was not already available to the press and public, but simply tried to casually explain the facts. What was Microsoft accused of? What was a monopoly? What does a breakup order mean? The trial team was so focused on the external press that we did not have an internal process, so I did the best I could.

I had little to offer by way of details. I took a lesson from a former test leader on the Windows team—a management lesson that permeated Microsoft, perhaps to the point of becoming apocryphal. David Maritz (DavidMa) was formerly an Israeli tank commander during his army service. His unit of tanks out in the desert would sit there in a defensive posture in the dark of night. If the radio was silent for too long, each of the tanks started to worry something was wrong with the other. Panic might sweep across the unit. David said the way they avoided this was for him to check in with the other tanks and periodically let them know that everything was OK—even though he didn't know himself. He taught us with that anecdote that even when leaders have no information, communicating something was better than nothing.

In between describing the intricacies of the legal process that would play out over years, people were worried that we were being immediately broken up, as in over the course of the coming weeks a spouse, partner, or roommate might work at "the other Microsoft." I reiterated that there were still many things that could happen before this order could become a reality, and that much was still unclear.

At least there was humor in the situation. No one in the atrium was clear on the legal goal of splitting up Microsoft between Windows and Office. As engineers and employees on the ground, it seemed kind of nuts. Presumably, the issue was that Windows and Office were working too closely, even illegally together, and that needed to stop.

In reality Office and Windows could barely get anything done together. That situation was literally the topic of every meeting across the executive team. Different schedules, different customers, different system requirements, and more reinforced how far-fetched this idea was. More than crazy, by some measures this could have the potential to be a huge relief. Office might finally be treated as a vendor, like Lotus, which we always believed received better placement at Windows developer conferences!

For a decade there were rumors that the Office team accessed secret Windows source code that no one outside of Microsoft could see and that somehow that was an advantage. There were rumors of APIs in Windows that were secretly used by Microsoft to make Office better than competitors. There was no proof of any of this, though it made for a conspiracy theory. Back in the earliest days of a tiny Microsoft, with just tens of developers on big projects, we didn't even have the technology to secure code from each other even if we wanted to. Ironically, many on the Office team remember diving in and trying to make Windows products work, not the other way around; whether it was Windows graphics for charts in Excel or printing in OS/2, it seemed that the advantage flowed to Windows. In the atrium, people were asking about this topic, and it brought a sense of levity to an otherwise unique situation because most were not around for the early days of Windows 2 and 3, or even Windows 95.

After a brutal series of motions, briefs, and other legal warfare, a year later on June 28, 2001, a federal appeals court reversed the breakup order, reprimanding and removing Judge Jackson and appointing a new judge. As often happens in these complex cases, the judge, Colleen Kollar-Kotelly, pushed to have the parties resolve their differences outside the court. By September 2001, the plaintiffs withdrew their effort to seek the breakup of Microsoft. By November, the case worked out a settlement, which Judge Kollar-Kotelly ruled served the public interest. There were no issues in the settlement regarding Office directly, though later when I moved to Windows in early 2006 some of my immediate responsibilities included complying with the terms of the settlement, which was scheduled to end in November 2007. We voluntarily extended that by two years, which meant the first release of Windows that I worked on included making sure it followed the consent decree.

While much speculation has gone into how the legal issues impacted Microsoft execution and product strategy, my view, even on the front lines back then, was that by far the biggest issue was not in the workplace specifically, but outside of it. Even though they had nothing to do with them, everyone on the team endured the negative comments about the company and its business practices. That's where the litigation and scrutiny truly caused difficulty. Consider those holiday dinners and family gatherings where an engineer on the team was called to the carpet to explain or defend Microsoft. Similarly, when recruiting college students, I frequently found myself on the phone with parents of candidates walking them through the case and the culture of Microsoft while also defending us.

Those side effects of litigation were more difficult than the specific structural and regulatory remedies.

In just a few years I would find myself on Microsoft's other side of this case, working on Windows. I would manage the last years of the consent decree, but the real challenge was cultural and bringing us back to the days of doing what was best for customers and not pre-judging every action through a legal process we on the development team were hardly expert in.

064. THE START OF OFFICE V. NETDOCS

The demonstration within the multi-hour series of keynotes was billed as a "sneak preview of something that hadn't been demoed before…technology that embodied the dot net user experience…this is real code…this technology will apply very broadly in the future across Microsoft products such as Windows.NET [pronounced Windows dot net], Office.NET as well as the consumer subscription service." What followed was a 15-minute demonstration of word processing, spreadsheet, email, calendaring that looked like Office. The demonstration was easier to use, sleeker, and more connected. It featured enthralling technologies like "universal canvas" and "XML." What's not to like?

Within a news cycle the technology demonstration had ballooned to *Office.NET* and was the future of Office. Within Microsoft, especially in Systems, nothing was higher praise than being the future project and conversely nothing was worse than being the past. The world of dueling code names had been brought to Office, except now it was Office.NET and whatever I was working on, aka Office10. What had been shown was being built by a separate team, an organizational peer of the newly christened old Office.

What was this and where did it come from? Was anyone building a product called Office.NET? Was this planned? I certainly knew the code being demonstrated, but the idea that it was presumed to be the future of Office was newsworthy, even though we did not say that directly and had not intended to leave that impression as far as I knew. Nobody wants to Osborne[20] the most profitable part of Microsoft. Weird.

Starting in early January of 2000 coinciding with SteveB's promotion to CEO and BillG assuming his new role of Chief Software Architect, BillG and PaulMa began working on a series of strategy offsites, meetings, brainstorms, memos, and more called *Next Generation Windows Services*, or NGWS. There was even a new leadership team formed called the TLT, *Technology Leadership Team*. Everything was kicked off with memos from both BillG and SteveB highlighting NGWS. BillG explained in a memo *Opportunities in the "Software Decade"* that NGWS was a bet on par with the graphical interface in both the transformation and opportunity. By now, I was seeing this as a familiar playbook. If you want to say something is big, then compare it to the graphical interface. SteveB also had a memo, *Changes and Opportunities*.

These memos, Bill's detailing the technology at a very high level and Steve's articulating a customer and business focus put forward an innovation agenda for the company. The goal was to let Microsofties know the company was committed to innovation, especially with the rise of dot-com companies and the huge valuation of anything internet in the public markets. It would be a few months until the market corrected itself, but Microsoft at this juncture was generally in a defensive posture. A broad re-branding was intended to create a new narrative for the company, supported by a next generation of technologies designed for the internet from the ground up, at least starting from Windows.

Just days after Bill's memo, there was a call for participation in the NGWS planning sessions. A detailed series of offsites and meetings were scheduled. Literally, the invitation stated the work was to figure out the details of NGWS as introduced in the memos.

In other words, we had a brand before we knew its meaning. That is not entirely fair because there were at least two key strategies under development. A series of projects defining consumer internet services such as email, calendaring, and identity were being developed by a group of the most senior leaders previously of Windows NT and others from around the company, an effort that would later become known as *Hailstorm*—consumer-focused experiences that also provided a platform for developers. A second effort encompassed the creation of a new programming platform for building internet applications on the server, which was just becoming known as .NET, dot net. This initiative included a variety of tools and platform work that built on the lessons from the first generation of internet applications.

To confuse matters, the .NET branding was starting to be picked up by a range of groups and products, including the next release of Windows NT Server which was sometimes referred to as Windows.NET, which was originally code-named Whistler, then later Windows Server 2002, then finally Windows Server 2003. The .NET name was also used for the APIs and programming tools which would collectively be called the *.NET Framework*, for programming both servers and desktops. If you're confused reading this, then you were not alone. NGWS was an umbrella term for everything, and .NET was intended to be a technology term, but we sort of ended up with two umbrella terms. The .NET branding was one of the more chaotic and self-inflicted product naming efforts. Was it .net, .NET, or .Net? Before or after the product name? With a space or without?

Like BillG's previous memo on software as a service, this memo also lacked any mention of Office. I was beginning to see a pattern. Only now that I was managing Office I started to wonder if I was somehow contributing to this. Whenever I reviewed drafts of these memos, I did not seek to include Office out of a reflex to fly under the radar and to avoid making promises for work that was not even underway, a strategy reinforced by my time working as BillG's technical assistant. The team always noticed, and I found myself doing my best to explain the virtues of being left out of the strategic fray. Should I have lobbied or been more forceful about including Office? Many would be naturally inclined to run towards the limelight, but so far in Microsoft's history that proved to be less than helpful. The Cairo OS project was a top-of-mind example.

PaulMa and the platform teams planned a strategy presentation for the press and industry analysts detailing Microsoft's internet-centric developer strategy. Originally scheduled for early June 2000, the event was delayed several times because of the looming court ruling in the antitrust trial. The NGWS working groups welcomed the extra time. The evangelism efforts did not slow, however, and the first half of 2000 was a steady stream of stories about what NGWS might be along with the implications of the looming court ruling on NGWS, or perhaps speculation that NGWS was an effort to end-run the potential court ruling.

The Windows team generally loved these strategy days as a key part of the culture. PaulMa would often describe them to me as a "forcing function," which meant a way to coalesce disparate groups into a shared plan. In this case, the planned event would force upon us a collective definition of NGWS.

The industry loved these events too. These were made-for-press events. Stories would run describing what could be announced in the lead-up (called curtain-raisers) and after the event there would be ample analysis. As was almost always the case, the event would gain a nickname or acronym. The event almost always included a new strategy with its own name or acronym. On the heels of *Internet Strategy Day* and *Windows DNA* (Distributed internet

Architecture), the press was anxious to learn what else was on the way. Frequently, such event days would get scheduled with only a vague idea of what would get talked about and shown. This was one of those events.

The weeks leading up to the event were chaotic and high stress. While the goal was to present a coherent strategy, the process of creating the strategy was more important—the forcing function. This was how Platforms came together as a team. Whether a PDC (Professional Developer Conference), a workshop, or a strategy event, Platforms used the process of creating the presentations the same way Office used memos and the vision planning process. Only Office spent months and involved a broad cross-section of the team across disciplines whereas Windows spent weeks and usually involved the *key people*, however that might be defined. Instead of detailed plans and schedules like we created in Office, the output consisted primarily of bullet points and architectural diagrams in PowerPoint.

Dubbed *Forum 2000*, the event proved a seminal moment in the evolution of Microsoft's platform and quickly came to be known as *.NET Strategy Day* or *.NET Day*, and SteveB would refer to it as "most ambitious undertaking since Internet Strategy Day in 1995." The event aimed to be almost a "mother of all demos", in reference to the legendary 1968 demonstration of the first graphical interface, hyperlinks, video conferencing, and mouse.[21]

At this point, Microsoft's approach to strategy presentations was adept at mixing a combination of BillG-style architecture slides with short and slickly produced video vignettes complete with keyed in screen mockups. The series of scenarios envisioning the future of software enabled by .NET formed the heart of the strategy articulated at Forum 2000. They featured the gamut of nascent technologies that were frequently talked about including tablet/pen computers, handwriting, wireless, voice control, video chat, location awareness, presence awareness, notifications, mobile devices, and so much more. The scenarios and designs had a decidedly consumer feel including the bubbly buttons and logotype used in MSN.

There was a slight problem in that the gap between what the audience saw in those demos and what any team might have been working on was, well, significant. It was not that many technologies were decades away from possibility, but only bits and pieces of a product were being worked. The role of a platform strategy is to inspire, however, not necessarily detail everything that is available in short order. Like the 1994 *Information at Your Fingertips* keynote, these sketches of the future were prescient and designed to create a *north star* for the company (a favorite expression) and even the industry. So, while it was a challenge to be so far out, it was intentional. Unlike previous visionary presentations, Forum 2000 was far more specific in terms of product and roadmap. That was the problem.

Today one might look at these presentations and the underlying products that emerged as evidence of many ideas where Microsoft was early, but for one reason or another fumbled in the transition to the modern world. It would be fair to say Microsoft was early to many shifts over the years, but as was so often the case being early ends up being wrong as well. When one is early and fails, the problem was usually that the culture or technology underpinnings are not yet mature enough to support the vision or the market was simply not ready. One could go through each of the technologies shown to realize the decade that would be required to bring them to market. A Tablet PC required screens and processors that did not exist. Handwriting recognition had been stuck at a level of reliability that was more frustrating than useful. Mobile devices would undergo a huge transformation with touchscreens and ubiquitous data connectivity. The services talked about would ultimately arrive with an entirely different architecture than Microsoft was building out at the time. Technologies such as XML would be widely used, but as commoditized as plain text files have always been and confer no real proprietary advantage as Microsoft hoped. Other technologies, such as virtualization that were key to the early cloud era had been rejected and would not play a part in Microsoft server strategy for another 5 years. Early efforts tend to be pointed in the right general direction, but the small errors or incorrect initial assumptions compound over time and ultimately diverge far too much from what eventually makes it to market.

Strategically, the comparison to the transition to the graphical interface was front and center and was used several times throughout the presentation. Our shared desire to repeat that transition and the success that followed provides evidence that being early is good. Windows arrived before the computational power and memory capacity could run the software we built. Taking time for technology to catch up did not deter us. Perhaps what would ultimately trip us up, however, was the grandeur and interconnectedness of our collective plans that left little room for execution error or for influences from the outside world and what was transpiring on the internet at a rapid pace. As many would note critically following the event, it was still about Windows at the center and to truly be a new strategy the conventional wisdom held that Windows needed to be abandoned. It is not at all clear to me that was the mistake, though it does make a simple narrative.

This was the peak moment for the catch phrase developed in response to the antitrust complaint of integrating software into Windows—*integrated innovation*. We overachieved on integrated innovation in that everything was integrated with Windows as we thought we should be permitted to do. Our defense was also our strategy, and also our technology foundation.

Nevertheless, the industry was excited by all this big talk. If there was a theme to the day, it was innovation. Every section of the day featured an explicit slide calling out innovation. This was a subtle jab at the critics and regulators who felt Microsoft achieved a dominant position and grown subsequently complacent. Innovation highlights were provided for .NET Services, .NET User Experience, .NET Programming, Small Business, and Business Users. That's a lot of innovation! In addition to the videos, we showed live demonstrations of code: the earliest Tablet PC prototype and handwriting recognition, a new browser-based service for small businesses, and the technology demonstration described earlier.

Perhaps more abstractly, the day was about a new era for Microsoft. There were the existing products and from this point forward there were new products built in new ways that would solve the problems the old products had built up. Everything was going to be faster, take less memory, reduce administrative burdens, and provide new levels of capability and convenience for customers. Microsoft clearly divided the world into old and new. That was bold and companies almost always lack the fortitude to make such statements clearly.

Competitively and concretely, .NET (using the term broadly as everyone did) was Microsoft's answer to Java for server programmers. That was the big battle driving the platforms strategy. Java had captured the hearts and minds of developers building web server applications. The .NET technologies for enterprise software development would go on to create the platform that dominated in-house enterprise IT software, creating a generation of .NET programmers who today are more than comfortable with Microsoft as a provider of cloud infrastructure, even if it is Linux and not Windows. While the .NET programming tools would launch over the next year, this was the first real stake in the ground. On the PC desktop and client, we had won with Internet Explorer and felt confident, which allowed the vision for the user experience portions of the presentations to move forward with fewer constraints and a focus on what was done on the PC but also supported in the browser—a desktop-first strategy.

It took 18 months before the first product release with the .NET architecture, Visual Studio .NET which was the first product to use the .NET name. The server product line underwent a pivot to support the new capabilities. Ultimately, .NET and its companion and proprietary programming language C# were enormously successful for Servers and Tools and came to define the era of enterprise client/server computing—so much so that most of today's leaders in IT were products of the .NET era and, as a result, Microsoft created a generation of business IT leaders strongly connected to the company. Much of Microsoft's strength today in enterprise accounts can be directly tied to IT leaders that rose up the ranks by betting on .NET.

Closer to home, the session on "User Experience" which was really about Office featured a presentation by a group building what instantly became known as *Office.NET* even though there was a clear demarcation of "technology demonstration"—we loved to think these small changes in wording brought us air cover or permitted distinction between products and directional demonstrations. To clarify, the technology demonstration did not claim to be Office.NET but the roadmap slides of product releases we presented at the time used the name and provided a "2002+" ship date.

The technology came from BrianMac, creator of Outlook, who upon leaving Outlook started up a new team called *NetDocs*, for network documents. NetDocs reported to BobMu, my manager at the time as well, though Brian and I had not crossed paths all that much since Outlook. We were both focused on what we needed to get done separately.

BrianMac formed the NetDocs team much the same way he built the Outlook team, growing the team to over one hundred in short order. The vision for the product was expansive and included many hot, new technologies. It was also being written in the latest technologies, including the latest magic technology XML (eXtensible Markup Language, which was becoming increasingly popular as part of programming for the browser) and, more importantly, it was using many of the new capabilities in Internet Explorer. XML also the latest *magic beans* technology that took on capabilities much greater than reality. Brian had a knack for constructing expansive visions assembled with the strategic technologies as we saw with the creation of Outlook. As with Outlook these technologies were new, unproven, and unfinished. Outlook did quite well.

The scenarios enabled by the NetDocs vision subsumed Office, particularly Outlook, Word, Excel, and more, but with a decidedly modern take. By modern, the implication was that people no longer needed to worry about which Office app to use as there was one single document type, the universal canvas, that worked equally well with words, numbers, graphics, and email, and was easier to use because of that. This was not a new vision and in fact the idea of integrated packages had a history of attempts from both Lotus and Ashton Tate in the pre-Windows era, as well as Microsoft's Works application, a modest success and much-loved product for price sensitive customers. The all-in-one application was a favorite among the first generation of PC users and BillG in particular who routinely complained about overlap and redundancy across the various "modules" in Office, modules being his favorite way to describe an app in the suite. Would this time be different? Did the processing power and memory finally enable this? NetDocs set out to prove it could.

I was skeptical, but from my position in Office skepticism was viewed by others as defensive and territorial. I wasn't being defensive. I just didn't think it could work. Others projected it could be a $1 billion business within three years.

A running joke at the time was that every new product idea somehow included digital photos, and Forum 2000 was no exception. Every demo included digital photos in some form. Digital cameras were the hot consumer item and sharing photos on the internet was becoming mainstream. NetDocs not only included photos, but to illustrate the importance of photos, a product that was extremely innovative but languishing at retail without sales and marketing support, Microsoft PhotoDraw, was reorganized into the NetDocs team. This method of building a new team by acquiring other internal teams and jettisoning their existing product was a strategy employed with Outlook as well. I was a big fan of PhotoDraw and to me it was one of many examples of innovative tools Microsoft created that we were unable to capitalize on because it was too small on its own and too niche to be part of Office—this will become a familiar theme shortly.

There was another running joke that every new product idea being dreamed up somehow also included electronic mail—email was the anchor of the internet and became a big deal for AOL, Yahoo, and MSN. Microsoft was a clear email leader with Exchange, but that was for business. For consumers, Microsoft's MSN division acquired Hotmail in 1997, the first web-based, viral, and free internet mail. The number of email users on that service was approaching 100 million when the entire internet population was roughly 300 million. NetDocs also became email. That should not be a surprise given the roots of the team and leaders.

Photos, email, calendaring, XML, word processing, spreadsheets…that's a lot, a lot to like.

NetDocs also enabled a new subscription business model. There was nothing particularly technical about doing this work, though convincing customers to *rent* software (as people thought of it at the time) was new. The team was working on a new technology to provide seamless updating of the NetDocs Windows desktop application over the internet. Seamless updates might convince customers of the benefits of rental over ownership as the product could be enhanced without purchasing anything new. Customers were struggling to deal with updates, most of whom were not yet able to use the Windows Update service that is now standard on every PC.

Given my early experience getting the first version of Outlook to customers, I remained skeptical of NetDocs achieving all that was sketched out, especially without the kind of constraints being part of the Office release imposed on Outlook originally. The amount of code to write, the ever-changing scope (and resistance to constraints), the huge challenges of building some compatibility and interoperability with Office, as well as the fragility of the technology foundation—as the latest and greatest always seem to be—were not usually a recipe for success and seemed familiar. The success Outlook achieved, due in no small part to being free and bundled with Office and more importantly the only client for Exchange email, provided a halo of sorts for NetDocs. This is a good lesson in how success in a big company can take many forms beyond customers laying out their cash for a product.

I had not paid attention to NetDocs (nor NetDocs to Office) and now suddenly and without warning, NetDocs was front and center strategically for the company. NetDocs was filling a void in the strategy, at least internally which was that for the .NET platform to be successful it needed a killer Office application. I should have internalized that strategic point going to the NGWS meetings, but I did not. I managed the Office10 project aware of the costs of choosing to lay low—that people would view Office as failing to support the platform or even to acknowledge the future. In an industry (and especially a company) where the next version is always way better than the current version and new platforms always require the leading apps to support them, it was challenging to take this approach.

This old versus new dynamic always creates tensions in a large company. Echoing *Innovator's Dilemma* (again), a series of press stories played out over several months. While there were grumblings, overwhelmingly people on the respective product teams were not consumed with potential overlap—Microsoft had a long history of next generation projects that fizzled. When will NetDocs replace Office? Will Office stand by and allow NetDocs to replace it? Will customers be confused? How will the market deal with two kinds of Office products? This was a far cry from the Cairo versus Windows NT, or the Windows NT versus Windows 95 battles that played out over years, at least I thought that to be the case.

During these times that the negatives the market perceives of the incumbent are amplified irrationally—software bloat, nothing left to add, slowing growth in the business, and more. Simultaneously, the perceived positives of the new product are amplified irrationally: sleek, modern, simpler, faster, lighter weight, innovative, and new. Microsoft was great at setting up this dynamic. I had been the poster child for old technology and resistance to change more than once (Java Office, component Office, web Office), and while I could brush it off, in the case of NetDocs and Office there was quite a bit of bashing externally of a product that was half of the company's profits. The internal tension was significant, but not because of a deliberate product competition or organizational competition for resources, but because there's no way to constructively align the past Office with an ever-expanding vision. Regardless of the strategy, NetDocs could have laid low and first spent a couple of years building a product. It just wasn't in Microsoft's culture to do so at this time given the demands to put a big vision out there.

Nothing could stop the Forum 2000 train. This was exactly what NGWS needed. There was broad satisfaction with the event, even though ongoing legal challenges clouded the strategic presentations and strategy. The future was .NET everything including Office.NET.

Deciding to show NetDocs at Forum 2000 was controversial, at least with me, and probably not many others. I was usually the most conservative about showing products or features with an uncertain path to shipping, let alone version 1.0 products built on version 1.0 technologies accomplishing new scenarios that often didn't pan out. There were also legitimate concerns that word of a modern Office.NET could slow or halt progress on Enterprise Agreements, in an extremely touchy post-dot-com bubble business environment.

After many email threads prior to the event, NetDocs ended up showing some basic features, such as typing into a word processor-like screen, summing a column of numbers without launching a spreadsheet, and a calendar scenario that used XML technology to merge a personal calendar with a Seattle Mariners calendar. The session painfully reiterated the "technology demonstration" aspects of the demo and never used the phrase Office.NET, though the prominence of Office.NET on the roadmap left few dots to connect.

To mitigate the risk to Enterprise Agreements, the demo was said to be relevant to Microsoft's new small business offering, briefly called *bCentral*. For almost another decade, the Office strategy for the web and internet targeted small business starting with bCentral and always using branding to show a distinct separation from Office for enterprise. This compartmentalized a new approach to the less risky market segment where Microsoft had more upside than downside. For big business, they were pushed to see things through the lens of Windows Server and the software housed in company data centers along with desktop Office, all available with an Enterprise Agreement. This was a defensive approach but was consistent with how customers thought about Microsoft products. Word and Excel were indispensable tools for small business, and increasingly Outlook, especially with many add-ins, was the preferred tool for small businesses to manage sales and customers. Customers could not buy Exchange and set up Windows Active Directory and file/print servers fast enough. In practice, operationalizing the transition outlined was more practical and somewhat defensive, echoing the *Innovator's Dilemma*.

The Wall Street Journal was quick to pick up on the potential challenges as well in a story by Rebecca Buckman shortly after the event "Microsoft Readies a New `Office' While Renovating the Old Standby" where she wrote:

> *What does a company do when its single-biggest product is in danger of being eclipsed by new technologies?*
>
> *If that company is Microsoft Corp., and the product is Office, it sets up a stealth team of crack engineers to dream up a brand-new version of the software suite — while continuing to crank out the old standby. It's a tough, two-track strategy that has pitted a "today" development team against a "tomorrow" team, as one person close to the teams puts it — and it's still unclear, he says, "how today and tomorrow will meet."*

As we know now, the danger of being eclipsed did not materialize. We deliberately and somewhat nervously made that bet, as previously described. The teams were not pitted against each other, not yet anyway.

PCWeek reporter Mary Jo Foley loved the NetDocs story and wrote about it many times. By the end of the year, a few months after Forum 2000 she said in a story "Netdocs: Microsoft's .Net poster child?" where she described the product as:

> *Netdocs is a single, integrated application that will include a full suite of functions, including e-mail, personal information management, document-authoring tools, digital-media management, and instant messaging. Microsoft (msft) will make Netdocs available only as a hosted service over the Internet, not as a shrink-wrapped application or software that's preloaded on the PC.*
>
> *Netdocs will feature a new user interface that looks nothing like Internet Explorer or Windows Explorer. Instead, Netdocs will deliver an integrated workspace based on the Extensible Markup Language (XML), where all of its application modules are available simultaneously. This interface is based on .Net technology that Microsoft, in the past, has referred as "Universal Canvas."*

There was nothing sinister or even that planful about what was going on. It was just…going on.

We were busy, and well into building Office10. At the very least, until NetDocs was usable (self-hostable) by more people, the best thing to do was let them keep writing code and hope they stopped trying to recruit people from Outlook.

NetDocs versus Office was just going to simmer for a while. There was no way around that. Because we were in the midst shipping (eight months to go) and NetDocs now had a deadline of sorts, there wasn't room to attempt to reconcile the products, have them relate strategically, or really do much of anything. I was happy to work heads down and not worry about it.

Putting Forum 2000 in perspective, SteveB sent an all-company follow-up email briefly laying out the strategy and timeline we were undertaking. He reinforced the huge change by referring to the strategy as "Microsoft .NET" (the space after Microsoft was important), coming very close to rebranding or even renaming the company around this new strategy:

> *Microsoft .NET will be delivered in three forms: a new user experience; infrastructure and tools; and a set of programmable .NET Building Blocks. This is a long-term strategy, one that will take years to execute fully, so it is critical that we all stay focused – not only on our goal but also on the daily steps it will take to achieve it.*

The Office team was focused on Office10. We would worry about NetDocs later.

065. SHAREPOINT: OFFICE BUILDS OUR OWN SERVER

"We need an 'Office' server" was another one of those drive by lunchroom conversations with SteveB before he became CEO. It was a concrete expression of an abstraction. What he was really saying was that Office needed to think broadly about how to solve the problems information workers were having. That business card he used to make a note of "find me all the stuff about France" was now looking like a product issue for Office. We were all-in on the opportunity and were well ahead of Steve, having been thinking about this from the moment we saw FrontPage. We made it through the 97 and 2000 product cycles and FrontPage had established itself as a favorite tool of Internet Service Providers. We were ready to build on that foundation and expand the little web server we had been using to share product documents on the team. An Office server was a key part of the Office10 vision. The path from vision to RTM was not going to be a straight line.

The first half of the year 2000 was nothing short of eventful:

- Microsoft and customers survived the looming Y2K apocalypse. Despite dystopian fears, except for a few trivial and humorous problems, nothing went wrong at midnight.
- Windows 2000 shipped.
- Microsoft rose to an astronomical $500 billion market cap.
- Then the NASDAQ dropped more than 2,000 points with the dot-com bubble becoming a defining event of the rise of the internet.
- Judge Jackson declared Microsoft a monopoly that violated the Sherman Act (causing a 15 percent post-bubble stock price drop), and then later ordered the split of Microsoft.
- Office was attacked by a massive virus, resulting in the disabling of core product features.
- Capping this off, Forum 2000 was a landmark event in the evolution of Windows Server and introduction of what would become *Hailstorm* in an effort to rebuild Microsoft as an innovator in the internet era.
- PaulMa retired from Microsoft after having had an incredible influence on the company's operating systems, platforms, and enterprise transformation.

It was also the start of SteveB's tenure as CEO. Many believed this would mean little or no change given how SteveB was known widely as the "third founder." SteveB would lead sales and marketing leadership and overall company execution. BillG would lead on technology vision and strategy. This seemed a formalization of what we always felt was the case. On the other hand, how could someone so different keep doing things the same way?

Earlier in the Spring of 1999, there was a *BusinessWeek* cover story about the remaking of Microsoft. It featured a photo of Bill and Steve together and the subheading "While Bill Gates plots strategy…Steve Ballmer shakes up the culture."

With so much going on, Steve's first reorganization as CEO seemed relatively minor even expected given how the sales force he created reorganized almost yearly. It didn't seem like much of a "remaking of Microsoft" as the headlines touted months ago. There were some new people, but the big changes were in financial reporting.

Jeff Raikes (JeffR) returned to Office in the role of group vice president of the soon-to-be-renamed Productivity and Business Services (PBS) division. It was noteworthy that the name included *services* as per the end of 1999 strategy mail from BillG. JeffR was among the most tenured executives and led the original "Office" organization, the Office Business Unit, OBU, home to Word and Mail. Jeff joined Microsoft in 1981 when the company was 100 or so people, recruited from Apple by SteveB for a product role in Apps, where he led marketing for the original wave of Macintosh applications and also shared a house with Steve for several months. On his PocketPC he used to keep a "days at Microsoft" Pocket Excel sheet he would open up when talking about how long he'd been at the company. Jeff was frequently mistaken for BillG, as both sported the requisite Microsoft uniform of loafers, khakis, and collared shirts, but it was the '80s plastic-rimmed glasses that sealed the deal. He grew up in Nebraska, often describing his beloved family farm, an aerial photo of which hung in his office. Before Apple, Jeff attended Stanford. Jeff was the earliest of advocates of pen and tablet computing, leading those as part of Microsoft's first foray into what was then called *Windows for Pen Computing*, which was also my first booth duty demonstration using C++ to code for a pen. Jeff also wrote an early memo describing the scenario that would become Excel pivot tables.

Prior to leading PBS, JeffR was the leader of the global sales force, having taken over for SteveB upon his transition to president. He pioneered the mid-year review process, which became a staple of the fiscal year planning process with its all-day meetings held through the entire month of January, all around the world. Among the sales team, Jeff was a legendary leader and stood shoulder-to-shoulder with SteveB in the evolution of sales at the company.

With his success in the field, Jeff was more a product of the SteveB perspective on problems and solutions owing to his most recent experience scaling the enterprise field sales organization. As Bill's longtime friend, he was probably the only executive that was equally well-versed in both BillG and SteveB.

Jeff brought with him a team of support personnel. There was even a chief of staff, a role standard in the field but foreign to the product groups. This was hard to escape notice as we had quite a few offices and a big conference room taken *offline* (reserved) when in 2004 we eventually moved into the new building 36 that we had fought hard to occupy. Part of assembling the staff ended up taking a good chunk of the top floor of Building 36, which was designed to maximize space for the team, including window offices and already maxed out with the dev team. Space was always the subject of intramural skirmishes.

As part of the staffing of the PBS organization, for the first time, the Office group had substantial and dedicated finance and HR teams front and center of the organization—a seat at JeffR's leadership team meeting. Some little things that were normal in the field seemed awkward or at least different in the product groups—like routine emails drafted by a staff member to be sent by Jeff for various planning or process tasks or scheduling meetings months in advance. JeffR scheduled everything, so spontaneous chats or walking by the office to talk became less the norm. Instead of PeteH stopping by my office, CollJ (our executive assistant) would get an email from JeffR's assistant "Can you make sure your exec is available for..."

It was natural though not necessarily mature of me to be skeptical of seemingly trivial changes, but these took place in the larger context of SteveB changes. I was not sure the new processes were consistent with a product-development team culture that was casual, ad hoc, and direct, but perhaps that was the point. During the transition I recalled a story that a former SteveB field staffer told me after he moved to Office marketing. He described how when SteveB moved from the Windows HQ product group to lead Sales, SteveB shifted his hardcore perspective on budget accountability. He changed to believe the field should be responsible for marketing dollars rather than the headquarters (product) group that needed additional discipline, a complete reversal from his days in HQ. As SteveB changed perspective, the problem area moved too. I started to feel we were a problem and Jeff's role was to fix something. I wasn't sure what or who was the problem.

Almost right away, JeffR pushed us to better equip the field to sell a big vision for the future of knowledge workers. This had been a long simmering tension point around Office, where I always felt squeezed between making sure we did not cause problems with customers timing Enterprise Agreement (EA) sales and customers wanting to know the future so they might sign up for an Enterprise Agreement. There was always that looming problem of future releases sounding so exciting, customers would choose to wait. Office was under a lot of pressure to get customers to deploy the current version and not wait. It seemed logical that talking about the future would only slow down deployment. This was clearly something that needed to be fixed. In fact, there were echoes of the SteveB 100 one-on-one meetings where he pushed me on this topic. Overall products were still late to market, and we'd just put ourselves out there massively with the expectations set by Forum 2000.

What the field wanted were more materials like Forum 2000, not better demos and whitepapers about Office 2000. The new head of Office marketing explained to me "when I used to work at IBM, we sold more products today based on slide decks about the future, then on any demonstrations of what today's products actually did."

I still admit I have a difficult time with that logic, but I am grown up enough now to know it is the reality of enterprise selling. I was uncomfortable selling the future. I was forever hung up on making promises we could not keep, or at least were not sure we could keep. I also felt selling the future was fraught with opportunities for misunderstanding. I've seen customers extrapolate features in directions we'd never go. It is obvious in hindsight I was just an engineer and naïve to the ways of sales. I was stuck feeling too high integrity to sell. I was silly.

There was one exception. We found a way to craft our own version of the future that was so far removed from product specifics, that it could not be mistaken for future product versus a futuristic vision.

To show customers (and JeffR) what Office was going to be like, we created a whole experience, almost a Disney-esque Future World of Productivity. MikeAng (now leading product planning) and the design team set up an *Office of the Future*. The team literally built an entire onsite immersive experience called the *Center for Information Work*. It occupied several large rooms (2600 sq ft) in a space next door to the EBC, Executive Briefing Center. Inspired by the soon-to-be blockbuster film *Minority Report* starring Tom Cruise (dystopian vision aside), the CIW offered guests a giant wall projecting status of the business—metrics for manufacturing, orders, and more. By a careful combination of scripting and clicking of wireless remotes, the demo revealed wall-size status reports, alerts, problems, and resolutions.

The CIW had a mock-up of an airplane cabin, long before there was Wi-Fi. There was a car of the future, where work and important decision-making continued *en route*, something that was just starting to take hold with wireless headsets, BlackBerry phones, and PDAs. Mike had listened to me go on and on about my new Toyota Prius hybrid and how futuristic it felt with an oddly mounted gear shift and big touch screen, so he secured a Prius dashboard and front seat, making the auto portion of the exhibit forward-thinking, and for me, super cool. Mike briefly regretted humoring me when SteveB's main account, Ford, showed up and gave us grief over the car choice.

There were several workstations at the CIW with a wraparound, curved, 180-degree-view display, with the screens partitioned for monitoring activities, work, and collaboration. Curved displays weren't available to buy but, working with display manufacturers, a curved perspective was created by stitching together flat screens with no bezels—innovative at the time.

The centerpiece was a Microsoft Research project called RingCam developed by Anoop Gupta's team (AnoopG, who was also a BillG technical assistant), which was a combination of hardware and software for conducting remote meetings, in 2000! The camera sat in the middle of the table seamlessly capturing the audio and video of all attendees. It featured a fancy array microphone that combined with software to detect the speaker and switch the video image to them. At each chair in the conference room there was a Wi-Fi-connected Tablet PC. The PC was an integrated part of the demonstration—documents were signed, spreadsheets were examined, and notes were taken on this device of the future. As if to emphasize the permanence and paramount importance of tablets, the conference room table featured integrated, angled stands for the tablets designed for hands-free viewing and notetaking.

For the first time, I felt like we had an opportunity to get ahead of the constant demand for the future of Office. We revealed no dates, no specific features, but successfully put forth a vision for the seamless use of technology to enhance collaboration, improve decision-making, and integrate data into daily work.

Over the next months, CIW became a meeting place for CEOs, heads of state, VIPs, press, and customers considering Enterprise Agreements visiting Microsoft. Soon there was a team that ran tours nonstop. Over 1000 customers per month made their way through the exhibit.

We found success for the field by creating a story about what we might build one day presented like a World's Fair exhibit that in no way could be confused with a product roadmap or plans.

JeffR's new leadership team embarked on its first group project—to identify areas for growth in the business. The business was growing high double digits, but we were forever paranoid about peaking and the bottom falling out. JeffR and the new finance and business development team engaged a major consulting firm to develop a market map for the whole of the business productivity space. Where was all the money on business software going? This project became known as the *opportunity map* as we crafted a vision for PBS—not a vision like Office or CIW but a plan for determining what new categories of software to enter or serve.

Outside of Microsoft broad horizontal tools like word processing and spreadsheets, the software industry was in an expansion phase driven by the rise of server computing and the web. Businesses were building out data centers and adding server-based applications for sales, marketing, finance, human resources, and more. These tools were domain-specific capabilities that often featured integration with Office, particularly Outlook and Excel, and were generally much more expensive per user than Office, though used by fewer people. The opportunity map was designed to capture the amount of revenue flowing to the rest of the productivity software space.

The map, unsurprisingly, looked as much like a set of opportunities as it did like a set of all the tools that integrated with Office or all the tools that weren't Office. Categories like Customer Relationship Management (CRM) were highly dependent on using email and integrating with Outlook as the user interface. Business intelligence for finance analyzed vast amounts of transactional data from SAP, or Oracle products to be sliced and diced in Excel, even if they worked to provide analysis in a web browser. While the market need existed to solve these product areas and scenarios, we always struggled with bringing to market domain-focused products while also running the risk of competing with partners who were telling their customers to buy Office.

The question arose as to how we would sell any new products. Would we add new dedicated salespeople for new products, bundle those products with the existing EA, or just add features to Office? We could add features to Office but charging more for them rather than leveraging those features to drive EA renewal and upgrades was something we faced many times. The pull of bundling more and more into the core value proposition was relentless and the path of least resistance. Even creating an upsell SKU by holding back specific features was a battle against just making sure the customer renewed their EA. Equally difficult was marshaling a new field sales process should we have an entirely new product to sell. Everything was a tradeoff against either finding new EAs or ensuring renewals. I had run into this buzzsaw before and was skeptical, even with Jeff's command of the field, that we would be able to find ways to sell whole new products.

It also didn't help that most of these market map businesses relied heavily on consulting and professional services, something Microsoft steadfastly avoided. BillG was not a fan of consulting just as he long disliked product support or anything that could scale by only adding more people. As we kept learning, most of the integration with Office was less about the strengths of Office and more about trying to be part of the sales momentum and ubiquity of Office—using Microsoft's distribution channel potentially afforded by Office. The makers of these tools did not necessarily want more software integration from Microsoft. Rather they wanted to find a way to insert their products into the massive Microsoft sales engine. If this sounds at all familiar, it is the dynamic we hear today time and again from SaaS companies.

Document Management was a market map opportunity that served customers such as law firms and pharmaceutical companies producing huge numbers of documents, requiring a detailed history of changes to those documents. Customers were always clamoring for a solution from Microsoft in the hopes it would be cheaper, or even free with Office. The existing market was a typical domain-specific product with high prices, low volume, requiring consulting or value-added resellers.

Aiming to enter this market while also broadening or redefining it, a server product under development in a different organization since 1998, Tahoe, planned to cater to the new space of *knowledge management*, a growing category of software for white-collar workers. The capabilities planned for the first version included managing a company's Office documents, collaboration, versioning, profiling, and security. These features were to compete with products used in document-heavy professions such as legal and research. Tahoe was also going to be a server for an intranet that supported professional content management tools, web search (like Yahoo but for your own information), and more. Tahoe was going to do quite a bit, perhaps too much. Jeff Teper (JeffTe) led Tahoe and this new product team.

Tahoe. a codename, was a good example of a product arguably designed from the field sales organization out. As an example, at one tumultuous presentation to sales leaders I attended, Steve was anxious backstage to deliver a message to the field that Redmond had heard his calls for an Office server. The work we had done with Office Server Extensions and FrontPage in Office 2000 was not enough. We needed a product for the new generation of *Chief Knowledge Officers* (a new job big companies were creating) to compete with Lotus/IBM Notes, later renamed Domino. He knew of the Tahoe plans, but it didn't seem like enough. There were existing plans for other products with code names (Grizzly, Polar) and even a side project known as "Digital Dashboard." In a classic reaction, he was saying we needed more, and sooner.

In what I can only remember as a blur of a tension-filled few moments, all the roadmaps for those products were realigned with components moved from one to another. It was confusing and I had only the vaguest idea of what would get produced. I just knew deciding backstage at a sales meeting probably would not stick. There was a confusing clarification issued after the meeting which remains difficult to parse. I struggled quite a bit because I knew we were in the space with code, dates, and a plan for Office10, but it lacked a certain strategic glow that the other products had. Our execution focused plan could not compete with big visions to dominate an entire ambiguous category of knowledge management. We just wanted to help people share and collaborate with Office. Our products were simple and, effectively, non-strategic.

That glow was that the envisioned product relied on and connected our entire server product line: Windows Server, Active Directory, Exchange (including the new release code-named Platinum), and SQL Server. What the field and strategic people loved was that knowledge management from Microsoft used (or required) all the servers too. Such strategic connections were great for efficiency of sales resources and messaging. The whole package could be bundled up as knowledge management and the sales process focused on that high-level message, and not product-focused messages across five different areas. This approach spoke to CIOs and their strategy, not to line executives and execution. In a sense, this approach solved for knowledge management by creating another bundle, but not one designed and built together.

That such a product would be next to impossible to deliver and almost certainly fail to work well, was unfortunately a secondary concern.

In parallel with Tahoe (and the other products), the Office server we were building for Office10 had already survived a tumultuous run-up to get to solid plans. We based the project on FrontPage and the solid market foundation we had built. To handle key scenarios, we needed an additional place to store data beyond standard Windows file servers. For example, customers might want to label a document for marketing and another for sales and then quickly sort or select documents for only one category. The obvious solution to this was SQL but we were organizationally much closer to Exchange, the mail server, especially because of Outlook. Selling Exchange was slightly more important than selling SQL, owing to the battle with IBM/Lotus and the long-term advantage we would gain from an Exchange win.

We spent months going around in circles trying to make Exchange work. At one point I had a showdown with the development manager leading the incubation, Mike Koss (MikeKo, an original Excel developer working in the FrontPage team), who was dead set against using Exchange. He would have known because he was also the original development manager on Outlook. I couldn't even get him to experiment with Exchange, which left me to defend our non-use of Exchange to the various executives involved. It was part of my job but not pleasant. Of course, I knew he was right, and I was trying to at least bring data to our decision. He thought I was foolish for even considering pushing Exchange on him.

The innovation underpinning our server product was a simple database, a *list*. Everything was going to be a list. There were lists of people, lists of dates, lists of announcements, lists of documents, lists of comments about documents, even a survey/poll feature for developing custom questionnaires to use, and more. Each list had all the same capabilities in that lists could be customized with different columns, sorted, filtered, and in general treated just like one would treat a list in Excel (or the Access database) while doing all of this from the comfort of Internet Explorer or Netscape Navigator.

We also had features being developed separately to publish office documents to a web server and maintain discussions about them, receive email notice when documents changed or were added (today we call these notifications), and more.

Though we started off with multiple teams, we reconciled the different approaches and arrived at one single plan. We called the product OWS, for Office Web Server, again no exciting code name. We were deeply concerned about cost and complexity to deploy it, so we also made sure it worked with the free version of SQL, thus maintaining the free distribution of the Office Server Extensions from Office9. Backed by a full server and the full version of SQL, the product could support hundreds of users (including the entire Office team) but was easy and lightweight enough that groups of 5-10 could easily use it.

OWS was incredibly simple, yet wildly powerful. Even today in researching this section, I ran "SETUPSE.EXE" from the Office XP ("Office10") CDROM on a standard Windows XP computer. With just a few clicks I had a full team web site up and running. Playing around with the resulting product brought waves of great feelings for all that we had built. Office built a server, a really good one.

Much of this simplicity obscures a remarkable program management effort in addition to the engineering work to build OWS. Program management started in the FrontPage team where JulieLar led the creation and incubation of the original efforts. In order to achieve the breadth of features and tight integration with Office, she partnered with another team in Office (the Office Product Unit) that delivered on integration with applications (for example opening and saving files to OWS) and other features already planned by them—this team was led by Richard Wolf (RWolf), an original champion of the concepts behind an Office server going back to the FrontPage acquisition. The connections across the team also included features built in Word, Excel, and PowerPoint. Creating such a highly collaborative PM environment to deliver integrated products was a hallmark of the new Office team, and OWS exemplified the work.

The full set of features would fill a whole other post. Even during pre-release press briefings, we would show up with a single laptop to show off a server at a time when server demos required multiple hefty computers. Many demos started in the server and flowed to Word and Excel then back to the browser. The excitement was such for the product that we ended up (through no small effort) connecting Word, Excel, PowerPoint, and Outlook to the server in a variety of novel ways—no one had really connected desktop productivity tools to a web server. When it came to mail, document authoring, presentations, and spreadsheets—the core of business productivity—those desktop files were like islands the internet could not reach. To the readers that wonder why we did not finish the job and do everything in the browser, I would note were still more than 7 years before Google would acquire its first web-based editing tool (Writely) and the Office team starting the web browser versions of Word, Excel, and PowerPoint. The web browser was not yet up to the task.

Apologies for a bit of indulgence by including the following list. Marketing's final product guide for the release listed four pages of features including:

- Team Web Site
- Lists with sorting, filtering, custom views, notifications via email, import from Excel, and support column types including single line of text, multiple line of text, numbers, currency, date/time, multiple choice, checkbox Yes/No, internet link, picture, and the ability to choose from an item in a separate list
- Announcements
- Events including Outlook integration
- Contacts including Outlook integration
- Tasks
- Links
- Surveys
- Discussion Boards
- Document and Web Page Discussions (discussions within Office documents or about any web page)
- Document Libraries
- Save/Open dialog integration with Office
- Search using Windows web server built-in Search
- Full customization with the new FrontPage

OWS worked easily through a web interface. It even worked with Netscape Navigator, which drove a lot of Microsoft people kind of crazy.

There was a big problem though, particularly with the document library feature. OWS and Tahoe overlapped quite a bit. Where Tahoe targeted IT managers with enterprise infrastructure, Office10's OWS targeted teams and individuals, though required IT to set up a server and deploy it.

While Tahoe was progressing through its development cycle, Office10 was finishing up. We began deploying OWS to teams and the feedback was incredibly positive. We knew we were on to something.

Despite being asked to, there was no way to reconcile the strategic overlap. Office10's server was easy, lightweight, and had few requirements. It was designed like an Office product in that it implemented a focused set of features, simply. Tahoe was complicated, had significant infrastructure requirements, and required a lot of work to set up, customize, and integrate with the rest of the infrastructure. It was complex and not particularly suited to end-users, arguably by design. That was exactly perfect for what the field wanted—a big investment to get something working and integration with all the other servers they were selling seemed far more strategic than Office's previously free server download.

During a one-on-one with BillG he really let me know how he felt. The meeting was set up to push me to reconcile the Exchange versus SQL storage debate. As CSA, Bill's most critical project was achieving what he called "storage unification" across our products. He wanted to get everyone to use a single data storage engine, eventually called WinFS, detailed in a future section. In the meantime, deliberately shipping collaboration that did not fully utilize one storage system was a high crime. In the heat of this discussion, Bill said that it wasn't that OWS lacked strategy, but rather it was "anti-strategic." It was as if OWS was a net negative for what we were trying to accomplish.

Ugh.

The more we talked things through, the more we found an opportunity—and by opportunity, I mean opportunity for me to avoid a drawn-out battle between conflicting products that created nothing more than grief and a lot of meetings and no happy customers. The more we found an opportunity to avoid simply shutting down a project for lack of strategy and leaving us exposed in the market for what (at least I believed to be) an enormous space in web-based collaboration for regular information workers. The most useful parts of Tahoe, from my perspective, were the ability to search across a company's disparate information sources, and to manage published intranet content sites and dashboards. We could thread a needle between otherwise overlapping products.

At the market map offsite, having had several heated email exchanges prior, Tahoe and Office (JeffTe and I) crafted a strategy, a napkin strategy—literally. Every company should deploy Office10 OWS for any team to use. All IT needed to do was set up a small server or two, and people in a company could create a team site—inside a company someone could visit a web server and, in a few clicks, have a custom team site up and running in a self-service manner. We started using this internally and it was instantly a hit, so much so, Microsoft IT became worried about the proliferation of all these sites. Just a year or so after shipping, we had over 3,000 SharePoint Team sites inside of Microsoft.

Enter Tahoe.

Every company could buy Tahoe and use it as the portal to all the OWS team sites that would proliferate around a company. The Portal category was gaining steam and came to represent the implementation of knowledge management. The more OWS sites a company created, the more valuable Tahoe became in order to search across them, keep a directory of them, and so on. For huge companies, Tahoe had other capabilities such as published sites for the company with news, information, the ability to search other important corporate information, even emails stored in Exchange, and an architecture to build corporate dashboards that were all the rage with IT. We navigated our way to a strategy of freemium with an enterprise upsell, like so many products in today's SaaS era. Looked at another way, we created a classic enterprise *arsonist-firefighter* strategy whereby we at once distribute a free product that proliferates and another product, a revenue positive one, to manage that proliferation.

The *SharePoint* name, created and secured by the Tahoe team, proved easy to use for both Tahoe, now *SharePoint Portal Server* (SPS), and *SharePoint Team Services* (STS), formerly OWS. SPS provided synergy with the server strategy and hot features like dashboards that CIOs wanted. STS provided the departmental and end-user appeal where work happened. I thought this naming to be particularly clever—SPS and STS. I was horribly wrong and when combined with the full name was unwieldy. Officially known as Microsoft SharePoint Portal Server 2001 and Microsoft SharePoint Team Services, while legally we could not use SPS and STS. This was another classic example of Microsoft product naming. My apologies.

We agreed that SPS would ship at the same time as Office10 as well, which was exceedingly important. Throughout the release we worked to have a unified experience to the degree we could. SharePoint would become a symbol of JeffR's new organization and the broader value of Office products to corporate customers.

SPS was a perfect product for an era of complex server products. The industry was blossoming with products from companies such as SAP, Siebel, Cognos, and more. Microsoft spent tens of millions of dollars and hundreds of person-years, including consultants, to roll out SAP. The same with Siebel. Such heavyweight products were state of the art in enterprise software. SPS embraced and reflected those attributes. SPS became a symbol of JeffR's new organization and the broader value of Office products to corporate customers.

STS was an emotional product for me. It was the end of a journey that started with making a web page with our specifications for Office9 and using FrontPage running on a server under my desk. The FrontPage team enhanced the server extensions to create the foundation for STS. The product was pulled in many directions for strategic reasons, but we stuck to it. More than once, I had to go to meetings where we debated killing STS because it conflicted with some strategy such as Windows Server, Exchange, or bCentral.

The idea of Office extended by a website for each Office user and team was incredibly important simply because it made using Office better. It was also a vision we had from the time we acquired FrontPage—everyone should have their own place on the web where it is easy to keep their work and share it with others. We were clearly too early. As we will see it was not just that the world was not ready, the world was anti-ready. SPS fit with the products of the era that remained top-down, complex, and under the full control of IT.

We struggled to turn what we built into an asset—the company, or mostly the field, thought of Office as the desktop EA. Getting the right skills to communicate and sell a server was not part of the Office sales motion. It was frustrating to watch companies introduce products that did the things we did and receive credit with analysts and press, or even customers asking if they should use them. We were inundated with requests to do business partnerships with team collaboration products all while, essentially, building a good one in relative silence.

The expression my former managed ChrisP used was "magic beans." It was a way of describing how some people in the company, no matter what they were doing, seemed to be able to summon magic beans and make products look much larger than life. There was something about STS that lacked magic beans.

We had big plans for STS down the road in the next release. STS was the foundation for extending Office to subscriptions and software as a service.

STS was not without controversy on its own. The company had not yet warmed up to web pages, especially as user experience. I realize how crazy this must sound. In 2000, the company was still of the view that the web is the type of experience for "reach" and the "rich" experience is what happened on the desktop. BillG especially was still hoping for a Win32-like experience for everything we did that used the internet. As an example, the discussions feature of STS also worked from directly inside the applications. It was a ridiculous amount of work we took on just to reinforce this view. Other features such as a Tasks list and Contacts List, which were simply trivial lists in STS, were viewed harshly by BillG because those were supposed to be in Exchange and Outlook. We also did the work so they could be accessed from Outlook.

During the traditional demos with the team, Bill got to see SharePoint (SPS and STS) of course as it was a pillar of the release. We left that section of the demo with him grumbling to me in person, "I hate that UI." Years went by with him saying "SharePoint? That thing I hate." Every time someone mentioned SharePoint or sent him a link to a SharePoint document (oh, the links did have horrible URLs that were crazy long and meaningless) he would grumble if I was there or forward me the mail complaining about the link or the UI. I concluded this was much more about the idea of a commoditized HTML-based interface than any specific choices for STS, that even today are fairly benign.

Regretfully, STS was oddly lost in the shuffle. CIOs and thus our field were far more excited by the prospects of enterprise-wide dashboards and other SPS scenarios. The team collaboration was almost backburnered. Where SharePoint really made a name was with an army of consultants who saw SPS as a big opportunity for value-added reselling. The fancy web interface for digital dashboards was both slick and required custom programming for every customer. Combine that with the purchase and management of server hardware and there was a great business for consultants. JeffTe and the new SPS marketing team started a SharePoint conference which turned out to be a cornerstone event for the PBS organization and the field loved everything SharePoint.

Internally during the beta of Office10 we worked with Microsoft IT and created a self-service STS. With a single click, any person in the company could create their own STS site. IT would manage it, back up the data, and keep it all running. It was an enormous hit. Every time a team had a project or an event they would create and STS site. Teams that were already managing their own internal web sites with custom hardware and web development were switching. STS was a huge win for IT, who had a new product they could offer their internal Microsoft customers. We had hoped to replicate this at every big customer. Why not? The rollout of SPS, while exciting to MSIT, did not go as smoothly. The search capabilities were slow, limited, and frustrating to use. The dashboards were difficult to create and slow. It would take some time to transition content publishing sites to the SPS model. The high-end document management features did not replace the domain solutions in place. It was tough.

Even as we came close to shipping, all was not so great. Sometimes it can be difficult to really understand success and what was actually achieved.

Around the internet today, Google Drive, Box, and Dropbox are all products in which I see STS, though not literally of course given how much technology has changed. There are a dozen start-ups building products today with the features like those STS had in 2000, even using the "everything is a list" metaphor such as Notion. The foundation of STS remains a key part of Office 365 today, but still more than likely underutilized by customers given the rise of so many viable alternatives or even the difficulty of finding SharePoint capabilities. Of course, a great many people and organizations rely on modern SharePoint as a key place for storing documents and files. As BillG used to say in exasperated moments, "yet another place to put files." The potential for tools to improve team collaboration beyond file sharing was mostly obscured by the complexity and weight of the whole offering.

Being early is sometimes the same as being wrong. Being in a bundle is sometimes…not being at all.

A bit after launching the whole wave of products, at the annual sales mid-year reviews SteveB was pushing one country on their Office numbers. As I recall, the country manager began to complain that they pushed SharePoint, but it wasn't landing. The manager said they are doing a bang-up business and the channel (those value-added resellers) and CIOs love SharePoint, but customers aren't using the product. I froze. I knew for sure I was about to get pounced on by SteveB in front of everyone. Instead, Steve looked at the me then the room, and agreed. He said, "I get it, no one anywhere is using SharePoint." Others in the room disputed that, perhaps out of concern for leaving a bad impression for the SharePoint brand they loved.

The conversation continued and Steve turned to me and mouthed again "no one is using it."

He knew. He was right. As popular as the product was, the part we were selling and what led the conferences, the excitement from industry analysts, and reseller activity, just wasn't what people were using inside of companies. The team collaboration parts of the product, STS, didn't receive the attention or visibility so those were under-utilized as well. Was the product a failure?

No, the business results were clear. SharePoint all up had succeeded competitively and by expanding the overall push of servers into the enterprise. This wasn't the only time customers were buying what we used to call *shelf-ware*. The Office business benefitted enormously from the upsell of Office Standard to Office Professional. Office Pro added the Access database, another wonderful product with an incredibly fierce and loyal following. The only problem was that it was used by a single-digit percentage of users, even though half and soon nearly all customers purchased it. We didn't intend for that to be. It was a win, but bittersweet. It can also confuse what success is in a big company.

Microsoft had a talent for creating a success out of a product that still wasn't quite a success, as if through sheer force of will and the power of distribution. We issued momentum press releases citing statistics in the millions. A single major company logo deploys a mission critical application which we reference relentlessly. We can even garner support of resellers around the world who will gladly take the business we send to them, even if the result is simply a showcase application. SharePoint was even touted as the fastest product to one billion dollars in revenue, which given Microsoft's revenue mechanisms is an awkward datapoint. These were the tools of the era. Today, the techniques of growth hacking are the norm such as user-interface that triggers use of a feature that may or may not be intended, or defaults that drive apparent usage of features. All of these are used with bundled products, because absent the specifics of customers directly acquiring a product, Microsoft had no genuine indication of market success. The nature of the big enterprise bundle makes knowing reality difficult.

What really matters is if people are using the product naturally, termed organically, and the usage is improving, though not necessarily more, but decidedly more valuable. We lacked the tools in the early 2000s to really know, but SteveB's intuition was never doubted. Today we think of this as lacking a clear understanding of product-market fit, a state of existence when the market literally pulls the product out of the company.

We did have exciting moments with STS to be sure. We had an inbound support incident from Japan where a customer was hitting limits for how many documents could be added to a single document folder. We had not tested it with more than thousands and learned the customer was unable to add over 100,000 documents while converting all their file servers to SharePoint. Yikes.

The lesson of the bundling things together (STS bundled with SPS, SPS effectively bundled with Exchange and SQL) should have been clear to me by now, having lost the battle over Outlook and soon some other products. I should have admitted defeat and recognized that new things go in the existing product bundle and the economics always make sense—meaning that not charging more doesn't matter because customers continue to value what they paid for already. We just really dislike building shelfware. Winning with shelfware doesn't feel like winning.

Every time we were deficient competitively it was to an unbundled product. Even our own unbundled businesses of Visio and Project were almost one billion dollars. Even worse, the unwieldy size and scope of the Office bundle all but guaranteed most customers would never know or experience most of what we do. That's the fate of most every successful bundle in business software from Microsoft, Oracle, Adobe, SAP, and more. Any success, or defeat of a competitor, comes from an overwhelming mass of software. I was simply naïve to think customers don't appreciate free, which after all is the same as adding more to the bundle means. I eventually came to think about this as customers paying $300/year for Word, Excel, PowerPoint, and Outlook and everything else was just free and of little ascribed value. The very reason new or startup competitors can win is because there is a price attached so customers know about a product.

With a bundle as features are added and customers keep buying, the value of the bundle appears to be reinforced. The act of bundling is correlated with growth, but there's no causal link. Conversely, when something is not bundled but the entirety of the sales motion is with the bundle, then the company concludes the unbundled product was a failure on its merits. Again, that is only a correlation not a causation. The presence of growth hacking and so-called vanity metrics distort available metrics, causing even more clouded judgements. Bundles make for great value and efficient sales engine but make it extremely difficult to know if you're doing the right thing or building a good product. Bundles make it easy to be lazy when it comes to building a fantastic product. Bundled products don't have to be great to win, just good enough.

I once vented to BillG about this, and his view was more sanguine. He said to think of the whole as a portfolio and to just make sure each release that the total value was what it needed to be. Bill was big on the portfolio approach to management.

In a similar conversation, SteveB was also right about the fact that sometimes the bundle wins, even with an inferior product, because the winning product is not just a product but the value of the product, distribution, and ecosystem around it.

The product confusion did not end. The Windows Server team that sold file sharing servers was deeply concerned they were being pushed out by STS, which did provide a much better way to share files. After many rounds of discussion, the best course to solve this strategy problem was to include STS in Windows as well. More distribution is better I thought. Due to antitrust scrutiny of any bundling choices, we ended up renaming STS to WSS, calling it Windows SharePoint Services. What seemed very clever only further served to marginalize or fracture the product.

This was killing me. I could not figure out what was going wrong or what I was doing wrong. It seemed to be so hard to get traction bringing this to market. I know not everyone shared my view of how cool STS was. What was cool was being measured differently. It was like we valued momentum or strategy more than usage. It couldn't be that building more complex products that were harder to use and more difficult to deploy and manage was the right answer?

At times I wondered if I personally lacked magic beans, but I didn't obsess about it. I was able to guide large products, lead teams where people were generally happy (as measured by the ever-present MS Poll survey on employee satisfaction, which SteveB re-emphasized significantly), and to get done what was promised without much dirt flying. None of my managers ever commented on the innovative work the team accomplished—things like SharePoint—or the risks we took, like how we shifted the team to build Office, or even the Office Assistant. "Failure is good," BillG said often. Rather, the conversation was always thanking me for keeping the trains running on time. Yes, it was great Office shipped on time when almost nothing else did, but it was so much more. The team deserved credit for doing more than *just* shipping.

My mentor Jeff Harbers (Jeff) and I were once talking, and he offered me a way to think about this. Leonard Nimoy's autobiography, *I Am Not Spock*, detailed all the things he did besides that one role—that one role everyone knew about. Many thought he begrudged Spock and was not appreciative of the role like fans were. I felt as though shipping was cool, but the team, and I, were so much more. A decade after his original book was published, Nimoy wrote *I Am Spock*, in which he embraced the role as part of him and explained how people misunderstood the first book. Later JeffR even lifted my Spock analogy in one of my performance reviews. It resonated. I reached peace thinking about that duality.

Later, working on Windows, I completely embraced it.

066. KILLING A KILLER FEATURE IN OUTLOOK, AGAIN

JeffR, my new manager and executive vice president, send me a note "LIS: Wow, the story just gets worse and worse…Let's kill it." He pushed to resolve this festering issue and suggested a meeting with BillG. This would be the second time we cut this feature, having shipped Office 2000 without it.

It was December 2000. In a hastily arranged lunchtime meeting (a BillG must was to always have hot lunch at noon), we sat in the Board Room where we normally met with him. It was a deeply technical meeting, the kind he liked. There were senior people from Exchange, Outlook, and the company experts on data storage that have been meeting as part of Bill's project to improve the storage data strategy. The meeting was to decide whether or not to abandon the work on LIS, or the Local Information Store, feature of Outlook and Exchange. The meeting was very tense. The broad view was that this feature was absolutely key to competing with IBM/Lotus Notes. The Exchange Platinum release was late with an uncertain ship date. Office10 was less than three months from being complete, and the code was essentially frozen.

After a tense hour that ran over, BillG said he would think about it, leaving everyone in a state of limbo. It was unusual for him to not reach a conclusion immediately. That meant he was either going to take an unpopular stance, perhaps try to keep the feature alive, or he knew it was a pretty grim situation and was going to avoid confrontation in the room. Counter to what many might have believed, Bill did not like to get involved in binary decisions that leave little room for optionality or win-win outcomes.

An hour later he sent mail saying it was a difficult decision but "I am for killing it because less than 5% of customers would end up using it." Counter to what many might believe, Bill did not like to get involved in binary decisions that leave little room for optionality or win-win outcomes.

What followed was the rollout of a brutal cut, which included drafting mails for another month, communication with the field sales group, and removing dependencies on the code.

This recounting made the process seem straightforward, but in fact it was one of the most challenging last-minute product changes I experienced. Going through this surfaced many of the most difficult product strategy and cross-company execution challenges Microsoft exhibited.

During the meeting with Bill, I was not worried or concerned. I was frustrated and it almost certainly showed. There was no need to have this meeting. The feature basically cut itself. There were no options other than delaying products for perhaps a year to complete this feature. This was the "physics of shipping software."

Even though the classic by Frederick P. Brooks, Jr., *Mythical Man-Month*, was over 25 years old and found on every Microsoft engineer's bookshelf, when decisions made it to the executive ranks, especially when they involved cross-group and strategic initiatives, the lessons from the book were forgotten.

BillG would ask if we could allocate more resources from either team to speed things up. We all knew that there was neither the expertise nor the available resources to do that. Plus, we all knew what the *Mythical Man-Month* said about that, "The bearing of a child takes nine months, no matter how many women are assigned."

BillG would offer suggestions on how we could scale back on some of the features or scenarios in order to require less work. We had been doing that for months. The feature had been scaled back so far that even if we shipped what we discussed at the meeting, it would not have moved the needle on competing with Notes. Quite the contrary, it would have disappointed.

BillG would say it would be acceptable to simply add some more time to the schedule, perhaps three months. Physics of shipping this amount of software meant that three months was hardly any time at all. Given all the work to test, stabilize, and for servers getting feedback from customers, adding three months was about the same as adding a few weeks of engineering at best. Besides, even without this feature Exchange Platinum would likely not ship until the end of 2000. Office10 was all but complete and "re-opening the patient" as we said was not an option. It was just physics.

There was something about how the company was working that we permitted ourselves to go through this sort of exercise when there really weren't any options. Generously it was a process to come to grips with a difficult failure to deliver. Alternatively, it was a way of spending energy exploring options that didn't really exist anyway. That's why I was frustrated. It was decision theater. The bottom line was we didn't deliver and there was no rescue mission.

There are times when these meetings can yield a new outcome. Projects have constraints and if BillG (or anyone in a position to do so) could relax some constraints—the broadly-defined trinity of ship date, features, or quality—then there is a new path to take. Usually, teams that forgo examining and changing these assumptions on their own tend to have other problems as well. Shipping software is managing the trinity and adjusting along the way, not blindly following constraints that aren't working.

What was this feature and why was it so important? LIS was a new way to store all the email on a PC. This of course seems crazy today because no one wants email on their PC where it could be lost or stolen or worse. LIS was a new model of email where the PC would maintain a copy of the email that was on the server and keep the copies in sync. This made it possible to work without an internet connection while also enabling a rich level of capabilities to build apps on top of email that ran on the PC. This replicated storage was a key feature of Notes.

Underlying the feature was a new data storage architecture. Here's the challenge. This model of software requires the code on the PC have the *exact* same capabilities as the code on the server in order to realize the benefits. Notes accomplished this with a smart architecture designed from the start. Exchange and Outlook evolved without such an architecture, and we were trying to retrofit a much more elegant architecture on top of Exchange. To do so would have required building a PC-based system with the same capabilities as the one running on big servers, but able to run with PC-level hardware not the much faster and more capable server hardware. The result: even by December 2000, LIS in Office10 was very best case 20% or more *slower* than Outlook 2000 and required a high-end PC. No one was accusing Outlook 2000 of being speedy, so this was a significant negative.

There were many other features that were slated to be delivered. Some of them were highly requested by customers. One was the ability to store email using the new UNICODE characters so one email storage file could easily have mail from any language. One feature that might be strange (or poorly architected) was that LIS was going to make it possible to connect from Outlook to the mail server using the web protocol HTTP and not the Windows networking protocol, which was really important for scalability and security. LIS aimed to provide a badly needed search capability that Outlook completely lacked. Another was the ability to store more than 2GB of email on a PC. This might sound crazy, but the cost of storing email on servers was so expensive that most Exchange customers were limiting email to 25-100MB, megabytes! The rest of email could be stored in a separate file that existed only on a PC. The implication of such an architecture was that Outlook needed to be unbelievably rock solid and never ever damage that mail storage file. Any bugs or fragility in the code might mean a customer would lose all their email, permanently. The idea of inserting an entire new data storage format into the product at this late hour bordered on crazy.

Developing this feature was never going to be easy. It was another case of two major products with different processes, approaches to work, and schedules trying to align. Kurt DelBene (KurtD) was always calm and a great partner with the Exchange team leader Gord Mangione (GordM), but the tension over this work was palpable the entire release. The two products, while built by separate teams, were inescapably linked. Microsoft's email strategy relied completely on both teams delivering an integrated product, while also serving another larger strategy—Exchange working with Active Directory, Outlook as part of Office.

The bet was even bigger for Office beyond Outlook. We had made a major bet on delivering "Office and Exchange for Corporate Groupware" as a significant pillar of the vision. While our vision process was still new (this was the second time we used it), the idea of losing a whole top-level focus area really hurt. In addition to Outlook, Office created a new tool called *Designer*, staffing an entire team of experienced engineers specifically for end-users to create applications like those in Notes. It was to be the cornerstone of Notes compete. Without LIS, there was no Designer—the work of that team would not ship at all.

The marketing team briefed important customers about the whole set of LIS deliverables including the features, Notes compete, and the new Designer product. There was a lot of excitement. It was easy to generate excitement with slides and mockups, especially when it made closing a big Exchange deal easier. Unwinding that excitement was brutally painful. Each customer meeting is incredibly difficult for the account and sets the relationship and business back. Immediately discussions turn to potentially turning to IBM for a solution to collaboration. Customers were tuned to escalate these failings straight to SteveB who in turn would again ask if there was anything to do or what he could say or offer. There was nothing. It was physics. The field hated physics. Customers did not understand physics. The press equated a missing feature with vaporware—software that never really existed except to muddy the competitive waters. How could Microsoft, the largest company in the world with the best software engineers anywhere not deliver? What did it mean for the future?

There were no answers, easy or otherwise. One way to say this was we failed to deliver. The lesson was not as simple as a failure to execute. Israeli military postmortems remind soldiers that there are no failures in battle only failures in intelligence. In software, failing to deliver was not a failure in writing code, but a failure in planning what code to write and how to write it. We were still planning products like the primary audience was retail customers or hobbyists who were more than happy to work through messy details, wait a little longer, or have some bugs as long as there was new stuff. Enterprise customers with their huge spend, multi-year planning horizons, and 5-10 year usage plans, were in no position to absorb this sort of attitude. We failed to plan, so our plans failed.

It took most of holiday season 2000 to make rounds with customers and all the teams to let them know we had cut the feature. The reactions across the company were varied depending on the team. The different cultures make quite an appearance at times like this.

The Office team already knew the feature would be cut by the time we told them it was official. More than anything they wondered why it took so long for Kurt and I to admit, finally, what they knew to be the case. Even our marketing team was somewhat relieved as this simplified our collaboration message to SharePoint and our email message to Exchange, without any redundancy. The Designer team, a whole new team, took it in stride as they knew it wasn't coming together. I do not want to downplay the stress and strain on the individuals who committed a product cycle to the work. It was not their fault—they were at the receiving end of this failure.

The Exchange team was in a different state of mind. They tended to see things through the lens of Office decommitting at best or at worst Office was never committed. When a consumer of a dependency cuts a feature, it was often perceived as though they never really believed or somehow did not try, any evidence to the contrary. The presence of what was seen as a backup plan (SharePoint for collaboration) only made it seem as though there was a plan all along to "fail." Exchange had a right to be anxious because they owned the Notes compete story and this was a big blow. It would take another couple of years, but Exchange would handily win in the market. The idea of building applications moved to the browser as quickly as customers decided they simply needed great email and scheduling more than applications, and Exchange plus Outlook was superior there. Competing with Notes, by 2000, was about skating to where the puck was as hockey legend Wayne Gretzky might say.

There was no escaping that the wounds were deeper on the Exchange team. Cutting LIS surfaced years later in a story highlighting Microsoft's perceived morale difficulties. In the story in *Forbes Magazine*, "Microsoft's Midlife Crisis", a former Exchange engineer was quoted "They sent me a 200-page document that said our technology had to be 100% better than the current stuff. Then it failed, of course, so they did it themselves."[22] The Outlook team would say (and did) that it just needed to be the same, not 4-5 times slower and bigger. Nothing was easy and when it doesn't work and when failure is poorly managed, people can remember the worst parts in the worst way as they seek accountability.

There were hundreds of technical account managers who were anxious to begin to build Notes-like applications who reacted horribly to the cut. To them this was another case of Redmond not understanding what customers needed and worse failing to deliver what we said we would deliver. In the field, where salespeople have quota that they make or not, where general managers either make their numbers or find a new company to work for, failing to deliver what was promised was a first order failure. I attributed much of the enthusiasm and support of SharePoint for collaboration and Notes compete to the lack of an Exchange story. The enterprise team in marketing spent the better part of the next six months smoothing over each country and market, one at a time.

BillG was disappointed of course. Something he always did extremely well was bounce back from these setbacks and not put the team or leaders in any sort of penalty box. I previously shared the story of AFX, my first project, and how we wasted a year and got nothing done while Steve Jobs's NeXT was on the rise. Bill was as anxious then as he was now and in a similar way—was there anything we could do sooner, more people, or a little more time? I bounced back. We bounced back. In this case, it is fair to say Bill re-doubled his efforts on the major project of the early 2000's, data storage. In his eyes the failure of LIS only made it more critical to solve the company's "storage problems."

We held a big meeting in the atrium and announced the cut to the whole Outlook team. Everyone knew. This was a formality. As we were easing the team into the final decision, I thought of Andy Grove's *Only the Paranoid Survive*. In the book he recounts the long process it took to come to grips with the need for Intel to exit the DRAM business only to come to understand the middle managers had long ago realized what was inevitable and made resource allocation choices in that direction. It was as if Grove was the last to really know. The team knew. We all knew. It just took a while to get there. It was the physics of cross-group collaboration, not just the physics of software.

A final reminder to the team was that we don't market the features that didn't make it into the release. No one was going to know there was something we did not do. In fact, the list of things we did not do was infinite. We did what we did, and it was going to be great.

I learned a lesson (again) about pre-committing to customers when basic engineering prudence said otherwise. With LIS out of the way, and Watson streamlining development, we were on a path to ship. We were feeling good. Like the end of every project, we were in the period where most people came to work and did nothing but make sure no one else did something rash. For a change, this holiday was going to be enjoyable and free from any project time crunch.

Cutting is shipping. We proved that once again.

Countdown to RTM blast-off and 3/2/01. At least I thought so.

067. MYR-CDG: PRODUCT MEETS SALES

In the classic book *Flow: The Psychology of Optimal Experience,* Mihaly Csikszentmihalyi demonstrates that a genuinely satisfying experience takes place in a state of consciousness called *flow*. During flow, people typically experience deep enjoyment, creativity, and a total involvement with life. While the book uses many examples, the concept of getting in a groove resonated with me. Flow is how programmers spend hours writing code and how our best customers spend hours creating satisfying documents with Office.

Reading *Flow* helped me, but my job was changing…a lot. The demands to be present in the newly added building 34 executive suite overwhelmed me at times. The pressure to spend so much time ruminating with other executives ran counter to what I came to believe and what I experienced as flow. It didn't used to be like that. I know because I used to see the execs I worked for most every day, casually.

Flow was how I felt writing a vision or the interactions I had as I walked the halls. This was especially important at Microsoft where everyone had a door. The criticism of private offices was that people get shut out of collaboration and spontaneous discussions in favor of the concentration and quiet focused work afforded by doors. I never believed that to be the case, because we had a culture of door open/door closed that implied a willingness to chat spontaneously or a need to focus. Since my first days at work, the richness of hallway and drive-by discussions were most useful and memorable.

The idea of connecting spontaneously and learning what was on the mind of a member of the team was something I viewed as my job—so much more than sitting in a conference room with other executives or reading slides presented by managers but prepared by people not even in the room. Making eye contact, not in a hurry, discussing someone's work and seeing if I could put it either into context or simply offer perspective on something going on in a bigger picture—that was flow for me. Everyone was always wrestling with something—bugs, recruiting, implementation choices, and more—and while I didn't want to walk around fixing things, I could support, learn, and connect. Most importantly, this was a way to connect with less senior members of the team 1:1. Even today, I can recount some of my favorite moments and best connections coming from people I was able to learn from by walking the halls, a phrase made famous at least in the tech world by Intel's Andy Grove.

Doing so was not the norm for many execs, especially outside Apps or the product groups. The vast majority kept to a Microsoft exec workflow of a reserved conference room across from their office and a steady stream of meetings all day. Even 1:1s were often held in bigger conference rooms.

The 8 a.m. meetings, the meetings to prep for meetings, the emails written by staff to communicate the meetings, the rescheduling of the same, were all starting to pile up. I felt I was becoming detached from the team—I was losing flow. I was uncertain of whether I was a poor fit for the role or if my role was defined wrong. I struggled trying to understand what changed in the landscape that required such a change in how to manage. We weren't facing new problems or new concerns—there were no new competitors or competing technologies. We had ideas to grow to new areas and were executing, and the enterprise sales process was yielding absurdly good numbers. What was I missing? Or, how could I convince people that managing 2,500 people was an investment in time that might be different from how a huge subsidiary GM or marketing VP ran things? Others in similar positions felt differently. They seemed to gravitate towards this new Microsoft culture. Perhaps I was wrong or underestimated what was needed to operate at scale and that was the driving force behind this perceived shift.

The field's annual *Mid-Year Reviews* (MYR), the process JeffR pioneered, were the most coveted meetings for field teams to attend. If there was a culture-defining element to the growing and incredibly successful enterprise field it was MYR, and it could not be more different than anything we did in the Redmond BGs. *Business Groups,* as we were called to imply we were separate businesses rather than mere product teams. BG was the new term for the teams in Redmond and everyone loved to say it as a differentiator to the field. Everything seemed to come down to the BG *versus* the field. It was as if Microsoft was a constant struggle between a BG brain and a field brain.

To say MYR was a production would be like calling the Olympics "some people playing sports." Over the course of three weeks or more in January, the company's collective leadership focused entirely on syncing up at various locations around the world and presenting mid–fiscal year results. Each year the process became more elaborate, took longer, involved more people, and became more all-consuming with ever-increasing import. Every country, though some were presented in regions, marched through a standardized slide deck slicing and dicing sales budgets and forecasts, finding holes, ferreting opportunities, and sharing best practices. These meetings were tense, terrifying, and a test of thinking on your feet under the harshest of business conditions.

To be extremely clear, this seemed an absolutely fantastic way to run the sales force. To me, this was their version of vision meetings, bug triage, and daily builds. The field was scaling up to tens of thousands of people pushing with a relentless focus. The military precision and standardization were obviously brilliant. My own love of *flow* was exactly what made me appreciate this process. The scale was mind-blowing.

But *I* didn't need to see it to appreciate and understand it, any more than I thought the field needed to attend spec reviews or triage meetings. Product groups saw each other every day and maintained a tightly integrated effort in continuous adjustment starting and ending with Redmond. The product teams integrated across many levels almost constantly.

The field was a geographically, linguistically, and culturally dispersed organization of massive scale tuned to be with customers operating on its own, focused on goals decided at the start of a twelve month execution process. The field was the definition of an organization tuned to thinking and acting locally. Each fiscal year, the global team regrouped and realigned for the next. MYR was the halfway point, checking in on all the assumptions and results that defined the fiscal year and fixing what needed fixing.

The connection between corporate and field was essential. There are many ways to connect—MYR was not the only time to see the field. I visited subsidiaries, connected with PSS routinely, (still) attended executive briefings, and we engaged marketing and planning essentially full time with counterparts in headquarters and subsidiaries, and directly with customers in forums like the OAC. The field headquarters staff was where the planning and coordination of the subsidiaries and regions coordinated full-time. Issues and resolutions bubbled up from the field to HQ for solutions in real-time with the BGs. Every year since becoming a vice president in 1998, I made a point of attending some MYR reviews, just not all of them. In the latter part of the 2000s, attendance became tightly controlled and required an invitation and resulting assigned seat. Failing to show (thus wasting a slot) was deeply frowned upon and clearly visible by a name placard and empty chair. For many, attendance became mandatory, and despite the protests, attendance was viewed as career progression.

What was an MYR like?

Meetings were usually held offsite, often in an airport hotel meeting room, and started at 8 a.m. Wherever we were, the room was always filled to the brim and oxygen was soon replaced by stale air, usually extremely cold air with that breeze of hotel air conditioning. Seating was assigned around a big rectangle of worktables. SteveB sat at the head of the table and fanned out from him on either side by *rank* were the field executives, followed by leaders from sales segments such as enterprise, education, small business, OEM, retail, and others, along with an army of finance people from corporate and the subsidiary and the region. Across the room from SteveB sat the subsidiary leadership guiding the meeting, with the GM sitting in the center and then a mirror of subordinates on their side, also by rank with the exception of a chief of staff or business manager right next to the GM as owner of the *MYR Deck* of slides. There was a gallery of the HQ business divisions on one side—usually the head of marketing and the senior product leader, such as me. Outside sat (or loitered) everyone else who could not fit into the room but was on hand ready to provide backup materials should they be urgently summoned.

There was a slide deck, but it was not made of slides so much, but rather posters printed in 8 – to 10 – point type on 17 x 22-inch paper, spiral bound. The pages were fully packed with rows, columns, bullets, numbered callouts ("as you can see at callout number 7…"), and a lot of heat maps, or mini spreadsheets with cells colored coded red, yellow, and green to indicate severity of issues. Every year brought innovations to the decks from better data integration on the back end to the use of color. A most prized possession was the databook, which was essentially a cheat sheet for the whole process that was available to the field executive leadership and SteveB—it contained global and regional summary tables, making it possible for comparisons to be discussed mid-meeting.

Each page was easily eight slides worth of data. Deck preparation began in the fall and was practically a full-time job for a team of people—in the big subsidiaries, dozens were deep in preparation. The slides were almost all data—data pulled from sales systems and reconciled across, and up and down, all the subs. Once all the numbers were right, the teams went through the decks and compared the actual numbers with the start-of-year budgets. Preparation was knowing exactly *why* for every variance, positive or negative. Outlying data was identified with a callout and a concise explanation was at the ready. Why did you sell fewer education PCs this year? Why are enterprise renewals behind budget? Why have you not met your hiring goals? Why did you rent such an expensive venue?

Every. Single. Number.

Intellectually, I knew for me to sit in this meeting watching what was going on was akin to a salesperson pondering the endless discussion about a single code change in a bug triage meeting. Emotionally, it was another story.

SteveB and the sales leaders were relentless and disciplined about accountability. An inability to explain a number credibly, or worse missing that a number was off, was bad, really bad. Every GM knew that this was not a meeting, but a performance review. Meetings that went poorly were legendary. Everyone was aware of the story of that time a meeting went so badly that when it was finally time for a 15-minute lunch break at 3 p.m., upon returning the seat the GM held before the break was vacant and his name placard was gone. Did that happen? Not quite. But the legend was all that mattered.

When a page turned in the book and the speaker changed, on to OEM sales for example, everyone briefly looked at the page (with a ruler and magnifying glass) and noted the circled numbers and carefully placed arrows. Then suddenly, usually, SteveB pointed to some specific number amid a giant grid of numbers and asked, for example, why business PC laptops were so low last quarter. Missing an outlying number was a crime, and it was shocking to watch what happened as a result. Panic ensued. An important skill among sales leaders is the kind of inherited capability the cheetah has to pick out the camouflaged prey from among all the small creatures in the veldt. Picking those outliers are the small prey of sales executives. SteveB was Jedi master of finding out what was important or determining the opportunity in a grid of otherwise indecipherable numbers.

This, unlike a standard meeting, was an ultramarathon. For a major subsidiary, like the United Kingdom, France, Germany, or Japan, or an important growing one like Korea or Russia, a MYR meeting could go on for 10 or even 12 hours, even though they were only scheduled for half workdays. And when it finally seemed over, the next team showed up. Jetlagged, suited up, hungry, and tired, they could have been waiting half the day in the lobby, but then they were *on*. We sat there the entire time, and while we broke for a meal, we usually brought food back to the table, which made the whole room smell of food and tired humans. We finished most days past midnight in the early hours of the morning and were right back hours later for 8 a.m. or earlier if the next meeting was already looking like it would go long.

An MYR was to me like what being on a space flight must be—long stretches of nothing and then a moment of terror when some instrument buzzer went off, warning lights strobed, and then the everything turned a red hue of emergency situation. That was these meetings. The buzzer was a subsidiary saying something about Office, the product or business, that was either negative or non-supportive. Then all heads turned and looked right at me. If my head was down in a laptop (or flat on the table asleep, "Bueller…Bueller") then everything about that moment of terror was amplified. The cardinal sin: "I'm sorry. I did not hear what you said." Leaving to go to the bathroom or to get a drink at the wrong time escalated into a "bad MYR."

While most of the slides were financial and focused on clear, sales-oriented accountabilities, for many years there was a qualitative section called *Feedback to Corp.* Usually offered by a GM, the feedback was candid, addressing areas that needed improvement that only BGs in Redmond could fix. Topics ranged from a single product bug that cost a big EA contract, to marketing materials not appropriate, to the sales motion, to resource allocation guidelines that were not right, to broad product feedback usually connected, to a big and challenging customer. The field was run diplomatically, so ambushes weren't supposed to happen.

The months-long preparation provided time to socialize the feedback so the BG could have a properly prepared response to recite at that point. These meetings were, in many ways, theater—for both sides. As an example, at the end of a meeting SteveB and the execs offered feedback, which was usually a series of messages about how to approach the second half of the year. By the third major subsidiary, messages were not only honed, but the subsidiary staffs shared them with the downstream subs and everyone knew what to expect and was on the lookout for even the slightest variations. It was the variation from the script that encoded the real feedback. Dedicated staff judiciously tracked every question and potential follow-up, entering information into a tracking system that later pinged the relevant parties with email until an issue was resolved. Over the years this tracking system was automated and targets of feedback received reminder mails for months until an issue was marked as resolved.

MYR 2001 for major EU subs was at the Hilton at Charles de Gaulle Airport. By day three, I had my fill of French hotel food and was longing for the McDonalds that I knew was in Terminal 1. I knew I needed to find time to hop on the shuttle to get there. The shuttle circled from the hotel to the gates and back at regular intervals, taunting me each time I imagined it passed. It was cold and dreary outside. I had no idea what time it was as we'd been in meetings for days on end. Modafinil wasn't in use yet, which is the generic name for Provigil a non-narcotic prescription drug originally used to treat narcolepsy now a favored pharmaceutical for traveling executives. We'd already gone through the United Kingdom and France. Germany was up. Germany and a dozen other countries loitered anxiously in the lobby for two days, in the hopes of picking up some G2 about questions and drill-downs.

The NASDAQ crashed one year earlier, and many countries were in rough shape. MYRs reinforced the adage that "when the United States sneezes the world catches cold." Still, PBS was generally doing well, though there were concerns that growth was slowing. In reality, we were going through a transition from choppy retail licensing to greater and smoother revenue through Enterprise Agreements. We were riding the year of deploying an enterprise-standard desktop of Windows 2000 with Office 2000, and Exchange 2000 just released. There was plenty of exciting enterprise software and strong initiatives.

The other thing that became clear was that changing the whole world market takes time. While the United States moved to enterprise licenses, the rest of the world was lagging. At the extreme, another decade would pass before Japan was fully enterprise licensed. Germany was in the middle, especially because its market dominated by giant manufacturing companies moved deliberately, meaning slowly. The implications were twofold. First, the enterprise section of the review was tense—HQ was putting pressure on sales to get big customers signed to EAs. Second, most of the Office teams in subs still viewed a retail launch as the big driver, something HQ made second fiddle for Office 2000 and which for Office10 was even less of a priority. While Office planned a single big worldwide launch event, the primary effort was on 100 local North American enterprise events. The strategy was to replicate this in each major market at appropriate scale.

When it finally came time for the PBS section of the meeting, I tried to perk up, still thinking how much I wanted to get on the shuttle. There was some back and forth conversation happening over enterprise selling and the difficulties of customers in the manufacturing and autos sector. There was some friction over the ever-troubling state governments who wanted lower prices on Office and perennially threated to switch to Linux and open source if they didn't get it.

Everything seemed normal. Then it was time for *Feedback to Corp* and, with it, an ambush.

Germany decided to make a big deal out of an Office10 retail launch. Our BG guidance was to spend marketing dollars on the enterprise launch with the large number of local events to drive IT awareness of SharePoint and business value. We planned a global launch event in New York, with BillG in attendance. While the event proposed by Germany was different, if the field made its numbers (all of them) then it was empowered to do what it believed was right. For all the top-down planning, execution was remarkably empowered with the field.

The rub was the German team was in contract negotiations with an expensive venue for the retail event and needed a solid commitment for software availability. They literally needed an immediate certain date for when volume quantities of German Office10 could be available through all German retailers. This was January 2001 and we were scheduled to RTM three months later. They knew we could commit—how could we not? They didn't like our scheduled date, though, and wanted an earlier one. Our actual *boxes in stores* date was May 31, which gave us buffer and was the plan.

We scheduled down to the day for everything, but we were not operating the team as though this was a date-driven release at the level of manufacturing. I was 90 percent certain of RTM on March 2, 2001 or the snappy 3/2/01. Our worst case, we thought no later than March 16 which was only two extra weeks. We could slip because of a bad bug that took time to track down, or if there was a production hiccup such as a bad master CD, a virus in an image, a delay in collateral for the box. Beyond that there was time needed to complete localization. We were not yet to the point where English and German versions were done on the same day, but we compressed that difference down to a week or so, especially for German. We always did German early because the words are really long and that was a good test for the product visuals, plus GrantG leading testing was a native German speaker. The final step was manufacturing the CDs, which happened in Japan, and then getting those assembled into boxes and distributed. Any time lost on this step could be made up by spending money on air freight and expedited shipping if really needed.

Such logistics steps and concerns raced through my head in the fraction of a second it took the entire room to turn and look at me like I was the last human in *Invasion of the Body Snatchers*. Then I committed a fatal error. I did not say, "Yes, book the venue for that date and we'll make it." Instead I said, "I can't be certain of that [earlier] date. We have a schedule, but we are not operating to guarantee retail boxes in stores in Germany on that date. Given what I know and how we're working, I would do this at the end of May as planned." I suggested we might finish early. That was the single worst thing I could have done on top of my first worst thing. We already communicated our end of May date in the leadup/socialization phase MYR, but they wanted an earlier date for local reasons and chose to make that case in the MYR forum—it was that important to them. I said a lot of words I should not have bothered saying.

My words were met with silence. I felt like that moment in outer space disaster movies when the alarm is off and all that remains is the silence of space and the red emergency lights. I'm certain I was perspiring.

Because of their venue choice, none of what I said was "acceptable," I was later told. They wanted that venue, on that date, and were forcing the issue—managing me in front of JeffR whom they knew super well , and SteveB whom they knew sided with them. The back-and-forth continued and I kept digging myself a deeper hole—at some point my spirit rose above the room and I watched the mess unfold.

Most of all, what was on my mind (that I could not share) was that we were still in the middle of figuring out a product name. The corporate branding team was working to come up with a name that spanned Office10 and the next Windows release. Without a name we could not finish the software and we could not make boxes, marketing materials, or even announce the product to retail partners. The lack of a name was becoming a sore spot with the engineering and localization teams. We were three months out and literally did not have a product name. Shocking for Microsoft, I know.

As of MYR, there was no name and corporate was suggesting we slip the Office product so they could have time to come up with one. They were working on a Windows timeline, with *scheduled* end of summer ship date. It bugged me that they were nonchalantly considering a slip of Office so Windows could have more time to come up with a name. As if I needed a reminder that Windows was the lead dog. I was being a good citizen and not throwing that team under the bus at MYR. In the process, I stepped in front of or under the bus myself. Heck, I threw myself off the bridge at the bus.

Neither of us could see the other's point of view. They were asking me for a favor: Make it happen. Germany could not see that I was trying to avoid an embarrassing event with no software and had no idea that I was working to avoid embarrassing corporate branding or shifting blame to them. I kept thinking that the team back in Redmond was doing so well, the last thing I should do as the manager was come back from a three-week hiatus to create a fire drill over the retail launch in Germany when we prioritized the worldwide enterprise launch for two years, especially when they were in a holding pattern on naming.

Germany and HQ called a truce and accepted the feedback, and marketing agreed to work out the details. The body language directed at me from the SteveB side of the room was painfully clear.

Following the conclusion of the meeting, JeffR pulled me out into the lobby of the hotel where I stood longingly watching the shuttle bus to Terminal 1 roll by every 15 minutes of this ad hoc 1:1. He was obviously livid though maintained a calm delivery—we had only been working together for a few months. Without asking any questions he said, "That *cannot* happen." He said we were obliged to deliver. He told me I handled it wrong. This went on for what felt like an eternity—look, there's the shuttle again. The entire time I assumed my name placard was being removed.

In that moment, I welcomed being put out of my misery.

When we returned to the main room, my name card was still there. I sent some mail back to the United States to say we needed to make Germany happen. Grant believed we could do it, but he could not guarantee that date. We told them to go ahead. Everything was fine.

Except me.

The biggest cultural difference internally was that MYR was the field's moment to shine. It was a chance for them to overtly manage the HQ organizations, so long as they had the facts straight. The field took direction from HQ on good days and put up with shoddy work and poorly executed marketing and product on bad ones. For 50 weeks of the year, they absorbed everything. Each country wanted its chance to be in charge and their MYR meeting was when they had the upper hand over the BG.

Until this MYR in 2001, I hadn't grokked the power dynamic. The idea of being managed in front of a room was so opposite the old Apps product group culture that for the longest time I simply thought I was being bullied. JeffR taking the side of Germany in the meeting was him taking part in the ritual of the culture when he sided against me in front of everyone. It is always weird to experience your new manager not supporting you in a big public meeting. I wondered if this dynamic was different or crazy or a bit of both?

One thing was clear. My job was different. Same software. Different job. I had some learning to do.

068. THE XP EXPERIENCE

In early 2000, branding and naming the next release of Windows was all gummed up and that slowed down Office, which needed a name in order to release on time in March. Whistler, the code name for Windows, was scheduled to ship about six months after Office10. An August ship date for Windows was achievable, and no one wanted to mess that up. The name, perhaps to the surprise of many readers today, was a long pole in the release as it touched code in many places and could impact localization, manufacturing, printing, and packaging. We needed a name. How hard could that be?

Windows trying to settle on some variant of "experience" because the main thrust of the release was to finally bring the Windows 95 experience of peripherals and consumer software to the enterprise-focused NT code base of Windows 2000. In addition, we collectively concluded the year names were not working (hence Windows *Me*) because of the difficulty of keeping ship schedules and customer confusion over what products worked with each other, both issues were entirely predictable and frequently discussed at the time. The branding team was thinking of something like *Windows EXP* or *Windows XPR,* and finally *Windows XP*. My concern in an endless email chain was not this product but the next one. Would the next name have a roman numeral, go back to adding version numbers, a superscript, or add descriptor *Edition* branding? At one point, someone mocked up *Windows XP* ^{2} which made me wonder if I was being made fun of, especially in the Spanish release.

The corporate teams settled on and cleared the name Windows XP, and what immediately followed was the question as to whether Office10 should be named be Office XP. The corporate branding team and sales teams were in favor. The Windows team, however, did not intend for other products to add an XP suffix. This seemed to be another .NET in the making, which was still nowhere close to being resolved. The branding powers demanded evidence in the product that supported co-branding.

We held many meetings during development about aligning the releases of Whistler and Office10, but the products were on wildly different schedules. From our perspective, Whistler was about finishing Windows 2000 without much new for Office. Besides, Office was going to run perfectly well on the new corporate desktop of Windows 2000 anyway. Windows 2000 had been years late, so it was not unreasonable early in the process to doubt the next Windows schedule. Whistler was making a ton of progress and we were self-hosted, so any worst thoughts were not going to happen. This was a first for Windows! Still, there was no significant release synergy. Office ran on Windows XP, and realistically not even as well as it ran on Windows 2000 PCs with the same amount of memory.

At one of these meetings the topic of naming them the same became heated, if not awkward. BillG wanted to know what was interesting in Office10 and what was unique when it ran on Whistler. Baked into this assault was the belief that Office was not exciting on its own and more importantly that Office failed at exploiting the latest Windows release. This was the view that came from the perspective that innovation from Microsoft emerged first from Windows.

My answers were not satisfying as I restated the series of meetings, lack of APIs, and our system requirements. I chose to highlight the work we did to align with Windows Server for SharePoint, totally irrelevant to the conversation in this context. BillG expressed frustration at "another release of Office that relies on Windows to make it exciting," which honestly didn't make much sense and bordered on insulting. By and large we were not looking to the Windows desktop to innovate for Office. In reality, many innovations in user interface flowed from Office to Windows for years already. That wasn't interesting to Bill in this moment.

Windows really wanted the XP name to be unique to Windows. Office really didn't want to look like it required or was matched to Windows XP. We learned that lesson when Office 97 arrived and many consumers at retail were wondering where the matching Windows 97 was or even if Office 97 ran on Windows 95. After more time back and forth, Office marketing and corporate branding agreed to, no surprise, a compromise of a name—Office XP with a "Version 2002" prominently displayed on the box. The apps were called Word 2002, Excel 2002, etc., not Word XP or Excel XP because branding didn't want to overuse the XP moniker. Windows did not have such a version on the box or in the software. Also, the boxes didn't look at all similar. This meant customers calling product support or using the web site would need to search for "2002" and not XP, unless they used Google which got it right. I can't make this stuff up, but just wait until the next release of Office.

We had a name. We were on track for March 2 and we had a date for launch and boxes for Germany. We signed off on 3/2/01 just like we planned. It was magical to do that. We beat the Excel record from more than a dozen years ago and hit our planned ship date. I know this sounds ridiculous—product development schedules are supposed to work, but it simply did not happen with software projects. We were so happy.

For launch, marketing planned one main US event, which we expected to be covered globally. BillG headlined the event at New York City's Manhattan Center Ballroom aimed at getting broad media coverage, while around the country and world there were hundreds of local events targeting enterprise IT professionals. There was no effort to get people lined up at stores or any sort of midnight madness, though local offices around the world did some of that and we did have BillG greet the early buyers in New York. A fixed launch date is a great forcing function (there's that phrase again) to get everything ready for press tours, reviewer workshops, and enterprise product information.

For enterprise customers the main features of the release going back to the original product plan were collaboration and integration with the just-shipped Exchange 2000. SharePoint Portal Server 2002 (there's that naming again) released a few weeks after Office XP which included SharePoint Team Services and also served as a collaboration platform. Our collaboration story was as complex as predicted in our vision statement, a result of targeting the same scenarios to two different back-end infrastructure products.

For system administrators, we enabled new scenarios, such as installing Office XP from a website and ever-more controls and customizations for deployment. There was a lot there and it was all new for enterprise customers. Industry analysts were having a great time digging into the idea of Office shipping servers.

Through some incredible outreach efforts by marketing and the field, more than 500,000 enterprise customers used the product in pre-release. The internet made it easy to distribute the product, and because of Watson we not only knew (anonymously) that people were using the product, but we were fixing bugs based on their usage and knew the release was high quality. We really knew that, not just hoped. Shipping software had radically changed using Watson. The availability of data forever changed what we worried about when shipping.

The traditional tech press and mainstream media continued to struggle with explaining, or making broadly interesting, heavy enterprise features like collaboration. I was still smarting from the reviews of Office 2000 and was determined for us to get credit for the personal productivity features. We built a great set of capabilities that worked with or without servers, and as was common at the time with or without a broadband internet connection, though by that point most every customer was connected.

Office XP introduced several novel features we believed gained notice including the first features that worked seamlessly using an internet connection from within the apps. Building such features was a fascinating lesson in team transformation. With many stories from the early days of the internet about traditional print-based offerings unable to transition to the web, we set out to do something new and innovative with the thousands of pages of training materials and the vast library of content we shipped on CDROM. Jeff Olund (JeffO) began his career in "user education" creating the written materials that accompany a product. He became a leader in building reference and training materials for Office and then led the worldwide localization team based in Dublin, Ireland. With JeffO's leadership, content went from a cost center to an asset for the business. The Dublin team went from taking almost a year to localize Office into a dozen languages to localizing Office into 100 different languages in just a month or so.

The next step in content to help customers was to use the internet to provide endlessly growing features such as adding images or clip art to a document, templates, how-to, and more. As an example, before Google pioneered image search, it was luck that enabled an author to find suitable clip art. Especially in large corporations, most of the clip art we shipped with the product was eliminated to save disk space. In Office XP we introduced an *Insert ClipArt* feature that used an ever-expanding and easily searchable collection of internet images much larger than anything on a CD. The idea of tens of thousands of images available for free was quite cool for business users of PowerPoint tired of *angry person* and *idea lightbulb over head person*.

In hindsight, a product having a website seems obviously trivial. But at the time, we were deeply concerned about adding a website to a product used (and liked) by hundreds of millions of people. The web was still flakey (and slow) and while novel, sites routinely did not work. We did so much work in quality, the thought of having toolbar buttons or menu commands leading to strange errors from unavailable sites was horrifying. Websites needed to be new and fresh all the time, and always work.

The help system was no longer limited to what was written and shipped with the product but could also search a large and growing library of how-to articles on the web, including an under-the-radar hit called *Crabby Office Lady* who offered tips with an irreverent tone ("advice with attitude"), authored by a professional writer on the team Annik Stahl (AnnikS.) Annik's column was wildly popular with hundreds of millions of views. She was interviewed by local newspaper tech columns (often writing similar content) and even had television appearances, as herself, not the character. The character and personality Annik created even drew some inquiries from the VP of Human Resources over concerns of stereotyping. Annik's goal was to take aim at the perceptions of the Office product, not the Office customer and she had full control over the project she initiated. We saw this approach used to great effect with a series of books such as *Word Annoyances*, which had become one of the most popular books on using Office products. So popular was the Crabby column on the site that Annik also went on to write a book and was part of several behind the scenes stories.

We created a new online services team under JeffO's leadership. AndrewK moved from OPU to lead program management to help focus on content reporting to JeffO, who reported to me. Seasoned managers Mike Kelly (MikeKell) and Randall Boseman (RandallB) had to create new processes and tools to go from zero to a one hundred million web visitors seemingly overnight. The Content team developed schedules for creating, localizing, and releasing content at regular intervals, something we had only previously done on multi-year release boundaries.

Between online content, Crabby Office Lady, and the introduction of a new *sidepane* user interface, plus the ongoing ridicule aimed at the Assistant we also made some big changes to Clippy. The plan for the product cycle was to provide even more options and administrator controls to reduce Clippy's visibility, including making sure that by default Clippy no longer appeared, though it could be summoned if desired. Importantly, the message for Office XP was that it was so easy to use that "...Clippy is no longer necessary, or useful."[23] That might have been spin, perhaps.

Lisa Gurry (LisaGu) in marketing thought up a clever idea to make the most of this change, and to embrace the opportunity to be self-deprecating in the process. She planned a formal *retirement* for Clippy. Instead of tacking the feature change on to the press tour in April, she planned a web-based celebration. Gilbert Gottfried, comedian and voice of dozens of animated characters, was enlisted in a set of internet Flash videos (these were all the rage then) of Clippy trying to insert himself into the daily lives of people. On retirement day, Lisa issued a press release and dressed another member of the team in a giant Clippy suit as we strolled Union Square in San Francisco, complete with a cable-car ride.

While this was the least corporate approach to PR, it set a high-water mark for intentionally cool viral marketing. To this day, the "retirement" still gets a laugh.

Laughs, however, were not part of the marquee feature, known as *Smart Tags*. Smart Tags were a set of buttons shared across Office applications appearing when and where the user needed them (such as when a user made an error in an Excel formula, when Word automatically corrected a user's action, or when a user pasted some data), providing options to adjust the chosen action or fix an error. Smart Tags appeared when pasting text into Word, giving a choice of whether to match formatting or not, a common need with the rise of taking text from web pages. Smart Tags made it easy to undo (or never do again) when Office autocorrected something incorrectly, like convert a row of dashes to a typeset line.

While there were many different features across the product, Smart Tags provided a single and consistent unified interface. From a marketing perspective, Smart Tags felt like toolbars in their ability to be a visual symbol of innovation in the release.. The screen shot was used all over the place.

It was Office at its best. We thought.

In press tours and reviews, Smart Tags proved a novel interface approach and were demonstrably innovative. Surprisingly, it took us several years to achieve—this idea was in the works going back to the original Office interoperability work in 1994, but before we could execute new ideas we needed to clean up the old implementations of menus and toolbars, which we did.

Smart Tags were also extensible. A corporation could recognize an order number or a shipping code and make it easy to link directly to those websites or systems. Browsers, especially Internet Explorer, and tools like free email programs or websites, were not yet universally inserting automatic links by recognizing the text of http://, phone numbers, dates, or other common strings. The most well-known was the use of 1Z as a prefix for a United Parcel Service tracking code (tracking was a new thing for consumers), which with a Smart Tag enabled that text to act like a link to UPS, if Internet Explorer or Outlook used Smart Tags extensibility. Phone numbers, addresses, dates, and more were all candidates for Smart Tag actions. We computed the time saved by the use of Smart Tags to be an insane number of millions of hours—pure marketing.

We thought this such a clever idea and an opportunity to show off synergy with Internet Explorer that we created a Smart Tag add-in for IE that recognized many common potential links. It seemed useful and synergistic and was included in the Internet Explorer 6 beta test. The IE team thought this was clever too—this was before browsers could be customized with add-ins and web pages were mostly static HTML, with the exception of occasional blinking or marquee text.

It wasn't long before JimAll (the leader of Windows) called to tell me that people were freaking out. By this he meant that the press tour for IE was not going well. Concerns about Smart Tags were expressed within the context of IE. While there was some hyperbole, the concerns boiled down to feedback expressed stridently by Walt Mossberg, who wrote in *The Wall Street Journal*, "In effect, Microsoft will be able, through the browser, to re-edit anybody's site, without the owner's knowledge or permission, in a way that tempts users to leave and go to a Microsoft-chosen site—whether or not that site offers better information."[24] The terminology isn't aging well, but the idea was simply that links would appear on HTML pages that were not authored by the site owner. This in effect could be viewed as editing the site, where editing means adding new links to a page authored by a third-party.

This notion of "re-edit" went beyond what we considered or even thought of the feature. There's some irony in that today browsers and mail clients (and many products) do this for a whole host of special strings and even Apple computers provide reference lookup to Apple sources. At the time, it was routinely pointed out that the climate of 2001 was filled with concerns that Microsoft might *leverage* one part of Microsoft to benefit another poorly performing or just poor part of Microsoft. Smart Tags in IE surfaced those concerns. Perhaps exactly the right feature, at exactly the wrong time, from exactly the wrong company. Conspiracy theories felt real to many perfectly rational people in the industry.

To make that point, Mossberg concluded, "Microsoft's Internet Explorer Smart Tags are something new and dangerous. They mean that the company that controls the Web browser is using that power to alter others' Web sites to its own advantage. Microsoft has a perfect right to sell services. But by using its dominant software to do so, it will be tilting the playing field and threatening editorial integrity."

We did not think through the potential abuse of the feature, though even in the worst case it was not precisely what was suggested by some. Sites were not being rewritten and links were not getting replaced. Neither was it benign nor free from potential exploitation. We did not consider how someone with bad intentions might develop a Smart Tag add-in that could at best be annoying and at worst recognize text and offer a link to a nefarious web site. As a result, IE removed the feature, which spared us the challenges. It appeared as capitulation, and the press was not shy about expressing that. As a broader point, the company, particularly under the new leadership in our corporate legal group, preferred and encouraged capitulation, especially for anything that might catch the attention of its constituents, the regulators.

Office XP and the press materials still had this marquee feature, using the name Smart Tag everywhere for consistency. Was the name tarnished, though? There wasn't anything we could do other than downplay the name and issue Q&A and FAQ documents to the marketing teams around the world. This was an unfortunate side-effect of not having thought through the implications in the browser.

The Smart Tag incident took place at what was perceived to be the height of Microsoft's power and potentially negative influence on the industry. The fact that we relatively quickly backed down has been viewed as a milestone moment. The incident was even portrayed in a widely read profile of Walt Mossberg in *WIRED*, May 2004, titled "Kingmaker." It was an example of "dozens of companies that have redesigned products in response to Walt's unsparing criticism." Walt was right. I viewed this incident as the system working—the reviewers acting as a check on poor product choices.

Finally, we always reminded people we made the product more stable each release. With Office XP, however, this was provable. We equipped the press and field with statistics and descriptions of the Watson curves and buckets so they could understand our new approach to improving product quality. Watson was industry-leading and pioneering. Every time I represented this work, I am sure I beamed with pride, even though showing it off meant using a tool we wrote for demos that forced the product to crash, again.

The reviews of Office XP generally reflected the positives of the product for both consumers and businesses. The industry was going through a post-dot-com consolidation and, while tech was still enormously popular, the slow but certain decline of print journalism (and the dot-com bubble) affected reviews. First, the budgets in time, people, and hardware for the kind of testing we used to see at *Byte* and *PC Magazine* were reduced or gone. This led to a decline in reviews based on usage of new parts of Office, especially the hard-to-test parts like SharePoint. Second, the web itself favored shorter and faster *takes* on what was new. People wanted reviews at the time of release. While we gave ample lead-time and supported embargoes, other pressing demands made it difficult to spend time in research mode prior to a product release. With the PC deep in middle age, in-depth reviews of technology products were replaced by more instant analysis of meta topics, such as the impact of the product to the company or a take on whether the product should be deployed or not. Hint, they always said to stick with a current version unless that was old.

In that context, Office XP provided a glimpse of what was in store for the business. Every review evaluated the product in the context of the value of the upgrade. The assumption for Office was that everyone with a PC owned it and, while this was far from true, it might have been true among those reading tech press with their up-to-date PCs at work, but not all PCs by any measure. Enterprise customers already owned Office XP and were by all accounts only upgrading with a PC refresh cycle. Reviews almost always included benign comments about the product from IT managers along with a quote about not being clear if there was enough value to upgrade at the time, but certainly the future looked good.

The decline of awards like *Editor's Choice* and in-depth 10-page reviews with benchmarks was, honestly, sad. It was as though the world cared less about what we did. The internet was the new focus for consumers and businesses. It was no longer the PC and new desktop software.

The enterprise field fully engaged on an XP desktop motion, meaning Windows XP plus Office XP, even with Windows months from finishing. As an aside, Windows XP was the first Windows release to have a plan and schedule that remained steady, and the product finished on plan late summer. Office XP and Windows XP were better together for the enterprise. That reduced the sales surface area for the field from two products to one, so to speak, which was greatly preferred. In that sense, the timing of the two products together reinforced a core belief of BillG's, that new applications provided excitement for a new OS, which created demand for new applications—a virtuous cycle.

Our glitzy launch event in New York at the end of May 2001 featured BillG leading an enterprise-focused event but with enough consumer demonstrations to capture headlines. The focus on productivity was illustrated by a broad though relatively unsupported statement, that by "making Office just 10 percent better we can save hundreds of millions of man-hours."

We were joined by some special guests that day. Chief among them was the founder and CEO of a relatively new Seattle-based company called Amazon.com. Jeff Bezos joined BillG on stage to demonstrate searching for Office XP on Amazon and buying it with Amazon's new *One-Click* ordering feature. A box even arrived on stage for Jeff and BillG to open.

But my mind was already deep in navigating what should come next for the product and the team.

2001-2003

The turn of a new century and survival of "Y2K" begins a massive expansion of the Office product line, a dramatic change in the products we built, and a reinvention of how we market Office, while simultaneously tripling and quadrupling down on enterprise customers. The result of this transformation sets the stage for the most formative years culturally for the Microsoft that takes us to today's products (365, Azure), but unknowingly constrained us going forward

069. MEGA-SCALE, MEGA-COMPLEXITY

One early company meeting as the CFO Mike Brown (MikeBro) was going over the numbers he had a chart of the Fortune 500 showing that Microsoft finally made it into the rankings. He showed the top 5 companies or so, which dwarfed Microsoft then just barely in the top half. Sitting next to my first Microsoft friend KirkG, I recall asking him if he thought there would ever be a software company the size of AT&T or General Motors. His answer, "hell yes."

Though Microsoft was number 84 by sales, it had achieved the unimaginable as the largest company by market capitalization. Thinking about that even today is still difficult to fathom—bigger than the oil companies, bigger than the entire auto industry, bigger than the phone company. It was obviously more than humbling. It was terrifying.

There was, nevertheless, a swagger across the company. Sure, the trial and settlement were still going on, but the worst seemed over. There was such an incredible wave of success from the new enterprise business, both the licensing of enterprise agreements and the product offerings on the Windows/Office 2000 platform, along with Exchange and several other key products. For product people these were the magical product releases. There were "investments" as SteveB called them across every imaginable product category. The combination of Microsoft pivoting to internet technologies, the dot-com crash, and simply winning against competitors is what I believe really caused a change in how we thought about ourselves, by rising to the moment and vanquishing competitors: Netscape, Sun, and Novell on servers, Apple on desktops, Borland on tools, Lotus on email, and so many other smaller companies. We saw success in everything we were doing. It became difficult even to find competitive products to get the team sincerely fired up. The biggest competitor was no one company but alliances such as anyone using Java or open source, but these were diffused and fragmented battles. Microsoft's oxygen came from competing and winning and we'd sucked all the oxygen out of the market by winning so soundly. The market capitalization was a realization of that.

It would be a mistake to think success would not change how we built products. When you chase a competitor, even if you've got better ideas for how to express, implement, or sell a product as we did for Excel versus 1-2-3, the idea for the product in the first place came from the competitor. Microsoft didn't invent from whole cloth many products. Most every product has a lineage of some form, so this is never an entirely fair way to judge. Most every successful product could be traced to a direct competitor with scale. On the other hand, many of our biggest failures were products that lacked a competitor where we would often get lost on a meandering journey trying to figure out what to even build. The Blackbird internet authoring tool previously described was a good example of this.

We had competitors of course, and some were spectacularly good. Oracle would forever remain the top SQL database company. Linux and open source were clearly a huge issue, but as should have been anticipated they would not win head-to-head but would only win when a paradigm shift—cloud and mobile—enabled them to flourish in business software. We had huge blind spots. SAP and the whole space of software that ran the back office of enterprise and CRM software escaped us even with their deep connections to Office and email.

Increasingly Microsoft's strategies became so daunting and all-encompassing it was nearly impossible to imagine a single competitor that could offer anything close to our strategy slides, and equally impossible for any single person to track. We were in a constant state of tuning the message and product line. Platforms lurched from *Distributed interNet Architecture* (DNA), to *Next Generation Windows Services* (NGWS), to *.NET* to *.NET MyServices* (aka Hailstorm), with stops along the way such as putting "+" on the name of every new endeavor, for example COM+, or adding XML to expand an existing strategy. At each iteration, everything was rebranded, expanded, and re-factored. An area like accessing data stored in a database cycled through acronyms representing increased capability and complexity, and varying compatibility and tools support: ODBC, OLEDB, DAO, ADO, ADO.NET, RDO, and more. The complexity of naming was only matched by the increasing complexity of software. The original Windows 3.0 APIs numbering about 350 had expanded to a literally uncountable breadth of platform services. No single developer could comprehend this. Definitely no one in Office, and we began to feel distant from the very platform strategy we depended upon. Office had historically been the source of killer apps for platform strategies, but now the platform team looked to the biggest consumer web sites and largest commercial web applications as the desktop and client were deprioritized.

The evolution of the much beloved Visual Basic provided a lesson in this divergence. Office had just managed to add VB to all the products with solid performance, a major cross-company success. VB was in the process of being updated, really replaced, by a newly rearchitected product called Visual Basic .NET or VB.NET, which gained synergy with the .NET strategy and new iteration of the language for use on servers. This product was so different from the classic and wildly popular Visual Basic that one of Microsoft's own and much-loved MVP supporters (the leaders in the community carefully selected to offer the best knowledge and support for products) dubbed the new product *Visual Fred* in an infamous blog post that rallied the community but divided it from Microsoft. Other posts began to meticulously track the differences in the new product and the time and effort required to migrate existing projects. [25]

Office could not possibly retrofit this incompatible tool into the product—customers would have lost their minds as we had just completed migrating from the legacy programming languages—leaving the carefully crafted cross-group collaboration in somewhat of a Cold War. The VB team's best response to the trade press asking about VB.NET was that we had "some difficult choices to make, as it's tough to move from the PC-centric computing model to the Web-centric .Net model."[26]

Were we losing touch or were we trying to do bigger and better things that would naturally and unfortunately alienate our best fans? [27] Were we growing our ability to create strategic enterprise products or were we over-reaching on what we could (or even should) deliver? Was disruptive innovation happening in real time like it should, or were we just being disruptive?

Broadly, we began the decade far more inwardly focused than ever before. An expression that was often used was "smoking our own supply" or I might have said, "Microsoft was creating our own bubble." Everything we did was relative to everything else we did which was relative to the feedback we got from the enterprise customers we already won, who were champions for anything we did. I thought often about the very first technical conference I attended which happened to be the last global DECWorld on a cruise ship in Boston in 1987. Digital Equipment

Corporation, DEC, was the famed makers of the VAX and VMS operating systems I used in college. I was a new graduate student and drove to Boston for the day.

The conference felt like the most grownup event I'd ever seen—everyone was twice my age. It seemed like everyone wore a suit and all they talked about was DEC. What I recall vividly, however, was that the sessions I went to were so advanced and so deep into the specifics of DEC and never mentioned anything else—in particular, I didn't understand how they only talked about VMS and not Ultrix (DECs Unix variant) which was what we were moving to at UMass—I went to learn about Ultrix. I realize now both how naïve I was to the idea of an industry conference, but also how much of a bubble that conference was. Not long after, DEC began a rapid decline and about 10 years later was no longer a standalone company. It was no surprise that shortly after DEC collapsed the book *DEC Is Dead, Long Live DEC: The Lasting Legacy of Digital Equipment Corporation*, was widely read across Microsoft. Being on top of the world in technology can be so fleeting and the descent so rapid, even if the products are loved—if only regulators could understand that point. BillG knew that. The competitive nature at the core of Microsoft existed for that reason. But what happens without a competitor? That's how DEC acted—it built products as though there were no competitors, or more precisely that the customer saw the world only through DEC products.

A company that was on top of the world in 2000 was Sun Microsystems, but it was also starting to struggle post the dot-com crash that impacted so many of their customers. There was no cloud computing, so starting a company meant buying a lot of Sun computers, but the crash stifled the creation of new companies and those purchases. Scott McNealy, the outspoken cofounder and CEO had said that people bought more Sun computers when the economy was good so they could grow and more when the economy was bad so they could be more efficient. He did not anticipate what Windows NT would do to those expensive computers though. McNealy never held back in his commentary on Microsoft. He reserved his harshest critiques for BillG or SteveB. McNealy's rivalry with SteveB seemed a bit personal, perhaps because they attended rival private schools in the suburbs of Detroit. As Office XP was making its way to customers, McNealy unloaded on Office, taking aim at the ever-present topic of bloat when it came to, apparently, banning the use of Office at Sun. [28]

> *Why did we ban it? Let me put it this way: If I want to tell my forty thousand employees to attack, the word "attack" in ASCII is forty-eight bits. As a Microsoft Word document, it's 90,112 bits. Put that same word in a PowerPoint slide and it becomes 458,048 bits. That's a pig through the python when you try to send it over the Net.*

Nevertheless Sun continued to use Office in finance, presentations, and more. Sun was still a strong company, though that would change in due time, coincidently as their use of Office declined. McNealy held an influential position, particularly when it came to internet technologies. Like Microsoft, Linux also took its toll on Sun.

To bolster his anti-Office stance, in 1999 Sun acquired a maker of a clone of Microsoft Office, a German company, Star Division GmbH. The rumors were that it was cheaper to buy the company and attempt to standardize on its software than it was to buy Microsoft Office. StarOffice was working to be fully compatible with Office and available on all platforms, especially Sun's Java which had consistently shown that it was not up to the task.

The engineers on the product were adamant that it was a "perfect copy" of Office, copyrights, trademarks, and patents aside. At a trade show, when they were still an independent company, I saw a demonstration at their booth. I was younger then and not concerned about the ramifications of obscuring my badge and affiliation. The demonstrator said they were a member of the engineering team while describing the keen attention to cloning Microsoft Office, "even the toolbars", they said. I pointed out some, um deficiencies. He launched Microsoft Office on their demo machine and shockingly I was correct. He summoned a coworker and after exchanging some thoughts in German told me to come back later in the day to see that they corrected the mistake. I came back and sure enough they did, and I properly introduced myself. Amazing.

With Sun's ownership and financial support, Star moved from a low-priced product to a free and open-source product. In keeping with the apparent desire to needle SteveB as much as possible, McNealy and team created OpenOffice.org, a philanthropic-sounding consortium to support open-source contributions and distributions of an Office competitor. What started off as an odd and failing strategy turned into an annoyance.

Highlighting StarOffice as an alternative to Office was one way enterprise customers expressed increasing frustration with bloat. Depending on who you asked the products indeed had many flaws. What we began to consider was that we were now being evaluated on and held to an absolute scale. It was no longer enough to be better than a competitor we vanquished or a new competitor like Star. We needed to be great on our own, an absolute standard.

Despite the flaws, customers continued to buy, and continued to sign up for multiyear agreements. It was difficult to be a serious global company and not be using the full Microsoft platform for PCs, document creation, email, and enterprise infrastructure. Office and Windows were the very definition of product-market fit—we just could not lose a deal. Even in markets where software piracy was the norm, Office and Windows still won against free (and legal) alternatives. This created a disconnect that was difficult for product groups to fully grok.

Winning didn't necessarily mean we had built the best product. Winning is a combination of product, price, place, and promotion and can come from any or all of them. At least for Word, Excel, and PowerPoint it wasn't simply that our products were the most satisfactory sold by Microsoft, dominated industry reviews, and consistently won against competitors. Microsoft's global sales force, product support, and complete product line were all part of a winning equation. Winning led to more winning when it came to familiarity, training, and cross-organization standards. Whatever products do win are by definition the best product.

Microsoft was a big place, and as we grew there were more and more people with ideas who were organizationally disconnected from execution. It was not difficult to find someone putting forth a proposition suggesting *this or that* risked ending a franchise: the browser, Java, open source, Linux, competitors using one or more of those, or customers rejecting Office due to bloat, poor quality, or complexity and cost in the enterprise. It was too easy to cast aspersions at the parts of Microsoft executing on what it takes to sell billions of dollars of software. These cross-group dynamics between the big money-making products and the new products or the groups simply incubating ideas with ample time to criticize introduced a new kind of tension in the company—one between those that were shipping and those that weren't, yet.

In the world at large, Windows and Office were becoming listed resume skills and that enabled them to become the punchline to jokes on late night TV, sitcoms, and a constant stream of syndicated cartoons such as Dilbert. Earlier I described when late-night TV host Conan O'Brien did a funny number on Clippy. "Come on, Bill, Microsoft got off easy compared to what the government did to Clippy, that *annoying* icon that pops up in Word all the time." Then followed by an animated gunshot and Clippy's demise.

We laughed—how could we not? Perhaps it was a rationalization to say that people always hated the tools foisted on them at work. I certainly remember how much people hated all the IBM mainframe software in use at my summer aerospace job and then the MS-DOS software used throughout Cornell. People loved the Mac, until it ate their file at midnight.

Our answer, and my answer, to all of this—the flaws, the increasing expectations, the late products, the quality issues, the jokes, and more—was to execute. Thinking back to that 1:1 when SteveB became president, ever present in my thoughts was what happens when a large development team loses focus and spins out of control. Considering how large our team had become with the addition of SharePoint, my concerns grew deeper. I had no idea just how real this concern was about to become.

As we were planning the follow-on to Office XP, the Windows team was starting to lose control after so carefully maintaining it. Windows XP shipped on August 24, 2001, within weeks of the original goal and six years after Windows 95, and then sketched out a grand vision for the next two releases. The first was code-named *Longhorn* after a bar in Canada between *Blackcomb*, which was the code name for the next release, and Whistler, the original code name for XP. Longhorn was planned to be a scaled back version of Blackcomb available sooner, which was being planned simultaneously as Windows traditionally did. Don't worry, I couldn't keep track either. There was so much excitement about the plans for Blackcomb that BillG kept pressing and the team was receptive to accelerating the long-term work for Blackcomb into the near-term Longhorn. It was typical to attempt this when planning two releases in parallel as the second release always appeared more exciting.

Nevertheless Longhorn was slated to be finished in a reasonable timeframe. Windows generally did not have specific completion dates as much as ranges though there were clear dates for early milestones. The release had a set of four strategic initiatives and grand long-term aspirations. These four initiatives were BillG's self-declared main projects for the next 5 years (two releases) and included major advances in storage, code name *WinFS*, user interface platform and graphics, code name *Avalon*, networking, code name *Indigo*, and a major set of new developer APIs, code name *WinFX*. Longhorn would embody the biggest and broadest platform strategy ever attempted by Microsoft. I began to share copies of my favorite book on massive engineering, *IBM's 360 and Early 370 Systems* by Emerson Pugh, detailing the history of the biggest and most enduring computing platform ever built. Could we top that? I probably should have noted more of the history of the project that came before the 360, code-named *Project Stretch*, which went so poorly the project leader was ostracized within IBM, only to find redemption with the 360 mainframe product.

A really (really) big problem brewing was that Windows XP was struggling in the market, having received muted reviews it often proved difficult for enthusiasts to upgrade and required a significant uptick in PC hardware from OEMs. More alarming though, the virus and malware criminals and troublemakers that attacked Office moved their focus to Windows XP and Windows Server. Those products with significantly more surface area were under assault. The Windows team was scrambling to patch a relentless onslaught of bugs. There was ample consternation over the rationalization that the product was behaving as was intended while also deep concerns about breaking third-party software. If this challenge sounds familiar it is because it is exactly the situation Office was in years earlier.

Windows developed a plan to implement a fast-turnaround service pack that addressed the major holes in the product and to complete it in six to nine months. From my vantage point, having a 50 percent error rate on the estimated schedule completion of a short-term project was already a sign of a team that was not operating in control. The scope of the work, the resources, and the schedule were not aligned. The update to Windows XP was going to need more time, more people, and more work.

There was some good news in how the update progressed. Windows XP as it released was outfitted with Watson technology from Office. For the first time a Windows release was getting real-time information on crashes. The Office team continued to run the Watson service while Windows was able to isolate and fix a very large number of common crashes, as Office did while shipping Office XP.

Six months turned into twelve. Then more. More and more of the team, especially management, were being pulled into security challenges. An annoyance erupted into an existential threat to Windows. Even more importantly, the security issues threatened to prevent Microsoft's .NET strategy from taking hold and earning product-market fit before even reaching the market. All around the world, the value proposition of only a browser and web pages with code on the server—the strategy espoused by Sun's McNealy and Oracle's Ellison—was looking more attractive. At stake was Microsoft's reputation with enterprise customers.

A favorite saying in the Office hallways was that it is not enough for the leading product to drop the proverbial ball, but someone had to be there to pick it up and run with it. While there were many challenges in market with Windows XP, the real concern was that it was increasingly apparent that the network computer and browser were there to pick up the dropped ball.

There were endless debates over how far to go. I had a long email thread with a VP of Windows sharing my experience asking if "fixing" Windows was even possible? No matter how much was "broken" the architecture was fundamentally open and extensible and thus subject to ongoing assault. I had my doubts this problem was solvable based on my experience in Office. I would return to this topic in just a few years when I moved to Windows.

The definition of product-market fit ultimately prevailed—Windows was the winning product, and the market could not get enough of it, even with security issues and incompatibilities. All Microsoft needed was to respond. The company needed to show it was taking the problem seriously.

Following the September 11, 2001 tragedy, Craig Mundie (CraigMu) led an effort to cement Microsoft's response to security threats. CraigMu, from his position as chief research officer, went around the world representing Microsoft to governments, universities, and enterprise customers. He was deeply in touch with the public sector perception of products and the nature of the existential threat. Working with BillG, Craig and his team authored a memo called *Trustworthy Computing* (TwC), released in early 2002 and dictated a new set of priorities and new way to develop products. In addition, CraigMu further developed Microsoft's Security and Response Center and led it to first-class citizenship in the world of *cyber defense*.

Often the press and outside world extend too much credit to BillG with something big like TwC. In this case, enough credit cannot go to Craig. He was early to this challenge and brought together the product groups and technologists in Washington, DC and around the world, academics, and other domain experts. He navigated these communities and found a way to frame the problem they were expressing so it could be addressed by the disparate organizations at Microsoft including engineering, sales, legal, product support, and more. Even the phrase trustworthy computing was no doubt influenced by the government commissioned report of that same name, which included participation from members of Microsoft Research and Craig's advanced products group. Bridging the regulatory and technical gap became Craig's specialty and proved enormously transformative for Microsoft.

TwC brought increased attention to cybersecurity as a boardroom issue for companies, beyond the damage done by viruses and malware. This was something existential to all companies and their customers, not just technology providers. Microsoft's Executive Briefing Center added sessions on TwC which served to further entrench Microsoft as a thought-leader with enterprise customers. This was a significant turning point in the establishment of deep customer relationships.

The TwC memo also saw broad external distribution and would even be celebrated at decade milestones.[29, 30] Along with establishing the center, mandatory security training for engineers, and a host of commitments to enterprise customers, we also made security a first priority in everything we did. While many offered input and additions to the memo, I was always proud of pushing what I learned from responding to the Word and Outlook viruses. The January 2002 memo prioritized security over features as we did for Office years before—a strong signal to enterprise customers that we would be, essentially, making incompatible changes.

> *So now, when we face a choice between adding features and resolving security issues, we need to choose security. Our products should emphasize security right out of the box, and we must constantly refine and improve that security as threats evolve. A good example of this is the changes we made in Outlook to avoid e-mail-borne viruses. If we discover a risk that a feature could compromise someone's privacy, that problem gets solved first. If there is any way we can better protect important data and minimize downtime, we should focus on this. These principles should apply at every stage of the development cycle of every kind of software we create, from operating systems and desktop applications to global Web services.*[31]

Message received. We were going to break a lot of stuff. Customers loved the TwC message, but the compatibility concerns would become a constant source of frustration for decades to follow.

Unfortunately executing the product changes to secure Windows XP turned into a 36-month journey (including an interim Service Pack 1), releasing Windows XP Service Pack 2, XP SP2, on August 24, 2004, three years after RTM and much longer than a quick turnaround. There were several major security incidents over the course of this, which either motivated more changes or slowed down releasing broad product changes, depending on perspective. When people say the regulatory climate distracted Microsoft and slowed execution, all I can think about is how much more responding to security did. While not everyone was working on compliance, every single group with code in Windows, Server, Office was making changes, fixing bugs, or investigating potentially risky areas to improve security of products while continuing to function correctly with the changes Windows was making. PC OEMs and independent hardware vendors (IHVs) contributed immensely by updating all the software installed on new PCs and required by hardware devices.

While the first couple of years were rather difficult with Windows XP, it emerged to become a deeply loved and fixture of a PC operating system. When I was working on Windows, we ended up extending official support for the product to nearly 13 years, three years longer than any other product.

Office was in a different place. We did not face the security challenges to the same degree but faced the needling of Scott McNealy, softening demand for new Office features, and high-friction upgrades from enterprise customers, and the ever-present risks of browser-computing.

More importantly, we were on the verge of understanding how Office could be a full participant in "services." We began crafting our plans to finally deliver on those offsites from almost a decade ago where we were asked the question of how to turn software into an "annuity" business.

We faced the challenge of forging into new areas and doing new things. Everybody had ideas, which meant saying "no" became a big part of the process. But who would say no and to what and why?

070. OFFICE.NOT

In the fall of 1999 Microsoft held its annual Company Meeting at the old Kingdome where a stage was set up over second base. While most of the world was fixated on the rise of internet sites or more likely the looming Y2K crisis, both SteveB and BillG used their time to begin a transformation of Microsoft—the transformation to a software services company, which would later be called cloud computing. Few even in the industry knew what this meant. Pioneer Salesforce.com was just months old and the original cloud infrastructure company Loudcloud started by web browser pioneer Marc Andreessen and former Netscape executive Ben Horowitz was incorporated just a week before the Company Meeting. This was very early, but it was also very big. Even though Microsoft was at the peak of success and the most valuable company in the world, the company was going to be reinvented. It was powerful.

BillG spoke first. His opening was dramatic—a reinvention of the core mission statement for Microsoft—the title slide was "Changing the World of Software." From the meeting transcript:

> *The vision statement that many of you have heard, year after year after year, we actually decided to change. That statement, a PC on every desk and in every home, running Microsoft software, is still true. It's a great vision. It really drove the company for the twenty-four years that we've been in business. But in some ways it's outdated. Not outdated because it's wrong. But outdated because it's not revolutionary. When you hear that statement today, you say yeah, of course, what else is new. PC's are in sixty percent of U.S. homes already. The prices are coming down to a point where increased penetration is very, very easy to predict.*
>
> *But Microsoft is a change agent. We're not just about taking the software we've done and making it a little bit better. We're about changing the platform. Taking the kind of risks we took when we bet the company on graphical interface or bet on a Windows NT. We're embarking now as big a bet, or I would say, a bigger bet than any of those. It's captured in this new vision statement. Empower people through great Microsoft, internally we say Microsoft, externally we just leave that as implicit thought, great Microsoft software, any time, any place and on any device.*
>
> *Now when some people in the company heard that they thought is that all really that much different? Is it something completely new? And just in the last month, Steve and I with a lot of help, from other people, have come up with a way of taking this vision and explaining what it means to our software in a way that is quite revolutionary. And that is by saying that from 1975 to 1998 the whole vision centered around the PC. It said the PC is getting more powerful, there is more and more things people are doing with it, just get the applications on to that PC and we'll continue to lead.*
>
> *Well, now we're saying that although the PC will continue to be important that it's actually the capabilities that are delivered through the internet, the services across the Internet that people will be thinking about.. They won't be thinking about managing their files on an individual machine. They'll want all their information stored in the network in such ways that any device that they pick up, a PC,*

> *a phone, a TV, a small screen device, they have access to the information they care about. That takes storage of file system that was purely PC-centric and makes it much more internet-centric.*[32]

This was classic Bill. There was a bold statement. An assumption that the company was willing to take on huge risk. Embracing success while saying we could do much better. Then pivoting to a very specific technical scenario, and no surprise it was data storage. He did this exact pivot when celebrating the Office XP launch with the team—great job, now about unified storage. There were demonstrations of web scalability on Windows, the new collaboration features in Exchange, including the Web Store discussed in previous sections. In something unusual for Bill, he ended his keynote by going through the newly created *Microsoft Values*, talking to Innovation, The Customer, Partners, Integrity, Diversity, Community, Entrepreneurial Culture, and People. A memo was authored describing these values, distributed to the company, and leaked to the local press, who often hung outside the Kingdome listening to the meeting anyway.

These ideas did not spring up for the meeting. A couple of years earlier Bill wrote a memo where the concept of a *WinTone* was put forth—something akin to a dial tone where your computer was always connected to a Microsoft server (actually called a *MegaServer* in the memo) where files would be stored and where PC updates could be distributed. Technically this sounded a good deal like a typical Unix workstation and was similar to ideas being espoused by Sun and NeXT.[33] By the time the Company meeting rolled around, these ideas had been much discussed and the Orwellian nature of them toned down. It is interesting to note that these perceptions would change dramatically, and the same ideas introduced today are not only typical but expected.

SteveB came next. Going from Bill's almost monotone delivery to Steve's energy filled enthusiasm was always fun. Steve's keynote was titled "The Power to Be Strong: The Wisdom To Be Wise." Where Bill was describing what we should aspire to, Steve was providing the emotional call to action, the aircover to go and act on what Bill said, while also taking us through the detailed business reasoning. Steve came bounding on stage to some song that meant a lot to him that he carefully picked to get him in the perfect mood. Where Bill was measured and deliberate, diving deeply into technology, Steve pounded on "services." He said the word almost 200 times in the keynote. The key slide was "Reinventing Microsoft: Software As A Service." Like Bill he started off describing our success, though Steve was even more hardcore from a business perspective:

> *As Bill said, the PC is not new to the revolution anymore. People wanted to know in some senses, what is it? The PC has been it for us for twenty-five years, and we have exploited it, and we have built it, and we have designed it and we did it better than any company in the history of the world! One vision, one technology model, one revenue model, one partner model, and we just went, and we went, and we went, and we went after it! And you know what? Here is the good news, it's still got some mileage left in it! And I like that a lot. But it doesn't have as much mileage to come, perhaps as the mileage it has brought to us in the past. And so when we talked about a new vision, people kept asking —but what is the new it?— The PC has been it, and the PC will remain it, but what's the new it?*[34]

I don't really think people expected that at all. Here we were on top of the world and Steve was telling everyone the party was over. This was Steve and he was going to take us on the emotional journey and was working towards showing us all the opportunity that was ahead. Steve pitched the company on the why of both services and PCs and an echo to "software *and* services" that would follow. He explained that Application Service Providers (ASPs) were the new developers to focus on. Then using the model, he was most comfortable with, he went through each Microsoft customer segment—enterprise, small business, consumer—and described the value proposition and how we would approach the opportunity. Who are the competitors and how would Microsoft compete? Steve had a list and made sure even in the face of regulation challenges, it was OK to compete vigorously. He even had a pro-forma P&L describing the way revenue would transition to services. Like Bill, Steve also concluded emphasizing the new company values.

It was a remarkable presentation and strategy. The presentation and details were the first draft what would become the months of meetings for the *Next Generation Windows Services* (NGWS) task force and presaged the Forum 2000 strategy day the following June. The 2000 wave of products (Windows, Office, Exchange, SharePoint, and many more) were announced at COMDEX just two months after the company meeting to over 340,000 people and created the product foundation for the company that would carry us forward as Steve described. These new products—the foundation of Microsoft for a decade—were positioned as old news before they even shipped. I loved it.

Unlike the internet strategy, especially the *Internet Tidal Wave* memo, this services strategy was ahead of the market. Microsoft was leading and no big company was heading there yet. It was, at best, a Silicon Valley startup strategy. When it came to services, Microsoft was incredibly early. Were we too early?

Windows and Office both created the XP products over the next 18-24 months while theoretically the new services infrastructure was built up. That wasn't quite the plan, as really both teams were polishing/finishing the 2000 wave, but it worked out that way. There would be an absolute ton of meetings about Services over the next two years. The big project being worked on was Hailstorm, also known as .NET MyServices. The services topic and getting more done and sooner was top of mind.

In Office we had already spent a couple of years on SharePoint and FrontPage and were more than convinced that services were the future for us—so many of the scenarios described by Bill and Steve were easily enabled by using a browser, HTML, and a web server. It was abundantly clear that any remnants of the old way of working were in the rear-view mirror. A long list of technologies were better suited to being redesigned for a web architecture including file servers, "net use" to share files, directly connecting to databases from Win32 apps, having all your files on one PC, and even obscure features of roaming settings and customizations.

We had many difficult balancing acts in front of us such as how much could work in a browser (very little in 2001) or who would buy services from us (we had no idea) or how much would a service cost (would it cost more or less than a box of Office.) We had been talking for the whole of the XP product cycle about a mythical product "FrontPage.NET" since every next version product or code name had a .NET suffix by summer 2000 and would be an app-less app. Simply go to a web site and sign in and start creating a new web site. We'd seen self-service collaboration sites take off with SharePoint Team Services. I compiled a list of a dozen or more competitors who were making browser-based products for sharing and collaboration. No one was really doing anything significant for document creation, yet. Outlook was achieving a huge level of interest in the browser version being done by the Exchange team, so much we'd move that team to Office to better align Outlook in the browser and Outlook on the desktop. We were ready for services.

In the spring of 2001 after Office XP released with the rise of the new .NET developer platform inside of Microsoft, Office shifted its gears to deliver what BillG referred to in an earlier memo, *Office as a Service*. Customers loved the idea of infinite clip art, endless templates, ever-expanding online help, even sending Microsoft bug reports. We had so many more ideas.

As Steve and Bill set the stage to transform the company, it was my turn to transform the Office team. We had almost 2000 people on the Office team. That's a huge management challenge, even with the air cover from the company meeting two years earlier. There's only so much a few hours in a stadium can do. My job was where the strategy and words needed to start turning into code and product.

To get there as a team, we needed to scale our planning process. Our mantra for planning had become "the best of top-down, bottom-up, and middle-out", but in truth we were far more tilted in the direction of middle-out, meaning gaining alignment across the various app and shared teams, and bottom-up where everyone contributed to feature ideation and prioritization. The top-down planning we did was around resource allocation and the big shifts to the suite and enterprise. The transition we're talking about here needed a much more prescriptive top-down effort. Somehow, I needed to find a way to do so without being rejected out of hand or worse being called "too much like Windows." Finding an enhanced way of planning that allowed for more senior management coordination and, yes, control, was hugely stressful.

I settled on a process of memos over a course of months that would lead to increasingly detailed priorities and ultimately an organization (aka a re-org) to execute on the plan. Along the way there would be countless 1:1s, skip-level 1:1s, group meeting presentations and Q&A, email threads, and hallway chats. Drafts were shared. Changes were made. The idea was that even the top-down was a product of bottom-up and middle-out. I admit that is an idealized view and some would disagree, but the goal and the work put in was intended to do that. At the very least we were running a version 1.0 process.

The process would take a bit more than 12 months from the first memo to the team meeting rolling out the vision (the plan), starting well before the current release even shipped. That seems like an insufferably long time in today's environment. Aside from the obvious notion of "boxed" software versus an ever-changing service, there was a crucial difference with today. Office was a single product, with a single strategy, which would all be made available on the same day, spanning the work of some 2000 people each of whom would deliver their contribution on that day, complete and working. There are many enormous, far bigger, projects today, but they are rarely delivered in this manner. Even today Office itself no longer delivers products this way. Today, a single new feature in Office might roll out over the course of a year even in one module, and the same feature might come later in another part of Office, for example, today's dark mode. It isn't just that the feature is released before it is done, but even after it is done there is a long tail of delivery.

In April 2000, 11 months before Office XP shipped, I sent out the first memo in the series, *Next Generation Office*, or NGO. Essentially on the heels of the Company Meeting and just before Forum 2000, I wanted to offer the Office analog to NGWS. The fact that this was just after the dot-com bubble was important context. While the stock dropped precipitously, it was nothing compared to most of the tech world. The introduction set the stage for a big change:

> *Office is at a crossroads—we are on the brink of shocking changes in the technology priorities of our customers and are facing a substantial disconnect between our product and what customers want. For two releases customers have been telling us that they don't have the need for upgrades and can't imagine what else is left to do with Office. At the same time we have continued to innovate roughly along the same path started back in 1992 with Office 4.x—improving the basic document process. As we close upon the development of Office10, the signs are upon us that we are truly at the end of one era and at the start of another, and if we don't act deliberately and precisely we run the very real risk of missing the transition. We have accomplished amazing things with Office, especially Office10. Over the years we have developed a product that is in daily use by perhaps 200 million people and each one of those customers gets tremendous value from our work.*

It went on to describe what I called "The Big Bet" which was about developing an "internet user experience" for Office:

The Next Generation of Office is not just an incremental addition to our "client-side" code, nor is it about developing stand alone server applications, or isolated "free services" [This is a vague but pointed reference to the dot-com crash and all the companies doing free software and planning on making it up in volume]. *The Next Generation of Office is about creating a compelling Internet User Experience built on top of the Next Generation Windows Services (NGWS, an early document from SteveB.) NGO is a product that is the seamless integration of our client, our server software, and our services. When we speak of "Office as a service" we mean that Office is the combination of a Windows application (like the world knows and loves) plus a wide variety of hosted services (extrapolate from Office Update) plus a range of significant server software (such as OWS or mail boxes.) Although we might also include some element of support or custom engineering, "consulting", or other people-based services, our bet does not explicitly require that—we are a software company through and through. We will fail if we do not deliver on that powerful combination.*

> The memo paints a complete picture of the many challenges Office 2000 faced in the market. I referred to this as the *innovation disconnect.* The perceived cost to deploying, training, absorbing new features continued to rise, while the perceived value of those features declined. In other words, we were digging a deeper and deeper hole for ourselves by simply doing what we were doing by adding features. The bottom-line on this observation was a dramatic number I placed on what were termed traditional innovation, or features in the desktop apps, which was only 20% would go to "guarding the core enterprise agreement." Such a statement proved to be enormously controversial with our team and as the marketing team which at the time reported to me. As we'll see the controversy did not end there.

As I came to learn, in a big company (and especially Microsoft) when people read memos from executives there's an ever-present expectation of a reorg. In Office our re-orgs had become routine and predictable. After a release we'd realign resources, shuffle the shared feature teams in Office proper, and make sure everyone had a chance to do something new or sit tight. It wasn't stress-free, but it wasn't a scary free for all. In reading NGO, many suspected a much bigger change. There was not. Instead, what we really needed was to create a whole new type of job. Our historic reliance of the magical trio of dev, test, and pm (software design engineering, software design in test, and program management) could not account for the important role of operations The contemporary title of devops was a decade away. Part of writing this memo was to have guest speakers come to group manager meetings and to share industry practices from some of the hot startups. For example, Tim Brady, the first non-founding employee at Yahoo spoke about prioritization, keeping services running, and the like. I met him at a Harvard Business School event when I was there on sabbatical teaching. In many ways the biggest change in NGO would be creating not only an operations team, but an operations mindset.

The real purpose of NGO was not to provide answers to what the product was, but to tee up the questions or to frame how the release should look. In the next iteration we'd call the memo at this stage the *framing memo*, because it framed the release. It wasn't nearly as prescriptive as BillG would have written because it was more of a management tool than a bulleted list of features that he tended to favor. In that sense, sending these memos up the chain was often frustrating for the recipients and a bunch of work for me. I had to learn how to use the memo to gather their feedback on the framing, not features.

Over the next months there would be any number of offsites and discussions about what should come next. Teams were using many new startup products out on the market, reading a great deal, and learning new technologies, like .NET. This enabled the next turn of the crank and many more specifics. Rather than putting forth a framing, the next memo said at a high level what we would build. It was still not features, but themes. I called it *Creating Office.NET: Next Steps in Creating a Vision for Productivity.* It was clear that the vision, the actual plan would follow, and this was not the plan. The goal, however, was to be something of a rough draft of the vision. The team would begin to fill in the details and thus own the actual plan. Again, this is solving for the lack of accountability that comes from simply telling people what to do. Plus, I had no idea what every feature should or could be.

> *This memo is about creating the next generation of Office. Not a vision statement, this memo outlines the business situation and the clear direction we are taking the Office product, and the bets we are making (a vision statement will follow soon.) This memo is also about creating a new product—one that takes the enormous success of Office and melds it with new functionality and new technologies to create an exciting new product. We will call this product Office.NET. Office.NET is the essential set of tools and services that empower individuals to get their work done with a personal computer.*

Without saying what the product did, the memo defined what success looked like. Again, this was either empowering or frustrating depending on the mindset of the reader. It is easy to lose sight of the work going on to change mindsets, not just accounting for what features to do. Office had almost no developers working on .NET, HTML, XML, and other new technologies. The memo continued:

- *Customers move beyond the view that Office is "just" a word processor, spreadsheet, email client, graphics, web authoring, and database.* ***Office.NET adds whole new services and applications to the toolset that we build and sell as Office****. Think of the service and services elements of Office.NET as "puzzle pieces." When we release Office.NET people will use our product to get work done in new ways that they might not have thought of and certainly did not think of using Office.* ***Office.NET is not "Office 11."***
- *Customers not only use our new suite of hosted services but customers come to rely on Office.NET services as a critical element of getting their work done. Office.NET services are not about gimmicks or "dumb PC/ internet tricks" but about being simple, elegant, and useful additions to getting work done. For customers,* ***Office.NET is about saving hours, not mere seconds.***
- *The glue that holds Office.NET together is integration and integration is what makes the value of our product greater than the sum of the pieces.* ***Customers using Office.NET see an unprecedented integration between their tasks****—whether those tasks are Office.NET services, desktop productivity tasks, browser-based services, third-party services affiliated with Office.NET, or Microsoft's own MSN services. Integration is the key that allows a customer to solve real-life problems, such as sharing a document with a partner outside the firewall or merging a work calendar and a private calendar. Many would say that one beauty of the internet is the elegance at which a large number of valuable tools interoperate saving time and effort—we will bring that elegance to Office.NET's services.*
- ***Office.NET provides a new level of "customer service"*** *by keeping the software updated, enriched, and "running" for customers. No longer will customers feel like they are "cut off" from Microsoft after they buy the product or feel like they have to wait a year for a 30MB patch to fix things. Of course, Office.NET doesn't change this from the first day a customer gets the product, but we will over time build up the service relationship. Customers no longer view buying Office as a one-time transaction, but rather* ***customers subscribe to Office.NET because Microsoft is making a commitment to back our software and services with the highest level of support possible.***
- *Customers who use Office.NET can do so with full faith and confidence that* ***Office.NET provides a safe, secure, private, and reliable service.*** *We will go to extremes to insure that customers can trust their important work to the tools and services offered by Microsoft. Everyday one hundred million people trust their work to Office, so we're in a good position to extend this trust to a new level of support. This will not come easy, but we will make it so by making it the highest priority in everything we do.*
- ***Office.NET is good for business.*** *The great American philosopher, Steve Martin, once had a moment of enlightenment when he realized "it's a profit game." For most of the history of Office, it has been more than good enough to maintain a clear focus on improving our engineering and building products that more often than not continued along the path of incremental improvement and that led to an amazing business. Office.NET is about building a new product and selling this product in new ways. We are making these choices because everything we know says that they will be good for business—just as we thought building Windows applications was going to be good for business. We will run a service business with the same focus on efficiency and cost that we have had in building our packaged product business.*

The text is rather self-explanatory today. It reads like common sense. At the time, each one of these points had controversies. Even the mundane such as providing software updates was broadly unacceptable to enterprise customers that wanted full control over what changed and when, and they still do. While writing the memo and talking (and talking) I could sense an increasing level of excitement. Bringing the excitement of the rise of the internet home to what we work on and how we work in Office was motivating. To put things in the era, many people were just starting to order books from Amazon and track stock quotes and news on Yahoo, though we were still 5 years from the rise of *Cyber Monday*.

Important to this memo was setting a bounding box around some important project attributes. This is the pure top-down aspect of the plan. This included setting time frames for the release, the number of milestones, system requirements, and more. The real deliverable (as with the operations team from the previous memo) are a set of carefully worded and coordinated "Focus Areas" which would be used by program management. These will anchor the process of feature ideation, prototypes, and scenarios. The memo outlined the following planning focus areas. These came with brief descriptions to answer the why, but were designed to ask the question how, not define the specifics of what we would do:

- *Accessing My Information from Anywhere, Any Time*
- *Creating a Personalized Office Experience*
- *Building Effective Communities and Teams*
- *Growing New Opportunities for Office*
- *A Note About "Traditional" Features*

The framing memo went out to the team in October 2000, about 5 months before most everyone was done with Office XP. A few weeks after that, the third memo in the series went out which was the adjustments to the organization. I like to remember this as relatively uneventful, though no org changes ever are for anyone who gets a new manager. In fact, the team had gotten so good at this re-shuffling after the release that it became somewhat of a game to go from the framing memo to the new org—clever people could guess the new shared teams or realignments that would happen from the way the focus areas were lined up and how the ideation progressed.

Program management created working teams based on these themes, and smaller groups based on specific scenarios. The features would emerge from these efforts—this is the bottom-up and middle-out planning work. PM led by HeikkiK drove this process, working across teams. If there is one magical step in all of Office, it was this particular part of our elaborate process that I came to value the most—we came to call it *participatory design*. It wasn't just that features and scenarios seemed to emerge as if by magic, but the scale and alignment that came with those features. Anyone can (and did) have great lists of features they planned on doing. In Office when we published a list or specifications, we viewed them as team commitments. Heikki was coordinating a couple hundred PMs, designers, product planners, who in turn were partnering with developers to make sure that what was being talked about could get built. Everyone above mostly just watched. I'm not exaggerating. I will learn just how special this process was when I try to import it to Windows in a few years.

By May 2001 we had a full product vision—a product plan—for Office.NET. This whole time I had been sending the memos and talking with BillG and SteveB. In the middle of this process the executive VP leading Office changed from BobMu to JeffR and I walked through this process and all these memos with him. I realize now that must have been like sitting down and trying to untangle the true meaning behind the sales Mid-Year Review (MYR) process in a few meetings and by looking at 100 country and segment-specific slide decks. This oversight on my part will reveal itself shortly.

The pillars of Office.NET included:

- *My Office*
- *Team And Corporate Productivity*
- *Keeping in Touch*
- *No-Brainer Upgrade*
- *Unlocking Information via XML*

Phew. We were getting close.

A side note on the process described above is warranted. In talking about what we did I have always struggled to express the iterative nature of the ongoing work. Almost universally, the process is viewed through the artifacts (the memos) and that has the unintended effect of making the whole of the process seem like a traditional, and loathed, waterfall, as described in Chapter VII. When the process is illustrated in PowerPoint, I tended to use a lot of arrows to show off the constant state of iteration. The memos are not the work, they summarize the work. The work is best thought of as the communication, alignment, and learning constantly taking place.

The other concern often expressed by taking an artifact view is that there is so much planning time, or even dead time while people wait for the plans. In reality, the process came about to avoid any dead time at all. Many in PM are able to peel off while dev and test are finishing the product, up to a year before. From the end of Office XP until the vision is in place was only two months, and two more months until coding the project started. During even that four months, the engineering tooling is updated, the codebase is cleaned up (the removal of so-called technical debt), and because of Watson we initiated a mini-milestone devoted to addressing top issues. The waterfall versus agile debate would follow me around for many years, an irony for sure given the ability for the Office team to *promise and deliver*, compared to so much overpromising going on. I even created a slide that attempted to convey the iterative natures of the process and what we felt was unique. I used this slide for many years.

After a decade of offsites and memos about subscriptions and annuity, we finally worked our way to a product that could truly be offered as a subscription. Quoting from our vision, "Office.NET is a software service consisting of the best combination of software and services that provides a personal experience in creating, communicating and collaborating anywhere and anytime."

The learning from the Office XP services emboldened us to embark on plans to host a broad set of productivity capabilities on the internet. We assumed if the MSN team could do it, then we could as well. We set out to define a new role on the team, on par with development, testing, program management, and design, called *operations* and led by Arthur de Haan (ArthurdH) as described months earlier in the original NGO memo. Arthur was leading the testing of enterprise cost of ownership shared team in Office and was one of Office's most senior test leaders with many years on Excel previously and international. He brought with him a calm demeanor and the attention to detail required to grow a new job function for Office. He was eager to learn, and the mental model of testing and operations were, we believed, a great match. We were all learning.

SharePoint Team Services anchored Office.NET. Every subscriber to Office received his or her own team site, much the same way IT enabled a self-service setup to create new sites on demand in our enterprise product for a new project or something. We called this site *My Office*. From My Office, a subscriber received the features of SharePoint (a place to store documents, calendars, surveys, to-do lists, and more), all accessible from any web browser. In addition, subscribers could download Office (Word, Excel, and PowerPoint) and "activate" it with their subscription. Hotmail offered email. Imagine how cool it would be if files were stored in a website, available from any PC with a browser, including if Office was needed it could be installed. In 2002, when we were dreaming this up, it was entirely workable but seemed like science fiction to customers.

We thought we were on top of these new challenges for the business and customers. We were naïve.

The first and marquee pillar of the vision was My Office, a home page for every Office customer available in a browser integrated all the information relevant to their Office experience: documents, mail, calendar, SharePoint lists, and more. From the start the intent was to support analogous features for enterprise customers installing and managing their own Windows Servers Today we would say this is having both cloud and on-premises offerings. IT could set up SharePoint servers, could distribute Office via browsers, and, in addition, have much improved email with major improvements planned for Outlook. My Office was a gateway to all the communication and collaboration features in the product. The adoption of hosted services by enterprise customers was so early as to not even be in consideration yet.

The plan was great. We were days away from our all-hands vision meeting that HeikkiK owned. We created the vision document (all posted online), a one-page summary everyone received at the meeting, a mock press release, and design built elaborate full-motion demo scenarios to illustrate each of the main themes.

Throughout the process, I sent drafts of the documents and status updates to JeffR, BillG and others. I met 1:1, requested feedback, sent mail, and so on. JeffR told me that it was critical that we schedule a review meeting to again go through the vision with SteveB. This made me uncomfortable because I had already learned the difficulty of reviewing an entire product plan in one meeting. I watched Windows fail at this many times going all the way back to working for BillG as technical assistant. This was nothing like reviewing the goals of an entire subsidiary in 8 hours. It would be more like reviewing every account manager's plan for their accounts and how it mapped to the subsidiary marketing plans and then to those goals—in 2 hours. Navigating a meeting of this scope—the work of 2000 people on a creative endeavor with a ton of unknowns that would be resolved over the next 18-24 months was, at least in my view, impossible.

While we were incredibly comfortable with our plan and the team was marching almost on autopilot, I wildly misunderstood my job description and accountability. We were planning this product since long before RTM of Office XP, with the elaborate process of memos and public milestones I discussed with JeffR 1:1. Reviewing a whole vision in one meeting at the end is an impossible task—the document was a work product of the team with nothing surprising by the time we rolled it out. Any changes this late, however, would be a surprise to the team. The empowerment that came with our participatory design process meant that management was not allowed to spring things on the team. Any big changes that the team did not participate in would be, um, poorly received.

Jeff and I took the shuttle over to SteveB's office, the other big office next to BillG. Once the discussion got underway, I quickly realized this was not a casual check-in.

I began to run through the vision slide deck and the demos—the materials that would be used at the team meeting in just a few weeks. The first demo was My Office. There was enormous tension in the room. All I heard was, "We can't do this product…it will put us out of business." The rest of the meeting remains a cloudy memory.

I was perplexed. This was not simply a feature, but it was the core of Office.NET delivering Office as a service, as planned and described for months. It was just what both Bill and Steve described at the Company Meeting over 18 months ago. Our capabilities were not being doubted, rather it was the strategy. Was it a statement about subscriptions? Or was it a bet against SharePoint services? Did we not even want to do an internet user experience?

It was clear that a collective mind was made up, and perhaps had been long ago. The idea of offering internet-dependent Office was deemed simply too big a risk to the enterprise business. Essentially, they were concerned about what might happen if an individual started using this and then it was appealing to enterprises but not sold or supported by our enterprise sales force. It could even undermine Enterprise Agreement growth. It could cause customers to question the role of enterprise servers and cause troubles for the new and fast-growing Windows 2000 business.

I tried to craft answers explaining how I was certain that enterprises were not ready for this sort of service, and that our sales and marketing effort was aimed at small businesses and individuals—a long underserved market. The idea of internet hosting SharePoint offering downloadable Office was exactly what we had communicated earlier as a long-term goal for what was branded bCentral (an internet product for small businesses that included among other things email and communication), only adding productivity tools, Office code, and data center that could deliver that—done by the Office team as a core business bet, not a separate offering off to the side attempting to build new capabilities around Office rather than into it.

Could this moment have been avoided? I don't think so. In hindsight, SteveB and JeffR were both focused on the enterprise sales motion—big accounts needing to close deals, enterprise thought leaders from Gartner, and most of all the field leaders. By their accounts, Office needed more "enterprise value" not what the IT industry had dubbed consumer services on the internet. And Office needed to reduce bloat. There was great love for the XML features, so more of that.

Should they have raised these points sooner? I incorrectly gauged their need to have more in person discussions. Their expectation from the field was that the process of planning and getting approval was a series of meetings. My expectations were based on writing ("writing is thinking"), and I found it ineffective to use a process that tried to agree on vast plans of thousands of people in person, with uneven engagement and unpredictable focus. My history, and that of BillG and MikeMap, was writing and communicating with strategy documents, detailed status reports, and transparency of process. But that wasn't the field's preferred method of engagement.

I failed to understand how much I was supposed to be managing up. This was my fault entirely.

At scale, a field organization is a much more top-down and prescriptive process than a product team. While a product team needs to scale execution (shipping quality code on time), defining what code to write is a different type of creativity than account planning or sales resource allocation. Field organizations tend to scale with HQ-centric strategy and planning teams that are there to work directly with executives—generally a clear separation between strategy and execution. Development organizations generally avoid distinct roles—those planning the strategy also execute it. As a result, there was a lot less bandwidth and interaction with management. We designed that into our organization, and it was appreciated.

In my case, it meant that I left a big gap in the way I managed the strategy *up* the organization, especially considering what they were used to.

As the meeting went on, I answered the concerns expressed, but I had mishandled the process. We would address bloat by not adding a bunch of features and keeping the core products the same. In other words, I unintentionally pointed out there would not be many new features in the core apps, except for enterprise capabilities, such as using the new-fangled XML technology. We intended to expand the value of Office with entirely new modules, one for pen and tablets and one for business processing and forms, a deeply enterprise scenario. The enterprise product was a superset of the Office.NET style product that would be deployed and operated by IT.

To be clear, I had said the enterprise product was *the* product. We were not selling a subscription, but we endeavored to beef up the free services offered with Office. I said the right words about the right priorities, and it was made clear that there was no subscription for Office that competed in the enterprise. But discussing that was not in the cards. Never had a product feature or strategy received a straight verboten before, so I left the meeting saying I was on top of it.

The vision for "Office.NET" reads well even today. In hindsight I should have seen this as a lesson in moving too soon or being *early* in May 2001.

> *Office.NET represents a major new vision for Office: integrating web services with the rich client to deliver unprecedented value to our customers. Office.NET also represents a major shift in how the product team approaches the Office product development cycle. Office.NET is* ***not*** *"the next version of Office." It is an entirely new focus for Office where we will start fresh and extend our software into new and unexplored areas—software services. Office.NET will introduce a new business model, integrate with other strategic Microsoft technologies, and make much of the company-wide .NET vision real.*

As of this writing, I still find the time the most puzzling few days in my career. I was too worried about the team and my constant fear of unraveling (as the Windows team was doing) to spend any effort on figuring out if there was a gap in understanding. I viewed this as an edict from above and executed as such.

I came back to the office and discussed these changes with Heikki. My state of mind was such that I did an exceptionally poor job of explaining what transpired. He was as puzzled as I was.

Since everything was essentially baked, we changed the body language of what we were doing. Where once again we started by planning the release not building *the next Office*, we ended up feeling incremental again. The step-function changes in the product—a subscription and internet offering—were scaled back, and our focus was back on IT and strategic enterprise value, to the exclusion of other work. Most everything we planned on doing as a hosted service we kept on doing, only as a server product using SharePoint. We would have many services as part of the core experience of the product (as previously described, such as templates, assistance materials, bug reporting, updates) and we would develop many new services along the way that would get us ready for a future.

For now, the snazzy sign up for a subscription with a credit card service was going to be the job of the bCentral team creating services exclusively on small business customers. Ironically this team, and its descendants, would spend the next 10 or more years working to scale SharePoint, Exchange, and various telephony products to work first in Microsoft hosted servers (essentially as an application service provider) first in a product called EHS, Exchange Hosted Services offering security and reliability services for a customer's Exchange servers, and then a suite called BPOS, Business Productivity Online Service. By the end of 2008 there were about 500,000 mailboxes protected by EHS, with some big names driving a large set of those. Then by 2010 there were about 1,000 paying companies on BPOS with 2 million mailboxes, again, highly concentrated. [35]

Therein lie the roots of today's Office 365 offering Exchange and SharePoint services. The browser-based implementations of the Office apps would come with the next full release of Office.

Hindsight is super clear for this issue. The timeframe for enterprise customers to be ready for Office.NET was not early 2000's. It would not even be 2010 or even 2015. Running essentially the same enterprise products but on Microsoft servers, the cloud as we call it today, would have in fact been insane in 2000. The killer application for the enterprise cloud was…simply scaling and running Exchange email for large customers. The product had become so complex and yet so mission critical that essentially only Microsoft could effectively operate it. It would take about a decade to build a product that customers would even begin to evaluate.

But in 2001 sitting in SteveB's office, the enterprise was in no way ready for the cloud model—not even close. In fact, they were uniformly against the model. That's how early we were. Would it have put us out of business? Probably not as most customers would have ignored the offering and thought we were crazy. That's how most felt even after 2010, and BPOS was essentially running dedicated servers for each customer. Steve was right, however, in that it would have been confusing to customers just as BPOS was in 2010.

The immediately visible change was that we re-code-named the project Office11 instead of Office.NET. For the moment, at least the corporate branding people were relieved. We presented the vision, only finessing the idea that the design sketches needed to be representative of an enterprise aesthetic.

Office.NET as an internet experience for consumers was essentially dead.

Personally, this was a really tough few weeks in early 2001. Around the same time, Steve was pondering making changes to the Windows CE/Mobile group. He spoke to a lot of people as he always did. Among those, he spoke to me and two other good friends that were also "product leaders." We also spoke to each other, that's how we know we all had basically the same input on what to do. We were getting killed by the new BlackBerry and our phones were nowhere near credible even though we'd been at it for almost 10 years. Unknowingly, we all said the same thing to Steve—we need to build our own phone and completely reset the operating system for that hardware. That was not the answer the company wanted then as we were totally committed to building out phones as we did the PC ecosystem. That meant no first party hardware and a software-only business selling the operating system to many phone makers. That also meant none of us would have been welcome additions to the team.

As a postmortem, I met up with one of my friends for dinner to talk about the situation and the state of the products, especially the phone situation we found ourselves in the middle of. I managed to inhale an entire slice of Metropolitan Grill 9-layer chocolate cake. Yeah, I was in a bad spot.

A few years earlier I had a wonderful and enriching sabbatical teaching on the east coast. I gave a lot of thought to the idea of switching gears. It didn't get to the point of discussing it. I'm glad I kept quiet, but that didn't make it any easier.

We had a slightly different product to build.

071. RESOLVING NETDOCS V. OFFICE

I was still working through the stages of grief over a product getting killed or at least wounded, considering what happened to Office.NET rapidly renamed Office11 at the last minute. Karma was about to come back around and bite me for, ostensibly, doing the same. Since Forum 2000 in June, the NetDocs product continued development. The team expanded, absorbing products, and broadening the mission. BrianMac used the same approach and much of the team that created Outlook.

The team was fired up but going in several different directions. Depending on who you asked on the team, NetDocs might be something different. What originally started as a new style of document creation tool, blending aspects of word processing, spreadsheets, and databases, expanded into a full-blown email program to replace Outlook, a photo editor, and even a web browser. It was also using the latest (unfinished) and most strategic technologies. Sensing the excitement over XML, the product also found itself deep in that strategy and brand-new code. NetDocs was also using the latest reusable code from Internet Explorer, which was great for the IE platform but also meant it was not exactly what most customers thought about as a browser-based implementation. Along the way, it created some of its own technologies such as the ability to install updates easily over the internet. There was a lot of excitement over a product that does…everything. How could there not be?

On paper, this was quite something. During the early days of MS-DOS, these all-in-one products always struck a chord with techies and regular people alike. The idea of using only one tool to get everything done, including email, was insanely appealing. In a demo, everyone, especially BillG, got excited. The idea Microsoft could finally crack the all-in-one category with a professional tool would be huge. ChrisP had a name for a design demo that incorporated "all the best of everything in one easy-to-use app." It was called *Uniprog Deluxe*. That's what we came to call this expansive vision. It wasn't meant to be cynical as much as it was meant to imply an *unachievability*.

Importantly, NetDocs was also a key part in the nascent strategy to use XML everywhere. XML was being pushed heavily by BillG. Despite being a simple text file format, Bill had let XML take on the role of providing a proprietary advantage to Microsoft in some way. This was a difficult topic to discuss because it conflated several aspects of implementation (such as where the actual intellectual property or code was) and appeared to assign proprietary value to a simple text file. Much of the excitement around XML (and thus NetDocs) was because of the concerns over the now ubiquitous HTML format and lack of proprietary control Microsoft had over a format. In short, XML was the way to regain a proprietary control over an internet technology. Whereas HTML was viewed as a display format, XML was viewed as a structured data format. I had a difficult time with the magic attributed to XML, especially because Office was already invested in HTML. I was holding on to the notion that HTML would remain human-readable at some level, whereas XML was brand new but already super complex. XML advocates would say it was never meant to be human readable. We planned on a significant amount of XML work but viewed it as interoperability more than proprietary advantage. For example, Excel would be able to import XML data from SQL databases.

There was one big problem. And a lot of little ones. The big problem was creating yet another email program—while NetDocs did try to do a lot of things, everything emanated from being an email and scheduling product. Microsoft went through several years of a comical email client strategy that was confusing and frustrating to customers. Email was literally the most important product the company was building and the most important enterprise product. Not only was it the key server product, but it was also the key new Office module. Perhaps that is why we had so many email products in the market and in the works—something important attracts a lot of attention from development teams looking to do important work. In a world where we were just establishing enterprise credibility, having multiple email programs was a disaster, especially when our flagship one wasn't so well-received, yet.

When something is hot, however, every project converges to that product. So, everything had to do email.

We had Outlook, which was struggling to become a great product for Exchange and enterprise email. After the initial release that just made it into Office 97, there was the split and the creation of Outlook 98, which was either a not-so-great Exchange client or a not-so-great internet mail client, but not both. Then for Outlook 2000 and then again with Outlook 2002 (XP) we failed several times at becoming a more reliable Exchange client with a new storage engine. Finally, with Outlook11 we committed to addressing the problems, come hell or high water.

We also had the new browser-based version of mail, which we named Outlook, technically Outlook Web Access, even though the relationship to Outlook was zero when it came to code and only acceptable when it came to user experience and features. The inability to share code and limited capabilities of rendering all of Outlook in 2000 era web browsers caused this divergence and inefficiency. Customers were extremely enthusiastic for the promise of browser-based email with Outlook Web Access.

In 1996, the Windows team released Internet Mail and News, or IMN, which became a much-loved internet mail program. It was part of Windows and Internet Explorer, made by the same team. IMN was plugging along doing great things for the internet when it became clear to our enterprise sales efforts that we could not have a first-rate internet mail and so-so Exchange mail. The solution was—and I'm not making this up—to rename IMN to Outlook Express.

This was a decree that neither the Outlook team nor the Windows team liked, but the theory was that it clarified the products for customers. The IMN team did not want to be tainted with yucky enterprise Outlook, and the Outlook team didn't want to be confused with free or, for that matter, the internet. Customers called everything Outlook and were, basically, always confused. Product support was confused. Reviewers were confused. Most of all, normal people were confused. It was a silly, self-inflicted mess that continued for more than a decade, except for the reality that in 2001 work on both Outlook Express and Internet Explorer stopped, and improvements were dependent on the future Windows Longhorn. There were no plans to update either on Windows XP. Those capabilities were going to exist in some new form on Longhorn.

We had Outlook, Outlook Web Access, and Outlook Express. The branding and naming relationship was much deeper than any technical one.

To complete the mail strategy, we also offered Hotmail, the web-based email acquired in 1998. Hotmail was both a mail "client" and a mail "server" in BillG architectural diagrams. MSN mail was trying to converge to Hotmail, but was also building a client-side application to compete with AOL and thus a client mail experience. Hailstorm was slated to provide or connect to a set of these email experiences, but it used a different protocol.

If you were to try to build a matrix of mail clients and mail servers and which connected to which, you'd have a matrix with many holes. Our strategy was a mess.

Many reporters (and customers) at the time looked at this mess and thought of teams competing and some sort of bloody "there can be only one" battle within Microsoft. From inside, it was not that at all. In fact, by and large the teams did not care what each other did. In its own way, each team thought they would win out in the way they expected and the others simply wouldn't be relevant to the battle the way they defined it. Outlook Express was certain they would win against Eudora (the leading classic internet email program) or Netscape Communicator, if for no other reason a bunch of people weren't going to pay for Outlook. Reviews at the time uniformly reported that Outlook was in no way competitive with Eudora. They were right, and the Outlook team put little energy into competing with Eudora or Outlook Express. MSN was going to win with their own subscribers and be the best (and only) experience for their dial-up customers. Hotmail was going to become advertising supported and win in browser-based email. Outlook proper anchored itself in the corporate market with Office, and made all the money.

There was a competition and that was for people. Recruiting and hiring was a source of conflict. Often when a new group spun up, recruiting kicked into high gear. There were neither rules nor much of an internal system that managed individuals moving between teams. Most moves happened by word of mouth. Teams would routinely bump up against the norms (not formal rules) by implying the potential for promotion or broader responsibility with a move. More often than not an employee would get caught in the middle of one manager recruiting heavily and another manager trying to hold their team together in the short term.

Such staffing skirmishes uniquely impacted Office where the vast majority of our hires came from college (hundreds per year) and we maintained a strong culture of finishing a release that was started. Luring people away from the team mid-cycle was something we deeply frowned upon at a cultural level. New hires with even a partial release of Office could join a team having gone through valuable training and initiation by Office. At release boundaries, Office proved a strong net exporter of people to other teams, renewing our own teams with even more college hires the next year. Since there was no coordination by HR, more than anything it was this cross-recruiting that introduced friction between teams.

If there was drama it was mostly constrained to the boardroom where the complex matrix of what worked with what, and who was using the latest technology were BillG's main discussions. Most of the time the problems were not anyone's fault, as much as the teams thought it unnecessary to implement something because their customers didn't care.

Yet the strategy from the top of Microsoft was to resolve these architectural "impurities" and to strive towards rationalization and consistency. Still, that did not create competing groups as much as a set of groups that all thought the other groups weren't doing their part to increase synergy. There wasn't anger, hostility, competition for resources, or anything substantial. Mostly, it was just eye-rolling and exasperation at a lot of meetings followed by long emails over how impossibly difficult some alignment would be technically.

The post-2000 Microsoft (after Windows XP and Office XP, with the arrival of the enterprise business) was a period of extensive meetings around synergy and strategy. At the extreme, groups could spin out of control on their own by signing up for too much synergy and strategy. At another extreme, groups could stay focused on shipping. Leading the former meant receiving high praise and attention internally while failing to deliver or delivering what was perceived as suboptimal. Groups of the latter type shipped and often received poor marks for lacking strategic alignment while developing a reputation for being difficult to work with. The reader is invited to guess which type Office was closely identified with and I came to personify that. Nothing occupied my psyche more than this reality I lived. Shipping is really difficult, even more so at scale. As ChrisP used to say in his "Shipping Software" talk from the early 1990s, it is like everyone comes to work every day to prevent a team from shipping. "Everyone" can be many people in a big company.

Every once in a while, something would get so visible and so tricky that a decision would have to be made and we could not just let some notion of passive-aggressive Darwinism decide.

NetDocs was another mail program, one that would in theory work for both Exchange and internet mail, and maybe even Hotmail, MSN, or new Hailstorm mail. Over the intervening years, since the NetDocs team was formed, Outlook won over corporate America and gained an enormous number of features—very difficult to code features. Everything from handling attachments to scheduling meetings across time zones, shared mail accounts, recurring events, sharing calendars with coworkers, SPAM protection, security, looking up other employees in the corporate address book, plus to-do and task lists, and personal contacts, and still more. Those features were built in Outlook; in fact, many weren't even available in the web version of Outlook Web Access, thus adding to the complexity of our mail story.

To software architects, the code implementing the semantics and capabilities of the Microsoft email solution was in Outlook running on the desktop, not running on the server. It was architected in a decidedly old-school manner, mostly out of necessity but also because of history. The problem (the big problem) was that there was no way for NetDocs to implement all those features either on its own or by sharing code with Outlook. It would be like trying to use Word's code for footnotes in PowerPoint, without dragging along all of the Word code. Code doesn't work that way. Getting all that right in the new NetDocs code base was a long project. Infinitely long. The team knew this, primarily because it was made up of many members of the original Outlook team. They were not worried. Their intent was to introduce NetDocs and add features over time.

There were nearly countless smaller features and implementation details to worry about. Being built on all the latest and greatest technologies from .NET and Internet Explorer was great in theory, but in practice most of those technologies themselves were far from being complete. In a commercial product for hundreds of millions of customers, they expected the product to handle typing in the world's languages (left to right, right to left, vertical and switching between)—a particular hot-button for Office given how much work we put into this area. They expected it to understand how dates, time zones, and other locale-specific data worked, which was especially important in calendaring, and they expected it to work with accessibility tools for people who needed assistive devices to read the screen or used alternatives to mice and keyboards. Customers wanted the product to work on the hardware they owned with the amount of memory and processor they already had. These "abilities" as we called them were a long list of requirements to just release a product that carried the Office logo. Many of these might make sense to readers today because the operating system, particularly mobile phones, provide this auto-magically by simply using the platform as intended and this is verified in the App Store submission process.

In a series of meetings and demos to BillG, SteveB, JeffR (who managed both NetDocs and Office), and many across the company, it became clear we were heading for something a big company never wants to happen—a decision meeting with consequences. I often referred to a line from the movie *Wall Street* when Gekko (Michael Douglas) sighs, "Showdowns bore me, Larry. Nobody wins." It is never a good thing when there are only two options on a substantial decision and a deadline, forcing one side to walk away a winner and another a loser. Management is all about avoiding these situations in the first place. The Microsoft of this era didn't make choices early, and for good reason—the original Windows project was exactly the kind of thing that could arise if you let ideas flourish. Windows NT was essentially a side project. Windows 98 (98 SE, and Me) took on the role of side project. The whole company was built on what were rebellious side projects.

It is easy to skip this point or to take the point of view that conflicting side projects are a cultural disaster that eats a company from the inside. It is very easy to say that. In practice, projects that might conflict also create optionality. Great CEOs treasure optionality. BillG was one of those. The risk is not having too many options, but too few. The other risk is that all the options being developed converge on products that look too much like what we already have versus new approaches. That is the mistake Microsoft made with some frequency. Too many photo sharing tools. Too many data access technologies. Too many mail clients. Each of which was similar, but different while not anchored in a scenario that introduced a step function change in the trajectory of a category. The key indicators of potential trouble are usually obvious in hindsight. First, the project plans become especially expansive and generally can't be scaled back because every feature area is critical. Second, the team size becomes especially large. Rarely do small teams cause big problems.

In this case, NetDocs worked super hard and made a ton of progress. Between two alternatives of fully replacing Outlook in the next release of Office or adding a fourth mail program even one that was potentially exciting to Microsoft's already confused mail strategy, there was no good answer. Not wanting to decide immediately, a question was how much more time it would take to be a full replacement for Outlook. Brian and team wanted to release a product and grow into the market, rather than wait and wait perhaps suffering from *the enemy of the good is the perfect* syndrome.

Unfortunately, catching up over time seemed like an unbounded problem as well—Outlook and Exchange were evolving. These products were still early in their lifecycles. For example, the major work to improve reliability was about to start and that could have a broad impact on all the code already written for NetDocs. Across Office, everyone was working to integrate with Outlook. In the competition with Lotus Notes, we continued to try many new features to embrace programmability of mail. It was not simply replacing a static view of email but plugging into an entire collaboration strategy. We already failed twice trying to use the new storage system for Outlook, would NetDocs be able to make it work?

The only thing we could do, and have a rational email strategy, was decide not to ship NetDocs and find a way to create a new product that did not try to replace Outlook. That's what I wanted to do and advocated. The past few years of trying to stabilize Outlook left an impression on me. I didn't see a path where NetDocs could ever catch up and was deeply concerned about customers perceiving the need to choose between NetDocs and Outlook, knowing how much of the Office value proposition was built around communication scenarios using Outlook.

For all the good ideas and hard work, a clear decision was needed. We discussed alternatives with the leaders on the team. There were well-deserved mixed feelings and some significant pushback, and honest emotion. The leaders on the team knew the facts and challenges, and so did most of the team.

Brian met numerous times with BillG and SteveB. Along with the NetDocs leaders, JeffR, Brian, and I met with BillG to decide on a plan to ship NetDocs with Office or not, and not shipping probably meant shelving the project. Bill hated this kind of meeting. Showing up with two options always meant debating a third option. When it came to this level of technology and product, however, it was increasingly difficult for Bill to have the best or most informed opinions. The company was made of so many brand-new products and technologies, no one could keep track. The NetDocs team was exhausted. They had worked tirelessly for the weeks leading up to these meeting to see just how much they could get done. Knowing them well, I could sense the resignation.

It was too tall an order to deliver on all the new things while maintaining compatibility with Exchange and Outlook, while advancing in all the ways they intended. It might sound like we could finesse having two products, but not for the Office business, not against Lotus Notes, certainly not for enterprise customers with new Enterprise Agreements, and definitely not for industry analysts and the press. Our credibility as a company was on the line and too much was at stake too soon in the adoption curve.

The team tried to do too much, too soon. Brian agreed with Bill that team should have focused more on XML seeing how important that had become to the strategy, and that it would have been too difficult to have a sort of slow burn email strategy where it took several releases to surpass Outlook. There were better ways to have a bigger impact, and sooner. Bill was clear he should have provided more direction to the team on priorities. There was ample humility and professionalism to go around. As painful as this transition could have been, much of the difficulty was mitigated by the level of accountability Brian and Bill demonstrated.

Brian pushed to have the refocusing of the product to XML scenarios happen within the Office team.

We held an all-hands meeting with the NetDocs team in the cafeteria, led by JeffR. While the decision was made between BillG and BrianMac, there was no escaping that some perceptions of this were about how I held control over the Office "box" and thus I ended up bearing the brunt of it, especially for those who thought NetDocs was closer to realization than not. Any meeting like this was going to be tough. Still, cancelled and redirected projects are a part of engineering and often turn out to be important lessons for many. I had just gone through a last-minute reset as well.

Few engineers make it far into a career without enduring at least one major project reset.

I was caught off guard by how much the press had continued to portray this as a battle, my battle. There were so many difficult situations, differences of opinion, and product challenges, but this wasn't one of mine. I experienced a friction between teams, primarily over hiring, and some regarding product claims when it came to working with Exchange. The irony of the situation was the friction was mostly rooted in the history and connections so many of the engineers on the team shared. It was as if members of the old Outlook team started building a new Outlook to take on their earlier creation—perhaps a second-system syndrome[36] as detailed in *Mythical Man-Month*.

When a project goes through a big change or reset, the feelings come out. When a project is in the press too early in its life, then these feelings make it to the press too. I knew enough to understand that people want to find a clear point of responsibility, even blame. I was an easy target. It would not be the first time.

It was also ill-advised to engage the press on these stories, leaving them to be based on whatever perspective was tipped to one of the Microsoft beat reporters. I understood it was clearly part of the job for me to take on accountability for things that don't go well, even when it feels like a stretch to call something my fault. I watched every manager or mentor I had (BillG, JeffH, ChrisP, MikeMap, PeteH) do that more times than I could count. Like so many difficult situations, the NetDocs transition proved a valuable learning experience.

Many on the NetDocs team used the project reset as a chance to stick their heads up and see what other opportunities were going on around the company and beyond. More specifically, there was a noticeable exodus of middle pyramid people in this era. The core group that remained earned a unique opportunity to create an entirely new product for Office11 focused on maximizing the value of XML. That was the constraint. My view was that if they were close enough to spend all this energy on NetDocs shipping in this timeframe, then they could ship the less complex product (without email) while still having the full Office11 schedule to work. They would be able to use the Office shared code to bootstrap the entire app, which would save a huge amount of time and also make consistency and synergy much easier.

From NetDocs, Don Gagne (DonGa, previously from Outlook and part of the formation of NetDocs) would lead a newly formed team called XDocs, short for XML documents, along with Rajesh Jha (RajeshJ) leading program management. XDocs was NetDocs repurposed to an end-user tool using the XML technology using the core NetDocs code base—at a high level NetDocs without email and calendaring. There was much work to be done in that regard including the difficult work of right-sizing the team for the task at hand. PPathe would step up as a VP to provide additional leadership in helping to integrate and shape XDocs. He brought with him a deep understanding of the history of SGML (the predecessor of HTML) and the way Word embraced HTML, which would come in handy when it came to XDocs integrated across Office.

During the project, NetDocs had expanded scope broadly so as to include the universal canvas, XML editing, XML data transformation, new user interface, a mail and calendaring client supporting both old and new protocols, and much more. To support these the team grew to a significant size—over 500 people. To put that in perspective, the entire Office team was about 2,000 people including everything sold under the Office umbrella. At the break between releases, Office maintained a long history of letting people move around the different teams or staying put if they chose. That is exactly where we were which enabled many to easily move to other parts of Office or other teams. Don Gagne (DonGa) who previously led Outlook and then moved to NetDocs would soon find a huge role in Office, so it was rather fortunate he stayed on.

The team went through a fast process to identify where XML technology in NetDocs could be reused. XML generated a ton of buzz in the industry as a way of exchanging data between applications. We increased support for XML in Excel. For example, the SEC began requiring companies to release quarterly earnings in an XML format, making it easier to import into spreadsheets or databases for analysis. BillG was now actually excited about XML in Office11.

Leading the effort to create a vision for XDocs was Judy Lew (JudyLew.) Judy joined Microsoft about five years earlier out of the University of Michigan MBA program. She attended Columbia University as an undergraduate and her pace in words and action was more New York than her Utah upbringing. She was thoughtful, analytical, and persistent, traits which served the team well in pivoting to an entirely new product.

Her research identified a tool for companies to create forms—expense reports, invoices, surveys, and more. She envisioned enabling a much more elaborate experience and including programmable logic, data validation, and connectivity to other data sources to make it easier to fill out forms—a significant benefit, it could function without being connected to a network using offline email, which was a huge win at a time when getting online was incredibly difficult. Such a product could help in competing with Notes.

XDocs showcased SharePoint to share forms and store the results of the data collected. Competitively, IT developers were starting to use web browsers for many applications and were often seeing limitations of HTML compared to how these problems might have been solved with tools like Visual Basic.

To put XDocs in today's context, it was designed to solve many of the problems solved by DocuSign today. Before web browsers were as capable as today, having a desktop application where the form to be signed and manipulated came together was a good idea. As it would turn out, leading customers were perfectly happy dealing with the limitations of browsers and HTML if it meant not deploying a desktop application. There was an extremely important lesson in there. The era of looking to solve new problems with a new Windows application was over. I was increasingly convinced of this fact. Not only was this an unpopular opinion inside the company, but the company strategy also assumed this was decidedly not the case. The problem for me was the Microsoft bubble with influential enterprise customers and the strategy bubble inside the company were protective enough that it would be years before the reality of our situation would be shared.

If having to outright cancel projects was rare, rarer still was the opportunity (or ability) to pull from the ashes of a cancelled project an entirely new product that, at least at the time seemed strategic and viable. The team, and the broader Office team, were excited by the work. Judy Lew's efforts were remarkable as was the execution for the remainder of the team. It was not our best product (in fact, it was a failure in hindsight, the right problem to solve but the wrong technology approach) nor was it the most exciting to work on but going from a long trek of not shipping to creating a credible product so elegantly was a noteworthy accomplishment. The team left behind a consumer subscription product for email to build an enterprise business process tool using XML. They delivered and that was a huge accomplishment in this era—so many new ideas failed to gain escape velocity. As Brian said in his mail to the team announcing the changes, organizing in Office would be a huge opportunity to ship on time and to maximize the potential impact of the product.

InfoPath, the final product name, shipped with Office11 as a full-fledged module in a business SKU. It showed off a strategic new technology, XML, along with SharePoint and Outlook, and it helped to compete with Notes. It provided the kind of strategic demo of business value that the sales force appreciated. It was the kind of product that Microsoft Press, Microsoft's book publishing subsidiary, pursued aggressively resulting in a book even before the product released. I fondly recall stopping by Rajesh's office when he showed me the book, beaming with pride.

InfoPath was bundled in an Office enterprise SKU. Doing so brought great distribution but made it difficult to realize the true value. As with Outlook, the desire to support the bundle was greater than any incentive or perceived opportunity to create a new business. JudyLew's work clearly identified the revenue opportunity and specialized customers for this type of product. Reaching them, as was often the case, required an investment in new sales and marketing people and programs.

Sales and marketing did not share those views—the priorities there were to increase the perceived value of Office, particularly signing new and renewing enterprise agreements. XDocs had the beauty of being a high-end tool for IT while being useful to every desktop in an organization, which fit in well with the EA.

From my perspective, I faced another round of being on the hook to deliver organic innovation that expanded to new categories, only to see the work turned into incremental innovation to support the existing Office bundle. The pressure to drive upgrades was greater than the need for more organic growth, yet it was clear no one was going to upgrade for InfoPath more (or less) than for any other feature in the bundle. The difficulties in upgrading were unrelated to the value proposition of any part of the suite. The complexity of the overall platform of Windows and Office cemented a view that any change introduced upgrade friction. As we saw with browsers, if something interesting came along that was entirely new rather than simply an upgrade, customers were more than happy to consider adding to their standard deployment. We never got the chance to see if InfoPath was interesting enough to consider as a new addition to the enterprise platform. It was just more bloat.

I was disappointed that we chose to simply add more bloat to the perception of Office, as reviews would say, rather than strive for new business opportunities. The revenue for Office kept going up, either demonstrating I was wrong or perhaps proving that with the product-market fit we achieved for the core suite, nothing else we did could impact the suite business.

Still, this was difficult for me. Clearly, I was responsible for what ultimately transpired in the NetDocs to InfoPath transition, at least to the degree that I advocated for the only rational choice technically and in the context of EAs and the business. On the other hand, I was not the one who let the product go on for a couple of years nor was I the one who insisted on the demo at Forum 2000 and numerous other demos to all sorts of industry people. NetDocs had enough external exposure that it was clearly perceived as a super cool product under development—at least based on that cool demo at Forum 2000. Why else demo it? Would it have been better if it were permitted a slow burn over several years? I have my doubts, as the technology seeds that it contained were inside the Microsoft bubble, not where the industry was strongly heading. Instead of a Win32 app and proprietary XML, Office would double-down on browser-based tools starting in the next release of Office. Ultimately, the product just was neither different enough from everything going on nor did it take a radically different approach that could come from a new technology.

Thanks to *me*, I suppose, NetDocs was one of several products on every list of legendary Microsoft products that never made it to market. Much later, another one of those products caused me and the company a considerable amount of grief.

Stay tuned.

InfoPath was not the only new product in Office11…

072. NOTES ON TABLET PC INNOVATION

I should have been prepared for what transpired following the unveiling of our Tablet PC. I was not.

The line to enter Bill Gates's keynote at the November 2001 COMDEX snaked through the hotel and required metal detectors and body searches following the events of September 11, 2001. Themed *Digital Decade 2001-2010*, it was set to be a highlight of the week—discussing bringing digital innovations across industries and emphasizing increases in productivity, richness of business infrastructure, and significant changes in home entertainment.

Previously at Fall COMDEX 2000, Microsoft unveiled the Tablet PC, showing a prototype tablet created by Microsoft, highlighting BillG's personal favorites of pen-based handwriting capabilities and online document reading. At the time printing was still the standard for sharing business information. The prototype was how we hoped to convince OEMs to build similar PCs.

A recurring theme for the Windows business was to use big trade shows to demonstrate exciting new PCs across the ecosystem. JeffR joined BillG on stage to show off multiple innovative PCs running the new Windows XP Tablet OS, many of which were to be available later in 2002 with the tablet-capable version of Windows XP. As with all things Windows, the strength in bringing the product to market was emphasized by a broad array of hardware of different sizes, shapes, and price points. Building off the first party prototype demonstrated the previous year, the keynote brought the full strength of the PC ecosystem to this new form factor with support in the new variant of Windows XP.

Alan Kay, a pioneer in visualizing and prototyping the concept of a tablet while at Xerox PARC, conceived of the Dynabook, perhaps the original tablet. The Dynabook was envisioned as a "personal and portable information manipulator" described in his amazing paper, *A Personal Computer for Children of All Ages* from 1972. Of the launch of Microsoft's Tablet PC in 2001, he told Newsweek's Steven Levy, "Microsoft's Tablet PC [is] the first Dynabook-like computer good enough to criticize."[37] In PARC-speak, that was a high form of praise, not a backhanded compliment.

The quest for a PC tablet was not new and perhaps dates back in our memories to Captain Kirk on the bridge of the starship Enterprise with his tablet and pen. In the 1980s and 90s the PC industry was buzzing with innovative large screen computers based on tablets and pens from the likes of IBM, GRiD, Momenta, NCR, Compaq, and Asian companies like NEC, Samsung, and Toshiba. Small screen computers arrived (and departed) as well. Palm had a breakthrough with its Pilot, while Apple failed with its Newton. Windows CE devices were blessed with a stylus as well.

What Microsoft envisioned to do differently was to build a new class of computer. The Tablet PC would be a full notebook sized computer, but better. It was a notebook PC in power with the convenience of an actual notebook and pen. It was also fully capable of running the latest Windows and Windows software. This was not only the core of the Tablet PC strategy but the core of everything Microsoft was doing with the "scalable Windows architecture", or "one Windows, with many implementations."

Microsoft's new Tablet PC group, led by Alex Loeb (AlexLoeb), reported to JeffR's division rather than Windows to streamline delivery of a killer productivity solution. As the original manager of the pen computing effort a decade or more earlier, JeffR had a longtime passion for pen input. Some personal history was that my first trade show booth duty was showing off C++ support for *Windows 3.1 for Pen Computing 1.0* at Spring COMDEX 1992. Jeff was an early fan of PocketPC devices, never missing a chance to use the stylus to jot down notes or show off the latest financials in Pocket Excel.

While the connection to information work was clear, this organization structure was a tacit admission that the Tablet PC might require more end-to-end design and implementation than a typical new Windows PC. To build a complete experience required integrating product design and engineering efforts across Windows, Office, research groups where the ink and handwriting technology was being developed, as well as hardware engineering for digitizers and working with PC makers. Coordinating marketing and partnering with OEMs introduced another aspect of the end-to-end effort.

Technology for digital ink progressed significantly, primarily as a result of the increasing focus on screens and digitizers—the technology that picks up a signal of some form from a pen and converts it to a series of datapoints representing what is drawn on the screen. Flat panel displays for notebooks were progressing quickly. The Tablet PC was timed well to capitalize on these innovations as display and touch/ink sensor-equipped panels proved to be the limiting factor for building even a marginally acceptable experience.

From its earliest days, Microsoft Research was working hard to make handwriting recognition a reality. Handwriting recognition had long been one of the fundamental linguistic technologies (along with language translation and bi-directional speech) that were always 5 years away since the mid-1950s. Our state-of-the-art approach was fascinating in hindsight. Improving digitizers were able to capture many more points (coordinates) as the pen moved across the screen, even when moved quickly. These points were used to connect dots, which could then be smoothed out to look like a continuous line of ink. Meanwhile, the starting point, ending point, direction, and other data were to guess the letter being drawn. Recognition was obtained by comparing the series of captured points along with direction and speed of the pen to a library of pre-collected samples. This was done letter by letter, building up recognition based on pairs or triads of letters commonly occurring together. Then when a collection of letters was detected, something like spellcheck was used to recognize an entire word. It was rocket science, the kind of rocket science BillG loved because no one could possibly duplicate the effort to develop the technology. The researchers managed to attain some almost useful level of accuracy, perhaps 90 to 95 percent, enabling ink to be searched as though it were plain text or to be selected and pasted into Word as plain text. This physics-based approach was used for decades with slow progress, but state of the art in 2001.

Fast-forward 10 years and handwriting recognition was upended by an ingenious use of machine-learning image recognition advanced by research at AT&T Bell Labs in 1989 led by Yann LeCun. In a heartbeat 50-odd years of attempts turned into something that worked 99 percent (or more) of the time and was vastly easier to implement. The advances in machine learning represent the most fundamental improvement in computer science I've seen in my career.

A most exciting step with a new Windows release are new form factors. An even more (super) exciting hardware innovation was dubbed the "convertible," which was a laptop that looked at first glance like a normal clamshell notebook, though smaller and thinner than most available at the time. Through a presto-change-o flip, the screen rotated and covered the keyboard to become a full-fledged tablet that resembled what Captain Kirk used on *Star Trek*, likely in size and weight too as the 8.5x11x0.8" device weighed 4lbs/1.8kg. In tablet converted mode, using a pen became the primary way of interacting, instead of a keyboard and mouse or integrated pointer. Techies have always loved and continue to love transformer PCs—presto-change-o is always a crowd pleaser.

The convertible form factor was particularly attractive to typical Office customers who craved mobility and could opt to use a keyboard and mouse when required for "full productivity." This contrasts with a slate form factor, which (like an iPad today) is a screen-only computer, requiring a pen for all input and manipulation. Perhaps surprising, the idea of using a touch interface was not pondered primarily because the existing screen technology did not work with a finger, nor did handwriting for input. As we will see, even when rumors of Apple building a tablet surfaced (a pun) the biggest question on BillG's mind was how they acquired handwriting technology, or did they build their own solution which was bound to be inferior.

The dual personality modality was a significant source of tension across JeffR's Information Worker division—does the design assume a convertible in which case Office was fine as it was, or do you design for a pen user interface? How productive did it need to be relative to how frequently the pen would be used. Every demo of a Tablet PC created questions (or concerns) about whether Office was participating in this future. There was no using Office without a keyboard and a mouse. Full stop. Microsoft's DNA was such that a new OS required apps to push the OS to succeed, and the lack of Office was readily apparent. Worse, Office did not commit to "full support," whatever that might imply.

Program managers across Tablet PC, Office, and Office applications spent months of meetings, prototypes, and discussions trying to understand each other. What did full support look like? In the best case, how should Excel work with a pen? Where and how would one input numbers and formulae? Did the Office user interface work well when navigated with a pen instead of a mouse? We were in a circular platform-apps debate—the platform said it needed input from apps to finish the platform, while apps said it needed guidance on what the platform was enabling. The dividing line between platform and app is always tested when the organization represents that split. The same dynamic happens with front-end and back-end in web applications.

The platform believed it was enabling a particular scenario while the apps don't value the scenario or had a thousand reasons why the scenario is way more complicated, and the platform should go back to the drawing board so to speak. In the case of supporting a pen as a replacement for keyboard and mouse, the list of what was impossible to do in a standard Windows app seemed impossibly long. There was a seemingly irrational insistence that every place one could type could also accept ink input, converting that to text. Being able to ink into the Excel formula bar was both awkward and a technical nightmare, with little benefit.

The only way to have pen support, I believed, was to build a pen-capable app from scratch. Unfortunately, the implication of that was that this new platform did not get Excel and there can't be a new platform without Excel. Except this new platform was also just plain Windows and ran Excel perfectly, so long as there was a mouse and keyboard. Though requiring a convertible PC was out of the question because of the svelte attractiveness of the screen-only slate form factor.

Regretfully, the perception became that Office was stuck in the mud or resistant to change or influence. This was at least equally, if not more so, a problem of a platform searching for validation from Office without clarity for how apps should work. There seemed to be a great deal more work to do on the very basics of user-interaction before validating that with the most complex applications around. As would prove to be the case for a host of innovations around Windows, adding something on top of, or on the side of, Windows was not a sound method of creating either a new product or market, no matter how much we wanted the new market to be based on Windows, and more importantly to have compatibility with existing Windows applications, especially Office.

Beyond the technical integration was the ever-present go to market challenge. Was the new version of Windows for tablets a separate SKU and if so, was it more expensive, or were the tablet features simply extra features that would light up if the hardware supported them and likewise was there a special version of Office or did Office just light up with new features. We should not forget the ever-present tension over putting everything in the enterprise bundle versus monetizing new innovations.

The desire for optionality, both for Microsoft and OEMs, almost always pulled the product towards a strategy where features would be active if hardware supported them. That way third-party developers could always assume the APIs were available on any Windows PC, making it safe to use without concern for system requirements. On the other hand, this also reduced the incentive to use those features (APIs) because doing so introduced complexity into a product where it had to test if features were available or not and behave appropriately. These challenges are why BillG always believed in the magic solution where developers used one and only one API and the conditional or variable implementation was hidden away in the API. Making this concrete it might mean a place in a product expecting typed input would magically transform into a place where a pen could be used for input. No one knew how to accomplish this in practice except for extremely limited scenarios that were more demos than reliable approaches. This was reflected in another classic tension point, which is how much of an application is simply a repackaging or use of Windows capabilities versus creating new capabilities in the application code? Recall earlier discussions over the role of text input and creation where Windows was woefully deficient which pushed Office to build significant capability in how text was entered. This would be repeated across every major component of the user experience—Office simply did not use much of what Windows had added over the years. The implication was that even if such magical transforming APIs were invented in Windows, Office would need to reinvent them for much more sophisticated and capable features that existed only in Office, including text input.

The disappointing truth would prove to be that innovation didn't move from the platform to the applications, at least when it came to Office. Innovation was flowing from Office to Windows, while Office was no longer looking to Windows for direction. The dynamic of leading applications scaling to a level where they are both dependent on but separate from the platform was a sign of platform and app maturity. It would be a while before we'd learn how problematic that was for both Windows and Office. Right now it was a Windows problem.

Collectively, these lessons failed to contribute to evolving Windows for other markets including mobile phones and home entertainment. It would prove to be an amazing struggle for me in a few years when I worked on Windows.

In this case, Office, at the core, used a mouse and keyboard and did so in every single facet of design. Equally at the core, the pen was designed as an alternative to a mouse not as a reimagined interaction model. It was a pointer, like a mouse, and the fact that it also wrote on the screen was added to the side. In any existing Windows software, writing was done in a small window that popped up and allowed for a few short words to be written at a time. Those words were converted to typed text and inserted into the application. That's how ink worked in all existing Windows products. Switching between ink for text input and typing was awkward, while ink remained inefficient.

The question was how to make the pen when used with apps like Excel work more like ink on paper. No one really knew because the first requirement was to shoehorn pen computing so as to require as few changes as possible to the existing code base. The theory was, and BillG strongly believed this to be the case, that the pen should just work. If this sounds familiar it is because "should just work" was a common refrain for Bill. This contrasts subtlety with Steve Jobs saying "it just works." The right architecture and abstractions should enable whole new implementations to appear above or below a given bit of code and like magic new capabilities appear. Programmers know this is great in theory but almost never works in practice. My rule for this type of capability is that unless the operating system ships having tested a particular type of replaceable layer then it doesn't exist and if one attempts to use it all the problems will eventually surface. Outlook connecting to internet mail, Word converting to/from WordPerfect, Excel/Access connecting to Oracle database, Windows replacing the file system, and on and on there are too many examples to list.

There were so many challenges, we simply did not know where to start. Some of the problems were hardware related, such as while a typical screen might be 60 or more typed characters across, handwriting was more like eight to ten. All the on-screen places one might type characters, from simple numbers in a date to file names to formulas in Excel, all the way to full pages of text in Word, were too small for ink. Making them all larger was simply the first step in an entire redesign of the product.

While we were debating how to make the pen work, keyboarding was becoming a native skill replacing handwriting in schools. Kids were learning to type at the earliest ages, and handwriting was viewed as optional. Smartphones were not yet ubiquitous but sending SMS by triple-tap captured the imagination of teens around the world and replaced the proverbial handwritten note slipped under a desk. Maybe the opportunity for pen computing was generational…a boomer scenario?

Bigtime bosses were very excited by the prospect of pen input. In the EBC and with execs in general, taking an existing typed document and marking it up with ink annotations captured their imagination. They loved this. In fact, I loved it. I reviewed significant memos this way—printed them out and wrote on them in red like a teacher. I took notes at meetings on printed out PowerPoint decks. Yet even I was skeptical that such a scenario justified an entirely new computer. It did not even need a new version of Office. The easy solution could take an image of the document (a PDF!) and support ink on top, exactly what the Tablet PC team's notetaking app, called *Journal*, did. It was a fantastic solution. There were still limitations, such as that the ink writing was huge compared to what was easy to read text. In fact, about all that could be done effectively compared to a real pen on real paper were gross annotations like arrows, circles, or crossing out with an occasional "bad idea" scrawled. The technology was not a replacement for the commonly used paper markup scenario. Not even close. It did not help that using a PDF-based solution was completely off the table as far as Bill was concerned. His feelings about PDF had not changed in the intervening 7 years since I first confronted him about the advantages of the format.

Even with those obvious limitations, BillG wanted those annotations and comments to use the semantically rich comment and annotation features that were part of Word, Excel, and PowerPoint—the track changes features used by lawyers. There were many problems with this including training people to use proofreading marks to change text versus typing using the existing keyboard features. The screens weren't big enough, digitizers weren't accurate enough, and handwriting recognition not good enough for these features to work.

The Journal app remained the closest we had to a killer app within the Tablet PC team—simply using ink as ink, with occasional translation to text. They made a cool feature where you could print a document to Journal and then mark up on top of it as though there was an acetate layer over a document, spreadsheet, or slide. It had all the limitations above, but the demo was perfect for executives.

Several Microsoft executives were early adopters of the new tablets. While they were effusive about the benefits, there was an aspect of them was difficult to escape. The amount of focus and attention it took to take notes with Journal was excessive. It was a head down, blinders on sort of focus. In meetings with people using the tablet maybe the notes were good, but it was a strain on engagement. As if to emphasize the limitations, executives that liked to print out their notes and file them soon discovered that a full screen of notes in Journal printed out cartoonishly large on standard paper due to the relatively low resolution of screens.

In early tests with the tablet across the company the feedback was uniformly positive, surprisingly so. As we kept digging into it, what was clear was that despite the heft of the early devices they were much lighter than the typical Microsoft issued laptop, which came in at 6lbs or more. It wasn't necessarily the use of a tablet that people were positive about, but simply having a 4lb laptop. The early tablets were designed as premium PCs, which meant they were light, thin, and very expensive. It wasn't merely the extra hardware for the pen that made them expensive, or the fancy hinges. The PCs used the latest in chips and displays too.

No matter what limitations, or frankly impossibilities, were raised, it always came back to Office being stubborn or resistant to features from other groups. Microsoft's inherent bias was always to suggest that the new group with the product that wasn't done yet was in the right and the existing group was resisting—in many ways this was a correct diagnosis and the right bias to avoid stifling innovation. Such a bias left little room for acknowledging that something new might not yet, or ever, work as intended.

It was clear, by collective body language and explicit direction, that Office was on the hook for something. Aside from adding ink to Word and Excel, what we needed was an Office version of Journal. The idea for a free Journal that came with Windows and a fancy version that was part of Office was exactly like the original strategy of having the mini word processor, Write, with Windows and Word in Office. Could we take a pen-centric approach like Journal and create a new category of productivity app, designed for ink but integrated with Office? Perhaps a Journal that also worked with Word and Excel? Or Word and Excel that worked just like Journal? Should Office build a product specifically for one kind of hardware that would likely sell in small units at first? Would such a product make defining SKUs challenging? We already had a half dozen SKUs and customers routinely expressed frustration with the complexity even though the bulk of our business transitioned to enterprise agreements where SKUs don't matter much. So many questions about what seemed such a simple request…this type of routine program management was difficult and not particularly suited to executive-level strategy discussions.

There were many potential categories for Office to enter as we understood from JeffR's opportunity map, but none seemed uniquely suited to tablet or convertible devices. Notetaking, however, was perennially on the minds of journalists and reviewers, implying anything we did would get a lot of personally motivated (though potentially nitpicking) coverage. Press encounters were also an opportunity to do research on information work. How did the reporter take notes? What tools were used to organize stories? How did they structure the writing process? By 2000, reporters were mostly using a Windows XP luggable with a big power brick in tow, while using Word to take notes during discussions. At most press events we often set up elaborate strips of outlets (and dangling network cables) attached to tables so the power-draining laptops of the era could plug in and file real-time stories. Invariably, reporters bemoaned the inadequacy of Word and Windows for the sort of juggling they did, working with notes, interviews, emails, documents, and later photos. Office didn't offer a tool to work with these in one place.

In the old days, this category of software was sometimes called personal information managers, or brainstorming tools. It was never a big category and fragmented among the many small players. It was almost exactly the kind of software we tended to avoid. There didn't seem to be a winner-take-all strategy, nor did there seem to be a ton of revenue. On the other hand, if we could somehow develop an innovative product that caused people to rethink the category there was potentially a broad and horizontal product that could yield much-coveted organic growth. We discussed the idea that all the Office tools were about producing final and permanent documents, but we lacked a tool for ephemeral information. This seemed to be a potential anchor for a new product. I was under a good deal of pressure to provide innovation in a new category that might lead to new revenue.

Notetaking was definitely worth a try. What's old was new again.

Trying to navigate the urgency to engage on a pen application and have something consistent with Office, I sent an email to Chris Pratley (ChrisPr), the leader of Word program management, to frame the need for a solution to notetaking. Chris was a Waterloo graduate hired to work on Word products who had previous experience living and working in Japan. He was instrumental in the transformation of Office to an extremely successful worldwide product, especially in Japan. Chris was also one of Microsoft's earliest contributors to UNICODE standards. Aside from his East Asia experience, Chris was an exemplar of Office program management when it came to defining products and executing.

Our biggest concern was that we would embark on notetaking only to end up with a subset of Word, re-creating the problem of Outlook and Outlook Express, but with the anchor tenant and most used Office app. We wanted to innovate without developing a confusing subset of Word. Customers were already using Word for notetaking but adding a notetaking mode to Word to address missing features would have been a horrible mess and bloat for most customers.

Innovator's Dilemma would say to create a new team to target new customers, but that almost guarantees a collision with Word as we saw with Publisher. In our world, any time a new team was chartered they will invariably spend

90% of their initial time revisiting basic user interaction models and duplicating basic infrastructure of the main competing product—such a dynamic was rampant at the company in the early 2000s with every new team creating their own variant of menus and toolbars with a web-like twist under the guise of being easier to use and innovative.

The other option was to ask the Word team itself to develop the product as they would be most sensitive to colliding or overlapping. But would that impossibly constrain the team and create an odd product that spent too much energy not duplicating Word, even if it made sense? Again, so many questions…

Most products dedicated to taking notes proved to be subsets of Word, where using Word bullets, numbering, and outlining would suffice. Scenarios were changing, however, and notetaking was expanding to include collecting snippets from the web, links, photos, and even audio and video from new laptops incorporating cameras and microphones. To differentiate notetaking from Word, we needed a novel approach to the problem that went beyond typing (and inking) and basic text entry. Tailor-made for user research, notetaking was the kind of thing researchers loved to study. Suddenly, the hallways were filled with examples of notes, the flow of notes for different authors using different tools of Office, notebooks and ways people organized them, notes for students in classrooms, notes for home and work, and more.

The team was excited and quickly converged on prototypes and an approach that was ink-centric yet also text-centric and highly differentiated from Word—in other words they took on all the work to design a product that seamlessly worked with ink or with a mouse and keyboard, or both. Peter Engrav (PeterEn) joined to lead software development. PeterEn, a rare Bellevue, Washington, native, was one of the most thoughtful development leaders on the team—he was also a founding member of JonDe's Office development team working on Escher graphics. Our offices were next to each other during the Office11 project and he and I often discussed the choices he was making into the late hours of the evening. The team picked a code name even though Office tended to shun code names, *Scribbler*.

ChrisPr took the team through a planning and vision process just for Scribbler. The team had sketches, prototypes, and a vision, Scribbler.doc. Perhaps a most impressive aspect of this process was how closely the concepts and details outlined in the original vision made their way to the final product.

From the outset, Scribbler intentionally did many things differently, as expected. We viewed it as a chance to pioneer some new approaches. While not as freewheeling as it might sound, the team would definitely say they would bump up against the culture of Office more than once—ironic given that PeterEn was a founding member of the Office development culture.

Scribbler built a native XML file format with next-level robustness, as one of those new approaches. Scribbler's files could have multiple people edit a file at the same time and almost immediately see the changes made by others. Editing by multiple people seemed crazy for a personal notetaking product, but early on the idea of shared notes or group notes became a hallmark of the innovation. To enable shared editing, Scribbler would eventually be able to use SharePoint and, for one of the first times in a Microsoft product, data was stored on the internet, what eventually came to be the cloud. While we abandoned many of the MyOffice internet experiences, Scribbler eventually offered a key demonstration of native internet services.

Scribbler was able to focus on truly differentiated features because it was the first new product to make use of the *MSO.DLL*, or the Microsoft Office library of shared code. For the five previous years, Office engineered a platform of shared code for Word, Excel, PowerPoint, Outlook, and others, but no new product tried to use this code starting from a clean slate. Remarkably, PeterEn and the development team were up and running in short order by using this code—normally it would take months of work for a new application to take shape. With minimal effort, Scribbler inherited all the basic capabilities of an Office application, such as menus, toolbars, localization, Watson recovery, fancy graphics, enterprise deployment and management, plus engineering and test tools, and much more. This let the team focus on the core task of taking notes. It was exciting to see MSO in action and, most importantly, to show that in middle-age Office reached a significant level of operational maturity. InfoPath, discussed previously, also used MSO.DLL.

The novel experience of Scribbler and the key differentiator for users was the ability to write or type anything anywhere on a page. Just like on paper, one could simply tap the screen with the pen and start writing or click the mouse and type in that spot on the screen—delivering on the promise of the NetDocs universal canvas demo from Forum 2000. If one thinks about each of the apps, Word documents are bottomless, starting at the top and continuing down with a fixed page width. Excel is an endless two-dimensional grid. PowerPoint is a fixed-sized rectangle that allows anything to be put anywhere. Scribbler was bottomless, two-dimensional, and it also let users put anything anywhere simply by clicking and typing or tapping with a pen and writing. Ink and text were seamlessly and effortlessly mixed. Content like photos, videos, and audio could be added anywhere on a page. In a hint at the future of all applications, Scribbler also let users mostly ignore files and the tension-filled process of saving data and simply organize thoughts as one did with a paper notebook, with tabs, but with the advantage of software. Reorganizing and quickly searching across all the notes brought the power of software to note taking.

One area where Scribbler diverged from the way the Tablet group thought was integrating handwriting recognition. ChrisPr and team found in working with early adopters that recognizing ink as text was of little utility—people rarely wanted to convert their ink to text. In fact, people loved leaving ink as ink. Where recognized text was most valuable was in searching through the ink notes. Scribbler constantly recognized the ink converting it to text for search, but rarely did that ink get used in other places. Journal had taken the lead from BillG who was literally obsessed with converting ink to text and was generally against leaving ink as ink. It was a debate he and I had many times when looking to expand the use of ink in Word and Excel.

There were many seemingly small but novel touches in the product such as the ability to create a table by typing, hitting tab, typing, tab, typing, return, and poof, a table appeared. Scribbler also created checklists—list items that could be marked as to-do items, checked when completed, for shared or personal use. Scribbler supported photos, drawing shapes, and a whole range of outlining features.

The most eye-popping demo was when taking notes on a new Tablet PC, whether typing or using a pen, Scribbler could record the audio of a meeting and keep track of what notes were taken during the recording. One could easily hop from a note to the full recording of the meeting or vice versa across pages of notes. In another demo, easily drawing diagrams using a pen on a PC with the same ease as on paper was unimaginably cool.

Despite all that it offered, and as important as I thought it could be to the Office franchise as a growth opportunity, Scribbler would become the next innovation to get caught up in the challenges of bringing new revenue-generating capabilities to market with Office. Should Scribbler be a new category of software with dedicated marketing and sales yielding new organic revenue, or should it be added to the Office product enhancing the suite for every user? We faced this challenging decision so many times: Outlook, FrontPage, SharePoint, and now in Office11 with Scribbler and InfoPath.

Scribbler was designed to be a core part of the Office suite, a broadly horizontal product, not for a small or specific segment or narrow selling proposition as we saw with InfoPath, Access, Visio, Project, or Publisher. Yet, in an ironic twist, Scribbler did not make it into the suite and was destined to be a new category.

Normally this would be a great idea. A new category meant a real revenue opportunity. That opportunity was only realized with a dedicated sales effort. A dedicated sales effort for a broad, horizontal product would be nearly impossible because those same resources would be selling the Office suite and upselling to EAs or more expensive suites. Recall, however, that the notetaking category was known to be fragmented and small. Such a category has a low return on investment. Customers are hard to find and the efforts at reaching them don't scale well. When you do find those customers, because there are so many alternatives, there is little pricing power.

Adding Scribbler to an existing suite would make the product available to everyone, which would be great, but would not alter the sales motion unless it became the key reason to upgrade or sign an EA. There were no such plans. In fact, the formal Office 2003 product guide mentions the new product exactly twice in 170 pages. One mention is a trademark footnote and the other in the SKU table, whereas Outlook is mentioned almost 200 times.

Scribbler was a product for everyone but marketed and sold to no one. The only suite Scribbler was added to was Office for Students and Teachers, used as a way of communicating that the low-priced suite was poorly suited for business enterprises because it included a notetaking product. In fairness to marketing, Scribbler had done some pioneering work with students at the University of Washington to support notetaking in college courses. Students loved Scribbler, which was also a testament to the product design for a version one product.

It would be reasonable to ask why I did not force the issue with marketing. Primarily, my view was that SKUs were entirely a marketing decision and accountability. With a dozen individual applications to mix and match, marketing spent the better part of a year picking and choosing combinations. The development team invested in features to make the production of different suites easy. I would be remiss if I didn't mention that to consolidate marketing across the entire information worker business, JeffR took on marketing as a direct report as well. Packaging literally wasn't my job or accountability.

Right up until the last minute, we had trouble coming up with the commercial name for the product. Scribbler was a good name the team loved, but we were unable to secure the rights. Eventually, the marketing team settled on OneNote, a perfectly good name but the one that left the product team somewhat bummed at first. Over the course of the product cycle, Scribbler really grew on the team and came to mean a great deal to them. Most (including the press) had a first reaction when hearing OneNote as it reflected the common expression "one note wonder" as in lacking range. It was a name where common usage reflected poorly, shades of DIM Outlook. In a small form of passive protest, some on the team mockingly referred to the official name as *Onay-No-Tay*. Fortunately, this name led to a tagline "One place for all your notes" and that made everyone happy. Like every naming exercise I experienced, eventually everyone warmed to it.

The product went on to be much loved by a core set of customers and received many super positive reviews. Ed Mendelson of *PC Magazine*, a longtime (very longtime) reviewer of productivity tools, called OneNote "breathtakingly well-designed."[38] Paul Thurrott, also a longtime Microsoft commentator and often a critic (especially of me), said, "In my mind, OneNote is one of the best applications Microsoft has released in years."[39] He and other reviews bemoaned the fact that OneNote was not included in the typical Office suites they bought.

The Tablet PC group was both happy and disappointed with OneNote. On its own OneNote showcased the new convertible Tablet PCs. Reviewers who loved OneNote were anxious to get their hands on one of the new devices, and certainly all the device makers were anxious to show off the capabilities using OneNote. At the same time, the existence of OneNote was viewed as some sort of cop-out relative to solving the big problem of using ink as a first-class input in Office apps. Perceptions aside, we invested disproportionate engineering effort to implement ink support in Word, Excel, and PowerPoint.

I viewed that criticism as harsh and a way of dodging the real question, which was whether ink was broadly suited to productivity or simply a way of trying to use software to emulate an old way of working. Was it the equivalent of controlling the first motor cars like a horse or was there something deeper about the benefits of ink? Was using a pen and ink something that seemed natural to a generation that had to learn to type later in life? Was handwriting a skeuomorphic answer to human-computer interaction that long outlived its need as a technology bridge? It might be an ironic twist that finally after decades of research and development handwriting, which was always the next big thing just five years out, improved to the point that it worked but the market that might have existed moved on.

We are 20 years through continuous investment with massive improvements in recognition technology and first-party hardware that supports pen input, yet the usage remains *de minimis*.

I have such a warm place in my heart for OneNote. The team did such a wonderful job. It was a breakthrough product, taking advantage of the latest operating system, while leveraging the latest hardware. Failing to capitalize on it with the field and business left me feeling that I let the team down. Microsoft couldn't capitalize on a horizontal, pure-play productivity tool—the sales team and Office bundle wanted IT-centric, and enterprise-focused products like InfoPath. OneNote was a distraction.

The good news: There was no shortage of complicated features for IT professionals.

073. **DO NOT FORWARD**

"I'd like to present to the witness *Exhibit 6508*, Bates number 0017811. Mr. Sinofsky, do you recognize this email that lists you as the sender?"[40]

To anyone involved in modern litigation, especially being deposed, there's a sinking feeling that comes with being presented an old email. A similar feeling arises when receiving a call from a reporter starting with, "I was just anonymously forwarded an email about..."

Email became ubiquitous across the corporate world by the early 2000s. With the rise of companies moving ever faster came "business at the speed of thought" (that was the name of Bill Gates's second book from 1999) or "flattening organizational hierarchy," to name two of the many touted benefits of email. In the early days, while senior managers at non-tech companies were still having email printed out for them and assistants transcribing email replies, not much thought was given to the permanence of email or the instant impact of an employee innocently (or not) forwarding email outside the company.

Every company that deployed email and embraced an email culture eventually wound up with a company policy on the use of email, likely explaining the ramifications if one were to be less than scrupulous in his or her use of email.

Born out of this were automatic disclaimers placed at the bottom of email, "THIS INFORMATION IS CONFIDENTIAL," or my favorite, simply writing in red letters across the top of a message (perhaps the first use of rich email formatting) "CONFIDENTIAL." We should not forget putting "**DO NOT FORWARD**" before the subject line of the email. We all knew that those emails were the important ones, and these warnings weren't even worth the bytes they took up—copy/paste and printers still worked. Just in case there was a button on every keyboard since the first PC "Print Screen."

Outlook featured commands that implied "Confidential" and "Do Not Forward," though these did little more than offer a fancy version of red text and, worse, were invisible to recipients reading the mail on systems other than Outlook.

Maintaining the corporate confidentiality of email became the Achilles heel of the platform, except that email found such incredible product-market fit that there was no putting the toothpaste back in the tube. Customers wanted a solution that protected email misuse, or more clearly made Outlook enforce a company email policy or intent of the sender.

Over the previous several releases of Office, we steadily improved the ability to encrypt Office documents. Office always had the ability to add a password to documents, and for years a top call to customers calling PSS was trying to retrieve a lost password. Microsoft provided no help, but a search on the internet quickly led to a variety of tools that worked with trivial effort up until about Office 97, and incidentally those search results were a common way to spread malware. We eventually added true encryption that made it increasingly difficult to read a document that was not yours to read. This level of security eventually became minimal as the ability to break encryption techniques had steadily improved.

A peak effort and an early test of our platform capabilities for encryption was working to win approval for Outlook and Exchange to be used in the Defense Messaging System in the Department of Defense in the United States. Implementing the required encryption was useful only to the Defense Department but we eventually added it anyway. That was not before the head of North American sales, Orlando Ayala (OrlandoA) made his case to me by standing on top of a table in the briefing center begging for an update to support the DoD. I was terrified. The customers were impressed. We did the work.

The core of implementing encryption was an ongoing collaboration between Windows and Office, as well as Microsoft Research. Encryption was not exactly one single thing or feature, but a complex *platform* that required servers, user identity, and a lot of sophisticated math. It was exactly the kind of infrastructure that enterprise IT was gobbling up in the early 2000s. The old days of encryption were rapidly being supplanted by the need to encrypt information that flowed across the public internet and used public internet infrastructure. It was no long as simple as a closed network with known proprietary endpoints.

Protecting files (and messages) with encryption was not without controversy, and without exaggeration for some technologists it was a line in the sand—crossing it put one squarely in the camp of *the man*. Encryption often collided head-on with the libertarian roots of the software field. Encryption was something of a third rail in the counter-culture elements of software.

The rise of the internet for online commerce created a brief moment where software vendors got caught up in the intricacies of import/export laws related to military products, specifically munitions. For a few years, the basic encryption algorithms—the results of widely-published academic research—were classified as munitions by US law and thus restricted for export. The hardcore technology advocates created a t-shirt featuring the code that implemented encryption with the implied threat that wearing such a shirt through a border crossing might subject the individual to law enforcement action of the highest order. The result was a headache for software vendors who maintained a secure version of products for the US market and a markedly less secure version for "export." President Clinton signed an executive order ending this awkward situation and at least one type of encryption flourished.

Broader awareness of encryption came about because of the iPod, surprisingly, because of how Apple chose to protect digital music downloads from being copied or pirated. The music industry embraced digital rights as a way of protecting the world from another Napster, the online music service that institutionalized either digital distribution of music or mass-scale theft of music depending on which side one was on. Essentially, using *digital rights management* (DRM), Apple's iTunes service ensured that the person who purchased a song was the only person who could listen to it and could only do so on devices authorized by Apple's iTunes.

Such usage restrictions had shades of authoritarianism harkening back to the early days of commercial software. In the first years of MS-DOS, software vendors routinely encrypted software in such a way that only the licensed user could install it on a PC using serial numbers that would unlock the floppy disk and permanently assign it to a given user. Vendors also made it difficult to impossible to make copies of the software disks forcing buyers to be extra careful with their $500 purchases. So annoying was this to even legitimate buyers, that I spent several weeks one summer internship writing a low-level assembly language program to make copies of Lotus 1-2-3 disks for a huge defense contractor. Historically, Bill Gates was at least on the side of the honor system by and large though he believed strongly in active enforcement of legal ownership of software.

The industry collectively backed off from rights enforcement during the high-growth years, particularly at the urging of upstarts such as Borland, who used the absence of anti-piracy measures as a selling point. Then, as piracy of Office and Windows increased, so too did the use of serial numbers and activation codes, which were then labeled DRM by some, as if to further inflame consumers seeking legitimate use of their license. Thus, any feature using any software use restrictions was going to enter the maelstrom of tech enthusiast ire. BillG was particularly unphased by the pushback, widespread negative news coverage, and relentless hostility online in just about every language of the world taking place just after resolution of the antitrust saga.

For many in the tech community DRM in music was the devil's technology. DRM prevented "fair use" of music and video all in the name of profit. The music and visual arts communities did not see it that way. Anything that looked like any combination of encryption or restricted use of digital information was labeled DRM. Anything called DRM came under intense scrutiny with the potential to backfire as features capitulating to authoritarian forces.

Nevertheless, enterprise customers were quite enthusiastic about a "Do Not Forward" button that worked. As one can imagine, in Microsoft's top-down selling motion, it was the C-suite executives most interested in protecting the rights of their own email and documents. Even though we knew the idea of protecting email from being forwarded had all the makings of being labeled DRM and building the feature would utilize previously militarized technology, the allure of solving such a clearly articulated need was enough to overcome such resistance.

During the early days of building out the Microsoft enterprise infrastructure stack, customers were perhaps unknowingly open to enormous amounts of complexity to implement new features. Our sales force actively embraced complexity if it meant opportunities to link products together in a cross-selling motion, especially across Windows Server and Office. Office11 *Information Rights Management* (IRM) did not disappoint. We called it IRM as if to distinguish it from DRM, kind of. We knew we were walking straight into a messy feature. In an early nod to the complexity of the feature, the Windows infrastructure used by IRM was called the Windows Rights Management Service (RMS), thus implementing our DRM-like features called IRM used RMS. Phew!

Customers were already annoyed that they could lose a password to a document and Microsoft could not, or perhaps they thought would not, help them. IRM, in the eyes of detractors, implied that Microsoft held the keys, literally, to documents and somehow positioned themselves to become gatekeepers of email and documents. Or perhaps, as some customers thought, Microsoft did not hold the keys to documents and email and somehow a company's own information would be subject to some sort of super-password that even they might not be able to unlock. What if there was a bug rendering the company information inaccessible? The questions were endless.

There was something inherently untrustworthy about the potential of using a content protection feature that could render the content unreadable. This was not theoretical. Many were already experiencing owning a library of rights-managed music, only to find it inaccessible when a company went out of business. Stories of lost music players and accounts disconnected from the rights were endlessly populating support sites. Whether these cases were real or not, they all contributed to a distrust of rights management. At this point in the company's history, Microsoft was not always viewed with the most latitude in terms of doing the right thing for customers.

IRM proved to be one of the most complex features we ever shipped, perhaps overly complex, but in many ways it was symbolic of the overall complexity we were delivering to customers, whether it was IRM, SharePoint, or even the base infrastructure of Windows Server.

During vision planning for the release the feature was proposed so an Office shared team was created to tackle the implementation of IRM for Office11—the team aimed to implement the feature across the suite of products, not simply a one-off for just email. They had a bold vision for a future where companies could have much more control over their corporate information.

Lauren Antonoff (LaurenA) led program management, and with her prior experience on the Windows platform side she was great at navigating the extensive collaborations across the company to make this feature possible. Mark Walker (MarkWal), a veteran of several releases of Word as well as SharePoint and one of the most consistently smart and broad-thinking engineering managers, led development. Brian Wiese (BWiese) led testing, perhaps the most complex interoperability test responsibility we had created to date.

From the start, even when sketching out the original feature, IRM was a big feature. All we were aiming for was that "Do Not Forward" button, but to the surprise of many we overachieved.

IRM had to handle a plethora of edge cases, as testers called them. What if the users lost their PC? What if they wanted to read a message or documents on a rental PC in a hotel? What if they wanted to use IRM with a trusted partner who was on a different email system? What about access on a BlackBerry? What about wanting to open a file on an old version of Office? What if in the future someone needed to open a file on some not-yet-existing *Office15*? Then lawyers started asking if documents were part of legal discovery orders? How would screen readers used by the blind work? Or what if an employee was terminated? These what ifs went on and on. Every time I stopped by LaurenA's office I learned about another case they were working on.

The strategic changes at the start of Office.NET seemed to be the kind that might reduce the complexity of this feature, because we no longer needed to worry about a parallel implementation of enterprise and outside the firewall, as we generally called it. The feature, however, needed to work outside the firewall if, for example, executives were to be able to read protected information on the road. The team took on the mission. We ended up doing much of the same work as we did for a hosted service but in bits and pieces, enabling IRM to work for customers using Hotmail in a browser, as long as the customer used the latest version of Internet Explorer.

As each development milestone progressed, M1, M2, M3...the complexity continued to rise. IRM added code to Office, SharePoint, and Internet Explorer and required additions to Windows Server and to Active Directory. Administrators needed to learn to manage and distribute encryption keys, something that was making its way into enterprise infrastructure.

Along the way we experienced surprises that questioned the notion of Microsoft implementing IRM at all. Historically, many third parties—companies building products that relied on Office files or email—relied on being able to change documents or read them without launching the app by directly modifying files. Screen readers for the blind were one such example. Many document management systems relied on reading the contents of Word documents. Financial systems routinely read the contents of spreadsheets pulling out specific cells or data. Such behavior should have been impossible because the files were encrypted. Ultimately, the team designed capabilities to enable these "hooks" but at the expense of even more complexity. The depth of the feature was astounding.

The operational flowcharts created by the IRM team were legendary. The team rose to the occasion, producing untold volumes of written materials for corporate admins, partnering with all the teams at Microsoft, and coordinating the documentation across the writing teams that made this feature possible. Setting up IRM remained a monumental task.

IRM's *pièce de résistance* was the addition of administrator-created rights management policy templates. It wasn't enough that a message could be marked "Do Not Forward" or a document could only be opened by a fixed set of people. Office11 enabled IT to create new document policies that expired (like Snapchat, but 15 years earlier), or for documents to be forwardable but only within a company. Several combinations of permissions could be set via policy.

The keepers of secrets in enterprises, especially those sending mail on behalf of big bosses, were super happy. IRM was an enormous hit in the Executive Briefing Center. Emails on corporate reorgs or M&A PowerPoint decks could finally be shared worry-free.

Then came the debate to end all debates. In an early customer briefing about Office11 the details of IRM were discussed. With all the work going on to secure Windows XP SP2, marketing and the field thought it prudent to refer to IRM as a security feature. The problem is security features imply a promise of robustness in an absolute sense. Either a document or email message was secure, that is it could not be read or forwarded, or it was not. We had those nasty details to contend with such as the Print Screen key or the more cryptic Prt Scr key on laptops. What if someone was reading a document and took a screen shot? That was a "security bug" according to the customer. The field sales reps were frustrated. The documents and emails were more secure because they were encrypted, but they were not absolutely secure from all forms of attack. Nothing is. After a scramble, work was done to disable screen capture involving the Windows team and marketing repositioned the feature away from security, we thought we were set. At least we thought so.

Once Office11 was available to Microsoft globally in pre-release, IRM quickly became an oft-used feature. Routinely, the most interesting mails were rights protected. Re-org announcements, strategy changes, schedule shifts, anything to do with sales numbers, staffing adjustments, and more were reflexively rights protected. Employees started rights protecting snarky threads commenting on other rights protected threads. Along the way, many learned an inescapable workaround for capturing the text of a protected message. Using another new Windows feature that allowed one to remotely log on to another PC, all one needed was a second PC to remotely log into your primary PC. After connecting, just read the message normally on the remote PC while capturing the screen on the second PC where the session was started. This was not something we could address. Most people didn't have a second PC so we felt reasonable about this and if administrators wanted, they could disable this capability, primarily used for servers anyway.

The feature, however, came just as mobile phones were gaining cameras and suddenly photos of screens were passed around with the latest news about a reorg or product schedule slip. Mobile phones would prove to be a huge challenge, especially non-Microsoft phones. Microsoft implemented support for protected content on Windows Mobile in a reasonably timely manner and released it to an anxious Microsoft workforce. Those of us still on BlackBerry or Treo devices, however, would have no idea what juicy secrets were sitting in a protected message we received while at the movies or out to dinner. We'd rush home to check out the message on a full PC as soon as we could. The proliferation of mobile devices only amplified the complexity of rolling out IRM to an organization. Almost fifteen years later, I joked with the founder of Accompli, a company that Microsoft acquired in 2014 and rebranded as the mobile Outlook client for iOS and Android, that among his first Microsoft duties would be to add IRM support to his product. A request that quickly materialized.

IRM could in no way protect anyone from discovery and litigation. Administrators had all the requisite tools to comply with courts. It was the start of a new era of information control. The era at least in Microsoft, of mail that frustratingly could not be forwarded. A feature of IRM was not just that the mail could not be forwarded but even the attached documents in mail received the same protections as the mail message. Documents could be saved in SharePoint where entire document libraries could be protected against unauthorized sharing. In fact, long memos could be protected so they could not even be printed. Those email attachments had to be Office documents, however, as people quickly learned. Photos or PDF files that were attached to protected messages did not receive those same restrictions.

Office IRM gained many fans inside Microsoft especially with the sales team who simply loved the way it connected all the major company initiatives of Office, Windows, SharePoint, and Windows Server.

Customer usage, however, was far lower than we hoped. This was perhaps in part because most end-users didn't want to invest the time and effort into dealing with the restrictions and no doubt IT departments could not absorb the complexity to deploy and manage the feature. It was likely that the only team that was able to run much of Microsoft's mid-2000s era infrastructure correctly, securely, and reliably existed in the 425 area code and carried blue Microsoft badges. Setting up, deploying, and training end-users was beyond the reach of most customers who were struggling to keep PCs functioning and patched with all the latest updates.

Setting up and deploying IRM in a company was an enormous undertaking. Once Microsoft successfully deployed IRM, a *Showcase IT* whitepaper detailing how MSIT implemented the feature stretched over 40 pages. For an average company to deploy the feature, they would need to invest in hardware and skills training across the Microsoft product line. On top of the typical deployment for desktops with Office and Exchange email, a company needed the Windows RMS server (or several), a Windows Server running Microsoft SQL Server, an SSL Certificate server (the encryption infrastructure), as well as to configure numerous externally facing web addresses for access outside the company network. While these products could be covered by an extensive Enterprise Agreement, typically adding these components was an upsell.

We were creating features that were, for all practical purposes, impossible to consume.[41] More than anything, this defined the era we were enabling. The problem was not that we created these features, but that customers and the sales force were embracing them—not so much deploying the features but embracing the underlying strategy of the features. Complexity was empowerment for the enterprise IT leaders, so it seemed. While there was continued backlash about bloat on the desktop and bloat within Office, the newness of servers and server infrastructure made features that relied on servers seem cool, and they were given a free pass regardless of complexity. The routineness with which IT succumbed to "standing up another server" was incredible. The enterprise account managers did not hesitate to push features that required more infrastructure—doing so was showing more value to customers and good for Microsoft's bottom line.

IRM was an incredible collaboration across the company. Development teams including Office, Windows, Server, Research, and more contributed to building the feature, while sales, support, and Consulting contributed to selling and working to deploy the feature. It was an amazing sense of pride of execution capability, that I wish was met with as much enthusiasm to deploy and use the feature as routinely as we would have hoped. Today's Microsoft 365 and Azure made the feature somewhat more accessible and perhaps more usable, though the decisions of an architecture from decades ago still linger in an underlying complexity that was probably good at the time in theory but not good relative to first principles.

Somehow, we had gone from simplicity as the guiding light to complexity as a sought-after competitive advantage. The story of IRM is both one of successful implementation and a cautionary tale of too much focus on customers to the exclusion of what is usable and desirable.

The world turned upside down, or sideways, or something.

074. OUTLOOK PRIDE, FINALLY

Outlook barely worked. Still.

Such was the product-market fit of Outlook that enterprise customers owning the latest in all the Office tools were routinely deploying the newest Outlook while leaving old versions of the core Office apps on the PC.

Five years and three releases from the debut of the product, Outlook remained fragile, bloated, and too difficult to use. It wasn't as though the team hadn't executed, releasing Outlook 97, Outlook 98, and Outlook 2000 in the span of just over three years. Rather the team, through little fault of their own at least after Office 97, whipsawed through strategic initiatives. First, they had to split the product into internet and corporate modes. Then they had to merge the product back together while attempting to integrate with Office and the deployment tools of Office 2000. Then they had to charge up the hill of unified storage for the second time, only to cut the feature again at the tail end of the project. As if this wasn't enough, the past couple of years saw the rise and unveiling of NetDocs which pivoted to a potential Outlook replacement, only to see that vision meet reality.

Marc Andreessen, founder of Netscape, wrote in 2007, years and a generation after the release of Outlook and long after the demise of Netscape, "The Only Thing That Matters."[44] This short piece codified product-market fit. Essentially, he said that the market pulls a successful product out of the company, "[t]he market needs to be fulfilled and the market will be fulfilled, by the first viable product that comes along." Outlook was such a product. Coupled with Exchange the market simply needed the combination to exist and to be provided by Microsoft. No matter what, the market was going to make the offering successful. It simply didn't matter what Microsoft did or did not do, Exchange and Outlook were going to be successful. Once customers saw enterprise-grade email running on Windows Server with a single integrated mail and calendaring solution, all from Microsoft, everything else was set aside: bugs, bad user interface, poor performance, and missing features. The combination clobbered IBM Lotus Notes. The rest is history.

We (or I) could not overcome the internal forces driving Outlook's strategy in order to give the team space to focus on building the product it needed to be. It was weird to achieve so much success with such a challenging product. That really throws one off balance. Product people, so to speak, like to think that being a great product is what matters in the market. This belief drove so much of the dialog internally and across teams it is hard to think of any other factors that were ever discussed—the battles were over what makes for a great product. We battled features, architecture, performance, competition, and more. We never really debated the other aspects of the 4 P's of the marketing mix beyond product: price, place, and promotion. Outlook was the right price, available through the right channel, meeting an articulated need exactly the right way. Oh, and Outlook email and calendaring kind-of-sort-of worked.

Still as a product development organization and leader, I really wanted to make Outlook work. We really wanted a release of Outlook we could be proud of in a product sense. It was a mission.

Standing in the way, more strategy.

The stars were aligning to allow us to focus—Exchange 2000 shipped and was stable, and Windows simply moved on from Outlook Express to aim for a grander and more unified Longhorn plan. the successor to Windows XP in the early stages as of this time. Yet, we found ourselves in the middle of a *Hailstorm*.

Hailstorm was the code name for a set of services announced shortly after Forum 2000 that built on the announced .NET strategy. Hailstorm would provide email, messaging, notifications, storage, and more, aiming to be the foundation for a broad set of consumer internet services.

That hardly stopped the corporate strategy motions. No sooner had Office XP shipped than the Hailstorm juggernaut took aim at Outlook. Once again, the classic Microsoft platform play entered the picture—a platform needed apps, and apps needed to demonstrate the value of the platform as the first and best adopters. Plus there was that other part of the strategy play, which was that the platform wasn't even close to complete. Pushing apps to support a new platform sooner accelerated its completion. Such a dynamic worked once, with Excel for Windows 2.0, but Windows was under development for several years before Excel really began to drive the platform with feedback. Plus, Excel had already made GUI work on Macintosh. This approach did not work with OS/2, though maybe IBM shouldered some of that blame. It could be said that Outlook contributed to Exchange success, but that was not a feeling shared across teams who did not see Exchange success as a client as much as success of a server. I disagree. Hailstorm managed to get a mandate for Outlook support, old-school Windows-Excel style.

Outlook was going to get beaten with the strategy stick once again. There was, however, one problem.

The Hailstorm platform was marginally more than memos and specifications, and few understood how it would diverge from Exchange (or Hotmail)—in other words Hailstorm implied supporting a new mail protocol for a client that only understood Exchange and was still not very good at internet standards. There remained an old-school belief that the world would accept a new proprietary mail protocol for internet scale email. Hailstorm was going to build on Hotmail infrastructure, but somehow introduce a new scale platform. Underlying this was the assumption that Outlook was architected to accept plugins supporting any email protocol so long as some small amount of protocol-specific code was written. This classic Microsoft miscalculation on the utility and viability of such architectures caused many cross-group skirmishes and much finger-pointing.

What many never really understood about Microsoft's email strategy and execution was that Outlook and Exchange were tightly coupled, just as Lotus Notes and later Gmail were for their respective clients and servers. They are essentially one product built by two teams. Even though Outlook could sort of support other mail servers, such as Yahoo or Hotmail, using those was never as good as when using Exchange—many features in Outlook required Exchange, with users mostly shouldering the burden of figuring out which features worked or not. Importantly, vast numbers of features were not expressed in the industry standard email protocols that existed and exist today. Hailstorm tried to build a mail server without a client. Supporting Hailstorm amounted to rewriting Outlook to support whatever it was that Hailstorm decided to implement as email, calendaring, contacts, and more.

What became clear was that the three-year Enterprise Agreement train that the Office11 schedule demanded would not be enough time for Hailstorm to deliver a working, solid, and scalable platform for Outlook. Hailstorm needed more time. Beyond Outlook even, Hailstorm proved to be too much, too soon for the many partners it needed.

The world of consumer companies was starting to warm up to advertising on the internet and saw the internet and software broadly as an extension of customer awareness and acquisition. The digital transformation that came to characterize most industries a decade or more later was far beyond what most companies were considering. Hailstorm concepts such as digital payments, customer identity, and even customer support happening through an array of software tools seemed wildly out of step, and, more importantly, concerning, as most companies were not looking to trust 2000s era Microsoft with those interactions.

In fact, many companies and organizations were so concerned, the thought of Hailstorm generated complaints to regulators resulting in a series of Congressional hearings. While many theories about regulations gumming up Microsoft existed (I disagree that was the case), in practice Hailstorm was an example of the specter of regulatory oversight slowing down or even outright killing product development. Whether Hailstorm would have been a success or not is easily debated. Certainly, all the capabilities described continue to exist.

The primary failure or resistance, however, came from customers and their concerns about owning data and customer relationships. These same potential industry partners eventually found themselves in the web of Facebook, Amazon, Google, and the likes of PayPal.

It was a grand vision that proved to be exactly right—and about 15 years too early and from exactly the wrong company.

By the time the fate of Hailstorm was sealed, we were only through the early stages of Office11. This gave the Outlook team time to regroup and renew the focus on making Outlook work. The team was already deep into the designs and features but cutting support for Hailstorm was a gift of development schedule hours to the two main innovations in Outlook11: rearchitecting the basics of mail delivery and reshaping the user experience.

Like many technologies in Office, from working on long documents in Word to recalculating large Excel spreadsheets instantly, delivering and storing mail was not the most electrifying feature in the product, but getting it right was something that Microsoft accomplished uniquely well. Before the rise of cloud-based email, mail delivery systems meant downloading email to a PC where it could be read and filed away—mail was stored locally on a PC hard drive and everyone was responsible for backing up their own email. It is not difficult to see how problematic that might be. Such effort was required primarily because storing and backing up mail on a corporate server was expensive (very expensive and time consuming) especially for a corporation with tens of thousands of employees. As an indication for how routine it was for IT to offload critical business functions to end-users, few considered the distributed costs and risks associated with every end-user at a big corporation acting like their own IT department. During the early days of corporate email, another limitation was connectivity (Wi-Fi was not yet ubiquitous)—employees were often disconnected from the network, especially information workers with laptops. Routine business travel was a constant hunt for hotels with wired networking in rooms or guest network cables at customer and partner offices. Of course airplanes and airports were disconnected experiences. Customers were offline and disconnected quite frequently.

The previous two Office releases attempted to address offline using the idea of a new storage technology, the Local Store, or LIS. Outlook supported a clunky way of working offline (rooted in old-school dial-up support), which the team improved marginally, but it needed much more work to be broadly usable by road warriors. Working online was how Outlook was built. By online, I mean Outlook worked best when it was connected to an uninterrupted, reliable, high-speed network.

As mobile work increased, working offline became much more the norm. This reality is difficult to imagine today, but two decades ago connectivity was the main topic of conversation almost everywhere there was a laptop. Connectivity, or lack thereof, was a major point of contention at sales Mid-Year Reviews (MYR) where country managers genuinely believed Redmond's product designers had no idea how poor connectivity was in other markets. They were mostly right, and even when we visited would had no problems paying $35 per day for wired connectivity in a business hotel. It would be ten years before Starbucks would offer free Wi-Fi.

Offline was the key to making Outlook vastly more reliable and responsive. Everything that a user experienced in Outlook would operate on data that was already downloaded from a server, which was not how it previously worked. If there was no network connection Outlook was still snappy and responsive and every feature just worked. When a network became available, Outlook seamlessly and silently connected, receiving any new mail, sending all the mail that was drafted while disconnected, and filing away emails in the right folders. A key detail was that an individual's PC was no longer the only storage for email but was a copy of all the email stored on the server. If a laptop was lost or a person wanted to use two computers, mail remained up-to-date and exactly the same. Outlook was a cache or copy of Exchange, which is why we called this *cached mode*. Through today's perspective, this is exactly how the Mail application on an iPhone works when connected to Gmail.

In Outlook 97 through 2002, online mode, when it worked (which was not always), worked incredibly fast, and instantaneously. When the server received new mail, Outlook instantly showed the new mail on a PC. That mail was fetched from the server then displayed, which, if the network was perfect, was snappy. Even a small network hiccup (as the CEO of Boeing experienced on a business jet) and Outlook would hang, and almost never recover gracefully. Email was novel and speed of delivery was a feature, so even then customers remembered how fast it all seemed during demonstrations. The important detail was that the mail still existed in storage only on the mail server. The PC was a rendering of the server. That's why mail delivery seemed so fast—the mail itself did not travel over the internet, just the visible portion of the screen.

With cached mode, Outlook11 changed how email felt. Suddenly, when new mail arrived on the server, the PC silently fetched it, waiting for a good network connection. It was fast, and not always instant, but predictably mail arrived when it could. When it did, the entire mail message, including attachments, was there. Mail with larger attachments took longer to appear. To big customers impressed by the speed of previous Outlook, Outlook11 felt slow and sluggish. With the rise of Wi-Fi on laptops, Outlook could sense when connectivity was available and, without crashing or hanging, continue to work seamlessly.

We were caught in the middle of crazy conversations with customers who could not get past it feeling slower, even though it was not, and it was more reliable. BillG even complained to me several times about how slow Outlook seemed, wondering if we would fix it as product development progressed. Again, we faced how changing small factors in a running system led customers to believe the changes were bigger and worse Word introduced background printing and saving, and sure enough the absence of a progress indicator scrolling across the screen led people to believe Word slowed down as well. Cached mode, background save and print, and many more changes that improved Office in an absolute sense convinced customers it was slower, more difficult to use, or different and thus worse.

When I was working on the first release of Visual C++, we were deeply concerned about performance when creating Windows programs, new for most developers, especially compared to the speedy Borland Turbo C++. I added a feature to rapidly display a count of lines of code as they were processed or compiled. Much to my chagrin, my code to draw that ticker technically slowed down the process. In usability tests, however, developers always thought being able to see the line count whiz by was perceived as faster. So, we left the line count in, even though overall processing time was slower.

Perception matters. The performance of an interface can depend on perception of the design as much as stopwatch time, though it isn't always obvious which matters more.

Office was no longer in the realm of tech enthusiasts anxious for every change. It became business infrastructure and like the floorplan of a factory or cost centers in accounting changing infrastructure was not done on a whim.

The middle-age of the PC was a period during which each change, obvious or not, was viewed with skepticism. It used to be that Office was difficult to upgrade because of the cost of upgrading disk space and memory, but such expense was viewed with a bit of excitement or even pride of accomplishment. Then upgrading Office became difficult because customers did not want it to change at all. Change was different and different was assumed to be bad, especially for Office, which was not the cool place IT was willing to invest time and effort. The complexities embraced on the server and in the datacenter were driving a movement to maintain status quo on the desktop. Change was actively discouraged when it came to the desktop and Office.

Still the user experience of Outlook remained horrible. It was Byzantine and bloated and had the reviews to prove it. Even today, searching for "Byzantine Microsoft Outlook" yields almost one million hits. Outlook11 aimed to recraft Outlook based on what we had learned over four releases and four years since Outlook 97. We were going to take the time to make it right so it could properly share the stage with Word, Excel, and PowerPoint. Each app in Office deserved to have a release where it stood out and was recognized for being great.

Jensen Harris (JensenH) was asked to lead program management the first broad, and much-needed, reshaping of the Outlook user experience. Hardly the typical computer science hire, Jensen joined Outlook from college where he majored in music. Previously, Jensen attended Interlochen, the prestigious performing arts school, with fellow classmate Jewel. When not composing for all the instruments in a piece or performing, Jensen was programming. Jensen was among the best of a new generation of program managers on the team and he seemed to know as much about how Outlook was coded as even the most senior developers. These skills were put to the test in sweeping changes to Outlook11—a process that, if successful, could prepare Jensen and the Office team for even bigger changes in the future.

While we made many small or incremental changes in user interface in each release of Office, Outlook11 would be the biggest changes to any one product to date. We would also make these changes in the context of the change-resistant enterprise customer base, especially the email administrators in IT that saw Outlook as a necessary evil supporting their beloved Exchange servers.

To say the changes were sweeping and high-risk only makes sense in the context of the time. First, many small features of Outlook that piled on over the previous years were rationalized, sanitized, streamlined, and in general made better and more accessible. Second, and more importantly, they came at a time when email was the most critical and mainstream tool being added to the workplace. Using email and Outlook often meant taking a training course, buying a book, or simply struggling to master a few scenarios and little else. Email was still in an expansion stage, leaving ample opportunity to make it better for new users not just change the user experience for existing users.

That context is important because so many of the paradigms we think of in email today were pioneered or refined in Outlook11: message flags, preview pane, switching between calendars, contacts, mail, message thread view, junk mail filtering, integration with instant messaging, and much more.

The most acute pain point in using email, any email not just Outlook, was unsolicited mail, junk mail, or SPAM. The rapid rise of email brought with it an exponential rise in the morning ritual of deleting unwanted mail offering everything from get rich quick schemes to fast college degrees, and even offensive sexually oriented offers. Everyone felt invaded by the onslaught. Unfortunately for Microsoft, the rise of Hotmail with hundreds of millions of accounts was both a source of junk mail and the target of junk mail senders. The junk mail problem on Hotmail was so bad that @hotmail.com addresses became synonymous with spam. It wasn't just an inconvenience, but email was losing its utility for businesses to communicate with customers as primitive junk mail technology too aggressively filtered out legitimate mail.

In one of BillG's most successful (and perhaps last) great cross-company technology initiatives, a working group from Microsoft Research, Exchange Server, and Outlook convened over many months with Bill insisting we collectively make improvements in junk mail filtering. The work from Microsoft Research was one of the early applications of the same technology used in the Office Assistant, Bayesian probability, advancing beyond typical keyword filtering that falsely flagged messages. Junk mail senders adopted their language rapidly to get around filters, substituting alternate spellings for words such as S3X instead of SEX or S1NGLE instead of SINGLE. Meanwhile, Exchange server pioneered some of the first cross-industry efforts at verifying legitimate senders. Outlook took advantage of MSR technology used in Hotmail to apply it to the desktop application so it could work for any email service customers used. The Outlook features were so well received that almost every review mentioned them, though they also mentioned Hotmail as the biggest junk mail headache.

So successful was the feature in the previously released Outlook Express that I found myself along with several lawyers in a San Jose courtroom defending the right of Outlook to even have junk mail filtering. A popular electronic greeting card company (yes, web sites that created a JPEG birthday card were a big thing for a short time) sued Microsoft for falsely flagging some of their free greeting cards as junk mail. I spent several weeks creating new mail accounts and collecting the junk mail that would routinely arrive even before using the account for legitimate email to show the judge as we entered arbitration. The lawyers made a great case for the right to protect consumers, but in the post-DOJ era the David v. Goliath environment was too difficult. We settled the case for an astonishing amount of money. The good news is that over time it paved the way for the industry to legitimately offer junk mail protection, if for no other reason than everyone with email recognized the junk mail problem.

In applications, the way to signify a major update is to change the user interface substantially. Doing so signals to the world how big the change is. BradWe, our product design leader, referred to this as the ten-foot test. Looking across at a PC screen ten feet away, could a typical customer see the difference in the product. This is surprisingly difficult as most people see typical screens as an array of meaningless graphics. On the other hand, when it comes to using a product up close even the smallest changes elicit massive feedback. The rise of Outlook in a few short years created a good deal of muscle memory, even though the product was awkward and complex. Most customers were not just learning Outlook but learning email, to many Outlook was email. Changing Outlook was changing email, and email had rapidly risen to be a core part of work. No one likes their daily workflow changed for no good reason. These conflicting goals set the bar high for JensenH and team to deliver on a vastly improved, and iconic user experience for Outlook.

The team answered this challenge with an entirely new layout for the main Outlook window, one that would pass the ten-foot test. The screen was divided vertically into three columns: folders, mail messages, and a single message open to read. It was a clean and logical design that was…broadly panned during beta testing. The visceral reaction to seeing a narrow column of the inbox subject lines and that the view was showing each message with two rows led beta testers to think less email was shown on the screen, and less email meant less productivity. Similarly, the relatively narrow reading view of the message led to a conclusion that less text of a message was shown on the screen. These observations were hotly debated on the newsgroups and the subject of many outcries from testers.

Yet, these observations were not true, and easily demonstrated. Jensen and team were hyper-analytical in the design and measured everything about the interface—in particular, the design showed a much higher level of information density on the screen, while apparently making people feel like less was on the screen, which would make it easier to read and less tiring. Brilliant. Over a few weeks the outcries were settled with volumes of screenshots and posts to the newsgroups, leaving a design in place that is routinely used by all email clients today. This was another example of visceral perception of user experience versus actual experience.

Outlook users tended to be either *pilers* or *filers* when it came to managing email. Pilers, like the BillG I knew, let their inbox grow, seemingly without bound. Inbox was where mail was read and also stored. When a piler wanted to find a message, they used Outlook search, which was slow and deeply unsatisfying, or more likely they sorted thousands of messages by sender or date or subject, which was fast. Filers created elaborate hierarchies of storage folders and messages. Advanced filers created email rules, moving messages to folders even before they read them. One reporter I knew maintained a folder for every company, and a folder within that for each contact at that company. He worked with all the folders visible and the whole hierarchy expanded, watching for unread messages.

There's a challenge when customer knowledge of the past makes improving for the new, faster-growing base of customers super difficult. The customers we heard from in early testing were those with knowledge and time to engage. They raised issues and engaged in debates that others happily let product design work out for them.

We came to learn that many of the tech elites were avid filers, making use of email rules. When a customer goes through the effort to create a rule, mail messages are automatically placed in a desired folder as they arrive in the inbox based on criteria such as the sender's name or company name, or perhaps keywords in the subject line. The general concept of advanced tech thinkers embracing hierarchy was consistent with how people made use of folders of files on their PC. Typical users often had desktops filled with files including what they were actively working on, whereas techie users tended to have elaborate folder hierarchies and store documents in the right place from the start.

Studying how customers used Outlook, rather than listening to how they thought they used Outlook, revealed a spectrum for how the onslaught of email was being handled. Customers tended to self-report how they wished to be perceived rather than how they used a product, something we learned over the years with the instrumented versions. As an example, customers routinely self-reported sending far more mail than they actually sent or would rarely get the number of messages in the inbox approximately correct. BillG, the piler, used to wax poetically about his love of filers as though he was one primarily due to his fondness for hierarchical lists, but also to make a point about the future of storage that would support hierarchy. He also exaggerated the amount of mail he sent and received.

Business books are filled with stories and strategies about learning from customers, getting feedback, and doing what customers want. In technology products, and in Office in particular, in the more than a decade I worked on the product, much of that feedback would have frozen our product where it was and prevented us from moving forward. Staying true to learning the reality of what customers experience was such a key lesson reinforced with Outlook11. The lesson was one for the ages and one that impacts every technology product, including, as I would learn, Windows.

Showing Outlook11 to the press and reviewers was not just a demo, but a story. We incorporated the data about how customers used the product in reality and showed the analytics behind the product. It sounds obvious, but it just wasn't something done in the industry because prior to the internet no one really knew. We had surveys and focus groups, and the early data about quality, but with Outlook and Exchange we had real data about real people doing real work. This story-telling approach dramatically changed not only how we designed and communicated product changes, but our willingness to take risk to make bigger changes that met customer needs.

As the success of Office continued, we were fast approaching the point where most everyone that wanted Office owned it, legally or pirated. PC sales in 2002 (post dot-com bubble) were nearly 130 million units, growing at an anemic rate of 3 percent or less. There was a fear that we had peaked and that conservatism in making changes should have ruled how we thought of the product. Some thought we should have been focused on listening to customers and not rocking the boat.

Except we were listening to customers.

There's a famous saying falsely attributed to Henry Ford suggesting that when potential customers of the Model T car were asked what they wanted, they said a faster horse, not a car. No customers wanted a graphical interface with a mouse, or an integrated suite of productivity tools, or even for those tools to evolve with the changing nature of work and the internet.

Finding a balance between listening to customers, while also moving forward with technology, is the most difficult challenge any successful technology company faces. Microsoft was no exception.

075. SCALING AND TRANSITIONS

Over the course of building Office11, Microsoft began to see cultural transformations that in hindsight were the product of trying to mature as an organization while not taking on the risk of changing as an organization. It was as though we wanted to add all the benefits of a coordinated, multi-dimensional-thinking, well-executing, mature company while at the same time not taking away the hardcore, code-centric, engineering-driven culture that got us to where we were. The goal was laudable. How could it not be? The only surprise was how long it took us to get to this point.

Around the company we were not executing well, not even a little bit. To some, however, it felt like we were executing. That was only because we had so many activities going on. Everyone was very busy (just try scheduling a meeting with someone) with launches, pre-releases, community gatherings, partner events, PR outreach, ecosystems, big reorgs, offsites, slide decks, spreadsheets, reporting systems, and more. The airmiles were accumulating at a phenomenal rate. A big company has an ability to show a great deal of activity even with little progress. What wasn't happening was new product innovation, except financially. That distinction is important. The money was coming in but that was for all the products we had already built, in some cases several years earlier.

Microsoft saw less than stellar success across most of our new initiatives. If the primary goal was to gain market share, then we were losing. SteveB used to say, "share is air." Whether it was phones, consoles, web sites, advertising, and so on, the first few years of the millennium looked like the dot-com startups we had ridiculed. To clarify our new initiatives, Microsoft began to report earnings across seven operating segments: Client home to Windows, Server and Tools including Windows Server, SQL Server, Exchange, and Visual Studio, Information Worker with Office, Microsoft Business Solutions including Great Plains/Dynamics, MSN owning the "consumer online" properties, Mobile and Embedded Devices including Windows Mobile), and Home and Entertainment including Xbox, consumer hardware. Every earnings call and cover story about Microsoft asked when these new businesses would become "profitable." The calls for "when will you win" were deafening.

Such a question was a naïve approach to how business worked, but that's how bringing visibility to a product under development is talked about. Anyone who has run a business knows that new products are not profitable at the outset and take years for a full P&L view to look profitable, but that's not how people comment on earnings. At company meetings or routine team meetings, SteveB had a great series of slides where he emphasized the long-term nature of Microsoft's approach and what it means to invest in the future—"investing" Steve would always emphasize. As a reminder, Windows took at least six years and three major versions for it to become a significant product. Had Windows been reported separately from MS-DOS it is not clear Wall Street would have been forgiving.

The new businesses were still much newer and were part of a vastly larger landscape than Windows or Office were years earlier. Combined, the four investment-mode new businesses (MSN, Mobile and Embedded, Home and Entertainment, Business Solutions) had a (FY 2003) **negative** operating income of $1.6 billion. Windows, Server and Tools, and Information Worker had an operating income of $17.9 billion, on total revenue of $32.2 billion. In other words, there was no material risk to the company due to these investments, nevertheless losing money or failing to pay off began to permeate the whole of the company's operating model and external narrative. Culturally, we weren't used to negative numbers.

There was an additional problem that drove operational changes. The Windows team began to have the signs of a product spinning out of control. Those were my words. The company was experiencing in real-time what SteveB and I discussed in his first series of one-on-one meetings when he became president a couple of years earlier. Big projects can seem to go from execution to out of control in a flash—there is a fragility in large-scale software projects that we had yet to fully grok. The time it took to complete Windows XP SP2, the resulting desire to produce separate releases for Tablet PC, Media Center, and Windows Server, and expanding strategic inputs from BillG shaping Windows development created a situation where the Windows XP follow-on release, Longhorn, was either "at risk" or "out of control" depending on who you asked. In practice, some still believed it was a typical Windows product cycle.

Beyond the new businesses described by segments, Microsoft had a seemingly infinite breadth of new products under development. Few areas of software went unnoticed without a Microsoft group claiming to be in the space. Yet, we lacked clear strategic view or even line of sight view to all these projects, if or how they fit in, when they might deliver, or what progress they were making. A skeptic would say this was an additional level of potential negative ROI hidden underneath the success (or not) of each segment. Optimists would say this was entrepreneurial thinking at its best. The challenge was that as primarily an enterprise company, the customer demand for a strategy, unification, and clarity were ever-present.

Seeing these challenges drove a shift in how the company operated, at least I believed that was a root cause. A pendulum swung away from autonomy and lack of rigorous strategic and execution oversight at the top-level towards a more centralized approach to planning and execution. In any business environment I've seen, when things aren't working the inevitable solution is to swing the other direction of some easily identified pendulum. In our case, that meant more corporate standardized processes.

I found such a change challenging (for me in Office) in two ways. First, it felt to me that Office didn't have these problems. We were executing well and had been for a long time. We had processes and delivered results—even when our projects were late, they were not unbounded, and we promised and delivered on plans without any gaming or redefining of deliverables. Second, the problems seen in these new businesses could look like execution problems, but as we'll see over the chapters that follow, they were fundamentally strategy and manager (versus management) issues. It wasn't enough to work to get the trains to run on time if there was no understanding of where the trains should run. Some of the projects were running well, but the destination was poorly understood.

That was my perspective. It was not shared by everyone for two reasons.

First, just as with any business if one wants to make a bear case then that would be possible for Office. What if customers rejected a new version? What if open-source OpenOffice took share? What if web-browser Office became a thing suddenly? What if we were out of control and just didn't know it? We just weren't going to be blindsided by those in 2003, but there was no way to prove that. Any attempt just sounded defensive. I sounded defensive far too often and that was not good.

Second, the company model for all the new businesses was to be a platform. What do platforms need? They need Office to build on the platform to prove it out. Any lack of success in the new businesses was therefore strongly connected to something the Office team was not participating in. As such, their problems were indeed Office problems. They were my problems. I didn't really believe they were my problems, and my rolling eyes or audible sighs were the tell.

I was busy finishing Office11. That's what I knew needed to happen, deep down. Putting up with all that was going on around me I thought added a second job. The Office team had gotten so good at planning and execution that there were plenty of cycles remaining for me to focus on those goings-on, even if I did not find doing so pleasant.

Was this the moment when dreaded bureaucracy was settling in? If only Microsoft would have realized as much, might we have avoided a "lost decade" that followed? The expression "lost decade" became a popular way to describe overall stock market returns in 2010 since the dot-com bust. The press started to refer to Microsoft's own lost decade. In contrast to the broader market Microsoft had a "popularity problem" to quote *The New York Times*, which said "the company hasn't received credit for its almost-half-full glass: the 40 percent of its business that is not Windows or Office…its enterprise software business, formally labeled *Server and Tools*, as 'an incredible business' accounting…for about 24 percent of the company's revenue and with an operating margin of 40 percent."[45] We were putting up the numbers but unlike Yahoo and Google we did not have a consumer business, and because of the internet and the rise of Google that was all that mattered. Yet, that was by design. We were not putting in place an arbitrary bureaucracy or processes, but the logic behind the changes was to try to have it all: an enterprise business, a consumer business, competitive products, and an overall technology strategy. We were not lost as much as trying to do a lot. Maybe too much. We were Microsoft and we thought big. What's wrong with that?

Dealing with these processes was challenging for me and it showed. Some aspects were always going to be my style. I did not have a staff (a business manager and/or chief of staff for example) who could spend full time in the preparation meetings for the larger meetings. I made slides I was responsible for by myself and got them done on time, but without endless iterations and sweating over every point that can come with a staff working full time on slides. In doing so I wasn't always part of the month of pre-meetings leading up to meetings and did not always have the context for when something new became a hot topic amongst the staff such as what is the Office answer for "healthcare" that came up in an earlier meeting or what are we doing about "small business" that was in that mail thread from UK. It was obvious to me that the processes were an effort to bring the rigor of the Mid-Year Review (MYR) process used by the subsidiaries and field to product development. It was never clear to me, however, that sort of process would work for the creative and uncertain aspects of product development. I was frustrated that no one ever asked for input over what we were being asked to do.

I believed that tired cliché about building products, which is you can't know everything before you start but you can cause everything to grind to a halt by asking questions at every step or thinking success can be known before we start. I held that romantic view that building products is an art, and no quantity of meetings could turn it into a science. Perhaps the most frustrating (to others) belief I held, was that questioning too much after a product started was a sure-fire way to bring chaos. That's what I saw happening.

I agreed with the problems that preceded these process changes. I didn't see processes as the solution. We were not going to fix things by having better slides or box diagrams. We weren't executing because we lacked the planning infrastructure and organizational structure that was required to deliver. Such a point of view, however, was difficult to prove because the very nature of the processes we were going through (with names such as Business Plan Review or BPR) was to surface the planning and org structure issues so they could be fixed. We were caught in very tricky loops.

"Competing with Linux" was a long series of meetings that was top of mind for the Server and Tools business and illustrates this point. I was running Linux at home. It was comfortable for me as it brought back muscle memory from college and graduate school (that was technically Unix, just to be completely accurate), but importantly it brought back a lot of technical reminders about the architecture of Linux. Office also experienced the rise of Linux through FrontPage, which achieved far more success connecting to Linux servers on the internet than anywhere (or anyone) else. This would serve me well in the product-led discussions, as would the feedback from internet service providers all running FrontPage on Unix and not Windows NT.

Strategy and execution meetings about Linux were overly focused on the immediate crises of head-to-head sales losses. What should be our pricing? Are we positioning correctly? Do we need a better partner? Many in product groups (the development teams) were familiar with the technology, many deeply so, but the product plans did not reflect Linux as a competitor when viewed through the lens of resource allocation and feature lists. It was as though there was broad acknowledgement of the competitive issues without responding with product plans. The basic idea was that we could win if we didn't change any of the product plans, where the list of must-do features for enterprise customers continued to grow. The real problem was that the business results made this look like the right decision. The sales of Windows Server continued to rise, and Linux was still free as in free like a puppy. We were winning at least in appearance.

From any objective distance, it became difficult to see the difference between how Windows and Office responded to Linux or competitive risks in general. If I suggested Linux was a real product competitor requiring a significant change in product features over what we would do if Linux wasn't on our radar, then I could just as easily be challenged over responding to OpenOffice..."you lost that sale to the German government didn't you?" they would knowingly ask. A response claiming it was different just made me look like I too was dodging the issues around Office or something akin to *whataboutism*.

One Linux review meeting reached a surreal phase when the whole of the all-day meeting with hundreds of slides and many presenters boiled down to a request for headcount in order to effectively compete with Linux. As a matter of practice, that was not how meetings were supposed to go. Headcount requests were for another meeting and process. As though it was to emphasize the matter, the actual headcount ask was for two, yes just 2, heads. The entirety of the strategy to compete with Linux from a 10,000-person division required asking for two heads. It was as crazy as it sounds. To his credit, SteveB was not happy with the ask and the team was not happy with the response.

I hesitate to write the above because my experiences at this time could not possibly reflect experiences of the thousands of people during this same transition. It is not even clear to me today what were causes versus correlations of the challenges we faced. Frankly, some of what seemed so wrong then turned out to not matter at all to where Microsoft is today. Such are complex stories. Such is product-market fit, which is likely the most important lesson. We had the most amazing product-market fit, which (at least according to theory) meant it hardly mattered at all what we did.

Through these new processes I reluctantly learned to be pretty good at telling the Office story with respect to execution. I became well-versed in explaining how we worked, organized, planned, collaborated, and executed. I spent an enormous amount of energy detailing these topics to anyone that would listen. Even very small details such as knowing how many people worked on a given project, something we routinely did for years, would take on almost mythical status as SteveB would ask other groups for a report that looks like the one from Office. They would often ask to connect with the staff that created a chart only to find it was usually just me. There were no secrets. We just did the work, but it did have a cost.

There was some personal history to my desire to do a good job explaining resource allocation within the context of this new business planning framework. Back when we organized for Office9 (Office 2000) one of the significant decisions we made was to allocate resources even more towards Office suite-wide development and also to what would become SharePoint. In doing so, the number of developers on Excel, for example, reduced from an historic high of 50-55 to just under 20. There was controversy and disagreement within the Office team, but that was no match for how BillG viewed such a decision as nearly irresponsible. Yet in a short time it became clear that reallocation for products that had won was a much better approach than to continue to incrementally pile on resources. In real-time, both BillG and SteveB got to see the culture difference between Windows and Office when it came to embarking on new projects. Everything in Windows always seemed to be incrementally new headcount (like Linux compete) and everything in Office was a reallocation. I didn't realize it at the time but using today's terminology I relied on the product-market fit achieved by Word and Excel. We just weren't going to lose in the overall Office business because of incremental features we failed to add to those products, even in 2001.

Counting developers became an obsession with me. Starting in Office 2000 I even did a census where I asked each developer to add a row to a spreadsheet saying what they worked on in their own words so I could compare it to the schedule, the vision, and what team they were on. After that we even started using unused columns in the SAP employee database to record what part of the project a developer worked on—that way the information was always available live and could be kept up to date as employees moved around the team. Any time someone asked me how many people were working on some aspect, I just brought up http://headtrax (the internal front end to SAP data) did a few queries and there was an answer. For data across the whole team, I'd just export to Excel and create a pivot table.

Such attention to resource allocation was seemingly encoded in my Apps Division DNA. It came from a reality that it didn't matter what a team said they were working on, rather it only mattered what developers were actually assigned to. As the company grew and cookie-licking became more common—when teams declare they own or are driving a critical initiative but are doing so without the work or resources to support it—the need to bring clarity to those discussions became even more important. I only wished at the time that more teams had clarity of resource allocation reflected in SAP.

Managing personal time was just as important as clarity on developer allocation. Following a lesson I learned from SteveB for the past few years I tracked where I spent time during the day. How many 1:1s, product meetings, customer and partner meetings, skip-level 1:1s, team meetings, and so on. I did this in a very lightweight manner attaching a category to Outlook schedule items. Every quarter I exported my calendar and created an Excel pivot table of hours spent on these categories. Over the course of developing Office11 I noticed that I was spending more time in what I labeled "process", the corporate driven planning and coordinating meetings and that was taking away from ad hoc time just talking with people in the hallways or more structured time with the team. I found this disappointing, if not depressing. When I discussed this with my manager or Steve in a skip-level, usually the feedback I received was that I was not spending enough time on corporate. Somewhere between too much and not enough was probably a better answer. I had reached that point where I felt caught in the middle and failing both of my constituencies. My algorithm for addressing this concern was that the team always won out, whenever it could. I just felt so much more useful in working with the team than in corporate rituals. It was easy to feel good because we were making a ton of progress, especially comparatively.

The team was doing a fantastic job finishing Office11, which was formally named Office 2003. Well, not exactly. With new marketing leadership in place and a mission to be more aggressive along with license to spend more doing so, the product branding was brought more into an enterprise perspective. Office suites sounded so small. We had so much more software. The entire collection of Information Worker software was branded "more than what it used to be" as "Microsoft Office System", "now an integrated system of programs, servers, services, and solutions." The suites of Office programs typically bought were called Editions. This meant Office11 was officially known as "Microsoft Office Professional Edition 2003" or as humans called it, Office 2003.

JeffR approved a major advertising campaign to go with Office 2003, over $150 million, five times the $30 million spent on Office XP. It was one of those campaigns where even the campaign itself gets a PR push and stories about it—marketing of the marketing team. The campaign covered print, online, television, and more, such as airplane video. Called "Great Moments At Work", the campaign a playful take at workplace successes as though success was celebrated like sports complete with pile ups and high-fives. The ads were fun. The print ads used photos of the same scenes but emphasized the sheer breadth of Office System software.

Breadth was an understatement. The sheer volume, or mass, of software being released as one product at one time was overwhelming for customers and the press. It wasn't just that it was overwhelming in quantity, but the features individually were so deep, so complex, that few could really understand them well-enough to provide detailed reviews. The product guide we distributed to reviewers and the press was 170 pages, a book! The *Microsoft Office System Evaluation 2003 Enterprise Edition* kit consisted of 11 CDROM discs and two discs filled with various technical and overview documents, demonstration videos, and an entire disc-based website of Macromedia Flash content. It seems easy to make fun of this today, but then one look at the web site for Office 365 and I guess one could long for the finiteness of a bundle of CDROM discs.

Outlook was the hero of the release, with a little bit of OneNote from the press as expected. From junk mail to the new user interface and especially more reliable mail delivery, Outlook finally achieved status as a first tier Office application. It was a story that started in the mid-1990s and took Outlook 97, Outlook 98, Outlook 2000, and Outlook 2002 before we finally got it right in 2003. Through all the strategic twists and turns, organizational changes, and internal competition it had been quite a journey. With 2003, the product finally made it.

A huge amount of software, and Outlook. That is how I remember the release. We so over-achieved on building enterprise software that even marketing, which by and large picked out the end-user features to promote in previous releases, went all in on enterprise to market the release. In the above Evaluation Kit for example in the included "Top 10 Reasons to Upgrade" four of those top reasons had to do with XML, magical XML.

To that end, the release came across as one deeply committed to the new XML technology, our fifth of five priorities when we planned the release. The problem was that we used XML as an implementation detail, not as an end to itself—we had built a platform not a solution, and it was too soon to tout the uses of the platform that had yet to see adoption. The company was overall was so committed, so enamored with XML technology, that it took on a life of its own. It became the destination. The Office marketing team was drafting off the incredible amount of XML evangelism being done by the Server and Tools group, where XML was a key underpinning of the .NET platform. It was still a text file, but we were going to make it seem magical.

If previously Office 2000 focused too much on cost of ownership and deployment to the exclusion of end-user features, then Office 2003 focused too much on a technology enabler or platform technology to the exclusion of doing more with the technology that enterprise customers could use immediately. Looking back at the vision, clearly the big change at the start of the project removed the bulk of the end-user appeal—the vision of Office.NET as an end-user service. The corporate version, "Team and Corporate Productivity" in the vision from May 2001, delivered well but suffered from the complexity and slow deployment of SharePoint as previously discussed.

Large projects are indeed a portfolio and with something as large as the Office System it is essential to build a product such that each constituency has something significant to grab on to, almost selfishly. This is an intentional part of the planning process—we look at the features we are building through the lens of critical stakeholders and make sure everyone has something. I measured our success on delivering on value by constituency.

Enterprises, medium businesses, IT professionals, channel partners, developers, integrators, and more had the full weight of the Office System. It was what they wanted. End-users, typical reviewers, and the individual "power users" (influential end-users in our taxonomy) were left behind, though with Outlook and OneNote there was enough, just not an overwhelming amount. The reviews showed that.

Rob Pegoraro a seasoned reviewer for the Washington Post wrote, even with some stinging criticism of some specifics in Outlook, "If e-mail rules your world, Outlook 2003 offers tough competition for pretty much every other program around…But the rest of Office 2003 is a yawner. Most people at home can comfortably sleep right through this upgrade cycle."[46] That's what most of the reviews were like. Individual reviewers representing typical Office users struggled to make sense of XML, SharePoint, collaboration, and the rest of the massive Office System. The thing is, those individuals just weren't our business anymore. Enterprise was our business. Those reviews were incredibly strong.

While we were nine months late, we were never out of control or unclear on where we were in the project. We just had a ton of software to get built. Nine months might seem too long, but with the original schedule finishing in late

September that really meant a late January launch anyway because launching over holidays isn't something you can do with enterprise software. So really it was just 6 months, a cup of coffee. The unanticipated long tail at the end of the release gave us more time to plan. My thoughts were wandering to bringing real excitement back to the product while solving the problem of the heft of the Office System.

The launch was a huge worldwide event. I chose to go to China for their launch. Shortly after the launch, I would use a sabbatical to live and work in China for the subsidiary full-time, on the heels of SARS no less. It was an amazing time in China as the markets were opening up, welcoming us, and anxious to expand business connections. The climate of optimism and collaboration was unique.

The launch was difficult, however. For all we had done to execute well, the last-minute change in the product plans away from a consumer service made the release difficult for me. Most people didn't obsess over or even think about the change, but it lingered for me. Perhaps because I took it as a personal failure in how I managed the planning effort or perhaps, and more likely, I felt it would have been incredibly cool to deliver on the vision of an "online Office."

I began to think about what would come next for Office and was clear that the product needed an end-user focus. The enterprise momentum had run its course. We were not going to lose for not being enterprise enough. We needed to regain the end-user. I thought to myself about the commitment to do that after Office 2000 and the moderate success we had in development but that did not translate into the way we sold the product. Office 2003 was to remedy that but the start of the project solidified the all enterprise approach. We faced real competition now and the reviews showed we had real problems for the humans that used Office, not just the organizations.

More than anything, the launch was bittersweet not just for me but for many on the team. Just as the product was going to beta test (summer 2002) the team received some devastating news.

Reader note: The following contains an emotional description of the loss of a Microsoft employee.

On Thursday August 22, 2002 (almost exactly one year before we released the product to manufacturing), I received a call on my landline at home from Steve Shaffer (SteveSh), the HR generalist for Office. A call from HR to my home never happened so I knew something was up before I was able to discern the shakiness in his voice.

"I have some terrible news," he said. "It is Heikki. He's gone."

I was not able to process what he was saying and was silent for what I am sure seemed like an eternity. I managed to ask what happened. Details were thin, but there was a fatal car accident in Monroe, Washington, about 20 miles north of the Microsoft campus in a relatively rural area. While trying to pass a car, Heikki's car collided head-on with a large vehicle. The roads were clear and dry and there were no visibility problems. It took a few weeks, but we learned that there were no drugs or alcohol involved. A young mother of two was also killed in the crash. The children and their father and grandmother survived.

The sudden death of a coworker, a direct report, long-time colleague, and friend was both a personal event and a team event, and a Microsoft event. Heikki was a towering and immense presence on the team, and many people were deeply affected. Microsoft was still a young company and, while we experienced some tragedies, this was the most sudden loss of a senior leader.

Heikki's family lived in Finland and made their way to the United States as quickly as they could.

We were all in shock. Yet we got through, in part, by thinking about how Heikki would have guided the team. Heikki in his most Finnish stoicism would have insisted we pick ourselves up and stick to the mission at hand. That was Heikki, Olympic-caliber athlete, submariner, sailor, and friend.

We were not ready for the loss. There was little about a technology workplace that prepared anyone for tragedy.

The memorial service was held at the Finnish Lutheran Church in Seattle. With Seattle's strong ties to the Nordic region, it was fortunate that he had found this community. There was an enlarged photo on display of Heikki enjoying his beloved boat. The church was filled beyond capacity, and we arranged a satellite broadcast for campus and a memorial gathering after the service. Speaking at church, out of admiration for his work family, I shared an expression that meant so much to him and one we often spoke of as a description of the kind of leader he was. "The sign of a great leader is that when the goals are achieved, everyone says things just happened naturally."

Heikki always said that he took on the mission and "did what needed to get done."

Back at work, everyone slowly began to move forward. Asking ourselves "What Would Heikki Do?" helped keep status mail going out and project communication across the team.

But there was a void to be filled. Heikki held the most critical communication and coordination role on the entire Office team, and we were at the most critical point for the project to come together. Big teams have succession plans, but they almost always assume some period of adjustment.

No one was expecting to do anything other than finish Office11 on plan. Antoine Leblond (Antoine) agreed to take on program management. In the same announcement, Don Gagne (DonGa), from Outlook and NetDocs, moved to lead Office development. It was what needed to be done and we were so fortunate to have a leadership that could adjust. The team continued the work while mourning the loss of a friend. It was most certainly what Heikki would have wanted.

The RTM milestone, a muted one for many, almost exactly a year later was a reminder of Heikki and all he had contributed in his time with us that was cut so short. Everyone thought of Heikki often, but especially on that RTM day knowing how proud he was of the team every time we shipped.

2003-2006

As we approached the launch of the massive Microsoft Office System 2003, it was time to plan a new release and that started by drawing a proverbial line, at least I felt so. We pivoted way too much to enterprise and clearly lost the "personal" in "personal productivity." It was not that we needed to go back to just building features for individual users editing documents, but our entire product was just too enterprise focused. While the product group owns responsibility, the whole company focus on enterprise meant that no matter what we did, as the product filtered through marketing to global sales to subsidiaries it became even more enterprise (as we saw with XML rising to the top of the release positioning, for example.)

As I later told a Microsoft Board Director, betting on enterprise customers is a Faustian bargain—done right and the business is fantastic, but when you do it right products become rigid, complex, and diverge from the end-user. This next release of Office, Office "12" or Office12, was a chance to rethink the complexity and refocus on end-users.

076. BETTING BIG TO FEND OFF COMMODITIZATION

Chasing The Low-End Product

In 1999, Steve Wildstrom, a widely respected BusinessWeek technology journalist, wrote a series of columns postulating a product called "Office Lite."[47] The first appeared June 13, 1999 "Office Lite: Less Would Be More." He wrote one brief column based on a discussion I had with him that spawned a second column and a bit of a letter-writing campaign from readers. It was a classic populist move in the world of tech to solicit readers for their wishes, though usually reserved for the annual "what would be the perfect laptop" column most writers did at the year end.

BusinessWeek printed a few letters but took advantage of the relatively new web site and shared dozens more online. In just about every way the letters showed passion for the concept of a smaller, lighter-weight, more tailored version of Office. What could be better than an Office that was easier to use, consumed fewer system resources, and performed better…and cost less?

Readers of the column in addition to Wildstrom chimed in with what features of Office to remove. Word has no need to support complex page layouts. No need to support embedding spreadsheets in word processor or videos in a presentation. Remove Visual Basic from the apps as that is really for corporates and even if it isn't used it adds complexity no one needs.

One reader provided details on the product in the form of a specification "(1) creating, formatting, saving, and printing a document (2) Creating, formatting, saving, and printing a worksheet and a graph (3) Inserting a graph and an image within a document (4) Creating tables within a document using a worksheet and/or a database (5) Creating and updating a database, and generating a report."

Also important were what features to keep. There should be a full suite of a word processor, spreadsheet, and PowerPoint, much to Wildstrom's surprise. Each of those were deemed essential. The file formats should be compatible with "big" Office. One reader insisted Lite include "free spell/grammar checkers in multiple languages for those of us in Europe who still write occasionally in French, Spanish, and German." And another pointed out "why did you leave Access out of you [sic] suggested suite? I think Access is equally as important to a home user as PowerPoint or Excel."

Also, it should be cheaper. Wildstrom suggested it cost less than $499, though noted the availability of less expensive Office suites.

A common point expressed was who would benefit from Office Lite. Sometimes readers pointed out they would not use it, but they thought it would be better for their kids or retired people, or just non-technical users. We previously discussed the challenge of feedback when it offers an idea that is good for others, but not for the person offering the feedback. That's gracious but almost always a sign that the product is heading for poor reviews. Coincidentally Wildstrom wrote in his positive review of Office 97 that the Office Assistant, Clippy, would be great for other people, just not him.

This column caused quite stir within the Office team especially in marketing. Honestly, it hit a nerve. For many individuals Office had become too much software. It also touched on the fact that the PC itself had become too complicated, too fragile, and too hard to keep working. Many readers used the word "bloat" to describe Office, a word that appeared a half dozen times across the stories and letters. In the next section we will develop a more complete definition, but suffice it to say between too many features, slow, fragile, complicated, and difficult there is an answer to be found. Customers expressing the concept of bloat was hardly new to us. Our own concerns go as far back as the earliest Macintosh applications when we added "Full Menus" and "Short Menus" to reduce the product's perceived overhead.

Reading the letters in detail, one could see they made just about every argument as to why such a product didn't stand a chance in the market. Every person writing in had a different idea of what features should be in such a product and why their features uniquely made sense. Wildstrom included what I shared with him about the use of features in the product relaying "that most people use only a fraction of the features in a program such as Word. But everyone uses a different fraction, so there's no way to design a simplified program with broad appeal." His readers made that very point in their own way.

In my numerous discussions with Wildstrom over these columns (and basically at every meeting) I would point out that we already had "Office Lite"— called Microsoft Works. That was my refrain for years when it came to the need for a low-priced, slimmed down version of Office. In the mass of letters to BusinessWeek someone else, someone with an informed opinion, agreed with me in their letter:

> We'll [sic], you're right to be championing "Office Lite," but you're wrong to be dismissing Microsoft Works for the job. Sure it has many inadequacies, but saying it needs features X, Y, and Z to warrant your recommendation is to set your steps in the direction that led to Office 2000 bloatware.
>
> Peter Norton
> Los Angeles
>
> Norton is a pioneer PC programmer and author of numerous books on PC software.

We offered Works at about $100 and Office SKUs at different price points ranging from about $149 to $499, including Student & Teacher, Small Business, Standard, Professional, Developer, and Enterprise. By most definitions in pricing architectures, we were meeting customers at low, medium, high, and very high prices with products offering different value propositions. It should be apparent, however, there was hardly a consensus among the press and its readers on what an alternative price and value structure might look like.

Microsoft Works was an early success, a genuine hit product for the company. Version 1.0 was released in 1987 and joined the ranks of the wildly popular category called all-in-one or integrated software. The category aimed to take the popular modules of productivity and bundle them into a single, easy-to-use, and low-priced product, usually including a word processor, spreadsheet, and database. Works included a communication module as well.

The basic assertion was, and keep in mind how early in the PC era this takes place, that the full-priced products were too expensive and did too many things (had too many features) and most people needed only a fraction of the product. This was bloat even in the earliest days of computing. Works sold for about half of what a single full-priced product cost and ran on very basic PCs with merely 384K of memory. Works was hugely popular outside the US and was localized into dozens of languages, often a tricky proposition in the days of MS-DOS software. Works was a marvel of engineering built with great passion by a small team, and thus extremely profitable.

In 1991, Microsoft released the first Windows version of Works, for Windows 3.0. Again, this product proved popular, though not as much globally where Windows was a slow burn due to hardware requirements. Works for Windows, or WinWorks as we called it, introduced some of the early toolbars and wizards. It was developed in the Consumer Division, home of those inventions and to product teams entirely focused on the home and student markets. WinWorks also supported OLE (Object Linking and Embedding), the enormously complex to implement capability to include data from other applications inside of documents and even included an early Microsoft drawing program to show off that capability. Microsoft made works available for less than $200 at retail and often for only $10 to PC makers looking to include basic software with a new PC. By 2003, Works included a broad range of software for the home user in addition to the all-in-one product including personal finance, maps of the world and major cities, an encyclopedia, a sophisticated photo editing program (PhotoDraw), and somewhat surprisingly the full and current version of Microsoft Word.

On the surface Microsoft had addressed the classic marketing problem of low-end and high-end with price support at the low-end. We could sell Works to price-sensitive customers and Office to everyone else. With the PC manufacturing channel, we could even tactically go after market share for certain PC models aimed at home and small business customers. Like all good marketers we would only sell Works when we had to, with all marketing and sales efforts aimed at selling Office. Even the Works customer would see opportunities to upgrade to Office. That seemed simple enough. On paper this looked like a great spot to be.

There were two problems. First, Works was not compatible with Office. It was only marginally similar in how the user interface worked and not at all compatible with files created by Office, nor was Office able to read Works files. Why would this matter in a world without networking or email? It didn't. Any given person would just use one or the other and it would be fine to print documents when they were finished with their work. But in our world, the press would ask questions and then make assumptions that all products from the company would interoperate, and by the early 2000s emailing documents was becoming a scenario for many home users. This product limitation led to the eventual inclusion of Word, though not Excel or PowerPoint, in the Works bundle. We failed these tests and too often the product was labeled as incompatible, and in the PC world incompatible is a big blow. Customers expected compatibility from Microsoft.

Second, and this gets to the heart of the matter, people didn't desire the product that did less. They wanted all the bells and whistles of Office. They just didn't want to pay full price, or they didn't have a computer with enough power to run Office. They wanted a more powerful computer and would almost certainly invest in that rather than stop-gap software for their current computer. We had a classic revealed preference problem in customers saying one thing but choosing to take a different action. There was no way around this—customers just wanted more product for less money.

This second point is the marketing challenge everyone with a successful product in software faces at some point.

The natural inclination is to remove some capabilities and charge less. Usually, it is possible to remove features that only a certain customer segment wants (enterprise for example) and that keeps the price low for customers that do not need such features. Today we see this as routine practice where a low-end or even free version of a product is used to upsell to increasingly expensive and feature-rich versions. Again, on the surface this is what we had for varying suites of Office, but we did not have that for the individual applications in Office.

We had a pricing problem. We did not have a product problem in the sense of getting value for the money paid. Customers wanted the value, just not the price. They also wanted the product to be better and sometimes they equated the high price with the reason it was not better, as if a lower price would require less disk space or be easier to use, for example.

Office also faced a competitor with a much lower price, free. Such a competitor is an especially acute problem when that product has a comparable feature set, whether that is real or simply perceived as such. OpenOffice claimed to be compatible and was certainly more compatible than Works, and it also claimed to have the features of full Office. If it was missing features, they promised to add them as soon as possible, just as I personally learned when they changed the product on a tradeshow floor to be more like Microsoft Office.

The scary question for us was would Office be susceptible to defeat in the market by a direct clone. Borland had been successful at making a dent in Lotus 1-2-3 sales and with the relaxed view of copyright law in the courts this seemed a legitimate concern. Still, the technical requirements to acceptably clone Word, Excel, and PowerPoint seemed insurmountable. We knew this because of how much effort it took us to maintain compatibility and document fidelity between our own versions with our own engineers.

In an interesting twist, some enterprise customers equated the low or free price of competitors with low-quality.

In other words, our pricing challenge was not as straightforward when looked at broadly. This mattered because software did not have highly specific distribution channels like cars or mattresses where we could control which channel sold which products.

The legendary author and marketing guru Geoffrey Moore visited Microsoft in the early 1990s to meet with a few of us to talk about Office. This was before Windows 95 and 32-bit computing, before Office had "won." Our minds were on adding features and getting new features to market to compete with the category share leaders that dominated the industry by revenue. The conversation was deeply interesting when I look back, though at the time it was not as relevant to Office as one might have thought.

According to Moore as per his *Crossing the Chasm* framework and book, the PC was still in the early adopter phase. Moore suggested as per the framework that we needed to consider products for specific subsegments of early adopters (legal, financial, consulting, education) providing versions of Office for each of those in succession as we grew the market to later stages of technology adoption. We were worried about price support versus Works, not against a competitor selling a different product specific to bankers or something. Tailoring Office for specific customers, however, was in some way the role of Works, except rather than job title it was skill level or distribution channel. The real mismatch, however, was that we were not struggling to gain adoption with the personal computer. We didn't have a crossing the chasm problem. We just had to wait for people to have enough money to buy a PC and pay for the software. We didn't have a segmentation problem. Everyone wanted Office. We did have a revenue maximization problem. We didn't want a lot of people buying Works.

One problem we did have was software piracy. It was long a bane of Microsoft's as the company was founded on the premise that software should be paid for just like hardware. Piracy of Office had grown astronomically. We estimated that perhaps 1 in 10 PCs paid us for an Office license, but more than half the PCs out there had at least one major Office application. It was technically easy to pirate Office as we did not employ any countermeasures as were common to software products in the 1980s. With the release of Windows XP (Windows too had a significant piracy problem), Microsoft put in place a global software license enforcement program much to the chagrin of tech enthusiasts and early adopters, not to mention small businesses that often bought one copy of a product and just assumed it would work for a workplace with a few PCs. To say this program was met with mixed results would understate the uproar. Some whole countries prohibited the use of anti-piracy measures and others mandated different mechanisms or terms of use. China officials famously lectured many of us (me personally) by applying lessons from the writings of Confucius (always said with erudition), "software is like a book; it is selfish not to share." I never looked up if that was an actual quote, but ministers and vice ministers lectured me enough I took it as such.

The result of high piracy? In many markets, customers simply stuck with the older and easy to pirate version of Office. On trips to markets from Italy to South Africa to China, members of the team would invariably return with a CDROM filled with Office 97 and everything Microsoft made five years ago bought on the street for $5. On a trip to China during the launch of Office 2003, I went to a tech market where I was offered a form to fill out where I picked what software I wanted up to the 650MB limit of a CDROM (Office 97, Windows 98, and so on) and within an hour I received my custom CD for just 20 kuai, less than $2.

Absent Microsoft corporate backing off from anti-piracy, something the field salespeople desperately wanted us to do, the calls for a cheaper version of Office were constant. They weren't quite sure what that would be, but they didn't want people to like it so much they would buy it instead of the Office that carried a sales quota. Many of the subsidiaries would try to make a case that people could not afford software, even though I saw the price of PCs at the market mirror those in the US, or in some markets such as Brazil PC prices were even higher. The issue was there was a way not to pay, not a lack of ability to pay for software. SteveB loved to point out that the computer market was located near an imported car dealership complete with Lamborghini and Ferrari on display.

The PC itself was also under attack for being too expensive. The *One Laptop Per Child* (OLPC) initiative out of the MIT Media Lab started in 2005 to address this concern with the goal of providing an extremely low-priced computer running free software for students in emerging markets. Windows quickly followed with their own effort to build an even cheaper version of Windows. This will not be the last of this challenge for me or the industry.

Given this context, the refrain for a low-end variant of Office had been echoing in Redmond for years but now was reaching almost deafening levels. I didn't really have a choice but to start a project and see where it went. I kicked off a unilateral skunkworks project (without marketing or broad buy-in) to see if we could come up with something that would end this endless discussion. The project even had a code name, *Firefly*. You can always tell when I wasn't wild about something when I gave it a code name. The team needed to go through a process to bring closure once and for all. With most of the effort centered on the user interface and access to features, Julie Larson-Green (JulieLar) led the effort from Office program management where she was now leading the shared user interface team, moving over from FrontPage.

We completely understood how every other product from cars to microwaves to stereos had a cascade of price points for basically the same product. The difference for Office is twofold. First, software is soft, and the marginal cost of more features is zero and customers readily see that. Second, interoperability between price points is key in a networked world and maintaining interoperability when different users can be editing a document with what amount to different tools all at the same time was technically difficult to imagine getting right.

I kicked off project Firefly, which quickly became known as Office Lite, knowing (perhaps that is too strong, I mean assuming) we would go through the exercise of figuring it out only to conclude that no one at the company really wanted it. No one would want to be responsible for releasing a product that was either so bad no one wanted to buy it and the Office brand would get devalued or so good that our enterprise customers would insist on having the Lite version of Office for much less revenue.

The reason I picked a code name was because the mere expression of Office Lite (or Office ES, or Office Prime, or any other marketing moniker) would cause customers to say, "that's the one I want." They would do so by attaching all positive attributes to the product: just the features I need, easier to use, boots and loads faster, takes far fewer system resources, and because of those attributes it is also less buggy and won't crash. There's something about how low-end products always garner catchy names. Sure enough the name "Office Lite" leaked to the press and customers early in this process.

Our new leader for Office marketing was hired from Adobe. They had not only faced the same problem but tried to do something about it. With its PDF product, Adobe had been struggling with the classic strategy of a free viewer and a paid-for product with the ability to create PDF and a better viewer. The problem they faced was that creating PDF was rapidly commoditized and free (this is the topic of a future section in this chapter as well) and few people needed the advanced viewing features, and certainly not for hundreds of dollars. With their flagship Adobe Photoshop product, Adobe had been trying to seed the low-end market with Photoshop Elements (there's that catchy name) side-by-side with Photoshop. This product still exists today, so we can assume it works for them. I'd say it works so well because you never see it being used. Of course I have no data on the real usage and am just speaking anecdotally. This Adobe experience led me to believe that Office would be viewed through this same lens by marketing.

The first step in developing Office Lite would be to go through an exercise where we removed a bunch of features from the product. Doing so technically is not difficult, one would think, but in practice the list of hypothetical problems gets very long very quickly. As an example, someone creates a template in Word that makes a document look a certain way. The document is then sent to someone else who has Word Lite. Can they see the new look? Can they edit the new look? What if they try to modify text within the context of formatting that looks a certain way? How do formulas work in Excel? Does Excel Lite have all the same formulas? What if a spreadsheet with a Pivot Table is sent to an Excel Lite customer, can they pivot it? The list goes on and on.

The fun part of this exercise was just how easy everyone thought it would be. Almost to a person, the first things to be removed for Lite were VBA, Mail Merge in Word, Pivot Tables in Excel, animations in PowerPoint, then circle back to Word and remove features like table of contents and legal citations, track changes/revision marks, and so on. Everyone brainstorming found it easy to make their own list of easy to lose features.

There's a core assumption these features aren't used and so it is easy. That's the problem. Everyone had an easy time removing features they believed they didn't need. How does that reconcile with creating a product that the enterprise customers would *not* want? It doesn't. In the next sections we will dig into the realities of what features are used or not as we design the next release—we had the real-world data on usage. For now, suffice it to say that it is very easy to make a list of features to remove but very difficult to remove any features that cause customers to feel they need the full version of the product. Those are painful decisions.

Some discussions became almost comical. One of my favorite examples had to do with documentation. For years, Office produced weighty tomes of printed books of documentation that more often than not served as ergonomic monitor risers if the end-users even got to see them. With the rise of enterprise agreements, we moved most documentation online. With the internet we were very excited to have always improving documentation available directly from within the product. One of the key differentiators for Office Lite was a proposal that the only documentation be available as a printed book that would come with the product and no online documentation or connection to the web. We no longer had the ability to produce printed documentation, and before I knew it someone in marketing already put out bid proposals to publishers to create the book for us. The cheap to make Office Lite was getting to be more expensive and have a higher bill of materials than the real Office.

One person who was hardcore about what not to remove was BillG. I exchanged mail with him over some of the rumors he heard about Office Lite and he came back to me saying exactly what I predicted he would say, which is we can't remove any platform features, such as VBA. A lesson learned the hard way with platforms is that platforms must be consistent for developers to choose to use them. While it is fine to adorn the platforms differently for various price points, anything a developer might want to use must be in the baseline SKU. Otherwise, they will work around it and either implement something on their own without using the platform or simply not have a feature. That's why every Windows API is in every Windows SKU where developers can always count on them being there, as detailed in the Tablet PC discussion.

Cameron Turner (CameronT) on the product planning team developed a framework for the brainstorming efforts for Office Lite. I gave up calling it Firefly. These goals included: great for creating simple documents, a great viewer for all Office files regardless of where they were created, effective competitive response to low-end competitors, smallest delta from full Office to reach design goals.

The team also developed a view of who the product was not going to be for. Office Lite is not for: group collaboration, data analysts, developers, online communicators (no Outlook), "beginners", or multi-language document creators.

The Office team was long expert at resolving what appear to be impossible to resolve challenges such as shipping on time versus shipping with quality. The Office Lite goals, however, were almost certainly, perhaps mathematically, unsolvable. Even something that to Americans seems simple like not supporting multi-lingual documents, becomes problematic for sales even in neighboring Canada. The most unsolvable constraint was that the product wasn't for beginners. If not for beginners or the home and not for specialists in finance or law, then who was the product for? Who is this broad middle and what are they doing? In this stage of PC expansion, there were tens of millions of customers getting their first PC and first use of Office at work. They were beginners too.

Rumors about Office Lite started making their way around Microsoft. Marketing teams across the company were getting very excited at the prospect of a low-priced Office because for some time they had wanted to have the Office brand associated with their product, but the price was too high. The Windows OEM group, the team responsible for selling Windows to PC makers, wanted nothing more than Office attached to every new PC "socket." They hated selling Works because it was so cheap. OEMs expected Office Lite to be only marginally more than Works. The emerging market teams loved the idea of a cheaper Office.

Then people started to think through the issues and how revenue would suffer. Not just revenue, but the sales quotas carried by each subsidiary and sales segment.

It didn't take long before the Office small business marketing team would come to realize that if every Dell Small Business PC came with Office Lite presumably because the OEM team was successful, they'd never make their numbers for selling the Office Small Business SKU. There weren't enough small business PCs to make it up in volume.

The MSN, Microsoft Network, team was working hard to develop a paid offering because the advertising business was not yet large enough to sustain the investment we were making, recalling the pressures mounting on the investment businesses from the previous chapter. They were very excited about being able to bundle Office Lite with a new MSN subscription. We had not yet arrived at a price, but it was obvious that like OEM they though it would add $1 or $2 to the monthly subscription, which was a Works level of pricing, not Office.

Then the other shoe started to drop. Not just the BillG shoe but the global enterprise field. Suddenly my inbox was filled with subject lines "Rumors about Office Lite," "Concerns about Office Lite," "Office revenue goals and Lite." These emails expressed incredible reservations about the potential for tanking the existing business in favor of a product that, by knowing only the name, the salespeople thought was too desirable for too low a price. My good friends in MSKK (Microsoft Japan) sent me a note directly stating they decided not to offer Office Lite in their market. They were so against the idea they just presumptively closed off any discussion in the most non-Japanese way I could imagine.

Problems such as these could be solved. Many businesses solve them all the time. Cars have low end models with a magical suggested retail price, but they do a fantastic job constraining supply of that model. Consumer electronics including PCs almost always have good, better, best, but these are often easily distinguished based on capacity measures including memory, watts, screen size and by distribution or where the products are sold. Imagine if Word Lite limited documents to 10 pages or Excel Lite had row and column limits.

Software, especially when exchanging data files and documents in a network, do not lend themselves to these artificial constraints. Those that grew up with IBM mainframes know the frustration of IBM upgrades when customers would request a higher-priced hardware upgrade and a tech would show up and simply crack open the case and turn a screw to enable the upgrade costing thousands of dollars per month. This didn't really happen, but the stories were legendary.

Unlike these other products we were also squeezed at the high end. Office for enterprise customers is designed to be a bundle with everything we sell. As discussed with the addition of Outlook, SharePoint, OneNote, and InfoPath, there was no support for adding more expensive enterprise "bits." Today many cloud software applications save enterprise capabilities such as security and management for the high-priced (or just priced) SKUs. With Office, 80% or more of the revenue was already coming from the enterprise SKU. There was no appetite to move up with higher prices, which could make the lowest priced SKUs more price friendly.

The process of planning the SKUs for Office 2003 was an exercise in chasing our own tails, so much so that we spent a significant amount of engineering time to create a push-button feature that enabled the production of a new SKU (a different combination of the 11 different applications) to be created without additional code or testing. This came in handy as the Office System 2003 Editions were rolled out with seven different SKUs.

We started to toy with the idea of being able to dynamically enable or disable different features in this same way so we could make progress on whether Office Lite was even possible. At the plumbing level this was not difficult but with thousands of features and product design elements such as toolbars that depend on features existing, it was not practical.

The design started to go from brainstorming to an actual product offering in a table form. Suddenly, Office Lite did not look so good. After all the sessions over features to remove, the desire to remove features faded away. The team created a table comparing the proposed Office Lite product to competitors. The resulting table was a disaster. It looked like one of those magazine reviews where a product gets clobbered for missing all the checkboxes. After getting feedback from the subsidiaries and hearing their lack of desire to even offer Office Lite, the risk of the subs failing to make their numbers and blaming Office Lite became real. The reality that Office Lite would be a non-competitive product versus our free competitor sucked all the excitement out of the potential offering. It didn't matter what we removed from the product, OpenOffice could just add it to their product, and charge nothing.

Office Lite was dead. Again. We had to win in the market with a better product that cost more. We had the product people wanted and we needed to sell it harder if that's what it took. Today we know we had product-market fit and a little thing like pricing was not going to be our biggest problem. By comparison, the Office price of $499 for a perpetual (runs forever) license of Office or the roughly $150-200/year for an enterprise 3-year agreement is comparable to an Office 365 today that can easily cost an enterprise more than $650/year per license, though Microsoft is running Exchange and SharePoint in the cloud in these plans.

What was not dead, however, was what got us talking about Office Lite in the first place. The customer concerns were not really about price. Price was a proxy for bloat. We needed to address bloat. We tried before but now it was critical.

What the heck does bloat mean?

077. WHAT IS SOFTWARE BLOAT, REALLY?

In 2001, Jon Stewart, the legendary host of *The Daily Show* on Comedy Central, performed a hilarious and brutal takedown of a redesign of CNN's *Headline News* show. In the segment, he took to task the departure from the traditional talking head, as epitomized by Walter Cronkite and the evening news and Jon Stewart. He mocked Generation Y, now called Millennials, for favoring a seeming onslaught of disparate information at once rather than one camera and a single story at a time. Stewart referred to a new look that " . . offers a great way to find out everything without the pressure of retaining anything."

The punchline, almost 20 years later, is that the redesign Stewart mocked became standard across every medium, web, broadcast, cable, Bloomberg, YouTube, and today's phone apps. We can bemoan such a change or accept the fact that people prefer consuming information differently than they did a generation earlier. The reality back in 2001 was that people were leaving TV news in droves in favor of on-demand, concise, and always available internet-based news displayed on crowded home pages.

Around the same time, the TV show *24* was considered both a breakthrough and critically panned for a similar departure from the tradition. The show was fast paced, had a complex narrative, and featured dozens of characters moving in and out of each other's story lines. Critics said the narrative was overly complex. The same generational change was afoot, and the MTV Generation was raised on fast-paced video, clipped dialog, and rapid cutting between scenes. To this new audience, *24* seemed entirely consumable. The single-camera sitcom was in its twilight.

Design, whether functional or aesthetic, is a product of the context of the times. When contexts change—meaning the people and their needs and the available tools and technologies—designs need to change as well.

File, Edit, View, Insert, Tools, Window, Help.

Like the catchy lyrics to a well-worn pop song, in Office we knew the top-level menus appearing consistently in each of the applications. We spent almost 10 years convincing, cajoling, and aligning each other around these words as though they were carved in stone. In fact, these words were the product of compromise—first a compromise between Microsoft and Apple on the original Macintosh applications and then a compromise between our new Windows applications and Macintosh versions. Finally, there was a compromise across Office to reach consistency. As with many compromises, no one was particularly happy with the result and there were plenty of exceptions, but nobody was all that unhappy either.

It wasn't perfect, but it was our menu structure and our customers liked it. So much so, it was widely emulated across the industry. That made it carved in stone. It was like so many arbitrary design choices that somehow develop a lore of great design, like QWERTY keyboards or P-R-N-D in a car.

While rather adaptable creatures, humans tend to react poorly to change imposed upon them—a new stoplight, a new layout for a website, or the most heinous of all modern changes, a new software user interface for an existing product. Unexpected or imposed changes are viewed at best as arbitrary and at worst as bad, incredibly bad. It is exceedingly rare in the world of software to see existing users embrace major changes to mature products.

Consider something that most of us would today think of as rather benign, a change in the layout and typography of a print-based magazine. Magazines would devote a few pages explaining the design and rationale or perhaps even TV commercials as The Economist did with their 2001 redesign. Such "bold" (they always called them bold) redesigns would often become the subject of weeks of letters to the editor complaining about the failings of the effort and calling for a return to the old design, followed by the inevitable subscription cancellations.

Even if a product makes it through a big change, there often remains an undercurrent harkening back to the good old days for a long time. Whether it is simply conservatism or as some express a true loss of efficiency or effectiveness with a product, change is hardly ever free of controversy.

Yet, we live in a constant state of change. What is it that separates the changes that cause an uproar from the changes that happen with little notice? Technology is changing all around. Consumer behavior and work norms are regularly evolving. Competitors with new perspectives arise frequently. Often competitors with a fancy new design might even compete directly with a small portion of a larger established product with a tired design. Perhaps the new product even garners outsized attention because of that new design, less so than the features it brings. Failing to change remains the biggest mistake technology companies can make.

And as I'd soon learn, failing to change correctly is the second biggest mistake technology companies make. There are no rule books or guidelines that govern how much a product can change and when. There are many books telling you if you don't change, you're doomed. There are also a lot of books telling stories of changes going haywire. Note to readers, this work is both of those.

Office became a bit like the old evening news, not so much Cronkite's CBS but more like CNN. It was ubiquitous. It was reliable and predictable. It did not draw much attention to itself. Younger people knew about it but didn't talk about it the way older people did. It was comfortable.

Still, each release was more successful financially than the previous and rated higher in customer satisfaction. Our customer base grew, and they continued to be happier with each release. The Office brand anchored several important traits of Microsoft representing "easy to use" and "professional."

But comments about bloat continued unabated. Was it insider talk? Were people overall happy and the beltway of tech journalism was searching for something, anything at all, to criticize in the face of success? How could customers be so satisfied, and the business be growing if we were making increasingly bloated products? We theorized that analysts, reviewers, and reporters, those most typically calling out bloat, were users of a small subset of Office compared to typical knowledge workers. One reviewer of a major national outlet would not review Excel because of the view that most people didn't need a spreadsheet.

As we discussed in creating Office Lite, a pervasive view existed that the product suffered in usability and quality because it had too many features. Specifically, there were too many features for how any individual said they used the product. Too many features lead to a complex experience and bugs, so went the theory.

Another theory was that PCs, not just Office, were becoming increasingly fragile and flaky. Bloat might be a PC problem and the ubiquity of Office simply an easy way to express the problem.

Three factors contributed to a feeling of a declining PC experience—sort of like a car that needed a tune-up to get rid of the engine noises, reduce the squishiness in the ride, and improve performance.

First, PCs were decreasingly interesting to purchase. The newest and best PCs lacked the excitement, and budget, that made consumers want to rush out to buy a new one. The pace of improvement in hardware arguably slowed, but so did the pace of software. By 2004, we were three years into Windows XP with no new release of Windows in sight. Longhorn was perennially under development. Without a new Windows, the need for a new PC was minimal and certainly not worth the pain of moving files and programs to a new computer. It is important to note that buying a new PC was the fastest way to reset the PC experience, cleaning out all the gunk. Without a PC purchase, such a spring cleaning was technically impossible.

Second, the rise of the internet turned everyone into a software downloader. Every first Tuesday of the month Microsoft sent updates to hundreds of millions of PCs to keep them secure—product changes that closed holes that could be exploited by malware and viruses. The creation of Patch Tuesday, as it was called colloquially, was rooted in *Trustworthy Computing* and was a major innovation in system security and reliability. The seemingly constant stream of product updates only served to emphasize the fragility of the PC. The required and poorly timed reboots wasted time or worse and left a bad impression of PC reliability while also providing great explanations for a PC slowing down or failing to restart.

Users were downloading software constantly as well. It wasn't only the next version of a browser that remained interesting but the latest media player software, software to control the newest device to plug into a PC, utilities making the aging Windows XP easier to use, and more. From Napster to BitTorrent to Adobe Acrobat, plus an onslaught of games, there was an endless stream of software to download. Software installed on Windows had free reign over the system. Installed software could interfere with performance, memory usage, battery life, or even conflict with other previously installed programs causing all sorts of mysterious problems.

Tech enthusiasts had names for these problems. *DLL hell* referenced programs that failed to run if the wrong version of a file known as a DLL existed on the PC. *Bit rot* was the slow decay of the overall system. My favorite was *registry corruption* which was a mostly meaningless term referring to the slowing performance and potential fragility of a specific part of the operating system due to adding too many programs with too many settings. These conditions led to a new class of software designed to clean PCs, freshen them up, and recondition them. But these utilities only further exacerbated any problems and served to reinforce and accelerate the problems that PCs faced over time.

Finally, PCs in the enterprise were locked down by system administrators with an arsenal of software to secure the machines. These included firewalls, antivirus, virtual private networking (VPN), not to mention intrusive scans and analyses of the PC, slowing down every work session, especially just logging on. The fragility and risk to typical users on PCs created the need for more software, ever more invasive software, to mitigate those risks.

A typical office worker faced a choice of a lethargic PC at work with disabled capabilities or a PC at home that became increasingly flaky as members of a household continued to pile on an assortment of downloaded software.

As real as all of these were, none were relevant to Office which by and large was well-behaved. We needed to dig deeper. Bloat was our biggest competitive problem. Office still lacked a major competitor, but increasingly the cost and heft of Office were viewed as liabilities or targets. StarOffice was free and continued to be an annoyance. Piracy of older Office was far more of a competitor, and by virtue of its age was more fragile and prone to viruses and security problems thus worsening the perception of Office.

Startups were beginning to experiment with the latest browsers and the technology pioneered by Microsoft known as AJAX—a style of programming web pages so they behaved more like a typical Windows program with interactivity but with all the benefits of simply being a web page in a browser. Across the web there were startups building simple word processors and drawing programs this way, and even a few spreadsheets and presentation programs. Intuit (makers of Quicken) shipped a browser-based database to compete with Microsoft Access called QuickBase that won an editor's choice for workgroup software. Microsoft invented AJAX for Outlook Web Access, but the depth of features made it useful for only occasional mail not the all-day transaction processing style of usage in Outlook. AJAX seemed far off for building a full-fledged productivity tool. Nevertheless, Office was investing heavily in making portions of the product browser-native, such as pivot tables in Excel and databases in Access, in addition to Word and PowerPoint documents.

The question in the air and among tech elites was chilling: Was Office finished and were the alternatives to Office *good enough*? This phrase good enough drove me crazy. It was as though there was something about productivity software that people should just settle for what gets enough of the job done today. Like a middle-aged person fighting off what seemed to be inevitable weight-gain was it slowing metabolism or was there actually a change in behavior? I used to ask rhetorically, "is Word (fill in the version) the peak achievement for humankind when it comes to writing?"

The snide comments about bloat were getting old.

The internet only served to magnify what used to only surface in a review. Along with terms like *MicroSloth*, *Micro$oft*, and *Windoze*, every time a tech writer mentioned Office, positive or not, a chorus of bloatware filled the comments section or as we saw old fashioned letters to the editor.

Bloat was an amorphous concept with numerous manifestations. We needed to get to some actionable definition if we were to make progress—the heart and soul of the brand was at stake.

In spite of bloat, we heard endless requests for new features. At one point we compiled the most recent requests and something like 90% of them were features already in the product. Ouch.

What really got under our collective skin was the constant whine that Office had too many features, most of them unused. We worked hard on all those features and every one of them was traced to solving some problem customers asked about. At least that is what we'd tell ourselves.

This bugged us because the data was entirely conclusive: Most of Office was used. But no one person used the entire product. As if to emphasize this point, most people didn't know or care what buttons they clicked on or menus they chose so long as it was working for them—and that meant when asked, "Did you use X?" most people couldn't recall. To a skeptical press or IT manager (and they all were) that meant unused features.

We measured usage for a decade, first with the laborious and entirely manual process of the instrumented version described earlier. With the arrival of the internet and Watson technology, we extended the instrumented product to every Office customer, everywhere. Enabling the telemetry of the product was via opt-in only, totally anonymous, and no identifiable information was collected. Several data points were recorded: what commands were used; if a command was invoked by a keyboard shortcut, menu, or toolbar; how long an operation took; and, importantly, what sequences of commands were executed. Things we guessed at 15 years earlier were knowable in what could be called a census of usage. While some people didn't opt in, a large enough majority of users (meaning an unbiased and large sample of the population) provided us with data upon which to decide how to evolve the product.

We called the extensions of Watson (previously used for crashes and system hangs) to usage data Software Quality Monitoring (SQM), or "skwim." SQM was the buzz of the hallway and became the *linqua franca* of the program management team. SQM was how we settled debates over who used what, how much, and what was most important. The insights gained from SQM were as exhaustive as the volumes of charts, tables, and graphs that filled our collective inboxes.

Decades later, the idea of using data to design products is a well-understood approach. At the turn of the millennium, it was new and radical, and a strategic advantage. We focused on using data to figure out how to get things done faster and with fewer clicks. Web sites were using data to figure out how to get people to buy more online, read certain articles, or to click on advertisements. Here we were using data to help people use the product less.

What we were learning with SQM, however, was that people were futzing a great deal with Office. While the most common commands were the obvious (Print, Save, Copy, Paste, Bold, and a few others), with astonishing frequency users were hitting Undo, Redo, Undo sequences trying to figure out how something might work. Seemingly common operations like creating a chart in Excel or a table in Word were tiresome and endless sequences of trial and error. A trivial task in PowerPoint, such as aligning two shapes in a drawing, was done by nudging with arrow keys and eyeing the result, rather than using the built-in alignment tools that were a few (too many) clicks away.

We called the futzing document debugging, and it created a frustration that the product was powerful yet overwhelming. People believed a specific result was achievable but getting from point A to B seemed impossible or unlearnable. The idea that documents were being debugged mirrored the complex dialog boxes for adjusting formatting. These user interface elements had incredible series of buttons, measurements, and options available with no indication of what to use when. The picture positioning dialog in Word featured a dizzying array of horizonal and vertical alignments with many options always greyed out, and no simple way to indicate a desire to stop moving everything around so much.

There were routine offenders like trying to fix the spacing between paragraphs or position an image in Word, or the impossibility of altering a chart in Excel. The mere mention of bullets and numbering would be followed invariably by a groan. Arguably, the worst offenders were the infrequently used idioms: creating labels used for holiday cards or the one time when a table called for alternating bands of shading in rows or columns. Inevitably, a person sat there looking at the screen trying to recall how they did it the year before.

None of this was new. A decade earlier, I was taking notes at a planning offsite with the Systems team. The laptop I was using was connected to a projector so everyone on the team could see the notes. In a quick sequence of keys, I created a blank page, a heading, and then followed that with subcategories and bullets. I didn't leave the keyboard. My breakout group watching me insisted on knowing what sorcery I conjured to create an outline in such a way. That was typical for anyone skilled in Office.

Every plane trip was a usability test opportunity for Office. Watching a seatmate analyze sales in Excel while simultaneously using a calculator was typical—and spectacularly difficult to watch. The daily work of using Office to create great-looking documents was filled with moments of, "If I could only figure out how." A common task for many, something like a product description page with a photo with text flowing, was impossibly confounding.

The specific user interface for these and other scenarios were an array of options, terms, and choices that are meaningless at best and destructive at worst. Even finding the right place to make a change was a leap in logic for typical users who did not have the benefit of software design expertise or the constraint of just trying to figure out where to squeeze it into the product. Offenders such as the paragraph formatting or picture layout in Word or the Excel cell format options appear to most people to have the same level of complexity seen in the cockpit of an airplane.

It was as painful for us as it was for customers. We sincerely believed we made things easier over the years. We had come a long way since the first reviews of Word 1.0 for MS-DOS that called it "difficult to use." We came to realize that after a decade, our user interface mapped directly to the implementation of the product—literally the data structures and structure of the code—and not to the results that a person was aiming to achieve. This was incredibly important for us to internalize.

It was not as though we were the first people to stumble upon the idea of making computers easy to use. It was more that after a good run of nearly two decades of trying to make products using a graphical interface easier, we needed a new approach. The irony was that the graphical interface itself, with its friendly mouse and menus, was supposed to finally make computers easier to use. Instead, more features and capabilities went underutilized and over time no one was around to remember just how impossible to use early software really was.

The earliest days of the graphical interface and the pioneering belief of Office was that consistency was the fastest path to easy. This was especially the case because Office was rooted in a collection of historically different applications. If a customer invested the time in learning one module of Office, then consistency made it easier to learn the next, and the one after that. An entire generation of reviews and industry analysis (and even my competitive analysis of Lotus SmartSuite) dove deep into consistency as a positive benefit. When computers were new to the world, it might have been that consistency felt safe and easy. Even IBM documented a consistent interface for the OS/2 operating system called Common User Access (CUA) that was to span mainframes to PCs, with a rack of design books for developers to follow. They did not.

The internet changed this for everyone by being wildly inconsistent. The web quickly evolved to a cacophony of user interfaces. The text and pictures, with blue links to navigate to the web, transformed into an environment as diverse as a stack of Gen-X magazines. The important lesson for us was that people didn't notice. Yes, there were sites that were difficult and sites that were easy, but people adapted to adapting. No powers were calling for a standard interface for the internet. As the essayist Ralph Waldo Emerson said, a "foolish consistency is the hobgoblin of little minds." This saying was used in an influential academic paper on the pros and cons of user interface consistency that appeared in 1989. Several times as a program manager I made copies of this paper and distributed it.[48]

While the Office Assistant was the last major attempt and failure to make software easier, by Office 2003 the product was filled with a series of widgets and affordances designed to surface features in a more helpful manner. Office became a stage for every designer and program manager idea to make things easier at a micro-level, one addition at a time. What started off as something simple, like keyboard shortcuts and dialog boxes, ballooned into context menus, wizards, panes, and toolbars, all customizable, floating, docking, and resizable. The next section will detail some of this history.

Bloat wasn't that products did too much. The marginal cost—in dollars, memory, disk space, or vague notions of complexity—was not bloat. We tried reducing bloat by hiding features as discussed previously, but that only added to the mystery of the product. Mac, Windows, and Office all went through periods of "simple means fewer" and tried mechanisms such as short menus, simple mode, or adaptive toolbars. But that frustrated or confused people. No one really wanted to use a simple mode and there was always one command missing that was needed, so simple mode became a complicated way to do that one thing that made someone's work unique.

We began to consider that bloat was the inability to feel mastery of a product, knowing that the product was capable of something while seemingly impossible to figure out how to make it do that something.

Two important lessons from the product planning and research team solidified our collective view of bloat and formed the foundation of designs.

The first lesson emerged from sifting through usage data. Cameron Turner (CameronT) and others studied the depth and breadth of usage of PCs, such as how many programs and how often for each, and also features within Office, such as which features were used. CameronT was an early PowerPoint program manager hired from Stanford who later left Microsoft to start a company focused on analyzing software usage, long before data science was a hot topic.

Watson crash reports trained the team well to work with the 80/20 rule, and Cameron applied this same analysis to features and commands used across Office programs. Looking at features used by everyone (those who opted-in to anonymous telemetry), 80 percent of the users shared only two commands, Copy and Paste. Said a different way, Copy and Paste were the only commands used by 80 percent of users. In other words, even at the most basic level people used the products in different ways, which was counterintuitive for most observers. At the same time, there were many commands that most people used such as Copy, Paste, Save, and Print. Even then, some commands were not used by even a majority of users, such as Open from the File menu, indicating that a good deal of work happened by opening email attachments or from folders on the desktop. When critics generalized about feature usage in Office, we learned they were almost always wrong.

Importantly, and also counterintuitively, nearly all the commands in the product were used by at least someone somewhere. There was not a lot of dead weight in the product, even accounting for accidental usage or the random case where it was clear a given customer was trying every single thing.

The histogram of usage was steep. There was a small set of commands that represented 80 percent or more clicks and a long Pareto tail for the thousands of other commands.

This second point was obvious to those on the front lines with customers—technical account managers, customer support, and our own sustained engineering teams. Routinely we saw what most would call esoteric use.

The breadth of usage was a major selling point of the product as well. At the high level, while someone might not create a spreadsheet model, that same person might receive one in email. At a deeper level, most in a company might not use a feature such as Track Changes (or Redlining) in Word. But their lawyer would. And contracts or legal letters might arrive via email for review. Rarely used features became part of the work of others. This network of usage was a key advantage of Office and a significant reason behind our ability to win corporate-wide enterprise agreements.

Just as the crash data became an obsession with development and testing, the SQM usage data became an obsession with the designers of our products. In fact, developers also loved SQM data. It gave them a way to push back on program management when they thought spending energy on a feature was a low-yield effort.

The second lesson was about how an individual experienced Office. In parallel, Tim Briggs (TBriggs) was one of the early user researchers to join the Office research team. He began to employ (then) sophisticated eye-tracking studies with volunteer test subjects in our labs. In eye-tracking studies, the test subjects sat in front of a PC and performed a series of typical scenarios. Special cameras were trained on their eyes monitoring where on the screen they looked. A program manager or designer watching the test saw a typical PC screen with Word or Excel running and a little dot flying around the screen representing the subject's eye focus. The test software drew tracking lines, like a route across the screen, and compiled statistics on the amount of movement, total gaze time, or even how much a subject seemed to look around trying to find something—rocket science at the time.

The results of this technique on Office 2003 were shocking. For basic tasks, if people did not know what to do, they scanned the entire screen in a seemingly random pattern, often for many seconds. They played hide-and-seek with menus and toolbars as they searched for something. The test software generated a heat map, a color-coded view of the computer screen showing where the subject looked most frequently—deep red for the hot areas looked at the most all the way to blue where subjects looked the least. The Office 2003 screen looked like a sea of solid red across the main toolbars and menus. Our test subjects looked everywhere for a long time.

The user interface carefully crafted over a decade was in no way helpful. It was bloated.

Ages ago in ancient Microsoft history there was a debate on the original apps team about what it means for something to be a bug. Is it a crash? Is it data loss? Is it a typo in an error message and so on? Out of that was created a notion of bug severity, a measure for how serious a bug might be from losing all data all the way to simple cosmetic issues. However, when it came to talking about bugs with product support or ultimately customers the definition of a bug was very simple "a bug is any time the software does not do what a customer expects." This definition created a discipline of documenting everything reported about the product and always making sure every issue was looked at, even if a code change did not result. The key lesson was how helpful an expansive definition was.

In past experiences with bloat, we only focused on two measures. First, we tried to reduce the user interface surface area by simply hiding commands behind context menus or full/short menus or even toolbars to some degree. Second, we spent countless cycles reducing the amount of disk space and memory consumed by Office to reduce the notion that Office was big or slow.

These are both bloat but that is a narrow and technical definition, one that is engineering focused and not particularly useful to customers. It didn't really matter if the product used too much memory or disk space, as those seemed like symptoms of the whole computing experience.

In the eyes of customers in practice, bloat comes from the fact (using that word on purpose) that Office does so many things that customers just assume the product can do whatever they need it to do. Despite that fact, customers have no idea how to make the product do what they need. This feeling of helplessness that leads to frustration is what it means to deliver a bloated product. It did not matter how many ease-of-use features we added, all that did was compound the problem of too many placers to click. What good is a new wizard or task pane if a person has no idea how to access that or if accessing it will yield the desired result.

Bloat is owning a product that you cannot master. No one felt they could master Office.

How is it that Office managed to get to this point and when did it become a problem?

078. A TOUR OF "YE OLDE MUSEUM OF OFFICE PAST"

How did we get to Office 2003 with a menu bar, toolbars, context menus, keyboard shortcuts, task panes, dialog boxes (with tabs), widgets, buttons, and pop-up commands?

We got here by solving customer problems. We got here by making the product easier to use. We got here by listening to the market. We got here by winning reviews. It was that simple.

Or was it?

It is easy to see what happened in hindsight. We added new features, one after another. To make features easier to discover and use, we added additional user interface. Layer after layer, or solution after solution, we built up an array of user interface elements that when looked at in totality created bloat. But it is just so easy to say that in hindsight.

One simple observation was that to win in the market when Microsoft started making applications, we had to win reviews. These reviews meant everything in a world with many competitors, retail distribution, and little word of mouth and no internet. Reviews were giant checklists of features. For example, *Software Digest* compiled yearly reviews of all products in market. The 1984/5 edition of their 200-page book on just word processors had a 4-page fold-out checklist of 50 features and a dozen abstract criteria. Fail any of those and the overall score sank. A losing score meant no ability to advertise winning, no recommendations from salespeople, and then the next release and review started in a hole. So, for a decade we made sure to always have those features. There was no choice other than to win reviews. And we did.

When should we have stopped and taken a first principles approach? When would the upside have exceeded the potential downside? When would the market and reviews have tolerated a big change? What if the market rejected a solution we tried? We would have reverted to the old way and delayed addressing bloat for how long, another decade? It drove me bonkers when people thought bloat was obviously caused by too many features. It also drove me bonkers when those that should know better would so quickly conclude that we were making things worse by winning reviews.

There is no easy answer to asking when the right time is to make a wholesale change in a product. Anyone in product development saying it is obvious hasn't really lived through the risk of making a bad choice or is simply applying hindsight.

Innovator's dilemma and disruption make it seem so easy to identify and act at the right moment. They also make it so easy to make fun of the leaders who are terrified, I mean literally shaking scared, to make a dramatic change to a product. No one ever gets fired right away for not making a big change. Many people get fired right away for making a big change at the wrong time. The worst part? So many big changes are eventually proven correct over time.

In the case of evolving Office, we were going so fast cranking out releases no one stopped to ask anything big. Customers were buying our product as fast as we could press new CDROMs, so to speak. We were winning reviews. Our biggest competitor was ourselves. We were so ubiquitous that we were punchlines on everything from David Letterman to Saturday Night Live to Dilbert.

Then suddenly, we were boring, bloated, and not particularly interesting. So much so that a buggy, poorly implemented, sort-of clone became a symbol of everything we had apparently done wrong. The world was saying that StarOffice was good enough. Ugh. Our sales, however, were not dented even the slightest. But could they be? We did lose that deal in one city in Germany. StarOffice was a German company so maybe it wasn't so bad. Then there was a medium-sized US government agency loss. When do you panic when something like this happens? There's no playbook.

Hemingway wrote in *The Sun Also Rises*:

> *"How did you go bankrupt?" Bill asked.*
>
> *"Two ways," Mike said. "Gradually and then suddenly."*

We became bloated gradually, and then suddenly it was too much. The product was collapsing under its own weight.

It was time to revisit from first principles everything we'd done and ask why. And to come up with a better approach, a wholesale reinvention.

The aim of this section is to briefly cover the history of those innovations that got us here so that we have the necessary context in the next sections on the design of Office12. When it came to telling the story of Office12 once he showed it to customers, Jensen Harris (JensenH) dubbed this his tour of "Ye Olde Museum of Office Past." Please join us on a tour.

Comparing a typical command in Office from the time it was introduced to a release decades later is a great lesson in the compounding complexity of products. Making text bold debuted in Microsoft Word 1.0 for MS-DOS in 1983. Text was made bold simply by selecting the text (actually, it wasn't simple at all since few had a mouse, but I digress), hitting the escape key, the letter F for format, the letter C for character, and finally the letter B for bold. For those with a fancy monitor, which not everyone had at the time, the text became bold on the screen. Choices at each step were limited to approximately five.

Commands also had keyboard shortcuts from before the mouse as an affordance for touch typists. Early keyboard shortcuts were simple, like using INS(ert) key to copy text from the scrap, the clipboard. WordPerfect, and other early MS-DOS apps, devised schemes that were nearly impossible to memorize. Most people had some sort of cheat sheet nearby or keyboard overlay to help remind them of keyboard sequences. Lotus 1-2-3 had a highly structured command architecture known as slash commands as navigating the character-based menus began by striking the forward-slash key for example, to open a file /WFR for slash, (W)orksheet menu, (F)ile menu, (R)etrieve command. Competitively, the two behemoths in productivity software of the MS-DOS era, WordPerfect and Lotus, arguably clung to their keyboard methods while the industry shifted to the graphical interface, even maintaining compatibility with those keystrokes during the rise of the mouse and standardized menus.

Macintosh, with menus and a mouse (and later Windows), aimed to simplify all this. In Microsoft's Word 1.0 for Macintosh, text was selected with a mouse and Bold was chosen from the Character menu, like what Apple did in their MacWrite 1.0. MacWrite had about 35 menu commands in total. Menus were mostly a direct mapping of the features to the product code. The whole product could be described by showing screenshots of all the menus in a two-page magazine spread as *Popular Computing* did in 1984 when Macintosh was launched.

Over time more and more formatting options were added: subscript, superscript, underline, different fonts, color, and so on. Excel was even more complicated because it supported formatting cells as dates or currencies, plus single underline, double underline, accounting underline, and more. This was great—we listened to customers, observed what they were trying to do in the real world, took advantage of new hardware, such as laser printers, color ink-jet printers, and fancy screens, and were adding features like mad. Soon, though, the menus got too long for even basic formatting.

Microsoft's early Macintosh applications introduced dialog boxes, which were windows that popped up and showed all the formatting options. This was inconvenient for routine formats, so the menus had a mixture of common commands like Bold and Italic, and then a menu to "bring up that complicated dialog box." This was the start of hide-and-seek with features.

Excel realized these challenges about the same time Microsoft Publisher did and created toolbars. There's a history of debate over toolbars—what is considered one, and which team or even company invented them. Many on the Excel team were hardcore about their version of the story. Toolbars were used for common commands, like Bold and Italic, as well as Print, Save, and Copy. In 1990, the front of the Excel 3.0 box and associated advertising displayed giant toolbar with buttons for Bold and Italic. Toolbars were such a big deal. Eventually, toolbars were so popular everyone wanted their favorite commands on them, so we created more toolbars and made it easy to rearrange the buttons and hide/show different toolbars.

Under development at the same time as Excel 3.0 was Word for Windows 1.0, Microsoft's first word processor for Windows. I'm omitting the venerable Microsoft Write included with Windows, which by the standards of MacWrite was every bit a word processor. Word for Windows also had toolbars, two of them, and a graphical ribbon which was the defining user interface element in word processors, owing to the skeuomorphic interpretation of the margin scale of a Selectric typewriter. Word 1.0 also fit on a screen 85% the size of today's HD television.

Word 2.0 released in 1991 nearly doubled the number of buttons on the toolbars but maintained the same layout and screen dimensions. While each iteration showed substantial gains, the transition from Word 1.0 to 2.0 marked a move from character to paragraph and document-level operations in the main user interface. There were now buttons for inserting tables, columns, charts, and graphics/shapes. The addition of inserting charts, for example, represented the rise of Office-wide technology connecting the applications which was strategically important even if not every customer used the features. Each of these features represented more than single attributes on a character. For example, adding a numbered list encompassed indenting the paragraph, an automatic number, hanging indent for multiple lines, and spacing after the list. These steps could have been executed manually but getting them right each time was error prone, assuming one could get it right the first time. As each of these features were more complex, Word introduced dialog boxes that had buttons on them to summon further dialog boxes, or nested dialogs. This really led to the creation of "where is that?" within the user interface. Designers and program managers worked enormously hard to position choices and options within these nested dialogs, but no user maintained this level of conceptual knowledge of the product. What was the problem we were solving? There was literally nowhere to put all the new features. Menus and toolbars were constrained by working on screen resolutions typified by 15" CRT monitors or first-generation laptops.

By Word 6.0 the race was on. The version number skipped from 2.0 to align with the ongoing MS-DOS version of Word which accelerated its version number to align with share leader WordPerfect—yes that's how the industry worked. Word 6.0 was a breakthrough product, even more so when brought together with Excel 5.0 and PowerPoint 4. as Office 4 in 1994. At that time, Office 4 was a monster of a product as no company had competitive products in all the major categories. Within the categories each Office application was at least tied with the nearest competitor. Office 4 was the last release entirely designed for individuals as the product was quickly becoming a standard business purchase.

That said from a design perspective, the relative heft was obvious. Word 6.0 added 6 additional toolbars and a host of new user interface affordances for accessing commands, while also increasing the baseline screen size by 25%. Word (and Excel and PowerPoint) added right-click contextual menus, tooltips, tabbed dialog boxes (a welcome refinement of the nested dialog), toolbars on bottom of screen, and wizards. What was already a difficult to master set of commands accessible by one action (point and click) became acts of hunting and discovery. Tooltips, helpful text explaining what a graphical toolbar button did, popped up when the mouse was hovered over a button. Some toolbars only appeared when invoking certain features, though they didn't always go away.

Right-click context menus are worthy of some historic context. Paul Allen (PaulA) Microsoft's co-founder was a huge fan of the right-click, drawing his inspiration from the original Xerox Smalltalk when he created the first Microsoft Mouse with two buttons. Steve Jobs rejected two buttons in favor of a simpler Macintosh mouse, and for years bemoaned the use of the secret Ctrl+click added to Office applications, simulating right click. Windows had not entirely caught up with its use of right-click but with Office 4, Apps added right-click with abandon. With right-click, relevant commands for a character, a selection, a picture or even a paragraph appeared by right-clicking the selected object. The laudable goal of these commands was that by carefully curating the user-interface the right commands would be available and there would be no need to cruise around the product to figure out what might work. The menus were called context menus for this reason. The feature was marketed heavily, so it was no surprise that sometimes we snuck commands into the context menu that were important strategically, though not always the most likely to be used.

We had our early usage telemetry for Word 6 that came from a specially coded version and data collection via floppy. I vividly recall the data coming back about context menus showing they were frequently used. I shared this data with PaulA who was active on the board still. It was quite a vindication of the two-buttons. The more fascinating datapoint was that for a typical command such as copy/paste the usage of the menu, toolbar, keyboard shortcut, and now context menus were split roughly evenly. A given user did not exclusively stick to one affordance. We learned early on that adding secondary and tertiary affordances to commands was a convenience picked up by a set of users, not a replacement for the old ways. Importantly, and reviews showed this, technical users heavily bought into the notion that user-interface should be available multiple ways for maximal efficiency. While we curated and designed the context menus, it was no surprise that these same technical users wanted to customize context menus because they had their own ideas for what might make sense. The popularity of context menus put pressure to add even more commands over time, eventually obscuring content or forcing awkward positioning on small screens.

It was always the case that menu items that were not applicable at a given time were disabled or greyed out. As commands and buttons began to encompass high-level abstractions, disabled commands started to become a mystery. Why couldn't I insert a table inside a table? Why didn't bold work on a chart? And so on. This proved even more frustrating than hide-and-seek. These "greyed out" commands aways seemed to be needed just when they didn't work. People had no idea why a command was greyed out. Even today searches for "Word menu item greyed out" have hundreds of millions of results.

Recall that the design of Word 95 (technically Word 7.0 for Windows 95) required we not change the file formats. This significantly constrained what features could be done since most formatting and document commands would result in a file format change. Word 95 innovations were mostly focused on IntelliSense, features that just worked with little if any user interface. We previously discussed background spelling and AutoCorrect as examples of these features. While the product did not gain bloat by way of pixels, the sense of product mastery was reduced. IntelliSense features introduced us all to "what just happened" when using the product. Typing a few dashes across the screen and pressing return yielded a clean horizontal line. Pressing backspace was a clever way to undo that so long as that was the next key pressed. This loss of control or as we now know an inability to fully master a product came about by the introduction of features specifically designed to be useful without having to learn a command. Hundreds of hours went into designing interactions such as how to begin and end a bulleted list or using an asterisk or hyphen at the start of a paragraph to begin, and a second return to end a list. Even with a dedicated effort, we could not be right 100% of the time. We began to consider the hypothesis that automatic features might need to be so perfect that they worked 100% of the time, and if we guessed wrong just 1 time out of 100 then to the user the feature was always wrong. Think about this in the context of today's iPhone AutoCorrect.

Word 97 was the first release using shared code across all of Office for deep architectural features. One of those features discussed earlier was command bars, our first shared code for this critical user interface affordance. The availability of shared code and ample time to develop new features led to an explosion of command surface area in the product. Thanks to 32-bit computing and Windows 95, the base screen resolution expanded to 1024x768, three times bigger than our original target for Word 1.0. An explosion in user interface correlated to the product being labeled a winner, a juggernaut, and competitively overwhelming. But it was not bloatware, yet. Just by toolbar count, the product was twice as big, jumping to 18 toolbars and each one had more buttons because of the screen size. For completeness the list of new user interface widgets included: toolbars on every side of the screen and floating, menu bar that can be docked on any side of the screen or floating, drag and drop any command anywhere, hierarchical and multi-level menus and context menus, icons on menus and context menus (the preceding all came as part of the new shared code), Office Assistant ("Clippit"), green-squiggle grammar checking, even more IntelliSense (including on-the-fly spell correction), along with more wizards and more multi-function commands on toolbars.

IntelliSense in Office 97 was as much a point of view as it was code in the product. Some of what was designed as IntelliSense was trying to do the right thing with the user interface elements that routinely appeared. We would try to anticipate needing some functionality and pop up the user interface. Often this puzzled the user, and they would quickly move it out of the way. The obvious addition was a check box "Never show this to me again." The significant problem with this option is figuring out when to show that user interface in the future. If we guessed and showed it again, we were ignoring the user choice. Absent that, the chances of a user finding where to uncheck the checkbox they just checked were slim. The chance of even knowing that is what was required was probably zero. In other words, whatever we popped up was effectively gone forever. This type of intelligence in the design proved to be incredibly frustrating. I'd offer a tip for readers that are designing products: a checkbox offering to never show something again is always a bad idea, the EU GDPR inclusive. Showing it in the first place was the problem.

Word 97 was both our last release aimed squarely at the retail consumer and technology enthusiast and our first release with an eye towards the volume purchasing business customer. It was also the last release that was done without thinking deeply about the impact of complexity on corporate customers. In hindsight it is probably right to look at this release as the start of an overwhelming Office but only because customers would soon be pointing to Office 97 as bloatware. At the same time, by today's standard the set of features and capabilities were not at all overwhelming, just ahead of the curve for most people. For example, PowerPoint dramatically added photo, drawing, and graphics capabilities which also appeared for charts in Excel and drawings in Word. It is entirely clear these are representative of mainstream scenarios today.

Hearing the early concerns of complexity and bloat from our new enterprise customers deploying Office 97, we looked to a cosmetic/graphic design approach to reducing bloat. Along with the enterprise feature set in Office 2000 we employed the use of the doctrine of "make it simple by hiding it." We used our command bar infrastructure to implement the personalized menus, where commands were hidden by default in both menus and toolbars. This was detailed in Chapter VIII. The feature proved a failure and would be an important part of informing our design for Office12.

In another visual trick, we used the space made available by hiding toolbar buttons by default to place the two main toolbars adjacent to each other rather than on top of each other, called rafting. The contextual toolbars introduced in Office 97 described above were further tuned so they would hide and show automatically in the hopes of returning some control to the user.

I'd offer another tip for readers that are designing products: invisible and hidden commands are in no way at all simpler or more streamlined, though they are frustrating.

The Windows team encouraged us to change our apps to have one distinct window for every open document, with each window showing up on the Windows taskbar at the bottom of the screen, a design long-standard on Macintosh. Previously only the application showed up on the taskbar and multiple documents for the same application were available as separate windows only through the application's Window menu. This was deemed complicated and not consistent with the direction of Windows. The result especially for Outlook was a ballooning in the number of windows on the taskbar each with ever-decreasing amount of text showing the title as they were cramped together. In other words, a change meant to make things easier turned out to scale particularly poorly when applied to real-world application usage.

By the time we shipped, Word 2000 added five new toolbars.

Office 2002 (aka Office XP) aimed to vector some efforts back to delivering end-user features. With the failure of the Office Assistant and Clippy's retirement due at the time we shipped, we introduced two features aimed at offering ease of use surface areas. In hindsight, both were poor choices, one of which continues even today, after being removed from Office12.

The first relatively minor change was to make our new internet-connected help system available all the time with a simple "type your question here" box at the top of every screen on the same level as the menus. This rather innocuous addition set a precedent of cluttering the menu bar for additional commands. The awkwardness of the affordance as a place to type questions made it a particularly poor choice. Typing in the menu bar is just weird.

The task pane described in Chapter IX allowed us to greatly expand the surface area of the user interface. The design choice was rooted in the rise of the web. Unlike menus and toolbars which are concise word-length command descriptions, the web evolved with sentences describing the steps, such as "After selecting your dates of travel click here for the best fares." Many on the design team favored moving Office to a more descriptive user interface as a way of reducing complexity and explaining actions in context. The task pane started as an experiment for a few key long-standing problems. The "New Document" task pane finally gave us more room for the user to choose from a list of previously opened files, document templates, and more. The "Reveal Formatting" task pane was an advanced feature long favored by technical users which showed all the formatting applied to a given selection of text. Historically this was also a feature to compete with WordPerfect.

The task pane would prove to be a frustrating experience for customers, especially on small screens where it took over a good chunk of the side of the screen. It is worth noting that laptops had started to switch to wide-screen format (16:9 aspect ratio)—screens remained about the same height but were wider to accommodate a standardized HD (720p) and Full HD (1080p) resolution being used for video. Theoretically the wider screens would offer more space for user interface arranged vertically. Tech enthusiasts became enamored with the idea of stacking the Windows taskbar on the side for this reason. Feedback was mixed. At the very least a large portion of our enterprise customers were still using standard 4:3 aspect ratio screens.

In total, Word 2002 created eight task panes and added another seven toolbars, bringing the total number of toolbars to 30. Task panes were a key part of marketing Office XP, exceeded only by Clippy's retirement.

Office 2003 as described in the last chapter was characterized by heft. We delivered more new "programs" than in any prior releases, plus services and servers—the entire Office System. The expansion of the user interface continued as well.

The task pane from Office XP proved extremely popular, even considering the feedback from Office XP. We believed that the continued standardization of wide screens would show that using the task pane for user interface was a good use of the extra width. We added 11 (yes, 11) new task panes bringing the total number of task panes to 19.

The task panes received a technology improvement adding support for more user interface elements and richer display. The task panes themselves were essentially mini-web sites within the product.

We didn't stop there. We added a second window aligned on the side for showing online help which would cause a jarring realignment of the whole application shifting everything to the side to make room.

Looking back at each of these releases one other point is worth noting. Each product cycle as we aimed to make things easier, some commands moved around and to users the changes in the interface felt as though the whole product moved around a bit. These small moves were designed to make the product a little bit better, but to users it was often the case that the product was more than a little bit different. Small changes have just as much of a negative impact on the feeling of product mastery as big changes, but a minimal effect on ease of use.

With Office 2003 we reached a point that the was envisioned in David Pogue's 1994 column as "Word 15.0, due to ship in 2004", give or take. A mock-up of such a future version of Word illustrates the article showing an enormous number of toolbar buttons filling the screen, leaving little room for editing any document.

Two more escape valves in the design of Office proved to be sources of bloat as well, even as they served to solve problems for our own designs and customers: customization and program settings or options.

In the early days of the products, we added the ability to customize most of the choices we made. End-users or system administrators could move commands to customize the product for their unique use. Over the years we continued to improve the ability to customize. By Office 2003, we had the capability of placing any command anywhere along with the ability to create as many toolbars and menus as required. This customization was embraced by those creating custom programs running within Office applications using Visual Basic.

Many tech enthusiasts took great pride in having a perfect toolbar for themselves or their business. One customer I visited, a big consumer product goods company in the Midwest, spent months planning the rollout of Office such that there were specialized arrangements of the menus and toolbars depending on an employee's job function. A lawyer, marketer, salesperson, or finance person saw different customizations. This might have seemed nifty, but it also meant the company needed to rewrite the documentation and help for the product, leaving employees with existing product knowledge or those who were using how-to books lost. We invested significantly in making it even easier to customize the product, believing that if more people could customize the user interface maybe it would be easier. We really needed to stop digging.

No discussion of bloat would be complete without mentioning "Tools Options" the settings for an application. These settings would increase every release. A "setting" is most often a choice somewhere in the code that we made in designing a feature, but for some reason we anticipated that customers would make a different choice. Some choices might be preferences or user information, such as default fonts or initials to use in marking document revisions. Others were often obscure compatibility choices such as the most famous of all, operating as though 1900 is a leap year or not. This is an option because the first versions of Multiplan and Excel (Microsoft's products) and Lotus 1-2-3 incorrectly coded 1900 as a leap year. Not to nitpick, but Lotus was incorrect and Multiplan then Excel maintained the error for compatibility with industry leader 1-2-3.[49]

Tools Options was also a place to cover the sins of indecision among program managers. When Excel pioneered the wheel on the mouse in Excel 97, between Word and Excel we could not agree on whether the wheel was meant for zooming or scrolling. To compensate for our own inability to agree we added a checkbox to change the default.

The Tools Options dialog, much like the control panel in Windows or system settings on Macintosh, is often the first stop for reviewers or techies. With over 200 choices there was plenty to keep an eye on. The presence of choices is empowering. At some point, however, empowerment turns into bloat. We reached that point.

Sure, the choices were overwhelming, and people were finding them difficult. But we were also speaking an entirely different language than customers, one they weren't interested in learning. They had work to do. They knew what they wanted when they saw it but describing what they wanted or even spending time exploring the product was time wasted. We used to joke that if we did a usability test to English speakers using the German version of Office and asked them to do something complicated, they were no more efficient in their native language simply because the words on the menus weren't words at all. What is "Mail Merge" or "Pivot Table"?

During the design of Office12 we conducted many usability tests where we asked subjects to pick where a command should go in the existing menu structure or to arrange related commands in the same place. Some of our menus had become almost dumping grounds for commands that didn't obviously fit somewhere. The problem with such a design is that if we don't know where a command should go how in the world would a normal person guess where it should go? Or even if they got lucky once would they remember it the next time?

Returning to how we became bloated, it was two ways. First slowly, then suddenly.

I hoped to make the case that at each generation of Office we were considered in where those features went. The thousands of hours we spent deliberating the names, entry points, and visualizations for every new feature were symbolic of our commitment to getting this right. We were proud of each the default user interface experience of product cycle. Screen shots were our currency, and we were always happy to see the new screen shots in the press. One thing we noticed was that even with all we added and improved, the ability for customers and the press to identify the new product versus the old from screen shots was rather limited. The product was so overwhelming most people could not tell the difference. We had a design language consisting of a lot of stuff on the screen, but to most people it looked like a bunch of buttons and computer stuff surrounding their work.

An analogy we often used was key to understanding a way forward for us. From crime and police dramas, most are familiar with the role of the sketch artist—the detective who takes a verbal description of a suspect and turns into a drawing that is used on the streets. It is difficult to describe another person as most of us lack a vocabulary for facial features necessary to reconstruct a face. That is why creating such sketches is a highly expert art. Over the years, the use of software to show options to a witness has become the standard for constructing a sketch. People do a much better job describing something from examples than they do from a blank sheet.

Office needed the equivalent of a library of choices rather than an overwhelming vocabulary of features they did not understand.

But how?

079. COMPETING DESIGNS, BETTER DESIGN

Microsoft always maintained a competitive culture. It started at the top and flowed down from there. Any doubts, ask one of the early morning basketball leaguers who played against SteveB.

Generally, one place we did not compete was on products. That was wasteful. To be sure, cookie-licking had a way of making it seem like there was competition, but those involved knew the reality. We'd seen IBM intentionally set groups after each other and it was ugly. Back when I was technical assistant, I had a call with an IBM technical assistant (a very different job it turns out) who asked me about how the company managed competing groups "so effectively" he said, and I thought he was speaking a foreign language. Later I would realize from his view he thought of OS/2 and Windows as competitive, but we didn't quite see it that way.

While competition rarely occurred across groups by building products that were addressing the same goal, at times it happened accidentally, such as when C# and .NET evolved to bump up against Visual Basic, or even NetDocs taking on email after starting from a word processor. There were also technology transitions resulting in a current and forward-looking product, such as Windows 95 and Windows NT, which was not resolved until Windows XP. Originally Windows NT was a server operating system, but over time it became abundantly clear it was the future general-purpose operating system.

The Windows competition was painful. It was not particularly secret, but once NT went from a side project to a real product and then to the strategy it is fair to say the competition was difficult on all involved. No one who went through that would ever think about having competitive groups on purpose. At least if we did, we gained lessons in how we might go about it. The resolution of this situation was painful for everyone.

Microsoft's culture was to avoid being wasteful of resources or internal energy, and to focus on one solution, getting to market, and iterating to get something right, in three versions or so. As we've seen when confronted with intentional redundancy, we typically dealt with it before products got to market. If there was a competition, shipping first was one way to fix it.

Many companies, like IBM, famously maintained cultures of competition. Often these companies sent two or more groups off to build solutions to a specified problem, frequently unbeknownst to each other, hoping a clearly superior solution emerged. For an engineer, that was an immensely frustrating approach and rarely resulted in a clean win. Executives had a way of looking at competing projects and determining that the best path forward was to remove the negative attributes from both choices and use the good from each. That forced merger of two formerly competing groups usually marked the start of a long, friction-filled journey to market. Worse, tell me the boss of the new merged effort and I could tell you the winning technology. Such was another reason to dislike that approach Incidentally, one thing we got right with the Windows 9x/Windows NT era was in moving code from one to the other.

The task of redesigning Office to address the challenges described was so high risk and difficult that it seemed sensible to try a few different approaches despite the difficulties of doing so. The questions were how to quickly try multiple designs and if one team could sincerely experiment in an unbiased manner.

The user interface was one part of Office12. The next section will outline the full scope of the release.

Julie Larson-Green (JulieLar), leading the UEX (User EXperience) program management team reporting to Antoine Leblond (Antoine), settled on investigating two approaches in parallel. Julie knew she wanted to experiment but was acutely aware we did not have a year to wallow in design alternatives. We shipped Office 2003 at the end of the summer 2003. We needed a couple of months on the engineering side to release worldwide products, refit the engineering process with improvements, and to plan for the next release. The rough schedule called to start coding for Office12 in early spring 2004. Less than six months to have a firm feature list, a robust engineering plan, and above all a new cross-Office design framework for a product used by hundreds of millions of people over the past 15 years. That's all.

Julie's Office 2003 team began iterating with designs before the release finished early in the year. The second design came from members of the team that moved over from Outlook in the late spring 2003. Movement across teams between releases was encouraged and planful, with program management starting moves a couple of months before RTM. Our resource realignment or reorg process was routine at this point and began uneventfully with a memo from me in late May 2003.

The two groups shared the same hallway with knowledge and awareness of each other, like OneNote and Word previously. JulieLar's leadership on this project across all of Office would prove immense. Her own evolution as an engineering and product leader set the stage for this project, starting from when we met at a C++ event at Microsoft Press more than a decade earlier, through her growth to leading the engineering team that created Visual Studio (an outgrowth of single-user Visual C++), then on Windows through the chaos of the browser wars, and back to Office to FrontPage and the incubation of SharePoint Team Services, and most recently to the shared user interface team for Office 2003, then called UIS. While decidedly among the best product leaders at Microsoft, it was her natural skills at bringing teams and people in conflict together that would prove to be the magic behind this risky and complex challenge.

The two teams were each staffed by very solid product leaders with strong but differing views on the evolution of user interface. The teams started from different constraints or assumptions. Julie aimed to arrive at one clear choice, not a nonexistent mix of two options or a committee compromise. That way the designs and specs could be finalized in time to start coding.

Few outside of Office fully understood the scope of the product's thousands of features—the prevailing view was neither could anyone nor did anyone care about all of the features. While we (in Office) could light-heartedly make fun of our 4,000 different commands across five main products, with very few exceptions there were no other products out there that had such a surface area. The only thing that came close was the Adobe suite of products and perhaps Visual Studio, but both of those were used by professionals who were specifically schooled in those products. Even big web sites on the internet were no more complex than the online help for Office. Recall during the most recent redesign of the Office user experience (the introduction of command bars for Office 2000) we had a full-time program manager just keeping track of all the commands, buttons, and keyboard shortcuts. This was a huge redesign, a jumbo-jet cockpit level design.

The world wide web introduced an entirely new metaphor to the world with blue underlined hyperlinks, big buttons, and a good deal of text. It was a radical departure from overlapping windows, menus, dialogs, keyboard shortcuts, and all the other widgets described in the previous section. A key question for Julie was should the web influence the new user interface for a productivity tool as expansive as Office?

One team was heavily influenced by the early design directions of Longhorn, the next release of Windows, which was at that point two years into its somewhat interrupted schedule due to Trustworthy Computing. Longhorn was starting to feel a bit of mission creep. Working to extend the traditional Windows desktop to incorporate weblike metaphors, the Longhorn design wanted to achieve the feel of browsing web pages while launching programs and working with files and settings.

The resulting designs made extensive use of textual descriptions and a task-oriented interface. Rather than verbs such as Save or Bold, the experience was much more like shopping on the web with categories like Collaborate, Share, and Edit. There were even command favorites (favorite commands?) and history like a browser, as well as buttons and menus within a wheel of commands, sometimes called a radial menu. A radial menu, a favorite of designers (and in movies), seems to surface every 10 years or so even though it has a host of problems with scalability, discoverability, and general ease of use. It also happened to be quite popular with the fans of pen computing.

One of the consistent challenges the Windows team faced was designing a user interface paradigm for all apps developers without themselves really having an app to design. The desktop, managing files and folders, launching programs, and the control panel are interesting but relatively minimal in scope, says this apps person. As discussed in the Windows 3.0 era, Windows benefitted enormously from the Excel team's input into what was required by Windows.

The first Office team's design, called OfficeSpace, felt futuristic—graphically it looked like something from a movie. The name derived from the generalized notion of a command space from Longhorn and happened to (perhaps by no accident) reflect on the 1999 Mike Judge film *Office Space* that quickly achieved cult status among Gen-X. It aligned with a stated direction of Longhorn, which was quite appealing. Alignment between Windows and Office was always viewed positively, especially by enterprise customers, even if we didn't always deliver on the details. In early 2000s, aligning with Windows was still a prime directive from BillG. We had just managed the impossible, which was to ship Office XP and Windows XP in rough proximity and the XP desktop would rival the 2000 desktop in excitement from field sales.

The OfficeSpace team created a high-fidelity interactive prototype called Strawman. It had a feel of Longhorn with a good deal of text in the interface describing commands in a command well that was like a taskpane. It also, however, featured traditional toolbars and menus. It was a strong design, but it felt additive to what we already had. The incremental addition of new affordances was described in the previous section and was how we ended up where we were in the first place.

The second team took a clean-slate approach. They started from the problems Office customers faced, rather than starting from a design language or set of abstract principles. The first thing they asked themselves was, "Why are things the way they are?" This simple question frequently proved liberating. Leading this questioning were Jensen Harris (JensenH) and Clay Satterfield (ClaySatt), both of whom joined Julie's team from Outlook, fresh off its complete and successful redesign. JensenH insisted on trying something entirely different. Julie gave him that latitude. Jensen brought with him a depth of Office product knowledge that far exceeded his tenure at Microsoft, something that was an absolute requirement to making this project work.

Jensen and Clay asked themselves the "why and what for" of the top-level menus: File, Edit, View, Insert, Tools, Window, and Help, along with the many widgets. It became clear to them that product history was no longer relevant. A button that was a hot new feature a few releases back, or that a program manager insisted upon long ago, didn't necessarily have a place in this version, nor did the widget that was added in an effort to make finding a command easier. Despite a deep understanding of what we aimed to do, those designs were rooted in the arbitrary history and evolution of the implementation of Office. This is why the history of Office as detailed in the previous section was such an important input to this design.

Taking a step back, as great product designers often did, the team concluded that features could be grouped in a much more systematic and logical way and, more importantly, by operations that were more familiar and easily labeled for human use. A reorganization was needed more than "pixel pushing," as HeikkiK used to say. Imagine the level of boldness required to suggest moving not just a few but every command in Office. This sounded like "Who moved my cheese?" on a grand scale.

Julie let the process run for a bit more and then it was necessary to drive towards a single unified design. She was determined not to simply pick a winner herself but work a process so a shared winner would emerge. This was brave and not the norm for Microsoft. She essentially told both teams to lock themselves in a conference room and arrive at a shared result. There was a risk of compromise or design by committee, but she knew that going in and wasn't going to let that become the result.

The teams hated this, as they should. It is exactly what no good product designer wants to do. As expected, there really wasn't a compromise. This did in a sense force Julie's hand. The purity of the latter design was great, while many questions remained about Longhorn's text-heavy approach. At first Julie finessed the choice, but it is fair to say even years later that at that moment there were those that felt like they won and those that didn't. Perhaps there really is no alternative with competing designs. The designs, however, gave us all much more confidence in the direction, having fully explored two radical alternatives.

Over the course of the next few months Jensen, Clay, and team created many visualizations. They created hundreds of prototypes. JensenH estimated that over 25,000 renderings were created. The teams used every level of fidelity from paper to Photoshop to Flash. Yes, that was still a thing as we shall see.

Why did we have so much confidence though? Who makes such a huge change to such successful products? The user interface was the product and "who moved my cheese?" could result in an unmitigated nightmare for end-users and a disaster for the business.

Early in the process, Jensen's team design centered on a small number of important concepts—concepts that provided an enduring framework for how the interface should be designed and evolve over time as the product expanded. Starting with PowerPoint, they sketched out a design that reflected their set of principles. Envisioning a design where each app had a dominant color consistent with the app's existing icon, the sketch of PowerPoint had a ripe red tone, and so they dubbed the initial design language Tomatoey (tom-ah-tooey), because it was a tomato-ish user interface. Get it?

The original renderings were compelling, albeit a bit too colorful. The work was unbelievably impressive. I often stopped by their offices in our shared hallway to see the designs evolve and hear what they were up to, especially in the evenings when they seemed to work best. Jensen was still new to the team, and young, and he was a little leery of my walk-bys, but he and Clay were both often working in the late afternoon or early evenings, the best time to chat and see updates. These discussions continue today except they happen over text and we're talking about the WWDC or latest hardware. I can say without hesitation that I had not had more interesting late-night conversations about technology since my days of AFX and talking to RickP about the early code in Excel and Windows. To be honest, given the risk of the overall effort, these conversations and talking to Julie and Antoine almost every day were part of my own risk mitigation therapy.

Tomatoey was the kind of design that people tried to poke holes in and find problems with but just couldn't. It was not just a rendering or a rearranging of the commands—it was an entire system and framework for how the product could exist and evolve. We were still very early. When you listened to Jensen and Clay go through the thinking and when they showed demos it was abundantly clear they were onto something. Normally when a design is early and one asks questions, the answers can be vague or bring on a feeling of unease. In this case, it wasn't just that answers exuded confidence, but the answers were often more thoughtful than the questions.

Too often the graphical aspect of software designs over-shadow the key tenets of functionality. We see this today in how designs so often start with or are communicated via graphics, or widgets, versus the problems solved or functional aspects of the solution. Even the names chosen for designs too often reflect graphical or aesthetic choices in the work such as Aero or Luna.

I asked Jensen how serious they were about this design and he said, "Very serious...We really went whole hog."[50]

Everything had a place, and there was a place for everything.

Even at this early stage there were a set of widgets or controls as the operating system called them. It would be easy to define the design by these mechanisms, but that would be incomplete and miss the whole point.

From the earliest days of the design, Jensen and Clay had a full framework and rationale for every choice, across every Office application. Early on the choice was to focus on the three main document creation apps, Word, Excel, and PowerPoint. The omission of Outlook proved to be frustrating for reviewers and those measuring us on consistency. Other document applications were pleading to get the new interface, but the need to focus was paramount.

The design was sweeping and all-encompassing. Considering the scope of the design this was an incredible accomplishment. Almost every system redesign I can think of started from a single dimension or metaphor—transparency, control palettes, a new command hierarchy, or our own command bar idea. The very notion of the first principles of Tomatoey was itself incredibly significant. As a reminder, the scope of this design was 4000 commands across three major products each used by hundreds of millions of people for some of the most critical work of their professional lives.

Jensen referred to this as a *results-oriented design*. The crux of the design was to pivot from thinking about individual commands and where they should go to planning the results of the document creation process. The design presented aggregates of commands at a higher level. The original bullets and numbering toolbar button in Word 6.0 was an early preview of this sort of approach, synthesizing a feature out of many commands that already exist in the code. Features are illustrated by results they obtain, not by a name. Instead of a Chart Wizard, illustrate the charts that can be created and do so using galleries. Users are far more likely to get the end-result they want by getting to an approximation quickly and then using visual choices to further customize it.

While the interaction design was one aspect of this work, and in general we tell stories about Office from the user to the feature choice and design then to engineering and quality contributors, I would hate for readers to think that I am failing to account for the immense impact of software engineering and testing to this work. As talented as JensenH and the whole PM and product design teams were, they had their match in equally talented engineering counterparts. They worked side-by-side at every step of the project—there was no handoff, but a crazy amount of iteration every day of the project. JulieLar's peer in development Dave Buchthal (DaveBu) led the development team. He started at Microsoft in 1992 and was an early member of the Office Shared team. Igor Zaika (IgorZ) was a development lead reporting to Dave and an informal tech lead for the project who also had more than a decade of Office development experience. Sean Oldridge (SeanO) led the testing and quality team, putting his decade of experience to work. The engineering, not just on the code to implement the design but the high performance and backward compatibility across Word, Excel, and PowerPoint, represented the most intense re-engineering efforts the entire Office team ever attempted, even to this day. I hope all the design and feature discussion doesn't take away from the engineering and quality aspects of this project.

The purpose of this section is not to be a tutorial on design, as much as I would like. There is a 2006-era blog (this will be described in a future section) as well as videos from JensenH's various conference presentations that are available online. Many are linked to at jensenharris.com.

When it comes to saying why the early design seemed so good, I would say was it a new reality where the Office user interface engaged users in a much more captivating way and users could see their work coming to life versus debugging the document. Capabilities existed in only one place and never moved around—and at the same time every feature was accessible by an equivalent to Office 2003 or less (!) amount of command distance. Gone were the days of tunneling into dialogs or playing hide-and-seek. Embracing web paradigms, the design took advantage of longer, more conventional text labels (longer than tooltips) and a livelier interface that showed the results of a command even before choosing it, enabling users to pick from choices like a modern sketch artist. The design even took up less space and worked on a wider range of screens consistently. The focus was on features and results. Going back to our cockpit analogy, the design essentially programmed the capabilities of Office rather than just putting a bunch of mechanisms out there to find commands. It was radical. It also worked extremely well.

They called the design the "Ribbon." The team described the design as visual, tactile, and responsive.

The Ribbon seemed not only to solve Office's bloat challenges but to create an interface paradigm that would be the best, and most enduring, design for the desktop era. While we were normally optimistic before we began coding, it was rare to have this level of enthusiasm so early in a project. There was something special about what was transpiring, even with a list of issues that continued to grow.

Still, we only had the early design for the Ribbon. We needed to finalize that and an entire release of Office to be built by a few thousand people.

080. PROGRESS FROM VISION TO BETA

Organizationally, we had become a (relatively) well-oiled machine. Procedurally we knew how to work. We also knew what was required at the high level and individual teams knew how to fill in the details with plans. Writing this all down and communicating to the organization—the Vision for Office12—was the next step.

Transitioning from Office 2003 to Office12 was happening across more than 2,500 engineers. In every respect we were building a coherent and collaborative plan with little dirt flying and no injuries, as the old MikeMap description of Office went.

By spring 2004 we had a complete product plan in addition to the user experience redesign described previously. Even with excellence of execution, this was not a lather, rinse, repeat release. Collectively, we learned some lessons from the previous releases. We learned more is not better, and that it was time to rethink, or, as we said in the vision, redefine the user experience. We learned that blindly following the enterprise path could lead to stasis, and in technology failing to innovate or standing still was equivalent to going backwards even when the best customers were telling us of the high costs of change. And finally, we had a firm grasp of how the product was going to evolve beyond document creation—the role of servers, services, email, and more were all important parts of Office12.

The question was not whether we had a good plan or even if we could execute, but would the results live up to our goals…finally. There was also a huge risk to making a big bet on changing the user interface of the product—an incalculable risk. It is the kind of risk you either accept and go for or don't try at all. Many people inside the company, and even on the team, immediately saw the risk of such a big bet and absolutely wanted to know the risk mitigation plan. There wasn't one. Any risk mitigation plan would only result in a compromise design, because at every step someone would be saying not to worry, we always have a fallback. Backup plans on big bets have a way of permeating the whole product development process and ultimately deny the resources required to achieve the goals, reduce the appetite for risk, and simultaneously dilute the efforts to achieve the bet itself.

From my perspective Office12 was all about that opening sentence of the vision document and a single slide shown at the team meeting for the vision. It read, "No More Good Enough," with a big red circle slash. Surrounding that PowerPoint SmartArt on the slide were reviewer quotes about bloatware and competing with Sun's free OpenOffice, along with some juicy analyst quotes about technologies that still weren't going to pan out. It was not that we set out to compete with a free product that had yet to make inroads, but we needed to reset the narrative that Office was complete, old, boring, and, worst of all, bloated. We had to show that there was deep thinking in the product and the paradigm of document creation was ripe for innovation, and by doing that we could demonstrate to the market that productivity tools were not commodities.

In the conventional wisdom of the day, Office was ripe for disruption. There was a less capable product claiming to be a substitute for less money. We took the initiative, intent on doing the disrupting ourselves and not letting something like OpenOffice, or our old products, do it to us. Not to race ahead, but one thing they don't tell you about in disruptive theory is that losing to a head-on competitor is almost never what happens. Head-on competitors end up, well, running head-on into the entrenched product and that is exactly what happened with OpenOffice.

Google's future suite would initially make this same mistake, but we were at least a decade before they would begin to address that false start, and three years before even their first release.

The redesign of the user experience was more than one part of the product or strategy. It was so visible and so potentially disruptive that we knew no other aspects of the release would rise above it, certainly in the initial product reception from beta through release. Managing the team and project knowing this reality was JulieLar's mission.

The overarching importance and the inherent risk of the redesign was not lost on the team. We had become accustomed to working together and collaborating. This was the sixth major release of the product and we'd been executing as a single team, not siloes of app teams, for a decade. The team was not fighting the shared redesign effort as much as it was rallying around it. As teams saw the design make it into the product, rather than point out how it might not work and cause it fail to make a point, teams came together to make it better. It wasn't everyone at first, but over time that was the case. Among thousands there would always be doubters and honest skeptics, but mostly there were legitimate concerns that required more work.

Success has many siblings and failure is an orphan as the saying goes. Time has certainly reduced the number of doubters across the team and company. Those working on the Ribbon have many stories of people across the rest of Office and Microsoft expressing extreme doubt and risk, but those too have softened over the years as people came to realize the different roles people play during a time of change. Suffice it to say, some of the doubters were hardcore and neither quiet nor necessarily even-handed in criticism. The same could be said of supporters. Anyone going through a big bet with massive downside would need to learn this lesson. It would come in handy for me.

The product vision process really came together. After the very rough start for Office 2000 followed by the over-correction in Office XP, and then again by another over-correction back to enterprise in Office 2003, we hit stride. The process very much became our culture and defined a new way of building Office. The output of the process, after just a few months of planning, included a robust vision document—the plan—over thirty-five pages containing details for all critical stakeholders. We covered the breadth of the 4 Ps of the marketing mix across product, price, place, and promotion. From a culture perspective we dove deep into the core tenets of the release, the non-debatable points meant to streamline discussion and reduce debate. We did so in a unique Office manner by offering tenets that themselves often contradicted each other. I had a favorite example of that. We had one tenet "Security trumps everything" followed immediately by a tenet "Privacy also trumps everything" which was a clear message to the team to be smart about resolving issues even when they contradict. The goal of the vision was to communicate the product but to also serve as a decision framework—it was not a detailed product specification, intentionally so. The full set of tenets is quoted below.

> ***Security trumps everything.*** *No feature will be important enough that it justifies exposing our users to malicious code.*
>
> ***Privacy also trumps everything.*** *Office12 will not compromise our users' privacy for anything.*
>
> ***OS and Hardware requirements remain the same.*** *Office12 will target the same versions of the OS as Office 2003.*

No new system components. *Office12 will work with the Office 2003 level of system components and redistributables.*

Instrumentation for all features. *Any work that doesn't include usage instrumentation will be considered incomplete.*

Performance counts. *Performance of key scenarios will not degrade with the new version of Office.*

Flawless forward compatibility. *Solutions, documents, and other content from Office 2003 will migrate to Office12 flawlessly.*

Office12 is a true language-independent binary. *No language-specific work will be built into the Office12 binaries.*

Full accessibility. *Office12 will comply with the current and future accessibility and privacy regulations flawlessly.*

Watson throughout the lifecycle. *We will be addressing Watson issues throughout the development of Office12.*

The main themes of the release provide insight into the cross-organization nature of the plan. We worked hard to keep the plan from reflecting the org chart. While obviously different scenarios had a locus of technology in the organization, by and large everything important involved multiple teams across Office. One challenge this process always had, and Office12 showed this as well, was addressing scenarios broadly defined as database or data access. This deeply technical area had many strategic partners across the company, but also a unique relationship to Excel, which organizationally shared an executive within Office. Interestingly, we always struggled the same way most modern-day data-intensive applications struggle. All data eventually ends up being pasted or opened as a text file into Excel. Figuring out how to avoid that manual step eluded us just as often as it did for customers or third-party software.

As with previous releases the teams created sketches of the vision by each product pillar as will be described. These sketches serve several key purposes. First and foremost, they are a tool for the team that owns an area to commit to delivering what is shown. These are not aspirational or directional but are supposed to represent commitments. The rest of the company was swimming in prototypes with a lack of clarity over when or if they were planned products or simply documenting thoughts. Second, the sketches served to inform the team about what everyone was working on and to provide a holistic view of the product end-state. Finally, these sketches help us to see the product end-to-end in a way that helps us to evaluate the plan for each customer segment. Ideally the sketches are not far off the final release of the product, just as the mock press release we created should be close to the real thing at the launch. With all the changes to the user experience, we did not have the production bandwidth to make sure each sketch had the most current designs, making the sketches a bit uneven in this regard. When I reflect on this, I'm glad we never over-produced the vision and importantly did not delegate the production to a distinct group, but rather we kept the low production values and saved our energy for the product.

The new user experience encompassed two vision areas. The first was "Redefining the Office Experience" representing the mechanisms and mechanics of the interface design. The second, intentionally the second, was "21st

Century Documents" which emphasized the customer facing benefit of the design and the kinds of cool and important new documents that could be created. Having two big, bold, and modern goals as the first two was an intentional effort to up the ante.

The next vision area brought together our collaboration efforts for teams and enterprises, mostly SharePoint. By this time, the business of SharePoint was still catching up to its strategic importance. We still had far more traction with sales, marketing, and partners than we did with deployment and usage, but that wasn't going to slow down iterating. It usually takes three times to get something right, and this would be the third release of the product.

For brevity, the remaining items are quoted below, including investments around data access which encompassed XML (again) and connecting data in SharePoint to desktop tools.

> ***Redefining the Office Experience.*** *Office12 will redefine the experience of using our applications through a bold new UI, more streamlined tools, and a deeper integration with the shell for system and document-level tasks.*
>
> ***21st Century Documents.*** *In Office12, documents will not only look dramatically better but will also integrate much more efficiently and dynamically with the systems and processes of which they are part.*
>
> ***Effective Teams and Organizations.*** *Office12 will fulfill the promise of group productivity, making organizations more effective through enhanced collaboration tools, better access to corporate assets, and stronger integration with the desktop.*
>
> ***Manage Your Time, Work and Relationships in One Place.*** *Office12 will bring together improved e-mail, calendar, task, and contact management tools, enabling our customers to manage their time, work and relationships in powerful new ways.*
>
> ***Unlock and Incorporate Business Information.*** *Office12 will make it easy for customers to collect, find, view, and analyze relevant data, communicate their findings to others, work together to make decisions, and measure the results of their actions.*
>
> ***Breakthrough Quality and Satisfaction.*** *Office12 will be the most trustworthy and easy to deploy version of Office ever, and will mark a leap forward in increasing the value of our digital connection with our customers.*

The schedule started in May 2004 after shipping Office 2003 in late summer / early fall 2003. We presented the vision in March, giving everyone about 8 more weeks to finalize the specific features and development schedule for each milestone. While we were anxious to begin, a big risk landed on us at the last minute. The primary reason for this would be our old friend Windows and Longhorn.

Days before releasing the project schedule for Office12—not a schedule I just made up in my Office or DonGa the Office development leader dreamed up, but a consensus across the leadership—there was a panic about Office missing the opportunity to align with Windows. JeffR, the executive vice president of Information Worker products, called me to his office to talk about the late-breaking issue. We just finished Office 2003 and at the start of that release there was a fire drill to align schedules between Windows Longhorn and Office 2003. Here we were again being asked to align around that same Windows release, with our next release of Office. The optimism Windows had in late 2000 now had a couple of years of work and it was abundantly clear the project was not where it needed to be. My head began to throb.

The elephant in the room was once again the Windows schedule only this time it was their alignment of the Windows desktop and Windows Server releases. The Server just finished a release in April 2003 and Windows XP SP2 was still about six months from completion, partially why Longhorn was adding risk as well. While the core operating system was the same code for both the desktop and Server, the differences and additions created a bottleneck to getting both done on the same schedule. As a result, Windows had to admit that getting both the desktop and Server products done at the same time—something highly desirable from efficiency and go to market perspectives—was not possible. They put together a schedule with Longhorn desktop finishing in the second half of 2005 and the server shipping 6-12 months later, or second half 2006. Since Office had both server and desktop code, trying to synchronize that presented an immediate problem, besides the reliability of a schedule with multiple 6-month ranges built in. This seemed to me to be a rather theoretical discussion given the history of Windows ship date ranges versus actual single ship dates.

The approach I took was to suggest releasing in sync with Server (aka Longhorn Server) which aligned with our proposed RTM date based on the detailed vision plan of May 2006. That seemed reasonable given the stated goal of alignment with both. Most everyone was really irritated with me for lack of flexibility, which seemed odd given the constraints. Much to my frustration this came across as a desire to ship above shipping the right thing, even given the realities of the situation. I just had to accept this characterization and let events play out.

Writing this I am sure some recall what ultimately happened, at least the headline. The Longhorn desktop project would go through a big "reset" (they called it that) and eventually shipped in late 2006 for an official street date of January 2007 for Windows Vista. The Server team became frustrated and chose to ship Windows Server 2003 R2 (comprised of a Server 2003 service pack and optional components) in December 2005. The full Longhorn Server released in February 2008. As for Office, our May 22, 2006, date turned out to be aggressive and we ended up shipping on August 15, 2006. We were 12 weeks late.

Looked at another way, from the start of planning releases after Office XP in May 2001 and Windows XP in August 2001, Office shipped both Office 2003 and Office12 (Office 2007) before another release of Windows or Windows Server shipped. It is not unfair to say I received a ton of grief at the time for putting us on both the Office 2003 and 2007 schedules, which I still think was unfair as it was abundantly clear at the time how the schedules would unfold. Nevertheless, there is no joy in being in the right when others ran into problems.

The most interesting aspect of this type of history is to consider an alternate scenario. What would have happened if Office just slipped along with Windows? Would it have mattered if we never shipped either of those releases and just eventually aligned around what became Windows Vista (Office Vista)? From a business perspective, it is almost certainly the case we would have continued just fine due to the compelling nature of product-market fit as described earlier. Office XP could have carried us for another ten years, just as Windows XP could have and sort of did. From a product development perspective, however, I could easily make the case that it would have been disastrous for Microsoft. Technically, we would have lost out on the long-term investments in servers and services, and a host of other important architectural efforts (including alignment with Exchange Server and the browser-based apps) so incredibly key to the anchor of today's Microsoft Office 365. The much deeper impact would have been to the lack of maturity we gained in the product development process to operate at scale. The team would have just been wrecked. I don't think I'm being dramatic to put that out there.

Rather than point out that we read the landscape correctly, I wanted to share what it felt like to plan and execute in this environment. These challenges were one thing faced from my position in Office and little did I realize at the time how important this experience would become as I moved to Windows.

With our plan in place and the whole team charging ahead with a great deal of energy and excitement, what followed was night and day from Office 2003. Where Office 2003 felt like a slog, perhaps bloated like the product, Office12 seemed to cruise along. While there were daily debates over the ever-changing interface, the fact that the product was changing so dramatically was, for most on the team, incredibly energizing. It was also nerve-racking. There were exciting moments along the way such as seeing the first right-to-left Ribbon design, as we'd ship to Hebrew and Arabic speaking countries.

Two of the more substantial issues the first two vision areas had to work through were performance and exposing more features of the apps in a manner that truly tapped into the potential of the new user-interface.

In terms of performance, we were pushing the limits of what thought would work in our apps. For the history of Office, formatting and changing the appearance of documents happened one single command at a time. Developers worked super hard to optimize this to be as fast as possible, but the user would only perceive it in extreme cases, for example changing a chart type with hundreds of datapoints. Live previews, a feature of the Ribbon, proved to be an enormous engineering challenge—never before had the products computed so many alternatives while a user simply hovered a mouse over choices. With a live preview, the Ribbon showed dozens of potential outcomes of applying a command in a gallery, while also showing the results live in the document, to save users from endless loops of trying and undoing commands. There were many opportunities for the product to be slow and non-responsive. Some on the team said the design was too difficult and we should abandon the hope of delivering previews. It would have been easy to give up. From a pure engineering perspective, live previews were an incredible accomplishment. For the press and reviews, the feature brought the strategy of results-oriented front and center making it very easy to visualize the concept. End-users could experience a whole new level of trying out a look without the dreaded undo-redo command sequence. Features such as paragraph styles in Word or new graphics capabilities in PowerPoint were brought to life in a show-me-first manner never before available.

Releases always have surprises along the way. Usually, the surprise is that the release is taking longer than planned. Office12 was the kind of release where the surprises were how much better things were going to be than even we thought. The battles, and I'm using that word on purpose, between the UEX team and the Word, Excel, and PowerPoint teams over how much to use the new user interface and for what features were difficult and really stretched the teams. The longer debates raged the less we could get done, and if you're looking to not do something then a delay tactic is a great way to get to a point of "would love to talk about this more but at this point the schedule is locked anyway". That's an awful "process win" we did not like. Each time a new aspect of the user interface came online in daily builds, internal friction was reduced a bit and some cross-group cooperation was unblocked.

BillG always complained about the fact that each Office "module" (he always called them modules and we called them apps) had some form of tables, with different features and substantially different user interfaces. The Ribbon gave us a chance to bring similarity to these while also showcasing the depth and capabilities latent in the product simply because the user interface was too complex or inaccessible. By latent, the features were unused because people could not find them or did not know they existed. The Ribbon gallery made it so simple, trivial even, to have a fancy table with colored rows and columns, even totals by columns. Who knew Word had spreadsheet formulas? These were also consistent across the applications as well. It was easy to change and customize. Since almost every document and deck had a table, it was easy to spot an Office12 document from across the room simply because of the cool table formatting made possible by the Ribbon. To eyes like Bill's, it looked like we had more shared code and aligned the implementations.

Across Word, Excel, and PowerPoint, documents were dramatically cooler and more modern, a word we used, and overused. The process of creating documents was blazingly fast, mistake free, and easy to change. Not a day went by when we were not blown away by the new capabilities of Office.

The design had a fascinating effect on new features. As the Ribbon was implemented, many features simply got better because of the way the Ribbon could expose them. In using the product over many years, Excel users figured out clever ways to make cells red, green, yellow, or some other coding, depending on the values, for example if sales growth was negative then color the cell red. The manual steps required were laborious and automating this mysterious at best. The Ribbon placed new *conditional formats* front and center—with clear, colorful labels showing exactly what could get done with the gallery. Suddenly everyone easily added color coding based on cell values with a single click. This only made the new features even better such as cells with small up/down/sideways arrows or miniature graphs of values.

Surprisingly, ancient features were given a new lease on life and brought front and center. Generations of writers had long been traumatized by the ritual of pasting a picture into Word and trying to understand how to wrap text around it, or not. The Ribbon exposed the existing features for images and using the gallery made it trivial to select a picture and then choose among the set of choices for flowing text. It only took 20 years, but finally everyone could easily paste pictures into Word and make the text wrap around or align with the image.

This ribbon dividend significantly improved the ability to market the product as both new and improved as well as getting more out of what was viewed as underutilized.

The team also set out to quantify the results of the Ribbon. It would not be enough for us to simply feel good or just know. The usability team explored every aspect of the design in our test labs. Hundreds of tests were conducted at the most micro and macro levels.

TBriggs on the user research team repeated earlier eye-tracking studies over the course of development, revealing how much less tiresome it was to find features. The deep red blob of eye-tracking marks was replaced by a calm and ordered browse of the Ribbon. Subjects left tests talking of how much less stressed they were using Office12 compared to the previous releases and how much less time they felt they were blindly searching for what might work. In general, people expressed much more mastery of the product rather than confusion or frustration.

Any change comes with a cost. While we knew learning would take time, encouraging news emerged. After the one – to two-week learning curve that caused productivity to diminish, there was a significant productivity increase. People created richer, more expressive (and more modern) documents in less time. The increased use of the product translated into better work outcomes and more success with the very work they intended to do. This went beyond fancier documents, too—people created documents for a reason: to persuade, deliver bad news, sell products, run projects, and more. Doing so more effectively was a huge benefit to the information worker, even if economists were not able to measure this for a generation of PC users.

We loved the Ribbon.

By the fall of 2005, about 18 months after Vision Day, we were ready to show the work to the world, or at least beta testers.

These early adopters would have some feedback for us. If we expected them to simply fall into line and cheerlead, we were mistaken.

081. FIRST FEEDBACK AND A SURPRISE

We'd been working on Office12 for almost two years and the product had made enormous progress. The team was buzzing, and everyone was very excited. This product was different. We were building something we could all feel. It was a product that was good for individuals, not just organizations and people. Still, no one outside the company had seen it or knew of monumental change we were making to the product. The user interface in Office was not just a user interface for the PC, for many many people for the past 15 years it had been **the** interface for the PC. We were quite confident. JulieLar was confident and prepared. This was a big moment, the first public showing and then the first feedback.

The first lesson of interface redesign: Do not unveil the design with static pictures.

The second lesson of interface redesign: Do not unveil the design with static pictures.

At the 2005 Professional Developers Conference (PDC), Chris Capossela (ChrisCap), Corporate VP of Information Worker Marketing, joined BillG on stage for a sweeping demonstration of Windows Longhorn along with the first public reveal of Office "12." The quotes with a space became the official way of writing the name. ChrisCap and the marketing team zeroed in on the positioning of "Better results, faster," while also pointing out that Office was "New, but feels familiar." The demonstration zipped across Excel, Word, and PowerPoint, showing all the elements of the redesign and dozens of new features, along with many others previously undiscoverable. I was sitting anxiously in the very back of the room gauging how people reacted. I did not have to listen too carefully as during the demo someone shouted out to the stage, letting everyone know how they felt.

"Ship it!" they yelled.[51]

We were still two months away from the first public beta, but this felt good. Only afterwards watching the tape did I realize we were being made fun of. Chris inadvertently missed a beat in the demo. His words describing what should happen did not match what was happening on screen. It looked like a bug and "ship it" was a classic Microsoft reference to shipping something with bugs. Nevertheless, the reception for the demo was quite positive.

The excitement spread through the industry.

Technorati, a tech news site that measured the important or high impact blogs on what was then called the blogosphere, was the place to be seen in the press. Our redesign made that home page, a first for plain old Office.

Despite the excitement of the moment, we learned a good lesson.

The video of the keynote was posted, but in 2005 not everyone was hip to consuming video. That meant that the still images (from Treo phones and the like), screenshots from the event, and JensenH's later session made their way around the blogosphere. That proved to be a mistake. The spread of simple static screenshots for such a major change in user interface was not the way to communicate the redesign.

Almost immediately we were confronted with a wave of comments proclaiming the Ribbon to be too big and that it took up too much of the screen—assertions made by comparing screenshots to the current version of Office and making snap judgments. Attendees at the developer conference were counting pixels but not considering the full scope of the design or the experience. Besides, there really was the same amount of room for content—that was a key point of the design.

We did not anticipate this level of dissection, and that was a mistake. This immediately reminded us, especially JensenH, of his redesign of Outlook and the furor over the layout. Recall from the previous chapter that we had a spirited debate among early testers over whether the layout displayed fewer or more email messages. The question being asked was whether the ribbon took up more space than the toolbars and menus previously there.

We had some work to do.

Lost in all the comments about how big the Ribbon seemed to appear was the fact that we eliminated the row of menus entirely. Some comments and blogs slowly absorbed that reality over the course of the day as the magnitude of the design began to sink in. The Ribbon was not, as people thought by looking at a static screenshot, a big, fat, tabbed toolbar. It was so much more.

Also missing from this discussion were the differences between tech enthusiast or developer use of the product and typical users. We knew the typical user interface experience from instrumentation. Most users ended up with two rows of toolbars, the main menu, plus toolbars floating around the screen, and the side pane (that innovation from Office XP) each obscuring the document or squeezing in on the user's work. By contrast, a very small number of tech enthusiasts prided themselves on purposely designing and maintaining a very select set of commands, often in a single floating tool palette, itself a very poor choice unless you have a giant screen, which many developers did. This was not the real world or even the base case, though we would eventually craft an answer for even this hyper-customized form of user interface.

In hindsight, letting the static shots out without video or animation was a rookie move that we corrected eventually. We were at the earliest days of real-time reactions to product launches.

Microsoft had recently begun using video as a means of connecting with the tech enthusiast community. The Developer Relations Group (DRG) created an online video site, *Channel9*, hosting videos with product leaders from across the company. JulieLar initiated the ground-level engagement as a companion to the PDC by recording a casual and friendly 40-minute discussion along with demos from her office.[52] This video made a huge difference and began engaging the techie crowd with a good deal more information.

Simultaneously, JensenH began his new blog. Blogs were the rage among product leaders. Many of us maintained "external blogs", or blogs that were visible to anyone, something that seemed risky for big companies at the time. Jensen shared his first Office12 posts after his PDC afternoon presentations. The blog was titled, *Jensen Harris: An Office User Interface Blog*. Portions of his blog can be found on a Microsoft site[53] with a table of contents, but unfortunately Microsoft changed platforms and all the images have been lost. Individual posts can be found on archive.org.

JensenH had many talents beyond his obvious software skills and his regular performances with the Seattle Symphony. He was also a fantastic writer, a style he honed while writing a column in high school for *USA Today*.

His posts detailing the Office12 redesign were not only incredibly well executed but ultimately served as a model for how a product could and should engage discussions on building software at scale. Through the course of the remainder of the release, and even today, these posts serve as reference materials for one of the most substantial redesigns Microsoft ever undertook, so far. While obvious today, the press and reviewers were also following the posts carefully—something we took note of and proactively communicated with them. We never edited, cleared, or otherwise scripted posts. Jensen did this all on his own and under his own supervision, with the goal of detailing "why we're changing the UI, not just how we're changing it."

Incidentally, this became another story of an Office process spreading virally across the company. I was often asked to point to the team in marketing that was doing our blogging and to the blogging strategy deck. It was one of those moments when I recognized parts of the company were scaling or growing up differently than Office. In other parts of the company, something like a blog would be a team, a budget, and a process with meetings and so on. We had none of that. It was just JensenH (and others) writing. We'd occasionally talk about topics to cover but otherwise it was an entirely organic effort. The key was that there was no strategy or oversight or overthinking, but just telling the actual story of the design and responding to the legitimate questions about it. Nevertheless, Gavin Shearer (GavinS) on the product planning team wrote up a blogging whitepaper so the rest of the company asking could see that we had some structure. Gavin met with several of the team's bloggers to see how they worked and turned that into a guide for the future. It makes for an interesting historical record contrasting with today's carefully crafted and managed communications. It served as a foundation for how we would later manage the larger task of writing about Windows, more on that soon.

Among JensenH's first posts about the Ribbon were pixel-by-pixel discussions of the size, even discussing alternatives that had been suggested in other articles and comments. In a post called "Mythbusters" (the TV show with the same name was popular at the time) he helped readers to see why the Ribbon was far more than a fat toolbar or why the layout was organized by usage frequency and scenario, not implementation category. For each of the main areas of innovation in the design, Jensen walked through in detail the design in a calm and factual tone, along with humor, and colorful (and embarrassing) comparisons from past releases of Office. The posts were wildly popular and served as a model for much of the future blogs our team would author.[54]

The two months from the PDC to the technical beta went by quickly—a good deal of product work was needed, but time flew by because of the incredible interest in what we were cooking up. Fairly low-key beta tests were the norm and only moderately interest. Suddenly techies clamored for access to the release, which we limited because of our own views of quality and inability to support full-time usage of the product.

We got some early instrumentation on usage that started to confirm much of what we hypothesized with respect to the design. It is worth noting that these early users were intentionally trying out many parts of Office they might not routinely use. Those who got hold of the beta were clearly exercising a lot of the product and trying it out. It had been a long time since there was so much excitement about a pre-release version of Office.

In November, we released the technical beta, which was open to developers, enterprise customers, and the Microsoft MVP community, Most Valued Professionals, who played a key role in the beta process of the Office12 redesign. Most enterprise customers did not tend to pick up early technical releases for evaluation.

Who are these MVPs? We were briefly introduced to this group of supporters when they initiated something of a protest against the new VB.NET, referring to it as Visual Fred because of the lack of relationship and compatibility with their much loved Visual Basic. As we'll see, compatibility and respect for the past are super important to MVPs who pride themselves on deep knowledge of Microsoft history and products.

The MVPs are an elite selection of consultants, educators, writers, and generally independent thinkers who are deeply committed to Microsoft products. Each of the major products has a group of MVPs from around the world assigned to it, with the MVP program managed by a central corporate team. Becoming an MVP involves a rigorous nomination and selection process along with reapplication when a term is up. MVPs take great pride in their role and commit significant effort, and often their livelihood, to Microsoft products. It is such a big deal that most readily identified their MVP status in email signatures, resumes, business cards, and today on LinkedIn profiles.

The MVPs are super important to the product once it is released. Many books, training videos, and courses on products are created by MVPs. Many command large audiences online and are the key creators of how-to content in many forms. While the program is centrally administered, including a yearly MVP conference, the product groups all have people assigned to serve as liaisons to their MVPs.

Over the years, the Office MVPs grew a little anxious in that they generally felt they did not receive enough insider information on planned features and ship date. My sessions with the MVPs sometimes had a bit of an edge because I did not use the forum as the first or earliest disclosure event. There was frequently some tension between the promises made by the managers of the MVP program and the product groups like Office in how they positioned the program relative to disclosure and influence on products. Office was perhaps unique in designing for a broad audience of many stakeholders. The most engaged MVPs were like the close-knit IT managers the Windows Server team managed with minimal risk to their IT-focused disclosure and business. I was always cautious of over-indexing on specific customers, especially when we knew they were a deviation or two from the typical user. One of the more challenging aspects of Office was how everyone tends to believe their use is widely representative of others, even software professionals who know this tendency but sometimes have trouble resisting the temptation to represent themselves.

I wanted to find a way to address this gap while also recognizing our responsibility to enterprise sales and customers. Regardless of the forum, I never wanted to be in the position of over-promising with a risk of under-delivering. I strongly believed sharing was committing and failing to deliver to customers had a high cost. Before the November beta, at the yearly gathering of MVPs in Redmond, we had a special session for the 50 or so Office and SharePoint MVPs.

They were invited but didn't know it was special.

After JensenH did a never-before-seen talk on the Ribbon, I walked to the front of the large meeting room and sat on the speaker's podium at the side of the stage.

"There's a feature in Office that everyone has wanted forever and been asking about for as long as I could remember," I said. It was a feature all our competitors provided, and some even claimed it to be a huge advantage over Office. I continued, "available in the public beta in a few weeks, **Office12 would provide full support for saving**

files in Adobe PDF format." We simply called this Save As PDF, exactly what everyone would have called it no matter what we named it.

The room went crazy.

I hopped up onto the stage and showed a click-through demo of the feature working exactly as expected. PDF was another file format option in the File Save As flow. I showed PDF in Publisher, Visio, and Word.

In today's context this sounds supremely dumb. How could our best and most informed users get so excited over PDF? Today PDF is an utter commodity. Everyone uses PDF and no one thinks for a moment if it cost extra. Companies from DocuSign to Google and every institution from banks to hospitals and every government create PDFs and enable their customers to create PDFs. Every browser supports PDF. Every tool creates PDF. But in 2005, Microsoft alone was not in the PDF business yet the whole world was using Microsoft creation tools. It was a big deal, and the world was a silly place.

I then shared that the work was done by the Publisher team and they took on the work to implement it in all the Office applications. At the time, it was a remarkable maze (or thicket) of legal and regulatory challenges: a feature that our competitors supported, that utilized an open and published standard, and that was an entirely obvious customer need. We were receiving more than 30,000 comments per week on our own Office website requesting PDF support. The code was only half the battle. Would regulators view PDF as anticompetitive? Would implementing PDF in Office and not charging money for it be predatory pricing? What would Adobe think or even do? Would there be intellectual property challenges?

It was this last concern that kept us awake. A patent dispute claimed on Office got very expensive very quickly.

Adobe invented PDF more than a decade earlier. Recall, when I was working for BillG, the idea of creating viewable files was a key initiative passed on from my predecessor. Even before PDF, BillG did not want to do a file format that could not be edited and still did not. Adobe distributed a free PDF viewer on every computing platform, but to create PDF required a license, except on Steve Jobs's NeXT operating system where it was built in, and thus eventually on Macintosh and iPhone too. Over time, however, as the internet made PDF more useful, Adobe got pressure, especially in Europe, to make it possible for third parties to create PDF legally, for free. This was already happening, but technically such work risked violating the PDF license or intellectual property. Adobe, perhaps a bit too clever for its own good, published an open specification in a European standards body. We built our feature using only the open specification in a metaphorical clean room.

Adobe was extremely concerned by our support even though we relied exclusively on their open specification submitted to the European standards body.

Except we were Microsoft. Even our largest and soon to be most evil of competitors, Google, and our main Office competitor Sun, were using PDF to compete with us. In fact, the only way to print a document created with Writely, the browser-based word processor that would be acquired by Google, would be by outputting it to PDF which they announced shortly after this event. OpenOffice created PDF by a simple Save As command.

It was the peak period of fear and the assumption that everything we did had a potential for an evil twist, and as such the legal team was predisposed to capitulate to any regulatory skepticism by simply not shipping a feature. In fact, Save As PDF was completely benign and customer driven, but in the climate our motives were always questioned. Erich Andersen (ErichAnd), our fantastic head lawyer for Office, Alan Yates (AlanY) in marketing, and many others spent weeks briefing regulators, trade press, industry groups, standards bodies, and more, laying the groundwork for the feature. ErichAnd spent countless hours with his fellow Microsoft lawyers and those in the antitrust group convincing them we were on firm ground and delivering PDF was going to be OK when their reaction was to avoid regulatory scrutiny at all costs. Perhaps the biggest lesson from the regulatory era was that a company in a dominant position can't always do the things that are perfectly acceptable with a lesser market position.

We were so worried that something might backfire in the antitrust or patent worlds that we designed the feature so we could easily remove it with a small update or reissue Office without the feature. If any party chose to litigate, it would not do so until after Office was commercially available to maximize the inconvenience for us and the damages owed to them.

Still nothing is ever easy, suddenly all those working hard to create or use our expanding XML file format were concerned we were sending a mixed signal to the market. XML was intended to support some of the scenarios PDF could, at least technically. The program managers working on XML authored a series of clarifying mails to be shared with the field on this topic. Under the hood, a key initiative for Office12 were the new XML-based file formats, the "x" in .DOCX, .PPTX, .XLSX. These formats would eventually be published as open standards as well, a fact we also used to deflect any potentially conspiracy theories regarding our use of PDF.

One other wrinkle was that the Longhorn team was doing its own PDF competitor, called XPS. Of course the X stood for XML in XML Paper Specification. We used the same code path we created for PDF to support also XPS. Peter Pathe (Blue) the VP leading the effort let the Windows team know we would support XPS, which they had previously pleaded with us to do. They were very excited to hear the news, but their excitement was considerably tempered by our additional support of PDF. Supporting both reinforced our claim as Office that we were trying to help customers by including multiple technologies.

We prepared an enormous package of briefing materials—all for a single feature. We had a whole media plan, Q&A with me on Microsoft's main web site, a long set of RUDE FAQ especially over the Longhorn XPS format, and even a draft email to send to influential press and partners. It was a production.

Save As PDF was so popular that it quickly became part of the standard demo flow—a feature that exported a document out of Office, not into Office.

Save As PDF was very well done. We supported all the key features of PDF, such as accessibility, fonts, images, and more. Never had we done something so obvious and yet so difficult to release to market. The fact that the lightly resourced Publisher team delivered PDF was a special bonus, and development manager Ben Ross (BenR) did an amazing job. PDF support, through the work of people on the Publisher team like Cherie Ekholm (CherieE) in test and test manager Tammarrian Rogers (TRogers), also furthered Office efforts in accessibility and worldwide government standards.

We received emails extolling the virtues of Save As PDF from dozens of MVPs. It was so rare in a business of our scale to deliver something so immediately positive without cynicism or skepticism. The most elite members of the press from Walt Mossberg at *The Wall Street Journal* and Michael Miller at PC Magazine reached out to congratulate or mostly to thank us for adding support. PDF was crucially important to their workflows, and this made their lives simpler.

It is weird to think, but a feature that seems so dumb today was easily the most friction-free and joyous addition to a product I think I ever did, except maybe for the widget that counted compiled lines in Visual C++ that made everyone think the product was faster. Peter Pathe (Blue) our VP of Word and Publisher overseeing the work was equally happy, especially considering his own personal history in typography and publishing technologies, not to mention studying at the MIT Media Lab during the heyday of e-books.

A few weeks after the MVP conference, the Office technical beta was released. The MVPs received a lot of attention and were anxious and ready, and also feeling good about the insider scoop they received. This would be the first time anyone would have their hands on the code to use day in and day out—and the product was ready for that.

Once the beta went out, we immediately began monitoring the private newsgroups (using the old NNTP protocol) the MVPs used to talk to each other—these newsgroups were the closed-door and NDA (non-disclosure agreement) meeting place for MVPs and part of what they valued most about the program. The product groups were on the hook to monitor the dialogs and respond to issues. The beta proved to be the source of many emotional and heated discussions.

The good news was that these discussions were mostly the arguments we heard following the PDC. The MVPs were a slightly different crowd than the PDC developers. They were dedicating their careers to Office. They had a lot to discuss.

Almost immediately we were again confronted with the feedback that the Ribbon took up too much of the screen. They were sending us screenshots of their customizations of Office—carefully removing much of the default user interface and relying heavily on keyboard shortcuts. To such a setup, the Ribbon was huge and wrong. Some showed us their dual monitor setups or how they arranged windows for multiple documents on a screen in skinny columns that did not work well for the Ribbon. Others had wide screens and sent us proposed renderings of the Ribbon oriented vertically on the screen to "save screen real estate."

We recognized that many of these were personal preferences. We knew we were making a major change and major changes that undid knowledge of the most knowledgeable power users almost always received significant push-back. Through the course of this writing, I've shared several such stories such as the introduction of the new setup technology in Office 2000.

We filled our replies to the comments with data from our telemetry about how Office customers used the product: the screens they had, the number of toolbars and task panes that were routinely visible, and so on. At each juncture, the discussions devolved to a point that we were asked for options: options to move something around, hide something, or be able to change something. This was a normal reaction to change. Essentially, those resistant to change do not battle the change as much as request the ability to not experience it...to turn it off and go back to the old way.

Articulating that the redesign was a programmed user interface, like the cockpit of a plane, not a set of parts to be assembled, was our challenge—essentially rethinking the ancient design point of a customization-centric product. We changed the whole model and made it much more productive, and, in a real sense, moved the customer base (not only the hardcore technical users) to a higher level of expertise and mastery. We did this the very same way the graphical interface itself made software easier, by improving the abstractions. The graphical interface technology of pull-down menus with a mouse replaced arcane and seemingly arbitrary keyboard shortcuts of early character interfaces. The Ribbon replaced the user interface that essentially mapped every feature directly to an implementation and constant document debugging and futzing with higher-level abstractions that regular people could understand.

There was one raucous private newsgroup debate that came to symbolize the challenge of the thesis of operating at a higher level and even of the Ribbon itself. It started when one of the MVPs posted a message ranting, sorry raising the feedback, about "sub-second keyboard access." The post explained that the reason the Ribbon wasn't satisfactory was because it required the mouse, and what was needed was sub-second access to any command. MVPs often customized Office to provide unique and highly tuned access to commands. With the Ribbon this level of tuning was not (yet) possible. The MVP simply stated:

> *Advanced users have ******got******* [emphasis in original] to have convenient — that is, sub-second keyboard access to all dialog boxes and many common commands. Without that capability, Excel 11 never will be uninstalled, because using it will be so much more efficient than using Excel 12.*

As challenging (annoying, actually) as the comment could be interpreted, I resisted the temptation to immediately dive into the debate, as I was often impatient with this type of comment (threat) from insiders. I would forget to remind myself that while we had debated these very points for the past 18 months, the MVP was seeing everything for the first time. Instead, I commiserated down the hall with Billie Sue Chafins (BillieSC), one of the key program managers on Julie's UEX team, reporting to JensenH. Billie Sue moved over to UEX from JeffO's web services team where she was hired in the middle of the Office XP project. Like many (but not all by any stretch) program managers, she was a trained computer scientist, having put herself through school after moving from rural Kentucky, where she was born and raised. Unlike most program managers, Billie Sue was also a teacher, having been a university lecturer of computer science before heading to Microsoft. As a key member of the UEX PM team she was in a perfect spot to drive engagement with the MVPs who were extremely interested in the Ribbon. Billie Sue kept an eye out for hot issues and made sure the team was handling the traffic.

The "sub-second keyboard access" feedback stumped us. Once when I stopped by her office, we looked at each other trying to understand what that could possibly mean, because no one could type and execute commands that quickly. She knew debating the premise of his question would be futile. When forum participants smelled weakness, a pile-on followed. Suddenly, everyone needed "sub-second keyboard access." Billie Sue drafted one of many responses on the thread and eventually provided enough data on usage, customization, and more to at least explain why the design worked.

The larger point she made was how the design committed to providing full keyboard access to all the commands, without having to customize the product to do so. In fact, part of the innovation of the Ribbon was to make sure everything was accessible via the keyboard. In addition, she pointed out that existing keyboard shortcuts remained compatible and customizable. This thread gave Billie Sue the opportunity to acknowledge the feedback and commit to improvements. We already planned on having full keyboard access. We just did not have it in the technical beta.

For every "sub-second" post, however, there were many threads not only defending the Ribbon and experience but calling it brilliant. Some of the more entertaining, if not parochial, comments asked if the Office team might go over and help the Vista team out. More on that later.

Customization continued to be a topic in the newsgroups simply because the MVPs were the people who customized the product the most. The data we offered showed how few people customized (or how often customization happened by accident and could not be easily undone), but there was no telling that to an (or the) audience of customizers. Experts always want customization options, but options have an enormously high cost in the short and long-term that impact customers as much as Microsoft. This is especially true when it comes to customization of user interface—something we were freshly experiencing as we worked to fully support the customizations that developers had become used to for creating custom applications hosted within Office. What doesn't make the product too complex today, will certainly make the product more complex tomorrow when the combinatorics of all the various customizations conflict with each other. What always seems like a simple preference or switch turns into a testing and compatibility matrix from hell.

We were in the earliest stages of the design of what we thought of as a customization escape valve, a place for those strongly committed to customization or, frankly, where the usage model was so far from typical. The Quick Access Toolbar (QAT) was a row of buttons that could be turned into any command from anywhere in the product. The MVPs could have full customization control over this feature. I admit to forcing an expansion concept of the QAT on the team for the power user customization scenario. It was kind of ugly and broke the model, but it was also a life saver with a specific set of customers. The brilliance of how the team designed the original QAT was how minimal the impact was on the overall Ribbon model and design.

The QAT, which is the tiny little row of buttons at the top-left of the title bar (at least through Office in 2021), had buttons for Save (the classic disk icon), Undo (the back arrow), and Redo (the forward arrow.) The QAT was meant to have the very top used commands always accessible regardless of what part of the Ribbon was visible. We were so worried about how dumb it might look for Save (of all things) not to be visible since it was from the first toolbar, that it was placed in the QAT. Much to the disappointment of HP, printing began its slow decline in the early 2000s and given the telemetry it was not on the QAT.

Surprisingly, none of the participants, so many well versed in history, drew the analogy to a feature in Macintosh Word called the Work menu (I believe going back to version 3.0 in 1987, the second Macintosh version), which was precisely the same idea—a menu that could be customized to contain any command in the system. Sometimes what is (very) old becomes new again and is even better when its reemergence goes unnoticed.

In the very early days of Excel, a command called "Set Print Area" was moved off the File menu and it immediately jumped to the top of the customer support call issues. Today this command is mostly automatic, but also readily available in the Ribbon. Fast forward to 2007, JulieLar and I were invited to join with a Harvard Business School executive education session being taught a case study on the user-interface redesign. The students were asked to prepare their notes for class using brand new Office 2007 (the official name of Office12), which none of them had yet been using given the pace of corporate deployments. As soon as class started a student/executive raised their hand and asked Julie "How do I print?" as the rest of the class groaned in support. The omission of a Print button on the initial QAT might have been the biggest oversight of the entire project. It was certainly an embarrassing moment.

The beta was solid enough that thousands were using it every day, and it was clear more of the product was getting used, quality was high, and we were on a path to finish. This, however, was the technical enthusiast audience.

Our next step was a broad release, including the core business users, specifically IT managers, who generally didn't react well to change and could be very vocal about it. The press and reviewers would also be testing out Office12 and most of them used Word and Excel for hours every day.

082. DEFYING CONVENTIONAL WISDOM TO FINISH OFFICE

Nearly every country's "Feedback to Corp" slide at the grueling field sales multiweek Mid-Year Reviews (MYRs) in January 2006 published the same bullet point:

- Office "12" – Need Classic Mode

What was this big, and clearly coordinated push for something called classic mode, and why now? We, of course, knew what it was but we did not know why this was happening now. It was very late in the schedule, post-beta testing. We were just months from scheduled completion as we just went through the final validation of the product—when the team is changing as few things as possible for the last few months, certainly not making any design changes.

A broad public beta went out to most enterprise customers as well as the technical press. More people enrolled in the beta than we expected or could even imagine. There was a great deal of interest in such a bold direction for Office.

As with the technical beta, the reactions came swiftly and clearly, often based on little more than the first few minutes with the product. Reactions from the press arrived in three waves—straightforward news of the release, first looks or reactions based on first experiences, and then, after a week or so, deeper dives into the product.

The first looks wrote themselves as we expected. Office12 was a sweeping change, and the obvious commentary or controversy questioned whether customers or the market were ready for it. Would it work? How difficult would it be to learn? Almost always the point of view of why the change was made was reflected, but the tone was skeptical. That was kind of annoying, but entirely expected.

For example, CNET's Ina Fried who is always fair and balanced, said, "The radical revamp could help the company as it seeks to stave off competition from OpenOffice and others, but it also risks alienating those who like things the way they are."[55]

Computer Reseller News, the trade publication focused on small and medium business, went to great lengths to express concern. "While most users will welcome the additional features, Microsoft's decision to teach its customers a new user interface for accessing commands and functions could be a risky proposition. Once the beta testers (and the bloggers) have registered their opinions, some Office 12 design points could be in for a course correction."[56]

A more detailed expression of concern came from CNET's editors. "In the past, Microsoft has sabotaged itself by unrolling too many new features to Office too fast. We're keeping a lookout for problems; after all, Office 12 was in its storyboard stages just a few months ago. If you've spent the past two years mastering Office 2003, prepare for a steep learning curve."[57]

These articles generated the MYR feedback. The enterprise account managers, essentially all our revenue except for Japan, were on the verge of freaking out. They saw the Ribbon as pure friction in the way of revenue and nothing less. They cited doubts expressed in the articles, reprinted in every language around the world, as evidence of deep concerns over the direction Office was taking. They did not want to spend energy selling Office where the assumption was we'd already won. They wanted to focus on selling the big server strategy, where we were losing to open-source Linux and a host of smaller competitors. So why put up a barrier, they asked.

As if to highlight these enterprise customer concerns even more, in the spring of 2005 Office marketing rolled out worldwide a series of advertisements as a follow-on to the "Great Moments" campaign previously described. Attempting to inject humor into the extremely enterprise Office 2003 wave and to encourage customers to digitally enable knowledge workers, marketing developed a new advertising campaign affectionately called "Dinosaurs" though formally called "Evolve." These ads featured humans in the office but with oversized, cartoonish dinosaur heads, implying those who have not yet embraced a digital workstyle including running Office 2003 were dinosaurs. In other words, we called nearly all our customers dinosaurs. At least the ads were popular in Japan, a market known to appreciate a good mascot, where the company distributed a large quantity of small plastic dinosaur heads.

Very quickly what felt like a magical release suddenly seemed to be worrisome to the sales force. That was not acceptable.

We obviously took on a significant risk in choosing a complete redesign of Office to address our "good enough" challenge. In hindsight sometimes I can hardly believe we did so. Now that we had 18 or more months of time to develop the product, we were genuinely confident.

Our previous attempts at addressing bloatware or the belief the product simply did too much each failed. These approaches were rooted in the conventional wisdom of different stakeholders:

- **Reduce User Interface**. From the earliest days of the product, the path to simplicity was to minimize the amount of interface visible on the screen. The conventional reaction to bloat was to proclaim less is more, as we often read about in reviews and analyst reports. We did our best to avoid removing features. Instead we twice tried a few design tricks, one was Intelligent Menus and the second was the technique of rafting toolbars.
- **Office Lite.** The business view looked at price points and wanted to meet good enough with a lower priced offering without upsetting the main revenue stream of course. The way to compete would be to have a stripped down, easy to use, easier to administer, lighter-weight version of Office, that cost less. We solved for this problem by changing the composition of SKUs to create lower price points, rather than chasing the low end as previously described.
- **Customization**. Customization was always the easy way out. If a customer or IT group didn't like something in Office, they could just rearrange it. The tech enthusiast users and those early in the beta process said they would be fine with the Ribbon, so long as it enabled full customization by rearranging the tabs or contents of the interface. We addressed this with the customizable Quick Access Toolbar, complete keyboard support, and support for creating custom add-ins.

As we have seen, each conventional approach was fatally flawed and by and large amounted to half-steps to addressing the challenge of bloat or good enough.

Instead, Office12 would take the perceived liabilities of Office—the depth and breadth of features—and turn those into assets. The strategy was to make the product better by not just redesigning but reprogramming the user's experience for a modern era.

Office12 could easily be viewed as taking the contrarian approach to conventional wisdom and feedback at each step. In early 2000s Microsoft, the idea of not "listening to customers" was decidedly counter-intuitive to put it nicely.

Most of our Office buyers were vocal and visible. Enterprise account managers regularly brought IT managers and executives to Redmond for briefings. Along with a direct line to SteveB, they were never far away, nor were their expressed concerns about products. As previously discussed, the growth areas of the Windows Server business hinged on directly listening to and acting on feedback from IT pro customers.

In the consumer business, Microsoft's new online services were increasingly enamored with A/B testing and experimentation, substituting data for intuition.

And here we were in Office being radical. To many it looked like we were either ignoring customers or not using data. We were just working the old way.

The MYR feedback added a new challenge. Customers, especially our prized enterprise customers, would simply demand we not ship the redesign at all. Even if we chose to there should be a way to easily revert to the previous design, at least for administrators.

Whether enterprise customers installed and tested the beta or not, this concern rapidly spread through the world of IT directly to our account managers. Budgets, dollars and headcount were reserved for back-end servers and data centers, for which we offered SharePoint and the full spectrum of Microsoft servers. In this environment, the resources that were allocated to PCs for individual knowledge workers were used almost entirely to keep PCs running, free of viruses and malware, and handle catastrophes such as breakdowns and stolen laptops. The budgets and resources for training materials, helpdesk, and even how-to courses all but vanished from the corporate world.

Given that context, any major change to Office was costly and unbudgeted. Even though customers were paying for years of Office, they had stopped factoring change into their IT budgets. For most in IT, Office was viewed as complete. Office was good enough. At the most extreme, a new version of Office would be fine if it added a few more menu items or commands, but mostly the best release of Office was one with no changes at all, but with better virus protection, reduced system requirements (Office already consumed the least amount of system resources of most anything running, even browsers), and even more administrative controls especially to turn off new features. Whatever lock-down we saw back in 1999 that first time visiting enterprise customers was now an ever-increasing new normal.

According to conventional wisdom among Microsoft followers, Classic Mode (CM) was the answer. CM was not part of Office12 and never was, but almost on cue the early punditry and enterprise teams assumed it would be in the product. The feedback or request was more of a Microsoft reflex. The term originated from Windows, referring to a switch or mode that flipped the new operating system to the look and feel of the old version. Windows had historically taken this to extremes. For example, in Windows 95 it was still entirely possible to run the old Program Manager and File Manager instead of using the new Start menu and Explorer. In fact, those still run today on the 32-bit versions of Windows 11. Windows also included visual themes that emulated the old graphic design, which made the product look…old or comfortable. This provided a comfort for IT managers concerned about training. It was marketed as an option, but it was heavily documented in many deployment and IT-focused publications as an asset or even preferred way to use the product. Technically, CM meant Compatibility Mode in Windows, but it was referred to colloquially as Classic Mode because it referred to the old, and presumably loved version of Windows. These were thin veneers on very easy to use features, but customers were comforted by the gesture.

It was therefore entirely logical that these same IT managers (and the field sales managers) assumed Office12 came with a switch that turned Office12 into the standard or conventional user interface design—Classic Mode. Both Classic and Compatible are interesting word choices in that both imply the new product is less than a classic or not compatible.

The absence of classic mode was a surprise to, well, everyone including BillG and SteveB. While at one point super early on it was something we thought we might do, in hindsight, it was never more than a consideration with a place-holder specification.

Still, I had to be careful not to say that at MYR. I learned long ago not to drop hints or to be vague at MYR. My action item was dutifully recorded and in due time I would get back to the field staff with our plan.

We had so many reasons why CM was not possible let alone desirable. First and foremost, the requests for CM were based on the assumption that existing Office products were as easy to use as our marketing implied. While customers overwhelmingly associated ease of use with Office, in everyday usage, the product was complex, maddening, and fragile. Each day millions around the world had moments of dissatisfaction. The old products were familiar, but no one thought they were easy in any absolute sense. There was room for innovation to save untold hours of grief. No sane person would debate the maddening frustration that came at some point when using Office.

The user interface for a product that does as much as Office goes well beyond aesthetics. The design of Office 2003 was functional, and as a design the product was failing customers. Many people were squeaking by as long as they used the small set of capabilities they previously learned. And the tiny percentage of people who mastered the product would not credit design for their success, but rather their fortitude and investment in learning the product. A product designed for a single profession, like Adobe Photoshop or Autodesk AutoCAD, could remain mysterious to outside users because those in need learned it as part of their professional training. Office needed to be different. It was a tool used by hundreds of millions of people who learned with little to no formal training.

The goal of Office12 was to be more human and less computer. The design language for the PC era's first two decades was primarily about utility and consistency—as in, making everything just function. We were at a point in time where we wanted to make the products work for people and to do so with a new sense of mastery and ease.

In early 2005, JensenH wrote *The Office User Interface System*, a document detailing the rationale and design for Office12. This document covered the motivations, problems being addressed, and the detailed philosophy behind each of the elements of the design. Even to this day, it amazes me that we had this document a year before release, and it still stands as an incredible accomplishment by the UEX team.

There was no looking back. CM was about looking back. As a practical matter, there were three major technical hurdles to classic mode.

First, there was literally no room left in the product. One could easily project out the future of Office as having hundreds of toolbars and task panes. Office would literally collapse in on itself into a giant black hole of buttons with little room left for content. The screenshots meant as jokes ten years ago were looking more like predictions or designs. Any new feature was like parking at the mall the day after Thanksgiving. Except instead of circling the parking lot in a car, program managers would be circling the hallways in search of an empty spot on a toolbar.

Second, and less obvious, was that the Ribbon design fostered a new and more modern interaction between user and features—live previews, extended text descriptions, galleries, contextual user interface, and high-level grouping of commands. New capabilities in Office were designed knowing they could be offered to users in this more modern experience. There was nowhere to do that in the old interface. That meant we would either not have those features or we would need to develop yet another mechanism to provide those new features in an old way, somehow.

Third, and most critically, everything we knew about customer behavior said that once a customer turned on CM, they would never turn it off. They would expect CM not just for Office12 but for every release after that. When one considers that Office is supposed to be compatible release over release, then it is obvious CM becomes part of a permanent compatibility story. CM would introduce a fork in the Office product where everything is done twice, once the new way and once the compatible way. An easy solution to this was to simply run the old release of Office forever. Microsoft had a way to make this possible as well.

The debate over CM, in my view, trivialized the design of the product. While I was of course extremely empathetic with the change that would be forced (as some would say) on to customers, I could not help but think back to the early days of the project. At the start we talked about all the places in life and technology that change. People are frustrated for a time then recover and move on. We were going through one of the greatest changes in the history of the world with the internet. Every internet site was constantly changing. Why did Office have to be static? Static equals dying.

Why were people so nervous about this change? I was puzzled for a while. Then I realized, almost no one in power positions in the industry had lived through a major change to Office. Since about 1990, or almost 15 years earlier, Office was unchanged. Office was a constant. It was as if no one ever expected Office to change. Almost no one recalled the early MS-DOS applications or the pre-Windows era. Most of our own development team only knew Windows or Macintosh. Out of almost 2,400 people on the Office product development team, only 58 of them even worked at Microsoft before Windows 3.1 shipped and only 7 were at Microsoft before Macintosh Excel shipped. Over 80% of the team joined since Windows 95 shipped. Even our own team never really lived through the graphical interface transition or the 8-bit to 16-bit transition, except while they were in grade school. Most were hired from college and the majority had much of their early computing experience on Macintosh. Our new hires during Office12 were the first generation of web-natives, having had the modern internet since high school.

JulieLar had a strong point of view on dealing with this, as someone who did live through the graphical transition as an early Macintosh app developer on PageMaker. She often noted, "When you believe in a design, go for it." Some might interpret this as no compromise, but principled was a more appropriate way to put it. In many ways it was a new-to-Microsoft approach. The general manner Microsoft (and Office) approached change was to always support the old way, either with an option or to move on to a completely new product that solved the same problem differently, leaving the old product on the market. If you ever wondered why Microsoft had so many data access APIs or UI widgets or any other of a multiplicity of solutions for one problem, it is this latter approach. It is vastly easier to start from scratch than to reengineer something in place. The only problem is starting from scratch and creating a new product/technology rarely brought forward the myriad of tiny subtle details that existed in the original implementation. Complex products resulted from this approach. The products were either complex because everything had an option or alternate way to use it, or complex because multiple products claimed to solve the same problem but in non-overlapping ways. Teams often took the path easiest for their code base, defaulting to whatever had the least friction to adding new features.

It is worth noting how valuable customers found a high level, or perhaps perfect, level of compatibility. Today we joke about running Excel 2.2 on 32-bit Windows 10, but it does so 35 years later! Even early 1980s character mode MS-DOS applications continued to run through new Windows releases as late as 2010. This is decidedly different from compatibility at a user interface level. Whether one uses old Excel or old Multiplan, doing so doesn't impact using Office 2003 or Adobe Photoshop as the compatibility is just bolted on the side. In the case of Office, the old features were intermixed with the new and that was an entirely different level of complexity, an unachievable level of complexity.

Because of this history, JulieLar and I wound up on the front lines, so to speak, engaging with hardcore fans over compatibility mode from the early days of beta testing. In the private MVP newsgroups, I once wrote a very long essay, almost, about why change is OK reinforcing the history and context of our industry, including that most customers had simply never seen any material change in Office or Windows. I might not have convinced anyone at the time, but I did start to formulate the kind of arguments that would come in handy later in my journey. Quoting from the newsgroup post verbatim:

> *To believe that at any given time some technology is the ultimate in productivity and nothing should change is of course absurd. While many people have a massive investment in analog recording of video and audio, few would argue that the change in technology is worth it if you want to stay a leader in the field. Photography magazines are filled with "move to digital discussions". There will always be a few people who remain convinced that the technology they invested in is the be all and end all of the field and that moving to a new technology is not perceived as being better, and in fact is worse. As with any technology shift, it is *never* 100% better — digital audio does not sound as good to some people, digital photos are not as rich in quality or resolution as film, digital video looks different than film, etc. But new technologies have benefits that were not possible or not thought of at the time. So it is with the new user interface.*

The idea that CM was a short-term fix crystalized our collective point of view for how wrong-headed such a capability was. If we learned one thing over the previous few years of Enterprise Agreements, it was that if customers were offered a way to freeze infrastructure, or avoid anything new, they would take it. Not only would they take it, but they would embrace it and stick with it. How did we know? Many customers continued to run Outlook 97 even though we had several new releases and they had no interest in touching email on the desktop or retraining users. Windows NT 4.0 was still a dominant server running many Exchange mail systems and it was released a decade earlier. In fact, the most critical initiative in the field was to upgrade NT 4.0 customers to Windows Server 2000 or later.

With the 10-year support lifecycle in place, CM would mean customers would assume they could run the new release the old way for another decade.

We had always tried to honor past products with immense levels of compatibility that went far beyond any of our competitors on the PC. The lessons from changing the file format in Office 97 were clear, but so were thousands of accommodations or compromises we made over the years. Now, however, the combination of Enterprise Agreements and the 10-year lifecycle proved to be a huge leverage point customers had with product groups. So much so that customers always assumed that any changes to a product would be optional. Their ideal new product release was one that was the old product, just faster and easier to deploy and manage, and the new features would be available on an as-wanted basis.

That was not our plan with Office12 and the Ribbon. Ever.

The Mid-Year Review (MYR) where we were swamped with compatibility mode requests provided the best evidence for the excitement surrounding Office12. Many countries used the new visualization features of Excel to enhance their revenue, budgets, market share, and expense numbers. Every grid of numbers used the new features to automatically color code red/yellow/green or included tiny sparklines for a great visual effect. This time I knew how to accept the MYR feedback gracefully by empathizing with a commitment to get back to the teams.

I must admit I already knew the answer. We decided at the earliest days of the project, May 2004 precisely. It would be a few months from then before anyone would even ask about it.

During the early demos of Office12 when BillG went from office to office to see a select set of features, one thing he mentioned to me that I wrote down was "classic mode". He wanted to hear why we didn't show him CM. He thought doing so was "trivial" and was something we of course did, but maybe (as was almost always the case) we were going to add it later. He was prepared to make his case and we had to defend our choices. We had to do so knowing we had no backup plan. Any product changes would mean a product slip, but that was the least of the worries. Bill did not think in terms of product slips or schedules even, and often believed what he asked for would be easy to squeeze in. The scale of the projects was still something he was not entirely adjusted to.

JulieLar and her manager and leader of program management (and former leader of Office development) Antoine Leblond (Antoine) were the right people to go to follow up with BillG. In January, they walked him through the state of the design, how we would measure success, and what risks we saw. They answered his questions with the supporting data. They detailed specific scenarios that they repeatedly measured throughout the development process.

I wasn't at the meeting, but they told me it went well. Julie shared one direct quote from BillG, later shared in a Newsweek magazine story by Steven Levy. At the end of the demo Bill said, "I can't believe you convinced me to get rid of menus and toolbars."[58] It was also one of the last Office product meetings BillG would have as a full-time employee before he transitioned to part-time later in 2008. We were done talking about CM.

We hit Beta 2 and RTM only about 90 days off the original schedule of the two-year project. By our standards we became an execution engine, and with Office 2007, as it would be officially named, we also showed we could innovate in a big way.

There were many reviews, now many blogs, from the end of 2005 through early 2006. Reviews focused on the major overhaul of the product as expected. Also as expected, each put the question out there asking if it would be too radical or too bold. Nearly every review was positive to glowing.

A smattering of reviews continued to complain about the lack of a bridge to ease into the Ribbon, compatibility mode, or a way to turn off the Ribbon, which they just assumed would be there. Of course, there were customers who told us they were not going to upgrade, but for any release only about one-third did anyway. That was another problem entirely, and all the Ribbon offered was a convenient excuse that went beyond budgets, IT strategy, something else.

Personally, this release was the confidence builder I needed after a challenging Office 2003. It felt great to build the hot or at least interesting and innovative product people were talking about. This came at a good time for Microsoft given the Longhorn chaos and the cloud over the company due to the regulatory settlement.

Anil Dash was early in popularizing blogging. Today he would have been called an influencer. He authored a post I loved. It read, "Short and sweet, the Ribbon and new UI in Microsoft Office 2007 is **the ballsiest new feature in the history of computer software**." [*asterisks in the original*]

He also captured the risk that we felt for the preceding two years:

> *Now, most of us who like to prognosticate and pontificate about software like to say things like "It'd be easy to just..." or "It's trivial to add..." but the thing is, most of us aren't betting our entire careers on the little tweaks and changes we'd like to make to our productivity applications. Try making a mistake that jeopardizes a business that makes $250 million a week.*[59]

But something else was on our collective minds.

What came after the Ribbon would not be more features in traditional desktop apps, but more internet scale services, more use of the browser and mobile, and more connections to data. We built the equivalent of the *Cutty Sark*, the best of wind-powered clipper ships. Steam-powered ships were coming, however, in the form of smartphones and mobile-cloud computing, as long-time industry analyst Benedict Evans would later write in an essay "The best is the last."[60]

The era of formatting documents was ending. The Ribbon was a new paradigm for desktop computing (what we called Win32 apps) in a world rapidly being overtaken by the web.

We were also approaching the end of an era of software reviews. We could sense that as we went out on press tours. There would not be another release where a magazine would devote dozens of printed pages to Office, or Barnes & Noble would have a shelf of Office books. One review mattered above all for me personally and that was by Walt Mossberg at *The Wall Street Journal*. It wasn't just that he was the most influential reviewer, though he arguably was. Others would review every feature and have dozens of screenshots. Walt spoke for the typical customers, the non-techie, the person who just needed to get work done without futzing. Winning that review meant winning over that customer, at least by proxy.

No one expects a perfectly glowing review of any product from Walt because he makes a point of raising concerns that normal people will have from learning, to new file formats, and even the pricing. That said the headline alone was huge for us and it was a big enough deal that the WSJ placed it on the front of the business section with color screenshots— "Bold Redesign Improves Office 2007." There was that word, bold, just like we aimed for at the start of the release. He went on to write:

> *So, when Microsoft makes significant changes to Office, it's a big deal. And the latest version of the software suite, called Office 2007, due out Jan. 30, is a radical revision, the most dramatic overhaul in a decade or more.*
>
> *I don't use the word "radical" lightly. The entire user interface, the way you do things in these familiar old programs, has been thrown out and replaced with something new. In Word, Excel and PowerPoint, all of the menus are gone — every one. None of the familiar toolbars have survived, either. In their place is a wide, tabbed band of icons at the top of the screen called the Ribbon. And there is no option to go back to the classic interface.*
>
> ...
>
> *If you'd like to get more out of Office, especially in the area of how your documents look, Office 2007 is a big step forward and worth the steep learning curve it imposes.*

Of course, I personally fixated on the places he was critical. For the team this was a huge, huge, win.

While we gave new life to Office with the redesign and we created a foundation to continue to evolve the product incrementally, the next wave of innovations would (and should) be entirely different products. We disrupted ourselves. We made the previous releases of Office look old and underpowered. OpenOffice would continue to chase the old design, and the soon to be released Google Docs would do the same.

The world was changing though, and we knew it. It wasn't just the reviews going away or the rise of the web for consumption. In November 2005, just before the MYR process detailed in this section, I wrote the framing memo as I always did for what would be called Office14. Yes, we skipped Office13 though I was careful to note that 13 is unlucky only in some cultures. In *Aligning for Office14*, I described five "Big Bets":

> *The big bets we will explore as we begin aligning the team for Office14 include:*

- *Moving Up the Value Stack*
- *Office Web Companions*
- *Internet (Web-Based) Services*
- *Building on Windows Live*
- *Office's Enterprise Content Management Platform*

The first bet was about enterprise computing, as it should be. My heart was in the second bet, which was to build Office for the browser. I received immense pushback for suggesting such heresy. Often people used against me my own argument from years ago that the browser wouldn't work for "real productivity." The trajectory we were on was now clear and the time to start was now.

To ease people into the idea, I positioned (so cleverly, I believed) the idea of building Office for the browser as "companions" to Office and called them OWC, the Office Web Companions. As companions versus competitors or replacements they would not risk cannibalizing the real Office. The other challenge within Microsoft was the view that corporations would be running a Microsoft-centric "browser-based" platform using much more capable technologies that relied on proprietary Windows Server and Windows Longhorn such as successors to ActiveX. The broad consumer world would be running "web-based" solutions in a least-common denominator browser, a phrase always used when referring to HTML. It was a subtle difference in wording with huge implications strategically. So, I danced around both as I wrote and then evangelized the memo.

I was very excited to build on our 1990s strategies of embracing the web with HTML and then Office Web Server. I was already dreading what was sure to be a significant uphill battle across the company, not unlike what we had faced in building Office 2007 or using HTML or creating SharePoint. The company had a strategy and these bets seemed to run counter to it, but only at first glance. I thought a good deal about how Windows rose out of what was often branded internally as a side project, operating environment, or experiment.

It was going to be a journey to disrupt the desktop applications, but we needed to start.

My direct reports and our significant others gathered for a dinner at Assaggio Ristorante in Seattle to celebrate the final beta release. I hardly ever asked people on the team to do things outside of work hours, but this release was so special.

Months earlier in just a hallway conversation, Richard Wolf (RWolf), manager of PowerPoint and Visio, said that it was cool that the "last" release of Office was the one with a major UI redesign—it was almost poetic for him to say. Richard was the productivity philosopher among us, having worked at Lotus before Microsoft, a reflective person, and an early member of the academic community focused on productivity. He was right. There was no reason to think there would ever be another major redesign of Office that was necessary.

Innovation is like that. Microsoft was built on the idea of creating, grinding out improvements, then moving to a new platform to innovate. We were at that point. Everyone could see it. It was as if we each felt it in our own way. We had accomplished what we set out to do a decade and six major releases earlier.

We shared a toast (of a beverage of choice) to what the team accomplished. We were proud. And we were happy. We built the very best version of Office—a reinvention of the product—in a way that had never been done.

For most of the seasoned leadership team at this dinner, this was going to be their last release of Office. I think we each knew that.

Things were about to change for me too. As happy as it was at the time, it was also a bit sad. There was always a bit of a low after shipping. The grind of building suddenly stops. A sense of mission accomplished takes over. Also, I just turned 40.

Unbeknownst to me at the time, this would be my last release of Office. Something I never even considered.

That Office14 memo was my last work on Office.

2006-2007

The year was marked by cultural shifts. BillG announced he would step down as Chief Software Architect, a transition that would take two years. I was given a new role and faced multiple corporate and culture challenges, and outside of Microsoft the tech landscape was changing too. And fast. “To google” was added to the dictionary.

083. LIVING THE ODD-EVEN CURSE

By the start of March 2006 the Longhorn product cycle had been a chaotic five-plus years that included the security work for Windows XP, the release of Windows Tablet PC, Windows Media Center, Windows 64-bit, Server releases, and importantly, a major project change called the *Longhorn Reset*, essentially defining a new scaled-back product mid-flight based on the original Longhorn. The Windows team had been through a lot and was not finished. Longhorn had been receiving a lukewarm reception from users of a big *Community Technology Preview* release since the fall of 2005. The team, however, had started updating the product more frequently and momentum was indeed shifting by early 2006.

Windows Vista, as it was officially named, was still an unpredictable amount of time away from shipping. While not public at the time, a couple of weeks down the road, Microsoft would announce a final and just-decided delay to ship Vista for availability in January 2007. The team could not commit to making the release available in time for PCs to be sold for back-to-school or holidays 2006. Vista would eventually release to manufacturing in November.

Windows was still on fire with PC sales breaking through 200 million units in a single year for the first time, demonstrating extreme product-market fit. Both Servers and Tools were doing well, extremely well, except there was a nagging problem emerging from across Lake Washington called AWS, Amazon Web Services, a shift from companies buying Windows to run on their own server computers to renting storage and compute in the (or a) cloud. There was a good deal of tension between Windows team and the Server team. The Server org required the Windows org to contribute to shipping a new Server. This delayed a new Server product, slowing their release based on Longhorn until the next Windows release. The .NET framework and Visual Studio had become leaders for IT development within corporations, but the onslaught of Linux, Apache, MySQL, and PHP (later Perl/Python) continued to dominate the public internet and the university programs in computer science.

On the RedWest campus the investments in online services faced a myriad of revenue, cost, product, and usage problems that were not nearly as visible as the Windows challenges. Wall Street, however, was growing increasingly impatient with financial results, which seemed to punish SteveB for his transparency. There were dozens of Microsoft online services, some branded as MSN and others using a new umbrella name Windows Live, in every conceivable category from selling cars (MSN CarPoint) to chat (MSN Messenger) to finding Wi-Fi hotspots (MSN Wi-Fi Hotspots.) Microsoft seemed to be searching for a big win against Yahoo and a rapidly dominant Google in the world of internet advertising and consumer services.

Google was top of mind for many, not because so many groups across Microsoft competed with Google products but because of the aura the 2006 Google culture achieved. Google was fast. They were innovative. They were empowering. They had "20 percent time" when engineers could work on whatever they wanted one day a week. They had free gourmet food and a chef, all day long, compared to our grungy filtered water dispensers and subsidized airport food with limited availability. They had snacks and we still had noodles and one type of V8®. They had massages, while we had a multi-purpose sports field, but no towels. Note, towels returned in the summer 2006. We had individual offices and they had collaborative open plan cubicles. You read that correctly, Microsofties complained about having offices. They had a modern, flat organization with 50 reports to a manager, and yes you read that right too. In the blink of an eye to me, everything we held near and dear and made Microsoft an icon of business culture, seemed to be old, tired, and either wrong or inadequate, like wearing khakis, loafers, and a button down to Burning Man.

Google Chrome was still almost three years from launching while Internet Explorer had 90% share. The last new release, however, was Internet Explorer 6.0 launched five years ago with Windows XP frustrating users, web developers, and the market. Gmail was about to turn two and it was crushing Microsoft Hotmail with its superior junk mail filter and massive free storage. Microsoft just started to build its own web search product which would launch in 2006 as Windows Live Search into a market where Google had already overtaken Yahoo and grown to half the market while gaining a half point of share every month.

As Vista was creeping along, albeit faster these days, toward shipping, there was a much deeper problem in Windows that was symptomatic of the broader malaise or even open hostility across the company, especially in engineering. Even though the company kept putting up blockbuster numbers, the morale across product groups had declined. Vista had contributed to that. *Integrated Innovation* had as well. Integrated innovation was the expression at the CEO level of the desire and *right* to build integrated software, which continued to be challenged in the courts and among regulators. Internally, this was the opposite of what people wanted to hear because the feeling was integrated innovation, or synergy, was what had first gummed up Microsoft relative to Google. The yearly Microsoft Poll survey was a litany of complaints and issues from employees across most of the product groups.

In a semantic twist, the phrase was later morphed into *Innovate then Integrate*. That might not have helped. In reality the pressure for synergy had not relaxed at all as it was a cornerstone of Microsoft's (and BillG's) strategy and culture, even more so as the company became an enterprise company given how much enterprise customers and the enterprise ecosystem valued synergistic strategy, or maybe strategic synergy. Strategy was the anchor holding back Longhorn. A scathing cover story in the September 26, 2005, BusinessWeek, "Troubling Exits at Microsoft" painted a picture of employees departing, malaise, and the rise of Google. Even a longtime member of Microsoft Research's Technical Advisory Board, Carnegie Mellon University professor Raj Reddy, called for a company breakup to support more "nimble operations."

But the biggest problem was that we felt like we were losing, and Wall Street felt that way too and the stock price reflected that lack of enthusiasm.

We were losing to Google. We were losing to Yahoo. We were losing to BlackBerry and Nokia. We were losing to Sony. We were losing to Oracle. We were losing to SAP. We didn't have anything to compete with AWS. We were losing to Apple when it came to PC hardware. We had already lost to Apple's iPod.

> *In the years ahead, we will see accelerating change in the software industry, as the computing needs of our customers start to move beyond the PC into a "PC-Plus" world. The PC will undoubtedly remain at the heart of computing at home, work, and school, but it will be joined by numerous new intelligent devices and appliances, from handheld computers and auto PCs to Internet-enabled cellular phones. More software will be delivered over the Internet, and the boundary between online services and software products will blur. The Internet will continue to change everything by offering a level of connectivity that was unimaginable only a few years ago — and every home, business, and school will want to be hooked up to that incredible global database. —Annual Report, 1999*

Our competition with Apple was becoming increasingly sharp compared to past years where our view was essentially to ignore them, going way back to the launch of Windows 95 and the "C:\ONGRTLNS.W95" full page advertisement in The Wall Street Journal. In 1999, BillG wrote an Op-ed for Newsweek and a month later proclaimed in the 1999 Annual Report to Shareholders[61],[62] that the "PC-Plus" era was upon us. With this Bill described an era where PCs would continue to be central, but rather than part of every scenario they would be surrounded by devices that connect to a Windows PC.

This framing of the future became more visible and widely used across Microsoft communications as the temperature of the competition from all corners heated up.

The PC-Plus era is rooted in a response to what had been simmering among the tech press from as early as 1993 when Walt Mossberg first used the phrase "Post-PC." The first wave of connected devices began with the EO Communicator in early 1993 and then the Apple Newton available a bit later. In his review of the EO, Mossberg described the device as not "the kind of post-PC device that promoters of the PDA concept have promised: something with the price, size and battery life of a Sharp Wizard, but the smarts and communications ability of a good PC and an advanced phone."[63] Whereas in the review of the Newton he described it as "a post-PC device that streamlines data entry, links all of your information in intelligent ways and adapts to your handwriting and work habits over time."[64]

A few years later with the arrival of the Palm VII in 1999, the first truly connected and mobile-phone sized device, the punditry was running full throttle declaring the arrival of the Post-PC era. The trade press was filled with editorial and widespread usage of the term, much to our dismay at Microsoft.

Bill Gates, Paul Otellini, and others in the PC industry went on a bit of a campaign defending the PC and declaring the PC-Plus era. They executed a series of Op-ed pieces and other marketing efforts to thwart the notion that the PC was dead. In The Wall Street Journal in May 2006, just after I started working on Windows, they wrote an Op-ed explaining why and how the PC will continue to thrive.[65]

> *So, the next time you read about the end of the PC era, think about what you do when you get home from vacation and want to share the pictures on your digital camera with family and friends. Or where you go to download music and videos onto your iPod or MP3 player. Or how you synchronize the contacts, calendars and email on your handheld wireless devices. Or where you go when you want to find new music or search for that episode of "Lost" you missed last week.*
>
> *You sit down at your PC, of course.*

As this shows, the defensiveness around the PC became increasingly obvious and the technical justifications increasingly detached from where the industry was heading.

There was no shortage of problems on the Windows front, in contrast to Office which seemed on both solid footing and heading calmly to a new era.

Despite the chaos, upheaval, corporate strife, and my own apprehension, I was about to run towards the fire.

Office Hours

I was sitting in the guest chair in SteveB's office while he was standing, swinging his golf club. He stopped, finally, and said, "Thank you. Thank you."

With great enthusiasm, those were his words as he shook my hand with all the vigor of a salesman closing a deal. A handshake between product group Microsofties was so unconventional that it added to my uneasy feeling.

Uncertain as I was, I accepted the role of leading Windows product development.

But it would not be so simple. That also meant managing the struggling Hotmail, the new Live Search, and the loved and popular, though shrinking MSN Messenger, along with several other online services. I would report to Kevin Johnson (KevinJo), who had joined Microsoft from IBM in the early 1990s and risen up the ranks by building out the company's customer support arm and then to running the worldwide field organization. After Microsoft he went on to become the CEO of Juniper Networks and then Starbucks. Kevin would provide much needed stability across his enormous portfolio, which included all of Windows and Server, Tools, Servers, and online services. The big news was that Kevin was taking on a new and huge product development role, essentially everything except Office. The way I thought about Kevin's job was he was on the hook to lead competing with Apple, Linux, Google, Yahoo, now Amazon, and the rest of the internet. The key thing for me was that one person oversaw every major customer segment at the company: consumers, PC makers (Microsoft's largest source of revenue concentrated in about ten customers), developers (developers, developers), small business, enterprise IT, and now advertisers. It was kind of nuts for one person to be asked to manage all of that I thought. My job was to help him by making sure Windows was taken care of.

The Windows team had been divided into two big teams for quite some time. The core operating system was known as Core OS Division, COSD, pronounced "kahz-dee". COSD led the parade at creating Windows, drove the engineering process and culture, and was staffed with first among equals. COSD owned the operating system kernel, device drivers, file system, networking, security, and in general the guts of Windows. The team was where the original Windows NT architects all worked. When Jim Allchin (JimAll) created the COSD organization he and I spoke about how we built the Office team (the original Office Product Unit a decade earlier) and COSD was somewhat mirrored after that, at least they thought so. About half the Windows resources were in COSD.

The other half of Windows was known as Windows Client and embodied the user side of Windows including the graphical interface, the explorer, start menu, control panel, printing, faxing, and all the experiences from tablets to media playback, to Windows Media Center, and importantly Internet Explorer. What COSD was to process and hardcore, Client was to "doing cool stuff." A visit over to one of the Client buildings and you were likely to see displays of cool new media players, fancy gaming PCs, or the latest in wireless gadgets. There was always a cool demo to be had. Showing off COSD innovation was a lot more tricky.

There always seemed to be tension between COSD and Client. Whether it was about the schedule, testing, or different views of the engineering process. There was not a lot of love lost between them. This might seem weird to many. To outsiders, I am positive the early days of the Office Product Unit tension with Excel and Word would look identical.

For clarity, the Windows Server product worked closely with COSD but owned the product definition and the unique components differentiating Server from regular desktop Windows. Yes, it was a complex matrix.

Technically I was to manage Client. COSD was driving the Longhorn project even though Client was 100% engaged on that. No need to upset anyone with a new boss anyway. We would figure out the details of COSD at some future date closer to when Longhorn would ship. I also took on half of the Windows Live Services, which were also divided into two orgs as well, front end and back end.

If this sounds a bit halfway, that would be a valid observation. It was certainly confusing to outsiders searching for the new boss of Windows, which JimAll was previously. In total fairness, very large reorgs are never finished before they start to roll out. There is always a balance between completeness and fighting the inevitable leaks that prove even more distracting. The press release from Microsoft tried to detail the organization but from the outset it was complex.

Was I up to this job? Was the team up to me in this job? Could a person with experience only in "boxed" software work in the modern world of online services? An Office guy running (half of) Windows? That seemed like a punchline to a bad reorg joke.

And what did we need to accomplish? Tackling the challenges faced by Windows seemed, well, perhaps too late to the party. They still hadn't finished Vista after the Longhorn Reset and it wasn't clear when it would ship. Did I have to ship Vista first? What if Vista turned out fine and customers were happy? Or did Windows need to be reinvented? Brought back to life? Or both? And, if so, what level of urgency was even possible? What did the individuals on the team think were the problems?

I had never hemmed and hawed about a job change or negotiated any titles, terms, or conditions, and I didn't for this one—just two weeks going back and forth, mostly with BillG to get a sense for his candid thoughts. My new role marked his last staffing efforts with SteveB—the last "Bill person" to move into the Windows job. Though I was not ever going to be a "Steve person" because of my lack of field experience, we both worked equally hard to see each other's perspectives.

All the best choices I had ever made in life were counter to my exceedingly planful product execution, without strategizing, lists of pros and cons, or excessive deliberation. I just went for it. I was lucky in that regard having not really made a poor choice, yet.

But I was tired. I had been going nonstop since graduating in 1987 and had, for all practical purposes, given my 20s and 30s to Microsoft. Was I about to turn over my 40s?

This opportunity was sure to be all consuming.

A management transition for Windows was a material corporate governance event, and thus a formal announcement needed to happen quickly to avoid the potential of leaks to Wall Street. Plus, there were many anxious people across the company who had both a need to know what was going on with Windows, and a need to influence what was going on or believed those to be the case.

"Quickly" turned out to be an understatement.

The Vista team sent out a team-wide mail as well as communication to partners with an absolute RTM date of October 25, 2006, a slip from the previous August target. This was essentially external communication and would generate press. However, word already leaked to The Wall Street Journal about me moving over to Windows. The PR team began negotiating by trading verification of facts in an effort to delay the story. The story was going to run on March 22, 2006.

The clock was ticking to actually get an announcement done. The announcement scheduled for the morning of Thursday the 24th would not be moved even with the WSJ story.

Within minutes of accepting the job, I was informed that my first meeting was to be held immediately to go over the announcement tick-tock, an expression I had not seen used before inside Microsoft. I was also asked for my internal comms contact, my external comms contact, my human resources contact, my executive assistant, and my chief of staff. Time was short. There were almost 40 people on a mail thread summarizing the process.

I had no staff, so I replied, "Just ask me." I suspect everyone on the mail thread had no idea what to do with my response, but it sure cut down on the email traffic as there was a bit of a culture of fear in Windows when it came to sending mail to an executive, especially a new boss and one they had not worked with.

I forwarded the mail to our executive assistant leader Collen Johnson (CollJ) and then immediately walked into her office. I shook my head as if to ask, "What did we get ourselves into?" I knew Colleen was already buffering a huge amount of noise, mostly people asking if I really meant for them to ask me directly.

I arrived at a conference room in building 34, the big executive building, to a room of what appeared to be a re-org war room. There were easily 30 people, standing room only, more people than I think I'd seen in a meeting since we signed off on Office 2003, all to plan the announcement of my new role. The big conference table was covered with handouts of org charts, talking points, and draft press releases and rude Q&A docs. I didn't know most of the attendees. It was funny because this was not a restructuring or anything complex; it was news of a retiring executive JimAll, a new executive boss, KevinJo, and then me. It seemed that every vice president involved in this announcement sent two or three people to the meeting but didn't show up themselves. Questions quickly started mounting over messaging, email cascades, and heads up. The production values well exceeded the actual announcement being planned.

As much as I understood the importance of this announcement to the business world and to the team—after all, this was the retirement of legendary technologist and leader Jim Allchin and a material event for a public company—the craziness (and that's what this was) around a single announcement represented a microcosm of the entire situation. I was no longer in the comfortable garden MikeMap had created for Office.

With a lot of effort, the room managed to get the information that everyone wanted to go into this announcement down into a single email response to the official press release and filing, which I wrote, which came from me, and had one small set of talking points for any press calls that PR would handle. There was to be no email cascade—a new word for me that meant a process where an email went out from the top to the organization, and then every level of management forwarded that email (that people had already received) to the team(s) they managed with their own words interpreting the org change for them. Since there were parts of the Windows team that were nine or even 10 levels deep, the amount of interpretation that went into these cascades was mind-boggling in the depth and breadth of potential misinterpretation.

Turns out, we needed none of that with this announcement. Why? There would be no outreach or interviews by anyone at this stage. Most of all, literally nothing would change until Vista shipped.

That was the only talking point that mattered.

I was not joining Windows with some sort of secret master plan nor did we want the announcement of my job to portray me as some sort of Vista savior. Still, it played out a little bit like that in the press. There was an uncomfortable 36 hours between that WSJ story and the official announcement. That's what happens when things leak.

The Wall Street Journal said, "[Sinofsky] has a reputation as a meticulous manager who is adept at controlling large software projects." Paying homage to MikeMap, the article said the Office team culture was created by "an executive recruited from International Business Machines Corp., the Office group adopted a more management-heavy, disciplined culture..." The headline read, "Microsoft delays Windows Vista debut again; consumer version to miss critical holiday season; unit shake-up is expected."[66]

The rest of the week saw much of the press derived from the WSJ and the announcement focused on my new role in fixing Windows. There was no way to avoid this. It was broken. I guess it was also the truth. Business 2.0 ran with a headline "The Man Who Could Fix Windows: Microsoft's new OS chief has to get Redmond to embrace a new model of programming, in which software is constantly being improved instead of updated every 5 years."[67]

Inside the tech industry, one of my longtime favorite foils in the press, Mary Jo Foley of ZDNet, said, "Sinofsky has the reputation of a strict, schedule-bound manager who keeps the trains running on time." After all these years, and quite a bit of product innovation from the team, I was basically a strict project taskmaster. That stung, in a Spock-like way. But later the ZDNet editorial team added more, "The Sinofsky promotion (not sure we'd consider being named Windows *Mr. Fix-It* constitutes an upward career move) grabbed the most headlines."

And finally, everyone's favorite anonymous internet whistleblower, *Mini-Microsoft*, a widely read blog maintained by anonymous author calling themself *Who da'Punk* offered thoughts. To clarify the record once and for all, I was not the writer and have no idea who was though at least two reporters met the blogger in person verifying that fact. The post on March 23 had a headline that read:

"Sinofsky to the Rescue!...(?)"

The article said, "There's a new sheriff in town, and he's aimin' to gun down any rootin', tootin' varmi[n]t that can't deliver what he committed to. Maybe."[68]

It is probably important to detail Mini-Microsoft at this time because they were a fixture over everything that was going on at Microsoft, even if I chose to ignore them the rest of the Windows team and the company followed every word and so did the press. Mini, as in "Did you see the latest Mini?" or "Well, that really pissed off Mini" wrote about all topics Microsoft though seemed especially focused on the plight of typical employees struggling to make sense of what was going on. Mini was especially critical of typical big company problems such as organizational bloat, excess hiring, lack of innovation, performance reviews, promotions, salary, and more. Mini was also critical of our technical strategy and challenges around Longhorn. Like many claiming informal whistleblower status, the challenge was always there for an executive to respond to critiques, but it was so difficult to do so knowing Mini did not always have the complete context.

It is difficult to parse today but when reading Mini's posts one of the most interesting aspects is how they turn the phrases of Microsoft's HR and leadership back on them. From accountability to synergy to integrated innovation and even "I love this company" which was classic SteveB. Beyond that I proved to be a subject, directly or not, over the next couple of years in many of his (eventually their gender was identified in the press) over 100 posts. Mini even got himself a profile in BusinessWeek, as part of the much larger negative story about the loss of talent at the company.

I had no real direct reports at this point because everyone, including BillG, was finishing Vista. Still, I needed a way to quickly connect with a large number of people in a way that felt more...intimate.

To move forward, I chose a decidedly non-traditional path. The Microsoft way might have been a big all-hands meeting, a follow-up email with vague statements of support, or an immediate gathering of a staff meeting. Instead, given the need to both ship Vista and meet a lot of people I looked for a way to communicate broadly while connecting in-person with many, all while not getting in the way at all of Vista. This meant, for example, turning down all the escalations or crisis moments that people would bring to me. For example, in July AMD announced the intent to acquire ATI, the graphics card makers, which caused a brief panic in how to handle shipping ATI drivers in Vista. Given the future impact of this choice many tried to pull me into this crisis. This was a brilliant acquisition and noteworthy that Intel did not lead or follow up with acquiring then similarly-sized NVIDIA.

I browsed over to the internal SharePoint site and created a new blog called *Office Hours* in an effort to signify openness and a risk-free place where ideas could be shared. Blogging the goings-on proved to be the best way to reach a team of approximately 10,000 people and, as I would learn, the rest of the company.

Over the course of six-and-a-half years, I wrote more than 400 posts amounting to nearly three quarters of a million words (1,700 pages), answering questions, discussing the how and why of all we were doing, not doing, or considering, and detailing almost every aspect of the business. I wrote something substantial most every week, sometimes twice. Posts covered product strategy, organization structures, people management, competition, features, culture, my personal management, and just about everything in between. I posted the trip reports I dutifully wrote after conferences, recruiting trips, and customer visits. Many of these posts were included in a book I co-authored with Marco Iansiti of Harvard Business School, *One Strategy: Organization, Planning, and Decision Making*.

I had one last meeting with the Office team. We gathered the Senior Managers, the most senior 120 or so people, including the dev/test/pm triads as well as general management and discipline leaders across design, planning, localization, content, operations, in the big conference room where I shared the news that was about to break. Even to this day it was the most emotional day of my years at Microsoft. I looked out over the room and saw people I had all but grown up with professionally, many of whom I'd known for my entire time at Microsoft. Mostly I sensed they were worried about me—the look on their faces said no one goes over to Windows and lives to tell about it.

As I was packing up my office to move across the street to a temporary office in Building 50, Ross Smith (RossS) on Grant George's test team stopped by and delivered the most wonderful hand-made lightbox of Office logos and packaging over the past dozen years. It still sits on my shelf with the note Ross wrote. It means the world.

This was just my first couple of days. Even though for the time-being I had no direct reports, I still needed to figure out who and what would eventually be on my team. The team was incredibly anxious and clearly expected both a master plan and a reorg. I realized that many people had observed or become a fast study in how the Office team worked. Many were prepared with arguments as to why the way Office worked (at least their perception of that) would never work in Windows.

I had a sneaking suspicion that SteveB and BillG wanted a quicker "fix" than I might deliver. Even though I had not only lived the Windows challenges for at least a decade and many of the people were well-known to me through countless meetings, offsites, email exchanges, and more, the one thing that is certain is that talking about fixing something is a lot easier that actually fixing something.

084. WHO'S ON THE TEAM, EXACTLY?

When you move into a new job there are a lot of things that need to come first, too many. You want to touch base with the most critical individuals, but don't want to minimize the importance of those less so. You want to focus on the high priority areas of work, but it is times like this that the lower priority work hardly needs to be reminded of that fact. You're dying to ask a lot of questions, but people are dying to tell you things. Then there's the political reality that the many things pushed to you or that arrive in your inbox are often those least needing your attention, but most likely to notice a lack of attention.

I had all this to think about while both being reminded of Windows Vista every day and needing to let the team in place finish the project without interference, inadvertent or otherwise.

It was extremely weird to commit myself to learning about Windows and the Windows team. I had, after all, essentially grown up around it, just not in it. I knew the Windows product. I knew the Windows people. I just had no idea how the people made the product. I knew the organization at a super granular level from Windows 3.x and Windows 95 working on toolbars and app compat (compatibility) and the shell from C++ and Office. I knew things at a strategic and executive level.

I had a high-altitude view of the organization, and I knew a lot of individuals, but between a few feet off the ground and 50,000 feet above the ground I had a lot to learn.

Little was as it seemed, however, when it came to the details.

There's a well-known military principle on knowing the difference between lessons and lessons learned, between reading about something and having learned that same thing through the experience of changing how one operates.[69] Any management book will tell you to know the budget and resources on a team and that's a good lesson. In the Microsoft culture filled with cookie licking, shiny objects, and side projects my most important lesson learned is to actively track how many developers there are and what code are they writing. Every time I was uncertain of what a team was actually building or if a project was real, understanding the number of developers assigned to which code was the most valuable information to have and the most critical to keeping a project on track. I learned that with NetDocs, the Tablet PC, and so many 1990s internet projects long since passed. Everything other than actual working developers is just talk.

Therefore, the first thing I chose to do was to get a handle on the composition of the team. With the help of Kristen Roby Dimlow (KristenD) from HR, one thing became clear: I was in a new world. KristenD was previously our finance partner in Office, coincidentally, and brought with her a refreshing analytical view of the structural challenges I (now we) faced. Kristen began immediately trying to collect the data on who was doing what.

In Office, headcount, resource allocation, and org structure were readily visible and, for the most part, easy to figure out by looking at the company's online system *headtrax*. Windows was a different apparatus. While there was a headcount number, what they were working on, for whom they were working, and even their actual physical location, were all less clear, or fuzzy.

In keeping with Windows tradition of reorgs that "split the baby," or product organizations that were structured such that accountability and ownership were muddled, the job I was given was not as much the "Windows job" as most would at first perceive. This wasn't a surprise at all to me—I knew what I was getting into. This was the Windows Client team previously described. COSD remained separate as it was already.

To KevinJo and SteveB, accountability was clear, even if the organization structure and people were not. This was typical Microsoft accountability in the 2000s. I was their Windows "guy" and decidedly on the hook to figure out what comes next. Kevin had a huge amount to figure out. He was clear just how much he was hoping I could wrap my brain around with respect to "what comes after Vista?"

Along with the Windows client, there was Internet Explorer and the user facing side of Live services—the split of everything down the middle was alarming when it came to accountability, but just how alarming required more investigation.

The Live services represented a lot of headcount but the revenue numbers did not seem so big to me at the time. By Microsoft Online Services standards there was significant revenue associated with Hotmail and Messenger. Hotmail sold display advertising, perhaps $300-400M worth. The ads were intrusive "right rail" ads that took up the right side of the screen. The running joke was that the most popular ad was for a toe fungus medicine. The team was working hard to try to sell Hotmail Extra Storage, upgrading to 10MB (later 50MB) for $19.95 per year. Google's Gmail had no ads and essentially free unlimited storage. The unlimited storage was not a gimmick, Google invented a novel "infinite" and reliable storage mechanism enabling the capability. MSN Messenger was selling ads inside the client application (less than Hotmail), also intrusive, though the move to mobile phones and the growing competition from Skype were both problems. In other words, the few hundred million dollars in revenue was not remotely sustainable and at the same time the products were struggling.

Almost an after-thought in all the discussions about me taking this job was the fact that I would also manage the new homegrown Search product, which was recently branded as Live Search. It would not be Bing for another two years. The team was growing rapidly, up to almost 100 engineers, but was still very new and clearly a very distant competitor to Google with over 10,000 employees. The first beta test of Live Search started just weeks before I joined the team.

Christopher Payne (ChrisPa) was chartered with leading the team. He was the vice president and team founder and had returned to Microsoft to lead many of the MSN Services efforts. In a moment of boldness for a team under a great deal of fiscal pressure, in 2003 he proposed to BillG a massive effort (expensive investment) to build out a search product that would compete with Google. This included maps, instant answers, books, and more. At the time, as crazy as it sounded, Search across all of MSN was a hodge-podge of business development deals and outsourcing—to compete with Google. In his prior time at Microsoft, Christopher was a product leader on the first versions of the Access database product in Office and some of the early MSN properties. He later went on to run eBay North America and is currently COO of DoorDash.

Over two years or so, the Search team built an extremely credible effort, first releasing at the end of 2004. The team was the first fully organic one at Microsoft, tasked to build scaled cloud services, employ artificial intelligence and machine learning, and create the kind of tools Google had developed to automate and manage tens of thousands of servers in multiple data centers. Many of these pioneering efforts were critical to Microsoft's cloud data centers over the next decade.

While ChrisPa knew what he needed to do from a product and technology perspective, there were only two things holding the team back. The first was resources. The team needed to spend a lot of money on capital expenses for servers and data centers, as well as hiring more people. Second, the team needed to be given the time to build much more of the product and technology base before being pushed on revenue—they were far behind Google and the complexities of overlaying a new advertising business did not seem prudent at the time. Google was doing about six billion dollars of revenue directly on search that year, doubling year over year. It was already a juggernaut. In 2003 at the exec offsite, Payne said it would "take at least 18 months and $150 million dollars to even enter the race with Google, and that it was critical we own our own search infrastructure."[70] The first time ChrisPa and I met (as part of Search and Windows) he told me he needed an additional $1 billion just in capital equipment (data centers) next fiscal year and revenue was not yet a priority.

As I would learn, there was only so much patience above me.

Combined we called all of these "Windows and Windows Live" and my official title was Senior Vice President, Windows and Windows Live or WWL. I was already Senior Vice President of Office, another fact several people pointed to as evidence I was not up to the job. COSD continued to report to Kevin, though figuring out how to manage and organize it was all part of our ongoing efforts. That meant the broad view was that there was WWL and COSD, just as before there was Windows Client and COSD. To some this was comforting. To others they were waiting for the other shoe to drop.

To put some numbers on all of this: There were approximately 3,500 full-time R&D employees in over 30 cities around the world for WWL, with about 1,000 software design engineers. In Office, we worked using ratios that would translate to 1,000 software testers and 500 program managers, compared to WWL, which had 750 testers and 600 program managers. We had only a handful of managers to oversee multiple job functions. Office 2007 had about 10, but this organization had more than 40.

COSD was a bit larger with about 4,700 people (in most every country Microsoft did business), but more than 1,500 were part of a major push to move all bug fixes and servicing of old releases of Windows to India. This was a radical out of sight, out of mind move designed for cost-effectiveness, and something we did not do in Office. COSD also had about 1,000 software engineers, but over 680 program managers (and not much user interface) and about 1,000 software testers, which was about what one would expect. COSD had another 40 to 50 multidisciplinary managers.

The number of vendors and contractors and open positions in WWL plus COSD product development approached 10,000 people. Yikes. The number of open positions was astonishing, thousands upon thousands. Not only could they never be filled, but the question was also how would they have helped to ship Vista? That couldn't be more different than what we did in Office.

Perhaps the most surprising data point was that almost one third of the team was managers and there were easily seven, and often up to nine, levels in the management hierarchy. Office was about 20 percent managers and rarely more than five levels of hierarchy domestically. Another measure of complexity in the system was the number of cost centers. In Microsoft lingo, a cost center was a locus of financial controls, budgets, and headcount monitoring. In practice, it was a numeric field in SAP. According to finance the mere existence of a cost center was about $100,000 a year in operational overhead. In actual practice, every cost center was a headache as it was another place someone could come up with unique budgets, costs, and headcount, and when everything was considered for one product release, cost centers became overhead and bureaucracy. Windows had around 300 cost centers. By comparison, Office had about 30, and most of those were needed because people were paid in local currency and a cost center could have only one currency.

Mini-Microsoft was looking more and more accurate. I was beginning to understand why I thought Mini was so off base when I compared what they said about Office and Windows.

I completed an inventory of the products and projects that were underway, and resources assigned. Doing so felt a bit like an excavation. There wasn't a single place where the allocation was tracked. Finance knew how many dollars were budgeted by cost center which were created to essentially streamline accounting or sometimes to park open headcount. The projects underway were mostly tracked by multi-disciplinary managers, MDM, or equivalently PUM for product unit managers. The mapping of projects to products or a roadmap of product releases didn't exist. Finance had one view of open headcount which had little correlation to the view HR had for recruiting. It was quite chaotic. When asked, managers had a solid idea of what they were doing but that certainty did not roll up in either a strategic or fiscal sense. Compounding this were what I came to call "headcount gymnastics". In order for one group to rely on a contribution from another, groups engaged in headcount bartering where heads were offered or loaned from one group to another as a way of creating accountability or a reliable contract for work. Absent headcount gymnastics, partnerships or collaboration between teams would be subject to the whims of PUMs. I suppose.

I knew about these gymnastics because more times than I could recall, Office was asked to support something new in Windows and as part of the ask they would provide headcount to get it done. It should be readily apparent as to why this is just not going to work, but when you think about it even for a bit you realize just how absurd such a system is. It basically says that headcount is the tool for changing the priorities of a group. If you don't want to do something then you don't want to, and the idea that if you had more headcount then that thing you were asked to do is the thing you'd choose to do next is absurd. That's on the face of it. There's the second order problem that headcount is not the same as a human being, a developer. It means the receiving group, the one that signed up to do something it didn't want to do naturally, has now committed to do that very thing but has no person to get the work done. If one continues to play this out, then you ask all sorts of other questions about what schedule the work would get done on and what would happen if the work required changes to parts of a system that were not open to accepting changes (for a variety of reasons) at that time. I could keep going but it should be clear operationally why this is awful. Yet, this is how almost everything worked.

Let me indulge with a brief view as to just how broken headcount was and how key this was to the whole mess I was now facing. There are some basics of all software projects, among them there is always more that the team wants to get done at any given time than is currently planned and that adding more people once a project starts not only fails to help get more done, but likely will result in less efficacy. There's a simple corollary to these rules, which is that most every project will end up scaling back work as it progresses to finish on time. Said another way, projects don't get more done by the end than they said they would get done at the start. These basics go back to the *Mythical Man-Month*, one of the books issued to every new Microsoft developer going back to the earliest days.

Therefore, the basic way we worked in Office (also for as long as I could remember) was that projects were planned to use the number of people currently in place at the start of the project or milestone, the sub-unit of a full release. If you don't have a human who can start the work, then whatever work was under consideration doesn't get put on a project plan. Groups that were growing had open heads but did not commit to work based on filling those heads.

This makes it very easy to know what a project is actually going to accomplish because everything without a human assigned to it simply won't get done. It will only get done the next time the team regroups, builds a new plan, and starts. In the case of Office this took place every milestone (projects had 2 or 3 milestones) and in the large every release.

A big part of how we ran in Office then was to free everyone from ever thinking about headcount, ever. There was really no process to request headcount. We started a project with a known number of people. Every team could hire people to replace attrition. And then every new project cycle we assessed where we wanted to spend resources and increased, decreased, shut down, or created new efforts. Lather, rinse, repeat. We grew the Office organization from 350 to 2,500 over a decade using this deliberate approach, and never had thousands of open heads.

Whenever we wanted to do something entirely new the first step was to create the team by reallocating from our existing teams, in a significant enough way we could execute the whole project just as described above. This is how we created OneNote, SharePoint, InfoPath, and even the original OPU, Office Product Unit. By starting new efforts this way, we benefitted from having experienced people volunteering for the new work who were committed to seeing it through and we never went through a period of one manager telling us they are still hiring people to do the work.

Some reading this description would be critical and point out how this lacks agility. They might suggest that this does not allow for flexibility or entrepreneurial thinking. What if a really great idea comes up or a competitor does something requiring a response, people would ask? Easy, change the plan, allocate people to that new thing, and scale back or cancel something else. What if something is much more difficult than originally conceived and there's no way to get it done without more people? Easy, the team really messed up and either we immediately reallocate from elsewhere on the team or we kill the feature.

Why are all these so "easy" then? Because anything that relies on hiring, onboarding, training, and getting up to speed with people that don't currently exist has zero chance of getting the work done in conjunction with the rest of the product plan. If the business wants credit for the feature then it is going to want it to finish with a release on some schedule, be incorporated into marketing, and launch. Otherwise, it probably won't exist for customers anyway.

Were there complaints or grumbling? Of course and primarily along the lines of "we could do so much more" which was hardly specific to any single team.

There's a certain psychology that takes hold while building out a product plan once execution starts. There are people who always think about "just this one more thing" or "if only we could also do this too." They fall into the trap of believing that it is always one thing that makes all the difference. That one extra thing. But it is never like that. And on the outside chance it is, then it is far more likely that the whole of the plan was not that great in the first place. That one last thing is never considered in the context of the entire plan, rather it is just in that one moment. That's the whole flaw with planning by headcount rather than holistic plans based on people that exist, ready to do work.

Ultimately, the key for how we worked in Office was to remove headcount from ongoing discussions. There was never a headcount request or approval process. Everyone was expected, and did, simply work with what they had. The deal from management (at every level) was that we lived with the tradeoffs teams made along the way. Into that process of tradeoffs, we baked in a culture of commitment to partnerships across the organization so we avoided one group prioritizing locally at the expense of other groups depending on previously committed work.

Windows (and Windows Live) had almost the mirror image of this approach. Nearly every team ran with open heads that sometimes approached half their existing team size. It was not just that the team was always hiring (we were always hiring in Office too) but the team was also in a constant state of having no idea what would get done and when. This lack of clarity extended to cross-team collaboration where headcount gymnastics were still not enough to make good on commitments.

It was even a bit more insidious than I just described. As I began talking to teams about what they were planning on releasing, it was almost as though at every step I was running into a manager explaining that they had open heads. I would ask then if the feature was in the plan or not, and they would always say yes. I would follow up, asking when it would be done. The answer was that it depended on when they could hire someone. Yet if someone left the team (in general, Microsoft teams at this time were attriting at 6-8% per year, more so during Longhorn as per the articles in the last section) then the next hires were simply replacements for who had left.

None of this reality slowed teams down from working in a constant state of signing up to do more, requesting and being granted more headcount, and furthering the gap between what was sitting on slide decks as the plan from a team and what code was going to be written and delivered and when. Meetings with executives, aka me, were viewed through a lens of expansive slide decks and accompanying headcount requests.

The culture of headcount, as I called it, led to a world where people were seemingly rewarded for thinking up big ideas and making the case for more headcount to implement those ideas. It seems entrepreneurial—making a case for an idea and getting resources to build it. Everyone can make a case for resources to get something done, but the question quickly becomes what will actually get done. The process of circling back to those original proposals and checking in didn't really exist, other than meetings where projects went from expressing goals to expressing "non-goals" or what was no longer in scope. My inbox was filled with these decks offering to get me up to speed, or maybe to approve more headcount.

The flipside of the culture of headcount is just how much bloat it causes. People do get hired on to these teams and the teams eventually grow though never as much as the open headcount. Additionally, more headcount keeps getting added as the team expands the charter to do more, at least on paper. The problem is that as soon as people show up they are invariably added to the efforts that have already fallen behind and not scaled back. This is a big part of how the original Outlook and NetDocs projects got to be so large, both of which reached a point where in order to ship headcount was frozen and plans shifted quite a bit. In Systems, this explained the growth of the Cairo project which was ultimately cancelled.

The fiscal tracking systems in place only exacerbated the challenges this process created. The finance team trying to budget expenses gave up accounting by heads and simply tried to use actual dollars being spent on payroll and then literally guessed how many dollars might be spent the next year. In other words, rather than asking executives how many people were on the team, finance maintained a dollar-based Excel model of expenses that had little correlation to all those cost centers and headcount slots. When I would ask managers about their headcount, they would point me to finance who would then tell me a dollar figure for the team's expenses.

I did not intend to discuss headcount so deeply, but as I was listening to people tell me what was top of mind it literally drove me bonkers. All I wanted to do was make a list of what was planned and who was working on it, but all I could get back were big plans and open headcount. As it would turn out, this was one of the most visible signs that things could be improved and since I knew what to do it gave me a bit of hope when I needed it the most.

This might seem like the talk of a headcount tracking maniac. I am not. In fact, I spent almost no time on this topic *until I moved to Windows*. As the next sections will describe, we had a massive amount of remedial work to do on headcount management. I won't skip to the end, but a bit of foreshadowing is that we will ultimately get more done, ship on time, and with vastly more clarity by spending **hundreds of millions of dollars less** (in direct costs) and completely removing the whole concept of budgets and headcount gymnastics from the team. It was a huge headache and had we failed to deliver good products then the effort would have been used as a causal factor for failure, but it positioned us enormously well for the financial crisis that would seemingly appear out of nowhere halfway through our first product cycle as a team.

The easy access to the headtrax system gave everyone a ready benchmark for how other groups were perceived as growing faster and bigger. In times of rapid growth, it was easy to find people who thought "Micro-dollars" were to be freely "invested." Not in the back of my mind, but front and center, were my mentor Jeff Harbers' words about spending and treating Microsoft money as the shareholders.

That's the rant as to why the key lesson learned for me was that if you want to know what an organization is doing, then just count where the developers are and what they are working on. It really is that simple. Every financial control follows from the number of people actually working on the team. People love to say that building comes from small teams and of course there is truth to that. Building at scale, however, requires sizeable teams. The way to make a big team seem small-ish is to keep the teams focused on building and making the tradeoffs inherent in building and not on budget and headcount gymnastics.

In many ways, in a large company with many talented people and key product people in key roles, the unique and critical role of executive management is to decide and manage headcount so no one else ever even thinks about it and to drive the reallocations to get new things done, or adding headcount to be filled without the expectation or requirement to deliver in the current project. The only way to do that is by knowing what the headcount is actually building all the time.

Returning to the inventory of projects in the WWL organization, I counted 74 projects, each with about 13 developers on average for a total of 947 developers. There were only about 780 testers which was far short of what Windows software generally required. Some of this shortcoming could be explained by Search, which was using more developer operations owing to the modern web architecture, but even Windows which I would argue needed more testers appeared short-staffed. There were 440 program managers which was shy of the 2 developers for 1 PM ratio I might have expected. There were, however, over 40 people managing the small teams of a dozen developers and most of those managers were serving as the lead program manager as well. I realize I am already falling into the trap of using Office as a baseline, but absent that there was no baseline, no plan or strategy, from which to work.

The largest project teams, over 25 developers, in this whole organization were (in order): Search, Print server/drivers, audio/video platform, audio/video codecs, modern interface (including pen, ink, and language), and media rights management. While there is never a perfect correlation between number of engineers and strategy, it was abundantly clear either the resource allocation was off or at the very least was not aligned with strategy. Looking to Windows for some examples, there were only 13 developers on DirectX the core graphics engine for Vista and there were only 25 developers on the rendering engine for Internet Explorer and they were primarily fixing security and compatibility bugs until the recent emergency plan to produce IE 7.0 for Vista. That came about because there was whole new, non-HTML, browser as part of Avalon which is no longer in the Vista plan. Avalon, which would later be known as WPF for Windows Presentation Foundation was a cornerstone of the Longhorn plan had a total of 46 developers. While the specifics of what code was where might not have been totally clear (and certainly isn't today as I write this) the team was staffed inconsistently with respect to what seemed important.

Windows Live was organized as series of what seemed to be small projects relative to the overall scale. On the one hand, it might be easy to look at the allocation and think about each one as a cool startup inside a big company competing with a startup from Silicon Valley in a similar space. With that view, the teams were staffed well. Except Microsoft was not able to release things in a small way and grow them like a startup. Everything needed to work worldwide, include adequate accessibility, work across browsers, not just Firefox, and scale to all the users seeing the service on Microsoft.com one of the busiest sites on the internet. Microsoft's online services were spread across 30 or so projects each with less than 10 developers, at least for the front ends. The backends were still in a separate organization.

The difference in org structure and composition relative to Office had already begun to clarify some of the questions I was receiving.

While those differences were stark to me, I quickly realized the obvious. Comparing what I was seeing in WWL to Office was not a merely non-starter, it was insulting my new team. No one in Windows wanted to hear anything relative to Office. Windows was not just different. It was vastly more complex as I was repeatedly told. It was also more difficult. For more than a decade I was used to being reminded directly (or more subtly) that Windows was technically deeper than Office, but now I was hearing that Windows was also a more complex management challenge. I wasn't convinced but I was in active learning mode.

I had no other baseline. I knew Office. I knew development tools. I worked across the company for BillG. I'd studied tons of other companies As much as I knew I was biased in my thinking of Office, I also knew…it was just software. It could not be that different, I thought. I did not really believe Windows was either more technically challenging or more difficult to manage, but I had to resist the temptation to debate those points.

There were bigger issues. As much as I was focused on addressing Windows challenges, I realized the pain and anguish the Vista product cycle had brought to the broad employee base.

To many product group employees, the stock price slump reflected the product execution, and Vista was taking the brunt of that blame. The challenges were much broader and deeper, however, and it would take time for employees and other executives to gain an appreciation for the difficulties the company was facing in products. There's a tendency to view morale and employee issues (or broadly culture) as distinct from company execution and performance, but at least at this moment one thing was clear. The negative employee experiences were happening at the same time as customers were experiencing product issues and strategically the company seemed to be falling behind. It did not seem to me that one could fix the culture unless we built better products, executed more effectively, and transformed the business to be more competitive.

A favorite internal conversation for me was on a Tren Griffin (TGriffin) email discussion group, called LITEBULB. TGriffin was a former technology investor, a Seattle-area native, and early friends with the Gates family. He was one of the strongest strategic thinkers at Microsoft. Long a student (and author of books) of investing, Tren frequently posted news stories or questions about competitive markets, Microsoft's approaches, or other industry dynamics, and generated a rich discussion among a core group of contributors and a larger set of observers. Often the best discussions about Mini's posts or other press articles about Microsoft could be found on the LITEBULB distribution list, or his external blog *25iq*.

After a couple of weeks of listening across these many forums, I started to gain a full picture of what was going on. It was deeply emotional for me—a mixture of opportunity, as I said in many team meetings, "to work on the other greatest business in the history of business" (a not-so-subtle reference to Office I could not resist), and deep angst, which I also shared in many meetings. "So much of what I'm hearing are things I've seen, heard, even experienced over the past 15 years but from afar…and now these are my problems, and by that, I mean our problems to solve together," I would say.

I had moments of sheer terror. For a while, I tended to avoid people outside of the Windows team, especially my dear friends in Office, because they all wanted to know, "Are things really that bad?" I simply could not afford to be candid. Even going to yoga class or out to dinner resulted in sightings I wanted to avoid. Seattle was a one-company town back then.

Fifteen years earlier when Mike Maples (MikeMap) shared his description of two gardens, the Windows and Office gardens, I understood it intellectually from the experiences I had. Now I was experiencing the difference emotionally. Even to this day, I struggle to articulate just how different the cultures were, while both still achieved spectacular success. Somehow this came about all under one roof in a remarkable case of divergent evolution.

While I definitely experienced lonely moments leading Office, I was never as lonely as I was in the first six months of working on Windows.

I had to write to think. But I was not ready to write in public.

085. THE MEMO (PART 1)

The history of Windows releases was cursed when it came to product and leadership. Like *Star Trek* movies, Windows releases alternated between good and bad, odd and even. Line up the OEM products by availability date, and you'll see this is basically true—starting at Windows 3.0 and changing to the NT kernel with XP—3.0, 3.1, 95, 98, 98 SE, Me, XP, Vista. Compounding this, the curse says, no leader seemed to last more than two major releases of Windows.

My neighbor, a successful biotech entrepreneur, asked me about the curse the day he read the org announcement in The Wall Street Journal story saying that I was moving to Windows. He wished me luck.

After 140 scheduled 1:1s, 20 team Q&A sessions, over 30 hours of office hours, and countless hallway conversations in a dozen different buildings I had to do some thinking and organize what I observed, heard, and learned. That meant writing.

A dose of reality was needed with BillG, KevinJo, SteveB, and to some degree even the Board.

I did that with a 20-page memo titled *Observations, Aspirations, and Directions for Windows and Windows Live.* For me writing is thinking and I really had a lot to think about, hoping others would join in. I felt alone for long enough and I was certain SteveB was growing increasingly anxious for what would come next. I had been talking to KevinJo constantly over the past few weeks as he was doing a huge amount assuaging those that essentially rejected the idea of an Office person leading Windows.

The 20 pages were the most difficult I wrote in my entire career—to literally put these words down—I knew they would be impossibly difficult to read. I was deeply concerned that what I wrote would be viewed through the simple lens of setting expectations or painting as bleak a picture as possible so that I could be a hero later.

It seemed that everyone, especially SteveB, wanted the plan for getting things back on track and a product roadmap. He also wanted to be able to communicate to the field and bring comfort to customers, while continuing to support Vista when it shipped. Bill was especially keen to restart discussions over product investments that had been cut since the Longhorn Reset. Kevin was getting his footing across wildly disparate businesses including the massive money-losing online services.

I couldn't kid myself, however, as I too needed a plan. The team was still frantically fixing bugs, but in order to ship by October that would soon end. The bar for fixing bugs would rise dramatically by summer. Idle hands will make trouble for sure. Projects will start, code will be opened up to changes, and worse presumptive commitments to outside customers and partners would be made, and so on which was business as usual for Windows. For there to be a release that addresses any challenges I would need to orchestrate that every team at a project arrive at the starting line at the same time in order to finish at the same time. In other words, I had only about four months and one shot to get all this figured out.

Adding to the stress, the OEMs were extremely anxious as they were reeling from Vista missing both back to school and holiday selling seasons. They were used to hearing plans, or at least slide decks, about future releases so they too could plan, as much as that was worth. A January launch was painful for PC makers as it meant they had to stock up retail outlets with PCs unsure if the buzz over a new OS release would dampen Holiday sales or not, and then deal with upgrades new customers demanded on those PCs. It was messy.

In round numbers, fiscal year 2005 had revenue of about $40 billion and net income of about $15 billion. The Windows OEM business on its own was $12.2 billion (about 30% of Microsoft—incidentally it is not possible using public data to compare these to today's Microsoft, much as people claim to) and $9.4B in net income, about 63% of all of Microsoft. OEM revenue was highly concentrated in six major and global PC makers, each CEO with a direct line to SteveB and KevinJo.

My memo solved for none of these immediate issues. Instead, it was a lot of bad news and, in contrast to conventional wisdom or expectations, was less about strategy as it was about execution and culture. It diagnosed, without blame, the situation as I saw it. I provided a ton of data about the organization. I detailed structural problems that I was worried would feel trivial up the management chain. It was a lot of work to count the number of people and find out how much money was being spent on projects, not salary. It was disappointing that for all of the staff and managers, the most basic controls over dollars and headcount were not in place.

Something leader of COSD Brian Valentine (BrianV) once told me really stuck in my head years earlier. In his inimitable way he reminded me, "There's just a lot of *shit* going on in Windows *all* the time."

I was fast learning he meant that in every way possible.

There's an old business story usually called "The Three Envelopes" about an incoming executive taking over a dysfunctional team. The outgoing exec offers advice to the successor in the form of three envelopes, with instructions saying, "when things get tough, open them one at a time."

After a bit of time, things indeed got tough. The new exec opens the first envelope. It says, "blame your predecessor." They do and it buys some time. A bit more time passes, and things take a turn for the worse, so the second envelope is opened. It says, "plan a reorganization" which improves things. Some more time passes and desperate for help, the third envelope is opened. This envelope reads, "prepare three envelopes."

Good grief, I thought. I felt like I'd become the punchline to a business joke.

I promised myself I would never blame my predecessor and never ever did. I went out of my way to avoid that not only myself, but to remind people not to do the same. There was no escaping we were going to enter some new era as a team, hopefully for the better, but I was not going to permit our time to be defined as positive compared to a blame-worthy negative.

I was troubled, however, because I knew we were going to reorg. I really thought I could get through this change without becoming a living cliché, but as I quickly realized sometimes a cliché is born out of countless experiences. As it turns out, most of the time to fix a dysfunctional team there's going to be at least changes in leadership if not structure. With so many of the leaders choosing to make Vista their final release of Windows, I would need to hire replacements, so why not new jobs? The memo was a precursor to much larger changes and designed to motivate those changes with facts, not blame. Unlike most reactionary reorgs I had seen (at Microsoft and elsewhere) it was also not based on swinging a business pendulum in the other direction as is often the case.

I continued to be concerned there was a perception that if we could just get a good strategy deck then my job would be to do what I do, which was to be a tyrant—take the new strategy and execute. The strategy wasn't there, nor would it be, but I viewed that as a third-order problem. Besides, strategy without a product plan isn't really a strategy. As the saying goes, "culture eats strategy for breakfast" often wrongly attributed to guru Peter Drucker. I was under no illusion that the current team and structure presented with even a perfect product strategy could execute it.

The engineering culture was broken.

In fact, over the previous few years, while SteveB had been increasingly leading the company, he embarked upon initiatives that presumed execution was the key problem to address. Key among those was an updated performance review system based on "commitments." Everyone was required to document their commitments, or goals, objectives, tasks, and share them up and down the management chain for review and approval. On some level this is a solid approach, and in start-ups the concept often works well, such as the well-known OKR process used at Google. At scale, however, this type of process too often devolved into people gaming the system with vague commitments or aiming to set low expectations. I was not a fan. That wasn't going to help this team.

There was a special difficulty in diagnosing and sharing execution and management problems with two people who basically never had managers, BillG and SteveB. KevinJo, on the other hand, was an expert in scale management and a true ally in this regard. In fact, he had clearly orchestrated many more people than I ever had. Adding to the degree of difficulty was to what extent they would, especially Bill, take my assessment personally. I was quite concerned that I would come across as way off base on what needed to change, and even more concerned that this would not go well. Perhaps worse, they would think I was blaming their leadership and JimAll's as well.

I was having flashbacks to a mismatched conversation with SteveB about Windows Phone leadership (c. 2000) and what was needed back when Steve was looking to change phone leadership for the third time in as many years. He ended up talking to several other product leaders, each of us saying essentially the same thing—the phone needed a full reboot, in the team, business, and code, to compete with (then leader) BlackBerry. There was a mismatch that continued for quite some time.

Avoiding an early product strategy discussion was important. The easiest thing for execs to do in time of crisis is debate the specifics of product features. In those discussions, there's a strong desire for a silver bullet—one change, one addition, one synergistic initiative, or one deal—and then to ignore all realities and externalities and rush execute that. We were in the midst of the Vista project which itself was designed around both synergy and silver bullet features, such as WinFS and Avalon.

Above all, this would all be extraordinarily difficult for me because I'd been either watching or participating in this brewing problem for most of my career. I had come into this role not thinking there was a Vista crisis but thinking there was a Windows crisis, years in the making, with Vista merely the latest symptom. It was not just the odd-even curse of releases but the challenges we had collaborating because of the differing methodologies of the two gardens, which was difficult in the best of times. Not only would I have to break free of my own prejudice, but any visible display of prejudice would immediately snowball into a horrible situation that would be perceived as something of a hostile takeover of Windows by Office. Given that Office was always viewed as the subservient business and technology, this was not acceptable.

The risk of being rejected outright by the Windows team was very real, much more so than the external view of the savior arriving.

Working to my advantage were the ever-present "quality of life" challenges the team faced. Most every discussion—1:1, team meeting, or small group—was much more about the way work was done rather than what work was done. There was a deep-seated victim complex, and the perpetrators were management at every level and some specific managers/execs. I abstracted these concerns to what I considered three relatively mundane concepts, the kind found in any management book, and illustrated them for BillG, SteveB, and KevinJo with some concrete and dramatic numbers. The details on the Services teams were decidedly different from Windows, though the issues were largely the same. In fact, the challenges were identical, just manifested differently owing to the delivery of code and business model more than anything.

While I diagnosed three main areas to work on, areas that would motivate the proposed changes I was going to make, I spent almost five pages on a situation analysis. Writing about the way I saw things at the time I shared some of the following (summarizing from the original):

> ***Engineering Skill.*** *Windows has the industry leaders in PC technology, having invented much of it. In industry technologies ranging from Wi-Fi, USB, printing to Microsoft's own technologies such as Hyper-V or DirectX, the team has unmatched and extraordinary technical depth. Translating that depth into high-performance, secure, robust, production code has been challenging. The Longhorn project showed a great deal of technology potential but across the main initiatives there was a broad inability at every level to turn that into products.*
>
> ***Fatigue.*** *The Online Services team has been running non-stop for years, releasing every month and spawning new projects, but with little in the way of product success or share gains to show. The recent financial results causing a pullback on headcount growth have really left the team shattered. The Windows team is on year 5, though optimistically it is only year three since the reset. The recent schedule change all but cancelled summer and the holiday season for most of the team. The team is fried.*
>
> ***Maturity.*** *There is a decided lack of subtlety or nuance in how the team approaches problems. By and large even the most senior people think and act locally, almost in survival mode. In discussing the situation with senior people, they invariably jump to unsophisticated solutions such as cancelling projects or putting groups under a single manager. The idea of being both fiscally responsible and investment minded is difficult for most to grok.*

Bloat. *The organization is bloated with middle management. There are too many multi-disciplinary managers (PUMs) which (as will be discussed) create a deficit of senior engineering leaders. This creates an absurd engineering structure where small groups flail on problems too big to solve, escalating to a PUM who has the sole motivation to keep the decision local for fear of losing control while lacking the personal experience to adjudicate the issue. This bloat also caps the ability of the organization to grow senior engineers.*

Science Projects. *The organization is filled with science projects. These are projects operating as though they are building product features, but they have little chance of achieving critical mass and an even smaller chance of remaining sustainable over time, if they ship at all. One way to view this is how cool it is to be exploratory and entrepreneurial. The vocabulary used to describe these is always "delivering value to customers" which is far from the reality. These continue despite the broad view of a resource crunch.*

Hiring. *The lack of deep excellence in senior leadership for development, testing, and program management creates a difficult hiring situation. There exists a highly distributed hiring decision process and a large number of open heads. This pressures relatively junior people who are under the gun to deliver to onboard any "warm bodies" they can find and in doing so these hires are often over-leveled or over-compensated, creating a down-stream fairness problem for the whole organization. The PUM model often drives poor calibration for promotions simply because the PUM sees people only through the lens of a tiny team they are trying to hold together.*

Competitive Fire. *There is a curious lack of competitive fire relative to Macintosh, Linux, Google, and Yahoo. There is a broad and vibrant spirit around the concepts of providing software that competes with these companies, but a clear lack of understanding of how what we build stacks up and what we are doing about it. For the most part this shows as an organizational challenge since everyone thinks to be competitive everything must be under one person and nothing is today. This was particularly odd as I was already running Linux at home long before this job and posting unboxing videos of the iMac to YouTube. I saw few Macs, iPods, or Linux boxes anywhere. In fact, the team was even lobbying to prevent the use of Google search at Microsoft's firewall. Everyone is aware of these but thinks competing is the job of a mythical compete team or belongs in a compete lab, not just in daily use. This is not just at the top level, but at every subsystem where the technologists are not aware of how competitive platforms support an industry standard technology.*

Bureaucracy. *The engineering process is loaded with universally accepted yet loathed and mindless bureaucracy. For Windows, the processes pushed down to teams in the name of security, builds, quality, etc. are not yielding the results but forcing people to spend creative energy working around those processes hoping to get something done. In Services, thought and judgment have been replaced by a Rube Goldberg set of key performance indicators that themselves would make for a case study in how to make sure things don't get done. Even the most basic corporate administration work from finance, to legal, to administrative assistants seem over-staffed relative to headcount. Here again the tiny teams headed by a PUM create excess overhead.*

I was rather reluctant to share the above. I recognize just how harsh and potentially insolent these statements were. Any one of them could be taken out of context as too broad an indictment of too many or worse about specific people. For each I could offer specific examples if called to, but I so much wanted to avoid this becoming personal. I saved specific callouts for things that were clearly going well or simply stood out relative to these themes.

This was a brutal list. I remember meeting with BillG and seeing his felt pen markup, his callouts, all over this section of the printed memo—and we debated many points he did not agree with. SteveB was deeply in touch with the management challenges, and his unusually silent agreement spoke volumes as I felt he was disappointed to see these findings while also relieved, in a sense, that someone was willing to diagnose and address them directly.

The bulk of the memo documented three areas in need of attention: **decision-making**, **agile execution**, and **discipline excellence**. I presented a situation analysis with supporting facts and data. To avoid being super negative, I also suggested what our **aspirations** would be for each of these attributes.

Initially, these felt rather anodyne but soon became rather crisp talking points for what amounted to my stump speech as I began to engage a very small set of people such as Ray Ozzie (ROzzie) who succeeded Bill as CSA, and board director Dave Marquardt. I perceived a consistent feeling of uncertainty over what to do with my assessment. The questions were much more about what to do—when WinFS would get done, or what should we tell the OEMs. In KevinJo's case, he simply agreed and said we need to just keep moving and asked how he could help. He was so supportive.

Decision-making was the first topic to address. Windows was an organization that loved decisions. They loved having decision-making meetings. BillG and SteveB were always meeting with the team on important decisions. What could I possibly mean by decision-making and what should the team aspire to?

086. THE MEMO (PART 2)

Reflecting on this moment of both optimism and fear, today I look at the candor I expressed with a bit of amazement. I wrote with detail and assertiveness yet seemed to forget that I was writing about one of the most successful businesses ever created. I was writing about hundreds of billions of dollars of market capitalization. I was writing about many friends. At the same time, there was so much that needed to be improved or more specifically to be repaired. I think what really motivated me were all those 1:1s I did and hearing all the different people expressing their pain and troubles, knowing things could be better. This was not a team that was dug in ready to resist change. It was a team waiting for change. It just needed to be the right kind of change.

That reality made this much easier. I felt if I could document what was going wrong and the broad population agreed then I was on a path to addressing challenges. If I could articulate reasonable aspirational goals, then what remained was to build a product plan on that rebuilt foundation of trust in management.

I was quite worried that both the problems described and the aspirations I would document would seem cliché. With BillG in particular, over the years he had shown little patience for the broad topic of management. His world view was always that the business would be best served by taking on the most difficult technical problems and developers would be anxious to tackle such challenges. That recipe propelled Microsoft for twenty years of Windows but was failing us now. SteveB was never one for patience and while he would be receptive to these management challenges, he was far more anxious about a plan and the timeline for the next product to address the concerns that were mounting about Vista—the company hung in the balance. KevinJo had just orchestrated a massive restructuring of the global sales force before taking over most of product development. He was deeply in sync with the idea of identifying organizational problems then directly addressing those.

The memo, *Observations, Aspirations, and Directions for Windows and Windows Live,* proposed three main areas to address: decision-making, agile execution, and discipline excellence. Each was presented in a section with both observations and aspirations.

These points will sound like random musings from any generic book on management, both at the time I wrote them and reflecting on them today. The lesson learned, using the phrase from the previous section, is to demonstrate that these are more than clichés by citing specific examples that resonate with the employees who are being asked to operate differently and specifics on exactly how we will achieve aspirations.

Decision-Making

Across all of Microsoft, "decision-making" had been a constant and nagging issue. We discussed it after every MS Poll (the yearly survey of employee attitude and feedback), and each year I was left puzzled. It had never been an issue for our team expressed in the MS Poll and other feedback channels. I didn't understand what was so difficult about decisions. We made decisions all the time in Office, so many it wasn't even clear to me what decisions were so difficult.

Then I arrived in the Windows hallway.

There, it was an endless discussion of who "owned" a decision or who was "accountable" and, worse, people were asking me what "model" I used to make decisions. This was a reference to classic models of business function (or more aptly dysfunction) that use tools known as a *responsibility assignment matrix* (RAM, one such tool) for decision-making. One labels participants as: Responsible, Accountable, Consulted, and Informed, or RACI. Another such tool, OARP, stands for Owner, Approval, Responsible, Participant. These tools consistently proved frustrating and there was little evidence that decisions were made with less effort or more importantly, more staying power or higher quality.

The use of these tools arose as a defense mechanism against executives and managers who were prone to *swoop and poop*, a metaphor I learned as I assimilated into the team. As with birds, many managers seemed to show up at inopportune times, issue a quick opinion or edict, and not stick around for the mess they left behind. How much of this was actually a mess or simply a reaction to executive authority or inability to influence decision-making would take time to untangle. The expectation for me as a new Windows executive was that I had a tendency to employ this technique, no matter my own personal history or approach.

What I knew already to be the case turned out to be a big part of the problem, and that was a *culture of escalation*. In all software projects at scale, it is always the case that one team depends on another team—to provide code, consume code, integrate things together, and more. And this extends to sales and marketing connections. In Windows, escalation seemed to be the way most situations between teams were handled. It was a culture in which nothing was decided until people got in front of a VP, resulting in a culture where most of the middle management layer was biding time. And did I mention there were 7 or 10 management layers in Windows?

Weening the team off the culture of escalation proved to be one of the bigger cultural transformations I needed to make. It was also the root of challenges over many years of work between Windows and Office. In a culture of escalation, decisions made by people on the front lines, so to speak, rarely stick. In fact, escalation was done expressly to reverse lower-level decisions. If a Windows partner or collaborator doesn't like the situation then an escalation ensues, and rarely did things stay the same. Office loathed escalation. Decisions were pushed down and stayed down. When people tried to escalate, they were told to work it out. The result was that when Windows tried to escalate decisions in working with Office they rarely got overturned, which proved enormously frustrating to Windows. And when Office tried to make plans, they would often find them upended at executive escalation meetings with Windows.

In Office, escalations happened so infrequently I cannot even recall any specific instances. In fact, we in Office had a saying that "escalation is failure."

The primary downside of escalation is the way it shifts accountability. The winning side in an escalation feels an accountability not to the decision, but to winning the process of escalation. The losing side (and yes, they feel like they lost) does not feel bought into the decision and if it does go wrong, they too will join in the chorus of pushing blame up the chain. This is the exact opposite of what you want to happen in times of making difficult decisions. The second-order effect is the obvious problem that as decisions are pushed up the chain there is less detail on execution-related issues available, and usually that is where the trouble starts. These downsides were especially acute in mid-2000s Microsoft which was so much about improving accountability.

Given the crisis situation I was facing it would have been trivial to declare some sort of emergency and take control like a field general in a losing battle situation. Not only would this have been straightforward and arguably predictable, but it would also have fed right into the dysfunction that was already present. Sucking up all the difficulty would have been another management cliché, but one I could avoid.

Changing the culture surrounding escalation was going to be tricky. I decided to focus on consensus as a core tool for decision-making. I had to work hard to help people to understand that consensus was not the same as design by committee or groupthink—I'd always seen these as distinct when operating well. I also felt it was important to remove two tools that were all too frequently used to avoid either committing to consensus or collaborating, or to create dependencies between teams: *Agree to disagree* and *Non-goals.*

Agree to disagree gave each team the freedom to act how they would have acted prior to coming together to reach agreement, while also getting credit somehow for trying. The result was a product design/development conflict, which would fester through the development cycle and later be a customer problem.

Non-goals offer up a list of all the things a project won't accomplish, which at first seems helpful. I never understood how such a list could be finite since there was an infinitely long list of features and ideas not in the plan. In practice, it became a way to kneecap executive input on potential collaborations or connections to other parts of the product by simply stating them as non-goals up front.

Executive presentations often began with a slide stating non-goals. Such presentations often ground to a halt debating non-goals as a result. Often the non-goals ended up looking as though the team would get nothing done at all. There's a general rule to follow which is never offer negative goals up front. Recall the story from Office 97 when I spent weeks unraveling the damage done when the routine status report included a very long list of feature cuts, but no indication of what we were actually delivering. Bad idea.

My new team had an over-reliance on metrics and process as a mechanism to drive or force agreement on issues. This was exhibited by the constant drumbeat of red-yellow-green scorecard reviews in Windows or the KPI process in Services. These processes took an enormous amount of energy while also creating a sense of disempowerment in the organization.

The execution of these practices was fundamentally flawed. In both Services and Windows, the culture developed around having a policing team derive and measure the results, which only created an us versus them dynamic. As one example, in Services the small product planning staff organization actually believed it had the job of "determining the work that needs to get done by 800 FTEs" a quote from a planning manager. Yet most of the debate and discussion took place around "are these the right metrics" or "are we measuring this correctly" as expected. And when the organization wanted to do something, but the metrics did not all point in the right direction the org still moved ahead. The result undermined the entire KPI process.

I offered a specific example that was going on in real-time. The team was deciding whether to turn on a new HotMail user interface for all users. The KPIs established by the planning team clearly said not to do this, but the engineering team needed to for testing and scale. Thus began a discussion over "maybe it is OK to meet 2 of 5 KPIs" or "perhaps we should weight the KPIs." All the while when you think about it, this was an engineering organization, and it was unable to determine if the software was ready then that was some seriously deep trouble—and this was the largest flagship service.

These common techniques—decision-making frameworks, non-goals, agree to disagree, and metrics—were too often employed in forums for deciding and seemed to have the exact opposite result. These were, however, just obvious signs of poor decision-making. It was apparent we could improve everything about deciding if I personally modeled behavior and worked from the top-down to change the culture. With that in mind, the aspirations with respect to decision-making included the following (summarized from the original here):

- **Consensus among engineering peers.** To avoid escalation, the team needed to arrive at a culture where the experts in the code (no matter who their least common manager is) can together reach a consensus on what to do. Once a decision about what to do in code (design or test) brings in general management we have reached a failure point.
- **Consensus among disciplines.** A significant issue in decision-making was the failure of executive management to provide a framework for decisions. I saw too often that poor choices were the result of discipline silos or unsolvable situations. For example, executives pushing on development for a certain date while pushing on program management for more features while not giving testing enough time. To counter this, I offered an aspiration of reaching consensus across engineering disciplines before escalating while also committing to providing frameworks that allow for the unsolvable problems (schedule versus features for example) to be solved.
- **Agreeing to disagree is failure.** Too many decisions were actually never made. A key example I came across early was the big bet in Longhorn on Avalon or what became Windows Presentation Foundation. WPF was shelved for a future release, but development continued. Yet at the same time to ship Vista the use of WPF (or its precursor, managed code from the .NET framework) were specifically precluded from shipping in Vista. In other words, on the one hand a big bet did not pay off and was effectively put on hold yet on the other hand it was banned from inclusion in the product. This was a prime example of the kind of non-decision that was made at a time when the team desperately wanted and needed clarity. It would be only a matter of time until the Avalon team would just assume they would be part of Windows again and yet the whole Windows team that was shipping was making sure to never use the technology. Agree to disagree was a huge failure point.

Agile Execution

No topic caused me more personal grief and angst than the phrase agile execution. The concept of agile execution—seemingly a religion with terms like scrum, sprints, and stand-ups, as well as development process approaches that put experimentation on customers above all other methods—was top of mind on the Services teams. The team believed that the only way of addressing the poor results they were seeing was to move faster and become more agile. And while they were focused on this new methodology, the Vista team was gummed up unable to do things but somewhat irrationally believed that their problem was not taking enough time to get things done. The key leaders in Windows believed the problem with Longhorn was that the team was not given enough time, enough time to complete WinFS, Avalon, or other key initiatives.

The Services view was consistently expressed as "delivering internet services is entirely different than releasing boxed software." The use of "boxed" was always meant as an insult specifically aimed at me, even if occasionally said with a neutral tone. The implication was old, easy, and irrelevant. A key aspect I was informed about repeatedly was: "Services do not use the waterfall approach, but rather they must iterate in the market." Waterfall was another code word for old and dumb.

The problem with describing Office (or Windows) as waterfall was (and is) that this presumed a development process of writing specification and handing off to development and then later to testing—a sequence of discrete steps known as a waterfall. Implied was that there was never any notion of reevaluating what was going on, iteration, or that no work was done in parallel. Also implied was a perceived timeline of years. This was not how Office worked, but there was no chance I would change the minds of those arguing for agile. Whatever Office did, it was not agile, and the proof was that a product took 24 to 36 months. Still, Office iterated throughout the milestone process and also updated the product with hundreds of changes every month, and those were based on data of how the product was being used in the real world. But that was only evidence of maintenance not innovation, even though the vast majority of Services updates were simply to keep the services running and not new features—roughly equivalent in my book. There was little evidence of innovation in Services to counter this example.

As an aside, the concept of waterfall development has been misunderstood for generations. The first descriptions of the process came from Dr. Winston Royce and appeared in the Proceedings of IEEE WESCON from 1970 in an article "Managing the Development of Large Software Systems." Royce diagramed out what became the canonical waterfall process of gathering requirements, analysis, program design, coding, testing, and so forth. One discrete step after another. Royce, however unfortunate for us all, meant for that diagram to be what not to do. In the full text, he explained how critical it was to iterate at each step to be successful.[71] Yet because of that diagram generations of engineers treated the process as a stepwise and discrete, one after another. Also, maybe IBM was to blame too. Nevertheless, many on the Services and Windows teams perceived the Office planning process, including a vision document and milestones, as a waterfall approach in the classic and incorrect manner.

What I had learned as I gathered information ahead of writing my memo was that our use of these new agile methods was causing multiple real execution challenges. One example was the Spaces service, which was poorly architected for scale while racing to put features into market to compete with MySpace. In fact, they were asking me (the new person) for budget approval for a lot more data center spend because the costs per user on the free service continued to rise significantly and non-linearly—that is, each new user being added to Spaces was costing more than previous users. Clearly, that was unsustainable.

The most shocking example of management by self-induced crisis was Internet Explorer. In many ways IE was the symbol of a rapidly developed product, participating in the creation of "Internet Time" as it competed with Netscape 1995-1999. Once the original Longhorn plan started in 2000 to 2001, development on Internet Explorer was, for all practical purposes, shut down. In my first days on the job, I met with the recently reconstituted IE team who had been given a "hurry up and get a release done for Vista mission." A recognition that Vista needed a browser as part of the Longhorn Reset.

Internet Explorer 6 shipped with Windows XP in August of 2001. Here we were, almost five years later, and while there was a great deal of activity in terms of security fixes and supporting the myriad of Windows releases, nothing substantial in terms of product features was released. Ironically, perhaps, the intention in 2003 was to stop releasing standalone browsers to focus on integrating and synchronizing the browser with Windows. IE had effectively ceded the browser war to Firefox. Google's Chrome was two years away, but there were rumors of its development. IE was riddled with security holes due to the use of Microsoft's ActiveX technology and components which were not architected for the modern security landscape, while also falling behind on performance and web standards. IE had become a pariah on the internet and attracted scorn from the developer community. Realizing this, a crisis was created by the very people who ended development and essentially commanded an updated browser in time for Windows Vista. This amounted to a classic arsonist-firefighter dynamic within a culture that always seemed to love a good crisis.

The good news, if there was any, was that Dean Hachamovitch (DHach, former Word and Office PM of AutoCorrect fame) was leading the new team, reconstituted from across the company. In the first meeting I had with the team, all the managers fit into one small conference room. The team was woefully understaffed for the work it needed to do. This was nine months before the product was to be completed. Dean was already exhausted, but we found ourselves allies. In talking about IE with BillG, SteveB, and KevinJo, the irony was not lost—voluntarily ending work on browsing after a fairly well-known legal battle was an odd choice, to say the least, and one I did not spend time trying to understand.

There was also the idea that planning and being thoughtful were archaic and the modern way of building products was via lean methods, as they became known—get an experiment or something "minimally viable" to market and then iterate. Though by this time, the biggest successes of these agile methods had also mostly imploded as companies. On the other hand, most people were consistently surprised at how long even relatively thin-featured products gestated before becoming viable and then successful. Managing every product like it might be the next Google search made no more sense than managing every product like it was a NASA mission. There was a rational approach in between, especially for products that were mature or necessarily focused on enterprise customers.

This issue as I would later discover was one that none of my new management receiving this memo would quite know what to make of. The conversation would come back to needing a plan and me returning to the reality that the team hadn't ever developed and executed on a plan. That meant there was more needed than a slide deck with a set of features and a schedule, all while needing to find a way to agree to the highest level of development methodology.

It also meant that the odd-even curse around Windows might have been due at least in part to a lack of patience, and that regardless of my plan the team might not have the patience to see it through.

While on a recruiting trip I caught up with Sarah Leary (SarahL), the product manager who represented Office at the Windows 95 launch event. Sarah invited me to attend her class at Harvard Business School in 1998. Professor Marco Iansiti taught his classic case study on the development of Microsoft Word[72]—the one where the Word team was called the worst development team at Microsoft by my future manager JeffH. Marco and I got talking and he invited me to spend the fall of 1998 helping to teach that very class with his colleague Stefan Thomke, which proved to be an incredible learning experience for me.

Marco later helped us to articulate our aspiration for agility as defined by *Agility = Execution + Impact*. This was a way to talk about three challenges all at once without having to define what agility really meant or even that it meant fast or, worse, faster. By focusing on execution, I was able make clear the issues of simply failing to get things done, like MSN Messenger working correctly for people with more than one PC or big features of Vista that were cut. With the addition of impact, I would discuss the issues of the Services team spinning their wheels while not making any strategic progress. This definition also helped me to avoid picking a specific development methodology which was about as appealing as choosing to become ISO 9000 certified. That's a joke a few people will get. Instead, we would focus on planning, plans, and timelines using my favorite methodology of "promise and deliver."

To put a time scale on agility in my memo, I pointed back to ChrisP's *Shipping Software* mantra. Chris was my manager in Office and had joined Microsoft to work on Mouse 1.0, Windows 1.0, Word 1.0, and also led Excel engineering, then Word, before leading Office. I said we would aspire to a milestone-driven process, with more than one milestone, and a process to plan, execute, reevaluate, and iterate. I had a great deal of difficulty bridging my experience in product cycles lasting years with the perception of needing to last days, no matter how much we talked about how processes can scale while the absence of a process is still a process, known as chaos.

Across all teams there existed a cacophony of agile development that was defined as a cultural high-order bit. In many years of working with teams as they moved into Office or were aligned with Office, my experience was that there was some degree of correlation between teams executing poorly and a very specific development and engineering process that the team was overly proud of developing. Such a process was one the team pioneered and was deeply committed to, even to the exclusion of success. This wasn't a causal relationship, but rather a correlation often seen. Certainly, teams with a unique methodology also executed super well, but that probably wasn't causal though they believed it was.

The challenge, or properly my baggage that Office worked differently than Windows, was much more acute when speaking with the Windows teams. Windows felt they were not moving fast enough, but after six years of Vista the more general view was that they were not given enough time. This was rooted in the way that Windows NT was developed, with architects and a lot of upfront design, which in practice was much closer to a historic waterfall approach. The project, which started approximately in 1989, was not ready for mainstream usage until almost 2000. And to many on the team, a decade was the expected amount of time needed to build robust platforms at scale.

The Windows team had a belief that Office shipped releases mostly on time by "cheating" because it cut features from the product before it shipped. PaulMa (pioneering manager of Windows, including NT, and former CEO of VMware) often told me, "You just can't cut things from Windows like you can in Office." In any discussions about Office processes, I always felt a bit of OS snobbery directed at me. While this could have been my own inferiority complex, there always seemed to be that unsaid feeling that Office was the simpler product.

For what it's worth, back in the day, Office people always thought that Windows was a perfectly good product to have in order to launch Excel and Word, but not much else. This was reinforced externally because Office on the Mac operating system was equally loved. We had our own expression of snobbery in Office.

The two gardens continued to exist.

There was another truth that emerged as I researched and tried to sell my plan. There was overall perception of Office, and by consequence me: aside from cheating by cutting features, I was confronted with the perception that I was a tyrant, literally. The reason Office shipped on time and was so structured was because of how I ruled the team—by terror or by some sort of iron-clad grip on process. The more I talked to people the more I learned of what I thought were crazy stories about how the teams worked, and how I worked—hearing them was like learning about some exotic culture across a vast ocean, not just another part of Microsoft. Not my Microsoft.

It was the first time I had to face the perceptions people had of me personally but also had to reconcile how those perceptions could be so opposite of my reality. At times the disconnect between perception and self-awareness had me questioning my sanity. I understood how I could be intimidating just as any executive could be, but at the same time I felt the team knew I was fully supporting them and worked hard to avoid the trappings that contributed to that perspective.

It was, after all, Windows where the manager punched his fist through a wall. It was Windows where people (including me) were regularly chastised in front of big war-room meetings. It was Windows where managers often found out about changes to their schedule or plans via rumors or indirectly. I did none of those things. I didn't yell. I didn't skip over managers. I didn't escalate decisions or tolerate escalation. Generally, my biggest offense was writing lengthy emails late at night with too many points in them, and sure, an occasional barb, though I rarely replied-all and did my very best to focus on ideas and products, not individuals in emails. That and refusing to go to endless meetings, especially early in the morning or when they were scheduled at the last minute were where I regularly messed up. Besides, how could anyone hold a crisis meeting for a strategic discussion?

Whatever my flaws as a manager, what I thought was going on was that the Windows team was looking at how they worked and assuming that to achieve the results that Office achieved it must be doing what Windows did but just more, or better. So, more escalation, more big meetings, more VP decisions along with better PowerPoints and shorter lists of non-goals. Or is that longer?

That wasn't reality. But it was the reality I had to deal with, as out of body as it felt.

In hindsight I began to realize that the two gardens were not styles but deeply held beliefs. Each of Windows and Office operated the way they operated, and loved it. Each had achieved tremendous success in the market. Where

I thought Windows achieved success in spite of how they operated, they saw their success as because of it, and vice versa. It just so happened that the most visible cultural differences were also almost the opposites: planning versus crisis, consensus versus singular leader, cult of team versus cult of leader, promise and deliver versus over-promise and deliver, and on and on. Even today, it can be challenging to describe the gardens without sounding judgmental one way or another.

Top of mind during this transition were some of the more legendary efforts at cross-pollination between Windows and Office. Several extremely talented and senior people in Office had taken roles in Windows only to quickly return to Office sharing tales of their adventures. And while there were stories in the other direction, it often felt like we had more success with Windows people moving to Office. From the outset, I was deeply worried about that sort of rejection knowing I had nowhere to go back to.

Our aspiration, *Agility = Execution + Impact.*

Discipline Excellence

Despite having thousands of engineers with more seniority (as defined by salary level) than any other engineering team in the company, the team did not have the depth or breadth of talent (human capital) to build products of the scale being attempted. Sharing this observation was scary. It was both counterintuitive in thinking and felt like the height of arrogance. To BillG who valued IQ above all and prided himself personally on the IQ assembled to build Windows, to express this was, for lack of a better word, insulting.

I used data to explain it.

Something PeteH once explained to me: "You can't build a billion-dollar business out of 10 products each doing $100 million dollars." What he meant was that the characteristics of a billion-dollar business are different than a collection of smaller businesses. He was referring to the struggles Microsoft was having in the Microsoft Home division. That pertained to my challenge at hand: we couldn't create a product team at scale for billions in revenue with 100 teams of 25 people each. A 2,500-person product team operating in unison was qualitatively different than all those small teams added together, even if headcount was the same. Even worse, it was almost always the case that the bulk of the value delivered was due to a small number of those teams anyway, leaving most of the teams work essentially unaccountable or even squandered.

Windows was sold and experienced as one product, but it was organized as though 100 small teams came together to create that product while operating essentially independently. What was supposed to make Windows be Windows was how all the pieces fit together. There was no organization, however, to build that product. Simply put, the whole was not greater than the sum of the parts.

The driving force behind all the small teams was to empower people to work outside the complexities of the bigger team. The team had found itself caught in a negative reinforcing cycle. It was too difficult to get things done because processes were failing, which caused management to assign senior leaders to work out of band or off the books to get truly important things done (translation: make it a crisis), which made it harder to integrate those into the product and amplifying the overall difficulty of shipping the whole of Windows. The empowerment led to poorly integrated and architected products such as Media Center and Tablet PC, as well as disconnected core architectures such as DirectX graphics, Networking, and Security. The success of early Internet Explorer working this way reinforced this as a methodology, but all that came to a standstill once the goal of the product was to integrate it with a whole.

That would be challenge enough, but accelerating this cycle was the existing approach to managing. In order to conjure up these small, agile teams, management pulled people from the ranks and gave them responsibility for managing a team of developers, testers, and program managers—creating product unit managers, PUMs, or multidisciplinary managers, MDMs, the HR term. PUMs were a direct manifestation of the old list of people and problems, formalized to an org structure.

For a culture that loved a good crisis, the heroics of being a PUM managing a crisis became an aspirational job. As I was making the rounds talking with middle managers before writing the memo, a frequent topic raised was the desire to become a PUM, and my view of the career path to become a PUM in my new world. When speaking with PUMs, I heard time and time again, "I work best overseeing a small, multidisciplinary team." The problem was the lack of supporting evidence proving that point. Being a PUM was a career goal for nearly every mid-level engineer, not being a great engineer.

A direct result of pulling people from the ranks and promoting them to manage multidisciplinary teams was to cut off the pipeline of talented engineers and, more specifically, program managers. The very people who would be called upon to scale and manage larger teams of engineering leaders were robbed of the depth of discipline expertise that would train them to do so.

As if this wasn't enough, these new leaders were then responsible for hiring, mentoring, and growing the next generation of leaders in job functions they had not even done at any level of seniority or tenure. As a result, most of these teams had a management structure where the PUM was also filling the role as development manager or group program manager, the titles for the role of leading the job function. This further stunted the development of new leaders.

To illustrate this point, I compiled the statistics of the approximately 40 product units in the Windows and Services group not including COSD, but the numbers matched almost identically. It revealed that half of the product units were being led by people who would not have been senior enough to be discipline leaders (dev managers, test managers, or group program managers) in Office.

The lack of seniority was immediately recognizable in program management, arguably the most crucial role for achieving synergy in product design and features across a single product. Overall though, Windows had more senior employees than Office, but they were allocated to pure management roles, PUMs.

The quest for PUMs and autonomy had pushed all the relatively senior talent to be managers of managers or their managers. That was a shocking realization. This was also a generational problem because the presence of PUMs robbed the junior engineers of opportunity. The Windows team had been robbed of a generation of talent development.

Perhaps nothing was more shocking than the Software Test discipline, where, once again, I was up against a long-held belief, by BillG and SteveB in particular, that having testers was not a sign of success but somehow represented a failure of tools and processes in engineering. For many years, I tried to have this debate or discussion but simply ran out of ways to sound anything but defensive. But in truth: there was no engineering or manufacturing, in any field, without the role of quality assurance, and the more complex a product the more testing it needed. Software projects brought with them two unique characteristics not seen in hardware or manufacturing. First, Windows for the most part provided programming interfaces to developers who would do all sorts of things, some expected but most not. Testers came to work and found ways to exercise APIs by writing adversarial code against them. Second, every release of Windows shipped supporting every previous release and previous capability on all the hardware that existed and all the hardware that would exist. Of course, Windows had enormous libraries of automated tests and more being added all the time, but all they could do was tell you that you had not broken something that already worked the way you thought it should work. There is much more to testing. I understood that start-ups and smaller projects could do without testing, as Microsoft had in the early days, but complexity, extensibility, and backward compatibility caught up to every product.

Later, when I made my case after sending the memo, I experienced a lot of friction on the topic of testing because SteveB as CEO had been pushing teams to reduce headcount as a cost-saving measure. Both Services and Windows had reduced headcount by reducing testing and moving responsibility offshore or to vendors. The Services team, where there would normally be one tester for every software developer, had half as many. As we learned in operating internet services in Office, testing wasn't reduced but rather shifted to and shared with operations, which was also understaffed.

Tactically, our plan was to aim for two important structural changes. First, we would dramatically reduce the height or depth of the organization. This was something that SteveB would get excited about as he had been trying to get people to understand Jack Welch's General Electric approach to org span of control and depth. At this time, everything Jack Welch said was undisputed business canon. SteveB had run up against PUMs and the depth and minimal span of control that model imposed on an organization. This would dramatically alter the jobs and career paths of dozens of the most senior people on the team. It would be a very expensive change to undergo.

Second, I proposed reducing the number of pure managers, those with no line of responsibility but who had management oversight. They did not write code, specs, or tests but focused on the process. Some were needed, but the organization had too many, which contrasted with Office where even the most senior discipline leaders were managing people and writing code and/or fixing bugs.

At the strategic level I used this memo to begin what I knew would be the most important management journey of my career: restructuring the Windows and Services team into a functional or discipline-led organization.

A reality I could count on was that it seemed nothing could have messed up the Windows business, and hence all of Microsoft's revenue and profit, at that point. In hindsight, what Windows had was the greatest product-market fit in the 20th century, except maybe for oil. That stability enabled the company to thrive during macro issues of recessions and wars. It thrived throughout the largest antitrust trial in our lifetimes. It thrived through successive changes in leadership and company reorganizations. It thrived through a restructuring of the PC manufacturing industry. More than anything, it thrived despite products receiving lukewarm reviews at best and a lot of releases being broadly panned, and nearly every single product being released to market years later than planned with notable quality issues.

Windows had no trouble surviving the odd-even nature of flawed products and changing leaders. To date, there had been no credible competitors or alternatives.

As I write this today, I realize just how wild that sounds. It was, however, true.

In one exercise, my colleague Adrianna Burrows at our communications firm WaggEd researched key product reviews for all the Windows releases going back to Windows 3.0. Surprisingly, out of that selection, while some were glowing, especially Windows 3.0 and Windows 95, most were lukewarm to good such as Windows 3.1/3.11 and Windows XP, and many were quite painful to read, including Windows 98 and Windows Me. Windows Vista was shaping up for reviews akin to the latter. Looking back on the reviews solidified my opinion that there was much more of a Windows challenge than a Vista-only challenge. The business model and momentum were sustaining the product, not the march of consistently improving products and increasing customer satisfaction. At one point, I even suggested to SteveB that Microsoft would have been fine not shipping several of the Windows releases. Heresy. To be fair, in *Hardcore Software* I have pointed out that absent the contractual obligations and staggered adoption of Office, it was not entirely clear the same would not be said of Windows.

While I did not have the vocabulary of product-market fit, I knew that I had the luxury of being patient and deliberate. SteveB showed restraint, even though every bone in his body wanted something fast. I was not going to rush. I was not going to have a short-term tactical plan to show we were awake or listening—something that had been suggested many times by those more senior than me and in subsidiaries. I knew we would spend a lot of time in push-pull conversations, but ultimately, I believed I had the support to do what I thought needed to get done.

The goal was to have the whole organization collectively, including COSD, deliver one Windows product to customers, OEMs, and enterprise/business customers. The cardinal rule of having everyone finish at the same time was to have everyone start at the same time. But with the Windows team still finishing and also about to undergo a major organization change, I needed to develop a hybrid approach. This would also remove some of the pressure at the company level to show progress or, worse, to make sure we did not look like a few thousand engineers were going into hiding.

In this transition memo, sent to BillG, SteveB, and KevinJo (which I sent when Vista was still six months from shipping), I proposed an entirely new organization and a rationale for why we were going to operate together as one.

087. REORG! WHY ARE WE TOGETHER, EXACTLY?

Most big company reorgs are fairly routine affairs that nevertheless cause teams to drop everything, stress out over the weekend (because reorgs always happen on Fridays) and contemplate what might change. But then returning to work on Monday, little changes immediately except for somewhere up the org chain there's a new boss who will in a matter of time introduce some changes. Most reorgs are not nearly as big a deal as all the time and energy that goes into talking about them.

This was especially true at Microsoft which, at least to many, felt like it was in a constant state of reorg hell. In my early days at the company, I experienced several reorgs in the most senior (other than BillG) executive structure from having a president to not having one, to adding a COO to removing a COO, three-in-a-box (the BOOP, Bill and the Office of the President), back to a president, then a president and COO, then SteveB as CEO and BillG as Chief Software Architect, and so on. Office itself bounced between a few executives over the years as well. In fact, just as I was in the middle of planning this June 2006 announcement, BillG announced he began transitioning from Microsoft to spend more time at the Foundation. Ray Ozzie (ROzzie) would be appointed Chief Software Architect, CSA

The thing about reorgs is that most people are trained, best case, to scan the reorg mail and see if their team is directly affected by the change. Specifically, how far away is the new boss. If there's no immediate impact, then just go on doing what they were doing. In practice, most reorgs at scale don't affect most people directly or immediately.

The Windows and Windows Live changes were not like those reorgs. This was not a change at the top. This was a change for literally everyone in the organization. More than half the team would get new managers soon after Vista shipped, and everyone would have a new manager no more than three hops up the chain.

It was even more than just that. Jobs were changing and with that many mental models of career paths were being upended. Everyone who thought they had plans for what would be next would wake up to something different. Aspirational jobs as a PUM or an architect with no direct reports (or code) were no longer going to be available. We were an engineering organization, and everyone was going to be asked to focus their trajectory on building products. Even becoming a manager was deemphasized as we asked managers to take on more directs while we reduced the percentage of the team that were managers by one-third.

Then beyond that we had every intention of radically changing the way we would work. Everything from the planning process to daily builds to milestones. Even meetings with execs would decidedly change or mostly go away.

I spent May and June 2006 on two things.

I was mostly meeting more people on the team and figuring out who would be filling in the organization I am about to describe. These meetings were a constant reminder of the desire for change. They were also opportunities for ongoing reminders that Windows and Services are different and more difficult than Office. I probably wrote 500 long emails replying to questions about everything from the future of specific technologies (most of which I knew nothing about: USB, DirectX, virtualization, and more) or to suggestions for how we could improve. I received quite a few questions asking "how do you want us to…?" on everything from hiring to signing purchase orders. There were many questions that were very specific to situations and people that I knew nothing about. The questions always seemed to boil down to process and culture challenges, never about domain expertise. It was 7x24 from the end of March to the end of June.

To remain sane, I was also installing daily builds of Vista and Office 2007 which were both winding down. Not being in the daily triage meetings for Office was kind of sad for me. I vividly remember sneaking over to the ship-room meeting one time, which proved to be silly and indulgent on my part and a distraction to the team. It was, for me, a moment of sanity just to see the team working, and by that I mean not taking any code changes.

Mostly, however, I was genuinely scared. I had absolutely no doubts about what we needed to do, including how to structure the team and what to ask of them. I had a lot of doubt that I'd be able to pull it off and most days wondered if I was the right person to drive these changes. There was so much baggage coming from Office.

Something that I was keenly aware of was how many managers, myself included, viewed reorgs as something of an adversarial process. A reorg was something to protect the team from, not something that could help. Reorgs prevented work from happening and were a distraction. That's certainly how I treated a lot of what went on above me for most of my career.

Now it was my turn. The very last thing the company needed was for people to view the changes I was putting in place to be prevented or redirected. I was terrified.

Would people quit? Or likely, how many people would quit?

Would people run to the gossipy press or Mini-Microsoft?

How much email would be sent to SteveB or BillG? And, yikes, would they answer it?

What if no one wanted any of the new jobs I was proposing?

My first step was to figure out the new leaders. In picking those leaders I was also certain of how the overall organization would be shaped, my direct reports and their direct reports and so on. This structural change was the visible symbol of the reorg. It was a massive pivot away from a product unit organization to what I called a "functional organization." A functional organization is based on having discipline specific leaders reporting at the top and their teams consisting entirely of people within those disciplines of development, testing, and program management. Across each of the disciplines we would have mirror structures of group managers, leads, and individuals. I sketched out the math and knew we could build the organization out of about 40 teams of 25 developers each and 25 testers and a dozen program managers, under their discipline leaders. In due course, the intention would be to organize COSD this way as well though we needed to let them finish Vista for a bit more time.

I would love to spend more words in this section describing the inherent tradeoffs between these two organization types, but it would be a bit of a distraction from the story. Instead, I would refer the reader to *Functional versus Unit Organizations*, an essay I wrote in 2016 on this topic.[73]

In assembling a team of new leaders, I tried not to be the guy who brought "his people" from his old job, but there simply weren't any candidates in Windows that would champion the changes we needed. You're not supposed to show up with a team, but managers almost always do. I never understood why that was the case, but after living through this

I have a more visceral understanding. It is not about the personal connection, as most think, but in times of change you need to have a team of people who share the same world view by default without having to guide at each step. Without that, change is impossible.

I thought I wasn't going to be that exec, but I was. Only to a point, however. Within the team, I was able to find a balance of "natives" and "imports."

Here's how the leadership team shaped up: The Search team remained as it was, under Christopher Payne (ChrisPa) working on its own roadmap and plans, but with much more capital and more people and soon a functional org structure. Chris Jones (ChrisJo), a longtime executive on the Windows Client team, would lead program management, design, and research for Windows Live Experience, WLX. Leading development would be Steve Liffick (SteveL.) Steve had Windows Live deep in his DNA, but he had been a program manager his entire career and also grew up in Seattle, interned at Microsoft, and joined straight out of college the same summer as I did. The challenge facing the team was a lack of senior enough software engineering leadership to manage a team of several hundred, so he agreed to manage the engineering team and would prove to do an excellent job over time. Arthur de Haan (ArthurdH), a longtime test leader in Office who had built out the internet services operational infrastructure, also joined the team to lead test and internet operations.

The new name for Windows Client was the Windows Experience team, or WEX, pronounced *weks*. WEX needed a program management leader. In many ways this job was the program management job at Microsoft. Vista screamed out in need of program management—it needed a holistic view of the user, the customer, and the experience. Julie Larson Green (JulieLar) was ready for a new and bigger challenge after leading such an extraordinary effort redesigning the Office user interface. She was just recently promoted to vice president for that contribution on top of her long history of successful product development and team leadership.

Aleš Holeček (AlesH, which coincidentally is the proper pronunciation of Aleš) wore his Czech heritage proudly and maintained close connections to Prague, one of the most creative and vibrant tech communities in Europe. He also frequently, and inexplicably, wore bright red pants. AlesH was in the process of leading a rescue mission for large parts of the most visible portions of the Longhorn Reset. In short order, as a new hire to Microsoft, he had established himself as a strong leader and deeply knowledgeable and respectful of Windows as a third-party developer, but also clear on where Windows needed to go. After several discussions, I sent him the shortest of emails asking if he wanted the job leading WEX Development. An hour later we had a leader.

The testing role for WEX was going to be the most visible testing leadership job in the entire company. Windows, almost more than anything, was a product of testing. Grant George (GrantG) was busy completing Office 2007 and was so focused he was reluctant to even chat about what comes next—focus was one of Grant's defining traits as a test leader. In speaking with him, it was clear he was excited about the challenge. But he had also been much more deeply involved with Windows than I had considered, especially over the past few months, and hesitated because of his concerns about the culture. After a couple of weeks of being left to his own thoughts, he came back willing to sign up. This was a huge win for the team.

With a team in place, I penned the longest reorg mail of all time. In hindsight, this surprised nobody, but at the time it was, well, shocking. It was not just an announcement, but an explanation and justification for an organizational pivot—moving from product units to a functional organization with large groups of each engineering discipline and very few product unit managers. While not an intentional play on words, functional organization worked that way too.

On the last Thursday in June 2006 (breaking with the tradition of Friday afternoon reorg mails), I sent out a 3-page email with an attached 20-page memo with no org chart or diagram, and no to-be-hired spots. At more than 13,000 words the memo was titled "Windows and Windows Live: Organizing for agility, Competing with focus, Building must-have software."

I even did something I had never done before, which was to copy the mail to all of Microsoft's executive staff and their direct reports all around the world. There were about 150 execs at the time plus their directs and usually staff. I broadcast the mail, in the last days of the Vista project, to send a message that we were working and making progress.

As soon as this mail landed in the inboxes of about 6,000 full time engineers (and designers, localizers, planners, and more) they would all hear that their jobs would be different. But precisely how would take time. It would take weeks to build out the five or so layers of the organization, down from 7 to 10. There was no spreadsheet with all the answers for each person. Not even close.

In fact, taking a lesson from Office, we put in motion something that was yet another point of evidence of how different things would be. There was going to be a bit of a free market for people to stick their collective heads up and decide what they might want to work on next. Everyone had a job, working on their old area or perhaps trying something new. At the same time, the new execs would be choosing new direct reports who in turn would be choosing new managers and those people choosing new leads.

The previous two sections detailed the process I used to learn and the memo I wrote for an audience of three to crystallize my thinking. Now it should be clear it was a rough draft for broader communication. I moved from "Observations, Aspiration and Directions" to "Organizing" and as you look at both you can see the tone moving from analysis to action. In many ways I was employing the same planning process we use for software to design the organization—open a funnel to inputs, iterate, and at each step distill down the actions to what is essential for success.

But hitting send on this memo led to the most workplace stress I had ever experienced or would experience, not to mention the stress for all the new leaders who would be crushed with questions and concerns. Significantly, I knew how stressful this was for every individual. I felt or hoped that the messages would be read and considered even if not immediately validated, recognizing the emotional nature of so much change.

There was sizable pent-up demand for a reorg as that is what people were expecting, but I was terrified that somewhere in this memo I unintentionally offended someone, or that I perhaps expressed too much candor, offending a constituency in a deep and unrecoverable way. I was certain that I was going to immediately get an email from Mary Jo Foley at ZDNet, who was going to reprint the whole memo. I even had a "I am being transparent so don't make me regret it" plea in the mail message cover note. It worked. No leaks.

I diverged from Microsoft culture in ways many found shocking but was routine for me and Office. I sent out a reorg mail without a directed acyclic graph of the organization at the top of the mail. Even more shocking, there was no org chart at all. When people opened the mail, it was as if they had opened a box of Cracker Jack candy and couldn't find the prize. I received countless replies to the mail asking for the org chart, some of them not particularly supportive of this cultural statement which was simply perceived as incompetence or insensitivity. Additionally, the organization was complete in the mail, absent any open positions or to-be-hired.

On the other hand, I also received so many replies that were positive beyond words. The desire for something significant to put the team on a path to better results was clearly in the air. From my former co-worker in Office, Jeanne Sheldon (JeanneS), who is (even to this day) an absolute stickler for brevity and clarity in writing (a decade leading Word testing would do that even if originally choosing to work on Word because of this skill) had perhaps the kindest words. Jeanne replied to me saying "This doc is a masterpiece of clarity and focus. Although it is long, it could have been neither longer nor shorter. Wish you could do another employee poll tomorrow." I needed that.

Much to my relief, the mail received a rather heartwarming reception. I received hundreds of messages from people who appreciated the transparency—the mere heft of 20 pages, which I know most people did not comb over like the Code of Hammurabi or anything, provided some air cover. Some even complained about having to read a memo of such length—a complaint that would become something of my brand if it wasn't already. Being able to answer questions in town hall settings and then saying "there's more in the memo" became a bit of a rallying cry for me along with a pointer to the inevitable follow-up post on my Office Hours blog.

Still, I received a few dozen deeply emotional mails combined with one-on-one conversations. These were people who were the most affected, particularly by the perceived loss of status or career trajectory when it came to product unit management. I knew these conversations would be the most difficult and dealt with those the best I could. No one was being demoted in any way from my perspective and the organization had a place of equal level and opportunity for everyone. There were no formal staff reductions at all. Surprisingly, we fielded queries from the press about layoffs which were never considered. I was asking people to take on roles more directly accountable to engineering outcomes. For some, and it was a small number, it was just not appealing, and they moved on. Each one of these cases was enormously difficult. I'd like to say there was some emotional distance for me because I didn't create the situation we were in, but there's no way to avoid the feelings of the moment—I in fact did create this change.

With the mail and the memo, I went out on tour and so did each of the new leaders. The slides to explain the reorg were focused on the strategy of "Why are we doing this" and "Why are we together." KevinJo came up with a hierarchy that we used across his expansive world consisting of product lines, engineering areas, and feature teams. Kevin was used to organizing tens of thousands of people and had real insights in how to use hierarchy to communicate.

I answered the "Why are we doing this" question with a slide on "Goals of Organization Changes." This was the core of the discussion. I made people sit through my talking about this slide at length rather than, as usually done, emphasizing the structure or org chart of the team. The reasons behind the org were a direct reflection of the past 90 days of learning as I thought back to the first memo previously described. Many of the exact same words were used that I had written a month earlier.

In the description of product lines, we intentionally left off the name COSD but it was implied in the Windows/ Windows Live product area. People would get the message that COSD was part of Windows, not separate or even Windows entirely.

To address the question of why we were together I created a table of the engineering areas for WWL: Search, Live Experiences, Internet Explorer, Windows Experience. The "glue" as I said at the time was that Windows, as critical as it is, needed a series of connected services that were core to Windows. This was a subtle shift away from Services independently focused solely on advertising. This vision would take time to materialize. One can see how Apple was also just starting this same push with iLife and iWork on the Mac. Recalling the fits and starts of services connected to Apple products is a great learning exercise. What we know as iCloud today was originally launched in 2000 as iTools, which were desktop applications for photos, video, and productivity. In 2002 the addition of email and other online services came with the branding of the .Mac service. Then in 2008 (two years after our org change) the service was renamed to MobileMe and greatly expanded, which lasted until 2011 when it became iCloud. Phew. That is some journey to get right. We would struggle much the same. It is interesting when everyone seems to have the same idea of where to go but takes many years to get there and not everyone even arrives at the future the same way.

The other glue across WWL was Internet Explorer. This was the era when tuning online services to the latest browser was still important. The struggle to deliver great experiences via the web that matched desktop applications was significant, as was owning the "frame window" for delivering advertising and promotions. Due to the declining popularity of IE and lack of work on a new version, Search and WLX (and the rest of the internet) had pivoted hard to optimizing for Firefox. It is not without irony that as I write this in June 2022, Microsoft has just announced that Internet Explorer has been officially retired and replaced by the Microsoft Edge browser based on Google's open-sourced code.[74]

Each of WEX, WLX, Search, and Internet Explorer had sections that outlined the major themes to be investigated or worked on for the next products. There were no names of feature teams, no schedules, no user interface sketches. Astute readers could see where we were heading and how, as we dove into more understanding about these areas, it would inform the next level of the org structure and then specific product features would follow. This is what we had mastered in the past four releases of Office, so I felt confident we could scale it here.

Change started with this memo. I summarized this change as follows, quoting from the original memo:

> *This memo represents a change. Change is difficult. Change is uncomfortable. Changes that look good today might also have looked good before and failed. Changes that look good today might not be so great tomorrow. Change is risky. The changes outlined here are not just tweaks, but represent the first steps in working in a substantially different manner. Many of the issues raised by members of the team are about the culture of our organization—these are the aspects of "how we work" that must be addressed.*
>
> *This memo is about the top line changes—the organization and priorities—and over the coming months the way we work together will also change. We will push more decisions down. We will aspire to a more consensus approach to decision making, rather than an escalation approach. We will streamline our organization with fewer managers overall, and fewer levels of hierarchy. We will*

value our core engineering disciplines more and demonstrate this by building an organization that focuses on the role of development, testing, program management, with integral contributions across the product line from design, usability, planning, localization, business development, operations, and more. We will ask our teams to be clearly focused on deep technical contribution in a smaller number of well-defined areas, rather than breadth of coverage at too shallow a level. We will allocate resources more deliberately and generally in smaller teams. All of us may not operate with the same tempo, but we will all operate with a rhythm and not move from crisis to crisis. We will operate with a clear framework with a clear understanding of how we will define success, a framework that is flexible and has vast room for innovation, yet represents a commitment to customers that we will deliver.

These changes are part of the agenda of this memo and our organization moving forward, but will require all of us to learn and grow together. I am committed to doing my part. I will not dive into the middle of situations. I will not randomize your work. I will not be a bottleneck for decisions. I am here to work with the senior leaders of the team to provide the framework, define success, provide the resources that map to those, and make sure we have the right people with the right skills in the right jobs to get the work done that you commit to doing. That is my commitment to change.

A few weeks after this communication blitz (July 22), KevinJo announced that Jon DeVaan (JonDe) was going to lead COSD also reporting to him. Partnering with JonDe was going to make everything better—Microsoft was very lucky that Jon took on this role. This was a bit of a reunion for us. I thought back to meeting Jon the first time in the summer of 1989 when he pointed out so thoughtfully how interesting yet naïve (in a commercial sense) my views of memory management bugs were. Then through a few releases of Office as peers and then Jon as my manager, promoting me to vice president. Over the past few years while I remained in Office, Jon had been leading a new team called Engineering Excellence, which brought all manner of excellence company wide. Under Jon's leadership the team introduced and deployed tools and software for training and management as well as individual excellence. Largely not followed outside of Microsoft, the EE team was critical in scaling, training, and developing the company's engineering capabilities across every product line. It was the first substantial effort at training engineers since "Klunder College" (ADC) for new applications developers, which ended decades earlier. Jon was uniquely qualified given his lifetime of experience to re-energize the engineering culture of Windows. So loved as an engineering leader, an early 1990s pre-beta build of Excel once read "Excel DeVeloper Release" in the About box.

Jon created a top-level organization structure to parallel WEX by naming three senior leaders for development, program management, and testing, respectively Ben Fathi (BenFa), Chuck Chan (ChuckC), and Darren Muir (DMuir), each experienced Windows leaders, for a new team Windows Core Services, WCS. Their peers and counterparts in WEX were AlesH, JulieLar, and GrantG. In addition, Jon would have a team of architects (the original COSD architecture team) as well as the corporate resource team for security engineering, a.k.a. Trustworthy Computing, and a large team providing the fundamentals engineering, engineering tools and measurement, sustained engineering, and support for in-market products that would produce urgent, monthly, and regular service updates led by Wael Bahaa-El-Din (WaelB) called Windows Engineering Services or WES.

The WEX and WCS split of Windows was a first turn of the crank organizationally to building a unified Windows team. Jon and I were 1000 percent unified at the top. Our respective teams were unified. Still, it would be fair to say that the old rivalry or tension between Windows Client and COSD would continue to manifest itself until we were well into building the next product. Jon and I were working to create an organization of peers, but history did not see the teams that way. There was a lot WEX would need to prove to WCS in term of focus on performance and quality, and much WCS would need to prove in terms of building an exciting product. When tensions would arise so would the old names of Client and COSD—that's how Jon and I knew we still in the midst of a culture transformation. In practice, the COSD name stuck around for the release as we most always were talking about WCS and WES. =I will generally refer to COSD throughout this chapter.

In practice, this was all part of the slow-rolling process of changing the direction (the culture) of a giant ship. The structure is only the first change of many. I remember when I was relatively new to Microsoft and BillG created the Office of the President and announced it at a big meeting (well, it wasn't that big since all of Apps fit in the old Kodiak room back then—still hundreds of people total) and then went back to my office and kept working. An analogy I often used about change came to mind. The reorg was like how the Soviet Union fell and then the next day everyone was back at GUM waiting for winter coats to arrive, but over time there would be huge cultural changes. As interested (or perplexed) as people were with these changes, they wanted to know who their boss would be and what they were going to build. Reorgs always come down to the most localized interpretation possible.

Something I should say about this organization that is incredibly important. While I'm obviously as biased as can be, this was the very best team at precisely the right time to do exactly what Microsoft needed to get done. Perhaps that is a bit much to say, this was decidedly a collection of Super Friends, each of whom brought their own unique "super-power" when Microsoft needed it. For the remainder of this work, everything good that I will write about happened because of this group of leaders. The Microsoft of today owes them enormous gratitude, not just because of what they did from this point forward for Windows, but several were also foundational leaders of Office that so dominates Microsoft today. They ran towards the fire.

But figuring out what we would do was going to take another six months. Whether that seemed like a lot of time or a little was a matter of perspective. Teams that were done with Vista would just start doing what they thought should come next, likely what was just cut, rather than what might be optimal for a product plan. Whether the team wanted to acknowledge it or not, there was also a ton of work to be done on the basics of the engineering system.

The changes weren't over. They had barely started.

088. PLANNING THE MOST IMPORTANT WINDOWS EVER

SteveB loved to talk about his discussions with engineers as he tried to better understand the company's execution and culture challenges. He would say "I talked to this engineer on the team, and they told me 'Look, everything is completely screwed up and everybody telling you how to fix it is wrong.'" Steve would continue to listen to a litany of problems and why everyone was being "dumb" wondering what he could possibly do. Then the engineer would look up and say to Steve, "But I [emphasis on "I"] know exactly what to do and how to fix it."

My problem was I was also that engineer. I saw the problems and "knew" what to do. Except it was my job and I had to lead the team to fix the problems.

Fortunately, early on there was a set of like-minded engineers who were willing to sign up and take on the challenge of building a culture and now a plan for what comes next. From the very start it was not just me driving the cultural changes, but the set of leaders put in place from our big re-org.

Change across thousands of people, each of whom knows exactly what should be changed, is not a one-time event. Change takes repetition. It takes calendar time. It takes making some mistakes and using those as learning or teaching moments. While everyone was anxious for change, thousands of engineers must be given time to think and reach the point—on their own—of agreeing to a certain kind of change.

Every step over the next few months, from the time of putting an organization in place to starting the real building of products, we (the leaders) would be confronted with two realities. First, we had to remind everyone on the team consistently and repeatedly of the process we were using and how we aimed to work together. Every. Single. Communication. At times it felt like we were reading the inside of the box of a board game at every meeting. Second, every time we made a mistake and didn't ourselves follow that process, expect someone to point that out and for that to become a moment of humility.

It was a constant push-pull with so many wanting to know what we were telling people to build while we were busy pushing back and saying how we needed them to figure that out. At the same time what we wanted to do would look radically different from the past. It wasn't a top-down plan. It wasn't a disconnected set of innovations. It was not about consensus of design as in design-by-committee, but a coherence of a plan. The investments (as we would say) were going to fit together into a holistic product plan across our new organization: WEX, LEX, IE, and COSD. After every step in the process, we regrouped as a leadership team and not only talked about what parts of the process we needed to improve, but we turned that into coaching and more outbound communication such as my Office Hours blog. At the same time, we were continuously adapting to what was understood, misunderstood, and especially challenged when it came to process.

An example of cultural change that was front and center was a desire to match the old Windows team in terms of scorecards or KPIs by automating or operationalizing key requirements. I would be out there talking about vision and scenarios and collaboration—abstract concepts that need to be made concrete by the team—only to find out some people were trying to make a vision scorecard or building an automated testing tool to check if scenarios were complete or tools to red/yellow/green dependencies between different teams. We'd come across this and then would need to course correct and talk about how accountability works without constant monitoring by others nor overwhelming bureaucracy.

Every email and memo, every team meeting, every 1:1 was a not just an opportunity to reinforce the new cultural norms, but a requirement for us to do so. The first and most important test was developing a product plan for the next release following Vista. For us to get to the finish line with a coherent product all at the same time and all on time we would need to get to the starting line at the same time.

First, we needed a product name. By now you know I was never a fan of code names.

Windows had always had somewhat clever (too clever) code names with layers of meaning. As a consumer of these code names, they neither made for secrecy, as one could routinely read about the release code names in trade press, nor did they make it easy to remember what someone was talking about. "Is that in Nashville or Memphis? I can't remember."

Windows Vista was the sixth major release of Windows and it was version 6.0.6000 for techies. So, by fiat I christened the code name of the release *Windows 7*. I thought I was being the opposite of clever and we could simply move on, as we had done when we picked *Office 9*. Oops. Immediately I made two mistakes. First, did I reach consensus on this name? Second, did I even understand the ramifications of the name I picked unilaterally?

This sparked a debate that only geeks would participate in (at the time and once the name was made public), which was: How did we count versions of Windows? Technically, this was not the seventh major version, as some would debate. My view: Windows 1.0, Windows 2.x, Windows 3.x, Windows 95, Windows XP, and Windows Vista. But wait, there was Windows NT, and there was Windows 98, 98SE, and Millennium edition.

It turned out there were lots of ways to count and lots of ways to have more than six previous releases or fewer than six. Essentially, everyone could be right. I probably received two dozen emails with different algorithms for counting how many releases of Windows had been done, ranging from "well, it was really only four" to "at least a dozen."

I stuck with seven.

Crisis averted by executive authority. Temporarily.

The test and engineering system team informed me that we could not possibly "bump the major version number," as this would cause a whole slew of problems for application compatibility. It turned out many existing Windows programs were bad at checking what version of Windows was running and failed to run if the "major version" (that would be the first digit) was incremented. I knew this from Office 95 when we skipped several version numbers to align all the apps.

Marketing had input too: that we had to make it version 7.0 because if not the press would think we were doing a minor version and then enterprise customers would not see the need to upgrade. So even though the engineering system did not want the major version number changed, the marketing team did.

This whole notion of "major" versus "minor" as the press characterized releases would drive me nuts. It seemed as though a major release was one that broke a lot of stuff and finished late. A minor release was one that worked because it polished features and finished on time. My view, no surprise, would be based on resources. Did we have everyone working on the release or did we peel off a subset of people to work on something less for less time than a normal release? Windows 7 had everyone, 100 percent. And we were determined not to break things. And we were going to finish on time. It was a major release.

I had an urge to quit before we even started. If this trivial thing was going to be so consuming, imagine what the whole release was going to be like. Yikes.

Despite the uproar, we stuck with the Windows 7 code name, and the ultimate irony turned out to be that we eventually stuck with the name for the commercial product as well.

Planning moved forward, but it became clear that there was a new challenge at every step of the journey. There were two sides to every situation we faced.

Some people on the team wanted to be left alone, confident in what they would be working on and that there was nothing to be gained by delaying the start of the work. In some sense this was true because some parts of the product were known. We knew we needed to improve the engineering system, for example, and we knew we would do another turn of the crank on many areas, such as performance, device drivers, and security.

On the flipside, there were the people who wanted to be told precisely what to do, simply because they had frequently and repeatedly come up with ideas only to have the rug pulled out from under them by new strategies, scheduling, or resource constraints. Those people wanted to know what success would look like for them as individuals and on a granular level. The big picture was not their concern.

This made things tough.

It was tempting to remove constraints on the "correct" people and tell others what to do. It would feel quite good to be making progress and to be able to report work is happening, especially to the anxious executive team above me. Even identifying the right teams along these lines would fall into old behavior patterns we wanted to break, mainly, that there were always the elites in Windows who were given freedom to do what they felt was right, while other teams too often fell victim to management processes. I believed that we could do better if we followed the old *Shipping Software* adage and got everyone to the starting line at the same time. The goal was to get the maximum number of ideas on the table via broad participation of domain experts and create a holistic product plan from that—a Windows version of our Office approach to participatory design.

The planning memo was a tool developed in Office to begin the process of the release and to kick off a participatory design process. Over several iterations we came up with a format that provided a structure such that people could investigate what to build, without having the conclusion in advance and without necessarily having organizational ownership or structure in place. It was planning but without a pre-ordained plan arrived at by execs beforehand or retrofitted from known technology efforts already underway. It was a tool for empowering the team to ensure the best ideas came forward.

The organization needed to transform before we could transform the product and culture, but we would still need to avoid the perils of shipping a product defined by an org structure. Perhaps the biggest change we would make was the transformation of the next level of the organization away from the history of product units to a large group of feature teams of development, testing, and program management. Windows 7 (WEX, IE, and COSD) ended up being about 45 teams with about 1400 software engineers. In addition, there was a design and research team of about 100 people and about 20 product planners dedicated to Windows and reporting to JulieLar. We had a large team responsible for international versions of Windows coordinating the work with translation resources around the world.

The idea of less than 50 teams was important because each milestone would involve a meeting with teams and that needed to be manageable. I didn't think we could scale beyond that, but frankly I thought we had more than enough by way of resources to build a great product. If we could better organize, we could simultaneously tap more creative energy from within the team while improving efficiency and causing the whole to operate smoothly and pleasantly.

In the process of organizing the team we moved several significant-sized teams to the division that makes Xbox, including the Media Center, music rights management, and the non-platform elements of gaming. Some other teams, notably what remained of Windows Presentation Foundation (Avalon) moved to join with the rest of the .NET Framework, putting an end to a cross-division skirmish. A small subset of Avalon that also moved was building a cross-platform browser-plugin that supported video playback and conferencing, code name Jolt. That plugin would eventually be renamed Silverlight and offered as a competitor to Adobe Flash while also serving as a developer platform for a new Windows Phone. The resulting Windows team became much more focused on delivering and building for Windows and these divisions were excited to have more control of key technologies that did not need to be part of the Windows platform. I was very happy to do these moves.

While some were amazed that we could create $150 billion in market capitalization with only a few thousand engineers, I still thought the team was a bit large. Office created as much with 20 to 40 percent fewer people. I wasn't there to cut costs and never even thought about reducing headcount. Bloat, inefficiency, and lack of clarity in a product, however, come from too many people especially when poorly organized.

In the abstract, it is easy to see the attraction of small-focused teams tackling problems independent of each other versus a flexible and agile (though perhaps monolithic) group that adjusts to changing needs at scale. In practice, and especially at any scale, the small, multidisciplinary team rarely has an outsized impact in the context of a big business and always finds itself challenged to hire and grow deep engineering talent. Furthermore, when organized in such a manner the teams do not share in a larger mission and as a result the overall product loses the ability to shift resources around as needs arise. If a key feature team needs more resources, the head of engineering (AlesH or BenFa) can load balance across the whole organization without disenfranchising a multidisciplinary manager who would feel undermined by losing their resources to another manager. I was certain this would be important with Windows 7 because the teams had not previously done rigorous scheduling or hit a ship date.

This was a truism based on what Microsoft had achieved, not a theory or abstract concept, and was my rationale for why a structure of flexible feature teams wasn't a management fad that would swing back in the other direction down the road. Windows was one product, and we would organize and operate like we were building one product.

JonDe, JulieLar, and I, with important contributions from marketing and product planning, wrote the December 2006 memo, *Planning Windows 7 Client,* outlining the state of the business and putting forth product and business priorities. The planning memo puts a large bounding box around the release but is not yet the plan. It kicks off a process, inviting participation from everyone on the team. Using the familiar Harvard product development funnel, we were opening up the funnel to ideas.[75]

Who knew that hitting Send could be so stressful? Again.

Julie and her counterpart in COSD, ChuckC, would drive the planning process and own the resulting plan, which would be a document called the *Vision for Windows 7*. Julie, having been part of the process in Office several times, would be the key owner. Julie also wrote an outline of the overall vision process, a primer basically, that was sent and resent many times throughout the next few months. The first challenge was that a good portion of the PM team believed the planning memo was the plan, when it was a framework to think about what the plan could be. To others, this memo and process seemed to be bureaucratic or arbitrary process getting in the way of what everyone knew we needed to do. Out of the gate the need to talk about building a coherent and cohesive plan where everyone on the team was accountable to promise and deliver was our key leadership message.

The planning memo was over 30 pages, but the first two pages were essentially instructions for how it works or "the inside of the box" as we described it—another example of the ongoing repetition of how we will work.

The planning memo is where the business enters into thinking. With most of the team and audience engineers, we would use every product start to reiterate the business fundamentals and what levers were being explored.

It is in the planning memo we talk about the kinds of challenges the financial side of the business face, as we did in Office with respect to enterprise sales. In Windows there were multiple constituencies: PC makers (OEM) representing a huge portion of Microsoft's business concentrated in just a few customers, developers who make use of API innovations in Windows, ecosystem hardware partners who supply components to OEMs and peripherals to end-users, enterprise customers that run their business by deploying Windows desktops and laptops, and of course consumers and end-users. Also critical was the role the core Windows operating system played for Windows Server. Nearly every aspect of Windows impacts two or more of these directly and generally speaking it was not the type of challenge that had been pushed down to teams the way we were working to do.

The first section of the memo focused on the need of Windows to bring energy and health to the PC business, especially by finding scenarios where home users would have more than one PC and where business users would see value in more feature-rich editions of Windows. Unlike the Office business, the Windows business was much more sensitive to the sales of new PCs rather than the core value proposition to enterprises.

It is worth keeping in mind that "renewed growth" and "health" were somewhat counterintuitive to any business metrics readily visible to the team—Microsoft's history of paranoia was definitely present in our planning, and that was a good thing. There were no material signs that the PC expansion was slowing. We still had not seen the giant leap Apple would make in "personal computing" with the iPhone that was announced in January 2007.In the coming months (exactly 3 months) Steve Jobs would announce that there would be an SDK to build apps for the iPhone and iPod. Phones were getting smarter, but people were decidedly still reliant on PCs for the internet.

About three-quarters of Windows revenue came from sales directly to PC makers. While we talked about one billion Windows users, they were only our customers in an indirect way. People bought PCs and those PCs came with Windows, which was purchased by the OEMs. Even if a person had a problem with Windows on their PC, support was provided by the OEM and not Microsoft. Effectively, Windows is a business with fewer than 10 customers, but those happen to be Microsoft's largest customers by orders of magnitude. This idea of a buyer and a user being different parties with different influences on the product development process was quite familiar to me from the rise of enterprise customers in Office. Where in Office we had an ever-present struggle over the needs of the enterprise versus the needs of individuals across the product, Windows had a much more uneven approach. Some teams were extremely focused on OEM customers while others were entirely focused on end-users.

Contrary to most perceptions, the cost of Windows on a new PC (that is the price to OEMs baked into the final consumer-visible price of a PC) was a fairly low percentage of a PC price and the price had remained largely unchanged for years. This would soon become an issue with the introduction of Netbook PCs (to be discussed in Chapter XIII), but by and large the Windows license was both unchanged and a constant source of frustration from PC makers because of that inflexibility. For a variety of reasons, Microsoft lacked the kind of pricing power one might have expected in such a market. This was in contrast with the price of the Intel portion of a new PC, which was much higher and had increased over the years as Intel provided more and more integrated capabilities and provided more pre-assembled parts of a PC with each new processor generation.

PC sales in 2006 were about 240 million units worldwide. That was an astounding number and our responsibility to do the right thing and better things for all those units. The predictions for 2010 and beyond (from analysts such as Gartner and IDC) showed no end in sight for PC growth, breaking through 400 million in the years to follow. However, as frothy as that might have seemed, there were concerns that the growth rate was finally starting to slow. In fact, 2006 appeared to be the first year since economic downturns when the overall growth rate slipped and never reversed that trend with any staying power. Nevertheless, PCs were forecast to grow about 10 percent, adding 25 million PCs, or about the size of the entire global PC-installed base in 1990. The most interesting trend was a bottoming out of sales of desktop PCs—the laptop had supplanted the desktop PC in work, and totally dominated the home PC market. Computing was becoming ubiquitous, and laptops represented both mobility away from home and in the home. Gone were the days of computers taking over a whole tabletop permanently.

As a reference point, worldwide PC sales for 2019 were forecast to be slightly above 230 million following a pandemic surge approaching 325 million that appears to have receded.

To say the business was entirely dependent on OEMs would vastly understate the potential with business customers who would add the enterprise version of Windows to both new and existing PCs, which represented a substantial uplift in pricing and that translated directly to profit. As important as this was, it was much more a matter of packaging and pricing as the company had long ago shifted to developing a wide array of business-friendly features for Windows, starting with security and business networking, with much more in the works.

A significant evolution of the Windows business, rooted in both upsell and competing with Linux, was the release of a low-end SKU, called Windows Home, and a more expensive SKU, Windows Professional. Where Office had different applications (or modules), Windows had different features. The emphasis on these SKUs began with Windows XP but was put into full force with Windows Vista. This is a classic product strategy, but due to the nature of the Windows business the financial upside is enormous. A small percentage in unit upsell from Home to Professional is a price increase of tens of dollars multiplied by tens of millions of units, and all of that is essentially zero incremental cost to Microsoft. The leverage was magical. [To those keeping track of present-day Microsoft quarterly earnings, there's a consistent talking point about the role of business SKUs in Windows revenue.]

Unique to Windows was the desire to make sure developer APIs were consistently available in the most broadly distributed SKU. Everyone wanted every API to be in Home. This constraint is what made specialty SKUs like Windows Media Center or Tablet PC destined to fail with third-party developers—the APIs developers would use to target those PC form factors were only in those narrowly available SKUs with expensive hardware. Seeing the tiny sliver of market, developers would rather attempt to roll their own solution rather than ride the tiny coattails of a niche market. This would become important as we broadened Windows 7 to include touch, where most of that support existed only in the Tablet PC specialty SKU.

The Windows Ecosystem could be thought of as four sets of deeply dependent yet independent entities, each believing that they contributed an outsized effort when there was success while each believing the other parties had more than their fair share of responsibility when things were not going well: Microsoft, Intel making and selling CPUs and associated chips and storage, PC OEMs and hardware makers, Independent Hardware Vendors or IHVs, and software developers, Independent Software Vendors, ISVs. The mutual dependencies are illustrated by a cycle:

- PC and hardware makers depend on Intel and **Microsoft** to deliver a complete PC experience.
- Microsoft depends on **Intel** to continue to drive demand with faster chips and new capabilities while enabling PC makers to take advantage of those.
- **PC OEMs** depend on **IHVs** to enable all sorts of new hardware capabilities that will excite consumers and drive demand.
- Microsoft courts the fourth leg of this stool, the **independent software vendor** (ISV or "Developers, Developers, Developers" as SteveB would calmly state) such as Adobe, Autodesk, Intuit, or PC game makers to make applications for a new version of Windows with new APIs or that require new hardware (such as faster graphics cards), which in turn require new PCs.

A new version of Windows without cool new PCs or new PCs without cool new chips or hardware or new software that didn't take advantage of any of those were all reasons why the ecosystem could become unhealthy. This codependency created an enormously tense network made up of a small number of large public companies, each with quarterly earnings reports. Also, at the time, in the United States, Japan, and Europe, PCs sold through a large number of retail stores so companies such as Best Buy, Dixons, or MediaMarkt were also part of this equation, and they were ruthless champions of low price and opportunity for margin.

The second section of the planning memo outlined what were called big bets. We hoped this would engage the architects and long-term thinkers by laying out significant challenges that we knew would need to be scoped and refined. Intentionally, there was only a small number of these so as to scope them to a single release. The constant discussion on bets was about how to define a bet as a set of steps that could be accomplished over reasonable time periods and incremental success, rather than one giant leap a decade later.

One of the unique things about Windows being part of the PC ecosystem while also being an open platform was that when new hardware was available to integrate into PCs, PC manufacturers could build PCs with support for new devices or peripherals without built-in Windows support. OEMs would write their own code from device drivers through user interface to support a new hardware gadget, for example Wi-Fi or a fingerprint reader. Unfortunately, this created a problem. Too often, such support did not have great APIs for developers or was not always integrated into Windows in a way that allowed others to make the most of it. But with Windows releases not being so reliable and PC makers always looking for an advantage over the competition, waiting for Windows to figure out support for new peripherals never really happened. With Windows 7 we set out to get ahead of some classes of devices, such as printers, graphics, storage, and so on, with a big bet on hardware-driven innovation but would leave it to the planning process to identify areas where such an approach would work.

There were two other big bets of note. Virtualization was becoming a huge push across the industry. But on that front, Microsoft was falling behind. Interestingly, at many team levels, there was a deep resistance to virtualization because of security concerns that the whole system could be compromised. There were also business concerns due to the Windows business having a foundational belief of one Windows license for every CPU. All the while, virtualization was growing rapidly and on every CIOs radar precisely because of security. Their belief was that virtualization was inherently more secure. It was also the core technology that would enable cloud computing and as such it was critical that we get it right. Competitively, virtualization was critically important for the Windows Server business. VMware, pioneers of virtualization, was rapidly becoming a technology powerhouse under the leadership of Paul Maritz—yes, the former leader of Windows. Ironic moments such as this were in no short supply.

We also wanted a big bet for the typical Windows consumer, which would give us a chance to incorporate Windows Live services as a key part of the overall value proposition for Windows. Historically, Windows had duplicated services provided by MSN (the predecessor to Windows Live), ostensibly for a whole variety of reasons from legal to performance to security, and at the same time the MSN services did not do any work to shine on new versions of Windows. The ultimate achievement of this was the debacle when Microsoft shipped both Windows Messenger and MSN Messenger on new PCs and both had different sign-on, networks, and features. Another example was when the Windows Mail program did not do a good job connecting to Hotmail. This gave us a chance to say, "We will plan on not duplicating work," at a minimum, but also push to do great work that could potentially compete with Apple or maybe Google.

In order to account for the heavy lifting that would be required to build on the Vista foundation and yet also fix it to the degree we needed to, we defined a big bet that we called "continuing bets." This provided a catch-all to plan on the needs for improved PC security, 64-bit computing, and overall cleanup work. The fact that the release ultimately succeeded in cleaning up or completing this work led to the frustrating belief by some that Windows 7 was, in fact, a minor or cleanup release.

The traditional Windows view loved big bets—that felt like the kind of work we did for Longhorn. Many on the development side were perfectly happy to define a release by making progress on big bets, even if the manifestation of big bets would take years and the visible features not particularly visible.

From Julie's perspective, the plan or vision for Windows would be start with planning themes. Rather than a plan itself, the memo contained ten planning themes. A planning theme was a precursor to a specific main pilar of the release. Themes are an invitation for brainstorming and creativity within that theme. Prior to this there is a step to even pick these themes, but that is a small group and done relatively top-down. The planning themes were broad strokes. The introduction of those themes was really an invitation to begin a process whereby the specific groups of engineers (feature teams) work together to define what it might mean to deliver on that theme—a literal call to innovate and be creative. The themes for planning Windows 7 included:

- Refining the Vista User Experience
- Building Customer Confidence
- Embracing the Best of Web Development
- Helping OEMs and IHVs Win the Hearts of Customers
- Turning IT Pros into Windows Evangelists
- Making it Easy to Add or Replace a PC
- Lighting Up Everywhere with Servers and Services
- Finding Everything Easily
- Connecting Multiple Devices to Multiple PCs
- Embracing Hardware Advances for Better Multimedia Experiences

Over the next three months there were countless offsites, meetings, design sketches, and more to arrive at more detailed views of what features might be built. It was this part of the process that is both the most uncertain and nerve-wracking for me. I not only had no idea if the ideas being generated were good, but I didn't even know if the teams were converging. There's no way to even measure this. In the back of my head, I was also wondering if there were developers writing code for new features that we won't even want to ship while PM was off figuring out what to make. If the goal of the planning process starting with the planning memo was to bake a cake, then I just couldn't open the oven every 15 minutes to check without ruining the cake.

Over the three months from the planning memo to the creation of a product vision the team is not producing code. The PM team was producing slide decks, PM prototypes, design sketches, and even a little bit of prototype code. The development team participated in this part of the process but was also tasked with watching the market telemetry for Vista and fixing a lot of bugs. The test and development teams together were working to improve the daily build and test process—an enormous undertaking that GrantG referred to as building out "the factory floor." The 6 years of Vista development and the numerous side releases of Windows had made for a neglected engineering process. There was plenty of work to go around. Having the time to address these pain points and to do so together without a crisis enabled even this type of work to become part of the culture change. JonDe dug into every aspect of the daily development process, which he had become acutely aware of in his role leading Engineering Excellence. Fixing the factory floor would prove to be an enormous win for morale and efficacy.

Then suddenly the cake was ready. There was a vision. Reading this, one might really want to know what precisely went on for those months. How did the team go from brainstorming to a plan? The lack of a concrete description of this is why it has always been somewhat magical. It really isn't magic, but it is empowerment, accountability, and creativity. There was never an answer other than build a great product, but pieces had to fit together, and everyone had to agree and reach a shared view of what was being committed to and being built. Every offsite, prototype, and sketch were talked about, debated, and considered. Most were thrown out for any of a myriad of reasons.

There was, however, one bit of magic and it was connected to a cultural change. The typical (in Windows and elsewhere) executive management role is one where teams go off and generate ideas and come back with a plan, for approval. Invariably during a meeting for approval the plans would be changed with the incorporation of executive feedback. The problem I always had with this was the underlying assumption that an executive thinking on the fly about whatever specifics or details arose during one meeting for an hour after weeks (or months) of work was truly value added or just value changed. I never had that much confidence. We started from an assumption that the plan was already approved, and the meeting was a confirmation of the plans the team created and was accountable to. The magic was that leading up to those review meetings we were, JulieLar in particular, in a constant and iterative conversation about ideas, tradeoffs, and specifically adherence to the evolving product vision. This led to a much deeper sense of ownership and buy-in and avoided the historic problems of swoop and poop or simply random executive thoughts.

We called the transformation of planning themes to the product vision a pivot. Microsoft loved to use the word pivot in just about every context, especially because it had nothing to do with basketball. We were pivoting from a long list of themes with ideas of problems to be solved to a much shorter list of vision areas each with specific scenarios we would implement. This is why the vision represented a true product plan.

On July 27, 2007, we gathered the team at the Meydenbauer Center—yes, the entire Windows product team was invited—for a meeting where we presented the product vision. The all-team meeting was another step in the culture change. It would be the first time the whole of the Windows team got together to hear the entire product plan—the committed product plan—for a Windows release before coding started. It was so important to me that everyone really experienced what we intended to build and to have that moment when as a team we commit.

Just as we did with Office, the product vision consisted of a substantial memo (this time with a bit more up front on how to read the memo), a series of produced design sketches showing each of the main themes of the release **as we intend to develop them**, a mock press release created by marketing showing how the release would be communicated upon shipping, and my favorite the one page cheat-sheet for the vision.

Even though we had been together for more than year as a team, and Windows Vista had been in market for six months already, we were still transforming and growing as a team. While everyone really wanted to know what everyone else was going to build (by this time most people knew what they were going to start to build) I wanted us to continue to build the culture. I had a slide defining a successful Windows 7 as a set of key traits feeding into success (using Office SmartArt of course): promise and deliver, develop satisfying features + scenarios, create partnerships [not dependencies], participate and communicate, learn and iterate and improve. Still, we had one more slide articulated how to use the vision. At this point, if you're not convinced management is repetition...

Before JulieLar would take the stage and share the vision themes and features, we had a special speaker. Although now formally transitioned from his role as Chief Software Architect to philanthropist and Chairman of the Board, I thought it would be important for BillG to share a personal view on the role of Windows within Microsoft. He delivered a wonderful and improvised talk without any slides. It was a mix of history and enthusiasm for the most recent innovations lasting about 15 minutes. He spoke of the patience we showed in building Windows after the first releases that were too early and the bet on having Office for Windows which made Windows better and Office better. I did ask Bill to emphasize competition knowing that was near and dear to him, given I had already shared with him my view that there was a bit of a lack of fire in that regard. The iPhone was just weeks on market and the potential impact on the PC industry was just becoming clear and did not escape Bill's mention, including some speculation about a tablet-sized device for reading, which will be discussed in Chapter XIV. He also touched on Linux competition which was acute in the enterprise space and on servers. The highlight for me was when Bill held up the vision one-pager and reinforced that this was the product he was expecting, and he too would behave and not ask people about things not part of the plan—the team applauded and that made for quite a moment for me. That moment didn't last long as he then told the team it wasn't critical that we hit the ship date as long as we got all the scenarios working—that is the Office baggage described in previous sections where Office somehow cheats by cutting features to ship on time. There is a recording, but it is poor quality—just a camcorder in the back of the room.

JulieLar presented the vision itself. It was a work of art. From a dead stop after Vista she pulled the entire PM team across WEX and COSD through a foreign process, an Office process no less. I could see the excitement and almost amazement from the team as I stood in the back of the room doing all I could to get a sense for the vibe. The vision for the release had five areas:

- Specialized for Laptops
- Designed for Services
- Personalized computing for everyone
- Optimized for Entertainment
- Engineered for Ease of Ownership

Each of these were detailed with scenarios, business motivation, and a definition of success and then illustrated with a narrated design sketch.

Following this ChuckC, Julie's counterpart from the Windows Core System team in COSD, presented the project tenets. These were the non-negotiable aspects of the project:

1. Design for interoperability
2. Security is a key promise to customers
3. Runs with existing hardware
4. Application and driver compatibility
5. Getting ready for 64-bit only
6. Performance breakthroughs for key scenarios
7. Improved Reliability
8. Design for sustainability, manageability, supportability
9. Design for every market, every language
10. Improved accessibility for all users

Chuck outlined the project schedule which included three milestones—each an opportunity to re-evaluate, adjust, re-allocate resources, and adapt the plan. We would begin coding in 5 weeks, after the US Labor Day holiday. Windows 7 RTM was set for May 13, 2009.

Mike Sievert (MSievert), the CVP of marketing (and as of this writing, the CEO of T-Mobile) provided a detailed overview of the current state of the business and opportunity. KevinJo spoke about the importance of Windows Live, which was in the process of executing a plan to run on a shorter schedule and would have releases of services for Windows 7 at availability. He also addressed what was top of mind for both of us, which was adhering to the newly announced *Windows Principles* a series of proactive steps to managing the business that the legal team put forth on their own in hopes of setting a different tone with regulators.[76]

JonDe spoke to the deep technology shifts in the PC industry where the COSD team had historically focused their energy and where the big bets at the core OS level were critical, especially for Windows Server which shared the OS. He spoke to the work we needed to continue including:

- Multi-core and many-core
- Virtualization
- GPUs
- Wireless
- Storage and non-volatile memory
- Power management
- New and popular devices: GPS, biometrics, web-cameras
- Diverse form factors

To set an example, the meeting went like clockwork and lasted three hours, and there was even a break. After the meeting, I sent out the full memo to the whole team. I recently acquired a new ultra-wide-angle lens for my (then fancy) DSLR and took a team photo. Everyone was in their limited-edition color-coded t-shirts which was always done tongue in cheek but certainly plays like something one would see on a bad take of a tech on HBO. I still see these Windows 7 t-shirts around town, which amazes me. I even saw one in a yoga class in Silicon Valley, years after vision day.

I followed up with an Office Hours blog post expanding on my themes of what would make Windows 7 a successful release.

The day could not have gone better. I had been through many vision days in Office, but this one was truly a special moment. I genuinely felt like we had reached a milestone of cultural change within the team.

I was of course kidding myself. I only felt that way because for 15 months non-stop I had been saying the same thing over and over again gradually improving. But we were just now starting the real work. Other than my own fatigue, there was no evidence yet to support an assertion that we would get the release done. In reality, I remained terrified. I couldn't even hide it. KevinJo sent me mail after the meeting saying he felt the meeting was great, but he thought I seemed down.

I was not down—the day was really excellent. I was, however, worried. Would this be enough? Would we get done on time? Was on time even soon enough? We had so much to do. We had so much to fix, starting with the relationships with PC makers who were truly suffering with Windows Vista.

089. REBOOTING THE PC ECOSYSTEM

In the summer of 2007 six-months after Windows Vista availability as we rolled out the Windows 7 product vision to the entire team, the press coverage for Vista began to get brutal. I say the coverage, but this is really about the customer reaction to the product and the press simply reflected that.

Then the OEMs, large public companies with shareholders and quarterly earnings, started to do something almost unimaginable. They began to speak out about the problems with Vista. In a widely covered interview in the *Financial Times* discussing quarterly results, Acer president Gianfranco Lanci lashed out at Vista, saying the "whole industry is disappointed with Windows Vista" and stated that Vista had stability problems and he doubted that Microsoft would remedy the issues within the next six months. He went on to suggest that customers really wanted Windows XP knowing that in just a few months XP would be discontinued.[77] Much of what he said in public, the OEMs had been telling us in private.

I had been in my role for more than a year and still did not have much to say about what was coming next. How could I? We just didn't know and all my experience with customers told me that claiming I didn't know would not be acceptable or even credible. Still, pressure was mounting to show progress.

The Windows, or PC, ecosystem is made up Intel, PC makers (the OEMs), and creators hardware components and peripherals known as Independent Hardware Vendors. OEMs accounted for the vast majority of Microsoft's extremely lucrative Windows business. IHVs were the key ingredients the OEMs counted on for innovation. Intel, provider of CPUs and an increasing portion of the main componentry, was the most central in the hardware ecosystem as half of the legendary *Wintel* partnership.

Suffice it to say ecosystem was in an unhappy and untrusting state after years of product delays along with a series of feature, product, and pricing miscues. The delays had been extremely painful to OEMs and Intel, who counted on a new release of Windows to show off new PCs and drive growth in PC sales. IHVs had critical work to do enabling new PCs. They had to build software drivers that enabled new hardware that was compatible with the new features of Windows, such as 64-bit Windows or new security features. They also faced the increasing complexity of maintaining drivers for old versions of Windows as the time between releases increased and customers demanded new hardware support on both old and new platforms. The rise of Linux was spreading the Windows ecosystem further as demand for Linux support increased. Fractures were everywhere.

Intel contributed an increasingly larger portion of the PC, much as Microsoft continued to add features to Windows. With Centrino® for example, Intel added Wi-Fi support directly to the components they provided to PC makers. This greatly expanded and standardized the use of Wi-Fi in laptops. Intel was in the process of broadening their support for graphics as well, continuing to improve the integrated graphics chips they provided to PC makers. This was a particularly sore spot with Vista. Intel was able to better control pricing of their components, encourage specific PC designs, and shift PC makers to various CPU choices using a combination of pricing actions and co-marketing arrangements. Originally these "Intel Inside" advertising efforts were a huge part of how PC makers selected and marketed different models and lines of computers and was enormously profitable for Intel.

Microsoft's relationship with Intel had not been particularly happy, going way back to the 1990s when Intel began to embrace Java and other cross-platform technologies. Recently, however, the rise of Linux was viewed by Intel as a large opportunity, while Microsoft perceived it as a competitive threat. What Microsoft used to perceive as a moat, device driver support for Windows, was rapidly fading due to active efforts by Intel to support Linux to the same degree. The specter of desktop Linux seemed to be held back by just a few device drivers should Intel support them, or so we worried.

There was also a complex relationship between enterprise customers and Microsoft when it came to Windows. From a product and feature perspective, Windows was making increasing bets on the kind of features businesses cared about, such as endpoint control, reliability, and management. Microsoft did not always want to give away those features for free to retail customers where they might not apply. The fact that these features existed caused OEMs to consider ways to add them to the base Windows they sold, feeling that the base Windows was under-powered. In other words, features Microsoft added to premium editions of Windows simply served as starting points for features OEMs might look to provide with their own software on top of the basic editions of Windows, increasing OEM margin.

The response to the increasing gap between consumers and enterprise was another reason for OEMs to embrace, or at least appear to embrace Linux. At the very least, OEMs began to ponder the idea of selling PCs with free Linux and letting customers pick and choose an operating system on their own as a backdoor way to avoid the Windows license for every single PC. Microsoft did not want OEMs selling PCs without Windows when Windows was destined to be on the PC anyway, as that would only encourage piracy. This "Linux threat" was not as empty as the state of technology would have indicated as OEMs were actively starting to offer Linux on the desktop, especially if they were offering it on Server already. Some markets, such as China, which already had enormously high piracy pursued this path aggressively.

From the least expensive PCs for the budget conscious to the fanciest PCs for gamers, the Windows product and business depended on these partners, and vice versa. Any business book would tell you just how big a deal the Windows ecosystem was, as would anyone who followed the antitrust actions against Microsoft.

We needed to reboot the relationship with and across the Ecosystem. Doing so would be an important part of the planning process and run in parallel with planning the Windows 7 product.

The perspectives, insights, and data from hardware and OEM partners were only part of the input to the planning process. Another part was the usage data from tens of millions of Windows users. What features, peripherals, and third-party programs were used, how often, and by which types of customers. Vista had done excellent work to incorporate the performance and reliability measures of the system, especially for glitches like crashes and hangs, but usage data was inconsistent across the system. As we would discover, this data was not readily available or reliably collected across the whole product. We knew we would need as much as we could for Windows 7 and certainly down the road, so we began in earnest to implement more telemetry across the product during the planning for Windows 7. This data would form a foundation for many discussions with OEMs.

The feverish pace and tons of work over the six months that followed the re-org tackled an expansive set of potential areas and distilled them down to a product plan, the *Windows 7 Vision*. That six months would bump up against not one but two OEM selling seasons during which the OEMs would not get the news about "fixing Vista" they were hoping for. The planning memo came out in December 2006 even before Windows Vista availability. That timing, however, would be too late to impact the February selling season. The July 2007 Vision was too late to become requirements for PCs for back to school in August or September of that year. Even though PCs would not ship with Windows 7 for quite some time, every selling season we missed would make it frustratingly difficult for those PCs to be upgraded to Windows 7. This was a problem for every part of the ecosystem including Microsoft.

The relationships were difficult, but more importantly the quality of work across the ecosystem was in decline. Communication was adversarial at best.

Mike Angiulo (MikeAng) joined from Office and began an incredible effort at rebuilding the relationships with OEMs. Mike was not only a stellar technologist, but a strategic relationship manager, having grown up as a salesman within his future family's business. He was also a trained mechanical engineer who rebuilt and raced cars, a natural-born poker champion, and an IR-pilot who built his own plane.

He recruited Roanne Sones (RSones) to lead the rehabilitation of the relationship with OEM customers. She was a college hire from Waterloo's prestigious systems engineering program who had joined Office five years earlier. Having worked on projects from creating the Office layperson's specification, to synthesizing customer needs by segment, to analyzing usage data across the product, Roanne brought a breadth of tools and techniques from Office to the OEM problem space. Also joining the team was Bernardo Caldas (BCaldas) who would bring deep insights combining usage data, financial modeling, and business model thinking to the team.

Roanne quickly learned that a big part of the challenge would be the varying planning horizons the OEMs required. "Required" because they told us that they needed "final Windows 7 plans" in short order if they were to make the deadlines for a selling season. Whether they needed the information or not, the reality was they were so used to not getting what they wanted they simply made any request urgent and expansive.

Each OEM was slightly different in how it approached the relationship, but all shared two key attributes. First, they viewed Windows as an adversary. Second, they did not take anything we told them to be the ground truth. They were constantly working the Microsoft organization and their connections, which were deep, across the separately organized OEM sales team, support organizations, and more, to triangulate anything we said to arrive at their own version of truth or reality. They also had no problems escalating to the head of global sales or to SteveB directly, several of whom had known Steve for decades.

After a decade of missed milestones, dropped features, antitrust concerns, and contentious business relationships, the connection between Microsoft and OEMs was painfully dysfunctional. Considering Windows accounted for so much of Microsoft's profit, this was a disaster of a situation. It had been going on so long that most inside Microsoft seemed to shrug it off as just a part of the business or "OEMs have always been like this." It was no surprise to me that the relationships devolved.

We found little to love in most new PCs while at the same time Microsoft was rooted in a long history of believing, as BillG would say though this is misinterpreted I think, that "ten years out, in terms of actual hardware costs you can almost think of hardware as being free."[78] He meant that to imply that relative to advancing software capabilities, the hardware resources required would not be a key factor in innovation. I'm not sure OEMs heard it that way.

What was really going on other than Microsoft's lack of reliability as a partner, not to dismiss that perfectly legitimate fact? It goes back to the history of PC manufacturing and its evolution to the current situation. When Dell and then Compaq first manufactured PCs, they were rooted in engineering and design of PCs, and each built out manufacturing and distribution channels—PCs made in the US (Texas) and shipped around the world.

As the industry matured, more and more manufacturing moved to plants in Taiwan and China. Traditionally, components such as hard drives, accessory boards, and motherboards were shipped to the United States from locations around Asia for final assembly, including the addition of the Intel CPU manufactured in the US. Eventually, as more and more were made in Asia, it became increasingly efficient to aggregate components there for assembly as a complete PC, which could then be shipped around the world. This transition is one Tim Cook, now the CEO of Apple, famously took Apple through even though Steve Jobs resisted it.

Over time, these assembly companies aimed to deliver even more value and a greater share of the PC experience, as they described. They even began to create speculative PCs and sell them to the OEMs, such as Dell and HP for incorporation into their product lines after a bit of customization such as component choice and industrial design. The preference for laptops over desktops made it even more critical to engineer a complete package, which these new original design manufacturer partners became experts at doing. As the name implied, an ODM would both design and manufacture PCs and many other silicon-based electronics. The ODMs developed such complete operations that some even created consumer-facing brands to sell PCs as a first party, in search of margins and revenue.

In a sense, the headquarters of an OEM was the business operation and the ODM the product and manufacturing arm, managed on metrics of cost, time to delivery, and quality. In this view, Windows itself became just another part of the supply chain, albeit the second most expensive part, usually far behind Intel. That's why PCs tended to converge on similar designs. Some argued that the ODM process drove much of that with a small set of vendors looking to keep costs low and sourcing from a small set of suppliers to meet similar needs from US sales and marketing arms. Even though there were a dozen global PC makers, the increasing level of componentization and the ODM model caused a convergence, first with desktops and now we were seeing the same happen with laptops.

Effectively, ODMs were driving a level of commoditization. On the one hand, this was great for better device driver support and a more consistent Windows experience, as investments the ecosystem made were leveraged across independent PC makers. On the other hand, this led to margin compression for PC makers which put even more pressure on ODMs and Microsoft. Further, given all PC makers faced similar constraints, PCs tended to converge to an average product, rather than an innovative one. There were a few outliers such as Sony who continued to drive design wins, but with ever-decreasing volume. Sony sold off their PC business in 2014.

Roanne and Bernardo were treating the ODMs with the same level of attention as OEMs, something that had not been done before. The PC business was extremely healthy in terms of unit volumes, but the OEMs were all struggling to maintain profit margins and were looking to ODMs for leverage. There was a great deal of envy of Apple and its sleek new MacBook laptops made from machined aluminum, but, more importantly, the margins Apple earned from those PCs were impressive. The OEMs were pressuring the ODMs to deliver the same build quality with room for ample margins and a lower price than Apple, which was believed to be charging premium prices at much lower volume. In manufacturing, volume is everything so it is reasonable to assume that much higher volume could make lower prices possible, but only if the volume was for a small number of different models which the OEMs were not committed to. The ODMs thought this was impossible and continued to push their ability to deliver higher-margin and higher-priced premium laptops.

Early in my time at Windows, I went to Asia to visit with some of the ODMs to see firsthand their perspective on the PC and the relationships across the ecosystem. Visiting with the ODMs brought these tension front and center and proved informative.

The ODMs that served multiple OEMs were quite stringent about secrecy and leaks across their own companies. Each OEM had distinct and secured facilities, and the ODM management structure was such that information was not shared across facilities. Visiting a single ODM meant seeing buildings for any one of the major global manufacturers all identical on the outside, but each entrance was guarded as though the building was owned and operated by the specific OEM. Access was closely guarded and employees of the ODM never crossed into different facilities. I recall once having an Apple building pointed to in a manner that reminded me of driving by a building on the Washington, DC Beltway when everyone knows it is a spy building, but just remains quiet and doesn't say a word. An ODM even acknowledging they served Apple would jeopardize their business even though it was an open secret.

The ODMs themselves were struggling with margins, even though they benefitted from a highly favorable labor cost structure in Asia. Several were responsible for manufacturing Apple devices, and while they would certainly never, ever divulge any details about that process, we knew that much of the math they would show us, bleak as it was, was informed by what they were doing for Apple and other OEMs.

One of the larger ODMs that I also understood made Macintosh laptops—and was run by a founder and CEO who had grown the company from the 1980s—proved to be an adventure to visit.

I arrived for my tour and put on a bunny suit and booties, deposited any electronics and possessions into a safe, and entered through a metal detector. There were cameras everywhere. There were acres of stations on the floor of a massive assembly line, each one responsible for a step in the manufacturing process. Pallets of hard drives, motherboards, screens, and cases arrived in one end, and progressed through the enormous assembly line stopping at each station. One added the hard drive, while one was attached the screen. Another verified that everything powered up. The final assembly step was where they attached the *Genuine Windows* hologram that proved that the Windows software was not pirated and was purchased legally. The ODMs always made a point of showing me that step knowing their role in anti-piracy was something we were always on the lookout for. Then the machines were powered up and burned in for a few hours to make sure everything worked.

After seeing the line, we ventured to the top-floor of the building to the CEO's private office, which was the entire floor. On this floor was a beautiful private art collection of ancient Chinese calligraphy and watercolors. After a ritual of tea and tour of the gallery, the discussions of business began.

Instead of hearing about all the requirements from Windows, the CEO raised many issues about our mutual customers. We discussed the constant squeeze for margin, the pressure to compete with Apple without paying Apple prices, and what I found most interesting: the desire for flexibility, which precluded everything else. The OEMs, it turned out, were born out of an era during which desktop PCs were made from a number of key peripherals, such as a hard drive, graphics card, memory, and other input/output cards. Each of these could be chosen and configured at time of purchase. This allowed for two crucial elements of the business. First, the customer had a build-to-order mindset, which was appealing and a huge part of the success of Dell. Second, the OEM could bid commodity suppliers of these components against each other and routinely swap out cheaper parts while maintaining the price for customers. This just-in-time manufacturing and flexible supply chain were all the rage in business schools.

The problem was that this method did not really work for laptops and especially did not work for competing with Apple. Apple designed every aspect of a laptop and chose all the components and points of consumer choice up front. This gave Apple laptops the huge advantage of being smaller and lighter while also not having to account for a variety of components placing different requirements on software, cooling, or battery life. This integrated engineering was almost the exact opposite of how the Windows PC makers were designing laptops.

During one visit in 2008, after the MacBook Air had recently been released, it was all the ODMs could talk about. The only PCs that came close were made in Japan for the Japan market or achieved little critical mass in the US except among tech elites, such as the Sony VAIO PCG-505 or the Fujitsu LifeBook that I used. The Air's relatively low(-ish) price point would eventually lead to an Intel marketing initiative called Ultrabook™™ but as future sections will describe, it would be years before the PC ecosystem could respond to the Air.

From an ODM perspective, the requirements for the supply chain were driven by non-engineers or marketing from the OEMs back at HQ and seemed disconnected from the realities of manufacturing. They felt they had the capability to build much sleeker PCs than they were being asked. Always implied but never stated was the fact that some of them built devices for Apple.

Meeting after meeting, I heard stories of ODMs who knew how to build leading and competitive laptops but the US OEMs, even when shown production-ready prototypes, would not add them to their product lines. They wanted cheaper and more flexible. Or at least that was the frustration the ODMs expressed.

From a software perspective, I began to understand why PC laptops were like they were. For example, they were relatively larger than Apple laptops to enable component swapping as though they were desktops. Nearly every review of a Windows laptop bemoaned the quality of the trackpads—both the hardware and software—and here again the lack of focus on end-to-end, including a lack of unified software support from Windows and a requirement for multi-vendor support, made delivering a great customer experience nearly impossible. It was also the case for cellular modems, integrated cameras, Bluetooth, and more.

The desire for lower costs would preclude advanced engineering and innovation in cooling. This led to most Windows laptops to have relatively generic fans and overly generous case dimensions to guarantee airflow and cooling for a flexibility in componentry. The plastic cases filled with holes and grills were just the downstream effect of these upstream choices. So was the fan noise and hot wind blowing out the side of a Windows laptop.

Review after review said Windows laptops didn't compare to the leading laptops from Apple, and yet I could see the potential to build them if only one of the OEMs would buy them. They simply didn't see the business case. Their view was that the PC was an extremely price-sensitive market, and their margins were razor thin. They were right. Still, this did not satisfactorily explain Apple nor the inability to at least offer a well-made and competitive Windows PC. Though simply offering it would prove to be futile because of the price and limited distribution such a low-volume PC would necessarily command. We were caught in a bad feedback loop.

A larger initiative Roanne and team would take on was the infamous "crapware" issue, the phrase coined by Walt Mossberg years earlier. Tech enthusiasts and also reviewers tend to view crapware through that namesake lens as software that just makes the PC worse. OEMs had a decidedly different view and to be honest one that as I learned about it, I worked hard to be more sympathetic to. To the OEMs, additional software was a means of differentiation and a way to make their own hardware shine. We tended to think of crapware as trial versions of random programs or antivirus software, but to the OEMs this was a carefully curated set of products they devoted enormous resources to offering. While some were trials and services designed to have revenue upside, others were developed in-house and were there because of unique hardware needs. The grandest example came with Lenovo ThinkPads called *ThinkVantage Technologies* or TVT.[79] Under this umbrella the full enterprise management and control of the PC hardware was enabled by Lenovo. While I might have an opinion on quality or utility, there was no doubt they were putting a good deal of effort into this work and most of the features were not part of Windows.

Previously I described the OEM relationship as adversarial. That might have been an understatement. The tension with OEMs was rooted in a desire to customize Windows so that it was unique for each OEM or each product line from an OEM. Microsoft's view was these customizations usually involved "crapware" and that Windows needed to remain consistent for every user regardless of what kind of PC it ran on. It is easy to see this is unsolvable when framed this way. It was amazing considering how completely and utterly dependent Microsoft was on OEMs and OEMs were on Microsoft. This is a case where new people with a new set of eyes had a huge opportunity to reset the relationship.

What I just described was a few months of my own journey to understanding why PCs were like they were, and now I felt I understood. Because I was new, and we had a new team led by Mike, we were optimistic that we could improve the situation. There was no reason to doubt that we could. We believed we understood the issues, levers, and players. It seemed entirely doable. We just had to build trust.

The primary interaction with OEMs were "asks" followed by "request denied" which then led to a series of escalations and some compromise that made neither happy. This would be repeated dozens of times for each OEM for many of the same issues and some specific to an OEM. As with any dynamic where requests are denied, the result was an ever-increasing number of asks and within those an over-ask in the hopes of reaching some midpoint. If an OEM wanted to add four items to the Start menu, then the ask might be to "customize every entry on the Start menu" and a reply might come back as "none" or "no time to implement that" and then eventually some compromise. It was painful and non-productive.

There are two schools of thought on these issues. One is that it is obvious that Windows is a product sold by Microsoft and the OEMs should just pass it along as Microsoft intended it to be—relegating the OEM to a wholesale distributor. In fact, the contract to buy Windows from Microsoft specifically states that the product is sold a certain way that should remain. Given the investment OEMs made in building a PC, they did not see the situation that way at all.

The other is that it is equally obvious that the OEMs are paying Microsoft a huge amount of money and they own the customer relationship, including support, so they should be able to modify the product on behalf of their end-user customers. As it would turn out, the first view was on pretty firm ground, at least prior to the 1990s antitrust case. After settling that case, the conclusion was that the right to modify the product as an end-user would pass through to OEMs and Microsoft had limits in what it could require. If readers are thinking about how Android works with phone makers today, you have stumbled upon the exact same issue.

Perhaps using the word adversary as I have previously used was too blunt. In fact, the relationships were often far more complex and nuanced, fraught with combinations of aligned and mis-aligned incentives. It was entirely the case that the OEMs were our customers, but that was confusing relative to end-users who were certain they were buying a Microsoft product while also a PC maker's product, and often the Microsoft brand was paramount in the eyes of consumers. The OEMs were also Microsoft partners in product development—we spent enormous sums of money, time, and resources to co-develop technologies and the whole product—yet this partnership felt somewhat one-way to both sides. OEMs were often viewed as competitors as they ventured into Linux desktops and servers, while at the same time they viewed Microsoft as offering one of several choices they had for operating systems. We certainly viewed OEMs as the source our shortcomings relative to Apple hardware, yet the OEMs viewed us as not delivering on software to compete with Apple. Even as distribution partners, depending on who was asked, the OEMs were distributors of Windows or Windows was a distribution tool for the PC itself.

These dysfunctions or as most schooled in how the technology stack evolved referred to them as "natural tensions" had been there for years. There's little doubt that the antitrust settlement essentially formalized or even froze the relationship, making progress on any part a challenge. There was no doubt a looming threat of further scrutiny as the ongoing settlement-mandated oversight body remained. I met regularly with the "Technical Committee" and heard immediately of anything that might be concerning. Every single issue was resolved, and frankly most trivially so, but the path to escalate was always there.

At the conclusion of the antitrust case, the Final Judgement or Consent Decree (CD) formalized a number of aspects of the relationship, some surprisingly made it more difficult to produce good computers and others simply reduced the flexibility the collective ecosystem had to introduce more competitive or profitable products. While the CD was generally believed to focus on the distribution of web browsers and Java (or in other markets, media players and messaging applications) it also dictated many of the terms of the business licensing relationship. Many of these related to the terms and conditions of how Windows could be configured by OEMs, essentially extending the OEM rights beyond simply installing competitive browsers to just about any software deemed "middleware" as Java was viewed.

In terms of bringing Windows PCs to market, the CD had three main sections:

- **Non-retaliation**. The first element was that Microsoft could not retaliate against OEMs for shipping software (or middleware) that competes with Microsoft, including shipping computers running competitive operating systems. This codified the right of OEMs to ship Linux and even dual-boot with Windows for example. My how the world has changed, now that is a feature from Microsoft!
- **Uniform license terms**. Basically, this term meant all OEMs were to be offered the same license and the same terms. Historically, as most all businesses see with high-volume customers, there were all sorts of discounts and marketing programs that encouraged certain behaviors or discouraged others. Now these offers had to be the same for all OEMs. For the top 10 there could be one set and then another for everyone else. In many ways, the largest OEMs got what they asked for, but not the result they wanted since this put the best customer on the same playing field as the tenth best. This did not preclude the ongoing *Windows Logo* program described below.
- **OEM rights**. The CD specifically permitted a series of actions the OEMs could take with regard to Windows including "Installing, and displaying icons, shortcuts, or menu entries for, any Non-Microsoft Middleware or any product or service" and "Launching automatically, at the conclusion of the initial boot sequence or subsequent boot sequences, or upon connections to or disconnections from the Internet, any Non-Microsoft Middleware." These terms, and others, got to the heart of many of the tensions with OEMs over "crapware" or software that many consumers, especially techies, complained about. Now, however, it was a right OEMs had and Microsoft could do little to enforce that.

There were many other terms of course. Since we were "stuck" with each other, with Windows 7 we tried a nearly complete reset of the OEM relationship.

The bulk of this work was captured in the Windows Logo program—these were the instructions from Microsoft for how OEMs installed and configured Windows during manufacturing described in the OEM Preinstallation Kit (OPK) authored by Microsoft with ample compliance scrutiny. Given the above, one could imagine that most anything was permitted. However, Microsoft retained the rights to implement a discount program for strictly adhering to a set of constraints to earn the "Designed for" logo. Sometimes these were discounts and other times marketing dollars for demand generation, though these are equivalent and interchangeable pricing actions by and large.

We viewed these constraints as setting up a PC to be better for consumers. OEMs might agree, but they also saw them as hoops to jump through in order to get the discount, which their margins essentially required. These logo requirements ran the gamut from basics like signing device drivers and distributing available service packs and patches to how much to configure the Start menu. None of them ever violated the CD as per ongoing oversight. It was these aspects of Vista that were particularly adversarial.

We revisited all the terms and conditions in the OEM license (and logo) and worked to make the entire approach more civil. We wanted OEMs to have more points of customization while also building the product to more robustly handle those customizations—we aimed to reduce the surface area where OEMs could fracture the Windows experience. We also would spend a lot of energy making the case for why not changing things would be a good idea and in favor of lower support costs or more satisfied customers. A key change we made from the previous structure was to have the same team responsible for taking feedback and producing the logo requirements. This eliminated the organizational seam as well as a place for OEMs to see potential conflicts across Microsoft, and exploit those.

As an example, early in the process of building Windows 7 Roanne and team would present to the OEMs examples of where they were given rights (and technical capabilities) to customize the out of box experience (OOBE) when customers first experienced a new PC. In one iteration we showed a color-coded screens where the OEM customizable region was clearly marked indicating just how much of Windows was open to OEM customization. This type of effort was a huge hit.

The process of collaborating with the OEMs was modeled after our very early Office Advisory Council (OAC) that was run out of the same product planning group where MikeAng and Roanne were previously. Instead of just endless slide decks that spoke at the OEMs, we engaged in a participatory design process with the OEMs, a planning process. We listened instead of talked. We gathered feedback. Then we answered their specific questions.

We began the process of working with the OEMs just as we completed the Vision for Windows 7. We did that because by then we had a real grasp of what we would deliver and when, and at least what we said was rooted in a full execution plan. This was decidedly different than past engagements where the meetings with OEMs reflected the historic Windows development process, which meant that much of what was said at any given time could change in both features and timing. For the OEMs with very tight manufacturing schedules and thin margins, information that was so unreliable was extremely costly to them. At every interaction they had to take the information and decide to act on it, allocate resources, prioritize a project, and more, taking on the risk that the effort would be wasted. Or they could choose to delay acting on some information, only to find out it was critical to start work to provide feedback that might be significant. It was a mess.

What Microsoft had not really internalized was just how much churn and the level of real dollars it cost the OEMs with this traditional interaction. In fact, most involved on the Microsoft side felt, as I would learn, quite good about the openness and information being shared. I learned this both from the OEM sales team and directly from the CEOs of OEMs who were starting to get rather uncomfortable with the lack of information. They began to get nervous over my lack of communication (literally me and not the OEM team) as I had not provided details of the next release even after being on the job for months. I just didn't know the answers yet. Our desire to be calm and rational created a gap in communication that worried people. It was not normal. We had not set expectations and even if we had it wasn't clear they would have believed us.

MikeAng characterized the old interaction as "telling the OEMs what we were thinking" when we needed to be "telling OEMs what we were doing." By characterizing what we were going to improve this way we were able to avoid massive amounts of wasted effort and negative feelings. We also believed we would reduce the number of budget-like games when it came to requests. No matter how much Microsoft might caveat a presentation as "early thoughts" or "brainstorming," customers looking to make their own plans under a deadline will hear thoughts as varying degrees of plans. Only later when those plans fail to materialize does the gap between expectations and reality widen—the true origin of dissatisfaction. At that point the ability to remind a customer of whatever disclaimer was used is of little value. The customer was disappointed. This cycle repeated multiple times over the 5-year Vista product cycle, and many before that over the years.

With the Windows 7 vision in place, we began a series of OEM forums and meeting at least every month with each OEM. Each forum (an in-person workshop style meeting) would focus on different parts of the product vision or details about bringing Windows 7 to market. Roanne and team dutifully documented the feedback and interactions. We actively solicited feedback on priorities and reactions to the product overall. Then we summarized that work and sent out summary of engagement memos to the OEMs. In effect, the relationship was far more systematic, and the information provided was far more actionable. From the very start we communicated a ship date for the product and milestones, and a great deal of information about the development process. We reinforced our attention to the schedule with updates and information along the journey.

The entire process was run in parallel for the key hardware makers: storage, display, networking, and so on. We also repeated it for the ODMs. The team did an amazing job in a very short time, for the first time.

Over the coming months and really years, the reestablishing of trust and the effort to become a much more reliable, predictable, and trustworthy partner would in many ways not only change this dynamic and experience for OEM customers, but significantly improve the outcome for PC buyers. At the same time, OEMs were able to see improvements in satisfaction and potential avenues to improve the business. The PC would see many major architectural changes over the course of building Windows 7—the introduction of ink and touch panels, broad use of security chips and fingerprint login, addition of sensors, expansion of Bluetooth, transition to HDMI and multiple monitors, high-resolution panel displays, ever-increasing use of solid-state disks, and the transition to 64-bits. The Ecosystem team would be the conduit and moderating force between OEMs, their engineering teams, the engineering teams on Windows, and even Microsoft's own OEM sales and support team.

The Windows business faced a lack of trust from every business partner. The Windows team needed to move from chaotic process that promised too much and delivered inconsistently and late. Instead, we aspired to make bold but reliable promises—my guiding principle, the mantra of promise and deliver. While we talked big, the ball was in our court. We put in place a smoother and more productive engagement with OEMs. Throughout the course of developing Windows 7 and beyond, we consistently measured the success of the engagement with qualitative and quantitative surveys. Through that we could track the ongoing improvement in the relationships.

Promise and deliver.

Just as we worked to gain renewed focus with OEMs, Apple chose to declare war with Microsoft, and the PC, with clever and painfully true primetime television commercials. While the commercials began before Vista, the release and subsequent reception of Vista were exactly the material the writers needed for the campaign to take off.

090. I'M A MAC

"I'm a Mac."

"And, I'm a PC."

The "Get a Mac" commercials, starting in 2006, changed the competitive narrative overnight and were a painful gut punch welcoming me to Windows.

They were edgy, brutal in execution, and they skewered Windows with facts. They were well done. Though it always bothered me that PC Guy had a vague similarity to the late and much-loved Paul Allen (PaulA), Microsoft's cofounder long focused on science and philanthropy. Things that drove Windows fans crazy like "no viruses" on Mac were not technically true, but true in practice because, mostly, why bother writing viruses for Macs with their 6 percent share? That's what we told ourselves. In short, these commercials were devastating.

They probably bumped right up against a line, but they effectively tapped into much of the angst and many of the realities of PC ownership and management. Our COO and others were quite frustrated by them and believed the commercials not only to be untrue, but perhaps in violation of FTC rules.

They were great advertising. Great advertising is something Apple seemed to routinely accomplish, while Microsoft found it to be an elusive skill.

For its first twenty years, Microsoft resisted broad advertising. The company routinely placed print ads in trade publications and enthusiast magazines, with an occasional national newspaper buy for launches. These ads were about software features, power, and capabilities. Rarely, if ever, did Microsoft appeal to emotions of buyers. When Microsoft appeared in the national press, it was Bill Gates as the successful technology "whiz kid" along with commentary on the growing influence and scale of the company.

With that growing influence in the early 1990s and a business need to move beyond BillG, a huge decision was made to go big in advertising. Microsoft retained Wieden+Kennedy, the Portland-based advertising agency responsible for the "Just Do It" campaign from Nike, among many era-defining successes. After much consternation about spending heavily on television advertising, Microsoft launched the "Where do you want to go today?" campaign in November 1994.

Almost immediately we learned the challenges of advertising. The subsidiaries were not enamored with the tagline. The head of Microsoft Brazil famously pushed back on the tagline, saying the translation amounted to saying, "do you want to go to the beach today?" because the answer to the question "Where do you want to go?" in Brazil was always "the beach." The feedback poured in before we even started. It was as much about the execution as the newness of television advertising. Everyone had an opinion.

I remember vividly the many pitches and discussions about the ads. I can see the result of those meetings today as I rewatch the flagship commercial. Microsoft kept pushing "more product" and "show features" and the team from W+K would push back, describing emotions and themes. The client always wins, and it was a valuable lesson for me. Another a valuable lesson, Mike Maples (MikeMap) who had seen it all at IBM pointed out just before the formal go ahead saying something like "just remember, once you start advertising spend you can never stop… with the amount of money we are proposing we could hire people in every computer store to sell Windows 95 with much more emotion and information…" These were such wise words, as was routine for Mike. He was right. You can never stop. TV advertising spend for a big company, once started, becomes part of the baseline P&L like a tax on earnings.

The commercials were meant to show people around the world using PCs, but instead came across almost cold, dark, and ominous as many were starting to perceive Microsoft. That was version 1.0. Over the next few years, the campaign would get updates with more colors, more whimsy, and often more screenshots and pixels.

What followed was the most successful campaign the company would arguably execute, the Windows 95 launch. For the next decade, Microsoft would continue to spend heavily, hundreds of millions of dollars per year, though little of that would resonate. Coincident with the lukewarm reception to advertising would be Microsoft's challenges in branding, naming, and in general balancing speeds and feeds with an emotional appeal to consumers. Meanwhile, our enterprise muscle continued to grow as we became leaders in articulating strategy, architecture, and business value.

In contrast, Apple had proven masterful at consumer advertising. From the original 1984 Superbowl ad through the innovative "What's on your PowerBook?" (1992) to "Think Different" (1997-2000) and many of the most talked about advertisements of the day such as "C:\ONGRTLNS.W95" in 1995 and "Welcome, IBM. Seriously" in 1981, Apple had shown a unique ability to get the perfect message across. The only problem was that their advertising didn't appear to work, at least as measured by sales and/or market share. The advertising world didn't notice that small detail. We did.

Starting in 2006 (Vista released in January 2007), Apple's latest campaign, "Get a Mac" created an instant emotional bond with everyone struggling with their Windows PC at home or work, while also playing on all the stereotypes that existed in the Windows versus Mac battle—the nerdy businessman PC slave versus the too cool hipster Mac user.

The campaign started just as I joined Windows. I began tracking the commercials in a spreadsheet, recording the content and believability of each while highlighting those I thought particularly painful in one dimension or another. A Wikipedia article would emerge with a complete list, emphasizing the importance of the commercials. I found myself making the case that the commercials reflected the state of Windows as experienced in the real world. It wasn't really all that important if Mac was better, because what resonated was the fragility of the PC. There was a defensiveness across the company, a feeling of how the "5% share Mac" could be making these claims. I managed a bit of a row with the COO who wanted to go to the FTC and complain that Apple was not telling the truth.

Windows Vista dropped the ball. Apple was there to pick it up. Not only with TV commercials and ads, but with a resurging and innovative product line, one riding on the coattails of Wintel. The irony that the commercials held up even with the transition to Intel and a theoretically level playing field only emphasized that the issue was software first and foremost, not simply a sleek aluminum case.

While the MacBook Air was a painful reminder of the consumer offerings of Windows PCs, the commercials were simply brutal when it came to Vista. There were over 50 commercials that ran from 2006-2009, starting with Apple's transition to Intel and then right up until the release of Windows 7 when a new commercial ran on the eve of the Windows 7 launch. Perhaps the legacy of the commercials was the idea that PCs have viruses and malware and Macs do not. No "talking points" about market share or that malware targets the greatest number of potential victims or simply that the claim was false would matter. There's no holding back, this was a brutal takedown, and it was effective. It was more effective in reputation bashing, however, than in shifting unit share.

One of the most memorable ones for me was "Security" which highlighted the Windows Vista feature designed to prevent viruses and malware from sneaking on your PC, called User Account Control or UAC which had become a symbol of the annoyance of Vista—so much so our sales leaders wanted us to issue a product change to remove it. There's some irony in that this very feature is not only implemented across Apple's software line today, but far more granular and invasive. That should sink in. Competitively we all seem to become what we first mock.

Something SteveB always said when faced with sales blaming the product group and the product group blaming sales for something that wasn't working, was "we need to build what we can sell, and sell what we build." Windows Vista was a time where we had the product and simply needed to sell what we had built, no matter what.

The marketing team (an organization peer to product development at this time) was under a great deal of pressure to turn around the perceptions of Vista and do something about the Apple commercials. It was a tall order. The OEMs were in a panic. It would require a certain level of bravery to continue to promote Vista, perhaps not unlike shipping Vista in the first place. The fact that the world was in the midst of what would become known as the Global Financial Crisis with PC sales taking a dive did not help.

Through a series of exercises to better come up with a point of attack the team came up with the idea that maybe too many people were basing their views of Windows Vista on hearsay and not actual experience. We launched a new campaign "Mojave Experiment" that took a *cinéma vérité* approach to showing usability studies and focus groups for yet to be released and experimental version of Windows Mojave. After unsolicited expressions of how bad Vista was, the subjects were given a tour of Windows Mojave. The videos were not scripted, and the people were all real, as were the reactions. Throughout the case study, and the associated online campaign, the subjects loved what they were being shown. Then at the end of the videos, the subjects were told the surprise—this was Windows Vista. To those old enough to know, it had elements of the old "Folger's Coffee" or "I Can't Believe It's Not Butter" commercials, classic taste-test advertising.

The industry wasn't impressed. In fact, many took to blog posts to buzzsaw the structure of the tests and way subjects were questioned and shown the product. One post in a Canadian publication ran with the headline "Microsoft thinks you're stupid" in describing the campaign. This was right on the heels of the Office campaign where we called our customers dinosaurs. We had not yet figured out consumer advertising.

We still had to sell the Vista we had built. We needed an approach that at the very least was credible and not embarrassing, but importantly at least hit on the well-known points about Apple Macintosh that everyone knew to be true. Macs were expensive and as a customer your choices were limited.

Apple's transition to Intel was fascinating and extraordinarily well executed, releasing PCs that were widely praised, featuring state-of-the-art components, an Intel processor unique to Apple at launch, and superior in design and construction to any Windows PC. The new premium priced Intel Macs featured huge and solid trackpads, reliable standby and resume, and super-fast start-up. All things most every Windows PC struggled to get right. We consistently found ourselves debating the futility of the Apple strategy offering expensive hardware. The OEMs weren't the only ones who consistently believed cheaper was better, but that was also baked into how Microsoft viewed the PC market. Apple had no interest in a race to profitless price floors and low margins, happily ceding that part of the market to Windows while selling premium PCs at relatively premium prices. In fact, their answer to the continued lowering of PC prices was to release a pricey premium PC.

The original MacBook Air retailed for what seemed like an astonishing $1,799. That was for the lowest specification which included a 13" screen and a meager 2GB main memory, an 80GB mechanical hard drive, and a single USB port and obscure video output port, without an DVD drive or network port. For an additional $1000, one could upgrade to a fancy new solid state disk drive which was still unheard of on mainstream Windows PCs.

As it would turn out the MacBook Air was right in the middle of the PC market, and that's just how PC makers liked it, stuck between the volume PC and premium PC, neither here nor there. An example of most popular laptop configuration was the Dell Inspiron 1325. The 1325 was a widely praised "entry level" laptop with an array of features, specs, and prices. In fact, on paper many PC publications asked why anyone would buy an overpriced Macintosh. The Dell 1325 ranged in prices from $599 to about $999 depending on how it was configured. The configuration comparable to a MacBook Air was about $699 and still had 50% more memory and three times the disk space. As far as flexibility and ports, the 1325 featured not just a single USB port but two, a VGA video connector, audio jacks, Firewire for an iPod, an 8 in 1 media card reader, and even something called an ExpressCard for high-speed peripherals. Still, it was a beast, while the same width and length it was twice as thick and clearly more dense weighing almost 5lbs at the base configuration compared to the 3lb MacBook Air. As far as battery life, if you wanted to be comparable to the Air then you added a protruding battery that added about a pound in weight and made it so the laptop wouldn't fit in a bag. Purists would compare to the MacBook (not the Air), as we did in our competitive efforts, but the excitement was around the Air. The regular 13" MacBook weighed about 4.5lbs and cost $1299, which would make it a more favorable comparison. It was clear to me that the Air was the future consumer PC as most PC users would benefit from lighter weight, fewer ports, and a simpler design. As much as I believed this, it would take years before the PC industry broadly recognized that "thin and light" was not a premium product. The MacBook Air would soon end up priced at a $999 entry price, which is when it began to cause real trouble for Windows PCs.

The higher-end MacBook Air competitor from the PC world was the premium M-series from Dell Incidentally, I'm using Dell as an example, HP and Lenovo would be similar in most every respect. The Dell XPS M1330, the forerunner to today's wonderful Dell XPS 13, was a sleeker 4lbs also featuring a wedge shape. With the larger and heavier battery there was a good 5 hours of runtime. Both Dells featured plastic cases with choices of colors. It too had models cheaper than the MacBook or MacBook Air but could be priced significantly more by adding more memory, disk storage, better graphics, or a faster CPU.

A key factor in the ability for the Mac to become mainstream, however, was the rise in the use of the web browser for most consumer scenarios. A well-known XKCD cartoon featured two stick figures, one claiming to be a PC and another claiming to be a Mac, with the joint text pointing out "and since you do everything through a browser now, we're pretty indistinguishable."[80] Apple benefitted enormously from this shift, or disruption, especially as Microsoft continued to invest heavily in Office for the Mac. The decline in new and exciting Windows-based software described in the previous section proved enormously beneficial to Apple when it came to head-to-head evaluation of Mac versus Windows. Simply running Office and having a great browser, combined with the well-integrated Apple software for photos, music, videos, and mail proved formidable, and somewhat enduring with the rise in non-PC devices.

We were obsessed with the pricing differences. We often referred to these higher prices as an "Apple Tax" and even commissioned a third-party to study the additional out of pocket expenses for a typical family when buying Macs versus Windows PCs. A whitepaper was distributed with detailed comparison specifications showing the better value PCs offered. In April 2008 we released a fake tax form itemizing (groan) the high cost of Apple hardware—the "Apple Tax."

From our perspective or perhaps rationalization this was all good. Consumers had choice, options, and flexibility. They could get the PC they needed for their work and pay appropriately, or not. This thesis was reinforced by the sales of both PCs and Macs no matter what anyone was saying in blogs. The PC press loved this flexibility. Retailers and OEMs relied on the variety of choices to maximize margin. Retailers in particular struggled with Apple products because they lacked typical mechanisms to attach additional margin, such as upsell or service contracts, not to mention Apple's lack of responsiveness to paying hefty slotting and co-advertising fees.

Choosing a PC while a complicated endeavor was also the heart and soul of the PC ecosystem. Once Apple switched to Intel, there was a broad view that the primary difference between Mac and Windows now boiled down to the lack of choice and high price and lack of a compatible software and peripheral ecosystem that characterized Macintosh.

To make this point, Microsoft launched a new campaign the "Laptop Hunter" that ran in 2009. In these ads, typical people are confronted outside big box retailers trying to decide what computer to buy. A PC or a Mac? In one ad, "Lauren" even confesses she is not cool enough for a Mac while noticing just how expensive they are. Lauren is almost the perfect representation of a Mac owner. She heads over to a showroom with a vast number of choices and whittles her way down to a sub $1000 PC with everything she needs. Another success.

Not to belabor this emerging theme, but no one believed these ads either. Only this time, the critics and skeptics were livid as it appeared Lauren was an actress and that called into question the whole campaign. In addition, Apple blogs went frame-by-frame in the ad to "prove" various aspects of the shoot were staged or simply not credible. The tech blogs pointed out the inconsistencies or staged aspects of Lauren's requirements as being designed to carefully navigate the Apple product line.

Laptop Hunter offers some insight into how addictive (or necessary) television advertising became and the scale at which Microsoft was engaging. The television campaign debuted during the NCAA basketball tournament in the US, prime time. It was supported by top quality network prime shows (Grey's Anatomy, CSI, The Office, Lost,

American Idol), late night staple programming (Leno, Letterman, Kimmel, Conan, and Saturday Night Live) and major sports events and playoff series including NCAA Basketball, the NBA, MLB, and the NHL. Cable networks included Comedy Central, Discovery, MTV, VH1, History and ESPN. The online campaign included home page execution on NYTimes.com, as well as "homepage take-overs" (the thing to do back then) on WSJ, Engadget, and CNN. We also supported this with an online media buy targeted at reaching people who were considering a non-Windows laptop, a Mac. We linked from those banner ads to a dedicated Microsoft web site designed to configure a new PC and direct to online resellers, closing the loop to purchase. The level of spending and effort was as massive as the upside.

I could defend the advertising but at this point I am not sure it is worth the words. Besides, Apple responded to the ad with a brutal reiteration of viruses and crashes in PCs and that lots of bad choice is really no choice at all. It is rare to see two large companies go head-to-head in advertising and you can see how Microsoft took the high road relative to Apple, deliberately so. The ads worked for Apple, but almost imperceptibly so in the broader market. Apple gained about one point of market share, which represented over 35% growth year over year for each of the two years of the campaign—that is huge. The PC market continued to grow, though at just over 10%. Still that was enough of a gain to ameliorate the share gains from Apple, which were mostly limited to the US and western Europe.

As much as the blowback from this campaign hurt, we were at least hitting a nerve with Apple fans and getting closer to a message that resonated with the PC industry: compatibility, choice, and value.

For our ad agency, essence of the PC versus Mac debate boiled down not to specs and prices but to a difference in the perceived customers. The Mac customers (also the agency itself) seemed to be cut from one mold of young, hip, artistic whereas the PC was literally everyone else. It seemed weird to us, and our advertising agency, that Windows computers were not given credit for the wide array of people and uses they supported, if even stereotypically. We were proud of all the ways PCs were used.

To demonstrate this pride, Bill Veghte (BillV) the senior vice president of Windows marketing (also reporting to Kevin Johnson) led the creation of a new "I'm a PC" campaign that started in the fall of 2008 and ran through the launch of Windows 7. Rather than run from the Apple's "I'm a Mac" we embraced it. The main spot featured fast cuts of people from all walks of life, including members of the Microsoft community as well as some pretty famous people, talking about their work, creations, and what they do with PCs. The ads featured a Microsoft employee, Sean Siler a networking specialist from Microsoft Federal, who looked unsurprisingly like the stereotype PC users portrayed by Apple. These ads were us.

The advertising world viewed success through the creative lens so dominated by Apple. The ads were well-received and for the first time we landed spots (costing hundreds of millions of dollars) that we could both be proud while emphasizing our strengths.

The memorable legacy of the campaign would be the brightly colored "I'm a PC" stickers that nearly everyone at the company dutifully attached to their laptops. Meeting rooms filled with open laptops of all brands, colors, sizes all displayed the sticker. We made sure all of our demo machines featured the stickers as well. In the summer 2009 global sales meeting just before Windows 7 would launch, BillV led the sales force in a passionate rally around "I'm a PC" and the field loved it. He was in his element, and they were pumped. The Windows 7 focused versions of this campaign featured individuals talking about their work saying "I'm a PC and Windows 7 was my idea" building on the theme of how Windows 7 better addressed customer needs, which will be detailed in the next chapter.

By the summer of 2009, the back and forth with Apple seemed to run its course as we were close to the launch of Windows 7. *The New York Times* ran a 3000-word, front of the Sunday business section story titled "Hey, , PC, Who Taught You to Fight Back?" covering what was portrayed as an "ad war, one destined to go down in history with the cola wars of the 1980s and '90s and the Hertz-Avis feud of the 1960s."[81] There was even a chart detailing the escalating advertising spend of the two companies. The story even noted that the ads caught the attention of Apple who pulled their ads from the market only to return with new "Get a Mac" ads criticizing Microsoft's ads. In the world of advertising, that counts as a huge victory. On the store shelves, the campaign finally seemed to at least slow the share loss to Apple worldwide and definitely pushed it back in the US.

Nothing hit home more a few years later than the photo of the White House situation room in May 2011 during the raid on Osama Bin Laden. That photo was memed by the internet to illustrate the point of just who is a Mac and who is a PC. The meme featured some barefooted hipsters in a coffee shop captioned "I'm a Mac" and then the situation room featured secured PCs captioned "I'm a PC" with the heading "Any Questions?" We loved it. That seriousness was what we were all about.

The real battle with Apple was now about software. Windows 7 needed to execute. We needed to build out our services offerings for mail, calendar, storage, and more where Apple was still flailing even more than we were.

While I was entirely focused on Windows 7 and moving forward, the ghosts of Vista and Longhorn would appear. Promises were made that ultimately could not be kept and we had to work through those.

PS. The "Get a Mac" ad that hit me the hardest for non-product reasons was the "Yoga" spot, which was funny to me because when I moved to Windows in March 2006 I switched to practicing yoga after a decade of Pilates. In the spot, PC guy switches from yoga to Pilates.

091. CLEANING UP LONGHORN AND VISTA

Early in my tenure, I received an escalation (!) to "fund" Windows *Ultimate Extras.* I had never funded anything before via a request to fund so this itself was new, and as for the escalation…I had only a vague idea what Ultimate Extras were, even though I had recently returned from the Windows launch event in Brazil where I was tasked with emphasizing them as part of the rollout. The request was deemed urgent by marketing, so I met with the team, even though in my head Vista was in the rearview mirror and I had transitioned to making sure servicing the release was on track, not finishing the product.

The *Windows Vista Ultimate* SKU was the highest priced version of Windows, aimed primarily at Windows enthusiasts and hobbyists because it had all the features of Vista, those for consumers, business, and enterprise. The idea of Ultimate Extras was to "deliver additional features for Vista via downloadable updates *over time*." At launch, these were explained to customers as "cutting-edge features" and "innovative services." The tech enthusiasts who opted for Ultimate, for a bunch of features that they probably wouldn't need as individuals, would be rewarded with these extra features over time. The idea was like the Windows 95 Plus! product, but that was an add-on product available at retail with Windows 95.

There was a problem, though, as I would learn. There was no product plan and no development team. The Extras didn't exist. There was an Ultimate Extras PUM, but the efforts were to be funded by using cash or somehow finding or conjuring code. This team had gotten ahead of itself. No one seemed to be aware of this and the Extras PUM didn't seem to think this was an issue.

As the new person, this problem terrified me. We shipped and charged for the product. To my eyes the promise, or obligation if one prefers, seemed unbounded. These were in theory our favorite customers.

The team presented what amounted to a brainstorm of what they could potentially do. There were ideas for games, utilities, and so on. None of them sounded bad, but none of them sounded particularly *Ultimate,* and worse: None existed.

We had our first crisis. Even though this was a Vista problem, once the product released everything became my problem.

The challenge with simply finding code from somewhere, such as a vendor, licensing from a third-party, or something laying around Microsoft (like from Microsoft Research), was that the journey from that code to something shippable to the tens of millions of customers running on a million different PC configurations, in 100 languages around the world, and also accessible, safe, and secure, was months of work. The more content rich the product was, in graphics or words, the longer and more difficult the process would be. I don't know how many times this lesson needed to be learned at Microsoft but suffice it to say small teams trying to make a big difference learned it almost constantly.

And then there was the issue of doing it well. Not much of what was brainstormed at the earliest stages of this process was overly compelling.

With nothing particularly ultimate in the wings, we were poised for failure. It was a disaster.

We set out to minimize the damage to the Windows reputation and preserve the software experience on PCs. Over the following months we worked to define what would meet a reasonable bar for completing the obligation, unfortunately I mean this legally as that was clearly the best we could do. It was painful, but the prospect of spinning up new product development meant there was no chance of delivering for at least another year. The press and the big Windows fans were unrelenting in reminding me of the Extras at every encounter. If Twitter was a thing back then, every tweet of mine would have had a reply "and…now do Ultimate Extras."

Ultimately (ha), we delivered some games, video desktops, sound schemes, and, importantly, the enterprise features of BitLocker and language packs. The ability to run Vista in more than one language, which was a typical business feature. It was very messy. It became a symbol of a lack of a plan as well as the myth of finding and shipping code opportunistically.

Vista continued to require more management effort on my part.

In the spring of 2007 shortly after availability, a lawsuit was filed. The complaint involved the little stickers that read *Windows Vista Capable* placed on Windows XP computers that manufacturers were certifying (with Microsoft's support) for upgrade to Windows Vista when it became available. This was meant to mitigate to some degree the fact that Vista missed the back to school and holiday selling seasons by assuring customers their new PC would run the much publicized Vista upgrade. The sticker on the PC only indicated it could run Windows Vista, not whether the PC also had the advanced graphics capabilities to support the new Vista user experience, *Aero Glass*, which was available only on Windows Vista Home Premium. It also got to the issue of whether supporting those features was a requirement or simply better if a customer had what was then a premium PC. The question was if this was confusing or too complex for customers to understand relative to buying a new PC that supported all the features of Vista.

A slew of email exhibits released in 2007 and 2008 showed the chaos and tension over the issue, especially between engineering, marketing, sales, lawyers, and the OEMs. One could imagine how each party had a different view of the meaning of the words and system requirements. I sent an email diligently describing the confusion, which became an exhibit in the case along with emails from most every exec and even former President and board member Jon Shirley (JonS) detailing their personal confusion.

The Vista Capable challenge was rooted in the type of ecosystem work we needed to get right. Intel had fallen behind on graphics capabilities while at the same time wanted to use differing graphics as part of their price waterfall. Astute technical readers would also note that Intel's challenge with graphics was rooted deeply in their failure to achieve critical mass for mobile and the resulting attempt to repurpose their failed mobile chipsets for low-end PCs. PC makers working to have PCs available at different price points loved the idea of hardline differentiation in Windows, though they did not like the idea having to label PCs as basic, hence the XP PCs were labeled "capable." Also worth noting was that few Windows XP PCs, especially laptops, were capable of the Home Premium experience due to the lack of graphics capabilities. When Vista released, new PCs would have stickers stating they ran Windows Vista or Windows Vista Basic, at least clarifying the single sticker that was placed on eligible Windows XP computers.

Eventually, the suit achieved class-action status, always a problem for a big company. The fact that much of the chaos ensued at the close of a hectic product cycle only contributed to this failure. My job was to support those on the team that had been part of the dialogue across PC makers, hardware makers, and the numerous marketing and sales teams internally.

The class-action status was eventually reversed, and the suit(s) reached a mutually agreeable conclusion, as they say. Still, it was a great lesson in the need to repair both the relationships and the communication of product plans with the hardware partners, not to mention to be more careful about system requirements and how features are used across Windows editions.

In addition to these examples of external issues the Vista team got ahead of itself regarding issues related to code sharing and platform capabilities that spanned multiple groups in Microsoft.

The first of these was one of the most loved modern Windows products built on top of Windows XP, Windows Media Center Edition, WMC or sometimes MCE. In order to tap into the enthusiasm for the PC in the home and the convergence of television and PCs, long before smartphones, YouTube, Netflix, or even streaming, the Windows team created a separate product unit (rather than an integrated team) that would pioneer a new user interface, known as the 10-foot experience, and a new "shell"—always about a shell—designed around using a PC with a remote control to show live television, home DVD discs, videos, and photos on a big screen, and also play music. This coincided with the rise in home theaters, large inexpensive disk drives capable of storing a substantial amount of video, camcorders and digital cameras, and home broadband internet connections. The product was released in 2002 and soon developed a relatively small but cultlike following. It even spawned its own online community called "Green Button," named after the green button on the dedicated remote control that powered the shell's 10-foot user interface.

The product was initially sold only with select PCs because of the need for specific hardware capabilities. Later, with Windows Vista (and Windows 7), WMC was included in the premium editions. The usage based on both sales and the telemetry collected anonymously was low and the repeat usage was a small fraction of even those customers. Nevertheless, there were vocal fans, and we had no plans to give up.

WMC was hitting real challenges in the market, though, especially in the United States, where television was moving from analog CATV to digital, and with digital came required set-top boxes and a new and not quite available technology called CableCARD, required to decrypt the cable signal. Not only did this make things difficult for WMC, but it made things difficult for anyone wanting to view cable tv, as if the encrypted analog channels were not difficult enough already. Everyone trying to use CableCARD had a story of trying to activate the card that included essentially a debug interface, typing in long hex strings, awaiting a "ping" back from the mysterious "head end." The future for the innovative TV experience in WMC was looking bleak.

Additionally, WMC was bumping up against the desires of the Xbox team to expand beyond gaming. The Xbox team had recently unveiled a partnership with the new Netflix streaming service to make it available on Xbox.[82] Some of the key leaders on WMC had moved from Windows to the Xbox organization and began to ask about moving the WMC team over with them.

At the time, I was up to my elbows in looking at headcount and orgs and was more than happy to move teams out of Windows, especially if it was straightforward, meaning they could just pick up the work and there was no shipping code being left behind unstaffed. This quickly became the first debate, in my entire time at Microsoft, over headcount and budgets because the destination organization was under tight revenue and expense review.

The WMC team was, surprisingly, hundreds of people, but it also had dependencies on numerous other teams across networking, graphics, and the core user experience. We could easily move the core WMC team but getting a version of WMC integrated with the new engineering system and to-be-developed delivery schedule (which we were planning) was a concern. Of course the team wanted to move to Xbox but had little interest in delivering WMC back to Windows, especially as the overall engineering process changed. They literally thought we would just move all the headcount and team and then create a new WMC team. They had awful visions of being a component on the hook to meet a schedule that was unappealing. We could not just give up on WMC, even with such low usage, without some sort of plan.

I learned that moving humans and associated budgets was fine. But CollJ had been working with finance on headcount and was told we had to also move revenue, something I had never heard of. I had no idea how that might even work. In Vista, MediaCenter was part of the Home Premium and Ultimate SKU, and no longer a separate product like it was for Windows XP. How could one arrive at the revenue for a single feature that was part of a SKU of Vista? Perhaps back when WMC was a separate product this made sense, but at the time it seemed like an accounting farce. In fact, the judge in the Vista Capable lawsuit even removed class action status because of an inability to determine which customers bought Windows Vista because of which premium features.

Microsoft had been divided into seven externally reported business segments; each quarterly earnings filing with the SEC reported a segment as though it were an independent business. The result of this was more visibility for the financial community, which was great. Internally these segments did not line up with the emphasis on code-sharing, feature bundling, or shared sales efforts. For example, from a product development perspective there was a lot of code sharing across all products—this was a huge part of how Microsoft developed software. Costs for each segment could never accurately reflect the R&D costs. An obvious example was how much of Windows development could/would/should be counted in the *Server and Tools* segment, given that so much of the server product was developed in the *Windows* segment.

My view was that there was a $0 revenue allocation for any specific feature of Windows—that was the definition of product-market fit and the reality that nobody bought a large software product for any single feature. This was always our logic in Office, even when we had different SKUs that clearly had whole other products to justify the upsell. Office Professional for years cost about $100 more than Office Standard simply for the addition of the Microsoft Access database. We never kidded ourselves that Access was genuinely worth billions of dollars on its own.

Over several weeks, however, we had to arrive at some arbitrary number that satisfied finance, accounting, tax, and regulatory people. To do this, we moved the hundreds of people working on WMC to Xbox along with a significant amount of Windows unit revenue per theoretical WMC customer. It wasn't my math, but it added up to a big number moving to the *Entertainment* segment. In exchange, we hoped we would get back a WMC that had improved enough to satisfy an enthusiastic fanbase, knowing that the focus was shifting to Xbox.

Given the fanbase externally, including several of the most influential Windows writers in the press, there was a good chance that such a seemingly arbitrary organization move would leak. The move would be viewed by many as abandoning WMC. I used an internal blog post to smooth things over, describing my own elaborate home audio/video system, which included Windows Vista Ultimate and pretty much every Microsoft product. In doing this, I chalked up a ton of points from tech enthusiast employees, showing that I had a knee-deep knowledge of our products—something most assumed an Office person wouldn't have, perhaps like BillG not understanding why a C++ developer knew Excel 15 years earlier when I first interviewed to work for him. In practice, my post made it clear that keeping this technology working to watch TV casually at home was impossible. I hated my home setup. It was ridiculous.

As part of the final Longhorn cleanup, I also needed to reconcile the strategic conflicts between the Windows platform and the Developer Tools platform, and as the new person I found myself in the middle. It was a battle that nobody wanted to enter for fear of the implications of making the wrong technology bet.

The Developer division created the .NET platform starting in the early 2000s to build internet-scale, web server applications delivered through the browser primarily to compete with Java on the server. It was excellent and remains loved, differentiated, and embraced by the corporate world today. It crushed Java in the enterprise market. It was almost entirely responsible for the success Windows Server saw in the enterprise web and web application market.

The .NET client (desktop programs one would use on a laptop) programming model was built "on top" of the Windows programming model, Win32, with little coordination or integration with the operating system or the .NET server platform. This created a level of architectural and functional complexity along with application performance and reliability problems resulting in a messy message to developers. Should developers build Win32 apps or should they build .NET apps? While this should not have been an either/or, it ended up as such because of the differing results. Developers wanted the easier-to-use tools and language of .NET, but they wanted the performance and integration with Windows that came from Win32/C++. This was a *tastes great, less filling* challenge for the Developer division and Windows. In today's environment, there are elements of this on the Apple platforms when it comes to SwiftUI *versus* UIKit as searching for that debate will find countless blog posts on all sides.

It was also a classic strategic mess created when a company puts forth a choice for customers without being prescriptive or complete. Given a choice between A and B, many customers naturally craft the third choice, which is the best attributes of each, as though the code was a buffet. Still other customers polarize and claim the new way is vastly superior or claim the old way is the only true way and until the new way is a complete superset they will not switch. Typical.

Longhorn aimed to reinvent the Win32 APIs, but with a six-year gap from Windows XP it was filled by the above .NET strategy when it came to Microsoft platform zealots. The rest of the much larger world was focused on HTML and JavaScript. At the same time, nearly all commercial desktop software remained Win32, but the number of new commercial desktop products coming to market was diminishingly small and shrinking. Win32 was on already life support.

The *three pillars of Longhorn*, WinFS, Avalon, and Indigo, failed to make enough progress to be included in Vista. Together these three technologies were referred to as WinFX. With Vista shipping, each of these technologies found new homes, or were shut down. I had to do this last bit of Vista cleanup which lingered long after the product was out the door.

WinFS receded into the world of databases where it came from. As discussed, it was decidedly the wrong approach and would not resurface in any way. Indigo was absorbed into the .NET framework where it mostly came from. Avalon, renamed Windows Presentation Foundation (WPF), remained in the Windows Client team, which meant I inherited it.

WPF had an all-expansive vision that included a unique language (known as XAML) and a set of libraries for building graphical and data-rich applications. Taken together and to their logical end point, the team spoke of Avalon as being a replacement for HTML in the browser and also .NET on the client. This was the reason work had stopped on Internet Explorer, as the overall Longhorn vision was to bring this new level of richness to browsing. From the outside (where I was in Office) it seemed outlandish, and many on the outside agreed particularly those driving browser standards forward. Still, this opened a second front in the race to improve Win32, in addition to .NET. All along WPF would claim allegiance and synergy with .NET but the connections were thin, especially as WPF split into a cross-platform, in-browser runtime and a framework largely overlapping with .NET. When I would reflect on WPF I would have flashbacks to my very first project, AFX, and how we had created a system that was perfectly consistent and well-architected yet unrelated to everything, in addition to being poorly executed.

But what should developers have used—classic Win32, or the new frameworks of .NET, WPF, or something else I just learned about called Jolt? These were big decisions for third-party developers because there was an enormous learning curve. They had to choose one path and go with it because the technologies all overlapped. That was why I often called these frameworks "fat frameworks," because they were big, slow, and took up all the conceptual room. Importantly, the common thread among the frameworks was their lack of coherence with Win32—they were built on top of Win32, duplicated operating system capabilities. Fat was almost always an insult in software.

The approach taken meant the idea of both .NET on the client and WPF were built on the shakiest of foundations, and what we were seeing with .NET on the client was as predicted based on all past experiences. I had a very long and ongoing email thread (which I later turned into an Office Hours blog post) with the wonderfully kind head of Developers, S. Somasegar (Somase, aka Soma), on this topic where I pushed and pushed on the challenges of having fat frameworks emerge while we have a desire to keep Windows relevant. As I wrote the email, I was struck by how similar this experience was to the one I had twenty years earlier as we built, and then discarded, the fat framework called AFX. While history does not repeat itself, it does rhyme. Many would debate the details, but fundamentally the team took the opposite path that we did years earlier. I recognize writing this today that some are still in the polarized camp and even today remain committed to some of these technologies. One of the most successful tools Microsoft ever released was Visual Basic, which was an enormously productive combination of framework, programming language, and development tool. That was not what we had here.

Nothing with developers and Microsoft was ever simple. Microsoft's success with developers was often quite messy on the ground.

Along with large product development teams, there was also a large evangelism team responsible for gaining support or traction of new technologies with developers. This team was one of the gems of Microsoft. It masterfully built a community around developer initiatives. It was largely responsible for taking the excellent work in .NET for Server and landing it with thousands of enterprise developers. In fact, part of that challenge was that the evangelism team had moved to the Developer division where the org chart spoke more loudly than the overall company mission and the priority and resourcing of evangelism tilted heavily toward .NET in all forms over the declining Win32 platform.

As a counterexample, the evangelism team seeing the incoherence in product execution provided significant impetus to force the Windows NT product to fully adopt the Windows API paving the way for Microsoft's Win32 success. I previously shared my early days story as a member of the C++ team pointing out how Windows NT differed from classic Windows APIs in Chapter II, I Shipped, Therefore I am. Many of the lessons in how divergent the two Windows APIs were surfaced in the well-known Windows NT porting lab run by the evangelism team, where developers from around the world would camp out for a few weeks of technical support in moving applications to Windows NT or Windows 95, before both shipped.

Perhaps an organization-driven result was a reasonable tradeoff, but it was never explicit, as was often the case with cross-divisional goals. In many ways the challenges were accelerated by our own actions, but without ever making that a clear goal we would spend too much time in meetings dancing around the results we were seeing in the erosion of Win32.

The evangelism team didn't ever fail at their mission and reliably located or created champions for new technologies. It seemed there were always some outside Microsoft looking to get in early on the next Microsoft technologies. The evangelism team was expert at finding and empowering those people. They could summon the forces of the book, consulting, and training worlds to produce volumes of materials—whole books and training courses on XAML were available even before Vista was broadly deployed. Although WPF had not shipped with any product, it had a strong group of followers who trusted Microsoft and made a major commitment to use WPF for their readers, clients, or customers as authors, consultants, or enterprise developers. Before Vista shipped, WPF appeared to have initial traction and was a first-class effort, along with .NET on the client. WPF had an internal champion as well. The Zune team used early portions of WPF for software that accompanied their ill-fated, but well-executed, iPod competitor.

Things were less clear when it came to WPF and Vista. WPF code would ship with Vista, but late in the product cycle the shiproom command came down that no one should use WPF in building Vista because of the burden it would place on memory footprint and performance of applications. This caused all sorts of problems when word spread to evangelists and their champions. People were always looking for signals that Microsoft had changed its mind on some technology. Seeing the risk to WPF by not being performant, the Avalon team (the team was also called Avalon) set out to shrink WPF and XAML into a much smaller runtime—something akin to a more focused and scenario specific product. This was a classic Windows "crisis" project and was added to the product plans sometime in 2005 or early 2006, called Jolt, while the rest of Longhorn was just trying to finish with quality.

Jolt was designed to package up as much of WPF as could fit in a single ActiveX control, also called WPF/E for WPF everywhere, and then later in final form called Silverlight. This would make it super easy to download and use. Streaming videos and small graphical games to be used inside of a browser became the focus. Sound like Adobe Flash? Yes, Jolt was being pitched internally as Microsoft's answer to Adobe Flash. To compete effectively with Flash, Jolt would also aim to be available across operating systems and browsers—something that made it even less appealing to a Windows strategy, and more difficult to execute. I was of the view that Adobe Flash was on an unsustainable path simply because it was both (!) a fat framework and also an ActiveX control. By this time, ActiveX controls, which a few years earlier were Microsoft's main browser extensibility strategy, had come to be viewed as entirely negative because they were not supported in other browsers and because they were used as malware by tricking people into running them. The technical press and *haters* loved to refer to ActiveX as *CaptiveX*. As an aside, one of my last projects working on C++ was to act overly strategic and push us to adopt the predecessor to ActiveX, known as OLE Controls, and implement those in our C++ library affording great, but useless, synergy with Visual Basic.

For me, this counted as two huge strikes against Jolt. Imagine a strategic project, at this stage in the history of the company, that came about from a crisis moment trying to find any code to ship while also using the one distribution method we had already condemned for doing exactly the same thing previously. I did not understand where it was heading.

Somehow, I was supposed to reconcile this collection of issues. When I met with the leaders of the team, they were exhausted though still proud of what they had accomplished. When I say exhausted, I mean physically drained. The struggle they had been through was apparent. Like many who had worked on the three pillars of Vista, the past few years had been enormously difficult. They wanted to salvage something of their hard work. I couldn't blame them. At the same time, those weren't the best reasons to ship code to hundreds of thousands of developers and millions of PCs without a long-term strategy for customers. My inclination was to gently shut down this work rather than support it forever knowing there was no roadmap that worked.

The team, however, had done what Windows teams did often—evangelized their work and gained commitments to foreclose any attempt to shut down the effort. With the help of the evangelism team, they had two big customers lined up in addition to the third parties that the evangelism group had secured. In addition to Zune, the reboot of the Windows Phone (which would become Windows Phone 7) would have a portions of the developer strategy based on Jolt—not the phone itself, but it would use Jolt as a way to make it easy for developers to build apps for the phone operating system. Prior to this time, apps for the phone were built to basically use ancient Windows APIs that formed the original Windows CE operating system for phones. The Developer division wanted to bring WPF and Indigo into the .NET framework and create one all-encompassing mega-framework for developers but branded as the new version of .NET. The way the .NET Framework generally addressed strategic issues was to release a new .NET that contained more stuff under the umbrella of a new version with many new features, even if those new features strategically overlapped with other portions of .NET.

Given all this, the choice was easy for me. As they requested, the Phone Team and the Developer division took over responsibility for the Jolt and WPF teams, respectively. It was a no-brainer. Eventually the code shipped with Windows 7 as part of a new .NET framework, which planned anyway. Most everyone on the Windows team, particularly the performance team in COSD and the graphics team in WEX, were quite happy with all of this. The Windows team had always wanted to focus on Win32, even though there was little data to support such a strategy.

While this decision clarified the organization and responsibility, it in no way slowed the ongoing demise of Windows client programming nor did it present a coherent developer strategy for Microsoft. The .NET strategy remained split across WPF and the old .NET client solutions, neither of which had gained or were gaining significant traction—even with so much visible support marshalled by the evangelism team. Win32 had slowed to a crawl, and we saw little by way of new development. It was discouraging.

Again, many reading this today will say they were (or remain) actively developing on one or the other. My intent isn't to denigrate any specific effort that might be exceedingly important to one developer or customer, but simply to say what we saw happening in total across the ecosystem as evidenced by the data we saw from the in-market telemetry. One of the most difficult challenges with a developer platform is that most developers make one bet on a technology and use it. They do not see histograms or pie charts of usage because they are 100% committed to the technology. They are also vocal and with good reason, their livelihoods depend on the ongoing health of a technology.

With everything to do with developers, APIs, runtimes, and the schism in place, the problem or perhaps solution was this was all "just code," as we would say. What that means is twofold. First, there was always a way to demonstrate strategy or synergy. In a sense, this was what we'd disparagingly call *stupid developer tricks*. These were slides, demonstrations, or strategic assertions that showed technical relationships between independently developed, somewhat-overlapping, and often intentionally different technologies. The idea was to prove that the old and new, two competing new, or two only thematically connected technologies were indeed strategically related. My project to support OLE Controls in C++ was such a trick.

Technically these tricks were the ability to switch languages, use two strategies at the same time, or tap into a Win32 feature from within some portion of something called .NET. A classic example of this was during the discussion about where Jolt should reside organizationally. It was pointed out that Jolt had no support for pen computing or subsequently touch (among other things) since there was none in .NET or WPF to begin with. These were both key to Windows 7 planning efforts. Very quickly the team was able to demonstrate that it was entirely possible to directly call Win32 APIs from within Jolt. This was rather tautological, but also would undermine the cross-platform value proposition of Jolt and importantly lacked tools and infrastructure support from Jolt.

Second, this was all "just code," which meant at any time we could change something and maybe clean up edge cases or enable a new developer trick. Fundamentally, there was no escaping that Win32, .NET, WPF, and even Jolt were designed separately and for different uses with little true architectural synergy. Even to this day, people debate these as developers do—this is simply a Microsoft-only version of what goes on across the internet when people debate languages and runtimes. Enterprise customers expect more synergy, alignment, and execution from a single company. More importantly, developers making a bet on the Microsoft platform expect their choices to be respected, maintained, and enhanced over time. It is essentially impossible to do that when starting from a base as described, and as Microsoft amassed from 2000 to 2007.

As simple as it was to execute moving these teams, in many ways it represented a failure on my part, or, more correctly, a capitulation. I often ask myself if it would have been better to wind down the efforts rather than allow the problem to move to another part of the company. I was anxious to focus and move on, but it is not clear that was the best strategy when given an opportunity to bring change and clarity when developers so clearly were asking for it, even if it meant short-term pain and difficulty. It would have been brutal.

It grew increasingly clear that there were no developers (in any significant number, not literally zero) building new applications for Windows, not in .NET or WPF or Win32. The flagship applications for Windows, like Word, Excel, and others from Microsoft along with Adobe Photoshop or Autodesk AutoCAD, were all massive businesses, but legacy code. The thousands of IT applications connecting to corporate systems, written in primarily Visual Basic, all continued daily use but were being phased out in favor of browser-based solutions for easier deployment, management, portability, and maintenance. They were not using new Windows features, if any existed. The most active area for Windows development was gaming, and those APIs were yet another layer in Windows, called *DirectX*, which was part of WEX and probably the most robust and interesting part of Win32. Ironically, WPF was also an abstraction on top of those APIs. ISVs weren't using anything new from Microsoft, so it wasn't as though we had a winning strategy to pick from.

Further evidence of the demise of Win32 arose as early as 1996 from Oracle's Larry Ellison, who put forth the idea of a new type of browser-only computer, the Network Computer. Sound like a Chromebook? At the time, Marc Andreessen famously said that Windows would be become, simply, a "poorly debugged set of device drivers," meaning that the only thing people would care about would be running the browser. Years later, Andreessen would point out the original was based on something Bob Metcalf had said.[83] Eight years later we had reached the point where the only new interesting mainstream Windows programs were browsers, and at this time only Firefox was iterating on Windows and the only interesting thing about Firefox was what it did with HTML, not Windows. The device drivers still had problems in Vista. In fact, that was the root of the Vista Capable lawsuit!

Moving WPF and Jolt to their respective teams, while an admission of defeat on my part, could best be characterized as a pocket veto. These were not the future of Windows development, but I wasn't sure what would be. We in Windows were doubling down on the browser for sure, but not as leaders, rather as followers. We had our hands full trying to debug the device drivers.

XAML development continues today, though in a much different form. While it does not make a showing in the widely respected Stack Overflow developer survey[84] of over 80,000 developers in 181 countries, it maintains a spot in the Microsoft toolkit. XAML will come to play an important role in the development of the next Windows release as well.

With the team on firm(er) ground and now moving forward we finally started to feel as though we had gained some control. By September 2007 we were in beta test with the first service pack for Vista, which OEMs and end-users anxiously awaited.

The team was in full execution mode now and we had milestones to plow through. While I felt we were heading in the right direction and cleared the decks of obvious roadblocks, there was a looming problem again from Cupertino. What was once a side bet for Microsoft would prove to be the most transformative invention of the 21st century…from Apple.

2007-2009

The competitive landscape was changing at an astounding pace across every conceivable avenue. For the first time in many years, the desktop was under competitive assault and the server had an entirely new platform with which to compete. Lenovo bought IBM's PC business and Amazon offered consumers an entirely new way to read books with the creation of the Kindle. While just a few years earlier the addition of a camera to a cellphone was a big thing, along came the iPhone. And that changed everything.

092. PLATFORM DISRUPTION… WHILE BUILDING WINDOWS 7

The days of competing head-to-head with our own past releases or with vaguely similar products were over. Windows faced outright substitutes, and they seemed to be working.

The Windows 7 team was progressing through engineering milestones M1, M2, and M3 with the energy and momentum increasing along the way, all while computing underwent radical changes at the hardware, platform, and user-experience layers. Everything appeared to be changing at once, just as we were getting our mojo back.

Microsoft's products and strategy were being disrupted. We just hadn't, or perhaps couldn't, come to grips with the reality.

These disruptive forces appeared over the course of developing Windows 7, each one taking a toll on Microsoft's platform value proposition. Each contributing to a small but growing chorus of changing times that started with the iPhone.

The iPhone was announced in January 2007, six months before Windows 7 Vision Day. The phone didn't yet have an App Store, an app SDK, didn't run a full desktop browser, lacked push email for Exchange like a BlackBerry, and even omitted basic copy and paste. Nobody at the time thought this phone was relevant in a competitive sense to personal computers. Heck, it even required a personal computer for some tasks.

Nobody except Steve Jobs.

We didn't know the extent the competitive dynamic would shift a year later, creating a true and unforeseen competitive situation, an existential threat, for all of Microsoft.

I attended the iPhone launch event (rushing to it as it was the same week as CES that year) and walked away with a lot to think about for sure. It was easily one of the most spectacular launch events in the history of computing in my lifetime—after Windows 95 and the 1984 Mac launch and its toaster-size computer with a bitmap display that talked. Steve Jobs said one thing that proved to be incredibly important, with long-term implications overlooked by many [**emphasis** added, my transcription]:

> *We have been very lucky to have brought a few revolutionary user interfaces to the market in our time. First was the mouse. The second was the click wheel. And now, we're going to bring multitouch to the market. And each of these revolutionary user interfaces has made possible a revolutionary product—the Mac, the iPod, and now the iPhone. A revolutionary user interface.*
>
> *We're going to build on top of that with software. Now, software on mobile phones is like baby software. It's not so powerful, and today we are going to show you a software breakthrough. Software that's at least five years ahead of what is on any other phone. Now, how do we do this? Well, we start with a strong foundation.* ***iPhone runs OS X.*** [applause]

> *Now, why, why would we want to run such a sophisticated operating system on a mobile device? Well, because it's got everything we need. It's got multitasking. It's got the best networking. It already knows how to power manage. We've been doing this on mobile computers for years. It's got awesome security. And the right apps.*
>
> *It's got everything from Cocoa and graphics and it's got core animation built in and it's got audio and video that OS X is famous for. It's got all the stuff we want. And it's built right into iPhone. And that has let us create desktop-class applications and networking, right.*
>
> ***Not the crippled stuff that you find on most phones.***
>
> ***This is real, desktop-class applications.***[85]

Most reviews mentioned it, but it did not take up nearly as much airtime as the touch screen. In fact, the absence of support for Adobe Flash in the iPhone browser seemed to even undermine this important fact for most. This important fact was the technology underlying the iPhone—the use of the full operating system was a massively strategic, risky, and difficult choice. Using OS X enabled Apple to gradually enable many Mac features over iterative development cycles, knowing that the code already worked. Apple could do this because it had bigger ideas for how it would break compatibility with the Mac and a bold new model for supporting developers to build third-party software. From the very start, the iPhone was destined to be a complete PC, only rebuilt bit by bit with a modern architecture and API. Not only did the iPhone bet on ever-improving mobile bandwidth as many criticized at the time, but it assumed mobile processors and storage would at least reach parity with the personal computer. In other words, from the very start the iPhone had a truck engine, a reference will make sense in Chapter XIV.

Windows had been taking the opposite approach which was to base the mobile platform on a nearly decades-old version of Windows, stripped down even, with thoughts though not goals of perhaps of catching up to the current desktop Windows by adding new code over time. The incredible challenges this decision introduced will become readily apparent, but only with the release of a new Windows phone operating system to compete with the iPhone. The diverging paths of Windows for mobile and laptop/desktop had been cast years earlier.

That summer, I lined up at the AT&T store at Pacific Place in downtown Seattle and picked up my black 4GB iPhone. Who needed 8GB on a phone? Some PCs were shipping with 4GB of storage and all of Windows XP. At the time of the launch announcement, I was quite skeptical of the touch keyboard and said so in an internal mail thread, pointing out if touch screens would work then Windows Phone had already tried and mostly failed. I had been a hardcore BlackBerry (and later Palm Trēo) user since before general availability in the late 1990s. I was as much a *CrackBerry addict* as anyone. Some of the many Windows phones had a stylus like a Palm (or Apple Newton), but I never warmed to those and thought handwriting with a stylus was as dumb as Steve Jobs said at the launch. Within a few hours of having the phone and a browser, my worldview changed, especially about touch and especially about the evolution of operating systems. Even lacking copy and paste and relying on the slow AT&T 2G mobile network, you had to really try hard to not be impressed.

I remember emailing the co-founder of BlackBerry and asking when there would be a full browser and in a long back and forth thread, he tried to convince me of the implications on battery life, lack of capacity on the phone network, and even the lack of utility. While months earlier I might have been sympathetic, I was now staunchly on the other side of this debate.

Inside the company, the iPhone went largely unnoticed outside of small pockets of people, and of course the Phone Team. Not because it was not a breakthrough product, but because it did not fully connect to our corporate mail service, Microsoft Exchange, as it was configured and permissioned by Microsoft's IT group. Only those of us running on the testing servers, *dogfood*, were able to use an iPhone for email, and even then it had no support for our much-loved rights-managed email and Microsoft directory. There was a significant debate over whether maintaining this capability was good for self-hosting and competitive knowledge or bad for supporting competition. It was also about this time that support for using BlackBerry was disabled. I put up a huge battle over this only to delay the inevitable. Making it difficult to fully host on competitive products was short-sighted but impossible to stop, even as a senior executive. This was done to "eat our own dogfood" even if the result meant truly innovative and competitive products would only receive cursory use.

While SteveB's comments around the iPhone launch have become something of an historically bad take as he somewhat mocked the high price, it is crucially important to understand that he as much reflected as simply shared the collective viewpoint of the entire PC industry, and most of the mobile industry. Collectively, nearly every party underestimated the ability for Apple, with no experience in the mobile industry, to deliver a hit product while also resetting the norms of the mobile carrier business model—the same carriers that Steve Jobs described as "orifices" during an interview two years before the world knew about the phone.[86]

The two fundamental assumptions of the PC industry that guided it to nearly 300 million units a year were low prices with consumer choice and a horizontal layering of hardware and software. This business model and technology architecture together enabled the PC. For all the struggles between OEMs, Intel, Microsoft and more, the success was indisputable, especially relative to the Apple model of premium price, limited choice, and a vertically integrated, single supplier.

Before the iPhone, the mobile phone seemed to be coming around to the PC model, with the Windows phone appearing to make progress against Nokia and BlackBerry with many PC OEMs using a Windows phone software license to offer low price and choice to customers. Jobs would take this good news and make it appear bad by showing how Windows Phone was fragmented across phone makers, not a single OS. That drove the Windows Phone Team crazy, particularly when Jobs presented the market share as a pie chart in 2008 basically rendering Windows Phone as "Other." The iPhone would literally trounce the traditional OEM model. Choosing between a bunch of crappy devices is no choice at all, even if they all run a single platform. Jobs had long been making this point about PCs too, except now this all seemed to be working.

He was only partially right because in just a short time, Google would repeat the technical and partnership aspects of the Windows model exactly for phones, while upending the economic model and not charging for a software license, opting to further its advertising business model. Of note, the successful OEMs for Android turned out to be an entirely new set of partners, with none of the existing PC OEMs making the generational transition, perhaps in part because most had tried and failed when using Windows mobile software. The combination of iPhone and Android would leave Microsoft in a hopeless middle, with a shrinking partner ecosystem across OEMs and developers. The iPhone was not a broad or instant hit as is well-documented. History does not easily recall the bumpy first year because the following years went so spectacularly well.

Seemingly, at least for the moment, unrelated, there was that money-losing online retailer named Amazon.com led by Jeff Bezos plugging away on what Steve Jobs might have called a hobby or a side project. The company created Amazon Web Services, AWS, in 2002, though few noticed. The product was relaunched about a year before the iPhone with a new set of capabilities and two main new products: EC2 and S3, providing scalable on-demand computing and huge cloud-based storage. For developers, that marked the birth of the cloud era. Amazingly, perhaps, this new competitive front was not Google, which is where nearly all of our platform angst resided.

For Microsoft, this was all starting to sink in. We had competition on the client and at the infrastructure layer. We were getting squeezed on both of our platform businesses, Windows desktops and Windows servers.

Ray Ozzie (ROzzie) was leading a new project, code name *Red Dog*, with an incredible group of early Windows NT developers including DaveC. As Chief Software Architect, ROzzie was looking to the cloud to reinvent the future of Windows Server, Microsoft's dominant and extremely profitable business of running enterprise computing in customer-owned and – operated data centers. The running of important business functions in the cloud was still more than a decade away for Microsoft's enterprise customers, but Amazon's clarity of vision and the start-ups that gravitated to the approach were incredible. With the cloud, along came Linux as well. Microsoft already needed to catch up, but you had to look very carefully to believe that to be the case, as it was not at all obvious from a customer perspective.

Microsoft had invested a decade in building out Windows Server, a hardware ecosystem, databases, and the entire .NET stack along with a trained sales force. Suddenly AWS running on Linux with entirely new models of compute was the competitor. No salespeople required. To use AWS, developers just signed up online using a credit card and paid for what computing resources they needed as they needed. No hardware to buy. No servers to set up, maintain, and secure. No running out of disk space or network bandwidth. No need to buy more servers in case there's a rush on the web site. A whole business could run off from laptop with a browser connecting to Amazon's data centers in the cloud.

It was nearly impossible for many born of the Windows server world, whether at Microsoft or our customers, to fathom this approach. There were endless debates inside the halls and boardroom of Microsoft over whether this was crazy or fantasy. One of the most common debates centered around storing data and either how much bandwidth would be required to move data to or from cloud servers or how expensive cloud storage would forever be. To me these debates seemed rather like the debates over the browser taking over for Office—it is not a matter of if, but rather when everything aligned to make it possible and how different the resulting solutions would look from what we built today. The very existence of Gmail seemed to demonstrate the present reality with the most mission critical of all storage intensive workloads, email.

We got so tangled up on how customers would migrate to the cloud, we did not really consider how much larger the market would be starting from nothing and growing cloud native. The irony of us failing to predict this same type of massive upside was almost too much, in hindsight, since that is exactly what gummed up the mainframe computing world and even the character-based (non-GUI) world of MS-DOS as the PC, Windows, and Office platforms took hold.

Additionally, when faced with disruption while substantially new ideas are fast pulling the market and customers in new directions, the previous generation of innovation does not stop. That is what makes it even more difficult for the new approaches to take hold with incumbents. At every step, we thought we would keep adding features in the direction we were going to keep winning. We were winning big. Microsoft's revenue growth in 2007 and 2008 was 15% and 18% respectively, with 2008 revenue growing past $60 billion.

One example of this competitive pull was our focus on the biggest competitor to Windows Server, VMware. Why? VMware used virtualization to manage Windows Server and in doing so commoditized Windows as one of many alternative operating systems VMware could manage. It had started off as a brilliant invention for developers to isolate code under development on the desktop growing into a new components of enterprise infrastructure. We had been using it ourselves to simplify testing of Windows and even Office for several years already. If Windows Server could enable competitive virtualization, we could thwart the competition from VMware while also solving for the same scenarios Amazon seemed to be addressing with AWS but without Linux.

VMware was acquired (in a complex series of transactions) by a Windows partner, EMC, which soon after acquired a separate company started by Paul Maritz (PaulMa), the former leader of Windows. Paul transitioned to lead VMware as CEO, where he implemented the same enterprise playbook that helped to make Windows Server a success. VMware was rapidly becoming the enterprise standard for a new wave of enterprise datacenter management, which would turn out to be a stop along the way to a future of cloud. This mattered because it impacted the COSD team's contribution to Windows Server and put the team in between two different versions of the future, being implemented by two different teams at Microsoft, each with serious competition—Red Dog building out one roadmap and Windows Server another. While one view might be that this was a prudent strategy, another view was that it was a strategy guaranteed to slow our progress to an inevitable future.

Our remaining competitive challenge was faced by Live Services. Competition was constant and coming from all directions. Many competitors came and went quickly, as was the norm in consumer, ad-supported services. Switching costs were low and whole populations changed quickly—it appeared to be a hit-driven business, which was not something Microsoft was geared up to navigate, especially after a failed decade of trying to make consumer and home software a thing with CDROM titles and later web sites. MSN Messenger and Hotmail had hundreds of millions of users, but daily active users (DAUs) were declining and engagement (usage time) overall was dropping. There was a good deal of advertising revenue, hundreds of millions of dollars, but it depended on intrusive display ads that riled users, even though the services were free.

Gmail rapidly became the new *de facto* leader in "free" email, offering essentially "unlimited" email storage in gigabytes while Hotmail was trying to build a business charging for extra megabytes. Originally announced as an April Fool's prank in 2004 and released in beta, by the time the Windows 7 vision meeting took place Gmail had finally removed the exclusive invitation signup requirement. Though remained in beta, the service was exploding in use. While it would be a few years until Gmail surpassed Hotmail, Hotmail almost immediately stopped seeing growth and started to see a decline in engagement. Gmail was not a gimmick; under the hood was an enormously innovative database and operational capability. Gmail had no advertisements. None.

MSN Messenger, eventually Live Messenger, had become enormously popular around the world, especially outside the United States with hundreds of millions of active users. It too was facing an existential competitive threat. This time competition came from Skype, a Swedish, Danish, and Estonian invention that offered free voice calls from almost any platform, notably both PC and Mac. While Messenger was often used to arbitrage SMS fees, Skype was arbitraging voice and creating a movement that would permit much of the world to skip using landlines for overseas calls when mobile minutes were incredibly expensive. Video calling was introduced as well, and while Messenger already had this capability, the cross-platform nature of Skype, as well as the focus on voice connections to local land lines, made for a much more compelling offering. Microsoft would finally acquire Skype from eBay (who had acquired it in 2005) in 2011 when it reached almost 300 million users worldwide, more than Messenger had achieved. In 2007-2009, Windows Live was still competing with Apple, Google, Yahoo, Skype, MySpace, and a host of category leaders across photos, blogging, and video. That was a lot.

SteveB and Kevin Johnson (KevinJo) spent a great deal of time and energy on the potential of acquiring Yahoo, the dominant leader with which MSN competed. Such a deal would have added to my challenges given their email and messenger services were suffering much the same way. We might have gained in search and content services, but we would have added productivity services that were also losing share just as Windows Live seemed to be.

Apple struggled to find its way through the cloud and services world, even with the launch of iPhone. Apple's decidedly client and device focused approach was quite similar to how we saw Live Services and Windows evolving together. The services would be augmented by rich "desktop class" applications for photos, video, messaging, blogging, and even productivity. Apple for years had been selling a suite of creativity products, iLife, later adding new productivity tools, notably Keynote for slide shows, called iWork. A collection of web services was originally called iTools then later rebranded as the .Mac service (pronounced "dot" Mac) and included email, online storage, and backup. In the summer of 2008, the service was rebranded MobileMe in a very bumpy launch that was not widely praised. After eight years and a good deal of iteration, Apple continued to work to find its way even as iPhone success grew.

The most disruptive announcement from Apple came a year after the initial iPhone launch. In 2008, Apple announced and then brought to market a software development kit with APIs to build third-party apps for the iPhone. This also included an entirely new store for software distribution and economic model for developers, the App Store. It is almost impossible to overstate the leap the App Store brought to computing. The PC was drowning in viruses and malware because of the internet—the ability in a few clicks to download software seemed wonderful at first, but then quickly became a cesspool of awful software that at best simply degraded the PC experience. Additionally, the world of PC software had stagnated simply because it was so large that it became almost impossible for a new desktop product to gain awareness, distribution, and enough sales to support a pure-play software company. In fact, Skype might be the most innovative native, though cross-platform, application to break through outside of browsers, and we acquired it in 2011 before it was profitable. While some would view the App Store as a sort-of closed ecosystem, it was literally the solution to the problems plaguing the PC. The Apple bet on OS X meant that there was a robust and proven platform and toolset to serve as a foundation, plus software distribution and economics. Developers hardly had all of OS X, but they definitely had a lot of it and Apple could add more over time.

Microsoft was steeped in a competitive mindset across every generation of leader and from many perspectives. BillG never missed an opportunity to cite some positive attribute or significant asset of a competitor. SteveB brought his relentless sense of competition from childhood math camp and sports. MikeMap and JeffH instilled this in all of us back on my first team with an intense business rigor. In working with the Windows and Windows Live role, I was faced with competition from more directions and with more depth than I ever thought possible. The team, at first as I moved into the role, seemed to consistently minimize this new reality. It would be rude to say Microsoft was in denial. I don't think it would be unfair to say that after years of winning and even feeling like we had beaten back Linux and open source, Microsoft had become much more focused on its own universe of customers and their problems which was mostly immune to influences from outside that gravitational sphere.

In hindsight, that was what happened when two factors combined to create a step-function change in product trajectory.

First, the existence of a single massive product, Windows and the Intel PC ecosystem, Wintel, created constraints for those looking to build entirely innovative products. While many built products thinking of Wintel as an ingredient, amplifying the platform without posing a risk, a small percentage of risk-takers saw a different world. They saw the shortcomings of Wintel as an opportunity to reinvent. They built as though the leaders were not there and built what, in their eyes, the world should look like, whether they achieved critical mass success or not. Each of these new competitors had a worldview that revisited underlying assumptions about Windows and Windows Live and the PC ecosystem. Competitors assumed any web browser as the user interface, connected over the internet to Linux servers running open-source software—no Windows Server or .NET at all. Google, Facebook, and a constellation of start-ups in Silicon Valley embraced this model as though Microsoft never existed. Even when it came to Microsoft Office, most new companies in Silicon Valley operated as though it was an insignificant part of the software landscape. In 2008, while Windows 7 was in testing as we tried to bring Internet Explorer back from hibernation, Google released the Google Chrome browser and with it putting an end to even that sliver of Microsoft as part of the next wave of innovations.

Second, the incumbent leader had to mess up. Customers generally didn't spontaneously change, even if there was something better to switch to, because of processes, habits, and costs, and they don't change all at once. Leaders messed up by ignoring new technologies, especially as over time little technologies added up to something material. Also, a risk was a failure to execute and deliver new products to market, simply dropping the ball. Microsoft mired in the journey through Windows Longhorn and a executing a Windows strategy put forth in the mid-1990s had indeed dropped the ball. It was increasingly difficult to appreciate or even see changes to the technology landscape when the company's decision-making context is so dominated by goals, challenges, and issues entirely of its own making.

Waiting to pick up the ball was the competition born of the internet and web. While many wished to connect this potential disruption of Microsoft to the antitrust events and resulting settlement in the early 2000s, none of Apple's iPhone, Amazon's AWS, or Google's Search or Gmail had anything to do with the trial and resulting settlement. Where some like to claim Microsoft was distracted, they would be wrong. If Microsoft was distracted, it was by simply trying to finish Windows Vista or compete with VMware or IBM or even Linux, or executing on our own plans and growth and dealing with issues like software security and quality. This wasn't about the browser, the price of Windows, or even what software was installed on a PC. Those had already become old battles and irrelevant to the rapid structural changes that happened in software—the kind that produced Microsoft, then Windows, then Office in the first place. As fast as one company can rise to success, another can do the same in equally unexpected or counterintuitive ways. This was the argument or perhaps the defense Microsoft and BillG had put forth time and time again. No matter how many times BillG said this to the press, customers, or regulators none would believe him…even as it was taking place.

This was all happening as I was trying to get our house in order and make progress. Things just weren't as simple as they were in 2005 when OEMs were just waiting on a new release of Windows. The PC makers were looking particularly unhealthy and deeply concerned about the rise of mobile phones on top of normal concerns about the price of components, delays in Windows, and the chip roadmap from Intel—would phones be an opportunity for PC OEMs or would they prove to be a generational change in hardware leaders as well? Should they be considering Linux on the desktop as a replacement of Windows given its popularity on servers?

SteveB, and increasingly the Board, had a lot of questions and concerns surrounding the competitive dynamic. Some board members were close to the hardware ecosystem and would oscillate between certainty that the ecosystem would deliver and that it would not. International board members were using Skype to talk to their families. Everyone wanted to know how to connect from their iPhones to their Microsoft corporate email or Windows Live personal mail, or why iTunes was so slow on Vista, or why Mac Excel was so different from Windows Excel as new Mac owners were discovering.

In fact, they were all asking how long it would be before they did everything on mobile phones. There was also deep concern over browsers, knowing it had been five years since the last release of Internet Explorer in 2001 and work had all but stopped. All of them wanted a PC as cool as a MacBook. Microsoft board members had a budget for PC purchases and always wanted to know the most Apple-competitive Windows laptop to buy, and for much of the duration of Windows 7 we had no answers. Each time I attended a Board meeting, I had to respond to all of these questions again.

Like Captain Kirk in ST:WOK (*Star Trek: Wrath of Khan*), I would look around and think, "Please, please…give us time…the bridge is smashed, computers inoperative." We were rebuilding the team and trust with customers and OEMs. Windows 7 was going to pave the way for us to do big new things. There was little more we could do than get that done.

Whether it was desperation, a lack of alternatives, or simply misplaced confidence in the team, the questions kept coming yet there were few questions about Windows 7. Many were already looking beyond Windows 7, thinking, and plotting as though delivering Windows 7 was some sort of no-brainer.

Looking back, it was equally easy to ponder the radical idea of basically skipping Windows 7 and going straight for something to compete on these many fronts. We could theoretically catch up to these multiple competitive forces and not miss an entire cycle of innovation if everything was aimed at mobile and cloud. One big mega-strategy to build a new Windows, a new phone, and integrated cloud services.

That would have been absurd. It was the opposite of possible. The team was still recovering from the Vista release with its portfolio of stretch goals, to put it kindly, that did not go as planned. The last thing we should have even come up with was some sort of Longhorn-redo. Frankly, what we planned for Windows 7 was kind of crazy, given the recent track record. We planned Windows 7 and all the features with the assumption the team could deliver a major update to Windows, on time. Additionally, the Server team and its customers remained not only unconvinced of the cloud but actively campaigned against it. Besides, we had Red Dog. Windows 7 had to serve both of those.

The impact and the constraints of the past had long-lasting effects.

While the Board was anxious about the post-Vista landscape, the technical trade press, mostly made up of Microsoft watchers, remained tuned to Windows. It was the product with the most familiarity, and the Vista release was causing difficulties. But the double-edged sword of the beat reporters was that they covered what we were up to, but not so much what we should have been up to, until it was too late. It would still be a few years before most reporters made the switch to Mac, but the switch to iPhone was happening quickly bringing renewed attention to Apple laptops.

At the same time, any little thing we did was chum in the water for the dozens of beat reporters covering Microsoft.

In the summer of 2007 word leaked out about the impending service pack for Windows Vista previously described. It was not a horrible leak, but it scrambled our OEM partners and immediately froze the few Vista enterprise deployments in process. The field sales team was livid that they had not been briefed on the release, again arguing for more transparency from Redmond. The problem was we had just gone through five years of transparency and every constituent was annoyed, at best. I wrote a 3000-word internal blog post "Transparency and disclosure" where I tried to put forth the idea that being transparent isn't compatible with being good partners, but we needed to aspire to translucency. An excerpt follows:

> Transparent. *Easily seen through or detected; obvious.*
>
> Translucent. *easily understandable; lucid.*
>
> *One topic I have been having an interesting time following has been the blogs and reports that speculate about how Windows will go from being an open or transparent product development team to being one that is "silent" or "locked down". Much of this commentary seems to center around me personally, which is fine, but talks about how there is a Sinofsky-moratorium on disclosure. I think that means I owe it to the team to provide a view on what I do mean personally (and what I personally mean to do), of course I do so knowing that just by writing this down I run this risk of this leaking and then we'll have a round of phone calls and PR management to do just with regards to "Sinofsky's internal memo on disclosure". But I thought it would be worth a try.*
>
> …
>
> *Customers and partners want to know about SP1 for Vista. Actually they need to know. We want to tell them. But we want to do so when our plans and execution allow that communication to be relatively definitive. We are not there yet. So telling folks and then changing the plans causes many more challenges than readily apparent. While it might sound good on paper to be "transparent" and to give*

> *a wide open date range and a wide open list of release contents, we all know that these conversations with customers don't end with the "we'll ship by <x> date and we've prioritized <quality>". Folks do want to know "did you fix this <example> bug?" That is reasonable, but we don't have all those answers and thus we cannot have a reasonably consistent and reliable communication…yet. We are working towards that. While there is clearly a challenge in the near term in not offering details, this challenge is much less than if we get the wrong information out there and we have to reset and unset expectations. Even among our enterprise customers, for whom this type of information is routine, we have a long history of really scrambling these most valuable customers with "information" that turned out to be "misinformation". The difference we are trying to highlight is the difference between transparency in what we're "thinking" and transparency in what we're "doing". Everyone wants to know what we're thinking, but making it clear that those are thoughts versus "doing" is a subtlety lost on a mass audience.*
>
> …
>
> *I know many folks think that this type of corporate "clamp down" on disclosure is "old school" and that in the age of corporate transparency we should be open all the time. Corporations are not really transparent. Corporations are translucent. All organizations have things that are visible and things that are not. Saying we want to be transparent overstates what we should or can do practically—we will share our plans in a thoughtful and constructive manner.*[87]

This too leaked. It became known as the "Sinofsky *omerta*" (awful) and the idea of being translucent was always said snidely. We had gone nine-plus months without any substantial forward-looking discussion of Windows. The reporters covering Microsoft were restless. The leaked blog post only served to amplify any other leaks.

A college student-blogger in Australia, Long Zheng, who had become somewhat of a canary in tracking Windows evolution, happened to catch an October 2007 college recruiting talk at the University of Illinois given by Eric Traut (EricTr), a Distinguished Engineer and one of the senior architects in COSD and a core member of the Windows NT architecture team. Eric was a key inventor of the hardware emulation technology used by Apple as it transitioned microprocessors the first time in the 1990s and then an early pioneer of virtualization at a competitor to VMware, Connectix, that Microsoft acquired in 2003.

EricTr presented a wonderfully detailed talk on the role of virtualization in modern computing, describing the work he did along with a number of the most senior people on Windows. He described the architecture of a modern scalable OS and the evolution of Windows over time. He even showed some code.

To that blogger, he had just seen a demo of Windows 7 or at least exactly what Windows 7 should be.

Zheng saw the presentation on a video posted on Microsoft's own *Channel9* website and promptly wrote a blog post about the future of Windows 7, referring to the talk as a "demonstration of Windows 7."

It wasn't that at all. What was so exciting, though?

Over the years there was that constant murmur underlying the evolution of Windows and its expression of bloat—expansion of code size, decreasing performance, the requirement that PCs have more and more memory just to keep up. Everyone's PC got slower over time because of bloat. EricTr's demonstration inadvertently played into this narrative and provided a huge hope for improvements in the future.

To implement virtualization, the OS kernel was being worked on to further reduce the impact it would have on memory and CPU consumption. Eric demonstrated this new "minimal kernel," which he dubbed *MinWin*. This would be exactly the solution to every problem with PCs—if Windows was good but a bit bloated, then certainly a minimum Windows, or MinWin, would be what everyone would want. It would do everything Windows did but with minimal code. Who would not want that? If one set out to create an ideal branding to describe a release of Windows for every tech enthusiast, MinWin was it. As I read the blogger's account, I thought "Oh my gosh, this is Office Lite, but for Windows"—it was a hypothetical product that did everything it needed to do, but was easier, smaller, faster, and lighter. What's not to love? (See 076. Betting Big to Fend Off Commoditization)

Eric's talk was about virtualization and scaling Windows Server. It was not at all about Windows the way most people thought about it. Eric described what he was showing as follows:

> *We created what we call MinWin. Now, this is an internal only, you won't see us productizing this, but you could imagine this being used as the basis for products in the future. This is the Windows 7 source code base, and it's about 25 megs on disk. You compare that to the four gigs on disk that the full windows Vista takes up.*

Everyone on the team, most certainly a COSD architect, knew the blogger's description that this was Windows 7 was incorrect—Eric even said so. Even assuming Windows was bloated, the OS kernel wasn't the culprit. We ended up spending a lot of time with the press figuring out how to reduce the expectations and to not consider the next Windows some sort of "new kernel." This backfired because they heard us downplaying expectations for the release overall. With our silence, this made sense, given the Windows history of overpromise and underdeliver. As word spread, we began to hear from enterprise customers who thought that a new kernel would introduce compatibility concerns, especially in the server. This was neither a practical nor theoretical issue.

The challenge this created was indirectly related to bloat. Rather, it created a perception that Windows 7 was going to be substantially "less bloated" (whatever that meant) than Windows Vista. That prompted people to talk about comparisons to the now, post-Vista, much-loved Windows XP. Nothing in the product plan had changed, but there was suddenly a perception Windows 7 would be dramatically improved.

The public expectations for the release went up, as if they weren't already sky high. When the outer reaches of the company saw these stories, particularly where there were direct connections to customers, the optimism was contagious.

Scary? Sure. Except we already had thousands of people working on that very opportunity—making a leaner, more efficient Windows while also making it do a lot of new stuff.

The absence of information gave people ample room to create their own worldview. Many, especially SteveB and the OEM team, wanted to use this, or one of the other rumor cycles, to get out there with more information. The team was still in the early stages of executing, and we needed to make more progress. I did not want to be out there just yet. Besides, all I could do at that moment would be counter the now exaggerated expectations which would create more confusion and likely cause another news cycle condemning Windows 7 to be a limited or incremental update to Vista.

Just as the Fall computer selling season was gearing up, a new type of computer was all the rage in Asia and about to hit the US market. Maybe these "Netbook computers" would breathe some life into Vista and buy us some time before we started talking about Windows 7?

093. NETBOOK MANIA

When a project like Longhorn drags on, the business is going to miss important trends. The biggest trend in computing in 2005-06 was expanding the PC to the rest of the world, something Microsoft and others called "the next billion" as the existing PC model reached approximately one billion of the world's 6.5 billion people.

To outfit the next billion, many believed a new type of computer was needed. They were right. Many places where we would have liked to bring computers to the next billion lacked reliable electricity, air conditioning or heating, constant high-speed internet connectivity, and often had dusty environments as in Africa and much of Asia where I happened to have some of experience.

At the MIT Media Lab, Nicholas Negroponte, the lab's founder, spearheaded a project called One Laptop Per Child, OLPC, that launched at the Davos forum in 2005. The rest of the world would come to know this as the "$100 laptop" at a time when most laptops cost about $1000 or more.

The price of $100 seemed absurd given that was less than an Intel processor and only marginally more than Windows, and that was before the rest of the hardware. Therefore, the initial designs of the OLPC would ship without commercial software from Microsoft or hardware from Intel. Instead, partners from anyone but Wintel lined up to help figure out how to build the OLPC. Almost immediately, Microsoft and Intel were blocked out of the next billion.

The resulting device, a product of some extremely fancy, perhaps fanciful, industrial design was a key part of drawing attention to what became known as the OLPC XO-1. The device featured several technical features that were aimed at solving computing needs for children in remote areas while also addressing the goal of ultra-low cost. The software was open source with a great deal of influence from historic MIT projects aimed at learning computing and programming. The effort even created a non-profit where people could go to a web site and donate the price of a device to have one distributed. The OLPC XO-1 was so cool looking that many people wanted one for their own use, right here in the US. The rollout and communications were exactly what you'd expect from the Media Lab—exciting and broadly picked up.

Microsoft through the Microsoft Research team and Craig Mundie (CraigMu) leading advanced technology spent a great deal of effort attempting to insert Windows into this effort. The company made progress but at the expense of causing some well-known members of the OLPC project to resign once it became clear that proprietary software was involved. Microsoft for its part would embark on the creation of a version of Windows that was ultra-low cost and stripped of many features as well.

If there's a theme in this work, both from Microsoft and MIT, it is that the core idea was that to bring computing to the next billion, products would need to cost less out of necessity and therefore they would need to do less and be less powerful. Often in the process of doing this the products would also go through transformation to make them easier to use, because apparently that is something required too. This is a fundamental mistake made time and again when addressing what the financial and economic world call emerging markets. Individuals in emerging markets do not want cheap, under-powered, or worse products. They certainly do not need products that are dumbed down. In technology, there is really no reason for that as products do get less expensive over time. Yet in the immediate term companies get stuck with their existing price structures and economics. And people in emerging markets are not less smart, they simply do not have access to the money for expensive products. I saw this dozens of times visiting the internet cafes in the most rural and economically disadvantaged parts of the world where students had no problems at all using a PC connected to the internet.

Microsoft would really get stuck in China where the limiting factor wasn't hardware. People were buying huge numbers of PC components and simply assembling their own desktops that were on par with anything available from Dell or HP. They weren't running Linux or Open Office, they were just pirating Windows and Office. The Windows team (I was still in Office) created a whole group to strip down Windows XP and add a shell to make it "easier" for emerging markets, again a dumbed down product. These changes to software were as much as way to make products favorable to the new markets as they were to make the product unfavorable to existing customers. Eventually, Microsoft came up with a plan to offer Windows plus Office to emerging markets, and China, governments for a very low price, so long as the computers were purchased by the government. At $3 per license this sounds like an incredible deal, but in all honesty was not that different from prices in many developed markets.

Still, the idea that the next billion required much lower priced computers, and somehow the rest of the world did not, would not go away. The need to serve this market drove the next wave of innovation from Microsoft and Intel, much more so than serving existing markets.

As Intel was mostly left out of the OLPC project, at the Intel Developer Forum in Fall 2007 they announced a new line of microprocessors with at least some emphasis on making lower cost computers for an expanded market. Intel demonstrated this processor in what is called a reference design, a PC made by Intel as a way to influence their customers to build similar PCs. The Classmate PC was a pretty cool looking laptop somewhat influenced by the Apple iBook, which brought the rounded edges, colors, and translucency of the iMac to a laptop form factor. Some would say the iBook itself owed its design lineage to the Apple eMate, based on the Apple Newton, and sold to education markets in the 1990s. As a reference design, the PC shown could support a variety of screen sizes, storage capacities, and more, so long as it ran a new Intel low-power chip.

Also showing off the new chip in the 2007 Intel Developer Forum was the ASUS Eee PC—that's a lot of e's, which ostensibly stood for "Easy to learn, Easy to work, Easy to play" according to the box. The Eee PC was the first Netbook. It was also one of the smallest computers on the market. While there were many previous attempts at super small computers, such as the Sony PictureBook and Toshiba Libretto, they were years earlier and premium priced. This form factor and price were unique at the time. The first Eee PC 701 had the most minimal hardware specifications in any PC around and ran customized Linux and OpenOffice. It also had several games and entertainment apps.

The laptop was physically tiny as was the keyboard at 8.9 x 6.5 x 1.4 inches and under 2 pounds. It had a 7-inch display running at 800x480 pixels. For storage the Eee PC had only 4GB of solid-state disk (like an iPod) and just 512MB of RAM. The price was $399 when it finally made it to the US, though the initial reports were it would cost $189-$299. It is worth noting that the same Intel chip was also available at retail stores in a laptop with a 14" screen,

80GB drive, a DVD drive, and 2GB RAM for about the same price. This reality would not distract from the cool factor or that it fit in any messenger-style bag.

The software load was kind of a mess, at least I thought so. The hardware, however, caught the attention of tech enthusiasts who were quick to turn the Eee PC into a tuner platform, looking to modify and replace components. Soon, modders were replacing the storage or adding more memory. There were web sites popping up devoted to modding the Eee PC.

The device sold quite well through the holiday of 2007 and that got our attention. So did the fact that modders were doing their own work to strip down Windows XP (from 2001) and squeeze it on to a 4GB system. One such modder was ASUS itself which came to us wanting to officially modify Windows XP. There were three problems. First, they wanted Windows XP to cost the same as their Linux, which was $0. Second, they wanted to remove a bunch of XP just to make room on disk. What they wanted to remove was simply anything that took up space. It was kind of a free-for-all that reminded me of what enterprise customers did to Windows 3.x and Office 4.x back in the 1990s to squeeze on to 20MB hard drives.

The third problem was significant. Windows XP was done. We were over it. It was already seven years-old and we released Vista months ago. Vista was our bet. There was definitely no way Vista could be squeezed down, first of all. Second, Vista just went through the Vista Capable mess where the basic version of Vista became tainted in market and these chipsets were good enough only for Vista Basic.

If we began selling XP again for ASUS, then we would have to offer it for every Netbook. And if we offered it for Netbooks then what would stop OEMs and ultimately customers demanding it for every PC. Suddenly it was looking like a roll back of Vista, especially if we participated. We didn't really have a choice. Either we would lose the sockets to Linux, the modders would continue to pirate XP and hundreds of thousands of computers would be running a Frankenstein build of XP which already had tons of security problems, or we could suck it up and let the OEMs sell XP.

It turns out Intel was in a bit of the same situation. They were starting to worry that OEMs would want to make many more laptops out of the low power chips and that would take away sales of their more powerful and profitable laptop chips. Intel defined the Netbook category, and thus availability and pricing of low power chips, to require certain maximum screen sizes and configurations. This constrained what would technically be defined as a Netbook. Microsoft used these same definitions, chief among them the tiny screen size, to offer Windows XP. This had a side-effect of extending the Windows XP lifecycle even more. When we finally celebrated the end of Windows XP it was years longer than originally planned entirely due to Netbooks, though the industry would remember this as a story of the failure of Vista in general.

In the Spring of 2008 after what could be dubbed the ASUS Eee PC holiday season, Intel announced the name of the chipset to power Netbooks, Atom®. With that both Intel and Microsoft were all in on Netbooks, and so were all the OEMs. The collective positioning of Netbooks was as a companion to a primary computer, though that was just marketing. Intel called them MID, for mobile internet device, a third category of device that was neither a mobile phone nor a laptop but a highly portable companion computer. A lot of customers genuinely bought Netbooks as their new laptop.

The industry was filled with concerns over margins from these devices. Intel chipsets that cost around $100 for a laptop were half that for a Netbook. At under $400 there was little room for either margin or innovation. *The New York Times* wrote of these concerns in 2008, "[D]espite their wariness of these slim machines, Dell and Acer, two of the biggest PC manufacturers, are not about to let the upstarts have this market to themselves."[88] No OEM was going to be left out of what could potentially be a big shift.

Maintaining low prices, especially around $399, posed some problems, mostly the need to cut back on other components and capacities. Intel dropped many of the required aspects of PCs, such as extensible memory, large disk drives, and DVD drives, in an effort to develop the platform that ASUS and others would follow. The PCs would be like a phone—bare bones with all the components essentially built in with little official extensibility. They would have 10-inch or less screens, presumably because of the category but in practice because small screens were super cheap, and, importantly, Intel did not want to see PCs that might compete with profitable, mainstream 13-inch laptops.

The typical specifications of a Netbook were an Atom processor, 1GB memory, Wi-Fi, USB ports, SD card reader, a web camera, and 2GB to 4GB of solid-state storage, as opposed to a spinning disk drive. The screen would be an inexpensive LCD running at 1024x600 resolution, with graphics bumping up against the low-end Vista Capable designation. Windows laptops had not yet incorporated solid state storage at all, which made Netbooks rather novel for techies.

For those keeping track, every single one of those specifications was less than the minimum system specifications for the lowest-end Vista PC. Every. Single. One.

That was the rub. These were low-end PCs in every sense. Some of the specs were borderline awful, most notably the screen resolution of 1024x600 was at the limits of what Windows XP would correctly display. Many interactions with Windows would be tricky with so few pixels and much of the Internet and Windows applications would really struggle. By struggle, it was not uncommon to get into a situation where the button that needed to be clicked was off screen and simply unavailable having run out of display area. At times the display just didn't show enough rows, or the text was too small to read or edit.

HP, Lenovo, ASUS, and others released a flurry of devices all with nearly identify specifications. Even though the devices were identical at the processor and chipset and even power adapter, they differed in keyboards, display, and quality of storage used. These small differences were the full-employment act for tech enthusiast web sites that tracked every development in this hot new category.

Personally, I was really into my Netbook. I was already wedded to the 11" form factor having made a switch to use only super portable PCs anyway. The Netbook was tiny, but the low-end nature of the hardware became an ever-present reminder of the need to make Windows 7 work on much less hardware than Vista did. I ran on a Netbook full time for most of the Windows 7 development cycle. The photo in the previous section of me holding up a Lenovo IdeaPad S10 with "I'm a PC" sticker was my very own Lenovo which I even modded myself to 4GB of

RAM and a faster solid-state drive. I managed to blog a few hundred thousand words on the tiny keyboard as well. Where it really came in handy was how I constantly used benchmarks and slow operations to annoy the engineering managers. I loved it, but I was a willing subject.

Behind the scenes though something else was going on. The reality was that the root of the Netbook was not just OLPC and the next billion PC users, rather it was both Intel and Microsoft or Wintel's inability to transition to a mobile world. The iPhone that released just before the availability of the Eee PC was built with an ARM chip, which technically is a system-on-a-chip, or SoC. ARM chips were what powered the new generation of devices from portable music players to mobile phones to the new iPhone. A SoC packages much of the whole board of a Netbook into a single chip that specifically includes at least the microprocessor and graphics, resulting in a small and energy-efficient package. The Intel Atom line was not quite a SoC, though over time it would evolve to be one, at least in name. What made it possible to run Linux and Windows was the combination of compatibility with Intel instructions and the support for PC-style peripherals such as graphics and storage. Microsoft's version of Windows for ARM SoC was Windows Mobile, built on the aged Windows code base.

Intel's entry, or lack thereof, into mobile computing and building a system-on-a-chip components to power mobile phones contributed to the origin story for Atom. Intel had substantially invested in an attempt to bring the Intel x86 architecture (or IA, as they called it) to mobile phones. Famously, though, Intel ended up not collaborating with Apple on the iPhone, as CEO Paul Otellini felt Apple's required price was too low and by some accounts desire for control too high.[89] While the initial foray for Atom was aimed at OLPC, many would claim that Netbooks were simply an effort to make something out of the failed investment for mobile. Since they were fully compatible at the instruction set level with other chipsets, an idea was to build a new laptop—essentially to rescue their failed entry into mobile chipsets. Since these chips drew less battery power, were smaller in size, and less expensive, Intel decided to suggest OEMs create small and inexpensive PCs with them.

In essence, the Netbook arose out of a desire to make use of a low-end chip that originally was meant to compete with ARM and to be used for mobile. While it was compatible with Windows, it was by most accounts inadequate for modern Windows, especially when it came to graphics. The small screen size, while convenient as a demarcation for the Intel chip product line and Windows XP license, was also a necessity because the graphics chipset could not drive a much larger screen.

Nevertheless, Netbooks were flying off the shelves. They were the talk of the industry. Over the next six to 12 months, the sales of these low-end PCs skyrocketed to 40 million units a year—more than 15 percent of all PCs, which was exactly what OEMs loved, especially ASUS that made a big bet. Unfortunately for all involved, the profits were slim across the ecosystem, and worse, the exuberance was truly cannibalizing laptop sales, though not ASUS, which had the new, hot product and a much smaller laptop business. When I visited southeast Asia or Africa, for example, internet cafés had a half dozen Netbooks where a single PC once would have been—quantity of endpoints over quality of experience.

Over the course of 2008 leading up to mid-2009, Netbooks remained great sellers. Even if a Netbook was sold with Linux, the demand for Windows was such that pirated Windows XP that was hacked to fit on the available storage became the standard. That seemed to benefit Microsoft in the long run, I suppose. These PCs were seemingly falling from the sky in massive numbers and while the business side was worried about the pricing of Windows and piracy, the product side was happy with something new, finally. There were review websites entirely devoted to the Netbook craze, chronicling the latest developments. In a sense, what was not to love about low-priced computers if people were reasonably happy?

There was little Microsoft could or should do to thwart the momentum, especially because we did not want to lose to Linux. We would have loved nothing more than the likes of HP or Dell to work on Sony VAIO-style PCs that competed with Apple, but that was not to be for a few more years. The PC ecosystem was once again proving that a race to the bottom on pricing and experience was what drove it.

Over time Netbooks expanded in system specifications, OEMs constantly bumping up against the constraints both Intel and Microsoft put in place on what was a legit Netbook. Some added slightly larger screens, making them even slower because extra stress on the under-powered graphics chips. Some added full-size spinning disk drives. Some were able to be upgraded to 4GB of memory. The problem was that under the hood these were still Atom chips. They were not good PCs. Were they convenient, lightweight, and portable? Yes, but they were slow and had poor graphics. YouTube videos skipped frames and were jittery. Web sites that used Adobe Flash were mostly unusable. Games were too slow. Using Office was marginal at best. Even battery life was limited to three or four hours.

Netbooks, however, played an indisputably positive role in developing Windows 7. They institutionalized a low-end specification that was in-market and broadly deployed. We had to make Windows 7 work reasonably well on them.

The press had been needling Apple about lacking a low priced product to compete with the rapid rise of Netbooks, even well into 2009 as overall PC sales were flat but Netbooks leaped to 40 million units. Apple would not have anything to say for some time. (Source: CNET, Feb 27, 2009)

Peak Netbook could perhaps have been best described by questions about when Apple would make a Netbook, which Intel would have loved. Such an introduction would have legitimized the category. The mainstream business press just assumed Apple would enter the category because it needed growth, and it was missing out on the hottest new category selling tens of millions of units.

Steve Jobs's answer to Netbooks, in a uniquely Apple way, was the MacBook Air, which was announced in late January 2008 just after the Eee PC holiday season. Apple's answer to a $400 Netbook was a $1,799 premium Mac. Classic Apple. The "world's thinnest notebook," said Steve Jobs, and Walt Mossberg said it was "impossible to convey in words just how pleasing and surprising this computer feels in the hand."

It simply wasn't in Apple's thinking to release a sub-optimal product. Even the low-priced point products from Apple are fully capable with little compromise. Netbooks violated that core tenet of Apple and so there was no legitimate reason to expect anything other than for Apple to completely ignore this new category the way the industry defined it.

In April 2009, then Chief Operating Officer Tim Cook even took to their earnings call to trash talk Netbooks:

> *When I look at Netbooks, I see cramped keyboards, terrible software, junky hardware, very small screens. It's just not a good consumer experience and not something we would put the Mac brand on. It's a segment we would not choose to play in. If we find a way to deliver an innovative product that really makes a contribution, we'll do that. We have some interesting ideas.*[90]

At least through 2009, the MacBook Air remained Apple's answer to small, portable, and even low-priced computing.

There were, however, enough criticisms of the initial MacBook Air to allow PC makers to look the other way or actively market against it by pointing out the lack of ports and extensibility. In fact, they would continue this approach for several years, while Apple refined its new approach to making laptops. The result was rather crushing. PC elites quickly started running Windows on MacBook Air hardware simply because the hardware was so good, and Apple even provided instructions for how to do that. I can't even count the number of meetings with OEMs, email threads around Microsoft, and queries from the press I received, asking, "When will there be Windows PCs like the MacBook Air?"

The ecosystem stuck its collective head in the sand all while we rode Netbooks up and then, in a short time, straight back down. In hindsight, the Netbook runup hid the secular decline in PCs that had begun with the recession following the Global Financial Crisis. It would take years to recognize that, and a massive effort for the ecosystem, and Microsoft, to respond to the ever-improving MacBook Air.

Understanding and somehow addressing the relentless force driving the PC ecosystem to produce what most tech enthusiasts see as lesser quality devices (especially relative to Apple) remained one of our key challenges. Too many saw the rise of Netbooks as the answer to products from Apple while not being able or willing to respond directly. There was a fundamental difference between the volume platform appealing to the "masses" and the premium platform appealing to a smaller and more "well-off" segment of the market. That mental model held until the iPhone and MacBook Air. We had reached a tipping point.

With the iPhone, App Store, and MacBook Air Apple was not simply on a roll but the biggest roll of all time from 2006 through 2008.

At the same time, we were deep into building Windows 7 and starting to feel good about the progress. It was time to get out and share our optimism.

094. FIRST PUBLIC WINDOWS 7 DEMO

The second of three development milestones for Windows 7 was originally scheduled to end on March 26, 2008 which was eight months after the project start, Vision Day. We ended up finishing on May 9, which was a slip of 44 days. For any massive software project, this was fantastic. For Windows, it was doubly so.

It was even better than that. The new organization was starting to take hold. The product was emerging. The team was executing. We were building what we committed to build, and it was working. The "daily builds" were happening and by and large the team was running Windows 7 every day.

After two years in this role leading Windows, I finally felt like it would be OK to emerge and talk about what comes next. It is difficult to put into words the constant gnawing, sick-to-my-stomach feeling up until now wondering if we would deliver. We had definitely promised but for nearly 20 years I had seen leaders across the company say "the team is feeling good" or "we're making good progress" or "the milestone is complete" only to see the project unravel or simply recognize it was never actually raveled.

For months I had been under immense pressure from OEM partners, our OEM account managers, enterprise account managers, investor relations, Intel, retailers, not to mention SteveB, and many more to just articulate a ship date or some plan. Hardly a week went by without receiving a forwarded email detailing the costs of not disclosing what we were up to.

Yet I was perhaps irrationally concerned that I would put something out there only to have to recant or adjust what was said. Many told me I was being overly cautious. Many said that it is better to open up communication and worry about having to correct it later. I just couldn't shake the concerns. I felt Microsoft had one chance to make up for the issues with Vista.

Many perceived the Windows team was trying to become more like Apple and close off all discussion of a product until the moment it was announced. This was not the case at all. Windows is a different product, as described previously, and to bring it to market requires a huge ecosystem of support and that invests time and money. There's no way to surprise the market with Windows because an entire industry needs to know about it, prepare, and execute to bring new PCs, peripherals, and applications to market.

For months, Roanne Sones (RSones) and Bernardo Caldas (BCaldas) on the Ecosystem team had been in deep technical discussions with partners about what would come next but had not yet committed to a timeframe. Any hints of a specific schedule (or business terms such as SKUs or pricing) would immediately make it back to the business side of the house and then to SteveB's inbox. Even topics such as if there would be a 32-bit release (versus moving the ecosystem to 64-bit only) would have had broad implications for PC makers and Intel. We had to walk a fine line between being excellent partners and creating an external news cycle that impacted partners as much as us. We knew that release dates were the most likely to be leaked, and the most damaging. Finishing a product with a giant, hovering countdown clock had dogged many past Windows releases. Yet, the partners needed time to prepare, and we were closer to finishing than starting. Windows 7 would soon be fully disclosed with the OEMs.

When asked in any forum, we said our goal was to release Windows 7 "within three years of Vista." We were intentionally vague as to whether that meant release to manufacturing, available for enterprise download, first PCs in the United States, or some other market. Effectively, this gave us a buffer of about three months. And yes, that was sneaky, but it was the one concession I made to disclosure. I really hated that all people cared about was a date when a product was so much more than that. I understood, but still.

Then, in April 2008, BillG gave a speech, and inadvertently in one small part some believed he implied that Windows would finish in the following year. The press, who were there to hear about international finance at the Inter-American Development Bank meeting, ran with it and suggested Windows 7 would be ready much sooner than the previously planned three years from Vista. In fact, a year from April 2008 was sooner than our published schedule. That was not going to happen. Explaining that inaccuracy without stating the ship date was impossible.

It wasn't just that Bill said the next Windows would arrive "sometime in the next year or so." He also expressed his enthusiasm in what was certainly meant to be a throwaway line but came across to a tech industry desperate for any news when he said "I'm superenthused [sic] about what it [Windows 7] will do in lots of ways."[91]

We were close enough to completing the milestone that it was time to plan on officially talking to the press, who would be happy to talk off the record while also helping us to reduce the amount they would need to absorb all at once when it was time for stories to be written. In parallel the Ecosystem team began working with OEMs and ODMs on the detailed schedule and on software drops.

Our first stop, as it had been with every product I worked on since Office 95, was Walt Mossberg at *The Wall Street Journal*. Our meetings had become somewhat of a routine, perhaps for both of us, though by no means easy or predictable—I usually prepared an overly large amount of data to demonstrate how people were using our products out in the wild and hoped to both inform him while pushing for some positive recognition. Sometimes, yes, I went a bit overboard on the data. Walt was staunchly independent and would never say if I was persuasive, but he was always thoughtful in his questions and comments.

By this time, Katherine Boehret was joining Walt when he visited. She started with *The Wall Street Journal* out of college. By 2011 she had her own column called *This Digital Solution,* and also worked with Walt and Kara Swisher on the All Things Digital Conference, ATD. Katherine and Walt together were a formidable audience. They were both deep into products with their own unique perspective and would put up with absolutely no spin or marketing. They were advocates for their readers and strident in their desire to see PCs live up to their ease-of-use potential and played no favorites.

This meeting, about a month after BillG's speech, had a dual purpose. We wanted to at least try to diffuse some of what they had no doubt perceived (rightfully) as a mess with Vista without throwing Vista under the bus, while also setting the stage for Windows 7. If all went well, we might even secure time at All Things Digital that year for a quick Windows 7 demo at the end of an already scheduled BillG and SteveB joint interview.

It was stressful. It was Walt. And Windows 7 was not fully formed for reviewers yet. Joining for the meeting or parts of it would be Julie Larson-Green (JulieLar) for Windows, Dean Hachamovitch (DHach) representing Internet Explorer, and Chris Jones (ChrisJo) discussing Live Services.

Meeting in a conference room in building 99 with a half dozen demo laptops on the table, I started with our usual printouts of data, showing them an overview of Windows Vista in market. Walt's earlier review of Vista called it "maddeningly slow even on new, well-configured computers." Katherine's writings had been a bit less harsh, but not by much. I had to at least try to change their minds, but neither Walt nor Katherine was impressed. I took the time to talk about the landscape of PCs being sold and what was going on with laptops and Netbooks. In reviewing the original ASUS Eee PC, Mossberg concluded it was a "valiant effort, but it still has too many compromises to pry most travelers away from their larger laptops."[92] That led to a hot topic for all reviewers, but especially Walt who had praised the MacBook Air: When Windows would see a MacBook Air competitor? Walt, JulieLar, and I had discussed the MacBook Air at the Apple launch event months earlier.

My lack of an answer on behalf of PC makers was not satisfactory for them, or me. As described previously, the PC makers were much more focused on inexpensive devices like Netbooks and not eager to take on Apple or the premium PC market.

Browsers were much discussed in the late 2000s, though not the one from Microsoft. We didn't know it at the time but in hindsight it would be fair to assume they had been or were soon to be briefed on the forthcoming Google Chrome browser that shipped in late 2008. Still, Walt and Katherine wanted to know about Internet Explorer and privacy, a hot industry topic among a few, but especially them. We were woefully behind Firefox on core browsing capability, but we had a fantastic story to share about privacy features that DHach and team had developed, including blocking "tracking cookies." We showed them how mainstream sites, like *The New York Times*, were doing a poor job communicating to users how much information was being shared and with whom, but with only vague permission or even disclosure. We did not go as far as offering ad-blocking which many tech enthusiasts would have appreciated, but we did plan on releasing and showed a "Do Not Track" feature.

During development, a series of meetings with lobbyists from the advertising industry discussing the Internet Explorer privacy features had led to veiled threats about anticompetitive behavior by Microsoft against ad-supported Google. Such hints or even threats were common from anyone connected to the Washington or government communities. This was unrelated to the Consent Decree, though there were still a couple of years left on that agreement and the oversight meetings that I routinely attended. As a result, Internet Explorer 8's privacy features that were well received in this briefing would ultimately be scaled back due to an enormously frustrating push from the senior ranks of Microsoft's legal department to capitulate to the lobbying groups to avoid drawing attention of regulators and to spare our own nascent advertising business from having to comply with privacy requirements. Do Not Track was essentially shelved even before we started. Today, the capability is a core part of Apple's platform and the Microsoft Edge browser.

Our primary goal for the meeting was to showcase Windows 7. For the first time, we offered up a full disclosure of our overall goals and schedule. We trusted Walt and Katherine as we had built a great working relationship with them over the years, but, more importantly, because of their unmatched professional integrity.

After the requisite, but polite, reminder of the holes we had dug with Vista, we moved on to show some of the working features of Windows 7. After discussing Vista, Internet Explorer, and Live Services we moved to Windows 7 and the demonstration. Julie led a deep dive into our theme of "putting the end-user back in control."

We discussed improvements to the dreaded UAC experience. User Account Control was introduced with Vista as a mechanism to lock down a typical consumer PC and prevent software from being installed by accident. Unfortunately, the swift reaction to such a "nanny feature" was universal loathing. It became a symbol for the dislike of Vista. As it would turn out, this feature was only the first of what would become the typical smartphone experience in years to come but being first at getting between tech enthusiasts and their downloaded software also incurred their wrath. It was also the subject of one of the more biting "Get a Mac" television commercials from Apple. Shortly after Vista launch, the internet was filled with instructions to disable UAC, which we definitely did not appreciate. Julie demonstrated the improved, though still secure, experience, which was much smoother and well-designed and added options for enterprise admins and tech enthusiasts to control the feature.

Julie's demo succeeded in bringing together many concepts in the basic experience of launching programs and switching between running programs, and the array of distracting notifications and alerts. We were calling the collection of improvements to the Windows taskbar the new Superbar. With confidence, we compared the Superbar to the OS X dock, knowing we had solved problems that the dock had not.

We showed them the collaboration with PC OEMs on what would be new with Windows 7 PCs. The Ecosystem team had a long list of improvements to device drivers, supported hardware, and features to make the out of box experience for new PCs better for consumers.

And we had a surprise for them.

A big bet in Windows 7 was to implement a touch interface across the product, with features in the desktop experience and APIs for developers, as well as device and hardware management. We had been working closely with OEMs to define standards and configurations that would bring touch to Windows 7 PCs. OEMs were excited due to an entirely new engagement from MikeAng and team to enable quality touch in new PCs. They believed this would help differentiate from the Mac. We had an even bigger vision. We wanted this for all PCs eventually.

Months or more from broad pre-release and totally hush-hush, JulieLar demonstrated how we had moved applications from the original Surface table computer to PCs connected to desktop monitor touch panels. The Surface table PC, the original Surface, was a product developed in the Hardware division. It was not unlike an '80s arcade table, featuring a modified version of Windows combined with custom hardware enabling a new form of multitouch interaction. The table had found niche uses in Las Vegas, as information kiosks, and had been demonstrated by BillG at the previous year's ATD Conference. As it related to Windows 7, there were touch APIs and the foundation of hardware support. Our main demonstration was mapping software that zoomed in and out using multitouch (like on the new iPhone) along with a virtual touch keyboard, which combined would offer up many opportunities for developers. On Windows, touch went beyond just using fingers but also included the digitizer needed for pen computing. It was the only feature BillG consistently pushed for in the release.

While touch was a part of Windows 7 from the start, there were two reasons we chose to emphasize it as an early Windows 7 feature in this meeting. Showing touch early was counter-intuitive because it was totally new and could have easily remained secret, for an actual surprise.

First, we wanted to garner broad OEM support for touch which was a long-lead feature for them. No OEMs were selling touch screens which meant sourcing and developing a product was a significant investment and effort. Momentum from the conference demonstration would represent a key public commitment by Microsoft.

Second, there had long been ongoing rumors that Apple would add touch to Macintosh and with the success of iPhone this seemed more likely. Whether such rumors turned out to be true or not, the opportunity to both garner ecosystem support and get ahead of Apple while also showing off a BillG pet feature while he appeared at the conference seemed positive all around. To BillG and other pen advocates, it seemed "obvious" Macintosh would gain touch and handwriting support. Microsoft's Tablet PC was in market for years already and had not seen a competitive entry, so the logic went.

Neither Walt nor Katherine ever gave a thumbs-up reaction at a first showing, always reserving judgment until they used and wrote about a product themselves. Walt agreed to consider a demo of the touch features of Windows 7 at the ATD Conference a month later. They wanted to show more but we chose to keep the demo focused on what the ecosystem partners would value.

We had a lot of work to do, but we were nervous-excited.

With the ATD Conference pending, we were faced with a ticking clock, which meant we needed to disclose more details about Windows 7. The touch demo was too fragile and too elaborate to take on the road. We did not want to disclose details of the product without evidence, or, more importantly, a call to action for either developers or OEMs.

Adrianna Burrows (ABurrows after joining Microsoft) was the senior vice president assigned to the Windows account at the Waggener Edstrom communications agency. Adrianna drove the agency strategy for Office and was assigned to Windows when I moved. She was an astute communication and marketing pro, had a keen ability to create the right story at the right time, and was an elite distance runner and French speaker by upbringing. While she was at the agency, she was a key part of our senior leadership team. She was also the most competitive person I had ever known and would never accept second place.

People in communications rarely say not to talk when given an opportunity, at least that was the case in the 2000s. Reporters are going to write even without first-party commentary, and eventually whatever they write becomes more plausible than anything a company might later report. I had been quiet for too long. We were on the cusp of having a narrative created for us—one that would read something like: *Windows 7 is going to be a "minor" service pack rushed out the door to fix the woes of Vista, built on a smaller kernel, MinWin, as the key technology. While that might introduce some compatibility concerns, it would enable finishing the release in early 2009.*

Adrianna proposed a long form interview with a highly regarded Microsoft beat reporter, Ina Fried of the influential CNET. Ina was a thoughtful journalist with a wide-ranging understanding of the dynamics of the industry. She was widely read and by the right people. Adrianna was able to arrange to have a full transcript of an interview published along with Ina's story to reduce the risk of being edited. I thought that was a solid idea at that moment.

Adrianna created the perfect opportunity for us even though I didn't know what to say. More accurately, saying nothing was my comfort zone. While I never speak unprepared, I just did not work out answers that sounded credible for the questions I was obviously going to get asked.

I got on the phone with Ina, Adrianna right there with me in my office with the call on speaker. For an hour I did my best Muhammad Ali rope-a-dope. I acted as though I had been forced to make the call. I gave a lot of non-answers. I'm sure Ina was confused since we had initiated the interview. Adrianna was tensing up the whole time—I could see her eyes widen with each non-answer. The more I spoke, the deeper the hole I dug. My answers got shorter and my deflection increased—all I could think of was that I didn't want to talk yet because I was so unsure of what we would get done and when. I could not figure out why I was talking and what the call to action was for readers.

I was trapped. I felt like we talked for the sake of talking and lost sight of the lead up to the first demo as the purpose.

Ina's story ran the day after the call, right before Memorial Day, as we were heading out to the ATD in Carlsbad for our first public demonstrations of Windows 7. It was 3,000 words of me saying nothing.

The headline said it all: "In an exclusive interview, Steven Sinofsky offers up a few details on the new operating system and the rationale for why he is not saying more publicly."

Adrianna wanted to punch me. I had blown an opportunity. I felt bad, but the damage was far worse for the team, who were confused because the interview ended up pushing the needle back to opaque from translucent. I made a mistake and handled it wrong.

I learned the hard way that I should have either not done the call or done it well.

Fortunately, All Things Digital gave us a chance to undo the damage. Bill Gates and Steve Ballmer were to appear on stage together for one last time. The goal for Microsoft was to show an orderly turnover as Bill announced the end of the two-year transition from Chief Software Architect to non-executive Board Chair and would no longer work day-to-day at Microsoft. After questioning, they would turn the stage over to a "surprise" demo of Windows 7 from JulieLar.

Julie and a veritable force of a dozen people had been at work hardening the Windows 7 demonstration for ATD. All had been setting up the demo since the night before.

On stage, BillG and SteveB discussed the transition and answered questions about what would happen in a post-BillG Microsoft. Steve describes the early financial controls and conservative hiring approach Bill put in place that became the hallmark of Microsoft. There is a touching and relaxed retelling of the way Bill recruited Steve to join the company, including Steve's recollection of "a computer on every desk and in every home."

Later, in a pointed question, Walt asked Steve, "Is Vista a failure? Was it a mistake?"

"Vista is not a failure and it's not a mistake," SteveB said. "Are there things that we will continue to modify and improve going forward, sure. With 20/20 hindsight, would we do some things differently?" He told Walt and Kara undoubtedly, yes, but then added that Vista had sold a lot of copies.

Walt asked if Vista had damaged the Windows brand. Bill jumped in with, "Well, there's no product we've ever shipped, including Windows 95, that was 100 percent of what I wanted in the product...We have a culture that's very much about, 'We need to do better.' Vista gave us a lot of room for improvement." The audience, and especially Walt, laughed.

Then Windows 7 was up.

JulieLar walked on stage and did a slick, six-plus-minute demo. It was the product that we had always envisioned, executed from an off-the-shelf laptop as well as from a desktop with a currently in-market touch monitor running Windows 7 software. It was live and that was terrifying for all of us. Notably, the code was barely working—clicking or tapping in the wrong place could have been a disaster. Still, it was a smooth demo.

Walt and Kara were constantly reaching over Julie's shoulders and touching the screen to see what would happen. We had agreed to the scope of the demo and that we would not venture off and show or talk about other features.

Julie drew using a touch version of the venerable MS Paint and whisked through photo management, including "features anyone with an iPhone would be familiar with, such as two-finger zoom and slideshows."

At one point, Walt noticed that the taskbar (the Superbar we showed off at our HQ meeting previously) looked a bit different and asked about it. Julie replied, "You know we're not supposed to talk about that today."

The mapping application from Surface table PC was also shown but on Windows 7, including the live data for the Carlsbad, California, hotel we were in. The demo wrapped up with the playing of a multitouch piano application, which by coincidence was like one making the rounds on jailbroken iPhones. There was still no app store yet, but the technically savvy crowd figured out how to use the released developer tools to build apps and sneak them on to an iPhone.

Our demo was a success. Phew. Windows 7 was out there, at least in words, pictures, and videos.

The next step was getting pre-release code into the hands of developers.

095. WELCOME TO WINDOWS 7, EVERYONE

Seattle summers are notoriously difficult on product development. After a long spell of clouds and rains, the beauty and long days of Pacific Northwest summers arrive, neither are particularly conducive to coding.

Summer wasn't why I ended up here, but it certainly had an impact on me. On my first visit in 1989 during a dismal February, I saw the outdoor Marymoor Velodrome down the street from Microsoft and thought, this is going to be great. On TV it didn't look as difficult to ride as I eventually learned it was. I sort of rode it exactly one time and that was the day my bicycle arrived from Massachusetts.

But alas, product development demands don't end even with 15 hours of daylight.

It was going to get busy for the Windows 7 team. Our planned schedule called for the third development milestone to be complete by the end of summer 2008.

We were making progress, but the schedule was slipping. The code was getting better every week, but the overall game of schedule chicken that often plagued a large project was an historical concern. This was our first time as a new team going through this part of a product cycle. While we had a good deal of positive progress building a team culture, Windows was notorious for groups betting against each other's schedules and being less than forthright with their own.

When HeikkiK was running the Office 95 ship room, he declared that everyone should be working to finish first, not simply to finish second to last. We needed to get to the end of the milestone as a team working together without looking for one group to blame, since it is never one group. JonDe and I had this same concern.

Everyone spent the summer installing daily builds on every PC we could. At one point, I must have had eight different PCs between home and office and was installing on all of them nearly every day. Every night I was installing a new build at home while doing email and other routine tasks. Even though my home "service level agreement" called for no beta software, an exception was made for Windows 7.

I was working at two performance extremes. I went to Fry's Electronics and built my own "gamer" PC from the best components. I spent big bucks on a newfangled solid-state desktop drive (not common at the time), a crazy graphics card, fast memory, and the most ridiculous Intel chip available. I installed Windows 7. I was blown away by the speed as well as the noise and wind emanating from the mini-tower. Starting Word or Excel seemed instantaneous. Boot took low single-digit seconds. It reminded me of the first time I used a hard drive on my father's Osborne computer and how much faster it was compared to floppy disks. I used this PC when I sat at my desk at work, which wasn't often as I was always walking around the halls.

At the other end of the spectrum were Netbooks. To the degree I could, I had taken a fancy to the Lenovo Netbook, the IdeaPad S10, and carried it with me everywhere especially at my favorite breakfast place (Planet Java) or lunch place (Kidd Valley) where I did a lot of Windows 7 blogging. Every Netbook was close to identical on the inside, but the Lenovo had a good screen and a rugged exterior. I modified mine, replacing the spinning hard drive with a then non-economic solid-state drive to better emulate future laptops like the MacBook Air. It was my primary PC for writing blogs posts, email, spreadsheets, and browsing, and the like, which was most of what I was doing. When we finally got to the Professional Developers Conference, this was the PC I held up with a bright yellow "I'm a PC" sticker on it, stickers marketing created in a jiu-jitsu move embracing the blowback from the Apple TV commercials.

I was constantly on the lookout for memory consumption and the number of running processes, the signs of bloat in Vista—fewer processes and less memory were better. Each process was a critical part of Windows. The number of processes had soared with Vista, and each had overhead in complexity and performance. In contrast to Linux, Windows processes were much more substantial and important to track. Windows 7 was making impressive strides in reducing memory usage and process complexity. It served to make me feel connected to the engineering of Windows 7 and reminded me of counting bytes and seconds back in the day. I snapped screen shots of the Windows Task Manager and would bug JonDe and AlesH every couple of days.

Each day booting into a new build and seeing the progress was a great day. Each day revealed a crisis or challenge, but as a team everything continued to move forward.

Even though I was mostly an observer, the effort to improve performance was some of the best work of the release. It set a tone for making progress, but also for the ability of teams to work together. The conventional wisdom was that Windows Vista was inevitable and unavoidable as capabilities were added and the product grew which could not have been prevented. Windows 7 disproved that theory.

By midsummer, we had to slip the schedule based on our progress through M2 and M3. Originally our goal was to finish M3 and have a full beta in time for the previously scheduled Professional Developers Conference, PDC, in Los Angeles. We weren't where we needed to be, so we took about an eight-week slip. The build at the PDC would officially be pre-beta, terminology we just made up. This would be our last slip. JonDe and I were privately relieved at the degree of the slip, but frankly the team was excited to be clearly on track, relatively, for the first time in many years. Depending on your experience or the context, eight weeks can seem huge or literally nothing. It was nothing.

SteveB sent a memo to all of Microsoft outlining some of the work to date for the whole of the fiscal year. The company had made a lot of progress on many fronts. The topic that had occupied a great deal of discussion, and was a good portion of his memo, was Google and competing with it on the consumer front and the potential relationship with Yahoo. SteveB also described the emerging cloud strategy, and the fact that more would be shared on that topic at our upcoming PDC.

Fiscal year 2008 was quite a year for Microsoft. Revenue broke $60 billion and operating profit grew 21 percent to $22.5 billion. The numbers were incredible. Still, the concerns about the PC and catching up on consumer services dominated Wall Street's view. This memo was one of the early communications in a strategic shift to the cloud platform and you can feel the push-pull between cloud and the traditional model in the technology descriptions. It's important to say that it was still super early in the journey to the cloud for enterprise computing and the topic was not top of mind for customers, especially as the financial crisis began to take hold. In fact, the feeling that the cloud was architecturally inferior to private data centers was by far the most common customer belief. Their future enterprise computing model was a data center running servers using virtualization. In 2008, the idea that there would be something of a new cloud operating system was mostly a view held inside the halls of Google.

In the memo, SteveB announced that KevinJo was leaving to be CEO of Juniper Networks, and that JonDe and I, along with Bill Veghte (BillV) leading marketing, would report directly to Steve, a reporting structure that remained in place through the release without issue. This was a standard and expeditious way to handle a managerial change at this stage of a big product. Incidentally, Satya Nadella (SatyaN) had recently moved to manage Search and ads in March 2007 and would also report to SteveB in a similar move.

In the lead-up to the PDC we began blogging publicly about Windows 7. With the focus on tech enthusiasts, IT professionals, and the trade press, I created a blog called *Engineering Windows 7,* or *e7*. An extension of how we thought about blogging for Office 2007, the blogs were the primary first-party communication channel for the product. We authored long and detailed posts, thousands of words, about the implementation choices we were making and how we measured progress. We offered tons of data to describe real-world Windows use. Those were often my favorites posts. I authored posts but also introduced posts that other team members wrote, each expressing the design point of view and rationale. Many generated a great deal of dialogue and discussion and became news stories themselves. There wasn't really a Hacker News yet for Windows coverage, but the comments sections of many stories read just like Hacker News would have read. Tech enthusiasts loved to dispute the data provided then just as today.

While to some press the blogging came across as a carefully crafted corporate message, nothing was further from the truth. We were simply blogging. The posts did not go through any corporate machinery or apparatus. They were as authentic as they could be. And the tradition worked so well that after the PDC it became a significant part of the communication of Windows going forward.

There were two relevant industry announcements that at any other time would have caused a great deal of distraction. The PC world was entirely focused on the PC, to the exclusion of the world of mobile phones, and, to some degree, browsers were still distinct as a challenge to Windows because they still ran on Windows and had yet to incorporate much beyond rendering text and graphics. Yet both phones and browsers would have announcements that would radically alter the competitive landscape for Windows 7.

In June 2008 at Apple's WWDC (the World Wide Developer Conference, Apple's version of the PDC), Apple announced the much-anticipated and predicted iPhone SDK and App Store which was teased earlier in the year. Initially, it had 500 apps, small relative to PC apps, but that number would grow at an astronomical rate. More importantly, it solved many key problems that had plagued PCs. In the announcement, which was a short note from Steve Jobs posted to Apple's news site, he said "We're trying to do two diametrically opposed things at once—provide an advanced and open platform to developers while at the same time protect iPhone users from viruses, malware, privacy attacks, etc." This controversial change riled tech enthusiasts but also ushered in a new definition of computer, one that was safer and more reliable than anything a PC (or Mac) could offer.[93] The emphasis below is mine.

Third-party Applications on the iPhone

Let me just say it: We want native third-party applications on the iPhone, and we plan to have an SDK in developers' hands in February [2008]. We are excited about creating a vibrant third-party developer community around the iPhone and enabling hundreds of new applications for our users. With our revolutionary mulitouch interface, powerful hardware and advanced software architecture, we believe we have created the best mobile platform ever for developers.

It will take until February to release an SDK because ***we're trying to do two diametrically opposed things at once – provide an advanced and open platform to developers while at the same time protect iPhone users from viruses, malware, privacy attacks, etc.*** *This is no easy task. Some claim that viruses and malware are not a problem on mobile phones – this is simply not true. There have been serious viruses on other mobile phones already, including some that silently spread from phone to phone over the cell network. As our phones become more powerful, these malicious programs will become more dangerous. And since the iPhone is the most advanced phone ever, it will be a highly visible target.*

Some companies are already taking action. Nokia, for example, is not allowing any applications to be loaded onto some of their newest phones unless they have a digital signature that can be traced back to a known developer. While this makes such a phone less than "totally open," we believe it is a step in the right direction. We are working on an advanced system which will offer developers broad access to natively program the iPhone's amazing software platform while at the same time protecting users from malicious programs.

We think a few months of patience now will be rewarded by many years of great third-party applications running on safe and reliable iPhones.

Steve

P.S.: The SDK will also allow developers to create applications for iPod touch. [Oct 17, 2007][94]

The App Store also provided distribution and awareness to developers, a way to make money, and a way for Apple to vet apps that might be harmful to consumers. At the time the focus was on the fact that "30 percent goes to Apple." When we saw the store, though, we knew the change would be monumental. To find software for a PC, the best someone could have hoped for was a website such as download.com. There existed varying levels of trialware, freeware, spyware, and malware. Apple had solved the software distribution problem, made sure software was reasonably safe and high quality, and given ISVs a huge new avenue for creativity and money. All on the most exciting computer around, the iPhone. That was the bad news. The good news was that the world still viewed PCs and phones as totally different things.

The world other than Steve Jobs and Apple, as discussed in the previous section. History would later reveal through email discovery the internal conflict that surrounded opening the iPhone to developers so broadly. The success would also go far beyond even what Steve Jobs anticipated.

All that I could think was, *Time. I need more time.*

That was not all I thought. I also greatly admired what Apple was accomplishing. Like many who joined the Apps division in the 1980s, Macintosh was a crucial part of my early Microsoft work and the years before that. The old Mac ToolBox APIs are forever imprinted in my memories. Other than the die-hard fans, few generally acknowledged the consistent refinement and foresight in Apple's software design. Several of us on the team were "original" Mac third-party developers from the mid-1980s and had always admired not only the results but the patience of their process. The continuous iteration and complete execution of what they did was admirable. Apple's business in Macs was definitely not something we worried about, but their product execution was worrisome. I looked over their R&D spend and compared it to Windows and Office. In 2008, Apple for the first time eclipsed $1 billion in R&D for the year, a big uptick from the prior year, perhaps an indication of iPhone and iCloud ramp. The full Windows 7 team was spending about the same. There's a huge difference in R&D when it comes to having a full ecosystem but at the same time R&D for hardware is much more expensive. The main point is not only were they building breakthrough products, they were doing so remarkably efficiently compared to Microsoft.

The Mac might have been a better product, but Windows won, and the winning product becomes the better product in the market. It was not until the iPhone and SDK came to be that the true appreciation of all they had done with so relatively little was so broadly understood.

A more shocking announcement that hit closer to home came six weeks later. Google announced the Chrome browser with a blog post and a classically Googley online comic that accidentally dropped too soon. Chrome, ironically named due of the absence of user interface chrome, would prove to be monumentally disruptive to the browser world. Google had dramatically improved performance and security in browsing compared to IE 7 from Vista (or IE 6 that so many were running still) and current leader Firefox. They had committed to open source and brought an entirely new level of energy to the browser battle. In his blog post, Sundar Pichai (yes, then product manager for Chrome) wrote in a nod to antitrust that the "web gets better with more options and innovation. Google Chrome is another option, and we hope it contributes to making the web even better."[95] In some ways, we were straight back to 1996 again. This would be a huge problem for the newly reconstituted Internet Explorer team, both immediately and going forward. Within a short time, there was a massive share shift to Chrome. Much like Gmail, Google released a product, seemingly out of nowhere, into what was viewed as a stable space. And they took it over. It would be years before privacy, tracking, and all the "evil" stuff Google's browser would come to be, but at the time, a new competitive landscape was defined for IE. If our job was difficult before, it suddenly was even more so.

The PDC took place on October 27th at the Los Angeles Convention Center. Azure, the new name for Red Dog, was announced on the day one keynote. That proved to be both prescient and somewhat ahead of the curve for most attendees. Windows 7 was the second-day keynote and carried the bulk of the news for the show. In some ways the fact that most of the attendees did not seem to find Azure immediately useful made our jobs easier. Most attendees were still debating the proper way to pronounce Azure. The developer relations leader found the debate the night before particularly irksome as he was a Persian who had his own ideas of how to pronounce a word he claimed as native in origin. I was completely entertained by this late-night sideshow. Nevertheless, the fact that the attendees were somewhat puzzled by Azure compared to what they saw as vastly more interesting sessions on .NET,

Avalon, virtualization, or the Windows 7 desktop. The disconnect was a harbinger of the disruption challenges the entrenched Microsoft would face.

While the audience for the PDC was professional developers there to learn the latest in APIs, tools, and techniques from Microsoft, the front rows of the main hall were the all-too-familiar members of the press. Looking out from the stage, I could see all the stalwarts of Microsoft beat reporters and technology press who had been frustrated by the lack of information of Windows 7. We were doing a keynote for developers who spent a few thousand dollars to be at the show, but in reality we were putting on a show that needed to be understood by the mainstream media and conveyed through the expertise of the industry press.

Steve Jobs had upped the stakes with his spectacular keynotes, increasing pressure across the industry to put on a good show. The normal Microsoft keynotes, the kind pioneered by BillG, were long and detailed with complex architecture slides and many graphics. These were somewhat enhanced as we moved to enterprise computing with obligatory and infamous "partner videos" featuring senior IT professionals in front of architectural diagrams or racks of equipment extolling the virtues of Microsoft's strategy. The audience expected this type of keynote and expected us to write code on stage. By those measures, they keynote might disappoint.

Having said that, as we planned for my first keynote leading Windows, I knew that the biggest mistake I could have made would have been to try to emulate what I was not. Most importantly, I also had to find a way to apologize for Vista without throwing the product or team under the bus. I had to find a way to be excited about Windows 7, realizing we had holiday PCs with Vista still to sell. Above all, our announcement was for a pre-beta, not even an official beta, though it was ultimately a distinction without a difference.

For my part, I went with who I was—like Sammy Davis Jr. used to say, "I've gotta be me." The slides I showed were sparse and my words carefully chosen. While not one for grand entrances, I did choose "I Can See Clearly Now" by Johnny Nash as walk-on music. I was the only thing standing between the thousands of press and attendees, and seeing Windows 7 code. We knew people were there to see a demo, not a build-up or a long story. Just get to the clicks. I used just two minutes and not even 400 words then introduced JulieLar to step on stage and start clicking. I stepped down from the podium and remained upstage opposite Julie.

As soon as she brought up the screen on the monitor, people started taking pictures, some with their new iPhones, but most with Windows Mobile, and since they were live-blogging the event, we knew they were noting the build number that was visible at the bottom of the screen, confirming that our debate about what version of Windows we were working on would be part of the conversation. Within about a minute Julie got her first round of spontaneous applause and hoots. The demo was fantastic and every time she said "…works the way you want to," we could feel the excitement. She demonstrated all features with both a mouse and by using touch on a monitor, including showing an on-screen keyboard with predictive text and more. The bulk of the demonstration emphasized "putting you in control" of Windows.

Once she was finished, I stepped onto the center of the stage and got to say, on behalf of the entire team, something two years in the making.

"Welcome to Windows 7, everyone."

It was the perfect demo to introduce the product.

At some point in the keynote I needed address what everyone was waiting for which was what did Microsoft really think about Vista. While the press would no doubt take note, the credibility of what was said would rely on winning over the tech enthusiasts. More than any audience, the tech enthusiasts in the room were most disappointed in Vista and felt let down by the product. From March 2006 when I came to Windows, I promised to never be critical of what preceded me and I intended for that to be the case. It would have been so easy and so cathartic for the room to profusely apologize for Vista. It would have been equally wrong to pretend that we had not made some sort of mistake. I chose a path of subtlety and to acknowledge "feedback" in all its forms, including a few television commercials. With a slide titled "Transition from Windows Vista" I framed the work we had done since Vista released as providing context for the day's keynote:[96]

> *As we set out to build this release of Windows, we really did have to recognize the context with which we were releasing Windows 7 and developing it. And that's in transitioning from Windows Vista. We certainly got a lot of feedback about Windows Vista at RTM. (Laughter.) We got feedback from reviews, from the press, a few bloggers here and there. Oh, and some commercials. (Laughter.)*

As part of the session, we wanted to highlight some of the features that were specifically relevant to the developer and enthusiast crowd. I took a moment to show seven features (the number 7 was used a lot) that were chosen specifically to generate applause for the crowd including: 1. BitLocker disk encryption (previously in Vista Ultimate), 2. Mounting VHD (a virtualization feature), 3. High DPI (support for really big monitors and normal sized text), 4. Magnify (an assistive technology for low vision that is also useful for product demonstrations), 5. Remote Desktop across dual monitors (the first live dual monitor demo we ever did), 6. Taskbar Customization (anything with customization is a pleaser), 7. Action Center Customization UAC/Notifications, the improvements over Vista for enthusiasts.

There was a clear call-to-action for developers including moving to 64-bits, using Windows touch, and more, but mostly to download and install Windows 7 pre-beta. People were doing that as soon as the lights faded.

We wanted the keynote to be easy and approachable, not usually the norm at the PDC. That also meant we would leave out a good deal of the team's work and new features present in the beta build. To that end we created a massive "Product Guide" for the trade press. We would also follow that up with a workshop for them to attend where they would have a chance to ask questions directly of the product leaders. The full product guide ran 119 pages! The team promised and delivered, and you can see this from the prominence of the "Engineering Focus Areas" in the guide which were taken straight from the product vision and mock press release.

While we would not normally expect long-form reviews and deep dives in a pre-beta, Windows 7 was generating so much interest that the tech press was filing tons of stories as were individual bloggers who drilled into every aspect of change from Vista. YouTube was filled with demos created in short order. Windows 7 was the top of Techmeme, and not for messing up.

An example of the coverage was ActiveWin, a Windows-focused outlet, that wrote over 13,500 words plus screen shots on the pre-release. Andre Da Costa wrote the piece, releasing it on October 31 as the conference ended. They dove into seemingly every detail, even including their summary of the key goals of the release:[97]

Key Goals:

- *Under-promise and over deliver*
- *Reduce Compatibility problems and bring investments in Vista forward*
- *Reduce disk foot print and memory foot print*
- *Improve performance*
- *Secure, predictable*
- *Make the Windows and PC Experience easier*
- *Exceptional hardware and software support*
- *Bring future releases to market faster*
- *Personalized experience that defines you*
- *Superior mobility through reliable performance, power management*

ActiveWin concluded better than anything we could have written ourselves. Promise and deliver.:

> *It's safe to say I am overwhelmed, overjoyed and most of all excited about Windows 7. This is the release of Windows everybody has been waiting for, it's what Vista was meant to be and beyond that. Windows 7 puts the user first; it's about going back to the fundamentals of what an operating system must do. Managing and maintaining your PC is exceptionally seamless in Windows 7 and users will appreciate the tremendous improvements and advancements this update will offer on both existing and new hardware form factors in the future. Windows Vista set the foundation for a lot of what is happening in Windows 7 today. Windows 7 makes security Essential, but not aggressive like Windows Vista. The improved UAC will no doubt give consumers confidence in this feature, just the fact that you can tweak it to a certain degree is a welcome change. Businesses will appreciate the improvements to how the OS is managed and deployed while mobile users can get better experiences between their work and home environments. Home Networking has finally reached a level of ease of use that will make even the novice to make those PCs in the home talk to each other. There is still a lot of work to be done as this early glimpse shows. But Microsoft is on the right path with Windows 7, focusing on ease of use, compatibility, better ways of interacting with the PC and managing the personal data. This is an upgrade I am looking forward to and you should too.*

Posts on Windows 7 experiences across all sorts of different hardware appeared. Engadget, everyone's favorite tech blog, tried Windows 7 on an ASUS Eee PC writing "just as Microsoft demonstrated, the relatively lightweight Microsoft OS required just 485MB of RAM when Windows 7 was fully loaded, sans applications of course. Hot."[98]

The article's title was even great for all the work the team put into this specific metric, "Lightweight Windows 7 pre-beta on Eee PC 1000H looks very promising." I can personally confirm that memory usage number.

As a manager of a giant product and team there are, honestly, few truly rewarding moments that are also deeply personal. Nearly all the time there's worry about how the team is doing and if they are finding the joy they deserve. October 28, 2008, was one of those exceedingly rare moments for me.

On to RTM…

096. ULTRASEVEN: LAUNCHING WINDOWS 7

The months after the PDC were extremely intense. We had set out to promise and deliver, but the success of the PDC had managed to inflate expectations. These were not false expectations—the use of the product was widespread and broadly satisfactory. That success is what raised expectations. PC makers, Wall Street, third-party developers, and enterprise customers knew the product we had to deliver and were just impatient.

We made a significant number of changes from M3 to beta. With our improved engineering system changes were made in a controlled and collaborative manner. Each change was discussed by many people and then the code change reviewed—no holes were punched in the wall. With each passing day it was more difficult to make changes while we aimed for stability of the beta. The most important thing about shipping a beta is not that it is perfect but that it ships in a known state. If something isn't right that's OK, as long as it's known. In the case of Windows 7, we knew work and bugs remained but were highly confident that millions of people would try out the beta and have a great experience.

That methodical crawl to beta went on for weeks, each day making fewer changes and calmly making it to sign-off. Then it was time to ship the beta.

On January 8, 2009, at CES, the Consumer Electronics Show, in Las Vegas, SteveB announced the availability of Windows 7 beta. The venue and the announcement from the CEO made this a significant worldwide event. It was covered on CNN, BBC, and more. That was exciting and even felt a bit like old times for a moment.

I watched from back in the green room because we were getting ready to turn on the web site for download and had no idea what to expect. While the internet was old news, downloading a gigabyte DVD image was hardly routine, especially from home and not something the internet was yet equipped to handle reliably.

To have some sense of control, we set a limit of 2.5 million downloads. Back then, before everyone had gigabit internet at home, a massive gigabyte download was something that would stress out the internet. As the keynote was going on we watched downloads begin. They quickly reached our limit while the keynote continued. A few calls to Redmond and we removed the throttle and began to rewrite our press releases with ever-increasing numbers. We extended the beta downloads through the end of January and had many more millions of installs than downloads as the download made it to all sorts of alternate and backup sites. We also learned a lesson in distributed computing that day.

For the beta we issued unique product registration keys which became the scarce resource. We soon removed the limits on activating those keys as well. While the download site was structured to choose 32 – or 64-bit along with locale to then generate a key, many figured out the URL that went directly to the 2.5GB download and passed that along. We just didn't want to be overwhelmed with Watson and SQM data so capped the release at 2.5 million. That was silly but at least we received an indication of excitement. There was a lot!

Every day we tracked bugs with Watson and observed usage with SQM. Hardware vendors were providing updated device drivers that were anxiously downloaded by millions of testers, many seeing new drivers arrive automatically by Windows Update. More new PCs would arrive to be qualified. More legacy hardware would be retested. More of the over 100,000 apps in the wild would be checked for compatibility. More enterprise customers would tell us that they were anxious to deploy Windows 7.

Many reviewers chose to review the beta as though it was final or at least something regular people might care about. It would be easy to gloss over this but for me it was an important part of promise and deliver. It had been a very long time, perhaps never, when a first beta for Windows was considered broadly usable and also had customers asking if it was OK to deploy even more broadly. Promise and deliver.

David Pogue, hardly a fan of Windows, practically filled an entire page of *The New York Times* with his review "Hate Vista? You May Like Microsoft's Fix" where he concluded "For decades, Microsoft's primary strategy has been to put out something mediocre, and then refine, refine, refine, no matter how long and no matter what it costs, until it succeeds. That's what's exciting about the prospect of Windows 7. It's Windows Vista – with a whole heck of a lot of refinement."[99] Microsoft was back to making sure it got products right.

In *The Wall Street Journal*, Walt Mossberg said in another front page of the business section review "Even in beta form, with some features incomplete or imperfect, Windows 7 is, in my view, much better than Vista, whose sluggishness, annoying nag screens, and incompatibilities have caused many users to shun it. It's also a serious competitor, in features and ease of use, for Apple's current Leopard operating system."[100] He also posted a video review as part of some of his more recent work creating video reviews.[102]

All we needed to do was finish.

By July 13, 2009, build 7600 was pronounced final and signed off on by GrantG and DMuir, the test leaders for WEX and COSD.

Windows 7 was ready for manufacturing.

July 9, 2009 was also my 20th anniversary at Microsoft and the team help me to celebrate by dressing like me—jeans, v-neck sweater, t-shirt. At least I was predictable.

Shortly thereafter at the sales kickoff in Atlanta, the annual MGX, we surprised the global field sales force and created a media moment when SteveB, KevinT (COO), and I held up a "golden master" DVD (a gold DVD), symbolically signing it as we announced that Redmond had signed off on the Windows 7 RTM build. It was a release that 10,000 people worldwide had contributed to and would likely end up on over 1 billion PCs. It was complete with another photo of me looking uncomfortable celebrating with SteveB on stage at the sales meeting. The sales meeting was always a country-mouse/city-mouse moment for me.

Just as soon as that excitement was over, Microsoft announced what turned out to be the worst earnings in corporate history with a 17% drop in quarterly revenue in July 2009 the end of the fiscal year. [103] The tough part was we knew this was coming while we were on stage, which made our celebration much less about the past and more about hope for the future. While many would blame the economy or Vista and some would even cite the recently announced Google Chrome OS (the predecessor to the Chromebook), the truth was much more secular in nature. PC makers were struggling on the bottom line as the 40 million Netbooks as exciting as they were lacked profit.

The astronomical rise in Netbook unit sales discussed in the previous section led many to assume a bullish future. In fact, Netbooks masked a secular decline in PC sales. We would know more as the year progressed as new PCs were sold with Windows 7 during holiday season 2009.

After the celebration, the team collectively exhaled. It was August and time for vacations, but we didn't have a lot of time to waste. Come September, we had to get the team fully engaged to plan what was coming next or it would be a massive effort to regain momentum.

Our team of administrative assistants outdid themselves with a wonderful ship party held on the activity fields in Redmond. In contrast to other Windows events, I would say this one was less eventful and even comparatively subdued, but still enormously fun for the team. We had custom cakes and cupcakes, tons of food, family-friendly games, craft beers contained to a two-drink limit within an enclosed area, and even Seattle hometown favorite *The Presidents (of the United States)* as the special musical guest. They took their popular song "Cleveland Rocks" and wrote the lyrics as "Microsoft Rocks." I still have a bootleg recording of that.

The competitive issues we were facing weren't going away. The organization was about to change and clarify responsibility for dealing with those.

Launching Windows 7

We had a fantastic foundation to build upon and all we needed to do was deliver an odd-even result—meaning a good release after the Vista release—and each of our core constituencies would breathe a sigh of relief. Looking outward, however, it was obvious that the world was a very different place than when we started Windows 7. It was not clear any of those constituencies or even our own team were prepared.

There was still a product to officially launch, but not before some realignment at the top of the organization.

Bill Veghte (BillV), who had started at Microsoft right out of college and had overseen Windows 7 marketing through to launch planning, decided after two decades with the company that he wanted an opportunity to run a business end-to-end and announced his intention to depart Microsoft. After a transition he would join Meg Whitman at Hewlett Packard. With that, SteveB wanted to put all of Windows under one leader and asked me to do that. He really wanted to elevate the job title which I pushed back on because of the way Microsoft was structured (and remains so) we did not really have what most consider true ownership of a business. Nevertheless, that was the origin of the job title of divisional president.

One of my first tasks was to hire a marketing leader to take over from BillV, one who would best represent the collaborative culture we aimed to create. I wanted to bring finance and marketing together under one leader because the Windows business uses billions of dollars in pricing actions to fund marketing through OEMs. Tami Reller (TReller) had been the finance leader for the Windows business, reporting to the corporate CFO. When she joined Microsoft 10 years earlier following the Great Plains acquisition where she had been leading marketing. I got to know her then as the acquisition fell under my then manager, Jeff Raikes (JeffR.) She was the perfect combination of marketing and finance leadership for a business where those went hand in hand and brought a great deal to our management team.

Microsoft wanted (needed) a big launch for Windows 7 and so did the industry. As had become a tradition for me, I wanted to spend the launch in Asia while my peers led the US event. My connection to my Microsoft family in Japan, China, and Korea ran deep and the business for Microsoft in those countries was huge. I couldn't be in all places at once, so I chose to attend the launch in Japan. No one loves a retail launch more than Japan.

I arrived two days before the October 22, 2009 launch. I never worked harder at a launch event. From first thing in the morning (easy because of the time change) until well past midnight (well supported now with Modafinil) because of excitement at retail stores, we did press visits, interviews, broadcasts, met with customers, and more. We'd shuttle from event to event in a Japanese microvan—all of us in our blue suits and ties with a stack of name cards.

For years, even way back when I worked for BillG, I had been going to Yodobashi Camera in Akihabara (and Shinjuku) to see what Japanese consumers were buying and to buy assorted USB and power cables that are exactly the length I need. The size of the Yodobashi flagship is unimaginable. The evening before the event we got an incredibly cool behind-the-scenes tour of the store, getting a look at the entire operation at night as they prepared the signage that would blanket the store for our event there the next day, such as the big decals that covered the walls of the 5-story escalator. As someone who grew up in the shadow of Walt Disney World, the underground tour of Yodobashi was much like the underground of Disney, and about the same number of people visit each year I was told.

The team put on an outdoor event at the front of the store the evening of the launch with all sorts of famous-in-Japan anime/cosplay actors and tech celebrities. And when the first copy was sold that evening, we did a press event right there at the front of the store. All along the main street of the Akihabara Electric Town, Chuo Dori, there were events in front of the many stores selling PCs and software.

Microsoft Japan, MSKK, had come up with a crazy promotional partnership with Burger King. The chain created a seven-layer Burger King Whopper to celebrate Windows 7. It was five inches tall (13cm) with seven patties totaling 1¾ pounds (791g) of beef. It was unfathomable, even for a no-carb, protein person like me. The first 30 customers got to buy the burger for ¥777, or about $9 at the time. The launch team and I snuck over to the Burger King around the corner from Yodobashi and ordered the monster burger. None of us could eat it elegantly or even try to finish it, but we got some hilarious team photos of the attempt and general celebration.

At a hotel ballroom, we held the main launch event for the press, featuring all the new PCs from Japan PC makers. The event featured an *Ultraman* theme. Why? I knew about the movies but was not a huge follower. What I learned was that *Ultraseven* was the third installment of Ultraman from the late 1960s. It was still wildly popular in some circles in Japan. The launch had a cast of people doing choreographed battle scenes in Ultraseven and Ultraman outfits. It was something to see. I filed this away for another *Lost In Translation* memory.

MSKK hosted a both a casual user group meeting and a formal business launch as well. At the user group meeting we did demos and gave away a bags of Windows 7 logo gear among a series of demo stations at a cool Akihabara exhibition space down the street from Burger King. I wore a super cool Windows 7 windbreaker which I still have.

The business launch was a formal ceremony highlighting the broad support of both hardware and software for the launch. Joining Microsoft was the head of Dell Japan. Together with a group of MSKK employees and partners we participated in the traditional celebration *kagami-biraki* or cracking open a rice barrel with big wooden mallets.

I've had the privilege of experiencing many product launches in Asia, but this time, for Windows 7, it was next level. MSKK is a gem of Microsoft. When I am lucky enough to be in Tokyo, even years and years later, walking around Akihabara I have the warmest and most vivid memories of the launch and my friends from MSKK. And sometimes my stomach hurts a bit thinking about the Burger King, which recently closed just before the pandemic. The news coverage of the event in Tokyo which was amplified across the important Asian markets was wonderful.

Our confidence was high heading into reviews, which broke with availability of the product and new PCs in retail stores—we had plenty of positive reviewer experiences and no deep concerns. That's what came from being not just in beta but running as the primary OS on reviewers' and enthusiasts' PCs for months. We risked a reviewer becoming somewhat bored or even cynical with the release simply because there was little new from the beta and no product drama to speak of. Hundreds of positive stories broke across print and TV. Local reporters did a lot of product reviews and buyers' guides at that time. Waggener Edstrom worked tirelessly in the United States to feed them information and support.

Walt Mossberg's review evoked a positive tone that started in January with the beta release. For his RTM review he said, "Bottom line: Windows 7 is a very good, versatile operating system that should help Microsoft bury the memory of Vista and make PC users happy." The headline read, "A Windows to Help You Forget: Microsoft's New Operating System Is Good Enough to Erase Bad Memory of Vista."[104] There was little more we could ask for in a review.

Ed Baig of USA Today and one of the most widely read reviewers made it clear how positive he was on the product when he said "What you'll notice is that Windows 7 is snappier than its predecessor, more polished, and simpler to navigate. Screens are less cluttered. It has better search. Windows 7 rarely nags.…It sure seems more reliable so far."[105]

Windows 7 was the first major release of Windows not to double the requirements for memory and disk space. While the box maintained the same requirements (also a first) in practice the reduction in memory usage and focus on Task Manager paid off handsomely. As much as we were proud of the business success, the engineering success of Windows 7 was among the most significant in company history and the reviews reflected this improvement in core software engineering competency. JonDe brought his engineering excellence to all of Windows.

Major PC makers used the time from sign-off on the build to the October launch event to prepare the first Windows 7–ready PCs and get them into stores for holiday sales, including Black Friday in the United States.

Industry analyst firm Gartner declared the "recovery of the PC market on a global level," with preliminary numbers showing a 22.1 percent increase over the previous year. Their quarterly analysis was effusive relative to their own reports just months earlier that were doom and gloom. More than 85 million PCs were sold in the fourth quarter of 2009, up more than 10 million units from 2008. This even though we were in the midst of a global recession. One year earlier, the top line was that PC sales had crashed. By the end of the first quarter, Gartner would upward revise their forecasts for 2010 to almost 370 million units, growing nearly 20%. The primary reason was that mobile computing, including Netbooks, was on fire. Gartner concluded "It was the strongest quarter-on-quarter growth rate the worldwide PC market has experienced in the last seven years."[106]

It would be incorrect to assume cause and effect relative to Windows 7. There existed pent-up demand for new PCs to replace aging ones. Windows Vista had caused many, both at home and at work, to hold off buying new PCs, and the recession further slowed those decisions. Windows 7 brought many people back into the market. The shift to mobility was helping PC units, but the low cost of Netbooks hurt the profits of the major PC makers.

The competitive forces were real. Apple was doing very well in the US (and Japan) and finished the year selling 24% more units year over year. The strength in consumer sales was the headline supported by the so-called consumerization of IT, where consumers were buying their own preferred computers to do work rather than rely on stodgy corporate Windows PCs that were slower, heavier, and burdened with IT software.

It felt, at least to me, that I'd been holding my breath for more than three years.

I walked through Meiji Shrine and Garden early the morning of my flight home, a travel day tradition and one of my favorite places on earth. The world's economy was still in shambles from the Global Financial Crisis. The PC sales everyone was excited by were obviously juiced by the start of an economic recovery and by Netbooks. These were not going to last. When it came to Netbooks, the major OEMs were anxious to exit the market and return to their view of normal. The problem was, as it became clear, Netbooks were additive to a shrinking market. Consumers wanted portability. They were willing to try Netbooks, but the product could not meet expectations.

As the Narita Airport customs officer stamped my passport and I walked through the turnstile, I could finally exhale. I think my stomach still hurt from the attempt at the seven-layer Whopper. Everyone else was heading back from the New York launch events and, other than the coverage I read, I don't remember if we even took the time to share stories.

I remember having the same feeling I had when Office 2007 finished. As happy and proud as I was, it felt like the end of an era. With the huge shift happening in PC sales, PC makers, the internet and cloud, mobile phones, there was no denying we were in another era. When I looked at Windows 7, I did not have a view of "look what more we could do" as much as "we've done all we can do." With the extension of Windows XP years beyond its intended lifecycle, I knew that with Windows 7 we had built a version of Windows that would continue to be used and appreciated for a decade or more. That would offer us a chance to go in a new direction and consider how to build products for a new world.

When National Public Radio, NPR, reviewed Windows 7 in a very positive review, even the introduction espoused the end of the operating system, saying:

> *We are in the modern world now and, while Windows continues to be the default OS, everyone is talking about Mac OS X, Linux and the second coming of, wait, no, just the much-anticipated arrival of Google's Chrome OS.*
>
> *The future is the Web, not the OS, and everyone knows it.*[107]

What I do remember more than anything was talking to members of the team in the hallways, at meetings, remote offices, or over email throughout the course of the release. No matter what was going on and how difficult things got, I will always cherish all the people who shared their feelings about doing some of the best work of their careers—thoughts I still hear even as I write this. It was incredibly rewarding to hear. That wasn't about me, but about the system and the plans put in place by the team of leaders we assembled. The Windows team was a new team. It was so ready to take on new challenges.

With RTM everyone on the team received their ceremonial copy of Windows 7. It is nice to have something to put on a shelf reminding each of us of the project and what we accomplished. For many, the next stop is the Microsoft Store to get upgrade copies for friends and family—another Microsoft holiday tradition.

The growth in mobility and demand for quality played right into Apple's strengths, though not at first glance. The market continued to pressure Apple on low prices and did not see the weakness we did when it came to Netbooks. On the heels of the Windows 7 launch, Apple released several new Get a Mac commercials. Among them was the segment "Promises" which reiterated all the times at new releases of Windows when Microsoft claimed the new release would not have all the problems of the old release. This one wasn't accurate, but that didn't matter.

In fact, Steve Jobs and Apple had a product in mind even more disruptive to the PC than the iPhone or MacBook Air…while we were just starting the next Windows release.

2010

2010: Apple has its resurgence with the MacBook Air and suddenly Macintosh emerges as real competition, while the iPhone adds apps and becomes a wildly successful platform. We decide it's time for big bets, transformations, and putting an end to having past versions of Windows be the biggest competitors to new ones. Across web browsing, Windows 7, Office 2007 and a vast ecosystem of software and hardware, the PC has arguably reached peak PC, selling over 300 million units. Only in hindsight will Microsoft know if the PC was at the end of an era or will be reborn, depending on the choices we make.

097. A PLAN FOR A CHANGING WORLD

In the summer of 2012, I was sitting across from BillG at the tiny table in the anteroom of his private office on the water in Kirkland. The sun was beaming into my eyes. In front of me was one of the first boxes of Microsoft Surface RT, the first end-to-end personal computer, general-purpose operating system, and set of applications and services designed, engineered, and built by Microsoft. In that box sat the culmination of work that had begun in 2009—three years of sweat and angst. After opening it and demonstrating, I looked at him and said with the deepest sincerity that this was the greatest effort and most amazing accomplishment Microsoft had ever pulled off.

Later that same week, I had a chance to visit with Microsoft's co-founder, Paul Allen (PaulA), at his offices at the Vulcan Inc. headquarters across from what was then Safeco field. I showed him Surface RT. I previously showed him Windows 8 running on desktop using an external touch monitor. At that 2011 meeting he gave me a copy of his book *Idea Man: A Memoir by the Cofounder of Microsoft* and signed it. Paul was always the more hardware savvy co-founder, having championed the first mouse and *Z-80 SoftCard*, and had been pushing me the whole release of Windows 8 on how difficult it would be to get performance using an ARM chipset and on the challenges of hitting a low-cost price point. Years earlier, Vulcan Inc. built a remarkably fun PC called *FlipStart*, which was a full PC the size of a paperback novel. Surface RT with its estimated price of $499, $599 with a keyboard cover, and a fast and fluid experience, resulted in the meeting ending on a high note. I cherished those meetings with Paul. I also shared with Paul, proudly, my view of just how much we should all value the amazing work of the team.

What I showed them both was the biggest of all bets. While not "stick a fork in it" done, by mid-2012 Microsoft seemed to have missed the mobile revolution that it was among the first to enter 15 years ago. In many ways Surface RT set out to make a new kind of bet for Microsoft—a fresh look at the assumptions that by all accounts were directly responsible for the success of the company. Rethinking each of those pillars—compatibility, partnerships, first-party hardware, client-computing, Windows user-interface, and even Intel—would make this bet far bigger and more uncomfortable than even betting the company on the graphical interface in the early 1980s. Why? Because now Microsoft had everything to lose, even though it also had much to gain.

With Windows 7, we knew we had a traditional release of Windows that could easily thrive through the full 10-year support lifecycle as we had seen with Windows XP. Windows 7 would offer a way to sustain the platform as it continued to decline in relevance to developers and consumers, while extracting value from business customers with little incentive to change.

Microsoft needed a new platform and a new business model for PC makers, developers, and consumers. The only rub? Any solution we might propose wasn't something we could A/B test or release pieces at a time experimentally. Windows was the standard and wildly successful. It wasn't something to experiment on.

While the company was 100 percent (or more) focused on Windows 7, we had started (drumroll for the code name please) *Windows 8* planning five months earlier. We had the next step, a framing memo from me first. Then we had a planning memo from JulieLar, ready to go as soon as we all caught our collective breath after the release—no real time to celebrate more, and certainly no downtime.

Technology disruption is often thought of at a high level along a single dimension, but it is far more complex. Consider Kodak's encounter with digital photography, Blockbuster's battle with DVD-by-mail, or the news business's struggle with the web. Great memes, sure, but one layer down each is a story of a company facing challenges in every attribute of their business, and that is what is interesting and so challenging.

Digital photos were more convenient for consumers, that was true. But also, the whole of Kodak was based on a virtuous cycle of innovation developed by chemical and mechanical engineers, products sold through a tightly controlled channel, and an experience relying on a 100-year-old tradition of memorialized births, graduations, weddings, and more. At each step of technology change to digital images, another major pillar of Kodak was transformed, sliced, and diced in a way Kodak could not respond. The magical machinery of Kodak was stuck because not one part of its system was strong enough to provide a foundation. Kodak didn't need to also enter the digital market. The only market that would come to exist was digital. The only thing that made it even more difficult was that it would take a decade or more to materialize as a problem, and that during that time, many said, "Don't worry. Kodak has time."

While figuring out what to do next for Windows, we saw BlackBerry facing a "Kodak moment." BlackBerry was not just a smartphone, but a stack of innovations around radios, a software operating system optimized for a network designed for small amounts of data consuming little power, a business model tuned to ceding control to carriers, and a keyboard loved by so many. In 2009, BlackBerry still commanded almost 45 percent of the smartphone market, even though the iPhone had been out since 2006. That led many to find a false comfort in the near term and to conclude BlackBerry would continue to dominate. Apple's iPhone delivered a product that touched every pillar of BlackBerry, not only BlackBerry the product but BlackBerry the company. Sure, Apple also had radio engineers, but they also had computer scientists. Sure, Apple also worked with AT&T, but Apple was in control of the device. And Apple was, at its heart, an operating system company. BlackBerry had some similar elements up and down the entire product stack, but it wasn't competitive. At its heart, BlackBerry was a radio company. BlackBerry seemed to have momentum, but market share was declining by almost 1 percentage point per month.

The smartphone, iPhone and Android in particular, was disrupting Windows. Though, not everyone thought that to be the case. Some said that phones did not support "real work" or "quality games." The biggest risk to a company facing disruption is to attempt to dissect disruptive forces and manage each one—like add touch or apps to a BlackBerry with a keyboard. The different assumptions and approaches new companies take only strengthen over time, even if eventually they take on characteristics of what they supplant. The iPhone might never be as good as the PC at running popular PC games, but that also probably won't matter.

I'd lived through graphical operating systems winning over character mode, PC servers taking over workloads once thought only mainframes could handle, and now I found myself facing the reality that browsers could do the work of Windows, relegating Windows to a place to launch a browser and not even Microsoft's.

Every aspect of the Windows business faced structural challenges brought on by smartphones. Compounding the challenge, Apple was competing from above with luxurious and premium products vertically integrated from hardware to software. Google, with Android and Chrome, was competing from below with free software to a new generation of device makers. The PC and the struggling Windows phone were caught in the middle, powerless to muster premium PCs and unable to compete with a free open-source operating system.

The browser had already shifted all new enterprise software development away from the hard-fought victory of client-server computing. Anyone who previously thought of building a new "rich client" application with Visual Basic or some other tool was now years into the transition to "thin client" browser software. The Windows operating system was in no way competitive with smartphone operating systems. The way to develop and sell apps had been reinvented by Apple. The Win32 platform was a legacy platform by 2009, the only debate was how long that had been the case. A legacy platform does not mean zero activity, but it does mean declining and second or third-priority efforts.

The partnership between the Windows operating system and hardware builders had fundamental assumptions questioned by Android. OEMs supporting Android not only received the source code but were free to modify it and customize it to suit their business needs. That was exactly what Microsoft fought so hard against in the DOJ trial. The touch-based human interaction model developed by Apple and the large and elegant touchpad on Mac were far more approachable and usable than what was increasingly a clunky mouse and keyboard or poor trackpad on Windows. The expectations for a computer were reset—a computer should always be on, always connected, never break or even reboot, free from viruses and malware, have access to one-click apps, while easy to carry around without a second thought. That supercomputer in your pocket is connected to built-in operating system services providing storage, backup, privacy, security, and more. Like Kodak, many said to slow down, that change would not happen so quickly. Many said we could "add this" or "change that." But it was not that simple, nor was it going to be that easy. The market was moving quickly.

The march to the next billion shifted, in the blink of an eye, to smartphones and soon non-Windows tablets, entirely skipping the PC. The entrenched PC customers were as excited as ever to upgrade to Windows 7 by buying a new PC or upgrading their existing PC. Everything new in Windows 7 was viewed through the lens of the past. How did we used to do that and did Windows 7 make it easier? Those skipping the PC didn't concern themselves with improvements in a new version of Windows because they didn't know about the old version. PC enthusiasts were still asking for features to handle managing files and keeping multiple PCs in sync while phone or browser users were seamlessly connected to a cloud and gave no thought at all to where files were stored. Buying a second iPhone or replacing a broken one proved astonishingly simple, because of the integration with services.

Microsoft's answer to iPhone and Android 1.0 was still being developed. Windows Phone 7, originally code-named Photon, would be released a year after Windows 7. The mobile team was heads down trying to get that release done, which had been in the works since Windows Mobile 6.0 shipped in early 2007. By the time Windows Phone 7 shipped, the Windows 8 team would have completed the first of three milestones. The next full chapter will detail the challenges this lack of synchronization created. We had Windows Phone 7 on a mission to get to market and compete and in doing so was pre-booking the next release; Windows 8 attempted to plan a major release that in theory would lend support to the mission of modernizing the codebase which was desperately needed by Windows Phone 7 competing with the modern Linux kernel and OS X.

Meanwhile, there were few new customers being brought to the cash-producing business of the Windows PC. There we were with the metaphorical *Sword of Damocles* hanging above us. The best days of the PC were behind us. It wasn't just obvious technically—the value propositions of mobile devices were in no way compatible with the Win32 and PC architectures. The only question was when things would truly turn for the worst.

The risks were infinitely high. We could do something radically different, potentially choosing wrong and heading right into failure even accelerating what was inevitable. Or we could slow walk as long as possible, releasing incremental features for as long as possible hoping to find some future solution to our quagmire. Doing both is a classic upper management answer that with near certainty results in a combination of a bloated and confused near term that keeps trying to pull features from the new, and a brand new product that develops a major case of second-system syndrome. The latter is a classic defined in the standard developer book *Mythical Man-Month*, and what we experienced with numerous Microsoft projects from Cairo to Longhorn when the next generation attempts to solve all known problems at once.

It is why so many default to preserving the cash cow as the most logical strategy, maintaining the success already achieved. Usually this comes with raising prices along the way for existing customers, who are by and large captive. In the short term, things continue to look great, and a crisis will be averted while the crisis is left to a future team. In fact, in the short term our most ardent fans would continue to carry on as though everything is normal. They are part of the same bubble as us.

Either way, the world outside of the Windows PC shifted to mobile. We were at a fork in the road and had to pick a direction.

The thing about disruption when it is happening is that you alternate between over-confidence and paranoia. Financially, the Windows PC was secure. Emotionally, the Windows PC was fragile. From a product perspective, not only was there little left to do on the current path but doing anything would annoy both the disinterested customers and ardent fans more than it would encourage them or any new buyers. Over-confidence leads one to incremental plans, assuming the existing business is so strong as to not worry. Paranoia makes it difficult to identify the precise nature of disruption and to calibrate a response.

For all the insights that *Innovator's Dilemma* captured, the one thing it did not seem to predict was that even after disruptions companies can continue to make vast sums of money for years to come from those disrupted products. Technologists tend to think disruption causes products to sort of go away, but as any private equity investor will tell you, that is not the case. That's why a misplaced confidence in incrementalism almost always wins out over a bold, risky bet, at least for a while.

We were determined to find a way to do better than to slowly lose relevancy as we'd seen happen to IBM.

Planning Windows 8

We kicked off a planning process just as had been done for all the other releases described in this work—from Office 2000 all through Windows 7. By now this team had fifteen years of product planning and results that had transformed a set of bundled applications into a suite of interconnected products and then to a platform of products, servers, and services, and then reinvented the user experience setting these tools up for at least another decade. We then aimed this same process at the challenges of the Windows business, and by all accounts set that product up for another decade.

About three months before Windows 7 released to manufacturing, I sent out the first step in planning Windows 8, the obvious name. "Building on Windows 7" outlined the state of the business and product, suggested where we would invest for the next project, detailed competitive threats, and defined what success would look like.

As with all the other framing memos I wrote, this one began upbeat. How could it not? The release of Windows 7 was a super positive experience for the team, the company, and the broad ecosystem. The memo celebrated all we accomplished as a team and with Jon DeVaan's leadership significantly improving our engineering capabilities and productivity. Promise and deliver.

Then the reality. The recession had slowed the growth of PC sales and analysts were taking forecasts down. The damage Netbooks had done to pricing leverage was significant, resurrecting the Linux desktop and lengthening Windows XP in market. Netbooks also masked the secular weakness in PCs that was also seeing as lengthening of the PC refresh cycle in large companies. PCs were being tasked to last longer without loading a new version of Windows or Office. Emerging markets and software piracy were proving highly resistant to most every effort. The sabbatical I took living in China in 2004 taught me firsthand just how impossible it was going to be to thwart piracy of desktop Windows and Office, our primary sources of revenue. Windows Live was, as we say, making progress, but Google was making much more progress much faster, and our marquee products, Hotmail and Messenger, were losing share and fast. Releasing SkyDrive (now OneDrive) with excellent integration of the new Office Web Applications (Word, Excel, PowerPoint running in the browser with compatibility with desktop Office) was a significant bright spot, but it came with very high operational costs and immense pushback from Office that feared cannibalization. There were even changes in how PCs were being sold that were proving highly problematic. OEMs were increasingly relying on nagware or trial products, bloating the PC user interface, and putting a ton of pressure on the overall experience of Windows. The retail channel, struggling from the recession, was anxious because they had not yet mastered selling smart phones, the hot category, which increasingly looked like a carrier-specific play. This in turn caused retailers to become part of the equation of pre-loaded software, thus further eroding the experience.

Competitively, all I asked us to focus on was Apple and Google. Most would see Apple as a competitor through OS X, but as discussed OS X was now powering iPhone. The framing memo was not a plan nor was it even a plan for a plan, rather it serves to bound the release and help encourage the team to focus on specific technologies, competitors, and challenges. There was much for the team to collectively learn. At the time, I summarized Apple competition as follows:

> ***Apple***. *Apple OS X is a very strong product coupled with amazing hardware. The transition Apple has made from OS 9 to a modern OS architecture on Intel hardware is on par with the transition we made to both the NT code base and to 64-bits. From an OS technology perspective we see the strength of OS X among universities and administrators who find the Mac (Mach-based) kernel and associated shell, tools and techniques "comforting". From a user experience perspective, we cannot be defensive about the reality that Mac hardware + OS X + iLife continues to be the standard by which a PC + Windows 7 + Windows Live will be judged in terms of technology, and then [sic, how] the purchase experience, post-sales experience, and ecosystem have grown to be considerable strengths. While we*

have only some details, the hygiene work being done on Snow Leopard is likely to generate significant positive views as the OS becomes "leaner and more streamlined" and likely claims about being more modern with respect to graphics, 64-bits, and user-interface. As we describe below, the sharing of code and architecture, particularly for important strategic elements of the OS, between the iPhone OS and Leopard is technically interesting and certainly responsible for some elements of the platform success. Apple is not without blemishes, but in planning Windows 8 we must focus on their strengths and assume they will continue to execute well on those. Being deliberate and informed about competing with Snow Leopard and, relative to iPhone, making sure we build on the assets of Windows for our Windows Phones should be strongly considered.

Rather than describe Android directly, I chose to consider Android as another variant of Linux. At the time, the only Android phone was the convertible BlackBerry-like device, the HTC Dream. Android 2.0 with full support for multitouch would not release until Windows 7 launched to market about three months later. Note the caution about Google control of Android expressed even then—it was obvious this would be a tension point down the road. In this context the competition with Linux also included desktop Linux:

***Linux**. Like so many competitors we have faced as a technology company, just as we thought "this one won't reach critical mass" we saw two events provide a breath of life into "Linux on the desktop". First, the rise of Ubuntu, both the technology/packaging and the "movement", has created a rallying cry for OEMs and for the Linux community. Second, the low-cost PCs that initially came with Linux (due to the footprint "requirements") created a new incentive for OEMs/ODMs to find a way to make it work. While we were effective in establishing a value proposition for Windows XP on these PCs, the seed that was planted will continue to be revisited by PC makers and designers. They appreciate the potential for business model innovation, componentization, tailoring, and also the opportunities to differentiate using the open source aspects of the OS. It is worth noting the reality that Linux on the server continues to dominate in many important workloads and the server plans are going to inform the planning of the base OS work such that we are extremely focused on defining specific scenarios where we make significant competitive progress with Windows 8 against Linux on the server. Within the context of Linux it is especially important to call out Google Android which will likely be funded by Google for some time and represents an OS choice for mobile phones and phone architectures encroaching on the PC "from below." Android can provide OEMs with the opportunities similar to Ubuntu, however Google is walking a careful line in providing Android where they can possibly lower costs for OEMs, or even subsidize the bill of materials for a device, counterbalanced by OEM wariness that Google will take too much control of additional revenue streams.*

Perhaps most importantly were the two "non-traditional" competitors: "Browsers" and "Phones/Alternative Architectures." The rise of Google Chrome was proving highly problematic, not just because of the loss of share, but because of Google's determination to add anything and everything from a PC to a cross-platform browser runtime, which is still going on to this day.

The view of the phone is much more interesting considering how the world evolved. Speculating about Android would prove accurate in just a few short months. I was deeply concerned about the PC ecosystem and the potentially rapid convergence of PC and phone hardware in the direction of phones, as well as Apple's unified OS strategy. This was in stark contrast to where Microsoft began its mobile journey a dozen silicon-years earlier and where it was today.

> ***Phones and alternate architectures****. The iPhone is referred to by many as a new form of portable computer—"it has a real OS" many have said in reviews. The Google G1 phone running Android is likely to be made available in more PC or "handheld" form factors beyond the single-handed in-your-pocket screen. The desire for the ultimate device that has the power and capabilities of a PC along with the convenience of always on wireless connectivity is beyond alluring. It is what we all want as consumers. To deliver on such a vision many might say that Windows can never power such devices—perhaps that is a statement about "business model" or a statement about technology. Sometimes it is just competitors declaring "[Big] Windows will never be on a phone". The reality is there was a time in the history of Windows phones (CE, PocketPC, etc.) where the synergy between "little" Windows and "big" Windows was technically robust in reasonable ways. For a variety of reasons we diverged. Today we have hardware designers and phone company customers facing a choice between the OS that supports phone networks, voice, and other "phone" scenarios super well, but does not have the rich ecosystem support of Windows 7 and runs on a small set of hardware chassis, and Windows 7 running on a mainstream hardware platform with broad ecosystem support and openness. These platforms differ in bill of material costs, power consumption, and so on. Much like the "browser is all I need" statement there is a significant amount of extrapolation that both excludes Windows and assumes the Windows platform cannot compete. Our chip partners for Windows are working hard on bringing the x86 architecture "down" and we need to be there with Windows software.* ***And at the same time we will strongly consider how to run Windows on alternate hardware platforms and learn what that would entail—we will work to bring "big" Windows to mobile chipsets, but we have significant groundwork to do before we know the practicality of such an investment.*** *Our Windows 8 planning will most certainly take into account the role of sharing new code across Windows and Windows Phones, starting with the latest Internet Explorer as we are already working on.*

There were several technology bets in the framing memo, putting stakes in the ground for how we would think about significant efforts on the deeper technical challenges of the release including a big effort to evolve the PC. While I don't want to fast-forward, these abstract definitions are what will lead to the work on ARM processors (see emphasis above), a new application model, and ultimately first-party hardware.

The technology bets on evolving the PC included:

- Mobile Devices
- Converged OS between Windows PCs and phones
- Mainstream PCs and the market turn to laptops
- High-end PC form factors such as meeting room PCs
- Shared computing PCs such as we were seeing with remote desktop and cloud computing

Taken together with the work on cloud, the memo defined the "Modern Windows Experience" as including five key components. The original even included a fancy Office Art depiction. The use of "modern" became a touchstone of the release and how we describe Windows 8:

- **Base operating system**: the OS kernel, device management, connectivity, and storage
- **Graphics, Presentation, and Interaction**: the visual aspects of Windows including the APIs used by applications and the end-user experience
- **Browsing**: the technologies required for browsing the web, but also how those will be reused across the platform to build rich applications
- **Windows "Form Factor" Experience**: tuning the experience for different types and sizes of computers from handheld through laptops and desktops to servers and alternate form factors such as tablets and wall computers
- **Windows Live**: the broad set of cloud-based services that complete the Windows experience including identity, communications and messaging, storage, and sharing

As with past releases the framing memo went out to the whole Windows team. The bulk of the team was super focused on shipping Windows 7 and mostly appreciated the informational aspect of the memo. The real work for program management began with JulieLar's "Windows 8 Planning Memo" which she sent to the entire team just after Windows 7 RTM for most worldwide markets. The purpose of the framing memo was to establish the "bounding box" for Windows 8 and bring together the best of top-down, bottom-up, and middle-out planning. The framing memo was the top-down step. The planning memo develops potential themes for the release and explores those.

Julie outlined the following planning themes which would then be the structure used to facilitate brainstorming, prototyping, and then ultimately the product vision:

> **Blending the Best of the Web and the Rich Client**. Recognizing the declining role of Win32 development and the increasing dominance of web development and associated tooling, this area asked to develop solutions to building an engaging and useful platform for developers. What kinds of apps do they want and how would they be distributed? How could the capabilities of Windows enhance what we see as limited web applications?

Defining a Modern PC Experience. Julie wrote, "The basic elements of today's Windows user experience—the Desktop, Taskbar, Start menu, and Explorer—were introduced in Windows 95, and their success has made Windows the world's most familiar computing environment. But today's modern world is in many ways different from the mid-1990s world in which Windows 95 was designed." This area asked nothing less than to bring the Windows user experience up to a level that would support existing scenarios and provide a better solution for the next billion customers who see the smartphone as their first and potentially primary computing experience.

Extending the Reach Of Windows. The Windows model of licensing and OEMs served us extraordinarily well, but with the rise of smartphones there were new revenue opportunities and sales models for Windows that can be supportive of reaching the next billion customers. Key among these was the role of mobile operators ("telcos") in the sales process.

Connecting to Windows From Anywhere. Typically, the PC of 2010 operated in a world where everything is on the PC except what is viewed through a web-browser. PCs could be greatly improved by making use of cloud services available with Windows Live to make all your files, settings, communication, and collaboration easy from any PC or device. What role could the cloud play? Synchronization across devices was something the company has tried many times before though we had limited success. How could it work this time?

Helping IT to Deliver Work Anywhere Infrastructure. Most of Microsoft's revenue and much of the upside opportunity came from doing a fantastic job for enterprise IT. This theme asked questions about deployment, security, encryption, and even the mundane such as how to easily replace a lost, stolen, or broken PC.

Showcasing Quality the First 30 Days and Over Time. This area asked what have historically been the most intractable of questions about Windows. "The burden of ensuring that a new PC is running as well as it should is placed on the customer who purchased it. As a result, the first days of usage, rather than being a period of exploration and fun, were often prove to be labor intensive and exasperating." Julie added, "Making matters worse, Windows itself is not running at its best during the first days of ownership. ...Windows performs all of its initial self-tuning and post-out-of-box-experience tasks during this critical time." When compared to what customers were starting to see with smartphones, Windows looked downright archaic.

Synthesizing these together into the vision was the next step. While most of the planning team were brainstorming and prototyping, we had some significant engineering work going, the success of which would prove crucial in enabling our ability to achieve a breakthrough Windows 8, such as working out the feasibility of Windows on ARM.

A bigger worry, did we set out to do too much? We knew that the team would naturally gravitate to ideas that made the PC better in incremental ways. We also knew some people would push hard on extremely bold ideas. The risk for any large organization is obvious...trying to do too much. The less obvious risk...ending up with a plan that is a too much of the old and a little bit, but not enough, of the new. Inertia is one of the most powerful forces in a large company.

I was worried. We only wanted to spend a few months "just" planning, still an enormous undertaking. Windows 7 shipped in August, with this planning memo and associated work taking most of the Fall. It was looking like we would start the project in the Spring of 2010, which meant an aggressive RTM of Windows 8 in the summer of 2012. Still, that would be exactly three years between releases, something never accomplished before. Promise and deliver.

098. A SEA OF WORRY AT THE CONSUMER ELECTRONICS SHOW

In early January 2010, I was walking around the show floor at CES the evening before opening day as I had routinely done over the years. CES 2010 was a mad rush to build a giant city of 2,500 booths only to be torn down in 4 days. This walk-through gave me a good feel for the booths and placement of demonstrations. It was just two months after the launch of Windows 7. Walking around I made a list of the key OEM booths to scope out first thing in the morning. It wasn't scientific but visiting a booth had always been an interesting barometer and sanity check for me compared to in-person executive briefings. Later in the week I would systematically walk most of the show and write a detailed report. The next morning, along with the giant crowds, I made my way through a few dozen booths with the latest *Designed for Windows 7* PCs mixed in among the onslaught of 3D-television controlled by waving your hands which garnered much of the show's buzz.

The introduction of touch screens was a major push for Windows 7 and there was genuine excitement among the OEMs to offer touch as an option, though few, OK none, thought it would be a broadly accepted choice. Touch added significantly to the price. With two relatively small suppliers for the hardware, OEMs were not anxious to make a bet across their product line. TReller, the new CMO and CFO for Windows, made a good decision to provide strategic capital to one component maker to ensure Dell would make such a bet.

There were touch models from most every PC maker, but they were expensive—most were more than $2,500 when the typical laptop was sub-$1,000. For the OEMs this was by design. If a buyer wanted touch there was an opportunity to sell a high-end, high-margin, low-volume device. OEMs had been telling us for months that this was going to be the case, but it was still disappointing.

Taking advantage of Windows 7, and wholeheartedly, were a sea of Windows 7 "slates" all based on the same design from the combination of Intel and Pegatron, an ODM. These slates were essentially Netbooks without keyboards. They fit the new Intel definition previously described—MID or mobile internet device. They were theoretically built as consumption-oriented companions to a PC. They were shown reading online books, listening to music, and watching movies, though not particularly high resolution or streaming given the meager hardware capabilities. All of them were relatively small and low-resolution screens. To further emphasize the Intel perspective, they also launched AppUp for Windows XP and Windows 7, a developer program and early content store designed to support rights management and in-app purchase as one might use for books and games.

The buzziest slate was from Lenovo, not a product announcement, but a prototype model kept behind glass at the private Lenovo booth located in a Venetian Hotel restaurant. The "hybrid slate" Lenovo U1 was a 11" notebook that could also be separated from the keyboard and used as both a laptop and a slate. As a laptop, the Windows 7 PC used a low-power Intel chipset, a notch slightly above a Netbook. Detached as a slate, the device ran a custom operating system they named Lenovo Skylight based on Linux running on a Qualcomm Snapdragon chipset. The combination weighed almost 4lbs. The Linux tablet separated from the Windows-based keyboard PC somewhat like the saucer section of the Starship Enterprise separated from the main ship. Lenovo built software to sync some small amount of activity between the two built-in computers, such as synchronizing bookmarks and some files. Economically, two complete computers would not be the ideal way to go, bringing the cost to $1000. Strategically for Microsoft this was irritating.

NVIDIA, primarily known for its graphics cards used by gamers, was always an interesting booth. NVIDIA was really struggling through the recession and would finish 2010 with revenue of $3.3 billion and a loss of $60 million.[108] As it would turn out it was also a transformative year for the company, and for one of the most legendary founders in all of the PC era, Jensen Huang. To put NVIDIA in context, my very first meeting with Intel when I joined the Windows team in 2006 was about graphics, because of the Vista Capable fiasco. Intel was digging their heels in favoring integrated graphics and was not at all worried about how their capabilities were so far behind what NVIDIA and ATI, another graphics card maker, were delivering, which Intel viewed as mostly about games. The rub was that AMD, Intel's archrival, had just acquired ATI for $5.4 billion making a huge bet on discrete (non-integrated) graphics, which was what NVIDIA focused on. Intel seemed to believe that the whole issue of graphics would go away as OEMs would simply accept inferior graphics from Intel because it was cheaper and easier while Intel improved integrated graphics over time, albeit slowly. A classic bundling strategy of "a tie is a win" that would turn out to be fatal for Intel and an enormous opportunity for ATI/AMD, NVIDIA, and Apple. Intel could have acquired NVIDIA at the time for perhaps $10-12B if that was at all possible.

In their booth NVIDIA was showing off how they could add their graphics capabilities to the Intel Atom processor and dramatically speed it up. Recall, Atom chips struggled to even run full screen video at Netbook screen resolutions. With NVIDIA ION it was possible to run flawless HD video. NVIDIA made this all clear in a "Netbook Nutrition Facts" label that they affixed to Netbooks running NVIDIA graphics. This was a shot across the bow at Intel, but NVIDIA had an uphill battle to unseat bundled graphics from Intel. Nevertheless, we were acutely aware of the strong technical merits of NVIDIA's approach, Jensen's incredible drive, and the needs of Windows customers. This will prove critically important in the next chapter as we further work on non-Intel processors.

More disappointing was how the OEMs chose to demonstrate touch capabilities in Windows 7. We provided OEMs with a suite of touch-centric applications, such as those demonstrated a year earlier—mapping, games, screen savers, and drawing, for example. We even named it *Windows Touch Pack*. The OEMs wanted to differentiate their touch PCs with different software and viewed the Touch Pack we provided as lame. Touch had become wildly popular in such a short time because of the iPhone, and the iPhone was a consumer device used for social interaction, consumption of media, and games.

With that frame of reference, the OEMs wanted to show scenarios that were more like an iPhone. The OEMs were going to do what they did, which was to create unique software to show off their PCs. This is just what many in the industry called *crapware* or, as Walt Mossberg coined in his column, *craplets*.[109] To the OEMs this was a value add and important differentiation. Worst of all, there was no interest from independent software makers who had dedicated few, if any, resources to Win32 product updates, let alone updates specific to touch that was exclusive to the new Windows 7. We never intended to support Windows 7 touch on earlier versions of Windows—something developers ask of every new Windows API. This compatibility technique we often relied on but was a key contributor to Windows PC fragility and flakiness, also referred to colloquially as DLL Hell as previously described.

The overall result: Windows 7 provided no impetus for third-party-developers, and we failed to muster meaningful third-party support for any new features, including touch.

What I saw was a series of new OEM apps taking a common approach. These apps could be called shells in typical Microsoft vernacular, an app for launching other apps—the Start menu, taskbar, and file explorer in Windows constitute the shell. In this case, these new shells were usually full-screen apps that had big buttons across the top to launch different programs: Browsing, Video, Music, Photos, and YouTube. These touch-friendly shells did not do much other than launch a program for each scenario, the browser, or simply a file explorer. For example, if Music was chosen then a music player, created by the OEM or chosen because of a payment for placement, would launch to play music files stored on or downloaded to a PC. The use of large touch buttons was thought to give the PC user interface a consumer feel. The browser used part of Internet Explorer but not the whole thing, just the HTML rendering component; for example, it did not include Favorites or Bookmarks usually considered part of a browser. This software, as well intentioned as it was, would fall in the crapware category. This was expected, but still disappointing.

In booths with mainstream laptops we were offered a glimpse into the changing customer views of what made a good laptop. The Windows 7 launch was just a short time ago, so most laptops had incremental updates, primarily with the new version of Windows and perhaps a slight bump in specs. Some show attendees picked up the laptops and grimaced at the weight and thickness—these machines were hardly slick. It had been two full years since the introduction of the MacBook Air and the PC industry still did not have a mainstream Windows PC that fit in the famous yellow envelope wielded on stage by Steve Jobs. The prevalence of Wi-Fi in hotels and workplaces had changed the view that a work PC needed all the legacy ports present on Windows computers, and the fear of dongles had faded. Most every Windows PC still shipped with an optical drive, significantly increasing the height of the PC. Show-goers were openly commenting on the size, weight, and lack of portability of Windows PCs compared to the MacBook Air, which was what many were fully lusting for and based on the numbers had already switched to. For the two years since the MacBook Air launch the PC makers were pre-occupied with Netbooks.

Apple broadened their product line with an even smaller and lighter MacBook Air using an 11.6" screen. They also added MacBook Pro models that were more in line with Windows PCs when it came to hardware, for example they included optical drives and discrete graphics. These laptops were expensive relative to mainstream business PCs running Windows. For example, the Dell XPS 15 debuted in 2010 was praised by the press, though only relative to other PCs. Compared to MacBooks, the Dell lost out for a variety of reasons including noise, keyboard feel, trackpad reliability, screen specs, and more. In reviewing the new Dell XPS, AnandTech, a highly regarded tech blog, said:[110]

> *We've lamented the state of Windows laptops on numerous occasions; the formula is "tried and true", but that doesn't mean we like it…what we're left with is a matter of finding out who if anyone can make something that truly stands out from the crowd.*
>
> *Of course, if we're talking about standing out from the crowd, one name almost immediately comes to mind: Apple. Love 'em or hate 'em, Apple has definitely put more time and energy into creating a compelling mobile experience.*

If only there had been a Windows PC like MacBook Air for Windows 7. The closest we had was the low-volume and premium priced Sony VAIO Z that was new for 2010. This model featured a solid-state drive like the MacBook Air but was much heavier and larger than the famous envelope and could easily top $3000 when fully specified.

This knocked the wind out of me. I was happy that there were Windows 7 PCs at the show. But seeing the reaction to them only reinforced my feeling that the ecosystem was not well. I was hardly the first Windows executive to bemoan the lack of good hardware from partners, especially hardware that competed with Apple. Six years earlier, before the MacBook Air but also around CES, my predecessor JimAll sent a polemic, intentionally so, to BillG, *Losing our way*...in which he said, "I would buy a Mac today if I was not working at Microsoft."[111] As with many of these candid emails, this one made its way to an exhibit in a trial—it added nothing to the case, but such salacious mails that have little by way of legal implications are often used to attempt to gain leverage for settlements or stir emotions in a courtroom.

By the time the show ended, I wrote up my CES 2010 trip report as I had been doing since about 1992 or so. I loved (and still love) writing up these reports. No matter how down I was or how boring I thought the show was, I amped up the excitement as though it was the first CES I ever attended. I think it is important to do because otherwise the aging cynicism that seeps in—often seen in the press covering the event—makes it too easy to miss what might be a trend. My report ran 20 pages with photos and covered everything from PCs of all shapes and sizes to 3D television to iPhone accessories, lots of those.

Not lost on everyone at the show was how Apple loomed over the show even though it had zero official presence. The vast majority of accessories located the edges of the Sands Exhibition Center were cases, docks, cables, and chargers for the iPhone. The camera area was filled with accessories to turn an iPhone into a production camera, such as a Steadicam for an iPhone that I even mocked in my report, oops that was way off base. The real news, however, was that the gossip of a forthcoming Apple tablet was everywhere. Nearly every news story about the show mentioned the one tablet that wasn't there.

The week before CES in a classically Apple move, invites were sent to the press for an Apple Special Event to be held January 27, 2010. Leading up to the event, rumors swirled around how Apple would introduce a new touch computer and eventually converged on a 10" tablet to be based on iPhone OS. As we see today, the rumors were wildly off base, and only days before did the rumors mostly match the eventual reality.

After the first day of CES and our contribution to the main keynote by SteveB, that evening, I was in a mood and not a good one. I skipped yoga (at the awesome Vegas HOT! studio) and a previously planned celebratory team dinner that I arranged to write a memo. Maybe memo isn't the right word. It was another dense thought-piece from me, a 6000-word SteveSi special for sure. I think JulieLar, MikeAng, and ABurrows are still angry with me for missing that dinner.

I knew mainstream PCs were selling well. PCs from Dell, Acer, and HP met the sweet spot of the market, even among a marketplace overdosing on Netbooks. People were over the moon for Windows 7. Office 2007 was doing quite well, despite not having compatibility mode, which had receded to a non-issue. Windows Server and associated products were going strong even though cloud computing had taken over Silicon Valley. Even Bing was showing signs of life six months or so into its rebranded journey, which had been managed by Satya Nadella (SatyaN) for the past few months. These all made for the bull case that Microsoft was making progress.

For customers and the tech industry, well, their attention had by and large moved to non-PC devices, Apple versus Google in phones, and the potential new tablet form factor. Microsoft launched the HTC HD2 running Windows Mobile 6.5 at CES. It was a well-received and valiant effort while Windows Phone 7 progress continued even in a decidedly iPhone world.

I remained paranoid, Microsoft paranoid. The dearth of premium PCs to compete with Apple and the lackluster success with touch gave me pause. Even though we had tried to right all the wrongs of introducing new hardware capabilities with new approaches, we had failed. There were no Windows 7 touch apps. There never would be. It was totally unclear if the industry would ever come together to create a MacBook Air, and even if it did it was unlikely to have the low cost, battery life, and quality over time of a Mac, even though it too was running on Intel. The browser platform consumed most all developer attention, with iPhone and then Android drawing developers from the browser. Apple's App Store, 18 months old, had 140,000 apps up from 500 at launch, growing at a rate of 10 to 20 percent *per month*. To put that in perspective, during the Windows 7 beta I shared what I thought was an astoundingly large number—883,612 unique Windows applications seen across the massive beta test. By mid-2022, the Apple store had more than 3.4 million apps!

A sense of dread and worry came over me when I thought about our converging Windows 8 plans. It wasn't a panic attack. It was more me wondering if I failed to give clear enough direction to the team about how big a bet we were willing to make on Windows 8. Was I too subtle, which I was definitely known to be, and gave too much room for the plan to turn into an "and" plan? An "and" plan means we would do everything we would have normally done, "and" also take into account all the new scenarios. Such plans are easy to sign up for because they don't involve tradeoffs. At the same time, they force no decisions and lacked the constraints that yield a breakthrough design.

An "and" plan is what I saw across the CES show floor and even from Intel. It is a plan where the PC is a Windows PC and the new stuff, as though the new stuff is just another app one could take or leave. The extra launcher shells, content stores, and touch interface were bolted on the side of Windows and did not substantially alter the value proposition that was under so much pressure. Related, an "and" plan would also presume a traditional laptop or desktop PC as the primary tool, which itself would prove as limiting down the road as it was right then.

We needed a plan with a point of view about how computing would evolve. That point of view needed to be built upon the assumption that Win32 was not the future, or even the present. We needed to realize that an app and content store were of paramount importance. We needed to account for shifting customer needs in their computing device. We needed a plan that assumed the web is the defining force that changed computing and smartphones were themselves changing the web. We needed a plan that substantially changed the futzing, viruses, malware, and overall fragility of the PC so it acted more like a consumer electronics device. Most of all we needed a plan to engage developers in a new way to become interested Microsoft's solution this opportunity, and not the solutions from Apple or Google.

We had the ingredients of a plan that might be adequate to quell the forces of disruption. Would executing such a plan be possible within the context of Microsoft? What does a plan look like when it also involves Windows itself?

The Windows 8 Framing Memo I wrote and the Windows 8 Planning Memo and process JulieLar had started contained the core of a point of view. We had set out to investigate "alternative hardware platforms," potentially "distributing applications in a store," designing "a modern touch experience," and much more. As interesting and innovative and outside the box as these were, they all suffered the same risk. The problem was that for the team they were viewed as additions to Windows, as add-ons to the next release, as nice to have, an addition to. We had—and this is where the discomfort came from—created a classic strategy of the incumbent when faced with disruption. Our strategy treated the forces of disruption—in this case mobile hardware platforms, modern user interface, and the app ecosystem—as incremental innovations in addition to what we had. We were thinking that we would be competitive if we had Windows and other features.

This is not how disruption works.

Disruption, even as Christensen had outlined a decade earlier, is when the new products are difficult for the incumbent to comprehend and are a combination of inferior, less expensive, less featured, and less capable, but simultaneously viewed by customers as superior replacements.

As a team, we had faced this before, and I had spent the better part of three releases of Office fending off those claiming Office was being disrupted by inferior products built on Java, components, or browsers. In all those instances, I stuck to what I believed to be the case and defended, effectively, the status quo until we took the dual risks of expanding Office to rely on servers and services and then redefining the user experience for the product. Patience paid off then. The new technology threats were immature at best and a distraction at worst.

What gave me the confidence to believe, as they say, this time was different? Was it my relative inexperience in Windows of just one release? Naivety? Arrogance? Was it envy of Apple or Steve Jobs?

It was none of those things.

It was simply the combination of the shortcomings I was seeing on the CES show floor and the fact that we'd all been using iPhones. We were not talking about a theoretical disruption where someday Java Office could have all the features people wanted in Office or that someday all the performance and UI issues would be squeezed out of the browser. The disruption had already happened, but the awareness of that was not shared equally by everyone involved.

To use a phrase attributed to William Gibson, "The future has arrived—it's just not evenly distributed yet."[112]

Windows had 100% share of the Windows PC market and 92% share of the PC market. iPhone and Android (phones, and soon other form factors) were making a compelling case that the Windows position, as a percentage of computing, was declining. This decline in computing share would only accelerate.

In technology, if you are not growing then you are shrinking.

Holed up in my hotel room while the rest of the team had dinner, I banged away at my Netbook keyboard a screed about the future of the web, apps, and how consumers would interact with content—and, importantly, ways in which the PC was deficient. I wrote 6,000-plus words, making the case that the iPhone was so good the internet was going to wrap itself around the phone rather than the phone becoming a browser for the existing internet—the web would tailor itself to the phone via apps. The experience of the web was not going to be like it previously had been—the iPhone was not going to deal with the desktop web and attempt to squeeze it on to the phone. The browser itself would become a form of legacy, "the 3270 terminal" of the internet era. The 3270 is the IBM model number for a mainframe terminal, replaced by PCs and applications.

As the office workers I gave first PCs to in 1985 did not realize, the business forms they filled out with their Selectric typewriters would change to work on a PC, not that the PC would get good at filling out carbon paper forms. A key part of a technology paradigm shift is that the shift is so significant that work changes to fit within the new tools and paradigm. There's only a short time when people clamor for the new technology to feel and behave like the old.

I sent the memo to a few people that night. It received a bit of pushback because it felt like what we were already doing, only restated. I kept thinking this was how disruption really happened—teams went into denial, say "We got this" and believe adding a bit more would make the problem (or me) go away. IBM added a 3270 terminal emulator to the original PC for this reason, but that didn't make people want a PC more or even use it; rather, they complained that the terminal seemed more difficult to use than a standard 3270 terminal. The PC I most frequently installed in the summer of 1985 was the IBM PC XT/3270, a hybrid mess if there ever was one.

It was clear we were falling into the trap of thinking incrementally when the world around us was not only changing but converging. The Windows team could no longer think of modern mobile platforms as distinct from the PC. People's technology needs were being met by phones and were moving away from the PC.

This was not a call to turn the Windows PC into a phone. Rather this was a chance to up-level the PC, to embrace the web, embrace the app store model, embrace the shifting hardware platform and associated operating system changes, and embrace internet technologies for application development.

Most of all it was about "apps" except I couldn't quite find the right word to use. Apple talking about "apps" for the past couple of years really bugged me. When I was in Office, we were the Applications (or Apps) group at Microsoft and an app was just the techie word for another more broadly used techie word, program. Word and Excel were apps and I was trying to define a new kind of app. App was such a weird word that even our own communications team didn't think we should use it. Lacking a better word that night in the hotel, I called the memo "Stitching the Tailored Web" which was a horrible name and worse metaphor that took a lot of time for me to explain to people in person.

The key ingredients of this new world as I described it were a computing device, content store, and the tailored web itself. The computing device encompassed an interaction model for the device and for the new tailored apps. The content store is where users obtained apps created and distributed by developers along with consumable content such as movies, books, and music. The tailored web included the APIs used by developers and the OS platform, the new tools required by developers, as well as the core technologies of Internet Explorer used to create these applications and to browse the traditional web. All three came together to create what I described as the more "consumable internet." I even had a fancy diagram I made with PowerPoint to illustrate the point.

My main point was that mobile phones were so huge and such a force that even the internet would change because of phones, the iPhone in particular. The notion of going to web sites would be viewed as quaint or legacy compared to apps. Today, there are plenty of people who do not take this point of view to be where we landed. There are those that use desktop PCs and live in a desktop browser and defiantly believe that to be the only way to get real work done. They use the highest-end PC tools such as Visual Studio, Excel, AutoCAD, and Adobe Premier and did not (and still do not) see phones or mobile software replacing those any time soon. Yet there is no disputing the vastness of mobile. Depending on the source (and country) about three-fourths of all web traffic is mobile-based, and about 90% of time spent on a mobile device is in an app. With this dramatic change in how the web was used, it is fair to say that the web became a component of mobile, not the other way around. The browser-based Web 2.0 juggernaut would be subsumed by the smartphone.

The most dramatic expression of this would not happen for another 2 years. In the summer of 2012, Facebook, the posterchild of Web 2.0, dramatically pivoted from desktop browsing as the primary focus for the Facebook experience to the Facebook mobile app. That legendary pivot is often touted as both remarkable and responsible for the success and reach the company subsequently achieved.

The Tailored Web memo was much better delivered as a passionate call to the team. I waited until just after Apple's scheduled event and later that same day held a meeting with our senior managers, the 100 or so group managers across all of Windows, each the leader of dev, test, pm for a feature team. This was my favorite meeting and one I held at least quarterly going back to the late 1990s in Office.

Working with Julie, this became our own version of a pivot. It was not as much a pivot as simply a focusing effort. We still had about three months until the vision needed to be complete. This was by no means a major change. Rather it was relaxing the constraint that Windows 8 had to do two things, an "and" project, and it could focus on making sure we were set up for the future. The call to action was a call to prioritize the new over the legacy and interoperability between the legacy and new was not a priority. We wanted to break away from what was holding us back, a legacy neither of our primary competitors dealt with.

To the team, I wanted to make the case about apps by showing a series of screen shots of web sites versus Apps on various platforms and rhetorically asked "Which would you rather use?" Facebook on iPhone or a desktop? Crowded, ad-filled Bing on a desktop or the Bing search app on Windows Mobile? Outlook or the Mail app on iPhone? Reading a book in a browser or on a Kindle? A traffic map on a desktop browser or in the Microsoft Research SmartFlow traffic app?

The answer was obvious for all of us and remains obvious even today. The call to action was a doubling down on the developing planning themes "Defining a Modern PC Experience" and "Blending the best of the Web and Rich Client" with an emphasis on consumption and the internet. Specifically, it was "Windows, in all form factors, needs to be the best platform and experience to consume internet content while enabling ISVs and IHVs to build the software and hardware to do that."

It was early in the potential for this disruption, and it was easy to point to thousands of tasks, features, scenarios, partners, business models, ecosystems, and more that required a PC as we knew it. Every situation is different, but it is that sort of defensiveness that prevented companies like Kodak, BlackBerry, Blockbuster, and more from transitioning from one era to another.

It is easy to cycle from anxiety to calm in times like this. It was easy for me to look around and find affirmation of the "and" path we were on. Every stakeholder in the PC ecosystem would be far happier with incremental improvements to the status quo rather than embarking on huge changes with little known upside and significant immediate cost and potential downside. It would have been easy to fall back on the financial success we had and leave dealing with a technology shift for the future when technology specifics were clearer. It would, however, be too late as we now know. We would also lose the opportunity to lead a technology change that had just begun.

Worrying seemed abstract. Developing a clear point of view and executing on that seemed far more concrete and actionable.

The announcement from Apple and their tablet turned out to be far more than our poorly placed sources had led us to believe. What was it like in the halls of the Windows team on that day, January 27, 2010? It was not magical for us.

099. THE MAGICAL IPAD

For months, BillG and a small group of Microsoft executives believed Apple was going to release a tablet computer. It had been rumored for more than a decade. Originally, tablet shaped computers traced their roots to legendary Alan Kay's 1960's *Dynabook,* plus there was that one on *Star Trek.* There's a long-held belief among Trekkers that all *Star Trek* tech will eventually be realized. By 2010, Microsoft had a decade plus of Tablet PC experience, mixed as it was. With Windows 7 we brought all the tablet features into the main product instead of a special SKU, so every version of Windows could run effectively on any PC with tablet hardware, such as a pen and touch screen. What was different about the Apple rumors in 2010? What made us more nervous? Why, this time, did we believe these rumors about a company for which predictions had always been wrong? No one had predicted the iPhone with any specificity.

Microsoft and partners had invested a huge amount of time, energy, and innovation capital in the Tablet PC, but it was not breaking through the way many hoped, such as how we visualized it in the Office *Center for Information Work*. The devices for sale were expensive, heavy, underpowered, had relatively poor battery life, and inconsistent quality. Beyond the built-in applications, OneNote from Office, and a few industry-specific applications pushed through by Microsoft's evangelism efforts, there was little software that leveraged the pen and tablet. Many, myself included, were decreasingly enthused. BillG, however, was tireless in his advocacy of the device—and the fact that Apple might make one, and whatever magic Steve Jobs could bestow upon it, only served to juice the competition between companies and founder/CEOs. BillG remained hardcore and optimistic about the pen for productivity and a keyboard-less device for on-screen reading and annotation.

To BillG a PC running Windows that was shaped like a slate or tablet seemed inevitable. For many of the boomer computer science era, the fascination of handwriting and computing on a slate had been a part of the narrative from the start. Over the past 30 years, few of the technical problems had been solved, particularly handwriting but also battery life and weight. Then came the iPhone and multitouch.

That Apple would build such a PC was more credible than ever because of their phone, though by Microsoft measures the iPhone still lacked a stylus for pen input, something Steve Jobs openly mocked on several occasions. The possibility made us nervous and anxious, especially knowing Windows 8 was underway.

Collectively, and without hesitation, many believed Apple would turn the Mac into a tablet. Apple would add pen and touch support to the Mac software, creating a business computer with all the capabilities of Office and other third-party software, and the power of tablet computing. The thinking was that a convertible device made a ton of sense since that allowed for productivity and consumption in one device. Plus, techies love convertible devices of all kinds.

There were senior executives at Microsoft with very close ties to Apple who were certain of Apple's plans and relayed those to Bill. Bill would almost gleefully share what he "knew" to be the case, using such G-2 to prod groups into seeing the opportunity for his much-loved tablet strategy.

There were debates consuming online forums—rumors rooted in the Asian supply chain as to what sort of screens and chips Apple might be purchasing for the rumored product. Some thought there would be a "big iPod" and still others thought Apple would develop a product tailored to books, like the two-year-old Amazon Kindle. In other words, no one had a clue and people were making stuff up. Some were even calling it the iPad, not because there was a leak or anything but because it made more sense than iTablet or iSlate, and because at one point in the late 1990s Microsoft had something in R&D called *WinPad*. The industry had not even settled on the nomenclature for the form factor, cycling among tablet, slate, pad, MID, convertible, and so on.

At least in the months prior to launch, zero people, to my knowledge, thought that Apple had in mind a completely novel approach. An aspect of disruptive innovation is how incumbents project their views of strategy on to competitors without fully considering the context in which competitors work. As much as Microsoft primarily considered Apple to be the Mac company that happened to stumble into music players and then phones, by 2010 Apple had already pinned its future and entire product development efforts to iPhone and what was still called the iPhone OS, which was based on OS X, the Mac OS, but modernized in significant ways.

On January 27, 2010, at a special press event billed as "Come see our latest creation," Steve Jobs unveiled the iPad. I followed the happenings on the live blogs. This was one of the first Apple special events used to launch products, as the previous 2009 MacWorld was the last one in which Apple participated.

The event took place starting with the reminder that Apple had become the world's largest mobile device company, followed by Steve Jobs quoting, with a bit of a chuckle, an article from December in *The Wall Street Journal*, "The last time there was this much excitement about a tablet, it had some commandments written on it."

As part of his build-up to introducing the iPad, he pointed out that in defining a new category, a tablet needed to be better at some important things, better than a phone or a laptop. It needed to be better at browsing, email, photos, video, music, games, and eBooks. Basically, everything other than Office and professional software it seemed to me—though this would come to be known as "creation" or "productivity" by detractors who would posit that the iPad was a "consumption" device. As we will see, the Microsoft Office team was already hard at work at bringing Office apps to the iPad.

The launch event deliberately touted "latest creation" in the invitations, which I always thought was a bow to creativity as a key function. What many pundits and especially techies failed to appreciate was that productivity and creativity had new, broader, definitions with the breadth of usage of computers as smartphones. Productivity and creativity were no longer the sole province of Word, Excel, Photoshop, and Visual Studio. The most used application for creating was email and it was already a natural on the iPhone, only soon to be replaced by messaging that was even more natural.

As the presentation continued Jobs delivered his first gut punch to the PC ecosystem in describing what such a device might be, as he set up a contrast for what the new category should do relative to Netbooks.

"Some people have thought that that's a Netbook." The audience joined in a round of laughter. Then he said, "The problem is...Netbooks aren't better at anything...They're slow. They have low quality displays...and they run clunky old PC software...They're just cheap laptops. (more laughter)"

Ouch. He was slamming the darling of the PC industry. Hard.

The real problem was not only that was he right, but that consumers had come to the same conclusion. Sales of Netbooks had already begun their plunge to rounding error.

Jobs unveiled the iPad, proudly. Sitting in a Le Corbusier chair, he showed the "extraordinary" things his new device did, from browsing to email to photos and videos and more. The real kicker was that it achieved 10 hours of battery life—a flight from San Francisco to Tokyo watching video on one charge, recharged using your iPhone cable. It also achieved more than 30 days of standby power and like a phone, it also remained connected to the network in standby, reliably downloading emails and receiving notifications. This type of battery management was something the PC architecture struggled endlessly to achieve. The introduction concluded with a series of guests showing specially designed iPad apps in the 18 months old App Store, now with over 140,000 apps.

The eBook-specific apps really got under our skin given how much this had been the focus of many efforts over many years. Being a voracious reader, BillG championed eBooks for the longest time. Teams developed formats and evangelized the concept to publishers. Still Microsoft lacked a device to comfortably read books. Then there was Steve Jobs reclined on an iconic chair.

Games were the icing on the cake of despair given Microsoft's efforts on both the Xbox and PC.

But there was no pen! No stylus! Surely, it was doomed to be a consumption device.

Then they showed a paint program that could be used with the touch of a finger. They were just getting started.

There was no productivity! Doomed, for sure. Then they showed updated versions of the iWork suite for the iPad. The word processor, spreadsheet, and presentations package for the Mac had been rewritten and tuned specifically to work with touch on the iPad. Apple even intended to charge for them, though this would later change. Those tools had already been stomped by Mac Office, but they became unique on this unique device. The ever-increasing quality of the tools, particularly Keynote for presentations, quietly became a favorite among the Mac set in Silicon Valley.

All these apps being shown were available in the App Store. They were curated and vetted by Apple, free from viruses, bad behavior, and battery draining features.

Rounding out the demonstration was the fact that the iPad synchronized all the settings, documents, and content purchased with iTunes with a cloud service. This was still early in Apple's confused journey to what became known as iCloud, but as anyone who tried to sync between a phone and a PC then learned, that it worked at all was an achievement.

The iPad also came with an optional cellular modem built in—on a PC one would need a USB dongle costing a couple hundred dollars and an elaborate software stack that barely worked, plus a monthly $60 fee. On the iPad, there was an unlimited data plan from AT&T for $29.99. Apple and AT&T also made it possible to activate the iPad without going to the store or calling AT&T. Minor, perhaps, but this is the kind of industry-moving innovation

Apple almost never gets credit for achieving what was impossible to do uniformly on the PC. Even today, mobile connectivity on a PC is at best a headache.

The pricing was also innovative. Apple had previously been called out as a high-priced technology vendor and for a lack of an appropriate low-price product response to Netbooks. There was no doubt the iPad would be portrayed as expensive. In fact, after drawing out sharing the price, Jobs announced it would start at $499, a shockingly low price point which was close enough to Netbook territory. The price went to $829 fully loaded with storage and 3G, which remained the same as many loaded Netbooks. The price was hardly OLPC but it was low, with $499 viewed as a magic price at retail.

The product would be available in all configurations in 90 days worldwide.

I promptly ordered mine. I also ordered the keyboard dock described below.

It was all so painful. Each time Jobs said "magical" I thought "painful."

There were so many things iPad hardware did that the PC could not do or had been trying and failing to do for so long that suddenly made all the difference: incredibly thin and light, all-day battery life, wonderful display, low-latency touch screen, 3G connectivity, multiple sensors, cameras, synchronizing settings and cloud storage, an App Store, and so much more. My favorite mind-blowing example was the ability to easily rotate the screen from portrait to landscape without any user interface action. It just happened naturally. At a meeting with Intel, the head of mobile products took an iPad out and spun it in the air yelling at me with his thick Israeli accent "when will Windows be able to rotate the screen like this?!" My head hurt. All of this made possible because the iPad built on the iPhone. Yes, it was a big phone, but it proved to be so much more. It had so much potential because of the software.

It also had productivity software, and, to finally rub in the point, the first iPad even had a desktop docking station with a keyboard attached. Jobs didn't need to address the complexity of adding a keyboard, but having a keyboard that actually worked without the touch screen keyboard popping up and getting in the way was an important technical breakthrough and also one rooted in using the iPhone adapted OS X operating system kernel while also using a new platform for application software. This was one of many subtle points we picked up on that showed the foresight of the underlying strategy. It was obvious the keyboard dock was an "objection handler" and not a serious effort, but it motivated an ecosystem of keyboard folios and cases for the iPad until Apple itself finally introduced innovative keyboard covers.

The conclusion of the presentation reminded everyone that 75 million buyers of iPhones and touch iPods already knew how to use the iPad. There was no doubt from that moment that the future of the portable computer for home or work was an iPad or iPad-like device—the only questions were how long it would take to happen and how much Windows could thrive on simply supporting legacy behavior.

It was, as Jobs said, "The most advanced technology in a magical and revolutionary device at an unbelievable price."

The international magazine coverage of the iPad launch was mind-blowing. It was pure Steve Jobs, the genius. *The Economist* cover featured Steve Jobs as a Messiah-like character with biblical text over his head "The Book of Jobs:

Hope, Hype and Apple's iPad" as he held the iPad tablet not unlike Moses.[113] Time, Newsweek, Wired, and just about every tech publication that still printed on paper did a cover story. The global coverage squarely landed the message that the iPad was the future of computing.

From the PC tech press, the announcement drew skepticism. The iPad was, marginally, more expensive than dying Netbooks. It lacked a full-size keyboard for proper productivity. It didn't have a convenient USB slot to transfer photos or files, the most common way of sharing files at the time. The use of adjectives like "full" or "proper" or "truly" peppered the reviews when talking about productivity. This was all strikingly familiar as it sounded just like the kind of feedback the MacBook Air received from these same people.

There was endless, and tiresome, commentary on how there could not be productivity without a mouse, a desktop, and overlapping windows, which was generously called multi-tasking, technically a misnomer. The irony was always lost on the person commenting—there was a time when the PC did not have a mouse and, in fact, the introduction of the mouse was viewed as a gimmick or a toy entirely counter to productivity. Or the fact that for most of the Windows history, the vast majority of users ran with one application visible at a time just like on the iPad. I collected a series of articles from the 1980s criticizing the mouse. Fast forward to 2010, replace mouse with touch, and these read exactly the same. It was as if we had not spent the past three years debating whether one could use a smartphone with only a touchscreen.

Also, there were no files. How could anyone be productive without files? The iPad turned apps using a cloud into the primary way to create and share, not files and attachments. Apple would later add a Files app. Kids today have no idea what files are.

When they weren't making fun of the name "iPad" many were quick to mock the whole concept of an iPad as a simply puffed-up iPhone. Ironically, the mid-2010 iPhone was still a tiny 3.5" screen; it would not be until late 2014 when Apple would relent and introduce a larger screen iPhone and a year later would introduce a 12.9" iPad. Apple in no way saw the iPad as simply a larger iPhone.

Walt Mossberg set different tone in with his review. "Laptop Killer? Pretty Close—iPad Is a 'Game Changer' That Makes Browsing And Video a Pleasure; Challenge to the Mouse." Among the positive commentary, Mossberg said of the iPad Pages word processor, "This is a serious content creation app that should help the iPad compete with laptops and can import Microsoft Office files," and, "As I got deeper into it, I found the iPad a pleasure to use, and had less and less interest in cracking open my heavier ThinkPad or MacBook. I probably used the laptops about 20 percent as often as normal." He concluded with a reminder that this was going to be a difficult journey. "Only time will tell if it's a real challenger to the laptop and Netbook."[114]

Apple sold about 20 million iPads in the first year (2010 to 2011) while we were building Windows 8. As it would happen, 2011 was the all-time high-water mark (through this writing) for PC sales at 365 million units, or about 180-200 million laptops. The resulting iPad sales were not a blip or a fad in the portable computing world—10% of worldwide laptop sales in the first year! In contrast, Netbook sales fell off a cliff and all but vanished as quickly as they appeared. Each quarterly PC sales report was skittish as sales growth was slowing. At first the blame was put on the economy, or maybe it was a shortage of hard drives or the lack of excitement from Windows. It would be a while before the PC industry absorbed the impact of phones and tablets and later Google ChromeBooks. There was a brief respite during the first year of the global pandemic and work-from-home, but that too quickly subsided. It is expected that 2022 PC sales (including Google Chromebooks) will be about 300M units.

The iPad and iPhone were arguably the most existential challenges Microsoft had ever faced. While the industry focus and Apple's business were on the devices, the risk came from the redefinition of operating system capabilities and software development and distribution. Apple had created a complete platform and ecosystem for a new and larger market. This platform came not at a time of great strength for Microsoft, but a time when we were on our heels strategically fighting for our relevancy. The Windows platform had been overrun by the browser, including the recent entry from Google that would soon eclipse Internet Explorer as well as the recently announced ChromeOS. PC OEMs were in rough shape financially and had an uncertain future. Windows Server, as well as it had been doing, had failed to achieve leadership beyond the (large) enterprise market. Linux and open source dominated the public internet. Amazon Web Services and cloud computing consumed the energies of academia and start-ups. Windows Phone 7 had not yet shipped and Windows Phone 6.5 was being trounced by Apple from above and Android from below. Even hits from Xbox to SQL Server were not actually winning in their category but were distant second place.

If ever "It was the best of times, it was the worst of times" applied to a company, the summer of 2010 was it for Microsoft. When it came to financial success Microsoft was in a fantastic position, but strategically and in "thought leadership" we were in a weak position.

Perhaps Microsoft could have made better bets earlier and we squandered what could have been a potential lead? In October 2011, almost two years since the iPad was available, I received an email from a corporate vice president of public relations. He relayed a message from a reporter asking about an unreleased Microsoft tablet with the code name Courier. The reporter wanted to know, "Why did Sinofsky kill it?" According to the reporter, the Courier project had been going on since before the iPad was released (this was important) and it was only just now, 18 months after the iPad was available, it became clear that Sinofsky killed it.

Oh no, they found out, I thought. Crap.

The problem was that I had never seen this project. I'd hardly heard of it other than rumors of just another random project in E&D operating under the radar that had been cancelled more than a year earlier. There was a small story in Gizmodo tech blog when the project, which was a design sketch/prototype was cancelled shortly after the iPad announcement in April 2010, "Microsoft Cancels Innovative Courier Tablet Project":

> *It is a pity. Courier was one of the most innovative concepts out of Redmond in quite some time. But what we loved about Courier was the interface and the thinking behind it-not necessarily its custom operating system.*[115]

Courier was developed in E&D, Entertainment and Devices division, where Xbox and Zune were developed. It was, apparently, a design for a dual-screen, pen-based tablet. A conceptual video rendering of the device leaked, and the internet was very excited. It looked to be the dream device to techies—it had two screens and folded like a book! As fascinating as it was, all anyone, myself included as far as I knew, had to judge it by was an animation. The first time I saw the animation was on the internet just before the project was cancelled.

That video leaked (by whom we did not know) two months prior to the iPad announcement during the height of tablet rumors even before the CES show with Windows 7 tablets and early Android tablets. Gizmodo, who above praised it as one of the most innovative concepts coming out of Redmond, described the Courier interface relative to their favorite interpretation (or "what everyone expects") of Apple tablet rumors:

> *The Courier user experience presented here is almost the exact opposite of what everyone expects the Apple tablet to be, a kung fu eagle claw to Apple's tiger style. It's complex: Two screens, a mashup of a pen-dominated interface with several types of multitouch finger gestures, and multiple graphically complex themes, modes and applications. (Our favorite UI bit? The hinge doubles as a "pocket" to hold items you want move from one page to another.) Microsoft's tablet heritage is digital ink-oriented, and this interface, while unlike anything we've seen before, clearly draws from that, its work with the Surface touch computer [the tabletop described earlier] and even the Zune HD.*[116]

In hindsight, one just knows that Apple got a huge kick out of this device and the quasi-strategic leak from the team.

More importantly, I had to pick up the pieces with the PC OEMs who read the articles about this device and wondered if Microsoft was competing with them or undercutting their own efforts at new Windows 7 tablets. In the leadup to the first CES with Windows 7 and our work on touch and tablets, trying to generate support across the ecosystem, this kind of leak was devastating. Aside from the appearance of hiding important details from partners, it looked like one part of Microsoft was competing with our biggest customers or worse that the Windows team was part of the duplicity. In his CES 2010 keynote, SteveB had to call out and bring special visibility to a new tablet from HP just to smooth over the relationship due to the Courier leak months earlier. There was non-stop scrambling from the time of the Gizmodo leak until he stepped off stage. HP, as the largest OEM, was (and remains) directly responsible for billions in Windows revenue, and thus profit. Months later, HP bought Palm and its WebOS software for $1.2 billion with every intent of creating a tablet with its own operating system. It would not be unreasonable to conclude that HP pursued Palm because of the Courier project even with the history of OS development at HP.[117] Our OEM partners thought we were bad partners.

The group of Microsoft influencers on the internal email discussion group LITEBULB thought we were foolish for cancelling what would certainly have been the next killer device. One person said, on a long discussion thread contrasting Courier with money-losing Bing and Xbox, "In my view, our apparent unwillingness to lose money on a few innovative, sexy products that people drool over is part of the reason we are losing the public perception battle to Apple and Google."

Courier became a shorthand or meme for incompetent management at Microsoft. Given the climate around the company and a decade of a relatively flat stock price, such internal discussions contributed to a growing narrative of the death-of-innovation at Microsoft. For so many reasons it was readily apparent even if materialized as a real PC, Courier would have been as doomed as all the Tablet PC products before it, and even more so because of the dual-screen approach. My own team mostly thought I was foolish for not even knowing about the existence of Courier.

I looked unaware or dumb, or both, and along with all the powers at Microsoft had stifled innovation.

We thought this story was over and then more than two years after that leak we received the inbound indicating I was the culprit and the reporter awaited comment. When the video of the leak first surfaced, I sent an email trying to understand if the Courier project was related to Windows 7. Was it for sale? What version of Windows 7 was it running? Did OEMs know? I became concerned that there was a modified source tree of Windows 7 floating around and how would that be released and supported? Was this another Tablet PC or Media Center code fork and potential mess? I was told it would run Windows 7, but heavily modified. Xbox was originally the Windows source code so now knowing the team I became concerned that playbook would be used. We had just cleaned all this up with the release of Windows 7, but this new situation could turn into a real mess. We just spent three years on Windows source code and sustaining engineering hygiene, so this better not take us back from where we came, I opined. It was messy, but as it turned out the budgeting and management processes within E&D led to the demise of Courier and had nothing to do with the concerns I expressed after the fact.

My reaction was to just tell the reporter we would go on record that I did not have any role in "murdering" the Courier project and had no knowledge of it until I saw the leaked video. I said as much in email to the communications team. There was no shaking the reporter who was certain of his sources and simply concluded this was some sort of misdirection from me and Microsoft. Whatever. A decade later whenever a dual screen device shows up in the market the Windows fans return to Courier and remark "what could have been" and that acts like an SEO (search engine optimization) effort to join my name with killing innovation.

We looked bad from every direction: internal innovation watchdogs, OEM partners, as an executive staff lacking a coherent strategy, and most of all with our own Windows team. The innovation or lack thereof narrative at Microsoft was dutifully fed by cancelling this project, which given our experience with Windows 7 would of course not have been successful. There were so many problems. The entire experience shows the problem with demos, leaks, press sources, and what it is like to try to do (or not do) new things in the context of a broader narrative.

It is a decade since Courier was cancelled and people still hope to bring back this project and many still see it as symbolic of the company's tendency to stifle innovative projects. Surface released the Microsoft Surface Duo device, running a modified Google Android as a somewhat puzzling approach. Courier routinely shows up on lists of innovative projects killed by mismanagement. There's some irony in that latter view given Microsoft's penchant for continuing to pursue products long after they have failed to achieve critical mass, well-beyond the requisite three versions.

The debates within the team about the iPad were there. Would it replace or augment a laptop? Was it a substitute for a PC and users continue to do what they did on a PC, or would people use it as an alternative to do new things in new ways? Would developers build apps specific for the larger iPad screen? Would it ultimately be limited to consumption as many predicted or become a creative and productive tool? Would third-party developers optimize apps for the iPad? Would PC OEMs make a good tablet with the software we would design, or not? This last question was critical.

Amazingly, these debates continue today even with something like a half billion active iPads. The convergence of today's Apple Silicon Mac and iPad make the debate either more interesting or exceedingly moot.

Back in the realm of what the team could control and execute, we began planning Windows 8 in the Fall of 2009. We saw the disappointments at the Consumer Electronics Show followed by the surprise of the iPad announcement. Our plans came together in the Spring of 2010. For the new Windows team, it was a magical planning effort.

100. A DARING AND BOLD VISION

We never lacked clarity in what we intended to do—reinvent Windows for a new era. That meant a new experience, a new platform for developers, a new connection to services, and, yes, new hardware. Books about reinvention (or disruption) don't tell you that you can't just announce such intentions to the world. It turns there is the intention to reinvent and then a plan to build it, though when you decide to share a strategy is an entirely different matter.

I was old enough to have personally lived through the creation of the term *Osborne effect*[118] as it pertains to pre-announcing products. In high school I programmed my father's Osborne he bought to keep the books for the family business. We'd been using the Osborne daily since it launched and thought about buying an upgrade for the business. Then Osborne founder and CEO, Adam Osborne, pre-announced the Executive, a fancier model with more memory and a bigger screen. The only problem was it was far from being done. The prototype product was shown in 1983. Customers held off buying the original Osborne long enough that the company went bankrupt before delivering the new computer.

Apple faced a similar dilemma when it first transitioned from Motorola chips to PowerPC chips. The transition was announced in 1994. While it is difficult to tease out the impact of Windows 95 from the chip transition, Apple's share of the Mac/PC market would steadily shrink for another decade, and decline significantly in absolute unit sales, until the next chip transition to Intel.

Microsoft had long been relatively immune from pre-announcing products because the overall growth of the PC market combined with the breadth of the product line dampened any pullback in a single product. The PC needed an OS even if the next one was delayed. As we saw with Longhorn/Vista, businesses still continued to buy PCs in droves. That's why many Microsoft products seemed to be talked about long before they were released. There was an added benefit to this early sharing, or as we called it openness, which was used to generate platform momentum. With nothing to lose, Windows itself benefitted from a solid 5 years of momentum building in the early days before Windows 3.0. Back then it was all just an industry norm.

In our world, the Windows business had just survived the Longhorn mess and recovered with Windows 7. We now faced an entirely new market situation. Windows itself faced structural challenges—actual alternatives in the market in the form of phones, tablets, browsers, Intel-based Macs, and soon ChromeOS. At the very least, people could just stick with Windows 7, which was fine by us, except given new alternatives most customers would not even consider buying a new or additional PC, which was very bad for us.

Every bone in the Microsoft body would cry out to begin evangelizing Windows 8 as soon as we had plans. We were going to build a new platform and evangelists wanted time to articulate the strategy so developers could weigh their alternatives. But doing so would also run up against Windows Phone 7 and the platform they were evangelizing. The lack of strategic connection between Windows and Windows Phone was obvious but at the time was fraught with difficult choices, especially in the context of competing with Apple.

Then there was the biggest of all problems, again something they fail to mention in books. What if the big strategic bet we planned on making ran right up against our biggest partners and customers? The whole idea of advancing Windows without our partner Intel and the major PC makers Dell, HP, and Lenovo would be heresy, plain and simple. We are talking about Wintel after all. Not only were we planning on a chipset, but we knew we would offer something radical with respect to the actual computer we'd offer customers. Double heresy.

As a result, the vision we created for Windows 8 was not specific in the broad communication about the role that alternate chip platforms, SoC or system-on-a-chip, or new hardware would play in the plans. By using the term SoC we could account for both ARM, the then UK company that designed the chips used in all mobile phones and tablets, and Intel who continued to work to develop a competitive SoC with their Atom branded chips. While the engineering was well underway, the degree of the bet still needed a bit more data and experience to decide if we could execute specifically on bringing Windows to ARM. By using SoC, if the term leaked, we could always point to Intel's latest Atom chips as the goal. The cost of openly defying our own ecosystem and then failing to materialize would have been immense given the state of the PC market.

As far as how these alternate chips would come to market, we had not yet decided on a complete plan. Would we go the standard route which was to evangelize to the OEMs as we did with Windows Media Center PC and later multitouch support? Would we build a first-party demonstration device and use that as the basis of evangelism as we did with Tablet PC? Or would we commit to what was either unimaginable or incredibly dumb depending on if you were our customers/partners or BillG and design, build, and sell, our own new device? The vision would be silent on this. The plans were still being made and would be resolved just a few weeks after the product vision was communicated.

With the iPad announcement described in the previous section, the pressure on everyone to respond was immense. For some the rise of Android was even more worrisome, primarily because of the history of Apple being less of a real threat. Google caused more consternation because it was growing so large so quickly in an area entirely new to Microsoft. Either way, even though Microsoft was the among the first to enter the smartphone market, by 2010 our share remained in low single-digits and would never get much higher.

The app revolution underway in Silicon Valley was on the iPhone. And we were missing it. I learned this firsthand sitting in the pouring rain after a wedding in San Francisco in 2010, when everyone else was using a new iPhone app to summon a limousine late at night. It was my first experience with the UberCab on-demand car service, and we couldn't summon one on my Microsoft phone as we became drenched.[119] The app gap was just getting started. Every day it seemed like a new company released a new app for the new iPhone platform and none of that innovation was happening on Windows. I swear it felt a bit like what IBM must have experienced when everything new was on Windows and all that was on OS/2 was what they paid to have there.

Windows and Windows Phone: Alignment?

The Windows Phone Team was in the midst of the significant reinvention of the phone platform, originally code-named Photon, which became Windows Phone 7 or WP7. The fall 2010 release was more than six months from the rollout of the vision for Windows 8.

There were many challenges in entering, or re-entering, the smartphone business. Bootstrapping an ecosystem was chief among them. Finding the right hardware partners proved difficult in the face of competition for those same partners from Android. There was also the challenge of building a differentiated product when the high-end was so solidly iPhone while Android seemed to cover the breadth of the market. To many reading this, the market might appear analogous to the evolution of the PC market, except Android has the role of Windows and the premium niche occupied by iPhone is much larger than the eight share points Apple computers achieved.

WP7 faced several software challenges simply because the core operating system was so old. Support for the latest capabilities across graphics, networking, multicore CPUs, removable storage, and devices (such as the NFC reader required on Japanese mass transit) was becoming increasingly difficult to impossible, as was enabling the product to work worldwide across languages with complex characters and input methods. A hot topic on the heels of the product release was the rollout of 4G or LTE technology, especially in Asia, and the challenges WP7 had in building support in the operating system.

When it came to synergy with Windows the developer platform was the key challenge. Windows Mobile, Microsoft's original phone OS, supported a subset of the Developer Tools strategy which had a nominal relationship to Windows itself. Breaking with that platform, WP7 made a new bet on the nascent Silverlight project, a decidedly non-obvious strategy relying on a technology project essentially salvaged from the prior big bets in Longhorn as I described when I supported moving the team and early project out of Windows. As a competitor to Adobe Flash, it seemed most suited to lightweight games, video, and photos designed for a cross-platform experience. A significant class of apps, sure, but as a general-purpose platform, a Windows platform, Silverlight was inadequate and would face challenges in maturing to a complete platform. For example, there was little hope of building an email client or Office in any enduring way using Silverlight's capabilities as they were. That was certainly my opinion. They made a strategy that was first and foremost based on time to market and that leveraged a new initiative in Developer Tools that many were very excited about, including the evangelists. The use of Silverlight felt leveraged and very…strategic. This will be further discussed in the next chapter. Given the break from Windows Mobile, there was an opportunity for a strategic platform alignment that was not taken advantage of.

By the time it released, with its stark "Metro" tiles and hubs rather than apps, Windows Phone felt unique and differentiated, despite the potential limitations. The Windows community would develop a wildly enthusiastic following for WP7, despite the paucity of apps relative to iPhone. Walt Mossberg wrote a review with the headline, "Microsoft's New Windows Phone 7: Novel But Lacking." He concluded "…Microsoft has used its years in the smartphone wilderness to come up with a user interface that is novel and attractive, that stands out from the Apple and Google approaches, and that works pretty well."[120] Ultimately, he did not recommend it and said it was neither as good nor as versatile as iPhone or Android.

Sales for Windows Phone would peak roughly a month after initial launch of WP7 and would never match that launch spike.

From my perspective, Microsoft's phone business faced many challenges but chief among them was a weak platform for building apps, and related, an underpowered operating system relative to modern computing needs and competitors, even with the new WP7. After launch there were rising numbers of Windows Phone apps, but the vast majority were simply web sites hosted inside an app without much, if any, work from the owners of the web site. The flagship apps were mostly paid for or even supervised by Microsoft. The lack of enthusiasm from third parties did not match the optimism within the halls of Microsoft and from our biggest fans. Being the third choice in the market, even a Microsoft choice, was not enough.

I'd soon learn the size of the hill that needed to be climbed for a new Windows.

The industry, however, remained optimistic that WP7 would be a contender for the number two spot behind Android, as BlackBerry and Symbian (from Nokia) continued to decline, and iPhone was viewed expensive and low volume. IDC predicted even as late as 2011 that Windows Phone would go from about 3.8% share to over 20% share by 2015.

Regretfully, that 3.8% share was the platform's peak.

We planned Windows 8 while WP7 was still finishing. We were about nine months ahead, both teams working hard to achieve a shared view of plans with what might become both Windows 8 and Windows Phone 8.

The problem was Windows Phone and Windows did not share aligned schedules, which made most efforts at synergy optimistic at best or an academic exercise at worst. In a quest for synergy between groups, I long advocated to align dates, especially with respect to making firm commitments. In all Microsoft history the only time teams successfully collaborated was when schedules aligned from start to finish and shared a complete focus on that one goal. We seemed stuck, however, unable to align our differing views of how fast we could move and what should be a collective priority. Should we have stopped working on Windows or stopped working on a Phone? These questions seemed silly since obviously neither made sense at the time. I was fond of repeating a mantra that sometimes to speed up we first must slow down. To most that came across as dumb, especially in the context of gaining prominence of Google and Facebook leading with speed. When groups aren't aligned getting aligned is extraordinarily difficult and requires painful choices. Was Phone ahead of Windows? That couldn't be because it was built on an old code base. Was Windows ahead of Phone? That couldn't be because we had not done any of the work to be a mobile OS yet. Should we have not released WP7? Should we have stopped working on Windows 8 until after WP7? Would we then have done another new reset of WP7 instead of a fast follow-on release? These were non-trivial questions to ask.

Apollo, the code name for Windows Phone 8, would start well after Windows 8 had started, plus there was the interim Windows Phone 7.5 release, code-named Mango. We could have aligned on many things with a schedule where Apollo finished after Windows 8, but the Phone Team did not want a schedule to stretch out that far. Our planned Windows 8 availability was in June 2012. To the Phone Team, finishing Windows 8 code in April would not have allowed enough time to make holiday of 2012 with phones. From my perspective, our April 2012 date for

Windows 8 was aggressive. If Windows 8 were the next Windows 7 then in all likelihood we would have hit the date, but given the massive scope of the project I could not be so precise which reminded me of schedule chicken with my friends in Germany a decade earlier.

Absent alignment across the full schedule, at every step the teams would be doubting each other, making alternate plans, or hedging on alignment. In this case, Windows Phone appeared to me to have more confidence in their target dates than I did in mine. Depending on the scope of changes in the phone plans that seemed plausible.

What would an aligned plan look like?

It would be a Windows Phone built using the new Windows 8 operating system. A plan like this would address both the operating system shortcoming of WP7 and the limitations of the Silverlight platform. Executing would have been straightforward, assuming the Windows Phone business was comfortable with the schedule and doing the work to make sure Windows 8 ran on the hardware phone partners required. The effort to bring Windows 8, as planned, all the way down to a phone level of hardware was significant but with a fully committed effort from the Phone Team it was entirely possible—Apple proved that by bringing OS X to the iPhone.

A plan where Windows limited itself to what was in Windows Phone 7.5 amounted to simply delaying the start of Windows 8 for another two or more years. This quickly began to feel like Longhorn all over again. Besides the WP7.5 code base and developer platform were no starting point for a long-term platform play and the phone required far too much of Windows anyway.

This was another round of strategic handwringing or unrealistic thought experiments since no one wanted any team to slow down, stop, or rethink plans resulting in slowing down or stopping. No one.

I was certainly not going to force the issue. Another team's schedules were their business, and I had enough concern over executing our aggressive plans. I retreated from the debate. I wasn't willing to force my idea of a plan without more support from Windows Phone.

Everyone was concerned about time to market—who wasn't? Tens of hours in meetings were burned up on hypothetical conversations about aligning on overly specific features or creating seemingly impossible synergies where the whole conversation was built on a foundation of dates that were not accurate to more than three to six months. Creating mythical savings by shaving weeks off testing or partner releases was academic. These handwringing conversations drove me nuts, like my 8th grade science teacher's reaction when I used too many significant digits just because my TI-35 could display them. We needed a coarse and big bet, not trying to gerrymander a solution without disturbing existing plans, existing plans that were not getting us to a stronger position.

In these discussions, we found ourselves detailing minutiae of Bluetooth drivers and graphics subsystems and how to share those, which were good goals but entirely divorced from the broader challenges of alignment or step-function change required to earn a seat as a leader. We seemed unable to discuss the deeper strategic issues like the developer platform or the need to move all of Windows Phone to a new OS and that a new OS had to be built first. There was nothing specific to Windows and phones in this situation; rather, this was a typical Microsoft pattern of strategic dysfunction. When faced with a big problem, we'd devolve into a debate about tactics, trying to find some alignment with minimal impact, then we'd surface with disappointing or unrealistic plans. It was the classic big company dynamic where the PowerPoints got longer and more divorced from reality and then one person in the room had to step back and say, "wait a minute." That was usually me or JonDe.

Even within our own Windows team, there was a small group in JonDe's organization that wanted Windows 8 to bet on making a phone from the start. Several key leaders from the Windows NT era were now on the Phone Team and remained close to those in leadership roles in Windows, creating a natural collaboration point. It was a totally rational bet, after all, because that was what Apple had done when it reengineered OS X to be the basis for iPhone and iPad and it was also what Microsoft needed. Apple's mobile product did not, however, need to maintain its existing business and at the same time move it forward. It also lacked the heft of the Windows ecosystem and moving the product to SoC/ARM in a single release. It also lacked the reality of being third to market in a new and clearly defined category.

I give huge credit to those on the Windows team that pushed to build a phone. As audacious, and that's the right word, as our Windows 8 plans were shaping up to be, building a phone from within the Windows group was one step more than we could take alone. These were difficult conversations to be had. The team heard the desire to push harder and responded. Had the company been a bit more receptive in a real and committed, and not symbolic, way then perhaps I might have been convinced to reach even further than we did with Windows 8. No doubt I was already nervous about the Windows 8 plan and as such there's no escaping that adding one more constraint—not building a phone—was welcome.

Apple had the benefit of a clean break with nothing to lose when it built the iPhone. We just did not have that option, or at least did not consider it.

My feeling, and decision, was that competing with the iPad was an enormous leap for Windows 8. On paper, the idea of building an OS on ARM, a new developer platform, an app store, a new user experience, and working on a new generation of hardware seemed like an absurd bet for Microsoft to get done all at once with its flagship product. In big company lingo, it was a stretch goal for the ages. I was worried about the problems that befell IBM when it embarked on Project Stretch, trying to get too much done too soon. That was hubris.

Building a phone would have been an irresponsible effort from just the Windows team. By constraining the first release of Windows 8 to devices that were tablet sized, we had the chance to achieve success in an area that was already our strength, productivity and information work. Tablets had a bigger screen, more room for user interface, more area for battery, and a logical size for a keyboard. Therefore, during our planning for our team, I drew project boundaries at targeting a tablet device rather than a phone device. We knew we could do a phone in the next iteration. In fact, as we'll see the engineering leaders were already making proof of concept progress in this regard. That's why it felt rational to constrain now and expand later.

Why did building a phone now keep percolating up as an idea? Primarily it was because of the operating systems effort of leapfrog products. The old management view of developing two products at a time and in theory being able to spend more time developing a future release while doing tactical work in the immediate release. Recall this methodology from the sequence of Windows code names, Chicago/Cairo, Nashville/Memphis, Whistler/Blackcomb, and so on. Also recall, the second release never made it to market.

The idea of the Windows 8 team building a phone while the Windows Phone Team built its own Windows Phone on a different code base seemed to follow this logic. It seemed logical to a company that still held a collective, though slightly revisionist view of the past, which was how we cleverly worked on both the original Windows (16-bit) code base, transitioned that to 32-bits, while also building a native 32-bit Windows NT to become the real future of Windows. That is a great story, but leaves out a ten-year story of warring groups, competitive missteps, failure to deliver, and the pure luck that both IBM and Apple all but failed at everything they did, while all the apps worked across all those variations of Windows. We were in no position to endure or accomplish any of that—the paradigm shift was one we were responding to, not creating.

As we will see, it isn't clear that delaying one or the other product would have fundamentally changed the trajectory once the bet on WP7 was made, a bet that was made in the middle of building Windows 7.

As we pulled together and began to circulate the draft vision memo the excitement and chatter in the hallways increased. The team was anxious to start work. Microsoft was always at its best when it faced a crisis, and this was a genuine crisis. Those working on the deep parts of the operating system were super excited about "porting" to SoC (I mean ARM specifically as Windows already supported Intel SoC) as that goes back to the roots of Windows NT and supporting many chipsets. They were confident. Those thinking about building apps were extremely excited about building a new Windows API for modern secure, power-efficient, multitouch applications and the challenge to do so as a core part of Windows and not another "random" new runtime from Microsoft. The user-experience team had fully embraced the idea of melding consumption and productivity.

The one question everyone had was about the target computer—where was our iPad and who would make it? Everyone was asking, "Would Microsoft build a computer?" There was little faith the ecosystem could produce something as magical as the iPad. There was a great deal of hope that we would, as a team, actually do the thing everyone thought it would take to truly enter a newly competitive market and redefine what Windows could do.

Whenever asked I said, "I don't know."

I definitely wanted to, but we had not yet committed. I'd been lobbying for a couple of months to make that happen. I knew we had to and knew that not doing the hardware would be the same compromise Microsoft had always made and I was certain we would fail as we had in the past. I needed to be very careful about words and body language when it came to hardware. As I saw with the fallout of the Courier project, the OEMs (reminder: Microsoft's largest customers) did not take kindly to first-party competition. I would maintain this position for the start of the project.

Confidence was high. Our plan for Windows 8 was daring and bold, even audacious. As I write this today reading the plan and in particular looking at the prototypes from Vision day, I am struck by just how much we set out to do. Spoiler alert: we actually got most of what you can see in the videos done for the release.

On March 24, 2010, six weeks following the iPad announcement, 6,000 Redmond-based employees gathered at the Seattle Convention Center for the Windows 8 Vision Meeting. We invited execs from around the company in a VIP section in the front rows, including Office, Development Tools, Server, Mobile, Research, and more. As in the past, the Company's product executives received the Vision memo and even the opportunity for a small and focused version of the plans for their staffs if they wanted.

Julie Larson-Green led the Vision process and the resulting memo and plans. She and the team perfected the best of top-down, bottom-up, and middle-out planning. They also perfected distilling the plan down to something thousands could understand and presented it in a compelling manner.

The admin team once again did an amazing job getting transportation from Redmond to the downtown venue. They even secured the space that was already staged for the Microsoft TechReady field training summit. We just had to promise to end on time because they had booked the venue until the end of the day. We saved hundreds of thousands of dollars this way. So proud!

We had the full range of collateral for the vision: the 30-page long-form vision memo, the two-pager vision everyone would tack to their corporate-standard cork board, prototype or sketch videos for each of the six vision areas, and a mock press release. The only thing we were totally silent on was the big question of building our own device.

The Windows 8 mock press release was my favorite. With the headline "Microsoft Redefines the PC with Windows 8: Breakthrough Release Brings Customized Experiences for Consumers, a New Business Model for Developers and Strong Value for Businesses" the opening graph read:

> *Redmond, WA – RTM Date – Microsoft today announced the completion and Release to Manufacturing (RTM) of Windows 8, a breakthrough release focused on humanizing the web. Designed for more natural interaction with the PC, Windows 8 enables a consistent and comfortable experience across the screens and devices you use every day. The Windows 8 experience scales consistently across the broadest array of devices: from small-screen slates to PCs to large-screen TVs, yet with no change in system requirements from Windows 7. In addition to its groundbreaking user experience, Windows 8 enables developers to create compelling experiences faster, easier, and reach new markets quickly.*

The theme of the day was "8" of course. Everything was about the number eight, right down to the use of Saturday morning TV videos on the number eight—"eight, eight, eight let's sing a song of eight." The theme of eight continued with a walk-in video of trivia questions related to the quantity eight.

After a brief introduction I asked SteveB to come on stage to provide context on the importance of Windows to Microsoft. His energy level always exceeded that of most and was always difficult to follow as the next speaker. I did not tell him in advance, but for his walk-in video I used what became infamous, a Windows sales video from 1985. It featured him in a tacky plaid coat doing his best "and that's not all" description of all the features of Windows 2.0, "including Reversi," all for $99. There was a great line at the end. He announced that the offer was not valid in Nebraska, an inside reference to my former manager, original leader of the Word (then called OBU-Office Business Unit) team, and SVP of the sales force Jeff Raikes's home state. Most on the team had no idea this video existed and were puzzled by that line at the end. We also showed the now famous "Developers, Developers, Developers" rallying cry which was all too appropriate for the event. While intellectually I understand why some might make fun of these performances, not only are they classic Microsoft events they show the genuine and electric passion SteveB had for the company and the mission we were on. They are as much a part of the success of Microsoft as any software we wrote. Steve probably used the phrase and same passion 1000 times, but it was immortalized in this video. In a later discussion we had on the audio app Clubhouse, Steve discussed what it was like to galvanize thousands of people and why such passion was important as a leader.[121]

I remained backstage and after Steve exited the stage, we walked over to the front row and sat down. I was right behind Steve and would narrate and provide color to the presentation as it progressed. He had of course already read the vision and we had our usually back and forth. Steve was an active listener and always had lots of questions during a presentation. I had sent the written vision to BillG as well but did not hear back much other than a renewed emphasis on the pen and handwriting.

Entering the stage to the Schoolhouse Rock video "Crazy Figure 8" JulieLar presented the vision of the product. The words she used repeatedly were "modern" and "tailored web," which was our way of describing the new apps for Windows 8, the Windows runtime, and the tools required. The "tailored web" phrase was awkward and my doing, but we meant apps. It was meant to reflect our view that apps were taking advantage of the web platform, not just another runtime API on top of Windows—it was Windows.

Julie presented six vision areas. It is worth going through each one in this text. Note for the web version the vision area slides used at the time are provided and area's text description is followed by the video shown the team.

- Designed for a Tailored Web Experience
- Engineered for Tailored Web Development
- Connected and Ready to Use
- Enhanced with Services
- Approaching Consumer Electronics Quality
- Future-proofing the OS

While I was saying "chipset to the experience" we always started describing the product from the experience. In most every way the audacity of the release was most visible in the experience, though by no means contained within. From there we moved deeper into the implementation.

The descriptions below are taken from the Vision Memo. Each of these high-level descriptions was accompanied by detailed subpoints articulating specific features that were (for the most part) delivered in the release.

Designed for a Tailored Web Experience. In Windows 8, we will create an experience optimized for consumption scenarios, and the form factors and input methods that enable them. We will design a modern user experience that re-imagines the spirit and benefits of the web—connected experiences, informing in real-time, built on open platforms—but evolved for modern PC form factors. We will cultivate a new ecosystem of applications, optimized around multitouch, sharing, people, and connection to devices, which together will create a web experience tailored to Windows. We recognize that customers store information about their identity, people, and the services they use in the cloud, and we'll rely on Windows Live or other compatible services to complete our tailored experience.

Engineered for Tailored Web Development. In today's world, the web is an increasingly central part of how customers use computing devices. Given the broad customer reach, the ease of deployment, and the potential for monetization on the web, developers—particularly new developers entering the market—have focused intently on the web and have utilized the standards-based web technologies of HTML, CSS, and JavaScript. Today, Windows offers very limited value to web developers, who cannot use web programming models for reliable access to the capabilities of the rich client. In Windows 8, we will blend the best of the rich client with the ease of deployment and openness of the web platform and enable developers to easily create, sell and deploy applications that take advantage of native system capabilities such as touch, media, hardware acceleration, connection to devices and services, as well as the capabilities of specialized PC form factors. Windows Live continues to be an important showcase for our Windows offering and a growing part of our platform message. Windows Live focuses on being a premier developer for Windows and provides additional services, including Windows Live Connect, which developers can use as they build their applications.

Connected and Ready to Use. Connectivity is the oxygen of digital life. People expect to connect to people, websites, data, devices, and applications whenever and wherever they want. They don't want to think about connecting, they expect to just *BE* connected. They're frustrated if connectivity is cumbersome or unreliable. Windows 8 PCs meet these challenges by easily connecting to people, places and data over any network; making network and device connectivity snappy and responsive on a wide range of hardware; intelligently managing network resources; delivering on the promise of connecting to work or home from anywhere; creating rich and delightful scenarios with wired and wireless devices; providing hosters more economical options for scaling their services; giving organizations the network policy controls to meet their security and compliance goals; creating more opportunities for Telco, retail and IHV partners to participate in and profit from the Windows experience; and offering programmers the ability to use the most important functions of Windows network and device capabilities in modern applications.

Enhanced with Services. Web services are an established part of daily life, connecting people, devices and information in a diversity of contexts—home, work, and in between and in an increasing number of geographies. Seamless web services that understand context can move software from the mundane to the modern. Services help realize the promise of connected technologies, dynamically delivering digital assets—content, media, applications—into contexts that delight customers. Services enable feedback loops and improvements over time, demonstrating customer-driven decision-making, founded in data, and ensuring that the experience becomes increasingly relevant and richer. Services in Windows 8 enhance the customer experience when a connection is present, while respecting a quality baseline experience in a disconnected state. Windows 8 services help us connect with customers, understand their needs and pain points, and enrich their experience over time through dynamic, contextual delivery of content and applications relevant for their locale and in their preferred language.

Approaching Consumer Electronics Quality. In the early days of the PC, most people who owned a computer were hobbyists or technical enthusiasts. As enthusiasts, their expectations were generally low around how much extra maintenance, repair, and tinkering were required to keep PCs running well. In fact, the amount of skill and know-how to keep a PC in top shape was often the source of bragging rights and status among enthusiasts. The

Windows 8 PC is easy to own and operate, from the day it comes out of the box to the day the owner decides to retire it. Building such an experience starts with our partners, who design hardware, drivers and applications that are a considerable part of the customer experience. To deliver a great PC to customers, we ensure these partners have the tools and data they need to create and deploy Windows images, assess their quality and solve any problems discovered. In many ways this is a journey that started with Windows 7, where we took a major step forward with both in-box quality and with the work we did with our partners to deliver great systems. Windows 8 takes the next step, with additional capabilities built into Windows as well as tools to help our partners deliver high-quality systems. Hardware platform investments and shared bets with our silicon partners, OEMs, ODMs and IHVs increase system quality. These investments result in the most stable, responsive, power-efficient and low-maintenance Windows we've ever produced, running on systems that take full advantage to deliver a quality experience that matches that of consumer electronics.

Future-proofing the OS. One of the greatest strengths of Windows is its versatility. Windows runs on hardware ranging from Netbooks to huge multi-processor servers, in roles spanning touch-enabled PCs in the home to massive databases in the enterprise. To make this possible, we build Windows on a powerful set of core services that deliver performance, scalability, reliability and security across a wide range of form factors, user scenarios, and server workloads. And, as the industry innovates in the core components of computing—such as processors, networking and storage technologies, as well as device types—investments in the core of Windows 8 ensure that Windows remains the leading way industry innovations reach our customers.

There are several current trends that will have a particularly significant impact on the core of Windows in the Windows 8 timeframe. System-on-a-chip (SoC) vendors are delivering new offerings that enable emerging form factors such as slates to rival the capabilities of today's PCs. Virtualization technologies are redefining the boundary between the operating system and the hardware on which it runs and the way that companies deploy and manage both their servers and clients. Further, customers tell us their use of virtualization technologies will grow dramatically. The price of commodity storage is plummeting at the same time that storage use is exploding in both consumer and business settings. And new security technologies are emerging that will affect the way customers experience computing in the future. Our investments in future-proofing the core ensure we're well-positioned to compete with a wide range of innovative device types, take a leadership position in scalable computing architectures based on commodity hardware and devices, and strengthen Windows as a secure, trustworthy platform.

Sitting in the audience with our guests from around Microsoft and next to SteveB, I could not resist emphasizing or highlighting aspects of the meeting, especially the videos. There was a lot of excitement but there were many questions. The biggest question from SteveB to me was "What about Office?" In our demos of all that was new, particularly with the "Tailored Web", we did not show Office. For the whole of Microsoft enterprise business and much of the company history, the business was not just Office but Office **and** Windows.

Without Office there would be no Windows and without Windows there could be no Office—that reinforcing flywheel was essential to both but also essential to the ecosystem. A new Windows without a new Office would send a message to the ecosystem that the new release was not important. Office 95 and Windows 95, Windows 2000 and Office 2000, the XP wave. When Windows didn't have a new Office or when Office didn't ride on the coattails of a new Windows, we struggled. Either new PCs were not seen as exciting, or developers would not know what to do with a new Windows, or enterprises would not be interested in the effort to deploy just one of the two products everyone used.

Our answer was simple yet just as bold as the Windows plan—we needed new software from Office just like we needed new software in Windows. The existing tools would run, but the vision encompassed a new user interface, a new API for expressing apps, and a connection to online services. In addition, this API and the store for developers to use would impose a new model where an app did not take over the PC in the same way we were all used to.

One of the more animated discussions, right then and there at the vision meeting, was about the Office Ribbon. Steve wanted to know where it was in our demos. While we were still early, we knew the Ribbon was not the path forward for touch devices or smaller screens. We knew that because the people behind the videos we were watching were the actual people who designed the Ribbon. This was not lost on me but did not seem to resonate in the VIP section at that moment.

For me, the shift that was underway was going to be bigger than the transition from character mode to graphical interface. Just as Windows brought graphical interface while also carrying forward the existing character applications, we would bring forward existing graphical applications. We showed this time and again in the videos. The future, however, was in a new kind of application. In many ways we felt bringing forward classic Win32 applications, Intel hardware, and all of the ecosystem was an opportunity for Microsoft. It was decidedly a compatibility play and not one where we wanted Office to come to rely upon. Said more bluntly, Microsoft did not optimize the Windows experience for MS-DOS spreadsheets and word processors—they ran better than they ever had previously but it was abundantly clear new apps built on Win32 was the strategy.

The challenging part was there was little news in the vision meeting for those in the front row watching. The past year had been a march to get to this point. The internal partners and their teams had been part of the process to get us to this point. It was, perhaps, the shock of seeing it all in one place that suddenly makes it all real.

We were really making a very big bet. Yet one look around in the marketplace and it was obvious we had to. The bet to make Windows in the first place, announcing it one month before Macintosh was announced was equally bold. Like Apple with the iPhone, in 1983 Microsoft had nothing to lose. In 2010, there were potentially immense downsides to making a bold, but incorrect, choice for the next Windows. That made everyone a bit nervous.

SteveB, however, is every bit the optimist and also cheerleader. He left the meeting pumped. He had a million questions, but he was definitely excited. He also wanted everything to get done sooner than we planned. Me? I just wanted to get it done when we planned.

For the team, the meeting was fantastic. We had a vision, a plan, and a team ready to execute. Our ship date was set for April 4, 2012, under three years from the completion of Windows 7. When I look at these plans and the video today, all I can do is wonder at just how much we signed up to do and in just two years. As we'll see, we also got most everything done and practically on schedule.

We did not know it at the time, but PC sales were peaking—industry analysts forecasted that the 2010 rate of PC sales of 317 million units would rise to almost 500 million by the time we shipped Windows 8. We shared these estimates with the team at every step. We had to.

Confirming our worst concerns, that never happened. Not. Even. Close.

Emotionally, however, the external climate gradually darkened as PC sales flattened over the course of the release, and then began their decline. The forecasts of 500 million PCs selling in a year gave way to forecasts of tablets, particularly with the unit volume of Android tablets, overtaking laptop sales in two years. From the boardroom to the schoolhouse, the iPad was quickly becoming a fixture. People traveling routinely commented on the use of tablets on planes and the rise of iPhone docks and chargers, and even tablets, in hotel rooms. Cash registers, information kiosks, and even signs in elevators were rapidly becoming iPads. Smartphones surpassed PC sales due to the rise of Android—three years after the iPhone released, phones were outselling PCs and the dreams of emerging markets becoming a source for growth evaporated. Tablets as a substitute for PCs was a debate that raged on a decade later even as PC sales declined continuously and iPad sales grew. PCs were baked into the fabric of the workplace and to a lesser extent schools, but any new business capability or use cases were appearing in the context of a browser, almost always Google Chrome.

As we began Windows 8, PCs transformed from a unit-growth business to a replacement business, in the blink of an eye, making our bet far more existential in nature. Given the way PC sales were shifting to a replacement device in business, the comfort of having a Windows 7 foundation upon which to rest—or fail—was, in fact, comforting.

We started coding just weeks after the worldwide availability of the iPad. We were focused and on a mission. It was amazing.

Steve Jobs appeared at the All Things Digital conference the first week of June 2010, celebrating the iPad hit the company created. Riding this wave of success, Jobs seemed to have a great time being interviewed by both Walt and Kara, with Kara stating that Apple had surpassed Microsoft in market capitalization. I'm sure no one paid attention to such things, ouch. I cringed at hearing that from my front-row seat, a spot I rarely took, preferring to sit in the back.[123]

In the span of a few minutes, Jobs made the case for iPads as the future of the laptop clear, without even using the phrase "post-PC era" that had become all too common. He dismantled our Tablet PC strategy and even relegated the Mac to legacy.

Among the jabs, perhaps most directed at Microsoft's unique strategy was the role of the pen and handwriting, so core to BillG's Tablet PC vision. Jobs said, "handwriting was the slowest input method ever invented." He said, "If you need a stylus you've already failed." In his view, the Tablet PC failed because it was based on a PC, had all the expense of a PC, the battery life of a PC, all the weight of a PC, and, most of all, a PC operating system that needed the precise tip of an arrow of a cursor and mouse.

It would not end. He was right and the tough part was we knew that ages ago, but the iPad delivered the proof.

I sat there writing it all down. But I was also agreeing. Finally, he pointed out that a "PC operating system" can't be used with touch, because all the apps have to be rewritten anyway.

Bingo. That was the major lesson of Windows 7 and the entirety of the strategy for Windows 8 in one quip.

While it was still early, the strengths and weaknesses of both the iPad and our plan were materializing. The iPad had no legacy strategy—it was a total break from the past. Importantly, Jobs defined a new operating system with a new interaction model. An OS is more, though, and for the rest of the OS—the interfaces to hardware, memory management, storage, networking, devices, and more—as he himself said three years earlier at the iPhone launch, the iPhone and thus the iPad were in fact based on a PC operating system, OS X. Apple reimagined not the whole OS (though, to be fair, as we will see, much of the guts of the OS change as well) but the user experience, or what techies call the shell. That was exactly our plan for Windows 8.

As if to somehow call out to me to validate the plan, Jobs in his inimitable manner also shared some news that had never been shared before. The iPhone did not lead to the iPad, but rather the iPad was the original product under development years earlier. Upon seeing the technology, the phone became the product goal, but it took time for the hardware to catch up and for Apple to regain footing as a corporation. We already debated this choice, but knowing we intended to bring forward more compatibility and more openness of the platform, we started with a tablet.

In what turned out to be a metaphor for the ages, Jobs compared PCs (including Macs) to trucks, and the iPad was the passenger car for the masses. He said:

> *When we were an agrarian nation, all cars were trucks, because that's what you needed on the farm. But as vehicles started to be used in the urban centers, cars got more popular. Innovations like automatic transmission and power steering and things that you didn't care about in a truck as much started to become paramount in cars…PCs are going to be like trucks. They're still going to be around, they're still going to have a lot of value, but they're going to be used by one out of X people.*

The internet had a field day disassembling the metaphor in a sea of pedantry that only Reddit and Twitter can produce. People were quick to provide the history of production years of trucks versus cars, the shipments of each over time, the reality that suburban drivers buy tons of trucks, and on and on. Why? Because of exactly what Jobs had said—this was a huge transition, and it was going to make many people uncomfortable. The more someone grew up with a PC (a truck), the more difficult the transition, and the more Apple would need to prove it wouldn't work. This debate continues today.

Outsiders heard that Jobs thought Microsoft had missed every opportunity or made the wrong choices, and in a sense that was his point without saying so directly. What observers did not know was that Windows 8 approached the next steps with a new perspective.

Our goal was to reimagine what a PC could be—no stylus, no Intel chips, none of the OS baggage. From the chipset through developer opportunities to the user experience, we set out to build a new future for PCs by rethinking the assumptions that constrained our every move. We wanted to deliver better products for a modern era.

From the outside it would look like we were copying what had become Apple's proven success, but, in reality, it was parallel evolution, at least when it came to the tablet. The one thing we were not doing was precisely what we incorrectly thought Apple would do, which was to build a new tablet out of our old OS. We were building a new OS that happened to bring along the old OS. This was exactly what Microsoft had done from MS-DOS to OS/2, from that to Windows, and from 16-bit to 32-bit then to 64-bit.

Because of its phone strategy and execution, Apple was ahead of Microsoft. That Apple had nothing to lose because it had built such incredible success in non-PC devices left a good deal of room and no expectations for Apple to reinvent computing for a changing landscape.

Because of its phone strategy and execution, Microsoft was behind Apple. That Windows was mired in poor execution for much of this time left little room and high expectations for Windows to reinvent itself for a changing landscape.

Still, we were going to be late with tablets, the calendar will prove so. At the same time, we weren't making irrational or unproven choices, nor were we simply chasing Apple. First mover advantage as a strategy has mixed results so there was a good chance our tardiness could work in our favor.

Back when our vision meeting ended, I stood at the exit as thousands filed out. The optimism and excitement were everywhere. We could not be in a better position to execute.

Our goal was nothing short of reimagining Windows from the chipset to the experience. The plans were bold to the point of audacious. To do otherwise was to stand still and let the new era pass us by—no way I would let that happen.

2011-2012

With a Windows 7 big win at our backs, we find ourselves terribly behind on other fronts, specifically smartphones, and pretty desperate to catch up. But long before we even realized it, our fate on the phone front was sealed. Outside of Microsoft, people can remotely adjust their thermostat at home or board an airplane with a mobile boarding pass. And then, along came the iPad.

101. REIMAGINING WINDOWS FROM THE CHIPSET TO THE EXPERIENCE: THE CHIPSET

Windows is already a big project, but what we did with Windows 8 was to finally get back to Microsoft roots and instead of merely a product release we aimed to make Windows 8 an industry release and certainly a product of all of Microsoft. From every aspect of the ecosystem and for each of our main customer segments we worked to garner significant support and alignment with Windows 8. We built a vision with that in mind. We organized the team to build that vision. We created a calendar of public milestones to deliver it all to the market.

Organizing for Windows 8

We restructured the team in mid-2009 just before Windows 7 was generally available. It was a complete shift to a functional or discipline-oriented team for Windows and Windows Live services. Internet Explorer with its unique position as both a platform and an application that also worked on older versions of Windows was a separate product unit. We organized about 6000 full time product development team members (about 2000 software development engineers) into 55 different feature teams that had on average 35 software engineers and corresponding software test engineers and program managers.

To scale, we created a new management layer, "the directors." The way I thought of this was from a college hire perspective. A college hire (in development, testing, pm) had a line/lead manager, reporting to a group manager (the 55 teams, each with 5-8 leads), who reported to a director each with 4-7 teams, who reported to the VP of Development, Testing, or Program Management. We also had large teams for creating content and localizing both it and the product, product design and usability, product planning and research, the ecosystem which had engineering as well as partnership, marketing and communications, finance, and soon a hardware team. It was as flat and wide an organization we could come up with. It was quite a long way from when we thought the Word team with 55 developers was the biggest team we'd ever have on one product or the Microsoft Foundation Classes with 4 developers including the manager.

The organization proved remarkably effective and what would surprise most people, it was incredibly agile to massive unknowns and learning along the way. What I said with Windows 7 was always the case with Windows 8, which is even as of this writing I hear from people on a regular basis who talk about the work on the team being the best of their careers and most fulfilling. That means the world.

Public Disclosure and Events

It is easy to imagine Windows 8 happening as a chronology from the initial planning before Windows 7 shipped through to RTM, but that does not do justice to the scale of the effort and how much work happened in parallel. When we spoke of the "chipset to the experience" each of those pillars was both a huge effort by Microsoft to engineer the product and a massive contribution from ecosystem partners to complete the delivery.

Tami Reller (TReller) the corporate vice president of marketing and finance for Windows presented a slide at the end of the project at our all-hands Company Meeting where she outlined the major milestones for Windows 8. These external milestones are on top of the engineering led milestones, M1, M2, M3, Beta, RTM. There were 10 external events for Windows 8, each a major outreach included participation from partners representing a particular aspect of the ecosystem. That's a lot of events for one product. It was another era. While it helps to think of them happening serially, all of what will be described took place in parallel.

These events help to organize the sections that follow: chipset, platform, experience, and the ecosystem. In each of the following sections, we'll follow various events—the internal workings and the public events—that took place from January 2011 through the final product launch in October 2012. The technologists reading along can appreciate this approach as we traverse the project from layer to layer. Those with a marketing perspective will appreciate the journey by segment or channel.

We will dive into product details quite a bit—the highs and the lows as they say. In a blog post on Windows 8 just after the Consumer Preview milestone we described the goals we intended to achieve for the product experience. These were a distillation of the product vision as we iterated on and completed the scheduled feature set. Each of the sections that follow apply to some of these goals but do keep them in mind as they guided the whole project:

- Fast and fluid
- Touch-first (but not only touch)
- Long battery life
- Grace and power of Windows 8 apps
- Live tiles make it personal
- Apps working together to save you time
- Roam your experience between PCs
- Make your PC work like a device, not a computer

Chipset

The journey from Intel to also supporting ARM was one of the more extraordinary technical achievements in scope and execution by the reinvigorated Windows team. The implications of the work were on two levels. First, the immediate challenges were within the existing ecosystem, starting with Intel. Second, we were literally resetting the PC platform while in flight and doing so required a platform evangelism success on par with the original success Windows achieved in the late 1980s.

I hated that throughout the planning of Windows 8 described in the previous section, right up through the team vision meeting, we were, or specifically, I was uncertain over whether we would be able to make the right big and bold bet on ARM. It was so much work.

The Demo

On January 22, 2010, I walked over to Rich Neves' (RNeves) office in the former COSD buildings of the core Windows NT team—these buildings were built just after the Apps campus and were where much of the Windows and Server teams were housed. The Kernel Platform Group (KPG) team had been hard at work on the port to ARM for months—calling it a port is too small, as every major subsystem of Windows required deep architectural innovations—it was a major refactoring of the Windows code base, much of which began under the guise of the previously mentioned MinWin. One week before the iPad announcement, Rich and the team asked me to stop by their hallway for a look at what they had been up to.

These buildings were much larger and a different design than the WEX buildings—the traditional Northwest wood construction had been replaced by exposed and painted metal beams and glass in these more recent buildings. I made my way up to a conference-room-turned-lab, where at least six members of the team waited to anxiously show off the progress. They were anxious because the progress was hard to believe. And frankly, we just hadn't had that many interactions as I had only been their official manager for a short time and in the Windows culture, executives visiting offices was not at all typical.

They showed me Windows 7 running natively on an ASUS phone that was designed for Windows Mobile. Actual Windows 7. All of Windows 7. Windows Mobile at the time was built on a subset of the ancient 16-bit and 32-bit Windows code. They were running the modern Windows NT code base on a phone with an ARM chipset. It was nuts. It wasn't an old-school demo of the kernel or a command line, but the Task Manager, Solitaire, even the on-screen keyboard used for touch, and a command window. This was still the core OS team after all and a command window was more than expected.

I was speechless. I was incredibly impressed with the team and the work they had accomplished so early in the product cycle—we had not even completed the vision. It was a huge boost to the confidence in our plans. While I insisted we remain opaque and secretive about the work as the full vision came together, this visit made it clear we were on our way.

I took some photos of the screens with my Samsung Windows Mobile 6.5 phone. Two years later I used them in a *Windows on ARM* blog post described below, intentionally leaving the original embedded timestamps of the afternoon January 22, 2010, which the internet quickly discovered. That was just after the iPad launch and, for those who cared, it let them know we were working on tablets and ARM much longer than thought and were clearly serious. I know that hardly matters in the scheme of things, but it always made me feel better when we were accused of following in the wake of Apple.

Even the best porting projects—moving from one platform to another, in this case Intel to ARM—have a weird effect. Visible progress is quick, but the last 10 percent of the work takes 90 percent of the effort. There was always a risk that going from early demos to a product would become nearly impossible. The core OS team had the collective experience to know that, in this case, this was no parlor trick. Over the next year the whole of the division and much of Microsoft would be doing its part to bring the full Windows experience to ARM chips.

Rich sent a wonderful mail to the team after the demo. It was the start of something really great.

The question: What would this mean as a product? The answer required a different perspective.

What Does ARM Really Mean?

Windows engineering leadership, leaders of the former COSD organization, had significant experience in porting Windows—translating the code from one chipset architecture to another—across numerous architectures. That is why this was not as outside of the box as many perceived.

In fact, Windows NT code was designed from the start to run on many chipsets—the team was never particularly enamored of the Intel architecture. Porting Windows from 32 – to 64-bit chipsets was one of the most contentious times in the Intel-Microsoft relationship when the Windows team essentially sided with Intel rival AMD in the definition of 64-bit Windows—those "AMD64" references in the source code drove Intel crazy. On the other hand, the team spent a good deal of energy porting to chipsets, such as MIPS and DEC Alpha that proved to have no business case but yielded improvements in the architecture, making future ports easier. While porting Windows to ARM involved the whole team, the core OS kernel team drove the project and provided the deep technical leadership and expertise required to make it happen.

This new cross-platform effort was a break from Intel of significant proportions, the implications of which were important to the future of Windows.

It is worth noting the long history of cross-platform development at Microsoft. Many believe Microsoft was always wedded to Intel, and certainly from the advent of the IBM Personal Computer in 1981 that was obviously the case for operating systems. As described, the Apps or Office team had been committed to Macintosh heavily since that product was under development, and it wasn't until 1997 that Macintosh apps were even split from the main Windows Office development team. Before the IBM PC, the origins of Microsoft go back to providing BASIC and early apps such as Multiplan on a wide range of micro-computers running any number of operating systems. My own very first project was to develop the cross-platform libraries that emulated the Windows 16-bit APIs on Macintosh to ease cross-platform development. That project ultimately led to the poorly received Word 6.0 for Mac and some valuable lessons for me. Microsoft seemed to have a good track record for knowing when to ebb and flow with platforms. From the start the original Windows CE and Mobile efforts were on non-Intel chipsets.

The problem was we were now in astronomically deep with Intel and the entire ecosystem of PC makers, development tools, peripherals, and a constellation of vendors and manufacturers all of whom were integral to Wintel. It was not like the early 1990s when it was viewed by the outside world as a minor side project for Windows NT to work on some fringe chipsets.

Even if, and that was still not certain, we had all of Windows running on ARM chips, we still needed support for all the peripherals and devices, companies to make the chips and computers, and software development tools and support up and down the stack of features. Microsoft had long ago become reliant on the ecosystem for much of this work. Over the past ten years or so we had increasingly included support within Windows itself for common peripherals such as keyboards, mice, some displays, various forms of storage, and mainstream printers, and with Windows 7 we started supporting some sensors and trackpads. The ecosystem, however, still contributed a lot of code required for a basic PC. That was an asset through Windows 7 and would continue with Windows 8 for Intel. For ARM, however, much more of this would need to just work and Microsoft would need to deliver these capabilities.

Cross-platform development is inherently seductive to technologists in how straightforward it should be, highly desirable by business leaders who value the optionality, and easily a requirement by enterprise customers who always insist on the diversity of their needs. The odd thing about cross-platform is that no single customer really cares because they generally have a single computer. BUT, when it comes to the software, all it takes is one application that one customer needs and then the whole effort can fall apart. This was especially, and overwhelmingly, an issue for Windows which took enormous pride (and economic benefit) from running nearly every program ever written for Windows even on Windows 7.

While the porting effort would continue, the issues above in just making Windows work were enormous.

SoC was both a generic term and a specific term. For Windows 8 when speaking internally SoC meant ARM, the chips manufactured to the specifications designed by ARM Holdings, the then British company that created ARM. Unlike Intel, ARM designs chips but does not manufacture them. Companies license ARM designs and intellectual property, which they can customize, and then either manufacture the chips themselves or contract a manufacturer like TSMC, Taiwan Semiconductor Manufacturing Company. Texas Instruments, NVIDIA, and Qualcomm also license ARM and offer designs manufactured in house, or by other chip makers across southeast Asia. Intel, as they often reminded me, held an ARM license. Apple licensed ARM designs and customized them.

Intel had a SoC as well, known as Atom, the chips that were used in Netbooks. Strictly speaking, the Atom SoC was a system-on-a-chip in that the main components were in one chip. Atom, however, came to rely on the existing PC architecture and was entirely compatible with all of existing Windows and so, as far as Windows was concerned, it was a standard Wintel PC. Whenever we talked about SoC, we included Intel, though from a product and engineering perspective, Intel's efforts to make a SoC competitive with ARM was a longer-term goal, one which Intel never achieved, unfortunately.

We called Windows running on ARM SoCs *WOA,* pronounced woe-ah, Windows on ARM. In July 2010, Microsoft also became an ARM licensee, just like Intel and all the mobile phone companies.

The difference between ARM SoC and Intel SoC gets to the heart of a computer science debate and innovation dating to the 1980s, and one of the biggest topics in systems groups when I was in graduate school. ARM chips, at the most basic level, were designed to be simple and leave complexity to the software layer with the belief that simplicity would ultimately yield better performance, power management, and lower cost. They were rooted in the ideas of reduced instruction set computing, RISC. The Intel SoC was rooted more in the idea that chips would continue to increase in transistors, doubling the transistor count every two years according to Intel founder Gordon Moore, and the best use of that was to enable chips to do ever more complex operations at the hardware level. Intel and AMD chips in general were known as complex instruction set computing, CISC, and even the Intel SoC was technically a CISC. There's much more to this overly simplistic explanation or a ferocious debate and I offer two references in this footnote.[124]

The WOA efforts gave the core OS team a chance to rearchitect major subsystems of Windows to perform better, manage power better for longer battery life, support fanless devices, consume less memory, and to be more secure. A significant part of the value proposition for porting to ARM was that Windows would make step function improvements in these areas—the vision for behaving much more like a consumer electronics device depending on the improvements to Windows that could only be done on ARM.

The basics of connectivity, disk storage, and memory were rearchitected as well, using technologies required by ARM designs—technology that took much less physical space because there were no sockets, plugs, or cables as a laptop might have—everything was packaged on one circuit board. In addition, the team engineered support for a whole set of new peripherals that PCs never had, like a compass or accelerometer, which a sensor that indicates when a device is rotated. This work also applied to Intel-based PCs, which was kind of cool even though few, if any, devices would gain these peripherals any time soon.

Software engineers love a good porting project. Ports are finite, measurable, and every day is a day of progress, mostly. Porting Windows to ARM was a massive effort, but also a good deal of fun for the team. They built out a whole new lab and set of tools to test WOA hardware. They designed and built ARM motherboards that had enough connectors to diagnose performance and quality as well as to manage installing new builds of software and test at high volumes. At one point, we had hundreds of WOA circuit boards racked and stacked in the lab.

ARM Strategy Goals

The easiest product strategy would have been to simply complete the work and offer WOA as a unique Windows product much like Windows for RISC or Alpha, or even the 32-bit or 64-bit choices PC OEMs could make. As with any chipset, Microsoft would also provide tools so that existing Windows software could easily target the new chipset.

At the highest level, such a port seemed like a good idea. As if by magic, Windows would gain all the attributes of ARM, such as always-on mobile connectivity, cheaper components, extended battery life, fanless devices, and so on, **plus** all the existing benefits of Windows, such as Office, choice of hardware from many vendors, and even the vast library of existing software. Oh, if only magic were possible.

As it turned out, every constituency in the PC ecosystem had a different rationale for wanting WOA and a different view of what WOA could mean and deliver. Our job was to navigate what amounted to conflicting customer needs and desires. As one could easily imagine, the various perspectives collided and meant there would be tradeoffs that made each constituency unhappy in different ways. Our intent was certainly to deliver on the promises of ARM, but there was difficulty in delivering those along with the "plus" for three important reasons.

First, ARM devices were not architected like x86 devices. Normally, one could pop a DVD into a drive and install Windows. ARM devices, like smartphones and tablets, are built as a complete package of hardware and software. There are no separate operating systems for ARM devices due to the nature of ARM—the customization and choices made by device makers define unique devices. They then do the work in the OS to mate the device and OS together. Apple did this with the iPhone and the iPod and most recently the iPad. Smartphones from Nokia,

Samsung, LG, and so on all do this work whether designing for Android, Symbian, or some variant of an OS. For Microsoft to deliver WOA as a product we would have to specify the ARM platform to a great degree.

That was different than the OEMs might have hoped for as they would have liked to source chipsets and other components from a variety of suppliers while treating Windows as just another component. ARM from any supplier was already cheaper than Intel, a major plus for OEMs. If one were to take a cynical perspective, OEMs simply wanted ARM as a point of leverage to negotiate with Intel over the price of x86 chipsets. For too long Intel held all the cards and even with AMD it seemed there was little leverage. Additionally, with multiple suppliers of ARM chipsets the OEMs saw an opportunity to negotiate even better terms by competitive sourcing just for ARM. While this sounds awesome, it would have been unmanageably complex to deliver WOA such that the choices of what hardware it would run on would be made by many independent OEMs. WOA hardware needed to be determined at the start of the project. The Android ecosystem took such an approach, and by and large customers are left with devices to wither without updates and security fixes, simply because the complexity of delivering them across the diversity of devices is overwhelming.

Second, from an end-user perspective WOA PCs should behave better not just differently than an x86 PC. Windows NT ran on several other chipsets, but all but x86 (and x64) failed because there was no value proposition unique relative to mass-market chips—software makers did not see the volume that would drive them to spend energy porting their own software, while PC makers did not see unique software to justify switching their supply chain. Our work on WOA was rooted in creating a unique value proposition. This was a lesson from the early support in Windows for different chipsets.

Third, the assumptions built into the Wintel model of hardware and software needed to be revisited. The Wintel PC assumed a wide-open hardware platform where anything could be inserted, plugged, soldered, or connected to a PC or laptop and along with that install any necessary software to make a peripheral function. The ability of any hardware to require device drivers or kernel mode software was the bane of the existence of Windows already and the requirement that Windows accept all such software was a recipe for continued challenges with security, reliability, and battery life. Everyone loves the flexibility, but the overall cost had become an inexcusable burden as PC usage expanded to a billion people.

Creating a next-generation platform with this extensibility from the start would bring these weaknesses to WOA. Why bring everything bad about a Wintel PC to this new hardware platform while at the same time reducing the potential to surface the good? This constraint creates a significant break from the way OEMs and customers thought of a PC. Whether Windows wanted it or not, computing devices were moving from a "break open the case and do what needs to be done" to a "sealed case" design as is common with most all consumer electronics.

WOA was not just an alternative chipset for Windows the way we saw 64-bits, RISC, or Alpha, but an entirely new way to think about building a computer platform.

Taking a step back, we wanted to reimagine what Windows could be. We knew we would always have x86 PCs and those would always support the existing body of applications, hardware peripherals, and the ecosystem that provided them. There was little life left in the PC ecosystem. The industry's hardware innovation cycle was firmly planted in mobile—radios, sensors, cameras, rapidly improving processors, memory, and storage, and more. The PC ecosystem was essentially in legacy-support mode, vendors doing what they could to squeeze out costs and continue to win existing business, while trying to break into the high-volume mobile space.

Reading this today it is abundantly clear how the world has changed. Nearly all the innovation that expanded beyond memory, storage, and CPU happened and continues on mobile platforms. By and large, innovations in PC hardware now feed off what happens in mobile so long as the suppliers of both components and software can do the work for PCs. Nearly all organic PC innovation is driven by the market for mega-scale datacenter computers, which are very low volume and very high price. Quite simply, the market size for PCs is one fifth as large as the smartphone market in unit sales. PCs, while twice the size of the tablet market, do not benefit from smartphone innovations as do tablets.

The PC, however, was and remains woefully deficient in the very attributes that were so exciting with the latest smartphones. The list of smartphone attributes read somewhat like the list of all the shortcomings of laptops: long battery life, always connected to the network, mobile network connectivity, instant resume from standby, passive cooling, consistent performance no matter how many apps are installed, high-quality cameras, GPS, motion sensors, light sensors, identity sensors, and more. We summed this up as a consumer electronics level of experience, maintained over time.

An example of the contrast between ARM architecture and x86 architecture is the way an iPhone works relative to low power standby mode, something everyone knows has been historically one of the flakier aspects of a PC.

Phones made people accustomed to consumer electronics devices with very long standby and all-day battery life all while remaining connected to the network and able to light up to full use instantly when a new message arrives. By contrast, even in 2022 people walk around balancing unfolded Windows laptops out of a worry of losing work should the PC fail to resume successfully from standby with the lid closed.

The original iPad had 30 days of standby and 10 hours of usage. During that entire time the product continued to maintain a connection to the network to receive email, messages, notifications, and more. We take for granted the ability for the device to work instantly when we need it and to quickly blank the screen and dramatically reduce power consumption when we don't, reliably and without question.

Building this type of feature takes work at every single layer of the system from the chipset up through the OS and developer platform to the apps. It doesn't "just work" because of a change in chipsets. In the case of Windows, the variation across the ecosystem makes this even more intractable when considering what might be plugged into the PC or what components and supporting code the OEM might have chosen to use.

Our goal was to infuse Windows with these attributes so that new Windows 8 devices and future devices could have the qualities of smartphones and tablets that consumers were experiencing.

We did not set out to have lower-priced devices, to find competitive leverage against Intel, to make better Netbooks, or to simply have more choices to do exactly what Windows already did perfectly well with Windows 7.

The job of engaging the OEMs to achieve these goals was non-trivial.

Steve and Steven Call Intel

We had to break the news to Intel that we were working on moving Windows to their architectural rival—the one that beat out Intel for the iPhone just after the success of winning Apple as an Intel customer for Mac. We planned on an event billed as a "technology demonstration" at CES in January 2011.

This was earth-shattering, geopolitically significant news. Some would see it as, essentially, a fracture of the Wintel relationship even though in practice we were just expanding Windows as we had always done, just as Intel supported Linux. It would be like McDonalds breaking up with Coca-Cola to switch to Pepsi, though more realistically simply adding Pepsi and offering choice. An entire industry was built on the Wintel partnership. For our part, we were confident that for the foreseeable future we would not only be supporting but actively building Windows 8 for x86 devices. That's why this was different than the Osborne effect. It is also why Apple had a much easier time in their past chip transitions because they were fully moving to the latest chips. We indeed planned to run with both x86 and ARM at the same time, for Windows, and recognized how difficult this might be.

In mid-December 2010 as we prepped for CES in January, we huddled around the low coffee table in SteveB's office, eyes fixed on the Polycom, and Steve called Intel CEO Paul Otellini.[125] At Intel his entire career, Paul joined the company in 1974 straight out of graduate school. He rose through the ranks to become Intel's first non-engineer CEO, a position he held for more than five years. Paul was always polite and gracious in our meetings, which made things even more difficult. Our investment in ARM would prove a significant strain in the near term.

Steve took the lead, of course. This was not a technical conversation but about the partnership.

He said we had "some news."

"Paul," he continued slowly and deliberately, "you're not going to view this favorably."

Steve told Paul we'd made the decision that in addition to Intel we would target ARM chips with the next release of Windows and that we would be doing a technology demonstration at CES in January 2011, just a few weeks away. We would talk about Windows support for ARM without doing a full Windows 8 reveal.

Steve reiterated that Intel would continue to be our primary target and that we planned on the vast majority of PCs to be Intel-based PCs still. I chimed in with some words about ARM being the focus for SoC efforts for Windows and that Intel's SoC was also a target. Our announcement would be about SoC, not exclusively ARM, and would feature Intel SoC products. This would scarcely soften the news.

Paul was quiet for a bit. Steve had delivered the news perfectly. Steve and I kept looking at each other waiting for a response. Seconds seemed like minutes.

Finally, we got one.

At first, Paul said Intel's SoC would be more competitive, and we didn't have to do the work to support ARM. Then he asked two questions. "Would the ARM chips would be executing any Intel instructions?" In other words, would ARM be emulating Intel, thus making it compatible with Intel? There might have been several reasons he wanted to know this, but I would imagine protecting Intel's intellectual property was top of mind with this question. It was irrelevant because we had no intention of trying to achieve Intel compatibility—it would not have worked given the state of the art and our strategy. Intel was rather protective of attempts to emulate or reverse engineer their x86 instruction set and remained sensitive to how Microsoft reduced their influence during the transition to 64-bits.

Second, Paul asked about Office and what our plans were there. He knew that Office was the most strategic product for Microsoft on traditional PCs, and he also knew that if Office were part of the equation, then software vendors would be taking a lead from Microsoft. We knew this as well. Steve said we didn't have an answer as we were still working on our plans for Office. This was true and, in fact, the plans for Office were still an internal issue and a frustrating one for me.

I had the role to close out the call outlining precisely how we planned to show Intel SoC at the event and how we would be showing existing Windows applications on the Intel SoC as a key differentiator of Intel's efforts. He seemed pleased with that and offered to help us. We always included the Intel SoC, the Atom product, even though it lacked many of the qualities we saw in ARM-based chipsets.

Days later, I flew to Intel's headquarters and visited with David "Dadi" Perlmutter, leader of the Intel Architecture Group, essentially Intel's core chip business, and a longtime Intel employee and rumored CEO successor to Paul, thus making us rumor-mill equivalents. Dadi was always fantastic to work with as we could bond over challenges we each faced in our efforts while recognizing the overall complexity of the equation. We had a cordial meeting. He offered up many technical issues we might face, pointing out the fact that Intel had deep knowledge of ARM as one of the earliest licensees of the architecture. He too was focused on application compatibility and, while he had been briefed, was satisfied to hear everything again firsthand.

In many ways the call and visit were the culmination of both supreme technical work on the team and of the most incredibly difficult product choice I ever had to communicate. The relationship between Intel and Microsoft formed the cornerstone of the PC era—a partnership and set of personal relationships that compared to any in business history. The relationship always had some tension—the kind of tension seen between hardware and software since the start of computing. My feelings alternated between betraying a business partner and relief that we could move computing forward, depending on the moment. Ultimately, for Microsoft to be relevant in operating systems it needed to rely on new hardware.

That said, Intel had similar feelings and had simply executed them more openly. For Intel to be relevant it needed a much more concerted effort to woo our competitors: Linux in the data center and Apple PCs. Going way back, my very first meeting at Intel with BillG, Andy Grove, Gordon Moore, and others was one where the main topic of conversation was how openly and aggressively Intel was courting Java developers. This was a time when Microsoft viewed Java, a cross-platform tool, as competitive to Windows, while Intel viewed it as a slow platform that would benefit from faster processors.

Over the coming months Intel would aggressively counter our work on ARM. Public statements were clear and pointed and one could only imagine how the conversations went with their partners in private. Business can be brutally competitive. From CES through the release, Intel was on the field battling against Windows on ARM. They had to. We expected them to. Still, it was not helpful. In hindsight, I might even suggest they were successful in convincing OEMs of their perceived downsides of ARM. All is fair in business even with the best of partnerships. It was Andy Grove himself who used the term *coopetition* in his thoughts on the industry.[126]

One reaction from Intel was to further emphasize that Intel chips supported a variety of operating systems. In one slide we kept seeing pop up at Intel events, the company emphasized this by putting the Windows logo in a tiny box with Google and MeeGo (a Linux distribution) with the title "Unveiling 'Oak Trail' building upon the low-power 'Moorestown' platform to add OS Port of Choice to tablets and Netbooks." Another variant of the slide included every operating system in use at the time, including Apple. Putting Windows on par with these offerings and using the phrase "port of choice" definitely rubbed me the wrong way. All is fair in this type of competition, honest.

Once Intel was fully briefed, we were ready to head to CES where SteveB would lead the show with a keynote. We chose to have a separate event with just the press and our key ARM partners to be able to offer Q&A and a to be able to see the demonstrations in a smaller venue.

CES 2011 "Technology Demonstration"

There was no way around it, but the coverage of Windows embracing ARM would be seen through the lens of the implications for the Wintel partnership. Additionally, it would be seen as a failure for Wintel to secure a market position in tablets, the hugest of huge new categories created by Apple and now overrun with Android. This was the kind of event we had to hold after the stock market closed because some would overreact and think of a technology demonstration as tradeable news.

Mike Angiulo (MikeAng) and the ecosystem team created a showcase for the technology and partners behind ARM. This was the kind of event where the primary goal is to prove to partners we are committed to the work by making a public statement. We would work in the background to gain enough support so the partners at least agreed to be named, which would be an accomplishment. We're on stage but the success of the event looks like a slide with all the partner logos, which the team delivered. The team built out all the demonstrations which were, to put it kindly, in a very fragile state. This was one of those big tables of devices on display where we couldn't even have backups because there was literally only one device, often a test breadboard complete with wires hanging off. Amazing work!

We began by showing how hardware on SoC (ARM) mobile platforms had improved. I put up a chart showing how Windows had doubled system requirements every release from Windows 3.1—twice as much disk space and twice as much memory from 1992 to 2006. The takeaway was that phones and PCs had converged in hardware capabilities, and phone hardware was improving faster—in other words while Windows had finally leveled off in hardware specs, smartphones basically caught up to PCs in capabilities.

As we worked through the computers running Windows on ARM we showed a number of significant innovations—things that did not work on phones or tablets...yet. Mike showed ARM devices using USB storage, printing, and connecting to external displays. While these were mundane tasks for a PC, they were the kinds of basic features not supported on the iPad or Android tablets. We were tapping into the breadth of capabilities in Windows.

SoC was the driver for the innovation, bringing along with it benefits such as integration of many peripherals not available on PCs, lower power consumption, no loud fans to cool the chips, and much smaller devices. By showing off SoC devices running Windows and Office, complete with printing, USB storage, and good graphics, we made it incredibly clear that Microsoft was dedicated to bringing ARM to market. MikeAng planned and executed the whole show, including working with his team and aligning partners. To say it was masterful in the context of a wild announcement no one was expecting would be an understatement.

The press coverage of the event was worldwide and spanned the technology and business news. As expected, there was a focus on the implications for Intel. The coverage was anchored by the huge showing of Android tablets at CES and the success in the first months of the iPad. Ina Fried, reporting for the All Things Digital outlet, had a detailed live blog of the event covering minute by minute what was shown. Fried also had a follow up story that ran with the headline "Windows on ARM Is No Knee-Jerk Move" pointing out how long the work had been underway.[127]

Later in the evening SteveB held his much broader keynote including Xbox, Windows Phone, and a nod to SoC where he said "Whatever device you use, Windows will be there."[128]

Still, CES 2011 had been rather challenging or even lackluster for Microsoft overall. The main keynote the company delivered was primarily about the 2010 wave of products. Xbox was making big news with Kinect but there was a dearth of Kinect-enabled games. Android totally dominated phones and pushed aside what presence Windows Phone 7 could muster just months after launch—Android's open-source strategy (free OS software) and anything-goes hardware drove a broad range of low-cost smartphones and connected devices of all types. Plus, we were approaching two years since Windows 7 and there were still no laptops to compete with the MacBook Air, which had already been updated. The PC OEMs were not showing many Windows 7 tablets or touch PCs. Instead, they had turned their focus to Android tablets.

One of the biggest changes in the computing device landscape was underway and one that went largely unnoticed. While there is ample attention paid to the software battle for computers—meaning personal computers, phones, and now tablets—between Microsoft, Apple, and now Google, there was also a battle across the manufacturers of devices. There was a changing of the guard underway in making computers as the leaders of the PC era such as HP, Dell, and Lenovo, were losing to the new makers of phones from Apple, Samsung, HTC, and a host of new manufacturers and ODMs in China that never made PCs. The tech blog BGR tracked over 100 different tablets debuting at CES 2011 and while some traditional PC makers were on the list, they were overwhelmed by manufacturers mostly new to computing.[129]

From my vantage point, this only raised the urgency of Windows 8, specifically the pressure to deliver a new PC experience. Noteworthy was the increasingly gloomy PC sales numbers that continued to roll out.

Those sales numbers were announced after CES. Smartphones surpassed PCs in units sold in the first quarter of 2011. PC sales declined almost 2 percent year-over-year. Analysts who predicted almost 500 million PCs were declaring the death of the PC, and that we had passed *Peak PC*. PCs, they reported, had been supplanted by tablets like the iPad.[130]

Android tablets had risen from hacked prototypes a year earlier to dominating the show floor, even as the spirit of Apple dominated CES. Google was releasing Android builds at a furious and incomprehensible pace. Even support for tablet sized screens was uncertain as the cleverly named releases on the roadmap were added and features moved from one release to another, from Android 2.3 *Gingerbread* just released before CES but unavailable on tablets to Android 3.0 *Honeycomb*, which forked the code to support tablets only to become Android 4.0 to Android 2.4 *Ice Cream (Sandwich)* and more. Or something like that—no one could keep track.

For the next year, behind the scenes we continued to develop WOA with OEMs. It was a constant push and pull with OEMs. The OEMs had challenges reconciling their conflicting goals—they wanted ultra-cheap, low-priced, mass-scale devices that could utilize their supply chains. We were hoping the OEMs would join us in a new category of device—a more capable tablet.

Engaging OEMs

MikeAng's PC ecosystem team developed a strategy to engage the OEMs on WOA projects that at once constrained the variations in hardware WOA supported, while also enabling OEMs to define unique innovations they brought to market.

The OEMs were not happy with constraints to say the least.

The assumption from just about every ecosystem constituent would be that Windows would do the work to implement Windows on ARM and the resulting product would maintain all the properties of x86-based Windows. OEMs would then build PCs out of ARM or x86 as they saw fit. New ARM-based PCs would presumably have all the software capabilities and compatibility of x86 Windows plus all the positive properties of ARM appropriate for small tablets such as low cost and long battery life.

As nice as this sounds, such an end-state was impossible. The investment in ARM would only make sense if the ecosystem could rally around a new value proposition. We did not need another Netbook. We certainly did not need the confusion of two different chipsets that did the same thing only slightly differently in a seemingly random set of ways.

It was going to be remarkably difficult no matter how we approached the situation. On the one hand, building the first WOA devices would be technically demanding and require a significant up-front commitment from all parties. At the same time, the strategy for WOA would not immediately resonate with OEMs who traditionally think first about margins, assortment, segmentation, and minimizing investment to achieve those given their margin structure.

We saw WOA as a new type of intellectual property from Microsoft with a new go-to-market. Such thinking was not exactly welcomed by our established partners and best customers. It was the fact that these were our customers that made this even more difficult.

This plan involved working with the core OS team to define ARM hardware choices that worked with Windows, defining the specifications for hardware including the chipset maker and all the associated peripherals. Essentially, we defined three different ARM base platforms—each unique in what it could provide consumers. Mike and team worked close with three ARM chip makers, each viewed as a primary partner for WOA including Qualcomm, Texas Instruments, and NVIDIA. For example, Qualcomm offered great connectivity in their ARM products. Texas Instruments had an array of sensors and a long history of low-power ARM devices. The NVIDIA Tegra platform had the best performing graphics, expected given their expertise. Within each platform there was flexibility, and in deciding the platforms we engaged OEMs to include their ideas as well.

For each platform, we determined if there was OEM interest in building a PC and working with them on the specifics of the PC—determining if it was to be laptop, convertible, or slate form factor, what size screen, collection of external connectors, and so on. The strategy was designed to provide a lineup of ARM devices from the day we launched Windows 8, while at the same time avoiding the customer confusion and channel complexity that might result from having essentially identical devices from different OEMs. Where Intel aimed for volume from roughly identical Netbooks, we aimed to have higher quality and differentiated devices.

The worry that led us to this approach was that OEMs would simply repackage Netbooks, with their low-quality screens, plastic cases, and commodity manufacturing, to represent WOA innovation. Low-price and keyboardless represented their default point of view when it came to ARM. Since we had a new platform and surmised that investment would be relatively minimal, we suspected OEMs would want to reuse as much of an existing design as possible. We wanted WOA to stand for a reimagined, higher-quality, and modern Windows, not a cheaper, less capable, subset.

OEMs were receptive to the plan even if they did not see the problems with Windows we wished to address as acutely as we did. Still, they immediately saw ARM as an opportunity to cut Intel out of the equation. They wanted to know how much cheaper WOA was relative to Intel Windows—in other words, their perspective was immediately focused on providing even lower cost PCs.

Our concerns were realized early, but at least remained predictable. There was immediate pushback over the constraints within the system. The limits in their flexibility and requirements were viewed as a sign of distrust. Much to our surprise, however, the OEMs seemed more circumspect when it came to our own execution. Based on years of experience, they had many reasons to doubt we would even deliver, which granted was entirely fair. While they never directly stated it, it was clear from body language that some believed maybe we had ulterior motives for WOA, perhaps to gain leverage over Intel or something. I found this frustrating as we only wanted to deliver on a new Windows value proposition. Given our recent history, their feelings and doubts were understandable.

Over the course of executing WOA we would have many ups and downs delivering multiple devices involving multiple silicon partners working with multiple OEMs. We saw firsthand the difference in how partners approached or believed in the opportunity and how their organizations reacted to what we certainly believed was an attempt at building our own disruptive innovation.

Qualcomm for example was highly tuned to running experiments with OEMs. That was great. At the same time, their process relied on essentially sizing the market early on and introducing measured involvement based on the perceived run-rate of a device. They also had their own partner ecosystem and were anxious to reward good partners with a WOA opportunity even if that partner didn't have a deep interest in bringing a device to market. Windows Phone already partnered with Qualcomm which proved to send a mixed message about unit volumes. Our process for PCs paired one OEM with Qualcomm whereas Windows Phone had many OEMs. Qualcomm was more interested in working with many OEMs. These are just some of the complexities that come from three or more decabillion dollar companies partnering. We were all used to it, even if it wasn't great.

At the other end of the enthusiasm spectrum was NVIDIA. At NVIDIA, Jensen Huang, the founder and CEO, took a personal interest at every step and while he certainly didn't need to, he continued to prove why he is one of the industry's most visionary and uncompromising innovators. While walking the show floor of CES 2011, Jensen saw me and pulled me into the NVIDIA booth to express his personal excitement. He said, "we're going to nail this partnership and create a whole new category of device." He was excited, and his enthusiasm was infectious and so welcome. The NVIDIA booth was also jam-packed with their best-of-show Tegra products used in a variety of devices. ZDNet in their "CES winners and losers" roundup went as far as to suggest "NVIDIA looks like it could become the Intel of the next great wave of computing." Everything about working with NVIDIA was impressive, including the technology.

In that same CES roundup, ZDNet said of "loser" Microsoft, "This is beginning to sound like a broken record, but I'm still waiting to hear any hint of Microsoft's vision of where it sees the computing world headed in the decade ahead and how Microsoft plans to take us there." [131]

8,617 Words Describing WOA

In February 2012 a year after the CES announcement we published "Building Windows 8 for the ARM Processor" on our *Building Windows 8* blog, *b8*. We had already unveiled the Windows 8 user experience and held the first developer conference, but work on ARM, particularly the new hardware took more time. It was time to be clear with the market with about six months to go before RTM.

8,617 words.[132]

That's what it took to describe the technology under the hood to reimagine Windows for a SoC chipset, primarily ARM. The post was so long and overwhelming that among the PC press it remains a meme for lengthy writing and cemented my own reputation as a writer of many words, as if the hundreds of thousands of words herein were not enough. The post was almost three years in the making when we consider when the work initially began.

The detail provided was, intentionally, overwhelming. In sticking with promise and deliver, what we communicated were our commitments and what we would deliver. The post covered working with partners, apps for ARM computers, the hardcore details of rearchitecting Windows for ARM, even how we tested WOA, and then finally how WOA PCs will make it to market. Yet there were still questions. Yikes. It is easy to say it was my fault for not providing enough information, but it would be more reasonable to say that this is just part of the difficulty of changing assumptions of a massive market that established decades of precedent.

The tech blogs were anxious for information. At CES 2012 we provided little by way of update which was probably a tactical error given it was the announcements at the previous CES. This led to all the coverage taking a tone of "finally." There were over three dozen stories anchored off of the B8 post listed on the industry site Techmeme. The comments and questions ran the gamut.

AnandTech's Andrew Cunningham, however, highlighted the main news items as effectively as any outlet using their in-depth analysis as we'd come to expect.[133]

Up front there was, finally, clarity on the notion that WOA would come to market differently than traditional Windows for x86 processors recognizing what most had previously assumed but was not the case. Cunningham wrote:

> *Up until now, we've operated under the assumption that a new version of Windows called Windows 8 would be released this year, and that it would run on both x86 (32-bit and 64-bit – throughout this article I'll use x86 to refer to both architectures) and ARM processors – Sinofsky's post makes it clear that the ARM version of Windows, officially referred to as Windows on ARM (WOA), is considered to be a separate product from Windows 8, the same way that products like Windows Server and Windows Embedded share a foundation with but are distinct from Windows 7. Windows on ARM has a "high degree of commonality" and "very significant shared code" with Windows 8 – much of the user's interaction with the OS will be the same on either platform, and much of the underlying technology we've seen in our Windows 8 coverage so far will be present in both versions, but they're distinct products that will be treated differently by Microsoft.*

Then came the two main questions that were answered but now the debate would really begin in earnest. First, to the question of the "desktop" that is the traditional Windows desktop interface and applications requiring a mouse versus touch. In the next posts, I will describe the new touch interface and application model, but for now all one needs to know is that new applications were called "Metro" or "Metro-style," and the name of the API layer was known as WinRT. Important to this context is that the press and most technologists viewed tablets as entirely separate from PCs and the future. Even Steve Jobs had made that point. As we will see we did not design the product to have that distinction. The article continued:

> *One of the biggest recurring questions I've seen about Windows on ARM is whether the standard Windows desktop would be available for use on those devices as it will be on Windows 8 machines – the answer is yes, it definitely will be. The desktop can be invoked from the Start screen, and once there users can perform standard Windows Explorer operations, launch the desktop version of Internet Explorer, and other tasks either via touch (for which Explorer has apparently been optimized) or via keyboard and mouse input. The desktop will only consume resources when it is launched, meaning that there are no performance or battery life implications for users who stick with the Metro interface for everything – the desktop is there if you want it, but one of Microsoft's stated goals with the Metro interface is to make it so that you don't need to use the desktop as a fallback.*

This view captured correctly how we described and demonstrated the traditional desktop environment. As we will see, we had been having this conversation almost continuously from the first time we showed the full product user interface with the discussion highly polarized. There were those that thought in no uncertain terms that a tablet could not possibly have a desktop, and there were those that thought a computer for "real" productivity could not possibly be without the desktop along with a mouse and keyboard. The views were so polarized that almost everyone concluded regardless of which end you were on there was a hard line implying only one of those could exist. This is the positioning Apple chose for the iPad and given its success so far it had the luxury of defining the tablet market. My view was that we could offer a different definition of tablets that just happened to play to our strengths and not fix what Apple chose to make. It is fair to say this was one of the two most controversial decisions. This controversy will be discussed in depth in the next couple of sections on the platform and experience.

Finally, the article turned to what would ultimately be the other most controversial decision. Would WOA PCs run existing x86 applications? To do so would require some form of virtualization and emulation. I had answered this question at the initial briefing more than a year earlier and said this was not going to be the case. The article described this decision as follows:

> *... Microsoft is firm in its insistence that it will not support running, emulating, or porting existing x86 apps on the Windows on ARM desktop – apps can only be downloaded and installed through the Windows Store, and only apps written to target the new WinRT APIs can be distributed through the store (however, the store will be able to distribute and update both ARM and x86 versions of apps in the event that the app uses any code native to either architecture.) Microsoft suggests that current Windows developers should be able to take significant bits of their existing code and wrap them in a Metro layer, but acknowledges that bringing over existing apps will require a bit of work – WinRT is clearly the wave of the future where Windows is concerned, but it'll be up to individual developers to decide how, when, and if to bring their programs over.*

One could hardly overstate the shock most had at WOA taking this position. Microsoft sold the value of compatibility from the earliest days of the company, compatibility in all forms. BASIC programs for one PC ran on any other microcomputer. MS-DOS programs ran on any PC with MS-DOS. MS-DOS programs ran on Windows, even the oldest MS-DOS 1.0 programs. Windows applications for 16-bit Windows ran on all versions of 32-bit Windows from 1990 until Windows 11 shipped in late 2021 and still have several years of support left—nearly 35 years! Even in preparing this work, I routinely ran Microsoft Office 1.5 on a 32-bit installation of Windows 10. This type of compatibility was not just for kicks or fun nostalgia demos. Many used utilities or tools written by third parties that long ago stopped maintaining the software. In the enterprise or corporate world, Windows continued to run line of business applications written ages ago that were no longer under active development but were required for business. Quite simply, customers expected to run really old software just so they would not have to touch it.

And we just blew this up. To many it seemed like we just abandoned the entire ecosystem just so we could build a tablet. I heard many times that it can't be called "Windows" if it doesn't run everything on Windows.

Technology blogs were quick to point out the irony of some history. When Windows NT ran on new chips from Digital Equipment, it was possible to translate x86 applications so they could run. Apple transitioned from

Motorola to PowerPC and then to Intel, using forms of translation and virtualization at each step. In fact, that example was repeatedly cited. So why not Microsoft?

For sure there were technical reasons. The ARM chips of the era lacked the horsepower to translate from x86 to ARM instructions, which would be required. Taking as an example, the Alpha chips that powered NT in the 1990s were far faster than Intel chips of the era and could use the extra processing power to translate. Apple was in a similar position as they were intentionally moving to more powerful chips. Still, this rationale was not compelling, and many thought we were just being stubborn in some way.

Microsoft faced a far different situation. As rich, storied, and useful as the Windows application world was, it was stagnant and, frankly, legacy. No one was investing in it. What this implied was that any solution that included running these existing applications would need to continue to do so, essentially forever or at least a decade or more. We knew this because we'd seen the amount of old software in the population of measured Windows PCs. In our world of compatibility, if customers were given an option to keep running, they would do so and would never accept a deadline to update or convert applications. We knew this because of two experiences.

First, as discussed, when we changed the user-interface for Office 2007, we'd seen how customers viewed a compatibility mode. They insisted that we have it and then in the next sentence they would insist they would turn it on from the start and never think about turning it off. Come the next release of Office they would reassert the need for the now even older compatibility mode.

Second, about a decade earlier Windows began the effort to move the PC ecosystem to much more reliable and secure 64-bit drivers, that is code to support hardware and peripherals. More than 15 years of cajoling and even requiring OEM support for 64-bit drivers and it was not until Windows 11 in 2022 that Microsoft finally completed this transition.

We were so committed to compatibility that absent active mitigations taken to break existing functionality even viruses and malware continued to run across versions of Windows. Recall the story, and related outcry, when we broke macros in Word or attachments in Outlook to stop the spread of a virus. Every security situation in Windows is also weighed against maintaining compatibility.

Now that's customer commitment. That commitment was also a 16-ton weight holding us back on delivering a new value proposition for Windows in a modern era of computing as defined by smartphones and tablets.

A counterexample many would be quick to point out today is how Apple migrated the Mac PC line to its own ARM-based chips, Apple Silicon, in 2020. They did so by utilizing an x86 program emulation/translation layer and maintained compatibility with existing software. How did they do that?

Apple had several distinct advantages that Microsoft not only lacked but that ran counter to Microsoft's long-term commitment to compatibility, aside from the vertically integrated hardware and software that gave Apple much more control over the device and what code could run.

First, Apple had been through two other chip transitions on Macintosh and regularly rearchitected and removed older features and APIs from the operating system. Anyone who was part of Apple's transitions in the past as a developer knows that Apple has a rather heavy hand when it comes to deprecating (that's the word vendors use to signify operating system APIs that are no longer supported) and then removing features. This hygiene is part of what enables Mac to have a more stable and less flakey experience as a broad general statement. Windows took the opposite approach which is to introduce rearchitected features while officially deprecating the old and almost never following that with removal. Essentially, strong encouragement to use new capabilities but all the old remains and can be used. As the Mac operating system evolved the programs for it evolved to maintain a more modern approach to computing. Windows programs just kept running, becoming more out of step, less secure, and unaware of new use cases for portability, cloud integration, or power management.

Second, Apple planned on providing emulation/translation for a finite time. The emulation feature itself is something Apple introduces and then shortly thereafter deprecates and then removes in quick succession. When Apple transitioned to Intel chips in early 2006 with the MacBook Air, the Tiger version of the operating system (10.4) included technology enabling PowerPC software to run. By the Snow Leopard version of the operating system (10.6) just 4 years later that support was no longer available. Hardcore.

As the largest third-party developer of software for Apple platforms, Microsoft lived these transitions in the Mac Office group. Often these were contentious. The Mac Office business unit had customers to serve, features to add, and many were in enterprises. Yet from Apple they were being told, basically, to drop everything and begin transitioning. Even I would receive mail from Steve Jobs trying to influence the pace of change. Other third parties like Adobe were notoriously slow at meeting the demands of Apple. Yet every third-party did or they would simply fade away. Incredible.

Third, Apple had a huge library of software and community of developers working in their new ecosystem to counter what was otherwise an ecosystem as moribund as the Windows Win32 ecosystem. The success of the iPhone created a new ecosystem of developers for Apple—the largest in the world for client-side computing. Apple had the advantage that comes from that, including deprecating support for older APIs. Mac developers were the subject of a great deal of evangelism to find ways to support the new iPhone and iPad platform with their existing products. The similarities between APIs across devices was a significant advantage for Apple. Again, even the largest third parties were hardly immune from this. Adobe has a vast number of iPhone and iPad apps that it provides and are often demonstrated on stage by Apple. As we will see, the Mac Office product was quietly prioritizing their support for the iPad even while the events here were taking place.

What was our customer promise, then? Why were we so rigid in supporting only new "Metro" programs on WOA?

The underlying operating system, Windows on ARM, aimed to deliver system security, reliability over time, performance, constant connectivity, and low power consumption. These were quite literally the weakest aspects of the classic x86 Windows PC and, not surprisingly, remain so today. Achieving these goals was an all or nothing proposition. Microsoft has historically avoided such hardcore tradeoffs favoring a caveat emptor approach to variety, tweaking, and compatibility. That served the company remarkably well, to say the least. That approach had quite literally hit a wall.

For Windows 8 and ARM our goal was nothing short of ending the misery, mystery, and constant futzing that came from the first 25 years of the evolution of the Windows PC and Windows API. Competing with the iPad and Android tablets was a side effect of that, not the goal.

The next sections will cover the goals and promises of the user experience and the developer platform and fully answer the customer promise question.

So then, where did the Start menu go?

102. THE EXPERIENCE

We set out to reimagine Windows, but it is interesting to ask what exactly the product is to most people. This helps us to understand the thoughts behind making a major change. We saw this in the changes to Office—we recognized the value of Office was not as many might have thought, the file formats or the old File|Edit|View|Tools|Window|Help menu structure, but rather the inherent capabilities and implementation of those capabilities. In that spirit, we looked at Windows and saw much more than the specifics of the Start menu or any particular expression of a user interface. Windows at its core proved to be a remarkably resilient operating system and our goal was to tap that resiliency to bring it new capabilities for a new world of customers.

Fundamentally an operating system can be thought of as the software that allocates hardware resources, manages connectivity and devices, and defines the human to device interaction model. Beyond these technology distinctions Windows is also a culture of openness to developers and an ecosystem of partners that itself has proven resilient over time. Windows is no more one of those than a single feature or attribute above others.

As both a participant in and later a contributor to the evolution of Windows, I find the transitions that the Windows product has gone through to be a case study in the "soft" part of software and in the flexibility of the product team to engineer transitions from one evolutionary stage to another. Consider just some of the transitions the Windows OS kernel or core operating system have undergone:

- **GUI transition**. Windows itself was the product of a transition that many doubted could be made. Could an entire OS be built upon the "shaky" underpinnings of MS-DOS in the face of Macintosh? A remarkable amount of work went into the technology across the ecosystem, such support for 32-bit microprocessors, that made Windows 3.0 such a watershed product. Yet underlying that, customers could still bring forward investments in all those applications and peripherals from MS-DOS.
- **32-bit transition**. The transition to 32-bits was one that required a vast amount of change and brought with it the introduction of "plug and play" and the ability to run more sophisticated graphical applications and games of unrivaled qualities. The introduction of Windows 95 was a watershed moment for the whole industry. While in hindsight it looks as though it was a sure thing, many at the time proclaimed it would be technically impossible.
- **Internet transition**. Immediately after the release of Windows 95, the conventional wisdom quickly became that Windows would be replaced by a browser. Yet few would have argued with the fact that the presence of Windows—the support for networking, the introduction of graphical web browsers on Windows, as well as the openness of the platform all contributed to the transformation of the world of information technology. In 2010 we were just starting to see how the powerful graphics of Windows could bring standards based HTML5 to life in unprecedented ways. As we will see in the next section, the programming model and API of Windows was indeed still struggling.

- **Server Scale**. As we continued to evolve the client (workstation) OS we were using this same OS foundation to power the datacenter. With Windows Server we scaled the OS to support hundreds of computing cores and terabytes of storage. And along the way we created this OS for multiple CPU architectures driven by the demands of server computing (DEC Alpha, MIPS, Itanium, and 64-bit.) At each step most people believed that such flexibility was neither prudent nor possible.
- **Security and Reliability**. Through the above transitions, there was an undercurrent that Windows was "aging" and that it could not transition to modern computing needs of much larger memory architectures, multi-core OS support, improved reliability, and much better security. The introduction of Windows XP was a milestone in bringing our enterprise server and workstation OS to mainstream consumers. Ironically, at the introduction of Windows XP many thought we had reached too far, and that the OS was more than people would need or could even afford to power. Throughout this transition the introduction of Windows Update enabled the OS to stay connected to customers, provide code updates, and distribute software on behalf of the ecosystem.

These transitions were supported by consistently strong engineering efforts to refactor, rearchitect, and re-tune the Windows operating system. Windows also showed a broad set of efforts at the experience or user interface layer in the system as well. The various editions of including Windows Home, Windows Professional, and Windows Enterprise while often viewed as pricing and licensing efforts did in practice introduce a wide range of functionality tuned to different customer segments. Windows was able to reach up and down in complexity using the resiliency and flexibility inherent in the architecture.

Yet, at the experience level Windows also struggled to achieve critical mass in several important areas even with the capabilities of the team and assets in the code. In *Hardcore Software*, we've seen the difficulties of creating tablet computers (Tablet PC), handheld computers (Windows CE), home entertainment (Windows Media Center), industrial devices (Windows Embedded), and most recently the ongoing development of smartphones, Windows Phone 7.

What is it about the experience layer that has proved so difficult for Microsoft? There could be many possible explanations. Was Microsoft too early when it should have been patient? Was Windows code simply the wrong starting point? Did we bring out good products but had inferior marketing, sales, and distribution? Some would point to one of more of these.

I had my own theory and plan for trying something different.

My view was that Microsoft relied too heavily on the notion of architectural layering and believed that experience could always be layered "on top" of the operating system. This computer science view drove nearly every discussion on how things should move forward. It was viewed as they key to architecting Windows for these different experiences while maintaining the shared code of the actual operating system.

Microsoft systems culture (aka BillG) loved to believe that with the right architecture things in one layer could advance independent of another. I don't think I could begin to enumerate all the times we debated issues that boiled down to me suggesting the abstractions are in the way while Bill insisted that great architecture would solve the problem. The counter was that I was failing to consider building a great architecture before addressing the problem. I was merely suggesting that we might end up spending 90% of the time on 10% of the problem.

In my heart I am an "apps person" as I've noted many times. One thing that is conceptually different about apps from operating systems is that apps tend to be much less hardcore (or religious as some might say) about architectural layers while much more zealous about solving the customer problem even if that means breaking through well-considered abstraction layers. In an operating system there's a general tendency to view the layers and architecture as goals the system must achieve and moving forward the layers enable advances and are deeply respected. Whereas in apps the layers and architecture tend to be the starting point while innovation and moving forward usually involve breaking those very abstractions.

Each of the above attempts at expanding the experience of Windows were implemented with the explicit goal and architectural starting point of not interfering with the core of Windows. Importantly, the teams executed without organizational alignment across the Windows team or schedule. The essence of the former COSD division was to serve the main missions of Windows for desktops and for servers but generally favored the server mission for cultural and historic reasons. Whereas the Client division served the multiple experiences of Windows but did not generally prioritize experiences beyond the main client. To be clear I am not saying this was wrong at the time, rather it introduced tradeoffs that had side effects relative to other missions.

This to me was the kind of decision made early in a project that is difficult to work around. The inability of the Tablet PC to fully embrace native Windows implementations or for Windows Phone to tap into the available power of the Windows operating system support for devices and connectivity were examples I'd personally experienced. As an apps person in the "two gardens" sense, the same way we needed Word and Excel to share code and align around everything from the use of the Windows registry to HTML to drawing code to user interface, we needed Windows to align around these expansions and changes to the experience.

Windows was making a tradeoff at each of the junctures. There were two higher priority advances that needed to happen. First the work to transition from MS-DOS and 16-bit Windows to the full 32-bit operating system was an imperative that could not be compromised. Second, the need to continue to scale Windows up for the data center and to have a consistent client-server operating system was architecturally key. These were long term goals that were put in place and executed over at least two decades as discussed in 011. A Strategy for the '90s: Windows.

By 2010 we had achieved those goals. The achievement of those goals came, arguably, at the expense of losing out on tablets, phone, internet-scale cloud, and embedded devices of all kinds. Further, as we will see in the next chapter, we failed to align significantly in our developer tools and messaging about the Windows experience platform, further weakening our strategy vis-à-vis these new opportunities for software and devices.

When announcing the transition Windows was making to support SoC and ARM the resiliency of Windows was top of mind. So much so that the working name of the event was titled around "resiliency" and that was the script I prepared though that was rightly deemed defensive.

The event stopped at the chip layer, intentionally. I knew the history and what we had been deliberate about in planning Windows 8. Windows 8 was not going to simply stick to the architectural layers that were in place. This transition was much bigger and needed a holistic and consistent approach up and down the layers. We were specifically not going to bolt a new experience on top of Windows any more than Windows 95 bolted a GUI on top of MS-DOS as some might have said we did. If all we did was port Windows to ARM, then literally nothing would have changed, and the outcome would have been no better than porting to DEC Alpha or MIPS.

For Windows 8 to succeed and reimagining Windows for a new era we would need to have a new experience that matched a new operating system kernel combined with new capabilities for partners and developers.

With that goal in mind, we set out to rethink the computer that we all used each day. We intended to build on the resiliency of Windows, not to simply go all in on tablets, but to support the attributes customers were already seeing in tablets and smartphones with a wide variety of computers of all shapes and sizes. This was not a fantasy or a "leverage Windows" approach lacking in engineering reality. In fact, it was exactly what Apple did to bring the iPhone and then iPad to market, building on the resiliency of their approach only with a much more explicit end-to-end implementation. Apple even had a server product just as Microsoft did, though ceased to offer it as a separate product in 2011. Android did not take this fully integrated approach to the operating system and scenarios and the result we were seeing in market was showing the weaknesses of Android when it came to customer experience across different devices.

While there was no escaping the tablet focus of the world beyond our hallways, our goal for Windows was to embrace new paradigms and bring Windows forward. Even at the unveiling of support for ARM, we tried to be clear that we saw a convergence of devices not a distinct world of devices, no matter how much they might work together. Whereas Steve Jobs claimed that the iPad was an in between a phone and a Mac and had something special to do, we saw devices as a continuum. Specifically, Apple saw three discrete devices and we believed that the tablet and the PC could be a single device, a new kind of device. We didn't see this as a hybrid or an inefficient bundle, but engineering and design problems to be solved.

Where Apple, even to this day, sees as laptop as something without touch capabilities and a tablet as something with less than optimal "multi-tasking," we saw devices as sharing metaphors and paradigms the way we saw desktops and servers successfully sharing paradigms. I viewed Apple's line in the sand about the iPad as stubborn, especially considering the role of something as obvious as a keyboard, never mind plugging in a USB drive or external camera. Apple did not even introduce their own keyboard for the iPad until 2015 and a trackpad came in 2020.

As I said, though in not so many words, at the CES 2011 event; the advantages Windows provided are the ones that have brought success and customers to so many:

- Broad opportunities for developers
- Openness of the software platform
- Breadth of devices and peripherals

These continued to be the hallmarks of Windows as we designed the Windows 8 experience.

The Windows 8 Experience

Previously when describing the Office 2007 user experience, I shared that the team had developed a set of tools supported by a set of principles, rather than simply coming up with new variants of the various widgets. The Windows 8 program management team, again led by Jensen Harris (JensenH) reporting to Julie Larson-Green (JulieLar) took this same approach. Sam Moreau (SMoreau) led the Windows design team joined by the incredible Clay Satterfield (ClaySatt) who had worked on the Ribbon with Jensen, and Jeff Johnson (JeffJo) led the software development team. Given the breadth of this effort it feels awkward to call out only a few, but at the same time these members of the team were the force behind the work.

When something new is introduced as a replacement for a standard, there's a tendency to look at what is different and to believe in a "whole new cloth" approach to design. Very few products are like that. In fact, most new products that achieve greatness or ubiquity are a reassembly of what came before combined with new elements at the right time. Tesla did not make the first car, the first car with a screen, or even the first electric car. It did recombine many elements and some new elements, to change everything about how we thought about cars. The same could be said about the iPhone, which recombined the cell-phone network, the internet, music players which Apple had previously reinvented, and even the graphical interface by adding touch. Likewise, we have talked about how Microsoft Office was not the first suite of products nor was it the first spreadsheet, word processor, or graphics but a new and unique combination of parts. The common thread is that at each juncture the new product was also substantially different from the old, established leader, and diverged from where the experts thought the market was heading. That is innovation.

Observing this across many fields and having executed on these sorts of changes is what led to the principles behind the reimagination and approach in building Windows 8. The Windows 8 principles infused the design of the entire product, from packaging to advertising, and more:

- **Do more with less.** Windows simply has too many ways to do the same thing, and too often too many things required to do one thing. The Start menu is there to launch programs, but you can't switch between running programs that way and all you can see about a program is the name. Then there's the taskbar where you can switch between running things, find recently opened files (sometimes), and even execute some commands for an app. Then there's the notification tray on the taskbar, which is sometimes used to launch programs, sometimes used to tell you innocuous information, and sometimes used to control important features like the sound volume or Wi-Fi. None of those were particularly wrong on their own, but they were not built and conceived with the goal of simplicity or consistency in approach. That is not meant to take away from success or familiarity, but it does limit the expansion of the platform over time, especially when faced with a new way of working that does do more with less.
- **Authentically digital.** We can trace the history of how a computer looks to the evolution of display technologies themselves. The first Windows interfaces were limited to very low-resolution character screens and so by nature looked essentially like mainframes. As computer screens could display more colors, but not that many, we ended up with themes like Windows *Hotdog Stand* with bright red and canary yellow. Everything was a dreary grey, *Redmond Grey*, in Windows 3.0. By Windows XP and Windows Vista, PC

graphics had reached a point where drop shadows and then translucency were commonplace and filled the interface. Famously, Macintosh and then iPhone built on the desktop metaphor but literally. How many users of Macintosh in 2010 still used paper files and manilla folders, or kept addresses in a leather-bound address book? The Office save icon is one thing, but it wasn't as though Word had fired off a ding at the end of every line or required the use of a correction tape brush to backspace. Authentically digital was a principle that said to embrace being a computer, minimizing the visually tiring overhead that comes from trying to emulate a physical world. This came through from typography, colors, animations, and making room for the content that the user cares about, not the user interface we or app developers care about.

- **Pride in craftsmanship.**[134] Jensen and team were maniacs when it came to details. Every detail mattered: the text of every error message, the spacing of every word, the ordering of animations, and more. This pride was infused across the whole team from the start. Bugs that would have normally been postponed were considered, reconsidered, and not simply punted. In a talk he gave just after product availability, Jensen said "It's about caring about every, every, every, every, every, every, every, every, every, every detail. Because if you don't, who will? That doesn't mean you're always going to win. Sometimes you lose. Sometimes you fight for something and it's technically not possible or you're out of time or something else. But you should care, and you should feel ashamed when something, doesn't work out."[135]
- **Fast and fluid.** It was no surprise that the PC had become slow but worse it had become unpredictable. One of the main priorities in designing the new user experience was designing it such that everything was predictable, everything was interruptible, and everything that took time would let you know if there was real progress being made. These engineering challenges were inherent in the design and architecture of Windows itself. Touch interface must be vastly more responsive than a mouse and keyboard. Whether typing or swiping, your fingers can see even the slightest difference in milliseconds compared to what happens with a mouse. In this case the hardware became increasingly important as we will see in subsequent sections. There was much we could do in the experience, but this too was a challenge from the bottom to the top of Windows 8. Striving for fast and fluid was a requirement for touch and made a huge positive impact on mouse and keyboard usage.
- **Win as one.** No product the scale of Windows could be or would ever be designed by one person, but great designs combined with great executions tend to have a feeling that there was one point of view. In overcoming the architectural boundaries between the layers of Windows and development tools we would consistently assert the need to win as one.

With these principles in mind, I wanted to describe the main user experience affordances in Windows 8 that worked across all form factors and on ARM or x86 hardware. From the beginning of the project, we assumed Windows 8 would run on the broadest range of hardware from 7-10" ARM tablets to traditional laptops to all-in-one desktops to all-out gamer or creative rigs with multiple monitors and discrete GPUs. We self-hosted all of these across the team the entire project.

The affordances described below—the Metro-style interface—included the following elements: the **Start screen**, **Live tiles**, the **touch experience**, **charms**, and the classic **Windows desktop**. The next section covers the development of Metro-style applications and even more of the capabilities available in the experience.

While I will summarize these here, there is a vast amount of reading in the *Building Windows 8* blog especially the first post on the user experience. I've made these available on the Internet Archive project as they moved around quite a bit on the old Microsoft site and sometimes the images were lost.

The first thing everyone saw in Windows 8 was the new **Start screen**. Technically, many would see the new boot screen first when powering on a Windows 8 device, which as part of our pride in craft was an area of intense work through the whole ecosystem including partners. The Start screen was from the start (a pun) a massive change with a clear intent to do more with less.

The Start screen was a radical simplification of the combination of the Start menu, system tray, gadgets, and taskbar. Rather than a finnicky and difficult to navigate menu haphazardly organized into some folders and some icons, you'd see a clear place to click (or press as we'll see) and launch or switch to an application. It didn't matter whether the application was previously running or not.

Combining launching and switching was long overdue. In the early days of a PC, knowing which programs were running or not mattered. It was an under-the-hood detail that surfaced to end-users who did not really understand why but had to concern themselves with running out of memory or slowing their computer down due to running programs.

With Windows 7 the taskbar was enhanced to provide a way to launch programs the first time and to switch to them after running. Users did so by pinning the application icon to the taskbar. We saw in the telemetry of the product over time that most users were pinning most of the applications they used and the frequency of launching programs from the traditional Start menu location dropped. Beyond that the Start menu became a repository for installed applications spamming user as most applications installed a folder of accessories, top-level applications, prodded the user to pin the application to the taskbar while leaving a new shortcut to the application on the desktop.

Typically, tech enthusiasts would pride themselves on vast collections of software installed on their PC. Often, they spent considerable time arranging, categorizing, and organizing their Start menus. This extreme in use cases is not uncommon in software and poses a design challenge. How does one design for a broad base case and an extreme case that often comes with substantial complexity for the base case.

In practice, however, the design of the Start menu itself began to fail at both the extremes of smaller and more portable devices as well as the increased use of larger monitors with high resolution running greater than the 1080P of high-definition TV. The Start menu had a sweet spot of screen size and resolution that was common on desktops almost a decade earlier. As typical PCs loaded ever more software while not dramatically increasing screen size, even the out of box experience of the Start menu turned into a dexterity test of up, down, left, right navigation. New large screen monitors demonstrated the challenges of a menu design even further as the pixel-distances to move to the small targets of the Start menu increased.

The trend was clear which was that screens would soon improve beyond what a good deal of Windows software was capable of handling gracefully and that would not substantially improve.

The Start screen "took over" the screen to provide a surface to do more (with less) while also acknowledging that a very small menu with a difficult navigation paradigm had hit a proverbial wall. The launch **screens** of phones and tablets were showing another way that rapidly became the most used experience for more people.

Still, when I first saw the iPhone launch and the apps organized as an endless grid, my first reaction, speaking to JulieLar at the event, was to ponder how long it would take Apple to add folders. By iOS 4 in 2010, folders were added. That followed a period where people would endlessly futz to organize apps by personal folders, by App Store categories, or sometimes just by color. Then in iOS 15 in 2020 Apple added the App Library which was a way of list all installed apps alphabetically while providing for search and launch.

Windows 8 would skip these intermediate steps. The design of the Start screen included folders, arranging apps in any preferred order, and an All Applications view. There was also a search command for apps. Additionally, when the Start screen was visible simply typing would invoke the search command. When Mark Zuckerberg, of Facebook, visited and I showed him Windows 8, this particular feature resonated with him. This was just before their pivot to mobile but at the time he pushed on launching the browser from there by just typing a URL. We considered that but were a bit reluctant to add more entry points to launch the "default" browser.

Taking all these features together, we exceeded the capabilities of the combination of the Start menu and taskbar and did so by reducing the number of concepts required to understand.

Located deep in the Windows 7 taskbar was a notification area, the third capability integrated into the Windows 8 Start screen. This area had become somewhat of a dumping ground for a wide-array of always available tools from the volume control to connecting to Bluetooth devices to a sort of mini-application that served to notify users of some important information such as stock quotes, weather, or other information sources. Windows Vista had also introduced gadgets which were an enhanced form of mini applications to show information such as news headlines and the like.

We chose to significantly expand this capability with **Live tiles**. The easy to press launching and switching buttons could come to life with useful information available at a glance. We went a step further and made it easy for developers to add additional tiles for users of an application to pin additional information to the Start screen, called secondary tiles. This was a feature initially on Windows Phone 7 and enabled pinning a single contact or stock quote to the home screen. This capability made further customization of the Start screen possible, again something not possible with the combination of Start menu, taskbar, and notification area in any system-wide manner.

The Start screen was naturally navigated with a mouse scroll wheel or a trackpad or using keyboard arrow and page keys. The Start screen itself was always available just as the Start menu was available, which was to press the Windows key on the keyboard. Pressing it a second time returned to whatever window was visible before. In this sense the Start Screen behaved exactly as the Start menu did, except it filled the whole screen. It was sort of like using a Netbook, though absent the dexterity required for a 10" screen.

On hardware with a touch screen, the **touch experience** comes to life. Perhaps no other element garnered more attention as it was defining characteristic of the new tablet era and the implementation detail that Apple used to define the iPad as a distinct device from Mac. Our view was an expansion and decidedly a course correction from Windows 7. Touch was now central to the experience as we baked it in across the whole PC experience, rather than bolting it on. However, the touch experience was designed to succeed when it was required, be there when desired but not in the way otherwise, or not present at all if the hardware did not support it. Executing this design truly tested the win as one principle as everything from boot through setup through daily use needed to consider the presence of a touch-only computer. Even the Tablet PC assumed a keyboard would need to be plugged in at times.

The team created what they called a "touch language" to describe how the design would feel to users. The touch language included:

- Simple and consistent
- Fast and fluid
- Limited gesture set
- Direct manipulation
- Sliding gestures
- Reversible gestures
- Limit the use of timed gestures

My intent here is to continue to focus on the product strategy and not detail every aspect of the product design, but it is important to show how the strategy was reflected in some of these attributes.

Everyone wants their PC to be fast. As described in the principle fast and fluid, we aimed for a new level of performance. The change in hardware to high pixel count screens and higher screen refresh rates meant that a much smoother interface was possible. The introduction of touch created the imperative that the interface be much faster as well. The intimacy, and that is the right word, that one feels with a device using a touch interface is much deeper. The way your finger connects with user interface elements is not just about speed but about how objects move with your finger. The ecosystem liked to refer to this as a "sticks to your finger" level of quality. How swipe or tap or drag *feels* matters immensely. Engineering this experience involved all layers of the system and a deep understanding of how the elements of an applications—the buttons, lists, and icons on the screen—interact with content.

When the mouse was pioneered and implemented in the first Xerox PARC computer it had three buttons. Initially the concept of chording (as in a piano) was a key part of the design. Paul Allen thought that was too complex and limited the PC mouse to two buttons. Steve Jobs thought even that was too complex and Macintosh had only a single button. That did not last too long as many were soon connecting mice designed for Windows or using a keyboard modifier to get to the commands exposed when clicking the right mouse button—Office began supporting right clicking in Office 4.x which was widely used on both Macintosh and Windows. When Apple introduced touch, Steve Jobs proudly defined the interface as having only a single finger. That did not really last either as soon gestures were developed for a host of advanced, but often necessary operations. These gestures were mirrored to a degree on the Mac trackpad.

We knew from usage studies and telemetry in Windows, that the right click commands were frequently used. Beyond that, however, complex modifiers often went unknown by most users. We saw this with pen-based computing as well, where overloading the pen with complex gestures akin to those used by old-style proofreaders or combinations of clickable buttons on the pen were nearly impossible to discover.

The Windows 8 touch language designed a finite and limited set of gestures that encompassed all we believed would be required to be highly productive in a touch environment. The design intentionally avoided complex chording gestures that are difficult to remember and awkward to implement.

The entire touch language consisted of ten unique gestures, from simply tapping to perform an action to using a thumb and finger to zoom or rotate (that's two gestures) to swiping from the left (to switch applications) the right (for system commands) or the top and bottom (that's four of the gestures in total, for app-specific commands.) For an application developer, they only needed to worry about seven of the gestures, as three were only used within the operating system.

The initial reaction to these gestures as being difficult to "memorize" was quite common among tech enthusiasts and tech press. What we saw in putting people in front of the user interface for the first time was a natural ability to experiment and to quickly master these basic gestures. People would simply tap and swipe around and as if by accident trip into the gestures or simply try something that seemed natural such as dragging, and it would work. Whenever we would say to the aforementioned techies that people discovered something by "accident," they would counter that this was flawed logic, compared to being taught. Yet we had seen this same type of learning happen with right clicking the mouse. As if by accident, people discovered that the action led to a menu of the most important or relevant commands.

Today, every mobile platform exposes functionality by swiping from edges or even corners.

As we intended Windows 8 to be used for devices that were touch-only as well as no touchscreen at all, the gestures also had mouse and keyboard analogs. One of the more novel aspects of the mouse-centric execution was that we made use of the corners of the screen as touch equivalents for operations. The use of the corners was seen by some as obscure. In fact, at one point in the evolution of the product, we made a desktop background as a reminder of the corners, but mostly in gest. Why jest? There were two reasons. First, the corners were almost always found within a few minutes of mousing around experimenting. Second, to those in the design world the corners have special meaning as they are the easiest targets to reliably hit with a precision mouse—far more reliable that a single square button or even a menu command—by simply racing the mouse or moving on a trackpad without concern for stopping. The use of corners as hit targets is known as Fitts's law, where the principles of the model essentially say the corners serve as infinitely large buttons. In 2021 JensenH made a video detailing the model which is linked to in the endnotes though we also spoke of it extensively in the e7 and b8 blog.[136]

The touch experience also provided for a robust on-screen typing experience. This typing experience included predictive autocorrect and support for a range of now standard on-screen typing features such as emoji and diacritics. Owing to both the PC heritage and a realization that touch gestures for very common commands such as Copy, Paste, and Select All would be tricky the touch keyboard included a Windows Ctrl to use those commands, arrow keys to quickly move left and right while touch-typing, and an option to display a full PC keyboard. Microsoft's handwriting history also meant the on-screen keyboard could be used to recognize handwriting and insert text as though it was typed. No pen required! The first Windows 8 tablets came with wide screens and to facilitate typing a split keyboard was provided which could be operated with two thumbs.

The combination of the touch language and the new Start screen were a significant simplification and consolidation of concepts without a loss of flexibility or power-user features. There are a couple of common examples that almost no typical Windows user knew were possible with the Windows 7 world that were addressed by the design. Few knew, for example, that the Start menu could be rearranged by bringing up the menu and then dragging and dropping the icons and folders, or that an icon could be placed in a folder while dragging. Most just lived with programs in the wrong order on a crowded and hierarchical menu. These power-user features were valued but so mysterious as to be known by a tiny sliver of the user base.

There are many system-wide commands that have historically been obscured or awkwardly placed in Windows, or worse implemented repeatedly but differently across applications. The last element of the Metro-style interface was the Windows 8 charms which provided access to system commands. The name charms came about because the icons displayed for the system commands of Search, Share, Start, Devices, and Settings were reminiscent of the clovers, hearts, stars, and moons[137] of Lucky Charms cereal.

The center of Windows 8 were apps. With Windows 8 we aimed to do more than present a sea of apps, but to connect apps together easily. Most apps connected to each other by somewhat blunt constructs of the clipboard and files. Cross-application scenarios were often hard-coded by app developers who had little information about what other apps were on your PC. The charms in Windows 8 provided a connection for all apps to (appropriately) connect to both the system and other apps. The mechanism developers used to implement these connections will be discussed in the next section.

From a user perspective, the Search charm offered simple method to search not only your PC but the information available via your apps. In Windows 7 we provided file search that worked across basic file types. In Windows 8 we extended this to include using search to find apps installed on your PC and to allow those apps to search the information and content available to them.

The Share charm provided the ability to share content such as photos, documents, contacts, or any other data with other apps. If you were looking at a photo, a web site, or a document choosing Share would connect whatever app you were using to the selected app. For example, sharing a photo to a social network app would guide you through posting that app on the network. Apple added this capability to iOS 8 in 2014.

The Start charm was an always available mechanism to return to the Start screen. It works just like the Windows key if you have a keyboard.

The Devices charm provided the connection of your PC to other hardware and connected devices. The most common devices to connect to included printers, speakers for playing music, and secondary screens either attached by cable or the new at the time wireless screens.

Finally, the Settings charm was the new Metro-style control panel. We knew this was going to be controversial for two reasons.

First, the Windows control panel had evolved, or perhaps devolved, to be a catch-all for an array of mini-programs to manipulate all sorts of system settings. These programs could be complex such as full anti-virus suites or even the control panel for managing your mail accounts in Outlook, which clearly did not belong there. Many people had grown up navigating this complexity and were able to somewhat fumble around the arbitrary categories to find settings they sometimes needed to change. The Windows 7 control had a search feature, but it was difficult to deliver on the promise because so much of the control panel was provided by third parties and the vocabulary of the control panel amounts to a set of inscrutable technical terms unknown to most.

Second, and painfully, from the start of the project we knew there was no way we would completely replace the current control panel in a single release. We were certain modernizing the control panel would take several product iterations. We built the Metro-style control panel to encompass the most common settings that also had the property of not requiring any device or OEM specific code. To get to additional settings the existing control panel remained and could be further updated.

The final, and as many would soon be debating, the most important part of the Windows 8 experience was the Desktop, the traditional place for launching and switching apps, working with files, and the place many people stored files they worked with daily "on the desktop." The Desktop was the very icon of the modern graphical PC.

The design of the desktop in Windows 8 was straightforward—the Windows 8 desktop was the Windows 7 desktop, only much better. We improved the taskbar, file explorer, window management, the Task Manager, file copying, multi-monitor support, virtualization, and more. We even did what we could to embrace touch even more than we did for Windows 7. The improvements in the desktop experience in Windows 8 was probably greater in terms of developer hours than in Windows 7.

The reason for this was straightforward. The desktop was where customers run the millions of existing, powerful, familiar Windows programs that were designed for mouse and keyboard. Office. Visual Studio. Adobe Photoshop. AutoCAD, and many more. This widely used software continued to be feature-rich, powering the bulk of the work people were doing on their PCs, at the time. Browsing and mobile apps all but took over home and consumer computing scenarios with a precipitous drop in the use of Windows apps for desktop publishing, photos, home finance, and entertainment. Many debated if the browser on the iPad was complete or powerful enough for these scenarios. Bringing the desktop forward (along with the metaphors such as manual discrete window sizing and overlapping placement) was a huge benefit when compared to tablets without these features or programs. It was an explicit design goal of Windows 8 to bring this software forward, run it better than in any previous version of Windows, and provide the best environment possible for these products as they evolved into the future as well.

As the iPad grew in popularity the interest in traditional desktop apps grew with it. Many customers, particularly in business, wanted the power of apps like Excel or PowerPoint to accompany them on their lightweight, long-battery life, and travel-friendly iPads. There was a sudden rise in remoting solutions that could enable access to these tools. Unfortunately, for desktop apps touch was a poor substitute a for a mouse and keyboard, as we knew from Windows 7. Apple believed it would be a matter of time until these apps were ported or reworked for the iPad. We believed there was a role for a better operating system to support this scenario.

To some the desktop was a thriving ecosystem rich with software capabilities. We certainly wanted to believe that was the case. In that spirit we did not think of the desktop and the million (or millions) of Win32 apps as legacy. It was our greatest asset. That's exactly why in the last section the first question Intel CEO Paul Otellini asked us when talking about ARM was if we ran x86 software.

Specifically, we didn't view the desktop as "legacy mode" or "old mode" but simply as the interface tuned to running Win32 software with a mouse and keyboard. It was pretty simple.

The core questions we needed to answer during these early days was "What if someone only ran desktop/Win32 apps on a PC without touch?" and "What if someone mixed and matched Metro-style apps with desktop apps?"

We iterated almost endlessly on minute aspects of the design when it came to the main detail of going from the Start screen to the desktop itself. We blogged about the design choices and discussed them in many forums as the software was shown more and got in the hands of the first users.

The design settled on several core user interface elements. First, both desktop apps and Metro-style apps were first class apps. The way we thought of this was that ALT-TAB, the primary way desktop users switched between apps, showed every running app. We treated the desktop itself as a launchable app, from a large tile on the Start screen. This followed from the way that MS-DOS was launched from Windows when Windows was introduced.

Switching to the desktop was also available from more touch-friendly app switcher that was available via swiping from the left edge of the screen or mousing in the upper left corner. The desktop itself could be accessed by moving the mouse to the lower left corner, exactly where the Start menu was located. A user that instinctively scrolled or tracked to the lower left and clicked would be brought to the desktop.

Perhaps the most visible example of the desktop and Metro-style living together as equals was the way Metro-style apps could be snapped next to the desktop, mixing, and matching as one needed. The existing desktop-based Windows snap feature introduced in Windows 7 received some enhancements and continued as expected whether running only the desktop or with a Metro-style app snapped as well.

With these designs in place, it was time to show people outside Microsoft what we had been doing. We knew there was a lot to absorb and a significant amount of complexity to communicate. We decided to roll out the product in stages. Each stage aimed at a particular audience and sharing a particular part of the product. Recognizing the magnitude of the user experience change, we chose to begin the roll out at the most influential of industry events and almost simultaneously at the most important partner event.

I was a very weird combination of terrified, excited, and confident. I was terrified by just how much we had to communicate and how complex the message was. I was excited because the work was making so much progress and was so innovative. I was indeed confident because I'd seen how far we'd come and, frankly, I knew we had made the right bets given the state of the platform and what needed to happen to keep Windows relevant to a new generation of customers and strategic for the ecosystem.

We chose to unveil the first US demonstrations of Windows 8 at the All Things Digital: D9 conference in June 2011. Just prior to the conference we seeded excitement for the conference itself with a preview. Jensen and team recorded a rather "DiY" video from the UEX program management design room. This video introduced the Windows 8 user interface. We dropped this video and quickly millions of people watched it. That might not sound like a lot today, but in 2011 millions of video views for a demonstration of a new OS was a lot.

We also showed a preview of Windows 8 in Taiwan at Computex just before D9. We took advantage of the time change so both demos were essentially in the same news cycle. This show is where all the Asian manufacturing partners and worldwide OEMs gathered to see the latest that would make for new PCs in the coming months and year. MikeAng and the Ecosystem team were responsible to this community and put on the demonstration. As with the above video, the words and images of this demo raced around the world.

D9 was going to be incredibly special, but we were, frankly, terrified. JulieLar along with JensenH and a half dozen others were scrambling the night before to get all the pieces to work—it wasn't just the software, but we were going to show a bunch of hardware that also barely worked months before the official release.

I joined Walt Mossberg on stage for an interview as JulieLar prepared to demonstrate her team's designs for the first time. On stage, Walt peppered me with a lot of difficult questions about the state of Windows and even Microsoft. It was a particularly brutal year for Microsoft as the industry had coalesced around a notion of "Gang of Four" companies leading the future of technology, a phrase coined by Google's CEO Eric Schmidt, no fan of Microsoft. His view of technology leaders of the time included: Google, Apple, Amazon, and Facebook. Walt wanted to know what it felt like to be left out.[138]

"Well," I said, "nothing called 'Gang of Four' ends well." Only a few years later, that inappropriate moniker would be replaced by the annoying FAANG, again without Microsoft.

Walt pressed more on Microsoft missing mobile and Windows tablets not taking off and focused on them not really having a touch-centric operating system. What could I say? He was right. Where Walt really pressed was on the quality of PCs. I suggested that Windows could be a great tablet (especially on ARM) because it brought the great parts of Windows.

Later that evening, some said to me that Walt was particularly hard on Microsoft and me in the interview. I didn't see it that way. Everything he said was both true and exactly why we designed Windows 8 as we had. It was interesting to be on the empathy or sympathy end for once though. I wasn't sure how I felt about that.

Almost on cue, Walt asked how we would show off a tablet. It is important to note the context and the importance of tablets to the audience and industry. They were a huge new development, and everyone was super excited by them. Recall, Walt's review of the iPad and how he favored using it over his Mac or ThinkPad. That was Julie's cue and I receded.

Julie came on stage with a battery of screens and computers, all working and ready, with a team backstage, collectively fingers crossed. I hovered behind her out of nervous energy, while Walt and Kara Swisher poked at screens and asked questions while Julie tried to stay on her script.[139]

The team had created a Lucite stand for a bare 10.6-inch touch screen display and the insides of a laptop, making for essentially a see-through demo tablet, like one of those old Ma Bell telephones made of clear plastic. The screen represented an ideal design size for a tablet, wide enough for a full-size keyboard, enough pixels for an HD movie, and able to show two apps at once. It was also the typical resolution of over two-thirds of laptops being sold.

Running through a fast and fluid demo, Julie showed off every key aspect of Windows 8 and Metro-style: design and typography, Start screen, gestures, immersive apps, snap, touch browsing with Internet Explorer 10, the on-screen keyboard including a split view (Walt had not seen before), and of course the complete support of the desktop apps everyone uses.

Walt called this the "biggest shift in Windows." That was true. Julie finished the demo by showing the other PCs on stage, all Windows 7 PCs made better by Windows 8: a regular laptop, a slate, and a full convertible Tablet PC. Phew!

But once Kara and Walt asked the audience for questions, attention turned to the notion of "two modes"—desktop and Metro-style tablets—and a nagging concern planted itself in my head. How would this play out? What could we do better? They weren't really modes any more than MS-DOS programs were modes. Or were they? We didn't come up with a good way to explain it. And if we had to explain it, we were already in trouble.

To distill the feedback at the show and what we subsequently discussed in the b8 blog, the issue was that to some observers the desktop had been somehow relegated and obscured by the new Start screen, leading to three reactions. First, this created an impression that launching to programs (or files on the desktop) was an extra step away after starting a PC. Second, that going to the desktop was entering some secondary mode of Windows. Third, there was a visceral reaction that the Start screen was simply too big and got in the way.

The Start screen itself was (literally) a big Start menu and the desktop was (literally) still another program that was always running. In Windows 7 we even made the desktop show up when using ALT-TAB to switch between programs, a fan favorite, so the desktop already looked like another program. But making that clear was the challenge.

We continued to iterate and polish the design. Should we have a Start button or not? Should we have an option to boot the PC directly to the desktop? There were dozens of small changes made to the design and a series of several blog posts of thousands of words from the team discussing feedback, questions, and design choices and alternatives.

As with every past release of Windows there was disproportionate attention on the basic user interface for launching programs and manipulating files—I say disproportionate because absent applications these are the features used to evaluate a new release and compare to the previous one. These features are also disproportionately used by tech enthusiasts, particularly file management and organization. Windows 8 was no different.

This focus tended to overshadow that Windows 8 was moving up the stack so to speak and redefining the basic operating system to include innovation in the other essential ingredient of offering an end-to-end experience, internet scale or cloud-based services.

Operating on a different timeline through all of Windows 7 and then Windows 8, the Windows Live team steadily improved email, calendaring, storage, identity, and a host of other capabilities under the Windows Live branding, mainly bringing the capabilities of scalable (and cost-effective) cloud storage for every Windows 8 PC and customer, along with account management, email, photos and video, editing, and more. On their own each of these services aimed to be competitive within their categories, even going up against Google's Gmail after a long road to improve the scale of Hotmail, renamed to Outlook.com. Even cloud storage, launched as SkyDrive in 2010 and then rebranded to OneDrive in 2013 due to a trademark conflict, had essentially under the radar become an integral part of the Windows 8 experience for roaming files and settings across multiple PCs and mobile phones including Android. We also integrated the new Office web applications (Word, Excel, PowerPoint for browsers that were started way back when I was still in Office) with both storage and email.

At the 2007 launch of these services Paul Thurrott even went as far as to say, "Looking ahead, Microsoft is working on the next generation version of Windows Live, which it sees delivering as a set of software and services suites, one each for the browser, Windows PCs, and Windows Mobile-based devices. The browser suite will provide common branding and user experiences, and will work in both traditional, PC-based browsers as well as mobile phone browsers."[140]

There was much to be done, more than we had time for, but all the pieces were part of the plan and executing well. These services were shipping separate from Windows on their own schedule, with frequent updates and at the same time planning on aligning with Windows 8 as the critical cloud and service elements of the product.

The innovations (and inventions) across the experience and the platform prepared Windows for a new generation. The modern Metro-style experience in Windows—fast and fluid, immersive, touch-first, and connected—brought a PC up to the standards of the smartphone, which had defined a new level of interaction. Metro-style apps were a missing piece. Without apps, we had nothing but a nice project. We needed developers.

The experience described in this section was designed with a broad range of new operating system capabilities that would be made available to developers so they could build Metro-style apps—we called this the WinRT platform.

A couple of months after the iPad was available to customers, it was clear it was a hit product. By the June 2010 earnings call, after only 80 days in market, inventory constrained, and, still not shipping all models, Apple sold three million units for an estimated $2 billion. At the time it was the fastest-selling mobile device of all time. If I wanted to brush it off, I could have argued that PCs were selling that many units every few days or perhaps the iPad was just Apple's Netbook. But that would have been short-sighted. As we knew, the iPad and the iPhone (and to some degree Android) were drawing all the attention of developers. Developer attention meant there was durability to the platform. The iPad ran all iPhone apps, and rapidly apps were being tuned for the larger screen of the iPad.

It was our turn to woo developers. The stakes were high.

103. THE END OF WINDOWS SOFTWARE

The Windows platform and associated app ecosystem were sick. Across product executives we had a very tough time coming to grips with the abysmal situation. We definitely could not agree on when the situation turned dire or why or if it had. That meant doing something about it was going to be challenging.

Some were so desperate for good news that they grabbed on to any shred of optimism. At one of the infamous Mid-Year Review (MYR) meetings during the development of Windows 7, a country general manager proudly presented their results of the annual developer survey designed to show what platform developers are coding for and the tools they use. The head of the developer segment for India said they were seeing Windows rise to the top of the chart for the most interesting and targeted platform. Windows! Immediately the room woke up from its MYR-induced stupor. Questions and comments were flying, "What outreach did you do?" "Did you start in University comp sci programs?" "How did you use financial incentives?"

The optimism was misplaced. The realty was even more bleak than a benign survey outlier, a common occurrence when compensation and corporate metrics were attached to surveys. There was no surge in Windows development. Nope, it was the opposite. India had become a favorite location for companies to outsource their legacy Windows software development. We weren't measuring an uptick. We were literally measuring the final blow to the Windows development ecosystem as companies everywhere looked to place development out of sight and out of mind. I hate to say so, but it was obvious that's what the data showed. Microsoft itself had incented teams to transition projects to India, and not often the most strategic ones as I had learned when we had to reconstitute the Windows sustaining engineering team.

Through the 1990s and the rise of Windows, BillG hosted an annual dinner for the largest and most important Windows ISVs, the CEOs and founders of leading tech companies of the era. The dinner was always a star-studded affair featuring the legends of the industry including Philippe Kahn, Jim Manzi, Ray Ozzie, Paul and George Grayson, David Fulton, Fred Gibbons, Scott Cook and perhaps 50 more. These were the leaders of the new industry each presiding over companies with hundreds of millions or billions of dollars of revenue. The companies built the tools from my earliest PC days: Borland Turbo Pascal, Lotus 1-2-3, Lotus Notes, Micrografix, FoxPro, Harvard Graphics, Quicken, and more.

As Windows won, ironically the health of these companies declined. There was a natural consolidation. Many were acquired, and their products slowly faded. Microsoft had its competitive products and the rise of Office, Visual C++, Outlook, and others certainly contributed. Microsoft's singular bet on Windows and early success on Macintosh were factors as well.

It was, however, the internet and the web browser that really changed everything. The above ISVs started their companies in the 1980s on MS-DOS or in the early 1990s on Windows. Anyone starting a company, particularly in Silicon Valley, in the late 1990s started as a web company. Many startups created enterprise software, though we tend to remember the rise of Yahoo, Google, and later Facebook.

A look at the top software companies in 2010 read like a list of industrial giants more than pure play software. PwC published a list, *Global 100 Software Leaders*, that illustrated how the industry had changed. Among the top 100, there were only three that made tools or productivity software primarily aimed at Windows or Mac: Adobe, Autodesk, and Intuit. There were even more companies that built safety, security, or management tools addressing shortcomings of the PC: McAfee, Symantec, TrendMicro, Citrix, etc. Most of the companies were either transitioning or transitioned completely to web-based interfaces running against datacenter software.[141]

The real end of the ISV dinner happened for me in 1999. The Microsoft Business Productivity Group (BPG) led by Microsoft senior vice president Bob Muglia (BobMu) announced a deal to acquire Visio Corporation for approximately $1.5 billion, Microsoft's largest acquisition at the time. Visio was a profitable company approaching $200 million per year in revenue and nearly $30 million in net income. Bob was my manager though I didn't know anything about the deal.

The Visio Corp. founders were the fantastic team of Jeremy Jaech, Ted Johnson, and Dave Walter. Jeremy and Dave had previously co-founded Seattle-based Aldus Corporation where Ted later led the engineering for Windows PageMaker. Aldus was acquired by Adobe in 1994.

Visio was a wonderful product and from the very start engineered a strong affinity to Microsoft Office, often working jointly with us on marketing, sales, and even consistency of product design. The product, an easy-to-use diagramming application, pioneered many structured drawing tools we take for granted today such as stencils of shapes, the ability to modify shape geometry, and magnetic connectors between shapes. The company was headquartered in downtown Seattle when Microsoft didn't even have offices across the bridge.

Visio was the last poster child of the old ISV world left standing to have started out as a Windows software company. It was one of the first applications developed for Windows 95, a fact that was heavily promoted. Strategically it used everything Microsoft could throw at it from Visual Basic automation to data access APIs to OLE. Ted once joked with me that they would have used Clippy if we gave them the chance.

Ted, who stayed on for a bit with Microsoft and then later returned to work on Internet Explorer (TedJ), was always candid about their journey. He was wonderful to talk with and had the experiences of a founder, which was something I sought out. His view was clear that the days of being a breakthrough independent developer focused exclusively on Windows were over. It wasn't just the browser, but also the demands of building out an enterprise sales force and having a full product line exclusively devoted to being a Windows ISV. This was even before the rise of mobile.

I had a few conversations with BobMu and SteveB over whether it was a good idea for the health of the ecosystem that we participate in the ongoing consolidation. I think they heard what I was saying as a resistance to the deal because I'd end up managing the team—that wasn't it at all and I loved the team and product. Visio was a great addition to the Office family and brought a significant amount of expertise with a great team. For me, it meant the only remaining independent and relatively horizontal Windows ISV was Adobe. Should we buy them too? Then we'd be our own ISV ecosystem. It just didn't seem healthy.

On the other hand, it was inevitable. The Windows ISV world wasn't what it was, but why?

Microsoft wasn't standing still while this decline took place. We struggled to build both a coherent strategy and execute effectively. It wasn't a shortage of strategy, rather it was a combination of several strategies that ended up failing to reinforce each other and ultimately weakened the overall company strategy.

At the core was Microsoft's collective response to the internet platform—the browser and the server programming model. The Windows team fully embraced the browser as the future platform, pioneering and advancing HTML along the way. In the late 1990s, Windows even redesigned the Windows desktop to integrate HTML and browser technologies on to the surface of the desktop. Still there was no bridge between Windows and the web platform. Windows simply became a place to run a browser. In Windows 7, we finally took a step of relying on Windows itself for browser features when we integrated DirectX graphics that enhanced animation, video, and overall browsing performance. That came after Microsoft ceded the dominance it earned in an earlier era, unfortunately.

This entire time, the Windows desktop API—Win32—went under-nourished, so to speak. It did not really matter because anything done in a new release of Windows would be ignored by ISVs unless it also worked on older versions of Windows. Enterprise PCs continued to run older versions of Windows longer than even the 3-to-5-year upgrade cycle of Windows and PCs were lasting longer as well. No ISV was willing to invest in writing code specific to a new version of Windows for what amounted to tiny marginal gains in functionality or features. Some teams released new features that ran on the installed base of older Windows, further reducing the perceived value of a Windows upgrade. This cycle of distributing new features for the old Windows installed base increased the complexity and fragility of existing PCs by designing implementations of system-level features to work in the context of multiple versions of Windows. It was a mess. Windows had turned into a distribution vehicle for features without a coherent platform strategy.

The Windows Server team faced its own API battle distinct from the client side. In the 1990s the team developed high-performance and scalable web server capabilities such as Internet Information Server. This platform handily won the enterprise market that was buying servers to host web sites along with Oracle databases, Microsoft Exchange email, and corporate file servers. There was an entire new software industry built on servers running Windows that rivaled or even exceeded the size of the old end-user software industry. Companies such as SAP, Siebel, VMware, EMC, and more rose from this era. These companies were really the platforms of the server era as most also supported Unix, Linux, or even IBM mainframes.

The ISVs and developers of this era were also mostly inside of corporations or consultants, either independent or at shops of all sizes. Their business was in connecting and customizing these new server platforms one customer at time. While Windows along with a database (such as Microsoft's SQL Server or Oracle) could easily serve web pages, the real business was in building a commerce site, a customer facing catalog, or internal corporate portal and connecting that site to internal line of business systems such as SAP. Windows wasn't much of a platform for that.

The Developer division built that platform. The origin of .NET was to provide the platform and abstractions for the web application landscape.

Arising during the fierce competition for mindshare with the Java language from Sun, .NET was Microsoft's own answer to "middleware" or software that was neither an application nor an operating system. The success of .NET proved that a platform does not have to be an operating system but can be anything that developers bet their business on—something we in Office had been saying about Word and Excel for ages. The .NET platform provided for the new world of browser and web server computing what Visual Basic and SQL provided for the Win32 client-server era.

This strategy and execution were incredible. The dominance in the enterprise customer segment prior to the cloud era was unparalleled. The emergence of cloud computing, however, posed new challenges. What had been an annoyance competitively had become the platform of the cloud. The tools affectionately known as LAMP, representing Linux, Apache, MySQL, PHP/Perl/Python, and their progeny, defined how the new enterprise public cloud would be built. These were the building blocks of applications built on Amazon AWS as well. Almost as fast as .NET rose to prominence it faded to be the installed base. There's a footnote to this in that many of the .NET-based systems built and deployed in the early 2000s were mission critical business systems that will be used, maintained, and enhanced for a decade or more.

The story did not end there because in parallel with the rise of .NET for servers, the Developer Division, tasked with battling Java, also had to compete with the use of Java on the desktop. There was ample evidence that the *raison d'être* for Java on the desktop was doomed to failure, the mantra "write once, run anywhere" meaning that Java programs could work on any type of desktop such as any version of Windows, Mac, or Linux. That was not reason enough to let it go.

As a result, there was a wave of products designed to bring .NET to the desktop to write Windows programs. The languishing Win32 API was no longer receiving much support or innovation from the Developer division. My old product, C++ and MFC the preferred choice of professional ISVs using Win32, was relegated to maintenance mode. Instead, a new and constantly expanding set of technologies from the Developer division were evangelized as the preferred way to write professional Windows software. The names and differences between them are not entirely critical and my intent is not to start a debate over the relative prominence, target customer, or capability of any one of these. Some of the new desktop technologies included: WinForms, Forms[3], WPF/XAML, Silverlight, and others that were less visible or more oriented towards application internals.

A defining characteristic of each of the .NET technologies was a strong relationship to Microsoft's programming language developed for the .NET server platform, C#, pronounced *see sharp*. This language was designed by the highly regarded language designer Anders Hejlsberg (AndersH) at Microsoft. He was previously at Borland which had licensed his product that became the legendary Turbo Pascal. The use of C# was a dream for BillG who always wanted Microsoft to develop and own a proprietary programming language implementation.

The combination of the C# language and the above growing list of technologies would together be known, confusingly, as .NET. While it made sense from a marketing perspective to have a single umbrella term, it meant for confusing discussions with developers. Were we talking about a language or the API? Were we talking about programming the desktop or the server? Which client API specifically, since they were both discrete and overlapped? This mattered because few developers used the whole of .NET and so when engaging with them narrowing it down mattered.

Even with .NET branding, owning a language was not enough. In fact, as I argued with BillG going way back to C++, a proprietary language was neither necessary nor sufficient strategically. The only thing that mattered in a platform battle was owning the APIs and runtime. Languages are both easy to copy and easy to replace, but the use of APIs in code developers write lasts a really long time. The "P" in LAMP was showing how many languages were already native to cloud computing. As we see today, the poly-lingual era of computing is the norm for most large systems. Enterprises did not like this, nor did the consulting and ISV world that was well paid by enterprises. They wanted a homogeneous C# world they could leverage across projects. The Developer division strategy fed that need to the exclusion of building quality Windows applications.

The other defining characteristic of the new Developer division desktop technologies was the weak or lack of a relationship to Win32. These technologies certainly ran on Windows, but they were not Windows itself and did not have the performance or quality of Win32-based, or what we called native, applications. They were layered on top of Windows architecturally. The strategy was specifically to evolve these technologies separate from Windows so they could be provided across Windows versions and because the implementation was specifically designed to avoid interfering with Windows.

Building .NET this way ensured that the Developer division was not beholden to the slowing and unpredictable Windows ship schedule. The rift between Windows and Developer grew significantly from 2004-2006 as the Longhorn/Vista project progressed. Then, Windows leadership effectively banned .NET from Longhorn because of performance and memory management issues. The Windows team made a rule that no applications written with .NET would ship with Windows Vista.

This infuriated the broad developer community as it seemed like a classic case of "do as I say, not as I do" after years of evangelizing that .NET was the future of Windows. There was a strong sense of betrayal among the .NET community outside of Microsoft, particularly those developing desktop applications. This put them on the defensive, constantly on the lookout for signs that Microsoft was backing down from support of their preferred .NET technology. One member of the .NET developer community consistently checked pre-release builds of Windows Vista creating a nutrition label of sorts and concluded that no more than 4% of Vista used .NET code. That was substantially different than the promise of a fully .NET operating system they believe Microsoft promised them.[142]

Managing an ecosystem comes with a responsibility to maintain a consistency of messaging as well as to avoid undermining the financial investments people are making in that ecosystem.

Windows Server did not see .NET this same way. In fact, Windows Server fully embraced .NET and it became an integral part of the value proposition. Why was there such a difference when only a courtyard separated the teams? .NET was the Server platform, plain and simple. While there were some developers writing native code to the networking, storage, or kernel layers these were the rough equivalents of those writing device drivers for the desktop. They were an important part of the ecosystem, but a very small community. This would have been the right way to separate the different API layers on the desktop, but that was not the approach taken.

Instead, a deep schism was created between the Win32 and .NET APIs on the desktop. This schism went even further than that because .NET itself had non-overlapping technologies where any given development project would likely only pick one, for example Silverlight or WinForms, creating advocates for one part of .NET over another even as the evangelists painted a picture of a .NET family.

There were also various Win32 APIs that weren't clearly part of the formal definition of Windows, such as DirectX graphics, but were used by different parts of .NET in varying ways. Often .NET would use a technology in Windows, which seemed good on the face of it. Diving in one would find .NET used a subset of Windows that precluded using the full capabilities from within a .NET program. It was super confusing. Such details were often lost in the fervent online discussions and zealotry that surrounding this debate. I understand as I write the preceding that people would want to even debate the merits of these opinions or offer examples of how one could indeed mix and match API sets. Section 091 describes such "stupid developer tricks."[143]

While the bulk of the world of software developers were moving to or had already moved to the browser, those within the Microsoft sphere of influence were debating the merits of their preferred way to write desktop apps for Windows, so long as it was using C# and not using Win32. There would be few to no pure-play commercial software products for sale that used .NET, other than some tools to support specific hardware or other support products. The Zune desktop app was often used as the example from Microsoft. A rewrite of Visual Studio itself was often discussed in this vein as well.

For the bulk of world's developers, there was only one thing holding back the browser and HTML-only world so many developers desired, aside from bugs and inconsistencies between browser vendors and versions. Surprisingly, that was Adobe. Adobe acquired Macromedia Flash in 2005. Flash had become the way to bring the power of desktop computing to run inside the browser. It crushed Microsoft's attempt as previously discussed, called ActiveX. Primarily it won over the world of streaming video having been chosen by YouTube and also the advertising world where Flash was routinely used for obnoxious and intrusive flashing and flyover advertisements, browsing interiors of cars, and movie clips.

Recall that Silverlight, in the 2010 timeframe, had originally been Microsoft's answer to compete with Flash but had been repurposed to be the API for Windows Phone 7 and subsequently Windows Phone 8. Silverlight was related to the whole .NET umbrella term but came with its own set of constraints. It had little to do with our Windows platform. Silverlight was non-apologetic about running on not just old versions of Windows but also Mac and soon smartphones. Microsoft's evangelism kicked into high gear for Silverlight. Many Microsofties fondly remember Netflix using Silverlight in the browser in the early days of Netflix.

Adobe Flash would hit a big speedbump, or more correctly a brick wall, along the way. Apple. The iPhone never supported Flash. Many thought this would doom the iPhone as Flash had become so synonymous with the fun part of the web and the economics of the web. The iPhone team worked with Google and YouTube to create an iOS app that played YouTube videos. That was not only the right solution for customers but made clear a deep philosophical point held by Steve Jobs—operating systems are a "thing" not a set of "layers" and to build a good operating system one does not layer one operating system-like technology on top of another.

This view would be seen as somewhat contrarian in the halls of Microsoft since both Silverlight depended on such layers as did the rest of .NET. Outside of Microsoft, people would perceive Apple's stubbornness about Flash as simply Steve Jobs trying to control things. It was obviously frustrating for Apple. It got to the point that Apple and Steve Jobs needed to say something. The reason was that the iPad was about to hit the streets in mid-2010 and the tech press was hounding Apple over the need to support Flash on such a large screen browser as the iPad if it were to be a true computer and not a phone. It didn't matter that Adobe never delivered Flash to any phone, as Jobs pointed out, or that on Netbooks Flash ran so poorly as to be useless. They wanted Steve Jobs to fix this.

Steve had a better idea. On April 29, 2010, commensurate with US availability of the iPad, Apple published a missive *Thoughts on Flash* signed by Steve Jobs.[144] I thought it was brilliant. To this day I believe it was the most concise expression of excellent product strategy and appreciation of great engineering that any CEO anywhere had written during the PC era.

Jobs laid out one of the clearest and most well-articulated strategies for why Flash was not a good idea on the iPhone, or frankly, ever. In terms of strategic clarity in general this remains a standard by which to judge any strategy. He dismantled Flash in fewer than 1,700 words, detailing that Flash was closed, not really part of the web, performed poorly relative to reliability, security, and performance, had poor battery life, did not work with touch, and, most importantly, the whole concept of third-party runtimes is bad for everyone. Was it self-serving? Sure. Apple wanted people to build Apps for the iPhone using Apple's proprietary tools and platform and everyone knew it. But Jobs wasn't wrong. In fact, he was precisely right on the negatives, which killed everyone to admit. This was the technical buzzsaw at its finest.

As I read the polemic, I found myself nodding in violent agreement. The current choices we faced in building Windows 8 found us in the middle of the various .NET runtimes each of which shared shortcomings and limitations with Flash. The Jobs memo also took me back to my first product, Microsoft Foundation Classes, when we lived through making all the mistakes of building a C++ variant of a third-party runtime. We discarded the "Old AFX" project after explaining to BillG why what we built in 1991 was so big, slow, and unlike Windows. Everything about *Thoughts on Flash* resonated. I loved it.

I quickly circulated *Thoughts on Flash* and talked for a long time with Aleš Holeček (AlesH), by then a vice president leading the creation of the app platform for Windows 8 as the engineering leader of DEVX, the platform counterpart to the UEX user experience team. He had firsthand experience in this problem area having worked on a Flash-like competitor in the early days of the web. We shared a lot of nodding when discussing the Jobs memo.

What Jobs captured so well was that modern computing had moved in a new direction. The idea of a modern computing platform hosting another platform on top of it while that platform essentially emulated, but differently, the underlying native platform was patently dumb. It was a guaranteed way to drag down the whole of the experience across the gamut of reliability, performance, touch, battery life, privacy, reliability, and so on. For certain Jobs's memo was a full assault on Flash, but it was the whole concept of building platforms on top of platforms that was the problem.

The Developer division did not see the situation the same way.

The tensions and divisions that had been growing between Windows and Developer since the arrival of .NET in 2001 were reaching a breaking point, not just within Microsoft but the developer community as well. From their perspective, Windows 8 should make a big bet on the runtimes they had created just as they had been promised previously.

We were well-aware of this desire and the existing schism in developing Windows 8. JulieLar and I both were rooted in our own experience in the Developer division in the early 1990s. PJ Hough (PJHough) who led the amazing cross-group partnership between Office and Visual Basic to bring VBA to all of Office was now a leader in the division. Our connections were strong. There was a good deal of positive history.

Similar experiences can yield similar engineering results and like Apple we had early in the Windows 8 design phase concluded that Windows needed a new platform, not yet another set of libraries on top of Windows like Flash. The Windows 8 platform needed to be Windows 8 itself, not a library floating on top. We were also determined to build first party apps the same way we were going to seek out developers to build their apps. This "eating our own dogfood" would be a critical validation of the platform. The tools and platform would support a new set of modern needs for Windows 8, paraphrasing from pre-release developer documentation defining the platform attributes:

- It is written to take advantage of the Metro-style immersive experience:
    - It provides a UI / look & feel that is compliant with Metro-style including the app bar, animations, typography, layout, and so on.
    - It supports modern startup, shutdown, and hibernation, windowing, and process lifetime management.
    - It supports app contracts. App contracts define capabilities apps can follow to participate in Windows controlled UI experiences, such as: live tiles, snap view, splash screen, search, share, notifications, file picking, app settings, connect.
- It runs in an Application Container for security and is completely isolated from other apps.
- It is only delivered through the new deployment technology, the new App Store.
- It is installed per user, not per machine.
- It installs and uninstalls cleanly leaving nothing behind at all.
- It is impossible for an app change the state of the OS in an irreversible way.

Nevertheless, at our unveiling of the user experience in June 2011 we ran right into this sensitivity and brought the full wrath of the .NET community. It was just the omission of a couple of words and a lack of appropriate deference to .NET that set us up for a good deal of pain. In the course of the demonstration, with both Julie and I on stage, we said and echoed each other about a key aspect of the new Metro-style apps.

We said these beautiful, secure, easy-to-build, safe, reliable apps could be built using "our new platform with HTML and JavaScript." That was it.

It was just a reflex. It was in fact the news. Microsoft embracing the world's most popular and widely used programming languages for its flagship product was a big deal. It was a key part of how we would make building Windows 8 apps easier and more accessible to legions of developers. It was also differentiated relative to Apple's proprietary and un-loved Objective-C and Android's Java that wasn't living up to the hype. As if to pour gasoline on the fire, JensenH in his video viewed by millions said the same thing. Steve Ballmer even waded accidently into the fray simply repeating the statements made at the D Conference demo.

The problem was we inadvertently sent a message to a very sensitive and on-edge community that we had jettisoned .NET and finally made good on what the Vista team had essentially done by fiat. In an Ars Technica article documenting the assault on .NET the headline ran "Why Microsoft has made developers horrified about coding for Windows 8" and was so indignant it even quoted an extraneous "uhh" in Julie's statement, "our new developer platform, which is, uhh, it's based on HTML5 and JavaScript."[145]

This was a problem of our own making. The strength of this reaction was testament to our incredible evangelism efforts—the success of which greatly outpaced the impact of these technologies in the market. We knew the data from developer surveys and what people were using. We knew what programs were running on Windows PCs through our telemetry. We knew what technologies the new generation of cloud companies were using, and the world's universities were teaching. We knew that within the Microsoft bubble .NET was everything. While that is a big bubble, it was small relative to the whole universe especially with the rise of mobile platforms. We used to joke about the Developer division surveys that always showed dominance of .NET because of the well-known Microsoft echo chamber or bubble—the survey results said "100% of .NET developers use .NET."

There were many frustrations with our statement at the D Conference expressed through countless blogs and endless discussions about this transgression. Most began with the notion that HTML and JavaScript were immature and lacked the horsepower to serve as the foundation for great applications. Rooted in this commentary was a disdain for what were routinely dismissed as "script kiddies" or those calling themselves programmers who merely created static web pages or simply modified a few lines of a web pages and claimed expertise. This was from another era and reminded me of the age old "Real Programmers" meme from long before there were memes. The truth is by 2010 real programmers did use HTML and JavaScript. In fact, they were the most used, the most taught, and the most actively developed languages. Taking a buzzsaw to HTML was going to be a losing proposition, no matter the technical merits programming language experts might debate.

The main issue, however, was where this left all the other Microsoft technologies. Disrespecting HTML and JavaScript was simply smoke around the .NET fire. Specifically, where did we see Silverlight and its more feature laden parent WPF and the language C# fitting in. Developers were apoplectic about their investment in Microsoft .NET technologies not moving forward with Windows 8, whether those were WinForms, Silverlight, WPF, C#, or even C++.

Silverlight/.NET expert Mike James wrote, in "Dumping .NET – Microsoft's Madness" that if "the future of Windows apps is HTML5/JavaScript then Windows has no future." His post went on to explain his idea that Silverlight is Windows, it just runs inside a browser. He also explained how .NET improved the Windows API and making it more readily programmable.[146]

Our choice was to engage at the time without pre-release of code to test or validate what we were saying or wait it out for a Seattle summer when we would have code available. Obviously given the situation the concerned developer community would doubt every word we wrote. We knew once the pre-release code was distributed, we would have to answer these festering questions but could do so pointing to the product. I chose the latter and waited for our developer conference scheduled for September 2011. Engaging online discussions with an asymmetry of information in the context of such deep concerns would be a frustrating exercise for everyone.

Tim Anderson wrote in his blog, "Microsoft Refuses to Comment As .Net Developers Fret About Windows 8" and said, "In fact, it is bewildering that Microsoft is being so careless with this critical part of its platform, even if this turns out to be more to do with communication than technical factors."

Finally, we could always count on Mary Jo Foley of ZDNet to catch a leak from the Developer division and her sources clearly indicated "Microsoft needs to tell Windows 8 developers now about 'Jupiter' and Silverlight." Jupiter was the code name of the other part of our Windows 8 developer strategy—to use C#, WPF, and XAML. The article continued "Microsoft's longer-term goal is to align its various developer stacks, giving it a story that's comparable to Apple's. Because Apple supporting iOS on tablets and phones, Apple developers can write once and have their apps run in both places with relatively little modification." Just as many of the blogs stated, this article also concluded "Like many devs I've heard from, I don't believe Microsoft can't [can] afford to wait three more months to let its developer base know what its intentions are. So far, however, ill-advised silence seems to be the Softies' plan…"[147]

We had a plan. We had a new platform. It addressed these concerns. We also knew that if we started answering questions now, we'd end up in theoretical debates from June through the developer conference in September. The conference, a rebranding of the PDC to //build, would provide code, tools, and answers to these questions. I thought.

Off to //build to share the platform we built.

104. //BUILD IT AND THEY WILL COME (HOPEFULLY)

The iPad was out there and still had skeptics. Pundits continued to assert that tablets were not good devices for content creation. Techies saw it as a consumer toy for lightweight computing. This same thing had once been said of PCs, right up until they overtook computing. It was said of server PCs, right up until they overtook business workloads and cloud computing.

Steve Jobs, at the 2010 All Things Digital: D8 conference, reminded the audience that the iPad was just getting started and added, "I think we're just scratching the surface on the kind of apps we can build for it. I think one can create a lot of content on the tablet." By 2011, Apple was demonstrating increasing confidence in the path they had created with iPad. The iPad was already the preferred tool for the road warrior, the boardroom, and the back seat. The iPad and iPhone combined with the developer platform had become the most formidable competition Microsoft ever faced. As much as Android unit volumes concerned the Windows Phone team, there was no ignoring Apple. Some were deeply concerned about the tsunami of small Android tablets. Given what we went through with Netbooks, low quality devices, even in high volumes, concerned me less.

The PC was moribund. The situation in Redmond became increasingly worrisome. This was despite our solid progress on Windows 8 and the interim Windows Phone release, Windows Phone 7.5.

The chicken and egg challenge of platforms is well known. How does a platform gain traction from a standing start? Every platform faces this, but it is unusual for the established world leader to be wrestling with this problem. When I think of how the computer world had literally revolved around every utterance about Windows, it was downright depressing if not scary.

The challenge the company faced was the dramatic loss of developer mindshare. Between web browsers, iPhone/iPad, and then Android, there was no room left for Microsoft. Win32 was legacy, a solid legacy, but a legacy. The latest efforts for Windows Phone seemed to have stalled at best. While there was a rhythm of press releases about app momentum for Windows Phone, the app numbers were tiny relative to Apple and Google and the app quality was low. Phone units were small too, meaning attracting developers was becoming more difficult not less.

Every leadership team meeting provided another opportunity to debate the merits of using financial incentives to lure developers to the platform. And at each meeting I raised the reality of adverse selection that every competitor to Windows had learned over the past two decades. The Xbox team loved to talk about how much they spent on exclusives, but that was a walled garden world of intellectual property. In an open platform, once you're spending money to win over developers, the least motivated developers show up with the wrong apps creating an awful cycle where paying developers attracts more of the less desirable developers building even more of the wrong apps. But not spending money seems guaranteed to lose if there's no organic interest. This debate would become front and center with Windows 8 as we faced the same challenge.

The concerns over the specifics of competing with iPad and Android tablets and how Microsoft and partners would respond occupied an increasingly concerned board. We had our plans for Windows 8, but the obvious question was could Microsoft do something sooner? In the summer of 2011, we were a couple of months from our developer conference in September and certainly less than 18 months from general availability of Windows 8. I assumed we could wait that long and knew we could not finish sooner. I also assumed there was no emergency product development that could finish something useful before then. That didn't stop us from having a classic Microsoft hand-wringing series of meetings to attempt to cons up a plan. Time for yet another *Gedankenexperiment* as part of a series of meetings with some members of the board and others.

We were not yet certain of the how or who of delivering ARM devices, particularly tablets, though by this point we had test hardware running and we were deep in potential designs for our own device. As a result, I was my routinely cautious self in an effort not to over-promise, especially to this group. I was, perhaps wrongly, determined not to get ahead of our own execution. Such a conservative stance was my nature but also not the norm or even appreciated. I was happy to talk about our developer conference and what was possible. The specifics required to answer when and by whom there would be a mini tablet running Windows were well ahead of where we were.

I reviewed our progress on Windows 8, again. The problem seemed to be that we were not getting enough done nor was it soon enough. They were right. Who wouldn't want more and sooner? From my vantage point, if we finished when we said we would it would be impressive and historically unique, even on the heels of Windows 7. How quickly people can forget the past. It felt like "more cowbell."

Shaving time off the schedule was discussed—it wasn't a grounded discussion, just a wish. After that, Terry Myerson (TMyerson) and his co-leader Andy Lees (AndyLees) of the Phone team, shared the early plans for Windows Phone 8. Since Apple had made a tablet out of the iPhone, the natural question was, could we make a tablet out of Windows Phone? Of course, we could do anything ("It's just software" as we said), but which phone and how soon?

Some in attendance even asked if should do a "quick" project and build a tablet out of WP7 (or 7.5)? Could we take an Android tablet design and put Windows Phone 7 on it? Why not? Seemed so easy. None of these ideas could possibly happen. There's no such thing as a quick project. The last quick hardware project Microsoft did was Kin, a poorly received smartphone.

There wasn't much I could do. From one perspective, Windows was suddenly the product that was holding us back and Windows Phone was the new solution to our tablet problem. Given what we were seeing in the market, Windows Phone apps, and the technical challenges of the platform, this was a ridiculous spot to land.

Windows Phone 8, working with Nokia, introduced really big phones called *phablets*, pioneered by Samsung on Android. For a time, some analysts thought these larger phones would put an end to tablet demand because tablets were in between. Still, tablets continued to thrive for productivity and, as far as Apple was concerned, to become the future laptop. The iPad certainly thrived. It was the cheap Android tablets, the ones the Board was concerned about, that ended up on the trash heap with Netbooks.

Ultimately, there was no tablet market, just an iPad market. The iPad run rate soon approximated that of consumer PC laptops. It was difficult for Microsoft to see the low-volume player as the real competitor, especially when it was Apple and the last time it was the low-volume producer it nearly died. Android was shaping up to be the Windows ecosystem on phones—high volume, low profit, endless fragility, device diversity (or randomness), and so on, but with a new OS, new OEMs, new business model, and new mobile developers who were making apps on the iPhone, though the iPhone apps always seemed a bit better.

The Windows and Windows Phone teams would eventually go through a challenging period where in the middle of Windows 8, we on the Windows team learned that the Phone team had been taking snapshots of various subsystems of Windows 8 for use in the phone OS. This got the product to market but did not give us a chance to align on quality, security, reliability, and code maintenance. This wasn't done in any coordinated or even transparent manner. Had we, Jon DeVaan and Grant George specifically, not intervened the company would have been set up for significant issues with security and reliability given we were not finished with the code and there was no process in place to manage "copies" of the code. Jon worked through a better process once the team got ahead of the issue. I had a super tense meeting with SteveB and the co-leaders of the Phone team about this lack of transparency and process and why it showed a lack of leadership, or even competence, on our part. In the new world of security, viruses, vulnerabilities, and more the company could not afford to be cavalier with source code like this seemed to demonstrate. This was all in addition to the lack of alignment on the developer platform as the Phone team made their early bet on Silverlight as previously discussed.

More and sooner was a constant drumbeat throughout the Windows 8 development schedule. I was called to the carpet many times to explain where we were and why we were not finishing sooner. I was grumpy about doing that and I'm sure it showed. Schedules did not get pulled in or completed early. In the history of the company (and software), that never happened. We weren't going to finish Windows 8 early. We would be fortunate to finish on time, mid-2012 plus two months to reach availability on new PCs.

The leadup to the fall developer conference was a constant series of crises external to the development team but going on all around. It was stressful at the executive level for strategy reasons. Every meeting, every mail thread, every new online story was just more worry for us.

It was stressful at the team level because we had asked the Windows team to pull together most of the company for the release.

In particular, we wanted to fix—yes that is the right word—the schism of the past decade that had replaced what was once lockstep strategic coordination, the Win32 strategy, between the Windows and Developer product groups. The Windows team most accountable for success of the new platform was DEVX, the Developer Experience, and the counterpart to the UEX team. DEVX was led by Aleš Holeček (AlesH) in engineering, Linda Averett (LindaAv) in program management, and Yves Neyrand (YvesN) in testing. The breadth and depth required of this team was in every way as great as the user experience.

Just as Windows 8 designed a new and modern experience, we designed a new and modern new platform to go with it. This platform was designed with the intent of growing to the future Windows platform for all apps across all form factors and devices.

Prior to releasing to the public, we called the platform "Modern Application Model" and later the "Windows Runtime" and finally WinRT, which was the name we stuck with in honor of Windows NT. Like NT we never attached a meaning to RT and just said the letters. In this section, we'll use the term "modern application" for new

Windows 8 apps which had also been called Metro and Metro-style. We were still in the midst of resolving this legal dispute and frankly could not keep the terminology straight which confused everyone inside and out of Microsoft.

We've described the experience goals of Windows 8 and to realize these goals the platform for modern apps in the experience had the following goals:

- Native APIs for the new application model, realizing the benefits of the experience
- Rapid application development coming from great tools supporting an API that could be mastered with relative ease
- Amazing tools of choice, including both .NET and standard web technologies
- Broad distribution and a great business model for apps via a new Windows App Store (covered in the next section)

The importance of "native APIs" could not be overstated yet was also subject to many philosophical debates over what really constituted native. At one extreme, some believed native APIs simply meant they came from Microsoft and therefore first party was equivalent to native. At the other extreme native APIs implied written from the ground up from scratch, divorced from any existing capability and consequently all new. As with many debates along these lines, one could debate semantics or simply build the product and let it speak.

I was familiar with this debate from the earliest days of Windows programming. The advent in the 1990s of object-oriented programming called for a new era of APIs that were improved over the abstractions provided natively—in other words taking the native APIs and recrafting them so they would be easier and more amenable to object-oriented techniques. The story of approaching API development this way, and our failure, was documented in section *010. Our BillG Review*. In that story, we developed a new API for Windows that was much prettier and tuned to C++ but was also bloated and different than Windows. This failure led to a super lean, efficient, and Windows-centric API that became the standard for building professional apps for the Win32 era, the Microsoft Foundation Classes, MFC.

Without diving too deeply into the weeds of architecture, there is an important point about systems design to make. What separated MFC from the era of object-oriented frameworks was, as described previously, a bet on the underlying platform to do the work. Our framework did as little work as possible and specifically never duplicated Windows functionality. That strategy permitted only one implementation of any given concept to exist and thus defines native. In that case, Win32 remained the native API because of the choices we made in MFC.

These choices were the exact opposite of those made in the various .NET technologies, which liberally duplicated capabilities in Windows. This duplication created both inefficiencies and deeper problems. Incredibly difficult problems to solve such as security, accessibility, localization, and so on were made vastly more difficult when there were potentially two (or more) ways to accomplish the same task or worse one way in a framework that made partial use of the OS. In this type of framework there was complete ambiguity as to what constituted native.

In the modern context, this debate over native capabilities of a platform is the situation currently consuming the Apple strategy of SwiftUI. SwiftUI is a layer on top of the existing native operating system API, but it also reimplements functionality and provides different implementations of other capabilities. Apple is attempting to decree the SwiftUI the answer, but even struggles themselves in moving apps from the old way to the new way. In the context of this story, SwiftUI and the debates surrounding it have a ring of .NET familiarity. I've been surprised at the approach but not the result. Apple has the ability to drive change across existing code that we did not have as discussed in the previous section which might smooth out this strategy over time. On the other hand, this entire section describes the outcome of fracturing even the most robust of developer ecosystems.

The approach for Windows 8 was decidedly to define new native APIs and implement those APIs such that there was a single code path for all capabilities. Sometimes the code was brand new to Windows and other times WinRT relied on existing code paths and reused them. Taken as a whole, the set of capabilities represented the first version of the future APIs.

The first version of Windows with any utility, Windows 3.0, was about 540 APIs and documented beautifully in the book *Programming Windows* by Charles Petzold that occupied a rarified position on every developer's thick oak bookcase back in the day. Most of us just referred to the book as "Petzold."

When Windows 3.0 arrived, it was not exactly meeting a known market demand. The platform was intriguing for a class of developers, some of whom had been working on Macintosh apps and others who just saw opportunity in a new way to program user interface. These developers, much like on Macintosh, could pick up a copy of "Petzold" and within a day or so would find their way writing Windows programs, often as a hobby or side project to impress people at work. It was exciting and rewarding. Within a relatively short time the effort paid off with a solid mastery of the 540 APIs. While there was all sorts of complexity and wizardry in the way tools worked, the breadth was such mastery was achievable by a single person.

The property of mastery is an incredibly compelling part of any new platform and often overlooked. The ability to master the platform and to use that mastery to complete an entire project is when something magical can happen, often for a just one or two engineers working together.

By the 2000s, there was no mastery of the Windows API to be had, by anyone. At the very best, one could master a subsystem of Windows such as networking, DirectX graphics, or the file system. Of course there were some wizards, but most of them worked at Microsoft or soon would. Even the largest software houses would struggle with building reliable and optimal Windows software. When the complexity of the various .NET, data access, graphics, and networking APIs were added to the mix the system was insurmountable. A huge part of the attraction of various aspects of .NET, such as Silverlight, was the notion that one could master some subset and complete a project. Unfortunately, as discussed, these runtimes were limited enough that one often needed to venture into other parts of Windows to complete projects. There is no escaping that the explosion of headcount and lack of management accountability to that proved to be our worst enemy when it came to strategic platform coherence for thousands of APIs.

Our Windows 8 plan was to create a new API that covered the full range of development scenarios we expected (or more accurately hoped) to see in the 1.0 version of the modern app world. That API would be the equivalent of

"Petzold." Due to the increasing capabilities of the underlying OS and development tools, the resulting apps would be vastly more capable and easier to write and debug.

Over the summer as we completed the software build that we would distribute to developers, the DEVX team created "Elements of a Windows tailored app: The Developer Story" which captured the "as we built it" mindset and working terminology used by the DEVX and Developer division teams.

The team took a scenario approach cataloging many types of potential applications along with how the platform could be used to write them. It also detailed how to reuse existing code, such as line of business code, within applications. At 275 pages it represented the amount of material one could master as an individual or team of 2 or 3 people.

The modern platform consisted of three main pillars: modern application behavior, application connectivity, and modern application user interface. Within the context of our ever-confusing terminology, the platform is WinRT which we also called the Metro platform.

One of the biggest changes developers needed to understand was that modern applications did not take over the computer. While many had become increasingly aware of the security model of Windows, which prevented access to various parts of the system without a password, the modern approach to applications meant that there was no access at all to the hardware or to other parts of the system. Every application ran in its own "container" (sometimes called "sandbox") or essentially walled garden. Most requests to the operating system went through an intermediate "broker" to ascertain whether such an operation would be permitted. For example, in Win32 an application wishing to use the camera would simply connect to the camera as a device and start using it. In modern applications, the request depended on whether the user had given permission to use the camera and importantly whether the developer built into the app the proper requests of the user for permission. This was a dramatic change for Windows and was only just starting to make its way to phones, whereas today we are all too familiar with the endless prompts for permissions to devices. These constrains placed on applications created a new level of trust and security for Windows, though at the expense of the kind of flexibility and "anything is possible" that Windows developers had come to expect.

Applications also behaved differently relative to how they could consume battery power by constantly running. In Win32, every application ran all the time. It did not matter if the user expected the application to be doing something even if the user could not see the application, it was simply how applications behaved. Every little icon on the system tray, every application that created a "background" process, and every window on the screen could be running on the CPU while consuming power. In a modern application, if an application was not visible to the user, then it entered a new state called "suspended" and consumed no power at all. Only when the app was visible did it resume operating as normal. In the desktop computing model, every window must be constantly updated whether the user is looking at the contents or not with each update draining battery power.

This architecture was essential to reduce the power consumption of a modern PC. It was, somewhat surprisingly, controversial. Developers with their large screens envisioned a world with many tasks happening in many windows and work as keeping an eye on all the different windows. The billions on the verge of using phones and tablets, however, were using one app at a time and the screen filled with that app. They were immersed in the app. Switching between apps was instant and tasks resumed instantly when needed. By and large this style of usage so typical on phones mapped to how real-world customers used even current Windows laptops. Most all Windows users had for the longest time, and still, ran applications full screen and worked on one app at a time. Even switching between apps followed the way apps on phones worked. We built support for snapping apps side by side to provide two apps at once.

Still, creating only full screen apps with the new platform would be an ongoing debate or discussion with developers. It was the kind of change that was perfectly fine for the broad user base and certainly for future new users, but not what developers themselves wanted. For developers of course the desktop was still there where all their tools ran anyway. We expected developers to focus on the desktop and they did.

This was one of a number of issues where the initial audience seeing Windows 8 did not see the world the way we saw the next billion customers heading. They had their jobs to do. It reminded me of the early days of Word when the project was not going well and a Word developer asserted that they aimed "to please an audience of one. I write it for me. If I'm happy I know some cool people will like it." which was a rather limiting way to think of word processors in hindsight.[148]

A distinguishing characteristic of modern applications was how they connected to each other and to Windows. In Win32, apps had a limited way of sharing information with any other app and that was through the clipboard via copy and paste. To do more usually required applications to open up files from one app inside another. This led to all sorts of potential risks, unbeknownst to users, as we learned with Office. Apps could insert malicious data into other apps or apps could crash opening data files created with another app simply because they did not fully understand the other app's files. Worse, apps could simply navigate the hard drive and gobble up all of a user's files in the background without their knowledge.

Modern apps were therefore isolated from each other. This would be quite limiting if not for the invention of "contracts" between apps, and between the operating system and app. With contracts apps could easily tell Windows 8 they would accept or provide information to other apps. Windows 8 created super easy mechanisms for apps to share their information with other apps while at the same time accepting information from other apps. This all took place only when a user initiated an action. Across the system, inserting data such as photos, searching across apps, opening files, and sharing information within a file were all just a tap or click away. A key aspect of the design of the platform was to make it as trivial as possible for an app to add these features and access them via the charms.

There were other connectivity features for modern apps as well, all of which were implemented with security and privacy in mind while doing so with a minimal amount of code. Connecting to a printer, a speaker, or camera could be done with minimal code and trivially. One of our most common demonstrations showed how easy it was in the platform to add a live video feed from a camera with only a couple of lines of code.

There weren't just new-fangled architectural changes in Windows 8. Even the mundane such as how displays worked underwent a dramatic rethinking. At one of the early meetings on Windows 7 tablets when we first showed touch to the PC team at Intel, their ever-enthusiastic platform leader, Mooly Eden, had a question for Windows.

He couldn't just ask he had to show us. Mooly always had to put on a show. He stood up and started flipping a new Windows 7 slate in the air, spinning it. He wanted to know "when will the screen image also rotate?" He was right. Windows had no ability to do what the iPhone and iPad did so well, simply handle the rotation of the screen, essential for a handheld device. Supporting this first required integrating a sensor to detect the rotation, something that no PCs had though Windows 7 provided some early support. Second, the whole video subsystem needed to be reworked. While it was possible to switch orientation of a display in Windows 7, doing so was cumbersome and involved a great deal of flickering and prayers to the Windows control panel. With little fanfare, Windows 8 added this along with support in the modern platform for apps to easily manage the transition between orientations.

At the other end of the spectrum of screen sizes, Windows 8 built the correct architecture to handle the new high-resolution screens coming on market. These screens would come to characterize iPhone and iPad as retina screens. While they were available as external displays for Windows, they were always buggy and flakey. Buttons or text would show up super tiny or where apps would click would not match on screen where the click took place. This failure of Win32 was rooted in the inability to uplevel the whole installed base of hardware and software as the hardware advanced leaving the old software in the dust. Supporting these new screens was one of over 100 features in Windows that improved the desktop and one of many features that were newly native in the modern Windows 8 platform.

Most would judge the completeness of a new platform for how it enabled them to build the main features of their application. In many ways this was the equivalent of Petzold and included the platform for creating the interaction between a developer's app and their customers. Relative to Win32 and to the chaos of the .NET world, Windows 8 arrived with an incredibly strong story. Much of this came about because of our own efforts building applications for Windows 8 and the scenario planning for the product. Windows 8 provided a palette of over two dozen "controls" or user interface elements typically used in apps. While one could find these and more via third parties or counting everything offered by all of Microsoft's existing platforms, never had the Windows platform delivered the full set of required controls all at once. This resonated with me personally because of my own history. Back in the early 1990s when toolbars were invented and developers wanted to add them, Windows provided no support even though Windows itself had toolbars. For Visual C++ I worked with a developer on the Windows 95 team who wrote those controls and added them to MFC, using the Windows code. That developer was also part of the Windows 8 team, so kind of full circle.

A key part of modern apps was how they fit in with the design language for Windows 8 to provide a beautiful, aligned, and consistent experience. Such polish and attention to detail was not something Windows had historically delivered. By and large Windows deferred to the marquee apps like Word and Excel to define the proper look of Windows apps though did not support that look with code or APIs. Windows 8 provided developers with a broad set of tools for typography, animations, color selection, user interface grids to align applications, and more.

Fitting into Windows also meant providing the support for system-wide features such as Live tiles, notifications and alerts, as well as all the necessary infrastructure to easily install and deploy apps. These were also features that Windows provided piecemeal, if at all, in the past.

Finally, everything discussed above was designed from the start to be programmed from all of the programming languages and tools offered by Microsoft. Developers could build modern apps using web tools of HTML and JavaScript, C#, XAML, Silverlight, and even C++ or Visual Basic. Every demo we planned on showing at the upcoming conference included use of all of these languages. We were ready to atone for the lack of communication over the summer.

The platform as delivered to attendees at the upcoming conference was as complete as anything ever delivered by Microsoft all at once, and in the first version. We knew we had a good deal to learn and a list a mile long of what we could do in the future. That was a given. We were so excited though to deliver the future of the Windows platform.

We arrived in Los Angeles on September 12, 2011 for our Professional Developers Conference, renamed //build to be attended by 5,000 people and what seemed like the entire technical press community. Marketing for the new Windows 8 Start screen and the new //build logo was everywhere—those live tiles, colorful rectangles, and animation. It was a breathtaking sight. And we were excited to be there. Even the Denny's across the street welcomed Microsoft for breakfast, with a sign. A pre-show tradition for me is breakfast at Denny's.

Unfortunately, there was also a something of sense of dread about the languages and tools for creating new modern apps—our self-inflicted crisis created at the unveiling of the user experience and the omission of .NET before the summer. There was so much cynicism in how the various existing platforms had been talked about—always implying one worked well with the other when in fact they were all separate, all had limitations that were not said, and all had major issues. As a result, however, we created the opportunity for a set of people to spend the summer alternating between conspiracy theories and anger over the developer platform.

The effort to make every single Microsoft language a first-class tool for the modern Windows platform was an immense cross-division project. To say it was easy or lacked controversy would be a huge understatement. It was extraordinarily difficult because many inside Microsoft also either believed or even wanted to believe the conspiracy theories surrounding the deemphasis of .NET by Windows. In some sense they had a right to as they believed in their own work and lived through the alienation and schism that Vista created between .NET and Windows. Windows 7 did offer any relief though it also did not do anything to make it worse. In that sense it was hardly a conspiracy theory, but a fact of life in the .NET world.

Windows 8, however, was when the strategic issues of the past required resolution. There was no simple answer. Realistically, the answer would require a degree of subtlety that tested those on every side of the mess, myself included. We absolutely intended to move forward with the languages of the .NET world (C#, XAML, Silverlight, VB, C++) while at the same time there was no plan to simply move all the code created that used the libraries and frameworks of the .NET era such as WinForms, WPF, VB forms, or Forms[3] or third parties. This "technicality" would prove to be an enormous barrier to not only acceptance but even acknowledging the strategy we were embarking upon. To many, not being able to simply port their code to new Windows 8 apps was a non-starter. We had accounted for this by describing the difference between domain-specific code (for example all the code that connects to a remote database or cloud service) and the user experience code that would need to be reimplemented. Most all apps written in this world were divided cleanly in this respect. Not only that, this transition was precisely the one most had gone through to provide web access to the databases and cloud services they built.

We had two challenges. First, within the Microsoft bubble it was clear "everyone" used these technologies. The Developer division had created a bubble of the .NET developer world insulated, as previously described, from the world of HTML and the web browser. Within that world it was of course true that everyone used .NET. Anything we proposed that was not about leveraging that investment was by definition failing to leverage something everyone used. Arguing over how much .NET was used as a portion of total development or skilled developers was futile, especially because even defining terms was impossible as we'd learned for several years of Mid-Year Reviews and Developer Usage Surveys. Even discussing the lack of commercial software would only serve to exacerbate the challenges.

Second, the existing .NET world was the one that failed to account for synergy with Windows or address the problems we set out to resolve with a new platform. When it came to consistency with Windows, safety, security, reliability, battery life, or even basic attributes such as performance or accessibility, the plethora of .NET tools failed to achieve a level of performance or quality consistent with our main competitor, Apple.

These two challenges were not just external to Microsoft. The .NET bubble extended to the 50,000 person Microsoft enterprise organization that were the tip of the .NET spear and also the massive Developer division itself. Many people had spent a decade building out these capabilities and all was going well until, well, I came along.

It was no surprise that the whole time Windows tried to create the connections to the .NET languages to use the new Windows 8 platform we ran into discussions about interoperability or conflicts with the existing .NET platform and APIs. Each new advance in Windows 8 was met with an opportunity to debate the reuse a .NET mechanism to accomplish the same—there was a near constant effort to work to insert the old .NET into the new platform. Windows 8 had a strong point of view about a platform for the future that embraced a new set of qualities entirely absent from the existing .NET efforts.

We intended to deliver on that point of view. The good news, actually great news, was that the vast majority of efforts between the teams supported this mission. That didn't preclude grumbling along the way. There were some outright stressful times. The release of code would surface many of those, either internally or unfortunately externally via the press as well.

Since we know now that Windows 8 did not achieve the success we hoped, this is a reasonable time to point out that it is precisely at this moment that the efforts between teams created the "told you so" people. In Microsoft parlance this is done by opening up Outlook and searching through Sent Items and reliving these debates to prove that no one listened, or someone knew all along. Success has many parents and failure is an orphan. No matter what happens someone always said it would. This isn't about bitterness on any side, but I can promise many more people contributed positively at the time than seemed to contribute in hindsight. We'll return to this reality.

We had an incredible keynote planed for the first morning. It would feature a demo of Windows 8 experience from Julie Larson-Green, an incredible overview of potential Windows 8 devices from Mike Angiulo, for the first Chris Jones detailed the many cloud-based services integral to Windows 8 experience, and on-stage Antoine Leblond would build a modern app using HTML and Silverlight. Even I did a demo showing only features improved in the desktop. It was a two hour and fifteen-minute *tour de force* by the full Windows 8 product executive team.

I had been to a lot (a lot a lot) of Microsoft keynotes and conferences and launch events over the years. I participated in many as well. With as much sincerity as I can muster, the keynote for the 2011 //build conference was absolutely Microsoft at its best. The whole of Microsoft had never come together to deliver such a coherent and compelling message. It was all done live on real computers running real software. Nothing like it has happened since and it is clear we're in a new era where that 2011 presentation might have marked the end of the PC era live event. Even Apple would cease to take on the kind of risks we took on during that demo when it came to real products, demonstrated by real executives, in front of a live crowd while streamed around the world. It scares me now to think of just how crazy we were. It was by far one of my favorite days at Microsoft.

Within that favorite day were two favorite moments. Technically, three if you count the walk-on music at the very top of the keynote that I chose. I walked on to *Renegade* by Jay Z (with Eminem)—"No lie, just know I chose my own fate./I drove by the fork in the road and went straight." Certainly, over the top. But I felt we could have taken an easy path and just built yet another version of Windows doing more of the same, there were many options for how to do that the equivalent of going left or right. Instead, we created our own path and went straight. The short sound clip is not in the official video because of copyright.

Over the summer we had become increasingly concerned that developers would have no way to experience Windows 8 on the type of hardware we expected to exist in the future. We were working with OEMs closely to create PCs with touch panels, ink pens, and in a variety of form factors from pure slates to convertibles to laptops to all-in-ones. While we tried to have some of those machines for Windows 7, they were few and not commonly owned because Windows 7 lacked the value proposition to drive sales.

The Ecosystem team had been working closely with Samsung on an Intel-based PC that was a pure tablet form factor with an available docking station which could be used to connect a mouse, keyboard, external display, and wired network. The PC was powered by the latest low voltage Intel Core processor. Many of our demos and most all of the demo sessions (over 100) would use this PC at the show.

At the 2009 PDC we were excited enough by the prospects of touch computing that we provided attendees a free touch laptop. It was a new "thin and light" form factor which was just starting to come to market to compete with Apple. This announcement stunned the audience. Therefore, by the 2011 //build attendees were certain there would be another free laptop. As a point of information that stunt in 2009 cost millions of dollars more than even the revenue from the paying conference attendees.

In the keynote, MikeAng, ever the showman, walked through all of the platform capabilities that the ecosystem and developers could bring to life with Windows 8. Showing everything from ARM-based devices to liquid cooled gamer rigs the size of dorm refrigerators. Then he began to describe a new Samsung device. He said, slyly, the device was being produced in small numbers right now as a prototype. I looked at him and asked "so how many will they make" to which he replied "well, I've been told not to bring a cool PC unless we brought enough for everyone so there are 5,000 out on the loading dock right now."

And with that we announced the "Samsung Developer Prototype PC" to go with the "Microsoft Windows 8 Preview Build." And everyone went nuts. The key value of this PC was precisely to demonstrate the value of Windows 8.

With one PC running Intel developers could run and develop Windows 8 applications for both Intel and ARM devices. The Samsung came loaded with Windows 8 software, sample apps, Visual Studio pre-release, and more.

Little did the 5000 attendees know but over the previous week a team of about 40 Microsoft engineers had been unloading the Samsung PCs from crates air-shipped from Korea to install all this new software and configure them for distribution. In order to get them to Los Angeles in time, Samsung had to manufacture them before the software was complete. It was an heroic effort and made it all the more rewarding for sure.

Loaded on the Samsung were 17 new Windows 8 applications, the source of my second favorite moment of the day. In addition to the apps from Microsoft such as Mail, Calendar, Bing, etc. each visible on the Start screens shown throughout the week, these 17 apps represented a chance to have fun with the pre-release. The amazing feature of these apps were that they were built entirely by the interns over their 10-week summer jobs. We asked 17 groups of 2-3 interns to work together to build these fun apps from scratch and zero baseline understanding of Windows 8. Not only were they able to create these apps on their own, but they did so when neither the platform nor the tools were near ready and were constantly shifting. I was so proud to both announce and share their summer accomplishments. While for most school had already started we were able to find about 20 of them who were able to sneak away from school to attend the conference and even provide a scheduled sessions detailing their experience. It was as amazing for them as it was for me. It was a career highlight for me. They even made a video of their summer experience which we showed to all the show attendees in the keynote.

That this group took their ideas with an unfinished platform and tools to create new apps was a huge source of validation for the "Petzold" test we hoped Windows 8 would pass.

After providing attendees with a candid roadmap from this moment to final release, there was a short break. We were not done with amazing day one content though. There were two absolutely amazing presentations to follow. We overwhelmed attendees with depth and quality of presentations.

First, JensenH provided an overview from the experience perspective of what makes for a great Windows 8 app. This was the touchstone presentation that brought together all we had learned to date, since the unveiling and subsequent feedback as well.

Following this, AlesH brought things down to the metal and showed the developers in attendance the ins and outs of the Windows 8 platform. He wrote a ton of code and built live apps on stage ably assisted by John Sheehan (JSheehan) who was a senior software engineer on the platform. Importantly, they showed off building apps from scratch using Visual Studio, connecting to Windows 8 to share information and use devices, and also detailed the architecture that provided apps with a sandbox to run in for safety, security, and predictability. They even showed off how apps don't consume resources when they are not visible on the screen. Of course, they used all the .NET languages and showed the broad support for bringing forward that knowledge.

Even with all that incredible content, there was one slide we worked the most on and that was a boxes and bullshit, or politely boxology, slide showing the new Windows 8 platform and its relation to all of the programming languages and APIs Microsoft had to offer.

This was not a slide I dreamed up in my office, not even close. Aleš in his role as distinguished engineering leading DEVX and the Windows 8 platform worked for weeks to create this diagram, collaborating with every part of the whole project across Windows and Developer division. I thought it was a work of art.

Ales also made the slide a key part of his presentation. By the time he spoke the proverbial shit had hit the fan and he knew he had to somewhat rescue his slide. People had already written instant blog posts and the live blogs picked up on the diagram as well.

So, what happened?

Presented in all the glory of the Metro design style, huge and on stage, was as clear a diagram as we could have created describing the Windows 7 world being brought forward for desktop applications, including support for Internet Explorer, Win32, .Net, Silverlight, HTML, C++, C#, and more. Everything had a box, resting on top of the Windows Kernel, a.k.a. MinWin! New modern apps were shown in boxes with all the tools and languages available to build "on top of" WinRT, including that same list: XAML, HTML, C#, C++, VB, and JavaScript.

The diagram, created by dozens of people from nearly every team in the company, proved incredibly popular, but not in a good way.

To support the diagram, Antoine's full demonstration of building a Metro app went through all the languages and tools, in real time on stage, by building an app. He built several apps. He built an app in HTML. Antoine took sample code from Developer division vice president (and previously manager of Silverlight) Scott Guthrie's (ScottGu) famous (amongst .NET fans) XAML sample, and with no changes ran it as both a desktop app and a Metro app on WinRT. The new Metro apps were touch-enabled, integrated with search and sharing, and even showed off the beautiful graphical qualities of the platform by displaying nicely alongside the rest of Windows 8.

The problem?

Before I even got off stage, people were taking the image and redrawing their view of the architecture. Some were critical of precisely how their favorite tools were rendered. Others challenged the technical integrity of the diagram. Within the developer press there were even news stories and a quite a few blog posts dissecting the travesty that was this image. It all happened in real time before we had even finished.

There were blog posts that dissected the diagram and rewrote it. It was the technical buzzsaw applied to a conceptual diagram. The weirdest part for me was that this was a diagram we had created about our own technologies, but the .NET community thought of them as their technologies. They wanted Windows 8 to fulfill the .NET promises they believed were made, and even more so now that we were indeed delivering a new platform. There was little accounting for what we believed we needed to accomplish in righting the Windows platform or the necessary steps to modernize the Windows platform.

Some of the blogs centered around how much code was actually Win32 though repurposed, not because that would be bad but because of a theory that would undermine our argument about the modern platform being native or completely new. Others took aim at the use of the .NET languages versus the .NET runtimes or libraries. This issue was the whole point, unfortunately. Ironically for me this point also was one I made to BillG for years when it came to the value of owning a proprietary language versus owning the API. Now all those championing a language were learning the value was really in the runtime. Yes, that was always my point.

Emotions were running high. There were deep concerns about investments in existing code and porting it to modern apps. We didn't make this promise to the degree developers wanted and, as a result, there was a wave of feedback over Microsoft abandoning them and costing "millions" of dollars of lost revenue. That's what people said. To me, this had shades of past transitions, specifically, the major mistake Microsoft Word made in trying to reuse the code for character mode Word to build Windows Word. It did not work and cost the team years. It also felt like the carnage caused when much-loved Visual Basic switched to .NET.

The biggest mistake in platform transitions is attempting to deny that a transition is taking place or to believe a dramatic platform shift could be managed by incremental changes.

Not everyone writing about this diagram took such a negative approach. Several provided thoughtful views pointing out that there was a good deal to be excited about. In an in-depth view, Paul Thurrott wrote on his *SuperSite for Windows* blog:[149]

> *WinRT solves many of the problems of Win32, from an apps perspective, though it can't be used for certain things of course (writing NT services, drivers, and the like.) Apps created for WinRT are safe, secure, and sandboxed, can't wreck other apps, can't cause "Windows rot," and all install in just 2-3 seconds. They feature isolated storage, single folder installs (as per the Mac), and require user consent to access the general file system. When Microsoft says it "reimagined" every aspect of Windows, this new runtime, or application model, must be included as well. This is part of it, a modern, truly different app platform that is far more different, and far more capable, than many people understand right now.*
>
> *And in the same vein of blowing past peoples' expectations, virtually no app could not be written as a WinRT app. Many are imagining very simple, HTML-like apps, and while I'm sure there will be plenty of those, you need to reset your expectations up. WinRT is amazingly full-featured and not constrained to goofy utilities and simple games. The next "Call of Duty" could be a WinRT app, complete with support for Edge UIs and Charms.*
>
> *And here's something interesting: Virtually all of the Microsoft WinRT apps—Mail, Calendar, People, Chat, and so on—are all written in HTML and JavaScript, not C# or another supposedly superior language.*
>
> *And you laughed when they repeated "Windows reimagined over and over again in Tuesday's keynote. I'm starting to think they didn't push this point enough.*

Our main aim for //build was to put forth the message of a bold reimagination of Windows from the chipset to the experience. So many of the reviews of the pre-release product articulated the bold design, the attractiveness, the functionality across different types of PCs, and the compatibility with everything in Windows 7. The note of caution was always about the amount of change and how some users might be skeptical. Overall, the press and bloggers were excited and impressed with the leap we had taken, excepting those still debating the diagram.

After a month with the pre-release code, Ars Technica in its detailed review had the following to say in "Turning to the past to power Windows' future: An in-depth look at WinRT":[150]

> *Microsoft is taking a risk with WinRT, as developers may not follow it, but it's a calculated risk, and it's a low risk. The re-use and modernization of existing technology gives WinRT instant familiarity for developers, but also an easy path for Microsoft to extend the reach and capabilities (and ease the restrictions) should it need to. It's at once the embodiment of Windows' future and the embracing of Windows' past.*

I shared how I thought this event was Microsoft at its best. The press coverage following the event generally agreed. I recognize in hindsight this might seem to be a combination of delusional and revisionist. It was neither. There were over 1,000 original stories of which nearly 700 were what we called PRIME, an acronym defined by the PR agency for stories appearing by top writers in top publications. On average the stories were extremely positive. In a system the agency used to score the tone and message pick up of stories where 100 is neutral, we scored 124 in 386 news stories, 118 in 293 blogs, and 117 in 11 product reviews done in real time. Microsoft events routinely scored a negative sentiment during this era, meaning less than 100. The agency put together an *End of Event* recap that ran for over 120 pages. These were tremendous results, not solely because of the content by any stretch. Achieving these results required an amazing marketing and communications effort around the world.

With no intention of shaming any writers who subsequently revised their views or chose to come to different conclusions later, but some of the quotes that came along with the availability of code and the Samsung PC press loaners were positively effusive:

> *"I've never witnessed this much excitement in a Microsoft audience at a keynote before. It's electric." –Tom Warren, WinRumors*
>
> *"I might just become a developer considering how easy #Microsoft has made it to write things for Windows 8." –@reese305*
>
> *"my iPad suddenly became old fashioned #win8 #bldwin" –@martinsih*
>
> *"Hello, Windows 8? This is iPad. You win." – @thurrott*
>
> *"the Metro UI stuff is the best thing Microsoft has come up with in years." @thurrott*
>
> *"Here's the real feather in Windows 8's cap: Write once, run (mostly) everywhere software.", PC World, Nate Ralph*
>
> *"the experience still felt magic, and that's what really counts. Well done Microsoft.", RedMonk, James Governor*
>
> *"Apple bloggers were apparently so flustered by the platform that they resorted to bombarding Twitter with jokes about cooling fans and Silverlight instead of stopping for a moment to realize that Microsoft is showing us the future of computing.", BGR, Zach Epstein*

Obviously, it wasn't all positive. Surprisingly, some still questioned whether we would release "on time" though we did not provide a date we knew we would hit the fall. The real lingering question, and one that did not come up all that much at the event, was the "two modes" of Windows. Speaking for "users" many press would rhetorically ask if users would be able to understand the two modes of using Windows, the desktop, and the new Metro experience. Owing to the developer audience, they were not yet concerned about ARM and simply saw it as an opportunity. They would be running Intel because that is where development tools existed.

The issue of "two modes" was the one we needed to tackle. I wasn't sure of what else to do. Given the history of Windows "modes" and what we designed for, the complaint and answer were not easily reconciled. Would this become the focus of the release?

With all that, including the protestations around our box diagram, I had wrapped up one of my happiest weeks at Microsoft. It had been a long time since the whole of Microsoft came together as a team and delivered a strategy and produced an event with such clarity and developer excitement.

In under 24 hours we had 500,000 downloads of the *Windows 8 Developer Preview Release*. At the time there were perhaps three million professional software developers worldwide, total.[151]

It was Microsoft at its best, but the reactions turned out to be relatively fleeting. The developer community was but one audience. For all the dustup over .NET they were the home crowd at //build.

We had a nagging issue of competing with Apple not just on iPads but on laptops. Could we work with the ecosystem to muster something to compete with Apple's MacBook Air, finally after years of failing to even try?

What would mainstream consumers say with a much more polished release? What would developers say about the new Windows Store which we had yet to show them? What would we tell developers waiting to see how Microsoft Office would build for Windows 8?

105. NEW ULTRABOOKS, OLD OFFICE, AND THE BIG CONSUMER PREVIEW

Following the //build conference we were feeling quite good. Not to belabor the point, but I recognize how challenging it is to take such feelings at face value given where the product ended up. In writing this and helping people experience the steps we went through at the time in sequence, my hope is that what comes to light is that we were not bonkers and in fact much of the industry was excited by Windows 8 as it emerged. Of course, there were skeptics and doubters, even haters, but as veterans of dozens of major products we'd seen this before and the volume for Windows 8 was not disproportionate. If anything, the excitement and optimism were higher. So where did things take a decidedly different direction? It was when after product emerged from the Developer Preview and a series of events including the widely distributed Consumer Preview, or beta, when millions of people would experience the product. The leadup to the Windows 8 Consumer Preview in March 2012 included some important steps in the process as well.

New Ultrabooks

On the heels of the //build conference in September 2011 Intel began kicking off an effort to reenergize the PC industry with a response to Apple, finally. Intel developed a series of specifications, financial incentives in the form of marketing and pricing actions, as well as supply chain activation to deliver on a new class of laptop. Intel called these Ultrabook™ PCs. We called them a blessing.

Intel was best positioned to drive this type of advance. It was always difficult for Microsoft simply providing the operating system to dramatically alter the hardware platform, even though many thought by virtue of building Windows we held significant sway. We certainly had influence, but ultimately Windows was a wide-open platform which meant hardware to support any scenario was under PC maker control. The few times we had tried to tightly control hardware specifications, such as with Tablet PC and Media Center PC, did not go well at all. Worse, such controls angered not just PC makers but our fans as well who always wanted to build PCs on their own and experiment with hardware components.

Unlike Microsoft, Intel had a unique ability to influence hardware specifications and their influence increased over time compared to Microsoft's which waned over the years. Intel rallied the industry around Netbooks. While that was a failure, it provided a playbook that Intel could later follow. Before the Netbook, Intel almost single-handedly drove a consistent level of support for Wi-Fi with the Centrino line of chips, which bought both lower-power consumption and Wi-Fi to the standard business laptop. In these cases, and many others such as USB, SATA storage, integrated graphics, and more, Intel took on a broader role in determining components and building software drivers for Windows (and Linux) while making it easier for OEMs to adopt a complete platform.

The efforts were not pure altruism. Intel would use these complete component platforms to steer OEMs to specific price points for chips as well as unit volume commitments. With those in hand, Intel could broadly advertise the platform using their massive *Intel Inside* advertising budget. These financial incentives were eagerly embraced by

OEMs and a key part of their margin. Intel maximized its own margins as well by careful choice of CPUs in these platforms and enabling OEMs to upsell to even higher margin chips as appropriate.

This dynamic is why competing with the new Apple MacBook Air starting in 2008 followed by subsequent models and then Intel-based MacBook Pros proved elusive. Conspiracy theorists would believe that Intel was slow-rolling competitive PCs just to keep Apple and Steve Jobs happy. I never saw any indication of such a dynamic. Rather, it just seemed like PC makers were basically fat and happy in their share battle with each other. They had little worry about the 3-5% of share Apple had especially because they viewed Apple laptops and their customers as high-end, expensive, and premium. The PC business was all about good price and great volume. Being a pound heavier, an inch thicker, and plastic made little difference. As Apple share among influential customers, especially in the US, increased, the urgency from Intel and PC makers changed.

At the 2011 Intel Developer Forum (IDF) in Taiwan and in parallel with the //build Conference, Intel unveiled a new concept PC, the *Ultrabook*™. An Ultrabook wasn't an actual PC from Intel, but a series of specifications or requirements for a PC to inherit the Ultrabook label, and thus the CPU pricing and broad co-advertising that came with it.

Unlike Netbooks and Centrino, Ultrabook specifications were rather detailed and covered a broad set of criteria beyond even the components Intel provided. The tagline Intel chose was "Thin, Responsive, and Secure" which would be used quite broadly. Among the requirements to be part of this program, new PCs had to include:

- **Battery.** A good deal of the platform effort was a new type of battery that was not yet used broadly on Windows PCs. Ultrabook PCs required non-removable Li-Poly batteries of 36-41WHr designed to fit around components and a minimum of 5 hours of runtime.
- **Storage and Responsiveness.** While not required precisely, there was a strong recommendation to use solid state disk drives, SSDs, in Ultrabook PCs which would significantly improve performance. SSDs also made it possible to strongly recommend a wake from standby time of just 7 seconds, which for Windows PCs would be excellent at the time.
- **Chassis Design.** For the first time, Intel specified what amounted to innovative chassis design. For laptops with 14" or larger screens, the chassis needed to be under 21mm and for smaller screens 18mm.
- **Screen.** The Ultrabook specification included guidelines and requirements covering display selection as well, including detailed values for thickness, bezel size, viewing angles, pixel density, and power requirements. At IDF, Intel showed off displays from a number of display makers who were ready and able to supply screens.
- **Keyboards.** Even keyboards, far from Intel's expertise, received attention. Back-lights, spill resistant layers, key-travel and key shape were all specified in Ultrabook design. This was a significant departure for Intel and the requirements created the need for keyboard redesign for all laptops.
- **Sensors and devices.** Intel even included recommendations for devices usually seen far off the motherboard including: 720p webcam, accelerometer, GPS, ambient light sensor and more.

Intel really geared up the supply chain. This was crucially important during the huge ramp up happening with mobile phones where many suppliers were thinking of moving on from PCs. As it would turn out, Ultrabooks were the last gasp for innovative PCs.

Ultrabook laptops would turn out to be the ultimate devices for the road warrior running Office. These even led to the standardization of HDMI connectors in conference rooms after decades of VGA/RGB connectors. Windows 7 had introduced the command Window+P to make it easy to switch thus ending the need for degaussing and rebooting PCs to project…mostly. The stellar work at the device and OS kernel level to reduce power consumption, improve boot time, and even the unique features for SSD storage all contributed greatly to a fantastic experience for this new form factor.

Ultrabooks brought Windows hardware to the 21st century and were far more competitive with Apple laptops than we might have expected after waiting so long. In fact, Ultrabook PCs were downright cheap compared to Apple products. While most would retail for the magic number of $1,495 many could be had for the other magic number of $999. This compared to nearly 50% more for the similarly configured Apple laptops. All in all, this was a huge win for the Windows PC. Every PC laptop today owes its existence to this excellent work by Intel and the supply chain. A small benefit for tech enthusiasts and IT administrators was that the wave of Ultrabook standardization also made it possible to install Windows without requiring additional drivers to be downloaded from PC maker sites.

Ultrabook PCs rapidly diffused across the ecosystem from the board room to executive teams to consultants and eventually to students. I remember a 2011 recruiting visit to MIT and Harvard and while I saw a lot (perhaps majority) of MacBooks, the PCs I saw were all newly purchased Ultrabook PCs with their sleek, un-PC-like aluminum cases.

Many believed Ultrabooks would put a dent in iPad momentum. Once again, it is worth a reminder that Apple's iPad was absolutely top of mind for the industry. The iPad was the holiday gift for 2011. Apple sold over 32 million iPads in 2011 and the tablet redefined the baseline requirements for a road warrior productivity computing. Apple, hoping to sell every Apple customer on an iPhone, MacBook, and a new iPad remained relentless in the distinct use case for iPad while also continuing to tout the iPad as the future of computing.

It was this spike in demand for iPads that drove the difficult conversations with the Microsoft Office team about the role of Office on Windows 8, specifically Windows 8 on ARM processors, including the ARM device we were developing in-house that was quite secret at the time.

Old Office

We always knew going into Windows 8 planning that developing a new platform and new API meant also enlisting the support of the Office team. This was not some innovative thinking on our part, but literally the Microsoft playbook from the founding of the company.

A platform cold start requires a huge leap of faith from the consumers of the platform. The best way to seed interest in the platform is to have flagship applications that can be demonstrated to other developers to get the flywheel going. Cool apps on a platform attract more app developers which lead to cooler apps. Sometimes this is even labeled "killer application" though I think that is a bit dramatic since it doesn't kill but brings life to the platform. Having Lotus 1-2-3 on MS-DOS, Microsoft Excel, Aldus PageMaker, and also Microsoft Word on Macintosh cemented that platform. Excel and Word were crucial to validating Windows and even to Microsoft's ability to complete building Windows for significant applications. Ultimately Office on Windows 3.0 proved to be a tipping point for Windows. In a turn of fate, Windows also proved to be critical to the success of Office as a productivity suite. Microsoft not only came to define this virtuous platform cycle but benefitted itself with Office.

Platform shifts offer a unique moment when all bets are off, and the new leaders can emerge. It is why BillG was so tuned in to creating and betting on platform shifts and why Silicon Valley always seems to be seeking out these moments. Recall from the earlier section 011. Strategy for the 90s: Windows, that platform shifts can be so dramatic that even within a company people decide to quit over them. My first manager and programming legend Doug Klunder (DougK) famously left Microsoft in the early 1980s over the strategy change to build a Macintosh spreadsheet rather than ship the MS-DOS spreadsheet that he had built and was certain would beat Lotus 1-2-3. That spreadsheet and Doug's recalc invention (minimal recalc) formed a core part of Microsoft going forward and Doug later returned.

As discussed previously, many describe nefarious means to the rise of Office on Windows compared to Lotus 1-2-3 and WordPerfect among other leading MS-DOS productivity tools. Within the leaders of MS-DOS applications, none prioritized Windows above all other platforms. Instead choosing to nurture their existing MS-DOS successes and character-mode user experiences. Microsoft uniquely bet on Macintosh and then Windows, perhaps because it lacked the mega-successful MS-DOS applications business the others possessed. Nevertheless, Microsoft bet and bet big and bet early. The rest is history.

Little did I and the other leaders on Windows 8, **all** of whom had previously worked on and led Office, realize how the tables would turn. Here we were at the start of Windows 8, knowing that we would be introducing a new platform and fully aware of Microsoft's own playbook. We knew it would take convincing but at least for me I failed to fully internalize just how difficult it would be for Microsoft to collectively make a bet on a new platform.

At the Windows 8 Vision Meeting, I sat next to Steve Ballmer and the guests from across the company, including the leaders of Office. We showed Office running in the prototype sketches just as we showed Office running in January 2011 on ARM at the CES show and then later at //build. The Office everyone knew and loved running in the desktop. It was right then at the Vision meeting that SteveB leaned over to ask me about Office for tablets and the new platform.

I said, definitively, that we had a huge chance to build a new kind of Office application for this new world of mobility, tablets, touch, and more. It wouldn't be like the current Office, and it wouldn't be like browser Office—the project started back when I was in Office. We had a chance to define the new user interface paradigm for this new style of productivity, much as how Office came to define the user interface paradigm for mouse and keyboard.

We had many conversations with the Office team throughout building Windows 8. Our goal was simple—convince the team to build a new kind of app for the new Windows 8 platform. We did not want to port the existing apps to Windows 8 any more than we wanted any ISV to do that. Microsoft's own experience with the first version of Word for Windows, a legendary mishap caused by trying to port code from one platform to another, was enough of a lesson to create institutional knowledge of the risks of doing that. Even the early releases of PowerPoint on Windows suffered from the difficulties of trying to port from Macintosh. Many might remember the difficulties Microsoft had with Word 6.0 for Macintosh which did not fully embrace the look and feel of Mac and disappointed.

The world changed a great deal with iPad and web browsers. The historical strengths of Office focused on fine grained document control for printing gave way to multi-player (a recent nomenclature for multi-user) collaboration, sharing, and online consumption, and considerably less demand for formatting. There would be ample opportunity for a new type of application. Perhaps if we collectively developed that, we thought, we could avoid the pressure to provide Office per se for Windows 8, which we knew would be a massive undertaking for a new platform, even futile.

Office was eager to experiment with OneNote, which was supporting mobile, browser, and more and was widely praised for an innovative experience in an important scenario. Doing something more significant was proving a challenge and a bit frustrating for us. In order to understand the situation, it is important to recognize the situation Office found itself in in 2010 and what really drove strategic choices.

Historically, the biggest factor in weighing choices for Office has been the maintenance of the value of the overall bundle (Word, Excel, PowerPoint, Outlook, and the Access database) and with that the pricing. Key to maintaining that value was compatibility with "full Office" meaning the complete feature-set of desktop Office. In other words, when sales and marketing were confronted with either a lower-priced or less-featured variant of Office the response was to focus on backward compatibility for dealing with old files and email attachments from anywhere, on the familiarity with the user interface, aka the Ribbon, and on the value of the bundle. By 2010, the Office brand came to represent the Ribbon user interface, the full Office feature set, and support for documents and custom Visual Basic solutions that existed across thousands of enterprise customers.

Office continued to face somewhat acute challenges to the business from Google Apps, previously Google Apps for Your Domain, often colloquially called Google Docs, more recently G Suite, today known as Google Workspace. Google pushed Google Apps relentlessly through the incredibly successful Gmail launch, something we would do with Windows Live and the Office browser-based applications. Google Apps was making real progress in the academic market, where the product was usually free. Small business was also adopting Google Apps owing to the push via Gmail and the easy use of the apps after registering an email domain with Google. Most importantly, enterprise customers under budget pressures following the Global Financial Crisis also began to consider Google Apps. Use of a difficult economy to put price pressure on Microsoft was something I'd experienced through every downturn since the Gulf War. Customers not only had the option of Google Apps, but they could also maintain full compatibility with Office by simply sticking with the Office they already owned and not upgrading, putting the Enterprise Agreement renewal in jeopardy. Losing even a single deal had the appearance of a "share shift" and a series of 3 deals would likely be followed by industry analyst quotes or even press releases from Google, and suddenly there was a trend.

The presence of this competitive threat made offering anything at all new seem risky. A new product would call into question the value of "full Office" and certainly anything priced at app store level pricing would draw attention to the nearly $200 per year Office was receiving in enterprise agreements, which today could be over $40 per month for Office 365. With a few thousand Enterprise Agreement customers, taking on this kind of product challenge was a level of risk that the Office team was not going to be comfortable with all that easily.

Office for Mac, long mostly out of sight and out of mind, had become a lot more interesting of late. Back when I was in Office and following the release of Mac Office 4.x and Windows Office 95, the legendary Apple-Microsoft deal between Steve Jobs and Bill Gates was struck. Most recall this deal through the lens of antitrust and Microsoft throwing Apple a life preserver just as Steve Jobs returned to a company on the brink of bankruptcy. Microsoft indeed paid apple $150 million in exchange for patent rights which would ensure the end of litigation between the companies. In exchange, Apple also received a commitment to Macintosh and that Office would continue to support the platform. It was then we (in Office) created the Macintosh Business Unit (MacBU) staffed at 100 engineers to start. The goal for us was to stop kidding ourselves about doing a great job of cross-platform support and let the Mac team focus on Mac and the Windows team focus on Windows, with judicious code sharing as the MacBU, staffed with Office engineers, deemed necessary. From that time forward, August 1997, the Mac team went merrily on its way as did Windows.

Each of the subsequent leaders of MacBU were deeply connected to Apple, and discretely so. The business relationship required that. Most of Mac Office was sold not through Microsoft's typical enterprise accounts but direct to individual customers. As Apple's new retail stores scaled, the sales of Mac Office through that channel quickly became the primary means for Apple customers to acquire Office. MacBU found itself somewhat beholden to Apple for distribution, price support, and even launch PR. In exchange, MacBU dedicated its efforts to being a fantastic client of the Mac OS as it evolved. Such support had become increasingly difficult as Windows and Mac diverged and then as Mac became a diminishingly small part of the overall business, unlike the 1980s when it was more than half the business. The deal created a win-win for Apple and Microsoft, not to mention Apple customers.

Part of the relationship between MacBU and Apple included early access to Apple technologies under development, exactly as Microsoft had done for Windows with leading vendors. By offering this, Apple hoped to garner MacBU support for the latest platform technologies. The transitions Apple made to the new OS X and then later to Intel processors all but required Office to be present from the first days of availability. Apple knew this. MacBU knew this. Our industry knew this. It was the way platforms worked.

As part of this work, MacBU also began to migrate the Office code base from the older Macintosh operating system APIs to the new OS X APIs called Cocoa. As previously mentioned, Apple had a different way of evolving the OS compared to Microsoft. Apple not only strongly encouraged ISVs to move to new APIs, but it also obsoleted APIs thus requiring ISVs to move. Sometimes with their big code bases, the important ISVs would slow roll these moves. Adobe was (and remains) legendary for its slow pace of adoption. MacBU tended to be nimble, due at least in part to the ever-present connection in the Apple retail stores. Plus using the latest was a pretty cool thing to do in the Mac community.

As Apple's new tablet came into existence, MacBU had to decide what to do to support it long before the general public or anyone else at Microsoft was aware of the project. To its credit, MacBU guarded Apple trade secrets just as Apple would have hoped. No one outside MacBU was aware of this project. Apple lobbied the team to make Office for iPad. Part of the promise was that the new iPad APIs were reasonably close to the OS X APIs and the work would not be crazy, taking advantage of the migration to Cocoa.

Of note, this was decidedly not an approach taken by Windows 8. Apple had already spent a generation modernizing the APIs for the iPhone and pushing ISVs to adopt more modern approaches for Mac. In other words, they were way ahead of Microsoft.

It was not quite so simple though. Apple threw a few wrinkles in the mix. First, Apple had put a good deal of effort into its own suite of Mac apps, called iWork, which were direct competitors to Office. This proved frustrating for Microsoft and also provided leverage for Apple. If MacBU didn't follow an Apple strategy, Apple would for its own iWork.

Second, iWork was cheap. At the early days, iWork cost $79, substantially less than Office which usually sold for $150 but up to $280 with Mac Outlook. MacBU was no happier about a low-priced competitor than Windows Office was, but this was especially problematic because of the first-party nature of this competition. Whatever MacBU offered for the future tablet was going to need to be price competitive or face a real uphill battle.

Related to this, the iPhone app store already demonstrated that pricing for apps would be much lower and much less favorable (to ISVs) than selling boxes of software at retail. Few apps sold for more than $9.99 and all had a perpetual license for as many devices as someone owned. That was not close to the level of pricing (and margin) to support the MacBU R&D commitment, especially without significantly more volume.

Third, the iPhone OS and by extension this future tablet would not initially support "full Office" for all the same reasons that Windows 8 would not be able to. The security model, the user experience, and even the setup and distribution tools all were substantially less functional or at least different enough. Simply porting Office to the tablet was no more possible for MacBU than it was for Windows Office supporting Windows 8. Maintaining the complete meaning of the Office brand—and the name—along with the price point would be impossible.

The concerns over pricing, cannibalization, and the Office brand on the new Apple tablet mirrored those of the Windows Office team. Still, unlike the Windows team, the Mac team began investing in the new tablet and by the time we were deep in discussions about Office and Windows 8 there was substantial progress on Apple's new tablet OS. I did not know this at the time, but once the iPad was announced I was made aware.

This created an awkward situation. If there was indeed a new, or a port, of Office for iPad but not an equivalent product for Windows 8, Microsoft would look confused at best or dumb at worst. MacBU was caught between its own business needs and the strategic needs of Apple while the Windows Office team was caught between its business needs and the strategic needs of Microsoft overall.

Meanwhile the Windows Office team was doing great work retargeting Intel-based Office to run on ARM processors. This was not trivial or zero work but was super well-understood. Much like Windows NT, Office had for a long time been insulated from the specifics of chipsets and instruction sets. So long as the compiler could generate the right code and the Win32 APIs were available the effort was straightforward. Going as far back as the January 2011 CES meeting, Office had native builds of Word, Excel, and PowerPoint for ARM using Win32 and these were important to our demonstrations of SoC support.

Our plans, however, did not include making the Win32 API available to third parties on ARM. As described previously, the Win32 API for apps presented many challenges on ARM including power management, security including viruses and malware, and full integration with the Metro user experience such as contracts for sharing information. Outlook was particularly problematic when it came to its power usage due to all the background processing. After a decade of fine tuning, the power profile for Word, Excel, and PowerPoint were excellent, far better than most all Windows software.

We intended to provide the desktop for working with files in Windows Explorer along with the traditional control panel for settings. Admittedly, this would prove to be the source of more confusion than convenience. Still the situation was not unlike that of the MS-DOS command box on Windows to some degree, especially on the non-Intel versions of Windows NT.

The bigger problem would be how an ARM device would require a keyboard and mouse to use desktop versions of Win32 Office apps as well as the Windows desktop itself. While all ARM devices would support a keyboard and mouse, not all would have one readily available as some would be pure tablets like the iPad. The Office team introduced some user interface redesign to better support touch, but at a fundamental level Office required a mouse and keyboard for any sort of robust usage.

After a series of difficult conversations culminating in an executive staff discussion we arrived at an end-state where we would ship Win32 desktop versions of Word, Excel, and PowerPoint and Metro-style OneNote. It is not without irony that I reflected on the fact that OneNote exists because we (in Office, me and others) made a bet on the Tablet PC edition of Windows when the team building the OS failed to demonstrate user interface mechanisms or scenarios for how or when a pen could be used for word processing or spreadsheets. Not only did we feel we had ample user interface metaphors we also believed we articulated the type of platform changes around touch, cloud, and mobile that could be incorporated to build a new and unique productivity tool.

When it came down to it, the Office team did not want to invest in a subset of Office, reduce the brand value proposition for the apps because they would lack support for Visual Basic and other enterprise features, or take on the risk of developing something entirely new. The biggest challenge for Office on iPad would prove to be the same as many other existing ISVs faced, the iPad app pricing and licensing model. Office was early moving customers to Office 365 and on Mac the business was still the $150 perpetual license. There was no way to charge that much for apps on iPad at the time, especially with Apple apps priced at $9.95. The App Store rules would prove complicated for Microsoft as well, who would not want to cede subscription revenue to Apple. I'm sure there were many discussions with Apple that I was not part of.

Ultimately, the Microsoft Office team had the same choice to make for the iPad as it did for Windows 8 but chose one way for the iPad and the other way for Windows 8. It was the same type of platform choice faced 30 years earlier when the Microsoft Apps team faced building a spreadsheet for MS-DOS or for Macintosh and then Windows.

I obviously understood all these reasons deeply from my own first party experience. At the same time, the company's choice felt to me like the most conservative approach we could take at a time when we needed to be taking on more risk. The company was going through a difficult period and was getting beaten up for the risks it was taking by investing across search, gaming, web, and because of the inability to get ahead on smartphones and browsing. Reducing risk to Office at a time like this is what can happen when a company sees defending the existing business as the top priority over what could viewed as innovation or new opportunity. Platform shifts are extremely difficult for the existing leaders, and Office was a leader on both Mac and Windows.

On ARM devices the lack of Metro-style Office (also called Office for WinRT) would prove even more confusing to the market because it would appear as though we were holding back key platform capabilities by not making it so simple to port applications to the desktop. We knew there would be little interest in providing native ARM applications from third parties who would have to go through all the effort to port and support when there were plenty of Intel-based systems out there for their customers to use. Most desktop applications for sale that were under active development were also the kind of tools that required high-end PCs and were not optimized even for laptops, applications such as those from Adobe, Autodesk, Dassault, and the like.

Apple provided iWork for the iPad from the initial launch of the iPad in 2010. They used the iPad as an opportunity to purpose-build tablet apps. By 2017, iWork was free across all platforms. Apple had nothing to defend and only benefitted from the effort to support the platform, so I suspect this was all relatively easy for them to do.

During that executive staff meeting we had the difficult discussion about the existing iPad apps for Office as well. In this case, the same concerns expressed about Office for WinRT existed for Office for iPad. The only difference was that Office for iPad was well on its to being done by late 2011. The team was concerned about what to call the apps, the lack of Outlook for iPad as they had only built Word, Excel, and PowerPoint, and the feature differences between the apps on iPad and Windows. Outlook would follow many years later, based on an acquisition of a Silicon Valley startup. Office settled on a business model where the apps were free for existing 365 subscribers or a $99 in-app purchase. Non-subscribers could use the apps to view, but not edit, documents. It would be messy and frustrating for customers who were searching the Apple App Store for "Word" and "Excel" in huge volumes and finding nothing from Microsoft.

Collectively we agreed that it would be embarrassing for Microsoft to have tablet apps first on iPad and then never on a Windows PC. The subset of Office apps would be released for iPad in March 2014. In 2021, Microsoft released an all-in-one app called Office, which supported each of the apps in a single download as well as Microsoft's cloud storage, OneDrive.

The world was waiting for validation from Office for the new Windows 8 platform and would only see that through OneNote, which was a nice addition but not the killer app that platforms require. While I am certain there is no one aspect to Windows 8 that contributed more than any other to the market reception, the lack of Office designed for Windows 8 was a top issue.

BIG WINDOWS 8 CONSUMER PREVIEW

The march of external Windows 8 milestones continued.

After the //build conference that was so energizing we held an event highlighting the app store that would be part of Windows 8. We held the event in San Francisco and ran through the economics of the store and the opportunity for developers. Antoine Leblond (Antoine) led the entire event as he'd also led the team building the store from scratch.

The Windows Store was another part of the whole of Windows 8 that went from a blank slate to complete offering in the span of the release. By the end of 2011, just months after the //build conference we already had the store up and running and soon developers were able to exercise the app submission and approval process. As with the WinRT API we had the process and tooling well-documented. There were no major hiccups, and the store did what we needed it to do and did so gracefully.

From the time of the Store event through the broad beta test, the marketing and evangelism teams worked tirelessly to onboard developers of all sizes and get their apps into the store. Going from 17 sample apps from interns and the apps built by the Windows team (Mail, Photos, Calendar, Contacts, and more) to hundreds of apps available just after beta including many first-tier consumer apps was a huge accomplishment.

The final major event for all of Windows 8 was to release the broad beta test. Normally we would not have a special event for a beta but given the huge change and major effort involved in releasing a new platform we chose to use the massive mobile telephony industry meeting, Mobile World Congress (MWC), in Barcelona, Spain to announce and make available the Windows 8 Consumer Preview. This would be a downloadable release available to anyone right after our press event on February 29, 2012.

MWC was also the big event for Windows Phone and usually where there were big announcements. The 2012 show was between phone releases, with Windows Phone 7.5 already in market and Windows Phone 8 still under wraps for an end-of-year launch coincident with Windows 8 for PCs.

Therefore, the big news for Microsoft would be the broad beta test for Windows 8. We were excited. So far, while there were questions and certainly challenges, primarily bootstrapping the new platform, we'd seen positive results from developers, launched the Windows Store, and the product was solid. The Consumer Preview was a refinement of the Developer Preview, with no major strategic changes from the release less than six months earlier.

The event was only for press held in a jam-packed tent of about 200 people. We were feeling pretty good about the planned presentations. While there was no strategic news, we had made over 100,000 product changes since the Developer Preview.

Our primary message was the complete Windows 8 story: the operating system, apps, the Windows Store, and PCs and peripherals that would shine on Windows 8. While the world was fixated and obsessed about tablets, we continued to emphasize our message that computing devices were converging. Mobile platforms were rapidly gaining capabilities and in many ways such as power management and sensors surpassing Intel-based PCs. On the other hand, Intel-based PCs had a quality resurgence with Ultrabook specs and Windows 8 would bring touch capabilities and proper apps to Intel PCs with touch screens. I would always emphasize that we expected traditional laptops to incorporate touch screens and remind people that at some near future all their screens would have fingerprints.

Julie Larson-Green (JulieLar) and Antoine Leblond had a series of demonstrations including the Windows 8 experience and many apps that had been submitted by developers to the store. The progress in just a few months on the Windows Store and third-party apps was a positive sign for the platform overall.

Mike Angiulo (MikeAng) and I showed off a very exciting and broad range of Windows 8 PCs from small tablets through a giant Perceptive Pixel 82" touch screen, the kind used on CNN for election night. The emphasis was on how Windows scales across the form factors and price points all with a single operating system.

Following the conclusion of the event a press release went out detailing the availability of the Consumer Preview for download. Within less than a day, the release was downloaded a million times. The Windows team back in Redmond was more ready than we were at the Windows 7 beta, standing by for the download traffic. Everything went smoothly.

The press coverage of the event and importantly the reviews for the release were quite good. I know as you read this, you must be wondering if I had too much Cava in Barcelona. How could professional tech reviewers possible like Windows 8? They did. I swear. In the first couple of days, we had over 250 first looks and reviews. Nearly 70% of them scored over 110 on the PRIME score measuring overall tone, where 100 is neutral. There were 4 perfect scores at 200. Only 13% were scored 90 or less, and this is during an era where Microsoft typically averaged 90 on most product launches.

Like the Developer Preview, across mainstream media, tech enthusiast press, and even broadcast we received an incredible volume of positive to effusive comments. I sit here today writing this and I know readers must think there is either highly selective editing on my part or some sort of conspiracy to rewrite the past. I can assure you it is neither. In writing *Hardcore Software*, I made it a point of researching and rereading much of the contemporary press for every product, even Windows 8 product reviews.

We spent two weeks on the road with the press doing briefings and dozens of outlets received the Samsung tablet from //build and the near final Consumer Preview release. Unlike most previous Windows releases we did not run into technical problems, but rather I received quite a bit of private communication expressing positive impressions and almost a surprise at the combination of radical and yet comfortable the Windows 8 experience seemed to be. Once the release was available, reporters started to comment in their reviews, blogs, and even tweets:

> *"Brace yourself, Windows users. Microsoft's operating system is poised for stunning, dramatic change." —Christina Bonnington of Wired*
>
> *"By the time the final version ships later this year, it's clear that Windows 8 is going to be a remarkable, daring update to the venerable OS. It is a departure from nearly everything we've known Windows to be. You will love it, or hate it. I love it." —Mat Honan of Gizmodo*
>
> *"In short, Windows 8 is elegant, dynamic and beautifully created." —Jeremy Kaplan of FoxNews.com*

> *"It's an interface that's girding itself to compete with the iPad as much as the Mac, even though it's not an iPad knockoff." —Harry McCracken of TIME*
>
> *"Windows 8 is evidence that the old tech company is quite capable of bold moves and impressive innovation." —Michael Muchmore of PC Magazine*
>
> *"One thing is knowable now: With Windows 8, Microsoft has sweated the details, embraced beauty and simplicity, and created something new and delightful. Get psyched." —David Pogue of The New York Times*
>
> *"Don't confuse the friendly interface with superficiality. This is Windows and can do all the things we've come to expect on a Windows PC." — Wilson Rothman of MSNBC.com*
>
> *"The first beta of the next-gen operating system is eminently touchable, definitely social, and maybe just a bit sexy." — Seth Rosenblatt of CNET*
>
> *"Overall, I'm extremely impressed with the next version of Windows – the features, the new ways of interacting with a tablet, and the potential of it all." —Joanna Stern of ABCNews.com*

Even the first apps available in the Windows Store were receiving positive feedback. The quality of the apps available in the store was quite good. This was very early in the mobile apps era. This makes it difficult for most to think back to how relatively basic the software was at the time. Android apps were notoriously flakey and while there were huge numbers of iOS apps, most did not do very much. In evaluating the first apps from the Windows Store, Joanna Stern of ABC News (a new beat after moving from The Verge) tweeted "First impression: the apps I see for Win 8 are already 100x better than the ones for Honeycomb or ICS [Ice Cream Sandwich, the code name for the next Android release]. Very exciting."

Techmeme and Google News (which was the new cool place to look for headlines) were filled with coverage and positive headlines. Google News registered over 9,200 stories from the sources it crawls. This was our first Twitter-centric release and Windows 8 had almost 200,000 tweets in the first 24 hours, at peak there 20,000 per hour. It might not seem like a lot, but the Twitter-verse was relatively small in 2012, at just over 100M.

One of our perfect score reviews, a 200 PRIME and 5 on message pickup, came from David Pogue at the New York Times. Pogue was no fan of Windows and was super well-known as an author and expert on Apple products. He wrote books on all the major systems and devices but was always a bit grouchy when it came to Windows. I had flown down to San Francisco to meet with him and pre-brief on Windows 8. He gave me an earful and I was quite concerned about the pending review. I wanted to share a bit of what the review had to say:

> *It's a huge radical rethinking of Windows — and one that's beautiful, logical and simple. In essence, it brings the attractive, useful concept of Start-screen tiles, currently available on Windows Phone 7 phones, to laptops, desktop PC's and tablets.*
>
> *I've been using Windows 8 for about a week on a prototype Samsung tablet. And I have got to tell you, I'm excited.*

> *For two reasons. First, because Windows 8 works fluidly and briskly on touch screens; it's a natural fit. And second, it attains that success through a design that's all Microsoft's own. This business of the tiles is not at all what Apple designed for iOS, or that Google copied in Android.*
>
> . . .
>
> *Swipe from the right edge to open the Start menu (with Search, Share, Devices and Settings buttons.) Swipe from the left to switch apps. Swipe in and back out again to open the app switcher. Swipe down to open the browser address bar.*
>
> *If you have a mouse, you can click screen corners, or hit keystrokes, to perform these same functions.*
>
> *These swipes take about one minute to learn. On a tablet, I can't begin to tell you how much fun it is. It's evident that Microsoft has sweated over every decision — where things are, how prominent they are, how easy they are to access. (If you have the time, watch the videos to see all of this in action.)*
>
> . . .
>
> *But one thing is knowable now: With Windows 8, Microsoft has sweated the details, embraced beauty and simplicity, and created something new and delightful. Get psyched.*[152]

I want to be sure to capture both the grief he gave me in person and what he wrote in the review. Many reviews indicated that there could be potential for some to have difficulty using the product or even wanting to make a change, though the reviewers themselves did not express the difficulty. When it came to expressing the weaknesses of the Consumer Preview, Pogue said:

> *The only huge design failure is that Microsoft couldn't just abandon "real" Windows completely — desktop, folders, taskbar and all those thousands of programs. So on a PC, hiding behind this new Start screen is what looks almost exactly like the old Windows 7, with all of its complexity.*
>
> *In other words, Windows 8 seems to favor tablets and phones. On a nontouch computer like a laptop or desktop PC, the beauty and grace of Metro feels like a facade that's covering up the old Windows. It's two operating systems to learn instead of one.*
>
> . . .
>
> *Look, it's obvious that PC's aren't the center of our universe anymore. Apple maintains that you still need two operating systems — related, but different — for touch devices and computers. Microsoft is asserting that, no, you can have one single operating system on every machine, always familiar.*
>
> *The company has a point: already, the lines between computers, tablets and phones are blurring. They're all picking up features from each other — laptops with flash memory instead of hard drives, tablets with mice and keyboards. With Windows 8, Microsoft plans to be ready for this Grand Unification Theory.*

> *It's impossible to know how successful that theory will turn out to be. Windows 8 is a home run on tablets, but of course it has lost years to the iPad. (The Zune music player software was also beautiful — it was, in fact, the forerunner to Windows 8 — but it never did manage to close the iPod's four-year head start.)*

This is as perfect as a review can get. As a note, the scoring of reviews is done by a separate research and data team at the PR agency and it as scientific as one could be at the time. Like an Olympic sport they do not like to give out perfect scores as it makes their job more difficult down the road.

Even Wall Street got in on the positive sentiment. Normally I would not have paid any attention at all to a financial analyst view on product design, but the analyst community had become part of the cycle around an ever-expanding Apple and an ever-shrinking Microsoft. Citi research department reported the following on March 11, 2012, in a report I received:

> *We continue to view Windows 8 as a positive catalyst – Inputs since the Feb 29th Community Preview (beta) have continued to be positive with developer and IS momentum appearing to pick up. We continue to expect general availability of win 8 devices around Sept / Oct with ARM devices likely later (although MST and OEM goal remains coincident.) Given long-term secular concerns, share gains in tablets or renewed momentum in the PC market in 2H should be positive catalysts for shares. We acknowledge that the stock has a tendency to "fade" post release and thus we believe stock performance beyond that depends on tangible success of release.*[153]

What about the negative stories? There were some, just not that many. In fact, most of the truly negative stories were about specific features in the release. For example, one reviewer noted that ARM Windows 8 would not include Outlook, another bemoaned the lack of support for old-style enterprise management tools instead opting for modern mobile device management, and another was concerned about a keyboard change to the diagnostic boot sequence.

When there were negative stories, they did indeed carry the themes alluded to in the Pogue review. For example, Dan Acerman at CNET wrote in a review titled "Does Windows 8 diss the PC?":

> *According to NPD Group, PCs are still the largest category for U.S. consumer technology hardware, selling $28 billion worth of desktops and laptops in 2011 (a 3-percent drop from 2010.) Tablets and e-readers nearly doubled from the previous year, to $15 billion, but that was mostly on the continued strength of Apple's iPad. If you take iPad (and Android) out of the equation, interest in Windows tablets is still tiny. It will no doubt grow under Windows 8, but mostly because it has nowhere to go but up.*

So just remember, while watching everyone pinching, swiping, and tapping their Metro interface tablets and convertible laptops over the next several months in product demos, the real work is, and will continue to be, done on traditional laptops (and, yes, desktops) for a long time to come.[154]

From our perspective this notion of "two in one" was quite similar to the review of Windows originally in how it was first used as a way to simply run MS-DOS applications in character mode. The two decades of seamless Windows compatibility across 16-bit, 32-bit, and 64-bit perhaps created an expectation that compatibility was always essentially transparent.

Over the course of the Consumer Preview millions of people would download and test the product. Many would write blogs, tweets, and record YouTube videos about their experience. Almost immediately, developers began to hack away at Windows and introduce utilities to bring back their favorite look and feel from past releases. All of this was perfectly normal. We'd seen this before in every release of Windows.

One competitor took time during their own earnings call to comment on Windows 8, which frankly was quite surprising. What he had to say would definitely become a meme for the record books. In the call, a financial analyst asked the following question of Apple's Tim Cook:

> *I was wondering if you can talk about how you think about the markets for tablet and PC devices going forward. I think you've been fairly clear about saying that you believe that tablets will eclipse PCs in volume at some point. And I think you've also said they're somewhat discrete markets. There seems to be a lot of work, particularly on PC-based platforms, towards trying to combine the PC and tablet experience going forward in part because Windows 8 will be able to — is a touch-based operating system as well. Can you comment about why you don't believe the PC or the Ultrabook and tablet markets or your MacBook Air and tablet markets won't converge? Isn't it realistic to think in a couple of years we're going to have a device that's under 2 pounds with great battery life that we can all carry around and open as a notebook or close up in a clever way and use as a tablet? Can you comment on why you don't think that product might not come or why you believe these markets are separate? (Tony Sacconaghi – Sanford C. Bernstein & Co., LLC., Research Division)*

Tim replied as follows:

> *I think, Tony, anything can be forced to converge. But the problem is that products are about trade-offs, and you begin to make trade-offs to the point where what you have left at the end of the day doesn't please anyone. You can converge a toaster to a refrigerator, but those things are probably not going to be pleasing to the user. And so our view is that the tablet market is huge. And we've said that since day one. We didn't wait until we had a lot of results. We were using them here, and it was already clear to us that there was so much you could do and that the reasons that people would use those would be so broad. . . . I also believe that there is a very good market for the MacBook Air, and we continue to innovate in that product. And — but I do think that it appeals to [somewhat —] someone that has a little bit different requirements. And you wouldn't want to put these things together because you wind up compromising in both and not pleasing either user. Some people will prefer to own both, and that's great, too. But I think to make the compromises of convergence, so — we're not going to that party. Others might. Others might from a defensive point of view, particularly. But we're going to play in both.*[155]

There were indeed two operating systems, but no individual customer needed concern themselves with this except at time of purchase. The ARM-based version of Windows, named Windows RT, was in fact a different operating system than Windows 8 on x86 systems. Windows RT did not run any third-party or legacy Win32 programs, had a different security model, and did not support all the hardware and peripherals available in the x86 ecosystem. Windows 8 for x86 was the successor to Windows 7 and supported everything Windows 7 did though with better fundamental performance across all measures. As we will see, the fact that our new, innovative, and exclusive flagship device from Microsoft was tablet-ish and also ran Windows RT probably did a lot to emphasize this confusion of actual operating systems.

At no point in designing the product, as described here previously, did we think of modes any more than any previous version of Windows did. We saw Win32 or desktop applications as having the same prominence as those apps in the browser, Metro-style apps written for the new modern WinRT, or even character interface/command line tools used by so many. We saw devices running Windows along a continuum based on hardware capabilities, but able to all run the same modern applications, along with traditional PC devices able to run traditional PC software.

Where we did spend a good deal of time was designing the transition between the traditional Windows desktop, full-screen Metro-style apps, and the new Start screen. We had a new design to solve for, which was the program launcher was itself a full-screen application with icons to press to launch apps, switch to already running apps and display information as Live tiles previously hidden away in popups or the system tray. The Start screen could be accessed by hitting the Windows-key on the keyboard, Windows button on the tablet, mousing to the lower left corner where the old Start menu was, or swiping from the left or right. The work was to make the switching smooth and instant. It certainly was not going to be less jarring than the existing ALT-TAB or minimizing/maximizing from the taskbar. It was, however, a new experience.

How is it then did we end up with reviewers and beta testers focused on these two modes? One answer would be that I have no idea since we never talked about these as modes. That doesn't seem particularly convincing though. As I (and others of course) continued to discuss this with reviewers, beta testers, and industry analysts it became clear that our strategy or perspective was not taking hold. In fact, Apple was setting the agenda and their narrative had been cemented as the way devices would play out. That meant, just as Tim Cook said in his April 2012 earnings call, there was a world of iPhone smartphones, a world of Mac laptops, and a new world of iPad tablets. They were related and work together, but these were inherently different devices designed for different scenarios. In other words, according to Apple there was a "tablet world" and a "laptop world" and they were separate. Separate was by all accounts optimal. Microsoft was so used to setting the agenda that we were ill-equipped to arrive at a way of changing the narrative in our favor. We were stuck justifying why we had two modes which was confusing where Apple had two (or three) devices, which was somehow less confusing.

Then on March 7, 2012, a YouTube video dropped by Chris Pirillo, a video blogger, tech enthusiast, and former host of the cable show "Call for Help" on TechTV. There were other videos but for any number of reasons it was this one that caught on and went "viral" as the kids say. In short order it achieved 100,000 views which was a big number at the time. This video was "How Real People Will Use Windows 8" and started with "My dad tries Windows 8 for the first time" something we probably wouldn't do today because of the ageist implications of such an approach. The video was four minutes and 30 seconds of "Dad" fumbling around trying to use Windows 8 while Chris encouraged or narrated the actions off camera. To any people curious about Windows 8, the video proved to be a brutal takedown of the usability of the entire product and concept and specifically to the missing Start menu. This was particularly acute as the subject was apparently trapped unable to either leave the desktop or find the place to start a program even though they were a PC user familiar with prior Windows versions.

To those uninitiated to the world of usability testing or user studies it was brutal. To those who had any experience with the context free usage of a new software product, it was typical. Immediately our reactions on the team, individually and as we shared the video and reactions, was that this could have easily been a usability test for the initial iPhone or iPad or any new piece of software. Certainly, the first web sites, particularly those with image maps to click on for navigation, were prone to trapping people on a single page. We were all certain no product could endure such a test. That's a weak position to be in because everyone thinks products should be able to "just work" as Steve Jobs was known to say.

If you have to keep explaining something then it isn't that people aren't listening, it is that you have a problem. We had a problem, but we were also stumped as to what the problem actually was.

For me, my first reaction to the "where did the Start menu go" was almost a triggering experience. The iconic Start menu of Windows 95 famously suffered in usability tests because people had no idea how to launch programs. Towards the end of the product cycle after so many puzzled reviewers and questions, the team added a bouncing "Click here to begin..." prompt along the taskbar—an obvious user-interface band-aid. Indeed, there was a time when people would turn on their computers and have no idea what to do next, trapped staring at a desktop, because clicking the Start menu was so non-obvious. Then everyone learned and we moved on.

Two years after Windows 95 was released many tech enthusiasts and computing professionals continued to complain about the new Start menu. During the fevered early days discussing the Pirillo video Ed Bott, the highly regarded and experienced tech writer posted a recollection of a USENET newsgroup discussion where an experienced user continued to complain about features of Windows 3.1 missing from Windows 95.

In fact, those of us that were older remember that people had no idea even how to use a mouse. Usability tests of the mouse in the early days were notorious for people unable to comprehend the difference between single-click, double-click, dragging, selecting, and then later right-click when we added that in Office.

The first user manuals that came with Macintosh and Windows often contained several pages devoted to explaining how a mouse worked. Can you imagine actually reading instructions for how to click a mouse? Even the 1990 edition of the *Getting Started* guide for Macintosh contained four pages of mouse instructions. Windows 95 was for many people coming from MS-DOS their first experience with a mouse, and often that was not unlike learning how to shift gears in a manual transmission car when the only experience was an automatic. Again, we take for granted that people know this today, but it was a significant change for everyone.

A common thread to each of these was that for existing users of all skill levels there was a change, and people hate change. Those new to computing simply just start using the computer as though that is just how they worked. Existing users just adapt, albeit with some learning curve or disruption. Then over time those new users would become the existing users and this pattern repeats. If we did our job, the new way of working came with some benefit and not just a random change for the sake of designery thoughts or fancy strategery.

We had designed the Start screen to "just work" by using the muscle memory of the previous Start menu experience when it came to mouse and keyboard users. For touch users we counted on the same type of serendipitous and risk-free trial-and-error that smartphones were benefitting from. Obviously, something more was going on here and we were not reading the situation correctly.

One of the more interesting and unexpected challenges we faced with the Preview releases was that a significant portion of pre-release use took place in *virtual machines* or testing the operating system from within a Windows 7 PC and not installed directly on hardware as nearly every user would. When running in a virtual machine, Windows 8 appeared as a window within Windows 7 as just another running program. To simulate the real world, we did not run or test Windows 8 that way on the development team. Almost as soon as the release went out, we started to see bug reports that the corners were not active and dragging the mouse to the corner wasn't working as we said. It took us a moment until we realized that when running in a virtual machine the hot corners were not "infinitely large buttons" as Fitts's Law would predict, but in fact 1-pixel sized buttons. Many other things within a virtual machine did not reflect real-world use but running this way had become quite common for testing out software.

While this video was flying around the company and the industry, it would turn out I was having my own Start screen experience, only it was with a new car I just acquired. I was so thrown off by this experience and how similar I thought it was to the Start screen that I wrote an internal blog post of 2000 words on what happened and a second follow-up post based on questions and suggestions, both literal and figurative.

I had been driving the first-generation Toyota Prius from 2001, which for this illustration I will call *Car XP*. By 2012 I had to get a new car when the hybrid battery died out of warranty. I decided on the Prius C, or the *Car XP Upgrade,* without any consideration of alternatives and called the dealer to secure a pickup time. I arrived at the dealership hoping for an instant transaction. I had my down-payment in hand as instructed and like many really did not want to spend an afternoon being upsold on stuff I don't want. The salesman, a 26-year veteran of Toyota, appreciated that and had everything ready. In a few minutes I was ready to go. But then the salesman said he wanted to take me out to the car and explain how it works and everything I needed to know. I resisted and thought I had 25 years of car driving experience and I'm a technology savvy owner. I'm good to go. From the post:

I jumped in the car. I adjusted the seat and mirrors. I am ready to go.

Holding the key I look for the ignition. But wait, I can't even figure out the key. It doesn't open up like my old one (switchblade style.) I managed to disassemble the key to component parts, but that didn't help. I figure it must just be a square key so I am now looking for the place to insert the (backup) black plastic fob, figuring it was a key upgrade. I can't find it. My excitement is waning. I am not cruising. I glance over to the dealer and smile.

> *I am scanning the dashboard. Maybe the key is by the emergency break like old Saabs. Nope. There's no chance I am going to ask for help from the super nice dealer. I'm considering the manual but seriously, who looks at a manual for a car, especially a Car XP upgrade. As I scan the instrument panel I keep noticing the giant blue button that says "Start" that is the size of a Golden Nugget poker chip, but that doesn't quite register as a solution to my starting problem. Beginning to panic that I can't use my new car, I more rapidly scan around the steering wheel—left side, right side, underneath?*
>
> *My heart racing...my confidence waning...what the heck, I push the big giant button. Everything lights up. Apparently that is how I start the car. Go figure. I don't have to insert a key or turn anything. That whole process went away. I no longer have to worry about Car Shutdown (turn the key, remove the key, place in pocket.) I just touch the button and leave. The doors lock and I am free of a bunch of manual steps. The key never leaves my pocket. It is like a Car of the Future or something to me.*

I just experienced "Dad tries to use Windows 8 for the first time" and felt like an idiot. It was not unlike the first time I drove my 2001 Prius and experienced regenerative braking and unexpectedly lurched forward the first time I took my foot off the accelerator. Should have I insisted they add back a keyed ignition? Should I have rejected the car for not supporting how I was used to cars working? Of course not. It took a few minutes to adjust, and I adjusted. If you get a new car only once a decade this kind of thing will happen. I decided to get vanity license plates that read "CAR 8."

The experience of being a technologist outpaced by a technology change is familiar to all of us. Technology is always moving and the more of it in our lives the less open we are to changes, especially if we as individuals deem those changes inefficient or random. The aversion or resistance to change grows as we come to rely more on technology and the less we find joy in learning what is new or simply futzing with something new.

This Pirillo video kicked off a wave of feedback about muscle memory, workflow, tradition, professional tools, and more. One of the most common lines of discussion was that tablets were essentially different than PCs. Tablets were designed for lightweight consumption and PCs were designed for "real" work. The comments always spoke of real work of professionals versus the consumer scenarios centered around tapping on social networks and "lightweight" email. We remained trapped in Apple's narrative.

We were more frustrated than panicked. At least in these first weeks of the smoldering fury. What we, what I, failed to understand was that we could not regain our footing and indeed the seeds had been planted for what the market would see as the major issue with Windows 8, the removal of the Start menu.

Our first efforts were to think if we should make a video of our own. We had thousands of hours of usability tapes of people successfully using Windows 8. We quickly dismissed this because as a defensive tactic it would lack any credibility. We'd be accused of picking the best case or simply having rigged tests. The beauty of the Pirillo video was the perceived credibility it had as a natural and legitimate test of usability of a new product. I can't think of a product we all use that would have passed this test, but that was not the debate.

We considered all sorts of ideas like going to a shopping mall and filming unprepared people who were successful, or taking a competitive approach and doing the same "Dad" test but with an iPad, or even repeating the same test showing not everyone fails. Today we would have called any of those approaches "you're doing it wrong" so I'm very glad we did not try anything like these.

I put Windows 8 in front of my 11-year-old niece and she didn't ask a single question as she tapped away. So what.

Instead, the debate was about existing users and their adaptation to an "entire" new experience and a need for "retraining" and "education" in order to use Windows 8. Was this really the case? Even in hindsight I do not think so. We had too much data to show that people could use the product. Our problem was that a specific group of people did not like or prefer what we had built. Preference is a perfectly legitimate concern.

The question we had was who was expressing this preference and was there something we could do to improve the situation. This is where it got tricky, well, more than tricky. We found ourselves in a quagmire.

In each of the products described in *Hardcore Software* I wrote about the product vision. A key to the vision was identifying the various customer segments and the value proposition for each. We did so for Windows 8. Some product development processes define each segment with a representative persona or literal person for each segment whereas we named them generically. The vision had a record number of customer types to consider including: Mainstream Consumers, Enthusiasts, Emerging Markets, Small Business, Information Workers, IT Decision Makers, IT Pros, OEMs, Retailers, Telcos, IHVs, ISVs, Rising Star Developers. Windows was a complicated product to bring to market with many stakeholders. Reconciling conflicting inputs or opinions across them was always a challenge.

Who were the people expressing the most concerns? There are some constants in how segments react. For example, it is well-known that most in the IT segments react negatively to any user-interface changes. They always ask to be able to turn off or disable changes in user flow. In a sense that was baked into the plan, very much as we described previous changes in Office and not unlike the reaction described above to Windows 95. Most on the ecosystem team were indifferent to change and focused on what new investments they needed to make. The segments representing sellers or sales channels tended to embrace change as an opportunity to sell more of something new versus the same old products. Retailers for example simply loved the Start screen because of its iconic display. Enthusiastic retailers were gearing up to build in-store Metro-style displays. Emerging markets have unique concerns around hardware requirements and cost but given that they were clearly going to skip PCs altogether, the design similarity to smartphones was a significant positive.

We can debate regular people, just plain consumers, or as we called them during Windows 7 and Windows 8, humans. Was Pirillo's Dad a human in this taxonomy and were we failing to address his needs? Or were the humans in our studies more numerous and representative? Humans generally don't participate in pre-release testing, and they certainly don't make videos or opine in blogs about pre-release software. While we could debate whether we were successful in representing the response humans would have, it turns out not to be all that important because one other segment was far more engaged and set the tone for all others.

Enthusiasts were the group up in arms and expressing concerns at a visceral level. But not all enthusiasts, a specific type of enthusiast we called "the basement." This is a difficult phrase to introduce and please bear with me. The basement are indeed humans and there's no intent to make them less than humans. Most all engineers on software products are the basement. Those who test pre-release software for fun or on the side or at night and write about it and document it as a hobby are the basement. Chances are as a reader of this work, you're part of the basement. There is nothing derogatory about the basement.

The term comes from the 2007 film *Live Free or Die Hard* and the computer techie character Warlock played by Kevin Smith. In the film, Warlock is in the basement of his house surrounded by monitors running all sorts of tools with a variety of very technical user interface scrolling by rapidly. We're all the basement. The basement loves and cares about the product more than anyone else and are not afraid to let the product makers know that. Sometimes, though frequently in a derogatory manner, the phrase *fanboys* is used.

As it turns out the basement loves technology, but they dislike and distrust change. Part of the reason is because they have invested more into existing products than other segments. Not only do they know all the ins and outs of every product they use, they are also highly tuned to how to customize products for their exact use cases. Importantly, there is no debating with them whether customizations are optimal in any absolute way. How Warlock chooses to use a system is by definition the preferred and best way to get the job done. Changes to any product must thread the needle of improving the product while not impacting a highly tuned basement workflow.

When introducing changes, the best way and perhaps the only successful way to make it through this type of gatekeeper customer segment is to create changes that are layered on top of a system, can be pushed aside, and usually adopted in a piecemeal fashion as desired. The worst type of change for the basement is a "take it or leave it" change that simultaneously upends the workflow.

A key reason for this change aversion is because it is rooted in the basement's sense of mastery. Not just mastery for personal gain but within a community of users. This mastery extends to customizations, integrations across products, and muscle memory. We saw with Office 2007 the feedback around "sub-second keyboard access is required" even though no human could type that fast. We saw the feedback from the basement of the IT world when we released deployment tools for Office 2000 that required re-learning for a much more manageable and scalable mechanism. The cardinal sin of a new product release is reducing the basement's mastery.

So, what does this mean? It means designing a whole new user interface is going to run head-first into the basement. And we'd better have an answer. Since we knew this about designing products, we thought we'd be ok. JensenH and team, many members of the basement themselves, had done everything they could to preserve muscle memory, not take even a single additional click and in many cases use fewer clicks, and continue to support working the way they had always worked. In fact, at least by our accounting, we had actually improved the situation because the Start menu had become increasingly finnicky on the very large and high-DPI screens that the Warlock was using. We introduced a zero-click ability to launch programs via keyboard by just typing the name of the program, something that would become a primary launch mechanism on PCs and mobile a decade later.

We were wrong. The Pirillo video was the match in a dry forest. From there the basement took over. The basement often knows that their needs are not enough to drive a new product for billions which is why, just as IT managers do, they often couch their feedback not in first-person terms but in speaking for the broader user community. For example, much of the technical press by nature of their jobs are charter members of the basement, but they are the first to say they are writing for their readers. A thought experiment to consider would be how much less credible or potentially noticeable a video would have been if it were just the technologist Pirollo in a video of himself—there were many such videos already out.

The basement had a visceral reaction to the design language of Metro-style—the rectangles, solid and bright colors, and use of text. This would be surprising because the basement, specifically the basement committed to Microsoft, were huge fans of Windows Phone. The phone was monochrome, and we defaulted Windows 8 to more colors by virtue of our authentically digital experience. The basement quickly dubbed the look of the Start screen as "Fisher-Price" aligning with the view that tablets were for kids to use in the back seat, not for real work.

Then came the Pirillo video and it provided the needed evidence that the design didn't work for regular humans. This equipped the basement with a lever upon which to base the feedback.

There needed to be a reason why this change didn't work for other people. That's where the Apple narrative came in. It isn't enough to say something isn't easy to use for some people. It needs to be wrong. The reason Windows 8 was wrong was not because of Fisher-Price colors or because users would not be able to find the old Start menu. It wasn't because the desktop was not the first thing you saw after booting the computer. Those are all effects. The cause was that Windows 8 was designed for tablets. Tablets, as per how people use iPads, are not for real work and productivity but for lightweight consumer scenarios like social networking.

The Windows team was trying to turn Windows into a toy for consumers when its *raison d'être* was for the real work of computing professionals, programmers, system administrators, and Warlock. We were trying to force Windows to do something it had no business doing and was of little value. Worse, the view was that the strategy and resulting design were simply wrong.

At this point you might be getting a sense of a snowball turning into a thundering avalanche. We were not really getting feedback about the design of the Start screen. This was really about the essential nature of Windows. It was as though Windows was being taken away from them. It was more than disempowering or reducing mastery.

The most concrete statement of where the design seemed ill-advised was that it was for a tablet more than a PC. Consider the design as a point on a spectrum between endpoints of a pure tablet user interface and a pure desktop user interface, whatever "pure" means in this regard. The assertion was we were far too close to the tablet side and needed to move back to the PC side—where Windows belonged. I was reminded of a *Penny Arcade* comic that was modified and sent to me that made the joke that Windows had "Less pad than you expected" which originally said "Less bad than you expected" at the launch of Windows 7.[156]

The challenge we faced was melding this feedback with our view across two dimensions. First, the idea of a tablet was being portrayed as a hard dividing line and we did not see that same line. Apple at the time had a hard line at a 9.7" screen having only touch and then the 11.6" and up screen having only a mouse and keyboard. That was their world. Second, we saw most humans using computers to be using tablet/phone interface in ever-increasing numbers and PC interface in flat to shrinking numbers. As we know today, there are 1.2-1.7B PCs in use depending on what is counted. There are almost 7B smartphones in use. Apple experts estimate about 500M active iPads. In addition, Apple Mac "computers" are now running the same chips and share huge amounts of software with iPhone/iPad, differing essentially in touch support, though sharing more and converging every iteration. In other words, while the criticism of being too tablet in Windows 8 would be fair, perhaps a more realistic view would be it was too soon to be too tablet. Could we have done something different? Yes, of course.

The videos and the feedback, nevertheless, were clear. What we were trying to do was perfectly fine, but just not as part of Windows. It was clear we were not listening to customers. Customers needed a better Windows, not a different Windows. The forums filled with lists of features we had not done that would have made Windows even better: improve Task Manager, tabs on the file explorer, a better registry editor, reduce the disk space take up by the WinSxS folder, fully integrate Power Toys (a set of utilities built by Microsoft but only released as a separate download from Windows) and on and on.

Lacking any indication that we were listening, the basement began to craft their own narrative of how to fix the situation. This pattern where the basement develops their own design is a common pattern of feedback we see in the internet era. Within a very short time of the Consumer Preview we started to see tools that could be installed to bring back the Start menu. Stardock was a company that already made utilities for customizing Windows 7 primarily used the basement. Announced two days *before* the Pirillo video, the company would soon have a utility to return the Windows 7 user experience to Windows 8, called Start8. Many would point to this as a failure of Windows 8, though we had not ever given these utilities a second thought. They were fine by us and did not see them as insulting or compensatory. They were exactly the kinds of features tech enthusiasts liked about Windows. Microsoft made their own version of utilities along these lines this called Power Toys. By the time we released Windows 8, Start8 would reportedly sell 2 million copies which was a lot but not compared to the hundreds of millions of copies of Windows.

We were faced with a challenge or even a demand. When would we fix Windows 8 to accommodate the clearly aberrant design as per the basement? What did the basement want, and could we deliver it?

Our problem was that the basement just wanted Windows 8 to go away. They didn't want the apps, ARM support, WinRT platform, and certainly not touch. What we started hearing again were the calls to focus on tablets with one product and real PCs with another. Microsoft should have two products. The feedback was not flippant or dismissive but detailed and prioritized towards not delivering Windows 8 but delivering more of Windows 7.

We certainly considered some ideas. Should we have put a permanently visible Start button in the corner as we happened to have in the initial vision? Should we offer a switch to enable the desktop "app" to always run first? Should we do something more dramatic like have the taskbar visible all the time at the bottom of the screen to be more like a PC? There were these and other ideas. Because they felt like going backwards, there were few on the team championing changes, least of all me.

Each of these suffered from the challenge that they would never be enough to placate the overall feedback. When faced with the kind of upheaval from a key customer segment that is being so specific with feedback, there really aren't any options to move forward. The option that one goes with is to capitulate. To embrace the design of the basement and declare victory in terms of "listening to customers." Unfortunately failing to capitulate means the opposite. We were not listening to customers. All of them.

On a huge product a situation like this was not managed on a single front. Each customer segment maintained strong connections to Microsoft primarily through outreach organizations within the company that "manage" different communities. The basement was connected to Microsoft through the MVP program and a variety of insider programs managed at the subsidiary or local level. These programs had one objective, maintain the community's satisfaction with Microsoft. They were there to keep a community active, thriving, and happy. When the community did not like a product or direction, the managers in the programs, the Microsoft employees, became very nervous. Their performance was now being questioned and quickly they became part of the community they represent but with blue badges worn by full time Microsoft employees. Whatever issues were happening outside the company were now happening inside the company. Microsoft being what it was, escalation became the norm, and my inbox was overflowing with red exclamation mark emails about the crisis in various communities of MVPs, VIPs, Insiders, and more.

Even Intel inadvertently made things difficult. Seeing the success of Ultrabooks and the near arrival of Windows 8, they began touting what they called "2 in 1" PCs. These PCs with touchscreens and optional removable keyboards were meant to be distinct from Ultrabooks, which would enable yet another channel control mechanism for Intel. The form factor provided a way for Intel to isolate touch computers to one product line. In the process it clearly sent a message that Windows 8 was not one computer, but two computers in one. This was exactly the opposite of what we intended. I hated it.

The snowball was growing.

Some of the technology press long considered by us as charter members of the basement understood what we were trying to do and had clear explanations. They would certainly be in the minority. Paul Thurrott who today records a history of truly despising Windows 8 from the start had a very solid take as one of the first to take on the missing Start button in his post from February 29, the day of the release of the Consumer Preview. In "Windows 8 Consumer Preview: The True Story Behind the Missing Start Button" he wrote (emphasis is mine):[157]

> *In the past few weeks, screen captures emerged showing that the Start button, a fixture in Windows since 95 when it debuted in Windows 95, would be removed from Windows 8. Enthusiasts acted as if it were a betrayal, a final nail in the coffin of the desktop UI they just know is being herded out to pasture.*
>
> *None of it is true. Well, the Start button is being removed from the Windows 8 desktop, though as I wrote about in tongue-in-cheek fashion in Windows 8 Secrets: Windows 8 Is NOT Dropping The Start Button, any Windows logoed device or PC will have a Windows key (on the keyboard) or Windows key button (on the device itself) that will accomplish the same thing. What I couldn't tell you at the time, sorry, was that this is only part of the story.*
>
> *So here's the true story behind the missing Start button in Windows 8.*
>
> *As you will discover in my article User Experience Fit and Finish Improvements, Microsoft has largely completed the Windows 8 user experience in the Windows 8 Consumer Preview, adding full-featured keyboard, mouse, and trackpad interactions to the system that rival any of the touch-based stuff it*

first showed off last year. One of the goals of this nearly-complete user experience is that these input types will work consistently, and offer nearly identical capabilities. So there shouldn't be anything that's possible only with, say, the touch interface.

The other side of this coin, however, is that these different input types should work consistently and nearly identically in both of Windows 8's user experiences, the Metro-style Start screen the Explorer-based desktop.

Think about that for a second.

The Start button as we know it is a fixed, desktop interface only. And since there's no logical way to meld that Start button into the Start screen—which by design is a scrolling, multi-screen interface that launches full-screen apps that would hide such a UI—Microsoft needed to figure out a Start button replacement, one that would work consistently in both Metro and the desktop, and be respectful of the differences in each user experience.

So … wait for it… Microsoft is not so much removing the Start button as it is replacing it. Long live the Start button.

From any UI in Windows 8—the Start screen, a full screen Metro-style app, or the desktop—you can move the mouse down into the lower left corner of the screen, to an area that is largely the size of the Start button in Windows 7 and occupies the same place, and a Start tip will pop-up. This Start tip, which was also leaked in screenshots recently and widely misunderstood, is your visual cue that the Start button may have "disappeared" but that its functionality is still there. In fact, it's more powerful than ever.

In addition to working in all Windows 8 user experiences, this new Start experience, as Microsoft calls it, provides a way for mouse - and touch-based users to trigger Start functionality. Better still, power users will be excited to discover that they can right-click on this UI and unleash a whole new set of useful options. Go ahead, try it. I won't ruin the surprise.

And as was pointed out to me, those that simply cannot live without a visual Start button on the Windows 8 desktop will be able to easily add one via the innumerable third party utilities that will appear within days—perhaps hours—of the release of the Consumer Preview. All you need, as a developer is a very simple API called SendKeys that's been in Windows forever.

The truth is, I suspect, that most people won't care once they figure out that the new Start experience is available globally in such a consistent fashion. *A lot of the current controversy, such as it is, is really just a psychological issue with persecution complex written all over it.* ***The new approach simply makes more sense, sorry. And once you've used it, I think you'll agree.***

While that was a long and detailed excerpt, it is precisely what we had hoped more would have seen in the product. That was not to be the case, ultimately.

One action we took was to develop a video as the Windows 95 team had done. When first booting a new PC or signing in for the first time, a video encouraging you to "Click the corners" ran highlighting the basic user experience metaphor. It worked for Windows 95…

While we considered a good many small tweaks and changes, we decided all were simply too small relative to the specifics being sought. We chose not to change the design not out of abstract notions of design integrity or high-brow design rationale. We were not being stubborn. We (and I mean I) believed we were at the beginning of a journey to reinvent the product. We knew it would not happen in a single release. We also knew that Windows can't take small little steps and count on a long-term vision over time. Windows had been trying that for a decade and it is what had failed. We tried to execute on Tablet PC, Media Center, Ultra Mobile, Phone, and more as side projects. Windows needed to move the whole thing forward. We needed to take a big step reframing the future and then iterate with incremental improvements on that new baseline.

Apple had the luxury of nothing to lose and an execution strategy that let them jettison baggage in their platform every couple of years. We had the opposite. We had everything to lose and an execution strategy that never let us move on from the past. Windows 8 was about changing this. We were confronted with our own strategy of the past precluding us from moving forward.

As Microsoft grew a common expression, Microspeak, was to point out in a big meeting facing a big issue that "the hardest thing to do in a big company is to do something." For me we had faced this at the start of the project when we took the bold step of not just doing something but doing a lot. Now these very words were being used to point out to me that we were indeed not doing anything.

Many were suggesting we just build a tablet operating system and sell it separately. In previous sections I offered the situation in this regard. In order for Microsoft to bring only a tablet to market we would need a new OS beyond Windows Phone 7 (or 7.5 or 8.0) and we did not have that. We would need to build a developer value proposition so we could have apps. We could do that in a few more years, but it would look a whole lot like the Windows 8 product cycle only restricted to tablet devices. We would have had no base upon which to build such an effort. By 2012, the Windows Phone trajectory was clear. The peak Windows Phone share was low single digits at best and never went above that. In other words, a tablet-specific product from Microsoft could best case have a tiny sliver of a market to build on and enter the market a distant number three with no discernable advantage. That's why all along the Windows 8 strategy was to build on the ability to bring existing applications together with new applications and run them on new computers. The run rate of Windows 8 would not be comparable to smartphones much longer, but it was still hundreds of millions.

We did have a dramatic and never used alternative which was that Windows 7 was going to be perfectly good in market for another decade. We proved that with Windows XP. There was no reason at all for us to forget that and we thought we could have happily pointed people to use Windows 7, provide corporate "downgrade" rights for Windows 7 Enterprise, and even continue to sell Windows 7 at retail. We continued to sell MS-DOS separately from Windows all the way until Windows 95 shipped and then just released it for free on our new FTP server for download. Speaking this way was heresy but I was confident if we needed to we could resort to that as we did by extending the life of Windows XP for Netbooks. Doing this would have given us time to gain traction with apps or further iterate on Windows 8, which we knew would happen. It is worth considering exactly what the capabilities of the first generation of any new platform in the industry looked like. We remember platforms as they were much later than when they launched.

Those in the press covering the debate were tuned into the Apple narrative. That narrative peaked with Tim Cook 's "toaster-refrigerator" assault and since Apple was so clearly the leader, the category definer, and the more visionary company the situation rapidly deteriorated for us.

By the time David Pogue wrote his final Windows 8 review at general availability in October 2012, all the love he had for the bold design and approach was replaced with a horrible tale of two worlds "Tile World" and "Desktop World" in his review in the New York Times, he said:[158]

> *This may be the biggest week in Microsoft's 37-year history. The company is releasing its very first computer (the Surface tablet), a new phone operating system (Windows Phone 8), and, believe it or not, two PC operating systems.*
>
> *I'm not talking about Windows 8 and Windows RT, which are, in fact, two new and distinct operating systems from Microsoft. I mean the two different worlds within Windows 8 alone, one designed primarily for touch screens, the other for mouse and keyboard. Individually, they are excellent — but you can't use them individually. Microsoft has combined them into a superimposed, muddled mishmash called Windows 8, which goes on sale Friday at prices ranging from $15 to $40, depending on the offer and version.*
>
> ...
>
> *DESKTOP WINDOWS This is my name for the traditional Windows: the land of overlapping windows, menus and the taskbar across the bottom. Here, you can run any of the four million traditional Windows apps, which Microsoft calls desktop apps: Photoshop, Quicken, tax software, games.*
>
> ...
>
> *TILEWORLD The enormous, controversial change in Windows 8 is the overlaying of the second "operating system," intended for touch screens.*
>
> *(It's not really called TileWorld. But Microsoft doesn't have a good name for it. Insiders know it as the Metro interface — that was its code name — but Microsoft simply refers to it as Windows 8, which is so infuriatingly confusing you feel like firing somebody. I'm going to go with TileWorld.)*
>
> ...
>
> *TileWorld is absolutely fantastic for tablets. The tiles glide gracefully with a swipe of your finger. You can "pin" frequently used tiles to the Start screen: programs, Web sites, playlists, photo albums, people from your contacts list, mail accounts or mailboxes, icons from Desktop Windows, and, of course, apps. The tiles are fun to rearrange, resize, cluster into groups and so on.*
>
> ...

> *Even so, two worlds means insane, productivity-killing schizophrenia. The Windows 8 learning curve resembles Mount Everest.*
>
> . . .
>
> *Got it?*
>
> *Me neither.*
>
> *You know what would have been perfect? Keeping the two operating systems separate. Put TileWorld and its universe of new touch screen apps on tablets. Put Windows 8 on mouse-and-keyboard PCs.*
>
> *Presto: all the confusion would evaporate. And the good work Microsoft did on both of these individual operating systems would shine.*

That's how we ended up. I'm hardly burying the lede since every reader knows and it would be pointless to try to keep things in suspense.

However, we were still marching from Spring to RTM in August and then availability. We did have one more chance that no one, literally no one, knew about. From the start of the project, we knew Windows 8 was just the software and that to fully realize all Windows 8 was capable of we needed great hardware. Windows 8 was the performance, but we needed a stage for that performance. Perhaps we could surface a new product that could show we did not build a toaster-refrigerator?

107. CLICK IN WITH SURFACE

In 2010, operating in complete secrecy on the newest part of Microsoft's campus, the Studios, was a team called *WDS*. WDS didn't stand for anything, but that was the point. The security protocols for the Studio B building were strengthened relative to any other in the entire engineering campus. Housed in this building was a team working on one of the only projects that, if leaked, would be a material event for Microsoft.[159]

WDS was creating the last part of the story to reimagine Windows from the chipset to the experience.

When we began the project, it was the icing on the cake. After the Consumer Preview, it had become the one thing that might potentially change the trajectory of Windows 8.

As Windows 7 finished and I began to consider where we stood with hardware partners, Intel, the health of the ecosystem, and competing with Apple, I reached the same conclusion the previous leader of Windows had—Windows required great hardware to meet customer needs and to compete, but there were structural constraints on the OEM business model that seemed to preclude great hardware from emerging.

At the same time, the dependence on the that channel meant there was no desire at Microsoft to compete with OEMs. In 2010, the Windows business represented 54% of Microsoft's fiscal year operating income and Office was 49%—yes you read that correctly.[160] BillG used to talk about that amount of revenue in terms of the small percentage of it that could easily fund a competitor or alternative to Windows. The "Year of Linux" was not just a fantasy of techies but a desired alternative for the OEMs as well. So far the OEMs had not chosen to invest materially in Linux, but that could change especially with an incentive created by Microsoft's actions.

Like my predecessors, I believed Microsoft needed to build a PC.

Building PCs was something BillG was always happy to leave to other people. In an interview in 1992, Bill said, "There's a reason I'm the second-biggest computer company in the world...The reason is, I write software, and that's where the profit is in this business right now."[161] On the other hand, the legendary computer scientist and arguably father of the tablet concept, Alan Kay, once said, "People who are really serious about software should make their own hardware."[162]

Microsoft was founded on the core belief that hardware should best be left to others. In the 1970s hardware was capital intensive, required different engineering skills, had horrible margins, and carried with it all the risks and downsides that pure software businesses, like the one BillG and PaulA had pioneered, did not worry about. With a standardized operating system, the hardware business would quickly consolidate and commoditize around IBM-compatible PCs in what was first a high-margin business that soon became something of a race to the bottom in terms of margins.

Microsoft's fantastic success was built precisely on the idea of not building hardware.

BillG was always more nuanced. He and PaulA believed strongly in building hardware that created opportunities for new software. Microsoft built a hardware device, the *Z-80 SoftCard*, to enable its software to run on the Apple]

[. Early on, Microsoft created add-in cards to play sound. PaulA personally drove the creation of the PC mouse, the famous *green-eyed monster*. Modern Microsoft built Xbox, but also Zune and the Kin phone.

Apple built great hardware and together with great software made some insanely great products.

To build hardware in this context meant to build the device that customers interacted with and to build all the software and deliver it in one complete package or, in economist's parlance, *vertical integration*.

Mike Angiulo (MikeAng) and the ecosystem had the job of bringing diversity to the PC ecosystem, a diversity that Apple did not have. This diversity was both an enormous strength and the source of a structural weakness of the industry. PCs in any screen size or configuration one might need could always be found or even custom built covering any required performance and capacity. If you wanted something like a portable server or a ruggedized PC for a squad car or a PC to embed in 2 tesla MRI, Windows had something for you. Apple with its carefully curated line essentially big, bigger, biggest with storage of minimum, typical, maximum across Mac were the choices. Even a typical PC maker like Dell would offer good, better, best across screen sizes and then vary the offering across home, small business, government, education, and enterprise. Within that 3 x 3 x 5 customization was possible at every step. This is the root of why Apple was able to have the best PC, but never able to command the bulk of the market.

The idea of vertical integration sounds fantastic on paper but the loss of the breadth of computing Windows had to offer was also a loss for customers. It is very easy to say "build the perfect hardware" but the world also values choice. One question we struggled with was if the "consumerization" of computing would lead to less choice or not. In general, early in adopting a technology there is less choice for customers. Increased choice comes with maturity in an effort to obtain more margin and differentiate from growing competition.

One bet we were making was that Windows on ARM and a device from Microsoft was the start of a new generation of hardware. It would start, much like the IBM PC 5150, with a single flagship and then over time there would be many more models bringing the diversity that was the hallmark of the PC ecosystem.

That is why we never built anything as central and critical as a mainstream PC, and never had we really considered competing so directly with Microsoft's primary stream of profits and risking alienating those partners and sending them to Linux. The Windows business was a profit engine for the company (and still is today) and that profit flows through only a half dozen major customers. Losing even one was a massive problem.

Microsoft had also lost a good deal of money on hardware, right up to the $1.15 billion write-off for Xbox issues in 2007. Going as far back to the early 1990s and the original keyboard, SideWinder joystick, cordless phone, home theater remote, wireless router, and even ActiMates Barney our track record in hardware was not great. Microsoft's hardware accessories were at best categorized as marketing expense or concept cars. It was no surprise my predecessors backed off.

Like the mouse, the sound card, and perhaps Xbox, I was certain that if we were to succeed in a broad platform shift in Windows that we would need to take on the responsibility and risk of building mainstream and profitable PC devices. We tried to create the Tablet PC by creating our own prototypes and shopping them to OEMs as proofs of concept. We repeated this motion with the predecessor to small tablets called Origami, same as we did for Media

Center. Each of these failed to develop into meaningful run rates as separate product lines even after the software was integrated into Windows.

OEMs were not equipped to invest the capital and engineering required to compete with Apple. As an example, Apple had repurposed a massive army of thousands of aluminum milling machines to create the unibody case used in the MacBook Pro. Not only did no OEM want to spend the capital to do this, but there was also no motivation to do so. Beyond that, the idea of spending a huge amount capital up front on the first machines using a new technology until a process or supply chain could be optimized was entirely unappealing even if the capital was dedicated.

The OEMs were not aiming for highly differentiated hardware and their business needs were met with plastic cases that afforded flexibility in design and components. In practice, they often felt software was more differentiating than hardware, which was somewhat counterintuitive. The aggregate gross margin achievable in a PC software load was a multiple of the margin on the entire base hardware of a PC. The latest and coolest Android tablet was a fancy one made by Samsung, with a plastic case. The rise of Android, a commodity platform, all but guaranteed more plastic, lower quality screens, swappable parts, and the resulting lower prices.

The OEMs were not in a battle to take share from Apple. They were more than happy to take share from each other. Apple laptop share was vastly smaller than the next bigger OEM making Windows laptops. Each OEM would tell us they could double the size of their entire company by taking share from the other OEMs. That's just how they viewed the opportunity. The OEMs were smart businesspeople.

Thinking we needed to build hardware, then building it, was one order of magnitude of challenge. Choosing to bring a product to mass market was another. Hardware is complicated, complex, expensive, and risky—risky on the face of it and seen as risky by Microsoft's best customers.

The Surface team, organized within the Entertainment and Devices division home to keyboards and mice, finished the first release of their namesake computer. It was a Windows Vista-powered table like the ones popular in bars, pizza places, and hotel lobbies in the 1980s when they ran Frogger. The new platform software provided the cool demos for Windows 7 touch. Surface came about from a research project rooted in long term efforts around optics and display technology. The effort was *productized* as the original Surface, with Panos Panay (PanosP) brought in to help accomplish that from the peripherals group. Unfortunately, the commercial viability of the table was limited. RobbieB, the executive of the division (that also included Xbox and phones), was looking to offload the effort or better said make Windows pay for it.

We would move the team over to take on our hardware challenge if we could figure out an arrangement that would not torpedo the Windows business. It was this step that put a halt to all previous projects.

Managing what could become a first-party hardware effort from within the Windows team posed significant challenges, even obstacles. PC OEMs would rightfully become unglued if they believed the decidedly limited, information they shared with MikeAng's ecosystem team about their plans was shared with other OEMs. If their information were to be shared with a first-party team, that would be even worse. Some of the earliest concerns expressed to regulators about Microsoft had to do with the walls, or lack thereof, between different parts of the

Microsoft ecosystem and competitive parts in Microsoft, for example, between Windows and Office, where Office might have an unfair advantage. I had no desire to further a conspiracy theory.

JulieLar offered her own set of challenges, but almost the opposite in nature. She was concerned about having a first-party hardware team that acted like an OEM more than a part of Microsoft. She wanted our hardware to fully embrace, not mangle, the Metro design language. I hardly wanted a team that would embrace the economics of OEM, such as *crapware* and expensive accessories.

Collectively we wanted a decidedly non-OEM to be our OEM.

Both Julie and Mike spent a lot of time with Panos to help us all arrive at a structure and work process that was set up for success. Panos joined Microsoft in 2006, relatively recently, after working at NMB Technologies, an expansive 60-year-old Japanese maker of electronics components including keyboard switches and skateboard ball-bearings that I used to pay top dollar for in middle school. The complexities for Panos in jumping into the thicket of Windows were significant, not to mention the delicate nature of first-party PCs. The concerns for all parties were legitimate.

The idea of a whole hardware team moving over, rather than building one organically, was worrisome, but we did not have the time to start from scratch. By most any measure, the idea that in about 30 months we would have a new ultramodern PC built on all new components the industry had never used before by a team that had only made a table computer was crazy. Panos's commitment to being part of the massive effort was not just significant but deeply sincere. He saw the opportunity the same way we did—a chance to reimagine Microsoft.

Working for Mike, Panos would expand the team in every dimension. Hiring and growing engineers for hardware, firmware, mechanical, plastic, manufacturing, acoustic, industrial, and safety, with designers from graphical to industrial to packaging, along with all the support functions I neglected to mention in that long list. We even had to embark on some special construction in the buildings to account for the needs of the kind of equipment required to build a PC.

WDS was formed in June 2010 just as we were beginning to code Windows 8. We did not even send out an org announcement mail, keeping with the secrecy of the project. The name "Surface" moved over with the team and would naturally stick with the device when we were ready to bring it to the public. For now, codenames and codewords were in order. Not just one codename, but an entire system of codenames. We had codenames for every part including unique codenames used for each vendor – part combination. There were codenames for every presentation. Over the course of the project, we maintained over 200 codenames. Why? The secrecy was to maintain our commitment to keeping information separate.

It is worth noting, we were piloting ARM work on NVIDIA Tegra hardware and seeding any groups across the company with ODM-style tablets housing Tegra components. No one inside Microsoft lacked hardware for testing, evaluating, or betting on Windows on ARM.

The next 18 months were the most remarkable sprint in hardware development I could have ever imagined. Panos built an extremely tight and remarkably talented team to deliver products in relatively short time. Everyone stepped it up to a new level. One of the most critical aspects of assembling this team was his direct manager, MikeAng, who created a cocoon around the team, isolating them from all the forces internally. Mike also mentored Panos on the product development methods used to create Windows while apprising him of the best ways to integrate with the software team to avoid thinking like an OEM—the key problem we set out to solve.

One of the things that Mike had to do which was super valuable for the whole effort was to be the "vault" for information about Surface and information about the PC ecosystem. The two orgs, Ecosystem and Surface, could have absolutely no information leakage between them. In many ways, the integrity of the Windows business model was in Mike's hands. It was easy to trust Mike since I'd worked with him since he joined Microsoft out of college, and his post-Microsoft career included becoming a lawyer, so I think it is fair to say he was the perfect person for this role. As we'll see it was just a bonus that he was exactly the right kind of engineer for this role as well.

The core of the WDS team had previously worked together, but the scale of their previous projects was small by comparison—everything was bigger in Windows. The team doubled from the early days of mice and keyboards to a broad range of peripherals and most recently Xbox consoles. Ten years in, Xbox was selling about ten million units a year (about 800,000 in 2021) and the business remained roughly break-even due to console margins. We had much grander aspirations.

The story of the two devices, both tablet form factors, that became the first Surface PCs was one of incredible design and engineering efforts going through a remarkable series of iterations in an incredibly short time and then scaling to manufacture millions. It was also a blur. Creating a PC was new for me as well. It is not only fair, but important, to say that without the collaboration across Julie's product team, JonDe's engineering team, GrantG's test team, and Julie herself, we would not have Surface. Jensen Harris (JensenH) and the entire UEX development provided an attention to detail on everything from the BIOS boot screen the on-screen keyboard, sound scheme, to the out of box experience that rivaled anything Apple did. It is one thing to build a reference PC within the walls of Microsoft—something done many times before. It is entirely another thing to deliver the innovation and scale of products that we did, and then bring it to a worldwide market.

I cannot stress enough how much of a whole-organization effort Surface was.

We did not set out to build what the industry was calling a consumer tablet or a tablet for consuming information and lightweight computing needs, as many, or just Apple, characterized the tablet market relative to the PC market. The world did not need more of that. Microsoft's heritage and business rested with productivity, so the overarching goal was to create a PC that was great for productivity, creation, and mainstream information work. The PC would just happen to fit the current definition of a tablet, which was smaller than an 11.6" laptop and usable as a screen and a traditional laptop posture.

To justify building our own hardware we needed a unique point of view.

We believed that if we could build a tablet that worked fantastically well for the web and Office, while being ultra-lightweight and ultra-reliable, we could redefine the device that constituted the bulk of PCs used in school and work. One of our most significant challenges was that the narrative for new devices was a dominated by tablet, meaning a keyboardless slate focused on consumption. This created the situation that even if we achieved our vision technically, we had an enormous communications challenge.

The first Microsoft device, code-named GT or Georgetown for no real reason, was a premium ARM tablet able to deliver on the promise of PC-style mobile productivity. The whole point of building hardware as a first party was to do what the PC ecosystem would likely struggle or simply decline to do, and ARM was first among the challenges faced. The PC makers had all been struggling to enter the smartphone market, and ARM required a significant amount of product engineering and investment that was inconsistent with the low-priced mindset. Besides, they were fully occupied with Netbooks and later Ultrabooks and seeing little success with smartphones. As described in section 101, those OEMs working with ARM were genuinely enthused and supportive, but somewhat like Detroit's reaction to electric cars, the internal tension proved too great to create and bring to market ARM, at least for the launch of Windows 8.

Whether premium implied premium price along with a premium experience was an ongoing debate. Typically, in hardware designs, manufacturers work backward from a retail price goal, assuming a certain BOM, margins, volume to manufacture (impacting the BOM or bill of materials), marketing and sales costs, returns, and so on. As product makers, this makes intellectual sense, but it frontloads so many constraints that rarely do great products emerge. I chose to start from the user scenario and see how far we could go and what we could get for what price, knowing that as we converged difficult decisions would arise.

This was a point of constant discussion with SteveB, who—and this was not news or even unique to this project—favored low prices and high volumes. Gaining market share was always preferable and what had gotten Microsoft to where it was. I felt this time we needed to take a different approach—reimagine what a Windows device could be even if that meant we start at the high end, perhaps like Tesla was doing at the time with Elon Musk's famously not-so-secret secret plan to iterate to a lower price with greater scale, funding that iteration with earlier high-priced products.

Early in the process, Mike and Panos set the tone for the role WDS would play in the overall strategy for Windows 8. It was extraordinarily helpful. The mantra for the joint efforts of hardware and software coming together was expressed as, "our job is to build a stage, a stage for the operating system and software." This fit well with the whole design for Windows 8 software, which itself was viewed as a stage for apps and user creations. The idea that every layer of the system was trying to get out of the way of the other layers above aligned entirely with the Metro design language, and also exactly what no one ever did, especially OEMs. This was in stark contrast to typical PCs and even typical OS iterations of the past, which felt the need to announce themselves whether via branding (those *Designed for Windows* or *Intel Inside* stickers, for example, that don't even appear on Apple laptops because they drove Steve Jobs crazy) or via icons, popups, or notifications.

We were not designing the hardware experience after the software experience (or before); rather, we were designing the hardware and software experience together—a reimagined experience.

I tried to keep my own role in check. I'd seen many past hardware cycles within the company where there was so much going up and down the chain, so much approval, and so much tweaking by executives. Plus, it is crazy easy to have an opinion on a device and act like some enlightened big-shot executive. Panos's experience with executives at Microsoft rightfully made him wary of me at first. Executives often had an outsized view of their contribution while underestimating the amount of work, backchannel, and eyerolling they caused. Advertising, pricing, user interface design, and feedback on hardware were places that executives easily meddled. And for that, teams suffered.

I used a lot of different laptops. I bought nearly every iPad typing cover available and there were dozens as the choice from Apple was so limited. I was a road warrior, so I was real-time testing. I used browsing, email, and Office a lot. I could have probably justified my own opinions, and many times I really wanted to, but had to resist the urge. I had asked Mike and Panos to pull off what by any measure would be a Herculean task. My responsibility was not to meddle.

From my vantage point in developing the product, there were five inflection points in the design process—a high-altitude view since there were thousands of choices made in developing the product. At some level these were choices to be made or constraints. The project could have easily become impossible or careened off path with so many potential degrees of freedom. Anyone who looked at the typical roundup of PC laptop reviews for back to school or holiday was left browsing a dizzying array of specs, ports, dimensions, and component choices. It would have been easy to get lost in all these decisions to be made. Each one of those decisions is related to many others in an ever-complex set of linear equations to be optimally solved.

The team picked these key points in the design process: chipset, the productivity posture, typing, materials, and peripherals.

By establishing the initial platform of ARM and a sub-11" form factor many of the traditional "spec" issues of designing the device would fall out. But this understates just how many and how fast, Panos and team needed to put constraints in place—constraints that would maintain a point of view and deliver a product.

The chipset was perhaps the most straightforward choice for the team to make on technical grounds, though hardly without controversy or for lack of a better word politics. There was a good deal of pressure from the Windows Phone team and from some OEM partners who were still trying to build phones of their own (though on Android now) to go with Qualcomm. Qualcomm was viewed as a safe choice and the choice with the most intellectual property and lawyers to support that. On the other hand, the early hardware was far from ready to build a PC especially the graphics support which was so critical. It was the first taste of developing a product where the choices had implications beyond building the best experience. My own view from dealing with Qualcomm was that they were more concerned with the volume of devices we would commit to up front than with the quality or innovation we would deliver, even early in the process.

The teams working across Windows porting to ARM were favorable to NVIDIA given the choices we had. In particular, NVIDIA was strongest on graphics which were key to the Metro-style experience. The underlying graphics chips mapped closely to our DirectX API and made developing device drivers supporting the animations and effects we needed with the performance we required as straightforward as could be given all that was new. Aside from that NVIDIA was a joyful partner and great at working with ODMs to supply test hardware.

Ralf Groene (RalfG) led hardware design efforts for WDS. He joined Microsoft with a classic design education and experience at several marquee design houses in Silicon Valley. If we were casting a movie for an industrial designer, Ralf would be perfect. RalfG and the design team were cycling through prototypes of sizes and overall form factors at an incredible pace. Engineering for productivity and typing fell to the design team, with a very strong collaboration with the UEX team to make sure the software could gracefully adapt to the presence or absence of a keyboard and trackpad.

The kickstand was such an amazing choice. Yet I lack a clear recollection of the genesis of it, only that the moment I saw it I was convinced it was an inspired choice. Having a kickstand solved the main problem tablets had, which is how to keep using one when you wanted to put it down or more importantly to type. The kickstand could easily have been a gimmick but in fact it became an iconic element and one that served to further the point of view centered on the dual modalities of consuming content hands-free and full-time work on the go. The kickstand would have tradeoffs in real-world usability, especially with the larger devices to come later, but the for the first generation I felt it was exactly the tradeoff to make.

The design team iterated with a kickstand, something that had been found on some early media players and phones. Should the kickstand be two small legs, one fatter leg, or something else? Should it support both landscape and portrait? The team settled on a full-width kickstand, almost a fold-out foot that provided a rock-solid level of stability. That stability came from a unique hinge design, created entirely by the mechanical engineers on the team. Opening and closing the hinge had the feel and robustness of a luxury car door, a German one of course. As the hinge closed the air dampening effect would give the motion a soft cushion with a nearly inaudible, but intentionally there, sound of luxury. I once spent time in the lab with the mechanical engineer on the team amazed at just the complexity and number of choices that were considered in the design and fabrication of the hinge. It was a great example of how every small detail is vastly more complex than readily apparent.

The beauty of the hinge and kickstand were that they reduced the thickness of the whole productivity scenario by quite a bit—the plastic cases of the iPad including Apple's own cases were true compromises. The 2015 Folio, which added two layers of material in a complicated origami-folding design and later the 2018 Magic keyboard, which was just heavy at 600 grams or 130 grams more than the iPad itself, were both awkward. The latter keyboard added so much weight and thickness to the iPad that it was more practical to carry a laptop. Whereas Steve Jobs had to sit in a chair holding the iPad, with Surface one could hold it or flip out the kickstand and watch the move while enjoying popcorn, or having a video conference with the integrated HD webcam angled precisely enough so it would capture your head and not neck or below when placed on a table.

Important for the productivity posture was the overall size. When working, a screen can never be too big, but when traveling a screen can never be too small. Finding the balance was super important. The math would work out super well to have a screen that was 10.6-inch diagonal but with a widescreen layout of 16x9, the typical HD or Blu-Ray numbers. At 1366x768 the screen was equally optimal for the new Windows 8 snap view to show two apps side-by-side—GT as a stage for Windows 8—and also to display movies full screen without the drawbacks of letterbox modification that consumers hated.

There was quite a bit if a debate over 16:10 versus 16:9 aspect ratio and the possible screen resolutions. UEX favored the extra width of 16:9, though 16:10 offered more vertical space for productivity but could not support side-by-side apps. The availability of components and cost of using the UEX preference made it a tough choice. This was also an area where we were going against the iPad trend which picked a more traditional even old 4:3 aspect ratio used on NTSC TV and VGA monitors at 1024x786 which was also criticized in reviews for letterboxing widescreen video. The iPad was between wide screen video and the traditional trade book and Amazon Kindle aspect ratio of 3:2.

From a supply chain and manufacturing perspective, the choice was more complex. The supply chain for screens was following the volume of all manufacturers combined. No single manufacturer could simply order a size not being used by others without committing to volume. In 2011 the dominant size for tablets was a 10.1" screen with 1280x800 resolution, a 16:10 aspect ratio. We saw the 1280x800 resolution as a waypoint, picked for price by the Android tablet ecosystem. It was neither good for productivity in landscape nor good for reading in portrait mode.

We were deeply committed to having a screen that supported the side-by-side view of two apps in landscape. This came with a real tradeoff, however, in the usability as a pure tablet. In other words, even from the choice of screen we were optimizing for productivity. When used as a "reading tablet" the portrait mode orientation of 9:16 was particularly awkward. Reading with one hand holding the device was tiresome, like holding a college chemistry textbook in bed. Additionally, traditional laptops with 13" or 15" screens had moved in large numbers with Windows 7 to the 16:9 and 1366x768 resolution, indicating that resolution was an excellent design point for apps and would be around for years to come.

The screen had two other technical issues to work through with significant impact on the experience. First, the core display technology for LCD screens was in the midst of a transition from MVA (Multi-Domain Vertical Alignment) to IPS (In-Plane Switching) with the latter being the newer technology. Going with the newer technology would be preferred as a basis for applying a touch sensor, but that further constrained the potential supplies and sizes.

Second, the display panel would need an extra stage in manufacturing to attach a touch panel sensor. There were two approaches here as well. The standard approach, again for Android tablets, was known as air-bonding. In this technique the touch panel does not directly touch the underlying display panel leaving a small gap which eases manufacturing. Unfortunately, this also introduces parallax, an effect by which where you touch and where the sensor detects your touch do not always align in your brain. This is seen at check-out counters and ATMs which prefer the manufacturability and low-cost of this approach. While cheaper, it is a disaster for precision work on a PC. The newer approach, direct bonding, used by Apple and more premium tablets, directly bonded the touch sensor to the display. This was more expensive and had a non-trivial defect rate increasing costs as well.

The way you know from the supply chain that you are asking for something difficult is that the price goes up and delivery goes further out. The suppliers, all singing from the same page, strongly encouraged a 16:10 screen with 1280x800. Their view was that this was the volume tablet resolution. After many trips and many meetings, we were able to secure a high-volume supply of the 10.6", 1366x768, IPS, direct bonded screen. This was a tough choice and added early risk, but once you lock in a supplier as a volume partner risk finds a way of decreasing. I suspect over time even for the 10.6" screen we would have gone with a more comfortable aspect ratio, but by then we would have had more answers to windowing and productivity than we had with Windows 8. I'm getting ahead of myself.

Productivity without a keyboard is not really productivity. We were not confused about this point as they were in Cupertino. Productivity without a mouse or trackpad, on the desktop, was not even possible. Because Windows RT had the desktop and desktop Office, a trackpad was required. The 10.6-inch diagonal screen would create a case with a 10.1-inch long edge, which by no accident was wide enough for a nearly full-size home row of keys for touch typists. This could be a huge advantage over the keyboard for the iPad, which was only 9.5 inches across, making a big difference in key size and spacing. Our screen size allowed for arrow keys and a row of function keys with the trackpad. These small differences bring a world of benefits when designing devices with which people have such intimate reactions. This is decidedly different than a desktop PC or even a large laptop. There's something about a device that must be held that makes small decisions so much more important.

The keyboard presented a unique opportunity to innovate to maximize portability. Panos himself personally an expert in mechanical keyboards and part of Microsoft's own efforts in innovative keyboards was well-positioned to develop two keyboards we would introduce with GT.

Fundamental to the keyboard was the idea that it would be faster and more accurate than touch typing on a glass screen and include a trackpad for precision, or "professional," pointing as so many reviews of iPad noted was lacking. Since GT had a kickstand, the keyboard did not need to also serve as a redundant cover for the back but when folded to cover the screen would offer screen protection. The underside of the keyboard was covered with a layer of what I always termed northwest fleece with a soft woolen feel when carrying GT around in your hand.

Our folding keyboard could make an easy transition from productivity and typing to reading or watching while lounging around. The keyboard itself was a touch-based invention from Stevie Batiche (StevieB), who was the resident scientist/engineer leading all things touch and display, and a genius. We would also add a very thin mechanical keyboard, one of the thinnest mechanical keyboards ever released to market. Our hearts would be with the touch keyboard at launch owing to its productivity and on the go scenario.

StevieB's ultrathin keyboard invention was essentially a touch panel with ever-so-slightly raised key outlines impressed on the panel. The electronics were created by laminating several layers of materials including a touch sensor and all the "wiring" together in a hot press machine—sort of a touch screen sandwich. The keyboard, called Touch Cover, was a mere 3.2mm and weighed only 7 ounces and under 200 grams. Given the dimensions of the screen, Touch Cover was able to incorporate a trackpad on par with many small laptop trackpads and a complete set of laptop keys including dedicated keys for Windows 8 charms along the top row, which also doubled as traditional PC function keys. In US English even the F and J keys had slight outward impressions for traditional typists to find the home row. There would be many skeptics about the keyboard when it came to typing proficiency. While there were many risks in the entire project, at the time Touch Cover seemed like the riskiest part of the project. It would be so immediately visible and open to snap opinions. The press that typed for a living were used to their preferred "feel" when it came to laptop keyboards, often a sore spot for just about every Windows laptop review.

GT had a beautiful hinge and an incredible touch keyboard, but how to attach the keyboard posed another challenge. Because of the hinge the cover could not be attached to the back of GT, but that would be dumb anyway—adding weight with no purpose was what we saw on the iPad. Once again, the mechanical engineers had a go at the problem. They put magnets to work. Not just any magnets, but a series of magnets of exactly the right strength to support the device, even swinging it from the keyboard, while also easy to remove. The magnets did not just attach the keyboard to the tablet, but they were the connectors for the signal and power. Attaching the keyboard had to perfectly align the connectors or it would not work.

The magnetic keyboard was a more difficult to path to perfection and reliability. Upon first seeing it, just as most others, I was skeptical. Would it fall off? Would it properly align even when connected in a sloppy manner? Would flipping it around to use as just a tablet prove "goofy" or would it really work? Would Windows correctly enable the on-screen keyboard at the right time and get out of the way entirely when a keyboard was attached? Would it work just as well for the thin mechanical model?

The process of connecting the keyboard to the device proved to be more than just reliable but something of a signature. The first time we showed the Surface to the team that would lead creating television commercials they immediately connected with the "click" sound the engineering team worked so hard to get right. That click would become the centerpiece of the initial campaign along with the profile of GT and the keyboard. A subdued version of a magnetic connector also with a click would be used for the very small charging adapter. Ironically, Apple's pioneering MagSafe connector that was so popular on MacBooks was not used on iPad, which took its lead from iPhone for charging. Even today Apple continues to struggle with magnets when it comes to covers and keyboard cases for the iPad. The new 2022 iPad typing portfolio with a kickstand is kind of a mess.

The removable keyboard provided several advantages. To compete in the "pure" tablet market the keyboard could be priced optionally and also be reviewed as an accessory versus required. It also permitted personalization by choice of colors since the laminating process was able to substitute any color materials for the back or front. The back of the Touch Cover could be customized in both material and look, for example corporate logos or art as we later offered. Finally, StevieB's innovative touch panel was not restricted to keys and could be used to create any touch surface. Since it could be removed easily, we envisioned the potential to have specialized Touch Covers dedicated to specific applications. One example we showed early on was a synthesizer drum app mated to a custom keyboard. At a small, private event held one night in Los Angeles I even had a chance to watch actor/musician Zack Efron of *High School Musical* have fun with the prototype music generating cover.

The materials choice for inner fame and device case were almost always where the OEMs made choices that were best for the bottom line—plastic provided low cost, light weight, rigidity, ample room for cooling, and agility across component and peripheral changes. This is where Microsoft's ability to provide a significant investment could make a real difference in the final product. The engineering challenge with case materials is the triangle of cost, weight, and rigidity. Cost is not only the cost of the material, but the manufacturing cost of making the case, with all the curves, holes, and cutouts that make it a computer. Materials can be inexpensive and lightweight but too flexible to be durable—the screen is glass and needs structure to prevent it from flexing and breaking. Materials can be rigid and lightweight but cost a tremendous amount, such as ceramics used in fighter jets. Aluminum is lightweight and relatively rigid, but to bring the cost down Apple invested a huge amount of upfront capital in order to take blocks of aluminum and use mechanical milling to turn it into a PC.

We needed the device to be as thin as possible and from the start we considered every fractional millimeter we could save. We knew that bringing over Windows in one product cycle, including the desktop, would bring real challenges to our ability to compete with the nine hours of video playback possible on the iPad. We needed every available millimeter for battery. An innovation in materials could prove a game-changer.

In research, the materials scientists became intrigued by a relatively new process of injection molding a magnesium alloy. Such a material was expensive and the manufacturing process complex, but the resulting parts were lighter than machined aluminum, extremely rigid and strong, and created by more flexible molding. At this point, the injection molding process had only been used for small parts such as watch frames or jet engine components, but the materials partner, Mike, and Panos's team thought it possible to use for the much larger cases. The material could be readily colored via a permanent and robust vapor deposition process, which afforded other opportunities.

MikeAng, a mechanical engineer by training and certified alloy welder, dove into the process, visiting the factory in Asia. He returned with movies of cases being injection molded that looked like scenes from 20th century industrial America—sparks flying, molten flows of metal, giant machine presses.

Betting GT on this new process was one of the more uncertain aspects of the hardware design, and also very expensive, relatively. The high upfront costs made us all nervous. With any upfront cost, called NRE, or non-recurring engineering costs, the only way of justifying them is to make a lot of the product which spread the cost across many devices. That was certainly our intent.

The material would get the name *VaporMg*, pronounced vapor mag. Finished in a smooth, so smooth, black-gray, the material was another manifestation of the collective efforts of design, materials, and manufacturing coming together. While we originally planned to make the entire case out of VaporMg, supply constraints resulted in a more traditional aluminum frame with VaporMg used more sparingly. While that resulted in a bit of increased weight, the resulting scaled manufacturing and cost reduction were a good tradeoff.

There's no doubt that VaporMg was the most extravagant choice in the whole project and one I felt the most over-extended in considering. In a big company with plenty of money, it is not uncommon to see branching out into new areas take on almost comically bad cost controls relative to industry norms. Without experience or baselines to compare and with all the excitement of "those other people doing this must be dumb" it is so easy to do this. Across the product, Mike, Panos, and team had extremely good controls and constant attention to the BOM, bill of materials, and NRE. Mike was a product of our frugalness in Office and brought that to this project and team. The VaporMg choice was one I felt we should go with even though it was so uncharacteristic for me or much of Microsoft.

One thing we considered was that we could reuse the materials process and plant capacity with other OEMs and license it to them for whatever devices they wanted to build. The idea of acting as a source for various components was a step we considered for trackpads and touchscreens as well as we saw OEMs unwilling or unable to take on the NRE costs to create competitive laptops. Once again though, I probably failed to consider they also viewed such costs unnecessary when it came to their share battle competing with other OEMs more than competing with Apple.

VaporMg was so strong that the team turned a standard GT chassis into a skateboard, on a lark. As a former skateboarder this thrilled me to no end. At one of the many press events hosted on campus offering a behind-the-scenes look at developing hardware, I skated around the lobby of Studio A. Not to worry, I was wearing a helmet though it was a borrowed bike helmet we located just for the photos. We snapped some photos that continue to live on. To further demonstrate the strength of the material, we showed off the drop-test machine that simulated dropping a tablet with different forces and angles and even directly on the kickstand—each time GT performed admirably. Protected by the Touch Cover, the combination felt relatively indestructible. The screen was securely protected without any extra casing on the back maintaining the thin profile and light weight.

Finally, productivity for a premium laptops and tablets circa 2012 still depended on wires or more specifically dongles. Apple's MacBook Air approach of wireless everything was conceptually great but practically a pain, certainly in the early days. Carrying around dongles to connect to projectors or to USB devices was annoying and error prone. As a tool for productivity, GT needed to show up at a meeting and get handed the slides on a USB drive, pop the drive in, launch PowerPoint, and then connect to a projector, or handle devices like microphones and speakers. As a stage for Windows 8, we had optimized this type of flow from a performance and user interface perspective—get to the user's work product and get to work as quickly as possible.

Mike and Panos framed GT as a device that should connect in the way people needed it to connect. GT had a standard USB port, standard audio output, and a mini-HDMI port in addition to the dedicated magnetic-charging connector. The USB port was rather tricky as it set a minimum thickness that was not an issue on the iPad that did not have a universal USB connector. The fat USB port was a bit ugly and some on the industrial design team referred to it as a "missing tooth" in an otherwise sleek profile. At one point we were so close to the standard for a connector we risked losing the trade group designation and permission to use the logo. This in addition to strong support in hardware and software for all the current wireless protocols for Wi-Fi and Bluetooth including support for wireless speakers and displays. This array of connectivity defined the soul of the device and shouted out point of view that the device was not a peripheral but a full computer.

Power adapters had become the bane of my existence as someone who used a variety of devices at home and work and travel. It was still too early to have a standard connector—Apple was still using the wide pin connector, which was painful and finnicky despite the super nice magnetic connector. GT created an ultra-skinny magnetic connector. I was, however, much more interested in the power *brick*. I could not stand the typical PC that had a three-foot cord to the PC, then a brick, then *another* three-foot cord to the wall. It turned out people in Japan disliked those too and Yodobashi Camera came to the rescue with an aftermarket model, a single 2-meter cable with a brick at one end with folding prongs. I stocked up on those. I really wanted GT to have an adapter with simple folding prongs. I wanted this so much I didn't even bother to ask about non-US plugs. As a constant traveler, I was also cursed with hotel rooms with too few outlets. Back then I almost always had to unplug a lamp which usually involved moving furniture around. I often traveled with an after-market phone charger that had an extra pass-through outlet to charge a USB device. I needed this because PC USB ports did not charge when the PC went into standby, which I usually discovered at 6 a.m. local time.

OK, so I meddled once after complaining one too many times.

One day RalfG invited me over to the studio and brought me through dozens of models for power adapters. I knew as soon as I got to the studio that Panos was managing me, but in a way that was entirely OK given how close we'd become. As we walked from 3-D model to model, I opined and envisioned about what it would be like in a hotel room. They explained to me all sorts of stuff about thermals, tolerances, UL standards, and even patents. One company had a patent on prongs that folded into power bricks! I picked the smallest adapter with folding prongs and a built-in USB charger. I like to think this was another iconic choice. It was not. It was merely useful. Ultimately, GT did not have a USB port on the charger but did have folding prongs. The second device had the USB port I wanted on a slightly higher-powered charger.

From the project start we had been considering a second device. Early on, Mike had suggested to me that the team could build a desktop all-in-one using a screen with the next generation touch panel technology from the Surface table running an Intel processor. This device was the concept for a follow-on or successor to Surface table. It was a beautiful device. The prototype followed the same lines and hinge as would appear much later after many iterations as the Surface Studio all-in-one.

We really wanted to showcase desktop productivity, especially the all-in-one form factor, which had no presence with PCs. Apple made all-in-one Macs as their desktop Mac and those, as with iPads and MacBook Air, made their way into every movie, high-end retailer, and boutique office setting. An all-in-one with the GT premium aesthetic could put Windows in those spots too.

PC makers finally decided to wed the displays they were making with the laptop parts they made to create all-in-ones competitive with Apple iMac. Windows 7 saw a broad introduction of low-cost and reasonably performant all-in-ones, which was great to see.

The arrival of PC all-in-ones and the reality that the next generation screen technology was not ready, especially in a large size and at scale led to us abandoning the all-in-one product. A good deal of work had gone into the basics of developing an Intel PC, which presented us with an opportunity.

Standing around the now defunct all-in-one prototype, we discussed the idea of creating an Intel-based GT with the Surface BOM, or a derivative of it. At first, I thought this was entirely against the spirit of the project as it would simply compete with our OEM partners and cause more of a rift than not. At the same time, I'd been so happy with the progress we were making while equally aware of the limitations customers would see in ARM-based Surface. The early prototype tablets like the \\build Samsung had the promise of being great tablets for using and testing Windows 8 apps while also working as platforms to build those apps or use any existing x86 Windows development tools.

Would the existence of a Microsoft-branded Intel device help address customer concerns, or would it create more confusion? Would OEMs see such a device as an inspiration, or would it further annoy them? What would Intel think?

I had many concerns about forging ahead with an Intel-based PC coming from Microsoft. It did not seem prudent. Frankly, it felt more like an extra poke at OEMs when our main goals were embodied in the ARM-based device.

What could we offer uniquely as a stage for Windows 8? The Ultrabook investments were ongoing, but Intel's specifications called for them to be large-screen devices for Intel-specific channel strategies. Everything that was a tablet or Netbook-like computer, less than Ultrabooks, on Intel was running low end chips that had mediocre performance on Windows. What if we mated mainstream laptop chips, Intel Core, to the GT form factor? We would have an ultraportable Intel-based Windows 8 device in an ultra-convenient Netbook-sized package. There was nothing like it in market, an ultra-portable Ultrabook.

The team took this as an opportunity to up-level all the specifications from GT. More of everything including a full HD screen, faster USB, support for dual monitors, bigger battery, more memory, and storage, and by default it would use the Type Cover with mechanical keys. We were super confident in the Touch Cover, but we saw in early usage that it did not have the throughput for a full-time professional user on this professional-oriented device. We weren't going to be religious about it and quickly adapted.

The up-leveled GT could in fact contribute something that would help enormously to smooth over the risk of building hardware. We could offer a super high-quality pen experience, exactly what BillG wanted. Since the device would be more portable, resembling a typical paper notebook, lighter than scarcely available Tablet PCs, it might prove to be the ultimate pen-based notetaking device. The fact that we could focus an Intel SKU on the pen and handwriting and deliver a size that the OEMs were not considering provided a reasonable justification in favor of the device plan. The up-leveled GT filled an obvious gap in the whole ecosystem lineup.

Why did we not put a pen on GT? The power draw and thickness of another layer added by the current state-of-the-art pen digitizer would impact the competitiveness with iPad. Prioritizing the ARM device to be competitive with hardware specs of the iPad was a key factor, and a good tradeoff for us to make. Given my own reticence about the pen it was also an easy tradeoff, though I had to repeatedly defend it with BillG.

This was enough positive and with MikeAng we considered or gamed out how the OEMs would respond to an x86 device. Our main point was that the OEMs were focused on Ultrabooks in order to gain the advantages of Intel pricing. Our device would fall outside Ultrabook specs and thus prove more innovative and less part of the crowded Ultrabook space.

From my perspective, I viewed the device as an objection handler. It was a way to signal to the market that Windows 8, the x86 product, was well-suited to playing in this new world. Instead of a focus on ultra-mobile and all-day battery life, the focus was on power and all the needs of professionals in an ultra-mobile package. This reflected the early reviews of Windows 8 and the challenges we were having with the tablet narrative as put forth by Apple and reviewers.

GTX, or *Montlake*, was the code name for this second device. It looked bit like a puffed-up GT. Unlike GT, GTX would have all standard Windows PC components from the chipset to the BIOS to storage and RAM. It would also have a fan, and to mitigate that the team developed innovative cooling slots all around the device to keep internals from overheating or creating a hot-to-the-touch exterior. By virtue of it being Intel based, GTX had noise and heat that GT did not, and had about half the battery life more typical of the real-world numbers being seen for the first generation Ultrabooks, about 4-5 hours, compared to the 9+ hours we would see with GT.

GTX was about three months behind GT. I was clear that GT was the priority should trade-offs in any dimension be required. By the time we announced GT we would announce that GTX would be available three months later. For many that gap felt amateurish compared to the most recent Apple launches which had announced new devices on a Tuesday for sale on a Friday. As we know now, that was not the long-term norm for Apple nor was it how the iPad, Apple Watch, or other devices launched since. Nevertheless, Apple was doing everything right at the time so as agile as I thought we were, it was still less than was expected of us.

By the early spring of 2012, the manufacturing team started making small runs of test devices. It took months of work to scale up an assembly line, and it was expensive to make devices in any quantity for testing. Plus, everything was top secret. We had made about 1,000 test ARM devices partnering with NVIDIA, which were being used mostly in labs. They were also shared with teams across Microsoft contributing to WOA under the strictest security protocols. We never had enough of these test machines for everyone who might have wanted one to just check out, but we had enough to build the software across Windows, Developer, and Office. These devices cost over $1,000 each and were great to have but decidedly test machines. I was still using our NVIDIA test device, but, as with anyone who knew about GT, I was anxious.

Time was passing both slowly and quickly. We were closing in on finishing the Windows 8 software schedule, August 2012, which meant time was slow as each day fewer and fewer code changes were made. GT, however, was getting close to the point where it was time to commit to manufacturing. Spinning up a line means you want to ramp it to full capacity and not stop, otherwise we'd just be burning cash.

Surprisingly, there were absolutely no leaks. Even across Microsoft no one suspected anything, certainly not first-party hardware. With Windows 8 RTM approaching, the overall messaging for our reimagining point of view would start to diffuse through Microsoft. That meant talking about hardware. At a regularly scheduled Board Meeting I was asked to provide an update on Windows 8. As the code was essentially done and we had broad disclosure already there was little to do but assure the Board that we were on track and to discuss the worries we all collectively shared. The Board, however, had not yet seen the final GT hardware. In many previous meetings we discussed ARM and the strategy, including building first-party hardware, and I had previously shown demonstrations using the NVIDIA testing prototype. My sense was that the gravity of the decision to make first-party hardware had not really sunk in—the general view of "competing" with our OEM partners was still viewed as a challenge, especially because the Windows Phone Team had tried to create a phone but ended up partnering with Nokia, before later acquiring the company.

Whenever I spoke with the Board, I was always excited to show the progress of our product—so long as we were ready to, and it would not be over-promising or confusing. I would almost always drive a demo myself casually and without much fanfare—not only was this more authentic, but it also permitted a more casual interaction. With GT I did just that. At one point I just pulled it out of my bag and began to show it off just as we had been doing in incredibly limited ways. The pitch was easy because it was what we had aimed to build. Promise and deliver.

The Board and SteveB, however, were much more focused on the big decision to sell first-party hardware and the bottom-line impact to the overall Microsoft P&L and earnings. I think the Board was still smarting from the Xbox write-off five years earlier. This ended up being the discussion, which seemed awkward to me as we had articulated this as the strategy from the start of the project. At the meeting, I was starting to get the feeling that I had in 2001 when we suddenly backtracked on the fully-baked Office.NET product plan. Only this time I felt I had laid all the groundwork and had discussed this at several other meetings. In hindsight, I suppose it was the reality of seeing the actual device and that we were delivering that made it all seem that much more real.

There was a tense discussion about the costs, especially the hundreds of millions of dollars to build out the final assembly capacity and the balance of creating enough units to keep the cost down by spreading the non-recurring costs over as many units as possible but not too many that we'd flood the market. One thing I had done specifically was not play any games with the budget or expense approval. Many projects at Microsoft spent a lot of money by spending a little bit at a time so as not to exceed an executive's approval limit. My whole career, with the help of CollJ, I kept my spending authority artificially low. The spirit of my mentor JeffH was always looking over my shoulder reminding me it was Microsoft's money and not mine to spend. This meant SteveB had to approve all the spending and we would have to have the discussion up front. At the end of the meeting when the Board asked the final approver question, there was no doubt in my mind. At the same time, strategically and from the perspective of how well we had executed there was no doubt. I was accountable for the result and was certain we should move forward and said as much. SteveB and I would have several more discussions, mostly centered on the price point and volume before he hit approve on the invoicing tool.

Before the first public showing, I wanted to show the device to PaulA. Paul was an early advocate of Microsoft building hardware and had several forays into leading-edge hardware through his Vulcan Inc. company. I brought a device over to his office near the stadium used by the Seattle Seahawks. As someone who said he believed the old saying about those serious about software building hardware, Paul was excited to see what the team had accomplished. We spent most of the time in a deep discussion about hardware manufacturing, the bill of materials, and how Microsoft would scale the business. Paul's Vulcan Inc. had built an ultra-portable PC powered by a novel Transmeta chip, which aimed to be Intel-compatible and consume less power. He was profoundly connected to the challenges of making hardware and at the same time agreed on the need to do so.

We set a date for a public unveiling in mid-June 2012. Just two weeks before at the All Things Digital Conference, we wanted to make sure one reporting team got a bit of a preview, only one team. I was using my Surface RT all the time, but not in any public places, and essentially handcuffing my messenger bag to me. D10, the 2012 conference, featured Apple's Tim Cook, Mayor Michael Bloomberg, and a host of top-shelf guests, including SteveB, but no Windows demo, Phew.

We prepared to give a brief and private demo at the conference. We did not schedule any time but instead sort of set up a bit of an ambush outside on the terrace of the show's green room. I messaged show co-host Walt Mossberg and asked if we could find 15 minutes between his on-stage interviews to show him and Katherine Boehret something very cool and secret. He was intrigued and they both of course agreed.

JulieLar and I would meet them and provide a surprise sneak peak of Surface. This was the first showing to anyone outside the Microsoft "tent" to see it. I grabbed my top-secret messenger bag from the hotel safe and met Julie and our audience of two backstage.

I offered a brief lead up, reminding them of the Windows 8 vision and goal of reimagining Windows from the chipset to the experience. I then took out Surface RT from my bag and said, "So, we built a computer."

We showed them all the bells and whistles. And they were, at least by my account, speechless for a more than a brief moment. We just smiled while they took turns handling the fully functional sample.

Then they had a lot of questions. How much would it cost? What would the OEMs think? What was the battery life? When would it come to market?

Wait…would it even come to market? Katherine asked if it was a prototype or one of those PCs we built to encourage better PC design. We assured them that this was going to market as a first-party device.

Walt asked about one of his most significant issues with Windows PCs, the prevalence of crapware—that software added by PC makers to "enhance the value" by offering trials, advancing PC makers extra hardware (such as buttons to launch specific software), and other add-ons that you probably don't want but significantly impact performance. On this topic I was extremely confident in answering. The whole point of creating Surface was to show the marketplace what the very best Windows experience could be. Little did I know just how difficult it would be to maintain this seemingly obvious point of differentiation.

While I had many fun moments described here in *Hardcore Software*, this surprise for a team I respected so much was one of the highlights. I wish I had a photo of the moment.

Invitations were later sent out for a mysterious event in Los Angeles with no hints of what to expect and little notice. The venue was a Hollywood production facility, Milk Studios. More than 200 press, financial, and industry guests made their way to the sound stage the morning of June 18, 2012. Some were still complaining about the short notice, the time, the location, and the lack of detail.

On stage, SteveB introduced Microsoft's move to hardware, emphasizing that we would not let barriers between hardware and software prevent us from innovating and serving customers. At the end of his section, he unveiled Surface, not the keyboard or the kickstand or any specs. It was the CEO photo op lending all his gravitas to the event.

The stage was small but had been designed with a runway making an intimacy possible, which would become a hallmark of Surface events. The risers were beveled at 22 degrees, the same angle as the kickstand.

As I looked on, I stepped through the demo in my head for the 1,000th time. I had my Surface RT in hand with the screen polished as bright as a signal mirror, using a trick the team had of buffing with hand sanitizer and a microfiber cloth. As Steve was finishing, I touched the power button like I was supposed to and noticed the slightest little screen twitch. I brushed it off.

Rookie fucking move.

I walked out on stage, as excited as I could ever possibly have imagined. About 10,000 people had worked on what was about to be shown for the very first time. Microsoft had never done such a surprise announcement before. We had never spoken to a room of people without pre-briefing them. Everyone was on edge.

Proudly, after making my way down the narrow runway, I announced Surface, a stage for Windows 8.

Two minutes and thirty-one seconds into the presentation, I was showing the new Internet Explorer. As I touched the screen for the audience, nothing was moving.

I muttered "Oops" and skipped backwards up the runway to the demo table and grabbed the backup. What felt like ten minutes was nine seconds, the longest nine seconds of any demo I had ever done. Who crashes the hardware during a reveal we practiced two dozen times flawlessly? Me. The guy on stage who should have swapped out the machine when the screen twitched. I could physically feel Mike, Panos, and the demo team backstage cringing.

Then the teleprompter went out too.

I kept going. In a bit of stage craft, I introduced the magnetic connector and a nice cover with smooth fabric on the outside, jokingly referred to as "Fine Northwest Polartec®" (it was just nylon), an innovation as well. I attached the cover with a memorable click—that great work of the mechanical team.

I posited to the audience: Why shouldn't we do something more than cover the screen? To oohs and aahs, some gasps, and then applause, I extended the cover to reveal the full multitouch keyboard. At least that worked I thought.

The main reveals were complete. Phew. I made it through the crash. Backstage the team was despondent but also worried about how I would react. I was so disappointed in my failure to switch devices. That it happened at all still nags at me a decade later.

MikeAng then came on stage and flawlessly demonstrated the Intel-powered GTX, newly named Surface Pro, including writing on screen with a pen. I know that made a certain person back in Redmond very happy. Mike then introduced Panos. Panos detailed the team culture and design process: RalfG, StevieB, Pete Kyriacou (PeteK), Brett Ostrum (BrettO), and so many featured in a video Panos showed before a deep dive on all the technologies in the product.

We concluded and then opened up an area offstage where the press could experience the device. Despite my troubles on stage, letting them see the device in action proved the right call. It wasn't a free for all, but it was something.

As the press and guests filed to the open area, one of the best in the business stopped me. By all accounts hyperventilating, Joanna Stern then of ABC News had just one question, "How did you keep it a secret?" I like to think we got more done than that, but that was a remarkable accomplishment for Microsoft. Some inside the company would be critical of the secrecy, specifically critical of me, but especially for Surface the nature of the business required it. The test hardware running essentially the same componentry was available to all participating teams.

With the product in hand, I started to use it more regularly. Just after the show I made it a point to use it on my regular places around headquarters. I had a photo snapped while eating lunch at Kidd Valley, my favorite protein and low-glycemic index spot right by campus.

One of the most useful traits of Surface running Windows RT was how even if something failed it took only a few seconds to restart the device and get back to where I left off, especially while under development. That made it more worry-free than a Windows laptop, as we expected and designed for. It was also so fast to resume from standby, and the Metro Mail app connected to Exchange was constantly fetching email even when in standby.

When AnandTech's Anand Lal Shimpi reviewed Surface at availability in an extraordinarily detailed and in-depth review of almost 9,000 words, the conclusion was just what we hoped to achieve.[163]

> *I don't believe Surface is perfect, but it's a platform I can believe in. What I'm most excited about is to see what happens after a second or third rev of the design. [. . .]*
>
> *If you're ok being an early adopter, and ok dealing with the fact that mobile devices are still being significantly revved every year, Surface is worth your consideration. If you've wanted a tablet that could begin to bridge the content consumption and productivity divide, Surface is it.*

My first day of work I could not even get a PC the size and sound of a small refrigerator to connect to a network and run reliably. How far we'd come. I held in my hand a PC that could survive a 10-foot fall, rebooted in seconds, running the best software Microsoft ever created, weighed under 2 pounds travel weight, and easily connected everywhere. I could not be prouder of the work the team had done.

Over the summer as the product wound down, we began planning for what would come next. This almost sounds crazy with all that was going on. We had created a machinery for delivering products. It was incredible to be part of. To think that just five years earlier the team, mostly the same team, had just struggled for six years to create one release and we created two releases on time, with none of the stress and strain relatively speaking, and with very high quality. We needed to keep moving.

Windows 8 was a 1.0 release. Perhaps by many accounts it was a 0.9 release, at least for the reimagined part. The Win32 and Intel part of the release was incredibly solid. It was indeed Windows 7 plus more. The team knew we had set out on a multi-year, even decade journey. I knew we would need to operate completely differently.

There would not be a Windows 9 next. In a very short time over the summer, we organized and began planning on "Windows Blue" which is a name I picked to signify it was not another big release. We had a lot of finishing to do. Microsoft never got anything right in the first version, or even the second. We needed to move the team to think about acting with precision in a timely manner so we could, in Microspeak, crank out a release every year.

We created a vision and a schedule for a release to finish in one year. The entire goal of the release was to refine everything from RTM. Refine the platform. Refine the user experience. Refine the core built-in applications and service connections such as SkyDrive and Outlook.com. Decide on a long-term Surface roadmap. The list was very long. Above all we'd fix the things that were so obviously not complete, such as requiring a trip to the desktop to use files or change a PC setting. And yes, we would pay close attention to the reviews as they came out. Though I can say even today, we would not have planned on a full retreat, a redo, or a reset.

Microsoft takes three versions to get things right. We grew up with that reality. The world was moving ahead with or without us. We were determined.

On August 2, 2012, Windows 8 went to manufacturing. We finished 120 days late from our original schedule. The Surface assembly line went into operation. We had a fantastic event on campus. Once again, the administrative assistant team outdid themselves.

August was always a busy month at Microsoft. The field sales organization held their annual rally/strategic coordination meeting with almost all of the global staff. Microsoft usually held a company meeting around that time. There was also a Wall Street event or shareholder meeting. These events are the rhythm of a large corporation.

August 2012 was also a month when the company came together to get behind Windows 8. For all the concerns and issues raised as the product progressed, there was an electricity and a sense of excitement. People had seen the doldrums for the past decade. People had seen PC numbers declining. People had seen Microsoft lose in mobile, fall behind Linux, and not yet have a role in cloud computing. While the financials the company was putting up were fantastic by any measure, the buzz was gone. More than a buzz, the company wasn't a leader. The company wasn't, for lack of a better word, relevant. We all believed, and genuinely hoped, Windows 8 would offer a chance to be the industry leader again, not just the biggest company, but the most relevant company.

At both the global sales meeting and the company meeting we presented Windows 8 and Surface. The global sales meeting told the story of Windows 8 and why it could win. The field of course were worried about the missing Start menu. I shared some usage data comparing how the Start screen compared to the Start menu. Rather than trying to jam all the functionality into a tiny corner of the screen we showed how people saw the information from Live tiles and made full use of the screen, all maintaining familiar positional memory and muscle memory. It was just one point but the kind of message you send to the field that says, "we heard" and here's what we consider to be the case. It was not spin. It was what we believed.

What I remember though was not apologizing for the Start screen, but the absolutely incredible and over-the-top reception just when I walked out on stage. I have never felt so much gratitude from 30,000 people all at once. I got to stand there, head bowing, absorbing that gratitude for the team back in Redmond. I stood on stage to applause for nearly a full minute. Humbling doesn't begin to describe the feeling. I couldn't say it enough at the time, but I can once again say thank you to the global field team for that welcome and appreciation on behalf of the team. It was so genuine, so unexpected, and just so wonderful.

Just a week later we gathered at the Key Arena in Seattle for the company meeting. While much of the message was the same as MGX, this was headquarters and that means it was mostly the product development groups and company staff. They wanted to see the long version of everything. We did everything to deliver. We had the biggest hardware lineup of Windows 8 PCs MikeAng had ever assembled. PanosP came out and "debuted" Surface once again. Tami Reller walked everyone through all we had done to bring the products to market. We had an amazing and relaxed time. Once again, the reception was just over the top. It was amazing.

We had one more surprise even after all of this. One of the many great joys of being part of creating Surface was the chance to work with a creative team in Hollywood who would bring Surface to television and web advertising. The team was headed by movie producer Andrew Panay, brother of Panos. He assembled a team of creative people to write, visualize, and direct the television spots, the sound stage for the launch event, a worldwide street art campaign, and a plethora of other materials. Andrew was already a seasoned film producer (*Wedding Crashers*), and their early ideas and pitch made it easy to decide to collaborate with the team on a whole new approach. Andrew, with his keen eye for talent, brought in the director Jon M. Chu to create the marquee television debut for Surface, called *Movement*. The commercial featured the iconic "Click-In" sound, the hinge action, colorful touch covers, and a troupe of talented *au courant* dancers. Astute viewers and frequent travelers would later recognize some of the dancers from another well-known spot from Chu, the Virgin Atlantic safety video. Chu would later direct *G.I. Joe: Retaliation*, *Crazy Rich Asians*, and *In the Heights* among his dozens of credits.

We debuted the spot not only for all of Microsoft HQ, but for SteveB as well. Steve did not like surprises, but I had a strong feeling he would love this commercial. It was high energy like Steve, and it sold hard on the attributes of Surface. It was cool. It was hip. It was, well, everything Microsoft was not.

Steve, MikeAng, Tami Reller, Panos, JulieLar, and some others stood by the green room looking on to the full venue of 20,000 or so employees as the lights went down and the commercial debuted. The arena and SteveB went bonkers. Score another awkward high-five moment for me and everyone within a 20-foot radius. The commercial was a moment. The campaign went on to win awards in the advertising world as well, something that Microsoft had not accomplished in ages.

Both events really demonstrated that Microsoft's headquarters personnel were excited, optimistic, supportive, and a great many were direct contributors. Certainly, we had not experienced anything like that in the past decade of Microsoft.

For the October launch, the Microsoft Store team secured New York City's Times Square, for a Surface and Windows 8 block party celebrating the opening of the new flagship Microsoft Store. The launch event itself was in an enormous hall downtown. It was filled to capacity. For me personally it would be mostly anticlimactic like all launch events usually were.

Walking around Times Square that night among thousands of people at our own party was crazy. But my mind was not there. I was thinking about what was going to appear with reviews and more. The plan was to only sell Surface RT in Microsoft Stores. I was thinking about how we would sell all the Surface devices we built. Our plan was to sell exclusively through only the few Microsoft Stores. I did the math on that, and it was scary. I worried about the aggressive pricing of $499, or $599 with Touch Cover. I was thinking about the Start screen. The desktop. The App Store. The Windows team. Windows Blue. All those people who had done so much, given so much, done such a fantastic job.

I loved this company. I was also exhausted.

About a year before that big launch, I wrote an email that I would deliver on my last day of work at Microsoft. Unsent then, I knew it would go out in the not-far-off future. I stored it in my email drafts folder and held onto a printed copy, undated and unsigned, in an envelope in my Windows logo Timbuk2 bag along with my Surface tablet and my 16 pages of printouts of the vision, staffing, budgets, product reviews, compete info, and the dev schedule that I always had with me. I told nobody about that letter.

I wrote it after a big debate at a cross-division executive meeting over the degree to which Windows 8 would be designed to sell other parts of Microsoft—how many of those colorful Metro tiles would be pushed to customers, not because each was a good product choice but because we wanted to sell them something else. I was being excessively principled, as I was known to be, believing in the primacy of the customer experience. I believed others were being too flippant with our role as a platform provider and a significant reason why we could make a better PC for customers. "It is not the user's PC, it is our PC," one exec opined. "Sure, it is crapware, but at least it is our crapware" and "We fought the DOJ so we could own the screen" others chimed in.

Product cycles are emotional roller coasters. Anyone who has ever gone through one knows there are dozens of times when it just gets to be too much. The more seasoned one becomes the more one knows never to do anything precipitously. I knew it was time for a change. I intended to get through the launch. The plans were in place.

I was spent.

Equally clear to me was that the company was spent too. Microsoft needed to do things differently, without me.

EPILOGUE. THE END OF THE PC REVOLUTION

Windows 8 marked my final product at Microsoft which I believe coincided with a significant changing of the guard leading the technology world. The industry saw an enormous shift to mobile computing, the largest technology adoption in the history of the world. With that, a change in leadership as well, as Apple, by many accounts the inventor of the personal computer, is now the undisputed leader of computing. I want to reflect on the end of the journey of the PC.

WINDOWS 8 WAS A FAILURE.

Hubris. Arrogance. Lunacy. Egomaniacal. Pick any word to describe the product; it was likely used somewhere. No one knew, or felt, the weight of the product failure more than I did.

Nearly every successful Microsoft product had survived our *it takes three versions to get it right* modus operandi. Esther Dyson, a technology investor and journalist, writing for Forbes in an article "Microsoft's spreadsheet, on its third try, excels" said "It's something of an industry joke in the software business that it takes Microsoft three tries to get it right. There's Windows 3.0, Word 3.0, and now Excel 3.0."[164] She wrote that in 1991, reviewing the third version of Excel.

No Windows leader made it through the odd-even curse of releases, certainly not three major releases of Windows from start to finish.

My hope had been for a credible Windows 8 knowing we weren't finished, which was standard operating procedure for new Microsoft products. We knew where we wanted to take the product over time—the hardware, the software, and the apps. But none of that happened. For reasons I still do not fully understand, for the first time I could remember Microsoft quickly and completely withdrew and actively erased Windows 8 in an almost Orwellian way—even Clippy preserved its dignity. I try to imagine what would have happened had Microsoft given up on Windows the first time, or Windows Server, Exchange, Word, Excel, or PowerPoint. All of those took multiple iterations to find product-market fit, to win both hearts and minds.

Requiring three versions was not a Microsoft thing. It is a product development thing. Even in a big company you must ship the first version—shipping a "V 1.0" (v for version) is always a miracle. Then you need to fix it and that was version 2.0. Then by version 3.0 not only does the product work, the sales, marketing, positioning, pricing, and more work. Product development is always a journey. Always.

With years of hindsight including the new mobile market, the PC market, and Apple, many of the initial problems with Windows 8 were not nearly as egregious as much of the commentary made them out to be. Or maybe the commentary was right and what was egregious was not that we made a product that did what it did, but that we made Windows do those things? Or perhaps we simply did it all too soon? Or that we, surprisingly, lacked patience to get it right?

There was commentary on me as a leader, as a person. I knew that was borne of immediate frustration and not enduring. That's why I remained quiet and did not speak out in 2012 as I moved on to a new experience in Silicon Valley and working with entrepreneurs. I understood and even respected the emotion from where it came and the forces that produced it. Over time individuals who facilitated that commentary have since apologized directly. I was proud to be part of more than two decades of building products, processes, teams, leaders, and people—a culture—that were the highest quality, best equipped, and most talented at Microsoft in the PC era.

The problems we needed to solve with Windows 8 and Surface were readily apparent, as I strongly believed the moment we shipped. Nothing anyone wrote about either was surprising or news to those of us who had lived with the products. The commentary on the severity of the problems, and how and what to fix, was debatable.

Microsoft had become synonymous with the PC, but could it also reinvent the PC? That was what we set out to do. The problem was that the people who loved PCs the most weren't interested in a new kind of PC. They wanted the PC to get better, but in the same way it had for decades—primarily, more features for tech enthusiasts and more management and control features for enterprise IT managers. They simply wanted an improved Microsoft PC from Microsoft—launching programs, managing windows, futzing with files, compatibility with everything from the past, and more like that. They wanted more Windows 7.

Instead, they got a new era of PC, a modern PC, from other companies, and it would be called iPhone, iPad, Chromebook, or Apple Silicon Macintosh and they would be OK with that. Today in the US, Apple's device share is off the charts relative to any past. Apple holds greater than majority share of phones. Macintosh is selling at an all-time-high 15-20% of US PCs depending on the quarter. As for the iPad, the device loathed by so many who believed thinking about tablets was the underlying strategic failure of Windows 8, Apple has perhaps 500 million active devices and sells about 160 million iPads per year, or more than half the number of PC sales. The business and personal computing market is no longer the PC market, but vastly larger, and the only position Microsoft maintains is in the part that is shrinking relative to the whole and on an absolute basis.

The iPad is worth a special mention because of the tablet narrative that accompanied Apple releasing their product just as we started Windows 8. The iPad had a clear positioning when released—it was between a phone and a PC and great for productivity. It was an odd positioning considering it was precisely a large, but less featured, iPhone. Soon Apple would say the iPad was the embodiment of the future Apple sought. Since then, however, the iPad has been mired in a state of both confusion and poor execution. While taking advantage of the innovation in silicon and the undeniably impressive innovation in Apple's M-series of chips, the software, tools, frameworks, and peripherals directed at the iPad have, for lack of a better word, failed. For all the unit volumes and significant use as a primary device, it has not yet taken on the role Apple articulated. I would not have predicted where they are today.

Jean-Louis Gassée, hired by Steve Jobs and former leader of Apple hardware and later creator of BeOS, had this to say in his wonderfully reflective weekly newsletter, *Monday Note*:

> *The iPad's recent creeping "Mac envy", the abandonment of intuitive intelligibility for dubious "productivity" features reminds one of the proverbial Food Fight Product Strategy: Throw everything at the wall and see what sticks.*[165]

In competition it takes the leader to drop the ball and someone to be there to pick it up. Whether Apple truly dropped the ball with respect to the iPad or not, it is certainly clear that Microsoft in a post-Windows 8 environment was in no position to pick it up. That is a shame as I think Apple created an opportunity that might have been exploited.

Instead in the Windows bubble, as much as anyone might have wanted new features or improved basic capabilities, they wanted compatibility with all that had come before. Legacy applications, muscle memory, and preservation of investments were the hallmarks of Windows, not to mention the ecosystem of PC makers and Intel. Why question those attributes with a new release in 2012?

There was a comfort in what a PC was already doing and refining that while leaving paradigm shifts to other devices was, well, comfortable. Many saw the PC as both irreplaceable and without a substitute. Like the IT pros who knew the Windows registry, they were comfortable with their mastery of the product even if the world was moving on.

Unfortunately, what is comfortable for customers is not always so comfortable for the business. Without a dominant and thriving platform, Microsoft is like a hardware company or an enterprise-only software supplier—reliant on deep customer relationships, legacy product lock-in, pricing power, and big company scale to drive the business. Those can work for a time, and perhaps even bide time hoping to invent the next platform. IBM continues to prove this every quarter, much to the surprise of technologists who today don't even know what IBM makes or does.

Windows 8 was not one thing, and therein lies its main challenge. Windows 8 was not simply a release of Windows, some new APIs, and a new PC. Windows 8 was a paradigm—it could not be disassembled into components and still stand. If we had just built a Microsoft PC for Windows 7 that would not have changed the trajectory of the business, just as we have since seen with hardware efforts. We already saw how touch on existing desktop software didn't deliver. Moving from Intel to ARM without new software or worse just porting existing software was running in place at best and taking focus away from worthwhile endeavors at worst.

To shift the paradigm and to enable Microsoft to have assets and compete in some new way required an all-or-nothing bet. Everything we know about disruption reveals how companies do what they can to avoid those situations and try to thread the needle. I was totally guilty of aiming to avoid that.

The temptation to cling, or leverage depending on perspective, to the Windows legacy was constant. As I learned over every previous, and smaller transition, giving customers a little bit of the past—a compatibility mode or a way to opt out of changes—meant customers would take advantage it. The new product wouldn't be new to most customers. With Microsoft's decade-long commitment to supporting that new-old state, we would have been shackled to the very platform that was already in an anemic state—Windows and the APIs for apps, Intel and the ever-increasing transistor march, and an ecosystem of OEMs and ISVs focused elsewhere.

There were five hot buttons I felt weakened our all-or-nothing bet. There was no quick fix for these, even in hindsight. Worse, each proved more early than incorrect. In technology, however as I have noted several times in this work, early is the same as being wrong. People will debate these even as I write them years later. I think we will always have fun doing so. I certainly will. It is the nature of engineering to forever debate the causes and decisions that led to failure.

First, the Start screen clearly served as the emotional lightning rod for the release. It was, to some, as if we ripped the heart and soul from Windows. I didn't see it that way, obviously. I saw a mechanism that had outlived its usefulness just as we saw menus and toolbars outlive their usefulness in Office, or even character mode decades earlier. Despite being there in the summer of 1995, I did not see the quasi-religious significance of the menu. I saw something that people had mostly stopped using—the taskbar, ALT-TAB, search, email attachments, and browser tabs replaced launching and switching programs. Tech enthusiasts, however, had many more programs, dozens of utilities, and elaborate custom configurations. I know because they sent us the screenshots in protest. I would posit today that most tech enthusiasts are using the taskbar and search to find and launch programs, exactly as we designed Windows 8 to work. I also think they would have been fine turning off their computers with the power button and would have survived not having shutdown on the screen all the time, though they would miss the chuckle from the timeless hilarity of Start – > Shutdown.

Phone app screens grew to become the way computer programs are launched and managed. They take up the full screen and they are super easy to navigate, unlike the Start menu, which even with a mouse grew increasingly finnicky and awkward. Apple's home screen evolved to be more like Windows 8, including search and an All Applications view. Windows ultimately evolved to become more like a phone screen and far less like the formerly beloved menu, but nothing would have appeased people at the time. Nothing, other than providing (an option, of course, everything is an option) the Start menu back for "non-touch" or "Intel" PCs or something arbitrary like that—a compatibility mode. We had compatibility mode—it was Windows 7.

Second, the presence of the desktop in Windows RT, the version of Windows that didn't run any existing desktop apps. Additionally, the desktop not being the first thing to pop up after starting any version of Windows proved to be "disorienting" in ways that were more reactionary than actual. From the first demo at All Things Digital when we were asked about "two modes," I was not able to find the way to describe this feature. If a product requires explaining, it's already lost.

On Intel Windows, we wanted to remove a level of indirection and simply have a place to start. The desktop, with its cacophony of uses, had become a hairball. It did not roam between devices well (due to screen size and contents), and the slew of uses as a file cabinet, scratch pad, dashboard, and program launcher made improvement impossible. Alas, it was viewed as sacrosanct and another place where the world was changing but disproportionately less so for power users. The move to phones, browser apps, cloud storage, and multiple devices relegated the desktop for most. We were just too early.

Third, on ARM we faced another challenge: Our own desire to ship meant we shipped a product that was knowingly incomplete. We simply had too many places to return to the legacy experience. Apple chose to hide those capabilities on the iPad until they were ready and perhaps that would have been a better approach for us too. We should recall that the iPhone shipped without copy and paste, and the iPad was literally a big iPhone with fewer built-in apps and no phone capability. We wanted to embrace the capability of the operating system without compromising quality, security, and so on. For example, the iPad had no files or file management capabilities, including using devices such as USB thumb drives, until 2017. We supported those out of the gate, but that sometimes required using the legacy desktop and explorer. We didn't have time to build the WinRT file manager app we had already designed, as an example, or update everything in the Windows control panel. The vast ecosystem took time to move, but we had to begin a transition.

Many believed omissions presented a weird modality or duality. Our explanation that this was always how Windows evolved failed to satisfy or reduce perceived confusion. Windows carried the DOS box and command line (and still does) and even .INI files, for those who cared, for decades—and it was widely used by tech enthusiasts and administrators alike—even for copying files! Having some of the old along with the new had always been the Microsoft way. It just seemed so inelegant compared to Apple.

I, we, did not love that we had to do this. While we considered many alternatives, we didn't have a better approach without taking forever to ship. The enemy of the good is the perfect. The industry was moving away from Windows, and we had to get in the game. That is decidedly different than Apple releasing a phone to a market that was far from settled and expected little from Apple which had nothing to lose. We had everything to lose and were losing everything.

Fourth, there was one very significant reason we required the desktop and why it was not simply a bonus like the old command or DOS box.

Office.

The shift to touch, phones and tablets, and a modern operating system with new apps was much larger than any one of those individually. To decompose the strategy into components is to wield the technology buzzsaw or fall victim to taking on disruptive technology shifts like entrenched incumbents tend to when failing. To have a viable product, we needed to execute on all, simultaneously.

These shifts happened all at once not because the PC did not take on each feature individually, but because the PC model itself could not possibly address the shortcomings that built up over years. Loosely aggregated features, engineered across adversarial partners, combined into a product was well-suited to the invention of the personal computer, but not the optimization of the experience. The idea that the PC could move forward into a new era by simply adding touch, or some new user interface features on top of what was there or adding an app store while still supporting downloading code from the internet, or even adopting ARM, each as a point solution was simply the old way of solving problems, the PC way.

Surface RT was designed to be the epitome of productivity for mobile information work. We wanted Surface to be people's primary work computer, the way they used a laptop (PC or Mac), but with all the reliability, security, battery life, and mobility of an iPad. To accomplish that we needed Office: Word, Excel, PowerPoint, and (some would say) Outlook. The problem: I was not successful at evangelizing the new platform opportunity to the Office team. Let that sink in.

The hallmark of Microsoft's strategy had always been apps and platform, platform and apps, and if necessary, by force. Early on the apps were forced to work on Windows against their judgment, and then later Windows was forced to be good for the apps even when it thought Office was not the focus, and this see-saw continued for the benefit of the industry. It was like we had reached a point where both businesses were so entrenched that their own worldviews precluded a bigger, all Microsoft bet. Perhaps we reached a level of fatigue in cross-company bets after the Longhorn and .NET eras.

When we presented the Windows 8 vision years before, I sat next to SteveB and friends from the Office team that were invited. It was during that meeting that we began to make the case that the new runtime existed to build new apps—new ways of working, focused on collaboration, sharing, tasks, cloud storage, and less on massive amounts of formatting, scattered document files, and so on. The collective questions were more about how to maintain compatibility for Visual Basic for Applications, third-party add-ins, and the Ribbon. We never bridged that gap. The whole product cycle, Office wanted to port existing Office to ARM and run it. The biggest irony was that the entire time the Mac Office team was busy building Office for the iPad, which is why it was ready to release on the heels of Windows 8. There are two sides to this story. The Windows 8 leaders knew both sides because we were previously the leaders of Office. There was a view that even that cross-pollination contributed to the challenges. Ultimately, there was a need for both the old Office and a new set of tools. Silicon Valley was hard at work creating new tools for information workers—modern, mobile, cloud, web, SaaS tools for productivity—while Microsoft continued to pay the bills with existing apps, even if they sold under the 365 cloud moniker for much higher prices.

Office was part of a symptom, a fatal symptom, of having no WinRT apps, which was obvious. Everyone in the industry knows that if Microsoft is serious about something then Office will participate. If Microsoft was not serious, then there was no Office support. Desktop Office sent the clear message that Microsoft was not serious about WinRT. It didn't matter what we said as our actions spoke louder than words. We had OneNote and some experiments. But without Excel, there was no WinRT. We had many debates in executive staff meetings about juicing the ISV ecosystem. That whole ecosystem was focused on the browser while still suffering from the strategy fatigue from Windows Phone 7 (and soon 8) and the failed Longhorn strategies. We needed Office. We got OneNote. I still love OneNote to this day.

We chose not to build a phone first or simultaneously. Perhaps the entire platform strategy would have been different if we had indeed executed on the mythical plan of having a phone and first-party hardware out of the gate. Since that would not have finished perhaps until 2015, debating it at all might be irrelevant. By 2015 the world would be solidified around iOS and Android leaving little headroom for us, plus we would have had a couple of more years of failure of Windows Phone, services, and an aging Windows 7. Fans of Windows Phone will continue to debate and champion that legacy the way people fondly remember the Amiga or Newton, so this is one debate I intentionally avoid.

And fifth, Windows RT and even Windows 8 were the product names. Many argued that any product without a traditional Start menu and full compatibility could not be named Windows. More would argue that naming Windows RT as we did, "confused customers" as to what would run where. That was true, but Windows had long had variants that came with limitations or exceptions: Windows NT, Windows CE, Windows Embedded, Windows Media Center, even Windows 2000, and most recently Windows Phone. All of these were confusing in some relative sense, but all were given time to rationalize the confusion.

Should we have abandoned the legacy that was embodied in the Windows name? I certainly thought about that a lot. Here again, everything about disruption would have said absolutely name it something different. Heck, put the team in another building, get them new card keys, and so on like the Zune team did. That same theory also showed how no one ever does that because they look at the cost and effort, along with splitting all the energies of the company, and reject any such approach as heresy. As someone who grew up knowing that Windows NT or even Windows XP didn't really run everything Windows 95 ran, I felt like we could pull it off. I was wrong. I don't think a new name would have worked any better and would wager that any new name would have been cutesy and clumsy at the same time given Microsoft's history. Then again, many chuckled at iPad too.

There were a host of smaller reasons as well, some related to timing and others to just trying to get a product to market. The original Surface did not support LTE, which undermined our mobility and mobile chipset message. We chose a unique aspect ratio for the screen, which proved to just be wrong for productivity. SteveB pushed on this as he personally began to like eReaders on Android that had paperback book aspect ratios. We all agreed, but it was too late. The original Surface RT keyboard, the Touch Cover, was innovative but not productive. There were other software aspects as well, like my refusal include Outlook, which would reduce battery life by 1-2 hours simply because it wasn't a modern app and had incomplete connections to our services backend. The lack of support for traditional group policy irked IT Pros who felt they needed to secure any device using invasive methods used on PCs. Those methods were battery draining while opening up a host of Win32 compatibility requirements. Modern mobile device management tools are far better than what IT did at the time, and we built those capabilities into the first release.

I tend to look at the failures of the product strategy because that is where most of the focus sits. But I had failures in the go-to market as well. I am rather fond of pointing out that success and failure are elements of the *4 Ps* of product, price, place, and promotion. In the case of Surface RT, we got the price right assuming we sold a lot of them and surprised some people even in the face of super cheap Android tablets. We got the place, the distribution strategy, entirely wrong. The Microsoft Store retail team was insanely excited to have exclusive access to Surface, but there weren't enough stores to sell the number we needed or wanted to sell. I was unable to make the math clear to leadership. We literally could not sell all we made even if the stores operated at multiples of capacity, 7 x 24. I begged and pleaded to expand distribution, and so did our partners, right up until the end. In the process we angered our Windows retail partners around the world. Then we had a whole bunch left over, and in 2013 Microsoft took an inventory write-off to complete the erasure of Windows 8 from memory. I remain convinced, perhaps naïvely so, we could have moved many more units had we opened the retail strategy. That would have allowed for the potential to iterate to a second and ultimately third version.

No matter what happens, someone always said it would, and when a product fails those predicting that are quick to make themselves known. I admit I found it enormously frustrating to see the revisionist views appear, whether with the press or with people at Microsoft. President John F. Kennedy famously said, "Victory has a thousand fathers, but defeat is an orphan." I certainly felt alone in defeat. It is well-known that as a leader, a huge part of the job is to stand alone and absorb the defeat. I think I did that at least as well as making sure any successes achieved over decades were those of the team or specific individuals and definitely not mine alone.

While our issues are quite clear in hindsight, they were also visible at the time which only serves to further the *told-you-so* reactions. Every technology shift had doubters focusing on some specific issue, or challenge, rather than seeing a complete package like all those people who said the Macintosh was not a real computer because of the mouse, or how the iPhone touch screen would not work. Had the iPhone failed, it is easy to imagine the self-congratulations from those who noted in their reviews the lack of copy/paste, missing Adobe Flash support, incomplete push email, or the new on-screen keyboard.

I knew the feedback on each of the specifics, but also, and naïvely, hoped the whole system could be seen for what it was trying to do...and it would do if given a time and effort. The story of the ribbon in Office, one of the biggest and most successful UI reinventions undertaken in a product, was one filled with doubters inside Microsoft and outside as we discussed. Today some of those who were the most negative about the change even find themselves leaders in today's Office.

But why should people have been patient? They had the iPhone, iPad, Android phones and tablets, and Chromebooks all to choose from. They were happy to use those and just stick to Windows for all the familiar legacy work.

As we progressed to the October 2012 launch of Windows 8, a lot was happening that perhaps marred our ability to see clearly and, more importantly, collectively. It was an anxious time. We spent the summer in leadership team meetings gearing up for the yearly sales meeting ahead of a big launch year. The past ten years of flat stock price and lackluster product success had taken its toll.

The difficulties with Windows Phone were compounding, despite poorly grounded optimism. Phone apps were not gaining traction and worse the hacks to gain apparent traction were backfiring, such as paying developers to write apps or adding apps to the store that were simply web sites. Fingers were pointing. With Surface, the question became: Should we build our own phone? Should we kick off a *skunkworks* project like Zune (that team was available) to build a phone? Would that truly address what we were seeing in the market? The phone was the next platform, a platform for the entire planet, and we were not even registering as a viable third place. The opportunity to align Windows and Windows Phone long passed and there was still no appetite to weigh down the phone strategy with a full Windows-centric approach. It was always as if the phone was on firm footing, and it just needed to borrow a bit more code from Windows. It was never on a path to success.

The Windows Server team seemed to resist embracing the new Azure product, which remained organizationally distinct. In hindsight this proved reasonable as Azure came to be dominated not by Windows as hoped but by Linux. We were obligated to support them, so that was creating a lot of extra work for us, delivering for both the on-premises server and the new data center product. The enterprise server and server apps data center era, as we knew it, was over. It was archaic and unmanageable. Microsoft was barely able to keep its own Windows data center running. The future of the server business was the cloud, but our enterprise customers were strongly resisting, or more likely entirely unaware, of that fact. AWS was still almost entirely a Silicon Valley novelty. This made it easier to ignore.

Our commitment to online services, what I saw as a key component of the Windows platform as we knew it, from communications to identity to storage, were all seen as cost centers despite the obvious need to own and build widely used cloud services across devices. A complete device experience required services extended to the cloud, built natively for the cloud rather than ports of existing Windows and Office servers. The device experience as we knew it to be was coming to an end without services.

Microsoft's transformation to an internet company—well documented as one of the most successful pivots of all time—turned out to be great for our revenue but lousy for our platform technology. The level of internet savvy across the company paled in comparison to Google and Facebook, yet the much-sought-after Yahoo rapidly faded. Little, if any, Microsoft technology or platform were part of the rise of these huge new powers. The only organic internet scale business was Bing, which continued to struggle, though ironically has today found a niche disguised as the anti-Google DuckDuckGo.

Across Office, Windows, and Servers, the reality was our pricing power, distribution moat, and enterprise account relationships combined to provide comfort in the face of shifting platforms. The reality of business disruption was right in front of us. It was plain to see. Yet the business was apparently thriving, just as the classic book on disruption would predict.

Despite the massive revenue success and great numbers, the technology story looked bleak to me. I felt alone in that concern. I sent a memo to the leadership. It was a plea to develop a point of view that these technology shifts implied that went beyond defensive—*Without a Point of View, There Is No Point.* I tried to argue that we had been lulled into a sense of complacency by having succeeded through the dot-com bubble yet ended up weak in every technology shift that followed. We were losing everywhere, except revenue. We did not have a platform, which as a platform company was a big deal. My memo, which turned out to be the last one I wrote, was decidedly a polemic meant to stir people up.

I also wondered whether it even made sense to keep score, so to speak, with products and technologies. Maybe all that mattered was leading by business metrics like revenue, profit, and cash flow. There are worse things than being a huge money-making corporation.

Leading Microsoft to reimagine Windows had been accomplishment enough for me. I knew what I had signed up for more than five years earlier. It was much more than even I had planned on. But it was time. Ultimately, I could not break the odd-even curse.

After the October launch in New York, it was time to mark the end of my career with Microsoft. With great clarity, I knew it was time to use that resignation letter I'd been holding on to. One last meeting with SteveB, and some quick rounds across my direct reports, and then I hit send. Our split was undeniably mutual. I felt a sense of relief. Compared to leaving the Office team for Windows, I was much more certain this was the right decision. I was eager for a context switch.

Once the decision was made, moving on immediately was best. I never wanted a big send-off. Quite the contrary. I had gone through two years or eight depending on how one counts of Bill "transitioning" not that there is a comparison. Then there was the year transitioning through Windows Vista I experienced. I'd seen too many people stick around for too long, confusing the team and dragging their departure out.

What I failed to understand, and deeply regret, was that in our collective haste to move on I left behind the most superb team, ready to take over and move things to the next level, but not prepared for what would actually follow. I was selfish and the people who gave the most to create the new Windows team paid for that.

The "post-Sinofsky" unwinding of Windows 8, not just the product, but the organization and processes as well, became even more painful than market reception of Windows 8. I let the team and my best friends down. I left them to pick up the pieces I should have been picking up myself. The management above them failed to show them the respect they deserved. Nearly every one of them represented in these half-million words—the best leaders Microsoft created across every discipline—has left the company. So many of them are creators, entrepreneurs, and thought leaders in ways that Microsoft does not even participate today.

BillG had always been fond of saying that tech companies have a remarkably difficult time leading as technology crossed generations. Leaders of each era might maintain scale, rarely evaporating, but losing influence and presence in the market. Technology analyst and friend Benedict Evans wrote:

> *Tech monopolies tend not to fall like Rome. They fall like Venice. They're still there, and no-one actually invades them, but the trade routes moved, the things that gave them power and wealth stop mattering, and they become just another city, and then a backwater.*[166]

Every day of Windows 8 development, I worried about losing our audience of developers who hung on every word of not just what new features for Windows and Office were being shipped, but what code they could write, what business they could build, what customer problem they could solve by making a singular bet on Microsoft's inventions to power them. I'd seen the relevancy of Office fade even while the business grew. Many companies have core fan bases, but Microsoft was blessed with people and companies building businesses on our technology, uniquely and singularly, and many of them moved on. Developers are not the end, but a means to a force-multiplying economic relationship with billions of people. I'd seen how easy it is in a large organization to find a bubble to hide out in—a bubble where our products are as popular and relevant as they once were.

Paul Graham, fellow 1980s Cornellian, founder of the Y Combinator startup accelerator, and described as a "hacker philosopher" by author Steven Levy, wrote two essays on Microsoft that were rather prescient, if not spooky. They were written so early as to be easily dismissed or perhaps wishful thinking. In 2001, he wrote "The Other Road Ahead" a nod to the book by Bill Gates. In this essay he described the new Web 2.0 paradigm relative to the desktop computer. He aptly described the bubble Microsoft was in, that I was in, and we just didn't know it:

> *Back when desktop computers arrived, IBM was the giant that everyone was afraid of. It's hard to imagine now, but I remember the feeling very well. Now the frightening giant is Microsoft, and I don't think they are as blind to the threat facing them as IBM was. After all, Microsoft deliberately built their business in IBM's blind spot.*
>
> *I mentioned earlier that my mother doesn't really need a desktop computer. Most users probably don't. That's a problem for Microsoft, and they know it. If applications run on remote servers, no one needs Windows. What will Microsoft do? Will they be able to use their control of the desktop to prevent, or constrain, this new generation of software?*[167]

The essay is long and well worth reading for its predictive powers. While not every technical point landed precisely as described, especially the iPhone and apps, it is a brutal read that was aptly ignored by us at the time. As if to double-down, in 2007 he wrote another essay "Microsoft is Dead" wherein he described what took place in the mid-2000s that killed Microsoft. This was just after Windows Vista when it was easy and rather popular to assert an end. That was because of Vista, however, not because of the four factors in his essay: Google, the desktop is "over", broadband internet, and Apple OS X on new Macs. He concluded with a candid and brutal take:

> *Microsoft's biggest weakness is that they still don't realize how much they suck. They still think they can write software in house. Maybe they can, by the standards of the desktop world. But that world ended a few years ago.*
>
> *I already know what the reaction to this essay will be. Half the readers will say that Microsoft is still an enormously profitable company, and that I should be more careful about drawing conclusions based on what a few people think in our insular little "Web 2.0" bubble. The other half, the younger half, will complain that this is old news.*[168]

Despite Graham's dire predictions, people continue to rely on Microsoft and bet on the company today. Microsoft is an enormous business. It is undeniably a different kind of leader, more a comfortable companion than a guide taking you to new places.

It is popular to say that the operating system is no longer key, that the definition of a platform has changed, and that the battle is now above the OS. That's a great rationalization, and as Jeff Goldblum's character in *The Big Chill* said, "Don't knock rationalization. Where would we be without it? I don't know anyone who can go a day without two or three rationalizations." The biggest business at Microsoft remains Microsoft/Office 365, and as valuable as email and video conferencing are (and as important as transferring the capital and operational costs to Microsoft in exchange for a huge price increase was too), the unique intellectual property in Office 365 that defies competition is Word, Excel, and PowerPoint. These remain key tools used in daily mission critical work by perhaps 300 million information workers. Those people, at least 90 to 95 percent of them, rely on Windows to do that work, which is Microsoft's second largest business.

Bundling the new Microsoft Teams with the 365 service perfectly reflects this legacy approach, a well-worn strategy to support the existing business and pricing rather than risk building a new business and creating a new revenue stream. In this work I described the bundling of Outlook, OneNote, SharePoint in this same regard during the expansive period of enterprise software. Microsoft loved a good bundle. Customers did to. I suspect this time with Teams will end differently primarily because the computing world is in a different place and the requirement that customers settle for a bundled product is nowhere the same as it was in the early or middle stages of the PC era. Certainly, the macroeconomics of 2022 will provide a foundation for a bundle, but that has not proven sustainable.

The virtuous cycle of apps and systems envisioned by BillG in the 1980s stands as the hallmark of Microsoft, but it is not growing in users and is not part of a thriving ecosystem. New customers aren't coming to PCs with Office even at a rate to replace those that retire. Windows PCs are not benefitting from advances in a hardware ecosystem that transitioned to mobile. Developers aren't building new software for Windows. The cycles have been broken.

PC sales in 2022 will likely have declined 15-20% over 2021. Many will point to the economy or foreign exchange rates or length of a replacement cycle, or maybe even Apple's inability to figure out its own product strategy. At some point the only conclusion is that the PC, like the mainframe, minicomputer, and workstation before it, was a mature and saturated market. There will be good years and not so good years, but the PC or PC server running Windows will never be the platform it was. Even if people develop new products on it, those products will not take advantage of what a new PC has to offer, which is the definition of a platform.

The web and smartphones have assumed the role of the information platform for the world. This time is different, however. Together these two have touched every human on the planet. That hasn't happened with any other foundational platform, to use the term broadly, in history except for perhaps fire. All the amazing, connected platforms from the 20th century reached their limits long before reaching every person everywhere, including rail, car, roads, airplanes, telegraph, telephone, television, electric grids, sewage, and more. Whatever comes along next will also be the greatest technology displacement in the history of humans as it will replace the internet-connected smartphone for every person on earth. That is going to be an incredible innovation.

Craig McCaw, one of the earliest pioneers of mobile phones in the US via his namesake company and graduate of Seattle's Lakeside School a few years before Bill Gates, described humans as inherently nomadic when it comes to the technology they use. He first made this observation with respect to mobile phones compared to land lines that tethered users to a wall.[169] Technology is broadly adopted first when it meets their needs, and not before. Then over time when a product fails to meet their needs and something better comes along, they simply move on. Smartphones came along and when they became good enough, people simply stopped demanding new PCs.

BillG once said to me of another legendary company facing challenges that things always seemed brightest before a precipitous decline. That's what Windows PCs were facing. Windows 7 was peak PC the way Office 2007 was peak Office. Peak, not in terms of financial success, but peak in terms of influence, centrality, excitement, and general interest. Microsoft was in the midst of disruption, to use that overused phrase on more time. Not everyone agreed about where we were in the arc, and that was the problem.

Either way, it was the end of the PC era.

We knew that because we could read, watch, or hear about it all by swiping with a finger or by asking about it on that modern computer in our pockets or one of the hundreds of millions of tablets on sofas, in the back seats of cars, or in airplane seats. That computer was the reinvention of the PC. In no shortage of irony, the company that brought us this new computer was Apple—the company that for all practical purposes invented the PC in the first place.

Windows PCs are never going to reach 500 or more million or more units a year as analysts had once predicted. The question was not how high sales would go but how low could they fall—peak PCs ended up being the Windows 7 upgrade cycle that resulted from a combination of poor demand due to Windows Vista, delays due to the recession, and lengthening PC lifetimes. A market of 300 million PCs is a fantastic business (about the same as 2007), but it isn't two billion iOS devices in use or the more than three billion active Android devices. It certainly isn't the growth opportunity of bringing PCs to every home and desk across emerging markets in Asia and Africa like we had hoped a year or two earlier.

Did Windows 8 cause PC sales to decline because it was the wrong product for the PC? Or did the substitution of phones for PCs in the eyes of customers cause the decline in PC sales which made Windows 8 the wrong product? Years later all I can say with certainty is that those both happened at the same time, each correlated with the other. Importantly, would a more incremental and traditional release of Windows have really saved PC sales or even have spurred significant growth? Does anyone really think this today? I didn't then and certainly do not today.

Looking back, there are small things that I might have changed, though I can say with confidence that would not have altered the outcome. To date, no one has offered up a plan that would have had a better shot at helping Microsoft achieve the same level of impact and influence in this next era of computing. It makes for a fun column or *Gedankenexperiment* to explore the counterfactual, but I didn't really have a way to do that in real time. There's no A/B test in building Windows.

Microsoft was going to be big for decades the same way IBM had remained significant, but it deserved its chance to earn a spot as influential and central a platform to computing as it had been originally. The most obvious answer is also the most difficult for me to accept, which is maybe there just wasn't a plan. Maybe, unfortunately, where the world settled was inevitable. People moved on.

It is easy to poke holes in this sort of logic. We were not caught off guard or in denial. This was not *New Coke*. We did not see that the youth market liked a slightly different PC, so we tried to tweak the PC to make it more stylish and appealing. Our strategy was similar to what Apple had done, though our approach brought our unique perspective. There was a clear case of parallel evolution, but Apple came to market first (again!) and there were many reasons to believe being second would have advantages, as had been the case for the PC, Windows, Word, Excel, Windows NT, Exchange, and so many other Microsoft success stories. That was not the case.

When I look at the Tablet PC, Media Center, Windows Phone, or a host of other products, one thing is clear. Those products did not have the right substrate relative to how the market would evolve. There was nothing in those implementations that represented a first step in a progression to the products that did eventually dominate. It is fair to say the concepts were right, but the technical foundation was wrong because elements were simply not ready. Windows 8, in my biased view, had the right ingredients that were also market-ready.

There is one exception to Windows 8 having the right ingredients, and I don't know if the market gives Apple enough credit for what they have done. The Apple Silicon work is, at least for now, unparalleled. There was no likely outcome over the past decade that I think would have left Microsoft and likely NVIDIA in the position to compete with Apple Silicon, though a stronger Microsoft might also have influenced how Apple evolved. Apple Silicon was really in Apple's DNA from the earliest days and was almost an inevitable outcome of the failure of Motorola, PowerPC, and then Intel to contribute to what Apple saw as its destiny. I look at that work and wonder how we might have responded because we most certainly would not have gone down that path. It was one thing to assemble the components and PC and bring it to market. It would have been quite another to have the audacity to create a chipset.

Since leaving Microsoft at the end of 2012, I've spent many hours discussing and debating the specifics of Windows 8 with friends, former coworkers, current employees, start-up founders, reporters, and, well, people who are just curious. Most of the time is spent discussing platforms, ecosystems, and tectonic shifts that one faces after unimaginable success, at least when we're not just tackling my favorite topic and the bread and butter of Silicon Valley, which is growing and scaling innovative companies and teams. There remains a desire, especially among the reenergized Microsoft community, for more about specifics on the perceived misdirected product choices. In many ways that discussion is both easy and impossible. It is easy because there are only a few things to point to. It is impossible because if the situation could have been so easily addressed by changing something that was so readily identified, then that would have made for a quick fix.

Maybe wanting so much more for Microsoft's products was the bigger mistake, more than changing the Start menu or breaking with legacy compatibility. That apocryphal Henry Ford adage about cars and horses was meant to point out that people express their needs relative to what they understand the possible solutions to be. Windows customers wanted Windows, a faster Windows, but they didn't want something different…until they did.

There's an old USENET meme used to make fun of seemingly trivial problems by claiming something is the "hardest problem in computer science." It might very well be that the actual hardest problem in computer science is a company reinventing its own successful computing product for a new era in a way that existing customers are willing and excited to use. The irony is that those same customers always seem willing, and excited, to jump to the next era of computing using products from another company. Maybe that is a net positive and it is nature's way of restoring, even rebirthing, our technology foundation.

The impact of Windows 8 and the way Microsoft chose to move on so quickly did have one important and chilling effect. Not only did so many people leave or were made to leave, but the culture that replaced them became risk averse and one that rewarded not failing more than taking risk. There was a fear of repeating a Windows 8, whatever that might have meant. For all the focus on growth and the ever-rising stock price, that meant growth of revenue more than new customers, scenarios, or business approaches. Soliciting feedback, voting on features, listening to customers, or creating products for all platforms are not substitutes for a point of view or strategic moat, as our industry has shown time and again—as counterintuitive as that might be.

A decade has passed since Windows 8 and product releases from the company have done little to avoid the IBM fate, a fear of which BillG firmly implanted in my psyche.

Half will read that and mock me for suggesting any of it and that explains all that's needed to understand the failure of Windows 8. The other half will read that wondering who IBM was and when exactly they mattered. I started my career when IBM cast a shadow over every aspect of the technology industry and was fortunate to experience when Microsoft rose to that position. Bill instilled this very fear into all of us even before the internet or the split with IBM.

Ibn Khaldun, an Arabic philosopher during the Middle Ages, wrote that in war "the vanquished always seek to imitate their victors." In business it is often the other way around. The victors end up becoming what they vanquished, as victors inherit the same problems on a new technology and product base. It might take years, but creative destruction is just as certain to take place. My Harvard Business School friend and previous co-author Marco Iansiti once joked to me that the school considered rebranding disruption theory as physics or math, not simply theory.

Despite how the product landed and then crashed, Windows 8 was the most committed, skilled, and brilliant Windows team ever assembled and it had one mission: to give the PC a new direction for a new world. Ultimately, under my leadership and management we failed to build a product that would change the trajectory of Windows or PCs. We failed, however, with elegance, grace, and an amazing group of people doing their most memorable and rewarding work. Unlike many failed efforts at Microsoft, we had remarkable execution. Like many failed efforts at Microsoft, we had the right ideas but the wrong timing. The Windows market wasn't ready, but when it was ready, Microsoft was too late. Windows 8, therefore, was both too early and too late.

Windows 8 was the last product to be made by Microsoft's definition of *hardcore software*. Some will say that is a good thing. It is neither good nor bad, but simply is. It is how eras evolve and the torch passes from one generation to another.

I was attracted to Microsoft by the level of product and technology acumen of every single person I spoke with all the way up the chain to the founder and CEO, the office with a door, the free drinks, and the Pacific Northwest. What really got me was what I saw as the true nature of hardcore software.

To be hardcore is to be wildly optimistic about what can be achieved tomorrow while harshly pessimistic about what works today. Creating software is an art. It is computer science and engineering. It is inspiration, and perspiration. It is inherently individual yet relies on a team. Most of all, building software is a group of people coming together to conjure something into existence and turning that into a product used by billions.

And that is *Hardcore Software.*

IN OUR MEMORIES

Remembering executives, teammates, co-workers, and friends from my time at Microsoft. May the memories of all they contributed to the community with their work be a blessing.

Francis J. Gaudette (4/23/93)

Mary Maxwell Gates (6/10/94)

David Kruglinski (4/1/97)

Derek Yenzer (5/11/98)

Luan Phi Dawson (12/24/98)

John Neilson (5/29/99)

Don Corbitt (7/7/99)

Robert Norton (3/7/01)

Heikki Kanerva (8/21/02)

Joel Downer (6/5/2006)

Jeff Harbers (6/25/06)

Marc Olson (9/21/07)

Aaron Reynolds (7/24/08)

Cristine Knappett-Wittress (9/2/10)

Jim Gray (3/28/12, declared)

Judy Lew Dirks (8/28/12)

Bill Hill (10/18/12)

Bill Henningsgaard (8/9/13)

John Hopper (2/19/15)

Kent Diamond (2/19/16)

Chuck Thacker (6/12/17)

Paul G. Allen (10/25/18)

James Douglas (3/29/19)

Dennis Flanagan (5/6/19)

Pamela Anderson Wagner (7/28/19)

Manny Vellon (5/26/20)

William Gates Sr. (9/14/20)

Eric Engstrom (12/1/20)

Ann Riordan (3/5/21)

Ebbe Altberg (6/3/21)

Kim Cameron (11/30/21)

Leanora Sears (1/19/22)

Ken Dye (2/8/22)

Max Morris (8/16/22)

Alistair Banks (1/30/23)

Steven E. Kraus (2/21/23)

Steve Madigan (2/27/23)

David T. Jones (7/17/23)

Dennis Austin (9/1/23)

Lynne E. Russell (1/19/24)

EXTENDED BIBLIOGRAPHY

Perhaps you would like to read even more about Microsoft and related works? This is a reading list I compiled while refreshing my memory and researching other perspectives on events. I've included books primarily about Microsoft and selected books where the Microsoft perspective was particularly relevant. In the 1980s and 1990s, magazine covers were the currency of the day when it came to business and cultural leadership. I've included references to some of the key magazine covers featuring Microsoft, Apple, and technology in general. Books can be found online or via your favorite independent bookstore. Magazines are often available on eBay or sites dedicated to old magazines. Books available on Amazon (or your favorite retailer) have been compiled into the Amazon list linked to in the Endnotes.[170]

Books About the History of Microsoft by Journalists, Academics, Employees

Fire in the Valley: The Making of The Personal Computer (1984) by Paul Freiberger and Michael Swaine (2nd edition has an audio CDROM of interviews)

Programmers at Work: Interviews (1986, also 1989) by Susan Lammers

The Making of Microsoft: How Bill Gates and His Team Created the World's Most Successful Software Company (1991) by Daniel Ichbiah and Susan Knepper

Gates: How Microsoft's Mogul Reinvented an Industry and Made Himself the Richest Man in America (1992) by Stephen Manes and Paul Andrews

Hard Drive: Bill Gates and the Making of the Microsoft Empire (1992) by James Wallace and Jim Erickson

Computer Wars: The Fall of IBM and the Future of Global Technology (1993) by Charles Ferguson

Getting Past OK: The Self-Help Book for People Who Don't Need Help (1993, 2009) by Richard Brodie

Insanely Great (1994) by Steven Levy

Showstopper!: The Breakneck Race to Create Windows NT and the Next Generation at Microsoft (1994) by G. Pascal Zachary

The Microsoft Way: The Real Story of How The Company Outsmarts Its Competition (1995) by Randall Stross

Startup: A Silicon Valley Adventure (1995) by S. Jerrold Kaplan

Accidental Empires: How the Boys of Silicon Valley Make Their Millions, Battle Foreign Competition, and Still Can't Get a Date (1996) by Robert X. Cringely

Microserfs (1996) by Douglas Coupland (Fiction)

All I Really Needed to Know In Business I Learned At Microsoft: Insider Strategies to Help You Succeed (1997) by Julie Bick

Speeding the Net: The Inside Story of Netscape and How It Challenged Microsoft (1997) by Joshua Quittner and Michelle Slatalla

Barbarians Led by Bill Gates (1998) by Jennifer Edstrom and Marlin Eller

Overdrive: Bill Gates and the Race to Control Cyberspace (1998) by James Wallace

Microsoft Secrets: How the World's Most Powerful Software Company Creates Technology, Shapes Markets and Manages People (1998) by Michael A. Cusumano and Richard Selby

Business @ the Speed of Thought: Succeeding in the Digital Economy (1999) by Bill Gates

Competing On Internet Time: Lessons from Netscape and Its Battle With Microsoft (1999) by David B. Yoffie and Michael A. Cusumano

Microsoft First Generation: The Success Secrets of the Visionaries Who Launched a Technology Empire (1999) by Cheryl D. Tsang

The Plot to Get Bill Gates (1999) by Gary Rivlin

Renegades of the Empire: How Three Software Warriors Started a Revolution Behind the Walls of Fortress Microsoft (1999) by Michael Drummond

U.S. V. Microsoft: The Inside Story of the Landmark Case (2000) by Joel Brinkley and Steve Lohr

Inside Out: Microsoft-In Our Own Words (2000) by Microsoft Corporation (photos)

Proudly Serving My Corporate Masters: What I Learned in Ten Years as a Microsoft Programmer (2000) by Adam Barr

Breaking Windows: How Bill Gates Fumbled the Future of Microsoft (2001) by David Bank

World War 3.0: Microsoft, the US Government, and the Battle for the New Economy (2001) by Ken Auletta

DEC Is Dead, Long Live DEC: The Lasting Legacy of Digital Equipment Corporation (2003) by Edgar H Schein, Paul J Kampa

Bad Boy Ballmer: The Man Who Rules Microsoft (2002) by Fredric Alan Maxwell

Microsoft Rebooted: How Bill Gates and Steve Ballmer Reinvented Their Company (2004) by Robert Slater

Old New Thing, The: Practical Development Throughout the Evolution of Windows (2006) by Raymond Chen

I. M. Wright's Hard Code (2007) by by Eric Brechner

Microsoft 2.0: How Microsoft Plans to Stay Relevant in the Post-Gates Era (2008) by Mary Jo Foley

Burning the Ships: Transforming Your Company's Culture Through Intellectual Property Strategy (2009) by Marshall Phelps and David Kline

One Strategy: Organization, Planning, Decision Making (2009) by Steven Sinofsky and Marco Iansiti

Hackers: Heroes of the Computer Revolution (2010) by Steven Levy

Idea Man: A Memoir (2011) by Paul G. Allen

Built for Success: The Story of Microsoft (2011) by Nell Musolf

Sweating Bullets: Notes about Inventing PowerPoint by Robert Gaskins (2012)

Resolve and Fortitude: Microsoft's "Secret Power Broker" (2012) by *Joachim Kempin*

Fearless Genius: The Digital Revolution in Silicon Valley 1985-2000 (2014) by Doug Menuez (photos)

Strategy Rules: Five Timeless Lessons from Bill Gates, Andy Grove, and Steve Jobs (2015) by David B. Yoffie and Michael A. Cusumano

Xbox Revisited: A Game Plan for Corporate and Civic Renewal by Robbie Bach (2015)

Hit Refresh: The Quest to Rediscover Microsoft's Soul and Imagine a Better Future for Everyone (2017) by Satya Nadella and Greg Shaw

Microsoft Secrets: An Insider's View of the Rocket Ride from Worst to First and Lessons Learned on the Journey (2017) by Dave Jaworski

Beneath A Surface (2018) by Brad Sams

Valley of Genius: The Uncensored History of Silicon Valley (As Told by the Hackers, Founders, and Freaks Who Made It Boom) (2018) by Adam Fisher

The Microsoft Story: How the Tech Giant Rebooted Its Culture, Upgraded Its Strategy, and Found Success in the Cloud (2020) by Dan Good

Other Relevant Books

Mythical Man Month (1975) by Frederick P. Brooks, Jr.

The IBM Personal Computer from the Inside Out (1984) by Murray Sargent (later an employee) and Richard L. Shoemaker

MS-DOS Technical Reference (1986) by Bill Gates, et al

MS-DOS Encyclopedia (1988, 1989) by Ray Duncan

Programming Windows: The Microsoft Guide to Programming for the MS-DOS Presentation Manager, Windows 2.0 and Windows/386 (1988, 6 editions) by Charles Petzold

The Third Apple: Personal Computers & the Cultural Revolution (1987) by Jean-Louis Gassee

Inside OS/2 (1988) by Gordon Letwin

The New Hacker's Dictionary Hardcover (1991) by Eric S. Raymond (Author)

IBM's 360 and Early 370 Systems (1991) by Emerson W. Pugh, Lyle R. Johnson, John H. Palmer

Microserfs (1995) by Douglas Coupland (see also *Generation X*)

Writing Solid Code (1993) by Steve Maguire

Code Complete (1993) by Steve McConnell

Debugging the Development Process (1994) by Steve Maguire

Almost Perfect (1994, Prima) by W. E. Pete Peterson

Dynamics of Software Development (1995) by Jim McCarthy and Denis Gilbert

Where Wizards Stay Up Late: The Origins of The Internet (1996) by Katie Hafner and Matthew Lyon

Dealers of Lightning: Xerox PARC and the Dawn of the Computer Age (2000) by Michael A. Hiltzik

Leaving Microsoft to Change the Word: An Entrepreneur's Odyssey to Educate the World's Children (2006) by John Wood

Fearless Genius: The Digital Revolution in Silicon Valley 1985-2000 (2014) by Doug Menuez

Track Changes: A Literary History of Word Processing (2016) by Matthew G. Kirschenbaum

How the Internet Happened: From Netscape to the iPhone (2018) by Brian McCullough

IBM: The Rise and Fall and Reinvention of a Global Icon (2019) by James W. Cortada

Play Nice But Win: A CEO's Journey from Founder to Leader (2021) by Michael Dell

Ideas That Created the Future: Classic Papers of Computer Science (2021) by Harry R. Lewis (Editor)

The Founders: The Story of Paypal and the Entrepreneurs Who Shaped Silicon Valley (2022) by Jimmy Soni

Other Relevant Works

"The Software Column" by Bill Gates in *Personal Computing*, May-June 1977. Bill explained what an operating system would offer and lays out the future strategy for MS-DOS.

"When We Invented the Personal Computer..." by Steve Jobs in *Computers and People*, July 1981. Steve detailed the computer as "bicycle of the mind."

"A PC Exclusive Interview With Software Guru Bill Gates" in first issue of *PC Magazine*, Feb-Mar 1982 by publisher David Bunnell. Also https://www.pcmag.com/news/heres-what-bill-gates-told-pcmag-about-the-ibm-pc-in-1982

"A Spreadsheet Way of Knowledge" by Steven Levy (November 1984) in *Harpers*

"Interview with Bill Gates" from *Computer History Archive Project* (April 1987) youtu.be/BXGJEHEj-KA

"Susannah Simons interviews Bill Gates" from *Answering Back* (1992) youtu.be/o4IftvjUrVI

"Bill Gates Interview", transcript of video interview, *National Museum of American History*, interviewed by David Allison, 1993. https://americanhistory.si.edu/comphist/gates.htm

"The spreadsheet interface: A basis for end-user programming." by Bonnie A. Nardi and James R. Miller, in *Human-Computer Interaction: INTERACT '90*. Amsterdam: North-Holland, 1990. http://www.miramontes.com/writing/spreadsheet-eup/

"Inside Microsoft: The untold story of how the Internet forced Bill Gates to reverse course" by Kathy Rebello (July 14, 1996) in BusinessWeek

"Not Only Microsoft: The Maturing of the Personal Computer Software Industry, 1982–1995" by Martin Campbell-Kelly (2001) in Cited by 15 Volume 75, Special Issue 1 (Special Issue: *Computers and Communications Networks*)

"Oral History Interview With Mike Maples" in Charles Babbage Institute, https://conservancy.umn.edu/handle/11299/107465

"The Origins of Word Processing Software for Personal Computers: 1976-1985" by Thomas J. Bergin in *IEEE Annals of the History of Computing* (Volume: 28, Issue: 4, Oct.-Dec. 2006)

"The Creation and the Demise of VisiCalc," by Burton Grad in *IEEE Annals of the History of Computing*, (Volume: 29, Issue: 3, Jul.-Sep. 2007)

"The first killer app: a history of spreadsheets" by Melissa Rodriguez Zynda in *Interactions* Volume 20 Issue 5, September + October 2013 Pages 68-72

"Spreadsheets – How It Started" by Lazar Raković, Marton Sakal, Veselin Pavlicevic in *International Scientific Journal of Management Information Systems* 2003

"The rise and rise of the spreadsheet" by M. Campbell-Kelly in *The History of Mathematical Tables: from Sumer to Spreadsheets* 2003

"The first killer app: a history of spreadsheets" by Melissa Rodriguez Zynda in *Interactions* Oct 2013

Magazines

Bill Gates, Steve Jobs, Steve Ballmer, and other leaders of the rise of computing were featured dozens of times on the cover of the major news weeklies and of course the bi-weekly and monthly technology enthusiast magazines. Included here are most of the cover or major stories. Not included are the industry weekly tabloids, InfoWorld, MacWeek, and PCWeek cited often throughout this work, as well as issues where Microsoft was simply part of a list of companies. Unless otherwise noted, these are US editions. Listings by publication title and date.

ABA Journal, 8/1/1993, Legal Documents of the Future

Ad Age Magazine, 12/19/1994, Marketer of the Year – Microsoft

American Spectator, 7/1/1998, Open Season on Bill Gates

Atlantic, The, 7/1/1945, Includes "As We May Think"

Bloomberg Business, 1/24/2011, Apple without Jobs

Bloomberg Business, 1/16/2012, No More Monkey Boy

Bloomberg Business, 4/4/2016, Spawn of Clippy

Brill's Content, 9/1/1998, Making Bill

British Airways Business Life, 1/1/2004, The Patience of Jobs

Business 2.0, 6/1/2002, How to Beat Bill

Business 2.0, 10/1/2003, Baby Bills

Business 2.0, 1/1/2004, 101 Dumbest Moments

Business 2.0, 4/1/2005, What's Next for Apple

Business Month, 11/1/1990, The Silicon Bully: How Long Can Bill Gates Kick Sand in the Face of The Computer Industry?

BusinessWeek, 10/3/1983, Personal Computer: And the winner is IBM

BusinessWeek, 2/27/1984, Software the new driving force

BusinessWeek, 11/14/1984, Apple's Dynamic Duo, and their bold plan to take on IBM in the office.

BusinessWeek, 7/28/1986, IBM versus the clones

BusinessWeek, 4/13/1987, The Whiz Kid

BusinessWeek, 8/1/1988, Is your computer secure?

BusinessWeek, 9/26/1988, Intel: The Next Revolution

BusinessWeek, 10/24/1988, Can Jobs Do It Again

BusinessWeek, 3/6/1989, Computers: Is the Industry Maturing

BusinessWeek, 9/10/1990, Computers: Will they sell this time

BusinessWeek, 6/10/1991, Computer Confusion

BusinessWeek, 9/30/1991, Software Made Simple

BusinessWeek, 2/24/1992, Life at the top

BusinessWeek, 3/1/1993, Is Microsoft Too Powerful

BusinessWeek, 7/5/1993, Apples Future

BusinessWeek, 7/10/1995, Windows 95 and how it will change computing

BusinessWeek, 7/15/1996, Inside Microsoft

BusinessWeek, 8/18/1997, How Silicon Valley Really Works

BusinessWeek, 1/19/1998, Microsoft: How Dominant Will It Be?

BusinessWeek, 11/23/1998, Jobs Movie Mogul

BusinessWeek, 12/14/1998, Amazon.com the wild world of e-commerce

BusinessWeek, 5/17/1999, Remaking Microsoft

BusinessWeek, 5/31/1999, eBay vs Amazon

BusinessWeek, 6/14/1999, Office Lite by Steve Wildstrom and Microsoft Must Settle

BusinessWeek, 7/5/1999, Readers Sound Off on Office Lite

BusinessWeek, 10/4/1999, The Internet Age

BusinessWeek, 7/10/2000, Can amazon make it?

BusinessWeek, 7/31/2000, Apple, Yes Steve Jobs, you fixed it, Congrats.

BusinessWeek, 6/4/2001, Microsoft How it Became Stronger than Ever

BusinessWeek, 7/26/2001, Microsoft How to Prevent New Abuses

BusinessWeek, 10/1/2001, Rethinking the Economy (inside Review of Windows XP)

BusinessWeek, 1/21/2002, Cisco Behind the Hype (also "Can Microsoft Control the Living Room")

BusinessWeek, 2/15/2004, Showtime: Moving Beyond Computers

BusinessWeek, 4/19/2004, Microsoft: Can It Overcome Middle Age

BusinessWeek, 4/18/2005, IBM: Beyond Blue

BusinessWeek, 8/7/2005, Bill Gates Interview

BusinessWeek, 9/26/2005, I'm Outta Here: Why Microsoft Is Losing Key Talent

BusinessWeek, 1/9/2006, Intel Inside Out

BusinessWeek, 2/6/2006, Steve Jobs' Magic Kingdom

BusinessWeek, 11/13/2006, Amazon's Risky Bet

BusinessWeek, 4/28/2008, Most Innovative companies

BusinessWeek, 5/12/2008, Mac in Grey Flannel Suit

BusinessWeek, 5/19/2008, Ballmer v Google

BusinessWeek, 1/25/2010, Why Can't They Be Friends

BusinessWeek, 10/14/2013, Secret Amazon: Explosive Account of Bezos

Connoisseur, 10/1/1989, What's Next

Creative Computing, 6/1/1982, Focus on Word Processing

Creative Computing, 11/1/1984, Pioneers Speak Out

Economist, 5/23/1998, Delete Microsoft on cover in US

Economist, 6/13/1998, Compete Don't Delete

Economist, 3/24/2001, Son of Paperclip

Economist, 4/14/2001, Cloud Issue

Economist, 4/28/2001, A kinder, gentler gorilla?

Economist, 4/1/2006, France

Economist, 10/1/2006, Steve Jobs the Magician

Economist, 6/28/2008, The Meaning of Bill Gates

Economist, 1/15/2010, The Book of Jobs

Esquire, 12/1/1983, 50 People

Esquire, 12/1/1986, Rest of your life eWeek, 6/30/2008, Bil Gates End of an Era

Family PC, 3/1/1997, Bill Gates Tips for Family PCs

Fast Co, 2/1/2001, Andreessen's New Rules — Act II

Fast Co, 12/1/2007, Open Season on Apple

Fast Co, 7/1/2009, Amazon Taps It's Inner Apple

Fast Co, 5/1/2012, Lost Tapes of Jobs

Financial Enterprise, 9/1/1983, The Magician and the Manager

Forbes, 4/1/1991, Can anyone Stop Him?

Forbes, 12/16/1996, Gil Amelio's Plan

Forbes, 7/27/1998, Master of the Internet

Forbes, 10/19/1998, Welcome to My Store

Forbes, 11/1/1999, So What's Paul Allen Got in Mind?

Forbes, 2/17/2003, The China Syndrome

Forbes, 10/3/2005, Steve remakes Microsoft

Forbes, 5/11/2009, Jobs – Nobody Loves Me (Stock options), Wiring Medicine Microsoft

Forbes, 11/7/2011, The Next Game Changers

Fortune, 2/7/1983, Apple's Bid to Stay Relevant

Fortune, 3/7/1983, How IBM Stung Hitachi Personal Computer

Fortune, 10/31/1983, Mass-Marketing the Computer

Fortune, 1/23/1984, Microsoft's drive to dominate software

Fortune, 2/20/1984, Apple Bites Back

Fortune, 8/5/1985, The Fall of Steve Jobs

Fortune, 10/1/1985, Latest from Steve Jobs

Fortune, 5/26/1986, The Puny Payoff from Computers

Fortune, 7/21/1986, Deal that Made Bill Gates $350M

Fortune, 10/13/1986, High tec Race

Fortune, 1/5/1987, 50 Fascinating Business People

Fortune, 9/14/1987, Apple on inside

Fortune, 5/23/1988, Steve Jobs Next Act

Fortune, 6/8/1988, Bill Gates takes on Antitrust

Fortune, 8/1/1988, Computer Upheaval

Fortune, 10/9/1989, Jobs Links With IBM

Fortune, 8/26/1991, Future of the PC

Fortune, 12/30/1991, What I want US Business to Do in '92

Fortune, 12/28/1992, Bill Gates Next Challenge

Fortune, 12/12/1994, AT&T On Cover Cellular $12B

Fortune, 1/16/1995, Bill Gates: What Doesn't He Want

Fortune, 7/10/1995, Andy Grove's Dream

Fortune, 10/2/1995, How We Did It Paul and Bill

Fortune, 7/8/1996, Bill Gates and Andy Grove

Fortune, 2/1/1997, Andy Grove Profit Machine

Fortune, 6/8/1998, One Digital Day

Fortune, 11/9/1998, Jobs Next Trick

Fortune, 1/31/2000, Stevie Wonder

Fortune, 2/7/2000, The Men Who Would Be King

Fortune, 7/10/2000, Microsoft Shoots for the Moon

Fortune, 6/18/2001, Beast is Back

Fortune, 6/25/2001, CEO Pay Heist

Fortune, 5/19/2003, Steve's New Act

Fortune, 2/21/2005, How Big Can Apple Get

Fortune, 5/2/2005, Why Google Scares Gates

Fortune, 9/5/2005, Steve Jobs Gets Personal (Stanford Commencement)

Fortune, 7/23/2007, Gates Conquers China

Fortune, 3/17/2008, Trouble with Jobs

Fortune, 11/24/2008, The Genius Behind Steve

Fortune, 6/15/2009, Amazon's Next Revolution

Fortune, 7/20/2009, I want You to Get the Future

Fortune, 11/23/2009, CEO of the Decade

Fortune, 11/1/2010, Dream phone iPhone and Verizon

Harpoon, 5/1/1999, Bill Gates Monster or Messiah

George, 2/1/1997, JFK Jr Interviews BillG

Inc Magazine, 10/1/1981, This Man Has Changed Business Forever

Inc Magazine, 10/1/1987, Why I Fired Steve Jobs

Inc Magazine, 4/1/1989, Entrepreneur of the Decade: An Interview with Steve Jobs.

InfoWorld, 9/14/1981, IBM Gets Personal, Apple "Macintosh"

InfoWorld, 11/30/1981, InfoWorld at Comdex

InfoWorld, 2/13/1984, Apple's Bet on Macintosh

InfoWorld, 10/17/1994, Why Steve Jobs Still Matters

Kilobaud, 1/1/1977, The Small Computer Magazine

Life Magazine, 9/10/1945, Includes "As We May Think"

Macintosh Business Review, 5/1/1988, 100 Top Companies Where Mac Is The Choice

MacWorld, 4/15/1984, Macintosh Future of Computing

MacWorld, 10/1/1989, Steve Jobs is Back coverage of NeXT

Mad Magazine, 10/1/1985, Special Computer Section

Mad Magazine, 3/1/1996, Cream Bill Gates

Money, 11/1/1982, Choosing the best new PC for you

National Geographic, 10/1/1982, The Chip

National Review, 1/24/1994, He Built a Better Mousetrap —So the Cats Ganged Up On Him

New York Magazine, 6/25/2007, Steve Jobs iGOD

New Yorker, 12/14/1981, Marvin Minksy Interview

New Yorker, 1/10/1994, Email with Bill Gates

New Yorker, 5/12/1997, Bill Gates Favorite Geek

New Yorker, 2/1/2000, Inside the Leviathan

New Yorker, 5/28/2001, Absolute PowerPoint

Newsweek, 2/22/1982, Home is where the computer is

Newsweek, 1/30/1984, It's The Apple of His Eye

Newsweek Access, 9/1/1984, Newsweek Access w/ Steve Jobs

Newsweek, 9/30/1985, Fall of Steve Jobs as Apple Chairman / A Whiz Kid's Fall

Newsweek, 1/27/1986, Jean-Louis Gassée

Newsweek, 10/24/1988, Jobs is Mr. Chips

Newsweek, 7/26/1993, Inside "From Champ to Chump"

Newsweek, 7/11/1994, The Microsoft Magic

Newsweek, 11/27/1995, Exclusive excerpts from his new book: Bill Gates predicts the Future

Newsweek, 12/2/1996, Microsoft Century

Newsweek, 6/23/1997, Gates& Ballmer: How Microsoft Was Built Interview

Newsweek, 8/18/1997, Is Bill Gates Good for Apple:

Newsweek, 3/9/1998, Why We Will Win

Newsweek, 5/18/1998, A Freshly Polished Apple (inside)

Newsweek, 5/31/1999, What You'll Want Next

Newsweek, 8/30/1999, Bill Just Wants to Have Fun

Newsweek, 11/15/1999, Bill Takes It on the Chin

Newsweek, 4/17/2000, Gonzalaz on cover

Newsweek, 5/8/2000, Antitrust slug on cover

Newsweek, 6/19/2000, How Bill Blew It and Can He Save Microsoft

Newsweek, 4/30/2001, cover Tablet PC

Newsweek, 9/5/2001, American Genius

Newsweek, 2/4/2002, They've Given Away $24 Billion

Newsweek, 11/24/2003, Bill's Next Big Thing

Newsweek, 7/26/2004, iPod Therefore i Am

Newsweek, 12/4/2006, Moving into a New Office

Newsweek, 11/26/2007, Books Aren't Dead

Newsweek, 4/5/2010, What's So Great About the iPad

Newsweek, 9/5/2011, Steve Jobs American Genius

NextWorld Magazine, 1/1/1991, Premier Issue

NY Post, 1/5/1995, First Bill Gates Column

NY Times, 8/6/1998, Microsoft Says Internet Browser Idea Arose Before Netscape

Online Access, 11/1/1994, Will this man revolutionize the online world?

PC Computing, 4/1/1984, Steve Jobs on the Future of Apple Computer

PC Computing, 8/1/1988, IBM or Apple, Is DOS Dead

PC Consumer, 3/1/1984, Bridging the Generation Gap

PC Magazine, 2/1/1982, Premier Issue

PC Magazine, 4/1/1982, Boca Diary

PC Magazine, 6/1/1982, Chaplin Cover

PC Magazine, 8/1/1982, VisiCalc v SuperCalc

PC Magazine, 9/1/1982, Inside the IBM PC

PC Magazine, 10/1/1982, Making the Elephant Dance

PC Magazine, 11/1/1982, 20 Word Processors for the IBM PC

PC Magazine, 12/1/1982, Games, Games, Games

PC Magazine, 10/1/1983, When It All Goes Wrong

PC Magazine, 1/24/1984, The New IBM PCs

PC Magazine, 4/17/1984, Challenging 1-2-3

PC Magazine, 9/4/1984, Word Processors for your PC

PC Magazine, 11/13/1984, IBM Breakthrough PC XT

PC Magazine, 4/1/2006, Bill Gates Exit Interview

PC Magazine, 9/1/2008, Best & Worst Reader Survey

PC World Magazine, 3/1/1983, How Compatible is Compatible

PC World Magazine, 4/1/1983, Traveling with the Personal Computer

PC World Magazine, 5/1/1983, DOS 2.0

Penthouse, 5/1/1984, Young Millionaires

Playboy, 1/1/1983, The Word Processor by Stephen King

Popular Electronics, 1/1/1975, Altair Part 1

Popular Electronics, 2/1/1975, Altair Part 2

Popular Electronics, 11/1/1981, What's New in Personal Computers

Popular Mechanics, 7/1/1980, Building a word processor

Popular Science, 3/1/1984, Apple's Mighty 32-bit Mac

Popular Science, 1/1/1989, Steve Jobs' Revolutionary Computer

Portable Companion, April/May, 1983, Is Portability A Myth?

Programmer's Journal, Jan/Feb 1982, DOS

Red Herring, 2/1/1998, Is Microsoft Bad?

Red Herring, 9/1/2000, Gates Unplugged

Red Herring, 1/16/2001, Privacy issue

Red Herring, 8/15/2001, The New Media Player

Red Herring, 10/15/2005, We Thought We Had a Deal

Rolling Stone, 12/7/1972, Space Game

Rolling Stone, 3/1/1984, Interview on Macintosh

Rolling Stone, 4/1/1996, Fall of Apple Part 1

Rolling Stone, 4/1/1996, Fall of Apple Part 2

Saturday Evening Post, 9/1/1982, Computers in the classroom (Steve Jobs)

Scientific American, 3/1/1973, Bicycles (Bicycle of the Mind)

Seattle Times, 4/25/1999, Wake A Sleeping Giant

The Standard, 11/15/1999, Busted (Antitrust)

Success Magazine, 10/1/1998, Managing Creative People

Success Magazine, 6/1/2010, Steve Jobs Master of Innovation

Sunday Express Magazine, 11/22/1981, Mr Apple Computerman

Time, 1/3/1983, Machine of The Year

Time, 4/16/1984, Computer Software: Magic Inside the Machine

Time, 4/1/1995, Welcome to Cyberspace

Time, 6/5/1995, Master of The Universe

Time, 2/19/1996, The Golden Geeks

Time, 9/16/1996, Whose Web Will It Be

Time, 1/13/1997, The Private World of Bill Gates

Time, 8/8/1997, Inside the Apple Microsoft Deal

Time, 9/22/1997, AOL big Coup

Time, 9/7/1998, Insert: Time Digital The next Bill Gates

Time, 3/22/1999, Bill's 12 Rules

Time, 8/9/1999, Apple of His Eye

Time, 10/18/1999, Steve's Jobs

Time, 11/15/1999, Busting Bill

Time, 1/14/2002, Flat Out Cool

Time, 5/23/2005, Xbox

Time, 10/24/2005, What's Next

Time, 12/26/2005, People of Year

Time, 4/12/2010, Inside Steve's Pad

U. Magazine, 1/1/2005, Exclusive interview Bill Gates

Upside, 10/1/1999, Steve Jobs #1

US News, 7/8/1987, Stock Market Killings

US News, 2/15/1993, The New Rockefeller

US News, 11/25/1996, Torment of St Bill

US News, 6/1/1998, The Real Threat to Microsoft

US News, 10/19/1998, The Trials of Bill Gates

Vanity Fair, 4/1/2006, iPod Therefore I Am

Vanity Fair, 8/1/2012, How Microsoft Lost Its Mojo

Wired, 7/1/1993, Peter Gabriel Interactive CD-ROM

Wired, 1/1/1994, *Microserfs*

Wired, 4/1/1994, Oh No, Mr Bill

Wired, 2/1/1996, Steve Jobs the Next Insanely Great Thing

Wired, 6/1/1996, Mr. Bill Goes Hollywood

Wired, 6/1/1997, Apple Pray

Wired, 8/1/1997, This Lawyer Is Bill Gates's Worst Nightmare

Wired, 4/1/1998, Up the Ante: Bill Gates Playing with the Big Dogs Now

Wired, 12/1/1998, 83 Reasons Why Bill Gates's Reign is Over

Wired, 8/1/2000, LoudCloud

Wired, 11/1/2000, The Truth The Whole Truth And Nothing But The Truth

Washington CEO, 8/1/2000, The Gamble .net

INDEX

Symbols

1:1s 100, 314, 414, 441, 493
4 Ps (marketing mix) 533, 858
8-bit 26
16-bit 24, 60, 63, 73, 103, 156, 176, 187, 325, 337, 349, 353, 554, 726, 734, 738, 739, 752, 758
20 percent time (Google) 562
24 (TV show) 507
32-bit 24, 62, 63, 73, 95, 103, 126, 150, 165, 176, 181, 183, 309, 353, 371, 501, 520, 553, 555, 668, 726, 734, 738, 741, 751, 752, 756, 758
64-bit 62, 63, 562, 614, 617, 619, 629, 668, 684, 734, 739, 741
80/20 rule. *See* Pareto distribution
1984 Superbowl ad (advertising campaign) 631
3270 terminal 708
16011 NE 36th Way, Redmond, WA 98052 9
//build 781, 790, 792, 795, 797, 798, 799, 801, 807, 808, 887
demonstration 635, 673, 674, 681, 687, 738, 769, 770, 780, 790, 791, 792
.DOC 182, 188, 251, 294, 299
.DOCX 545
.Mac service 603, 654
.NET 281, 387, 388, 389, 390, 391, 394, 422, 431, 435, 440, 441, 443, 449, 455, 481, 494, 525, 562, 589, 609, 641, 642, 643, 644, 645, 646, 652, 655, 679, 774, 775, 776, 777, 778, 779, 780, 785, 786, 789, 790, 791, 793, 794, 795, 797, 888
.NET Framework 387, 562, 589, 609, 642, 644, 645
.NET MyServices. *See* Hailstorm
.PPT 188, 294, 299
.PPTX 545
.XLS 182, 188, 294, 299
.XLSX 545

A

AaronG 75, 79, 80, 122, 161, 299
A/B test 552, 692, 864
ABU 92
ABurrows 597, 672, 673, 705
accountability 52, 91, 178, 220, 251, 285, 287, 397, 412, 416, 443, 448, 457, 458, 471, 569, 572, 574
Acer 619, 664, 705
Acerman, Dan (CNET) 811
ACG (Applications and Content Group) 262
Acrobat 299, 374, 509
ACT 117, 124, 125
ActiMates Barney 829
Active Directory 112, 341, 476
ActiveWin 682, 886
ActiveX 216, 282, 559, 591, 644, 777
ADC 17, 18, 19, 20, 21, 22, 23, 29, 32, 60, 78, 368, 369, 604
adds/cuts 224, 287
ADO 342, 431
Adobe 299, 321, 348, 367, 374, 407, 503, 509, 526, 544, 553, 555, 609, 612, 644, 646, 650, 666, 709, 722, 754, 767, 773, 777, 778, 806
Adobe Flash 859
Adobe Photoshop 503, 553, 646
ADO.NET 342, 431
Advanced Windows 56
Aero 529
Aero Glass 638
A Few Good Men 316
AFX 45, 47, 51, 53, 56, 57, 58, 59, 62, 65, 66, 71, 73, 75, 76, 78, 79, 98, 166, 175, 281, 413, 529, 642, 778
agile execution 585, 590
Agility = Execution + Impact 592, 594
agree to disagree 588, 589
A Hard Line on Software (video) 336
AICG (Applications and Internet Client Group) 262
AJAX 510
Akihabara 687, 688
AkioF 323, 325
AlanY 545
Aldus Corporation 773
Aldus PageMaker 773, 801
AlesH 600, 604, 609, 676, 778, 784, 793
AlexLoeb 463
Aligning for Office14 (memo) 558
Allen, Paul. *See* PaulA
all-in-one PC 841
All Things Digital 669, 671, 672, 673, 732, 747, 769, 782, 814, 844, 855
D8 782
D9 769
Amazon 428, 445, 482, 562, 565, 648, 652, 655, 712, 716, 769
AMD 62, 183, 569, 703, 739
America Online 129, 198
Amiga 857
AnandTech 704, 847, 886
AndersH 775
Anderson, Tim 781
Andreessen, Marc 136, 148, 244, 380, 438, 480, 646
AndrewCr 16
AndrewK 222, 344, 425
Android 478, 626, 651, 693, 694, 697, 698, 706, 707, 716, 717, 718, 721, 722, 723, 732, 742, 746, 747, 748, 755, 759, 771, 780, 782, 783, 830, 857, 858, 859, 863
AndyLees 783
AnnikS 424
Answer Wizard 192, 193, 229
antitrust 21, 201, 298, 329, 348, 377, 379, 380, 381, 382, 387, 389, 408, 596, 621, 655
Antoine 14, 344, 496, 526, 529, 556, 791, 794, 807, 808
AOL 124, 126, 129, 131, 133, 134, 139, 141, 145, 150, 153, 198, 256, 273, 347, 371, 391
Apache 277, 340, 562
A Personal Computer for Children of All Ages 462
API 62, 63, 95, 103, 106, 177, 199, 201, 237, 295, 308, 342, 380, 422, 465, 728
Apple 4, 5, 6, 7, 9, 11, 20, 24, 26, 34, 39, 41, 44, 51, 57, 79, 82, 83, 87, 103, 107, 120, 125, 129, 131, 137, 140, 141, 156, 163, 174, 209, 212, 213, 229, 253, 370, 379, 396, 426, 430, 462, 464, 474, 507, 518, 563, 564, 565, 603, 611, 613, 622, 623, 624, 625, 626, 629, 630, 631, 632, 633, 634, 635, 636, 641, 647, 650, 651, 654, 655, 656, 657, 658, 662, 665, 666, 667, 668, 670, 671, 672, 676, 677, 678, 679, 685, 689, 690, 691, 693, 694, 696, 698, 703, 704, 705,

706, 707, 708, 709, 710, 711, 712, 713, 714, 715, 716, 717, 719, 720, 721, 722, 724, 725, 726, 731, 732, 733, 734, 738, 740, 741, 744, 745, 746, 747, 748, 752, 753, 754, 759, 760, 763, 764, 766, 768, 769, 771, 777, 778, 779, 781, 782, 783, 785, 791, 792, 796, 797, 798, 828, 829, 830, 832, 833, 839, 840, 841, 844, 853, 855, 856, 864, 868, 885, 886
Apple][4, 5, 829
Apple eMate 662
Apple iBook 662
Apple iMac 841
Apple Lisa 9
Apple-Microsoft deal 803
Apple Newton 125, 462, 564, 650, 662, 857
Apple Silicon 719, 753, 853, 864
Apple Special Event 705
Apple Tax (advertising campaign) 634
Apple v Microsoft, 1988 379
Application Service Provider (ASP) 347, 440
Applications & Internet Client Group 278
App Store 456, 649, 654, 667, 678, 706, 713, 849
AppUp (Intel) 702
Arabic 123, 537
Arae-A Hangul 304
ARM 124, 349, 665, 692, 698, 700, 721, 725, 726, 737, 738, 739, 740, 741, 742, 743, 744, 745, 746, 747, 748, 749, 750, 751, 752, 753, 754, 755, 758, 759, 761, 768, 769, 783, 792, 793, 797, 800, 801, 804, 805, 806, 811, 813, 815, 822, 829, 831, 833, 834, 841, 842, 843, 855, 856, 857, 887
Ars Technica 72, 780, 796
Art Committee, Microsoft 166, 220, 321
ArthurdH 447, 600
ASCII 11, 325, 432
ASCII Corporation 325
Ashton Tate 97, 390
aspect ratio (Surface) 836
Assaggio Ristorante 559
ASUS 664, 665, 738
ASUS Eee PC 662, 663, 665, 666, 670, 682
As We May Think 131
Atari 4, 7, 141
ATG (Applications and Tools Group) 262, 311
Athena 198, 267
ATI 569, 703
Atom 663, 664, 665, 666, 703, 740
AT&T 27, 28, 49, 50, 124, 130, 145, 260, 379, 381, 430, 463, 650, 693, 713
attrition 575
AutoCAD 367, 553, 646
AutoCorrect 99, 189, 193, 194, 304, 520, 591
Autodesk 348, 367, 553, 612, 646, 806
Avalon 434, 578, 582, 589, 590, 609, 642, 643, 680
AWS 562, 563, 652, 655
Azure 479, 679, 859

B

b8 blog 770
back to school 175, 218, 581, 621, 638, 834
bad actors 355, 357, 362, 375
Baig, Ed 688
ballsiest 557
Barnes & Noble 192, 557
basement (customers) 132, 328, 819, 820, 821, 822, 823
Bayesian 485
BBC 684
BBS 141
BCaldas 621, 668
bCentral 392, 448, 450
BDC 69
Beige 265
Bell Labs 463
BenFa 604, 609
BenR 545
BenS 153, 158
Best Buy 613
beta 62, 63, 65, 68, 69, 89, 105, 114, 136, 152, 160, 205, 212, 238, 263, 265, 292, 303, 309, 312, 315, 316, 320, 321, 324, 374, 405, 426, 486, 495, 533, 539, 540, 542, 543, 546, 548, 549, 550, 551, 552, 555, 559, 653, 676, 680, 684, 688, 706, 884
Bezos, Jeff 428, 652
BHerbold 313
BillG 12, 14, 17, 18, 19, 21, 25, 26, 30, 31, 33, 35, 38, 39, 41, 42, 43, 44, 47, 48, 49, 50, 51, 53, 54, 55, 59, 67, 70, 71, 72, 73, 75, 77, 78, 79, 80, 81, 82, 83, 84, 85, 86, 87, 88, 89, 91, 92, 93, 94, 95, 96, 97, 98, 99, 100, 101, 102, 103, 105, 107, 108, 110, 111, 112, 113, 114, 115, 117, 118, 119, 120, 122, 123, 124, 125, 126, 127, 129, 130, 136, 138, 140, 142, 143, 146, 148, 152, 158, 159, 160, 161, 164, 165, 166, 176, 178, 180, 182, 183, 197, 199, 200, 201, 207, 208, 209, 211, 212, 214, 224, 225, 226, 227, 229, 235, 236, 237, 243, 244, 245, 247, 251, 255, 257, 259, 263, 264, 266, 267, 276, 277, 284, 287, 289, 290, 291, 293, 294, 295, 297, 298, 299, 306, 308, 310, 313, 314, 321, 322, 323, 325, 330, 336, 337, 340, 341, 343, 346, 347, 349, 352, 356, 375, 377, 378, 379, 380, 382, 386, 387, 388, 390, 395, 396, 398, 399, 403, 405, 406, 408, 409, 410, 413, 418, 422, 423, 428, 432, 434, 435, 436, 438, 441, 443, 446, 447, 448, 449, 452, 454, 456, 457, 458, 459, 462, 463, 464, 465, 466, 467, 470, 473, 475, 483, 485, 486, 487, 489, 492, 504, 505, 527, 538, 540, 544, 553, 556, 563, 564, 566, 569, 570, 572, 578, 580, 582, 583, 585, 586, 591, 594, 596, 597, 598, 599, 605, 616, 622, 630, 641, 655, 656, 669, 671, 672, 673, 674, 680, 687, 692, 705, 711, 713, 721, 728, 732, 745, 757, 772, 775, 776, 778, 785, 794, 801, 828, 842, 860, 861, 862, 863
BillieSC 547
BillN 383
BillV 635, 636, 677, 686
Bing 572, 705, 709, 860
BIOS 832, 843
Bitlocker 638
Bit rot 509
BitTorrent 509
BlackBerry 377, 398, 451, 476, 563, 582, 650, 693, 710, 723
Blackbird 149, 150, 155
Blackcomb 263, 434, 726
BLampson 117

bloat 33, 46, 47, 48, 197, 256, 282, 300, 301, 302, 303, 304, 349, 392, 432, 433, 448, 449, 460, 468, 479, 480, 484, 499, 500, 506, 507, 508, 510, 513, 517, 520, 521, 531, 532, 551, 584, 609, 659, 676
bloat (definition) 515
bloatware. *See* bloat
Blockbuster 118, 693, 710
blog 1, 540, 541, 542, 568, 569, 579, 602, 641, 658, 676, 677, 712, 770, 794
blogging whitepaper 542
Bloomberg 507, 844
Blue 138, 152, 200, 356, 357, 371, 545, 546,
Blue Screen of Death. *See* BSoD
Bluetooth 624, 629, 724
Board Meeting 843
Board Room 409
BobMu 262, 311, 343, 390, 446, 773
Boehret, Katherine 669, 672, 845
Boeing 45, 270, 310, 312, 334, 483
bold 54, 87, 103, 189, 212, 297, 389, 439, 476, 508, 517, 520, 535, 550, 557, 558, 629, 650, 695, 700, 726, 731, 734, 737, 795, 809, 825, 826
BOM 833
Bonnington, Christina (Wired) 808
BookLink 153
BOOP 91, 95, 598
Borg 94, 245
Borland 38, 39, 45, 47, 54, 57, 65, 66, 67, 68, 69, 70, 71, 77, 79, 83, 97, 164, 168, 208, 380, 430, 475, 484, 501
Borland Resource Workshop 65
Borland Turbo Pascal 772, 775
Bott, Ed 816
Bouic (Barsi), Kim 357, 358, 359
Box 406
boxed software (insult) 590
boxology 793
BPG (Business Productivity Group) 262, 773
B.P.O.E. 207
BradCh 44, 45, 66
BradSi 83, 121, 125, 136, 278
BradWe 213, 270, 486
Brady, Tim 443
BrendanB 292
BrettO 846
BrianMac 234, 235, 390, 452
BrianV 581
Broadway 143
Brodie, Richard 75
Brooks, Jr, Frederick P. 409
Brown, Mayor Willie 327
Brown University 29, 131, 367
browser war 211, 591
BSoD 371
Buckman, Rebecca 393
Bueller, Ferris 417
Buffet, Warren 127
bug (definition) 514
bugs 18, 20, 22, 23, 24, 29, 30, 31, 117, 170, 171, 249, 292, 320, 356, 368, 369, 372, 374, 376, 414, 423, 435, 437, 596, 684
Building on Windows 7 (memo) 696
Building Windows 8 750, 762
BUM 92, 166
bundle 5, 163, 186, 188, 239, 257, 267, 334, 379, 406, 460
Burger King Whopper 687
Burning Man 563
Burrows, Adrianna. *See* ABurrows
Bush, Dr. Vannevar 131
Business 2.0 568
Business Plan Review 491
BusinessWeek 27, 158, 252, 395, 498, 499, 563, 569
buzzsaw 69, 148, 149, 164, 219, 221, 227, 275, 778, 856
BYTE 5, 36, 72, 88, 252
Byzantine 110, 280, 307, 484

C

C# 390, 525, 775, 776, 777, 780, 781, 790, 794, 795
C++ 1, 27, 28, 37, 38, 41, 44, 45, 49, 50, 51, 53, 56, 57, 58, 60, 61, 62, 63, 64, 65, 66, 68, 69, 70, 71, 73, 78, 79, 81, 83, 102, 107, 108, 120, 123, 135, 144, 151, 158, 164, 175, 235, 238, 298, 336, 396, 463, 484, 526, 546, 571, 641, 643, 644, 645, 772, 775, 776, 778, 780, 785, 789, 790, 794
CableCARD 639
cached mode (Outlook) 483
Cairo 100, 103, 104, 105, 106, 107, 108, 112, 113, 116, 121, 123, 125, 134, 145, 149, 152, 165, 200, 211, 235, 236, 237, 238, 263, 387, 392, 576, 695, 726
CameronT 504, 513
Canada 82, 271, 434, 505
Cape Cod 260, 264, 266
Capitol Hill 18, 44, 60, 143, 207
Capone 200, 201, 202, 235
Captain Kirk 229
CaptiveX. *See* ActiveX
CAR 8 (license plate) 818
CarlS 75
CarlT 345
Carnegie Mellon University 41, 96, 563
Carroll, Martin 50
CATV 119, 639
CC 55, 100
CDROM 62, 63, 302, 306, 401, 424, 493, 502
CellarTacker 375
Center for Information Work 397, 711
Centrino 619, 798, 799
CES 253, 349, 649, 684, 702, 705, 706, 707, 717, 719, 744, 745, 746, 747, 748, 750, 759, 801, 805, 887
CES 2011 746, 747, 750, 759, 887
Changes and Opportunities (memo) 386
Changing the World Together (memo) 347
Channel9 541, 658
CharlesS 18, 43, 60, 182, 367
charms 762, 766
Cheifet, Stewart 148
CherieE 545
Chicago 62, 83, 95, 103, 104, 105, 106, 108, 123, 124, 125, 126, 134, 136, 138, 143, 144, 145, 146, 150, 152, 153, 154, 163, 165, 176, 177, 178, 180, 181, 183, 187, 188, 189, 190, 191, 195, 196, 200, 201, 202, 203, 204, 237, 238, 263, 726, 888
Chief Knowledge Officer 400
chief of staff 314, 396, 416, 567
Chief Software Architect. *See* CSA
China 1, 495, 502, 622, 687
ChrisCap 540
ChrisJo 158, 600, 669, 791
ChrisP 51, 57, 121, 166, 167, 170, 174, 177, 200, 201, 203, 220, 223, 237, 238, 243, 246, 247, 248, 250, 259, 260, 405, 452, 455, 458, 592
ChrisPa 572, 573, 600
ChrisPr 468
Chromebook 646, 685, 853
Chrome (browser) 563, 591, 655, 670, 679, 685, 689, 697, 732, 814

Chrome OS 685
ChromeOS 720
ChuckC 604, 610, 617
Chu, Jon M. 849
Cinemania 89
CIT 133
CIW. *See* Center for Information Work
Clark, Jim 148
classic mode 550, 553, 554, 556
Classmate PC 662
ClaySatt 528, 529, 760
ClifS 49, 66
Clip-It. *See* Clippy
Clippy 192, 226, 229, 230, 231, 232, 233, 252, 253, 300, 366, 425, 434, 498, 522, 773, 852
cloud 76, 114, 116, 195, 207, 295, 341, 348, 469, 482, 562, 572, 613, 652, 653, 676, 705, 716, 771, 855, 857, 859
CNET 550, 672
CNN 507, 508, 684
CObject 60
Cocoa (API) 650, 803, 804
Cognos 404
Coke 332
Coke, Cherry 127
Coke, Diet 127, 141, 284
college hires 12, 13, 18, 454
CollJ 287, 318, 321, 567, 640, 844
COM 107, 108
COM+ 431
COMDEX 130, 153, 163, 213, 251, 349, 350, 354, 440, 462, 463
Comedy Central 507
Come see our latest creation (Apple) 712
command bars 225, 520, 527
Common User Access 124, 512
Community Technology Preview 562
Company Meeting 42, 79, 123, 213, 236, 320, 379, 380, 430, 438, 442, 448
Compaq 15, 24, 26, 49, 81, 140, 163, 349, 363, 372, 462, 622
compatibility mode. *See* classic mode
Composer 65, 66, 68, 70
CompuServe 124, 139, 141, 145, 149, 157, 371
Computer Chronicles, The 148
Computer Reseller News 550
Confucius 502
Connectix 135
Consent Decree 626, 670
Consumer Electronics Show. *See* CES
context menus 513, 515, 516, 519, 520
continuous integration 31
convertible PC 464
cookie-licking 105, 140, 153, 235, 492
Cook, Scott 772
Cook, Tim 622, 666, 812, 815, 826, 844
Cooper, Alan 70
coopetition 130
Corel 34, 208, 281
Cornell 6, 14, 29, 83, 120, 129, 132, 133, 134, 136, 137, 138, 139, 140, 151, 152, 168, 361, 434, 861
Cornell Synthesizer 120
corrupt file 249, 368
COSD 565, 566, 572, 573, 581, 595, 597, 599, 603, 604, 605, 606, 609, 610, 616, 617, 645, 653, 658, 659, 738, 739, 758
Coupland, Douglas 245
Courier 716, 726
CP/M 5, 6, 21
Crabby Office Lady 424
Cracker Jack 602
CraigMu 117, 145, 435, 661
craplets 703
crapware 625, 627, 703, 704, 831, 845
Creating Office.NET (memo) 443
Creative Writer 226
CRM 399
Cronkite, Walter 507
Crossing the Chasm 351, 501
cross-platform 20, 26, 27, 28, 42, 45, 48, 50, 60, 112, 609, 620, 642, 645, 654, 745
Crotty, Dave 4
CRT 5
CSA 386, 403, 598, 616, 652, 673
Csikszentmihalyi, Mihaly 414
CSL 18, 20
CUI 17
CUINFO 133, 134, 135, 136
culture eats strategy for breakfast 582
Cupertino 156, 208, 647, 837
CU-SeeMe 135, 141
customization 163, 271, 275, 402, 523, 547, 548, 741
Cutting is shipping 413
Cyber Monday 445

D

DABU 92
Da Costa, Andre 682
DAD 164, 166, 170, 171, 172, 174, 176, 178, 183, 186, 195, 206, 207, 208, 218, 223, 224, 225, 237, 238, 239, 262, 266, 267, 292, 309, 322
daily builds 105, 106, 224, 344, 415, 538, 598, 599, 668, 675
Daily Show, The 507
Daniel's Broiler 242
DanN 17, 19, 21, 369
DAO 342, 431
Dash, Anil 557
Dassault 806
Data General 9, 26, 117
DAU 653
DaveBu 530
DaveC 13, 62, 63, 64, 93, 652
DaveL 140
DaveWe 68
DavidMa 384
DavidTr 139
DavidTu 188
DavidV 112, 341
DavidW 21
Davis Jr, Sammy 680
Davos 661
Daytona 150
dBase II 5, 6, 8
death march 22, 29, 31, 44
Death Star 245
DebS 81
Debugging in the (Very) Large: Ten Years of Implementation and Experience 375
DEC 9, 13, 26, 55, 97, 739
DEC Alpha 739, 757, 759
DEC Is Dead, Long Live DEC 432
decision-making 178, 287, 352, 398, 585, 586, 587, 588
DECWorld 431
Del Boca Vista 206, 319
Dell 24, 26, 273, 505, 622, 624, 633, 662, 664, 666, 688, 702, 704, 705, 721, 747, 829, 886
Dell Inspiron 1325 633
Dell XPS 633, 704, 886
denial-of-service 360
DenisG 71
Denny's 790
Department of Justice. *See* DOJ
dependencies 172, 173, 612, 640
Designed for Windows (sticker) 833
Designer (Office product) 411, 412
Detroit 120, 272, 432, 833
device driver 620, 622
DEVX 778, 784, 787, 794
DHach 188, 193, 303, 304, 591, 669,

670
Dharma & Greg 130
dial-up 6, 69, 124, 129, 141, 146, 149, 273, 280, 310, 355, 371, 454
Dick's Burgers 127
Digital Dashboard 400
Dilbert 40, 44, 272, 434, 517
dinner 22, 45, 49, 132, 207, 244, 260, 559, 579, 705, 708
Dinosaurs (advertising campaign) 551
Dinosaurs (CD-ROM 130
DirectX 578, 583, 595, 598, 646, 774, 777, 786
discipline excellence 585
disruption 38, 151, 159, 214, 278, 279, 283, 286, 288, 293, 350, 354, 516, 532, 634, 653, 655, 680, 693, 695, 707, 708, 710, 720, 854, 857, 863
Distributed Authoring and Versioning (DAV) 310
Distributed interNet Architecture (DNA) 431
Dixons 613
DLL 219, 470, 509
DLL Hell 219, 509, 703
DMuir 604, 685
docking station (iPad) 714
DocObject 201
document debugging 511
DocuSign 544
dogfood 65, 115, 201, 651
DOJ 127, 201, 233, 377, 378, 485
DOJ Case, Conclusions of Law 378
DOJ Case, Final Judgment 377, 378
DOJ Case, Findings of Fact 378
DonGa 238, 458, 459, 496
Don't ship the org chart 264
donut chart 326
DoorDash 572
Dorling Kindersley 130
DOS/V 325
dot-com (bubble) 349, 386, 392, 395, 427, 430, 432, 442, 487, 488, 490, 860
DougK 17, 18, 19, 26, 45, 46, 75, 78, 148, 368, 369, 801
Douglas, Michael 456
DRAM 413
Dr. Dobb's 5
DRG 81, 541
DRM 474, 475
Dropbox 406
Drucker, Peter 582
DSLR 618
DTAP 140, 141
DuaneC 23, 26, 29, 267, 292, 369
DuckDuckGo 860
Dynabook 462, 711
Dyson, Esther 852

E

e7 blog 677
EA 257, 316, 330, 331, 332, 333, 334, 335, 337, 338, 342, 345, 392, 393, 397, 398, 399, 404, 417, 418, 448, 460, 471, 478, 481, 555, 556
eBay 572, 654
EBC 466. *See* Executive Briefing Center
eBook 712, 713
EBU 92
Economist, The 508
ecosystem 91, 94, 96, 103, 106, 112, 153, 159, 177, 178, 208, 262, 277, 348, 350, 355, 365, 408, 451, 462, 563, 610, 612, 613, 619, 620, 621, 622, 623, 624, 626, 634, 638, 645, 651, 652, 654, 655, 656, 665, 666, 667, 691, 705, 707, 710, 741, 742, 748, 783, 828, 830, 833, 854, 855, 857, 862
Eden, Mooly 788
EdF 200, 201, 243
Efron, Zack 838
Egghead 9
Elements of a Windows tailored app: The Developer Story (memo) 787
Elfman, Jenna 130
Ellison, Larry 282, 435, 646
eMachines 350
EMC 653, 774
Emerson, Ralph Waldo 513
EMS 110, 111, 112, 113, 114, 115, 116, 121, 125, 133, 149, 150, 199, 200, 201, 202
Encarta 89, 130
Engadget 635, 682
Engineering Excellence 354, 375, 604
Enterprise Agreement. *See* EA
Entertainment and Devices 830
ErichAnd 545
EricLev 296, 297, 373, 375
EricSc 58
EricTr 658, 659
ErinCu 147
escalation (in decision-making) 352, 587, 588, 593
Escher 220, 221, 222, 224, 225, 469
Escher, M.C. 166
ET++ 28, 29, 31, 35, 38, 40, 45, 47, 53
Eudora 280, 454
EULA 320
Evans, Benedict 861
Evolve. *See* Dinosaurs
Excel 13, 17, 18, 19, 20, 21, 24, 30, 32, 33, 34, 35, 38, 43, 44, 47, 48, 51, 58, 65, 75, 78, 82, 83, 84, 92, 94, 95, 99, 101, 107, 114, 115, 122, 123, 135, 137, 148, 154, 156, 163, 164, 165, 166, 169, 170, 173, 174, 175, 176, 177, 178, 180, 181, 183, 186, 187, 189, 190, 192, 194, 195, 199, 200, 203, 206, 207, 214, 216, 217, 218, 219, 221, 222, 223, 224, 225, 226, 228, 229, 230, 232, 234, 235, 239, 240, 241, 246, 248, 249, 259, 264, 266, 267, 269, 270, 274, 281, 288, 289, 290, 293, 294, 295, 296, 299, 302, 307, 313, 314, 318, 324, 326, 334, 335, 336, 338, 342, 343, 345, 369, 375, 379, 385, 390, 393, 396, 398, 399, 401, 402, 407, 423, 425, 430, 433, 447, 452, 459, 463, 464, 466, 467, 470, 472, 481, 482, 484, 492, 493, 498, 500, 501, 504, 505, 508, 510, 511, 512, 514, 518, 519, 521, 523, 524, 527, 529, 530, 534, 537, 538, 540, 547, 549, 554, 555, 556, 558, 566, 577, 592, 593, 604, 641, 646, 656, 675, 696, 708, 709, 712, 758, 768, 771, 775, 789, 801, 802, 805, 806, 852, 856, 857, 862, 864
Excel 2.2 555
Excel, Pocket 396
Exchange. *See* EMS
EXECSUPP 318
Executive Briefing Center 257, 269, 300, 311, 318, 332, 334, 436, 477
EXTRAVEL 318
eye-tracking 514, 538

F

FAANG 352
Facebook 134, 482, 655, 709, 723, 763,

769, 772, 860
factory floor 615
FAQ 229, 427, 545
fast and fluid 692, 761, 764, 770, 771
fat (software) 31, 48, 281, 541, 542, 642, 644
Federal Trade Commission 378
Ferguson, Charles 243, 244
FIDONet 6, 141
Fight Club 130
Final Judgement 377, 626
Financial Times 209, 619
Fincher, David 130
Fine Artist 226
Firefly. *See* Office Lite
Firefox 578, 591, 603, 646, 670, 679, 814
Fisher-Price 821
Flash (Macromedia) 425, 493, 528, 609, 644, 650, 666, 722, 778
FlipStart (Vulcan) 692
floppy 5, 14, 15, 23, 30, 64, 129, 132, 141, 157, 163, 171, 182, 195, 271, 675
Flow: The Psychology of Optimal Experience 414
FNH (Japan) 352
Foley, Mary Jo 393, 568, 601, 781, 888
forcing function 122, 387, 388, 423
Fordham, Neal 4
Ford, Henry 487
Forethought, Inc. 244
Forgaard, Randy 242, 244
Forms[3] 775, 790
Fortune 500 270, 340, 430
Fortune Magazine 76
Forum 2000 388, 391, 392, 393, 394, 395, 397, 440, 442, 452, 460, 481
foundation classes 58
FoxPro 772
framing memo 265, 266, 268, 443, 445
Frank and Ollie 231
FrankGa 91
Franklin Gothic 207
free like a puppy. *See* Linux
frenemies 130
Fried, Ina 550, 672
Frogger 830
FrontPage 234, 246, 247, 248, 284, 286, 293, 294, 299, 339, 358, 395, 400, 401, 402, 404, 440, 471, 491, 503, 526
Fry's Electronics 675
FTC. *See* Federal Trade Commission
FTP 139, 140, 146, 153, 154, 155, 825
ftp.microsoft.com 139, 157
FUD 77
Fujitsu 352
Fujitsu LifeBook 624
Fulton, David 772
futzing 16, 511, 547, 558, 706, 755, 763, 818, 853

G

Gang of Four 769
garbage collection 20, 27, 45, 50
GarthH 44, 45, 58
Gartner 253, 257, 258, 269, 272, 282, 342, 448, 611, 688, 886
Gassée, Jean-Louis 853
Gates, Bill. *See* BillG
GBU 92
Gedankenexperiment 783, 864
General Electric 49, 351, 596
General Magic 125, 131, 211
General Motors 257, 430
Generation, Greatest 206
Generation X 245
Generation Y 507
Genuine Windows 623
Gen-X 513, 527
Georgetown. *See* GT
Germany 253, 417, 418, 419, 420, 421, 423, 517, 724
Gerstner, Lou 281
Get a Mac (advertising) 630, 631, 636, 671, 690
Getting Started guide (Macintosh) 816
Gibbons, Fred 772
Gibson, William 707
Glærum, Kirk. *See* KirkG
Global Financial Crisis 632, 667, 689, 802
Glockenspiel 28, 53
Gmail 481, 483, 563, 572, 653, 679, 771
Go Get This Rock 283
Golden Gate Bridge 263
golden master (DVD) 685
Goldman Sachs 23
good enough 146, 175, 333, 337, 407, 444, 462, 467, 510, 532, 552
Google 120, 182, 207, 280, 320, 402, 406, 423, 424, 482, 490, 533, 544, 558, 562, 563, 565, 572, 573, 582, 584, 591, 603, 613, 651, 652, 654, 655, 670, 676, 677, 679, 685, 689, 693, 696, 697, 698, 706, 716, 717, 718, 721, 722, 723, 732, 746, 747, 748, 769, 771, 772, 777, 782, 860
Google Apps 802
Google ChromeBook 716
Google Drive 406
Google File System (GFS) 120
Google News 809
Gopher 133, 134, 136, 139, 141, 144, 150, 152, 153, 154, 156, 242
GordM 310, 411
GordonL 15
GPM 167, 170
Graham, Paul 861
GrantG 174, 219, 224, 267, 292, 344, 419, 420, 570, 600, 604, 615, 685, 784, 832
Grayson, Paul and George 772
Great Moments At Work (advertising campaign) 493, 551
Green Button 639
GregMa 79, 244
Gretzky, Wayne 412
GRiD 462
Grizzly 400
grok 42, 192, 240, 421, 433, 489, 583
Grove, Andy 82, 413, 414, 745
growth hacking 190, 407
grunge 18, 158, 207
GT 833, 835, 837, 838, 839, 840, 841, 842, 843, 844
GTX 843, 846
GUI 17, 18, 21, 27, 38, 39, 42, 44, 45, 47, 65, 66, 67, 110, 168, 169, 208, 236, 281, 481
GUID 358, 359, 360, 362
GUM 268, 605

H

Hacker News 366
Hailstorm 387, 395, 431, 440, 454, 455, 481, 482
handwringing 724
handwriting recognition 344, 389, 463, 467, 470
HankV 208
hardcore 3, 14, 19, 47, 48, 51, 62, 63, 87, 173, 272, 309, 320, 518, 547, 650, 711
Hardcore Software 3, 52, 757, 866
Hard Drive: Bill Gates and the Making of the Microsoft Empire 76
Harvard Business School 1, 44, 220, 248, 278, 443, 549, 570, 592, 866, 888
Harvard Graphics 772

HBO 618
HDMI 629
headcount 86, 167, 175, 254, 256, 318, 491, 492, 552, 571, 572, 574, 575, 576, 577, 581, 594, 596, 640
headcount gymnastics 574, 576, 577
headtrax (internal tool) 492, 571, 577
HeikkiK 186, 205, 249, 251, 272, 273, 344, 445, 447, 450, 495, 496, 528, 675
Hello World 60, 68
helpdesk 15
Hemingway 350, 517
HenrySa 139, 146
Hewlett Packard 686
high bandwidth 90, 91
high IQ 50
high-order bit 236
High School Musical 838
Hitachi 323, 324, 352
Hollywood Racetrack 206
Honan, Matt (Gizmodo) 808
Hood Canal 87, 122, 127
Horowitz, Ben 438
Hotdog Stand 760
Hotmail 198, 247, 348, 353, 391, 447, 454, 455, 476, 481, 485, 563, 565, 572, 613, 653, 771
Hotmail Extra Storage 572
Hot Truck 135
Houlihan's 9
House Science Committee 364
HP 13, 15, 548, 622, 633, 662, 664, 666, 705, 717, 721, 886
HP-16C 15
HTC HD2 706
HTML 87, 95, 136, 143, 144, 146, 149, 152, 153, 154, 155, 156, 201, 216, 242, 243, 247, 251, 280, 282, 283, 284, 286, 288, 291, 293, 294, 295, 296, 297, 298, 299, 301, 304, 313, 335, 339, 341, 348, 358, 373, 405, 426, 440, 443, 452, 458, 459, 559, 578, 641, 642, 646, 704, 729, 758, 774, 777, 779, 780, 790, 791, 794, 795
HTML5 756, 780
Huang, Jensen 703
Human Interface Guidelines (Apple) 163
humans 192, 193, 227, 282, 295, 296, 319, 417, 495, 507, 551, 640, 819, 821
Hungarian 18, 60
HyperCard 131, 136
Hyper-V 583

I

Iansiti, Marco 1, 570, 592, 866
IAYF 118, 130, 131, 134, 136
IBM 6, 7, 8, 11, 13, 20, 21, 22, 24, 26, 33, 34, 35, 43, 47, 49, 54, 55, 56, 76, 77, 79, 81, 82, 83, 84, 85, 88, 91, 92, 96, 97, 106, 107, 110, 112, 119, 120, 123, 125, 132, 133, 136, 138, 141, 143, 199, 208, 211, 216, 234, 237, 239, 240, 244, 273, 281, 282, 308, 310, 313, 325, 334, 340, 341, 342, 345, 346, 347, 351, 352, 366, 375, 380, 381, 382, 397, 400, 409, 411, 434, 462, 480, 481, 506, 512, 525, 565, 590, 631, 648, 655, 695, 708, 721, 725, 726, 739, 774, 828, 829, 854, 864
IBM PC XT/3270 708
IBM's 360 and Early 370 Systems 434
I Can See Clearly Now (song) 680
ICCD 267
iCloud 603, 679, 713
Idea Man: A Memoir by the Cofounder of Microsoft 692
IdeaPad S10 675
idle loop 196
IgorZ 530
IHV 612
iLife 603, 654, 696
ILOVEYOU 355, 363
iMac 584
I'm a PC (advertising campaign) 630, 635, 636, 664, 676
IMN 453
Inbox 198, 199, 200, 202, 234, 486
Indigo 434, 642, 644
infinite bugs 30
influential end-users 94, 289, 494
InfoPath 460, 461, 470, 471, 472, 506, 575
Information at Your Fingertips 388. *See* IAYF
information worker 539
InfoWorld 22, 88, 313, 327
Innovate then Integrate. 563
innovation 103, 375, 389, 439, 465, 559, 563
Innovator's Dilemma 278, 283, 284, 347, 351, 392, 393, 468, 695
Input Method Editor (IME) 326
integrated innovation 389, 563
Intel 7, 14, 15, 21, 24, 25, 53, 56, 62, 78, 82, 95, 97, 99, 103, 124, 183, 196, 333, 358, 378, 380, 413, 414, 569, 611, 612, 619, 620, 622, 624, 631, 632, 633, 634, 638, 651, 655, 656, 661, 662, 663, 664, 665, 666, 668, 675, 692, 696, 702, 703, 706, 714, 720, 721, 726, 731, 733, 737, 738, 739, 740, 741, 742, 743, 744, 745, 746, 747, 749, 750, 753, 754, 768, 788, 792, 793, 797, 798, 799, 800, 803, 804, 805, 806, 807, 823, 828, 833, 841, 842, 843, 844, 846, 847, 854, 855, 864, 885
Intel Developer Forum 662, 799
Intel Inside 619, 798, 833
intellectual property 143, 274, 379, 452, 544, 740, 744, 748, 782, 834, 862
intelligent agent 213
IntelliMenus 303
IntelliSense 99, 189, 190, 193, 194, 195, 197, 286, 303
Internet Explorer 153, 211, 216, 247, 267, 280, 282, 288, 294, 298, 304, 340, 348, 377, 378, 389, 390, 393, 401, 426, 452, 453, 455, 476, 563, 565, 572, 578, 591, 595, 603, 642, 655, 656, 669, 670, 679, 698, 704, 708, 716, 736, 751, 770, 773, 794, 814, 846
Internet Mail and News. *See* IMN
Internet Service Provider 395
Internet Strategy Day 244, 387, 388
Internet Tidal Wave 126, 151, 158, 440
Internet Time 591
interns 35, 51, 267, 288, 793
intranet 286, 328, 399
Intuit 245, 510, 612
Invasion of the Body Snatchers 419
iOS 478, 763, 766, 777, 781, 857, 863
iPad 464, 711, 712, 713, 714, 715, 716, 717, 718, 719, 721, 725, 726, 732, 733, 735, 738, 741, 743, 746, 747, 752, 754, 755, 759, 764, 767, 768, 770, 771, 778, 782, 783, 789, 796, 800, 802, 804, 805, 806, 809, 811, 813, 815, 816, 818, 822, 834, 835, 836, 837, 838, 842, 843, 853,

855, 856, 857, 858, 859, 886
iPadOS 813
iPad Pro 813
iPhone 20, 33, 483, 520, 544, 611, 616, 648, 649, 650, 651, 652, 654, 655, 657, 665, 666, 667, 671, 672, 674, 677, 678, 679, 690, 691, 693, 694, 696, 697, 698, 703, 705, 706, 707, 708, 709, 711, 712, 713, 714, 715, 716, 721, 722, 723, 724, 725, 731, 732, 733, 741, 743, 744, 754, 759, 760, 761, 763, 771, 777, 778, 782, 783, 784, 789, 800, 804, 815, 816, 822, 838, 853, 855, 858, 859
iPod 280, 474, 563, 643, 649, 712, 741
IQ 25, 117
IRC 134, 141, 152
IRM 475, 476, 477, 478
Isaac Asimov's The Ultimate Robot 89
ISDN 124, 130, 310
ISO 9000 592
ISV 612, 857
Italy 502
Itanium 757
iTools 603, 654
iTunes 474, 656, 713
I've gotta be me (song) 680
Ive, Jony 213
iWork 603, 654, 713, 804, 806

J

JabeB 75
Jackson, Judge Thomas Penfield 377
Jaech, Jeremy 773
JAllard 137, 138, 139, 140, 143, 147, 154, 158
James, Mike 780
January 27, 2010 (iPad launch) 705, 710, 712
Japan 82, 94, 146, 158, 230, 231, 253, 277, 306, 322, 323, 324, 325, 326, 352, 407, 417, 418, 419, 468, 505, 551, 612, 624, 687, 688, 689, 840
Java 244, 279, 280, 281, 282, 283, 294, 301, 302, 348, 389, 392, 430, 433, 620, 626, 641, 707, 745
Java Office 281, 282, 294, 392, 707
JavaScript 280, 281, 641, 729, 779, 780, 790, 794, 795
JeanneS 320, 345
JeffH 42, 43, 44, 45, 46, 47, 49, 57, 65, 67, 68, 73, 75, 78, 79, 98, 105, 113, 165, 224, 397, 408, 448, 458, 577, 592, 655, 727, 844
JeffJo 760
JeffO 424, 547
JeffR 396, 397, 398, 404, 408, 409, 415, 419, 420, 421, 446, 447, 448, 456, 457, 462, 463, 464, 468, 471, 493, 535
JeffTe 400, 403, 405
JennC 271
JensenH 484, 486, 517, 528, 529, 530, 540, 541, 542, 543, 547, 553, 760, 765, 769, 832
Jensen Harris: An Office User Interface Blog 541
JimAll 100, 107, 108, 426, 565, 566, 567, 705
JimMcC 73
jiu-jitsu 294, 676
Jobs, Steve 7, 39, 41, 42, 43, 47, 57, 61, 97, 107, 174, 209, 357, 413, 466, 519, 544, 611, 622, 649, 650, 651, 652, 666, 677, 678, 680, 690, 704, 707, 711, 712, 713, 714, 732, 733, 751, 754, 759, 764, 777, 778, 782, 799, 803, 816, 833, 835
JodiG 29, 238, 369
JohnLu 136, 137
Jolt 609, 644, 645, 646
JonDe 20, 26, 45, 51, 78, 121, 174, 175, 201, 208, 219, 221, 223, 224, 259, 260, 264, 265, 266, 267, 277, 278, 281, 292, 318, 353, 369, 375, 469, 604, 610, 615, 617, 675, 676, 677, 688, 696, 725, 784, 832
JonS 91, 258, 313, 638
Journal (Tablet PC) 466, 467, 470
JSheehan 793
Judge, Mike 527
JudyLew 459, 460
JulieG 78, 81, 160
JulieLar 71, 401, 503, 526, 530, 533, 540, 541, 547, 549, 554, 555, 556, 600, 604, 609, 610, 615, 616, 669, 670, 671, 673, 674, 680, 692, 699, 705, 707, 727, 728, 760, 763, 769, 770, 779, 808, 831, 832, 845
Juniper Networks 565, 677
Jupiter 781

K

kagami-biraki 688
Kahn, Philippe 38, 77, 772
Kaplan, Jeremy (FoxNews.com) 808
KarenFr 227
Kay, Alan 462, 711, 828
KayB 160
KayW 242, 296, 297
KeithRo 63
KevinJo 565, 567, 572, 580, 581, 582, 583, 585, 586, 591, 597, 602, 604, 617, 618, 654, 677
Keynote (Apple) 713
Khaldun, Ibn 865
kickstand 835, 837, 838, 840, 845
Kidd Valley 675
Killer app 137
Kin 783
Kindle 648, 709, 712
Kingdome 59, 438, 439
Kingsoft WPS 304
Kinko's 8, 60, 143
Kirk, Captain 462, 464, 656
KirkG 29, 45, 372, 373, 374, 375, 430
knowledge management 114, 341, 342, 399
knowledge worker 273
Kodak 693, 694, 710
Kodiak Room 287
Kollar-Kotelly, Judge Colleen 385
Koozie 207
Korea 253, 417, 687
KPI 588
KristenD 571
KurtD 310, 364, 411

L

Lakeside School 863
Lamborghini 323
LAMP (Linux, Apache, MySQL, PHP) 775, 776
Lanci, Gianfranco 619
LanMan 15, 84, 138, 316
Laptop Hunter (advertising campaign) 634
Las Vegas 251, 671, 684
Late Night with Conan O'Brien 233
LaTeX 9
Lauren. *See* Laptop Hunter (advertising campaign)
LaurenA 476
leak (press) 274, 337, 568, 641, 657, 712, 717, 718, 885

leap year (1900) 523
Le Corbusier chair 713
LeCun, Yann 463
Leno, Jay 207
Lenovo 625, 633, 648, 664, 675, 702, 721
Lenovo IdeaPad S10 664
Lenovo Skylight OS 702
Lenovo U1 702
lessons learned (US Army) 571
Letterman, David 517
leviathan 253
Levy, Steven 462, 556, 861
LEX 606
Liar's Poker 323
LindaAv 784
LinkedIn 543
LinkExchange 346
Linux 13, 50, 98, 110, 139, 277, 340, 348, 350, 389, 418, 430, 432, 433, 491, 492, 551, 562, 565, 584, 612, 616, 619, 620, 626, 627, 652, 653, 655, 656, 662, 663, 665, 666, 676, 689, 694, 696, 697, 702, 716, 744, 745, 746, 774, 775, 829, 859
Linux on the desktop 697
LIS 306, 307, 308, 310, 311, 312, 342, 409, 410, 411, 412, 413, 482
LisaGu 425
LisaJ 173
LITEBULB 579, 717
Live Free or Die Hard (film) 820
Live Search 565, 572
Live Services 566, 653, 654
Live tiles 737, 762, 763, 789
Local Information Store. *See* LIS
Longhorn 434, 453, 481, 489, 509, 527, 528, 535, 536, 540, 545, 557, 559, 562, 563, 566, 569, 576, 578, 580, 583, 589, 590, 591, 600, 614, 636, 641, 642, 644, 655, 657, 661, 695, 720, 722, 724, 776, 888
Longhorn Reset 562, 591
LORG 257, 263, 268, 269, 271, 272, 274, 288, 289, 290, 294, 303, 311, 313, 316, 348, 354, 367, 372, 373
LoriM 345
Los Angeles 845
Los Angeles Convention Center 679
Losing our way (Allchin email) 705
lost decade 490
Lost In Translation 687
Lotus 9, 13, 20, 21, 34, 35, 38, 79, 82, 86, 94, 95, 97, 110, 111, 112, 116, 121, 125, 137, 163, 164, 165, 166, 168, 169, 172, 174, 177, 188, 199, 202, 208, 211, 222, 228, 234, 235, 237, 239, 282, 290, 307, 310, 315, 340, 341, 342, 356, 380, 384, 390, 400, 409, 430, 456, 481, 512, 559
Lotus 1-2-3 9, 21, 38, 82, 137, 163, 168, 169, 170, 172, 228, 290, 356, 380, 474, 501, 517, 523, 772, 801
Lotus Domino 400
Lotus Notes 20, 34, 86, 111, 112, 114, 115, 116, 121, 125, 199, 202, 234, 235, 237, 239, 240, 307, 310, 311, 315, 341, 342, 409, 456, 457, 459, 460, 480, 481, 772
Loudcloud 438
Love Bug. *See* ILOVEYOU
LucyP 156
Luna 529
lunch 16, 22, 29, 31, 34, 117, 156, 206, 249, 260, 417

M

Mac 8, 11, 17, 18, 20, 21, 22, 39, 43, 58, 82, 92, 94, 111, 132, 133, 135, 136, 138, 139, 140, 169, 170, 172, 175, 176, 178, 190, 231, 434, 513, 593, 603, 630, 631, 634, 635, 636, 649, 650, 654, 656, 657, 666, 667, 671, 677, 679, 689, 694, 696, 705, 706, 711, 712, 713, 719, 732, 841, 856, 857
MacApp 28
MacBook 623, 656, 666, 667, 690, 691, 704, 705, 706, 715, 747, 830, 840, 841
MacBook Air 624, 632, 633, 666, 667, 670, 676, 690, 691, 704, 705, 706, 715, 747, 754, 797, 799, 812, 840, 841
MacBook Pro 704, 830
MacBU 803, 804
Mach 41
machine learning 124, 463, 572
Machine of the Year (Time Magazine) 4, 18
Macintosh 7, 9, 11, 13, 17, 22, 23, 24, 25, 28, 30, 33, 34, 35, 39, 41, 42, 43, 48, 49, 51, 53, 54, 57, 58, 83, 87, 98, 103, 107, 110, 120, 124, 125, 129, 131, 135, 136, 139, 141, 148, 155, 166, 167, 168, 186, 187, 198, 231, 262, 302, 331, 366, 369, 379, 396, 481, 499, 507, 518, 519, 521, 524, 544, 548, 554, 584, 623, 632, 633, 634, 672, 679, 691, 731, 739, 753, 756, 761, 764, 772, 786, 853, 858
MacMendeleev 28
Mac Office 4.x 803
Macromedia Flash 777
Mac ToolBox 679
MacWrite 9, 518
magic beans 390, 405, 408
MagicGate 306
Magic keyboard 835
magic quadrant 342
Magnum, P.I. 130
MagSafe 838
Mailgram 10
malware 353, 375, 434, 436, 473, 509, 552, 632, 644, 677, 678
Management Committee 124
Management Conference 81, 334
Mango. *See* Windows Phone 7.5
Manhattan Center Ballroom 423
Manzi, Jim 125, 772
MArcuri 303
Maritz, Paul (VMware) 613
marketing mix 480
market requirements document 266
MarkK 203
Markoff, John 357, 358, 359, 360, 362
MarkWal 476
Marquardt, Dave 585
MartinO 53
MartinSt 364
Marvel 124, 127, 146, 149, 150, 151, 155
Marymoor Velodrome 675
mastery 228, 513, 520, 523, 539, 547, 553, 786, 820, 821, 854
mastery (of product) 820
McCaw, Craig 863
McDonalds 418, 744
McDonnell Douglas Aerospace 9
MCE. *See* Windows Media Center
McNealy, Scott 197, 380, 432, 433, 437
McZee 226
MDM 595. *See* PUM
Media Center PC 721, 798
Media Lab (MIT) 661
MediaMarkt 613
MegaServer 439

Meiji Shrine and Garden 689
MelBG. *See* MelissaB
MelindaF 102
MelissaB 29, 31, 372
memex 131
Memory Stick (Sony) 306, 307
Memphis 40, 263, 607, 726
Mendelson, Ed 472
Mercury 111
Messenger 572, 613, 654
metadata 360, 362, 373
Metcalf, Bob 380
Metro 722, 770, 771, 794, 831, 833, 847, 850
Metropolitan Grill 451
Metro-style 751, 762, 766, 767, 768, 770, 771, 779, 785, 805, 806, 815, 819, 821, 824, 834, 887
Meydenbauer Center 615
MFC 59, 60, 62, 63, 64, 65, 66, 68, 69, 70, 78, 79, 238, 775, 778, 785, 789
MGX 685, 848
Micro$oft 510
Micro-dollars 577
Micrografix 772
MicroNews 158, 350
MicroRim 9
Microserfs 245
MicroSloth 510
Microsoft Access (database) 114, 165, 175, 510, 640
Microsoft Achievement Award 327, 443, 451, 495, 696
Microsoft Bob 226, 227, 229, 231, 253
Microsoft Campus
  Building 1 9
  Building 5 13
  Building 8 78
  Building 16 152
  Building 17 64, 78, 172, 188, 204, 220, 249, 267, 278, 287, 317, 321, 384
  Building 17 275
  Building 34 414, 567
  Building 36 396
  Building 50 570
  Building 99 670
  Northup Building 71
  RedWest 348, 350, 562
  Studio A 840
  Studio B 828
  Studios Campus 828
Microsoft Company Store 169
Microsoft Edge 603
Microsoft Exchange 86, 115, 211, 269, 341, 651, 774
Microsoft Foundation Classes. *See* MFC
Microsoft Home 594
Microsoft is Dead (essay) 862
Microsoft Mouse 519
Microsoft .NET 394
Microsoft Office System 493
Microsoft Poll 563
Microsoft Press 11, 14, 460
Microsoft Research 88, 117, 118, 123, 131, 192, 211, 212, 229, 319, 344, 367, 398, 436, 463, 474, 637. *See* MSR
Microsoft Secrets 245
MicrosoftSF 327
Microsoft Store 849
Microsoft Teams 862
Microsoft TechReady 727
Microsoft University 71
Microsoft Values 439
Microsoft Works 499
Microspeak 105, 111, 825
MID 663, 702, 712
middleware 627
mid-year review 396
MikeAng 201, 202, 397, 398, 621, 628, 671, 705, 746, 747, 748, 769, 791, 792, 808, 829, 830, 831, 832, 834, 839, 842, 846, 848, 849
MikeBro 430
MikeCon 186
MikeKell 425
MikeKo 343, 401
MikeMap 43, 47, 54, 56, 58, 67, 68, 85, 91, 92, 93, 96, 98, 99, 111, 121, 154, 164, 166, 171, 177, 206, 211, 217, 258, 314, 449, 458, 532, 568, 579, 631, 655
MikeMur 82
Milk Studios 845
Millennials. *See* Generation Y
Miller, Michael 546
Mini-Microsoft 568, 569, 574, 599
Ministry of International Trade and Industry (MITI, Japan) 325
MinWin 659, 672, 794
MIPS 62, 84, 739, 757, 759
MIS 140
MIT Media Lab 229, 502
MobileMe 603, 654
Mobile World Congress 807
Modafinil 418
modem 6, 129, 273, 310, 713
Modern Application Model 784
Modern Windows Experience (Windows 8) 699
Mojave Experiment (advertising campaign) 632
MOM 188
Momenta 462
monopoly 2, 155, 378, 381, 383, 384, 395
Montlake. *See* GTX
Moore, Geoffrey 501
Moore, Gordon 333, 740, 745
Moore's Law 117, 214, 301, 333
more cowbell 783
Mosaic 117, 136, 139, 141, 148
Moscone Center 62
MOSE 345
Mossberg, Walt 254, 327, 426, 546, 557, 564, 625, 666, 669, 672, 673, 674, 685, 688, 703, 715, 722, 732, 769, 770
Motorola 14, 260, 720, 753, 864
Movement (Surface commercial) 849
MSAA. *See* Microsoft Achievement Award
MSCOPY 148
MS-DOS 8, 11, 13, 14, 15, 16, 17, 18, 19, 21, 22, 24, 25, 29, 33, 34, 38, 39, 42, 44, 51, 53, 54, 56, 65, 82, 84, 91, 94, 103, 104, 110, 121, 129, 137, 139, 148, 164, 168, 169, 170, 174, 187, 190, 209, 218, 290, 325, 331, 355, 356, 357, 368, 434, 452, 474, 488, 500, 512, 517, 519, 554, 555, 653, 731, 734, 752, 756, 758, 759, 768, 770, 772, 801, 805, 812, 814, 816, 825
MSievert 617
MSKK 146, 306, 323, 324, 325, 326, 505, 687, 688
MSMOVE 39
MSN 159, 278, 336, 348, 349, 350, 388, 391, 444, 446, 454, 455, 488, 505, 572, 592, 613, 653, 654
MSN CarPoint 562
MSN Messenger 562, 565, 592, 613, 653, 654
MSN Wi-Fi Hotspots 562
MSPHONE 39
MS Poll 408, 586
MSR 96, 117, 118, 121, 485
MTV.com 141
Munchmore, Michael 809
Multiplan 17, 21, 26, 44, 523

multitouch 649, 671, 674, 697, 711, 717, 721, 726, 846
MurrayS 21
Musical Instruments 89, 130
Musk, Elon 833
MVP 365, 431, 542, 543, 546
My dad tries Windows 8 for the first time (video) 815
MYR 414, 415, 416, 417, 418, 419, 420, 421, 446, 483, 490, 550, 551, 552, 553, 556, 558, 772
MySpace 590, 654
MySQL 562
Mythbusters (blog post) 542
Mythical Man-Month 14, 316, 409, 458, 575, 695

N

Nader, Ralph 357
Napster 474, 509
Narita Airport 306, 323, 689
NASA 383, 591
Nash, Johnny 680
Nashville 263, 607, 726
NatalieY 73, 75, 79, 160, 161
NathanM 96, 100, 103, 117, 118, 119, 145, 146, 184, 212, 214, 284
National Public Radio 689
NCR 462
Nebraska 396
NEC 352, 462
Negroponte, Nicholas 661
NeilK 45
Netbook 611, 660, 661, 662, 663, 664, 665, 666, 667, 675, 685, 686, 689, 690, 696, 702, 703, 708, 712, 714, 715, 748, 763, 771, 798, 833, 842
NetDocs 386, 390, 391, 392, 393, 394, 452, 453, 455, 456, 457, 458, 459, 460, 461, 470, 480, 496, 525, 571, 576
Netflix 639
Netscape 68, 148, 185, 201, 207, 211, 234, 239, 242, 244, 245, 247, 277, 280, 283, 289, 291, 294, 298, 340, 348, 352, 377, 380, 401, 402, 430, 438, 454, 480, 591
Netscape Communicator 454
Netware 15, 133, 138, 146
Network Computer 282, 646
Network Courier 110
Newsweek 462, 556, 884
New Yorker, The 127
New York Times 88, 199, 252, 357, 360, 373, 490, 636, 664, 670, 685, 884, 885, 886
NeXT 413, 544
next billion 661, 662, 665, 694, 700, 788
Next Generation of Office. *See* NGO
Next Generation Windows Services. *See* NGWS
Next Release of Office. *See* NRO
NeXTStep 41, 42, 43, 45, 46, 47, 53, 57, 58, 65, 66, 67, 70
NGO 442, 443, 447
NGWS 386, 387, 392, 431, 440, 442
NIH (Not Invented Here) 219
Nimoy, Leonard 408
Nishi, Kazuhiko: "Kay" 325
NMB Technologies 831
NobuY 324
NOISE 352
Nokia 260, 563, 651, 678, 723, 741, 783, 843
non-goals 576, 588, 589, 593
Norton, Peter 499
NoSQL 113
Novell 146, 430
NRE 839, 840
NRO 337, 338
NSFNet 143
NVIDIA 569, 703, 740, 749, 750, 831, 834, 843, 864, 886
NVIDIA ION 703
NVIDIA Tegra 749, 831

O

OAC 274, 275, 276, 294, 303, 352, 415, 628
Object Linking and Embedding. *See* OLE
object-oriented programming 37, 49, 785. *See* OOP
Object Windows Library (Borland) 45
O'Brien, Conan 434
Observations, Aspirations, and Directions for Windows and Windows Live (memo) 580, 586
OBU 92, 175
ODBC 342, 431
ODM 622, 623, 624
OEM 84, 91, 146, 153, 198, 332, 333, 416, 417, 505, 580, 581, 597, 610, 611, 620, 621, 622, 623, 624, 625, 626, 627, 628, 629, 633, 638, 651, 656, 657, 660, 664, 665, 666, 667, 668, 671, 672, 697, 702, 703, 704, 716, 717, 718, 726, 741, 742, 743, 747, 748, 749, 750, 753, 767, 784, 811, 828, 829, 830, 831, 832, 834, 841, 843
Office 4 98, 99, 156, 163, 165, 170, 171, 175, 178, 179, 180, 182, 188, 189, 190, 250, 287
Office9 265, 266, 268, 275, 277, 278, 279, 283, 284, 286, 287, 288, 289, 291, 292, 293, 294, 295, 303, 305, 309, 310, 312, 315, 316, 317, 318, 337, 344, 404, 607
Office10 335, 337, 342, 343, 344, 353, 357, 359, 360, 367, 374, 375, 376, 384, 386, 393, 394, 402, 403, 418, 419, 422
Office11 450, 452, 458, 459, 460, 461, 469, 475, 476, 477, 481, 482, 496
Office12 517, 521, 522, 524, 526, 532, 533, 534, 535, 536, 537, 538, 540, 541, 542, 543, 545, 549, 550, 552, 553, 554, 556
Office14 558, 560
Office 97 232, 249, 252, 253, 254, 255, 257, 258, 259, 262, 263, 264, 265, 267, 271, 272, 277, 278, 279, 286, 287, 288, 289, 291, 292, 293, 294, 300, 304, 308, 309, 312, 316, 320, 321, 322, 339, 357, 358, 359, 369, 375, 423, 453, 473, 556
Office 365 114, 206, 341, 406, 450, 493, 506, 537, 862
Office 2007 536, 549, 557, 558, 559, 573, 599, 600, 677, 689, 691, 705, 753, 760, 863
Office as a Service 441
Office Assistant 230, 252, 322, 408, 485, 498, 513. *See* Clippy
Office for iPad 804, 806
Office for Mac 803
Office Hours 606, 618
Office Hours (my blog) 565, 569, 602
Office Lite 498, 499, 503, 504, 505, 506, 508, 551, 659
Office.NET 386, 390, 392, 443, 444, 446, 447, 448, 449, 450, 452, 476, 844
Office planning process 263, 590
Office Resource Kit 271
Office Space (film) 527
OfficeSpace (user interface) 527
Office System 2003 506

Office User Interface System, The (memo) 553
Office Web Applications 696
Office Web Companions (OWC) 558, 559
OFFPM 167, 201, 291, 319
OKR 582
OLE 107, 163, 186, 201, 216, 500, 644, 645, 773
OLE Controls 644, 645
OLEDB 342, 431
OLPC XO-1 661
Omega 30
OneDrive 1, 696, 771, 806, 848
One Laptop Per Child 502, 661
OneNote 216, 471, 472, 493, 494, 506, 526, 575, 711, 802, 805, 806, 857, 862
One Strategy 1, 570
Only the Paranoid Survive 413
OOF 49
OOP 26, 27, 49, 63
oopaholic 49, 51, 57, 60, 108
Open Letter to Hobbyists 379
Open Office 662
OpenOffice 433, 489, 491, 501, 506, 532, 544, 550
OpenOffice.org 433
open source (approach) 295, 418, 430, 433, 655, 661, 679, 697, 716
open-source (product) 133, 134, 152, 219, 277, 340, 433, 489, 551, 747
open standard 298, 545
operating segments 488
OPK 627
Opportunities in the "Software Decade" 386
opportunity map 398, 399, 468
OPU 166, 170, 171, 174, 175, 176, 178, 180, 181, 186, 188, 190, 194, 212, 218, 219, 220, 221, 222, 223, 224, 231, 235, 237, 238, 257, 259, 262, 265, 267, 277, 286, 287, 289, 291, 296, 303, 309, 314, 344, 373, 375, 425, 565
Opus 29, 30
Oracle 112, 113, 155, 258, 282, 313, 320, 340, 341, 352, 399, 407, 430, 435, 466, 563, 646, 774
order of magnitude 27, 830
Origami 829
OS/2 11, 13, 15, 17, 20, 21, 22, 24, 25, 28, 31, 33, 34, 35, 36, 38, 39, 42, 43, 44, 45, 48, 51, 53, 54, 55, 56, 66, 76, 77, 80, 83, 85, 92, 103, 106, 124, 198, 345, 385, 481, 512, 525, 721, 734
OS/2 3.0 56
Osborne 4, 5, 675
Osborne, Adam 720
Osborne effect 720
OS X 649, 650, 654, 671, 689, 694, 696, 712, 714, 724, 725, 733, 803, 804
Otellini, Paul 564, 665, 744, 745, 768, 885
Other Road Ahead, The (essay) 861
Outlook 97 254, 267, 268, 308, 365, 480, 483, 484, 493, 555
Outlook 98 267, 308, 309, 365, 453, 480, 493
Outlook 2000 309, 365, 410, 453, 480, 493
Outlook 2002 453, 494
Outlook 2003 494
Outlook Bar 239
Outlook.com 1, 771
Outlook Email Security Update 365
Outlook Express 267, 268, 453, 468, 481
Outlook Web Access 453, 455, 510
OWL 65
OWS 401, 402, 403, 404
Ozzie, Ray 111, 355, 585, 598, 652, 772. *See* ROzzie

P

Pacific Place 650
PageMaker 71, 102, 554
Palm Pilot 124, 158
Palm Trēo 650
Panay, Andrew 849
PanosP 831, 833, 834, 839, 840, 841, 846
PARC 18, 27, 75, 107, 117, 120, 182, 367
Pareto distribution 374, 514
Park Hyatt 323
participatory design 274, 276, 445, 448, 608
Patch Tuesday 509
patents 79, 379, 380, 433, 841
PaulA 26, 31, 98, 129, 209, 255, 519, 630, 692, 828, 844
PaulMa 65, 95, 98, 100, 121, 136, 160, 161, 245, 257, 258, 259, 278, 282, 314, 343, 386, 387, 395, 593, 653
PayPal 482
PBS 396, 398, 418
PC Magazine 72, 88, 252, 427, 472, 546
PCode 26, 281
PC on every desk 269, 438
PC-Plus 564
PC Week 22
PCWeek 393
PDC 62, 63, 64, 65, 68, 95, 105, 106, 388, 540, 541, 542, 546, 676, 677, 679, 680, 681, 684, 781, 792
PDF 182, 242, 299, 321, 374, 377, 466, 478, 503, 544, 545
Pegatron 702
PeggySt 271, 272, 274, 275
Pegoraro, Rob 494
pen computing 463, 466, 527, 645
Penny Arcade (comic) 821
Pentium 358
Perceptive Pixel (PC) 808
Perfect Office 304
Perlmutter, David "Dadi" 745
persona 819
Personal Technology 254
PeteH 99, 100, 121, 164, 166, 214, 223, 259, 396, 458, 594
PeteK 846
PeteMor 222
PeterEn 221, 469, 470
Petzold, Charles 786
P&G 313
PhotoDraw 391, 500
Photon 722
Photon (Windows Phone 7) 694
Photoshop 367, 528
PHP 562
physics of shipping 409
Pichai, Sundar 679
Pilates 636
pilers or filers (Outlook) 486
PIPC (Pre-Installed PC) 324, 325
piracy (software) 433, 475, 502, 620
Pirillo, Chris (blogger) 815
pivot 77, 98, 158, 235, 239, 313, 348, 375, 390, 396, 439, 492, 493, 504, 510, 530, 599, 601, 615
PJHough 779
Planet Java 675
Planning Windows 7 Client (memo) 610
Platforms & Applications Group 278
platform shift 801
Platinum 306, 307, 310, 315, 320, 336
PMF. *See* product-market fit
PocketPC 396, 463
Pogue, David 523, 685, 809, 814, 888
point of view 48, 57, 59, 116, 152, 254,

298, 300, 420, 456, 491, 521, 550, 554, 555, 677, 706, 707, 709, 710, 749, 761, 791, 812, 832, 834, 835, 840, 843, 860
Polar 400
poorly debugged set of device drivers 380, 646
POP3 198
Popular Computing 518
Post-PC 564
PowerBook 140
PowerPC 720, 753, 754, 864
PowerPoint 34, 47, 60, 85, 92, 107, 123, 156, 163, 165, 166, 169, 170, 175, 177, 180, 181, 187, 189, 190, 192, 194, 195, 203, 206, 207, 213, 214, 216, 218, 219, 221, 222, 224, 225, 228, 233, 234, 240, 241, 243, 244, 245, 246, 249, 266, 267, 270, 280, 281, 288, 290, 292, 293, 294, 296, 297, 299, 301, 304, 314, 318, 324, 335, 349, 350, 373, 375, 401, 402, 407, 424, 432, 433, 446, 447, 455, 466, 467, 470, 472, 477, 484, 498, 500, 501, 504, 510, 511, 513, 519, 521, 529, 530, 532, 537, 538, 540, 558, 559, 696, 709, 768, 771, 802, 805, 806, 840, 852, 856, 862
Power Toys 822
PPathe See Blue
Prague 600
press release 318, 319, 322, 344, 425, 447, 534, 568
PRIME score 796, 808
Pritchard, David. *See* DavidPr
privacy 360, 533
product-market fit 169, 407, 433, 435, 460, 473, 480, 492, 562, 596, 597, 640, 852
product requirements document 266
Professional Developers Conference 104, 540, 676, 790, 886. *See* PDC
PROFS 110
Programming Windows (book) 786
Project Stretch (IBM) 216, 434, 725
Project X 213
Project Xanadu 131
promise and deliver 31, 629, 682, 684, 685
proprietary 18, 38, 79, 88, 98, 108, 117, 144, 146, 199, 251, 280, 281, 294, 295, 297, 298, 306, 310, 335, 340, 379, 389, 390, 452, 460, 474, 481, 559, 778
protected mode 21, 23, 24, 95
prototype 216, 389, 462, 527, 614, 615, 702, 716, 720, 727, 792, 801, 809, 838, 841, 843, 845
Provigil 418
PSS 83, 157, 357, 365, 370, 371, 372, 415, 473
PST (file format) 308
Publisher 102, 123, 158, 227, 471, 518, 544, 545
PUM 574, 584, 595, 596, 598, 637
Puma Clydes 138

Q

QAT 548, 549
Qualcomm 702, 740, 749, 834
Qualcomm Snapdragon 702
quash innovation 378
Quattro Pro 380
Queen Anne (Seattle) 127
QuickBase 510
Quicken 245, 510, 772
QWERTY 507

R

Rachleff, Andy 169
Radio Shack 258, 313
RAID 18, 20, 31, 188, 370
raison d'être 775, 821
RajeshJ 458
RalfG 835, 841, 846
RAMJAC 382
RandallB 425
random 50, 86, 96, 122, 131, 192, 265, 356, 359, 514
Rashid 96
real artists ship 57, 65
real mode 23
Rebello, Kathy 158
Reddit 45, 69, 366, 733
Red Dog 652, 653, 657, 679
Reddy, Raj 563
Redmond Grey 760
ReedK 195
registry corruption 509
Release 1.0 23
R.E.M. 141
Ren 234, 235, 236, 237, 238, 239
Renegade (song) 792
Ren & Stimpy 199, 200, 202, 234
ReplayTV 118
Repo Man 292
Residence Inn 9, 12
responsibility assignment matrix 587
results-oriented design (Office 2007) 530
Revenge of the Nerds 76
RFC 143
Ribbon 531, 533, 537, 538, 539, 540, 541, 542, 543, 546, 547, 548, 549, 551, 554, 556, 557, 558, 731, 857
RickP 44, 45, 46, 47, 50, 51, 58, 60, 64, 78, 369, 529
right-click 196, 519
RobbieB 203, 830
RobG 146
RobPr 364
Rosenblatt, Seth (CNET) 809
RossS 570
Rothman, Wilson (MSNBC.com) 809
Royal College of Art 213
Royce, Winston 212, 590
ROzzie 341, 585, 598, 652
RSN (real soon now) 22
RSones 621, 668
RTM 30, 72, 79, 84, 114, 178, 203, 257, 292, 315, 322, 395, 413, 419, 436, 448, 496, 526, 536, 557, 560, 567, 617, 681, 683, 685, 688, 690, 843
Rube Goldberg 584
Ruby 70
runtime 70, 71, 642, 643, 728, 778, 857
RussS 129, 134, 146
RWolf 401, 559

S

SaaS 83, 399, 404, 857
sabbatical 327
Salesforce.com 438
SamF 323, 324, 325
SamH 230
Samsung 462, 742, 783, 808, 830
Samsung Developer Prototype PC 792
Sands Exhibition Center 705
San Francisco 62, 327, 425, 713, 721
San Jose Mercury News 55, 209
SAP 318, 352, 399, 404, 407, 430, 492, 563, 574, 774
SarahL 207, 592
SARS 495
Saturday Night Live 272, 517
SatyaN 677, 706
scalable Windows 103, 462

Schedule+ 86, 111, 199, 218, 234, 235
schedule chicken 59, 66, 292, 309, 334, 675, 724
Schwarzenegger, Arnold 123
ScottGu 794
ScottRa 12, 17, 23, 28, 41, 44, 45, 58, 65, 107, 369
Scribbler 469, 470, 471
SDK 38, 42, 231, 611, 649
Seattle Post-Intelligencer 76
Seattle Times 11, 300, 384
SEC 2, 143, 459, 640
Securities Exchange Commission. *See* SEC
security 337, 365, 436, 533, 595, 614
Seinfeld 118, 206
Selleck, Tom 130
Semiahmoo 81
Sent Items 791
Sent Items folder 351
September 11, 2001 435, 462
SGI 148
share is air (SteveB) 488
SharePoint 216, 395, 403, 404, 405, 406, 407, 408, 412, 418, 422, 423, 427, 434, 440, 447, 448, 450, 459, 460, 469, 471, 476, 478, 492, 494, 506, 526, 535, 543, 552, 559, 569, 575
SharePoint Team Services 404, 423, 440, 447, 526
shelfware 406, 407
shell 106, 108, 123, 200, 204, 227, 235, 236, 535, 571, 639, 704, 733
Sherman Antitrust Act 377
Shimpi, Anand Lal 847
Shinjuku 306, 687
ship meals 22
ship party 207, 322, 686
Shipping Software 51, 57, 455, 592, 608
Shipping Software On Time (memo) 51
Siebel 404, 774
Silicon Valley 1, 3, 16, 62, 156, 222, 248, 266, 281, 347, 349, 440, 578, 618, 655, 705, 713, 721, 772, 801, 806, 835, 852, 857, 859, 865, 868, 870, 871
Silverlight 609, 644, 722, 724, 775, 777, 780, 781, 784, 786, 790, 791, 794, 796, 888
Simple Finder (Macintosh) 302
SINDOGS 369
single-threaded 263
Sinofsky, David 4
Sinofsky, Jill 5
Sinofsky, Marsha 6
skateboard 840
skeuomorphic 472
SKU 95, 203, 240, 266, 332, 399, 447, 460, 465, 467, 468, 471, 499, 504, 505, 506, 612, 637, 640, 668, 711
SkyDrive. *See* OneDrive
Skype 572, 654, 656
slash commands 168, 517
slate 59, 126, 263, 274, 464, 465, 470, 528, 702, 711, 712, 770, 833
slate (tablet computer) 702
SLM 18
Smalltalk-80 9, 27, 28, 519
SmartFlow 709
SmartSuite 163, 164, 189, 237, 239, 282, 304, 512
Smart Tags 425, 426
Smith, Kevin (actor) 820
smoking our own supply 431
SMoreau 760
SMS 466, 654
SoC 665, 721, 725, 726, 730, 740, 741, 744, 745, 746, 747, 750, 758
Software As A Service 439
software as a service (SaaS) 332, 338, 339, 347, 405
Software Assurance 345
Software Digest 516
Software Quality Monitoring. *See* SQM
SOM 107
Somase 642
Someday you will. . . 130
Sony 253, 306, 307, 308, 327, 563, 622
Sony Metreon 327
Sony PictureBook 306, 662
Sony VAIO 308, 624, 666
Sony VAIO Z 705
South Africa 502
Soviet Union 268, 605
SPAM 455, 485
Spiff 265
Spock 229, 408, 568
SPS 404
SQL 112, 113, 114, 115, 274, 277, 308, 315, 327, 336, 340, 341, 342, 343, 400, 401, 403, 407, 430, 452, 716
SQM 511, 514, 684
Squire of Gothos 266
Stack Overflow developer survey 646
Starbucks 483, 565
Star Division GmbH 432
Stardock 822
StarOffice 304, 432, 433, 510, 517
Starship Enterprise 702
Start menu 105, 126, 155, 188, 189, 553, 625, 627, 700, 704, 755, 756, 760, 762, 763, 766, 768, 770, 810, 815, 816, 817, 818, 820, 821, 822, 848, 855, 857, 865
Star Trek 229, 266, 464, 580, 656, 711
Star Trek: Wrath of Khan 656
Start screen 751, 762, 763, 766, 768, 770, 790, 810, 815, 817, 819, 821, 824, 826, 848, 849, 854
State Route 520 71
Stern, Joanna 809
SteveB 12, 14, 42, 84, 91, 100, 115, 122, 138, 146, 157, 239, 249, 250, 259, 272, 283, 313, 314, 316, 317, 320, 327, 332, 334, 340, 346, 352, 353, 386, 388, 394, 395, 396, 397, 398, 406, 407, 408, 411, 416, 417, 419, 420, 430, 432, 433, 434, 438, 439, 442, 446, 447, 448, 450, 456, 457, 488, 489, 491, 492, 493, 502, 525, 552, 553, 562, 565, 566, 569, 570, 572, 580, 581, 582, 583, 585, 586, 591, 596, 597, 598, 599, 606, 612, 621, 632, 651, 654, 655, 656, 660, 668, 669, 673, 676, 677, 684, 685, 686, 705, 717, 727, 730, 731, 744, 746, 747, 773, 780, 784, 801, 833, 844, 845, 846, 849, 857, 858, 860
SteveGr 375
SteveL 600
SteveSh 495
SteveSi 12, 705
StevieB 837, 846
Stewart, Jon 507
stock option 10
Stranger in a Strange Land 192
Strategy for the '90s - BillG email 55, 76
strategy tax 180, 308, 481
streaming 119, 120, 141, 146, 639
STS 404, 405
stupid developer tricks 645, 777, 888
stupidest thing 50, 77, 101
stylus 124, 462, 463, 650, 711, 713, 732, 733
Sun 79, 107, 141, 155, 156, 157, 197, 258, 280, 281, 313, 340, 348,

350, 352, 380, 430, 432, 433, 435, 532
Sun Also Rises, The 350, 517
Sun Microsystems 197, 280, 380, 544
superenthused (BillG on Windows 7) 669
Super Friends 605
supply chain 622, 624, 712, 742, 798, 800
support lifecycle 556
Support Lifecycle Policy 345
Surface 1, 671, 674, 692, 717, 718, 826, 830, 831, 832, 835, 838, 841, 844, 845, 846, 847, 848, 849, 850, 856, 858, 859
Surface Duo 718
Surface RT 692, 844, 845, 846, 849, 856, 858
Surface table PC 671, 674
sustaining engineering 345
SwiftUI 641, 785
Swisher, Kara 669, 673, 732, 770
swoop and poop 587
Sword of Damocles 694
Symbian 723, 742
synergy 87, 123, 124, 176, 178, 182, 213, 246, 247, 265, 307, 311, 336, 337, 342, 404, 422, 426, 431, 454, 455, 458, 563, 569, 595, 642, 645, 722
system-on-a-chip. *See* SoC
system requirements 187, 384, 552, 638, 746

T

T3 124, 265
table pencil (Word) 326
Tablet PC 388, 389, 398, 462, 463, 464, 466, 467, 470, 472, 489, 504, 562, 571, 595, 612, 672, 711, 717, 718, 721, 732, 757, 758, 764, 770, 798, 805, 825, 829
Tahoe 399, 400, 402, 403, 404
tailored web 708, 728
Taiwan 622, 740
Taligent 125, 174
TAM 274
Tandy 7, 26
taskbar 188, 521, 522, 671, 674, 704, 760, 762, 763, 767, 810, 814, 815, 816, 822, 826, 855
task pane 515, 522
TBriggs 514, 538
TCO 208, 344
TechFest 319
techies 168, 254, 452, 542, 607, 716, 733
Techmeme 681, 751, 809
Technorati 540
TedJ 773
Ted Johnson. *See* TedJ
Tektronix 9
teleprompter 846
TeresaFe 271
Tesla 760, 833
testosterone-based development 269
TeX 9
tfc 229, 253
TGriffin 579
The Economist 88, 230, 714
The Only Thing That Matters (product-market fit) 480
The Presidents (of the United States) 686
Think Different (advertising campaign) 631
ThinkPad 93, 715, 770
ThinkVantage Technologies 625
ThinkWeek 122, 123, 124, 125, 126
Thomke, Stefan 592
Thoughts on Flash 778
Three Envelopes, The 581
three versions, conventional wisdom of 226, 852, 858
Thurrott, Paul 472, 771, 795, 823, 887, 888
Tiger 118, 119, 120
tight (software) 14
Tile World (Windows 8) 826
Time Magazine 76
Times Square 849
Titanium 336
TLT 386
T-Mobile 617
TMyerson 783
toaster-refrigerator 813, 826, 827
Tokyo 323, 688, 713
Tomatoey 529, 530
TomEv 111, 136
toolbar 78, 95, 163, 189, 190, 195, 222, 225, 273, 301, 302, 303, 344, 374, 426, 470, 511, 513, 514, 516, 518, 523, 541, 542, 546, 556, 854
Tools Options 523, 524
tooltip 222
top-down, bottom-up, and middle-out (planning) 264, 441, 699, 727
top-down, bottom-up, middle-out (planning) 286
Toshiba 462
Toshiba Libretto 662
Total Cost of Ownership 272, 302. *See* TCO
Touch Cover (Surface) 837, 838, 840, 842, 849
touch interface 464, 671, 678
towels 562
Tower Books 27, 48, 192
Toyota 398, 817
Toyota Prius 398, 817
trackpad 140, 624, 837
Transmeta 844
Transparency and disclosure (memo) 657
transparent 14, 100, 601
TReller 686, 702
trivial 2, 23, 26, 27, 101, 149, 193, 222, 272, 280, 347, 354, 359, 395, 424, 473, 511, 538, 557, 581, 865
TRogers 545
TRS-80 6
trucks 39, 733
Trustworthy Computing 509, 527, 604. *See* TwC
T-shirt 59
TSMC 740
TwC 436
Twin Peaks 130
Twitter 378, 638, 733, 796, 809
two gardens (Windows and Office) 94, 101, 121, 154, 161, 579, 583, 593, 758
Tylenol 363
Type Cover (Surface) 842

U

UAC 632, 671
UberCab 721
Ubuntu 697
UEX 526, 537, 547, 553, 769, 778, 784, 832
UIKit 641
Ultimate Extras (Windows Vista) 637, 638
Ultrabook 624, 798, 799, 800, 808, 812, 833, 842, 843
Ultraman 687
Ultrix 432
Underwriters Laboratory 357
undo 225, 229, 233, 367, 368, 425, 673
unearned revenue 330, 331
UNICODE 250, 411, 468

Uniprog Deluxe 452
Unix 9, 12, 13, 15, 26, 41, 49, 59, 62, 79, 95, 107, 139, 198, 247, 257, 277, 348, 432, 439, 491
Unsafe at Any Megahertz 357
usability testing 816
USA Today 207, 541, 688, 886
USENET 45, 68, 141, 150, 157, 158, 865
USENIX C++ Conference 49
User Account Control. *See* UAC
Utopia. *See* Microsoft Bob
UUNET 15

V

V8 562
van Dam, Andries 131, 367
VaporMg 839, 840
VBA 175, 223, 232, 312, 504, 779, 857
VB.NET 431, 543
VBScript 280
Venetian Hotel 702
vertical integration 829
virtualization 389, 598, 613, 617, 653, 658, 659, 677, 680, 681
virtual machine 18, 26
VisiCalc 5, 137
Visio 347, 407, 471, 544, 559, 773
Vision for Office9 287
Vision for Office10 342
Vision for Office12 532
Vision for Office.NET 446
Vision for Windows 7 610, 621
Vision for Windows 8 726
Vista 339, 536, 548, 562, 563, 566, 568, 569, 579, 580, 582, 590, 591, 592, 597, 600, 605, 613, 621, 637, 638, 640, 642, 643, 644, 646, 656, 657, 659, 664, 669, 670, 671, 672, 673, 674, 676, 679, 680, 722
Vista Capable 663, 703
Visual Basic 65, 70, 71, 112, 114, 116, 125, 173, 175, 199, 281, 282, 316, 335, 336, 431, 459, 498, 523, 525, 543, 642, 644, 646, 694, 773, 775, 779, 790, 795, 802, 805, 857
Visual Basic for Applications. *See* VBA
Visual Basic .NET. *See* VB.NET
Visual C++ 73, 281, 326, 526
Visual Fred 431, 543
Visual J++ 281
Visual Studio 71, 73, 336, 390, 488, 526, 562, 709, 712, 767, 777, 793
VMware 593, 613, 653, 655, 774
Vonnegut, Kurt 382
Vulcan Inc. 692, 844

W

W97M.Melissa.A 360
WaelB 604
WaggEd. *See* Waggener Edstrom
Waggener Edstrom 158, 357, 672, 688
walled garden 129, 134, 782, 787
Wall Street (film) 456
Wall Street Journal 6, 55, 80, 88, 209, 254, 300, 393, 426, 546, 557, 564, 567, 568, 580, 669, 685, 712, 883, 885, 886
Walt Disney World 687
Warlock. *See* basement (customers)
Washington Post 494
waterfall (development) 590
Watson 83, 97, 370, 371, 372, 373, 374, 375, 413, 423, 427, 435, 446, 470, 511, 513, 534, 684
WCS 604, 605
WDS 828, 831, 833, 835
webcam 306, 799, 835
WebOS 717
Web Store 306
Wedding Crashers 849
Welch, Jack 596
Welcome, IBM. Seriously (advertising campaign) 631
WEX 600, 603, 604, 605, 606, 609, 616, 645, 646, 738
WGA 201, 234, 235
What's on your PowerBook? (advertising campaign) 631
Where do you want to go today? (advertising campaign) 630
Whistler 263, 336, 337, 387, 422, 434, 726
White House 636
Whitman, Meg 686
Who moved my cheese? 528
Wieden+Kennedy 630
Wi-Fi 153, 398, 482, 483, 562, 583, 613, 619, 664, 704, 760, 798
Wikipedia 631
Wildstrom, Steve 252, 498
WillK 359, 364
Win32 62, 64, 73, 95, 103, 104, 106, 120, 177, 196, 208, 281, 348, 405, 440, 460, 557, 641, 642, 643, 645, 646, 694, 699, 703, 706, 731, 754, 768, 774, 775, 776, 777, 782, 784, 785, 787, 788, 789, 794, 795, 805, 814, 815, 888
Win32 API 775, 805
Win32s 62
Windows: The Next Killer Application on the Internet 137
Windows 1.0 11, 29, 33, 141, 166, 379, 607
Windows 3.0 20, 22, 24, 31, 32, 33, 34, 35, 36, 41, 51, 53, 54, 60, 63, 66, 67, 73, 80, 95, 103, 168, 345, 366, 369, 431, 500, 527, 580, 597, 720, 756, 760, 786, 801, 852
Windows 3.1 for Pen Computing 1.0 463
Windows 7 1, 187, 607, 608, 609, 610, 612, 613, 614, 616, 617, 618, 619, 620, 621, 627, 628, 629, 632, 635, 636, 639, 645, 649, 653, 655, 656, 657, 658, 659, 660, 664, 666, 667, 668, 669, 670, 671, 672, 673, 674, 675, 676, 677, 679, 680, 681, 682, 684, 685, 686, 687, 688, 689, 690, 691, 692, 694, 695, 696, 697, 698, 699, 701, 702, 703, 704, 705, 706, 711, 717, 718, 720, 724, 726, 727, 730, 731, 732, 733, 735, 736, 738, 739, 740, 743, 747, 751, 762, 763, 764, 766, 767, 768, 770, 771, 772, 774, 783, 788, 790, 792, 794, 795, 800, 808, 810, 813, 815, 817, 819, 821, 822, 824, 825, 828, 830, 841, 853, 854, 855, 857, 863, 886
Windows 8 1, 200, 692, 694, 695, 696, 697, 698, 699, 700, 701, 706, 709, 711, 715, 719, 720, 721, 722, 723, 724, 725, 726, 727, 728, 729, 730, 732, 733, 736, 737, 740, 743, 744, 747, 749, 750, 751, 755, 759, 760, 761, 762, 763, 765, 766, 767, 769, 770, 771, 778, 779, 780, 781, 782, 783, 784, 785, 786, 788, 789, 790, 791, 792, 793, 794, 796, 797, 798, 800, 801, 802, 804, 805, 806, 807, 808, 809, 810, 811, 812, 813, 814, 815, 817, 818, 819, 821, 822, 823, 824, 825, 826, 827, 828, 831, 833, 835, 837, 840, 841, 842,

843, 845, 846, 847, 848, 849, 850, 852, 853, 854, 855, 857, 858, 859, 861, 864, 865, 866, 887, 888
Windows 8 Consumer Preview 798, 807, 814, 823, 888
Windows 8 Developer Preview 797, 814
Windows 8 Framing Memo 707
Windows 8 Planning Memo 699, 707
Windows 8 principles 760
Windows 8 Vision Meeting 726, 801
Windows 11 553
Windows 95 1, 62, 83, 103, 126, 136, 153, 183, 185, 190, 198, 199, 200, 202, 203, 204, 206, 207, 208, 209, 211, 213, 232, 234, 236, 249, 251, 258, 267, 277, 291, 316, 333, 350, 371, 377, 379, 385, 392, 422, 423, 434, 501, 520, 525, 553, 554, 564, 571, 592, 597, 631, 637, 643, 649, 674, 700, 720, 730, 756, 759, 773, 789, 814, 816, 819, 823, 825, 858
Windows 98 211, 258, 279, 306, 315, 357, 359, 456, 502, 597, 607, 814
Windows 98 SE 211
Windows 2000 315, 316, 324, 327, 333, 336, 337, 347, 348, 349, 350, 353, 395, 418, 422, 448, 607
Windows and Windows Live. *See* WWL
Windows and Windows LiveOrganizing for agility, Competing with focus, Building must-have software (memo) 601
Windows Application Design Guide (WADG) 163
Windows Blue (8+) 847
Windows CE 117, 124, 349, 451, 462, 644, 739, 757, 857
Windows Client 565, 572, 573, 642
Windows DNA 387
Windows Embedded 751, 757, 857
Windows for Pen Computing 396
Windows for Workgroups 95, 199
WINDOWS.H 63, 64
Windows Home 612
Windows Live 558, 562, 566, 600, 601, 613, 654, 655, 656, 771
Windows Live Search 563
Windows Logo 183, 627
Windows Me 211, 258, 422, 597
Windows Media Center 489, 562, 565, 595, 609, 612, 639, 718, 721, 757, 798, 825, 830, 857
Windows Mobile 478, 488, 665, 680, 694, 706, 709, 722, 738, 771
Windows Mobile 6.0 694
Windows Mobile 6.5 706
Windows.NET 386, 387
Windows NT 1, 56, 57, 62, 63, 64, 65, 66, 67, 73, 84, 95, 98, 103, 104, 105, 107, 112, 114, 115, 118, 119, 133, 138, 139, 144, 145, 150, 152, 160, 165, 176, 181, 183, 187, 211, 247, 279, 315, 341, 342, 348, 371, 372, 387, 392, 432, 438, 456, 491, 525, 556, 565, 592, 607, 643, 652, 658, 725, 726, 738, 739, 742, 752, 784, 857, 858, 864
Windows NT porting lab 643
Windows Paint 59
Windows Phone 124, 582, 609, 644, 650, 651, 694, 706, 716, 720, 722, 723, 724, 726, 747, 750, 757, 758, 763, 777, 782, 783, 784, 807, 809, 821, 825, 826, 834, 843, 857, 859, 887
Windows Phone 6.5 716
Windows Phone 7 644, 694, 706, 716, 720, 722, 723, 724, 747, 757, 763, 777, 783, 857, 887
Windows Phone 7.5 723, 782, 807
Windows Phone 8 807
Windows Pioneer Award 111
Windows Presentation Foundation. *See* WPF
Windows Principles 617
Windows Professional 612
Windows RT 815, 826, 837, 847, 855, 857
Windows Runtime 784
Windows Server 101, 111, 120, 133, 155, 191, 269, 277, 307, 327, 336, 340, 341, 348, 387, 393, 395, 400, 404, 408, 422, 435, 475, 476, 478, 480, 488, 489, 491, 536, 543, 552, 556, 559, 566, 610, 613, 617, 641, 652, 653, 655, 659, 705, 716, 852, 859
Windows Store 752, 797, 807, 808, 809, 813
Windows Touch Pack 703
Windows Vista 317, 536, 562, 568, 571, 591, 597, 607, 612, 616, 618, 619, 621, 631, 637, 638, 639, 640, 641, 655, 659, 670, 676, 689, 860, 863
Windows Vista Capable 638, 640, 646, 664
Windows World Expo/Tokyo 99 323
Windows XP 56, 232, 325, 333, 336, 346, 401, 422, 423, 428, 434, 435, 436, 437, 439, 453, 455, 462, 468, 477, 481, 489, 502, 509, 525, 527, 536, 562, 563, 591, 597, 607, 612, 619, 638, 639, 640, 641, 650, 659, 662, 663, 664, 665, 689, 692, 696, 697, 702, 757, 760, 814, 825
Windows XP lifecycle 663
Windows XP Service Pack 2 436
Windoze 510
WinForms 775, 777, 780, 790
WinFS 403, 434, 582, 585, 590, 642
WinFX 434
Wings (television show) 260
WinHelp 131, 143, 144, 149
WinMail 110
WinPad 124, 712
WinRT 751, 752, 771, 784, 786, 787, 794, 795, 796, 806, 807, 813, 815, 822, 855, 857, 888
Wintel 619, 631, 655, 661, 665, 740
WinTone 439
WinWorks 500
Without a Point of View, There Is No Point (memo) 860
Wittress, Cris. *See* CrisWit
WLX 600, 603
WMC. *See* Windows Media Center
WM/Concept.A 356, 357, 360, 361
WOA 740, 741, 742, 748, 749, 750, 751, 752, 754, 843
Word 1.0 32, 106, 166, 512, 517
Word 6.0 for Macintosh 802
WordPerfect 9, 13, 34, 35, 82, 94, 97, 168, 169, 170, 174, 177, 178, 190, 208, 228, 290, 296, 356, 466, 517, 519, 522
word prosser 11
worm 361, 363
Worona, Steve 135
WP7. *See* Windows Phone 7 (Photon)
WP7.5. *See* Windows Phone 7.5 (Mango)
WPF 578, 589, 642, 643, 644, 645, 646, 775, 780, 781, 790
WPF/E 644
Writely 402, 544
write once, run anywhere 281
writing is thinking 357, 448, 580

WWDC 529
WWL 573, 577, 578, 603
WWPG 91, 93, 95
WWSSG 91
WzMail 110

X

x86 665, 698, 741, 742, 743, 744, 745, 748, 751, 752, 753, 754, 761, 768, 815, 841, 842
XAML 642, 643, 646, 775, 781, 790, 794
Xbox 201, 331, 488, 609, 639, 640, 641, 713, 716, 717, 718, 747, 782, 829, 830, 832
XDocs 459, 460
Xenix 13, 15, 18, 39
Xerox 18, 27, 28, 51, 75, 96, 107, 117, 119, 120, 141, 182, 367, 462, 519
Xerox PARC 27, 75, 462, 764
Xerox Star 141
XKCD 634
XML 299, 386, 388, 390, 391, 392, 393, 431, 443, 446, 448, 449, 452, 457, 458, 459, 460, 469, 494, 535, 545
XML file format 469, 545
XPS 545

Y

Y2K 309, 318, 321, 352, 353, 373, 375, 395, 438
Yahoo 207, 295, 349, 391, 399, 443, 445, 481, 562, 563, 565, 584, 654, 676, 772, 860
Y Combinator 861
Year of Linux 828
Ye Olde Museum of Office Past 517
Yodobashi Camera 306, 687
YouTube 507, 584, 639, 666, 704, 777, 812
YvesN 784

Z

Z-80 SoftCard 44, 692, 828
ZAW (Zero Administration Windows) 282
ZDNet 568, 601, 750, 781, 887
Zenith 26
Zero Defects 29, 30, 31
Zheng, Long 658
Zuckerberg, Mark 763
Zune 643, 644, 716, 717, 777, 829, 857, 859

ENDNOTES

1 https://www.tech-insider.org/windows/research/1991/0717.html

2 en.wikipedia.org/wiki/Alan_Cooper

3 Wall Street Journal, Pascal, B. G. (1990, May 21). Operating system: Opening of `Windows' shows how Bill Gates succeeds in software —- Microsoft founder bargains, frets, badgers engineers and never tires of games —- an early zeal for capitalism.

4 Rumsfeld's Rules: Leadership Lessons in Business, Politics, War, and Life, Donald Rumsfeld, Broadside Books (2013)

5 nces.ed.gov/programs/digest/d08/tables/dt08_432.asp

6 getfilings.com/o0000891618-94-000150.html

7 www.csmonitor.com/1994/0525/26091.html

8 www.newyorker.com/magazine/1994/01/10/e-mail-from-bill

9 www.theatlantic.com/magazine/archive/1945/07/as-we-may-think/303881/

10 elmcip.net/node/7367

11 "Managing the Development of Large Software Systems" (PDF), Royce, Winston, Proceedings of IEEE WESCON, 26 (August 1970)

12 store.hbr.org/product/microsoft-office-2000/600097

13 www.nytimes.com/1997/01/14/science/an-upgraded-leviathan-sets-sail.html

14books.google.com/books?id=r7w4vfOHVRUC&pg=PT9&lpg=PT9&dq=internet+division+that+would+be+-like+having+an+electricity+division+bill+gates&source=bl&ots=BkVSvj59AQ&sig=ACfU3U26N9OLRQZuSZ-R567zmbRdpFTzq-Q&hl=en&sa=X&ved=2ahUKEwiqqserkcPkAhXIpZ4KHavFDc0Q6AEwCXoECAkQA-Q#v=onepage&q=internet%20division%20that%20would%20be%20like%20having%20an%20electricity%20 division%20bill%20gates&f=false

15 twitter.com/StevenLevy/status/1165612620281536513?s=20

16 old.seattletimes.com/html/businesstechnology/2008020019_webgatesmemo277.html

17 worldhistoryproject.org/1976/2/bill-gates-writes-open-letter-to-hobbyists

18 AppleComputer, Inc. v. Microsoft Corp., 35 F.3d 1435 (9th Cir.1994).

19 Lotus Development Corporation v Borland International, Inc 516 U.S. 233 (1996)

20 en.wikipedia.org/wiki/Osborne_effect

21 en.wikipedia.org/wiki/The_Mother_of_All_Demos

22 www.forbes.com/2005/09/12/microsoft-management-software_cz_vm_0913microsoft.html?sh=68abd1165b91

23 news.microsoft.com/2001/04/11/farewell-clippy-whats-happening-to-the-infamous-office-assistant-in-office-xp/

24 WSJ 07 June 2001: B.1.]

25 web.archive.org/web/20010504053129if_/http://www.mvps.org:80/vb/index2.html?rants/vfred.htm

26web.archive.org/web/20031012194726/http://news.com.com/2009-1001-251154.html

27 web.archive.org/web/20010504053129if_/http://www.mvps.org:80/vb/index2.html?rants/vfred.htm

28 www.newyorker.com/magazine/2001/05/28/absolute-powerpoint

29 http://archive.wired.com/techbiz/media/news/2002/01/49826

30 https://www.microsoft.com/security/blog/2022/01/21/celebrating-20-years-of-trustworthy-computing/

31 www.wired.com/2002/01/bill-gates-trustworthy-computing/

32 From widely distributed unofficial transcript.

33 www.nytimes.com/1998/10/12/business/technology-microsoft-memo-offers-a-glimpse-of-gates-2.0.html

34 From widely distributed unofficial transcript.

35 rcpmag.com/articles/2010/04/01/the-evolution-of-microsoft-bpos.aspx?m=1

36 en.wikipedia.org/wiki/Second-system_effect "the tendency of small, elegant, and successful systems to be succeeded by over-engineered, bloated systems, due to inflated expectations and overconfidence"

37 www.newsweek.com/bill-gates-says-take-tablet-150561

38 "Freeform Information Managers Get Fancy." PC Magazine, Ed Mendelson, September 21, 2004.

39 www.askwoody.com/newsletter/microsofts-little-known-note-taker/

40 techrights.org/2009/06/25/bill-gates-office-patents/

41 www.techrepublic.com/article/control-your-documents-with-office-2003s-information-rights-management/

42www.itprotoday.com/windows-8/protecting-sensitive-documents-windows-rights-management-services

43and part 2 www.itprotoday.com/strategy/deploying-windows-rights-management-services

44 pmarchive.com/guide_to_startups_part4.html

45 "Even With All Its Profits, Microsoft Has a Popularity Problem", Stross, Randall, New York Times, 25 July 2010: BU.3

46 "Despite a New Outlook, Office 2003 Offers Little Reason to Upgrade" by Rob Pegoraro, The Washington Post, 19 Oct 2003, F.07

47 BusinessWeek, "Office lite: Less would be more," June 14, 1999, "Give us a simpler "Office,"" July 5, 1999, both by Stephen H. "Steve" Wildstrom

48 The case against user interface consistency by Jonathan Grudin, Communications of the ACM Volume 32, Issue 10, Oct. 1989 pp 1164–1173

49 docs.microsoft.com/en-us/office/troubleshoot/excel/wrongly-assumes-1900-is-leap-year

50 store.hbr.org/product/microsoft-office-2007-abridged/613061?sku=613061-PDF-ENG

51 youtu.be/kmZHPOU-FnA

52 www.youtube.com/watch?v=nueFbP9kP8Y

53 docs.microsoft.com/en-us/archive/blogs/jensenh/table-of-contents

54 web.archive.org/web/20060110150058/http://blogs.msdn.com/jensenh/archive/2005/09/15/467956.aspx

55 www.cnet.com/news/faq-looking-into-office-12/

56 www.crn.com/news/channel-programs/174300991/office-12-enters-first-major-beta-test.htm

57 www.cnet.com/reviews/microsoft-office-12-beta-1-preview/

58 Newsweek, December 4, 2006, Steven Levy "Moving Into a New Office"

59 anildash.com/2006/06/19/office_2007s_ri/

60 www.ben-evans.com/benedictevans/2016/4/20/the-best-is-the-last

61 Newsweek, May 31, 1999

62 Microsoft Annual Report, June 1999. www.microsoft.com/investor/reports/ar99/download.htm

63 “Personal Technology” by Walter M. Mossberg. The Wall Street Journal, 05 Aug 1993: PAGE B1

64 “Personal Technology” by Walter M. Mossberg. The Wall Street Journal, 20 May 1993: PAGE B1

65 “End of the PC Era? Hardly!” by Bill Gates and Paul Otellini, 15 May 2006, The Wall Street Journal

66 Wall Street Journal. Guth, R. A. (2006, Mar 22). Microsoft delays windows vista debut again; consumer version to miss critical holiday season; unit shake-up is expected.

67 money.cnn.com/2006/03/24/technology/business2_msftreorg/index.htm

68 minimsft.blogspot.com/2006/03/sinofsky-to-rescue.html

69 Establishing a Lessons Learned Program, usacac.army.mil/sites/default/files/publications/11-33.pdf

70 money.cnn.com/magazines/fortune/fortune_archive/2005/05/02/8258478/index.htm

71 Royce, Winston (1970), “Managing the Development of Large Software Systems” (PDF), Proceedings of IEEE WESCON, 26 (August): 1–9 www-scf.usc.edu/~csci201/lectures/Lecture11/royce1970.pdf

72 hbsp.harvard.edu/product/691033-PDF-ENG

73 medium.learningbyshipping.com/functional-versus-unit-organizations-6b82bfbaa57

74 blogs.windows.com/windowsexperience/2022/06/15/internet-explorer-11-has-retired-and-is-officially-out-of-support-what-you-need-to-know/

75 Revolutionizing Product Development: Quantum Leaps in Speed, Efficiency, and Quality by Steven C. Wheelwright, Kim B. Clark (1992)

76 news.microsoft.com/2006/07/19/brad-smith-new-america-foundation-windows-principles/

77 www.wired.com/2007/07/acer-president-the-whole-industry-is-disappointed-with-windows-vista/

78 www.neowin.net/news/bill-gates-hardware-to-be-nearly-free-in-10-years/

79shop.lenovo.com/SEUILibrary/controller/e/web/LenovoPortal/en_US/special-offers.workflow:ShowPromo?LandingPage=/All/US/Sitelets/Software/ThinkVantage-Technologies (via archive)

80 xkcd.com/934/

81 ”Hey, PC, Who Taught You to Fight Back?”, New York Times, August 30, 2009

82 news.microsoft.com/2008/07/14/microsoft-and-netflix-unveil-partnership-to-instantly-stream-movies-and-tv-episodes-to-the-tv-via-xbox-live/

83 www.wired.com/2012/04/ff-andreessen/

84 insights.stackoverflow.com/survey/2021#technology-most-popular-technologies

85 www.youtube.com/watch?v=vN4U5FqrOdQ My transcription via video 8:20 minutes in, emphasis added.

86 podcasts.apple.com/us/podcast/steve-jobs-in-2005-at-d3/id529997900?i=1000116189683

87 From “One Strategy” or the leak on Microsoft 2.0 www.microsoft2.net/2008/04/27/translucency-vs-transparency-blog-post/

88 Smaller PCs Cause Worry for Industry, New York Times (Online), Jul 21, 2008.

89 “Paul Otellini’s Intel: Can the Company That Built the Future Survive It?”, The Atlantic May 2013, www.theatlantic.com/technology/archive/2013/05/paul-otellinis-intel-can-the-company-that-built-the-future-survive-it/275825/

90 Apple earnings call transcript, April 2009

91 Reuters, April 4, 2008 “Gates sees next Windows ‘sometime’ in next year” www.reuters.com/article/us-microsoft-windows-gates/gates-sees-next-windows-sometime-in-next-year-idUSN0430179020080404

92 "Wall Street Journal. Mossberg, W. S. (2008, Jan 17). ASUS Offers Travelers Small, Mobile Eee PC, But It's Too Cramped

93 www.techmeme.com/071017/p57#a071017p57

94 Via Tidbits (tidbits.com/2007/10/17/steve-jobss-iphone-sdk-letter/) as the Apple posting on HotNews did not have a permanent link

95 "A fresh take on the browser" Sept 1, 2008. googleblog.blogspot.com/2008/09/fresh-take-on-browser.html

96 Transcript of Day 2 keynote from the Professional Developers Conference via Microsoft, news.microsoft.com/speeches/executive-keynotes-day-2-microsoft-2008/

97 ActiveWin "Windows 7" October 2009, activewin.com/reviews/previews/windows7/ via archive.org.

98 Lightweight Windows 7 pre-Beta on Eee PC 1000H looks very promising www.engadget.com/2008-10-31-lightweight-windows-7-pre-beta-loaded-onto-eee-pc-1000h-with-ver.html

99 Pogue, David, "Hate Vista? You May Like the Fix", The New York Times, January 22, 2009

100 "Even in Test Form, Windows 7 Leaves Vista in the Dust" Mossberg, Walter S.

101Wall Street Journal, 22 Jan 2009

102 www.wsj.com/articles/SB123258632983004629

103 "Microsoft Can't Evade Downturn's Tight Grip" Vance, Ashlee, New York Times, 24 July 2009

104 "A Windows to Help You Forget", Mossberg, Walt, Wall Street Journal, October 8, 2009

105 USA Today, Baig, Ed, October 16, 2009

106 Gartner press release, "Gartner Says Worldwide PC Shipments in Fourth Quarter of 2009 Posted Strongest Growth Rate in Seven Years", January 13, 2010.

107 "Windows 7: Microsoft's Lucky Number?" October 22, 2009, by Wright Bryan, www.npr.org/sections/alltech-considered/2009/10/microsoft_upgrades_with_window.html

108 NVIDIA finished fiscal year 2021 with revenue of $26.9B and a net income of $9.75 billion, with a market capitalization of $735.3 billion, with a b. via NVIDIA annual report and Q4/21 report.

109 ptech.allthingsd.com/20070405/pcs-mired-in-chores/

110 "Dell XPS L501x: An Excellent Mainstream Notebook" in AnandTech, November 10, 2010, www.anandtech.com/show/3999/dell-xps-15-l501x-review

111 blog.seattlepi.com/microsoft/2007/01/10/jim-allchins-mac-message-the-full-text/

112 Quote Investigator, quoteinvestigator.com/2012/01/24/future-has-arrived/

113 Also, an Economist Oxford comma.

114 Wall Street Journal. Mossberg, W. S. (2010, Apr 01). "Laptop killer? pretty close — iPad is a 'game changer' that makes browsing and video a pleasure; challenge to the mouse"

115 "Microsoft Cancels Innovative Courier Tablet Project", Gizmodo 4/29/2010, gizmodo.com/microsoft-cancels-innovative-courier-tablet-project-5527442

116 "Courier: First Details of Microsoft's Secret Tablet", Gizmodo, 9/22/09 gizmodo.com/courier-first-details-of-microsofts-secret-tablet-5365299

117 In the 1980s during the early days of Windows, HP had its own windowing system built on top of Windows. It was called HP NewWave and was the source of much consternation at Microsoft and a bit of legal back and forth with HP.

118 en.wikipedia.org/wiki/Osborne_effect

119 Note. We did not realize it at the moment in the rain, but upon returning I learned there was support for

hiring a car via plain SMS. Everyone around us using their iPhones only knew about the new cool new app. The SMS support was soon dropped anyway.

120 "Microsoft's New Windows Phone 7: Novel But Lacking" Mossberg, Walt, October 20, 2010, www.wsj.com/articles/SB10001424052702304741404575564300118397396

121 "'Developers, developers, developers!' Ballmer and Sinofsky talk Microsoft, memes, more in Clubhouse"

122by Kurt Schlosser, 2/12/2021, www.geekwire.com/2021/developers-developers-developers-ballmer-sinofsky-talk-microsoft-memes-clubhouse/

123 podcasts.apple.com/us/podcast/steve-jobs-at-the-d-all-things-digital-conference-video/id529997900?i=1000116189688

124 For an overview of the history of ARM see arstechnica.com/gadgets/2022/09/a-history-of-arm-part-1-building-the-first-chip/ and for my own recollections of the RISC v CISC debate see medium.learningbyshipping.com/risc-v-cisc-an-age-old-debate-79d859668d35

125 Paul passed away in October 2017. en.wikipedia.org/wiki/Paul_Otellini

126 For example, see the second point. 25iq.com/2016/07/29/a-dozen-things-ive-learned-from-andy-grove-about-business-and-strategy/

127 "Microsoft Talks ARM at CES" by Ina Fried, January 6, 2011, mobilized.allthingsd.com/20110105/live-microsoft-talks-arm-at-ces/ and "Windows on ARM Is No Knee-Jerk Move" by Ina Fried, January 5, 2011.

128 "Ballmer At CES 2011: "Whatever Device You Use, Windows Will Be There" by Danny Sullivan, Search Engine Land, January 5, 2011, searchengineland.com/live-blogging-steve-ballmer-at-ces-2011-60475

129 "Over 100 Tablets Were Unveiled at CES 2011", BGR, Zach Epstein, January 24, 2011, bgr.com/general/over-100-tablets-were-unveiled-at-ces-2011-heres-a-list-of-all-of-them/

130 "PC sales 'have passed peak'" by Charles Arthur, April 14, 2011, www.theguardian.com/technology/2011/apr/14/pc-market-has-passed-its-peak

131 "CES 2011: The biggest winners and losers", ZDNet, Jason Hiner, www.zdnet.com/article/ces-2011-the-biggest-winners-and-losers/

132blogs.msdn.microsoft.com/b8/2012/02/09/building-windows-for-the-arm-processor-architecture/

133 "Microsoft Provides Windows on ARM Details" by Andrew Cunningham, February 9, 2012 www.anandtech.com/show/5527/microsoft-provides-windows-on-arm-details

134 Some might consider this word failing in inclusiveness. I kept the original as we wrote in 2010. Microsoft Word today suggests artisanship or perhaps quality. I think "pride in craft" works as well.

135 UX Week 2012, August 2012, "The Windows 8 Story" by Jensen Harris, vimeo.com/52173464 or //build 2011 Conference, Sept 2011, "8 Traits of Great Metro-style Apps" by Jensen Harris, learn.microsoft.com/en-us/events/build-build2011/bps-1004

136 Jensen Harris, "The Hidden Way Plane Crashes Improved Your Laptop" via youtu.be/f52N1eZxF3E

137 …and now blue diamonds.

138 Microsoft Windows President Steven Sinofsky Introduces New Look of Windows by Ina Fried, All Things Digital, June 1, 2011, allthingsd.com/20110601/up-next-at-d9-microsoft-windows-president-steven-sinofsky-live-at-d9/

139 www.youtube.com/watch?v=kBHujE6DdrA

140 Windows Live 2007: A Look at the Next Generation by Paul Thurrott, SuperSite, June 27, 2007, www.winsupersite.com/showcase/wl_2007_preview.asp

141 "Global 100 Software Leaders" www.pwc.com/gx/en/technology/publications/global-software-100-leaders/assets/global-software-100.pdf

142 "Welcome to the 4% operating system" on Microsoft Vista and .NET www.grimes.demon.co.uk/dotnet/vista-AndDotnet.htm via archive.org

143 See "stupid developer tricks" in 091. Cleaning Up Longhorn and Vista

144 www.apple.com/hotnews/thoughts-on-flash/ This is no longer available online and was not archived as per prior note. See the Wikipedia article, en.wikipedia.org/wiki/Thoughts_on_Flash

145 "Why Microsoft has made developers horrified about coding for Windows 8" by ArsTechnica staff, June 12, 2011, arstechnica.com/information-technology/2011/06/html5-centric-windows-8-leaves-microsoft-developers-horrified/

146 "Dumping .NET - Microsoft's Madness" by Mike James, June 11, 2011, see www.i-programmer.info/professional-programmer/i-programmer/2591-dumping-net-microsofts-madness.html

147 "Microsoft needs to tell Windows 8 developers now about 'Jupiter' and Silverlight" by Mary Jo Foley, June 5, 2011, see www.zdnet.com/article/microsoft-needs-to-tell-windows-8-developers-now-about-jupiter-and-silverlight/

148 Microsoft Corp.: Office Business Unit, Harvard Business School case study, Marco Iansiti, Geoffrey K. Gill, 1990

149 WinRT Is Replacing Win32, SuperSite for Windows, Paul Thurrott, 9/15/2011, www.winsupersite.com/blog/supersite-blog-39/windows8/winrt-replacing-win32-140605

150 "Turning to the past to power Windows' future: An in-depth look at WinRT" by Ars Staff, 10/21/2012, arstechnica.com/features/2012/10/windows-8-and-winrt-everything-old-is-new-again/?amp=1

151 Occupational Employment And Wages, May 2012, US Bureau of Labor Statistics, www.bls.gov/news.release/archives/ocwage_03292013.pdf. Microsoft had traditionally taken US numbers and roughly doubled them for worldwide numbers. This rule of thumb no longer applies.

152 "A Review of Windows 8 Beta" by David Pogue, New York Times, February 29, 2012. archive.nytimes.com/pogue.blogs.nytimes.com/2012/02/29/a-review-of-the-windows-8-beta/

153 "Citigroup Positive on Microsoft's Windows 8" via Benzinga.com www.benzinga.com/article/2414539

154 "Does Windows 8 diss the PC?" by Dan Ackerman, CNET, February 29, 2012. www.cnet.com/tech/mobile/does-windows-8-diss-the-pc/

155 Apple earnings transcript, April 24, 2012 via finance.yahoo.com/news/apples-ceo-discusses-q2-2012-011004832.html

156 Penny Arcade, www.penny-arcade.com/comic/2009/10/30/in-the-seventh-house

157 "Windows 8 Consumer Preview: The True Story Behind the Missing Start Button" by Paul Thurrot, February 29, 2012, Windows IT Pro, www.winsupersite.com/article/windows8/true-story-missing-start-button-142338 via archive.org

158 "Windows, Revamped and Split in 2" by David Pogue, October 25, 2012, New York Times, www.nytimes.com/2012/10/25/technology/personaltech/microsofts-windows-revamped-and-split-in-2.html

159 Background www.anandtech.com/show/6385/microsoft-surface-review

160 Microsoft annual report 2010. Server and Tools contributed 22% but negative contributions from Online and Corporate segments balanced that out. It is not possible to compare these numbers to today as external reporting of "More Personal Computing" is not comparable to the 2010 "Windows and Windows Live" segment.

161 Bill Gates, Chicago Tribune, March 15, 1992

162 "Creative Think" by Andy Hertzfed on Alan Kay, July 1982, www.folklore.org/StoryView.py?project=Macintosh&story=Creative_Think.txt

163 "Microsoft Surface Review" by Anand Lal Shimpi, AnandTech, October 23, 2012, www.anandtech.com/print/6385/microsoft-surface-review

164 Forbes. Dyson, Esther. (1991, April 1), Esther Dyson, "Microsoft's spreadsheet, on its third try, excels."

165 "The iPad Mystery. New Episode: Food Fight Strategy" by Jean-Louis Gassée, November 20, 2022, monday-note.com/the-ipad-mystery-new-episode-food-fight-strategy-1aa7b11dfa7a

166 twitter.com/benedictevans/status/1127280727475679232?s=20

167 "The Other Road Ahead" by Paul Graham, September 2001, www.paulgraham.com/road.html

168 "Microsoft Is Dead" by Paul Graham, April 2007, www.paulgraham.com/microsoft.html or the abridged version "Microsoft Is Dead: the Cliffs Notes", April 2007, www.paulgraham.com/cliffsnotes.html

169 "Billionaire McCaw, Unfazed by Flops, Backs Wireless Internet" by Peter Robison, February 23, 2005, www.bloomberg.com/news/articles/2005-02-24/billionaire-mccaw-unfazed-by-flops-backs-wireless-internet

170 Amazon shopping list for books in the Bibliography, https://www.amazon.com/hz/wishlist/ls/YVTTJY0AFQI5